Twentieth-Century Literary Criticism

Guide to Gale Literary Criticism Series

When a patron needs to review criticism of literary works, these are the Gale series to use:

If the author's death date is: **You should turn to:**

After Dec. 31, 1959
(or author is still living)

CONTEMPORARY LITERARY CRITICISM

for example: Jorge Luis Borges, Anthony Burgess,
William Faulkner, Mary Gordon,
Ernest Hemingway, Iris Murdoch

1900 through 1959

TWENTIETH-CENTURY LITERARY CRITICISM

for example: Willa Cather, F. Scott Fitzgerald,
Henry James, Mark Twain, Virginia Woolf

1800 through 1899

NINETEENTH-CENTURY LITERATURE CRITICISM

for example: Fedor Dostoevski, George Sand,
Gerard Manley Hopkins, Emily Dickinson

1400 through 1799

LITERATURE CRITICISM FROM 1400 to 1800
(excluding Shakespeare)

for example: Anne Bradstreet, Pierre Corneille,
Daniel Defoe, Alexander Pope,
Jonathan Swift, Phillis Wheatley

SHAKESPEAREAN CRITICISM

Shakespeare plays and poetry

Gale also publishes related criticism series:

CONTEMPORARY ISSUES CRITICISM

Presents criticism on contemporary authors writing
on current issues. Topics covered include the social
sciences, philosophy, economics, natural science, law,
and related areas.

CHILDREN'S LITERATURE REVIEW

Covers authors of all eras. Presents criticism on
authors and author/illustrators who write for the
preschool to junior-high audience.

Twentieth-Century Literary Criticism

**Excerpts from Criticism of the
Works of Novelists, Poets, Playwrights,
Short Story Writers, and Other Creative Writers
Who Lived between 1900 and 1960,
from the First Published Critical Appraisals
to Current Evaluations**

**Dennis Poupard
Editor**

**Thomas Ligotti
James E. Person, Jr.
Associate Editors**

**Gale Research Company
Book Tower
Detroit, Michigan 48226**

STAFF

Dennis Poupard, *Editor*

Thomas Ligotti, James E. Person, Jr., *Associate Editors*

Mark W. Scott, *Senior Assistant Editor*

Earlene M. Alber, Sandra Giraud, Denise B. Grove,
Marie Lazzari, Sandra Liddell, Serita Lanette Lockard, *Assistant Editors*

Sharon K. Hall, Phyllis Carmel Mendelson, *Contributing Editors*

Robert J. Elster, Jr., *Production Supervisor*
Lizbeth A. Purdy, *Production Coordinator*
Denise Michlewicz, *Assistant Production Coordinator*
Eric F. Berger, Paula J. DiSante, Maureen Duffy,
Amy T. Marcaccio, Yvonne Huette Robinson, *Editorial Assistants*

Karen Rae Forsyth, *Research Coordinator*
Jeannine Schiffman Davidson, *Assistant Research Coordinator*
Victoria B. Cariappa, Robert J. Hill, James A. MacEachern,
Linda Mohler, Leslie Kyle Schell, Valerie J. Webster, *Research Assistants*

Linda M. Pugliese, *Manuscript Coordinator*
Donna D. Craft, *Assistant Manuscript Coordinator*
Colleen M. Crane, Maureen A. Puhl, Rosetta Irene Simms, *Manuscript Assistants*

L. Elizabeth Hardin, *Permissions Supervisor*
Filomena Sgambati, *Permissions Coordinator*
Janice M. Mach, *Assistant Permissions Coordinator*
Patricia A. Seefelt, *Assistant Permissions Coordinator, Illustrations*
Susan Nobles, *Senior Permissions Assistant*
Margaret Chamberlain, Anna Maria Pertner, Joan B. Weber, *Permissions Assistants*
Elizabeth Babini, Virgie T. Leavens, *Permissions Clerks*
Margaret Mary Missar, Audrey B. Wharton, *Photo Research*

Library of Congress Catalog Card Number 76-46132
ISBN 0-8103-0222-5
ISSN 0276-8178

CONTENTS

PREFACE

ιι is impossible to overvalue the importance of literature in the intellectual, emotional, and spiritual evolution of humanity. Literature is that which both lifts us out of everyday life and helps us to better understand it. Through the fictive lives of such characters as Anna Karenin, Lambert Strether, or Leopold Bloom, our perceptions of the human condition are enlarged, and we are enriched.

Literary criticism can also give us insight into the human condition, as well as into the specific moral and intellectual atmosphere of an era, for the criteria by which a work of art is judged reflects contemporary philosophical and social attitudes. Literary criticism takes many forms: the traditional essay, the book or play review, even the parodic poem. Criticism can also be of several kinds: normative, descriptive, interpretive, textual, appreciative, generic. Collectively, the range of critical response helps us to understand a work of art, an author, an era.

The Scope of the Book

The usefulness of Gale's *Contemporary Literary Criticism (CLC),* which excerpts criticism on current writing, suggested an equivalent need among literature students and teachers interested in authors of the period 1900 to 1960. The great poets, novelists, short story writers, and playwrights of this period are by far the most popular writers for study in high school and college literature courses. Moreover, since contemporary critics continue to analyze the work of this period—both in its own right and in relation to today's tastes and standards—a vast amount of relevant critical material confronts the student.

Thus, *Twentieth-Century Literary Criticism (TCLC)* presents significant passages from published criticism on authors who died between 1900 and 1960. Because of the difference in time span under consideration *(CLC* considers authors who were still living after 1959), there is no duplication between *CLC* and *TCLC.*

Each volume of *TCLC* is carefully designed to present a list of authors who represent a variety of genres and nationalities. The length of an author's section is intended to be representative of the amount of critical attention he or she has received from critics writing in English, or foreign criticism in translation. Critical articles and books that have not been translated into English are excluded. Every attempt has been made to identify and include excerpts from the seminal essays on each author's work. Additionally, as space permits, especially insightful essays of a more limited scope are included. Thus *TCLC* is designed to serve as an introduction for the student of twentieth-century literature to the authors of that period and to the most significant commentators on these authors.

Each *TCLC* author section represents the scope of critical response to that author's work: some early criticism is presented to indicate initial reactions, later criticism is selected to represent any rise or fall in an author's reputation, and current retrospective analyses provide students with a modern view. Since a *TCLC* author section is intended to be a definitive overview, the editors include between 20 and 30 authors in each 600-page volume (compared to approximately 75 authors in a *CLC* volume of similar size) in order to devote more attention to each author. An author may appear more than once because of the great quantity of critical material available, or because of a resurgence of criticism generated by events such as an author's centennial or anniversary celebration, the republication of an author's works, or publication of a newly translated work or volume of letters.

The Organization of the Book

An author section consists of the following elements: author heading, biocritical introduction, principal works, excerpts of criticism (each followed by a citation), and an annotated bibliography of additional reading.

- The *author heading* consists of the author's full name, followed by birth and death dates. The unbracketed portion of the name denotes the form under which the author most commonly wrote. If an author wrote consistently under a pseudonym, the pseudonym will be listed in the author heading and the real name given in parentheses on the first line of the biocritical introduction. Also located at the beginning of the biocritical introduction are any name variations under which an author wrote, including transliterated forms for authors whose languages use nonroman alphabets. Uncertainty as to a birth or death date is indicated by a question mark.

- The *biocritical introduction* contains biographical and other background information about an author that will elucidate his or her creative output. Parenthetical material following several of the biocritical introductions includes references to biographical and critical reference series published by the Gale Research Company. These include *Contemporary Authors, Dictionary of Literary Biography, Something about the Author,* and past volumes of *TCLC*.

- The *list of principal works* is chronological by date of first book publication and identifies genres. In the case of foreign authors where there are both foreign language publications and English translations, the title and date of the first English-language edition are given in brackets. Unless otherwise indicated, dramas are dated by first performance, not first publication.

- *Criticism* is arranged chronologically in each author section to provide a perspective on any changes in critical evaluation over the years. In the text of each author entry, titles by the author are printed in boldface type. This allows the reader to ascertain without difficulty the works discussed. For purposes of easier identification, the critic's name and the publication date of the essay are given at the beginning of each piece of criticism. Unsigned criticism is preceded by the title of the journal in which it appeared. For an anonymous essay later attributed to a critic, the critic's name appears in brackets in the heading and in the citation.

  Important critical essays are prefaced by *explanatory notes* as an additional aid to students using *TCLC*. The explanatory notes will provide several types of useful information, including: the reputation of a critic; the reputation of a work of criticism; the specific type of criticism (biographical, psychoanalytic, structuralist, etc.); and the growth of critical controversy or changes in critical trends regarding an author's work. In many cases, these notes will cross-reference the work of critics who agree or disagree with each other.

- A complete *bibliographical citation* designed to facilitate location of the original essay or book by the interested reader accompanies each piece of criticism. An asterisk (*) at the end of a citation indicates the essay is on more than one author.

- The *annotated bibliography* appearing at the end of each author section suggests further reading on the author. In some cases it includes essays for which the editors could not obtain reprint rights. An asterisk (*) at the end of a citation indicates the essay is on more than one author.

Each volume of *TCLC* includes a cumulative index to critics. Under each critic's name is listed the authors on whom the critic has written and the volume and page where the criticism may be found. *TCLC* also includes a cumulative index to authors with the volume numbers in which the author appears in boldface after his or her name. A cumulative nationality index is another useful feature in *TCLC*. Author names are arranged alphabetically under their respective nationalities and followed by the volume numbers in which they appear.

Acknowledgments

No work of this scope can be accomplished without the cooperation of many people. The editors especially wish to thank the copyright holders of the excerpts included in this volume, the permission managers of many book and magazine publishing companies for assisting us in locating copyright holders, and the staffs of the Detroit Public Library, University of Detroit Library, University of Michigan Library, and Wayne State University Library for making their resources available to us. We are also grateful to Jeri Yaryan for her assistance with copyright research.

Suggestions Are Welcome

Several features have been added to *TCLC* since its original publication in response to various suggestions:

- Since Volume 2—An *Appendix* which lists the sources from which material in the volume is reprinted.

- Since Volume 3—An *Annotated Bibliography* for additional reading.

- Since Volume 4—*Portraits* of the authors.

- Since Volume 6—A *Nationality Index* for easy access to authors by nationality.

- Since Volume 9—*Explanatory notes* to excerpted criticism which provide important information regarding critics and their work.

If readers wish to suggest authors they would like to have covered in future volumes, or if they have other suggestions, they are cordially invited to write the editor.

AUTHORS TO APPEAR
IN FUTURE VOLUMES

Abercrombie, Lascelles 1881-1938
Adamic, Louis 1898-1951
Ade, George 1866-1944
Agate, James 1877-1947
Agustini, Delmira 1886-1914
Aldanov, Mark 1886-1957
Aldrich, Thomas Bailey 1836-1907
Allen, Hervey 1889-1949
Annensky, Innokenty Fyodorovich
  1856-1909
Archer, William 1856-1924
Arlen, Michael 1895-1956
Austin, Mary 1868-1934
Bahr, Hermann 1863-1934
Barea, Arturo 1897-1957
Bass, Eduard 1888-1946
Benét, William Rose 1886-1950
Benjamin, Walter 1892-1940
Benson, E(dward) F(rederic) 1867-1940
Benson, Stella 1892-1933
Bentley, E(dmund) C(lerihew) 1875-
  1956
Berdyaev, Nikolai Aleksandrovich
  1874-1948
Beresford, J(ohn) D(avys) 1873-1947
Bergman, Hjalmar 1883-1931
Bergson, Henri 1859-1941
Bethell, Mary Ursula 1874-1945
Binyon, Laurence 1869-1943
Bishop, John Peale 1892-1944
Blackmore, R(ichard) D(oddridge)
  1825-1900
Blasco-Ibanez, Vicente 1867-1928
Blum, Leon 1872-1950
Bodenheim, Maxwell 1892-1954
Bojer, Johan 1872-1959
Bosman, Herman Charles 1905-1951
Bosschere, Jean de 1878-1953
Bottomley, Gordon 1874-1948
Bourget, Paul 1852-1935
Bourne, George 1863-1927
Brancati, Vitaliano 1907-1954
Broch, Herman 1886-1951
Byrne, Donn (Brian Oswald Donn-Byre)
  1889-1928
Caine, Hall 1853-1931
Campana, Dina 1885-1932
Cannan, Gilbert 1884-1955
Chand, Prem 1880-1936
Chatterji, Sarat Chandra 1876-1938
Churchill, Winston 1871-1947
Comstock, Anthony 1844-1915
Corelli, Marie 1855-1924
Corvo, Baron (Frederick William Rolfe)
  1860-1913

Croce, Benedetto 1866-1952
Csáth, Géza 1887-1919
Davidson, John 1857-1909
Day, Clarence 1874-1935
De Gourmont, Remy 1858-1915
Delafield, E.M. (Edme Elizabeth Monica
  de la Pasture) 1890-1943
Delisser, Herbert George 1878-1944
DeMorgan, William 1839-1917
Dent, Lester 1904-1959
DeVoto, Bernard 1897-1955
Döblin, Alfred 1878-1957
Douglas, (George) Norman 1868-1952
Douglas, Lloyd C(assel) 1877-1951
Dovzhenko, Alexander 1894-1956
Drinkwater, John 1882-1937
Dujardin, Edouard 1861-1949
Durkheim, Émile 1858-1917
Duun, Olav 1876-1939
Ellis, Havelock 1859-1939
Erskine, John 1879-1951
Ewers, Hans Heinz 1871-1943
Fadeyev, Alexandr 1901-1956
Feydeau, Georges 1862-1921
Field, Michael (Katherine Harris Brad-
  ley 1846-1914 and Edith Emma
  Cooper 1862-1913)
Field, Rachel 1894-1924
Flecker, James Elroy 1884-1915
Fletcher, John Gould 1886-1950
Frank, Bruno 1886-1945
Frazer, (Sir) George 1854-1941
Freeman, John 1880-1929
Freud, Sigmund 1853-1939
Fuller, Henry Blake 1857-1929
Garneau, Saint-Denys 1912-1943
Gladkov, Fydor Vasilyevich 1883-1958
Glyn, Elinor 1864-1943
Gogarty, Oliver St. John 1878-1957
Golding, Louis 1895-1958
Goldman, Emma 1869-1940
Gosse, Edmund 1849-1928
Gould, Gerald 1885-1936
Grahame, Kenneth 1859-1932
Gray, John 1866-1934
Guiraldes, Ricardo 1886-1927
Gumilyov, Nikolay 1886-1921
Gwynne, Stephen Lucius 1864-1950
Hale, Edward Everett 1822-1909
Hall, (Marguerite) Radclyffe 1886-1943
Harper, Frances Ellen Watkins
  1825-1911
Harris, Frank 1856-1931
Hernandez, Miguel 1910-1942
Herrick, Robert 1868-1938

Hewlett, Maurice 1861-1923
Heyward, DuBose 1885-1940
Hichens, Robert 1864-1950
Hilton, James 1900-1954
Hodgson, William Hope 1875-1918
Holtby, Winifred 1898-1935
Hope, Anthony 1863-1933
Howe, Julia Ward 1819-1910
Huch, Ricarda 1864-1947
Hudson, Stephen 1868-1944
Hudson, W(illiam) H(enry) 1841-1922
Hulme, Thomas Ernest 1883-1917
Ivanov, Vyacheslav Ivanovich 1866-
  1949
Jacobs, W(illiam) W(ymark) 1863-1943
James, Will 1892-1942
James, William 1842-1910
Jerome, Jerome K(lapka) 1859-1927
Jones, Henry Arthur 1851-1929
Khodasevich, Vladislav 1886-1939
King, Grace 1851-1932
Korolenko, Vladimir 1853-1921
Kuzmin, Mikhail Alexseyevich 1875-
  1936
Lampedusa, Giuseppi di 1896-1957
Lang, Andrew 1844-1912
Lawson, Henry 1867-1922
Leverson, Ada 1862-1933
Lewisohn, Ludwig 1883-1955
Lindsay, (Nicholas) Vachel 1879-1931
Lonsdale, Frederick 1881-1954
Louys, Pierre 1870-1925
Lowndes, Marie Belloc 1868-1947
Lucas, E(dward) V(errall) 1868-1938
Lynd, Robert 1879-1949
MacArthur, Charles 1895-1956
Manning, Frederic 1887-1935
Marriott, Charles 1869-1957
Martin du Gard, Roger 1881-1958
Masaryk, Tomas 1850-1939
McCoy, Horace 1897-1955
McCrae, John 1872-1918
Mencken, H(enry) L(ouis) 1880-1956
Meredith, George 1828-1909
Mirbeau, Octave 1850-1917
Mistral, Frederic 1830-1914
Monro, Harold 1879-1932
Monroe, Harriet 1860-1936
Moore, Thomas Sturge 1870-1944
Morgan, Charles 1894-1958
Mori Ogai 1862-1922
Morley, Christopher 1890-1957
Murray, (George) Gilbert 1866-1957
Musil, Robert 1880-1939
Nordhoff, Charles 1887-1947

Authors to Appear in Future Volumes

Norris, Frank 1870-1902
Olbracht, Ivan (Kemil Zeman) 1882-1952
Ophuls, Max 1902-1957
Parrington, Vernon L. 1871-1929
Pickthall, Marjorie 1883-1922
Pinero, Arthur Wing 1855-1934
Platonov, Andrey 1899-1951
Pontoppidan, Henrik 1857-1943
Porter, Eleanor H(odgman) 1868-1920
Porter, Gene(va) Stratton 1886-1924
Prevost, Marcel 1862-1941
Quiller-Couch, Arthur 1863-1944
Rappoport, Solomon 1863-1944
Reid, Forrest 1876-1947
Riley, James Whitcomb 1849-1916
Rinehart, Mary Roberts 1876-1958
Roberts, Elizabeth Madox 1886-1941
Rohmer, Sax 1883-1959
Rolfe, Frederick 1860-1913
Rolland, Romain 1866-1944
Rölvaag, O(le) E(dvart) 1876-1931
Rosenberg, Isaac 1870-1918
Rourke, Constance 1885-1941

Roussel, Raymond 1877-1933
Ruskin, John 1819-1900
Sabatini, Rafael 1875-1950
Santayana, George 1863-1952
Sardou, Victorien 1831-1908
Seeger, Alan 1888-1916
Service, Robert 1874-1958
Seton, Ernest Thompson 1860-1946
Shestov, Lev 1866-1938
Slater, Francis Carey 1875-1958
Solovyov, Vladimir 1853-1900
Spitteler, Carl 1845-1924
Squire, J(ohn) C(ollings) 1884-1958
Steiner, Rudolph 1861-1925
Stockton, Frank R. 1834-1902
Strachey, Lytton 1880-1932
Sudermann, Hermann 1857-1938
Sully-Prudhomme, Rene 1839-1907
Tabb, John Bannister 1845-1909
Takuboku, Ishikawa 1885-1912
Tey, Josephine (Elizabeth Mackintosh) 1897-1952
Tolstoy, Alexei 1882-1945

Turner, W(alter) J(ames) R(edfern) 1889-1946
Vachell, Horace Annesley 1861-1955
Van Dine, S.S. (William H. Wright) 1888-1939
Van Doren, Carl 1885-1950
Vazov, Ivan 1850-1921
Veblen, Thorstein 1857-1929
Verhaeren, Émile 1855-1916
Wallace, Edgar 1874-1932
Wallace, Lewis 1827-1905
Walser, Robert 1878-1956
Webb, Mary 1881-1927
Webster, Jean 1876-1916
Welch, Denton 1917-1948
Wells, Carolyn 1869-1942
Wister, Owen 1860-1938
Wren, P(ercival) C(hristopher) 1885-1941
Wylie, Francis Brett 1844-1954
Yonge, Charlotte Mary 1823-1901
Zangwill, Israel 1864-1926
Zoshchenko, Milchail 1895-1958

Readers are cordially invited to suggest additional authors to the editors.

Endre Ady

1877-1919

Hungarian poet, journalist, short story writer, and critic.

Ady is considered the father of modern Hungarian literature. Known primarily as a Symbolist poet, he addressed the need to revive Hungary's aesthetic and cultural spirit, and demanded the political, social, and economic reform of his Austrian-dominated homeland. His poetry is distinguished by an innovative system of symbols, a blend of archaic and modern language, and themes which were unique to Hungarian literature. Although Ady's achievements are unparalleled in twentieth-century Hungarian literature, the measure of his international reputation has been limited. Critics consistently attribute his relative obscurity in world literature to the difficulty of translating the poet's distinctive Hungarian imagery and subject matter.

Ady was born in the village of Érmindszent to an impoverished family of the lesser nobility. He was raised in a conservative Protestant tradition which he later rejected as an adult. Ady attended both the local Calvinist and Catholic primary schools. He received his secondary education at a Calvinist college, where he excelled as the school's best student and most notorious debauchee; his reputation for the latter persisted throughout his career. Ady studied law for one semester, leaving school to work as a journalist in 1899. In that same year he published *Versek*, his first collection of poems, a volume of sentimental verse which does not suggest the artistic quality of his later works. The turning point of Ady's career occurred while he worked at a small newspaper in Nagyvarad. There, he began a romantic affair with a sophisticated married woman, Adél Brüll Diósi, who served as the inspiration for "Léda" in his first significant poetry collection, *Új versek*. In 1904, Diósi encouraged Ady to join her in Paris, where he came under the influence of the works of the French Symbolist poets, most notably Charles Baudelaire and Paul Verlaine, and where the intellectual environment served to refine his reformist political and social ideology. After his return to Hungary in 1905, Ady published verse collections which introduced original themes with a candid approach never before practiced in Hungarian literature. Among his most important works of this period are *Vér és arany*, which presents both the good and bad aspects of materialism, and *Az Illés szekéren*, which expresses the hypocrisy of religious fervor devoid of forgiveness. In addition to his verse, Ady contributed political articles and short stories to the literary periodical *Nyugat*, becoming that journal's guiding force and Hungary's most controversial writer. However, his indulgent life resulted in continual ill health. Suffering from syphilis and alcoholism, Ady spent much of his time in hospitals until his death in 1919.

Critics often discuss Ady's poetry in chronological order, considering each of his volumes as a progressive step to the next, with all of his work forming a unified whole. The most salient characteristic of this unity is the poet's imaginative and original symbolism: Ady transformed typical Hungarian motifs into a system of symbols which convey a consistent visionary meaning throughout his poetry. In addition, his use of thematic and linguistic contradictions is an essential constant of his poetic style. Ady is also noted for his inventive language. Greatly

influenced by the Bible, he combined Biblical idioms with words used in everyday speech, thereby enhancing the mystical allusions of his symbolism. A dominant concern of Ady's poetry relates to the suffering of the Hungarian lower classes and the need for social reform. An important motif illuminating this concern, used repeatedly throughout his works, is his belief that Hungary's monarchist order was an anachronism in the modern world. Ady radically opposed the ruling class's imperialistic attitude that adhered to stringent class separation; he believed that it inhibited social, spiritual, and aesthetic growth. Critics agree that through the expression of this view in his poetry, Ady's works display a revolutionary spirit that transcends those of his Hungarian predecessors and contemporaries. In his later verse, he extends his concern for the fate of the Hungarian people to that of humanity; thus, he developed a wider range of themes that includes love, death, and the search for a new religious ethic. Prompted by the advent of World War I, Ady incorporated these themes into his antiwar poetry, which reiterates his concern with human suffering and the debilitating aspects of war. Many critics consider these apocalyptic poems the apex of his career.

Critics concur that Ady was one of the most original Hungarian writers of the twentieth century. His innovative style not only revived a dormant Hungarian literature, but inspired a whole nation to seek social reforms that were compatible with the modern world. Throughout his career, Ady received critical attention from both the bourgeoisie, into which he was born, and the radical, working-class groups who were aroused by his revolutionary spirit. Although several of Ady's works have been translated, he is little read outside of his own country. According to most critics, the translations cannot adequately express the mystical qualities of his poetry, nor can the foreign reader easily understand the Hungarian topicalities. In spite of Ady's lack of recognition outside Hungary, his major literary contribution within his country is summarized by Dézo Keresztury, who wrote: "He touched every painful, and disquieting sore in contemporary Hungarian life; it was this quality of his poetry that has made it an inspiration for the Hungarian reform movement, a Bible for the Hungarians at home and the Hungarians scattered through the world." For this reason and for his modern literary approach, Ady is remembered as the preeminent modernist in Hungarian literature.

(See also *Contemporary Authors*, Vol. 107.)

PRINCIPAL WORKS

Versek (poetry) 1899
Új versek (poetry) 1906
Az Illés szekerén (poetry) 1908
Vér és arany (poetry) 1908
Szeretném, ha szeretnének (poetry) 1909
A minden titkok verseiböl (poetry) 1910
A menekülő élet (poetry) 1912
A magunk szerelme (poetry) 1913
Ki látott engem? (poetry) 1914
A halottak élén (poetry) 1918
Az utolsó hajók (poetry) 1923
Ady Endre összes versei (poetry) 1930
Poems (poetry) 1941
Poems of Endre Ady (poetry) 1969
*The Explosive Country: A Selection of Articles and Studies,
   1898-1916* (essays) 1977

ENDRE ADY (essay date 1909)

[*In an essay written for the periodical* Nyugat, *Ady expresses his fear at being a creative artist in a world of "simple and second-hand" minds.*]

I am afraid, therefore I am; I am afraid for alas! life has been granted to me, and I can be so afraid that I am afraid even to confess this fear. (p. 208)

I know something which few people know today, and this is a sad and fearful state. Oh, just consider: there is a man who has an intense awareness of life, and sometimes he can produce fine confessions of this. And this man uses this awareness, does this, must do something with it: this is his life, indeed this is what he lives on. Consider someone who is compelled to boast of something which he possesses, and which our modern civilization rightly values little. Someone who tends and flaunts something which would make a sensible, modern bourgeois human being run off inevitably to the doctor to have it cured if at all possible. I have lived an awful lot, but how difficult it was for me to decide, for example, to write poetry. Yet this is something I can do, and if fear were not my superstitious faith and religion, I would happily flaunt this ability

of mine. But I am afraid, and the fact that I am talking about it here is also fear; I want to see how others as they tremble view this trembling fear. I have some very kind and good friends from my schooldays up to now, who maintain that I possess intelligence and logic, and more recently they declare that I even have ability. The fact that I have become the Hungarian showpiece of unintelligibility shows what a sacred, rightful law fear is. And oh, if only that were sufficient to indicate all that should or can be known about me! But since in business jargon I am on a campaign, I have a still more deadly fear that I shall be understood. One is thirty-two years old, does not like Horace and the court poets, and is accustomed to the death of a good poet before he has been noticed by many people. And then one sees that people do notice him, and in Hungary of course they give him an unprecedented drubbing, shout his name, caress him and see him. One must be afraid, and quite often nowadays I believe I am a humbug, a man who is almost a success.

How would anyone else in my position console himself, except that even those who understand him do not understand him? This is what I do, because in my great fear I am least afraid of banalities. And I philosophize too, because this is no bad habit, and likewise quite banal. I consider how this world would not exist if we always copied our predecessors and there were no exceptions at all. I consider how much better it would be to sense things as did the old races of mankind and to profess so. I really envy those who are simple and second-hand with all the audacity of the reformer, because perhaps they are right. And perhaps it is a finer vocation to recite the words of human souls unsullied by various sights, sounds and readings than those new words of new souls. With the sincere emotions of an honest and therfore very cowardly person, I openly salute those who are old-fashioned and monotonous. But—but I also consider sometimes that it is not necessarily a sign of mediocrity that my name is known in Hungary. They know about me, they know about me as about anyone else, but it makes them rather uncomfortable, and this is the main thing.

It is almost certain that I am not simply a poet, whose proper course would be to die like Gyula Reviczky. Indeed I despise my craft and I am frightened of my appearances even when I am appearing. I see myself as one of those Hungarians whom József Katona left out of the great conspiracy-scene. I see myself as a man, a Hungarian, who nods in his cups, silently, for a few centuries while his more wide-awake companions discuss Hungarianness and the tragedy of destiny. But in the end he lifts his head—and it is high time—and says something which is Hungarian and has something to do with the matter in hand. He says it fearfully; he says it powerfully, sometimes almost without knowing he has said it, but what he says is Hungarian and not entirely valueless. (pp. 209-12)

Endre Ady, "Fear and Writing" (originally published as "Félelem és írás," in Nyugat, November 1, 1909), in his The Explosive Country: A Selection of Articles and Studies, 1898-1916, edited by Erzsébet Vezér, translated by G. F. Cushing (translation © Erzsébet Vezér, 1977), Corvina Press, 1977, pp. 208-14.

FRANZ KAFKA (letter date 1921)

[*Kafka wrote the following letter to Robert Klopstock after reading a copy of* Auf neuen Gewässern, *a German translation of* Az új Hellász.]

Gradually, with a little outside help, this great man [Ady] is being unearthed here and there from Hungarian obscurity. However, a flock of false conceptions and false analogies also intrude upon the process. Such a translation reminds one somewhat of the complaints of ghosts over the painful incompetence of mediums. Here we have the mediumistic incompetence of reader and translator. But the prose is more direct and gives us a somewhat closer view of him. There's much I don't understand, but I take in the whole. As always in such a case, one feels happy that he is there and that one is in some way or another related to him. "Without antecedents," his work is said to be, and therefore we are also related in this respect. . . .

The epilogue also contains some new things, at least new for me.

> *Franz Kafka, in his letter to Robert Klopstock in December, 1921, in his* Letters to Friends, Family, and Editors, *translated by Richard Winston and Clara Winston (reprinted by permission of Schocken Books Inc.; translation copyright © 1958, 1977 by Schocken Books Inc.; originally published as* Briefe: 1902-1924 *by Franz Kafka, edited by Max Brod, S. Fischer, 1958), Schocken, 1977, p. 312.*

WATSON KIRKCONNELL   (essay date 1937)

[*Kirkconnell was one of the first to undertake the difficult task of translating Ady's works from Hungarian into English. In this essay he discusses the variety of themes in Ady's poetry.*]

It would be possible, by a tendencious selection of poems from [Ady's] output, to prove that he was a pagan or a Christian, a Satanist or a pietist, a proletarian or an aristocrat, a rebel or a mystic, a cynic or a sentimentalist, a neurasthenic or a man of iron, a cosmopolite or a patriot. Each of these facets of his personality would be authentic, but each, if isolated from the rest, would falsify one's estimate of the man. His is rather the poetry of totality,—the synthesis, in a thousand lyrics, of a thousand intensely realized aspects of modern experience. In so far as there is any dominating mood in his work, it is the tragic fever of a terrible, self-consuming spirit, "a wandering hell in the eternal sphere." He was a turbulent creative force that burned itself out in an effort to become incandescent with the intensity of its living. (p. 501)

[Ady] was consumed with an ambition to become the creator of a new lyric poetry for Hungary, a poetry which should express adequately the shifting currents and profoundly contradictory moods of modern life and thought. (p. 504)

In the very forefront of his poetic themes stands his treatment of love, a treatment in which he broke completely with that sentimental tradition which the Age of the Troubadours has imposed on Western Europe for the past nine centuries. In the passion of sex he found rather a gloomy compulsion, far nearer to the Black Aphrodite of Corinth than to the foam-begotten goddess of Paphos. He might, indeed, express a pagan joy in the gratification of the senses, but even in his psalms to the white body of "Leda" an ineluctable bitterness creeps in. Hedonism exhausted itself and found itself involved in sombre strife, full of shameful compromises and empty storms of passion. Thence came Ady's lyrics of penitence and confession, the realization of spiritual fall and of the need for spiritual expiation. He thus runs through the whole gamut of erotic experience. One is reminded of Catullus's poems to "Lesbia," but Ady had embraced a legion of Lesbias and his "love lyrics"

are, if possible, harsher and starker in their intermittent moods of disillusionment. (pp. 505-06)

Death, in Ady's poetry, is a theme almost as frequent as love, and one more august in its conception. It is the rare ebony coffin that enhances the value of his brief earthly pleasures, lying yet alive within it but soon to be interred forever. It is the invincible frost that sooner or later blights all human effort. It is an ocean of darkness on whose shadowy shore we linger for a brief while. It is a cavalcade ("**The Horses of Death**") that rides the roads by night, halting at unpredictable door after door with its austere summons. . . . (p. 506)

Religion entered likewise into his poetry, but under strange guises. Calvinism had permeated his youth in no uncertain fashion; and the Bible, his constant study throughout life, tinged with its fundamental colours nearly all that he wrote. More important still, there issued from his early training a tragic dualism of spiritual mood, for even amid his most riotous living the Prodigal could not free himself completely from the allegiance of an earlier devotion. He might deny God, and blaspheme proudly against Him, uttering black accusations against the Administrator of the Universe; but all this could alternate with sobs of contrition or with expressions of simple trust in the Divine. The Rt. Rev. Sándor Makkai, the Calvinist bishop of Transylvania, has actually regarded Ady as the most authentically religious of Hungarian poets; and there is a sense in which he shares in the spirit of the penitential psalms of that lovable blackguard, King David. . . . In **The Last Boats** [*Az utolsó hajók*], the sombre lyric that gives its general title to his posthumous poems, the mood, however, is one of tragic exhaustion—sans faith, sans fear, sans hope, sans everything. . . . Whether or not this represents the final position reached by the spirit of Ady, it is hard to say. With posthumous material, assembled by literary executors, it is almost impossible to assign dates to individual pieces or to give them their respective places in the progressive experience of their author. The most legitimate conclusion, however, is that we have here his last grim utterance, written on "the shores of waters of darkness."

Nature is often a favourite theme among lyric poets, but with Ady a real sensitiveness to nature does not seem to have been awakened until his sojourn under the alien skies of Paris had opened his eyes to the beauties of his native Hungary. Thence came not only wistful enthusiasm from a distance, but plenary inspiration when the Magyar countryside was revisited. A specimen of this rapture over his native fields in spring, reaching its climax in a masculine awareness of woman as a symbol of earth's beauty and fertility, is found in his poem "**After a May Shower.**" . . . (pp. 507-09)

Towards Hungary as a land and a nation, he was profoundly patriotic. That is not to say that many of his earlier poems were not trenchantly critical of his countrymen, even to the point of arousing bitter protest; but while he might be frankly faultfinding within the family circle, he was emphatic in telling the rest of the world of Hungary's achievements and Hungary's age-old martyrdom. . . . With the World War, however, his sense of the Hungarian tragedy grew deeper and more intense. He saw the Magyars drawn against their will into a maelstrom of death. He saw Austrian generals prodigal in their use of Magyar storm troops. Under the similitude of "**The Lost Horseman,**" his 1918 volume compresses the long, fateful annals of Hungary into a few melancholy stanzas. . . . (pp. 509-10)

Love, death, religion, nature and patriotism are thus among the major themes of his poetry; but these, even in all their

Protean forms, do not begin to exhaust the range of his interests. . . . More and more, in reading through the collected works of Ady, one is impressed by the universality of his experience. Twentieth century critics are prone to emphasize the impossibility of co-ordinating and integrating all of the spiritual contradictions of modern life. A fatal erosion of thought has tended to demolish the massive ideological structures of an earlier age, leaving Man to wander blindly among the ruins. Bitter, corrosive waters lap at the foot of walls once deemed impregnable. Vampire systems of long dead thought suck at the life-blood of the bewildered living, while new, amorphous worms of half-begotten concept writhe into greedy life. A metaphysical unification of all that is significant in contemporary thought is almost too much to hope for. In Ady, something of that integration takes place; but it is in feeling, not in thought—in an intensity of infinitely varied mood, not in a coherent and well-rounded philosophical system. There is a sense in which Ady is a Nietzschean *Übermensch*, consummating in his own person a combined and heightened version of all modern experience but burned at last to a charred wreck by voltages beyond human endurance. (pp. 511-12)

It is important, in conclusion, to comment on the intrinsic qualities of his poetry. He is not a great artist in the sense that János Arany and Mihály Babits are artists. His verse is not finely chiselled marble, but lava still warm from subterranean arteries of passion. He often achieves revolutionary ends by revolutionary means; his very power often produces the effect of monumental dignity; but one rarely feels that conscious planning has entered into the task of creation. His most notable quality is his command over vivid and unforgettable images. In this he is no doctrinaire exponent of an opinionated ''imagism,'' but rather a spontaneous spiritual brother of the English poet, William Blake. Vision and metaphor are the very essence of his thought.

One is reminded of Aristotle's magistral dictum with regard to poetry: ''The greatest thing of all by far is to be a master of metaphor. It is the one thing that cannot be learned from others; and it is also a sign of original genius, since a good metaphor implies the intuitive perception of similarity in dissimilars.'' Had he no other endowment than this, Ady would rank high; and it is by the application of this gift to a universal range of experience that he is a poet of world importance. As already noted, he is not a conscious ''imagist,'' ticketing prosaic little ideas with single, explicit little images. His is rather an inborn power over symbols and analogies that are complex and suggestive, assisting the mind to explore and chart non-measureable worlds of spiritual quality. (pp. 512-13)

> *Watson Kirkconnell, ''The Poetry of Ady,'' in* The Hungarian Quarterly *(reprinted by permission of The Hungarian Academy of Sciences), Vol. III, No. 3, Autumn, 1937, pp. 501-14.*

RENÉ BONNERJEA   (essay date 1941)

[Bonnerjea's essay discusses several of Ady's poems and stresses the originality of the poet's contribution to Hungarian literature.]

If we were to pass in review the names of all those poets noted for their originality we could hardly find one more original than Ady. His originality borders on eccentricity, and his subjectiveness on neurasthenia. In whatever mood he may happen to be the reader of his verses is not for an instant allowed to forget that the poet is born and evolves in a universe other than our own. He feels far beyond the life of experience and drags us back into the most unexplored and dreaded convolutions of our soul. Ady's poetry is more than strange: it is alarming. To the broad, smooth highway paved with tradition, he prefers the unbeaten labyrinths of virgin forests where the green-eyed monster of madness is day and night on the lookout for unwary pioneers. What Ady describes are images distorted and unintelligible for having been observed at too close a range and with a camera out of all focus.

Reading Ady we feel ourselves wrecked on an island where the conceptions and the habitual trends of thought of the Old World are unknown or long since forgotten. Symbolism is the lord of creation and master of our will. Ady is a visionary. He sees rather than composes, and jots down what he has seen. Like the Delphic oracle he is in a state of ecstasy whenever he speaks, and sometimes is not conscious himself of what he has uttered. Symbolists there were before him by the dozens, but we may safely say that none of them ever went as far as he did. Not only does he write, but he lives and thinks in terms of symbolism. Realities of common, everyday life are not real to his imagination until they have undergone a process of transformation in which they gradually lose their distinguishing characteristics and become signs in a world of enigmas. A few examples of his poems chosen at random by their very titles will suffice to demonstrate in what symbol-conscious channels the current of his thoughts flowed: **''Migration from Curses' City''**, **''The Cemetery of Souls''**, **''Burial at Sea''**, **''I kiss Miss—Kisses''**, **''My Coffin Steed''**, **''Homesickness in the Land of Sunlight''**, **''Weeping beneath Life's Tree''**, **''A Boat on the Dead Sea''**, . . . etc., etc.

The publication of **''New Verses''** [**''Új versek''**] was a slap in the face of Convention and a challenge to the Past. As such it received its full and just share of attacks. Critics literally pounced upon it. It was objected to from all points of view. But of the throng of writers who fenced with him Béla Tóth was the only one who struck him at the weak point of his armour. Tóth's criticism was cruel yet, from his standpoint, just and judicious. He accused Ady of raving, and said that his poems were a jumble of senseless and blatant rigmarole. It hit home, and Ady, stung to the quick, tried to parry by a riposte.

When the scum and slush of his life will have sunk into oblivion and when Ady will be read no longer prejudiced against for his revolutionary principles in politics and aesthetics, but for what he himself has to offer, the validity of Tóth's attack will still hold good. All of Ady's greatness depends on our decision on this point. It is a question of fundamentals. Accept Ady's premises and we shall find him to be a poet of rarest value; refute them, and his writings will make neither head nor tail. It would be as futile an undertaking to criticize his works from any other standard than his own as it would be to wish to understand Copernicus by the Ptolemaic system, or Kant's conception of space through Leibnitzian monadism.

There is—if we may express ourselves thus—a special ''Ady-World''. We must receive our admission into this land of wonders before we can ever hope to understand him. He is baffling and incomprehensible to the uninitiated. He is so subjective as to admit of no compromise on the part of the reader. We must either leave him alone and remain aloof from his universe, or we must let ourselves go and sink without logical restrictions to whatever he wishes to lead us into. We either rave with him or we stare at him as at an alienated. We *must* have that ''willing suspension of disbelief which constitutes poetic faith''. Every single poem of his is of the species brought into literature by "Le Bateau Ivre" or "Le Tombeau d'Edgar Poe". (pp. 7-9)

Depending on unlimited inspiration as he does Ady is often unequal in his output. Sometimes his Muse lets him down; more often, however, she grips his soul and carries him to regions into which no human being had ever penetrated before.

Of whatever reality he is speaking—no matter how slight the impression from which it was derived—he first makes it pass through a process of crystallization and then starts cutting and polishing the flashing jewels which stud his ideas. As we have already mentioned he is through and through a symbolist and, as such, obscure to many; yet those who are tempted to call his poetry decadent impressionism should think twice before doing so, for, when he wishes to, he can be as universally appealing as a Vörösmarty or a Petőfi. He has many poems which are simple and direct. What more touching in its simplicity than "**Saint Margaret's Island**" relating how the famous modern pleasure resort received its name? How pathetic is the picture he draws of the poet born in an environment too severe and far too discouraging for him to conquer ("**The Unknown Poet**")! No less does he make our very heart-strings vibrate in "**A Cross in the Forest**" where he shows us how life and experience have taught him to uncover his head before the effigy of Our Saviour. And how intimate and passionate his poem entitled "**The Lord's Arrival**". It is not without just cause that Bishop Alexander Makkai calls Ady Hungary's greatest religious poet. Interesting and original too are the poems in which he treats classical themes as "**Degenerate Nero's Death**" or "**The Death of the Poet Catullus**".

But Ady's greatest contribution to Hungarian literature consists in his introduction of a world of images never seen before. There are degrees in the depth of his inspiration. At times we skim with him gaily on a lake of delicious delight, at others, he grimly drags us down to the bottom of a sea of red horror. His poems are either allegories, symbols, visions or poetic trances. His sanest vision barely reaches the borders of waking life and his wildest transcends the last limits of dreams.

Sometimes with his fertile power of imagination he establishes a striking comparison which he gradually weaves into a picture clear and consistent throughout. Such is "**Old Ancestor Envy**", a *curriculum vitae* in words of fire. The meaning of poems like "**The Lake laughed**" with its underlying philosophy or "**Tender, Caressing Hands**" which reminds us vaguely of Browning's "Andrea del Sarto" is perfectly clear to us. Nor do we have any difficulty in invoking the images of "**The Tisza Shores**", "**The Thrown-up Stone**", "**Gare de l'Est**" or "**The White-Lady**". In "**Adam, where art thou?**", "**The Holy Caravan**", "**In Elijah's Chariot**" and compositions of this nature the situation is already different. Their comprehension depends on an insight into the writer's soul, since the pictures are incomplete and require an effort on our part to supply the missing parts. Thus, the reader's mind is gradually swallowed by a whirlpool of symbols. We no longer obtain definite reproductions of the known world, but circulate in an atmosphere of subconscious intuition charged with emotions too delicate for a normal heart to register. The full meaning of his symbolic poems cannot be divined. "**The Tale Died**" admits of as many explanations as we wish to give to it. "**Rise, Ebony Moon**" is the record of a mood where the opening bracket seems to represent the black moon. "**The White Lotus-Flowers**" takes us to a fairyland where castles slowly revolve on an immense duck's foot. "**The Compulsory Hercules**" escapes logical analysis. "**A Fight with the Great Lord**" is, like "**Old Ancestor Envy**", a combat between the poet and a fiend—this time not the past of his race, but gold and its purchasing value, symbolized by a dreadful monster half man, half swine. "**In Front of Prince Silence**" reveals the instinctive fear which we all have felt once at least in our lives of being followed and yet not daring to look back. . . . "**The Dance of the Widower-Bachelors**" is a wild dream in which weird, inhuman creatures, misunderstood in life, dance about at the hour of midnight when the restless bats are screeching and vanish at dawn, leaving behind them no traces of existence save a few drops of blood, a tear or two, and a sheet of mad verses. "**The Black Piano**" is the scapegoat of modern Hungarian literature, and is considered as a perfect example of Ady's ravings. Yet it seems that with a little good will and poetic feelings we should have no difficulty in understanding, if not all the words, at least the mood in which it was composed.

The reader of the poems contained in "**New Verses**" is either puzzled, shocked or exasperated. Ady gives us no time to breathe. From the very first line he discards the usual insipid images of his predecessors and throws himself body and soul into his own inaccessible world. The first poem of "**New Verses**" is perhaps one of the most difficult to understand for a foreigner.

"I am the son of Gog and Magog" he exclaims. This provides us at once with food for thought. What does he mean by claiming himself to be the offspring of such an evil power who, according to St. John the Divine, will rise to mutiny? Let us explain. In Ezekiel XXXV Gog is a mighty prince who menaces invasion at the head of a coalition of people. Josephus said that they were the Scythians. Later on, Christian writers, delving in exegetics, pinned the characteristics of these peoples on to the Asiatic races invading Europe among whom were the Hungarians. So Ady uses this line to say that he is a Hungarian seen through the history of Western Europe. (pp. 9-12)

Whether under the influence of the French *décadents,* or by his own genial intuition, it is an undeniable fact that he acquired specific conceptions of prosody unknown until then to the Hungarian public. He adheres to the principles exposed by Verlaine in his "Art poétique", the basis of which was the systematic use of impair syllables.

Ady is the Lucifer of form. His poems are consequent and as true to their own internal laws as to the severest of classical limitations. The regularity of his irregularity is imposing. (pp. 13-14)

> *René Bonnerjea, in his introduction to* Poems *by Endre Ady, translated by René Bonnerjea (copyright 1941 by Dr. George Vajna & Co.; reprinted by permission of René Bonnerjea), Dr. Vajna & Bokor Publishers, 1941, pp. 3-16.*

JOSEPH REMÉNYI (essay date 1944)

[*The following excerpt provides a critical survey of Ady's poetry. Reményi emphasizes the personal and poetic qualities which made Ady a literary innovator.*]

As a student of law in Debrecen and as a reporter in Nagyvárad, [Ady's] aesthetic taste was in accord with the problematical romantic effusion of his older poetic confreres. In his first collection of poems, entitled *Versek (Poems),* he succumbed to the falsehood of sentimental platitudes; in their nationalistic implications his poems did not differ from the glibly expressed patriotic impulses of other popular poets. He produced articles and verses with the quickness of his lyrical temperament, utterly unaware of his own possibilities. (p. 196)

After the publication of his second volume, entitled *Még egyszer* **(Once More),** Endre Ady showed signs of political orientation which was not his primary interest, but was sufficiently strong to center much of his attention upon the activities of those political and social forces which fought reactionism or conservative nationalism. Though his political intuition was keen, Ady's relationship to civic problems was first of all that of a humane poet whose sense of form would have felt alien to its purpose without an awareness of social injustice. Like Schiller or Shelley, his idealism assumed the realization of human values which from the standpoint of pragmatic politics seemed too complex to be too easily solved. His wisdom was humane; but it was also creative, transcending the horizon of those whose mental and moral range was solely political. (p. 197)

If Ady were but the embodiment of Western European poetic symbolism transplanted into Hungary, he would only signify newness in relationship to Hungarian literature. Hungary had great poets in the past, but previous to Ady there was no poet who found and suggested so much delight in verbal shades as this descendant of small landowners and Calvinistic ministers. He was a challenge to the poetic conservatism of his predecessors. He had qualities which overcame the limits of an isolated tongue and showed in proper perspective the paradox of a somewhat belated poetic symbolism. (p. 198)

Ady saw the anachronism of many Hungarian views and institutions. He himself was apt to dramatize his own "gentlemanliness." He was obsessed with inordinate pride, viewing the world through the nervous temperament of a poet. But he also had deep sympathies. His amour with a married woman whom he named Léda and later his marriage to a considerably younger woman were as much a part of his intense conflict with fate as his opposition to the interests of the Hungarian ruling class, or his awareness of the plight of the underprivileged in the framework of Hungarian society. . . . Between the first and second World Wars, literary critics in the Little Entente countries, surely not favoring the Hungarian *status quo,* found valid material and poetic wealth in Ady's work. Ady's eroticism, narcissistic sensitiveness, and occasional pointedness are proofs of the contradictory components of his character; his yearning for God shows a stormy soul in search of peace.

In his majestic poem, **"Az ős kaján" (The Old Malign),** Ady fought his ancient tempter and seducer. But there is also a gay, pagan melodiousness in this archenemy. In comparison with the decadent poets of the *fin-de-siècle,* Ady's personality seems more vital than theirs. His nation was not spared his indictments. His symbolism transcended the expression of the complicated ego of a highly impressionable individual; it unfolded the image of Hungary, victimized by outer and inner forces. This explains why Ady should be called the apocalyptic poet of modern Hungary. He rose above most of his contemporaries not through learning (Mihály Babits, the classicist, had more erudition and intellectual keenness), not through a balanced orientation in the wilderness of political, social, and economic problems (others were better equipped for scientific thinking and pragmatic understanding); he rose above most of his contemporaries because his utterances took the form of concentrated imagination and emotion and turned the pathos of his national and personal destiny into a constructive symbol. While the "sober"-minded rationalized the position of Hungary in the Danubian valley with the practice of experienced politicians

("the little men of the moment"), Ady sometimes seemed possessed in a Dostoevskian sense.

In discussing Ady as a poet it should be stressed that his expression records music and color. His words have a provoking magic. One can read much into them because of their intrinsic imaginative value. His ravaged spirit sometimes abandoned the desire to outsmart perilous traps; sometimes it induced him to renounce his own world and the world at large. But as a poet he had always enough stamina to remain loyal to the integrity of words. In his most enervated and enervating moods he had sufficient energy to translate the condition of his spirit into poetry. There is a peculiar Hungarianism in his cadence and blazing unhappiness which suggests a Magyar hearth turned to ashes. His poetic diction is Hungarian and Western European; it also shows reminiscences of the Hungarian-Calvinistic edition of the Scriptures and of folk songs. Here and there, mainly when he excels in tour de force, he aims to discover a remedy for his "modern ills" in Hungarian mythology. Some of these poems seem fabricated, suggesting an arbitrary escape from the Occident. Generally, however, his spontaneity or careful articulation is symbolized by the vocabulary of a sincere poet, whose mainspring of expression was the cleavage between his sense of values and the sense of values of those in power. (pp. 199-201)

The homocentric force of nationalism, probably as an accompaniment of a small nation's instinct for self-preservation, deterred Hungarian poets from consistently applying the doctrine of art for art's sake. The reappearing motif in the work of every Hungarian poet is the acceptance of a line of conduct that connects the poet with the rhythm of his nation. Even an innovator like Ady, an innovator who as a patriot and a poet exasperated many people, echoes the overtones of nationalism with a voice that would sound incongruous in the poetry of "pure poets" who live and create in the West under more favorable circumstances. (p. 201)

There is austerity in the admission of Ady that it would be deceptive for a Hungarian poet to emphasize solely his personal problems. When one studies his volumes in chronological order, the landscape of his spirit changes, except in one respect: the spirit always indicates a return to Hungarian roots. The familiar theme of patriotism, sometimes forced to rhetorical expressions, shows effects of a tradition which is stronger than the attributes of pure art. Ady rarely knew real peace for any length of time, but when he found it his wrestling spirit rested on the strength that arose from his village past. His complex character made him different from his ancestors, yet he found comfort in memories related to his birthplace. Nevertheless, he could not forget the lack of understanding and the sad fact that so many Hungarian values were destroyed in the material poverty and depressing aesthetic insensitiveness of life. A poem, entitled **"A magyar messiások" (The Magyar Messiahs)** is a revealing example of his fatal Hungarianism. . . . This romantic voice and prophetic fervor, this frightening uneasiness, characterizes much of Ady's work. Even in translation one senses that the subject matter of tragic despair urges the poet to examine and castigate himself and through himself his own nation, while creating poetry. (pp. 201-02)

The ideological and emotional components of his poetry show the contrast between the need for salvation and nihilistic indifference, sensuality and restraint, faith and lack of faith, vitality and aridity, a spiritual nostalgia for Catholicism and an adherence to Calvinistic dignity, a childlike need for God and a pagan separation from Christianity, a baffling simplicity and a phraseological artificiality. He sang with the voice of an accuser and a confessor. It is no wonder that his admonitions and his wrestling with the spirit of life confused his enemies and stirred his friends. He himself said, "I claim no relative." In the same poem he declared, "I yearn for the love of others." He experienced brutal or hypersensitive sensations with a sensuous imagery. But one must draw a line between unconcealed revelations of an almost fierce emphasis upon pleasures and the expression of real love that knew humbleness and gratitude. How well he understood the varied moods of nature; the grayness of the Hungarian dawn and the softness of twilight; the loveliness of a Parisian autumn; the colors of the Mediterranean Sea. The boundaries of his excitements were limitless; the ardor of his manner was that of a man standing at the precipice of destiny. When the *dies irae* seemed inevitable, when the day of punishment seemed to threaten Hungary with annihilation, he turned to God with a singleness of devotion, thus bracing himself against the death of his nation and his own death.

Throughout the years of his poetic evolution and maturity, constantly seeking escape from the burdensome stupidities and unfairness of his environment, there were two symbols that followed Ady with fantastic consistency. With a cursing madness he at times turned to sensuality and alcohol or sang about the pursuit of money of which he never had enough; then, with a brave fervency, he discovered nobility in the lot of a small nation and in the position that the poets of a small nation occupy. There was logic in Ady's seeming inconsistencies; it was the logic of a conscience struggling with dejection and with a will to live. It is apparent that his sentiments and his thoughts were human, all too human. The memory of a Hungarian Atlantis, confronted by the somber and careless reality of modern times, compelled his imagination to yield to the urge of expression, making of his perception and images the poetic protagonists of truth and justice. His weird lamentations, his desolateness, his shadowy and vital passions, his manners and mannerisms, have their parallels in Western poets. Ernest Dowson's desire for "madder music and stronger wine" and Charles Baudelaire's "accentuation of vice with horror" were experiences that also motivated Ady's spirit. But whatever is supreme in Ady's poetry, whatever expresses his total personality, defies the sick magnitude of his symbolist confreres. His humanitarian Hungarianism rebelled against the nightmarish symbolism of mere poetic self-centeredness. (pp. 202-03)

Ady's symbolism was not the technique of a clever versifier, trained in the particular poetic vanities, ennuis, or intricacies of the West. It was the natural expression of a poet's experience who interpreted life in tragic terms, and to whom in relation to truth and justice, images and subtle phrases, the freedom of verbs and adjectives and nouns, were as necessary as good taste is necessary to those whose attitude resents vulgarity but whose intelligence and candidness cannot ignore its recognition in the scheme of things. In other words, the "outer show and the inner fact" in Ady are not separated by a curtain of pretense. Had he been only a poet of faultless composition, or of a spiritual underworld poetically hypnotizing the inferno of the outer world, he would have been a minor poet endowed with a major sensibility; but his private and his poetic life was organically one. It was also one with the heroism, grief, and helplessness of his nation. He consecrated his life to poetry; but poetry, life, and his native land were inextricable parts of his being, equal in value and importance. Some of his poetry is outlived; more of it may be outlived in the future. Nevertheless, whatever is good and great in his work is perfection attained by means of an honest, uncompromising expression.

One discerns this absolute indentification between experience and expression in John Donne and William Blake. Ady more than any other poet in modern Hungary exercised the gift of human and poetic responsibilities on an identical plane.

In a critical and narrative interpretation of his work it is almost impossible to give an adequate picture of the identity of Ady's human self and poetic genius. An attempt can be made. His first significant book, *Új versek* **(New Poems),** contains a poem in which he apostrophizes himself as the son of Góg and Magóg, stressing his singing mission at the foothills of the Carpathian Mountains. It is defiant in tone, imbued with strength and vision; a yes-saying poem, vindicating its newness, its Hungarianism, and its victorious spirit. In his last volume, published while he was still living, entitled *A halottak élén* **(In the Vanguard of the Dead),** there is a pulsing, deep poem, **"Ifjú szivekben élek" (I Live in the Heart of the Young),** in which he tells of his eternal life that will find sanctuary in the heart of young people. Between the self-assertion of the first poem, conditioned by pride, and the latter, conditioned by humility, there is a vista of mental and emotional voyages, the beginning and the end. But the vatic voice remained true to itself. It was inherent in the character and temperament of Ady to comment upon things and events with a romantic intonation. His emotional intensity did not change, though it found release in wonders and beauties, in irony, and in despising the mean.

The restless symbolism of his first volume was followed by the stubborn materialism of *Vér és arany* **(Blood and Gold).** Ady was always terribly in earnest. His absorption with sensual materialism, his biting disgust with and derision for the ruling class that did not wish to alter its way of life, was balanced by his vision of rural loveliness and by his sense of Hungarian solitude finding sustenance in brave dreams. He could write with a Coleridge-like imaginative sensitiveness, as for instance his poem, **"Jó csöndherceg előtt" (In Front of the Silence-Prince)** indicates. (pp. 203-04)

In the volume *Ifal Az Illés szekerén* **(In the Chariot of Elijah),** Ady's religious nostalgia produced unexpected images, visualizing enduring values. He did not set himself apart from the rest of humanity; in fact, he expressed a noble view about man's place in the universe. Yet in the midst of his awakened religiousness he was unable to forswear his Hungarian bitterness. In a tender poem, **"A téli Magyarország" (Hungary in Winter),** he envisions the nearing sleep of his soul beneath the snow, and he tells about dreamless Hungarian homesteads; as dreamless as the world expects him to be. One is reminded of Gogol's words about nineteenth-century Russia. In this same volume Ady has his testament. He leaves the anger of his poor heart and the wealth of his love to someone who will be a good Hungarian precisely because his environment did not consider him a good one. Ady's personal worries, all his neurotic outbursts, seemed unable to overcome his permanent awareness of Hungary's tragic fate. This was the leitmotif of his poetry; this signified his uniqueness. He withheld nothing when his sorrow challenged the maniacal senselessness of wrong policies and conditions. He did not hate mankind as Swift did, but he hated inhuman thoughts and actions.

Some poems foreshadowed the centrifugal force of his later work, that is, the tendency to develop in the direction of God. He needed God as a comrade-in-arms, reassuring the poet in his just fight with his enemies. **"Ádám, hol vagy?" (Adam, Where Art Thou?)** is a manifestly successful expression of this state of mind. (p. 205)

In each volume, regardless of its characteristic pattern, the poet's allegiance to death is recognizable. It is a magic attachment, a reverence for the mysterious, a courtesy toward the unknown. His images have primeval quality; they are serene and subtle, poetic and dramatic. The poem "A halál lovai" (The Horses of Death) exemplifies that trait of Ady's spirit which shows a self-conscious artistic co-ordination with an intuitiveness which can produce suggestive meaning. (p. 206)

In the volume *Szeretném, ha szeretnének* (I Wish to Be Loved) all that has passed in his life, all that rhymed with pain and longing, with hope and disillusionment, with love and a shivering loneliness, returned with a sense of impending doom and a demand for the triumph of affection. The poet mastered his medium of symbolist expression; in some of his poems he rivaled the best of Western European poets. The hazy or sunny suggestiveness of his poems was an expression of lyric beauty, faithful to his ecstasy and emotional pensiveness. Ady sings about his lonely countrymen, meeting in small groups, tasting bitter tears. He sings about the old whom he envies and dreams about final silence. In "Séta bölcső-helyem körül" (Walk Around My Birthplace) he remembers his birthplace. . . . In the next volume, *A minden-titkok verseiből* (From the Verses of All Mysteries), he faces a stern eternity. He wants to believe in God, though he somehow lost this faith. Again his Hungarian consciousness returns. Sometimes we hear the high-pitched voice of Jeremiah; to be sure, of a very complicated Jeremiah. In this volume, and in the following one, *A menekülő élet* (Fugitive Life), there is strife and turmoil, but there are also gentle, *clair-obscure* poems, and meditative poems, bidding farewell to life, expressing great sorrow and an attempt to make peace with the inevitable.

The volume *A magunk szerelme* (Our Love) shows Ady as a poetic figure, hesitating and dreaming about the purpose of his pilgrimage. In a poem, "Fekete virágot lattál" (You Saw a Black Flower), he cries out with a sadness that comes from the depth of a despondent spirit. He sees his heart as a black flower on the market place; he sings about his exhausted heart, plucked by purity. In his volume *Ki látott engem?* (Has Anyone Seen Me?) he sighs with the burden of centuries, yet loves his people with a gentle acceptance of their lapses and defects. The poem "Ad az Isten" (The Lord Gives) is a direct expression of this feeling and state of mind. In the volume *A halottak élén* (In the Vanguard of the Dead) much of his sorrow lies unburied, much of his plight is the prey of hopelessness. But he knows it is his appointed task to safeguard beauty. The poem "Intés az őrzőkhöz" (A Reminder to the Watchers) shows the purpose of his suffering; he asks those who have placed their faith in him not to abandon their convictions. The most extraordinary poem in this volume is "Emlé-kezés egy nyáréjszakára" (The Memory of a Summer Night). It is a strong, profound, feverish poem, inspired by pacifism. The symbol of war is made analogous with a fantastic night, whose blackness devoured the universe. As if destiny did not know what to do; the poet sings, wide awake and restless; he sings of this strange night, when everything deeply alive was sleepless. Indeed, a strange night. The volume reveals an irreconcilable attitude toward trifles and toward quests that are meaningless; the poet is seen marching at the head of the dead, reaffirming his need for faith. He wants Christ, he wants love and life, he wants every experience that a human being is able to have. Finally, like a person acquitted after a long and uncertain cosmic trial, he consciously and unconsciously communicates with a symbol that one might designate as the mastery of mystery. He cannot be absorbed by the multitude; he

must be alone, but there is humbleness in his declaration, reticence about icy superiority, a tried soul's anguish and submissiveness in the presence of the incomprehensible, a consciousness of eternal realities. In his posthumous volume, *Az utolsó hajók* (The Last Ships), this vision is completed. (pp. 207-08)

Though his writings are definitely lyrical and display love and contempt for the world in a manner that mixes iconoclastic views with troubled innocence, in his study on Ady, Aladár Schöpflin, the well-known Hungarian critic, pointed out that there is also intense drama and a ballad-like quality in certain poems of Ady's. Other critics recognized the same characteristics. In a magnificent poem, "Harc a Nagyúrral" (Fight with the Great One), the poet records his gigantic struggle with the "boar-headed Mighty," the dreamless monster. There is tension and action in the ten stanzas of this poem, and sustained concentration. The momentum of the poem carries one in the direction of a pure heart, in fear of Moloch who expects every human sacrifice for the pleasure of his own power. The poem signifies Ady's insistence of his conviction that the materialistic demands of modern society make one's ego violent, shrewd, and ugly and pursue the human conscience with the tenacity of a slimy adventurer. Notwithstanding these dramatic and ballad-like qualities of Ady's poems, the majority of them should be considered lyrical in a concrete and an elusive sense. He either used the rhythmical structure of traditional Hungarian lyrics or the iambic meter, often in combination with other meters. He was apt to make use of irregular measures. His resourcefulness was metrically expressive. (p. 209)

The enigma of human life compelled him to express himself in a manner that in its tenseness and terseness reflected an eclectic disposition with a homogeneous direction. . . . Not only Hungary but the rest of Europe was in dire need of redemption. Ady was the poet who recognized and expressed this need for redemption in his native country.

He had no desire to sermonize, so he sang. In an age of disintegration he himself, as poet and as citizen, showed manifestations of disintegration. Sometimes his spirit walked on crutches, often it had wings. His contradictions were the mysteries of unhappiness; the unhappiness not of a weak person but of a strong man pursued by weakness that overpowered him. In retrospect so much of his sorrow and suffering seem the expression of a man purposefully driven into neurosis. From these chaotic conditions he emerged with the reputation of a true poet; so much so that for several years it was actually embarrassing to criticize anything he wrote, as his followers considered this almost sacrilegious. (pp. 209-10)

Ady's singular contributions to Hungarian literature are undeniable. His significance, as the poetic incarnation of twentieth-century Hungary and that country's relationship to her neighbors, is now admitted even by those who otherwise ignore poetry. Ady was not "modern" according to postwar "isms." The exponents of various isms and the younger poets adhering to the theory of neoclassical equilibrium were somewhat irritated by Ady's haunted and haunting symbolism. A Central European nation, at the borderline of the Balkans, is epitomized by Ady with such anxiety and courage that it makes one uncomfortable. But Ady also epitomizes the darkness of a civilization and culture that was in great need of a poet's love, integrity, and light. Much of his poetry and his journalistic and hectic prose is only biographically important; much of his work is apparently a versified erratic culmination of honest dissatisfaction and righteousness. Nonetheless, the sum total of Ady's poetry implies uniqueness, passion, delicacy, devotion, beauty, in many instances creative greatness. (pp. 210-11)

> Joseph Reményi, *"Endre Ady, Apocalyptic Poet (1877-1919),"* in The Slavonic and East European Review (© University of London (School of Slavonic and East European Studies) 1944; reprinted by permission), Vol. XXII, No. 58, May, 1944 (and reprinted in his Hungarian Writers and Literature: Modern Novelists, Critics, and Poets, *edited by August J. Molnar, Rutgers University Press, 1964, pp. 193-212).*

LÁSZLÓ BÓKA   (essay date 1962)

[*Bóka discusses Ady's distinctive use of a "system of symbols," which differs from the classic French Symbolism in that Ady's symbols consistently possess the same meaning throughout his poetry.*]

One of the characteristic features of Ady's poetry is that he wrote very many political poems. At least one, but sometimes even two cycles in his volumes of verse consist of poems with a political subject. And these poems on political subjects are not about general political ideals—liberty, national independence, social progress, etc.—but are linked to everyday political events. He cursed the prime minister with the passion of an Old Testament prophet, called the Minister of the Interior a lackey, wrote a menacing poem to the Chief of Staff on the occasion of some manoeuvres, and devoted a cycle in verse to a political demonstration. The West European reader—estranged even from Dante, whose political fervour constructed the Inferno, Purgatory and Paradise—, the present-day reader, bored by the political allusions of Byron himself, will find Ady's political poetry odd reading indeed, particularly if he is not Hungarian and requires explanatory notes to tell him that when Ady talks of a fool or a scroundrel, this must be understood to mean Count István Tisza, then Hungarian premier of the Austro-Hungarian Hapsburg monarchy. (pp. 83-4)

Another feature that has now also become an obstacle to Ady's international recognition is that a considerable part of his poetry is couched in the language of symbolism. As a literary trend, symbolism is now outdated and European poetry has long entered on different paths. But those Western readers in whom an interest in Ady has arisen thus find it peculiar that Ady should have appeared on the scene as a symbolistic poet towards the middle of the 'nineties and essentially remained one to his death, at the eve of the 'twenties. For symbolism had really flourished in the 'eighties and 'nineties, so that Ady's symbolism is felt to have been anachronistic even in his own age. Those who today endeavour to popularize Ady must also take this source of aversion into account, and of this your author is well aware. Before embarking on any account of Ady's poetry—for it is only through this that his symbolism can be explained—it is therefore necessary first to draw attention to this very anachronism and belatedness. Ady's symbolism is not identical with the literary trend that is hallmarked by the names of Mallarmé, Moréas, Maeterlinck, Yeats, Ruben Darío and Sologub. Ady's relatively late symbolism indicates that in his creative work symbolism was to some extent transformed. With him, for instance, musical effects, suggestive twilights, ambiguities and visionary effects no longer play anything like the decisive part they did in "classical" symbolism, and Ady's poetry was in direct contradiction to the aesthetic program of *L'art pour l' art* writing, of "*poésie pure.*" Those who are opposed to symbolism in general need have no preconceived aversion to Ady's poetry. (p. 85)

The young Endre Ady set out on his path without illusions and ideals, without appropriate aims or real opportunities, and he became what he could. He abandoned his law studies to become a journalist (beginning his career as the correspondent of Government and politely oppositional papers) and also set out on the path of literature, achieving success in official quarters. If we now, in the knowledge of the whole of his poetry, peruse his first two volumes of verse—[**Versek (*"Poems"*)** and **Még egyszer (*"Once Again"*)**] . . . —we may discover traces of the lion's claws that were to be the possession of the great poet of later years, but we can feel no surprise whatever that these little volumes earned official recognition when they appeared. As a whole they fit into the customary pattern of contemporary poetry, and Ady is here no more than a gifted epigon of epigon poets. It was not these poems that betrayed his gifts, but the fact that he himself rapidly became disillusioned with his first successes, wrote ever fewer poems, and in one of his own autobiographic essays openly declared that he had desisted purposely from writing because he had not been content with the results he could achieve by progressing along the conventional paths of poetry.

He began as an insignificant poet, but was then already an excellent journalist.

He was rendered an excellent journalist by qualities that were later also to play an important part in developing his poetical gifts. This young columnist, who rapidly advanced from being the correspondent of insignificant provincial papers to become a celebrated contributor to the largest Budapest dailies, had three virtues to distinguish him from the ranks of the foot-sloggers of journalism. It is now with amazement that we read the articles he wrote at the turn of the century in the isolation of a small township, and this mainly because they bear witness to such very broad interests and knowledge. He was interested in everything and able to become conversant with the salient facts in next to no time. What he had once learned was not acquired for a particular occasion only, but actively continued to persist in his thought, as though it had been incorporated in a special system of logic whose internal organization rendered it accessible at any instant. This wide-spread, rapid and lasting facility for acquiring information was accompanied by the lightning alacrity of a clever mind. He was matchless in his readiness to appreciate the special and singular consequences of general phenomena and to find the way from individual, apparently random events, to the general phenomenon. While his inquiring spirit was that of a newsman, his intellect was the philosopher's, using a uniquely dialectical approach to discover the link between the singular and the universal. It was his third quality, however, that made him ferocious as a columnist: his pen was guided by indomitable moral courage. . . . He struck no bargain over truth with either those who paid him or the mighty men of politics. He would not palliate even his harshest sentences and was obedient only to his pen—the "steel-nibbed devil."

Even if he had remained a journalist, our literature would have recorded his name. And for a long time it did, in fact, appear as though he would be no more than a brilliantly gifted columnist. (pp. 87-9)

The first scientific appraisal, written by János Horváth in [Ady's] lifetime, after the appearance of his first three volumes of poetry, and published in 1910, bore the title *Ady s a legújabb magyar lyra* ("Ady and the Latest Hungarian Poetry"). After Ady's death, Lajos Hatvany in 1924 began a powerful series of essays about Ady, entitled *Ady világa* ("Ady's World").

In 1949 Gyula Földessy published his commentaries on Ady in his book *Ady minden titkai* ("All Ady's secrets"). My aim is not to write about the philological literature concerned with Ady and I shall not, therefore, continue the list—it is to the titles that I should like to draw attention. The title of Horváth's work indicates that as soon as Ady appeared on the scene everyone looked upon his poetry as the opening of a new epoch and considered that its effect would be the hall-mark of his generation. The titles of the books by Hatvany and Földessy, moreover, show those who wrote in appreciation of Ady's work to have been well aware that the essence of this poetry was a kind of fullness and universality, that Ady cannot be appreciated by taking this or that quality separately, and that the value lies not in his work as a whole, but in the composed unity in which he wrote his works.

Ady's poetic works are—however strange it may sound to say this of a lyricist—a composition. Not a composition in the sense that a novel or a play are, but like a philosophical system, or a Baroque wall painting, or like a piece by Bach. Everything has its well-defined place and form in it. Does this mean that his lyrical poems are not independent, complete works but only parts of a string of poems? No. Each of his poems is an independent, lyrical unit, conceived in a unique mood. But beyond this independence, each poem somehow fits into a system of visions. There is a poem of Ady's called *A Tisza-parton* ("On the banks of the Tisza"), which was published in the first volume. (p. 94)

[The poem's opening stanza] is a regular, beautiful, symbolistic, lyrical image, with the exoticism of the distant Ganges' shores and the tremors of an enigmatic flower. The reader is not even struck by the strangeness of using the harebell's blossom as the symbol of a man's heart. Yet eight years after the publication of his first collection, in the volume entitled **"Our Own Love"**, one of his love poems begins thus:

> Black was the blossom you sighted,
> Strange to behold, so you plucked it,
> Pardon be granted by a libertine God,
> Sin if you thus did.

It appears from the poem that this black blossom is the poet's heart (the next stanza begins: "A heart you saw . . . My heart it was . . ."), and it is now obvious that in contrast to the stereotyped poetic imagery, here it is the man's heart that is the flower, and the woman who plucks it. **"On the banks of the Tisza"** is an early political poem in which the dreamland of the Ganges' shore is used to counterpoint the barrenness in Hungary, **"Black was the blossom you sighted"** is a late love poem, yet in the peculiar internal order of Ady's world it is always the poet's heart that is the strange flower to be plucked.

Even this single example is sufficient to suggest wherein Ady's symbolism differs from the poetic practice of the symbolists. Ady's were not individual symbols, but his poetry is itself one vast system of symbols. For the symbol appears not on a single occasion only, but consistently and always with identical meaning. (p. 95)

However, this extraordinarily well defined poetic world does not grow rigid or static, for the coherent force of the poet's view of the world is that of the "either-or" presentation—Ady's world is a system of dialectical opposites. He once called himself "Apollo, the faun-costumed," and on another occasion described himself as a "Nightingale-masked gull". (p. 96)

It is sufficient to read the titles of some of his poems for it to become obvious that the inner structure of this poetry is provided by setting opposites against each other. (**"Judas and Jesus," "Snowy Mountains and Riviera," "Blood and Gold," "Eternal Struggle and Honeymoon," "Mary and Veronica," "Ruth and Delilah," "Flower of Death: the Kiss," "Laughter and Tears," "Starling and Dove," "Kissless Living in Kisses."**) . . . It is not that Ady found special pleasure in seeking for opposites and setting them against each other, and in exacerbating extremes. One of Ady's special abilities was a by no means superficial dialectical approach which was sensitive not only to the obvious antithesis of mutually distant concepts, but also recognized the interior contradictions within apparently homogeneous phenomena and concepts that had seemed unequivocal. There is a poem of Ady's whose title fits in among those enumerated above and which sheds a penetrating light on this dialectically constructed world of the poet: **"Unbelieving I Believe in God."** Ady is a past master at this. No one has so consistently set forth the interior contradictions of contemporary man and of his complex spiritual life, with its unbelieving belief and doubting hope and the alternatives of individualism or collectivism, as he did. . . . (pp. 96-7)

And this dialectical approach was manifested in all the structural parts of his poetry, from the themes to the poetic idiom he used. Ady wrote the most militant, confident revolutionary poems that had appeared in Hungarian since [Sándor] Petőffi; but it was also he who wrote the most pessimistic poems, prophesying final destruction. Ady was the great bard of the mood of the outlying, mute Hungarian villages and sleepy provincial townships, but it was also he who first made the complex spiritual entity and the nervous vital rhythm of modern metropolitan man a lyrical subject in Hungarian poetry. He was the most consistent poet of anti-feudal, radical bourgeois revolutionism, but it was also in his verse that the anti-capitalist, socialist class struggle was first voiced in elevated, poetic tones. Ady was a haughty individualist and at the same time he proffered his heart to the masses in the tender lyricism of his love poems. And I must repeat that this strange dialectic was manifested down to the elemental particles of his poetic forms and poetic idiom. Ady remained immune to the strivings of his period for the disruption of traditional forms and never wrote free verse—he always wrote in close forms. Within this closeness of form, however, he carried out a veritable revolution in forms—almost each of his poems has a different stanza construction. According to statistics compiled by Gyula Földessy he created some eight hundred kinds of poetic structure, disrupting the traditional rhythms of the poems by making lines with even and odd numbers of syllables rhyme, and introducing startling dissonancies. In his poems the West European quantitative metre and the Hungarian stressed metre are constantly intertwined. The poetic vocabulary of his verse shows a similar strange duality—his poems are full of the common words of modern life, and he was not averse even to city slang, yet at the same time he also used the ancient, forgotten words of the Hungarian language and rarely-heard, full-flavoured dialect expressions. (pp. 97-8)

We have already spoken of Ady's peculiar symbolism. The function of symbolic expression in poetry is that the poet clothes a particular phenomenon, hard to define conceptually or in time and space, in a perceptible, visual symbol, whose mood suggests that which the conceptual definition cannot yet precisely define. The symbols with which Ady strove to express his new view of the world are mainly derived from three sets of ideas—the religious mythologies, the Hungarian historical and legendary past, and the names of characteristic Hungarian regions. Hungarian readers, who in Ady's age were well versed in Biblical lore, were familiar with the story of Hagar, Abraham's Egyptian servant, who was the embodiment of extramarital love and of alienness in Jewish mythology. Ady wrote one of his most profound confessions on the erotic love of modern man in his symbolic poem *A Hágár oltára* ("**The Altar of Hagar**"). One of the tragic figures of Hungarian history was György Dózsa, the hero of the greatest Hungarian peasant revolution, whom the state authority of his day, the feudal peers thirsting for revenge, burnt alive on a throne of fire. When Ady became the spokesman of the new revolutionism of the century, he began one of his first revolutionary poems by declaring, "I am the grandson of György Dózsa," and he frequently calls the proletariat "Dózsa's folk." (pp. 98-9)

The examples clearly show that we are here concerned with a consistent poetic method—the more unknown, the more strange to public thought, the more startling through its novelty the idea which he voiced in his poetry, the more he turned to the deepest, atavistic layers of common knowledge for his symbols. This corresponds to the dialectical approach that unites polar opposites, and at the same time by no means lessens the visionary and suggestive power of his symbols. To the public's mind Dózsa's name recalls a bloody revolutionary struggle, but when a twentieth century poet calls himself the grandson of György Dózsa, then, beside the automatic evocation of a revolutionary mood, the reader is also made to feel that he has now encountered a new, a different phenomenon, familiar, even in its unfamiliarity.

Another proof that this is a case of the poet's composition is the cyclic arrangement of Ady's volumes. They usually begin with a prologue, the striking of a powerful note, characteristic of the whole volume. This is followed by cycles of poems. The cycles, in a sense, respond to one another. In the volume entitled "**The Chariot of Elijah**" there is a cycle called "**Winter Hungary**" which contains poems on the terrible situation of the Hungarian people, while the response is a cycle "**The Song of the Street**," which is a collection of Ady's revolutionary poetry, linked to the labour movement. The same volume contains a cycle entitled "**Between Léda's Lips**" of his love-poems written to Léda, but the volume also has a cycle "**Flower of Death: the Kiss**," devoted to love in general, as a tragic feeling in life. There is a similar dialogue in the volume "**Desire to be Loved**" between the poems of the cycle "**Friend of Tamás Esze**" (Tamás Esze was a leader of peasant extraction in the Rákóczi rising, one of the Hungarian freedom movements) and those of the "**Whites of the future**" cycle, conceived upon the inspiration of the revolutionary labour movement. This, moreover, is how his love for Léda is recalled by the cycle called "**Two Holy Sailing Boats**" and the poet's views on love by the cycle entitled "**The Altar of Hagar**." It is clearly to be seen that this is not simply a case of a highly intellectual poet arranging his poems according to subject, but that—as the mutual responses of the cycles show—the poet confronts the special features (the fate of the Hungarians, his love for Léda) with the general (the world revolution and love).

It was by no means fortuitous for one of our critics to write that Ady's individual poems are beautiful, but that in the unity of the volumes, the unity of his whole life work, they are even more beautiful and significant, because in the system of ceaseless, mutually relevant responses established by the poet's composition, they are given the same radiance that musical notes and chords—melodious in themselves—acquire in the harmonic unity of a symphony. In the course of one of the debates concerned with Ady, his greatest fellow poet, Mihály Babits,

compared Ady's poetry to Dante's *Divina Commedia* and called it an edifice of symbols in which each tone, apart from its intrinsic value, has a value given it by its position—or, in the language of philosophy, a systematic value. (pp. 99-100)

Ady's significance as a poet—this is the significance of every true poet—is that he was able to put into verse his subjective experiences, conceived in the concreteness of time and events, in such a way that, a generation after his death, half a century after these experiences, we are able topically to apply to our own experiences forms and feelings with whose inspiration we no longer have anything in common. He was able to impart eternal forms to human emotions, because he moved among things eternal and wrote of fundamental human feelings. (pp. 107-08)

László Bóka, "Endre Ady and the Present," in The New Hungarian Quarterly *(© The New Hungarian Quarterly, 1962; reprinted by permission of The Hungarian Academy of Sciences), Vol. III, No. 5, January-March, 1962, pp. 83-108.*

MIKLÓS SZABOLCSI (essay date 1962)

[*Szabolcsi's essay focuses on Ady's poetic style and themes, stressing their uniqueness in the literature of Hungary.*]

Ady's poetical world is a self-contained world, his language one that is all his own; the range of his themes is an extremely wide one. One group includes themes like the revolutionary heroes and movements of Hungarian national history; the backwardness of Hungary—the shocking visions of the "Hungarian Fallowland," of the "Hungarian Moorland"; the agony of the poet fighting the "Great Lord with the Boar's Head." Another group of themes: the thousand and one aspects of love, the unashamed presentation of his love for Leda; songs of all the warped complexities of love; and evocations of passing, sensual love-affairs. Another strand is constituted by poems evoking death, fleeting time, fear and solitude; verses that convey the restlessness, the strain and worries, of the modern big-city dweller, his seeking of refuge in God, or his personal quarrel with Him. Lastly, two entirely new themes of crucial importance: the proclamation of his historical mission, a drawing of his own personality, and—crowning his work—the verses of the poet stretching out his hand to the working class.

This is a self-contained world indeed, an entirely new world in Hungarian poetry! In his poems he speaks of himself and of the world around him with a candour, with an ingenuous exhibition of his soul, and with an ardour, that are quite unparalleled in Hungarian letters before him. His poetry grew out of the contradictions of contemporary Hungarian society—and those contradictions it mirrors—and while his poetry and intellectual system undoubtedly owe a good deal to French influences (Baudelaire, Verlaine), and his philosophical system to that of Nietzsche and others, it is absolutely original and unmistakably Hungarian. His basic experience was formed from the sorry plight of the Hungarian people, oppressed, prostrate, exhausted, and the blackguardism of the "well-born cads" who lorded it over them; the haughtiness, the arrogance of the aristocrats of birth and of finance. This was a country, he felt, where you must either be stifled to death or change the set-up boldly, implacably, and although, at times, weariness and disenchantment would overcome him, his revolutionary fervour, his determination to transform conditions, increased steadily. His poetry is charged with the restlessness and suffocating atmosphere of the age, and burns with its yearning for better things, with its feverish revolutionism.

If one were to revert to political terms, one might say that, in a Hungary encumbered with feudal survivals, Ady was championing the cause of a democratic, popular revolution. He felt he was living in a "country all set for an explosion" where "all things are clamouring for transformation, for renewal." He had a deep insight into the problems of being a Hungarian and he felt himself one with his race; he scolded it, castigated it, that he might rouse it from its torpor, stir it to action—he wanted to see his nation advance once again into the van of world progress.

His was a great role indeed, and he played that role with awareness. He had a strong poetic consciousness, a strong sense of vocation; he was one of the race of poet-apostles; and, for all the touches of the Nietzschean superman and Baudelairean Satanism that are evident in his poetic make-up, he was the poet champion of the cause of the people. He was a great individual, a personality integrating sensuality and retirement into quiet love, the lust for money and a hatred for "counts and the rich," and an overriding yearning for a real, full life.

For his individual experience and theme he created a highly individual poetic language and world.

Ady's poetical world is one great forest of symbols. But it is not one in the sense of the Baudelairean *correspondance* and is only too far removed from the French symbolists of the late nineteenth century like Albert Samain, who was in vogue in Hungary. He created a system of symbols, and through them he surveyed the world. These symbols (or, more precisely perhaps, metaphors) were taken from the world of Hungarian realities, of common notions. Under this system of symbols, money become the "God Baal," or "the Great Lord with the Boar's Head," Hungary appears as the "Hungarian Fallow," the "Moorland," "the Slough"; the workers are referred to as "the White Ones of the Future." He built for himself a novel prosody: the accent of his verse is determined by its meaning, but it is pierced by the beat of the Western metre and of old Hungarian verse. On the whole, Ady's poetry is at the same time modern and ancient at the same time it is in the mainstream of the latest European intellectual trends and rooted in the time-honoured core of Magyar tradition. This perfect integration of progress and nationality is of great importance still. His poetical language, too, is new and full of surprise-turns teeming with words taken from the Hungarian linguistic heritage but at the same time endowed with metaphoric qualities. The richness of his store of adjectives, his verbal flow, and the multitude of his own coinages or revivals from the archaic vocabulary of the language combine into a fascinating idiom that is unlike anybody else's.

Following his *début* his poetry grew in power and gradually achieved fulness of development. . . . In Ady's lyrics, his longing for death, the note of fleeing, a feeling of frustration and solitude became more frequent. However, behind the tones of frustration and world-weariness there is always a lurking note of hope; and his poetry seems to grow clearer, more simple, more refined. There began the cycle of his *Kuruc* verses: he deliberately reached back, even in tone, to the Hungarian people's crushed independence struggle, in his desire to give expression to his virile grief over the downfall of the revolution and his fatherland. (pp. 194-98)

In his last poems—those of the volume, *In Death's Fore-ranks,* . . . and of his posthumous volume, *The Last*

Ships, . . .—we hear the voice of the poet, the lone giant, who suffers for the sake of mankind, which he loves passionately. This voice, increasingly simple and sombre, rings with the grim force of the Biblical prophets. It is the voice of a man yearning for peace and rest and at the same time of a poet ready to fight. (p. 198)

Ady's work is of crucial significance for Hungarian letters as a whole: his work could not be directly continued, only imitated by countless epigons, but it has served as the great heritage on which many distinguished later poets have been groomed. By now, Ady's work has come to assume its rightful place in the great heritage of Hungarian revolutionary poetry; and it is felt that the whole seething world of the early twentieth century, the mental struggles—and, in general, the cast of mind—of Modern Man is mirrored in his great work. (pp. 198-99)

> *Miklós Szabolcsi, "The Rise of Modern Hungarian Literature (1905-1914)," translated by István Far-kas, in* History of Hungarian Literature *by Tibor Klaniczay, József Szauder and Miklós Szabolcsi, edited by Miklós Szabolcsi, translated by József Hat-vany and István Farkas (translation © Tibor Klan-iczay, József Szauder and Miklós Szabolcsi, 1964; originally published as* Histoire abrégée de la littér-ature hongroise *by Tibor Klaniczay, József Szauder and Miklós Szabolcsi, edited by Miklós Szabolcsi, Corvina, 1962), Collet's, 1964, pp. 187-228.**

DEZSŐ KERESZTURY   (essay date 1969)

[*Keresztury surveys Ady's work and discusses three recurring themes.*]

The birth of modern Hungarian poetry is justly reckoned from the dates of publication of [Ady's] first three volumes [*Uj versek* **(New Poems)**, *Vér és arany* **(Blood and Gold)**, and *Az Illés szekerén* **(Elijah's Chariot)**]. . . . All the problems of modern existence are expressed in his poetry, with the help of a system of symbols in which elements of the most ancient and most modern mythologies, superstitions, faiths and symbolisms are combined. His is a poetic world at once imaginative and pro-vocative, unapprehensible and fascinating, prolific, yet crys-talline in structure. His language both flows freely and is as concise and mysterious as runes; now trivial to the point of banality, now majestic and arcane as mystical liturgies. The language of Ady's poetry is the idiom of modern poetry, com-plex, unhackneyed, allusive and oblique.

From this the reader may begin to see why this kind of poetry is so hard of access, and why in the renewed discussion on Ady's work the charge of "incomprehensibility" has been levelled once more, on two different grounds. In Hungary his poetry was received with astonished incomprehension or zeal-ous enthusiasm, but in both cases with the kind of perplexity all major innovators have to face. Abroad the specifically Hun-garian character of his poetry hampers or prevents understand-ing: not merely the fact that his poetry is full of references to contemporary topical events in Hungarian life, but also the fact that an integral part of his poetic system of symbols is unknown to the western reader. I emphasize "western" because, as I said earlier, the peoples of the Danube basin find him much more comprehensible, and easier to assimilate and his impact on them has consequently been considerable. To clarify every aspect of his poems would need the same sort of annotation and explanation for the uninformed reader as we need for the *Divine Comedy*.

In the last decade of his short life Ady's poetic horizon widened greatly. In his later volumes [*Szeretném, ha szeretnének* (**I Would Like to Be Loved**), *A minden titkok versei* (**Verses of All Secrets**), *A menekülaio élet* (**Fugitive Life**), *A magunk szerelme* (**Self-Love**), *Ki látott engem?* (**Who Has Seen Me?**)] . . . the themes of the first volumes appear again and again. This is all the clearer since Ady always organized his volumes around cycles of poems, and the same themes re-appear and show their resemblances to one another. Three of these themes, however, were particularly significant and developed in richer and more completely expressive forms.

The love themes became more concrete and imbued with even greater agony. He had married, and he seemed to have found repose in "the haven of young arms." But the shadow of increasing gloom and the resigned anticipation of death fell even on these poems of happy consummation.

His philosophical poetry might seem at first glance the disconnected, delirious confessions, ravings, prophecies of a wild barbarian sage. In reality they are the expressions of the metaphysical agonies, the contemporary frustration and search for faith of the whole of European civilization. "Unbelieving, I believe in God"—this might be said for all of them. These poems gave occasion for more than one critic to rank him among the great religious poets of the century; although, or because, this religious inspiration is free from all the limitations imposed by churches, and a kind of early existentialism plays at least as important a part in it as living Christian traditions. The system of symbols in these poems may therefore be more easily accessible to the Western European reader, since the symbols used are common to all Christianity, and are becoming increasingly well-known in modern literature, especially those found in the Scriptures and in literature, from Nietzsche to Rilke.

The third theme—the dilemmas of the Hungarian destiny—is less accessible, if indeed at all. In this sphere, I repeat, there are many symbols and allusions which are common to Hungarian and East European history. During the First World War Ady, turning against the new Behemoth, total war, warned and wept for Hungary and humanity slipping down on a doomed slope. As he was opposed to the authorities who waged the war he was unable to publish new volumes of poetry for several years. His last collection *A halottak élén* (**In the Vanguard of the Dead** . . .) published while he was still alive, contained a selection of the poetic harvest of those four years. This marked the peak of his career. Dying, he forced his people's destiny and his own to face the ultimate metaphysical powers, threw the authority of his genius into the scales against the horror of the war. His anti-war poetry reached its highest peak in these apocalyptic poems, which expressed the sufferings of the Hungarian people and mankind drowning together in a whirlpool of barbarism. (pp. 52-4)

It is difficult to draw a convincing portrait of Ady for the writers and critics of other nations. This is not merely because his problems, his system of symbols, and his idiom are closely involved with the life and history of the Hungarian people, but also because those values of his poetry which extend beyond this strictly limited world—those which are universal—have no parallel. In part, because the storm of time blew over them and fanned the sparks which had only barely begun to glow in his poems into flames elsewhere. Partly, however, because they represent innovations which have only reappeared in isolated examples of the newest poetry. His contemporaries considered him influenced by the French moderns. For a time he too regarded himself as one of the Symbolists, but in fact they acted on him rather as releasing agents. In Ady's mature poetry Baudelaire's ascetic adoration of beauty, Verlaine's softly vibrating music, Apollinaire's playful surrealism, Mallarmé's taut abstraction are all completely transformed. Ady was their contemporary, not their follower. (pp. 54-5)

Dezső Keresztury, "Endre Ady, 1877-1919," in The New Hungarian Quarterly *(© The New Hungarian Quarterly, 1969; reprinted by permission of The Hungarian Academy of Sciences), Vol. X, No. 35, Autumn, 1969, pp. 49-55.*

GYÖRGY LUKÁCS   (essay date 1969)

[*Lukács, a Hungarian literary critic and philosopher, is acknowledged as one of the leading proponents of Marxist thought. His development of Marxist ideology was part of a broader system of thought which sought to further the values of rationalism (peace and progress), humanism (which Lukács considered synonymous with Socialist politics), and traditionalism (Realist literature) over the counter-values of irrationalism (war), totalitarianism (reactionary politics), and modernism (post-Realist literature). The subjects of his literary criticism are primarily the nineteenth-century Realists—Balzac and Tolstoy—and their twentieth-century counterparts—Gorky and Mann. In major works such as* Studies in European Realism *and* The Historical Novel, *Lukács explicated his belief that "unless art can be made creatively con sonant with history and human needs, it will always offer a counterworld of escape and marvelous waste." In the following excerpt, Lukács assesses Ady's place in world literature.*]

Is Ady archaic in terms of style? Born and bred in a certain epoch, the idioms and the figures of speech of every poet are quite naturally typical of his age. This applies with equal force to Heine, Shelley, Petőfi and Baudelaire, and of course to Ady as well. I must admit that I take a poor view of all those categories of style, and particularly of *Sezession*, *Art Nouveau*, and the like when they are mentioned in connection with Ady. In the metaphors and the vocabulary of Ady obvious marks of the 1900-1918 epoch can be seen; the same, I think, is true of Babits and [Dezső] Kosztolányi, though of course in another form. Any intelligent critic could discover that Ady and Babits were contemporaries.

In analysing lyrical poetry particularly it is fair to say that there is no lyric poet whose poems all reach an equally high standard. . . . From the many hundred poems Ady has written there are—let us exaggerate—perhaps two hundred poems in which these find expression, and these two hundred verses are the intrinsic treasure through which Ady survives. Neither Ady, Petőfi nor any other poet ever became immortal through his collected poetical works. It is sheer rubbish to say Ady is obsolete: he is not out of date at all; but it is true, on the other hand, that he wrote verses in, say, a January issue of *Nyugat* that were already dead in February. This is no disparagement of Ady; it is true of all poets. I believe—and this is again quite another matter—that in Hungary, after the country has truly passed beyond the Stalin era and begun to build a living socialism which relies on a new proletarian democracy, there will be many more people who will become aware that Ady is the poet they like best. Since I read *Új versek* (**New Verses**) in 1906—that is more than sixty years ago—I have not lost touch with Ady for a single day. (p. 60)

Then why is it so difficult to break a way for Ady into world literature? In the first place it is far easier to introduce narrative and dramatic works into world literature through translations.

There are many million people all over the world whose favourite reading is *War and Peace,* the *Iliad* or Swift, of whom only five or ten per cent at most have read these masterpieces in the original language. . . . Lyric poetry, however, can hardly ever be reproduced; that is one of its characteristics. In my youth, when I was closely in touch with all things German, I read French poetry in German, translated by lyric poets of the calibre of Stefan George, and I have to admit that if I had not read Baudelaire in the original, the Stefan George kind of Baudelaire would never have impressed me at all. . . . There are certain things whose emotional accents in French or German are radically different. And this all holds good to an even greater degree in the case of Hungarian, the language of a small people, and its remote literature. . . . [Whether] a writer becomes part of world literature depends on various literary, social, linguistic and other circumstances, and it must be admitted that no Hungarian writer so far has really done it. Petőfi has not, and in Ady's case certain specific additional difficulties arise, for since many of his greatest poems take a profound knowledge of Hungarian development and history for granted, the text would demand a number of annotations if the foreign reader is to understand it and this, particularly in lyric poetry, is an almost unsurmountable barrier. Our particular age, moreover, must also be taken into account. A dislike of elevated style and any compromise with manipulations is a characteristic of modern lyric poets. As a result—with the possible exception of a certain group of French and South American lyric poets— the content of Ady's verse would sound very unfamiliar to contemporary poets. (pp. 61-2)

The great crisis that drew Europe into the First World War was echoed more or less consciously—through a variety of underground channels—in the entire literature of almost the whole world. It is my personal opinion that Ady was the first to react, and to react most effectively, and that Ady is supreme among all those who voiced recalcitrance and the necessity of revolution—hence, Ady is the greatest lyric poet of this age, both humanly and poetically. I have no fear of being branded a chauvinist for expressing this opinion. (p. 63)

> György Lukács, *"The Importance and Influence of Ady," in* The New Hungarian Quarterly (© The New Hungarian Quarterly, *1969; reprinted by permission of The Hungarian Academy of Sciences), Vol. X, No. 35, Autumn, 1969, pp. 56-63.*

LÁSZLÓ FERENCZI   (essay date 1977)

[*Ferenczi examines several of Ady's poetry collections, finding them as relevant today as when they were written.*]

[Ady] was a class-conscious nobleman with a clear conscience, and a Calvinist versed in the doctrine of predestination. As such, he wrote in the 1908-9 volume of the periodical *Szocializmus:* "This new literature, even if it does not seem socialist (it probably is not) from afar and in feudal and bourgeois heads, still exists through and by socialism. Its symbolism and alleged incomprehensibility symbolize what these people cannot and, what is more, do not want to understand. The devil knows only what will happen to this country near the Danube and the Tisza. The devil only knows what this Potemkin interest in literature will add up to. One thing is certain and the author of these lines senses it and acts by it: this literary war is an offspring of the social war—that is why so many fear it (so many and so movingly, ludicrously, a promising sign of beauty and great things for the writers and this sad country.)"

The "new literature" and the "literary war" are linked to the name of Ady. To avoid misunderstanding, Hungarian intellectual life was certainly not barren at the time when Ady appeared. (pp. 26-7)

Poetry was, however, still barren. Young men who pursued their studies at universities, were ready to come forward fully equipped after Ady's first important poetry was published. These perceptive members of the young and old generation made up the staff of the journal *Nyugat* (founded in 1908, wound up in 1941), whose leading member was undoubtedly Ady. *Nyugat* has often been called the Hungarian *Nouvelle Revue Francaise.* Ady's influence was vital from two points of view: he created a new kind of poetry, and changed the political and social views of the large public regarding the role and possibilities of poetry. (p. 27)

After publishing two insignificant collections of poems in 1899 and 1903 (he later wrote that for years he had been afraid to write more poems lest he "should make it to the college of meek poets"), the first really noteworthy book by Ady appeared in 1906, his *Új Versek* (**New Poems**). The book's prologue, which is a prologue to Ady's mature poetry, is a programme and provocation in one:

"I travelled the famous Verecke road, An ancient Hungarian tune still rings in my ear," (prose translation) says the poet, identifying with those said to have come that way a thousand years earlier to settle in present-day Hungary. The poet, returning from Western Europe now wants to break into the country "with the new songs of new times." And this song ". . .should it be condemned by Pusztaszer is nevertheless victorious, still new and yet Hungarian." Pusztaszer—where the conquering Hungarians held their first-ever legislative assembly in the country a thousand years ago—is the symbol of Hungarian backwardness and reaction in the poem. From then on the poet vows to be the "hero of tomorrow" who keeps on demanding "new and new horses" until he dies lest "I turn into a pillar of salt before the wonders of today," he writes in one of his last poems.

Not even Ady was left unaffected by the influence of Baudelaire. In the **"New Poems"** appeared the Hungarian translations of three of Baudelaire's sonnets. Later, in 1917, on the 50th anniversary of Baudelaire's death, he wrote: ". . .he is our suffering, mournful ancestor, Carducci, Swinburne, Dehmel, and the much smaller Bryusov are his direct and undeniable offspring. He encouraged me, as I did others, but I shook him off for his Gallic forms, even though I adored him for them." At the time of the publication of **"New Poems"** and *Vér és Arany* (**Blood and Gold**) . . . Nietzsche was another influence. Especially Zarathustra's creativity carried Ady away to the extent that he expressed from time to time his criticism of Hungarian domestic conditions with Nietzschean symbols. (pp. 29-30)

One of Ady's most personal, self-revealing confessions is to be found in an obituary on Ibsen. Let several passages from the necrologue **"Ibsen Is Dead"** stand here. In parentheses I will quote (in prose) from some poems of Ady to show that the poet reveals the same thing about himself or his nation that he says about Ibsen. They comment on some of his statements. "A grim and magnificent Messiah of the North rebelled for the last time and then died." (Ady called himself Messiah several times.) "The tragedy of his life and personality is twofold. That of the offspring of a ruined family and the son of a small nation." (Both problems worried Ady.) "Nobody has put up a more human and majestic fight with life than the apothecary apprentice of Grimstadt.'' (''We have fought our fight,'' wrote Ady of himself and his Hungarian political allies.) ''It is certain that he suffered much from hunger when young. It is certain that he went through all the calvary stations of exceptional souls. The life of a hundred persons cannot be as rich as his.'' (''He was free a hundred times in a hundred forms,'' he wrote of himself.) (pp. 30-1)

In May 1906 Ady wrote: ''Ibsen soared into the skies as an anti-Elijah: on the carriage of frost.'' In 1908 Ady published a collection entitled *Az Illés szekerén* (**On the Carriage of Elijah**): ''The Lord carries off like Elijah all / Whom he afflicts with his great love: / Their fierily whirling hearts are / Chariots of fire sent from above.'' (p. 32)

The collection was a turning-point in the then mature poet's career. Other collections like **''New Poems''** and **''Blood and Gold''** mainly contained love songs and political verse. Love had never been treated like that in Hungarian, not before Ady. As for the political verse, Ady called Hungary the ''big desert'' where ''the Hungarian Messiahs are a thousand times Messiahs.'' A special feature of the **''Blood and Gold''** cycle was the new tone concerning money in Hungarian poetry and prose, used by Ady. Money and sexuality were taboos which Ady ignored.

The **''On the Carriage of Elijah''** cycle was a turning-point for two reasons. The journalist Ady had from the beginning of the century dealt with the struggle of the proletariat and (more seldom) his own religious problems. But the fact that these problems can be subject of verse and the possibilities of poetry are richer than those of prose, was demonstrated only in **''On the Carriage of Elijah.''**

The second turning-point concerns the Bible. There had been earlier biblical references (''I am sitting by the waters of Babylon'') but it was from 1908 on that the Bible became a regular source of reference for Ady. For the first time the Bible was used to enrich the idiom of modern Hungarian poetry, i.e. the Bible in the beautiful sixteenth-century version by Gáspár Károli as well as Albert Szenczi Molnár's metrical psalms of 1606. From 1908 and rather from 1914 on, Ady declared himself to be the descendant of Old Testament prophets. He used variations and paraphrases of Ezekiel, Jeremiah, Joel, and Hosea among others to express the tragedy of the First World War. The last great period in Ady's poetry coincides with the Great War. His poems of the time are contained in the collections *A halottak élén* (**Heading the Dead . . .**), and the posthumous *Az utolsó hajók* (**The Last Ships . . .**). (pp. 32-3)

Tradition can put shackles on you, or it can inject a new lease of life into you. Tradition gives Ady new strength, he is released through tradition. All of tradition and not just a small fragment. (p. 33)

Despite his noble origin, Ady fought for a bourgeois Hungary, and looked ahead to socialism. He wrote an article on the possible alliance of Calvinism and socialism as early as 1902.

The prologue to the collection *A magunk szerelme* (**The Love of Our Selves, . . .**) is one of Ady's most important poems because he defines his own scale of values and interest in it. Only two things are vital to him: politics and love. (p. 34)

Ady was a contemporary of Freud. To the best of my knowledge, he never wrote his name down, though he must have heard about him. . . . I do not think it was chance that Ady never wrote Freud's name down since he could not have been

of interest to the poet. Freud regarded Nietzsche as the man who knew himself best—and Ady knew his inner self in a Nietzschean way. His origin, education, social position, sense of vocation enabled him not to lie to himself, and face the socio-moral, or as he called it, the ''pseudo-moral'' taboos. He discussed his sexual yearnings as openly as his V.D.

Sexual anguish, characteristic of the Vienna of Freud, almost completely lacked in Ady. Sexuality was not a problem of individual psychology for him, but a political issue. He wrote sarcastically: ''In this awkward country it is patriotism that determines a man's performance as a male.'' He was a proud, handsome male, sure of himself, who even dared to reveal his failures. His constant homelessness and search for companionship was not caused by the lack of sexual partners or by sexual problems. As a journalist at Nagyvárad, he was admired by women. Ady's problems originated apart from sexual issues. Despite the reminiscences of Baudelaire, his poems may be read as if they had been written after the sexual revolution.

All the nuances of mood in the man-woman relationship were recorded in his poems. Ady was yearning after women like Petrarca (he always had a soft spot for the Italian poet), he called women ''the lovely, sustaining'' ships who carry through life, of whom ''none was less—and none of them was worth more.'' He complained that ''Our stimulant, our real self woman has been torn from inside us.'' (pp. 34-5)

Dozens of Ady's love poems ought to be quoted only to intimate the rich variety of his poetry. But poems should inevitably have been cited here that tell infinitely more than any commentary. Experience suggests and Hungarian literary opinion holds that Ady's poetry is untranslatable. Should the future prove the contrary, what is it that does make his translation a tough job?

Ady wrote mostly in rhymed stanzas. There is no other Hungarian poet whose treatment of rhymes, use of stanzas, and within each stanza the length and rhythm of each line, is more varied than his. With some exaggeration one might say that no two poems use an identical technique. In a particular way he transformed the form of expression of seven hundred years of Hungarian lyrical poetry. His technique was influenced by the language of the psalms, the *Kalevala* and the modern French poets. His vocabulary is rich and has several layers, extending from long-forgotten words to the most up-to-date. What's more, he uses them arbitrarily. Ady drew for his images and idiom on the scriptures, classical antiquity, Hungarian folk poetry, the symbols of the contemporary labour movement, the events of Hungarian history, and the works of nineteenth-century poets and philosophers. Each of his poems is a synthesis of the content, rhythm and metaphor of many civilizations. Today, 100 years after his birth and nearly 60 years after his death one gets the impression when reading his best lines that Ady's special language and poetry are being composed under our very eyes.

Obviously no great poet can have an *alter ego*, but there are degrees. It appears to me that of all the Hungarian poets Ady is the least possible to mimic. Malraux says in the *Musée imaginaire* that the truly great artists are like next-of-kin. He probably meant that they are so rich, so versatile that they make the reader, spectator and admirer receptive to new vistas and possibilities. I cannot tell what Ady may possibly mean to readers abroad in 1977. But a Hungarian, thanks to him, becomes at the same time receptive to the past and present of Hungarian and universal culture. (pp. 35-6)

László Ferenczi, ''The Timeliness of Ady,'' in The New Hungarian Quarterly (© The New Hungarian

Quarterly, *1977; reprinted by permission of The Hungarian Academy of Sciences)*, Vol. XVIII, No. 66, *Summer, 1977, pp. 23-36.*

ERZSÉBET VEZÉR   (essay date 1979)

[*Vezér is the editor of Ady's* The Explosive Country *and the author of two biographies of Ady. In the following excerpt she emphasizes that Ady's works express the social atmosphere of the times. Vezér disagrees with such critics as László Bóka and Dezső Keresztury (see excerpts above) regarding Ady's system of symbols.*]

Poetry and writing on public issues were closely linked in Ady's case, so much so that for him the poet's calling, even at the zenith of his career, was committed to national and social causes with a sense of self-awareness rarely experienced in Hungarian literature. At the same time, the reality discovered during his journalistic years freed him from the patriotic cant and commonplaces that had tied the popular-national second-rate poetry to the yoke of false clichés. Ady was first and foremost a poet which was not only proven by elements of poetry in his journalism, his metaphoric style and personal tone, but by the artist's attitude, the way he looked on the world; always of this time and that place, but with universal implications. (p. 102)

His deep-rooted Calvinism became one of the decisive factors of his verse. His Calvinist faith in predestination suffuses his poetry. These poems revive with special force the language and the spirit of the Bible, and the transcendence of predestination always coincides in them with the secularism of the regularity of social progress. . . .

Because his revolutionary spirit is inseparable from his belief in his mission, his revolutionary spirit revolting against everything is, first of all, of Calvinist origin. That is why traditional religion is united with revolt in his case, bringing about the peculiar combination of tradition and revolution, expressed by him this way: "In the same branch I am emancipation and curb, protesting faith and missionary veto." He dialectically combines tradition and revolution, and it is the Calvinist origin of this which made him feel André Gide to be closely related. (p. 103)

The roots of Ady's symbolism were given outright in his mythopoeic imagination and an ability of expanding practically without limits the expressive possibilities and powers of the Hungarian language. György Lukács first pointed out that Ady's symbols appear complete, natural and as a sort of experience, and the most sensually concrete images express impersonally abstract ideas in a powerfully suggestive way. But as the process of the ideas turning into images is concealed from the reader, the symbols have the effect of myths.

That mythopoeic way of visualizing things was believed by contemporaries to be instinctive. Even the Catholic priest poet and professor Sándor Sik—at the time one of the best interpreters of Ady—demanded in a down-to-earth rationalistic form whether Ady really believed his own visions, and came to the conclusion that he did in the hours of the inspiration, but only on an instinctive, intuitive basis, and not through reason.

Ady was not instinctive at all, but a conscious creative mind. His poetic outlook was completely understandable, his most daring images and symbols are explicable on the level of concepts, if not always on the level of definite objectivity, i.e. not unanimously, with the concepts of a philosophical thesis.

What looked to the contemporaries as something incomprehensible, is easy for a secondary-school pupil of today.

It is a moot point whether Ady's symbols form a system or whether they are occasional. Although the cyclical grouping of the poems and the recurrence of the cycles in his successive collections warn the reader that he consciously strove to expand the cycle of themes, this does not necessarily mean a system. Only a systematic typological classification could decide the debate one way or the other. One thing is certain: the chain of symbols undergoes a change, a development in the poet's creative periods. His images simplify from the most daring to something translucent and pure, and his symbols turn more abstract, but also richer and fuller in thought. The same process of concentration goes on in his language in Ady's late period. His war poems are just about unsurpassable masterpieces of terseness.

As Ady's social and individual sphere are inseparable, even his most personal poems are closely linked to the social reality of his age. The torment of his love poetry was not only linked to his syphilis, but with a certain nervousness arising from the domestic political atmosphere that drove the poet to Paris, then back to Hungary. Ady's poems on God not only relied on the doctrines of Calvinism and the intellectual crisis of his age, but also reflected the state of mind of the pursued revolutionary, his relative loneliness, and a sensitivity bordering on paranoia owing to recurrent persecutions. The linguistic elements of his revolutionary poems could make up a dictionary of religious terms. To workers he sends an Ark of the Covenant as a token of solidarity, he welcomes revolutionary youth with hosannahs and in the coming revolution of the proletariat "every fighter is a Christ."

The reason for this apparent inconsequence is the poet's ever present endeavour and ability to re-live the world in its complexity and totality. That is why contrasts and contradictions play such a great role right from the linguistic elements of expression to the construction of cycles to the arrangement of cycles in a way that his contradictions can justly be regarded as one of the defining principles of his poetry as far as form is concerned. This accounts for the constant tension in his poetry. And this is also the reason for the very fact that readers encompassing all layers of society felt him to be their own, and his poems created a kind of consensus among readers. The suggestion of new, unknown, mysterious forces connected with symbols taken from myth, the dynamic and thrilling opening lines, and the language blending the unusual, the old and the new, and the individual, together account for the effect that made contemporaries either back him or oppose him. There had never been a Hungarian poet like Ady who could provoke such a clash of passions. (p. 105)

His volumes include cycles of poems on Hungary that shed a more penetrating light on the nature of Hungarian backwardness than many studies in sociology. In his castigation of the errors of his people Ady compares best with Heine. The pathos of these poems, apart from the alternation of confident and dejected moods, is fed by the same revolutionary belief that had arisen in him following the desolate state of affairs described in his first poems on Hungary.

Following an extensive explanatory campaign by the forces of progress, the stimulation of the Russian revolution of 1905 and the militancy of the Ady poems, extortion of democratic freedoms from successive weak governments was possible until 1913. At that date, however, the opposition suffered a crucial defeat owing to their own hesitancy, a fact marked by the outbreak of the First World War in 1914. Despite the dejected public mood Ady did not give up the fight. For him fighting and absence of compromise were moral commands from which he would not and could not escape even in a state of hopelessness and suffering. His self-mythologizing metaphors (the forced-to-be-Hercules and the tree of compulsion) apply to that militant role acted with a consciousness of moral obligation.

The catastrophe of the Great War exposed him to his hardest trial. Not for one moment did he doubt the senselessness and dehumanizing nature of the war. He was well aware, and he recorded this, that there can be but losers in the war: "All will lose out in the field." When the greatest minds of the age, Thomas Mann, Anatole France, Dehmel, or Verhaeren faltered, Ady paid tribute to the memory of the martyr Jaurès in one of his poems. He thought that all the values accumulated by the human race and his own people in cultural and material goods thanks to democratic progress would come to nought in the war. . . . His worry centered on the fate of the humanity instead of joining the masses in their chauvinistic hatred: "I keep suffering as a man and as a Hungarian." It was at that time that he put into words a moral command which could not become obsolete, that would in the hardest of times help a man retain his integrity: "Be a man in inhumanity."

Through the inferno of the war Ady managed to save in his poems the values worth saving: the ravished idea, beauties of life wherever found, the enthusiastic beliefs of progress of yesterday, and the hope of renewing humanity tightened under terror, now sleeping under the snow. Thus he kept the autonomy of his poet's personality despite the fact that he had been worn out by the war, both in body and mind. (p. 106)

Ady in the last years of his life reached the summits of the literature of his time but the world took little notice. A possible exception were neighbouring nations. Their poets started translating Ady in his lifetime and his poetry left a deep impression on them. But it must be admitted that his poetry is still unknown beyond these limits. Reasons should be sought in the difficulties of the language: apart from the fact that Ady's language is that of a relatively isolated community, it is loaded with very old tropes deeply rooted in the Hungarian historical conscience that do not raise the same connotations in foreign readers, making translation extremely difficult. But other obstacles hindering dissemination of Ady's poetry include the viewpoints of selection which may have been the guiding principles at the time, and still gain ground from time to time. The earlier selections placed the accent on Ady's first period, the poems

of which are often overornamented, rich in mythological symbols and Art Nouveau decorativeness, ignoring those poems that are modern in thought, and linguistic terseness which represent the unsurpassable Hungarian poet of the early twentieth century in the best possible way. Translating a poem of Ady into a foreign language thus requires special effort.

All this is important merely from the viewpoint of a universal impact. Ady does not depend on the quality of translations or the degree of his popularity abroad. A poet who has realized the need of human totality in his outlook in a very complex and contradictory age, is a universal phenomenon whether the world knows it or not. (p. 107)

Erzsébet Vezér, "Ady—Poet and Social Critic," in The New Hungarian Quarterly *(© The New Hungarian Quarterly, 1979; reprinted by permission of The Hungarian Academy of Sciences), Vol. XX, No. 73, Spring, 1979, pp. 101-07.*

ADDITIONAL BIBLIOGRAPHY

Auty, Robert. "The Danubian Ady." *The New Hungarian Quarterly* XX, No. 73 (Spring 1979): 97-101.
    Discusses Ady's literary influence on Hungary's neighboring states of Croatia and Slovakia.

Masterman, Neville. "Andrew Ady (1877-1919) and the Welsh Bards." *The Anglo-Welsh Review* 16, No. 37 (Spring 1967): 122-30.*
    Offers a biography and critical comments on Ady's poetry and political radicalism. The essay also includes Masterman's translation and discussion of Ady's *Two Kinds of Welsh Bards*.

Masterman, Neville. "Ady As Political Thinker." *The New Hungarian Quarterly* XIX, No. 72 (Winter 1978): 162-68.
    Reviews *The Explosive Country*, a collection in English of Ady's journalistic essays. Masterman maintains that a study of these articles would provide the impetus for understanding Ady's political thoughts and gain for him the significance in the Western world he deserves. In addition, this essay compares Ady's political views with those of two other journalists writing in the same period, Charles Péguy and G. K. Chesterton.

Nyerges, Anton N. "Endre Ady, the World of Gog and God." In *Poems of Endre Ady*, by Endre Ady, translated by Anton N. Nyerges, pp. 11-56. Buffalo, N. Y.: Hungarian Cultural Foundation, 1969.
    A detailed biocritical survey of Ady's life and work.

Vajda, Miklós. "Ady in Knightsbridge." *The New Hungarian Quarterly* XX, No. 73 (Spring 1979): 91-6.
    Overview of a 1978 London seminar on modern Hungarian literature. Vajda's essay focuses on the group's discussion of Ady and his poetry.

Konstantin Dmitriyevich Balmont

1867-1943

(Also transliterated as Constantin; also Dmitrievich; also Bal'mont) Russian poet, translator, essayist, novelist, short story writer, critic, and dramatist.

Balmont was one of the leading figures of the Symbolist movement in Russian poetry. He is famous for the musical quality of his verse and is credited with broadening Russian poetics by the virtuosity of his phonetic and metrical innovations. He was also a prolific translator who introduced previously unknown foreign literature to Russia. One of the few Symbolists to attain public adulation, he was most widely praised upon publication of *Budem kak solntse*, which is considered his masterpiece, but his later works of poetry were not well received. However, recent appraisals of Balmont's work have elevated his standing to that of an important contributor to one of the most significant periods in Russian poetry.

Balmont was born into an aristocratic Russian family. Known for his stormy temperament, he engaged in revolutionary activities as a student, and his conflicts with authorities resulted in expulsion from the University of Moscow and temporary exile. At age twenty-two, plagued by career disappointments and emotional problems, Balmont jumped from a third floor window in a suicide attempt that resulted in serious injuries and a permanent limp. His literary career began with the poetry collection *Sbornik stikhotvorenii*, which was privately published and gained little notice. It was his second collection, *Pod severnym nebom*, which earned Balmont public and critical attention. With the greater success of *Budem kak solntse* in 1903, Balmont became recognized as a leader in the Russian Symbolist movement. Some critics, notably the poet Valery Bryusov, proclaimed *Budem kak solntse* the apex of Balmont's career. His later works were largely ignored by the literary community. After supporting the 1905 revolution, Balmont left Russia in 1907 to avoid political persecution and in the same year published *Pesni mstitelia*, a political satire that demands revenge against the czar. An inexhaustible traveller and master of many languages, Balmont visited Europe, South Africa, Mexico, and the South Sea islands during his exiles, importing exotic descriptions and language to Russian poetry. He returned to Russia in 1912, but left for the last time after the October Revolution of 1917, settling in France. Ignored by both Soviet critics and the literary community in exile, Balmont continued to write until poverty and illness overcame him. He died in a French home for the aged in 1943.

Balmont's first literary works were translations of foreign literature, especially English and American poetry. He was not a strict textual translator and was often criticized for the looseness of his translations. His translations of Percy Bysshe Shelley, for example, distorted the originals so that the rhythmical and phonetic effects were emphasized. However, Balmont's translations of Shelley, Edgar Allan Poe, Walt Whitman, Oscar Wilde, Pedro Calderón, and others expanded the possibilities of Russian poetics while influencing his own work. In Balmont's earliest poetry, the influence of Afanasy Fet and Alexander Pushkin is reflected in the traditional romantic descriptions of the Russian countryside and the liberal political sentiments of civic verse. He breaks with tradition, however,

Ardis Publishers

in the internal construction of his poems. Acclaimed for the musical sound of their language, the poems of *Pod severnym nebom* stress alliteration and other verbal devices in a manner that was innovative in Russian poetry. Balmont also utilized the sonnet, free verse, and other stanzaic and metrical forms uncommon to Russian poetry. His work displays the influence of several non-Russian writers. For example, his use of internal rhyme and attention to sound in *Pod severnym nebom* and the collections that followed it reflects the influence of Poe. The works of this period also display Balmont's interest in mysticism, the unknown, and the erotic, as he abandons his former civic and pastoral themes in favor of those commonly associated with Decadent or Symbolist literature.

Balmont wholeheartedly embraced the Symbolist doctrine of art for art's sake. Escapism was an integral part of this philosophy and it became the dominant focus of Balmont's poetry in *Goriaschie zdaniia*, *Budem kak solntse*, and *Tol'kov liubov*. Throughout these collections, fascination with the concept of the god-like self and a glorification of the individual contrasts sharply with the themes of his early poetry. The Symbolist desire to transcend the limits of the psychological and social self is portrayed through dream imagery, transcendental allusions, and a mergence of humanity with nature. These poems also reflect Balmont's belief in reincarnation and his interest in theosophy. Religious symbolism, eroticism, and elemental imagery recur throughout these works, in which Balmont increasingly adopts the role of a seer who mediates between the supernatural and physical realms. However, while musical language and exotic subjects predominate, these works also convey Balmont's opposition to the czar and the oppressive conditions of Russian life. Publication of these collections gained Balmont acclaim as the most prosodically talented of the Symbolists. In his later poetry, early themes and stylistic techniques are developed more fully and maturely. *Sonety solntsa, mëda i luny,* for example, displays his ceaseless, skillful experimentation in extending the limits of the sonnet, while staying within the strict restraints of the form. The subsequent collection, *V razdvinutoi dali,* is more reflective than those of his tumultuous Symbolist period. An impressionistic realism and unusual word combinations characterize the poems, which are essentially patriotic and nostalgically autobiographical.

Early twentieth-century critics agreed that Balmont was the most technically adept Russian poet of his time. However, while he was praised by many for his innovations and additions to Russian language in his early works, his collections after *Budem kak solntse* were almost universally disparaged and have only recently undergone favorable reexamination. Modern critics, who have more closely assessed Balmont's later works, find them comparable, and many superior, in quality to the highly acclaimed poetry of his early career. In a major reappraisal of Balmont's works, critic Vladimir Markov has stated that Balmont "turns out to be a poet of consistent achievement who was growing and changing throughout his creative life."

PRINCIPAL WORKS

Sbornik stikhotvorenii (poetry) 1890
Pod severnym nebom (poetry) 1894
V bezbrezhnosti (poetry) 1895
"Russia" (essay) 1898; published in journal *The Athenaeum*
Tishina (poetry) 1898
"Russia" (essay) 1899; published in journal *The Athenaeum*
Goriashchie zdaniia (poetry) 1900
Budem kak solntse (poetry) 1903
Tol'ko liubov (poetry) 1903
Feinye skazki (poetry) 1905
Liturgiia krasoty (poetry) 1905
Zlye chary (poetry) 1906
Pesni mstitelia (poetry) 1907
Zhar-ptitsa (poetry) 1907
Palnoe sobranie. 10 vols. (poetry) 1908-13
Ptitsy v vozdukhe (poetry) 1908
Morskoe svechenie (essays) 1910
Zelënyi vertograd (poetry) 1910
Belyi zodchii (poetry) 1914
Iasen' (poetry) 1916
Sonety solntsa, mëda i luny (poetry) 1917
Marevo (poetry) 1922
Gde moi dom? (essays) 1924
V razdvinutoi dali (poetry) 1929
Golubaia podkova (poetry) 1934(?)

Translated selections of Balmont's poetry have appeared in the following publications: *A Book of Russian Verse; Lyrics and Songs from the Russians; Modern Poems from Russia; Modern Russian Poetry; Poems and Adaptations; Russian Poems; Russian Poetry: An Anthology;* and *A Treasury of Russian Verse.*

VALERY BRYUSOV (essay date 1903)

[*Bryusov, poet and critic, was the leader of the Moscow Symbolists, and his* The Scales *was the most important literary periodical of the period. The review from which the following excerpt is taken has received much attention by critics who believe it was instrumental in determining subsequent appraisals of Balmont's work.*]

In few people does [the] tremor of futurity so clearly and powerfully manifest itself as in K. D. Balmont. Others recognize perhaps more clearly the entire mysterious meaning of contemporaneity, but rarely does anyone carry this contemporaneity within himself, in his personality, or experience it more fully than Balmont. Balmont is first of all a "new man"; there is a new soul in him, new passions, ideals, expectations—different from those of earlier generations. To a certain extent he is already living that "tenfold life" about which another contemporary poet has dreamed. And it is this *new* life that makes Balmont a poet of the *new* art. He did not arrive at it through a conscious choice. He did not reject the "old" art after rational criticism. He does not set himself the goal of realizing an ideal rationally discovered at an earlier time. In forging his verse, Balmont is concerned only about whether it is beautiful in his own mind, interesting in his own estimation, and if his poetry belongs all the same to the "new" art, it happened without his willing it. He simply relates what is in his own soul, but his soul is among those that have only recently begun to flower in our land. It was the same with Verlaine in his day. Hence all the power of Balmont's poetry, all the vitality of its transports, although in the very same quality lies its weakness and limitation. (p. 164)

"I am consumed to ashes by each moment, I live in each betrayal," confesses Balmont. "Everyone knows how momentary I am," he says in another passage. And in individual images he lets you see as though with your own eyes those moments which absorb the whole world. (p. 165)

"Wandering through countless cities, I am always charmed by love alone"; these are Balmont's words. "Like that Sevillian Don Juan" he passes in love from one soul to another in order to see new worlds and their mysteries. His poetry glorifies and celebrates love, all the rites of love, its entire rainbow. He says himself that, going along the path of love, he can attain "too much—everything!" (p. 166)

Songs to the elements are one of the favorite themes in Balmont's lyrics. "I am unfamiliar with what is human," he notes. He writes hymns to Fire, Sun, the planets. An entire section of his book [*Let's Be Like the Sun*] is devoted to the "four voices of the elements." He calls the wind his "eternal brother," and the ocean the ancient "progenitor" of all human generations. (p. 167)

Four fundamental currents in Balmont's art are the thirst for the completeness of every moment, the awareness of the abysses surrounding us, the feeling of mystery in passion and mergence with elemental life. They draw all of his impressions into their channels. Indeed, they determine his literary sympathies as well ("We like the poets who are like us"). In quest of the full life, of integral, impetuous characters, he turned to Calderon, to the Spanish drama of the seventeenth century. **"The Awareness of Mysteries"** makes him akin to the poet of horror, mad Edgar; his attitude toward love, passion and women draws him close to Baudelaire and today's "decadents"; and finally his penetration into the life of the elements allies him with Shelley and Indian pantheism. Adjunctive to the basic currents are secondary ones; these are rather tributaries with semi-independent lives of their own, yet essentially nourished by the same currents. Hence, in consequence of his belief in the possibility of a "full" life, and thus its opposite, he hates life that is lustreless and temperate. This leads him to stinging, barely lyrical satires (e.g., **"In Houses"**). Hymns to the elements, on the other hand, often resolve into quiet childrens' songs—gentle, meek, and beautiful songs about fields, spring, dawns and snowflakes. But the four voices remain fundamental in Balmont's entire being and in all his poetry. (p. 168)

In Balmont the unconscious life predominates over the conscious. But, proud of his bright eye, this blind man who is recovering his sight depends too much on the power of his vision. He dares to venture upon the most forbidden roads, sometimes slipping pitifully and falling where many walk freely with a stick. Wherever there is power in consciousness and clarity of thought, Balmont is weaker than the weak. All of his efforts to achieve breadth of thought, to imbue his verses with broad crystallizations, to encompass centuries in a concise image, end in failure. His epic effort, the long poem **"Artist-Devil,"** except for several beautifully formulated thoughts, and a few truly lyrical fragments, is completely composed of rhetorical commonplaces rising from that scream with which singers strive to conceal vocal insufficiencies. And in his lyrics Balmont can never survey his creations with the impartial view of a critic. He is either in them or hopelessly distant from them. Hence Balmont can never correct his verses. His corrections are distortions. If he fails with a certain verse he rushes on to the next, satisfied—in the interests of association—with any kind of approximate expression. This obscures the meaning of some of his verses and the obscurity is of the most undesirable kind: it is occasioned not by the ambiguity of the content but in the imprecision of the selected expressions. In such cases Balmont is satisfied even with empty, hackneyed phrases that say nothing. For all the subtlety of the general construction of his poems he reaches the limits of banality in individual verses.

In one of his poems Balmont speaks of himself:

> I am the rarefaction of the leisurely Russian tongue;
> Other poets before me merely forerun.

If Balmont said this with his individual line in view, its musicality, he is right. Balmont's equals in the art of verse have not existed in Russian literature and do not exist. It might have seemed that in the melodies of Fet Russian verse reached maximal ethereality, but where others saw limits, Balmont discovered the boundless. Such an unattainable model of euphony as Lermontov's "On an Ocean of Air" pales completely before the best songs of Balmont. Yes! He was the first to discover "inflections" [*uklony*] in our poetry, to discover possibilities that no one had suspected, unprecedented "echoes" [*perepevy*] of vowels blending one into another like drops of moisture, like crystal ringing.

And yet Balmont's verse has retained the whole construction, the entire substructure of conventional Russian verse. One might have expected Balmont, in his impetuous craving for changing impressions, to surrender his verses to the will of the four winds, to shatter them, to cut them up into small glittering pieces, into a pearly dust.

But this simply has not happened. Balmont's verse is the verse of Pushkin and Fet—perfected, refined, but essentially the same.

The movement that created *vers libre* in France and Germany, which sought new artistic devices, new forms in poetry, a new instrument for the expression of new feelings and ideas, left Balmont almost completely unaffected. Moreover, when Balmont attempts to adopt the features of the new verse from others, his success is poor. His "broken verse" [*preryvistye stroki*], as he calls his meterless verse, loses all the charm of the Balmontian musicality without acquiring the freedom of the poetry of Verhaeren, Dehmel and d'Annunzio. Balmont is Balmont only when he writes in strict meters, correctly alternating strophes and rhymes, observing all the conventions developed during two centuries of our versification.

And new content far from always fits into the Procrustean bed of these correct meters. Madness, forced into an excessively rational stanza, loses its elementality. Lucid forms impart a vulgarizing clarity to all the vague, chaotic elements with which Balmont attempts to infuse them. It is as though he accepts Pushkin's "Until Apollo calls the poet . . ." in reverse. The Pushkinian poet's soul awakened like an eagle responding to divine summons. In Balmont it loses something of its power and freedom. Balmont is free and unlimited in life; in art he is fettered by and entangled in thousands of rules and prejudices. He is a "genius of the elements" and a "bright god" (his own words) in life, but in poetry first a man of letters. His transports and passionate experiences pale in passage through his art. For the most part only fading embers remain of the fire and light; they are still fiery and bright for us, but they are already wholly different from the sun that they were.

Such are the limits of Balmont's poetry.

Let's Be Like the Sun is Balmont's sixth collection of verse (if the one published in 1890 is not counted). His last collection, *Burning Buildings,* was a momentary flare, a glittering display of fireworks. It was almost entirely composed in a few weeks. It had the poignancy and tension of rapture. *Let's Be Like the Sun* is the art of several years. Here Balmont's poetry has spread out to its full expanse and apparently reached its eternal banks. Here and there it has attempted to splash over these banks in a kind of turbid, weak wave, but without success; it is fated to remain under this horizon. But in his own world Balmont will of course reach ever newer depths, for which he now merely yearns.

Let's Be Like the Sun places Balmont immediately after Tyutchev and Fet in the ranks of our lyric poets. He is their nearest and only successor. Among contemporary poets Balmont is indisputably the most significant, both in the power of his elemental gift and his influence on literature. All of his contemporaries will have to be careful first of all not to fall into the orbit of his gravity, to guard their independence. To vie with Balmont in the realm of the pure lyric is a dangerous feat. There is little hope of surviving even as a cripple, like Jacob. (pp. 169-70)

> *Valery Bryusov, "K. D. Balmont: 'Let's Be Like the Sun'," translated by Rodney Patterson (translation ©1972 by Ardis Publishers; originally published under a different title in* Skorpion, *1903), in* Russian Literature Triquarterly, *No. 4, Fall, 1972, pp. 163-74.*

NIKOLAI GUMILEV   (essay date 1908)

[*Gumilev was one of the founders and major figures of the Acmeist movement in early twentieth-century Russian poetry. The Acmeists reacted against the earlier school of the Russian Symbolists, whose work they criticized as abstract, diffuse, and alienated by mys-*

ticism from the beauties and value of the physical world. Gumilev and other Acmeists, including his wife Anna Akhmatova and the poet Osip Mandelstam, briefly established a poetics that demanded concise and concrete renderings of physical reality, emphasizing a Neoclassic formalism which contrasted with what the Acmeists considered the loose transcendental verbiage of the Symbolists. The following comments on Balmont's poetry were written just prior to Gumilev's full involvement with the Acmeist movement.]

So recently written, and already an historic book. Thus falls the lot of either very good or very bad books, and of course, **Only Love** belongs to the first category. In my opinion it most deeply reflects Balmont's talent, proud as the thought of a European, colorful as a southern tale, and pensive as the Slavic soul. In it he is that very Balmont-Arion whom they rightly called by the ancient tender name of the mellifluous poet. And the readers of Balmont's lastest works (are there many of them?) will read with sorrow this book, strangely beautiful, refined in thought and feeling, in which perhaps the germs of later decay already hide—the corruption of the virgin Russian word in the name of its wealth. There is something unmitigated in the melodiousness and imagery of these poems, but they are still timid, like a girl in the instant of her fall. Balmont said: "If I approach the abyss, lost in admiration of a star, / I will fall not regretting that I will land on stones." He has come immeasurably close to the star of pure poetry, and now the swiftness of his fall is merciless. **Only Love** concluded the brilliant morning of the renaissance of Russian poetry. At that time the formulas of a new life were only projected, of a literature united with philosophy and religion, of a poetry as guide of our actions. It was necessary to go over unexplored roads, to reveal hidden worlds in one's soul and to learn to look at things already known with a fresh and enthusiastic gaze, like on the first day of creation. Balmont was one of the first and most insatiable discoverers, but his thoughts were not confined to the Promised Land, he delighted in the charm of the path. But then, no one's hands picked such dazzling flowers, in no one's curls rested such golden bees. It seemed that his muse was not subject to the laws of gravity. And justly, before all other "Decadents," he gained recognition and love.

But when the time came for creative work, and the swords were beaten into plows and hammers, Balmont turned out to be alien to everyone. Came the time of the great sunset.

And these confused wanderings through the folklore of all lands and peoples which have occupied him recently, add nothing to his repute. (pp. 41-2)

> *Nikolai Gumilev, "Balmont" (1908), in his* Nikolai Gumilev on Russian Poetry, *edited and translated by David Lapeza (translation © 1977 by Ardis Publishers; originally published as* Sobranie sochinenii v chetyrekh tomakh, Vol. 4 *by Nikolai Gumilev, edited by G. P. Struve and B. A. Fillipov, Kamkin, 1968), Ardis, 1977, pp. 41-2.*

MOISSAYE J. OLGIN (essay date 1920)

[*Olgin offers a descriptive outline of Balmont's poetry and poetics.*]

The influence of Balmont upon the poetry and poets of our time can hardly be overestimated. Never since Pushkin has one great talent so completely revolutionized the contents, the tone, the language, the spirit of poetry, as does Balmont.

Balmont is the lyrical encyclopaedia of the modern intellectual man. "Nothing human is alien to me" could be put as a motto for all his works. No human mood, however fleeting, escapes his sympathetic attention. No phenomenon in the wide universe is too remote for his alert soul. At times it even seems that he is too diversified; that there are too many strings in his ever reverberating, supersensitive musical instrument. He started with moonlight motives, with half-tones, with passing echoes in the midst of mysterious silence, with vistas resembling a winter-forest where every branch and every twig is quaintly carved out of ice crystals and reflects a melancholy sun in numberless cold sparks. He spoke of existences half awake, half dreamy. He sang of the belladonna, the magic of poisonous perfumes, the somber depths issuing a strange radiance, the waves of subdued emotions in a state of mental intoxication. Soon, however, he published one volume of poems entitled **Let Us Be Like the Sun,** and another **Burning Buildings,** where the cry of red blood, the lusty hymn of sunshine, the all-dominating glory of fire is voiced in strong metallic verses. In these new poems, Balmont appears to be a heathen, a worshiper of elemental forces, a friend to the savage tribes who revel in the sight of red blood and in rushing over the primitive steppe on the backs of their swift horses. Balmont, however, does not dwell long in those moods. He soon passes to other experiences: pain, suffering, beauty, joy of existence, love for the near or love for the remote, passions, hell, demons, the torture of thought, hopelessness, prison-walls, physical and mental despair. This swift passing from one experience to another with complete abandon in each feeling is, perhaps, the most characteristic feature of Balmont. He speaks of "the joy of eternal changes." "I am the surface that breaks the rays, I am the playing thunder, I am the crystalline brook, I am for all and nobody," he declares in one of his poems. He admires the "miracle of his flaming thought," he knows that "whatever is in heaven, and much more, is in the human soul." "My heart is wounded by my reason," he confesses; yet soon he accepts absurdity because "in the abysses of absurdity mad flowers are living"; he is ready to greet even hell because "there is truth in suffering," yet he knows that suffering for him is not final: "I have burned my happiness, yet I doubted I might kindle it with a stronger flame."

Thus Balmont is the eternal wanderer in the jungles of human thought, feeling, and emotion. There are, however, a few points of concentration in his poetry, a few motives to which he returns with renewed fondness. These are the witchcraft of poetry, sun and fire, and eternal change.

"Verse is magic in substance," he writes in his essay on **Poetry as Witchcraft.** "Every letter in it is magic. The Word is a miracle, the Verse is witchcraft. The music that governs the universe and the soul, is Verse. Prose is a line, and Prose is a plane, it has only two dimensions. Verse alone has three dimensions. Verse is a pyramid, a shaft, a tower. In the rare verse of a rare poet there are even more than three dimensions: there are as many as there are in fancy." "The Universe is multi-voiced music. The entire Universe is chiseled Verse."

The power of sun and fire is perhaps the most favorite subject of Balmont's lyrics. The sun is "the creator of the world," "the giver of life," "the music of a beautiful tale," the hot blood "that makes the soul impassioned." The fire is "purifying, fateful, beautiful, imperious, radiant, alive." "O, thou shinest, thou warmest, thou burnest, thou livest, thou livest!" In fire all the qualities of poetry, including that of change, are combined.

Change for Balmont is life. "I live too quickly," he writes in his notebook, "and I know nobody who loves moments as I do. I go, I go, I go away, I change, I suffer changes. I give myself to the moment, and over and over again it opens before me new fields. And new flowers are blossoming before me forever." (pp. 171-73)

Balmont uses all the devices of modern art; schematization; symbolization; impressionism. His rhythms are rich in variety, in time, in timbre, in color. His language represents all shadings from the very powerful to the mellow, blending echoes of distant faint music. (p. 174)

> *Moissaye J. Olgin, "K. D. Balmont," in his* A Guide to Russian Literature (1820-1917) *(copyright, 1920, by Harcourt Brace Jovanovich, Inc.), Harcourt Brace Jovanovich, 1920, pp. 171-76.*

D. S. MIRSKY (essay date 1926)

[*Mirsky was a Russian prince who fled his country after the Bolshevik Revolution and settled in London. While in England, he wrote two important and comprehensive histories of Russian literature,* A History of Russian Literature *and* Contemporary Russian Literature. *In 1932, having reconciled himself to the Soviet regime, Mirsky returned to the U.S.S.R. He continued to write literary criticism, but his work eventually ran afoul of Soviet censors and he was exiled to Siberia. He disappeared in 1937. In the following excerpt from his* Contemporary Russian Literature, *Mirsky provides a brief overview and estimate of Balmont's poetry, citing his debt to Edgar Allan Poe and Percy Bysshe Shelley, and denigrating his translations of these authors. Oleg A. Maslenikov (see excerpt below) gives a more favorable appraisal of Balmont's translation of Poe.*]

[Balmont's] literary career begins in earnest with the publication in 1894 of *Under Northern Skies.* In the nineties Balmont was considered the most promising of "decadent" poets and was given a good reception by those magazines which piqued themselves on being reasonably modern. He continued publishing books of poetry, of which *Buildings on Fire* . . . and *Let Us Be as the Sun* . . . contain his best poems. After that commenced a precipitous decline of his talent, and though he has ever since published about a volume a year, all those that appeared after 1905 are worthless. In the nineties he had forgotten his schoolboyish revolutionism and was notorious (like the other Symbolists) for his "uncivic" attitude, but in 1905 he joined the S.D. party and published *Songs of an Avenger,* a collection of remarkably crude and violent party verse. (p. 184)

Balmont's work is very voluminous. But by far the greater part of it may be swept aside as quite worthless. This part will include all his original verse since 1905, most of his numerous translations (the complete metrical version of Shelley is especially bad; on the contrary, his translations of Edgar Allan Poe are quite acceptable), and all his prose without exception, which is the most insipid, turgid, and meaningless prose in the langauge. In so far as a place is reserved for him in the pantheon of genuine poets, he will be remembered for the six books of verse published from 1894 to 1904. Even in these books he is very uneven, for though he had at that time a genuine gift of song, he was always incapable of *working* at his verse, he could only sing like a bird in the bush. But he had a keen sense of form, and his poetry is pre-eminently formal; sound and tune are the most important things in his verse. In the nineties and early 1900's, he struck the ear of the public with a richness of rhythm and vocal design which seemed even excessive, disconcerting, and, to the stauncher of the Radical puritans,

wicked. This pageant of sound was a new thing in Russian poetry; its elements are borrowed (without any slavish imitation) from Edgar Allan Poe and from the Shelley who wrote *The Cloud, The Indian Serenade,* and *To Night*. Only Balmont is less precise and mathematical than Poe and infinitely less subtle than Shelley. These achievements went to his head, and *Let Us Be as the Sun* is full of assertions of this kind: "Who is equal to me in the power of song? No one! No one!" and "I am the refinement of Russian speech." These immodesties are not entirely unfounded, for in this peculiar quality Balmont has no rival among Russian poets. But of refinement there is precisely very little in his verse. It is curiously devoid of the "finer touch" and of the finer shades. He has a sufficiently wide scale of emotion to express, from the brave *fortissimo* of the most characteristic poems of the last-named book to the sweet, subdued undertone of *Wayside Grasses* or *Belladonna,* but in every single case the expression is simple, monotonous, all in one note. Another serious shortcoming, which he shares with Bryusov, and which is explained by the necessarily Western character of his poetry, is his complete lack of feeling for the Russian language. His verse has a foreign appearance. Even at its best, it sounds like a translation. (pp. 185-86)

> *D. S. Mirsky, "Balmont," in his* Contemporary Russian Literature: 1881-1925 *(copyright 1926 by Alfred A. Knopf, Inc.; reprinted by permission of the publisher), Knopf, 1926, G. Routledge & Sons, 1926, pp. 184-86.*

ERNEST J. SIMMONS (essay date 1943)

K. D. Balmónt . . . shared with Bryúsov the honor of being one of the first of the symbolists in the field by virtue of his early volume of verse, *Under Northern Skies*. . . . There is more sound than sense in Balmónt's poetry, which has nothing of the intellectual quality of Bryúsov's and very little of the symbolic quality characteristic of the whole school. Succeeding volumes, such as *Buildings on Fire* . . . and *Let Us Be as the Sun* . . . , added to Balmónt's reputation for possessing a sense of form and richness of rhythm almost unique among Russian poets. But in his voluminous later works, both original and translations, the richness began to cloy and the patterns of sound became monotonous.

Bryúsov and Balmónt were more interested in the language of poetry than in its content, and their symbolism was more a matter of theory than practice. (p. 28)

> *Ernest J. Simmons, "The Symbolist Movement," in his* An Outline of Modern Russian Literature (1840-1940) *(copyright, 1943, by Cornell University; used by permission of the publisher, Cornell University Press), Cornell University Press, 1943, pp. 27-35.*

OLEG A. MASLENIKOV (essay date 1952)

[*Maslenikov compares Balmont to Paul Verlaine for the musical quality of his verse and offers qualified praise of his translations, which D. S. Mirsky (see excerpt above) dismisses entirely.*]

In the first half of the 1890's . . . [a] star rose on the symbolist horizon. It was Konstantin Balmont, a lyric poet "by the grace of God." Although he had published his first book of verse in 1890, the amazing musical quality of his poetry did not become apparent until his second volume appeared, four years later. This won him not only the acclamation of the followers of the "new art," but also the recognition of many critics of the conservative camp. Although the older readers found Balmont's verses pleasing to the ear, not all of them were able to grasp the significance of his poetry. Tolstoy, a venerated representative of this older generation, on reading some of Balmont's verse is said to have exclaimed, "What charming nonsense!" remaining apparently deaf to the melody of the most musical of Russian poets.

Balmont was to Russian modernism what Verlaine was to its French counterpart. He elevated Russian poetry to hitherto unattained musical heights. Nor was this his only merit. Like many other symbolist poets, Balmont was well acquainted with Western modernist literature, which he translated for Russian readers. In his translations Balmont emphasized the poetry of the English-speaking peoples. He, more than anyone else, was responsible for popularizing in Russia Oscar Wilde, Walt Whitman, Edgar Allan Poe, and Shelley, to say nothing of Rosetti, Blake, Coleridge, and Tennyson. His translations of Poe are excellent on the whole, for Balmont was able to render much of Poe's musical charm into Russian. His translation of *The Raven*, which he did in competition with Bryusov, is particularly deft; in fact, the Russian version of Poe's refrain "quoth the raven—'nevermore!'" ("*kárknul vóron—'nikogdá!'*") sounds more sinister than the English original; sometimes, however, Balmont translates this line also with "*mólvil vóron—'nikogdá!'*" when a more melodious and less menacing note seemed appropriate. On the other hand, his translations of Shelley show unwarranted liberties with the original. Some wag from the daily press even dubbed him "Shelmont" for his efforts—a pun not only on the surnames of the two poets, but also on the word *shel'ma*, a Russian colloquialism for "rascal." Balmont did not limit himself to the English; his translations include verses from the classical Greeks, the Spanish, and one Italian (Giacomo Leopardi).

Balmont's influence on Russian poetry of the twentieth century has been very great. He showed the public and the poets alike the musical potentiality of Russian verse. (pp. 21-2)

> *Oleg A. Maslenikov, "The Early Phases of the Symbolist Movement," in his* The Frenzied Poets: Andrey Biely and the Russian Symbolists *(copyright © 1952 by the Regents of the University of California; reprinted by permission of the University of California Press), University of California Press, 1952, pp. 9-32.**

MARC SLONIM   (essay date 1953)

> [*Slonim was a Russian-born American critic who wrote extensively on Russian literature. In the following excerpt from his* Modern Russian Literature, *Slonim maintains that Balmont's minor talent was diffused and exhausted by an overabundance of poems written on an undiscriminating variety of subjects.*]

[The] capacity of becoming infatuated with the most diversified lands, objects, men, or periods was Balmont's salient characteristic. He never discriminated but simply responded to any external stimulus, and this ability for lyrical and poetic response seemed inexhaustible. He wrote thousands of poems upon thousands of separate themes. Instead of channeling his own flow, he dissipated it into trickling rivulets. He could not help it—this uneven, multi-voiced, often noisy, and frequently enchanting poet. His chief trouble was that he lived and talked in verse, and this talk degenerated into shallow chit-chat. His repetitions and verbiage became tiresome. Briussov was annoyed by Balmont's ability to learn and to forget with equal

facility. 'He can gulp down a library,' Briussov once commented angrily, 'and it will stick with him as long as water on a duck's back.' This ability made Balmont a prolific translator (he knew dozens of languages), but his translations of the collected works of Shelley (whom he adored), of Poe (whom Briussov also translated), of Whitman, of Calderon, of Lope de Vega, and ever so many others all too often turned these authors into so many Balmont phantoms; the translations were, nevertheless, highly popular in Russia.

He assumed a hundred guises, but two of his self-characterizations seem not inappropriate: he often compared himself with the wind, or with a sun-shot cloud. The charm of his poetry melts away like a cloud, and only a few of his poems, out of the scores upon scores of his volumes, have remained impervious to time.

The peak of his influence was between 1904 and 1910. He was known and loved much more than were any of his fellow Decadents, and was imitated by many poets. Even those who called him superficial, grandiloquent, raucous, or shallow could not deny his unusual craftsmanship, his musicality, his iridescent imagination, and the great role he played in the rebirth of Russian poetry. Yet his popularity was not lasting, and he was the first victim of the anti-Decadent and anti-Symbolist movements in poetry that sprang up during World War I. Since then, and especially in Soviet Russia, where he was tagged as a White Guard and 'reactionary *émigré*,' his name has become a synonym for formalism and frippery in verse. (pp. 94-5)

> *Marc Slonim, "The Modernist Movement," in his* Modern Russian Literature: From Chekhov to the Present *(copyright 1953 by Oxford University Press, Inc.; renewed 1981 by Tatiana Slonim; reprinted by permission of the publisher), Oxford University Press, New York, 1953 (and reprinted in his* From Chekhov to the Revolution: Russian Literature, 1900-1917, *Oxford University Press, New York, 1962, pp. 79-102).**

RENATO POGGIOLI   (essay date 1960)

> [*Poggioli was an Italian-born American critic and translator. Much of his critical writing is concerned with Russian literature, including* The Poets of Russia, 1890-1930, *which is one of the most important examinations of this literary era. In the following excerpt from that work, Poggioli analyzes the stylistic traits of Balmont's poetry and states that what distinguishes him from other Russian poets of the time is "the vitality and exuberance of his talent, and . . . his lack of self-consciousness and self-restraint."*]

Modesty was not one of Bal'mont's virtues, and he felt no compunction in praising emphatically his own contribution to the renovation of Russian verse. "I have shown what can be done for Russian poetry by a poet who loves music," he proudly stated in one of his prefaces. (p. 91)

The analysis of a single stanza, taken from a poem where the poet compares himself to the wind, will suffice to give an idea of Bal'mont's technique and craftsmanship. The meaning of its four lines may be literally rendered with the following words, where the reader will notice the overpowering presence of the pronoun "I," or rather, since the Russian verb allows the omission of pronouns, of verbal forms in the first person: "I am the free wind, I always blow; I stir the waves, I fondle the willows; I sigh amid leaves, silently I sigh; I lull the grasses, I lull the crops.'' The original reads thus:

> Ja vol'nyj veter, ja vechno veju,
> volnuju volny, laskaju ivy,
> v vetvyakh vzdykhaju, vzdokhnuv nemeju,
> leleju travy, leleju nivy.

Even a reader unacquainted with the Russian tongue may recognize some of the elements forming the sound pattern of these lines: the rich alliterations vol'-nyj, vol-nuju, vol-ny; the alliterative repetition vzdykh-aju, vzdokh-nuv; the simple repetition leleju, leleju; the anaphorical endings v-eju, voln-uju, lask-aju; the identical endings nem-eju, lel-eju; the consonance between the words travy and nivy, the one placed at the caesura, and the other at the end, of the last line. To this one must add the absolute symmetry of the structure: every line is divided into two parts, each one of which consists of a double iamb with a feminine ending. Finally, if we except the first line of this quatrain, and fail to count in the others the double appearance of a monosyllabic pronoun and the presence of a preposition consisting of a single consonant, we shall see that every hemistich is formed by two words of either two or three syllables, the one being a verb, and the other a noun.

The passage quoted reveals at once the positive and negative qualities of Bal'mont's diction and style, and suggests why his art was bound to degenerate, by an excess of virtuosity, into the vice which the critic Kornej Chukovskij was later to call by a Russian term which sounds more like ''bal'montitis'' than like ''bal'montism.'' This degeneration led to the triumph of an empty sonority, which denied by itself the poet's claim of his own ''musicality.'' . . . In poetry rhyme should agree with reason, and this is why one could repeat for Bal'mont what T. S. Eliot said of a poet whom the Russian resembles on many grounds: ''What we get in Swinburne is an expression of sound, which could not possibly associate itself with music.'' In Bal'mont as well as in Swinburne language and the object which it should represent ''are identified solely because the object has ceased to exist, because the meaning is merely the hallucination of meaning. . . .''

It is not only this aspect of his work that separates Bal'mont from the better among his contemporaries, who were, like Brjusov, more controlled, or, like Sologub, far more conscious craftsmen. What distinguishes Bal'mont from them, as well as from the poets of the following generation, is on the one hand the vitality and exuberance of his talent, and on the other, his lack of self-consciousness and self-restraint. He is the only Russian poet of his time who could sometimes indulge in a panic enthusiasm recalling D'Annunzio, or in a cosmic optimism which reminds one of Walt Whitman. Thus, at least psychologically, Bal'mont is far from being a Decadent, although the term reacquires its validity if used as a merely literary label, as a summary description of his literary experiences. By nature a neoromantic, Bal'mont becomes a Decadent by choice or by pose; but, unlike D'Annunzio, he fails to develop the dialectics of Decadence, which implies a paradoxical sympathy for the primitive and the barbaric.

Like D'Annunzio, however, Bal'mont sings the praises of life, understood as the triumph of nature and the feast of the senses. This is especially true of the work of his maturity, when he was tempted by more vital lands and warmer climates, and went, in words as well as in deeds, ''from the northern sky to the bright South.'' Bal'mont was often able to evoke the charms of winter and the subdued beauty of the melancholic landscapes of his native land, the ''languid tenderness'' of the Russian countryside, as he did in a poem entitled with an abstract word of his coinage, which reads in English like ''Ineffability''; and once he went as far as to proclaim: ''lovelier than Egypt is our North.'' Yet, all this notwithstanding, he will be primarily remembered as the poet of summer. Like the early Belyj, Bal'mont is the singer of the sun, which, however, he celebrates as a cosmic power rather than as a symbol of the godhead. Life is for him a solar experience. One of his most famous poems opens with the proclamation: ''I came into this world to see the sun and the blue horizon,'' and ends with the announcement: ''I shall sing of the sun in the hour before death.'' At least three of his books *Let Us Be like the Sun, Buildings Afire*, and *The Firebird* . . . , indicate by their very titles his worship of heat and light, his obsession with the sun as reality and myth. It is in the sun that he personifies himself, both as a man and as a poet, and Boris Zajtsev was right when he said that Bal'mont's poetry reflected, or even embodied, ''the face of Helios.''

Yet, like D'Annunzio, Bal'mont celebrated not only Helios, but all the elemental powers of nature, identifying himself with each of them. In the poem **''The Gospel of Being''** he preached the imitation not only of the sun, but also of the wind and the sea, enjoining all men to heed the commands he had received from those elements: from the wind, to be volatile; from the sea, to be everchanging; from the sun, to burn. As this threefold command easily proves, Bal'mont's poetry does not limit itself to the expression of the joy of being, although it is there that it achieves its highest feats. Some of the better poems of his later years evoke those moments of our experience when the fever of life seems to subside, when ''the unpurged images of day recede'' and give place to the night of the soul. Two good examples of such a shift of mood are two simple, allegorical poems, **''The Gull''** and **''The Swan,''** which take up again the romantic theme of the poet as a heavenly spirit exiled to this earth, but which express with calm resignation his all-too-human doubts and griefs.

Bal'mont's originality lies in two factors, both of which operate at the margins, rather than at the center, of his work. The first one is psychological, and has to do with his temperament, which seems not to differ too much from that of many modern poets of the West, but looks rather singular when compared with the personality types most frequently occurring in the history of Russian poetry. The second factor is technical, and concerns his exceptional virtuosity, which is an almost monstrous phenomenon, precisely because it works spontaneously and flows endlessly, led by no conscious aim, unchecked by any critical insight. In brief, we have to do with an originality founded on passivity: and this is why one could use as an emblem for Bal'mont's art Pushkin's lovely poem likening the poet to an echo responding to any call. Unfortunately, Bal'mont's poetry is incapable of responding to the appeals of life and reality with the simple and natural fidelity of an echo or of an Aeolian harp: it alters and reforms the sounds it hears, almost without listening to them; and it sends them back, magnificent, magnified, and magniloquent, with romantic reverberations, from the resounding cave of the poet's soul. Each one of Bal'mont's poems seems to grow hypertrophically, by assimilation and diffusion, rather than by evolving slowly from its own seed. This explains why this poet devoted so much of his creative activity to translation; this may even suggest that he behaved as a translator even when composing works of his own.

The implication that Bal'mont is a translator even as an original poet has nothing to do with the Romantic conception of *Poesie der Poesie,* according to which the poet gives voice to the mute and passive poetry hidden in the bosom of nature, nor with the Symbolistic view of the poet as a decipherer and interpreter of the mystical riddles of the universe. Bal'mont is a translator in the sense that he imitates nature and life without conscious artificiality, but with approximate and exaggerated images, where he mirrors himself even more than his objects. His genius is in substance that of an *improvvisatore,* as Bal'mont avowed in the poem where he defined himself as "the exquisite flower of the slow Russian speech." "I grasp all, I take all, depriving others," said the poet in another line of the same poem, with the selfish, uncritical pride which is characteristic of every virtuoso. In another piece he described with a naïve ostentation his own creative method, which is no method at all, as this passage may easily show: "Suddenly my strophe is born, another rises without hesitation; already a third shines from afar; smilingly, a fourth joins the race; whence and how many I never know. . . ." And the poet concludes, blissfully unaware of the implications of his statement: "Truly I never compose. . . ." In the poem where he claimed to be born into this world to see the sun, Bal'mont asked the rhetorical question: "Who is my equal in singing power?" and answered it simply: "No one, no one." Ultimately the improviser is but a performer; and Bal'mont may have failed to realize that his self-appraisal as a peerless singer was perhaps more than a flowery metaphor. Posterity may well take that definition literally, and view him as a maestro of *bel canto,* as the greatest tenor of Russian poetry. (pp. 92-6)

> Renato Poggioli, *"The Decadents," in his* The Poets of Russia: 1890-1930 *(copyright © 1960 by the President and Fellows of Harvard College; excerpted by permission), Cambridge, Mass.: Harvard University Press, 1960, pp. 89-115.*

VLADIMIR MARKOV (essay date 1969)

[*In the following excerpt, Markov reviews Balmont's career and counters the popularly held critical opinion that Balmont's later works are unworthy of critical attention. He concludes that an injustice has been done to the author and his reputation as a poet, since many of the later works are, in fact, superior to the early ones. Rodney L. Patterson's essay (see excerpt below) also offers a favorable reappraisal of Balmont's later poetry.*]

Balmont's literary career began with the publication of his first book of verse, *Sbornik stikhotvorenii (A Book of Poems),* in Yaroslavl in 1890. Later he came to be ashamed of this immature collection, and perhaps for this reason critics have been too ready to dismiss it, alleging a dominant influence by Nadson. This is not altogether correct: Nadson was only one influence—others were A. K. Tolstoy, K. R., and several other "romantic realists" of the second half of the nineteenth century. The clichés of theme, composition, and diction in *A Book of Poems* are obvious enough; yet on closer scrutiny these twenty-odd poems yield much that is familiar from Balmont's mature work: the theme of the moment, the image of the well (*kolodets*), and even his famous alliteration in rudimentary form. . . . On the whole these juvenilia show fluency but little variety, and are actually not much inferior to the pieces in Balmont's next book, *Pod severnym nebom (Under Northern Skies).* The main difference between the two collections is that the first (minus translations) is entirely within the Russian tradition and devoid of metrical innovations and contrivances.

It was *Under Northern Skies* that first brought Balmont to the attention of the public. The book, a slim volume of about fifty poems, was written during the winter of 1894 and is thematically a far headier mixture than *A Book of Poems.* The youthful romantic *Sehnsucht* and pictures of the Russian countryside à la Nekrasov are still there, as is the "civic" verse of the liberal journals (see especially the poem in memory of Turgenev), but occasionally old-fashioned romanticism can hardly be separated from decadence, and Nadson rubs elbows with Baudelaire. (pp. 222-23)

Strictly speaking, *Under Northern Skies* does not contain a single really good poem. In contrast, Balmont's next collection, *V bezbrezhnosti (In Boundlessness . . .),* is not only bigger (it contains about a hundred poems) but is also the best of the early books. It is also a more consistently "decadent" book, and its formal organization was to become typical of Balmont: from now on almost all his books were to be divided into titled sections, and epigraphs attached to the book itself, to each of its sections, and to many of the individual poems (which almost always bear a title as well). Often a manifesto-like poem gives the keynote to the volume; this "key poem" is printed in italics and stands outside the first titled section. Such is here the famous **"Ia mechtoiu lovil" (By Dreams I Captured).** The first part of the collection, "Za predely" (Beyond the Bounds), is the best, and also the clearest in its statement of decadent themes—swamps, death, remote and inhuman regions (the ocean bed, the North Pole) alternate with motifs of snakes, the moon, the cold, and vague shadows; occasionally there is a defiant declaration. . . . Even at this early stage we find flowers, winds, brooks, and the elements (*stikhii*), all of which occur with such profusion in Balmont's later work; these winds, incidentally, obviously come from Balmont's favorite poet, Shelley, whom he made an integral part of the Russian decadent movement. (pp. 224-25)

It is generally agreed, and the poet himself held the opinion, that [*Goriashchie zdaniia (Burning Buildings)*] opens a new period in Balmont's poetry. Ellis [L. L. Kobylinsky] even goes so far as to speak of "an almost complete transformation of life" which marks "an abyss between *Burning Buildings* and *Silence.*" The book was a triumph for the poet, and together with his next, and even more successful, collection, *Budem kak solntse (Let Us Be Like the Sun),* made Balmont the most popular poet of the decade. . . . Psychologically and, to a great extent, thematically, this bright-colored, loud-shouting book may seem at first an artistic *volte-face* (and obviously a more mature collection with more good poems than all the preceding books); on closer investigation of the verse texture, however, we may doubt whether any basic change has taken place. The presiding literary deities (Baudelaire among others) remain the same. (p. 228)

For Balmont *Burning Buildings* was the product of "a single wave" of inspiration, a self-realization, and more than that: he was convinced that he spoke for his contemporaries. It is for this reason that he subtitled the book "poetry [*lirika*] of the modern soul." In this sense it is part of that quasi-, or perhaps pseudo-, Nietzschean trend in Russian literature which includes, among others, Gorky. Possibly the central idea in Balmont's work at this time is what he called *otdacha mirovomu* (giving oneself to the universal). In this he may be echoing Tiutchev and Fet, who played an important part in his formation (while being, one might add, utterly alien to his poetic core), but there can be no doubt that a far more immediate source was theosophy, a movement which attracted so many intellectuals at this time. . . . A glance through the index of Mme. Blavatsky's *The Secret Doctrine* reveals numerous thematic coincidences with Balmont's poems, and suggests that her writings (and probably those of other theosophists) first pointed the way along paths (in particular, to India and Egypt, and to Maya and the old Persian *Zend-Avesta*) which he later followed to the considerable enrichment of his poetry. (p. 229)

For most readers and critics the peak of Balmont's achievement has remained *Let Us Be Like the Sun,* subtitled "The Book of Symbols" and published in 1903; it was several years in the writing and is twice the size of the preceding collection. One of the clichés of Balmont criticism is that with *Burning Buildings* the poet abandoned his earlier "moon" poetry and entered his "sun" period. This generalization is not entirely satisfactory, for the sun and moon themes are linked throughout Balmont's work, sometimes juxtaposed, sometimes interwoven. And in this, reputedly the sunniest of his books, the moon also casts its light. It must be said that exaggerated claims have been made for the originality and artistic quality of this book: it contains no new themes or motifs, and there is much in it that is weak (it would be hard to find something more tasteless and absurd than "**Danse Macabre**," for example). (p. 230)

In this book we may observe the crystallization of a few genres which were to be peculiarly Balmont's own: symbolic pictures, hymns of praise, visionary fantasies, and exhortations. The preacher of spontaneity becomes exceedingly rational at times, and then his verse falls into hollow rhetoric or mechanical jingling (sometimes both at once).

Despite all our cavils, *Let Us Be Like the Sun* remains the milestone of Russian poetry in this century that it is reputed to be, and there is much that is positive to be said about it. In the first place, the metrical experimentation is unceasing, especially in the mixing of lines of different meters (evens iambs with amphibrachs) and in the excursions into free verse. The section "Khudozhnik-D'iavol" (The Devil as Artist), which bears a dedication to Briusov (who disliked it, however), is a series of fifteen long poems written in terza rima, magnificent exercises in the decadent-grotesque with occasional hints of what we would·now call surrealism. Balmont's handling of terza rima is masterly; and since, at least on Russian soil, this stanzaic form (like the sonnet and ottava rima) predetermines style, his verse here takes on a fresh and novel aspect. In this book the poet's preoccupation with colors is also much in evidence; there are obvious examples, such as the Spanish poem "**Tri tsveta**" (**Three Colors**), which is about the colors black, yellow, and red. (p. 231)

The same year saw the publication of Balmont's next book, *Tol'ko liubov (Love Alone),* written during the summer of 1903, which Balmont spent on the Baltic coast in the company of the poet Jurgis Baltrusaitis. It differs little from *Let Us Be Like the Sun:* again there are paeans to the sun, epigraphs from Shelley (and from Balmont himself), cruel beauty, yearning for the transcendental; life is contrasted with "the inexhaustibility of dreams," "the shimmerings of dreams"; and the moon and the ocean bed make their inevitable appearance, together with a few manifestoes—"Ia nenavizhu chelovechestvo" (I hate humanity), "Ia ne znaiu mudrosti godnoi dlia drugikh" (I know no wisdom meet for others). (p. 232)

Yet, on the whole, this book is a more solid achievement than either of the two preceding ones. To reproach Balmont with banality is to miss the point—his banality is successful; one

might as well reproach Mayakovsky with rudeness. Where Balmont is less than successful is in his love poetry (plainly a product of his real-life flirtations) and in his attempts at philosophical verse in the cycles "**Mirovoe koltso**" (**A Ring of Worlds**) and "**Priblizheniia**" (**Approaches**), which are downright bad. It is in this volume, however, that one finds the famous "**Snezhinka**" (**Snowflake**) and "**Bezglagol'nost'**" (**Wordlessness**), the latter of which, for some reason, enjoys a certain prestige even among those who reject the rest of Balmont's work. . . .

We also find the theme of the poet's work as a harsh discipline, something one associates with Briusov rather than the "I-sing-like-a-bird" Balmont. He even tries to undermine his own melodiousness by the introduction of what he calls "preryvistye stroki" (broken lines)—really, on the whole, the four-stress *dol'nik* (or rather *udarnik*). We are given ample proof here that jingling Poe-esque trochees and ambitious hymns to the elements are not, contrary to prevailing opinion, the only Balmont; he was also capable of an "Acmeist" precision of observation. (p. 233)

Liturgiia krasoty (The Liturgy of Beauty), which bore the subtitle "Elemental Hymns," came out in 1905 and marked the beginning of the poet's fall from fashion. As might be expected, this sense of disappointment was first felt among the elite and took some time to filter down; the general reader was still as intoxicated with Balmont as ever. . . . While it cannot be denied that much of the book is mediocre, chaotic, long-winded, and tedious—especially the rehashes of old manifestoes and, once again, the love poetry—there are nevertheless some highly interesting pieces, such as "**Pliaska atomov**" (**The Dance of the Atoms**) and "**Lemury**" (**The Lemurs**). (p. 234)

It is [in *The Liturgy of Beauty*] . . . that the poet enters the field of the occult (although there had been hints of this before); this manifests itself in the epigraph from Apollonius of Tyana, the amulet theme, and the Pythagorean idea of numbers ruling the universe. The Slavic theme too, so important to Balmont's later development, is here sounded distinctly for the first time. Finally, the Mexico of the later books makes its appearance here in a single poem about a hummingbird. Attention must also be drawn to the long (and artistically unsuccessful) cycle "**Fata morgana**," which deals with colors and their combinations. There is no doubt, however, that the final section of the book, devoted to the four elements, is a remarkable, if uneven, achievement. (pp. 234-35)

It might be said that *The Liturgy of Beauty* is full of premonitions of approaching crisis, both in its artistic decline and in its groping after new themes. Another sign of these premonitions might be *Feinye skazki: Detskie pesenki (Stories About the Fairy: Songs for Children),* a slim volume of sixty-five poems. . . . *Stories About the Fairy* is both a discovery of a special world and a new demonstration of Balmont's range. Written for the poet's small daughter, these Victorian picture-postcard pieces about the Fairy and her pastimes, the insects and grasses which surround her, and her war with the King of the Ants are somewhat on the sweet side for modern taste; still, they are convincing in their way and are not without a certain old-fashioned charm. Balmont did have a purity of heart unique among his contemporaries (with the possible exception of Kuzmin). . . . Of course, the book is not perfect, there are clumsy lines and that general lack of "the resistance of the material" which is so typical of Balmont. (pp. 235-36)

The second part of the book, which abandons the theme of the Fairy, is an important stage in the development of Russian children's literature before its flowering with Chukovsky and Marshak, and cannot be omitted from any history of such literature.

We now come to a period in Balmont's poetry which has met with almost unanimous critical condemnation. Biographically it coincides with his second exile, which lasted from December 1905 until shortly after the amnesty of February 1913. During this time he lived in France (Paris and Brittany) and Belgium and also traveled extensively in Europe, Africa, Asia, and Polynesia. All his books were published in Russia in the meantime (though three of them—*Evil Spells, Poems,* and *Songs of an Avenger*—were confiscated because of their political poetry).

Zlye chary: Kniga zakliatii (Evil Spells: A Book of Exorcisms) was written in the spring of 1906 and published the same year in Moscow. It is a tired book, revealing the poet's sickness of spirit on almost every page, and hardly a single satisfactory poem is to be found in it. Stylistic incongruity, repetitions of Balmont's own and echoes of other poets' work (from Apukhtin to Briusov), fragmentariness, and downright vulgarity are some of the book's faults. . . . Nevertheless, the book is the first to develop on any scale Balmont's interest in Russian and Slavic folklore. (pp. 236-37)

More "constructive" and far more ambitious was Balmont's next book, written in Brittny during the summer and fall of 1906. . . . *Zhar-ptitsa (The Firebird)* bore the subtitle *Svirel' slavianina* (A Slav's Oaten Pipe). . . . The symbol of the firebird recurs throughout Balmont's work (there is a poem with this title in *Love Alone*), and, strictly speaking, there are no motifs in this mammoth collection that were not already present in *Evil Spells*—magic, precious stones, Russian folk poetry and Slavic mythology. . . . This time, though, there is much more folklore, and it is obvious that Balmont worked with collections of Russian *byliny* and *dukhovnye stikhi* open before him. (pp. 237-38)

With all its shortcomings, particularly in the area of lexical stylization, *The Firebird* is well worth studying, and its sources, themes, and meters await closer investigation. (pp. 238-39)

Pesni mstitelia (Songs of an Avenger) was the only book of Balmont's exile to appear abroad. . . . It contains forty-nine poems, mostly written in Britanny in the same breath as those of *The Firebird* and published earlier in Amfiteatrov's Parisian magazine *Krasnoe znamia*. The book astonished many by its subject matter (direct political invective and satire, calls to vengeance, paeans to the working man and revolution)—and by its poor quality. Actually there was nothing surprising in Balmont's turning to revolutionary themes: he was no ivory-tower aesthete, for all his professed individualism and love of pure art, and he had been involved in politics before. . . . The antitsarist poems in *Songs of an Avenger* are particularly abusive ("dirty scoundrel," "bloodstained hands," "monarch-thief" are some of the expressions used); indeed, he even goes so far as to threaten the tsar with the gallows. Certainly no Communist poet ever surpassed Balmont in heaping obloquy on a monarchist regime. (p. 239)

The next "crisis" collection made its appearance in St. Petersburg in 1908 under the title—"preposterous" according to one critic—of *Ptitsy v vozdukhe (Birds in the Air)*. Subtitled *Strokhi napevnye* (Melodious Lines), the book is in seven sections whose titles are echoed in the poems they contain. In the main, it develops or repeats old themes—some older than Balmont. . . . Here again are colors, numbers, and exorcisms;

and the imagery—in addition to the promised birds—includes sun, moon, wine, magic, rainbows, snakes, and bees. Folklore, too, is here with themes taken from fairy tales and pagan rites, with folk riddles thrown in for good measure. In **"Zolotaia parcha" (Gold Brocade)** Balmont finally succeeds in reproducing the true folk style. . . .

Even if most of these poems do not impress (occasionally one has the curious feeling of reading a fine poem in a poor translation), good poems can be found; a certain mellowness is in the air, and there is an unexpected trend toward terseness in the four-line poems. From now on, this will exist alongside Balmont's diffuse and flowing manner. (p. 240)

Zelënyi vertograd: Slova potseluinye (A Green Garden: Kissing Words), which came out in St. Petersburg in 1910, was the occasion of one of the greatest misjudgments of Russian criticism. Ever since *The Liturgy of Beauty* Russian critics had become so accustomed to dismissing every new book of Balmont's that they overlooked one of his finest collections. Briusov's word of admiration went unheeded, as did Balmont's own advice in one of his earlier poems not to be too hasty in "stripping the old idols." *A Green Garden* consists of almost two hundred imitations of the songs of Russian flagellant sectarians (*khlysty*), and it is a poetic miracle. Never before had Balmont maintained such a consistently high level, such long-breathedness (*shirokoe dykhanie*), such energy and swiftness, such lightness and simplicity, or even such metrical variety; there are no weak poems here. Perhaps this was what Balmont had needed from folklore in order to soar—not epic but lyrical models. The book is also exceptional in its arrangement: gone are the baroque trappings of preceding collections, with their elaborate divisions into epigraph-studded, elaborately titled sections (and let me remark here that Balmont was a baroque—or rather a neobaroque—poet not in an "impressionistic" or figurative sense). Here the poems do form cycles, but the reader is carried from one to another without any prompting from the poet; the cycles flow into each other—symbolic rivers, paradise, brothers and sisters, the Boat (*Korabl'*), ecstatic rites (*radeniia*), sacred sex, prayers, religious symbolism, culminating in a vision of the end of the world and eternal glory. Balmont can be both wild and gently colorful in the manner of a Russian Fra Angelico, and there is a richness of orchestration here which goes far beyond Poe-esque jingling all the way to Derzhavin. . . . He even brings off successful paraphrases of well-known prayers (such as the flagellants' version of the Cherubim Prayer)—an enterprise in which Pushkin himself did not come off entirely victorious. All is achieved without any betrayal of his poetic self: the familiar Balmont features are all here.

Khorovod vremën: Vseglasnost' (A Round Dance of the Times: All Voices), which was written mostly in Flanders, concludes Balmont's European period. It has, unfortunately, little to recommend it except variety of content. (pp. 241-42)

The books Balmont produced between 1906 and 1912, the years of exile, were almost unanimously condemned by the same critics who had been so vociferous in their admiration of *Let Us Be Like the Sun* and its companion volumes. (p. 242)

The first book to be published in Russia (by "Sirin") after Balmont's return was the large (two hundred poems), sumptuous, and very important *Belyi zodchii (The White Architect)*; subtitled *Tainstvo chetyrëkh svetil'nikov* (The Mystery of the Four Lamps), it appeared in St. Petersburg in 1914. In a sense, this is the culmination of the new Balmont, no matter how old some of his themes might appear. No other book of Balmont's approaches this one in variety of subject matter, ranging as it does from Russian folklore to the industrialization of Australia in styles that encompass self-parody and new sonorities. . . . Predominantly Balmontian themes, but often with a new "un-Balmontian" personality behind them, are what distinguish *The White Architect*. The outstanding qualities of this verse are tonal richness—especially in the sections entitled "Zolotye vëdra" (Golden Pails) and "Iuzhnyi krest" (The Southern Cross), where Balmont seems to enter successfully into competition with Viacheslav Ivanov—energy, virility, solidity, finish. (p. 247)

The same level of quality was maintained in Balmont's next collection, *Iasen': Videnie dreva (The Ash: A Vision of the Tree)*, which came out in Moscow in 1916. The book is not divided into parts and further consolidates the solidity attained in *The White Architect*. Balmont concentrates here on his symbolical mysticism and on the cosmological theme; both the sources and meaning of this book's symbolism require special investigation, and in this sense *The Ash* is perhaps the poet's most difficult collection. The main image—the Tree—derives from the Scandinavian Igdrazil and other mythological and legendary trees. . . . For the first time the cosmological Balmont is without the defects of artificiality, trivial musicality, and rawness sometimes apparent in earlier books. This poetry is austere, but it has scope and is built with weighty, meaning-packed words. Sharp outlines are provided by the occasional use of scientific terminology. . . . In this book Balmont explores an area, much closer to Russia, which he had previously neglected—Georgia (*Gruziia*). Very noticeable is the increasingly important place the sonnet now occupies in Balmont's work; it appears individually, in cycles and as "sonnet redoublé" (i.e., a chain of fifteen sonnets). (pp. 248-49)

In his book of essays [*Morskoe svechenie (Sea Gleams)*] Balmont had written: "The sonnet is like a knight's garb: always monotonous and eternally beautiful." Perhaps the best book of his whole career is *Sonety solntsa, mëda i luny (Sonnets of Sun, Honey, and Moon)*, subtitled "A Song of the Worlds" and published by Pashukanis in Moscow in 1917. . . . The book consists of two hundred and nineteen individual sonnets in addition to seven cycles (two of them "redoublé") and was "two winters and two summers" in the writing, as the poet himself says . . . , a time when he was "in the sonnet's sweet slavery." The book represents a unique achievement in Russian poetry and deserves to be admired, enjoyed, and studied. Balmont here creates an encyclopedia of his life's work in sonnet form, gathering together all his main themes and areas of interest (and adding China to his already impressive atlas). As in his previous book—and this becomes a habit from now on—Balmont does not separate his poems into sections; they do nevertheless fall naturally into groups, and the whole book describes a kind of arch, from fire and sun to night, moon, and death, encompassing a great variety of themes both little (cigarettes and children's drawings) and big (man as monarch of nature—a poem with which future Soviet "discoverers" of Balmont might well begin). The exclusive use of the sonnet form does not lead to monotony, and this is not only due to the thematic variegation. Balmont is constantly changing his perspective from the bird's eye to the microscope; lexically he obtains variety by employing scientific terminology, neologisms, and carefully placed long words. . . . Among the thematic cycles mention should be made of the one dealing with hunting and prehistoric life, and of the one devoted to woman (for the first time Balmont is convincing on this theme), as

well as of the sonnets on individual poets, painters, composers, and saints; the book also contains a cycle of sonnets on the sonnet. The saturated and honeyed lines of this verse . . . have not only a lovely clarity but also a marvelous sense of ease. Indeed, Balmont is so relaxed here that he can occasionally break his usual solemn tone with a conversational intonation—and without a hint of bathos. The sonnet disciplines Balmont and keeps his tendency to diffuseness on a tight rein; the two dangers which lurk most often for him—the amorphousness of the hymn and the equal, if different, amorphousness of the snapshot—are avoided by the very form of the sonnet. As a result, there is hardly a weak poem in the book, though it must be admitted that the clinching lines of individual sonnets sometimes disappoint (but this is something that even Shakespeare could not always escape). (pp. 249-51)

Balmont's first book to be largely written in emigration, and one which clearly marks a new poetic departure, was *Marevo (Mirage)*, which appeared in Paris in 1922. The ninety-five poems in this book are all dated—an unusual thing for Balmont—and divided into sections according to the time and place of their composition, which is also unusual. . . . *Mirage* is Balmont's first completely nondecadent book. It is a diary, a collection of mournful poems about Russia and her revolution. (p. 253)

The tragic atmosphere of the book reaches its greatest intensity in the last part, with its motifs of famine, fear, blood, and pillage, and Balmont finds images in the Gospel parables and the Book of Revelation for his macabre and grotesque visions. This part is also the most outspokenly anti-Soviet, with its images of the possessed, the blind leading the blind, the people enmeshed in a foul, blood-stained cobweb, and pus flowing from the Kremlin into the world; the poet calls for the execution of the executioners. For Balmont the events in Russia are simply madness, a case of the Dostoevskian demonic possession of a whole people. He is appalled by bloodshed and fratricide (as he had often been appalled by war in his earlier verse), and communism repels him not because of his political convictions, but because its sole eloquence for those who think differently is the bullet. . . . The relevant book of essays for this collection is the later published *Gde moi dom? (Where Is My Home?)* . . . , where Balmont carries great human conviction in lamenting the impossibility of writing poetry both in the Russia of the Soviets and the politics-dominated Russian Paris of the émigrés. (pp. 254-55)

The greatest surprise of Balmont's poetic career was *V razdvinutoi dali (Distances Drawn Apart)*, which appeared in Belgrade in 1930 (even though the title page bears the date 1929). This is the best, and the earthiest, book of his exile, and it is hard to understand how it could have been completely ignored by the critics. . . . One explanation is the book's somewhat unpromising start, with page after page of second-rate verse, mainly patriotic stuff probably composed with an eye to the poet's public appearances before none-too-refined Russian audiences in various émigré centers. The book proper begins with autobiographical poems, followed by some most interesting, Tiutchev-like, metaphysical verse, then by ocean poetry composed at Capbreton; scattered among these cycles are many individual poems which stand by themselves. We find here a Balmont who is enigmatic and elusive, magnificent and autumnally subdued—a poet, in a word, who cries out for critical attention and study. . . . Even in pieces which might be accused of banality there is a new weightiness in individual lines and unexpected combinations of words. A poem may begin obviously enough, then suddenly, after a touch or two, it becomes haunting. These poems do not strike or charm in the old Balmont way, but touch strangely with their deceptive simplicity. Thus, the pieces about sorcery—an almost irritatingly persistent theme with Balmont—are magical for the first time (see **"Donnaia trava"**). . . . In short, for all that Balmont had produced impressive, fascinating, and even perfect books before, it might be said that only in *Distances Drawn Apart* did he touch greatness. It is incredible after this that Adamovich and other émigré critics (who obviously never opened this book) continued to condemn "Balmontism" as false poetry. (pp. 256-57)

Balmont, who is habitually divided into early, famous, and washed-up (or appearance, flowering, decline, and nonbeing), turns out to be a poet of consistent achievement who was growing and changing throughout his creative life. (p. 259)

> *Vladimir Markov, "Balmont: A Reappraisal," in* Slavic Review *(copyright © 1969 by the American Association for the Advancement of Slavic Studies, Inc.), Vol. 28, No. 2, June, 1969, pp. 221-64.*

RODNEY L. PATTERSON   (essay date 1972)

[*Like Vladimir Markov (see excerpt above), Patterson claims that Balmont was consistently maturing throughout his career and that his later collections of poetry are among his best, a conclusion that contrasts sharply with the opinion of previous critics.*]

Konstantin Dmitrievich Balmont . . . was the best known poet of Russia's literary "Decadence." There were poets like Alexander Dobrolyubov who were able to don more demonic masks, but it was Balmont who was first and most successful in brewing an intriguing potion of Decadent exoticism, Fetian ambiguities and musicality, "European" sophistication, Romantic madness, ennui, pride, sense of doom and deviltry—and sonorously lacing the mixture with birches, nightingales, rustling reeds, endless steppes, marches and rugged mountains. In Balmont's poetry and personality there was something to titillate or outrage everyone. (p. 241)

Among members of the literary avant-garde he seemed the legitimate scion of "mad Edgar" Poe. Among elitists he was read as a European scholar-poet of deep, eclectic and hermetic learning, subtle and refined tastes, symbolic and exclusive language. To the progressives he seemed a man of strong (if inconstant) Nekrasovian cast who fearlessly chastised corrupt potentates (including the Tsar) and was often in serious trouble with the authorities. Among liberals his praise of Turgenev indicated a man of patrician sensibilities as comfortable at a Russian country estate as in the concert halls of Europe's capitals. His admirers were consequently disparate, ranging from Annensky and Prince Urusov to Gorky and the Bolsheviks.

In his youth he sedulously expressed a literary culte de moi no less outrageous in public opinion than that of Oscar Wilde's characters, who liked to expatiate on their own unique beauty. . . . (p. 242)

He was a prolific poet, translator and essayist (he also wrote a play, a novel and stories) with a mind drawing its main dimensions from libraries and countless hours of lonely contemplation of nature. Although his relationships with people were complex, he was always on more intimate terms with the ocean and the stars. His lyrical "I" often seemed blind to contemporary human beings. His poetry rarely depicts people; even his wives, mistresses and daughters appear synecdochi-

cally at best. His poetic vision seemed to pass through the quick in search of the dead; it was keener in explorations of the world as Adam might have seen it than in descrying the outlines of contemporary civilization (a noisy pollution which he loathed).

Addicted to alcohol, limping from an attempt to kill himself in 1890, knowledgeable about drugs, an inexhaustible worker, haughty and mercurial, Balmont was like one of those exotic birds that the Decadents so loved to place in their art. His early poetry, regardless of the circumstances in which it was written, portrayed the dangers of a literary movement along the brink of madness (to which he ultimately succumbed, as had his brother before him).

Oscar Wilde sported green carnations in his lapel; Balmont wore a large emerald in his cravat and his behavior shocked almost as many people as Wilde's had. Yet Balmont quickly won critical approbation—first (like Baudelaire) for his excellent translations and essays—and then for his own poetry. After a weak collection in 1890, *A Book of Poems (Sbornik stikhotvorenii)* published at his own expense, came a succession of steadily improving collections culminating in four or five outstanding successes: [*Burning Buildings (Goriashchie zdaniia), Let's Be Like the Sun, (Budem kak Solntse), Love Alone (Tol'ko liubov'), The Liturgy of Beauty (Liturgiia krasoty),* and *Stories about the Fairy: Songs for Children (Feinye skazki: detskie pesenki)*]. There was some talk about a "Balmont Age" of Russian poetry.

There followed a period in which Balmont's sincere affection for and deep study of Slavic folklore informed his own collections, which were more or less condemned out of hand as doing violence to their models and Balmont's own talents. . . . Balmont's alleged "decline" after *Let's Be Like the Sun* may well have been brought about less by the poet's literary faults than by a review of *Let's Be Like the Sun* written by his friend Valery Bryusov [see excerpt above]. Bryusov arbitrarily decided, before the publication of the allegedly faulty books, that Balmont's poetic waters had probably reached their eternal banks in *Let's Be Like the Sun*. Fortunately for Balmont, the general public continued to be fascinated by his work for another ten years and some writers refused to dismiss him immediately—e.g., Vyacheslav Ivanov, who still praised him in 1912.

With the advent of new schools of poetry and the increasing unanimity of critical disfavor, Balmont found it nearly impossible to find readers willing to forgive him for his supposed "excessive fluency" and lack of profundity. Consequently, he entered his final phase condemned to self-parody, insipid repetitiousness and crimes against folklore. A final blossoming of his art came and went with only a few poets (mostly non-Russian, except for Tsvetaeva) able to recognize his gifts. This premature lapse into oblivion was furthered by his defection from the Soviet Union in 1920, after which he became a nonperson in that country. It was not until 1969 that an anthology of his poetry was published in Russia, and this otherwise admirable collection is marred by the editorial subscription to the notion that Balmont's later works do not warrant serious consideration. (pp. 242-44)

Like Baudelaire, Balmont was fond of describing true artists as "straying planets;" he imagined himself a comet, ever in motion, confident that his course was charted by forces beyond his comprehension. Although he was uncertain about the number and nature of his anterior lives (he believed in reincarnation), he knew what he wanted from his present life: love and art ("I'll always sing of the reign [of love] . . .", **"Forever"** **["Navek"]**); the ancient wisdom both of the folk and of sophisticated Seers; an understanding of the nature and range of innumerable oppositions which he believed to be fundamental to all life; voyance; and a mystical-sensual blending of his personality with the elements. (pp. 244-45)

The voyant could hope to predict parts of the future by studying the past; this may explain why cosmology assumes such importance in [*The Ash Tree: A Vision of the Tree (Iasen': Videnie o dreve)*] (and in Balmont's later works generally). In poems like **"The Tale of the Moon and Sun"** Balmont wrote of the creation of the world, and he struggled to read nature's "runes" (e.g., in **"Snow runes"** **["Sngeovye runy"]**), in order to understand the world. In folklore he longed to hear the voice of Adam. Going back in time he looked for intimations of a lost Paradise, thus to anticipate the Paradise toward which he thought himself moving. That is why he journeyed so tirelessly through nature, folklore and real and apocryphal monuments (such as Atlantis) and personalities (such as Blake).

Balmont occasionally emphasized his integration with the motley throng of mankind, but it was more usual for him to express strong feelings of estrangement, which he associated with his special nature as poet-voyant: "I passed through the crowd like a drowsy shade, / Fascinated by the patterned motleyness" (**"Singing"** **["Pene"]**).

In *The Ash Tree* most of mankind is depicted as slumbering beneath a sea of illusions (underwater poems such as **"Beneath the Sign of the Moon"** are especially frequent in his early books, but they continued to appear later). The theme of despair, particularly in conjunction with the *odi profanum vulgus* theme, appears frequently throughout Balmont's works. But the later works reveal a reassurance rare in the early ones: nature's cyclical renewals (see **"Cerements"** **["Savany"]**) remind the poet that he, too, will thrive again.

Few poets have been more intoxicated than Balmont by each of nature's store of beauties—not merely the sunsets that poets traditionally glorify (and Balmont too, e.g., in the brilliant **"Transluscence"** **["Peresvet"]**), but every blade of grass, wings of insects, sparkling flecks of waves. Few more than he understood that the well of each unrepeatable joy was inexhaustible, yet he strove to drain it anyway. All the more interesting, therefore, is the fact that he blurred the personalities and incidents in his erotica, but treated his love for nature in great detail. Balmont's brother once said that the poet's eyes were constructed like an insect's, with 20,000 reflecting mirrors; the simile was astute if limited to his perception of nature.

The war and impending revolution seemed to demand an iron manhood of poets. Gumilev rushed away to win his medals. . . . But Balmont could not forsake the child in himself to play the man; in **"The Stubborn One"** (**"Upriamets"**), he declared that regardless of the war he would remain a child. Although he admired men of action (such as Napoleon, see **"The Renunicant"** **["Samorazvenchannyi"]**), and was capable of exceptional courage himself, there was a deeper fidelity to him in gentleness, simplicity and an inaction that seemed to lead toward spiritual dynamics (see **"Concentration"** **["Sosredotochie"]**). These aspects of Balmont's poetic vision were considerably deepened in *The Ash Tree,* for example in **"The Anchorite"** (**"Otshel'nik"**). Other poems present the poet's meditations on the necessity of accepting all the trials of life passively and in silence, submitting to the glory or the disaster

of each reincarnation with a humble spirit. Acceptance of life's numerous ordeals (see **"Ordalii"**) seemed to be made possible by the poet's idea that non-resistance to the karma of recurrent existences allows even the lowliest of humans to be the designing gods of their own macrocosms.

The Ash Tree is not an easy book to understand; Balmont's philosophy is not organic but accidental and associative, built up by accretion like the coral beds he liked to describe. He moved willfully through libraries, reading innumerable books at random or because they were mentioned in the book he last read. It is a formidable task, therefore, to reconstruct Balmont's symbolic systems, and the task is further complicated by the fact that the theosophists also sought instruction from various mahatmas, who attempted to help them develop understanding of their "latent inner senses responsive to the invisible chaos." What Balmont's inner senses told him in this regard is conjectural. In spite of its difficulties, the book rivals Balmont's best, suggesting in quiet sonorities rich, exciting abstracts through an elusive interplay of antiquity and futurity, quietude and love, the search for ipseity and the quest for the "keys to the mysteries" of existence.

Balmont worked on [*Sonnets of the Sun, Honey and the Moon: A Song of Worlds (Sonety solntsa, meda i juny: pesnia mirov)*] for at least two years. It is not unflawed; some of the 225 sonnets fail to combine the formal and thematic ideals of this demanding genre. But Balmont severely restrained his verbal flow, and sonnet after sonnet cannot be described without positive superlatives. Why the poet's reputation as a master poet was not immediately reestablished after *The Ash Tree* and *Sonnets . . .* is an interesting question. The critic D. Vygodsky, who had recognized an apex in *The Ash Tree,* severely castigated Balmont for lacking the courage, talent and wisdom to "seek a new route" after that collection (as though a book of sonnets was not a novelty in Russian literature), which the critic arbitrarily concluded was the *summa summarum* of Balmont's career. The critic predictably objected to the impetuosity and lavishness of Balmont's style, but he failed to understand the book's strength: mature and interesting thought expressed with a recognizably Balmontian ebullience and without irreverence for the sonnet's laws. The poet had clearly made an effort to demonstrate that craftsmanship need not sacrifice spontaneity. Writing in 1927, L. P. Grossman displayed some understanding of Balmont's skills in the sonnet by pointing out the "unexpected fluidity and . . . lightness" Balmont brought to the genre; but he was unwilling to allow Balmont much more credit than that.

The anthology sets a variety of themes against backgrounds ranging from the exotic to the drab, times from deepest antiquity to future epochs, and atmospheres crackling with violence or opiated with silence. Such contrasts are familiar enough to readers who know Balmont's poetry; what is characteristic of the poet's new voice is the more insistently recurrent attitude of tranquil reverence for a still, contemplative life and a purely human astonishment (reminiscent of Pasternak) at the miracle of natural renascence: ". . . Again the sigh of April breathes its flowers . . ." (**"Amber Preserved"**). As in earlier works, life is still dream-like, but the dreams are seldom like the nightmares of some of Balmont's earlier works (e.g., **"Artist-Devil"** in *Let's Be Like the Sun*), for the poet is surer now that his dreams are sustained by "beams of light, dew, quietude and knowledge" (**"Obelisk"**). That comforting knowledge came, of course, from his study of the mystics. In his mature spiritual state there was a new imperative: to express an increasing willingness to release his grip on life, for, "life's term is the term of a flake of first snow" (**"Relativity"** [**"Otnositel'-nost'"**]). (pp. 246-49)

Balmont's deep appreciation of a fraternity of voyant artists was periodically expressed throughout his career; in this collection he voiced his love for Leonardo, Michelangelo, Marlowe, Shelley, Poe, Rustavelli, Scriabin and Lermontov. These obeisances underline an important theme of the anthology: life is meaningless without love, renunciation of self and search for brotherhood. The brotherhood of artists was most important to him; he did not demand homogeneity of this company. He never bothered to conceal his own eclecticism, setting his candle "before every ikon" (**"The Candle"**). (p. 249)

Sonnets of the Sun, Honey and the Moon is Balmont's most unusual book; with consistent mastery he enclosed most of his philosophy, his self-portrait, many of his favorite poetic devices and his idols within a form that would not allow him room for weakness.

When *In Distances Drawn Apart* [*(V razdvinutoi dali)*] appeared in Belgrade in 1930, Balmont was sixty-three years old and living out a lonely old age (made worse by increasing poverty) in France. In Russia he was infamous (if remembered at all), and he enjoyed no popularity in emigre circles in France.

The book was not hailed by emigre critics, most of whom believed him defunct. . . . Few readers ventured to expose themselves to what they so wrongly assumed would be a tiresome rehash of stagnant tunes from a garrulous old alcoholic.

In these poems one of the central concerns of the lyrical "I" is to penetrate the "beyond," to wander as a shade through that holy "boundlessness" that the poet had so ardently sought since his youth. In this and many other respects Balmont was consistent from first to last; indeed, in spite of the fact that a large part of the public had been conditioned to expect deliberate inconsistencies from him and enjoyed viewing him as wholly irrational, Balmont had, as early as 1904, demonstrated an awareness of a master plan:

> From book to book, clear to each attentive eye,
> I have stretched a link, and I know that while
> I remain on Earth I shall not cease to forge new
> links, and that the bridge created by my dream
> is leading to free and beckoning distances. . . .

The book is virtuosic. At least a third of the poems are worthy of deep and lasting esteem, and most of the rest are good enough to bear reprinting. Even the weak poems such as the three entitled **"Russia"** are not spoiled by those excesses to which the young Balmont was prone (as in the lines his enemies invariably quote: V bereg b'etsia / Chuzhdyi charam chernyi cheln. "Alien to charms the black bark beats against the bank"). Their weakness stems from the fact that Balmont tried to express his patriotism in them, and patriotism usually blinded him to the imperatives of craftsmanship.

To be sure there are many echoes of Balmont's past. He still clings to his role of Seer, believes himself sensitive to preternaturally subtle hints . . . from the godhead. The *moment,* held sacred by an entire poetic generation in Europe, continued to exercise an irresistible attraction (". . . the moment is my home," he asserts in the tenth sonnet of **"The Foundation"** [**"Osnova"**]). An occasional brimstone-scented phantom from his decadent years lurks among debile plants exuding poisons (see **"The Deadly Nightshade"**), but they are of no great consequence.

Bryusov was right, in a sense, to view Balmont as a rural poet, for Balmont came to loath the "prison walls" of cities. If there was any redeeming virtue in metropolitan existence, in his view, it was the one already adumbrated by one of his idols, Dostoevsky: suffering is the way to God. He is content only when he can be wholly absorbed in nature, which in his hands yields an amazing variety of material. He is attentive to the work of bees and forest birds; like an innocent child he reacts to all the simple things in nature, and nature rewards him with love, quietude, mystery, inspiration and all this is necessary for a steady transcendence from the "world of will." This transcendence or its promise kept Balmont's eyes hypnotically focused on the sky throughout his life.

Certain formal elements characteristic of earlier stages of his career can also be discerned in this book. Alliteration is controlled, but the old musicality sometimes flares up again. . . . Evident in this book is Balmont's continued preference for the epithet rather than the simile or metaphor, but his figurative language is still better than it was in the books that brought him fame. One of the ways by which he circumvented the need for richer metaphoric stock was to continually expand his vocabulary; the many archaisms, neologisms and esoteric words in this collection contribute to a texture resisting facile comprehension. In his handling of syllabo-tonic metrical schemes Balmont remained traditional but always inventive, writing in measures ranging from dimeter schemes to amphibrachic heptameter (**"In a Distant Valley"**). The concluding *sonnet redouble* (**"The Foundation"**), an exceedingly difficult form, is a brilliant piece.

Balmont seldom succeeded as much as in this book in moving effortlessly through time and his visions: as an old man he raptly inspects the frozen beads of water that jewel a tree, and with the same clarity and ease he returned through many decades to his childhood to gaze at portentous wax settling to the bottom of teacups like heavy jewels (**"Winter Branch"**). The intensity of his gaze does not allow sensations from the "real" world that would inhibit his confusing falling snowflakes with white bees swirling from a silent hive (**"Silent Bees"** [**"Nezhuzhashchie"**]). The temporal matrix of many of these poems is not solid, the lyrical "I" slips away from the reader into nature's chaos or assumes disturbing guises. The lyrical voice of **"With Quiet Evening"** is anonymous, illusively melting from the scene of Salome's dance into garden thickets where the heavy mauves of sunset barely penetrate and strange nightflowers grow. The imagery is set upon more distant and engaging analogues than was the case in earlier collections, e.g., "The wind moves along the fence / Like a drowsiness along lashes . . ." And there are good metaphoric variations ranging from sunset as the severed head of John the Baptist to "An airy nomad's camp of clouds / Drank up the reddened grapes." (pp. 250-55)

Behind much of Balmont's later poetry there is a constant presence—a rumbling ocean rocking more than the bones of Atlantis. It is both a symbol of mystery, adventure, the endless excitement of artistic play with beauty—and a symbol of the eternal community of free spirits like Odysseus (**"The Unfading Blue"**). Like the "ocean" of the universe above, Balmont's oceans of salt water wait for the dust of all men only to spit it out, perhaps centuries later, in a different form, into a different adventure. It was also a catalyst of poem after poem, including **"Capbreton,"** in which Balmont bade a lyric farewell to all he loved. . . . In such poems Balmont seemed to anticipate (correctly) that his failing health and his poverty would soon force him to leave his beloved Atlantic retreat and return to Paris, which he loathed. . . .

Perhaps the same impulse is at the heart of **"Absolute Peace"** in which Balmont (whom Andrei Bely thought almost supernaturally youthful and described as a thirteenth-century troubadour who had forgotten to die in his own time), finally seemed to submit to senescence—at least in theory—as he seemed to be settling into that select company that has drunk deep and now simply waits for the bill. (p. 256)

The initial signs of Balmont's final mental illness appeared only two years after the writing of this collection. He paced the shore near Larochelle, waiting for death, reviewing his life, composing his complaints, and his farewells to the visible sun. One of the best expressions of this summing up is **"From the Sun."** . . . (p. 257)

In Distances Drawn Apart, like *The Ash Tree* and *Sonnets of the Sun, Honey and the Moon,* represents an impressive achievement in a career full of impressive accomplishments. Having read these books one finds it difficult to agree with those who insist on preserving the image of Balmont as a precious troubadour, a Spanish hidalgo, a brooding Hamlet, mad Decadent or strutting chanticleer. The old Balmont, although continuing many old themes, had an altogether different voice: quiet, self-contained, modest and often profound. The old poet, who had traveled the whole world and viewed its wonders with no more astonishment than that with which he looked into himself, eventually began to wait with only occasional impatience for death to come. He wrote his poems and studied the smallest birds and flowers as he had once studied whole libraries—still with the same objective—to see the opening through which he thought he would pass into another, more spectacular and satisfying life. (p. 258)

> Rodney L. Patterson, "Balmont: In Search of Sun and Shadow," in Russian Literature Triquarterly (© 1972 by Ardis Publishers), No. 4, Fall, 1972, pp. 241-64.

EVELYN BRISTOL   (essay date 1980)

[Bristol examines Balmont in the context of the Decadent movement in Russian literature, showing how its themes and theories are displayed in his work.]

In Russian literature, decadence became popular earlier than idealism, although the initiates of the inner circles were either dedicated to an idealistic revival, as was the case in St. Petersburg, or at least aware of the centrality of idealistic premises to Symbolism, as were its younger adherents in Moscow. The document now considered to be the initial polemic of the Russian movement, Dmitrii Merezhkovskii's essay, *O prichinakh upadka i o novykh techeniiakh sovremennoi russkoi literatury* (1893), called for a new literary mode that would both reflect the new idealism and be spiritually uplifting as well. And some of the coterie around Merezhkovskii in St. Petersburg showed more concern for the philosophical renaissance than for the literary one. But in the 1890s the public was won over by Russian poetry that was remarkably imitative of Baudelaire and Verlaine, and whose practitioners were primarily Konstantin Bal'mont in [*Pod severnym nebom, V bezbrezhnosti,* and *Tishina*] . . . and Fedor Sologub in his first two books. Valerii Briusov was still maturing as a poet, and Zinaida Gippius was as yet not as well known. All exhibited melancholias, frustrations, and a spiritual impotence in their verse, particularly

Bal'mont and Sologub, who depicted a character who is enervated, wilting, and neuraesthenic. . . . [Throughout Balmont's] three books nature itself is shown drooping and sorrowing. A resigned desire for death is displayed in some poems in his first two books, and in *Tishina,* in the section "Akkordy," we find an alternate decadent impulse, a paroxysm of splenetic revolt, which has a demonic character. (pp. 270-71)

Because Russian literary criticism has exhibited a puristic tendency to distinguish between idealistic and decadent poets, the doctrinal idealism of the so-called decadents, Bal'mont, Briusov, Sologub, and Gippius, has often been underestimated. Thus, in all three of his books, Bal'mont showed aspirations to the ineffable, and in the poem *"Zachem"* he complained that mankind is given a soul but denied spiritual attainment. He often wrote of weak things, himself, or nature, that strive upward to light, or life, or the elevated, and sink again into sadness and murkiness. In the section "Snezhnye tsvety" of *Tishina,* he rose to the experience of miracles and an identification with the eternal. (p. 272)

During the first several years of the new century, a general spirit of metaphysical optimism replaced the uncertainties characteristic of the 1890s. Not only did there appear a new wave of mystics, but ameliorating changes took place in the work of the decadents as well. Bal'mont executed a well-known change from passivity to self-assertion. In *Goriashchie zdaniia* . . . , he abandoned his neuraesthenia and alienation to become a passionate participant in life in its natural and divine aspects. The section, "Antifony," is a celebration of the idealistic view, in that he praised artistic creation, entertained visionary utopias, explored the solipsistic outlook, and identified with the springtime. In the sections "I da i net" and "Indiiskie travy," he became a pantheist and coursed upward to blend with the multiplicity of phenomena and with divinity. In *Budem kak solntse* . . . , he dwelt on his interchangeability with natural phenomena, which is the putative origin of his verse. This is the sense of his poem **"Ia izyskannost' russkoi medlitel'noi rechi."** (p. 273)

Bal'mont's revolutionary poems in *Pesni mstitelia* . . . , calling for the overthrow of the Russian monarch, appear to be unique among Symbolists in that they do not reveal any special connection to Symbolist theory. Zinaida Gippius, on the other hand, combined, like Sologub, political thought with philosophy. (p. 278)

In the early years of the century, as the movement gathered momentum, its polarities became more visible. Bal'mont created a drama in his work by becoming an exultant pantheist. Sologub dedicated himself to a distant, ineffable ideal. Gippius made her appearance as a Christian longing for universal salvation. . . . However, decadence could now more clearly be seen as an alternative to idealistic belief. Bal'mont, Sologub, and Briusov questioned the necessity and resented the very existence of evil. Bal'mont protested by identifying with violence, Sologub rebelled against heaven, Gippius succumbed to individualistic pride. . . . (pp. 279-80)

Symbolism as a movement did not survive the revolt of the Acmeists and Futurists against Platonic idealism, which had been its ideological core. But decadence had an existence of its own apart from the uses to which it was put by Symbolists. It can be seen both in the arrogant glamor of the Ego-Futurists and in the antibourgeois dandyism of the Cubo-Futurists. (p. 280)

> Evelyn Bristol, "Idealism and Decadence in Russian Symbolist Poetry," in Slavic Review (copyright ©

1980 by the American Association for the Advancement of Slavic Studies, Inc.), Vol. 39, No. 2, June, 1980, pp. 269-80.*

ADDITIONAL BIBLIOGRAPHY

Donchin, Georgette. "The Symbolist Aesthetics," "Themes in Symbolist Poetry," and "The Symbolist Technique." In her *The Influence of French Symbolism on Russian Poetry*, pp. 76-119, pp. 120-163, pp. 164-215. The Hague: Mouton, 1958.*
   Challenges Balmont's denial of French influence on his poetry. Balmont's main themes and poetic devices are examined in relation to the Symbolist movement in Russia.

Folejewski, Zbigniew. "Dynamic or Static? The Function of the Verb in Poetry." In his *Canadian Contributions to the Seventh International Congress of Slavists*, pp. 111-19. The Hague: Mouton, 1973.*
   Compares conflicting data on the effect of verblessness in creating dynamic or static effect in Balmont's poetry.

Gumilev, Nikolai. "Blok, Klyuev, Balmont, Verlaine, Veselkova-Kilshtet, Shershenevich, Genigen," and "Leaders of the New School: Konstantin Balmont, Valery Bryusov, Fyodor Sologub." In his *Nikolai Gumilev on Russian Poetry*, edited and translated by David Lapeza, pp. 97-105, pp. 172-74. Ann Arbor, Mich.: Ardis, 1977.*
   Reprints two reviews of Balmont's works. The first article, written in 1912, calls Balmont "a very great poet who can write very bad poetry." The second, written in 1918, gives Balmont credit as "the foremost" among the poets who renewed Russian poetry with his translations of Western literature and descriptions of his exotic travels.

Kipa, Albert A. "K. D. Bal'mont and Gerhart Hauptmann." In *Views and Reviews of Modern German Literature: Festschrift for Adolf D. Klarmann*, edited by Karl A. Weimar, pp. 51-60. Munich: Delp Verlag, 1974.*
   Discusses Bal'mont's translations of Hauptmann's plays into Russian, focusing on the Russian's attitudes toward the German playwright's work.

Patterson, Rodney L. "Review of: *Stikhotvoreniia*." *Slavic and East European Journal* 16, No. 1 (Spring 1972): 103-05.
   Favorable review of Vladimir Orlov's collected edition of Balmont's poetry. Patterson praises Orlov's attempt "to wipe some of the tarnish from Balmont's once resplendent image by reviewing some of the abundant and impressive accolades Bal'mont received during his career."

Schmidt, Tatyana. "Escapism As a Form of Revolt." *The Slavonic and East European Review* 47, No. 2 (July 1969): 323-43.*
   Discussion of the decadent Symbolists' reaction to Positivism and the nature of their self-created worlds. In Balmont, this escapism blended "revolt for its own sake and refuge in western thought."

Philip (James Quinn) Barry

1896-1949

American dramatist, novelist, short story writer, and poet.

One of the most prominent American dramatists during the 1920s and 1930s, Barry was best known for his sophisticated comedies of manners. His work combines witty repartee and amusing plots to satirize the values and mores of the upper class. Barry's dramas consistently examine such aspects of marriage as love, adultery, and divorce, as well as the "well-bred" individual's search for self-fulfillment. In addition to his comedies, Barry wrote several psychological dramas. Although these works were not as successful as his humorous plays, they deal with similar motifs and are praised for their innovative use of psychoanalytic techniques, such as role-playing and dream analysis, within the confines of drama. Barry's most enduring work is *The Philadelphia Story*, an urbane comedy of manners which continues to be enjoyed in theatrical revivals and in two film versions.

Born in Rochester, New York, to a middle-class Irish-Catholic family, Barry was educated in Catholic schools and at Yale University. While at Yale he contributed short stories and poetry to the *Yale Literary Magazine* and the college newspaper. After a year of service in the American Embassy in London during World War I, Barry returned to the United States and enrolled in Harvard's Workshop 47, a dramatic composition course conducted by George Pierce Baker. The well-known workshop was attended by several important writers, including Eugene O'Neill, S. N. Behrman, and Thomas Wolfe. It was in this workshop that Barry received the encouragement and training that helped him develop his play writing skills. In 1922, his drama *The Jilts* won Harvard's Herndon Prize, which included a professional Broadway production of the drama. *The Jilts,* retitled *You and I* for its Broadway engagement, was enthusiastically received by audiences and critics. It was the first of Barry's plays to deal with the frustration of unrealized ambitions. The serio-comic treatment of the subject and the lively dialogue throughout the drama are mainstays of Barry's work. *You and I* was the beginning of a career that spanned three decades. During that time, Barry achieved financial success as a dramatist and became well-acquainted with the social elite he portrayed. Though he was disappointed that critics preferred his comedies to his more provocative works, such as the psychological drama *Hotel Universe,* he continued to produce serious plays in addition to his more popular comedies. Barry worked in the theater until he died of a heart attack in 1949.

In a Garden, Barry's third play, is characteristic of the best of his comedies. The subject of freedom in marriage is comedically, yet sensitively handled. Adrian Terry, the egotistical husband of the drama, attempts to disprove the premise that "every man's wife is another man's mistress at heart." *In a Garden* is notable for another reason: in the play Barry employed a psychoanalytic technique when he had Adrian construct a garden setting in which his wife's first love affair could be reenacted. W. David Sievers considers *In a Garden* significant as "the first modern attempt to incorporate in a play the concept of psychodrama." *Paris Bound* was Barry's first overwhelming Broadway success. Divorce and adultery

are the subjects of this drama, which expresses an attitude toward marital infidelity that was unusual in popular art of the time. In *Paris Bound,* Barry proposed that the spiritual love of marriage is too important to dissolve because of a sexual dalliance. When both husband and wife realize the solemnity of their marriage vows, divorce becomes more of a transgression than adultery. Typical of Barry's work, the characters in *Paris Bound* are among the ranks of the upper class and "the comic felicity of the dialogue" reverberates in the drawing room setting. With *Holiday,* Barry left the topic of marriage to satirize materialism in America. When the protagonist of the comedy states that he will enjoy himself when he is young and work when he is old, the wealthy family of his fiancée is appalled. This humorously portrayed break with convention expresses Barry's view that money is not an end in itself. A timely drama, *Holiday* closed after a successful season shortly before the 1929 stock market crash. In *The Animal Kingdom,* Barry returned to the theme that marriage must transcend physical appetites to be a true union. His clever depiction of a lover's triangle reverses the roles of a man's wife and mistress. The wife seduces her husband into compromising his artistic ambitions for monetary gains, while the mistress offers him abiding love and respect for his life's work. Many early reviewers questioned the morality of *The Animal Kingdom,* because at the close of the drama the husband leaves his wife for the mistress. However, other commentators found the work highly moral and consistent with Barry's marital ideals.

Barry reached the apex of his career with the phenomenal success of *The Philadelphia Story*. During its Broadway production, this comedy of manners was seen by more people than any of Barry's other works. The portrayal of the rich and spoiled Tracy Lord—a classic Barry character—provided actress Katherine Hepburn, for whom the role was written, with her first critical success on the stage and in films. Beneath the comedic dramaturgy of *The Philadelphia Story*, morality and human frailty are central issues. Barry satirized the moral hypocrisy of the privileged class through Tracy, who is intolerant of human weaknesses, especially those in her own family. Tracy is enlightened, however, when, on the eve of her second marriage, she experiences a moral indiscretion of her own and realizes that it is love and people that matter, not position or class. Gerald Hamm believes the outstanding dramatic success of *The Philadelphia Story* resides in Barry's "seemingly unconscious sense of juxtaposition which enabled him to blend into a unit his rich dramatic technique, his supple dialogue, and his natural insight into character."

Barry's artistic departure from drawing room comedies produced the dramas *Hotel Universe* and *Here Come the Clowns*, his most frequently discussed efforts in psychodrama. These experimental works were not the typical Barry successes, for they perplexed both critics and audiences who did not expect cosmic considerations from Barry. In *Hotel Universe*, Barry gathered a group of troubled characters in a villa in Southern France. The action of the drama takes place on a terrace which seemingly becomes more and more like a nebulous wedge in space. On this terrace the characters are encouraged to regress to happier times, recall dreams, and role-play, eventually to return to reality, cognizant of what they have learned about themselves. Though *Hotel Universe* is criticized for its abstruseness, most critics praise Barry for his novel use of psychoanalysis within the work. Sievers regards *Hotel Universe* as "one of the truly original masterpieces of the modern American drama." Similar to *Hotel Universe*, *Here Come the Clowns* is a philosophical examination of existential questions. Good and evil are major concerns in this work which finds free will to be the greatest of life's gifts. Throughout the drama, Barry utilized psychoanalytic therapy to jar the subconsciouses of the characters—a motley group of vaudevillians. Although *Here Come the Clowns* was not a popular or financial success, critics agree that it is the work of an accomplished writer.

Barry's literary reputation rests primarily on his deft ability in the comedy of manners, and he is especially praised as a masterful practitioner of witty and clever dialogue. While some critics also laud Barry's humorous, often satirical characterization of upper-class individuals, others criticize him for limiting his characters to the drawing rooms of the wealthy. Though his career flourished because of these entertaining, sophisticated comedies, Barry expressed disappointment that his more serious works were not critically acclaimed. However, critical reevaluations of his work indicate that his experiments with psychodrama represent a significant contribution in the development of the modern theater. For this reason, and for a prolific comedic talent that continues to entertain audiences, Barry holds a significant place in twentieth-century American drama.

(See also *Dictionary of Literary Biography*, Vol. 7: *Twentieth-Century American Dramatists*.)

PRINCIPAL WORKS

You and I (drama) 1923
The Youngest (drama) 1924
In a Garden (drama) 1925
White Wings (drama) 1926
John (drama) 1927
Paris Bound (drama) 1927
Holiday (drama) 1928
Hotel Universe (drama) 1930
Tomorrow and Tomorrow (drama) 1931
The Animal Kingdom (drama) 1932
The Joyous Season (drama) 1934
Bright Star (drama) 1935
**Here Come the Clowns* (drama) 1938
War in Heaven (novel) 1938
The Philadelphia Story (drama) 1939
Liberty Jones: A Play with Music for City Children
    (drama) 1941
Without Love (drama) 1942
**Second Threshold (drama) 1951
States of Grace (dramas) 1975

*This drama is an adaptation of the novel *War in Heaven*.

**This work was completed by Robert E. Sherwood.

GEORGE P. BAKER   (letter date 1923)

[*Baker was the renowned professor of Harvard's Workshop 47. Of the fledgling playwrights he instructed and encouraged, Barry was one of the most successful. In the following excerpt, Baker comments on Barry's prize winning drama* You and I.]

My dear Barry:

With your accustomed consideration you ask me to write a foreword as you present this child of your brain, *You and I,* to the reading public. Certainly it is quite fitting that the child's godfather should share in the pleasurable excitement of the moment. I watched its birth in English 47A two years ago; I admired the fine yet kind exactingness with which you trained it from the ways in which the child wilfully, like all children, would try to go to the ways in which it should go. (p. 1)

Surely now, you don't expect critical comment on *You and I,* do you? Off and on, this past two years haven't you had enough of that? Moreover, is it not the well-understood duty of a loyal godparent to watch, to try to understand, to comment cautiously to the anxious parents and seal his lips for all observers? Certainly it is thus that I understand these duties. (p. 3)

It is not because thousands of people have been amused by *You and I* that I take pride in it. Rather it is because here you have written not a comedy of situation bordering on farce, but really a comedy of character. It is pleasant to go from your play with a renewed sense of the wholesome, fine-spirited people, who yet are keenly amusing, to be found all around us. Delicately, tenderly and with no sentimentality, you suggest the affection and understanding of father, mother and son. Most of all, I like *You and I* for the light, sure touch with which you reveal Matey's tragedy, the conflict of his business success with his artistic longings. When he first reveals his desires, there came from an audience in which I sat at the Belmont Theatre an odd, low murmur of male voices,—understanding, sympathetic, self-incriminating. That is the best testimony to the truth and the artistry of your play you could desire. Humorously, yet gently, you have revealed to your generation one of the little tragedies of us, your elders, whom they are disposed, ''murmuring Mid-Victorians,'' to waive aside as emotional rigidities. (pp. 4-5)

> *George P. Baker, in his letter to Philip Barry on May 15, 1923 (copyright, 1923, by Brentano's; copyright, 1922, by Philip Barry; reprinted by permission of Edwin O. Baker and George P. Baker, as living heirs of George P. Baker, and Ellen Barry as executrix of the Estate of the late Philip Barry), in* You and I: A Comedy in Three Acts *by Philip Barry, Brentano's Publishers, 1923, pp. 1-5.*

EDMUND WILSON   (essay date 1923)

[*Wilson, America's foremost man of letters in the twentieth century, wrote widely on cultural, historical, and literary matters, including several seminal critical studies. He is often credited with bringing an international perspective to American letters through his widely read discussions of European literature. Perhaps Wilson's greatest contributions to American literature were his tireless promotion of writers of the 1920s, 1930s, and 1940s, and his essays introducing the best of modern literature to the general reader.*]

You and I by Philip Barry is a partially interesting attempt to deal with an authentic theme and to study an authentic *milieu*. But it is badly spoiled before the end and I believe for the following reasons. In the first place, Mr. Barry takes the inhabitants of his country house for very smart and cultivated people when they are actually half-baked in the extreme. You think he is going to study them seriously, then you discover that he shares their view of themselves—that he is impressed by their suburban luxuries and ravished by their silly-clever wit—a wit which is only one of the means such people employ to make agreeable the banality of their lives—like curtains of flowered chintz and little electric wall-lamps. Furthermore, Mr. Barry, having set out with a real problem, proceeds to develop it with theatrical situations. The young girl who loves the boy so much that she is willing to give him up entirely so that instead of being obliged to support her he may follow his architectural dreams, but never offers to share his struggles or to assist him with her $2000 a year! The father who having smothered his own artistic ambitions by a money-making career allows his son to do the same thing just at the moment when he is himself most keenly feeling his own futility, and who after becoming at the end of years one of the mainstays of a large soap company is unable to take a year's vacation without being in danger of losing his job! . . . [The] whole thing reminded me a little of the late Clyde Fitch. Clyde Fitch was *par excellence* the virtuoso of the external: like the America of the time, his true gift lay in playing with it. When I think of his plays, I think of people being kept awake by banging radiators, trying to eat wax oranges, turning on the wrong electric lights, of men diving under the table after dinner to retrieve the things the ladies have dropped. I think of beings who speak on ordinary occasions in the very accents of life, but who as soon as they are moved by any strong emotion begin to talk like the theatre of fifty years ago. When Fitch was on the surface he was excellent: he was a master of the property and the ''line,'' but when he was serious he was almost always awful: his situations were wholly for and from the stage.—Mr. Barry has a gift not unlike Clyde Fitch's; let him

beware, as he hopes to be an artist, how he falls back on the same tricks. (pp. 100-01)

> *Edmund Wilson, in his review of ''You and I,'' in* The Dial *(copyright, 1923, by The Dial Publishing Company, Inc.), Vol. LXXV, No. 1, July, 1923 pp. 100-01.*

JOSEPH WOOD KRUTCH   (essay date 1927)

[*Krutch is widely regarded as one of America's most respected literary and drama critics. Noteworthy among his works are* The American Drama since 1918 *(1939), which analyzes the most important dramas of the 1920s and 1930s, and ''Modernism'' in* Modern Drama *(1953), in which he stressed the need for twentieth-century playwrights to infuse their works with traditional humanistic values. A conservative and idealistic thinker, he was a consistent proponent of human dignity and preeminence of literary art. His literary criticism is characterized by such concerns: in* The Modern Temper *(1929) he argued that because scientific thought has denied human worth, tragedy had become obsolete, and in* The Measure of Man *(1954) he attacked modern culture for depriving humanity of the sense of individual responsibility necessary for making important decisions in an increasingly complex age.*]

Much was expected of Philip Barry's **''John.''** . . . The author had previously written two failures rather generally regarded as too good for the public. . . .

The John referred to in the title is the man generally described as ''the Baptist,'' and the play is, or rather tries to be, concerned with the tragedy of his personal failure. Conceived by Mr. Barry as a man with all the passionate force and all the narrow limitations of most evangelists, it is his fate to be an instrument for the achievement of a purpose which he is incapable of understanding. A nationalist, a man of violence, and preeminently the prophet of a revengeful God, it is not within the compass of his soul to comprehend the Messiah whose advent he has been foretelling. He has seen Jesus, he has liked him even, but it has been so impossible for the two men to know one another that when John, in prison, is told of the new turn-cheek doctrine preached by his erstwhile disciple he can only set it down as a malicious lie, and though, at the moment of his death, he knows that Jesus is the Messiah he goes to that death gladly only because he is sure that the new leader will have the adultress Herodias stoned as the law commands and wield again the war-like might of the Jews.

Not only is the conception intellectually interesting but—and this is more important still—it has the stuff of great tragedy in it. This John is exactly the large but imperfect man of whom Aristotle spoke, and death, coming upon him in a moment of exaltation, affords exactly that sort of situation which we properly call tragic—one, that is to say, in which the moment of external catastrophe coincides with the moment of internal triumph and a man dies in the full possession of his soul. John has not failed for himself, and because he can accept death gladly we, too, can accept it with that exaltation which makes the genuinely tragic as far removed from mere pathos as it is from comedy. Nor does the fact that the peace of his soul is founded upon a misapprehension, that he accepts his fate because he does not understand it, do anything except intensify the interest of the situation. It complicates heroism with irony and it makes John not merely a triumphant failure but a glorious dupe as well.

The play fails, not because of any lack of spiritual insight on the part of the author but simply because he has not been able to manage his narrative. Exposition, often unnecessary, clogs his action, and his story will not move forward. There is a long, meandering first act that barely succeeds in introducing the subject, a second largely concerned with irrelevant affairs in the home of the Tetrarch, and then, finally, a concluding scene too short to do more than suggest how effective the play might have been. (p. 582)

> *Joseph Wood Krutch, "A Fiasco," in* The Nation *(copyright 1927* The Nation *magazine, The Nation Associates, Inc.), Vol. CXXV, No. 3255, November 23, 1927, pp. 582-83.*

CARL CARMER   (essay date 1929)

[*Carmer discusses Barry's potential for writing a play that is both important and popular. He maintains that the dramatist has thus far lacked an "overwhelming purpose"—the one factor necessary to create the "great" play he believes Barry is capable of writing.*]

To the critical appraiser Phillip Barry presents a curious anomaly. From the beginning of his career he has been favored of the gods of the American theatre. Without exception his plays have been presented by first line producers. . . . They have been interpreted by . . . experienced, competent, and well known players. . . . They have been furnished with settings designed by talented stage artists. . . . They have been produced outside of New York more frequently than the plays of any other American except Eugene O'Neill. Now they have been published in a uniform edition [*Plays by Philip Barry*]. And yet Barry is a playwright whose failures are more significant than his successes, a widely acclaimed dramatist who has yet to write a play both popular and important.

The American theatre has scarcely another devotee who brings as much to it in background and ability. Barry is young, intelligent, a graduate of a representative college, trained in the drama by the well versed and practical Professor Baker. Few would deny that he has a genuine talent for the theatre. He has a knack of true observation and a feeling for form. As for experience he has written seven plays besides *Cock Robin,* a mystery play written in collaboration with Elmer Rice (disregarded in this article as not a true index of Barry's abilities), that have been produced. He is, I suppose, most representative of America's academically schooled dramatists and makes an interesting contrast with the group of play-makers whose only education has been Broadway itself.

When the student prize-play, *You and I,* attracted the attention of New York audiences in 1923, critics vied with each other in predicting that this young man would go far. There is no reason to deny the prophecy now—except that several years have passed and he has not advanced as rapidly as the critics and, doubtless, he himself expected. *You and I* displayed Barry's most valuable talents. It was well made; it presented characters who could be differentiated and distinguished in American society quite as well as their prototypes in the comedy of manners of a more class-conscious England, and it put into their mouths with astonishing facility and truth the words that such Americans really speak. Moreover, despite the fact that it was a "first play", it acted well. Audiences found themselves readily sympathetic to this story of a business man who had once sacrificed an artistic career on the altars of love and expedience, and is determined his son shall not follow in his footsteps. With a serious theme, critics agreed, Barry could write a great play.

But *The Youngest,* which followed close upon *You and I,* though it was fairly successful, did not advance his banner. It seems less characteristic of its author than any of his works, a not very effective excursion into those fields of wholesome American domestic comedy, where bloom *The First Year, Tommy, Skidding* and others made popular throughout the land by travelling Chautauquas. The playwright was not living up to his lights. Still the drama with a theme worthy of his effort eluded him.

Apparently, someone, sensing the difficulty, must have advised Mr. Barry of this, for in his next play, *In a Garden,* the theme hangs rather heavily above the characters and the audience. It produces much the same effect as a Victorian "drama of ideas." An attack on the fundamental untruth of epigrammatic generalities, it ends by merely substituting a new rule for one outworn. "Every woman is the potential mistress of her first lover" is supplanted by—"You can't do that with people, Adrian. That's God's province. For you it's blasphemy." When Lissa leaves Adrian's house because he has dared to arrange circumstance in the effort to shape her life, her departure seems motivated upon as fallacious a basis as his attempt to keep her love. The play also shows one of Mr. Barry's major weaknesses . . . , his tendency to be "cute", to lay the whimsical humor on with too heavy a brush. *In a Garden* gives the impression of being carefully worked out, a thesis play with little spontaneity, a modern, immature *Doll's House* with neither the strength nor the natural charm of Ibsen. But it revealed a poetic quality, not very noticeable in Barry's previous plays, which, added to the gifts he had already displayed, augured well for the future.

It was this very quality which ran away with him in his next endeavor and prohibited the commercial success of what I believe to be his best play, *White Wings.* Here was a madly humorous, profoundly and grotesquely poetic interpretation of the never-ending battle between this day and the one just past. One might as well expect a play written in good poetry to make money as for *White Wings* to draw crowds to the box-office. The love story of a horse-loving White Wing Capulet and the daughter of a motor-minded Montague, told with a bizarre modernistic symbolism, bewildered auditors who were not wont to look upon the material things about them as having more than material meanings. The play demanded such an agility of mind and a *finesse* of intelligent appreciation as only a selected audience could be expected to have. Possibly, now that the mourning critics have written such golden elegies for it, it might successfully be revived. I doubt it. I am inclined to believe that a really good play must have enough of surface values to make it of more than ordinary interest to the auditor of mediocre intelligence. Shakespeare's technique, his knowledge of what is called today "good theatre", kept the groundlings breathless while his more sensitive hearers marvelled at the subtlety of his meanings and the beauty of his lines. But *White Wings* makes no concessions. Caviar to the general, it remains a museum piece for the admiration of connoisseurs.

Mr. Barry's next play, *John,* was a far cry from contemporary satire. It was a reverently conceived historical drama of the fiery prophet of the wilderness and his relationship to Jesus. The dialogue is written in a homely, salty, rhythmic prose that on stirring occasions (and apparently without conscious design) crosses the misty border-line into poetry. Some passages, indeed, if written in verse form, are reminiscent of sounding lines from the chronicle plays of the Elizabethan stage. . . . (pp. 819-22)

Modern audiences do not, as a rule, care for serious poetic dramas on religious themes. The application of the methods of recent biographers to John the Baptist may have seemed an admirable basis for a play but the translation of those methods into drama is not always easy. Moreover, the Baptist is a much more remote figure than Lincoln and Disraeli about whom successful plays have been drawn. Perhaps it was for these reasons that *John* ran but two weeks. Or possibly it was because of the average theatre-goer's fear of didacticism which must have seemed to him inherent in the subject. Whatever it was, much fine and sincere work was lost to the stage when the play failed.

In *Paris Bound*, a decided break in the line of commercial failures, the bars of the playwright's own standards seem to have been let down. It would appear that he wished to prove he could write a successful play if he chose. It is amusing but artificial comedy. While it does not seem Barry's best or most spontaneous work, there is much to recommend it. Returning to the scene of his first success, he gives us a picture of upper middle class Americans that is truer than any we have yet had. No one is better able to depict today's "younger generation" with its desperate frankness, its heroic effort to control sentiment and to ridicule sentimentality, its love of nonsense. (pp. 822-23)

The play handles the subject of divorce with a well administered compound of humor and intelligence. It is not a true comedy of manners, however, for the author is too much in sympathy with all of his characters to make fun of their inconsistencies and foibles. Moreover, he uses one comedy device quite as boringly as does contemporary society: his characters' satiric use of expressions made clichés by others. The following passage illustrates:

> FANNY: They say in Poictesme that she loves her husband.
>
> PETER: Will the gray hordes never cease? God! Are we too late?
>
> FANNY: Six weeks without him is just too much to bear, it's too much to bear.
>
> NORA: Never mind. To-morrow we'll have our old Mary back again.
>
> PETER: She had charm, that girl. Always a smile for everyone.
>
> FANNY: And now it's a curse or a blow.
>
> PETER: Love is like that.

Not one of these speeches is truly "in character." Each is a quotation from some familiar but un-named source. Certainly this method is not witty, for wit demands variety. It is dull as most fads are dull. It is simply a part of the transitory fancy for poking fun at sentimentalities, a fancy that last season lined the pockets of the producers of the Hoboken revivals with gold. (pp. 823-24)

This sort of thing is very tiring. The characters become really exasperating with their never-ending stock of second-hand speeches and attitudes. Nevertheless *Paris Bound* had real, if superficial, charm, and it was not lacking in interesting social purpose. It dared to take the modern viewpoint that adultery may not be so great a sin against marriage as has been generally supposed. It pictured smart people as they and those who would be smart like to picture themselves. It was eminently actable. And so it had a long run.

Holiday, obviously written as a follow-up for *Paris Bound,* is Mr. Barry's latest play. Here Peter and Nora of the first play go under the aliases of Nick and Susan, while Fanny masquerades as Linda. The theme, that riches are not essential to happy living, is not exactly novel, nor is it made so important as the divorce problem of the preceding play. The dialogue again is charming and rings poignantly true except in those scenes where all the characters play the game that Peter started back in *Paris Bound.* (p. 824)

Counteracting the scenes of silly humor, however, are sincere, moving passages of dialogue, speeches that have the rhythms of actual conversation and yet are dramatically constructed, sharply tipped with meaning. From the player's point of view they almost act themselves. This (with many actors' predilections for playing the roles of "nice people") probably explains the popularity of Barry's plays among actors, both professional and amateur, and accounts for their frequent production by stock companies and little theatres. In a play so slight in substance as *Holiday* this acting quality stands out very noticeably, often giving untrained players the opportunity of presenting a good performance. (p. 825)

Mr. Barry has had the best preparation that America can give. He has been educated by our professors and theorists and has built upon the foundation thus attained with experience in the hard school of Broadway. If he allows nothing to turn him aside from it, he may yet write a great play. His chief need at present, if I may be allowed a modest opinion, is to put aside his facile fooling and acquire an overwhelming purpose, a burning sincerity in his theme. There is none of his plays which does not seem to me to be saying: "Here is a great idea for a play!" instead of "Here is a great idea!"

His knowledge of technique, his ability to write sincere and moving dialogue, his poetic sensitivity, the acting quality of his work, his varied experience, all forecast an achievement of which America may be proud. (p. 826)

> *Carl Carmer, "Phillip Barry" (reprinted by permission of the Literary Estate of Carl Carmer), in* Theatre Arts Monthly, *Vol. 13, No. 11, November, 1929, pp. 819-26.*

JOHN MASON BROWN   (essay date 1930)

[*Brown, an influential and popular American drama critic during the 1930s, 1940s, and 1950s, wrote extensively on contemporary British and American drama. He had a thorough knowledge of dramatic history and his criticism often displays a scholarly erudition in addition to the qualities of popular reviewing. Although Brown praises Barry's deft ability to create witty dialogue and portray upper-class characters usually associated with high comedy, he comments that Barry's dramas do not maintain the acerbity of true high comedy; rather, they eventually rely on the whimsical or sentimental to convey their themes.*]

It is in his dialogue that Philip Barry shows himself to be more fully possessed of the comic spirit than is any other practising American playwright. He alone is able to fill his stage time after time with people who, while they belong in reality to this world, seem to be the gay property of a world of his own invention. To be sure his characters look and act like other people. They are warmed by the same sun, cooled by the same rain, and vexed by the same dilemmas that we are, even if they are not dressed by the same tailors or watered by the same watering places. But in facing their problems they speak a joyous, light-hearted language of their own which—at Mr.

Barry's best—cannot only obscure the sheen on a familiar situation, but lift a fact above its cold realities and push it over into that realm of glorious nonsense of which only high comedy is capable.

They play a game, a snobbish game if you like, that is meaningless, even irritating, unless you approach it in the spirit of gleeful ridicule with which they attack it. You cannot bring to it the sober standards of your Hamsuns and O'Neills. You must forget the red table cloths of your regional drama to enjoy it; and forget, too, those Calvinisms—both spiritual and presidential—to which as an American you have undoubtedly been exposed. You must forget them because this game of mad-cap banter which his characters play is never halted to make certain that you are in on it. It does not stop because its major premise—which is the major premise of all high comedy—is equality. Not that equality which was set down in Magna Carta, or in that other document to which the original John Hancock was appended, but the equality of the Social Register. It takes for granted not only that the author and his audiences are equals socially and intellectually, but, what is far more important, that they also share that greatest test as well as that most ultimate privilege of equality—the capacity for laughing at the same thing, at the same time and in the same way.

This game to which Mr. Barry sets his characters is played by well-dressed people who belong to that world of comfortable means which has always been—and must ever be—the background of high comedy. Its worries are the luxurious grievances that indolence and wealth alone can breed. For not only are its characters to the manner born (as modern America understands the term), but they are also to the manor born (as the word is understood in Westchester County and the East Sixties and Seventies). Moreover, they are, in their own way, cosmopolites who enjoy their intermittent flings at Paris, London, Antibes, Cannes, and St. Paul du Var. But, though they belong to what Upton Sinclair would dismiss as a stuffy world of moneyed respectability, neither they nor their world is stuffy by the time Mr. Barry has endowed them with his banter.

Certainly the game his men and women engage upon is not stuffy, in spite of all the shortcomings it may have. It is written by one of the few American playwrights who does not have to rent a dinner coat to write a comedy of manners, of a class that approaches the game as peers; slightly bored, fully aware of the failings of their kind, but possessed of its lucky ones who speak the same language and are ready for the same intellectual releases. It is a special world—undoubtedly trivial in its worries if you judge them by the loamy fundamentals of the giants of the earth and the empire builders. But it is young America, mannered, wise-cracking, collegiate; the world of the second and third generations of today, painted as personally in each play as if it were a first novel.

It is America just dwindling into matrimony as Congreve would express it; faced in *Paris Bound* and *In a Garden* with the problems of divorce as they present themselves in their most *editions de luxe* form. It is a world, as it shows itself in *You and I* or *Holiday,* or even in that far less successful farce-comedy, *The Youngest,* that is considerably aware of "Art" (spelled with a capital of course) and agitated by those clear-cut decisions which, according to Mr. Barry, must always be made by sensitive people between "Art" or "Personal Freedom" and "dat ole davil" of the contemporary theatre—"Big Business." It is a sensitive world, however, fed up with plenty, yearning for something else as in *Hotel Universe,* though usually for nothing greater or more profound than "finding itself."

But at least it is a world that feels an intangible awareness of its lacks which is deep enough to challenge its own facility of expression. Certainly Mr. Barry's treatment of it, witty and delightful as it is, is not faultless, either as plot material or as high comedy. But in each of the "above-stairs" comedies in which he has dealt with it, he has managed to restate this world in his own terms and to give it a style that is unmistakably his own.

He does this most especially by the bantering game of mock-heroics to which he sets his characters, and by the glib but meaningful dialogue he puts into their mouths. (pp. 19-21)

Watch Johnny Case in *Holiday,* for example, who is not rich enough, nor "fixed" enough, to walk with such assurance into that enormous Fifth Avenue living room and ask old Edward Seton, "financier and cotillion leader" for the hand of his daughter, Julia, and you see Mr. Barry in a typical moment, turning an old scene topsy-turvy by the ingratiating freshness and the mock bravado of his speeches. The great Mr. Seton is still at church. But the young Setons realize that their father's objections to the marriage are certain to be strong. More than that, they know him and his kind well enough to foresee exactly what they will be. Accordingly, Linda, Julia's sister who has never seen Johnny before, and Ned, her brother, prepare Johnny Case for his ordeal.

"See here, Case," says Linda, "I think you need some coaching. . . . Have you anything at all but your winning way to your credit?" "Not a thing," Johnny admits. "The first thing father will want to know," continues Linda, "is, how are you fixed?" "Fixed?" "Fixed—Are you a man of means, and, if so, how much?" "I have in my pocket now, thirty-four dollars and a package of Lucky Strikes. Will you have one?" "Thanks," says Linda, taking a cigarette from him. "But no gilt-edged securities? No rolling woodlands?" "I've got a few shares of common stock tucked away in a warm place." "Common?" cries Linda, feigning horror. "Don't say the word. I'm afraid it won't do, Julia. . . . He's a comely boy, but probably just another of the vast army of clock-watchers." (pp. 22-3)

It is a grand time that Mr. Barry gives his characters, allowing them to spoof to their heart's content, and providing for their spoofing dialogue which, on the whole, is more consistently fleet than any of our dramatists can write. Sometimes the lines are gagged with such obvious, but none the less laughable, undergraduatisms as "I didn't stroke the Vassar crew for nothing." Sometimes they are of that "bookish sort," which, as Thornton Wilder once expressed it, "people who do not read Charles Lamb imagine to be like him." Seldom, however, as Mr. Barry uses them, are they allowed to have amusement as their only goal. The reason is of course that his comedies, in spite of the gay mockery of their speech, are saddened, tender, whimsical tragedies at heart. They do not pillory an institution, "exposing," as Hazlitt said, "the follies and the weaknesses of mankind to ridicule." They may laugh at the absurdities of a class and poke fun at contemporary Americana, but their laughing correctives are incidental, not direct. Occasionally they may speak the language of high comedy, but almost invariably they are swayed by the emotions of sentimental drama.

Mr. Barry's characters have hearts, which is contrary to the tradition of sheerest comedy. They invite our sympathies rather than sway our reason. Beneath the veneer of their glibness most of them "lead lives of quiet desperation"; such lives of hidden self-pity as Matey leads in *You and I,* as the father does in *Paris Bound* and Linda in *Holiday,* or as that group of people do who assemble on a terrace in *Hotel Universe* to plumb the mysteries of life. They do not ask for those callous judgments by which we appraise the Witwells, the Fainalls and the Mirabells. They draw upon our compassion by reaching out to that very self-pity which most of us manage to bury deep within ourselves. Nor are they shadows raised above the moral law. Instead they are emotionalists who, for the most part, are its willing and expressive subjects. (pp. 23-4)

Though they are the products of an age in which men and women are rated as equals, facing life on the grounds of that sex equality which Meredith pointed out was necessary to all high comedy, neither Mr. Barry's men nor his women belong to the tradition of heartless comedy, which is the great tradition of all high comedy. They are too unfitted for independence, and too susceptible to love to make the battles of their courtships or their marriages more than petty skirmishes. They play an enchanting game with one another, instead of living coldly by the brittle radiance of their wits. His women, in particular, are not made of the stuff of which the Millamants and the Celimenes are made. They are not, in spite of their modernity, the self-reliant masters of their fates. On the contrary, they are, as Meredith would call them, "wandering vessels, crying for a captain or a pilot." They may laugh at their love in their speeches, but their very mockery of it is the surest sign of its existence, betraying as nothing else could their self-consciousness before it and anticipating their surrender.

Nor does Mr. Barry, like Congreve, "spread a privation of moral blight" over his world. For, in spite of its sophistication and the paradoxical manner in which he treats it, his is a very moral world. In each of his plays—with the exception of *Hotel Universe* which found him vaulting into the saddle and riding off as rapidly in all directions as if he had been a Stephen Leacock hero—Mr. Barry has approached this world of his with a definite thing to say, a theorem to prove, or a preachment to make. In *In a Garden* he shows how different are the motivations of life from the purely arbitrary motivations of literature. In *Paris Bound,* disguised by the comic felicity of his dialogue and his seemingly unconventional point of view, he preaches a most churchly sermon against divorce, basing it on the debatable idea that occasional infidelity is pardonable, when—and only when—a husband and a wife are truly in love, because then a mere physical transgression can have nothing to do with the real ties that bind them.

Mr. Barry does not as a rule take the chances with his underlying ideas that he does with the rippling banter of his dialogue. Because, though the conversation of his characters is based on the assumption that it is a game played by equals, the exposition of his ideas is not. They are baldly stated, hammered home with the nervousness of all democratic playwrights, said not once but twice, so that everyone is certain to be aware of what he is up to. Indeed it is only in the Freudian gropings of *Hotel Universe* that Mr. Barry is reticent about his underlying ideas. And then his reticence seems to be more the product of his own uncertainty than of anything else. Elsewhere, however, he not only writes his lessons clearly on the blackboard, but uses a ruler to point them out. In *Holiday,* for example, though the idea is considerably less didactic, even less substantial, than most of Mr. Barry's *motifs,* it is solemnly summarized by Johnny Case as, "You see, it's always been my plan to make a few thousands early in the game, if I could, and then quit for as long as they last, and try to find out who I am and what I am and what goes on and what about it—now, while I'm young and feel good all the time."

In each of his plays you will find that Mr. Barry ceases to laugh when he stumbles on the idea upon which the play is founded. His comedy fades from him, and his banter subsides into rather sententious plain speaking. Watch him in *You and I,* where youthful marriage threatens to stand in the way of a son's architecture just as it has stood in the way of his father's painting, and you realize just how solemn Mr. Barry can be when he is faced with his own solemnity. (pp. 24-6)

The mid-way channel Mr. Barry steers between wit and pathos, laughter and tears, and those good old enemies—reason and whimsicality—is perhaps best shown by the manner in which he refuses to confine his "smart people" to their drawing-rooms. Like the song writers in *June Moon,* who must invariably be going back somewhere—back to Dixie, back to Ole Virginny, or to Mammy—his characters are invariably going back to their childhoods. The reversion may be incidental as it is in *Holiday.* Or it may be the pivot upon which the whole play tries to turn as it is in *Hotel Universe,* that most pretentious of Mr. Barry's offerings. But it is pretty certain to occur, if for no other reason than that the past is the natural ally of a writer of fantasy.

Almost always Mr. Barry's people dodge the gossip, the prattle, and the malice of their parlors and flee to a room "upstairs" where the realities dare not enter. These attic rooms are their escapes, their refuges from high comedy, and Mr. Barry's complex. Because, rich as they are in their sentimental associations, they provide a ready-made setting for fantasy. (p. 27)

Twice so far Mr. Barry has deserted that special world, which is the favorite setting for his most characteristic comedies, to try his hand at other materials. In *John,* he broke with his whimsi-comical past to attempt a serious biographical drama about John the Baptist. In spite of the occasional beauty of his writing, it was an unsuccessful attempt, which failed because it was too prone to waver between the grand manner of historical plays and the trivial informality of more contemporary methods to achieve any coördinating style of its own. In the other play, however—*White Wings*—Mr. Barry conceived, even if he did not wholly write, one of the most hilarious and original of fantastic American comedies. He forgot the upper world of comedy and jubilantly descended into the lower world of travesty. In a setting as unusual as it seemed bound to be rich in comic possibilities, he restated the age-worn fight between the progressive and conservative spirits, choosing as his representatives of the old order, the Inches, a proud family of street cleaners who for years had followed the horses—with a broom. As his radicals he selected the Todds, the first motorists, whose horseless buggy came quite naturally as a threat to the dependent livelihood of the Inches. But, though *White Wings* was delightful as an idea, and gorgeous in stretches of its Rabelesian dialogue, it was, as Mr. Barry stated it dramatically, too slim to bear the weight of four long acts. It began to repeat itself, to run thin of complications, to seem a one-act distended to fill an evening.

The attic retreats that recur in the more typical of Mr. Barry's "above-stairs" comedies are not only the shelters that he seeks from the conscienceless ridicule of high comedy. They are also indications of the mixed mettles from which his comedies are made. For his are not pure comedies either by intention or in execution. They are too diluted in their methods to serve the Comic Muse unswervingly. They are comedies that laugh in order to preach rather than preach in order to laugh. They are comedies, too, that stoop to farce. . . . But more marked than either their descents into farce or their ascents into the pulpit is the fact that Mr. Barry's comedies are of a kind which cry into handkerchiefs instead of laughing behind fans.

They are whimsical comedies, not high comedies. And as such they are softened by the rose-colored lights of sentiment rather than being subject to the white glare of pure comedy. As such too they are written from the heart more than from the head, and find Mr. Barry pouring the champagne of his dialogue into tear bottles instead of serving it in the glasses that the purists would demand. In his mixture of sentiment and laughter, pathos and wit, however, Mr. Barry is but obeying one of the oldest of Anglo-Saxon theatre instincts. Most generally he compounds the two so that each works for the other's advantage. But occasionally his tenderness gets the better of him, deadening the fine buoyancy of his writing and robbing his dialogue of its necromancy. It is in those moments when he turns mawkish and is inclined to let his whimsicality slip over into what Mr. Nathan has rightfully objected to as "whim-whim," that Mr. Barry would do well to listen to the sound advice that his Mary gives the composer in *Paris Bound.* "Watch out," she says, "that your angel doesn't go whimsical on you." Mr. Barry should watch out, too. Because when his touch is purely comic, it is one of the most engaging that our theatre knows. (pp. 28-30)

> John Mason Brown, "The Playwright and the Amer-
> ican Theatre," in his Upstage: The American Theatre
> in Performance (copyright © 1930 by W. W. Norton
> & Company, Inc.; copyright renewed 1958 by John
> Mason Brown; reprinted by permission of the Lit-
> erary Estate of John Mason Brown), Norton, 1930
> (and reprinted by Kennikat Press, 1969), pp. 3-77.*

EDMUND WILSON (essay date 1931)

The plays of Philip Barry, like certain other products of New York—like the songs of Cole Porter, like a good deal of the *New Yorker* magazine—have the deftness and a glimmering of the comic sense that are cultivated in a high civilization, but, like other things of the kind in New York, they remain imperfect, uncertain, rather unsatisfactory, because they have no stable social system behind them and consequently no fixed code of manners or definite point of view. They flicker and float on the surface of the shifting heterogeneous city; are at their best when they reflect its queer mixtures and its disconcerting surprises. But to write a really first-rate comedy, you ought to have a set of standards, even if those of a small class or group, to refer people's behavior to. Eugene O'Neill, for all his faults, has these for the whole of humanity; Arthur Schnitzler has them for the sophisticated pre-war Viennese. But Philip Barry, who writes for a sophisticated class with little social tradition and little real education—[*Tomorrow and Tomorrow*] has no more to do with the Indiana town in which it is laid than Cole Porter's new musical show—has a very hard time getting hold of anything that will enable him to take a clear line in regard to all the curious things that he sees going on about him. (pp. 507-08)

> Edmund Wilson, "Schnitzler and Philip Barry"
> (originally published in The New Republic, Vol. LXV,
> No. 844, February 4, 1931), in his The Shores of
> Light: A Literary Chronicle of the Twenties and Thir-
> ties (copyright 1952 by Edmund Wilson; copyright
> renewed © 1980 by Helen Miranda Wilson), Farrar,
> Straus and Young, Inc., 1952, pp. 504-08.*

R. DANA SKINNER (essay date 1931)

[*Skinner, in a balanced assessment of Barry's early and middle plays, cites* Holiday *and* Hotel Universe *as two of the dramatist's finest works.*]

As to "**Holiday**," all one can exclaim is—Salutations to Philip Barry for the one well-nigh perfect comedy of many seasons! If ever there was a justification for the belief that a thoroughly honest play can also be highly diverting and enormously successful from the box-office viewpoint, "**Holiday**" stands forth as that justification. There is not an off-color line from beginning to end. Yet the comedy is clean, swift and high-spirited. The design is as simple as a landscape, yet the substance of human emotion is there in full measure. The play is firm, true and often stirring without once bordering on sentimentality. (p. 114)

The story, as I have suggested, is straightforward. A young lawyer, Johnny Case, who is on the verge of success, meets Julia Seton at Lake Placid. Julia is the oldest of Edward Seton's three children and very much wedded to her father's views on how the family and the world in general should be run. Her father—otherwise dubbed "Big Business" by his second daughter, Linda—is one of those conservative crustaceans thoroughly accustomed to having his own way in everything. He is somewhat horrified to discover that Johnny Case has no social background, but is slightly mollified by the fact that Johnny has just arranged a successful merger of public utility interests and shows evidences of making a name for himself. Serious trouble begins just after Mr. Seton has agreed to announce the engagement of Julia and Johnny at a large New Year's party. It then turns out that Johnny has some ideas of his own about relative values in life. Having made a little money of his own and being something of a vagabond at heart, he is rather inclined to take some of his leisure while young. He is fully prepared to stop business for a little while and to resume it only after he and Julia have had a period of leisure and travel. This comes as a bombshell of the maximum calibre in the Seton houschold—to all, that is, except the forthright and rebellious Linda and her younger brother Ned. The conclusion is, if you wish, obvious. The engagement is broken, and Linda, who has understood the vagabond in Johnny all along, finds her way toward him clear at last, after making doubly sure that Julia no longer cares for him at all.

Now, in many ways, we have here only a repetition of the familiar Cinderella theme. You could tell the story in a way to make it seem almost ridiculous. But Barry does not handle his material that way. In the first place, the Cinderella characteristics in Linda are well concealed by her abrupt, almost boyish mannerisms, her quick wit and apt tongue. She is the dominating figure throughout the play. Then, too, we find a perfection of characterization which convinces us that we are dealing with individuals and not with age-old types. There is authenticity in every detail, and many side touches give the picture depth and inner meaning. For example, there is the brother, Ned—well on his way to becoming a drunkard for the simple reason that the whole atmosphere of the stuffy household has jangled his nerves. He needs spiritual fresh air and plenty of it. There are Linda's best friends, Nick and Susan Potter, who, in their unassuming way, have made a real art out of life and extract plenty of amusement and meaning from it by using their sufficient means intelligently. They do not make accumulation of money or power an end in itself. There is also the constant battle of the two sisters, carried on in an undertone and rarely flashing into heat, but forever keeping before us the sterility of wealth as a thing in itself.

I am well aware that through description these things are apt to appear as mere platitudes and moralizations. The point is that Barry, with consummate art, has concealed their obviousness, given them fresh verbal expression, and surrounded them with a sensitive breeze of comedy that takes all the curse off of them. He never strains an emotional point to sentimentality. He never permits fierce denunciation. He lets the audience do its own thinking for the most part, and creates a complete illusion of real human experience. Perhaps the finest touches of all are in his handling of dialogue between the conflicting family groups. Linda and her friends know the worth of nonsense. They never lose the spirit of play—and in that alone lies the secret of the "moral of the play" never becoming tiresome. No American playwright can create such delicious nonsense as Barry at his best, and in this play he has given us the cream of those qualities which made certain parts of **"White Wings"** and **"In a Garden"** enchanting. He has avoided the main fault of those earlier plays, however, in not getting carried away entirely by nonsense and fantasy. He has set about to write a real play and has introduced whimsicality only where it serves a dramatic purpose.

To some people **"Holiday"** may seem a trifle thin and lacking in the flame of drama. But to my mind its very restraint is what gives it its universality. By keeping true to character it permits the audience to fill in the gaps, and to share in the decisions made by the characters. In brief, **"Holiday"** is a masterpiece.

In **"Paris Bound,"** which immediately preceeded **"Holiday,"** Barry also used just that touch of reality and genuine feeling which his earlier plays lacked, and managed to provide a diverting and occasionally serious evening in the theatre. It is, of course, a confusing play—so confusing, in fact, that one famous newspaper critic virtuously excluded it from competition for the Pulitzer Prize on the ground that it upholds adultery! As a matter of fact, it does nothing of the kind. It simply tries to make clear, in human terms, that a momentary weakness leading to adultery should not be sufficient grounds for immediate divorce. It states very clearly that marriage is a much greater thing than the merely physical relationship of man and wife, and that the companionship of years and the responsibility toward children should not be discarded in an instant.

On the other hand, Barry has opened himself to criticism by his method of handling the subject. The reasons he gives for maintaining the marriage union in spite of infidelity are, essentially, emotional reasons. He is, of course, writing for a mixed audience with highly varied moral standards, and for this reason it may be part of his deliberate intention to seek a common ground for argument. This leads him, nevertheless, into many bypaths and into an explanation of infidelity which undoubtedly seems to make light of the sin of adultery itself. When you try to show that a man may be unfaithful to his wife, under stress of temptation, and at the same time remain deeply in love with her and a devoted husband, you are certainly treading on dangerous ground and it is not at all surprising if at least half of your audience goes away with the idea that you are justifying adultery on the grounds that it is not a very serious offense.

Certainly no one who shares the belief that marriage is a life-long partnership for better or for worse can disagree with Barry's main theme. Understanding and forgiveness have saved thousands of marriages that were headed for the rocks. But it is one thing to argue this as a principle and quite another to argue it merely as a controlling emotion. Barry's wandering hero shows no signs whatever of remorse or of any consciousness that he has been unfair. This is what lends color to the assumption that Barry is upholding adultery. In his anxiety to show that it is not the only sin against married happiness, he

practically flops over to the other side by permitting the inference that it is no offense at all, or at the most, a very slight one.

We might summarize the play by saying that it is a good point very poorly made. It advocates the right course of action, but for the wrong reason. It is somewhat like saying that society should be merciful to a certain thief, not because all justice should be "tempered by mercy," but because the particular thief happened to have stolen from a rich man who wouldn't feel the loss very much. The parallel, in fact, is rather close, because Barry uses the object lesson of a particularly happy and devoted marriage from which the infidelity in question robs only a part of its beauty. There is a strong implication that if the marriage were otherwise less perfect, this particular climax might have been grounds for the inevitable divorce after all.

Aside from this cardinal error in handling the theme, the play is entertainingly written as to dialogue and situation, and the characters are quite the most real that Barry had at that time built up. It is rather too bad that he did so much good playwriting in a mood of confused moral values—for, whatever one's views might be on divorce, Barry does not establish his case on clear enough grounds to leave one with that sense of a sharp issue which it is the task of such comedy-dramas to create. Reverting to the familiar matter of the theme of a play, it should not only ask a question but should answer that question unmistakably. Half an answer is mere dramatic evasion. (pp. 114-19)

Another play which deserves more enduring recognition than anything promised to it by contemporary press criticisms is Philip Barry's **"Hotel Universe."** In its essence, it is unquestionably one of the finest plays Barry has had produced so far.

The play is in one long act without intermission. On this account, the objections made by many critics to certain details of play structure, to the awkward handling of certain scenes and to one or two incongruous episodes were perhaps well taken. The play lacks craftsmanship—as if it had been poured out in a torrent. But its central idea is so simple, so obvious and so coherent that one is amazed at any accusation of vagueness and confusion.

Barry has simply taken the old thought that we are often chained to the past, and so prevented from forging ahead, by the fact that our memory of the past is largely illusion, and that if we can once re-live the past in all its stark truth, we recover our faith in the present. In other words, a daughter may remember her dead father as one of the most entertaining and fascinating men on earth, forgetting that he was a worthless drunkard and an impossible egotist. Let some shock or accident bring back the full truth to her mind, and she is at once freed. We are always imagining the superior beauties of the past and neglecting the precious instants of the here and now. Barry has simply thrown together a group of people, each one of whom is suffering from this spell of an imagined past, and for that reason discontented or disconsolate—even to the point of intended suicide. Through the device of a mysterious old man, the father of one of the group, Barry has arranged to have a spell cast over all of these discontents through which each one re-lives the true past and so finds freedom and happiness and a return of lost faith. It is not a highly subtle idea, nor is it, as several critics hinted, a relic of Freudian psychology. It is pretty much ordinary common sense, applied with a fanciful touch, some highly engaging dialogue, and an intensity of hidden feeling which occasionally leads Barry astray in his technique. It is, if one may be permitted to use the word these days, a deeply religious play in the sense that true religion demands an acceptance of present reality as one basis of stalwart faith. Tender and mistaken illusions of the past only create a conflict in the present which, sooner or later, attacks the roots of faith, hope and love.

Plays of this sort are, of course, peculiarly difficult to write in a way that maintains complete theatrical illusion. Only such rare masterpieces as Ansky's ''The Dybbuk'' are able to lift you from the plane of gross realism to a plane where the supernatural or the extraordinary seems plausible. In many of his scenes on the veranda of an old house overlooking the Mediterranean, Barry has effected this sense of the plausible with considerable skill. But he has failed just often enough to account, in some measure, for the confusion the play has created in many minds. In spite of this, it is a work of real distinction which probes to the very root of many of our present-day confusions and distortions of values. If Barry has the courage to write more plays of this sincerity and restrained passion, he can go far toward obliterating the memory of his unfortunate **"Tomorrow and Tomorrow."** (pp. 145-47)

In this play, Barry has apparently come under the spell of psychoanalytical dabbling. From the gay charm of **"Holiday"** to the serious symbolism of **"Hotel Universe"** was a long step, but firmly and bravely taken. In **"Tomorrow and Tomorrow,"** however, he steps deep into a bog—the impetus, curiously enough, coming from the theme of Elisha and the Shunammite woman. He has interpreted this theme of nobility and faith as it might be interpreted by the combined efforts of Messrs. Erskine, Freud and Jung.

In the biblical story, the childless woman of Shunam is given a child through the prayers of Elisha, whom she and her husband have befriended and taken into their home. Later, the child dies from a strange malady and is brought back to life by the prophet. It evidently occurred to Barry that he could improve considerably upon this theme by substituting an itinerant lecturer on psychiatry for the prophet, a carnal love affair between the lecturer and the wife of his host for Elisha's fruitful prayers, and a brief psychoanalytic treatment, about ten years later, for the prophet's miracle in behalf of the child. Since Mr. Barry quotes the opening text of the biblical story on the program, the purpose of this modern ''rationalization'' can hardly be mistaken.

There can be no question of Barry's skill as a playwright. His dialogue is matchless. His unspoken dialogue is even better. He is one of the few living playwrights who knows the full implications of a silence. He can also convey minor shadings of emotion with a delicate pliancy that seems to heap meanings upon very minor incidents. For this very reason, the essential crudity of his present story has gone largely unchallenged in the critical columns. The play progresses from one maudlin absurdity to another with such outer grace and charm that its inner implications apparently pass unnoticed. (pp. 169-70)

If ever a well written play showed complete topsy-turvydom of moral and spiritual values, it is this one. Nor does it rate much better when it comes to plausibility of the action itself. Even a skilled psychiatrist might well be puzzled at the rapidity of the child's cure in the last act—in spite of long theoretical explanations of the psychic cause of the illness itself. Psychiatric treatment is seldom notably swift in achieving its results. To be asked to believe that a fatal illness can be cured in five minutes of honeyed words from ever so skilful a doctor is to have one's credulity tried too far.

I do not deny for a minute the sensitiveness with which Barry has delineated emotions. If plays had nothing to do with life and the experience of truth, one might be able to join the chorus of praise for an exceptionally well written play. One must even admit that there are many people who might act and think and feel as Barry's characters do. But they would not deserve the implied comments of the play itself. They would not be cast in heroic or exalted mould. Their essential disloyalty—the more pronounced because it brings no qualms—would not be held up for sympathy and admiration. It is in such cases that the intentions and viewpoint of the author play a large part in the ultimate valuation of a story. Robert Benchley, to his everlasting credit, is one of the few critics to pierce through the sham and trickery of this play, particularly in pointing out that Professor Hay never acts otherwise than as the perfect cad—one who knows, by professional experience, the effect of his words and actions, and never hesitates to take a bounder's advantage. Barry's excursion into experimental psychology has not been helpful. What some would call his ''mechanism of projection'' tells too many tales of a deep confusion in the only life values and in the only feelings of good sportsmanship that count.

Nor was Barry far more fortunate in one of his earlier plays that attracted much attention—**"In a Garden."** A better title for this play would have been ''Caught in His Own Trap.'' Barry, softly transposing Ibsen's ''Doll's House'' to another key, has tried to tell the story of a sensitive and spontaneous wife who has lived under the dominion of a playwriting husband who sees all life, including his own, in strict terms of the theatre. He would analyze his own romance at the very moment it was taking place. He would see his wife as a character in a play, and ''stage'' her life accordingly, for the jovial purpose of discovering her ''reactions'' and proving how perfect was his own knowledge of human emotions. He knows every one ''like a book''—meaning that he knows no one as a human being.

Unfortunately, Barry's own play indicates that he was, at that stage of his career, precisely that same type of dramatist. It has precisely the bookish quality he derides—shows the same undue fascination with a theme or thesis—and consequently carries no illusion whatever of reality. It is like a dull man telling you dully how dull he finds his next-door neighbor. Barry tells you artificially how artificial he finds the minds of some dramatists. If, by any unhappy chance, Barry is satirizing some particular writer of today's theatre, that victim can respond—''Praise be, thou too hast written a play!''

In the end, the wife in this play, failing to bring her husband to terms with reality, trots out the back door like Ibsen's Nora . . . , and the dismayed playwright vents his amazement in pulling down the flowers of a garden ''set'' which he had constructed in his own living room to further one of his domestic experiments. But where Ibsen at least wrote a strong play, with whose moral index one might take issue seriously, Barry's effort, because inconclusive, does not merit even serious pulling to pieces—so completely artificial is it, so mechanically motivated, and so heavily larded with false sentiment. The wife, as a character, has possibilities of reality. By herself, she is an excellent type portrait, easily understood and commanding considerable sympathy up to the last act, when the plot jumps in and robs her of reality. . . . We might call the play as a whole, elephantine—were it wholly fair to elephants, who are not limp and indefinite but alive, spontaneous and conclusive in their bulk!

We can match, then, the caddish implications of **"Tomorrow and Tomorrow"** and the vague artificialities of **"In a Garden"** with the calm wisdom of **"Hotel Universe"** and the impish delights of **"Holiday"**—and having matched them, all we can ask is, "Who and what is the real Barry?" I think he is by all odds one of our three or four most important playwrights. But will his fatal facility with words carry him away from strong values to an irresponsible mirage of wit and sophistication? We have urgent need of him—in the mood of **"Hotel Universe"** or in the mood of **"Holiday."** But in the mood of **"Tomorrow and Tomorrow"** he is a poor leader for earnest playwrights. (pp. 171-74)

> *R. Dana Skinner, in his* Our Changing Theatre *(copyright © 1931 by The Dial Press, Inc.; permission granted by The Dial Press), Dial Press, 1931, 327 p.**

MONTROSE J. MOSES (essay date 1934)

[*Moses discusses what he considers the central theme of Barry's dramas—the search for self-fulfillment.*]

It is difficult to place Philip Barry in a category. We hear from him at intervals with a play which bears the stamp of his own personality, which reveals his own lightsome style. (p. 223)

His plays are really Barry in quest of himself. There is no American dramatist of the same stamp. He cannot take life too soberly; he shadow-boxes with ideas and philosophies, he writes the most exquisite dialogue, he can be absurdly childish and delicately serious. His gossamer plays are shot through with patterns of ideas always in the bud, and the ideas are never given a chance to become full blown. His stories are spider webs of quaint spinning, with problematic knots which help to hold the dramas together. His seriousness is never left alone a minute; the puckered brow is chased by the inexhaustible good humor. If he should consider himself, Philip Barry would find his youth in his plays.

Which brings me to the point I have in mind. We must picture Barry as young: tomorrow he will be older, and while it will be difficult for him to alter his style, while his mind we hope will never lose its quaint conceits, while his dialogue will not, we trust, lose its facility, its ease and grace, he may recognize the importance of being earnest. Whatever the Philip Barry of the future, the charm of the young man will always be authentic biographical data; and only by that youthful portrait of the young man will we be able at a later date to judge his plays, from **You and I** through **The Animal Kingdom**.

Barry hovers over his plays with an unmistakable fancy wand, and even if he does not completely justify his means, they are holding as sheer entertainment. Problems have a fascination for him, but his mental habit is to toss them deftly back and forth in care-free dialogue; and he is not so much concerned with solutions as he is with wit and quick response. A quick retort turneth away wrath—and this tendency on Barry's part makes him a lovable writer, if not always a potent dramatist. I think sometimes there is method in his disjointed incidentals; unsteady thinking though it may seem, the flavor of a solution is often more lasting than the solution itself. Amidst tender confusion, positiveness is out of place. . . . It is because of fantastic fooling in **White Wings**—a breezy, pathetic picturing of the street-cleaning days of New York in the gay Nineties— that it lingered so short a while on the stage. Philip Barry was not at first a lucky star for the managers. But with the advent of **Paris Bound**—and the two plays that followed, **Holiday** and

Hotel Universe—he more definitely found a foothold in our theatre.

I do not know whether Barry ever thought, while writing these plays, that they might represent a trilogy of youth. But I take them as such. If so considered, they may stand together as commentary on his own era. They are held close by a similar mannerism, and certain fooling which sparkles in *Holiday* crops up again in *Hotel Universe*, showing a bitter agony which comes with immaturity. Once upon a time, Barry and Elmer Rice, exiled abroad in order to escape the cloying rush of American life, collaborated in a play called *Cock Robin*. It seemed strange to see a play of Elmer Rice's later on and to come away, thinking persistently of Philip Barry. But that is exactly what *The Left Bank* did to me—it made me ponder on the illusive charm of Barry and on the intellectualized, sober statement of reality in Rice, which Barry always so lightly evades. Both playwrights have dealt with the younger generation, have used their vocabulary. That vocabulary and the philosophies which were expressed by it nearly ran away with the group living under the roof of the *Hotel Universe*. Let us analyze the situation.

The younger generation which came out of the War had its bitter cracks against everything; they set out to repudiate the world as it was; they left from their calculations entirely any illusions that might have been ready at hand for them; they were not sure of anything, but they were willing and anxious to think of everything. What they knew for a certainty was that they had had enough of what they called the "older generation," which had bungled the world into a great social and economic mess; they were—in other words—out on a voyage of new discovery.

If they had taken anything with them in their mental kit other than rebellion, they might not have so easily fallen into morbidity. If they had been willing to pause by the roadside, to spend a weekend with themselves as they were fundamentally, and to chart the seven seas of existence, they might not have turned so violently against the life they finally came to live, after they turned against the life of the older generation. As I see it, that is the entire philosophical matrix in Philip Barry's plays. In *Paris Bound*, youth married gains its experience, becomes ripened in the spirit of compromise. In *Holiday*, youth fights against the pressure of life that would strangle the *joie de vivre*. In *Hotel Universe*, youth is fagged. Barry would substitute a sense of fun for the vacuous living of the older generation. "Life is exciting," exclaims Youth. "Life is an exacting business," exclaims the older generation. Barry's plays have about them the atmosphere of youthful excitement. In *Holiday* the exclamation is, "We are all grand at seventeen." What is the disillusionment in *Hotel Universe*?

Plays of the younger generation, with which we have been deluged for many years past, all seem to agree upon the restlessness of the rebel. *Holiday* is restless. But, even though the rebel, who repudiates the conventions of society, goes out to think bravely about life, he soon realizes that thinking about life is not living, and the two points of view sometimes end in disillusionment. So we have the poignant moments in *Hotel Universe*.

After the War, young people looked upon the world as hideous; they could not square their own questions with any of the answers offered by their elders. They became violently interested in the problems of why they were here and whither they were going. That is a typical youthful attitude of the past decade, of all decades. They have debated the morality preached in the pulpit and have been witness to the repudiation of that morality as exploited in the newspapers. So, the restless group that Philip Barry introduces in *Hotel Universe* is but the reflection of that awful drifting uncertainty into which rebelliousness so often takes us. Barry's characters express their doubts because they have only a smattering connection with the permanent things of the universe. They distrust any permanency whatsoever. They would not work on schedule time because they wish an untried schedule for life of their very own, that would make life worth living. In *Holiday,* the hero decides that it were best for people to let fresh air into life while it is young; to take a holiday first and to work afterwards.

In this spirit, young people are willing to risk everything. They are sometimes willing to risk death, and, in a moment of despondency, they are willing even to take life as a sacrifice. They do not yet know the value of ease; they only know that they must go quickly through the adventure. One of the characters in *Hotel Universe* contemplates killing himself, and an older, a wiser being tells him that things may change—why do it? He is sufficiently knowing of the younger generation not to say to this young person: "*You* may change. In this world there is a certain law of maturity which comes from experience; you are in a state of flux; you know nothing of the certainty of calm."

Not one of Barry's characters but is thus drawn rebellious. In most of his dramas, with a flash or two, he suggests that there is a practical side to life which, humorous though it may be in dialogue, serves also its purpose as a stabilizer of excessive energy. One of his people says: "While there is life there is rent to pay": in itself a wisecrack, but representing a point of view which might serve to bring back a rebellious spirit to a point of rest. For a point of rest is as necessary in life as it is, according to Ruskin and Coventry Patmore, in art.

After the War, the younger generation cried out: "We have had enough," meaning enough of the old-time bungling. Our dramatists are giving hint that in some respects that same generation, looking back on its rebelliousness, is again saying: "We have had enough. We will take stock of what we have gained, of what we have lost. There is time to recapture some of the things we hastily threw overboard when we rebelled."

All this tumble of living, discussed so sensationally in the papers of the day, is by no means steadying to the so-called younger generation. Philip Barry has reflected this unsteadiness in his plays. He has used both the positive and negative characteristics of the time. He does not answer any questions. But he gives the panorama with a thread of narrative that oftentimes is very thin; the reward is that he always has at his disposal a beautifully light touch of fancifully quaint humor. (pp. 224-28)

> *Montrose J. Moses, "Philip Barry," in* Representative American Dramas: National and Local, *edited by Montrose J. Moses (copyright 1933 by Leah M. Moses; copyright renewed 1961 by Leah M. Moses; reprinted by permission of Little, Brown and Company), revised edition, Little, Brown, 1933 (and reprinted in* The American Theatre As Seen By Its Critics: 1752-1934, *edited by Montrose J. Moses and John Mason Brown, second edition, W. W. Norton & Company, Inc., 1934, pp. 223-28).*

ELEANOR FLEXNER (essay date 1938)

[*In the following excerpt, Flexner discusses the "similarity of pattern" throughout Barry's plays, as well as his difficulty in fusing a serious style with a comic style. Flexner draws a conclusion similar to that of Montrose J. Moses (see excerpt above) when she finds that Barry's works usually portray an individual's revolt against social pressure.*]

The characteristic cleverness and "brightness" of Philip Barry's dialogue have tended to obscure the similarity of pattern of his plays. He deals for the most part with the individual's revolt against conventional pressure for social conformity and attempts to force him into a pattern of behavior to which he is inimical. Most frequently his antagonist is "business" and everything it stands for: its goal, way of life, its hostility to originality and individuality. To Barry "big business" represents everything he abhors in modern life.

The right to do as one pleases and the desire for leisure are two themes basic in most of his plays. They are the motives which successively impel Richard Windlow in *The Youngest,* Maitland White in *You and I,* Adrian Terry in *In a Garden,* Johnny Case in *Holiday,* Tom Collier in *The Animal Kingdom,* the Farley brothers in *The Joyous Season,* and Norman Rose and Tom Ames in *Hotel Universe* to turn their backs on success and prosperity and seek a more satisfying existence. Without such freedom—freedom of action outside, freedom of the spirit inside—life is unendurable; this is the principal tenet of Philip Barry's philosophy.

It is obvious that he does not go beyond one particular aspect of the problem of "freedom," that relating to persons whose only fetters are those of habit or acquiescence. As H. T. Parker, the distinguished critic of the Boston *Transcript*, put it, in a review of *Hotel Universe* [see additional bibliography], Barry's characters "need take no thought of the financial morrow, since their balances in bank are renewed like the widow's curse in Scripture. It is their privilege to rise up and depart, to sit down and linger, the world around, *as impulse without obligation may prompt.*" (Italics mine.) Gail Redman in *Tomorrow and Tomorrow* and Daily Sage in *The Animal Kingdom* are only exceptions to the general rule of trips abroad, ladies' maids and, the "general atmosphere of plenty with the top riveted down on the cornucopia" which constitutes Barry's favorite dramatic milieu.

In other words, though he poses the question of individual redemption from Philistinism, Barry limits himself to the spiritual welfare of a microscopic section of the population which appears to be making an injudicious use of its advantages. Like Miss Crothers, Barry would like to have his financiers and businessmen stop at a certain point in their accumulation of wealth, from natural judicious restraint, and turn to self-cultivation and contemplation. The real problem involved, and therefore the real reason why Edward Seton and Rufus Collier and the Farley brothers lack understanding or warmth, completely escapes him: that self-seeking at the expense of other people's elementary human rights destroys humanity and ideals no less surely than it increases the size of a bank account.

The limitations of Barry's point of view are clearly brought out by the people whom he designates as models of human behavior. There are the Potters, Nick and Susan, in *Holiday,* of whom Johnny Case remarks—

> It seems to me that they know just about everything.—Life must be swell, when you have some idea of what goes on, the way they do.

Linda Seton's opinion of them is equally rapturous:

> You've always seemed to me the rightest, wisest happiest people I've ever known—You're my one real hope in the world.

These are big words, all the more revealing when we hear Linda explaining the reason for her faith in the Potters: "They get more fun out of nothing than anyone I know." In comparison to Edward Seton and his daughter Julia, and to their cousins, the Crams, the Potters are certainly refreshing. At best, however, they are dilettantes who have made a fine art of living pleasurably for themselves, "like the dirty loafers we are," to quote Nick Potter himself.

Then there is Christina Farley in *The Joyous Season*. She is one of Barry's finest characterizations, and in her selflessness, her discrimination and vitality, she represents the highest type of Catholic. But she sees the degeneration of the Farleys purely in terms of their loss of adventurousness and joy of living. What they do is wrong only insofar as it affects them. The rich must be saved from themselves. Her understanding penetrates no further, and her weapons against greed and stupidity are only her religious faith and an ethical code of behavior.

Lastly take the philosophy which Stephen Fields in *Hotel Universe* recommends to his daughter's troubled friends. What goal, what hope, what discipline, does it offer them? To "accept" life, to "live" it. . . . Such an outlook, he suggests, will render them invulnerable to bewilderment and discouragement. But his precepts, noticeably, do not extend to a scale of values, to a suggestion that their neuroses may arise at least in part from undue self-absorption, and that psychological dislocations may exist, due primarily to social causes, which cannot be cured by the Freudian technique or a return to the faith of one's childhood.

Naturally the milieu to which he confines himself has determined the type of characters Barry portrays. Probably Barry himself is unaware of how significant is their unvarying similarity. Like Rachel Crothers when she came to devote herself to comedy in the higher social brackets, Barry can only reiterate himself: his men and women are of an appalling sameness. Lissa Terry, Mary Hutton, Cecelia Henry, Terry Farley, Ann Field—are one and all slim, immaculate, exquisite, poised, urbane. The same with the men: Adrian Terry, Jim Hutton, Tom Collier, Pat Farley, Gail Redman: they are invariably well set up, likable, straightforward young Americans, with slightly varying degrees of imagination. Even the few individual types whom Barry has created—Linda Seton, Johnny Case—talk just like the others. Only occasionally do we find life and feeling— in Christina Farley, in Eve Redman and Nicholas Hay. But the young artist rebels in *The Animal Kingdom* are stuffed caricatures, and in *Bright Star* hardly a single character gives the illusion of life.

Some of this weakness may be traced to Barry's absorption in clever dialogue for its own sake. His characters all talk alike, not the way people really do speak, but in phrases which have become the playwright's own mannerisms. He has no ear for the ordinary colloquial rhythms of speech. Instead, he creates his own, staccato and clipped to the point of stylization. (pp. 249-53)

Dramatically Barry's greatest weakness is his habit of imposing a situation or a line of behavior on his characters instead of allowing both to arise from the nature of the characters themselves. His approach is in fact exactly what he decries so strongly in life itself: he manipulates, he contrives, he is arbitrary instead of permitting his characters to develop naturally.

In *Paris Bound* . . . he struck what was to be his most successful vein: presenting an essentially serious idea in an amusing and sprightly fashion. In this case he contends that divorce for adultery is a much more serious offense than adultery itself.

In the case of really happy marriage, a transitory affair on the part of the husband does not infringe on his wife's province. The question is whether the younger Huttons will duplicate the tragedy of young Jim's parents. Mary Hutton starts her married life swearing that she will not be a possessive wife. Characteristically, Barry then shatters all our ideas of the kind of person Mary is (quite a different matter from showing up human inconsistency); hearing of Jim's affair with one of her ex-wedding attendants (whom she already knows has a strong attraction for Jim), Mary decides instantly to divorce him. She is only deterred by discovering for herself what Jim has experienced—a physical attraction for someone else, and the profound difference between such an attraction and her relationship with her husband. Jim's sudden return from abroad, his instinctive awareness of what has happened to her and his refusal to take notice of it stamps both episodes as irrelevant and carries them over the danger-point.

Regardless of the merits of such a point of view, we can see in *Paris Bound* an example of Barry's difficulty in fusing two dissimilar styles. He creates a charming relationship between husband and wife, but his tendency to express tenderness and deep feeling always in light comedy vein presages a time when he will be unable to write in any other. His penchant for underwriting handicaps him in his serious scenes, which are rarely written with sufficient fullness and clarity.

In *Holiday* Barry once again does violence to his characters. The cause of the misunderstanding between Johnny Case and Julia Seton would ordinarily become apparent in their first serious talk after their engagement. Instead, at the playwright's direction, they talk carefully around it until the moment when Barry wishes to precipitate a showdown. If we overlook this piece of hokum, and the limitations of Barry's social point of view, we can accept *Holiday* as his best play and one of the most amusing comedies of the decade. For once he has contrived an engrossing story and some brilliantly witty characterizations, and the figure of Edward Seton, "financier and cotillion-leader," ranks among the best caricatures in our drama. (pp. 254-56)

Holiday is Barry's last attempt at satire. *The Animal Kingdom* bogged down in the old conflict of wife versus mistress; his remaining plays have been serious in outlook despite the bantering tone which predominates in the writing. In fact, one of our best-known comedy writers has not written a real comedy in ten years, if we except *Spring Dance*, his most recent offering and an adolescent reversion which is more charitably ignored.

Instead, he followed *Holiday* with *Hotel Universe*, his most ambitious enterprise in the intellectual sphere. Actually what befuddled critics and audiences was, not its profundity but its inchoateness. For Barry permitted himself to veer from problems of individual psychological adjustment to metaphysical considerations of the human mind abroad in space and time which add nothing to the clarity of the play. Its very obscurity, however, enhanced its apparent significance, and thanks to an uncanny use of theatrical devices and some fine writing *Hotel Universe* held audience attention.

The setting of *Hotel Universe* is particularly effective—a stone terrace overlooking the Mediterranean, at dusk. The terrace itself sets the mood: beyond the low wall at the back and to one side, "Nothing is visible: sea meets sky without a line to mark the meeting. The angle of the terrace is like a wedge into space." . . . With great skill Barry builds up this unreality of atmosphere. As darkness increases, a lighthouse at sea throws its beam across the terrace at regular intervals, "like the finger of God.'' The characters all sense an eeriness of some kind: they recall the past with the immediacy of the present, they have chills of premonition, moments of acute sadness, and they are haunted by the recollection of a young stranger's suicide that afternoon on the beach—''off for Africa.''

The whole action of the play takes place on the terrace, without an intermission; like *Yellow Jack, Hotel Universe* depends on carefully created atmosphere sustained without interruption. Six people, the modern sophisticates whom Barry delights in depicting, are on a brief visit to an old friend, Ann Field, who is living in exiled solitude with her invalid father. They are leaving in a few hours, and one by one they reveal to Ann, who loves them dearly and most of all Pat Farley, their profound unhappiness and disillusionment with life. In the words of H.T.P.'s review, already quoted, ''Barry deals with the malaise of a time and a breed that lack illusions and want faith.—They have lost illusions and found nothing to replace them. They are at odds, in their own fashion, with living.''

Much of the obscurity of *Hotel Universe* derives from Barry's failure to make clear the causes for this frame of mind *in general*. . . . Barry sees each case of discontent and maladjustment as a purely *individual* affair—the result of an incident or an emotional experience in childhood or youth. Under the guidance of Ann's father, each of the characters goes through a dramatically compressed course of psychoanalysis which liberates him from his fixations; one by one we see them re-enact the episodes which derailed them, Stephen Field assuming the role of interlocutor. He plays the old Franciscan father to whom Tom Ames goes back to beg for renewed faith, the father whom Lily Malone feared and loved too much, the father of a young English girl who killed herself for the unrequited love of Pat Farley.

Unfortunately the continuity of scenes is so jumbled that we are continually confused. To make matters worse, Barry embellishes Stephen's particular brand of Freudianism with something that resembles most closely the philosophic concept known as ''serial time.'' (pp. 261-63)

By the time he came to write *The Joyous Season* . . . , any feeling Barry had possessed for clear-cut conflict and development had been dissipated; it lacked even the retrospective ''action'' of the psychoanalytic episodes in *Hotel Universe. The Joyous Season* surveys the immobile members of the Farley family, who in one generation have travelled from a country farm to the social eminence of Boston's Beacon Street. This transit represents the loss of a simpler way of living and of ruggedness of spirit and sensitivity to spiritual values, for a mess of potage. In his anxiety to ''keep the family together'' (which Barry regards as a typically Irish trait but which might just as well be Jewish or Italian) John Farley has been pampering and bolstering up the weaker members of the clan to the point where they have lost all desire to stand alone or adventure on their own.

Christina Farley, who left home under a cloud many years before to become a nun and who returns for a twenty-four [hour] visit, is the catalyst which shatters their lethargy. For two acts she observes her family, and they wait for her to decide whether she wishes to take their old home or their present residence for her holy order, a choice permitted her by her mother's will. She leaves without making a decision, which she puts up to them; and impelled by the new currents she has set in motion they decide to abandon the newer and shoddy life and go back to ''Good Ground.''

This sudden regeneration is completely unconvincing, as any sunburst finale is apt to be without adequate preparation. The reason for such a conversion ending as well as for its utter uselessness, is that we have never come to know a single character in the play except Christina. And this is inevitable, because to know people you must not only hear them talk but see them act, which is the one thing none of the characters in *The Joyous Season* ever do. They do not act because Barry himself does not know them; he has no idea how they would behave, and therefore cannot launch them into a situation requiring action.

As a matter of fact, each character contains the germ of an implicit conflict, a reservoir of dramatic possibilities, but the dramatist never taps it. Take Terry Farley and her husband Francis. Terry is confused and unhappy, another Eve Redman, or a character carried over from *Hotel Universe*. Her love for her husband, her faith in him, her interest in life, have gone. Why? We never find out. When she and Francis are reconciled at the conclusion of the play, the occurrence is as incomprehensible, as lacking in motivation, as their estrangement was in the first place.

Ross Farley might have been a fascinating character study; there is a wealth of potential conflict in the Catholic turned skeptic and Communist who reverts to the faith of his fathers. John and Martin Farley are typical businessmen. But Martin cherishes a hidden longing for the diplomatic service, and John is in love with his secretary. Less than twenty-four hours after Christina's arrival, Martin in on the verge of leaving for Washington and John of proposing to his secretary. But we never have the vestige of an idea of what either of these men is really like.

This is bad dramaturgy, and its cause is not far to seek. Barry has a knack of picking these disillusioned, bewildered worldlings out of a crowd, of suggesting their distraction in a few lines. But he only sets them into motion among one another. His sphere is the drawing room. Life outside it baffles or bores him, it is hard to tell which. Therefore their disquiet, which must perforce lie in this larger sphere, is arbitrarily ruled out of consideration. His plays take place in an artificial vacuum, where only small, set, secondary motions can take place, and consequently his characters become mere puppets.

This becomes finally clear in *Bright Star,* in which Barry tried to draw a man in close relation to the world of affairs—a ''man of action.'' It is a type he cannot encompass. Quin Hanna, part reformer and idealist, turns into an emotional freak and egoistic introvert. His social conflict is overlaid, and finally displaced, by fantastic emotional complications. For Quin, a man of ''too much head and too little heart,'' marries an angel from heaven who loves him to extinction. Unable to love Hope, he feels that he has wronged her, and his insensate career of political idealism, degenerating to chicanery, is nothing but a flight from self, from love, from guilt, in which he finally destroys himself.

Nothing is believable in *Bright Star,* not Quin Hanna's particular brand of Napoleonism, not his power to attract and hold friendship from the most unlikely people, not his social schemes, nor is Hope's redundant love and self-abnegation any more convincing. Hanna's Utopian dream of reconciling class antagonisms within the confines of one small municipality is a dream which harks back to the brotherly vistas of Robert Owen and Brook Farm. Like Hanna, Barry's attempt to grapple with reality miscarries because he is not equipped for such a venture. He has dwelt elsewhere too long. (pp. 268-71)

Eleanor Flexner, "Comedy: George S. Kaufman, George Kelly, Rachel Crothers, Philip Barry, Robert E. Sherwood," in her American Playwrights: 1918-1938 *(copyright © 1938, 1966 by Eleanor Flexner; reprinted by permission of Simon & Schuster, Inc.), Simon & Schuster, 1938, pp. 198-282.**

GEORGE JEAN NATHAN   (essay date 1943)

[*Nathan has been called the most learned and influential drama critic the United States has yet produced. During the early decades of the twentieth century, Nathan was greatly responsible for shifting the emphasis of the American theater from light entertainment to serious drama, introducing audiences and producers to the work of Eugene O'Neill, Henrik Ibsen, and Bernard Shaw, among others. Nathan was a contributing editor to H. L. Mencken's magazine* The American Mercury *and coeditor of* The Smart Set. *With Mencken, Nathan belonged to an iconoclastic school of American critics who attacked the vulgarity of accepted ideas and sought to bring a new level of sophistication to American culture, which they found provincial and backward. Throughout his career Nathan shared with Mencken a gift for stinging invective and verbal adroitness, as well as total confidence in his own judgements.*]

Once content to write at least an approximation to pure and unadulterated light comedy, [Philip Barry] some years ago became obsessed by the notion that, in addition to his talent in that direction, he was a creature of puissant brain and that it was his duty, along with his pleasure, to share its pearls with the public. From this hallucination there presently issued not only a quota of pseudo-philosophical opera that sorely grieved that portion of the public whose mental capacities were slightly in excess of those of the average ballet critic but, further, a proportion of comedies which were not satisfied to be merely comedies but which deemed it incumbent upon them to include a variety of solemn passages confiding their author's profundities on divers cosmic enigmas. The result was and is a species of entertainment that sacrifices light comedy to heavy platitudinizing and that in sum suggests an undergraduate at a small Methodist college wildly celebrating the completion of a cribbed thesis with a couple of beers.

This *Without Love* provides a sterling example. Borrowing the time-honored theatrical plot of a hundred or more marriage-of-convenience and marriage-in-name-only plays, Barry has overlaid it with political symbolism analogically having to do with English-Irish national relations. Therefrom it is his apparent idea to prove that a little hot love would not be and is not a bad idea in either case and, in the English-Irish case in particular, that it might lead to mutually profitably co-operation, especially in war time. (He elects to overlook that the platonic relationship between the two nations in point has been somewhat one-sided and that Ireland's frigidity has not restrained England in the past from seducing her good and plenty.) His stated argumentation in proof of his point is additionally so juvenile that even the most bellicose Anglophile would have some trouble in rationalizing it, taking as it does the vaudeville viewpoint that whereas everybody objects to Ireland's neutrality in the present war, nobody objects to Switzerland's and contending further that it is Ireland's duty to have consideration in a dire hour for a country which never showed it consideration in an almost equally dire hour.

Not only has such political brain exercise invalidated much of Barry's comedy but his comedy writing itself shows an in-creasing inner debility. Once not without some wit, it has now descended to such Balaban and Katz humors as alluding to an inebriated character as "my little tipsy sweetheart" and patriotically observing of a highball layout that "it has everything but Vichy." Once given to some originality, it now presents itself as little more than a pastiche of materials from its author's antecedent plays, as well as from the plays of others on end. (pp. 123-25)

If Mr. Barry regards what I write of his mental gifts as unkind, let me give him some comfort. Let him reflect that some of the best comedies the modern theatre has disclosed have been written by men of no especial cerebral voltage. Unlike him, however, they have duly appreciated the fact and have contented themselves with the achievement of merely very brilliant light entertainment. (p. 125)

George Jean Nathan, "The Year's Productions: 'Without Love'," in his The Theatre Book of the Year, 1942-1943: A Record and an Interpretation *(copyright 1943 by George Jean Nathan; reprinted by permission of Associated University Presses, Inc., for the Literary Estate of George Jean Nathan), Alfred A. Knopf, 1943, pp. 121-26.*

ROBERT E. SHERWOOD   (essay date 1951)

[*Sherwood was a Pulitzer Prize winning dramatist and friend of Barry's who undertook the revision of Barry's last play,* Second Threshold.]

Although Phil Barry had talked to me a little about *Second Threshold* in the last months of his life, I did not read it until after his death. It moved me very powerfully and excited me greatly. For I felt that he had at last begun to achieve the realization, or the synthesis, of his apparently but not actually discordant qualities: his Irish, impish sense of comedy, and his profound, and also Irish, sense of the ultimate sadness of life on earth, the "endless assault" of evil upon good. I think that the most obvious mark of his self-imposed limitations had been his fear that he must keep these two senses in airtight compartments, that he had said to himself, as he started a play, "Now I'll write a comedy (or potboiler)," or "Now I'll write a serious play (or valiant failure)"; and the comedies were far bigger than potboilers, and the serious plays were far bigger than failures. In *Second Threshold,* it seems to me, he began to reveal the mature discovery that life is indivisible, that bright comedy and dark tragedy must blend into the fluent half-tones which evolve between black and white and provide the endlessly varied coloration of all creation. The revealing of this discovery in *Second Threshold* makes his sudden death all the graver a loss to American letters. (pp. x-xi)

Robert E. Sherwood, in his preface to Second Threshold *by Philip Barry (copyright © 1949 by Philip Barry and Ellen S. Barry; copyright © 1951 by Ellen S. Barry and Estate of Philip Barry; copyright © 1951 by Robert E. Sherwood; reprinted by permission of Harper & Row, Publishers, Inc.), Harper & Brothers Publishers, 1951, pp. v-xiii.*

W. DAVID SIEVERS   (essay date 1951)

[*Sievers's* Freud on Broadway *offers a thorough discussion of Barry's innovative use of psychoanalysis within the dramas* In a Garden, Hotel Universe, *and* Here Come the Clowns. *He describes Barry as a "sensitive and deeply spiritual writer coming to grips with the psychology of his times and expressing a yearning for maturity and emotional wholeness.''*]

In a Garden . . . was the first of Barry's three major psycho-analytic plays (the others being *Hotel Universe* and *Here Come the Clowns*), all fantastic in form and all dealing with the repressed past which is exhumed and faced down. (p. 188)

In a Garden states a psychoanalytic theme in Barry's original, unhackneyed way, adding to it the fanciful conjecture that "Every wife is at heart another man's mistress" (which can hardly be credited to Freud). There is much that is subtle, tasteful, almost precious in Barry's handling of the motif of regression to a happier state. The garden may be intended symbolically as all happy states of wish-fulfillment. In a sense, the conclusion is anti-psychoanalytic, for Barry tests the prop-osition that to face down the force of the past will free one of its repressive power; as in *Tomorrow and Tomorrow* and *Re-union in Vienna*, the Freudian formula fails to live up to ex-pectations. Clinically, of course, the test if over-simplified, insufficient and inadequately evaluated to produce insight. But Barry seems indeed to be criticizing all pat formulas for human nature rather than psychoanalysis itself. (p. 189)

There are, to be sure, flaws in the motivation of *In a Garden*. Lissa's discontent is not entirely credible after the first-act picture of her married life and Adrian's offer to retire and take her away. She hardly commands our sympathy as a Nora Hel-mer. The motives of Norris, too, remain somehow unexplored in his clinging to an adolescent experience throughout his ma-ture life. *In a Garden* is of considerable significance for the drama, however, as the first modern attempt to incorporate into a play the concept of psychodrama. A psychiatrist, Dr. Jacob L. Moreno, pioneered in the clinical use of psychodrama, in which patients act out improvisationally their disturbing situations and play various roles to enlarge their insight. Mor-eno did not begin publishing in English until 1928 and whether or not Barry knew of Moreno's previous work in Vienna with the "Theatre of Spontaneity" cannot be ascertained. At any rate, Barry was the first to see the aesthetic as well as clinical possibilities of acting out a past experience as a means of freeing the individual of its oppressive influence.

In 1930 (still anticipating Moreno's major publications, al-though there had been several articles on psychodrama by Mor-eno and Trigant Burrow in psychological journals), Barry trans-muted the same materials of *In a Garden* into one of the truly original masterpieces of the modern American drama, *Hotel Universe*. That it should have baffled so many of the New York critics is strange, for its meaning is readily accessible with the key of psychoanalysis. But most of the metropolitan reviewers found it "vague," "off the deep end," "confused," and "mystic."

In one long act of irresistibly heightening mood, Barry assem-bles a group of characters in an old house in Southern France that used to be "Hotel de l'Univers," a mysterious, formerly deserted château where the past keeps cropping up in an unreal juxtaposition of people, places and time. Although the group has come to cheer up Ann, an old friend who is forced to devote herself to nursing her old father, their efforts produce anything but cheer. For they are a group of neurotic, anchorless souls, each with a drive or need which is barely understood on the conscious level.

Barry undertakes to release these bewildered and representative humans from their neurotic drives and bring them to con-sciousness by the use of psychodrama. (pp. 190-91)

No bare synopsis of the plot can do justice to *Hotel Universe*. Its genius lies in the subtle interweaving of *leit-motifs,* a mu-sical orchestration of the mingled yearnings and wishings of these compassionately drawn, deeply understood characters (though it is true that Barry can naturally penetrate deeper into the childhood emotional constellation of his Catholic Tom than of the Jewish Norman). But all of Barry's people are suffused with his unique humaneness, slipping in and out of the multiple roles that make up a complex adult with effortless artistry. Stephen plays four roles, Tom's priest-confessor, Norman's employer, Lily's father and the father of Pat's sweetheart; rather it should be stated in the converse: four individuals project their feelings toward the authority-figure onto Stephen. *Hotel Uni-verse* is truly a drama of role-playing, and if it was misunder-stood in 1930 surely it deserves to be re-staged today and evaluated in the light of modern applications of role-playing and psychotherapy.

Hotel Universe evokes the child within the adult, flowing from past to present, from conscious to dim unconscious with con-summate skill. The dramatist gives his characters the oppor-tunity not often afforded outside the psychoanalyst's office to return to childhood, to play "Under the Piano," and reevaluate past experiences in the light of reality. Effecting its catharsis on audience as well as on participants, the play is fantasy not because it is fantastic—for it is not—but because its pattern compresses many lifetimes into one mosaic and permits char-acters to act and speak without the reality-testing censorship of the ego. It may be called psychoanalysis transmuted into a work of art, dramatized on a far deeper level than literal efforts such as Flavin's *Tapestry in Gray*. To the Freudian theme of finding oneself by a regression to the past, Barry adds his own special whimsy, his generous feeling for people and his poetic certainty that there is continuity to human life. With the warm humor lacking in *Mourning Becomes Electra* and the subtlety lacking in *Strange Interlude*, Barry created in *Hotel Universe* possibly the masterpiece of the psychoanalytic drama.

The third of what might be called Barry's "regression-fanta-sies" was *Here Come the Clowns,* which in 1938 left the critics as bewildered as if there had been no *Hotel Universe* or *In a Garden*. The intervening years, however, made certain differ-ences notable. *Here Come the Clowns* was born of a mature playwright and thinker's perturbation about the meaning of life and the value of religion. Subjective and relatively plotless, it anticipated *The Time of Your Life* and *The Iceman Cometh* and has many similarities to the O'Neill play; both ask the question: Can man face himself without illusions? With a struggle that must have been as agonizing for the author as for his characters, Barry rejects religion, which fosters dependency, in favor of an active free-will. Man must be active in forming his own destiny, which he can only do when he is able to see the truth about himself clearly. This essentially psychoanalytic conclu-sion is not presented in Freudian terms; nor is the ending une-quivocal in its meaning, so that it is not difficult to see why the reviewers disparaged the play with the epithet "philo-sophical."

In the same general form as *Hotel Universe* (although this time with intermissions), Barry assembles a grotesque, almost Tou-louse-Lautrec collection of vaudevillians on the periphery of show business. In a café owned by a former female imper-sonator, a man named Ma Speedy, there is a ventriloquist and his dummy, a dwarf, a chronic drunk, a magician named Max Pabst, and a young couple who fear to marry because he is a foundling. There is also Clancy, a gentle, wonderfully kind, deeply suffering Irishman who had lost his beloved daughter and had gone away, returning after many years to a wife who doesn't love him. He free associates on a carnation, bringing to consciousness the repressed memory of a lemon tree and his mother who had taught him that carnations were the flower of God. (pp. 194-96)

If there is an inherent weakness in this bizarre group psychotherapy which Barry puts upon the stage, it is that the collection of characters is a motley one and cannot elicit the degree of empathy which one or two more fully developed roles might have. In that respect, the form of *In a Garden,* with its concentration on one individual's re-living his past, was more successful than the other two plays. The characters in *Hotel Universe* were more universal, more recognizable and sympathetic, while the Barry of *Here Come the Clowns* was in the bitter mood of the Munich years, and had to turn to a less savory and more warped assortment of human specimens. Clancy, who was potentially a great character, is given much less chance to grow to full tragic stature than Harry Hope, in O'Neill's comparable play. But his final awareness is greater and clearer than Hope's, for Clancy sees as he dies that in self-knowledge lies the road to freedom for the individual.

Although hardly apt to be a popular theatre piece, *Here Come the Clowns* is an important philosophical drama in which Barry predicates the only kind of religion which is acceptable to him—that which does not reduce man to a state of unconscious dependency. The device of the ventriloquist who uses his dummy to talk out the agonized confession that is too painful for him is a brilliantly original attempt to solve the same problem of duality for which O'Neill used masks, asides and two actors. If Barry's symbols seemed mordant—if humanity seemed to him only a side-show of clowns, ventriloquists, dwarfs and Lesbians, the play must be taken in the light of 1938 when the hope of the world was at a low ebb. (p. 197)

The themes that recur throughout the work of Philip Barry and which relate to Freudian psychology are: reliving the past in order to be free of it (*In a Garden, Hotel Universe, Here Come the Clowns, Foolish Notion*); regression to the security of childhood (*You and I, Holiday, Hotel Universe, The Joyous Season, Liberty Jones*); frigidity or the impoverishment of emotion (*Bright Star, The Philadelphia Story, Without Love* and *Second Threshold*); and finally, the search for self-realization or emotional maturity which is somehow related to the "victory over his own family"—in all of his work.

Certainly it falls far short to dismiss Barry as a witty writer of high comedy of manners, bantering, facile and superficial. He was that and more. Beneath his flippancy and his "chit-chat" was a sensitive and deeply spiritual writer coming to grips with the psychology of his times and expressing a yearning for maturity and emotional wholeness. No other American playwright was able to transmute the raw elements of unconscious life into a work of art so delicate, so subtly ingratiating, and so fresh in form, as did Philip Barry. If these are the criteria of greatness, *Hotel Universe* belongs among the great plays. (p. 211)

> W. David Sievers, "The Psychodramas of Philip Barry," in his Freud on Broadway: A History of Psychoanalysis and the American Drama (originally a dissertation presented at the University of Southern California in 1951; copyright © 1955 by W. David Sievers; reprinted by permission of David L. Sievers, Donna Rose Sievers and Sandra Louise Sievers), Hermitage House, 1955 (and reprinted by Cooper Square Publishers, Inc., 1970), pp. 187-211.

JOHN GASSNER (essay date 1954)

[*Gassner, a Hungarian-born American scholar, was a great promoter of American theater, particularly the work of Tennessee Williams and Arthur Miller. He edited numerous collections of modern drama and wrote two important dramatic surveys,* Masters of Modern Drama *(1940) and* Theater in Our Times *(1954). In this analysis, Gassner refers to Barry's "civilized" artistic disposition—a rare and refined temperament that helped to produce his urbane comedies. He also asserts that Barry's manner was one of moderation, that is "he was a moderate among dramatic extremists, and a reflective writer among raucous entertainers."*]

It is not surprising that [Barry] was frequently tempted to abandon comedy. If he did manage to become, with Behrman, one of our two most consistently successful writers of high comedy, his manner, nevertheless, distinguishes him from most European writers of comedy. Their steel is more tempered, their point sharper. They appear to be, at least on the surface, more acute observers of folly because less tender-minded. Barry seems to care too much for his characters to seem as astute as, let us say, Carl Sternheim. He could rarely sting.

When this record is carefully studied, it becomes apparent that Philip Barry was a scrupulous artist of the theatre who faced and assigned to himself the difficult task of standing between extremes—between social satire and vacuous entertainment, between social passion and theatrical tomfoolery, between crass realism and poetic drama. In all respects, he tried to arrive at a reasonable position in an increasingly unreasonable world that placed a premium on excess. Playwriting was much easier for farcical "debunkers" on one hand and for hammering social realists on the other hand than for a writer of Barry's disposition and calibre. He was a moderate among dramatic extremists, and a reflective writer among raucous entertainers. His talent being distinctly comedic and theatrical, he succeeded much more frequently when he was not inhibited by the large measure of reflectiveness and sympathy (and whimsy) that he had at his command. And the same inclination also blunted the edge of his satire and the sharpness of wit of which he was capable, for which reason even his best comedies may not yield their full effectiveness to the reader who does not follow them with a sure sense of how well they played and can still play on the stage.

There is, indeed, no great possibility of our now having other writers of comedy who can command his restrained expertness, and even less possibility of our meeting up again with playwrights who will attempt to effectuate themselves in his kind of moralistic yet refined drama. His talent was unique in this respect. It had, so to speak, one foot in a genteel society still secure and another foot in the quicksilver of society as we know it today. Barry was completely at home in the theatre. It is less certain that he was entirely at home in the world. His art sustained him; it could not integrate him. From this circumstance arose the dissatisfactions registered by critics, as well as the unevenness of his career in playwriting.

From this circumstance, however, also arose the distinctive savor of his writing, its truly civilized taste and its humane considerateness for people whatever their station in life and whatever their errors of impulse or judgment. There was no acid in the composition of his writing in spite of his amused attitude toward the social set so well expressed in Mike's line in *The Philadelphia Story,* "The prettiest sight in this fine pretty world is the Privileged Class enjoying its privileges." Despite such apt observations on the social scene as Dexter's reminder to Tracy in the same play, "You're a special class of American

Female now—the Married Virgin,'' Barry was not truly a satirist. In spite of his ability to write many amazingly well-turned lines in his plays, it was not even wit that he specialized in. His forte was something warmer, a suspension of judgment as a way of life. It is well expressed in *The Philadelphia Story:* in Tracy's jibe at that ''pin-feather in the Left Wing,'' Mike Connor when she tells him, ''You've made up your mind awfully young,'' and in her blanket statement: ''The time to make up your mind about people is never.'' If wit emanates infrequently from such an attitude, and excitement even less frequently, other qualities pertaining to high comedy, as well as to whimsy and fancy, do stem from it—amusement, of course, and also a feeling very rare in our theatre that one is in the presence of a civilized soul. It may not invigorate us, but it puts us at ease and in sympathy with humanity, which is one of the saving graces of Barry's art.

Barry's was a healing art at a time when dramatic art was mostly dissonance. Perhaps Barry felt the need for healing too greatly himself to add to the dissonance and to widen the rifts in the topography of the modern, specifically contemporary American, scene. Whatever the reason, and regardless of the risk of indecisiveness, Barry sought balm in Gilead, found it somehow, and dispensed it liberally—and with gentlemanly tact. It does not appear that the future, at least the immediate future, belongs to dispensers of balm. Nor is it either gratifying or feasible to accept it from most givers, since their manner is apt to be maudlin and their palms are often uncomfortably clammy. It was not the least of Barry's merits, a mark of both his breeding and manliness, that his manner was generally bright and brisk and that the hand he stretched out to others, as if to himself, was as firm as it was open. For all the cleverness that won him popularity and for all his theatrical deftness, his considerateness never failed him, and his tolerance never succumbed to either cynicism or indifference. This is a great deal to find in a contemporary playwright, even if there are also greater virtues to be sought in dramatic writing. The word for this quality of Barry's work on the whole is not easy to find. It is not the word that comes most readily to mind; it is not mere urbanity. ''Civilizedness,'' that state of grace which being inwardly civilized entails, is perhaps the most accurate word for Philip Barry, and civilizedness, regardless of the penalty one pays for it, is to be treasured in the theatre that nowadays rarely makes a virtue of it.

The limitations that have been generally charged to Barry were themselves the consequences of his disposition and the causes of whatever distinction he was able to attain. As the gentleman-playwright *par excellence*, he tended to be too partial to good society, and his partiality accounts for the mildness he exhibited in comedy and fantasy. He was reluctant to shake the foundations upon which stood the charming and articulate people who provided him with comedy. And he either transferred them to the more or less metaphysical world he favored, as he did in *Hotel Universe,* giving more attention to their neuroses than the effort was worth, or allowed their voices to susurrate in the world of moral conflict, as they did in his too gentle religious plays and in the semi-morality play *Here Come the Clowns,* in which the war between good and evil was somewhat too subdued. (pp. 326-28)

[He] was often aware of the ennui and emptiness of the social set even while giving its members some measure of his own scrupulous humanity. *Holiday* and *The Animal Kingdom* are especially charged with discontent. Nevertheless, it was his burden in life to carry the world of the social set with him, whether or not he entirely approved it. The rebelliousness he introduced into his plays always seemed to me symptomatically lukewarm, as if the author himself could not go beyond a palace revolution.

Even for comedy of manners one could have desiderated a stronger animus than any Barry employed or was perhaps capable of mustering into the service of his playwriting. And for that reason alone, if for no other, most of his work seems to belong to a vanished period—almost the mauve period—of American life and theatre. But the amiable disposition Barry brought into his writing cannot lose a certain grace attendant to his humanity. Without that grace—and it was a grace of mind, too, quite often—both theatre and life could probably go on, but in some state of impoverishment that some of us would regret. (p. 328)

> John Gassner, ''Philip Barry: A Civilized Playwright,'' in his The Theatre in Our Times: A Survey of the Men, Materials and Movements in the Modern Theatre *(copyright © 1954 by John Gassner; used by permission of Crown Publishers, Inc.),* Crown, *1954, pp. 322-28.*

MONROE LIPPMAN (essay date 1956)

[*Lippman discusses the social and political themes in Barry's dramas.*]

Philip Barry is not chiefly concerned with the presentation of a socio-political viewpoint, as is frequently considered to be the case with such dramatists as Lillian Hellman and Clifford Odets. He has written only one play in which the major theme is primarily based on a political, social, or economic issue. But there are others of his works in which he does disclose such a viewpoint by evincing definite critical attitudes toward certain social or political phenomena, even though the presentation of his viewpoint may not be essential to the major theme of the play in which it occurs. In several of his earlier plays his favorite target is Business (with a capital B), and in some of his later works it is fascism as a threat to democracy.

Barry's attitude toward Business if first revealed in his earliest produced play, *You and I* . . . , where the attitude is one of amused tolerance. Any allusions to Business and its practices are oblique rather than direct, but there is no mistaking the fact that Barry looks upon the average successful Big Business man with something approaching contempt. G. T. Warren, the big business man in *You and I,* is not malicious; on the contrary, he is a warm, expansive, not unlikable Babbitt. But he is a man with no intellectual or cultural interests, whose entire life revolves around his business, and whose judgment of a serious piece of painting is based entirely upon the wide popular appeal he senses in it, and upon its consequent value as an advertising medium which might stimulate increased sales of the soap he manufactures. Although we cannot dislike Warren, he comes off very poorly in contrast to the other major characters in the play: Maitland White, an artist turned business man, and his wife; Ricky, his son, who is planning to study architecture; Ronny, his son's fiancée; and Geoffrey Nichols, a friend who is a writer—all people with an awareness of and interest in things beyond the realm of commerce.

In his next play, *The Youngest* . . . , Barry manifests a somewhat sharper distaste for Business, although this is neither a play about that subject nor a play of social criticism. Rather, it is the story of the youngest in the family, a potential writer, rebelling against his elders in a fight for the right to live his life as he wishes. But in a sense, perhaps Business might be considered the antagonist, for the young hero's elders wish him to devote his life to the family business, a pin factory which has been the basis of the family's position as the social and industrial leaders of the community. Here again the representatives of Business are portrayed as stuffy people, concerned with nothing but their own affairs, and completely scornful of such dubious tastes as an appreciation of literature and a desire to write.

Barry's disdainful attitude toward these representatives of Business is expressed through his young protagonist, Richard Winslow. "Industrial Progress—more business—bigger and better business," scoffs Richard, "Agh! 'S if there wasn't too much business already." Again, while addressing the employees of the pin factory in a Fourth-of-July address normally made by the oldest brother, Richard says, to the dismay of his elders, "What the world needs if more leisure 'n' fewer alarm-clocks—less do-as-you're told 'n' more do-as-you-please." (pp. 151-52)

Although at least one Barry play was produced in each of the seasons intervening between 1924 and 1928, it was not until that latter season that he again gave us a play in which there is a strong element of social criticism. The play was the highly successful comedy, *Holiday,* and again the target was Business. *Holiday* opened in late November, 1928, just eleven months before that fateful day in 1929 when the stock market crashed with a force that shook the world. During the season of *Holiday* the big boom was still on; money was still America's god, and anyone who possessed it in sufficient quantity was to be admired, especially if he had acquired it through such respectable channels as Big Business.

Edward Seton, the Big Business man in *Holiday,* is definitely a less likable person than G. T. Warren, his predecessor in *You and I.* He is successful, pompous, cold, cocksure, and imbued with a reverence for riches. When informed of his prospective son-in-law's lack of interest in making too much money, Edward is stunned, but recovering his equilibrium, says bewilderedly, "Too *much* money?" It is clear that to Edward Seton and all other right-thinking men there simply is no such thing. This attitude is shared by his older daughter, who assures her fiancé that "there's no such thrill in the world as making money."

When Johnny Case, the young man in question, presents his scheme to make just enough money to retire and enjoy it till it's gone, and then work when he's older, Edward recoils at the thought that there is a red-blooded man alive who doesn't want to make enough to enable him, as his younger daughter satirically puts it, to live well "on the income of his income." This entire attitude of Johnny's, his unwillingness to devote his life exclusively to piling up money, is characterized angrily by Edward as "deliberately un-American," and there is little doubt that if there had been an un-American activities committee at the time, Edward would have reported Johnny as being subversive of the American system of free enterprise.

In the ten years following the season of *Holiday,* six Barry plays were seen on Broadway, but it was 1938 before Barry again concerned himself with criticism of the existing order. By this time he was through with Business as a target, for times had changed, and there were other more immediate problems. Nineteen thirty-eight, it will be remembered, was the year when Hitler marched into Austria and made it a part of greater Germany; it was the year of the Munich agreement which brought Czechoslovakia's Sudetenland under the rule of the Third Reich; it was the year in which many people in this country were forced to realize that the titanic struggle between democracy and fascism had in fact begun, although the outbreak of the great war was still a year off. . . . Barry's awareness was revealed in the somewhat obscure fantasy, *Here Come the Clowns.*

Although this play met with general critical approval, there was some bewilderment on the part of critics and audiences alike as to its meaning. The action occurs in a cafe in back of a vaudeville theatre named the Globe because it represents, according to Barry, a "small cross-section of the world." Occupying the cafe at various times during the action of the play are such performers as a ventriloquist and his Lesbian wife, a song-and-dance team, a midget, and others. Into their midst comes a Mr. Pabst, a somewhat Freudian illusionist with a central European accent who, by persistently and maliciously prying into the innermost problems and worries of these people, succeeds in ruining their lives. Just before meeting his death, Clancy, a bewildered stagehand who is Barry's protagonist in search of Truth, turns on the illusionist with this revelation: "I see now it's no will of God things are as they are—no, nor Devil's will neither! It's the will of all them like yourself, the world over—men bad by their *own choice*—and the woods full of 'em!"

If the application of Barry's play to the then-current problems of the world is not readily apparent from the script (as it is not to this writer), at least we have the playwright's word that it was intended to be, for in an article which Barry wrote for the New York *World Telegram* of December 10, 1938, just three days after the play's opening, the playwright stated, for the benefit of those who had failed to grasp its meaning, that it was concerned with the battle with evil being fought throughout the world. He further clarified his viewpoint by saying that "it is infinitely better to die in this struggle than it is to live in fear or in the questionable security which follows any compromise with all these things in government and human society that we know in our hearts to be wrong." That Barry felt it necessary thus to explain the meaning of his play seems to indicate that his first effort to deal directly with an international political issue was not eminently successful.

It was over two years before Barry again turned to protest, this time with *Liberty Jones,* an allegorical play with music. When this play opened in February, 1941, World War II was in its seventeenth month. . . . [In] the United States, the nation's first peacetime draft had gone into effect, reserve units had been called up, and there was steadily increasing tension. Although it was still ten months before the attack on Pearl Harbor, the feeling that we should take our stand against fascism was being shared by an increasing number of Americans, among whom was Barry, whose sentiments are evident in *Liberty Jones.* Of all Barry's plays, this is the only one which can accurately be considered a protest play, for it is the only one in which the playwright projects through his major theme a definite point of view on a political, economic, or social issue; and in this case, since the play concerns the struggle between fascism and democracy, all three of these issues are involved.

As the play opens, we are introduced to Miss Liberty Jones, a young girl who lies in bed afflicted with what is feared to be a fatal illness. Her Uncle Samuel is much too busy directing his vast industrial empire in the manufacture of "needlesses" to be sufficiently concerned with the state of health of his niece; her Aunt Gloria is too occupied with numerous matters of only superficial importance to heed adequately the girl's condition. Hence, largely because of neglect, Miss Liberty appears to be on her death bed, although she herself is not quite willing to give up. When informed that she is merely an idea to the people and consequently is dying, she replies with some fervor: "I'm *not* just an idea, a word in a book, a far-away dream, a long-ago memory. . . . A girl is what I am—and their own girl! Theirs for every day in the week . . . and I shan't die yet. . . ." When asked what it is she wants, she says, "I should like to speak my mind freely. . . . Pray my own prayers. . . . When I sleep, sleep in peace"—a reaffirmation of our basic rights. (pp. 152-54)

If this only protest play of Barry's is one of his less successful works, it is perhaps because of three major faults: his characters are pallid and unreal, even for a musical allegory; his usual bright and entertaining dialogue is missing; the treatment of theme degenerates into rather dull propaganda. In comparison with certain other plays which treat of the same general theme, such as *Watch on the Rhine, Thunder Rock,* and *The Gentle People,* it is not difficult to understand why *Liberty Jones,* labeled by Barry as being "for city children," did not appeal greatly to city adults.

In only one more play did Barry manifest a strong interest in a national or international problem. This play, *Without Love,* reverts to the formula of such earlier works as *The Youngest* and *Holiday.* Primarily, it is a comedy built around the romance of two highly engaging people, but a current political issue is considered in a sort of secondary story. The action of *Without Love* occurs in 1940 and 1941, although, when the play actually took the stage in November, 1942, we had already been in the war for nearly a year. A major concern during the time in which the play is set was the fear that Germany would try to reach England by an invasion of Eire, which was stubbornly maintaining its neutrality despite pressure to allow England to establish air bases in Ireland, in order to be able to fight off a possible invasion. It was this situation which Barry used as a sort of minor theme in *Without Love.* (p. 155)

From the standpoint of dramaturgy, it is not vitally important that the issue involving Ireland fails to be resolved. If this were a true protest play, the issue would be of major importance; but in this play, although the introduction of the issue lends a strong feeling of timeliness and indicates Barry's awareness of a live political problem, it is not the major concern. Hence the somewhat nebulous disposal of the problem is acceptable if not completely satisfactory, for it does not interfere with the play's major conflict and the resolution of that conflict in the romantic culmination of a marriage of convenience, which had been originally planned "without love."

In all the plays considered here, except *Liberty Jones,* Barry's social or political viewpoints are secondary, if not incidental. They permit him to indicate his own attitude toward the problems involved, and they sometimes give the plays a quality of contemporaneity. Aside from this, they are not basically important to structure, at least as far as major themes are concerned, although they may sometimes serve as a factor in the plots. In view of the lack of success of his one protest play, it is perhaps well that Barry did not usually attempt plays of protest, but was content to approach obliquely whatever criticism of the political, social, or economic scene he might choose to present. (p. 156)

Monroe Lippman, "Philip Barry and His Socio-Political Attitudes," in The Quarterly Journal of Speech (copyright 1956 by the Speech Association of America), Vol. XLII, No. 2, April, 1956, pp. 151-56.

JOSEPH PATRICK ROPPOLO (essay date 1965)

[*Roppolo is the author of the only available biography of Barry. In the following excerpt, he offers an overview of Barry's literary techniques.*]

Behind each of Barry's plays lies the teaching of Professor George Pierce Baker. Barry learned and clung tenaciously to Professor Baker's broadest concepts—of interest, of action, of unity, of real life as a source of inspiration, and of hard, persistent, unrelenting effort. . . . But, Professor Baker insisted, a play presented special problems to the playwright, who must keep in mind always that he was neither a novelist nor an essayist. A play was meant to be produced before a heterogeneous audience, and to be successful the playwright had the primary duty of being entertaining. He must interest his audience from the very beginning, and he then must maintain or heighten that interest through the remainder of the play. *You and I* and *Second Threshold,* produced twenty-eight years apart, are examples that Barry learned and applied this lesson. Both begin with a scene involving a young man and a young woman who, before the play ends, will be destined for marriage; and both scenes move swiftly into the serious problems of the older characters. More sensationally, Barry begins *Here Come the Clowns* with a man who dares to seek out God, to challenge him with questions about the necessity of evil in the world.

Professor Baker insisted upon action, also, and Barry complied, but in his own way. Action to Barry did not mean violence. His plays are almost classically Grecian in their avoidance of on-stage bloodshed. Young Christian in *Tomorrow and Tomorrow* is injured in an off-stage accident; and the curtain falls in *John* before the Baptist is decapitated. The shot that kills Clancy in *Here Come the Clowns* reverberates shockingly in Barry's otherwise almost gunless world; and Clancy alone of Barry's protagonists dies before the audience.

Lesser modes of violent action are rare in Barry plays, too. Except for the clash between the Three Shirts and Tom, Dick, and Harry in *Liberty Jones* and the always imminent threat of physical conflict in *Here Come the Clowns,* Barry relies entirely on the conflict of ideas for his action, much in the manner of George Bernard Shaw. And, as with Shaw and Oscar Wilde, wit is his substitute for weapons. In this realm, and in that of language generally, Barry goes beyond Professor Baker to achieve distinction and complete individuality.

Sophisticated, racy, poetic, natural—Barry's language is all of these and more; and to these characteristics critics paid tribute throughout Barry's career. Perhaps Barry's strongest trait is his ability to record the language of the young, preserving at the same time a freshness that resists the years. *You and I,* for example, was produced in the early 1920's, a period vibrant with the slang of the Jazz Age. But in Ronny and Ricky, the young lovers, there is very little of the Jellybean and the Flapper. With an astoundingly acute ear, Barry chose for them slang and colloquialisms that were both appropriate and enduring: "Hang it," "in a pig's eye," "You can't get away with that," "Life shouldn't be all gravy," "I could swing it," "I'd better shove off," and "They're full of red ants." Not one would be inappropriate in the mouth of Thankful Mather in *Second Threshold,* who nevertheless has her own slang, equally enduring and appropriate: "I'd perish," she says; and "I'm completely all wore out." And Thankful has a little trick of omitting words: "Goodness, what an *attractive* man," she says. "And knows it, I expect. They usually." (pp. 112-14)

Barry reveals both character and emotion with language, and he moves easily from humorous word play through whimsy, to tense and frequently poetic seriousness. His skill reaches its highest point, however, in his use of what has been called the "unspoken word" to reveal deep feeling. This device, in which casual, even trivial, conversation covers and, for the audience, intensifies emotional climaxes, is especially effective in the love scene between Eve Redman and Nicholas Hay in Act II of *Tomorrow and Tomorrow* and in the dismissal scene between Tom Collier and Richard Regan in Act II of *The Animal Kingdom.* (p. 114)

Language is also a vehicle for symbolism in all of Barry's works, but he does not rely on words alone. Properties, characters, even the setting itself become symbolical in some of the plays, most notably in *Hotel Universe* and in *Here Come the Clowns.* In the latter play the Globe Theatre, representing the world, is discussed but not seen. The Café des Artistes, a segment of that world, is the single set. Concannon, never seen, is a God figure; and Pabst, the illusionist, represents not Satan but the evil that stalks the world in man himself. *Liberty Jones* is unashamedly allegory. The girl Liberty is the idea Liberty, and Tom, Dick, and Harry are representative of Everyman; but the allegory is not strictly maintained. Other symbols, overwhelming in their numbers, multiply, intensify, and even confuse Barry's meanings.

As early as *You and I,* Barry had developed his use of symbols to a high degree. The setting itself, described carefully at the beginning of Act I, is meant to be a full commentary on the life which Maitland and Nancy White have led; and "The Studio" in the attic is a retreat, a place of withdrawal—for Maitland White a place of withdrawal to his youth. (pp. 115-16)

Unity was one of the virtues which Professor Baker stressed, and in most of Barry's plays this virtue is present. Even in plays which deal with the fragmented stories of several characters, like *Hotel Universe,* unity is provided by the overall theme. Only in *Without Love* does Barry fail. In this play two stories are told, one of a marriage, the other of international politics. They are meant to be parallel, with the love story reinforcing the political lesson that Barry wished to teach; but the love story moves on to its expected ending, while the political one has necessarily no ending at all. The parallel exists and is both understandable and reasonable; but the two stories touch only occasionally, and Barry found no way to force the lesson of the marriage to the attention of his politicians.

Every Barry play is "about something"—marriage, divorce, family solidarity, the conflict between tradition and progress, the presence of evil in the world, the meaning and value of life. And Barry is careful to state his theme clearly, so that no audience or reader should be misled. In *You and I* Maitland White generalizes with a quotation from Thoreau: "Most men lead lives of quiet desperation." In *Second Threshold* Josiah Bolton refers to the Bible to justify his lack of interest in life: "If the salt has lost its savour wherewith shall it be salted? It is thenceforth good for nothing but to be cast out and to be trodden under foot of men." Maitland White's "quiet desperation" exists because he has "jilted" art for marriage; Josiah's, because he has cut himself off from life and has become useless. These reasons give Barry the opportunity to explore a variety of sub-themes and motifs: the relationship of parent and child, marriage, individual responsibility, family responsibility, work, art, and love. In all these themes, Barry's first and last Broadway plays are remarkably similar. It is as if

Barry had deliberately stated in his first professional work all, or almost all, of the major themes that he hoped to deal with and had, in his final work, attempted to restate them and to give his final and considered judgment on the value and meaning of life.

Of the sub-themes that appear in *You and I,* marriage is the one most frequently (and mistakenly) regarded as dominant in Barry's works. It is true that without exception Barry's major characters have been, are, or are about to be married. It is also true that in many of the plays Barry comments clearly on the meaning of marriage and that in three—*Paris Bound, Tomorrow and Tomorrow,* and *The Animal Kingdom*—this theme is dominant. (pp. 116-17)

In none of these "marriage plays" is Barry specifically Catholic. He becomes so in two, *Here Come the Clowns* and *The Joyous Season*—and the emphasis is the same. In *Here Come the Clowns* Clancy insists that marriage is a sacrament, and in *The Joyous Season,* Christina, a nun, points out that a marriage is void if the sacrament is taken with reservations.

The relationships between parent and child and, on a larger scale, the family as a unit are, like marriage, sub-themes that are apparent in most of Barry's plays; and once again Barry's conclusions are soundly moral. In *You and I* there is love between parents and son, but Maitland White resists the idea that as a father he has "given hostages to fortune" and that he is responsible for the welfare and happiness of his children. In *Second Threshold* Josiah Bolton deliberately rejects the love of his children and insists, in his emptiness, that there is no debt on either side. Maitland accepts responsibility finally, and Josiah learns to accept and return love.

White Wings presents a family, the Inches, which is bound by tradition and to which the son, Archie, is almost sacrificed. And *The Joyous Season* emphasizes the idea that the family has spiritual links as well as physical and that unity and mutual support extend beyond the walls and roof of a home. In both these plays and in *The Youngest,* Barry demonstrates that the role of the family should be to encourage development of the individual, rather than to inhibit individuality. (pp. 118-19)

During the 1920's Barry's work focused on the individual— the individual's responsibility to himself. Barry insisted in *The Youngest* that the individual had the right and the duty to develop in his own way—to achieve fulfillment regardless of the pressures of family and society. Such pressures were in fact violations of the human soul, and therefore sacrilege, as Barry says in *In a Garden.* On this point, Barry's views are comparable to those of Hawthorne. *Paris Bound, White Wings,* and *Holiday* further Barry's study of individual responsibility to self. In *White Wings* the enemy is family and tradition, here symbolically identical. In *Paris Bound* and *Holiday* the enemy is society. In each of these plays, the individualist is the victor. (p. 120)

In the 1930's and in the 1940's, Barry's focus remained on the individual; but, as *Here Come the Clowns* demonstrates, he elaborated on the individual's responsibilities to others. Self-fulfillment becomes a means not merely of satisfying or pleasing one's self, but of rendering greater and truer service. Christina, in *The Joyous Season,* leaves her family to enter a convent; but it is she who holds the Farley family together. Tom Smith, in *Liberty Jones,* demonstrates that there is a time when the strongest individualists must band together, fight, and die to protect individual liberties from danger—specifically, in this play, the encroachment of totalitarian ideas. Responsibility to self expands to embrace responsibility to family, to society, to the nation, and to the world. (p. 121)

In his recognition of free will and responsibility, Barry removed himself from the quest of his times. He is not, and never was, among those who strove to create new values for a world which apparently had none. Despite doubts, Barry's world was essentially moral; and, despite certain unconventionalities, Barry's morality remained essentially Catholic. Like Whitman, Barry believed that the kelson of creation is Love. Love of husband and wife and of parents and children dominates *You and I,* and love is the answer to Josiah Bolton's despair in *Second Threshold*—love given, returned, and accepted. (p. 122)

The majority of Barry's plays fall into the category of conventional three-act drama, but *Hotel Universe* is unique in that it was written and presented as a full-length drama in one act with no intermissions. *Cock Robin* and the earlier *White Wings* present interesting reversals of a single set. *Foolish Notion* offers two innovations: an invisible fourth wall which is reflected visibly in a large mirror and characters who, in the Broadway version if not in the script, enter the fantasy sequences by walking backward. *Liberty Jones* is a daring, if not entirely successful, attempt to unite drama, song, dance, music, and rhyme in a single patriotic allegory. And surrealistic effects, along with a striking use of lights and the noise of automobile horns, are apparent in *White Wings*. In almost every instance, Barry uses novelties with restraint. For him, the play and the theme were important. Experiments and innovations were employed only if they contributed to the desired effect, never for their own sakes.

Not all of Barry's innovations were successful. The dreams who walked backward in *Foolish Notion,* for example, were derided by more than one critic; and the lack of intermissions in *Hotel Universe* brought discomfort to some. But Barry had discovered early in his career that it would be impossible to please everyone. He was criticized even for his language, although from the beginning most critics agreed that his way with the English language was one of his greatest strengths.

A more telling criticism leveled against Barry was that he was not concerned with the social problems of his day. Even the most socially conscious of his critics, like Miss Flexner [see excerpt above] admit, however, that Barry's savagely hilarious picture of the capitalist in *Holiday* ranks with the best of those drawn in the 1930's; and his concern with the totalitarian threat during the 1930's and the 1940's and with the Allied war effort is obvious in such plays as *Here Come the Clowns,* and *Without Love.* Barry beat no drums for organized movements. Instead, and always, he found the answer to the world's problems in the individual, who, with his free will, was the source of all the evil in the world and the potential force to conquer that evil.

A second criticism leveled against Barry is that he was limited to writing of the privileged classes—the sophisticated, educated, work-free rich. There is some truth in this, just as there is some truth in the same charge leveled at Henry James; and the defense is the same for both. The limitation, when it occurs, is deliberate. By confining himself to the privileged, Barry is able to isolate a problem and to probe it cleanly, without the complications that poverty or the necessity of labor would introduce. (pp. 123-24)

All people were important to Philip Barry, as he himself said in defending *Here Come the Clowns;* and he was in awe of the unrealized potentialities of the human individual. Despite what he saw in the world around him—the frenzied search for plea-

sure in the 1920's, the despair of the Great Depression in the 1930's, and the horrors of World War II—Barry remained hopeful, even optimistic. Man can triumph; man can prevail; over and over, in comedy and tragedy, in farce and serious drama, Barry played on this theme. He was not swayed by mass movements, by leftist trends, or by biological, environmental, or psychological theories which reduced man to a helpless plaything of forces he could neither control nor master. To Barry, man remained morally responsible for all his actions; a creature of God, made in God's image, he was capable of illimitable self-improvement. Barry's voice was affirmative, and perhaps that is why it has been all but lost among the shrill negativism that characterizes much twentieth-century drama. (pp. 124-25)

Joseph Patrick Roppolo, in his Philip Barry *(copyright © 1965 by Twayne; reprinted with the permission of Twayne Publishers, a Division of G. K. Hall & Co., Boston), Twayne, 1965, 158 p.*

WALTER J. MESERVE (essay date 1970)

[*The author of several books on American drama, Meserve focuses on the philosophical aspects of Barry's plays. He believes that they represent the dramatist's own search for meaning in life and that in his last play,* The Second Threshold, *Barry finds a satisfying answer to his cosmic reflections.*]

As a dramatist . . . Barry was motivated throughout his career by a single idea—man's need for freedom—which he found basic in man's constant attempt to understand himself, to discover truth, to find something in which to believe.

Quite simply, Barry wrote about people who were consciously or subconsciously trying to discover something. As the characters in his plays live and learn, they make certain discoveries which may be distinguished either as dramatic and technical, that is, necessary to the conclusion of the play, or philosophical. The more common discoveries are simply necessary to the plot and good Aristotelian dramaturgy. In *Philadelphia Story,* for example, Tracy Lord learns something about herself and, as a consequence, expediently directs the denouement of the play. The same is true for Mary in *Paris Bound,* John in the play by that title, and the major figures in *Joyous Season.* Yet the characters may also make a philosophical discovery. This kind of discovery is significant in Barry's personal search for something in which to believe but is satisfying, either in terms of his play characters or of Barry's search, only in his final play, *The Second Threshold.*

It is this second type of discovery which constantly haunted Barry. In most of his plays, for example, the dominant characters have a driving interest which they describe as a concern for living or knowing life. Johnny Case in *Holiday* illustrates this very clearly: "I want to live every which way, among all kinds—and know them—and understand them—and love them—that's what I want!" For Barry, wanting to live was the first step in man's search for meaning in life. Obviously, however, man must have the opportunity to find out about himself. And individual freedom was the means by which he might live and discover something, perhaps even the truth, although most Barry characters only suggest this end and simply want something which they cannot really define. In these plays the characters do one of two things: either they discover that they are frail human beings requiring personal freedom and, consequently, change to become more tolerant of the world; or events in the plays force them to make decisions which they generally describe, but never specifically, as "seeking freedom" or "knowing life." The more specific Barry tried to be in explaining this "freedom," the more obtuse his plays became, sometimes reaching a point where they were essentially discussions of his own inner doubts and dissatisfactions. Although in his light comedies he could solve a dramatic situation by having a character make a discovery which seemed to set him psychologically and personally free, in his more thoughtful plays he had great difficulty explaining what freedom was and what it could allow man to discover.

Even a cursory reading of a Barry play reveals this theme of individual freedom—the first step in man's search for meaning in life. *The Youngest* . . . , although a weak play with unreal characters, stilted language, and a very dated attitude, has a theme of independence. Foreshadowing Barry's next two plays, it warns that man must not try to control other people—an idea expressed in *In a Garden* . . .—and demands, as Barry did in *You and I* . . . , that man must be allowed to find himself. In the climax of *The Youngest* Richard finally does become free and even asserts his new-found freedom to ask Mary to marry him. *You and I* seems to present a life in which one may eat his cake and have it, too. At the final curtain Ricky will go to Paris to study architecture, but he will also marry Ronny, completing the romantic concept of *You and I*. The thesis of the play, however, is that man must be free to do what he wants, an *I* alone discovering who he is. And he must do this early in life, or he will never make it. Barry considered the end of this play tragic—Ricky's freedom is destroyed: the *you* will always come before the *I*, and man only fools himself if he thinks otherwise.

In *Paris Bound* . . . Barry treats his theme most effectively in the story of the ballet—the angel and the germ who are lionized and, therefore, controlled by society and who subsequently commit suicide. In the ballet story as in the main plot of the play man must have a certain freedom. The ballet shows that without this freedom man will die, while in the play the wife expediently, and with a certain wise sophistication, accepts this idea of freedom. The next year, 1928, Barry built an entire play around the idea that man wants to live and be free. Johnny Case in *Holiday* must be allowed to live and dream; the alternative that Barry sets up is the tradition of social and economic pressures where one dies, as did the angel and germ in *Paris Bound*. Although *Holiday* dramatizes only Barry's first step, there is the underlying suggestion that man, free to discover himself, should discover truth. In this play, however, Johnny Case is not sufficiently penetrating as a character to understand what he really wants.

Although Barry was never commercially successful with the plays in which he tried to go beyond this first step and find an answer to life's questions, these plays obviously express his most earnest thoughts. It is true that he was not a philosopher, but he was a thoughtful and serious man, bothered by what he saw in life. He was also a very religious man, a Catholic who believed in the power of Christian love and felt an overwhelming need to force life into an agreeable and optimistic pattern. Almost every Barry play ends with a suggestion of optimism. His ultimate question, however, was "What is man?" or "What is reality?" And in his conclusion, which he took a lifetime to reach, he had to find something compatible with his basic religious beliefs. Interesting to any thoughtful man, Barry's progress toward these conclusions reveals a modern artist struggling with man's most serious problems.

Barry first posed his question seriously in *In a Garden* in which the climax dramatized the chaos he felt if people could be reduced to intellectual rules. Adrian Terry, the protagonist in the play, had thought that a person could be controlled simply by one's discovering the Guiding Idea behind that person's actions. In this play, however, Barry showed not only that such a discovery was impossible but that the person who assumed the godhead was doomed to defeat. For Barry, at this time, man was free, mysterious, and beyond explanation.

The following year in *White Wings* . . . he tried his hand at an explanation, but the farcical nature of the play evidently did not allow him to see the penetrating quality of his observation. Or perhaps he was not reconciled to the answer which this play posed. Beneath this rather silly farce about people who follow the horses—with a shovel—there is a serious thesis. Both the Inches who sweep the streets and the Todds who made the automobile, want to live, and living means seeing the truth. The problem comes in discovering what the truth is. For the Inches the truth was simply the reality of the horse who would always need their services. Consequently, they were forced to maintain this truth and the pathetic beauty of the past through worn-out traditions quite dramatically staged and silly promises about the dignity of their work and the nobility of the horse. Poor old Mr. Inch! When he was finally converted from a street cleaner to a garbage collector, his call of "Sloppo!" always sounded like "Strawberries!" But man must go forward; he must live and search for the truth. In this play love, tenaciously dramatized by Mary Todd, provides the only way by which man, rather pathetically presented by Archie Inch, can discover truth and achieve happiness. He alone among the Inches seems to distinguish truth from illusion, accept the auto, and enjoy the feeling of driving it. And the purity of unquestioning *love* is clearly the determining force.

John . . . , concerned with the personal failure of John the Baptist, also deals with the question of man and truth, but Barry's first attempt to face the question clearly and seriously was in *Hotel Universe*. . . . In this long one-act play Barry presents man as confined and defeated by society and by illusions before he frees him—with the help of Freud. In a place where "time went sort of funny," where the beam from a lighthouse crosses the terrace "like the finger of God," and before a man, Stephen Field, who is "supposed to have some kind of power" over people and can "set the hour-glass on its side" and rest for a moment, Barry presents a group of young people of the Lost Generation who can find no values in life. "Nothing matters a damn anyway," is a shared opinion. All have at least contemplated suicide, and none reject death. To these people, each with his own problem, Stephen reveals what Barry has discovered: "a simple thing: that in existence there are three estates. There is this life of chairs and tables, of getting up and sitting down. There is the life one lives in one's imagining, in which one wishes, dreams, remembers. There is the life past death, which in itself contains the others. The three estates are one. We dwell now in this one, now in that—but in whichever we may be, breezes from the others still blow upon us."

Each of these people, with the help of Stephen, metaphorically or with Freud's assistance, walks back in time and dramatizes his or her problem. All are disillusioned and dissatisfied. All want to go somewhere, to find something! As Barry's answer to the various problems of lost faith, lost love, lost opportunity, Stephen tells each to give up his illusion and "come through alive." . . . [The] play shows Barry's interest in man's difficulty in finding himself and in distinguishing truth from illusion. At this point in his life Barry reiterated the insight that man must be free and reached the tentative conclusion that whether through religion and love, art, or the recognition of the real world man is the sum of his possibilities. In an existence where "everything has meaning" man has the potential to know truth.

Joyous Season . . . shows a more positive conclusion on Barry's part as he contemplates life. The opening scene presents a family overwhelmed by greed and desires of social advancement. Then, Christina, a sister in the family and a Mother Superior in a Catholic order, arrives and with her strong faith directs each member of the family to what is meaningful in life. Each must achieve the freedom to see himself or herself clearly and to do what is best. The main conflict in the play involves the family's decision to leave the city and return to "Good Ground," the old homestead. The symbolism of the name, of course, is obvious, but it is significant that religious faith is the catalyst which brings each person to the right decision. The fact that Christina really wanted "Good Ground" for her religious order, and could have made the choice but did not, only emphasizes Christian and therefore sacrificial love as central in a search for meaning in life.

An interest in religion was also dominant in *Here Come the Clowns*. . . . One character says of Clancy, the protagonist: "He was always very religious. I hope it helps him." But Barry himself was then unsure of that help, and confusion and inconclusiveness mark not only the ending of this play but many of its scenes. Whether as literature or theater the play is weak. Characterization is poor, and the play becomes a philosophical discussion with illustrations of man's selfishness, his fears, his perverseness. (pp. 93-7)

In *Here Come the Clowns* . . . , which is his most pessimistic point in his search for meaning, Barry shows that man has a confused idea of both truth and God. Man still has his pride, however, and his own free will. This is important. And he is still searching, a point which dramatizes the optimism inherent in Barry's approach to life.

It would seem that in his final play, *The Second Threshold* . . . , the writing of which was spread over the last ten years of his life, Barry started off at about the point *Here Come the Clowns* ended. Josiah, the protagonist who at 42 years has come to the end of "his soul's rope," makes this observation: "Life to the letter: brutal—intolerable—appalling—how do we endure it?" At another point he describes his situation in a more metaphorical manner: "—you are standing on the second threshold—a doorstep into the final ante-room that separates life from death. Maybe it is an enormous room, the end of which cannot be seen, maybe it is a stuffy little alcove." But through another character Barry suggests an answer: "Maybe there's one leading into a new life, not death." It is this discovery which Josiah must make, and does, when he learns that his daughter does not want him to die and would kill herself if he chose suicide. It is that discovery which Barry accepts as an answer to his many questions of the past. *Hotel Universe* suggested the potential of man; *Here Come the Clowns* ended with Clancy still searching; and in *The Second Threshold* man has learned. What is the answer that makes man want to live? that gives meaning to his days? Love! The intellectual question "What is man?" has become "What is Man that Thou art mindful of him?" Although Barry discussed Christian sacrificial love many times before, he had seemingly never quite acknowledged it as the answer to his philosophical questions. Accepting the fact that this last play occupied much of his later years, one can see *The Second Threshold* as an answer to the vagueness of *Hotel Universe* and the confusion of *Here Come*

the Clowns. It is also interesting that this final play which satisfied him philosophically was also the play which combined most successfully the wit and sparkle of his light comedies with a serious thesis.

Barry's career suggests the problems of the sensitive artist in a society shaken by conflicting ideas. Some of his plays, particularly *Here Come the Clowns* which is thematically similar to *The Iceman Cometh* and *Tomorrow and Tomorrow* which is sometimes compared to *Strange Interlude,* suggest those of Eugene O'Neill. Both were Catholic, but Barry kept the faith which O'Neill renounced. He stopped struggling and accepted. Like O'Neill, Mann, Camus, or Pirandello, Barry dramatized the saga of modern man, and his answer is one aspect of our culture. He was concerned; he thought, he doubted, and finally he believed in man on faith without fully understanding him. (pp. 98-9)

> Walter J. Meserve, "Philip Barry: A Dramatist's Search," in Modern Drama (copyright Modern Drama, University of Toronto), Vol. XIII, No. 1, May, 1970, pp. 93-9.

FRANCIS WYNDHAM   (essay date 1975)

[*In his discussion of the more successful of Barry's comedies of manners, Wyndham examines the father-daughter relationship that is basic to several of these plays.*]

The native school of drawing-room comedy which flourished on Broadway in the years between the wars never recovered from the death-blow delivered in the late 1940s by the first successes of Tennessee Williams and Arthur Miller. If George Kelly was the most original exponent of this vanished genre, Philip Barry was certainly the most distinguished, and [the Barry collection] *States of Grace* is a reminder of some of its more attractive qualities. . . .

Although twenty-one of his plays were produced on Broadway, only a handful were hits: *Paris Bound* (not included in this collection), *Holiday, The Animal Kingdom* and *The Philadelphia Story.* All four were made into films (*Holiday* and *The Philadelphia Story* twice) and all four were drawing-room comedies. . . .

Barry was himself prouder of his serious flops than of his tailor-made successes, but (to judge from the examples of both in this collection) the verdict of *Variety* and the Broadway public has been sadly justified by the passage of time. *White Wings* is a heavy-handed expressionist fantasy about the motor-car taking over from horse-drawn carriages; the Chekhovian *Hotel Universe,* with its cast of plangently discontented bright young things stranded on a terrace in the south of France, bears a closer resemblance to *Outward Bound* than to any more lofty model; and *Here Come the Clowns,* an allegory of Good and Evil played out by the freaks, homosexuals and similar misfits in a run-down vaudeville theatre, may have mystified the public in 1938 with its intimations of metaphysical despair, but today appears all too embarrassingly explicit. It seems that the frankly artificial framework of drawing-room comedy was necessary to preserve the frail but genuine spark of Barry's talent: when he ventured into freer forms, its originality was extinguished. Timid "experiment" is doomed to date: masterly exploitation of a well-worn tradition may, with luck, transcend its context and achieve unexpected longevity. . . .

In his best plays about the rich (and his best plays *are* about the rich) Barry seems to be writing not as an outsider trying to crash the country club, but as an insider casting wistful glances at a happy-go-lucky artistic bohemia outside. Writers, painters and musicians—what Dorothy Parker ironically called "people who do things"—are seen in such glamorous terms that one finds oneself forgetting the self-evident fact that Barry belonged in their company himself. *You and I* . . . , his first successful play, was originally called *The Thing He Wanted To Do*—and the thing that its hero, a middle-aged advertising executive, wanted to do was to paint. "To look at him", run the stage directions, "you might think him any one of a number of things. You guess that he is in business and you know that he is successful. His hands—long, slender and restless—and a kind of boyish whimsicality in him, are all that betray the artist." (There are moments when Barry himself betrays the influence of his near-namesake, the author of *Peter Pan*.) . . .

Linda, the heroine of *Holiday* . . . , is a rich girl stifled by her family's stuffy conventionality: her favourite friends are a decorously crazy couple called Nick and Susan Potter ("They get more fun out of nothing than anyone I know"). The part of Nick Potter was based on Barry's friend, Donald Ogden Stewart. . . . Johnny Case, the hero, falls in love with Linda's snobbish sister Julia without realizing that she is an heiress; when he *does* realize this, he wants to go off with her to Europe and "do nothing" instead of joining her father's business firm, and only Linda sees his point. Again, business is the enemy—of what, is never made quite clear. "I want to live every whichway, among all kinds—and know them—and understand them—and love them—*that's* what I want!" cries Johnny. Like most of the sympathetic characters in Barry's comedies, he wants to have fun—and fun has nothing to do with making money, only with spending it in a gracious and tasteful way.

The Animal Kingdom . . . is an ingenious reversal of the standard triangle drama of the period: here it is the wife who is the scheming gold-digger and the mistress who is the understanding sport. The hero is a publisher who says things like: "His work is the only true mistress a real artist ever had. When he takes on the world he takes on a whore." His wife seduces him into publishing trashy novels called *Indian Summer* and *Young Ecstasy* for financial gain. His mistress, Daisy Sage, works for fashion magazines but, like Maitland White, wants to "paint." . . .

Daisy Sage is a great Barry heroine: bohemian but monogamous, proud but vulnerable, awesomely intense but never quite abandoning the light touch. She has something in common not only with Tracy Lord of *The Philadelphia Story* . . . but also with Macaulay Connor in the same play—the cynical reporter for *Destiny* magazine who has published a book of short stories. ("They're so damned beautiful", Tracy tells him. "The one called 'With the Rich and Mighty'—I think I liked *it* best.") Everything is wrong with the man Tracy thinks she wants to marry: he is a "man of the people", a careerist, a humourless snob who doesn't believe in having fun. Neither, for much of the play, does Tracy herself, a "virgin goddess" whose standards of taste and grace are impossibly high. Her sin is to disapprove of her father's embarrassing involvement with a show-girl; her punishment is to believe, erroneously, that while drunk she slept with Macaulay Connor; her reward is remarriage with the rich playboy C. Dexter Haven. The play ends with a crucial exchange between Tracy and her erring father:

"How do I look?"
"Like a queen—like a goddess."
"Do you know how I feel?"
"How?"
"Like a human—like a human being!"

Barry was exceptionally happily married, with two sons, but the father-daughter relationship for some reason obsessed him. It is prominent in *Hotel Universe,* basic to *The Philadelphia Story* and dominant in the play he was working on when he died, aged fifty-three, in 1949. *Second Threshold* was posthumously performed in a version completed by Robert E. Sherwood; it is printed [in *States of Grace*] as Barry left it. Interesting, imperfect, almost painfully personal, it appears to be a study of what would now be called the "male menopause" but shirks the issue halfway through: the successful, cultured, urbane elderly lawyer is only pretending to be suffering from a crisis of confidence. His aim is to prevent his devoted but over-intellectual daughter, significantly named Miranda, from marrying a "boring" Englishman old enough to be her father. The ruse succeeds, and when Miranda falls instead for a young American "in his mid-twenties, spare, rangy, with a humorous, likable face, not at all handsome", she is congratulated, like Tracy, on "joining the human race".

The incestuous undertones are all the more disturbing for being nervously camouflaged beneath an air of conservative complacency unusual in Barry's work. Johnny Case of *Holiday,* who refused to be "made over" in the image of Wall Street, has matured into Josiah Brook of *Second Threshold,* bitterly aware that the civilized values he has lived for are threatened by the horrors of the modern world. It only takes a generation for cheeky hedonism to harden into peevish reaction.

Why did Barry apparently long, like Mr. Dearth in *Dear Brutus,* for a "dream daughter" he never had? I think the answer is that he had fallen in love with his own composite heroine—Linda, Daisy, Tracy, Miranda—daring, chaste, highly bred, independent, fastidiously witty and fundamentally decent: the image so potently purveyed by the personality of Katharine Hepburn. And the only possible relationship with this ideal creation would be that of a proud father gazing, as into a magic mirror, at his beautiful, arrogant, momentarily rebellious but ultimately obedient child.

*Francis Wyndham, "Dreams and Drawing Rooms,"
in* The Times Literary Supplement *(© Times Newspapers Ltd. (London) 1975; reproduced from* The Times Literary Supplement *by permission), No. 3849, December 19, 1975, p. 1507.*

ALBERT WERTHEIM   (essay date 1978)

Philip Barry is one of the few masters of the American comedy of manners. The world of his plays, a twentieth-century version of the Restoration *beau monde,* is comprised of witty, urbane, spoiled, and very rich, American east coast bluebloods. As all comedies of manners do, Philip Barry's demand a great sense of style from actors and actresses who must demonstrate the wit and urbanity that wealth and social position can foster, yet at the same time show the foibles and failures that exist despite social prominence and material well-being. (p. 273)

The Philadelphia Story portrays a range of upper-class social types, but centers on the figure of Tracy Lord, a morally uncompromising and consequently brittle and even priggish young woman. Beneath the cool poise of her regal manner, beneath her alabaster surface resides a flesh-and-blood human being, and it is the business of Barry's play to bring Tracy Lord a comic insight that will enable her to harmonize her social poise with her inner humanity, to blend her restrained classic beauty with tolerant playfulness, to produce, in short, something akin to Barry's idea of true human grace. In *The Philadelphia Story,*

Barry expresses that idea through the boating term *yare:* "Easy to handle—quick to the helm—fast—bright—everything a boat should be." Implicit in this graceful flexibility is a sense of give and take, both interpersonal and sexual. Tracy, on the verge of a second marriage, comes to recognize in herself the meaning of *yare* through the juxtaposition of her fiancé, George Kittredge, who worships her as a flawless social leader, and Mike Connor, a reporter come to do a story about the wedding, who is attracted to Tracy as his sexual conquest. Discovering that she has both social self-possession and sexuality, Tracy makes a stunning return to C. K. Dexter-Haven, her first husband, who understands the meaning of *yare.* (pp. 273-74)

Barry's aim was at least in part a revaluation of the merits and basic humanity of the upper class after the flogging it received at the hands of the social revolutionary playwrights of the Depression years. After an analogous flogging of "the establishment" in recent years, the production of this play seems to plead for a binding of social wounds as much now as it did nearly forty years ago. (p. 274)

> *Albert Wertheim, in his review of "The Philadelphia Story," in* Educational Theatre Journal *(© 1978 University College Theatre Association of the American Theatre Association), Vol. 30, No. 2, May, 1978, pp. 273-74.*

ADDITIONAL BIBLIOGRAPHY

Brown, John Mason. "The American Barry." In his *Still Seeing Things,* pp. 30-7. New York: McGraw-Hill Book Co., 1950.
  Reminiscences of Barry. A drama critic and friend, Brown discusses the dramatist's talent as emanating from two worlds—one in which the sophisticated Barry produced high comedies, and one in which the "experimentalist" Barry searched for metaphysical answers.

Clark, Barrett H. "Philip Barry." In his *An Hour of American Drama,* pp. 100-13. Philadelphia: J. B. Lippincott Co., 1930.
  Balanced critical review of Barry's works from *You and I* to *Holiday.*

Dickinson, Donald Hugh. "Mr. Eliot's *Hotel Universe.*" *Drama Critique* I, No. 1 (February 1958): 33-44.*
  Explores similarities between the psychological dramas *Hotel Universe* by Barry and *The Cocktail Party* by T. S. Eliot.

Downer, Alan S. "From Romance to Reality." In his *Fifty Years of American Drama: 1900-1950,* pp. 39-75. Chicago: Henry Regnery Co., 1951.*
  Discussion of *Hotel Universe* and *Here Come the Clowns.*

Dusenbury, Winifred L. "The Failure of a Love Affair." In her *The Theme of Loneliness in Modern American Drama,* pp. 86-112. Gainesville: University of Florida Press, 1960.
  Comparative study of the love affairs in Barry's *Tomorrow and Tomorrow,* Eugene O'Neill's *Strange Interlude,* and Clifford Odets's *Rocket to the Moon.*

Gagey, Edmond M. "Comedy—American Plan." In his *Revolution in American Drama,* pp. 175-231. New York: Columbia University Press, 1947.*
  Survey of Barry's domestic dramas.

Gild, David C. "Psychodrama on Broadway: Three Plays of Psychodrama by Philip Barry." *The Markham Review* 2, No. 4 (October 1970): 65-74.
  Discusses critical reactions to Barry's psychodramas *In a Garden, Hotel Universe,* and *Here Come the Clowns.* Gild considers these plays the best of Barry's serious works.

Gill, Brendan, ed. "Biographical Essay: The Dark Advantage." In *States of Grace: Eight Plays,* by Philip Barry, pp. 3-47. New York: Harcourt Brace Jovanovich, 1975.
  Biocritical introduction to a collection of Barry's dramas.

Gould, Jean. "Philip Barry." In his *Modern American Playwrights,* pp. 78-98. New York: Dodd, Mead & Co., 1966.
  Traces the development of Barry's creative work in this biocritical survey.

Hamm, Gerald. *The Drama of Philip Barry: A Dissertation in American Civilization.* Philadelphia: Privately printed, 1948, 91 p.
  Valuable study of Barry's life and work.

Krutch, Joseph Wood. "The New American Drama and the European Tradition." In his *The American Drama since 1918: An Informal History,* rev. ed., pp. 3-25. New York: George Braziller, 1957.*
  Examines "high comedy" in Barry's plays.

Lavery, Emmet. "The World of Philip Barry." *Drama Critique* III, No. 3 (November 1960): 98-107.
  Survey of Barry's work which finds similarities between his comedies and his serious plays. Lavery also recalls a meeting with Barry.

Parker, H. T. "Green Grow the Lilacs: *Hotel Universe.*" In *American Drama and Its Critics: A Collection of Critical Essays,* edited by Alan S. Downer, pp. 116-27. Chicago: The University of Chicago Press, 1965.
  Reprints Parker's 1930 criticism of *Hotel Universe.* Parker was the drama critic for the *Boston Transcript.*

Quinn, Arthur Hobson. "*Paris Bound.*" In his *Representative American Plays: From 1767 to the Present Day,* rev. ed., pp. 1059-1100. New York: D. Appleton-Century Co., 1938.
  Short critical survey of Barry's works to date, in this chapter which reprints *Paris Bound.*

Salem, James M. "Philip Barry and the Spirituality of Love." *Renascence* XIX, No. 2 (Winter 1967): 101-09.
  Discusses the treatment of love and marriage throughout Barry's plays based on the dramatist's view that the spiritual relationship in marriage transcends the physical. Salem regards Barry as one of the most contemporary writers of comedy dealing with the problems of adultery and divorce.

Louis Bromfield

1896-1956

American novelist, essayist, short story and novella writer, dramatist, and screenwriter.

Bromfield was a Midwestern writer whose works—like those of Sinclair Lewis, Booth Tarkington, and Sherwood Anderson—expressed the author's efforts to understand and to protest America's transformation from an agrarian to an industrial society. Bromfield addressed this issue in two distinct areas of literature, each of which attracted an enthusiastic readership. During the first part of his career, as an expatriate living in post-World War I France, he wrote several critically acclaimed novels which examined the destruction of the Jeffersonian ideal of an agricultural society as it was overtaken by industrial materialism. Prominent among his early novels are *The Green Bay Tree, Possession,* and *Early Autumn: A Story of a Lady,* which won the 1926 Pulitzer Prize in literature. Bromfield returned from France to establish and operate a large experimental farm in the rural Midwest. In the second part of his career Bromfield continued to write novels, but concentrated on writing books which combined practical farm lore, new agricultural theories, reminiscences, anecdotes, and fanciful retellings of folktales concerning the Ohio farmlands. Although he lost many of his readers when he wrote such nonfictional accounts of farming as *Malabar Farm* and *Pleasant Valley,* he gained a new audience whose concerns had never before been addressed so inventively and entertainingly.

Bromfield was born in Mansfield, Ohio, at a time when the town was completing its transition from farm community to small industrial city. In the late 1880s, Bromfield's father had to sell the long-established but failing family farm. Forced to take a series of jobs in Mansfield, he instilled in his son a hatred of the impersonal standardization of industrialism and a desire to return to the agrarian lifestyle which had supported the Bromfield family until the late nineteenth century. Bromfield studied agriculture at Cornell University for one year, but during that time a series of setbacks caused his family to abandon their plans of becoming farmers again, and Bromfield transferred to the Columbia School of Journalism. When World War I began, he enlisted in the United States Army Ambulance Corps, attached to the French army. He served for two years and was awarded the Croix de Guerre. After the war, Bromfield moved to New York, married, and worked for a number of news agencies and publications, becoming one of the original staff members of *Time* magazine. The immediate critical and popular success of his first novel, *The Green Bay Tree,* in 1924, led to his decision to become a full-time novelist. A "vacation" in France, made possible by the proceeds from his second novel, *Possession,* lasted nearly fourteen years. During this time Bromfield produced a novel almost yearly.

The Green Bay Tree was the first in a series of "panel" novels, each depicting an aspect of the period of American history that most concerned Bromfield—the era that saw the defeat of agrarianism and the rise of industrialization. Characters and settings from *The Green Bay Tree* recur in the next three novels, *Possession, Early Autumn,* and *A Good Woman.* These novels also display Bromfield's tendency to portray predominantly strong, determined women and weak, ineffectual men.

Courtesy of Prints and Photographs Division, Library of Congress

He later wrote that these first four novels could be considered collectively under the title of "Escape," since escape from the stifling effects of narrowly-bounded town life is the theme of all four. Beginning with these earliest works, critics consistently praised Bromfield's ability to construct believable and memorable characters. Bromfield's next novel, *The Strange Case of Miss Annie Spragg,* proved a departure from his usual themes, though not from his familiar settings. A framing device sets the novel in Italy, but a series of flashbacks places most of the action in the American Midwest. This novel explores mystical and mythic themes rather than the historical concerns of the earlier novels, and introduced a supernatural element that was new to his work. Critics found in the fresh subject matter and characterizations of *The Strange Case of Miss Annie Spragg* indications that Bromfield was achieving new depth of insight as a novelist. His next novel, *The Farm,* remains one of his most critically successful. It is an account of the struggles and eventual triumphs of two families, very like Bromfield's ancestors, as they settle and farm the Ohio countryside. Critics note in *The Farm* a certain homesickness on Bromfield's part for the ways and places of his youth. During his residence in France Bromfield occasionally returned to the United States for lecture tours, vacations, and, in 1930, for a brief stint as a Hollywood screenwriter. He bought out his own contract when he found himself unsuited to such work; however, many critics thereafter noted a tendency in his novels toward flamboyant characters and involved, action-packed plots in the manner of the Hollywood screenplay.

Bromfield realized a lifelong dream when he returned to the United States, purchased several run-down Ohio farms, and combined them into Malabar Farm. This venture became one of the world's most famous pilot farms for experimental agricultural techniques, and drew up to fifteen thousand visitors annually. Bromfield's new life as a farmer inspired a new phase in his writing, as he produced both fictional and non-fictional works focusing on life at Malabar Farm. *Pleasant Valley* tells of Bromfield's acquisition of the land, and of the project's first six years of development. The book combines autobiography, technical advice about farming, and essays discussing local legends and folk traditions. Bromfield's biographer, David D. Anderson, called *Pleasant Valley* "Bromfield's *Walden*" and described it as "the microcosm of man's experience as he attempts to find his place in the natural order." *Malabar Farm, Animals and Other People,* and *From My Experience: The Pleasures and Miseries of Life on a Farm* share the entertaining piecemeal construction of *Pleasant Valley.* Bromfield's most technical work is *Out of the Earth,* an exposition of modern experimental agricultural practices. While farming and writing about farm life increasingly occupied his time, Bromfield continued to publish novels, short stories, and novellas until his death. Though all his later fiction sold well, it never attained the critical standing of the novels written prior to Bromfield's return to the United States.

Edmund Wilson scathingly and somewhat unfairly summarized Bromfield's career as a novelist when he wrote in a review of *What Became of Anna Bolton* that Bromfield began as "one of the younger writers of promise" who moved into the ranks of the second-rate with the publication of *Twenty-Four Hours,* and "by unremitting industry . . . had gradually made his way into the fourth rank, where his place is now secure." David D. Anderson, however, argued that *What Became of Anna Bolton* is "not a bad novel; it is merely so incredibly weak that it is insignificant. It was certainly not deserving of the attention that Edmund Wilson gave it when he used it as the basis of a strong attack on Bromfield." Although critical response to his earliest works indicated that Bromfield's career as a novelist was a promising one, critics have noted that several elements combined to flaw the later novels. First, he developed a tendency toward shallow Hollywood-style characterization, when fine character delineation had once been his strong point. Secondly, his growing involvement with the Malabar Farm project occupied his attention, often to the exclusion of all else. Finally, Bromfield seemed to lose interest in writing fiction for art's sake, and began to regard his novels as an outlet for delivering his agricultural, social, and political theories. Most critics concur with Anderson that an evaluation of Bromfield as a novelist should focus on those works written during his years of residence in France, when novel writing was his main concern.

Within the small sphere of the Midwestern farm novel, Bromfield remains a significant figure on the strength of his earliest novels, which effectively portray the final years of America's agriculture-based society, though these works have been overshadowed by those of such contemporaries as Sinclair Lewis, Booth Tarkington, and Sherwood Anderson. With his unique farm books, Bromfield provided useful information on experimental agricultural techniques to farmers and entertained many other readers.

David D. Anderson wrote of Bromfield that "the many shortcomings that had prevented the fulfillment of his early promise are serious enough to keep him out of the first rank of American novelists. But at the same time he deserves a much better literary fate than he has received, because of his effectiveness of style, his character portrayal, and his narrative technique that are his most consistent strong points; because he has made substantial contributions in individual works; and because of his effective and intelligent interpretations of the American scene and American life."

(See also *Contemporary Authors,* Vol. 107; *Dictionary of Literary Biography,* Vol. 4: *American Writers in Paris, 1920-1939;* and Vol. 9: *American Novelists, 1910-1945.*)

PRINCIPAL WORKS

*The Green Bay Tree   (novel)   1924
*Possession   (novel)   1925
*Early Autumn: A Story of a Lady   (novel)   1926
A Good Woman   (novel)   1927
**The House of Women   (drama)   1927
The Strange Case of Miss Annie Spragg   (novel)   1928
Awake and Rehearse   (short stories)   1929
Twenty-Four Hours   (novel)   1930
A Modern Hero   (novel)   1932
The Farm   (novel)   1933
Here Today and Gone Tomorrow   (novellas)   1934
De Luxe [with John Gearon]   (drama)   1935
The Man Who Had Everything   (novel)   1935
The Rains Came: A Novel of Modern India   (novel)   1937
It Takes All Kinds   (short stories and novellas)   1939
Night in Bombay   (novel)   1940
Wild is the River   (novel)   1941
Until the Day Break   (novel)   1942
Mrs. Parkington   (novel)   1943
What Became of Anna Bolton   (novel)   1944
The World We Live In   (short stories)   1944
Pleasant Valley   (nonfiction and reminiscences)   1945
Malabar Farm   (nonfiction and reminiscences)   1948
The Wild Country   (novel)   1948
Out of the Earth   (nonfiction)   1950
Mr. Smith   (novel)   1951
Animals and Other People   (short stories and essays)   1955
From My Experience: The Pleasures and Miseries of Life on a Farm   (nonfiction and reminiscences)   1955

*These works were published as *The Louis Bromfield Trilogy* in 1937.

**This drama is an adaptation of the novel *The Green Bay Tree*.

CHARLES C. BALDWIN (essay date 1924)

Since I am self-confessed a clown I may as well drag in Balzac—his is the first name that comes to mind on reading Mr. Bromfield's *The Green Bay Tree*. Here is the crowded canvas of *La Comédie Humaine* and here in all her glory is Balzac's *la femme de trente ans*. Chapter follows chapter; a whole family life develops; a generation passes along the way to dusty death; they wax rich and powerful; they decay and are forgotten. They have their little day, their influence, their pride; and they see that pride humbled and made a mockery. And the writing is thick and vivid, colorful. The effect is realistic, as in *Père*

Goriot, like some busy faubourg in the Paris of before the war. There is intrigue and a clash of wills. And, best of all, there is no psychoanalyzing. There is no going beneath the surface to dissect motives and peer with a microscope into emotions. Life is accepted as mysterious. The characters live by their own right; and their histories are reconstructed from bits of gossip, from confidences, gestures, tones of the voice, from things they say and do. *Gott sei dank [God be thanked],* Mr. Bromfield does not write with one eye peeled on the medical profession and both ears listening to the wails of suppressed desire. Mr. Bromfield is (you can shout it on the streets of Ascalon, if you will) an artist. Land knows we have waited long enough for his arrival. (p. 46)

"I have seen the wicked," said the Psalmist, "in great power, and spreading himself like a green bay tree."

Such a state of affairs upset the Psalmist, but it does not upset Mr. Bromfield. He goes calmly to work. He studies the wicked— or one generally accepted as wicked, the mother of a child born out of wedlock—and decides that she is just a little bit of all right; that, first-off, she is a beautiful woman, a charming woman; and that perhaps the father of her child, while all right as a lover, would not measure up to her requirements in a husband. Perhaps she knows this? (p. 48)

Mr. Bromfield does not speak in parables. He has no lesson to teach, no moral to bring home to us. Two things, he says, inspired the writing of *The Green Bay Tree,* both of them reactions: one against the conventional drab presentation of the Middle West and the other against the psychoanalytical presentation of character development. He was born in the Middle West and he knows there is a tremendous amount of romance there. What is more romantic than the passing of one era and the rise of another, the destruction of a pleasant life by the growing-up of a monstrous industry? This is what has been going on in many a midland city for a quarter century past; and in some cities the struggle is over, the monster triumphant.

Mr. Bromfield is not fascinated by the perversities and delusions of adolescence. He wants a full life, a good life—and it is a full life he gives to his characters. All the humanity of the French lies between him and Nathaniel Hawthorne. (pp. 49-50)

> *Charles C. Baldwin, "Louis Bromfield," in his* The Men Who Make Our Novels *(reprinted by permission of Dodd, Mead & Company, Inc.; copyright, 1919, 1924 by Dodd, Mead and Company, Inc.), revised edition, Dodd, Mead, 1924, pp. 46-51.*

STUART P. SHERMAN   (essay date 1925)

[*Sherman discusses the aim and scope of Bromfield's "panel novels," and compares the author's works with those of several other writers of the day.*]

[It] is a pleasure to turn . . . to an author like Mr. Louis Bromfield, of whom one can say confidently to the general novel-reading public: "You should know him"; and to novels like **"The Green Bay Tree"** and **"Possession,"** of which one can say with assurance to this same wide public: "You should read them. They will please you." (p. 1)

We are told that he has deliberately shunned competition with youngsters of his generation. We are told that he has deliberately written and shelved in manuscript no less than three of those "first novels" such as bubble out of authors at two-and-twenty like water from a spring and sin from the unredeemed heart of man—precocious first novels, in which the author, barely escaped from college, "naked and unashamed," confesses the deficiencies of his parents and the defects of his upbringing and reveals to the public how many times he was drunk and how many times in love before he was twenty. Mr. Bromfield sweated all that out of his system before he invited the world to consider whether he is a novelist.

There can be no question now that he has an authentic calling to produce prose fiction. I am rather appalled by the shining completeness of his equipment, by the early mellowness of his tone, the envelopment of his "atmosphere," the smoothness of his texture, the bright fluency and ease of his manipulation, his abundance and range and the confident largeness of his design. When could he have experienced all the life of this generation which was in full blossom when he was in the cradle? He has known how to make his imagination *work.* And so he has entered the field, not as a "promising young man" but as a *maestro* whose initial performance showed such finish and such virtuosity that one's only doubt was whether he would ever be able to do anything better. To that doubt he now gives the interesting, if not wholly satisfactory, reply that he intends to do something very much larger.

It was in the spring of 1924 that he made his first appearance as a novelist with **"The Green Bay Tree."** His second novel, **"Possession,"** is independent of the first, yet is related to it, as it treats of the same times and places and reintroduces several familiar characters. In the foreword to this second novel he makes an announcement. "The two," he says, with a significant image, "are what might be called *panel novels in a screen* which, when complete, will consist of at least a half-dozen panels, all interrelated and each giving a certain phase of the ungainly, swarming, glittering spectacle of American life." Let us speak a little of the large design.

Upon the many-paneled screen Mr. Bromfield intends to depict the civilization of that generation which flourished in America between the Homestead strike and the World War. When, taking the hint from him, I say that he is painting a social history upon a many-paneled screen, I wish to suggest at once the elaborateness of the design, the swift light-handed execution, and my sense that the effect, especially on the second panel, **"Possession,"** has occasionally been too facilely sought, that the paint has run a little thin in spots, that certain of the figures—Callendar, for example, in **"Possession"**—were rather hastily visualized than deeply felt and imagined. Merely a pictorial mystery, this Callendar, with a pair of eyes—I forget the color—and an "olive" skin. However!

You see in a general way what looms in Mr. Bromfield's lucid and well ordered day dreams. He intends projecting a vision of American society which shall be comparable with that vision of English society contained in "The Forsyte Saga" and shall perhaps be even more extensive. (pp. 1-2)

Mr. Bromfield shows us representatives of three generations dwelling [at Shane's castle] side by side. It is decidedly an indication of his imaginative power that he portrays grandfathers and grandmothers and stout, set, middle-aged people with insight and with gusto. He has already given us a half-dozen interesting old men and women—Grandpa Tolliver, Mrs. Tolliver, Mrs. Callendar, Mrs. Harrison, Mrs. Abercrombie, for examples—and Julia Shane, the lady of Shane's Castle, seems to me a penetrating and memorable piece of characterization of the grande dame type.

But Mr. Bromfield, like the rest of us, has a great curiosity to know what is coming out of the society which the Shanes and the Tollivers and the Harrisons made. And so he is going to study with chief concern, I think, the discovery of the younger people in his community that the material conquests in which their forbears triumphed leave them cold, that the religion of their grandparents is incomprehensible to them and that the Western frontier which formerly tempted to fresh adventures has vanished. He is going to depict—he is already depicting—the predicament of young people in the doldrums, restlessly turning eastward again, to New York, to Paris, to Munich, seeking new outlets, new objectives, new modes of self-realization.

In each of the "panels" I surmise that we shall have the story of some selected hero or heroine setting out on some typical quest for the "meaning of life." Taken all together, these stories will constitute Mr. Bromfield's summary of what civilization between the Homestead strike and the great war amounted to for the most purposeful and the most adventurous members of that generation.

In **"The Green Bay Tree"** Lily Shane, daughter of the notable Julia Shane, is the heroine of a quest for "self-realization" through the luxurious expression of her physical beauty and her personal charm. Those who are acquainted with the work of Miss Cather will understand just what I mean when I describe her as Mr. Bromfield's version of the Lost Lady. She is occasionally mentioned as the "sinner" of the Shane family; but it is clear that her creator adores her, and her distinction, like that of many of her sisters in current fiction, is that she sins and does not pay—not much, nor more than she can easily afford!

Lily herself, tall, red-bronze hair, voluptuous shoulders, languorous, selfish, egoistic—quite! but seductive, daring subject to fine bursts of generosity and courage—Lily herself is not a novelty in American life or in American fiction. Mr. Bromfield portrays her with the gusto and ardor of our younger generation for all adventurers whose grace and beauty and charm triumph in the teeth of opinion. A thing happens to Lily which—"happens only to servant girls," but she deals with the incident in the fashion of the Du Barrys, the companions of popes and kings. She is not a novelty, but Mr. Bromfield enlarges her interest by his elaborate development of her relationships to other people at home and abroad. He uses her as an indicator of changing standards and values by showing us her image in the eyes of all the sorts of people who make up his generation, from Irene, her ascetic sister, through the Polish labor leader, to her titled French lover.

In **"Possession"** I think one does not feel quite the intensity of energy which was applied in **"The Green Bay Tree"** to the initial task of establishing in our imaginations the reality of Shane Castle and the odor of its gardens, the taste of its foods and wines, the color and feeling of its furniture and fabrics, the gleam of its jewels, the suave contact of fine silks and skins, the tension of teas and parties, the stir of servants, the rolling of carriages, the sensuous murmur of life. Having once thoroughly constituted the background, Mr. Bromfield inevitably relaxed his attention at that point. In compensation, he has wrought diligently to realize for us the house and the social setting of his Americans in Paris.

In this second novel Ellen Tolliver, cousin of Lily Shane, emerges as the heroine of a quest for self-realization, supposedly through art. She becomes, it is alleged, a celebrated pi-

anist. Again I can suggest to Miss Willa Cather's readers the sort of character Ellen is intended to be by describing her as Mr. Bromfield's version of Thea (in "The Song of the Lark"). Now, in the respects which I have indicated, Mr. Bromfield's Lost Lady, Lily Shane, is a more complex, highly organized portrait than Miss Cather's Lost Lady, Mrs. Forrester: Lily Shane is *socially* illuminated, Miss Cather's heroine in the little Nebraska town is, so to speak, imaged in poor fragmentary mirrors by the light of kerosene lamps. But Mr. Bromfield's portrait of Ellen Tolliver as artist is, on the contrary, far less highly organized than Miss Cather's Thea. As the portrait of an artist, Ellen is, in my judgment, immeasurably inferior to Thea, who is, to be sure, an almost unrivaled representation.

Mr. Bromfield himself has unconsciously explained why he has failed to make Ellen "convincing" as an artist: "The author, knowing that much which pertains to the life of the musician is boring and of little interest to any one outside the realm of music, has endeavored to eliminate all the technical side of her education."

He has been only too successful in a misdirected effort: he has eliminated the material evidence that Ellen was a musician or, for that matter, that she was any sort of passionate artist. The root of the thing does not appear, nor the "sacred flame." Mr. Bromfield's references to the playing of Brahms, Chopin, Debussy, have a perfunctory air. The art is thinly washed over this character. I am no musician, can merely carry a tune, play no instrument, but I found Thea's music lessons in "The Song of the Lark" of breathless interest, intensely exciting; and the portraits of her two or three music masters at work were not merely brilliant portraits: they carried one into the very passion of art, of all art, and they contributed extraordinarily to the heroine's extraordinary effect of authenticity. Now, by eliminating all the detail, which Miss Cather gave us supremely well, of the artist's discovery of her talent, her relations with those who educed it, her growth in musical culture—by eliminating all this Mr. Bromfield has reduced his alleged artist to a kind of "go-getter," a climber with a hard-mouthed Scotch-Irish intention to be famous.

She is a type, too, right enough, common enough, heaven knows. But my guess is that Ellen Tolliver was not really an artist. She was a woman who liked playing the piano pretty well and wanted desperately to get on in the world. She is not an artist—she is a ruthless female force. Her portrait does not seem to me equal to that of Lily Shane. In her relations with the olive-skinned Callendar her effectiveness derives from him a theatrical hue—the effectiveness of things seen, but not experienced in the actual quick of the consciousness.

The spots in which she "comes alive" are those in which she is the will of her generation to get what it wants before it dies and to regret only the desirable things which it has not done. In her, in various of the young people who "don't want to miss the war," there is "Gargantuan desire to devour all the world within a lifetime." The musical tour which she is planning in August, 1914, is to be her chance, not to create beauty, but to devour Paris, Berlin, Munich, Vienna, St. Petersburg and London. She is effective as a symbol of appetite. She is impressive as the voice of deep, insatiable hunger. In her youth of old Grandpa Tolliver lives again, his greedy indulgent youth, over which, in his old age, he is still smacking unrepentant lips. . . . (p. 2)

As yet I think Mr. Bromfield has seen no touch of frost, no sign of withering, in the umbrageous branches of his green bay tree.

I return now for a moment to the general charm and interest of the first two leaves of his many-paneled screen. Zest is somehow the note of it, zest in all the processes of life and of death. Mr. Bromfield's zestful pleasure in the suave surfaces and harmonious color of the spectacle abides as a kind of distinction among our contemporary satirists, revolters, and experimenters in new ways of penetrating to the internal flame of life.

In method, temper, point of view, he reminds me very seldom of Mr. Dreiser and Mid-Western naturalism, of Mr. Lewis and Mid-Western satire, of Mr. Anderson and Mid-Western symbolism; he is not naively naturalistic, his talent is not satirical, nor is his manner "journalistic"; he is not mystical nor experimental, nor stylistically "personal." He reminds me little of Arnold Bennett and his rather strident middle-classiness. He does not in the least remind me of Mr. Wells; he is not a propagandist, not "sociological," not a pamphleteer, not a savior. He does indeed shrewdly appropriate, almost exhaustively appropriate, the "sure-fire" interests of current fiction: sex, business, religion, wealth, politics, labor, foreign types, luxury, art, Paris, mistresses, titled society, war; but he *insists* on none of them; he interweaves them all in a glamourous flowing movement which affects me like the cantabile style in music.

In the personal sympathies which he, like every novelist, betrays between the lines, he seems a typical superior "young man of the hour." But as a writer of prose fiction, he is distinctly on the "conservative" side—old school with quickened tempo. I suppose his striding ambition—an exhilarating thing at twenty-eight, when there is obviously going to be something to stride on—will be pleased if he reminds his readers now, or presently, of Mr. Galsworthy and Mr. Walpole and such others of our contemporaries as look with respect upon the performance of Trollope, of Thackeray, of Balzac—old fellows who painted social life and manners on a grand scale, because social life and manners pleased them, excited and absorbed them, and then flowed from them abundantly, in a strong stream, rhythmical and murmurous as the music of rivers. (pp. 2-3)

> *Stuart P. Sherman, "Here Is a Novelist Who Will Please You," in* New York Herald Tribune Books *(© I.H.T. Corporation; reprinted by permission), October 11, 1925, pp. 1-3.*

HENRY B. FULLER   (essay date 1927)

[*Fuller was an American novelist of romance* (The Chevalier of Pensieri-Vani) *and realism* (The Cliff-Dwellers). *This latter work, concerning life in Chicago, is recognized as a pioneering contribution to the American city-novel. Fuller also wrote book reviews for the Chicago* Evening Post, *the Chicago-based magazine* Poetry, *and other periodicals. He found escape to be the primary theme of Bromfield's first three novels,* The Green Bay Tree, Possession, *and* Early Autumn. *Below, he praises Bromfield's characterization, particularly that of his women characters, and finds him skilled in depicting settings as well. The critic objects, however, to "Bromfield's recourse to simple fornication" which "is too frequent and too facile."*]

To an elderly writer, now retired from the field of creative activity, the salient feature of Louis Bromfield's equipment might appear to be his energy—a boundless vigor with its concomitants of momentum, pertinacity, and self confidence. With a hard head and a stout heart he adventures gallantly in his chosen fields—which, up to the present, comprise industrial

Ohio, New York City, Paris (unescapably), and more recently a New England of his own free and unfavorable imagining. . . .

His prime impulse, thus far, would seem to be necessity for escape. Escape from a barbarized Western Reserve, escape from an enfeebled New England. Escape, on the one hand, from too crude and violent a growth, and, on the other hand, from too deplorable a decadence. For Bromfield, the west (outlet of so much American energy) is closed; the frontier is abolished: the only liberation for the descendants of the Puritan and the pioneer is eastward; and one can find one's true, free self in Europe alone, with a vast preference for the capital of France.

One after another, most of his heroines get their education in Paris; and it is to Paris that many of his men, old, middle aged, and young . . . go to recapture the past, to enjoy the present, or to sacrifice the future.

His women rather outrank his men. His Aunt Cassie and his old Thérèse Callendar are successes; his Michael O'Hara—Roman Catholic and Democratic politician—is not. In general, his admiration is all for the woman (preferably young) who bursts the bars of an invidious American locale and who, taking "a firm hold on life", makes it "a glittering success". This success can mean only Paris—or perhaps, secondarily, New York. Boston? Never! . . .

If these women are young, well and good; if they are approaching middle age, none the worse. . . . I can think of no present day novelist who approaches women with a greater show of interest and self confidence—and mostly he succeeds with them. Women, in the end, rule his books and their action. (p. 200)

[A] writer so conspicuously "called" to the novelist's career as is Bromfield, is sure to succeed as well with his places as with his people. Locale, milieu, environment, are all at the easy disposal of this diversified talent. He renders well the New England landscape as its bleak face appears to his vision and tones in with his purpose. He renders equally well his New York apartment house on Riverside Drive and the portentous mansion of the Levantine Callendars on Murray Hill. He is especially successful with those settings that persist throughout—what the Italians, I believe, call the *scena stabile*, the set scene. Such settings have a curious, satisfying quality of permanency; whether the scene is before us at the moment or not, it continues to live with a life of its own. (p. 201)

As most readers now know, his *œuvre*, up to the present and regardless of the promises of a teeming future, consists of three novels: **"The Green Bay Tree", "Possession"** (titled rather inadequately and over-ingeniously), and **"Early Autumn."** These, taken together, are full, solid, and highly varied, as well as interdependent. They form a firm mass that is calculated to endure, and perhaps to repel, assault. All the same, I shall attempt to present a bill of exceptions.

To one who was early established in the decent, if antiquated, tradition of Howells (a practice calling for reticence and decorum), it seems that Bromfield's recourse to simple fornication is too frequent and too facile. Such indulgence is the initial and obvious motif of **"The Green Bay Tree",** and it is the postponed and latent consideration which conditions **"Early Autumn".** Data of this sort, when really fundamental, may be accepted readily enough as among a novelist's prime necessities; but one may protest the employment of such a motif when it comes to seem, as it often does, frivolous, incidental, mechanical, superfluous. . . . Yet Bromfield now and then restrains himself, and when he does his success is all the greater. Witness his "big" scene in his first book—and the biggest in all three—where the two sisters, the unmoral Lily from Paris and the tense Irene (not yet immured in her French convent), contend over the wounded young Ukrainian steel worker who leads the strike. Here there is no mechanical recourse to mere sensuality, as to a convenient counter. All such feeling is sublimated, so far as it exists at all, into something better and higher, and the gain is great. The pre-Howells day is doubtless gone, never to return; yet one good test for the up-and-coming novelist is the ability to weave the plain, level fabric of life without too great a dependence on the kinks and snarls that interfere. Of course, even the most sober and conscientious artificer must be allowed an occasional tangent, but the serious observer in the social field does well not to over-indulge. (pp. 201-02)

While Bromfield sees in advance much of his broad scheme as a whole, and accounts for everything, and leaves no loose ends, one experiences, on the way through his three books, a growing perception of conscious and rather obtrusive contrivance: he manages things too thoroughly and too well. This habit tends to grow, I think, being most apparent in **"Early Autumn"**, where his poor New England, lighted up from but one side, seems to figure as a victim of the arbitrary. The French, I believe, have a word for arrangement that is too onesided and too obvious. Mr. Bromfield may know better than I if the word is *voulu*. (pp. 202-03)

As for Bromfield's diction, it serves its purpose. Though there are passages of extreme felicity and intensity, they are brief and infrequent. A comprehensive social study requires a style that is sober and not too ornate—the Bromfield novels, thus far, are to be read more for their substance than for their manner.

That substance is solid, abundant, varied, and picturesque. I have read all these novels more than once, with undiminishing interest. Considering their various qualities, and their author's qualifications, I tend to regard Louis Bromfield as one of the chief among our present hopes in American fiction. . . . Note . . . that **"The Green Bay Tree"** and **"Possession"** run side by side; neither is imbedded in the other, and neither continues the other; each has its own proper heroine, who is subordinated when her rival has the better claim; environments and chronology are shared in common—an equal division of alluring Paris and of impelling Ohio; each book helps, with no missteps, to bring the other out, and each is as completely readable (whether the two be taken together or apart) as its mate.

Perhaps it is this cooperation (acting like the two lenses of a stereoscope) that gives them an advantage over their successor. Clever and attractive people indeed return from Paris for social and matrimonial adventures among the country houses of the New England shore, but the clear keenness of a double line of sight is not quite replaced. However, a book is better, from one point of view, for standing erect by its one sole powers. This **"Early Autumn"** does, besides providing an intensity of situation and of intrigue all its own. (p. 203)

Henry B. Fuller, "The Bromfield Saga," in The Bookman, *New York (copyright, 1927, by George H. Doran Company), Vol. LXV, No. 2, April, 1927, pp. 200-03.*

STARK YOUNG   (essay date 1927)

[*An American playwright, poet, and novelist, Young was a prominent member of the Agrarian group of Southern poets with Allen Tate, John Crowe Ransom, Robert Penn Warren, and several others, from 1928 until the mid-1930s. The aim of this school, as stated in its manifesto* I'll Take My Stand *(1930), was to preserve the Southern way of life and the region's traditional values. The Agrarians were concerned with social and political issues as well as literature; in particular, they attacked Northern industrialism and upheld the value of the South's agricultural economy, drawing upon the thought of Plato, Thomas Jefferson, and Thomas Carlyle in support of their views. Young served for twenty years as drama critic for such journals as* The New Republic, Theatre Arts Monthly, *and* The New York Times, *and the best of this criticism is collected in* Immortal Shadows *(1948). He is especially acclaimed for his translations of Anton Chekhov's dramas. Below, he offers a mixed review of* The House of Women, *a play derived from the novel* The Green Bay Tree.]

The chief and best thing to be said about Mr. Louis Bromfield's earlier novel, **"The Green Bay Tree,"** is that it is carried through very much *con amore*. It essays, and with genuine gusto, great themes: an old woman's life, high and cynical, crossing the lives of her two daughters, one of them nun-like, the other glowing with sensuous beauty, in a grand house where the factories of a new age crowd the ancient gates, remarkable passions that go still to the fascinating, loved and hated dead man, John Shane, not to speak of themes like the changes in ideas, politics, fashions, tyrants, Europe, Rotarians, America, the War, a battle, life in France, an illegitimate child that is the fruit of its mother's curiosity about life and a politician's animal fires, and so on and so on.

It is a romantic, realistic novel built on enthusiasm and on the methods familiar in literary schools, that range from the patient, abounding detail of Arnold Bennett to some of the old-style glamors of De Morgan—though Mr. Bromfield may have read much or little in either of these particular instances. About all this there is a certain engaging current, if you like; **"The Green Bay Tree"** may very likely be passable reading. But the sum total is perfectly unimportant; the galaxy of themes, motivations and characters is never created; the book has nothing of reality to it, not as actual transcription of the day, social record or human detail, nor as prismatic fantasy or romance.

The play that the author has somewhat too casually struck out from his book limits itself to the crux of the three women in the house, as their lives work out inside each one of them and in relation to the other two. . . . On this main theme, however, the focus established by the dramatist is very loose indeed; the effect is too often one of getting the novel's business done; we are always learning things and rarely seeing them come alive. The lines are often pointless for the theater; the essential lack of creation in the novel appears now in their continued lack of any living rhythm or infectious beat; they often merely defeat the players trying to say them. Some of the scenes are not written at all: the supper at the end of the second act, for example, where there is a crisis in the turn of the play, has no edge and apparently no stage intention. You feel that Mr. Bromfield, safe in the casual comforts of fiction writing, does not even suspect the glaring finalities of the theater art.

Nevertheless, there are fine places in **"The House of Women,"** such as the sister's frantic prayer at the curtain of the first act, or the death of Julia Shane in the last. And there are two things most interesting to observe, one of them to the credit of the theater, one to Mr. Bromfield's. The first is the way in which things that are third-rate on the printed page of a novel become second-rate when created in terms of acting, voices, footlights, audience. The second is the richness of texture, so far above the average drama, that the presence of ideas and complicated emotions lends to **"The House of Women."** (pp. 236-37)

Stark Young, " 'The Green Bay Tree'," in The New Republic (© 1927 The New Republic, Inc.), Vol. LII, No. 672, October 19, 1927, pp. 236-37.

DONALD DAVIDSON   (essay date 1928)

[*Davidson, with John Crowe Ransom, Allen Tate, and Robert Penn Warren, was a member of the Fugitive group of Southern poets from 1915-28. The stated aim of the Fugitives was to create a literature utilizing the best qualities of modern and traditional art. After 1928, the four major Fugitives joined with eight other writers, including Stark Young and John Gould Fletcher, to form the Agrarians, a group dedicated to the preservation of the Southern way of life and traditional Southern values. The Agrarians were concerned with social and political issues as well as literature; in particular, they attacked Northern industrialism as they sought to preserve the Southern farming economy. Ransom, Tate, and Warren eventually left Agrarianism behind and went on to become prominent founders of New Criticism. Davidson, however, was fiercely partisan to the Agrarian cause and continued to promote the values of the Agrarians throughout his career. Davidson firmly believed that the antebellum South was the best of all possible worlds; for that reason his poetry and critical writings have been alternately characterized as anachronistic, as a voice from the past unwilling to submit to the anonymity of modern life, or as the conscience of a lost civilization. In the following essay, Davidson prefaces his evaluation of* The Strange Case of Miss Annie Spragg *with a discussion of irony in art. He examines both Edith Wharton's novel* The Children *and Bromfield's* The Strange Case of Miss Annie Spragg *in terms of their ironic content.*]

Among American novelists, irony is rare. The popular mind which wants to be charmed and not puzzled (Socrates was executed for puzzling people) is always at first glance drawn to the unironical. . . . But, since it does not want always to be merely amused, instinctively it finds out at last the serious artist. . . . Louis Bromfield, though as yet more brilliant than mature, has irony in most of his writing, and it is this and not his enormous facility and keenness as a reporter that makes his novels distinguished. (p. 84)

Mr. Bromfield's novel, ***The Strange Case of Annie Spragg,*** has a less subtle irony [than that of Edith Wharton's *The Children*], more easily detectable, rougher and more primly humorous (if also pathetic) in its action. The intent of the book is apparently to show how widely separated series of events in lives far aloof from each other, both in geography and in social strata, may, by the peculiar operation of the cosmos, at last all draw together to an intense focal point, and how those lives and events combine to show that the spiritual and the sensual are closer than we think, or that paganism and Christianity or the primitive and the cultured, still exist side by side in modern civilization. Maybe this is not wholly a serious intent; Mr. Bromfield's cool amusement with his own characters leads me to think he may be half joking.

And the book is in fact the more curious mixture, almost a hocus-pocus, a regular prestidigitation of people and events. A statue of Priapus, unearthed in an Italian garden owned by a desiccated "new thought" devotee, has a most happily disturbing effect on her companion, the suppressed Miss Fosdick, and on an English bachelor, the well-behaved Mr. Weatherby, who wrote poems for the *Yellow Book* and has spent his life

on a magnum opus about miracles. Miss Annie Spragg, of American origin, a primitive Methodist, daughter of Cyrus Spragg (whose practices quaintly resemble the alleged ways of the "House of David"), dies in an Italian city with the marks of the stigmata of St. Francis on her body; and the Catholic Church debates whether she is a saint or not and buries her in consecrated ground. Like St. Francis, Miss Annie Spragg had an unaccountable way with birds and animals; but in her strange case," too, there are hints both of diabolism and of the old primitive earth-magic associated with the rites of Priapus. There are other diverse lives, too, that her death affects: the priest, Father D'Astier, and his simple-minded son who is killed by the Fascisti; Anna D'Orobelli, wistful and suffering princess of not too good a fame; Sister Annunziata, the ugly but devoted nun who believed that St. Francis had personally spoken to her through Miss Spragg.

I cannot detail these complicated strands. Mr. Bromfield weaves back and forth from Europe to America, with side excursions to British "pubs" and Victorian pursuits; folklore and religion, Greece and Italy, religious fanaticism and religious disillusionment are strangely mixed. You hardly know whether to accept the book as serious. It looks almost like a parody, with its study of separate lives that come together in one critical event.

But it has irony—an irony which tends to show that neither simplicity nor guile, love nor madness, religion nor mysticism, are quite what they seem on the surface. As it depends on mechanical means for its composition—that is, the more or less arbitrary relation of various series of events and characters to one another—it is naturally more artificial than Mrs. Wharton's irony, which depends solely on the elements of character and on acts proceeding from character. The irony of ***The Strange Case of Annie Spragg*** makes it a provoking rather than a satisfying book; but it also gives a robustness and strength, which lifts Mr. Bromfield's work, even in a book which may be considered somewhat inferior to his series of "panel" novels, above most contemporary performances. (pp. 86-7)

Donald Davidson, "Other American Fiction, Irony: Edith Wharton, Louis Bromfield" (originally published in The Tennessean, September 23, 1928), in his The Spyglass: Views and Reviews, 1924-1930, edited by John Tyree Fain (copyright © 1963 by John Tyree Fain), Vanderbilt University Press, 1963, pp. 83-7.*

CLIFTON FADIMAN   (essay date 1932)

[*Fadiman became one of the most prominent American literary critics during the 1930s with his often caustic and insightful book reviews for the* Nation *and the* New Yorker *magazines. He also managed to reach a sizeable audience through his work as a radio talk-show host from 1938 to 1948. In the following essay, Fadiman provides an early indication of the current critical assessment that Bromfield's best novels are those preceding* A Modern Hero. *This point is acknowledged by Bromfield himself in a 1942 interview with Robert Van Gelder (see additional bibliography).*]

Isabel Paterson said recently of Mr. Bromfield that he was the sort of author one enjoys reading but shrinks from rereading. The comment focuses the dissatisfaction with which the last page of his novels leaves us—the feeling that somehow we should be much more moved by his ambitious stories, his large-scale characters, his "scope," and his "vitality" than we actually are. It is not that he is fooling us—he has written only one thoroughly dishonest book, **"Twenty-Four Hours"**—but rather that he is fooling himself. He hides his head in the sand to escape facing the bitter question: Is this the uttermost, the absolute uttermost, that can be done with this material? Again and again, in "**The Green Bay Tree**" and "**A Good Woman**," and now in "**A Modern Hero**," he projects themes of Balzacian, or at least Galsworthian, proportions, works at them with the greatest energy—but somehow fails to load them with the tragic weight their dimensions call for. At the crucial moments in each of his novels everything deserts him save sheer narrative skill. Conflict weakens to melodrama; his insight suddenly stands revealed as the intelligent cynicism of a superior man of the world; the carefully built-up characters flicker out as the "problem" of the novel emerges with painfully simple clarity; and one closes the volume quite ready to telephone the second-hand book dealer. . . .

Today even the most fervent admirers of his early books find themselves a little puzzled at his lack of progress; for "**A Modern Hero**" is surely less interesting than was "**The Green Bay Tree**," and cannot even be compared with "**The Strange Case of Miss Annie Spragg**." At times, in fact, it comes perilously close to dulness. Why is it that the talented young writer who was hailed at the outset as "a new fixed star in the American literary firmament" should have dimmed so rapidly?

It is because the star has remained fixed. Mr. Bromfield has learned nothing new since his first novel. His geographical knowledge has increased—mainly some small annexations in the Park Avenue and Sutton Place regions—but nothing else. A few stock themes and "strong situations" still fascinate him: the spectacle of the aging, once attractive woman; the tragedy of the strong male ruined by too many females; the superiority of Parisian salon culture to American provincialism; the psychic domination of American women. All these themes he has treated with the worldly intelligence of a high-grade clubman. None of them has he really come to grips with. None of them has he pursued to their deep roots in our social and economic structure. None of them has he grasped *historically*. An adept at recognizing surface social phenomena and types, he gives them that apparently portentous and actually sentimental overtone which sends thoughtless readers into a sweetly solemn reverie—the voluptuous brooding, the and-life-goes-on mood. . . .

His latest novel shows up nicely his truncated talent. It deals with the tragedy of the exploiting temperament. The central character is Pierre Radier, a circus rider of romantic antecedents who possesses that peculiar come-hither dark handsomeness and that introspective egotism with which non-Jewish novelists inevitably endow their Jewish or partly Jewish heroes. . . . Pierre Radier's life is ruined by his desire for power, by the fatal attraction he exerts on women, and by his inability to extract any final values either from them or his own career. This is a perfectly good subject—in fact, Theodore Dreiser did pretty well by it some years ago in "**The Titan**" and "**The Financier**"—but Mr. Bromfield does very little to make us believe either in the personality of his hero or in the symbolic importance of his tragedy.

In the first place, the problem of representing the two chief traits of Pierre's character—his sexual and personal charm and his ruthless ability to rise in the world—is shirked by the author. Pierre encounters a succession of women—and what stock types they are: the farm girl, wise in her strong, stoic simplicity; the anemic, repressed industrialist's daughter, bound up in her sour domestic banalities; the middle-aged woman of the world, tender, understanding, sacrificing; and the hard, coldly erotic, calcu-

lating, high-grade international adventuress. All these women make a bee-line for Pierre. Why? We are told he is the typical *homme fatal;* but though the results of his fatal charm are stated again and again, the charm itself is simply chucked at us without convincing demonstration. As for his rise from bareback rider to capitalist, Mr. Bromfield gives us the whole story minus a shred of evidence. (p. 40)

Mr. Bromfield's failure is one of intelligence, which is to say, it is a failure of conscience and of nerve. The problem of the exploiting temperament, particularly as it manifests itself in our industrial society, cannot be solved by the projection of half a dozen "vivid" characters or by the elaboration of a picturesque plot. If Mr. Bromfield is going to call his book "**A Modern Hero**" he must be prepared to expose, in all its tragic detail, the irony of the title. That is what Theodore Dreiser did when he called his novel "An American Tragedy." . . . But Mr. Bromfield cannot bother to study those forces which make possible his Pierre Radier. He is afraid to touch on the real weakness of Pierre, to expose its roots in a rotting social system. He refuses to see that Pierre's egotism is not only a defect of personality, not merely a picturesque and exciting vital urge, a convenient character trait with which to generate a story and produce a melodramatic catastrophe— but a blindness that is part and parcel of the whole competitive post-Civil War industrial system. The roots of Pierre's failure lie not merely in his unstable biological inheritance but in that unthinking economic *arrivisme* which is the peculiar expression of the stupidity of the petty bourgeois, as fake cultural *arrivisme* is the expression of the stupidity of the big bourgeois.

Had Mr. Bromfield's intelligence, his conscience, his nerve been equal to the task of really writing a book about a modern hero in these terms, he would not, as the genteel critic might say, have turned out a "sociological novel." He would have created a character seen as a historical totality, a character set roundly and solidly in his time, a "modern hero" in every sense of the phrase. Either Mr. Bromfield recognized the problem and was too modest to attempt its solution, or—this is more likely—he did not see it at all. (pp. 40-1)

Clifton Fadiman, "A Modern Novelist," in The Nation *(copyright 1932 The Nation magazine, The Nation Associates, Inc.), Vol. CXXXV, No. 3497, July 13, 1932, pp. 40-1.*

ERSKINE CALDWELL   (essay date 1933)

[*A novelist and short story writer of the Deep South, Caldwell is best known for his novels* Tobacco Road *and* God's Little Acre. *Traditional concepts of the family, race relations, and moral values are brought into question in many of his works, some of which have been unsuccessfully censored. In the essay below, Caldwell notes the lack of "a single outstanding character" in* The Farm, *a view that contrasts with most early criticism of Bromfield's works, which had praised his characterizations. Caldwell is the first critic to remark upon Bromfield's growing tendency to write novels resembling screenplays (see excerpts below by Arthur Calder-Marshall and Edmund Wilson).*]

The subtitle of Louis Bromfield's new novel could be "the story of four generations of an American family," and there are no other nine or nine hundred words better suited to indicate its unevenness, brilliance, and tedious detail.

The unevenness throughout "**The Farm**" leaves the reader with the impression of having read two books at the same time. The long stretches of dull prose read as if Bromfield had sat day after day over his writing pad working with gritted teeth to fill in the hundred-year outline or to die in the attempt. The lines and paragraphs of brilliant writing scattered over the 346 pages are something else; the reader is here brought face to face with a writer who moves us as only a few novelists in America have the power to do. If these passages are not the work of a superior talent, then there is no such thing as creative writing.

But the detail—the tedious detail! Perhaps it is the average reader who demands this itemizing in his novels. The popularity of such novels as **"The Farm"** would point in that direction; but why must the rest of us be choked with minute descriptions of clothes closets and kitchens, wearing apparel and thoughts? Not even the solitary traveler who unsuspectingly stumbles into one of Bromfield's forest clearings can escape until he has been subjected to the embarrassment of being catalogued from beaver hat to union suit.

"The Farm" is one of the better examples of the novel without characters. In this instance, regardless of what can be said for or against the tendency to write about masses of things rather than specimens of humanity, there is little lack of interest on that account. Bromfield's scores of walking characters—which is to say, characters who come and go without adding to or detracting from the story—are too fleeting to make any lasting impression, good or bad or indifferent, on the reader. Rather, we are held and urged on to the next page by the feeling of a seething mass which, we innocently hope, may break open on the following page and reveal men and women real enough to thrust forward a hand to greet us. And strangely enough, when we turn the final page, we discover that we bear no resentment against Bromfield for having told us a story merely about things, without the help of a single outstanding character.

It is to be hoped that Bromfield will institute a more intensive search in his next novel for the source and causes of America's regression. In **"The Farm"** he touches lightly on the more obvious symptoms of decay and decadence; and so, well and good. But since the future of the novel lies in its willingness or unwillingness to utilize its unique medium of expression, it is to be hoped that novelists like Bromfield will render the form secure by writing intelligently on peculiarly American expressions of morals, religion, and economic relationships.

In the meantime **"The Farm"** will find a large and readymade band of readers, not a few of whom will be disappointed because dirt-farming is squeezed out by detailed descriptions of knickknacks. But, as if by chance, the story resembles the script treatment of a Hollywood screen play, and at some future time the disappointment may be assuaged by a faintly familiar version of **"The Farm"** accompanied by process shots of cows and chickens and fade-ins on the farmer's daughter.

> *Erskine Caldwell, "Brilliant and Tedious," in* The Nation *(copyright 1933 The Nation magazine, The Nation Associates, Inc.), Vol. CXXXVII, No. 3557, September 6, 1933, p. 277.*

GRAHAM GREENE (essay date 1934)

[*Greene, an English man of letters, is generally considered the most important contemporary Catholic novelist. In his major works, he explores the problems of spiritually and socially alienated individuals living in the corrupt and corrupting societies of the twentieth century. Formerly a book reviewer at* The Spectator, *Greene is also deemed an excellent film critic, a respected biographer, and a shrewd literary critic with a taste for the works of undeservedly neglected authors. In a review of* Here Today and*

Gone Tomorrow, *Greene compares Bromfield's fiction to that of Vicki Baum, whose novel* Falling Star *was appraised in the same essay.*]

Mr. Bromfield and Miss Vicki Baum are both primarily entertainment purveyors rather than novelists, and the superiority of Mr. Bromfield arises from a certain agreeable cynicism. He has done good work in his time, and if he now feels the lure of popularity, he preserves an agreeable air of knowing exactly what he is about. In literature he is like one of his own racketeers, sentimental, wise-cracking, as hard as nails at the core. The first story in his book [*Here Today and Gone Tomorrow*] is an example of how good mere entertainment can be: the story of Miss Mehaffy, the middle-aged provincial, who, visiting New York, falls into the company of crooks and gangsters and finds herself delightfully at home. This is the best kind of American burlesque, with the glitter and brittleness of a Woolworth diamond. The other stories in his collection are inferior because they appeal to the Baser Passions. I mean sentimentality and self-pity. In all of them pathos goes berserk with rather terrible results, though the last story, *No. 55,* is worth reading for the sketch of the elderly refined school-teacher, who is engaged to teach Mr. Beppo Bianchini, gangster and night-club proprietor, how to speak elegant English. "She leant across the table and in a confidential whisper said, 'You mustn't say "a lady tried to shoot me." You must use the word "woman." Ladies don't shoot people.'"

> *Graham Greene, in his review of "Here To-day and Gone To-morrow," in* The Spectator *(© 1934 by The Spectator; reprinted by permission of* The Spectator*), Vol. 152, No. 5527, June 1, 1934, p. 864.**

JOSEPH WOOD KRUTCH (essay date 1935)

[*Krutch is widely regarded as one of America's most respected literary and drama critics. Noteworthy among his works are* The American Drama since 1918 *(1939), which analyzes the most important dramas of the 1920s and 1930s, and "Modernism" in* Modern Drama *(1953), in which he stressed the need for twentieth-century playwrights to infuse their works with traditional humanistic values. A conservative and idealistic thinker, he was a consistent proponent of human dignity and the preeminence of literary art. His literary criticism is characterized by such concerns: in* The Modern Temper *(1929) he argued that because scientific thought has denied human worth, tragedy had become obsolete, and in* The Measure of Man *(1954) he attacked modern culture for depriving humanity of the sense of individual responsibility necessary for making important decisions in an increasingly complex age. In the following excerpt, Krutch scathingly reviews the drama* De Luxe.]

In one of our tabloids I notice the report that a play called **"De Luxe"** . . . is a "society hit." Perhaps the tabloid doesn't know what "society" is, but if it actually does, then that mysterious entity is even worse off than this play about some of its members implies. For society's judgments I have no exaggerated respect, but I am loath to believe that even the best people can be taken in by anything quite so completely phony as this preposterous piece of romantic nonsense in which a group of gaudily unconvincing degenerates talk about their lost souls and wish, between drinks, that they could do "the decent thing."

"De Luxe" is portentously labeled "a play about the end of an epoch," but it is hard to believe that Louis Bromfield really took very seriously his part in its composition. Few persons, I should have supposed, are still very much interested in the more drunken expatriates reeling about Paris, but that is not the point. However unimportant they are, it would doubtless still be possible to write convincingly about them, and there certainly never was a time when a play like the present could have seemed other than the taudriest of inventions. Sometimes when the characters come out with biological remarks of extreme simplicity one seems to detect the hand of a rather retarded sophomore; at other times it is difficult not to suspect intentional burlesque, as I could hardly help doing when the irresistible Don Juan explained to a young girl bent on experiment that he might be a rotter but that he still had a respect for innocent virginity. Another big moment occurs when the leading nymphomaniac goes to "the wisest woman in Paris" to seek advice on the management of a restive lover and is told—you would never guess—that she ought not to let him see so clearly how much she cares. Surely reputations for wisdom must be easily acquired in Paris.

Possibly I do not know life. Possibly the worst of the expatriates really did behave like this, but I get my ideas from such sober authors as Michael Arlen, and his personages are not only prim but highly credible by comparison. Elsa Maxwell, obligingly played by herself, was to me the only character in the play who seemed at all authentic and in retrospect even she appears a little bit improbable.

> *Joseph Wood Krutch, in his review of "De Luxe," in* The Nation *(copyright 1935* The Nation *magazine,* The Nation *Associates, Inc.), Vol. CXL, No. 3637, March 20, 1935, p. 342.*

A. CALDER-MARSHALL (essay date 1940)

[*In a review of* Night in Bombay, *Calder-Marshall finds not "a single human being . . . All are characters for the film." This criticism is very similar to that made by Erskine Caldwell regarding* The Farm *(see excerpt above) and Edmund Wilson (see excerpt below). Calder-Marshall casts an imaginary film version of the novel.*]

Bromfield in Bombay, a Book Society Choice, you know what to expect. "Maharajahs, business men, harlots, missionaries, saints and wastrels crowd the stage of this astonishing novel!" burbles the blurb. And by Akbar, it's true. There isn't a single human being between page one and page three hundred and fifty-three. All are characters for the film. Can we cast them? For Carol Halma, ex-Miss Minnesota, ex-showgirl, heart of gold harlot, surely Ginger Rogers of *The Primrose Path*. Robert Young for Bill Wainwright, "Goodtime Charlie," the oil-magnate's son making good. Priceless for India school worker, Homer (Buck) Merrill to be rescued from a mysterious disease by the love of Carol . . . give Ralph Bellamy a break, his eyes would be perfect in Technicolor. . . . Sabu as Ali, the blind son of the mahout; and, why not? Peter Lorre with coffee make-up as Colonel Moti, the brilliant Indian scientist.

It's an all star cast; and boy! what a setting! Bombay, hub of the Orient, where East meets West in all its glamorous lubricity! *Night in Bombay* has got everything, suicide and stolen rubies, gambling in pleasure palaces and champagne by the case, cool Indian dancers and voluptuous women. (pp. 279-80)

Most interesting departure from the accepted feuilleton is the sex life of the villains. Take the Maharajah of Jellapore (Jelly as he is known on every racecourse, in every casino of Europe). You'd have expected that he was going to seduce every girl he set eyes on. Not a bit of it. With all that money, the poor fish is impotent. So is his brother. So is the evil Parsee, Mr.

Botlivala. In fact the only coloured character who isn't is Colonel Moti, and even he hasn't succeeded in giving his wife children. It seems, if scenario-writer Bromfield is to be believed, that Bombay is the paradise for any good-looking girl who'd like the wages of sin without the labour. In this fascinating city, blonde gold-diggers can find emeralds big as walnuts, just for the trouble of going to the races with a coloured gentleman.

I need not add that as the reader follows the brilliant characters through their gorgeous rout, he need never have a moment's doubt that love in the end will find a way. "No one knows his India like Louis Bromfield," states the blurb, "—not the India of Viceroys, nor the India of agitators, but the India of everyday people, with its passionate *tempo* of existence, its fierce romance and no less fierce vices, its strange medley of Eastern and Western desires." It would be egotism on my part to say that *no one* wants to. (pp. 280-81)

> *A. Calder-Marshall, in his review of "Night in Bombay" (reprinted by permission of the author), in* Life and Letters To-Day, *London, Vol. 26, No. 37, September, 1940, pp. 279-81.*

E. B. WHITE (essay date 1948)

[*White is an American essayist, poet, humorist, and author of books for children. He is often considered one of the finest American prose stylists of this century. White's essays, characterized by their wit, directness, and unrhetorical observation, appeared regularly in* The New Yorker *and* Harper's Magazine. *Below, White provides a poetic summary of Bromfield's autobiographical* Malabar Farm.]

Malabar Farm is the farm for me,
It's got what it takes, to a large degree:
Beauty, alfalfa, constant movement,
And a terrible rash of soil improvement.
Far from orthodox in its tillage,
Populous as many a village,
Stuff being planted and stuff being written,
Fields growing lush that were once unfitten,
Bromfield land, whether low or high land,
Has more going on than Coney Island.

When Bromfield went to Pleasant Valley,
The soil was as hard as a bowling alley;
He sprinkled lime and he seeded clover,
And when it came up he turned it over.
From far and wide folks came to view
The things that a writing man will do.
The more he fertilized the fields
The more impressive were his yields,
And every time a field grew fitter
Bromfield would add another critter,
The critter would add manure, despite 'im,
And so it went—ad infinitum.
It proves that a novelist on his toes
Can make a valley bloom like a rose.

Malabar Farm is the farm for me,
A place of unbridled activity.
A farm is always in some kind of tizzy,
But Bromfield's place is *really* busy:
Strangers arriving by every train,
Bromfield terracing against the rain,
Catamounts crying, mowers mowing,
Guest rooms full to overflowing,

Boxers in every room of the house,
Cows being milked to Brahms and Strauss,
Kids arriving by van or pung,
Bromfield up to his eyes in dung,
Sailors, trumpeters, mystics, actors,
All of them wanting to drive the tractors,
All of them eager to husk the corn,
Some of them sipping their drinks till morn;
Bulls in the bull pen, bulls on the loose,
Everyone bottling vegetable juice,
Play producers jousting with bards,
Boxers fighting with St. Bernards,
Boxers fooling with auto brakes,
Runaway cars at the bottom of lakes,
Bromfield diving to save the Boxers,
Moving vans full of bobby-soxers,
People coming and people going,
Everything fertile, everything growing,
Fish in the ponds other fish seducing,
Thrashing around and reproducing,
Whole place teeming with men and pets,
Field mice nesting in radio sets,
Cats in the manger, rats in the nooks,
Publishers scanning the sky for books,
Harvested royalties, harvested grain,
Bromfield scanning the sky for rain,
Bromfield's system proving reliable,
Soil getting rich and deep and friable,
Bromfield phoning, Bromfield haying,
Bromfield watching mulch decaying,
Womenfolks busy shelling peas,
Guinea fowl up in catalpa trees.
Oh, Bromfield's valley is plenty pleasant—
Quail and rabbit, Boxers, pheasant.
Almost every Malabar day
Sees birth and growth, sees death, decay;
Summer ending, leaves a-falling,
Lecture dates, long distance calling.

Malabar Farm is the farm for me,
It's the proving ground of vivacity.
A soil that's worn out, poor, or lazy
Drives L. Bromfield almost crazy;
Whether it's raining or whether it's pouring,
Bromfield's busy with soil restoring;
From the Hog Lot Field to the Lower Bottom
The things a soil should have, he's got 'em;
Foe of timothy, friend of clover,
Bromfield gives it a going over,
Adds some cobalt, adds some boron.
Not enough? He puts some more on.
Never anything too much trouble,
Almost everything paying double:
Nice fat calves being sold to the sharper,
Nice fat checks coming in from Harper.
Most men cut and cure their hay,
Bromfield cuts it and leaves it lay;
Whenever he gets impatient for rain
He turns his steers in to standing grain;
Whenever he gets in the least depressed
He sees that another field gets dressed;
He never dusts and he never sprays,
His soil holds water for days and days,

And now when a garden piece is hoed
You'll find neither bug nor nematode,
You'll find how the good earth holds the rain.
Up at the house you'll find Joan Fontaine.

Malabar Farm is the farm for me,
It's the greenest place in the whole countree,
It builds its soil with stuff organic,
It's the nearest thing to a planned panic.
Bromfield mows by any old light,
The sun in the morning and the moon at night;
Most tireless of all our writing men,
He sometimes mows until half past ten;
With a solid program of good trash mulch
He stops the gully and he stops the gulch.
I think the world might well have a look
At Louis Bromfield's latest book;
A man doesn't have to be omniscient
To see that he's right—our soil's deficient.
We've robbed and plundered this lovely earth
Of elements of immeasurable worth,
And darned few men have applied their talents
Harder than Louis to restore the balance;
And though his husbandry's far from quiet,
Bromfield had the guts to try it.
A book like his is a very great boon,
And what he's done, I'd like to be doon.

> *E. B. White, in his review of "Malabar Farm"
> (copyright 1948, 1976 by E. B. White; reprinted by
> permission of Harper & Row, Publishers, Inc.; orig-
> inally published in* The New Yorker, *Vol. XXIV, No.
> 11, May 8, 1948), in his* Poems and Sketches of
> E. B. White, *Harper & Row, 1981, pp. 56-8.*

EDMUND WILSON   (essay date 1950)

[*Wilson, America's foremost man of letters in the twentieth century, wrote widely on cultural, historical, and literary matters,
including several seminal critical studies. He is often credited
with bringing an international perspective to American letters
through his widely read discussions of European literature. Wilson was allied to no critical school: however, several dominant
concerns serve as guiding motifs throughout his work. He invariably examined the social and historical implications of a work
of literature, particularly literature's significance as "an attempt
to give meaning to our experience" and its value for the improvement of humanity. Though not a moralist, his criticism displays a deep concern with moral values. Another constant was
his discussion of a work of literature as a revelation of its author's
personality. Related to this is Wilson's theory, formulated in* The
Wound and the Bow *(1941), that artistic ability is a compensation
for a psychological wound; thus, a literary work can only be fully
understood if one undertakes an emotional profile of its author.
Wilson utilized this approach in many essays, and it is the most
often attacked element of his thought. However, although Wilson
examined the historical and psychological implications of a work
of literature, he rarely did so at the expense of a discussion of
its literary qualities. Perhaps Wilson's greatest contributions to
American literature were his tireless promotion of writers of the
1920s, 1930s, and 1940s, and his essays introducing the best of
modern literature to the general reader. Below, Wilson details
the plot of* What Became of Anna Bolton *at length, noting especially poor characterization, which was previously held to be
a strong point of Bromfield's writing. Wilson concludes that Bromfield was obviously writing novels geared to the motion picture
industry—an opinion shared by A. Calder-Marshall and Erskine
Caldwell (see excerpts above).*]

In the days of *The Green Bay Tree* and *The Strange Case of Miss Annie Spragg,* Mr. Louis Bromfield used to be spoken of as one of the younger writers of promise. By the time he had brought out *Twenty-four Hours,* it was more or less generally said of him that he was definitely second-rate. Since then, by unremitting industry and a kind of stubborn integrity that seems to make it impossible for him to turn out his rubbish without thoroughly believing in it, he has gradually made his way into the fourth rank, where his place is now secure.

His new novel, *What Became of Anna Bolton,* is one of his most remarkable achievements. The story begins in the London season of 1937, and in a succession of brilliant scenes which, for the density of the social picture, recall the opening of *War and Peace,* Mr. Bromfield makes us acquainted with a vivid and varied company from that international haut monde about which he writes with authority. (p. 153)

Mr. Bromfield, in *What Became of Anna Bolton,* has accomplished something in the nature of a miracle. In hardly more than sixty thousand words—a story that recalls, by its length, *A Lost Lady* and *Ethan Frome*—he has produced, by severe compression, a small masterpiece of pointlessness and banality. Most novelists of Mr. Bromfield's rank have some hobby about which they become interesting, some corner of life which they know and about which they have something to tell, some humor or infectious sentimentality or capacity for creating suspense; and it must have cost Louis Bromfield a rigorous labor of exclusion to achieve this smooth and limpid little novel in which there is not a single stroke of wit, not a scene of effective drama, not a phrase of clean-minted expression, and hardly a moment of credible human behavior. (p. 159)

[The] book reviewer is baffled when he attempts to give an account of a work which has already turned its back on literature and embarrasses him on every page by stretching out its arms to Hollywood. He comes to feel that what he ought to have done was simply to pass it along to the movie department. For the characters of Louis Bromfield are hardly even precisely stock fiction characters: they are blank spaces like the figures on billboards before the faces have been painted in. When their features are finally supplied, they will be the features of popular actors. Mr. Bromfield seems to have made it easy, by giving Anna a similar name, for his heroine to wear the face of Ann Sheridan, who, not so very far back, in *Kings Row,* was playing just such an Irish girl from the other side of the tracks, in love with a rich young man; and in the same way Eric von Kleist can merge readily into Erich von Stroheim. No doubt the public will see them soon and will not mind if what they are and do has no logic and no motivation, no likeness of any kind to life. But the book reviewer is rather up against it, since he has to have something to take hold of, even to say that a book ought to be better, and *Anna Bolton* completely eludes him because it is really sub-literary and proto-film. (pp. 159-60)

> *Edmund Wilson, "What Became of Louis Bromfield" (originally published in a different form in* The New Yorker, *Vol. XX, No. 8, April 8, 1944), in his* Classics and Commercials: A Literary Chronicle of the Forties *(reprinted by permission of Farrar, Straus and Giroux, Inc.; copyright 1950 by Edmund Wilson; renewed © 1978 by Elena Wilson), Farrar, Straus and Giroux, 1950, pp. 153-60.*

HAL BORLAND (essay date 1955)

[*The critic, a resident of rural Connecticut, praises Bromfield and his final autobiographical book,* Animals and Other People.]

There's something about life close to the land that makes a wise man aware not only of his own transience but of his tenantship rather than ownership of his acres. His is by no means the only life sustained there; unless he understands this and accepts it he will find that life barren and sterile; for there is an interrelationship between man and his environment that is inescapable, particularly in the country.

Louis Bromfield, when he went back to the land in Ohio, knew this. . . . In all the books he has written about his Ohio country and Malabar Farm this has been apparent. Now he has brought together parts of these books, added new material about his animals and birds, wild and tame, and assembled **"Animals and Other People."** The animals include dogs, cats, geese, rabbits, skunks, raccoons, cows, bulls, horses, goats, turkeys and pigs. Especially dogs and pigs. . . .

There is a temptation to quote extensively, for Mr. Bromfield writes vividly and fluently. Instead, certain chapters will be cited. The poignant and eloquent one about Johnny Appleseed and blind Aunty Mattie. The one about people who are "teched," with eccentric Phoebe Wise its chief character. The one about Walter Oakes and the farm he called "My Ninety Acres," which is full of warm and simple drama.

There is a good story about the death of Prince, a favorite boxer, and a chapter about the farm pond and the fish. Mr. Bromfield tells of the goats who finally got so rambunctious they weren't content to sleep in the porch swing but had to get inside any visiting car and make themselves at home. There is also a love letter to the land in an account of Malabar—and how it was changed from an area of eroded, worn-out land into a flourishing farm. This chapter alone deserves a place on any shelf of farm books and a special place in any farmer's home.

"Animals and Other People" adds up to a constantly readable book about people and other animals, most of whom anyone would like to know. Most anyone, at least. Some people don't even like dogs, let alone Guernsey bulls and Nubian goats and hogs. This book isn't for them, and they will know it from the very first page.

> *Hal Borland, "A Man Who Doesn't Kill Woodchucks," in* The New York Times Book Review (© *1955 by The New York Times Company; reprinted by permission), November 20, 1955, p. 47.*

MORRISON BROWN (essay date 1956)

[*Brown surveys Bromfield's short fiction, nonfiction, and dramas.*]

Individually the stories [in *Awake and Rehearse*], with a few exceptions, did not rise much above the level of mediocrity. Collectively they offered proof that Bromfield could write compact stories even though his novels gave little evidence of it. Since the stories all touch on death in some way there was a kind of unity about them that made it suitable to include them all under one title. There were many examples once more of Bromfield's great range in both character and scene.

Justice, written in 1925 and therefore first in point of time of composition, is one of the best stories in the collection. It tells of the trial and conviction of Willie Fallon by a jury of 'impartial' citizens who find him guilty of a petty robbery because he looks like a thief and because society needs to be protected. They have only the weakest kind of circumstantial evidence against him, but they know he is guilty just the same. The narrator, a member of the jury, holds out for a while but is finally browbeaten into agreeing to the verdict of guilty. A light goes out of Willie Fallon's eye as sentence is pronounced. The story is a good one, having succinctness, clarity, and a thought worthy of attention. One cannot fail to recall, however, that Galsworthy wrote a play called *Justice* in 1910 which concerned itself with a similar theme. (p. 62)

The Life of Vergie Winters is also a fine story. This story is another instance of Bromfield's great talent for character portrayal. (pp. 62-3)

For a pure picture of the decadence of European society at the end of the first World War that had been bolstered up by purchasable nobility and wealthy American dowagers, it is difficult to imagine a better view than that which one gets in *The Apothecary*. The story is artistically sound as well. If most of the stories were of the calibre of the three mentioned, the collection would be superior, but unfortunately the majority of them have little about them that is memorable. (p. 63)

Here Today and Gone Tomorrow consists of four short novels. . . . The stories are *No. 55, The Listener, Fourteen Years After,* and *Miss Mehaffy.* Taken together they give us a rather good view of the social life of the late 'twenties when the speakeasy flourished and the flappers were just starting to age a little.

In *No. 55* we have an inside view of a speakeasy that has been established in an old fashionable brownstone house just off Fifth Avenue in New York. . . . The story is in no way unusual but it is technically sound and does give a good picture of the speakeasy.

In *The Listener* a story is told that is reminiscent of the actual Ivar Kreuger story. . . . There is a rather good picture in Olivia Jenkins of the wealthy old lady who has no interest in life except in those who gather in the lobbies of famous hotels, but on the whole this is not one of Bromfield's best stories.

Fourteen Years After is probably the poorest story of the four because it does not have even plot to sustain it and presents no characters that are memorable. The events of the story centre around the activities, in one night, of the various passengers on a ship returning from Europe to the United States. They are mostly the somewhat aged members of what was the lost generation that grew up during the first World War, who are 'always rushing round and round, never getting anywhere'. Every move seems to be a move of desperation.

In *Miss Mehaffy* Bromfield has told the best story of the lot. Miss Mehaffy, daughter of Two-Gun Joe and Big Annie, has lived quietly in Winnebago Falls for most of her life without ever experiencing any of the excitement that was the daily life of her parents. When she suddenly decides to go to New York to see Baby Peterson, the excitement she has craved comes her way. . . . Miss Mehaffy is an individual, and, as such, becomes the one bright spot in the book that displays otherwise a rather colourless although competent effort.

Here Today and Gone Tomorrow brought more cash than credit to the author. . . . (pp. 74-6)

From the time that Bromfield had been a drama critic in his early days in New York, he had a desire ultimately to write some plays. His dramatization of *The Green Bay Tree* . . . which had been no great success, had not dulled his interest. Apparently he thought it was time to make his big try in the drama in late 1934 and early 1935. By March he had two plays opening in New York; one which was called *De Luxe,* written in collaboration with John Gearon, had to do with 'the decadence of end-of-the-line expatriates in Paris' and the other was an adaptation of Edouard Bourdet's *Les Temps Difficiles,* which Bromfield called *Times Have Changed.* Neither play was much of a success although Bromfield spared no pains in trying to have them presented well. Both plays had casts that were superior, but they could not overcome the fact that the plays were not too interesting in theme and were not technically good drama.

Bromfield liked a great deal of space in which to present his rambling novels; he did not seem able to construct a tightly woven play where compression and movement were simultaneously a necessity. The theme of the decadence of the postwar group was no longer of interest, and caused one commentator to call his play an 'unfragrant corpse of an unmourned epoch'. The story of *Times Have Changed* was a little more palatable in its study of the decadence of the Pentlands of New England and their unsuccessful attempt to head off ruin by having a daughter of one of the members of the family marry a half-wit son of a multi-millionaire. However, it too had no great appeal, and both plays were off the stage in less than a month. (pp. 76-7)

During the year 1939, Bromfield was much in the news. In January a short pamphlet entitled *England, A Dying Oligarchy* was brought out by his publishers. It was a very blunt attack on the men who headed the British Government, especially on Chamberlain, who was accused of selling out to Hitler so that the shops might stay open in Britain. He predicted that war, should it come, would put a sudden end to the oligarchy that was leading the British down the road to ruin. He maintained that what Britain needed was a great leader. There was much critical comment in the United States and in Britain concerning the vehement attack, but subsequent history has on the whole dealt kindly with Bromfield in this matter. He also predicted in the pamphlet that war would open in the East when Japan was ready, a prediction that also helped to keep Bromfield's score as a prophet relatively high. (pp. 89-90)

During the year Bromfield also found time to assemble *It Takes All Kinds,* another collection of four short novels and five short stories. . . . It makes a sizeable volume, 690 pages, but has not too much to recommend it except technique and finish when we compare it with a book like *The Rains Came.* One of the short novels, *Bitter Lotus,* is interesting because in it Bromfield takes Lady Heston, Lord Heston, and Ransome from *The Rains Came,* puts them in a new setting with a different background and new background characters, and lets the story develop in the new environment. This story . . . was, according to Mr. Bromfield, 'a technical experiment'. The events and atmosphere are even more romantic than they were in *The Rains Came* and the shorter novel suffers in comparison with the original tale.

McLeod's Folly, another of the short novels in the collection, is quite interesting in that it displays rather well Bromfield's knowledge of the newspaper business. The plot is commonplace, however, having to do with the building up of a widow's newspaper business by the unrecognized son of an owner of a string of big dailies. . . . Although none of the stories strikes one as being extremely significant, the literary skill which is displayed in them is very great. J. P. Marquand probably summed up the situation adequately when he called *It Takes All Kinds* 'a case book of literary craftsmanship which anyone in the profession will be better for studying.' The success of the film *The Rains Came* probably helped the sale of the book considerably. (pp. 90-1)

The stories [in *The World We Live In*] have to do largely with people in Europe and America during the build-up for the second World War and during the war years. There are six stories connected with the war itself, and, in spite of a kind of intolerant attitude toward anything German, they are interesting because they reflect a tremendous knowledge of men and movements that could only come from unlimited personal contacts with a great variety of people in this troubled time. We get an intimate view of German industrialists and political opportunists who set the stage for Hitler, of men and women passing back and forth across borders as they engage in the business of espionage, of wealthy American women who are caught in the maelstrom by their involvement in foreign marriages, and of many simple, ordinary people who get swept along by the current. Some of the characters are unquestionably built up by the use of a vivid imagination, but there is an air of reality about most of them that must have been suggested, at least, by real people.

Especially memorable in the collection are *The Pond,* which though somewhat extreme in its mystical basis does present clearly some fundamental human relations; *True Love,* which maintains an atmosphere of tense excitement as two spies waver between their human feelings and their duty; *Thou Shalt Not Covet,* which pictures the depravity of the political associates of Hitler; and *Death in Monte Carlo,* which deals with a woman who loses all human dignity in her greed for money. *Up Ferguson Way,* one story not connected with the war, is concerned with a Richland County legend—the legend of Phoebe Wise, who shot her lover through her kitchen door. . . . This latter story looks ahead to the kind of thing we are to encounter in the dozen years from 1944 to 1956 in the writings of Bromfield. The entire group of nine stories in *The World We Live In* attest to the fact that, although Bromfield is not one of the world's great masters of the short story, he is indeed a very fine storyteller; the stories as a whole lack only depth to make them great—all of the technique of good writing is in evidence and the interest factor is always high.

In this period between the purchase of Malabar in 1939 and the publication of *Pleasant Valley* in 1945, five books appeared. In addition to books there were quite a number of stories and articles sent to various magazines throughout the country. . . . Throughout the entire period of five years there was what almost amounted to a flood of original articles in the *Reader's Digest,* most of them having to do in one way or another with the farm operation or the Ohio countryside. (pp. 103-05)

When we consider whether Bromfield's farm-inspired books or articles were more important to him than his fiction in the last years, there is little question that the farm writing was the closer to his heart. His interest in agriculture had apparently completely submerged the novelist and short story writer. In 1940 he was reputed to have said, 'I make my reputation with a pen, but my heart is with the spade.' . . .

In *Pleasant Valley* . . . Bromfield began the story of his farm adventure which was later to be continued in additional books. It was an immediate success. . . . (p. 107)

The book was unquestionably directed toward those who either had a love for the land and for farming or could be influenced to become intrigued by the mystery of the soil. Its appearance was coupled in time with one of the greatest gardening movements in the United States, brought on by the scarcity of food during the war. (p. 108)

Pleasant Valley was not only a record of the trials and successes of an intelligent amateur engaged in building a home for himself and his family and in restoring a farm, but it was an intimate picture of the fundamental thinking of a man who had travelled the wide world over, had had unusual success at his chosen work as a writer, had been a part of the world of glamour and glitter, and who withal had lived deeply in spite of the confusion of his life in the centre always of much activity. It was the picture of a man eternally in search of significance in a world that had continually thrown roadblocks in his way by giving him too much success and adulation. (p. 109)

Kenny, [a] short story collection, was made up of three stories: *Kenny, Retread,* and *The End of the Road.* (p. 113)

There is nothing very unusual in any of the three stories; they are not on a par with Bromfield's best short stories of former years.

Colorado is one of Bromfield's 'misunderstood' books, according to the author. It was his intention to write a satire on 'Westerns' and on Westerners. He was tired of hearing about a Western aristocracy from his friends in the West as well as other 'general hogwash' concerning the development of the West. Bromfield called it a 'story without social consciousness or self-consciousness'. Through exaggeration of incident and character, Bromfield displayed the history of the Meaney family from the humble early days of P. J. Meaney through his rise to power in Silver City and then through the advance of his son Dick to Washington as the revered senator from Colorado. (p. 114)

Taken as a satire, the novel is quite interesting and is a clever piece of writing. Through its exaggeration there are innumerable scenes that are highly entertaining. Like most of Bromfield's novels the story is fast moving and holds the reader's attention even though he knows that what he is reading is just delightful nonsense. It is understandable how many of the reviewers missed the satire and considered the story as an attempt to write a real 'Western'. Bromfield seems to get carried away with the events of his own creation and the characters, who are supposed to be caricatures, sometimes take on a reality that makes it difficult to catch the tongue-in-cheek presentation. All in all, the book that was never meant to be anything too significant is an entertaining piece of writing, and that is all the author wanted it to be. (p. 115)

[*Malabar Farm*] brought the story up to 1945, continuing what had been previously told in *Pleasant Valley.* The rather loosely connected chapters are held together by two letters to a make-believe sergeant at Okinawa, one at the beginning explaining that the author is writing a book to answer the many queries of people like the sergeant and one at the end making apologies for sins of omission and commission. . . .

The nature of the letter to the imaginary sergeant sets the tone for the book. There is a move away from the familiar essay pattern of *Pleasant Valley,* which had an appeal to quite a wide audience, to a narrower kind of informational essay that appeals primarily to those people who seek material on land reclamation and general farming practices. It is true that many people have read *Malabar Farm* who are not farmers and never expect to be, but it is plain that Bromfield, although he did not exclude these armchair farmers, did have in mind, as he wrote, the reader who might make some practical use of the successes and failures at Malabar. (p. 116)

Along with valuable information for those working with the same kind of agricultural problems as the ones faced at Malabar there is pictured further in *Malabar Farm* that which was the very heart of *Pleasant Valley,* the appealing kind of life that is possible in the country. We get further insight into the pleasantness of a situation that provides an abundance of good food, a house large enough even for the Bromfield circle of friends from near and far, space for a great many large gatherings at reunions and barn dances, animal friends and pets of all kinds—and all in the environment of one of the hill-and-valley sections of the most beautiful part of Ohio. Bromfield had a great knack for picturing those things that seemed beautiful or important to him in a way that enhances their appeal so that the reader has the feeling that he too would like to share such experiences or such scenes. This appealing description is a solid part of the value of *Malabar Farm.* Probably no other reviewer caught the essence of this attraction better than E. B. White, who wrote his humorous review in the form of a 100-line poem . . . [see excerpt above]. (pp. 117-18)

[*Out of the Earth*] was the most serious book of the three [Malabar books], concerning itself as it did for the most part with the technical aspects of the New Agriculture, particularly as it had been practised during the preceding ten years at Malabar. (p. 122)

It was Bromfield's intention in *Out of the Earth* to follow in detail the various practices that were used at Malabar to bring worn-out land back into full production and to present the theories and reasoning that went along with these practices. . . .

It was Bromfield's purpose, in the first place, to put those theories and discoveries that held promise into practice at Malabar, and then, finally, to write of his high adventure in agriculture with both clarity and the kind of imaginative language that would 'spark' the somewhat dormant interest in those who might become converts. (p. 123)

In *Out of the Earth,* which is a quite well organized book, Bromfield describes in great detail some of the basic theories that he found possible to accept, tells why he accepted them and how they worked out in practice on the farm. (p. 124)

Just how much *Out of the Earth* is 'literature' in the narrow sense is a question, but no one can consider [the] book to be merely a technical manual. . . . There is no question of Bromfield's having been able to clothe his thoughts on even the most prosaic subject with imaginative language that causes one to fall under his spell, and like him see what is sometimes a rather dull world through his rose-coloured glasses. (p. 125)

[The play *Helen of Memphis*] makes its bid as entertainment on the thesis that reducing the story of Helen and Paris to modern vaudeville is likely to produce a hilariously funny situation.

Bromfield was quite enthusiastic about the play during its preparation and after it was finished. His previous failures in the drama in the 'thirties had been forgotten, and he was certain that Broadway would be all agog when it got the latest masterpiece. . . . But after the cool reception in New York early in 1951 when he took the play there, his enthusiasm for the theatre subsided as suddenly as it had risen. (pp. 127-28)

Bromfield . . . turned to the troubles of the nation in a piece of non-fiction, *A New Pattern For a Tired World,* which came out in March of 1954. In it he first tries to show how the United States has failed in her attempt to lead the world to peace, and then he presents a plan that he thinks might ultimately be successful. (p. 133)

A New Pattern For a Tired World had weaknesses, as a book of this kind would be bound to have. In spots it tended to be too unkind to those who had anything to do with the recent Democratic administration of Roosevelt and Truman and often seemed to be too much dominated by the political philosophy of ex-Senator Robert Taft. The basic concept of the nature of our present difficulty was, in all probability, perhaps a little too pat; there were spots where few of us could agree with Bromfield's reasoning, but that was to be expected in a book of this type. The least that could be said of it would be that it was a book that made people think, and, even if it served no other purpose—and it may well be that it advanced the suggestion that will be followed ultimately as our foreign policy changes—the resulting thinking would be of enough worth to make the writing of the book a satisfactory effort.

Although *A New Pattern For a Tired World* was not a book that was drawn directly from the farm experience, it had its development while its author walked the Malabar acres. As time had passed it had become ever clearer that Malabar Farm was more than just a 'terrible rash of soil improvement'. Just how the farm operation fitted into the Bromfield story was a matter of speculation until late in 1955 when Bromfield himself tried to bring things into focus in the first and last chapters of *From My Experience.* It is true that there is nothing in the two philosophical essays that give this book its substance that could not be read between the lines of previous utterances, but here Bromfield puts the story of the quest into words that speak directly.

It is a quest that has for its goal the finding of significance in a materialistic world. (pp. 135-36)

Of all the things that were near to his heart, Bromfield's animal friends had a very special place. As far back as he could remember he had a great love for all living creatures, and they usually responded with a devotion equal to his own. Scattered here and there throughout his farm books were stories of the antics and demonstrations of the affection of these animals. Finally Bromfield decided to bring most of these stories together, with additions that came to his mind, in *Animals and Other People.* . . . In the book we are told again the story of the eccentric Phoebe Wise, who was the first person to bring to Bromfield's attention that there were certain people who had a strange affinity with nature which she termed being 'teched' and that he was one of those special people to whom the term could be applied. . . .

Bromfield speaks, in *Animals and Other People,* of his favourites from among the more than fifty dogs which he owned during his lifetime. (p. 138)

To the average reader, *Animals and Other People* might not have too much appeal because there was not much that was new in it, but to the 'teched' it was very nice indeed to have all the stories in one place. Certainly we can see in this book a reflection of the extreme warmth and kindness that Bromfield extended even to his animal friends. (p. 139)

[In *Out of the Earth*] he gave in effect his reasons for finding the experiment at Malabar so fundamentally satisfying:

A lot of things have changed on the farm of to-day, but the essence of the farm and the open country remains the same. The freedom is unchanged and the sense of security and independence and the good rich food and the beauty that lies for the seeing eye on every side and, above all, that satisfaction, as great as that of Leonardo or Shakespeare or any other creative artist, in having made something great and beautiful out of nothing. The farmer may leave his stamp upon the whole of the landscape seen from his window, and it can be as great and beautiful a creation as Michelangelo's David, for the farmer who takes over a desolate farm, ruined by some evil and ignorant predecessor, and turns it into a Paradise of beauty and abundance is one of the greatest of artists.

(pp. 150-51)

Morrison Brown, in his Louis Bromfield and His Books: An Evaluation *(copyright, 1956, by Morrison Brown; reprinted by permission of the author), Cassell, 1956 (and reprinted by Essential Books, Inc., 1957), 165 p.*

DAVID D. ANDERSON (essay date 1964)

[*Anderson is the founder of the Society for the Study of Midwestern Literature. He has written critical studies of such figures as William Jennings Bryan, Brand Whitlock, Robert Ingersoll, and Bromfield, as well as several important works on Sherwood Anderson. In the following excerpt, Anderson finds the quest to attain some form of the lost Jeffersonian ideal of a self-sufficient, agrarian democracy to be a concern which unifies Bromfield's canon. Anderson's argument runs sharply against the beliefs of such critics as Erskine Caldwell (see excerpt above), who saw Bromfield's agrarian works as a sharp falling-off in the career of the hitherto promising realistic novelist.*]

At Bromfield's death it was widely believed that there had been two Louis Bromfields: the promising young novelist who had gone on to commercial success in a flamboyantly fashionable world before disappearing, and the conservative middle-aged farmer whose dirt-stained fingers wrote convincingly of agricultural practices and alarmingly about economics. . . .

At the time of his death his literary reputation was as varied as his audiences. Among recognized literary critics, he was not taken seriously in spite of kind comments by some reviewers about his last fiction. With the reading audiences of the book clubs and the public libraries, interested in fast-moving stories rather than in form and ideas, he remained extremely popular: and with the readers of his agricultural works he was controversially regarded as almost anything from a charlatan to a prophet. In spite of this diversity of audience and opinion based on the apparent dichotomy in his writing career, it is obvious that no such dichotomy exists. Bromfield's lifelong writings were actually the record of a consistent romantic search, and the apparent breaks in his career were merely tactical movements that he hoped would bring him closer to its end.

This unity behind his apparently different careers is evident from the consistency with which he sought to define and to attain a Jeffersonian ideal that had apparently become an anachronism in a society dominated by industrial materialism. (p. 171)

[Bromfield's] first novels taught him that the triumph of the natural aristocrat was appearance only because it was essentially a victory based upon the terms of materialism and because, in gaining it, his natural aristocrats had lost the touch with humanity and nature that is essential for fulfillment. But this realization came slowly, intensifying in each of the novels, until in *A Good Woman* his protagonist suffers obvious defeat rather than apparent victory. In *The Green Bay Tree* Lily Shane had apparently escaped the dehumanizing influence of the town, but at the end she has nothing with which to fill her life except melancholy waiting; in *Possession* Ellen Tolliver is completely dehumanized by the goal she has attained, and she is as dominated and isolated by her music as the people of the town are by materialism. In *Early Autumn* there is no victory but a graceful defeat as Olivia Pentland finds herself trapped by dead tradition. *A Good Woman* marks the ultimate defeat as Philip Downes seeks his fulfillment in death after having recognized the transience and the meaninglessness of a victory gained at the expense of human values.

When he recognized the futility of the attempt to escape through adapting the premise of natural aristocracy to a modern, post-Darwinian world, Bromfield had no choice but to abandon the attempt and the rest of the series of projected panel novels. Attempts to escape the modern world through success in the arts could only mean a success on the world's own meaningless material terms. In seeking to provide a meaningful victory, he turned in *The Strange Case of Miss Annie Spragg* to a deliberate rejection of material success, and he sought a new kind of victory based on his instinctive perception of man's ultimate relationship to the natural order. But this approach was equally romantic, and it was complicated by a mystic quality that he could not explain, although he permitted it to dominate the novel. (pp. 172-73)

At this point, as his fiction between 1929 and 1935 shows, Bromfield was baffled; having rejected the idea of the triumph of the natural aristocrat, he continued his preoccupation with the personal qualities inherent in the type. Consequently, his fiction of these years is philosophically unresolved as well as apparently unresolvable. The result is the ambiguous material and the emotional triumph of the natural aristocrats in *Twenty-Four Hours* and the complement of that novel, the equally unsatisfactory emotional and material defeat of Pierre Radier in *A Modern Hero*. In spite of the excellence of *The Farm* of this period, Bromfield presents its subject matter as a re-creation of an ideal that has been destroyed. It can never be revived except as an impossible nostalgic dream, and the futility of that dream, or of any dream, is emphasized by the ironic emptiness of *The Man Who Had Everything*.

The decline of Bromfield's literary reputation began early in these years, and it was intensified both by the unresolved dilemmas of his fiction and by the events in the world around him which his philosophical floundering forced him to ignore. Because Bromfield's work during the 1920's had marked him as one of the period's romantic rebels against modern materialism, he had been regarded as a young man to watch. But in his personal dilemma he was not interested in manning the barricades in the economic crisis of the early 1930's; hence to the prevailing critical view, led by reviewers in *The Nation* and *The New Republic*, he had become a reactionary. (p. 173)

[Because writing fiction] had brought material success without personal fulfillment, he began to regard it as merely another means of earning a living, and not a particularly satisfying one when compared to the life he had been seeking so long and had finally found.

This attitude produced a number of poor novels and other fiction, notably *Night In Bombay, Wild Is the River, Until the Day Break,* and *What Became of Anna Bolton,* primarily because Bromfield had begun to regard fiction as a utilitarian tool for propaganda rather than as a medium of artistic expression. But the same period produced *Mrs. Parkington* and *The Wild Country,* novels that were almost as good as his best, an indication that Bromfield found much more satisfaction and meaning in writing fiction than his contrary statements imply. However, by this time it was no longer his major interest, for he devoted most of his energy to restoring the soil of "Malabar Farm." (pp. 174-75)

In all his works Bromfield is very much a Midwesterner and an agrarian romantic in spite of the veneer of sophistication that overlies so much of his fiction. He belongs properly in the stream of American literature that came out of the Midwest in the first thirty years of the twentieth century and for a while came close to dominating American fiction. In spirit Bromfield is very close to Sherwood Anderson who, like Bromfield, came out of Ohio to seek the meaning of the individual in an industrial age and eventually was forced to withdraw to the Virginia hills where he could come closer to a simple society that materialism had made impossible elsewhere. Bromfield was never the artist that Sherwood Anderson was; and he did not, perhaps could not, create a *Winesburg, Ohio.* But in philosophy, in faith in his fellow man, and in his rejection of the phony and the material superficiality of American life, he was very close in spirit to his fellow Ohioan. Bromfield's quest, like Anderson's, has been largely misinterpreted. But whereas the misinterpretation of Anderson's has led to loose categorization of him as a naturalist rather than as the romantic idealist that he was, Bromfield, condemned as being commercial, has suffered a worse literary fate through the misunderstanding of his work.

In spirit, too, Bromfield is closely related to the Midwestern poets of his time—Vachel Lindsay, Edgar Lee Masters, and Carl Sandburg; but again his artistry suffers when compared to theirs. Like them and like Anderson, he was a romantic who sought to discover what had happened to the dream of the perfect society that had been brought over the mountains from the East almost a hundred years before any of them was born, and had then been lost in the same human frailties of greed, misunderstanding, and puritan morality that had prevented its achievement in the East. (pp. 175-76)

To assess Bromfield's contribution to American literature is not difficult: the many shortcomings that had prevented the fulfillment of his early promise are serious enough to keep him out of the first rank of American novelists. But at the same time he deserves a much better literary fate than he has received, because of his effectiveness of style, his character portrayal, and his narrative technique that are his most consistent strong points; because he has made substantial contributions in individual works; and because of his effective and intelligent interpretations of the American scene and American life.

The decline of American individualism and agrarian democracy, the growth of industrialism, the unique role of the strong woman in American society, and the egalitarian nature of a country that permits a young person to rise above his social origins, are themes with which Bromfield dealt significantly and well; in his use of them in his work, he came close to the essence of America as thoughtful Americans know it. That he

did not go on to chronicle the rise of an industrial democracy, as has been protested by his major critics and detractors, but attempted instead to return to the past, does not detract from the effectiveness with which he handled these major American themes. Rather it strengthens them as he reiterates the human values on which the country was built rather than the material values with which it asserts world leadership, and he emphasizes the need for those values in a world devoted to things.

Among the substantial literary contributions that he made, one must include the four panel novels, all of which combine to document in human rather than sociological terms the impact upon the individual of sweeping social changes and of perverted values. These novels are valuable, too, because they illustrate Bromfield's narrative talents: a forthright, effective, and literate style; an ability to draw characters that are both human and intense; and a talent for first-rate storytelling—all of which combine into well-constructed, fast-moving novels that are both readable and believable.

To these novels must be added his best single work, *The Farm; Twenty-Four Hours,* a remarkable *tour de force* of control and intensity in spite of its melodramatic lapses; and *The Rains Came,* certainly the most dramatic as well as the most philosophically unified of all his novels. From the last group *Mrs. Parkington* must be included as an intensely human portrait of a magnificent American woman; and *The Wild Country,* too, in which he came close to defining the American Midwestern experience as it reached the peak of one phase of its development and was about to enter another. These, together with a number of short stories—most notably **"The Life of Vergie Winters"**—compose a respectable and substantial body of work in spite of the lapses and failures that marred his career. Were they all he had done, they would have been considerable.

In addition to these achievements one must take into consideration Bromfield's contributions to the literature of nature, of folklore, and of agriculture. . . . This phase of Bromfield's career is certainly the most frequently ignored in spite of the fact that it is a delightful, informative, and important part of his total literary output. Certainly **"The Cycle of a Farm Pond"** deserves a major place in the history of romantic nature writing, and such essays as **"My Ninety Acres"** and the others in which he probes the close kinship between past and present, man and nature, are examples of what the modern re-creation of folk legend can be but so seldom is.

Finally, and perhaps most importantly, Bromfield must be regarded as important for his contributions to the field of agriculture and to its literature, a field of activity that for too long has been dominated by the charts and graphs of profit-loss ratios that ignore love and respect for the land and the soil. Assessment of his specific contributions to agricultural theory and practice is beyond the province of the literary historian and critic; and perhaps it is difficult for the agricultural scientist without the further verification and experimentation that scientific judgment demands. As literature, however, his agricultural writings are significant because they occupy such a prominent place in the Bromfield canon and because they provide clear-cut examples of the philosophy of The Enlightenment. That philosophy is modified by the impacts of romanticism and of Darwinism, but nevertheless it is recognizable as the logical intellectual descendant of that great tradition. The spirit of The Enlightenment has largely disappeared under the assault of material philosophies, but Bromfield provides valuable insight into its meaning and continuance. Furthermore, these agricultural writings are for the most part examples of what technical writing can be when it is lucid, free of jargon and unnecessary scientific terminology, and written with an imagination and insight that give it life. Much of it is a permanent and valuable addition to the literature of science.

These, then, are the contributions that Bromfield has made to American literature. While they are not enough to justify a high place in the history of that literature and while it is easy to protest that he might have contributed a great deal more, protests and their implied or actual denunciations are futile. Bromfield was what he was: a man plagued by a personal philosophical dilemma that could not be resolved or removed through literature; and he was forced to look elsewhere for a solution. Such a fate has been common to writers in the mainstream of American literature from Herman Melville to John Steinbeck, and perhaps Bromfield was more fortunate than most in the effects of the search beyond literature; certainly he achieved a sense of fulfillment and justification that has eluded a great many writers considered to be more significant than he, and at the same time he also contributed to agriculture, a field vital to America and the world. (pp. 177-79)

In his accomplishments and his failure Bromfield epitomizes much that is wrong and much that is right in twentieth-century American writing. He provides a graphic example of a man who could and did write too well too easily, thus making it easy to comply with the demands of publisher and public, both of whom were insatiable for his work. He illustrates, too, the adverse effects of early commercial and critical success, both of which, while pleasing to the young writer, force him to live under the shadow of demands that not even an old professional can resist.

Most of all, Bromfield represents the typically American problem that results from the inability to reconcile the American dream with the American reality. Bromfield's commercial success enabled him to avoid the usual unpleasant results of that problem because it permitted him to escape into new areas of concentration that would absorb his romantic energy and insight; in this respect, he was far more fortunate than most American writers. But the problem is evident in the works of serious writers from Sherwood Anderson to the post-World War II group, all of whom sought futilely to transcend the gap between the world as it is and the world as they would have liked it to be.

In the final analysis Bromfield is worth reading today if only because he was willing to meet most of the major problems of his era head-on in his fiction and at the same time to attempt to explain or resolve them in terms that are at once romantic and rational. His approaches to solutions are certainly questionable in many respects, but his refusal to take refuge in easy solutions or pat answers in response to his critics is commendable. But, more importantly, Bromfield is worth reading because at his best he was very good, because he told a good story well, because he had the gift of constructing characters that are both believable and memorable; and because he was the master rather than the servant of the words that form the basis of his craft. These are not common abilities in any literary age. (p. 180)

> *David D. Anderson, in his* Louis Bromfield *(copyright © 1964 by Twayne Publishers; reprinted with the permission of Twayne Publishers, a Division of G. K. Hall & Co., Boston), Twayne, 1964, 191 p.*

DAVID D. ANDERSON   (essay date 1980)

[*In a lengthy biocritical study, Anderson examines Bromfield's dream of Jeffersonian agrarianism. He traces the unifying features of time, circumstance, and theme—the theme of defeat of agrarian idealism by industrial materialism—through Bromfield's first five novels. Several later works are also discussed.*]

[In] the fall of 1916 Bromfield entered Columbia to study journalism. (p. 65)

Before the academic year was over, America was at war; and Louis enlisted in an Army Ambulance Unit, the sooner to get overseas, where he began a love affair with France and the French that was to last the rest of his life. Behind him, too, were the experiences and ideas that were to provide the substance of his best fiction in the future: the Jeffersonian dream of agricultural self-sufficiency and the harsh reality of industrial power; the new values of the post-agricultural town; the nature of the natural aristocracy that rose above those values; the strong women who direct the course of much of human affairs; and, above all, the dehumanizing effect of industrialism as it destroyed the dream that had brought Americans across the Appalachians to open up the Ohio country. The best of his works in the remarkably productive decade between the publications of *The Green Bay Tree* in 1924 and *The Farm* in 1933 are rooted in the experience of his twenty years in Mansfield: the destruction of the dream and the determination of his people to make a new reality in a new age.

Remarkably evident in most of the works—certainly all of those that originate in the town and move to the greater world beyond—is the depth of Bromfield's conviction that the dream of Jeffersonian agrarianism was just that and no more; that his people could rise as natural aristocrats only in the world of reality; and that in that new age their success was limited. Only by adopting the values of the new industrial-material age, at the same time insuring the destruction of those of the old could their success become complete.

During this decade, Bromfield's best fiction was unified not only by time and circumstance—the uniting feature in the first four novels which he called "panel" novels—[*The Green Bay Tree, Possession, Early Autumn,* and *A Good Woman,* as well as in *The Strange Case of Miss Annie Spragg*] . . .—but also in theme: the defeat of agrarian idealism by industrial materialism and the attempt of the natural aristocrat to triumph in the new age. But in each case that triumph was elusive if not impossible: in *The Green Bay Tree* Lily Shane escapes the values of the town but finds at the end only melancholy waiting; in *Possession* Ellen Tolliver is as isolated by her music as others are by materialism; in *Early Autumn* Olivia Pentland is trapped by dead tradition; in *A Good Woman* Philip Downes finds his only escape in his own death.

With the emptiness of individual victories over materialism clear in each novel, Bromfield turned to a different manifestation of that same struggle in *The Strange Case of Miss Annie Spragg;* and in so doing he found a new symbiotic relationship by which the individual might rise above materialism: the relationship not between man and the values of his time but between man and the natural order of which he is a part but which he so seldom understands. And in so doing he returned to the eighteenth century of his intellectual origins. But it was not the eighteenth century of an agrarian utopia; it was that of a conviction that man, as part of the natural order, must learn to live according to its rules and must accept the inevitability of his own fate and that of the world and the society he creates. Conversely, that natural order was, in its fragility, susceptible to material inroads that were destructive not only of the order itself but of man as he sought to make it something other than it was.

Bromfield epitomized this destruction of the natural order in *A Modern Hero* . . . ; and he personalized its destroyer in the novel's central character, Pierre Radier, a man who rises from circus performer to industrial magnate, and who, through his partnership with the small-town financial magnate of New England origin, despoils the Midwestern countryside with his creation, Rader Motors, at the same time that he makes mockery of its human values through seduction and violence.

In spite of its melodramatic dimensions, *A Modern Hero* is one of the most important of Bromfield's works because it marks the end of his concern with the fact of the destruction and its cost in human terms. Writing the novel also taught him a lesson that he had failed to learn in the earlier novels in spite of the consistence with which his central characters were left isolated, frustrated, and unfulfilled at the end of each: that in the modern industrial, material society, the natural aristocrat could not rise, that success in terms defined by the new age could only be achieved by the Radiers and the Flints—destroyers in the guise of builders.

At that point Bromfield made two abrupt shifts in his writing and thinking. The first was that, although he accepted industrialism as the fact of modern life, he would never again use its rise or its reality as the subject of his fiction, nor would he seek ways by which he or his people could rise above it and redirect it to humanistic ends.

Furthermore, although he knew that the old agrarian values were gone forever, he determined that they—and the people who believed in and lived by them—would be the subjects of his future fiction. Neither the values nor the people could live in fact, but they could and would in his imagination. It was at this time that he began to write *The Farm* as a memorial to and a record of what had been. (pp. 65-7)

[*The Farm*] is neither fact nor fiction but a form that draws from something of both. Like Sherwood Anderson's autobiographical writings of the same period, it attempts to recreate not the facts of the past but the spirit that lies behind them. He uses what Northrop Frye has called "the only possible language of concern," that is, the language of myth, in Frye's terms, having "more to do with vision and with an imaginative response than with the kind of belief that is based on evidence and sense experience." (pp. 67-8)

In *The Farm* Bromfield used the subject matter and the people that he knew and understood best as the substance of the work. This is the story of his own family, of his great-grandfathers, both of whom had their origins in the eighteenth-century East and came across the Appalachians to the Ohio country in the early nineteenth century, bringing with them the Jeffersonian dream—actually in their day a rational plan to construct a reality by which wilderness might become agrarian order as the basis for a free, orderly society in which nature's aristocrats, persons of talent, ability, and energy, might rise to positions of leadership. The narrative of the book describes the means by which they and three generations of descendants worked to bring about that reality and were, in turn, shaped by it: the people of integrity and idealism described in his prefatory letter.

It is the story, too, of the land that those emigrants encountered and reordered to resemble and support the ideal as it became real, as the ideal and the real became one. (p. 68)

The Ohio country, as Bromfield depicted it, had been destined to become an ideological battleground, the warfare to be waged by weapons that were political and economic as well as ideological; and, in a sectional war fought for the noblest of motives, to extend the domain of human freedom in the nation, the outcome was assured. (p. 69)

Bromfield describes this transition in *The Farm* in three vivid scenes, vignettes of the same setting, a meandering stream, as seen by three generations of the farm dynasty. The first scene is that of the stream seen by the founder as it flows clear through lowlands on its way to the river. Quiet and shallow as it curves around tree covered hills, its corruption, yet invisible, has already begun. It is called Toby's Run after an Indian who had gotten drunk at the blockhouse, fallen in, and drowned.

The second vignette of the stream is that seen by the founder's son-in-law on the verge of the Civil War. The trees have disappeared from the hills and the town has spread over them. But the stream still flows free and clear, although it has just been bridged by a railroad; and cinders and gravel have begun to find their natural way down its banks.

The third vignette, that seen by the great-grandson of the founder, is at the beginning of World War I. The stream, flowing among factories and workmen's hovels, has become an open sewer carrying debris and corruption into the countryside to the river. Only its name remains unchanged to commemorate the introduction of corruption into the wilderness. . . . (p. 70)

But *The Farm* is neither the social history nor the ecological tract that this recapitulation suggests, nor is it a retelling of the story of the rise of industrialism in Ohio. *The Farm* is about people, about the apparently random quality of human life and experience, about the natural order of which human life is intrinsically a part, and about the growing awareness of a pattern of meaning that controls, reorders, and interprets the natural order and man's place in it.

Bromfield uses, in other words, the substance of this ideological warfare and the human experience that carries it on and in turn is caused by it to create a meaningful pattern that at once unifies and explains human experience in the Ohio country as it passed from wilderness, from eighteenth-century natural order, to civilization, to twentieth-century material domination. In so doing, he creates a myth of nineteenth-century Ohio, a myth of the Ohio frontier.

To do so, Bromfield uses a convenient device not unlike that used by Sherwood Anderson in *Tar: A Midwest Childhood:* the growth of a boy's awareness as he passes from youth to maturity. The central character, a member of the fourth generation of the family, the first generation to be forced off the farm and into the town through economic necessity, is a boy named Johnny Willingdon, who grows to maturity in the course of the book. Bromfield moves freely from past to present and back again as he records a hundred years of family history as the boy learns it through his growth of awareness from his earliest sense impressions—impressions of security and well-being—to the last conflict in the book, that in which he participates and which drives the family off the farm, presumably forever.

In spite of the looseness of the book's structure, it does move forward as the boy learns about the past and its relationship to his own experience. At the same time changes continue to occur in his own lifetime—in himself, in the family, in the town, and in the countryside. Finally, with the triumph of the new order complete and the farm itself about to be absorbed by the town, the boy has become a man; and he goes off into the world to seek a new meaning and a new purpose in his life.

With him, however, Johnny Willingdon carried values, attitudes, and traditions which, however unpopular or unfashionable, were to provide much of the meaning and direction of his life and the substance of his work. Johnny carried with him, in other words, the myth that Bromfield has created in the book as he reorders and interprets human experience through Johnny's growing understanding. That myth was to control Johnny's attitudes, his beliefs, and his actions in the future, as it was to control Bromfield's own future, eventually leading him back to Richland County to create what was to become *Malabar Farm* little more than five years after the book's publication.

As mythmaker, as creator of a myth of the Ohio country as it passed from wilderness to industrial empire, Bromfield created an image of an ideal society, of its origins and growth and of its decline and fall, a myth unique in Ohio and Midwestern literary history. . . . Bromfield's myth [is] the result of failure, of frustration and defeat, as are other myths of the Midwest. . . . It created, in other words, a reality for Bromfield and the others who accept it, a reality of its own against which human experience from the point of its creation to its inevitable disappearance must be weighed and measured.

Bromfield's myth is complex: it is an attitude, a way of life, a pattern of behavior, and a relationship, all of which merge in an ideal that has its own subjective reality rather than the objective reality of the world around it. Its attitude, as he comments in his preface, is based upon what he calls the American characteristics of integrity and idealism, abstractions that became real in their relationships between men and between man and nature.

Bromfield's ideal stems directly from the philosophy of Thomas Jefferson, but in *The Farm* it is transmuted into mythic reality through the unfolding of human life and experience. Its basis is Jefferson's faith in progress and in the perfectibility of man and his institutions and in the freedom and fulfillment that are possible for each human being. It is based, too, upon the growth of the farm from wilderness to self-sufficient entity, the definition of the abstraction in human terms as men and nature work in harmony to bring about a new order that emulates nature. (pp. 70-2)

In *The Farm* Bromfield had recreated the past and redefined its meaning for himself, his children, and his readers as the twentieth century began its third decade. He had recreated values and a way of life that had been lost but not destroyed and that had not yet lost their validity; and he was convinced that they never would. He had defined and articulated a philosophy that he had imbibed and used but had never before consciously formulated, and in so doing he had found for himself a new sense of intellectual and emotional stability. (p. 73)

> *David D. Anderson, "Louis Bromfield's Myth of the Ohio Frontier," in* The Old Northwest *(copyright © Miami University 1980), Vol. 6, No. 1, Spring, 1980, pp. 63-74.*

ADDITIONAL BIBLIOGRAPHY

Anderson, David D. "'Shane's Castle': Myth and Reality in Louis Bromfield's Fiction." *Northwest Ohio Quarterly* XLII, No. 4 (Fall 1970): 38-46.
> Interprets Bromfield's works as a protest against the dehumanizing factory system and industrialization, while reaffirming "older Jeffersonian and agrarian American values."

Anderson, David D. "The Search for a Living Past." In *Sherwood Anderson: Centennial Studies*, edited by Hilbert H. Campbell and Charles E. Modlin, pp. 212-23. Troy, N.Y.: Whitson Publishing Co., 1976.*
> Examination of Bromfield's place in the "Revolt from the Village" myth—a movement of Midwestern writers to reject the villages of their youth.

Bromfield, Mary. "The Writer I Live With." *The Atlantic Monthly* 186, No. 2 (August 1950): 77-9.
> Account by Bromfield's wife of his physical appearance, personality, and habits.

De Jong, David Cornell. "Louis Bromfield and a Malabar Farm Weekend." *The Carleton Miscellany* VII, No. 1 (Winter 1966): 14-27.
> Personal reminiscence of a hectic weekend spent at Bromfield's Ohio farm.

Field, Louise Maunsell. "Louis Bromfield: Novelist." *The Bookman*, New York LXXIV, No. 1 (April 1932): 43-8.
> An early survey and overview of Bromfield's career.

Geld, Ellen Bromfield. *The Heritage: A Daughter's Memories of Louis Bromfield*. New York: Harper & Brothers, 1962, 204 p.
> Noncritical biography, concentrating on the years Bromfield spent developing Malabar Farm.

Marquand, J. P. "Bromfield Omnibus." *The Saturday Review of Literature* XX, No. 25 (14 October 1939): 7.
> A generally favorable review of *It Takes All Kinds*.

"Pulitzer Awards are Made for 1926: Bromfield's *Early Autumn* and Green's *In Abraham's Bosom* Get Novel and Play Prizes." *The New York Times* (3 May 1927): 7.*
> Announcement of Bromfield's novel *Early Autumn* winning the Pulitzer prize. His other three novels to date are described briefly and some biographical facts are given.

Redman, Ben Ray. *Louis Bromfield and His Books*. New York: Frederick A. Stokes Co. Publishers, 1929, 16 p.
> An early biocritical study, sympathetic to Bromfield.

Sisto, David T. "Pérez Galdós' *Doña Perfecta* and Louis Bromfield's *A Good Woman*." *Symposium* XI, No. 2 (Fall 1957): 273-80.*
> Examines thematic and structural similarities between the two novels.

Stein, Gertrude. "After the War—1919-1932." In her *The Autobiography of Alice B. Toklas*. New York: Harcourt, Brace and Co., 1933.*
> Very briefly mentions Stein's casual acquaintance with Bromfield and describes a lunch during which Stein and Bromfield discussed gardening and discovered "they first liked each other as gardeners, then they liked each other as americans and then they liked each other as writers."

Van Gelder, Robert. "An Interview with Louis Bromfield." In his *Writers and Writing*, pp. 265-68. New York: Charles Scribner's Sons, 1946.
> Acknowledgement by Bromfield that his early novels are better received critically than later ones. Bromfield also discusses the workings of his cooperative farm, his method of devoting two hours a day to writing, and his latest novel, *Wild is the River*.

Willa Cather

1873-1947

American novelist, short story writer, essayist, journalist, and poet.

Cather combined a regional knowledge of Nebraska with an artistic expertise reminiscent of the nineteenth-century literary masters to create one of the most distinguished achievements of twentieth-century American literature. In novels such as *O Pioneers!* and *My Ántonia*, Cather portrayed the lives of Old World immigrants on the American Midwestern frontier in a manner that was at once realistic and nobly heroic. For her, the homesteading German, Danish, Bohemian, and Scandinavian settlers of that region were the embodiment of the artistic and cultural tradition she cherished. In her Nebraskan novels, courage and idealism are juxtaposed with modern materialistic values. In other works, such as *The Song of the Lark* and *Youth and the Bright Medusa*, Cather equated the spirit of the artist with that of the pioneer, and depicted these same qualities in characters such as Thea Kronberg, a "pioneer of the imagination." Cather's sensibility, her high regard for the artist and European culture, and the emphasis on technique in her later novels link her with Gustave Flaubert and Henry James, while her vision of the wasteland and her alienation from modern American society link her to the "lost generation" of Ernest Hemingway and F. Scott Fitzgerald.

Cather was born in Gore, Virginia, in 1873. When she was nine years old her family moved to Red Cloud, Nebraska. The desolate Nebraskan prairie and the diversely cultured European settlers that Cather encountered strongly engaged her youthful imagination. Years later, her early experiences were reproduced in the settings and the characters of her fiction. Specific incidents recollected from her childhood often became the basis of stories. For example, the suicide of the Bohemian violinist in her first short story, "Peter," was based on an actual occurrence. Cather attended the University of Nebraska at Lincoln, where she edited the student magazine, the *Hesperian*. In 1892 *The Mahogany Tree*, a Boston magazine, published "Peter." Encouraged by this, Cather began writing fiction on a regular basis. She also began to write drama criticism for the *Nebraska State Journal*. Youth and idealism made her critical standards high, and she could be ruthlessly outspoken in her views. In consequence her criticism soon drew her into a controversy: the Des Moines *Register* praised her for raising the standards of theatrical criticism in Lincoln, while travelling players from coast to coast labelled her "that meat ax young girl." In 1896 Cather left Red Cloud and went to Pittsburgh to work as an editor for *Home Monthly* magazine, and later for the Pittsburgh *Leader*. In Pittsburgh, Cather made the acquaintance of Isabelle McClung, the well-to-do daughter of a local judge. The two women shared an interest in the arts, and Cather was soon invited to move from her boardinghouse into the McClung mansion, where she could have the necessary quiet and leisure time to pursue more serious writing.

During this period, Cather produced her first book, *April Twilights*, a volume of poetry. Although these poems reveal a certain technical competence, critics agree that they lack originality. Most are nature lyrics fashioned too obviously after

the *Shropshire Lad* verses of A. E. Housman, whom Cather admired and whom she had met on a trip to Europe. The publication of her second book, a collection of stories entitled *The Troll Garden*, brought her to the attention of S. S. McClure, the brilliant, often eccentric editor of *McClure's Magazine*. From 1905 to 1911 Cather worked as an editor for McClure's magazine, and served as the ghostwriter of his autobiography. In 1911, spurred on by the persistent promptings of novelist Sarah Orne Jewett to give up her editorial duties and devote herself entirely to her own writing, Cather left *McClure's*, ending her journalistic career. Thereafter, until her death in 1947, fiction writing was her only occupation.

The influence of the great prose master Henry James, whom Cather considered "the perfect writer," is nowhere more apparent than in her four short story collections. Cather had studied James's style, and, in attempting to emulate his artistry, produced some of the finest short stories ever written by an American author. The themes of these collections, which were written at various stages of her career, reflect her own changing attitudes toward life and art. The stories in *The Troll Garden*, her earliest collection, deal primarily with the struggles of artists in culturally impoverished environments. Often, as in the story "The Sculptor's Funeral," this environment is the Nebraska prairie. The madness, failure, and frustration depicted in this collection reveal the mixture of fascination and fear with which Cather still contemplated Midwestern life. In *Youth and the Bright Medusa,* Cather reprinted four of the stories from *The Troll Garden,* along with four of her more recent efforts. In her newer stories she explored a more positive side of the artist's existence by examining the meaning of artistic success. The "bright Medusa" of the title refers to art—"Life's bright challenge"—and the stories portray artists who have chosen either to use art to achieve wealth and popularity or to labor toward the fulfillment of their talents. Cather's passionate idealism and her disdain for materialistic aspiration leave little doubt that, in her view, it was only perfection that should concern the true artist. Cather continued to exalt spiritual over material values in the stories of *Obscure Destinies.* Cather's posthumously published collection of short stories, entitled *The Old Beauty, and Others,* focuses on the theme of remorse and atonement for past wrongs. The doubts and regrets that Cather experienced late in life over the many sacrifices she had made for her career are echoed in the note of irrecoverable loss in these final stories.

As critics have long acknowledged, it is Cather's novels that constitute her major contribution to literature. *Alexander's Bridge,* her first novel, was highly derivative, both in its form and its sophisticated subject matter, due to her desire to write in the manner of Henry James. In subsequent works, such as *O Pioneers!* and *The Song of the Lark,* however, she returned to the Nebraska background that had provided her with the settings and characters for many of her early stories.

Cather's prose style in these novels has been universally praised by critics for its elegance, its radiance, and its almost uncanny ability to evoke an immediate image in the mind of the reader. Moreover, as Cather grew older, her style grew steadily more polished and her craftsmanship more adroit. Late novels, such as *Shadows on the Rock* and *Sapphira and the Slave Girl,* which most critics regard as seriously flawed in other ways, are nonetheless appreciated for the beauty of their prose. The thematic content of Cather's novels is identical to that of her short stories. Although she is best known as the author of "pioneer" novels such as *My Ántonia* and *O Pioneers!,* Alfred Kazin has observed that "she did not celebrate the pioneer as such; she sought his image in all creative spirits—explorers and artists, lovers and saints, who seemed to live by a purity of aspiration, an integrity of passion or skill, that represented everything that had gone out of life or had to fight a losing battle for survival in it." Cather achieved the fullest expression of this theme of struggle and triumph in her masterpiece, *My Ántonia,* which celebrates the triumph of life itself over the harshness of nature and the pettiness of small town society. In other works, such as *The Song of the Lark,* she portrayed the struggle of the artist to maintain personal integrity in a materialistic culture.

Like many other artists after World War I, Cather was disillusioned by the social and political order of the world. With the publication of *One of Ours,* for which she won the Pulitzer Prize in 1922, an underlying mood of despair entered into her novels, and a motif stressing the need to escape from contemporary life. There is little question that at this time, as Granville Hicks has said, Cather "switched from creating symbols of triumph to creating symbols of defeat." This pattern appears in such late novels as *A Lost Lady* and *The Professor's House.* It is absent in *Death Comes for the Archbishop* and *Shadows on the Rock* only because Cather's desire to retreat from the modern world led her, late in her career, to write novels about historic figures to whom she could once again

attribute heroic virtues. As she grew older, Cather also became increasingly outspoken in her social criticism. Money and property in the later novels became symbols for the overriding spirit of materialism that she saw destroying much that she valued. Some critics, including Clifton Fadiman and Granville Hicks, have condemned this change in Cather's mood as a symptom of her refusal and inability to deal with contemporary realities. Others, like Kazin, have chosen instead to see it as a dignified retreat, necessary to preserve a "rare and exquisite integrity."

Some recent critics have detected political overtones in much of the negative criticism that accompanied the appearance of Cather's last novels. They argue that Cather's blunt condemnation of materialism in such works as *A Lost Lady* and *The Professor's House* was interpreted as an endorsement of socialism in the politically sensitive decades of the 1930s and 1940s. For this reason they believe that these books may not have been assessed fairly by critics at the time of their publication, and they are now beginning to reexamine them. Cather's willingness to experiment with new forms, her technical mastery, and the superb prose style in evidence in these works have generally led today's critics to take a more positive view of them than that held by Cather's contemporaries. Cather's unique stylistic and thematic contribution to American letters and her importance as an early modernist writer are now widely recognized.

(See also *TCLC,* Vol. 1; *Contemporary Authors,* Vol. 104; *Dictionary of Literary Biography,* Vol. 9; *American Novelists, 1910-1945;* and *Dictionary of Literary Biography Documentary Series,* Vol. 1.)

PRINCIPAL WORKS

April Twilights (poetry) 1903; also published as *April Twilights, and Other Poems* [enlarged edition], 1923
The Troll Garden (short stories) 1905
Alexander's Bridge (novel) 1912
O Pioneers! (novel) 1913
The Song of the Lark (novel) 1915
My Ántonia (novel) 1918
Youth and the Bright Medusa (short stories) 1920
One of Ours (novel) 1922
A Lost Lady (novel) 1923
The Professor's House (novel) 1925
My Mortal Enemy (novel) 1926
Death Comes for the Archbishop (novel) 1927
Shadows on the Rock (novel) 1931
Obscure Destinies (short stories) 1932
Lucy Gayheart (novel) 1935
Not under Forty (essays) 1936
The Novels and Stories of Willa Cather. 13 vols. (novels and short stories) 1937-41
Sapphira and the Slave Girl (novel) 1940
The Old Beauty, and Others (short stories) 1948
On Writing: Critical Studies on Writing as an Art (essays) 1949

*This work includes a portion of the earlier *The Troll Garden.*

THE CRITIC (essay date 1905)

There is real promise in these half-dozen stories [in *The Troll Garden*]—studies, in reality, of different phases of the artistic temperament. The extremes are shown in the striking "**Sculptor's Funeral**" and in "**The Case of Paul**"—a sympathetic study of one form of sin to which "temperament" is liable. Doubtless the best of the group is the opening story—("**Flavia and Her Artists**," which is good—very good. With Flavia's type we are, alas, familiar: she is of the race of climbing, would-be social powers that prey upon genius, as intent and skilful in her chosen field as a Wall street broker on stocks or a good bird dog on the quarry. Clever, exceedingly clever in exhibiting herself clad in a kind of appliqué culture—impressions obtained at second hand, but with no more capacity for fellowship, no more community of feeling with a true artist than a hen has with a skylark. Utterly different, but pathetically true to life, is the "**Wagner Matinée.**"

Miss Cather has sincerity, and no small degree of insight. In fact when she writes her novel one may venture to predict it will be far too good to be among the "best sellers" of the month.

A review of "The Troll Garden," in The Critic, *New York, Vol. XLVII, No. 5, November, 1905, p. 476.*

FREDERIC TABER COOPER (essay date 1913)

[*An American educator, biographer, and editor, Cooper served for many years as literary critic at* The Bookman, *a popular early twentieth-century literary magazine. In the excerpt below, he criticizes Cather's* O Pioneers! *for its loose construction and its overall lack of interest. For a later interpretation of this work read the 1975 excerpt below by David Stouck.*]

[*O Pioneers!*] is a study of the struggles and privations of the foreign emigrant in the herculean task of subduing the untamed prairie land of the Far West and making it yield something more than a starvation income. Miss Cather has an unquestioned gift of observation, a keen eye for minute details and an instinctive perception of their relative significance. Every character and every incident in this slow-moving and frankly depressing tale give the impression of having been acquired directly through personal contact, and reproduced almost with the fidelity of a kodak picture or a graphonola record. And yet the net result strikes one, on second thought, as rather futile. The story opens practically at the deathbed of a middle-aged Swede, permaturely worn out with his vain struggle against inclement weather, the failure of crops and the burden of mortgages. He leaves behind him some incompetent sons and one splendid, dauntless amazon of a daughter, Alexandra, who dedicated her youth and strength and beauty to the hopeless drudgery of carrying on the task, that had slain her father. We get brief glimpses of her early blunders and discouragements; the grudging help and secret antagonism of her brothers, and the departure of her young neighbour, who, although a lad several years her junior, was the only person who gave her sympathy. Now, the story of how Alexandra fought her battle and won it might have been well worth the telling; but this is precisely the part of her history which Miss Cather has neglected to chronicle. Instead, she has passed over it in leaps and bounds, and when we once more meet Alexandra, it is in the midst of prosperity, with all her brothers save the youngest happily married, her land increased by hundreds of acres, all yielding fabulous harvests, and Alexandra herself on the threshold of her fortieth year, and, with all her success, keenly conscious of the emptiness of her life, the craving for the love of husband and of children. Of course, it requires no keen guesswork to foresee that the young neighbour of her youth will ultimately return and the discrepancy of their ages will be forgotten. But somehow the reader cannot bring himself to care keenly whether the young neighbour returns or not, whether Alexandra is eventually happy or not,—whether, indeed, the farm itself prospers or not. The conscious effort required to read to a finish is something like the voluntary pinch that you give yourself in church during an especially somnolent sermon. The book does have its one big moment; but it is due to an incident that lies outside of the main thread of the story. Alexandra's youngest brother falls in love with Marie Shabata, the wife of a big, hot-tempered Bohemian; and one night the two forget discretion and are found in the orchard by the infuriated husband, who wreaks prompt vengeance. The swift, sharp picture which follows has a touch of Maupassant in it. . . . But this incident, perfect as it is by itself, lies outside the main story, outside the history of the conquest of prairie land. And for that matter, the whole volume is loosely constructed, a series of separate scenes with so slight cohesion that a rude touch might almost be expected to shatter it. (pp. 666-67)

Frederic Taber Cooper, in his review of "O Pioneers!," in The Bookman, *New York (copyright, 1913, by George H. Doran Company), Vol. XXXVII, No. 6, August, 1913, pp. 666-67.*

H. L. MENCKEN (essay date 1920)

[*From the era of World War I until the early years of the Great Depression, Mencken was one of the most influential figures in American letters. His strongly individualistic, irreverent outlook on life and his vigorous, invective-charged writing style helped establish the iconoclastic spirit of the Jazz Age and significantly shaped the direction of American literature. In the brief review below, he considers Cather's collections of short stories* Youth and the Bright Medusa *and* The Troll Garden *and praises their author for her firm grasp of character, her ability to write with "ease and grace," and her mastery of the art of evoking the reader's feelings. For a more fully developed discussion of Cather's short stories see the excerpt below by E. K. Brown.*]

[*Youth and the Bright Medusa*] is made up of eight stories, and all of them deal with artists. It is Miss Cather's peculiar virtue that she represents the artist in terms of his own thinking—that she does not look *at* him through a peep-hole in the studio door, but looks *with* him at the life that he is so important and yet so isolated and lonely a part of. One finds in every line of her writing a sure-footed and civilized culture; it gives her an odd air of foreignness, particularly when she discusses music, which is often. Six of her eight stories deal with musicians. . . . Four others are reprinted from *The Troll Garden,* a volume first published fifteen years ago. These early stories are excellent, particularly "**The Sculptor's Funeral,**" but Miss Cather has learned a great deal since she wrote them. Her grasp upon character is firmer than it was; she writes with much more ease and grace; above all, she has mastered the delicate and difficult art of evoking the feelings. A touch of the maudlin lingers in "**Paul's Case**" and in "**A Death in the Desert.**" It is wholly absent from "**Coming, Aphrodite!**" and "**Scandal,**" as it is from *My Ántonia.* These last, indeed, show utterly competent workmanship in every line. They are stories that lift themselves completely above the level of current American fiction, even of good fiction. They are the work of a woman who, after a long apprenticeship, has got herself into the front rank of American novelists, and is still young enough to have her best writing ahead of her. I call *My Ántonia* to your attention once more. It is the finest thing of its sort ever done in America. (pp. 9-10)

H. L. Mencken, "Four Reviews: 'Youth and the Bright Medusa'" (originally published as a review of "Youth and the Bright Medusa," in The Smart Set, *Vol. LXIII, No. 4, December, 1920), in* Willa Cather and Her Critics, *edited by James Schroeter (copyright © 1967 by Cornell University; used by permission of the publisher, Cornell University Press),* Cornell University Press, *1967, pp. 9-10.*

EUNICE TIETJENS   (essay date 1923)

[*Tietjens was an American poet and long-time editor of* Poetry, *the first periodical devoted primarily to the works of new poets and to poetry criticism.*]

[*April Twilights*] is a book of poems by a great literary personality, who well deserves the Pulitzer prize—but not by a great poet.

Willa Cather is, to my thinking, one of the few authentic voices among the prose writers of today. Her novels and short stories are as sweeping and indigenous as her own western prairies, as full of hope and heart-break as the immigrants she knows so well, and as pathetically courageous as the flame of youth in city slums. Her stories are unforgettable. They etch themselves into your consciousness and you can no more escape them than you can escape your own memories. They are an integral part of this our mother country.

But Miss Cather is not at heart a poet. She is not at home in the medium. Much of herself comes through, as is inevitable since she has so much to give. The same humanity, the same sense of drama, the same directness of vision are in this book which are in her prose. And they are almost as hard to forget. Eighteen or twenty years ago I read several of these poems, two in particular, *Grandmither, think not I forget,* and *The Tavern,* and as I read them now they are as familiar as old friends.

Yet now, examining them in the cold light of later knowledge, I see that I have loved and remembered them because of the humanity, not because of the poetry. And this is not alone because they are in the manner of another day. In 1903, when this book was first published, English poetry had not undergone the cleansing and revivifying that has since come to it. Conciseness was not a virtue; rue and rosemary, minstrels and Helen of Troy were still legitimate lyric symbols. And it is inevitable that we should find them here. Yet if the form alone stood between Miss Cather and the reader accustomed to the idiom of today, the second part of the book, in which she speaks a later language, should reveal her as an authentic poet. But to me it does not.

She is simply not at home in the medium. Her thinking, for all its directness, is cramped and clouded by the song element, not released by it. (pp. 221-22)

Yet for all this, the book is welcome, for it reveals a less known phase of a great literary personality. And some of these poems, especially the earlier ones, will surely be remembered when another twenty years have added themselves to the first twenty, for their human drama and their sympathetic understanding of the stuff of life. (p. 223)

Eunice Tietjens, "Poetry by a Novelist," in Poetry *(© 1923 by The Modern Poetry Association; reprinted by permission of the Editor of* Poetry*), Vol. 22, No. 4, July, 1923, pp. 221-23.*

RENÉ RAPIN   (essay date 1930)

[*In the following excerpt, Rapin gives a lukewarm response to Cather's* The Song of the Lark, *arguing that though the novel is poorly constructed and quite sentimental it presents an excellent portrait of the western landscape and its unique characters.*]

The Song of the Lark takes us through nearly five hundred crowded pages from Thea Kronborg's early youth in Moonstone, Colorado, to her twenty-seventh year or so, the year of her first triumphs as a Wagner singer at the Metropolitan Opera.

Willa Cather has a tender spot for musicians. Of all musicians, however, operatic singers seem to interest her the most. . . . There are portraits or sketches of them in several of her works. The German Wagner singer in *One of Ours,* Kitty Ayrshire and Cressida Garnett in *Youth and the Bright Medusa.*

The Song of the Lark, the story of such a singer, is an "account of how a Moonstone girl found her way out of a vague, easy-going world into a life of disciplined endeavor." . . . (p. 27)

The Song of the Lark is only Willa Cather's second full-length novel and . . . must have presented many difficulties and problems for her which only a more experienced novelist could have solved.

The novelist's craft calls for gifts not always found together. Besides the essential gift, that of creating life, your novelist must have others. He must be able to tell a good story, to paint good portraits and landscapes, his characters and his intrigue must be such as will bear critical inspection, pass successfully the test of credibility and of truth. In Willa Cather, who has the essential gift (didn't she create such well-defined personalities as Alexandra Bergson or Thea Kronborg?), the analyst and technician were at first much inferior to the narrator and to the landscape and portrait painter. She could manage the short story (the *Troll Garden* stories and *Alexander's Bridge* are structurally perfect) but the more unwieldy novel still resisted her. (p. 40)

Willa Cather's "earlier novels seem not to have grown from a germ but to have been put together," *awkwardly* put together. Prof. Whipple's remark [see *TCLC*, Vol. 1] is true of *The Song of the Lark* as well as of its successor and its predecessor.

One can well imagine *The Song of the Lark* as having come to Willa Cather as a series of visions: Thea at Moonstone, Thea struggling in Chicago, Thea in Panther Canyon, going back to her youth and to her deeper self, Thea singing at the Metropolitan Opera, visions of inescapable clarity and truth, absolutely convincing.

Willa Cather's trouble began when she had to piece the visions together. That called for other gifts, the logician's, the analyst's. Being neither, Willa Cather went to work painfully, deserted by her inspiration, misled by sentimentality once more. To give Panther Canyon to Thea she invented Fred Ottenburg. To reward Fred Ottenburg's generosity she gave him Thea's love. But, as the vision clearly showed Thea, once the canyon episode was over, once more treading the narrow, rising path of art, Fred Ottenburg had to go, and Willa Cather concocted the absurd story we know. (p. 41)

With the canyon episode *The Song of the Lark* is practically over. There are still one hundred and fifty pages to come, it is true; Thea's departure for Germany on Dr. Archie's money, and her return to New York, seven years later, to sing at the Metropolitan Opera. Through conversations between Dr. Archie and Fred (they have become fast friends now that Dr. Archie has lost his wife, and left Moonstone and the practice of his art for Denver and business) we learn something of Thea's struggle in Germany, her mother's death and her plans and ambitions. At last we see Thea herself, in her hotel apartment and on the stage, and finally witness her triumph as an interpreter of *Fricka* and *Sieglinde.*

There are still some beautiful scenes (the scene, for example, when Thea, having come home tired and cross, is suddenly called upon to "come down and finish *Sieglinde*" . . . , the famous singer who is singing the part having broken down at the end of the first act), but *The Song of the Lark* never recovers from the falsity of the *dénouement* of the canyon episode. Willa Cather seems to have lost her sure hold of her subject and of our attention. We see less and less of Thea herself, more and more of Thea as seen by Dr. Archie and Fred Ottenburg. Her struggling days are over. We do not accompany her to Germany, and, when she comes back, her fight for recognition by the leaders of the Metropolitan Opera is as nothing in comparison with her fight against herself and against the world in her Chicago days. Then like *O Pioneers* and *My Ántonia, The Song of the Lark desinit in piscem.* Not only is the last part less interesting than the rest but the book does not even end on the powerful and beautiful scene of Thea's first great triumph. . . . A superfluous episode brings us back to Moonstone and to the grotesque figure of Thea's Aunt Tillie.

Yet of *The Song of the Lark* . . . we can say that it is a great book. A great book, and a very rich one. A masterly study, in its first three hundred pages at least, of the artistic temperament and of its building, an unforgettable evocation of the desert (page after page of the first part flashes with the hard dry colors of the Colorado desert), of the small town "set out in the sand and lightly shaded by gray-green tamarisks and cottonwoods . . . , the light-reflecting, wind-loving trees of the desert, whose roots are always seeking water and whose leaves are always talking about it, making the sound of rain" . . . , of the sheer drop of the canyon, its "great wash of air" . . . , its human memories.

There is youth in the book, its delight in itself, its adventures, its bitterness and its doubt. There is a warm sympathy for the "foreigners in our midst," the Germans, Mexicans, Hungarians, with their sensitiveness to music, the natural harmony of "their movements, their greetings, their low conversation, their smiles" . . . ; a corresponding criticism of American life with its fear of expression, its habits of hasty classification, its contempt for the simplicity and spontaneity of the Mexicans: a criticism all the more striking as it is couched in very moderate terms. There is a great, ennobling feeling of solidarity with the past, a feeling typically Willa Cather's, born of the deep, complex emotion that rises in her when she contemplates the vast Western landscape, a landscape great and awesome in itself, but made greater and more impressive to her by memory, and intense visualization, of man's passage upon it.

Then there is that gallery of living individualities grouped around the central figure—Mr. and Mrs. Kronborg and Thea's brothers and sister, Aunt Tillie, Dr. Archie, Old Wunsch, his friends the Kohlers, living a peaceful, harmonious life in the shade of the European lindens they have made to bloom in the desert,

Ray Kennedy, the Tellemantez, the Chicago Swedish pastor (he might have come straight out of *Elmer Gantry*!), Harsanyi, Bowers, Fred's Jewish friends the Nathanmeyers, people of taste and of means with an intelligent and passionate interest in the arts . . . Their milieus have the same air of reality. Characters and environment are in harmony, both stand out in striking outline, the characters, seldom analyzed, unfolding themselves in dialogue and in action.

The greatest of them, the most *nuancé,* is of course Thea herself. Though not a complex figure (Willa Cather hardly drew one until she created Prof. St. Peter), Thea has the fulness and variety of life. Like most of Willa Cather's heroes and heroines she has both beauty and strength, the beauty and strength of a healthy, full-blooded animal. No weak intellectual she. In fact she is not an intellectual at all. The world around her, the meaning of nature and of life she never grasps with her intelligence. She divines and feels. Neither very quick nor very bright, when in trouble she painfully works her way out. By sheer Scandinavian doggedness and an unperturbed concentration on the goal she has set before herself she carries her points. She never turns an obstacle, she charges at it. She makes up her mind to become an operatic singer. Neither family ties nor love must stand in her way. Once she has set her heart on something she is like a mastiff or bulldog whose jaws you cannot force open. Egotism carried so far compels admiration, it is not usually provocative of any tender emotions. Yet, as witness Ray Kennedy's, Dr. Archie's, Harsanyi's or Fred Ottenburg's experience in the book, men not only admire Thea (their weaker natures bowing to her strength), they actually love her. For Thea *is* lovable. She is lovable because she is so intensely alive, so constantly "pulsing with ardor and anticipation" . . . ; lovable also because, however ruthless her devotion to her aims, her ideal is a high one, and there is no littleness in her, only an unqualified giving of herself to the realization of the best in her; lovable because of her quick instinctive appreciation of passion and of beauty, her utter disregard of prejudice and conventions, her powerful and delicate imagination. . . . (pp. 43-6)

> *René Rapin, in his* Willa Cather *(copyright, 1930 Robert M. McBride & Company; reprinted by permission of the Literary Estate of René Rapin), McBride, 1930, 115 p.*

CLIFTON FADIMAN   (essay date 1932)

[Fadiman became one of the most prominent American literary critics during the 1930s with his often caustic and insightful book reviews for the Nation *and the* New Yorker *magazines. He also managed to reach a sizeable audience through his work as a radio talk-show host from 1938 to 1948. In the excerpt below, he severely criticizes Cather's late novels, particularly* Death Comes for the Archbishop *and* Shadows on the Rock, *for their unrealistic presentation and their failure to treat contemporary issues. For Fadiman, Cather's work has steadily retreated into an idealistic past and, therefore, has lost its credibility with the modern reader. For a similar reading of Cather's work see the excerpt below by Granville Hicks. For other, more positive interpretations of her middle and late publications see the excerpts below by Alfred Kazin, David Stouck, Paul Comeau, and Merrill M. Skaggs.]*

To classify the novels of Willa Cather is to make clear her remoteness from the problems which engaged most of her contemporaries. First there are the novels dealing with the Western pioneers of foreign birth or ancestry, and with the generation which directly followed them. Her finest works (**"O Pi-**

oneers!," the first half of "**The Song of the Lark**," "**My Ántonia**," "**A Lost Lady**," and "**Obscure Destinies**") fall roughly into this class. Then there are those less successful novelettes, influenced by Edith Wharton and Henry James: "**Alexander's Bridge**," some of the stories in "**Youth and the Bright Medusa**," "**The Professor's House**," and "**My Mortal Enemy**." Possibly in reaction to the earthy simplicities of her Western novels, these treat isolated emotional conflicts in the lives of the well-bred. Finally, we come to the two recent novels ["**Death Comes for the Archbishop**" and "**Shadows on the Rock**"]—legends would be more correct—of outright withdrawal into a kind of dream history.

These three interests bound the field of her artistic activity. Reflect upon them and it becomes clear why, in satisfying them, Willa Cather has been led farther and farther away from contemporary life, deeper and deeper into the past. There is a way of treating the past so that it links with the present and illuminates our own lives. The novels of Evelyn Scott, for example, dynamic and forward-looking, have this power. Miss Cather's mind is basically static and retrospective, rich in images of fixed contours. Her evocation of the past can be beautiful and moving, and even at its most ethereal can transport us to a world of pleasant reverie. But few will affirm that it bears any relationship to our present-day conception of history.

One recalls at once Miss Cather's West, which she has made so wholly real that many have taken it to be wholly true. It is a West filtered through a very special and selective temperament. It is not false; it is merely partial. She decks her scene with a narrow range of good people—stoical, warm-hearted peasants, Christian souls like Alexandra and Ántonia and the mild, likable Ray Kennedy. Her business men are always gentlemen. Railroading is romantic—and it *was* romantic, no doubt, except that it was also other things. Although her finest book tells the story of a servant girl, she prefers ordinarily to place her characters in comfortable middle-class surroundings. Thus "**O Pioneers!**" is not about pioneers at all, except for the first fifty (and best) pages. It deals with the second generation of prosperous farmers far removed from the sweat and toil and heartache which went into the conquest of the soil. In general, Willa Cather sees her West through a lovely haze, abstracting those qualities in people and even in landscape which lend themselves to her special idealistic bias.

Those who have studied the winning of the West in its less picturesque and Rooseveltian aspects may find little interest in Miss Cather's treatment. On the other hand, if one accepts her very special point of view, it cannot be denied that "**The Song of the Lark**" and "**My Ántonia**" are as moving today as when they were first published. No one has better commemorated the virtues of the Bohemian and Scandinavian immigrants whose enterprise and heroism won an empire. These books are safe for many years. Can one name another modern American novel whose emotional quality is so true, so warm, so human as that of "**My Ántonia**"?

Such books as these spring from their author's admiration for the quality of moral courage. But it is usually—and here too Miss Cather is at variance with her contemporaries—a moral courage acting in harmony with convention. It never takes up arms against the social order. The idealism which was so full and fruitful in "**My Ántonia**" shows its weaker side in a kind of reserve which of late has come perilously close to gentility. In part this may be due to Miss Cather's religious faith. Her allegiance limits the moral problems she may face and imposes upon her an attitude of submission. Catholicism lies quite openly

at the heart of her last two novels. They are books from which the very idea of moral conflict is excluded. Not that there is any deliberate falsification of life in them—naturally, one does not expect moral struggle to enter very intimately into the lives of archbishops and fourteen-year-old girls—but they reveal a growing tendency to select from the great array of human emotions those which do not call up conflicts that are difficult to resolve. If this tendency is indulged, Miss Cather's remarkable and precious talents may end in a cul-de-sac; and we shall have to fortify ourselves against works of piety dressed up as novels.

It is perhaps in her treatment of the relationship between men and women that this emotional caution is most clearly revealed. When . . . "**The Song of the Lark**" was published, the Victorian compromise, at least in intellectual circles, had already broken down. But its hold, probably against the author's own will, was strong in this book, and has grown stronger in her later ones. When Miss Cather tries to project a vigorous male character she is hardly convincing. Fred Ottenburg is a case in point. By an overemphasis on his feats of eating and drinking and his general physical vitality, she tries to compensate for her inability to present him as a complete male. The love relationship between Fred and Thea is faded and unreal, though the opposite effect is intended. To tell the truth, the unspoken, non-sexual, half-unconscious love between Thea and Dr. Archie is, in comparison, warmly and vividly portrayed. Relationships of this order, loves from which the body is barred, are common in Miss Cather's writings: Jim Burden and Ántonia, Dr. Archie and Thea, Captain and Mrs. Forrester, Mrs. Forrester and Neil come readily to mind. (pp. 563-64)

Miss Cather's conception of passion is broad. It includes passion for one's work, one's children, one's friends, one's land, one's memories, and for beautiful objects and experiences. But it does not extend, except formally, to sex. There is something very oblique, sparse, over-delicate about her infrequent treatments of even the slightest sexual irregularity. This is not so true of her early work—"**O Pioneers!**" for example—but it has become increasingly evident. Her most recent stories are constructed so that such matters will not naturally intrude. The love affair in "**Shadows on the Rock**" has no more substance to it than a fairy-tale romance. Though Miss Cather cannot be accused of prudery, there is unquestionably in her a strong vein of puritan reticence. In a book like "**My Ántonia**" this may be transformed into an artistic virtue. But it can also too easily degenerate, as "**Shadows on the Rock**" shows, into mere sweetness and twilight.

The characteristic quality of Willa Cather's mind, however, is not its puritanism or its idealism, but something deeper in which these are rooted. She is preeminently an artist dominated by her sense of the past, seeking constantly, through widely differing symbolisms, to recapture her childhood and youth. A sort of reverence for her own early years goes hand in hand with her Vergilian ancestor-worship; and out of this has flowered her finest work. "**My Ántonia**" is one long gesture of remembrance. The most remarkable parts of "**The Song of the Lark**" describe Thea's childhood, especially her friendships with Spanish Johnny and Ray Kennedy. Once Thea reaches Chicago, she becomes the heroine of a novel. The more she triumphs as a mature artist, the less interesting she becomes as a personality. Only at the very end, when she returns to her childhood home to sing in church, the book suddenly breaks once more into beauty and reality. "**A Lost Lady**," too, owes much of its quiet emotional power to this same Vergilian quality of reminiscence. All her books are filled with throw-backs of the memory. Give one of her characters half a chance and he will begin to recall his youth. Pierre Charron in **"Shadows on the Rock"** says: "You see, there are all those early memories; one cannot get another set; one has but those."

Although this preoccupation with the past bore fruit in two beautiful and significant novels, it has also been responsible for Miss Cather's continuous diminution of vitality since **"A Lost Lady."** For while it is the fountain of her inspiration, it may also function as a chain limiting her freedom of movement. The greatest novelists, such as Proust, draw simultaneously from both worlds, that of the remembered past and that of the fully realized present. The purely retrospective artist is faced with a simple difficulty—his material begins to lack significance unless it is constantly renewed by contact and comparison with the life about him. Soon he may find himself telling the same story over and over again. This Miss Cather has not done, though she has frequently repeated characters. But once she had fully exploited her early Western recollections, there were only two courses open. She could go forward into the present— or she could retreat even farther, call history to her aid, break contact with contemporary minds, and evoke rather than create. She has taken the latter path, one hopes not irrevocably.

Somewhere Miss Cather speaks of "the world of the mind, which for most of us is the only world." It is a perilous phrase. That world of the mind can be a small or large one, depending upon the depth and frequency of its meetings with other minds. It may be a closed world or an open world. Of recent years Willa Cather has been pensively drawing the shades and fastening the shutters. It is quite true that her prose, considered solely as an instrument, has gained in precision and a certain minor poetry of phrase; but it has lost, many feel, some of the fresh morning vigor and warmth of her earlier work. In sheer power of invention the last two novels are inferior to her earlier ones. They have fewer characters, no changes of scene, no richness. **"The Song of the Lark"** is too long, but one has an admiring sense that it could easily have been longer, that the author had all she could do to keep a rein on her imaginative faculty. But in **"Death Comes for the Archbishop"** and **"Shadows on the Rock"** there is something precious, over-calculated. The effects are somehow parsimonious. Life is gently set in a sanctuary and viewed through a stained-glass window. They are, indeed, hardly novels at all, as we understand the word, but reworked legends, acceptable additions to the lives of the saints.

No one may dictate an artist's subject matter or his point of view. His own feeling for what is vital and important, his own sensitiveness to the forces which move his fellow human beings will point the road for him. There is a very real danger that Miss Cather may, quite simply, lose contact with life. Her hypertrophied sense of the past may permanently transport her to regions where minor works of art may be created, but major ones never. And this is a sad thing to contemplate, for the author of **"My Ántonia"** and **"The Song of the Lark"** was not a minor writer, but a major one. These books will remain classic in our literature and stir the imagination of Americans when her archbishops and her shadows have long vanished from memory. (pp. 564-65)

Clifton Fadiman, "Willa Cather: The Past Recaptured," in The Nation *(copyright 1932 The Nation magazine, The Nation Associates, Inc.), Vol. CXXXV, No. 3518, December 7, 1932, pp. 563-65.*

GRANVILLE HICKS   (essay date 1933)

[*In 1934 Hicks published his famous study* The Great Tradition: An Interpretation of American Literature Since the Civil War *and quickly established himself as the foremost advocate of Marxist critical thought in America. Throughout the 1930s he argued for a more socially engaged brand of literature and severely criticized those writers, such as Henry James, Mark Twain, and Edith Wharton, who he believed failed to confront the realities of their society and, instead, took refuge in their own work. Hicks was shocked by the effects of the Great Depression and felt that events demanded a new commitment on the part of writers to clearly understand and express their times. In Marxist terms this meant that all American artists should comprehend the growth of capitalism and its negative side effects, such as war, periodic depressions, and the exploitation and alienation of the working class. Thus the question Hicks posed was always the same: to what degree did an artist come to terms with the economic conditions of the time and the social consequences of those conditions. What he sought from American literature was an extremely critical examination of the capitalist system itself and its inherently repressive nature. After 1939 Hicks sharply denounced communist ideology, which he called a "hopelessly narrow way of judging literature," and in his later years adopted a less ideological posture in critical matters. In the following excerpt, he, like Clifton Fadiman (see excerpt above), criticizes Cather's writing after* A Lost Lady *for the way it retreats into romance and the nostalgic past rather than confronting the realities of contemporary society. For a more positive account of Cather's later novels and stories see the excerpts below by Alfred Kazin, David Stouck, Paul Comeau, and Merrill M. Skaggs.*]

In her first representative book, *O Pioneers!* . . . , Miss Cather clearly indicated the subsequent development of her career. After experiments, some fortunate and some not, in the short story, and after the failure of *Alexander's Bridge,* her one book that betrays the influence of Henry James, she found her distinctive field of literary activity and her characteristic tone. *O Pioneers!* contains all the elements that, in varying proportions, were to enter into her later novels.

We observe first of all that the very basis of *O Pioneers!* is a mystical conception of the frontier. (p. 703)

Miss Cather, too, is concerned with [the] past era, and she looks back at it with nostalgia. "Optima dies. . . . prima fugit" might as well be the motto of *O Pioneers!* as of *My Ántonia.* Alexandra retains to the end the spiritual qualities of the pioneer, but the novel depicts the general disappearance of those virtues after the coming of prosperity. The coarsening of Lou and Oscar Bergson and the confusions of Frank Shabata and Emil are the fruits of change. (p. 704)

Even in little things *O Pioneers!* is prophetic. We find, for example, in her depiction of Amédée's funeral service, the same fondness for the colorful ceremonies of the Catholic church that dictated so many passages in *Death Comes for the Archbishop* and *Shadows on the Rock.* We find, also, in her scorn for the agrarian radicalism of Lou Bergson and Frank Shabata, the political conservatism that is implicit in all her works. And we find the episodic method, the reliance on unity of tone rather than firmness of structure, that is so marked in the later novels.

The two successors of *O Pioneers!*—*The Song of the Lark* and *My Ántonia*—closely resemble it, especially in the qualities we have noted. Both depend upon a mystical conception of the frontier, and both look back longingly to the heroism of earlier days. The more successful portions of *The Song of the Lark* are those portraying Thea's girlhood in Colorado and her visit to the cliff-dwellings. Both of these sections are developed at greater length than the part they play in Thea's life warrants, as if Miss Cather could not resist the temptation to expand upon her favorite theme. *My Ántonia* is exclusively concerned with the frontier, and the heroine retains the pioneer virtues in poverty and hardship, even as Alexandria and Thea do in success. All three women are triumphant products of the pioneering era; in them the mystical essence of a heroic age, now unfortunately passing, is embodied.

But if these three novels were merely mystical and nostalgic we should have less to say about them. After all, Miss Cather saw at first hand the Nebraska of the eighties and nineties, and her accounts of the life there are not without authenticity. However much she emphasizes the heroism and piety of the pioneers, she does not neglect the hardships and sacrifices. And heroism and piety did play their part in the conquest of the frontier. Miss Cather's proportions may be false; she may ignore motives, conditions, and forces that are altogether relevant; but there is nevertheless a basis in reality for the picture she gives.

That is why *O Pioneers!* and *My Ántonia* have their importance in American literature. Although the story of *My Ántonia* is told by Jim Burden, with his concern for "the precious, the incommunicable past," the book does create credible pioneers in the Burdens and Shimerdas and does give convincing details of their life. In the latter part of the book there is a passage in which several daughters of immigrants tell of their homes in the first years in Nebraska, and we realize that Miss Cather can appreciate the bleakness and cruelty of this land for the travelers from across the sea. She can understand their eagerness to escape to the towns, and she knows, too, the monotony and narrowness of the prairie city.

Against this background Miss Cather presents the unforgettable picture of Ántonia, more human than Alexandra because of her weaknesses, more likeable because of her defeats. (pp. 704-05)

From the first, it is clear, the one theme that seemed to Miss Cather worth writing about was heroic idealism, the joyous struggle against nature sustained by a confidence in the ultimate beneficence of that nature against which it fought. In her own childhood she had actually seen such heroic idealism in the lives of Nebraskan pioneers, and in writing of those lives she achieved not only personal satisfaction but also fundamental truth. One may feel that she deals with the unusual rather than the representative, and that what she omits is more important than what she includes. One may be conscious that the haze of regretful retrospection distorts innumerable details. But one cannot deny that here is a beautiful and, as far as it goes, faithful re-creation of certain elements in the pioneering experience.

But after *My Ántonia* was written there came a crisis in Miss Cather's career as an artist. She obviously could not go on, painting again and again the Nebraska she had once known. The West was changing, as she had been forced to admit in *O Pioneers!* and the others. Could she learn to depict the new West as she had depicted the old? The story of this new West could scarcely take the form of a simple, poetic idyll. Heroism and romance, if they existed, had changed their appearance. Characters could no longer be isolated from the social movements that were shaping the destiny of the nation and of the world. She would have to recognize that the life she loved was disappearing. Could she become the chronicler of the life that was taking its place?

At first she tried. The earlier chapters of *One of Ours* describe a sensitive Nebraskan boy in the years before the war. Claude Wheeler, who as a youth flinches before the coarseness and materialism of his father, suffers almost as much from the narrow religiosity of his wife. The joy and beauty that are so prominent in the lives of Alexandra and Ántonia have vanished from Claude's Nebraska. Though he seems capable of a heroic idealism, his life is miserable and futile. Then the war comes, and he enlists, goes forth to battle in heroic mood, and dies a hero's death. Thus Miss Cather, thanks to a romantic and naïve conception of the war, was able to approximate her favorite theme. But the second part bears no relation to the issues raised in the account of Claude's unhappiness in Nebraska. For Miss Cather, as for Claude, the war provides an escape from apparently insoluble problems.

Insoluble indeed, Miss Cather found these problems, and as she looked at the life about her, her despair grew. Once she had created symbols of triumph in Alexandra, Thea, and Ántonia, but now she concerned herself with symbols of defeat. Of all the books between *My Ántonia* and *Death Comes for the Archbishop*, *A Lost Lady* is the most moving. Why Marian Forrester is lost Miss Cather never explains, contenting herself with a delicate and pathetic record of that descent. Captain Forrester has in him the stuff of the pioneers, but his wife, though one feels in her capacities for heroism, is the product of changed times, and she abandons her standards, betrays her friends, and encourages mediocrity and grossness. She is the symbol of the corruption that had overtaken the age.

But *A Lost Lady* is merely a character study, and Miss Cather felt the need for a more comprehensive record of the phenomena of decay. St. Peter in *The Professor's House* is alienated from his wife and family; he has finished the work that has been absorbing him; he realizes that he must learn to live "without delight, without joy, without passionate griefs." That, Miss Cather seemed to feel at the moment, was what we all must learn. Heroism and beauty and joy had gone. For St. Peter these qualities had been summed up in Tom Outland, dead when the story opens, and perhaps fortunately dead: "St. Peter sometimes wondered what would have happened to him, once the trap of worldly success had been sprung on him." But Tom lives in St. Peter's memory, and his story occupies much of the book. Tom is the pioneer, vital, determined, joyful, sensitive to beauty. In telling his story Miss Cather escapes from her gloom and writes with the vigor and tenderness of her earlier work. But in the end the animation of the Outland narrative only serves to accentuate her melancholy, and she is left, like Professor St. Peter, in a drab and meaningless world. (pp. 705-07)

Her despair increased, and Miss Cather made one more study of defeat, in *My Mortal Enemy*. But obviously she could not continue with these novels of frustration and hopelessness. One may risk the guess that, while she was writing her studies of despair, she personally was not particularly unhappy. Her reputation and income were both established on a reasonably high level. As a person she could be as contented as anyone else who enjoyed comfort and security, and as indifferent to the woes of the world. But as a writer she had that world as a subject, and the contemplation of it filled her with sadness and regret. It was not a world in which her imagination could be at ease, for her imagination still demanded the heroic idealism of the frontier. She could deal with that world only by portraying, in a few tragic lives, the corruption and defeat of what she held dear. She could not understand why evil had triumphed or how good might be made to prevail. All she could express was her conviction that something of inestimable value had been lost. (pp. 707-08)

Miss Cather has never once tried to see contemporary life as it is; she sees only that it lacks what the past, at least in her idealization of it, had. Thus she has been barred from the task that has occupied most of the world's great artists, the expression of what is central and fundamental in her own age. It was easy for her, therefore, to make the transition from *My Mortal Enemy* to *Death Comes for the Archbishop*. If she could not write as she chose about her own time, she could find a period that gave her what she wanted. The beauty and heroism that she had found in pioneer Nebraska and that seemed so difficult to find in modern life could certainly be attributed to life in mid-nineteenth century New Mexico. And thence she could turn, in *Shadows on the Rock,* to Quebec about 1700. Once more she could show men and women who were neither awed by the savageness of nature nor unappreciative of its beauty. Once more she could deal with "the bright incidents, slight, perhaps, but precious," that are to be found whenever "an adventurer carries his gods with him into a remote and savage country."

Death Comes for the Archbishop, which describes the life of two Catholic missionaries in the Southwest, is highly episodic, and the episodes are so chosen as to make the most of the colorfulness of the country, the heroism of the characters, and the contrast between the crudeness of the frontier and the religious and cultural refinement of the archbishop. As one reads, one seems to be looking at various scenes in a tapestry, rich in material and artful in design. At first one is charmed, but soon questions arise. One asks what unity there is in these various episodes, and one can find none except in Miss Cather's sense that here, in the meeting of old and new, is a process of rare beauty. What significance, one goes on to inquire, has this beauty for us? Does it touch our lives? Is this really the past out of which the present sprang? Did these men and women ever live? Is there anything in their lives to enable us better to understand our own? We ask these questions, and as we try to answer them we realize that we are confronted by the romantic spirit. Miss Cather, we see, has simply projected her own desires into the past: her longing for heroism, her admiration for natural beauty, her desire—intensified by pre-occupation with doubt and despair—for the security of an unquestioned faith.

What is true of *Death Comes for the Archbishop* is also true of *Shadows on the Rock.* Miss Cather has again created her ideal frontier and peopled it with figments of her imagination. The construction is even weaker, the events even more trivial, the style even more elegiac, the characters even less credible. The book has a certain sort of charm, for Miss Cather's dreams have beauty and are not without nobility, and it has brought consolation to many readers who share her unwillingness to face the harshness of our world. But for the reader who is not seeking an opiate *Shadows on the Rock* has little to offer. Compare Cécile with Alexandra and Ántonia; compare Pierre Charron with Tom Outland. What Miss Cather chiefly tries to do is to throw over her Quebec the golden hazen of romance, and she succeeds so well that her characters are, to the reader's vision, obscured and distorted almost beyond recognition.

Apparently it makes little difference what Miss Cather now attempts to do. The three stories in *Obscure Destinies* are more or less reminiscent of her earlier work, but the honesty and enthusiasm have disappeared. As if she were conscious of some

lack, she finds it necessary to rely on direct statements. In **"Neighbour Rosicky"** she underlines the harshness and rapacity of the city and exaggerates the security of the country, and she introduces Doctor Ed to point the moral of the tale: "Rosicky's life seemed to him complete and beautiful." **"Old Mrs. Harris"** is so lacking in unity that its point has to be explained in the closing paragraph: "When they are old, they will come closer and closer to Grandma Harris. They will think a great deal about her, and remember things they never noticed; and their lot will be more or less like hers." **"Two Friends,"** concerned with two "successful, large-minded men who had made their way in the world when business was still a personal adventure," teaches that politics is much less important than friendship. Twenty years ago Miss Cather had no need of exposition, for her themes were implicit in her material, but now her romantic dreams involve the distortion of life, and she cannot permit the material to speak for itself.

The case against Willa Cather is, quite simply, that she made the wrong choice. The nostalgic, romantic elements so apparent in her recent work were present in her earlier novels, but they were at least partly justified by the nature of her themes, and they could be introduced without the sacrifice of honesty. But once she had to abandon the material her Nebraskan childhood had so fortunately given her, she had to make her choice. She tried, it is true, to study the life that had developed out of the life of the frontier, but she took essentially marginal examples of modern life, symbolic of her own distaste rather than representative of significant tendencies. And when time had shown how certainly that path would lead to impotence and ultimately to silence, she frankly abandoned her efforts and surrendered to the longing for the safe and romantic past. (pp. 708-10)

If, to the qualities Miss Cather displayed in *O Pioneers!* and *My Ántonia,* had been added the robustness of a Dreiser or the persistence of an Anderson, not only survival but growth would have been possible. But the sheltered life seldom nurtures such qualities. She has preferred the calm security of her dreams, and she has paid the price. (p. 710)

Granville Hicks, "The Case against Willa Cather," (copyright © 1933 by the National Council of Teachers of English; renewed 1961 by Granville Hicks; reprinted by permission of the publisher and Russell & Volkening, Inc. as agents for the author), in En-glish Journal, Vol. 22, No. 9, November, 1933, pp. 703-10.

ALFRED KAZIN   (essay date 1942)

[*A highly respected American literary critic, Kazin is best known for his essay collections,* The Inmost Leaf *(1955) and* Contemporaries *(1962), and particularly for* On Native Grounds *(1942), a study of American prose writing since the era of William Dean Howells. Having studied the works of "the critics who were the best writers—from Sainte-Beuve and Matthew Arnold to Edmund Wilson and Van Wyck Brooks" as an aid to his own critical understanding, Kazin has found that "criticism focussed many—if by no means all—of my own urges as a writer: to show literature as a deed in human history, and to find in each writer the uniqueness of the gift, of the essential vision, through which I hoped to penetrate into the mystery and sacredness of the individual soul." In the excerpt below, he considers Cather's middle novels* A Lost Lady *and* The Professor's House *two successful portraits of the "physical and moral destruction" of the pioneer tradition Cather so admired. Unlike Granville Hicks (see excerpt above)—who sees Cather's middle stories as uninspired "symbols of defeat"—Kazin calls* The Professor's House *"the most persistently under-*

rated'' of her novels, and in general considers her middle period a time when Cather consummately, and even ironically, captured the passing of a great and novel age in American history. Kazin even goes so far as to exonerate Cather for her "romantic submission to the past" by concluding that she fought a losing battle which "no one of her spirit could hope to win." See the excerpt above by Clifton Fadiman for additional discussion of this matter.]

The climax in Willa Cather's career came with two short novels she published between 1923 and 1925, *A Lost Lady* and *The Professor's House*. They were parables of the decline and fall of the great tradition, her own great tradition; and they were both so serenely and artfully written that they suggested that she could at last commemorate it quietly and even a little ironically. The primary values had gone, if not the bitterness she felt at their going; but where she had once written with a naïvely surging affection, or a rankling irritation, she now possessed a cultivated irony, a consummate poise, that could express regret without rancor or the sense of irretrievable loss without anguish. She had, in a sense, finally resigned herself to the physical and moral destruction of her ideal in the modern world, but only because she was soon to turn her back on that world entirely in novels like *Death Comes for the Archbishop* and *Shadows on the Rock*. In the person of a Captain Forrester dreaming railroads across the prairies, of a Godfrey St. Peter welding his whole spirit into a magnificent history of the Spanish explorers in America, she recaptured the enduring qualities she loved in terms of the world she had at last been forced to accept. These were the last of her pioneers, the last of her great failures; and the story she was now to tell was how they, like all their line, would go down in defeat before commerce and family ties and human pettiness. (pp. 253-54)

The theme [of *A Lost Lady*] was corruption, as it was to be the theme of *The Professor's House*. It was as explicit as Marian Forrester's dependence on her husband's frontier strength and integrity, as brutal as Ivy Peters's acquisition of Marian Forrester herself. And at the very moment that Willa Cather recognized that corruption in all its social implications gave its name and source, she resigned herself to it. It had been her distinction from the first to lament what others had never missed; she now became frankly the elegist of the defeated, the Amiel of the novel. The conflict between grandeur and meanness, ardor and greed, was more than ever before the great interest of her mind; but where she had once propounded that conflict, she now saw nothing but failure in it and submitted her art almost rejoicingly to the subtle exploration of failure. In any other novelist this would have made for sickliness and preciosity; now that she was no longer afraid of failure as a spiritual fact, or restive under it, her work gained a new strength and an almost radiant craftsmanship.

The significance of this new phase in Willa Cather's work is best seen in *The Professor's House*, which has been the most persistently underrated of her novels. Actually it is one of those imperfect and ambitious works whose very imperfections illuminate the quality of an imagination. The story of Godfrey St. Peter is at once the barest and the most elaborately symbolic version of the story of heroic failure she told over and over again, the keenest in insight and the most hauntingly suggestive. The violence with which she broke the book in half to tell the long and discursive narrative of Tom Outland's boyhood in the Southwest was a technical mistake that has damned the book, but the work as a whole is the most brilliant statement of her endeavor as an artist. For St. Peter is at once the archetype of all her characters and the embodiment of her own beliefs. He is not merely the scholar as artist, the son of pioneer

parents who has carried the pioneer passion into the world of art and thought; he is what Willa Cather herself has always been or hoped to be—a pioneer in mind, a Catholic by instinct, French by inclination, a spiritual aristocrat with democratic manners.

The tragedy of St. Peter, though it seems nothing more than a domestic tragedy, is thus the most signal and illuminating of all Willa Cather's tragedies. The enemy she saw in Ivy Peters— the new trading, grasping class—has here stolen into St. Peter's home; it is reflected in the vulgar ambition of his wife and eldest daughter, the lucrative commercial use his son-in-law has made of the invention Tom Outland had developed in scholarly research, the genteel but acquisitive people around him. St. Peter's own passion, so pure and subtle a pioneer passion, had been for the life of the mind. In the long and exhaustive research for his great history, in the writing of it in the attic of his old house, he had known something of the physical exultation that had gone into the explorations he described. . . . Now, after twenty years of toil, that history was finished; the money he had won for it had gone into the making of a new and pretentious house. The great creative phase of his life was over. To hold onto the last symbol of his endeavor, St. Peter determined to retain his old house against the shocked protests of his family. It was a pathetic symbol, but he needed some last refuge in a world wearing him out by slow attrition.

In this light the long middle section of the novel, describing Tom Outland's boyhood in the desert, is not a curious interlude in the novel; it becomes the parable of St. Peter's own longing for that remote world of the Southwest which he had described so triumphantly in his book. Willa Cather, too, was moving toward the South, as all her books do: always toward the more primitive in nature and the more traditional in belief. Tom Outland's desert life was thus the ultimate symbol of a forgotten freedom and harmony that could be realized only by a frank and even romantic submission to the past, to the Catholic order and doctrine, and the deserts of California and New Mexico in which the two priests of *Death Comes for the Archbishop* lived with such quiet and radiant perfection. Her characters no longer had to submit to failure; they lived in a charming and almost antediluvian world of their own. They had withdrawn, as Willa Cather now withdrew; and if her world became increasingly recollective and abstract, it was because she had fought a losing battle that no one of her spirit could hope to win. It was a long way from the Catholic Bohemian farmers of Nebraska to the eighteenth-century Catholicism of the Southwest, but she had made her choice, and she accepted it with an almost haughty serenity. . . . It was now but a step from the colonial New Mexico of *Death Comes for the Archbishop* to old Quebec in *Shadows on the Rock* and the lavender and old lace of *Lucy Gayheart*. Her secession was complete. (pp. 254-57)

Alfred Kazin, "Elegy and Satire: Willa Cather and Ellen Glasgow," in his On Native Grounds: An Interpretation of Modern American Prose Literature *(copyright 1942, 1970 by Alfred Kazin; reprinted by permission of Harcourt Brace Jovanovich, Inc.),* Reynal & Hitchcock, 1942, pp. 247-64.*

E. K. BROWN (essay date 1953)

[*Brown's* Willa Cather: A Critical Biography *is an important study of Cather's life and work. In the following excerpt from that book, Brown discusses her short stories, suggesting Henry James's influence on her first collection,* The Troll Garden, *and focusing on Cather's correspondences between the artist and the western pioneer. For a more detailed discussion of James's influence on Cather's work see the excerpt below by Edward A. Bloom and Lillian D. Bloom.*]

[Cather's] first book in prose [*The Troll Garden*] contained two groups of stories. Three of the stories, the first, the third, and the fifth, present artists in relation with persons of great wealth. Alternating with these sophisticated tales is another series, comprising the second, fourth, and sixth stories, in which an artist or a person of artistic temperament from the prairies returns to them in defeat. The collection closes with **"Paul's Case,"** the story of a sensitive Pittsburgh youth, for which there is a subtitle: "A Study in Temperament." (p. 113)

Willa Cather was under the spell of Henry James at this time and quite possibly was struck by the manner in which he always arranged his short-story collections thematically. If one were to seek a parallel to **The Troll Garden** in James, it is to be found in his volume *The Two Magics* . . . , in which he juxtaposed a tale of black magic ("The Turn of the Screw") with what might be considered a tale of white magic ("Covering End")—the one baleful, filled with suggestions of nightmare and evil, the other bright, sunny, cheerful, fairy-tale-like in substance and denouement. So Willa Cather's two strands in **The Troll Garden** are the baleful and the sunny, the evil-working goblins and the industrious trolls. Her stories of artists creating "things rare and strange" amid the wealthy belong to the trolls and to that "fairy garden". . . . The fairy palace and the fairy garden are the preserves of art; and the trolls are artists or persons with artistic temperament. In each of the stories the trolls come into relation, and usually into conflict, with those who live outside the preserves of art or trespass upon them. The tales of the defeated artists from the prairies are tales filled with an undercurrent of malaise and a sense of nightmare: those who venture into the goblin market, that great and exciting yet treacherous world beyond the prairies, risk eating of the poisoned fruit. The goblins will "get them"—if they don't look out! The sensuous fruits of life and of luxury can be tainted with evil. Success somehow exacts an ominous price. There is always the danger of having to retrace one's steps, back, back into the open stretches. This is the equivalent of death: the stony death that lies in the deceptive stare of the Bright Medusa. The attitude toward the aspect of the prairies, toward the people who live on them and form the ideas that prevail there, is still hard.

The first of the three tales of the "troll" series, **"Flavia and Her Artists,"** is the story of the wife of a manufacturer of threshing machines. Lacking any aesthetic responses, and unaware of her lack, she collects artists and intellectuals so that from the phrases she forces from them she can make an appearance of cleverness before the rest of the world. An ironic story might have been written about Flavia's parasitic relation with her artists; and that story is in fact here, but entangled with much else. It is entangled, for instance, with the presentation of her artists—some of them persons of the first rank in performance—as sorry, stunted human beings. The crux of the story comes when a French novelist, just after he leaves the house-party, gives an interview in which Flavia's type is ridiculed; everyone who remains, except Flavia, sees the report of the interview; and her loyal husband, believing that what Monsieur Roux has said the rest of the artists think, rebukes them at his own table. . . . An ironic story might have been written also about the chasm between the artist's devotion to beauty and what is sordid and trivial in the rest of his life; there are fragments of that story here, in the crude manners of

one, the simper of another, the "malicious vulgarities" of a third; but only fragments, for just where this story required definition and elaboration, in the rendering of Roux, it evaporates. There does not seem to be anything wrong with Roux except that he is candid where the laws of hospitality require silence or a lie. The center shifts from Flavia to her artists and then to her husband, not with development, but only with vacillation.

The second in the series, **"The Garden Lodge,"** is essentially a record of an inner conflict. Caroline Noble questions whether the practical stodgy life she lives in reaction against the fecklessness of her musician father and painter brother is not a negation of life. In the rendering of Caroline's bitter, anxious mood one can feel not only Willa Cather's personal sense of the value for one's life of devotion to art, but no less, and for the first time in her writing, a sense that sustained labor, when forced upon one by ambition and determination and directed toward a nonartistic goal, threatens the very core of personality. This was an opinion that Sarah Orne Jewett was soon to preach to her; her own experience was already leading her to feel its force.

The third and most Jamesian of the tales, **"The Marriage of Phaedra,"** tells of an artist's visit to the studio of a fellow artist after his death and his discovering there an unfinished masterpiece. . . . The story is filled with Jamesian echoes, and notably of those of his tales of artists and writers which appeared during the 1890's. As in **"Flavia,"** the author writes from a recent superficial absorption of the material. The process Stephen Crane described, the "filtering through the blood," had not occurred, had not begun to occur.

From the group, the work of an author who had been thinking about the arts more than about anything else for fifteen years, it is unexpectedly difficult to derive any theory, any general idea. Artists do not often appear practicing their art, or theorizing about it, and never do they attempt either theory or practice at length; they appear in their relations with others, usually either with nonartistic persons or with persons who are merely appreciative. One may safely derive the idea that artists are crucially unlike other beings; Roux's discourtesy is an outcome of his radical honesty, his need to tell the truth whatever may fall; Treffinger loved his wife, but he sacrificed her as he sacrificed everything else that threatened his art; the emphasis on the unlikeness of the artist runs through all the stories. The unlikeness often brings havoc into the lives of those who surround the artist. The emphasis on the enriching force of an artist's personality also runs through the stories, and Willa Cather has made no attempt to weigh the havoc and the enrichment in the balance: she is content to suggest that both are real, both weighty.

The most promising source for a general idea about art is **"The Marriage of Phaedra,"** for here one artist is seeking to unravel the artistic method as well as the personality of another. The narrator discovers that Treffinger was guided toward his method and the range of his subjects by an older painter from whom he learned as much as an artist of genius can learn from anyone; in order to paint his masterpiece he needed to add to what he had learned the fruit of painful intimate experience. The clue to Treffinger's greatness as an artist is in the fusion of experience with instruction. Simple as this formula may be, it is not superficial. It applies generally to Willa Cather's writing— to the few promising pieces she had done before **"The Marriage of Phaedra"** and to the works she was to do.

The stories in which art and the prairies are brought together were of quite another sort, as Willa Cather herself recognized when she reincorporated them into *Youth and the Bright Medusa*. These stories arise from old memories, they have the richness that long preoccupation can give. They have been filtered through the blood. In **"A Wagner Matinée"** the deep source is in Willa Cather's brooding over the life of an aunt for whom the years on a farm in Webster County were a form of slow suffocation to which she was almost inhumanly resigned; in **"The Sculptor's Funeral"** the source is in her sense of her own differentness, vulnerability, and value during her years in Red Cloud. The incidents scarcely matter, and there is no contrivance in the arrangement of them: the stories take their life and also their shape from the force and fineness of the feelings poured into them. The quality that animated those passages in **"The Garden Lodge"** where the theme is the woman's feelings about the crucial and irremediable mistake in her management of her life sweeps through **"A Wagner Matinée"** and **"The Sculptor's Funeral."** For **"A Death in the Desert"**— the title derived from Browning—one cannot say the same. It is like the other two stories about art and the prairies in the rendering of the foreground; but in the background is the world of **"Flavia and Her Artists,"** evoked as the dying singer and the brother of the great composer she has loved talk away her last afternoons in the Colorado summer, with the same chasm between the artist's devotion to beauty and what is ugly and small in his personal life. The fall in force from the scenes in the foreground to those in the background is always palpable. Only in the rendering of the Western elements is there an effect of moving authenticity or of depth.

In a very direct manner these tales are saying what Thomas Wolfe expressed more crudely as "you can't go home again." An image of "home" creates the tense and emotional climax of **"A Wagner Matinée."** . . . The burden of **"The Sculptor's Funeral"** is that even in death the artist cannot escape the harshness and hostility of his home surroundings where he is fated to be remembered as "queer" because he never conformed, and because he fled to unfamiliar worlds undreamed of by his family and friends. (pp. 114-20)

Although different in setting and material, **"Paul's Case"** is of a piece with these tales. It has been the most widely read of Willa Cather's short stories; for many years it was the only one she would allow to be reprinted in anthologies or textbooks. A surprising number of the aspects in her experience of Pittsburgh are gathered into **"Paul's Case."** Paul is a student at the Pittsburgh high school; and in the early scenes the life of the school is given in classroom vignettes and in one long disciplinary incident in which the boy is under attack from principal and staff. The neighborhood where Paul lives has the petty-bourgeois dreariness that Willa Cather had resented during her years of boarding-house living: the ugly dirty plumbing, the kitchen odors, the unbuttoned laziness of Sunday afternoons, the everlasting sameness from house to house and street to street. . . . From the routines of home and school Paul's regular escape is to the symphonies and pictures in Carnegie Hall; and for him the great "portal of romance" is, as it was for Willa Cather, the stage entrance to the downtown theater where a stock company plays. The doors to the Schenley Hotel . . . make another such portal: Paul is drawn to them not only because they are the approach to luxury but because the singers and actors with whom he identifies himself are always passing through them. Like Willa Cather and so many others who lived in Pittsburgh, he felt the pull of New York, the wish to exchange Carnegie Hall for the Metropolitan Opera, the Schenley

for the Waldorf, to feel himself in the center of "the plot of all dramas, the text of all romances, the nerve-stuff of all sensations."

The first half of the story describes Paul amid his circumstances in Pittsburgh, the second his yielding to the pull of New York, stealing a thousand dollars from his employers, buying everything one should have to mingle with the millionaires, and after his few days at the Waldorf carrying out the last phase of his plan by taking his life. In the end Paul too can't go home again; he has burned his bridges and has no wish to rebuild them. The Pittsburgh scenes are vivid beyond anything in the series of sophisticated stories, with sharp strokes from experience both of outer objects and of personal states, never multiplied in excess of what the effects demand. New York is drawn in a contrasting manner, for which there is not a parallel in any of the other stories, as a dream city, snow-covered, with a beautiful thick impressionistic haziness that suits the setting for the dreamlike climax of Paul's life. (pp. 121-22)

> *E. K. Brown, "Troll Garden, Goblin Market (1902-1905)," in his* Willa Cather: A Critical Biography, *edited by Leon Edel (copyright 1953 by Margaret Brown; reprinted by permission of Alfred A. Knopf, Inc.), Knopf, 1953, 351 p.*

JOHN H. RANDALL III (essay date 1960)

[In the excerpt below, Randall calls A Lost Lady *one of Cather's best works and attempts to demonstrate how the novel works effectively on two different levels, one literal, the other symbolic. Literally, the novel simply relates the story of a woman's demise following the death of her husband; symbolically, it tells the story of the disappearance of the pioneer spirit and its replacement by the spirit of commerce and materialism.]*

From *One of Ours* through *My Mortal Enemy* Willa Cather's protagonists become increasingly preoccupied with one problem: how to lead the comely life in the modern world. They endeavor to engage in the search for the comely life and become more and more frustrated in this by the very nature of modern times; in particular by the triumph of commerce, which she sees as identical with institutionalized greed. In a society grounded upon organized hoggishness, she seems to be saying, there is no place for the cult of beauty. And since she holds beauty to be the highest good there is, once she becomes convinced that the comely life cannot be lived in the modern world, she turns against that world. Rejection of the present becomes for her an act of virtue.

This is clearly seen in [*A Lost Lady*]. . . . It has for its heroine a lovely woman who can exert her charms only in a society which recognizes her worth. That society is represented as passing away with the death of her husband and the approaching old age and helplessness of his friends. Marian Forrester does not herself turn against the present—this is why she is lost— but Willa Cather makes it perfectly clear that it would have been much better if she had. Thus the revulsion against the modern world which was implicit in the ending of the previous novel [*One of Ours*] becomes explicit in this one.

A Lost Lady is one of Willa Cather's best novels and is central to her thought. In compact prose and in the brief space of 174 pages she manages to present as much as she ever could of what she felt to be the nature of life and the meaning of civilization, as well as give her interpretation of the history of an epoch. The book is an excellent example of that kind of writing which is at the same time realistic and highly symbolic; the story runs along perfectly credibly on the literal level and yet every incident and almost every spoken word stands for more than itself and tells another tale. What Willa Cather has done is to present the story on two different levels, and much of the artistic beauty of the work comes from the fact that in large measure the two are united, that action and significance, symbol and meaning, are one.

On the literal level the story is about the decay of Marian Forrester, a charming lady, after a crippling accident has made an invalid of her once powerful husband, the Captain. On the symbolic level Willa Cather was writing social allegory expressing her view on the significance of the history of the West. To her mind this history was no less than that of the creation and destruction of a civilization. *O Pioneers!* and *My Ántonia* had centered on the problems of founding and consolidating a civilization. In *A Lost Lady* the cycle is completed. It shows the decay of the pioneer spirit and its replacement by the spirit of commerce, the decline of the broad imaginative vision that created the West and the substitution for it of the narrow goal of petty self-aggrandizement. The two opposing principles are identified with successive generations and are embodied in the contrasting figures of Captain Forrester, the aging and crippled railroad builder, and the shrewd young shyster lawyer, Ivy Peters.

The fact that she is writing social allegory does not detract in the slightest from Willa Cather's fascination with her heroine. . . . The disintegration of her personality under the influence of Ivy Peters and his generation is but another fictional portrayal of the suffering inflicted on the creative spirit at the hands of a petty commercial Philistinism which has been presented to us so often in the European and American literature of the last one hundred and twenty years. Marian Forrester, pining for the fashionable life of the winter hotels at Denver and Colorado Springs but forced by the Captain's infirmity to spend the remaining years of her youth in a small Nebraska town, first takes lovers, then alcohol, and finally bogs down in a mass of debt which involves her with the town's most unsavory character, Ivy Peters. On this level Mrs. Forrester is a Middle Western Madame Bovary, although her troubles do not drive her to suicide. (After the Captain's death she manages to escape to Argentina.) Willa Cather and Flaubert present the same picture of a soul thirsting for beauty set down in a bourgeois world filled with ugliness and incapable of coping with it; she lavishes the same meticulous care on Marian that Flaubert did on Emma. Both authors manage to make their characters very appealing while still maintaining a certain aesthetic distance from them (something of Keats's negative capability applies here since both heroines are treated sympathetically but without sentimentality). After reading *A Lost Lady* one is not at all surprised to find that one of Willa Cather's favorite novels was *Madame Bovary*.

The social allegory in the novel is deliberately made apparent from the very first page. Briefly, the Lost Lady represents civilization in the West, for all the amenities of gracious living which can make life the agreeable and charming thing which at best it can be. Her husband, the Captain, is a pioneer railroad builder. . . . He embodies all the virtues which Willa Cather has led us to expect in a pioneer: the imagination to see, the strength to achieve, and an absolutely incorruptible moral integrity. Willa Cather is saying that only when civilization is wedded to moral values can it amount to anything more than a beautiful parasitic growth. But Marian Forrester's union with the Captain is threatened by forces from without and within.

Not only does the change in civilization threaten the moral values on which the marriage is based, but the deterioration of Mrs. Forrester's character imperils the union and also reflects the social disintegration brought about by the rising tides of commerce. (pp. 174-77)

In spite of her spiritual estrangement from post-World War I America, Willa Cather found herself in agreement with the new literary generation on at least one important point. This was in her sense of malaise and dislocation, the feeling that modern man had somehow lost his bearings and must try desperately to find them again. Like many of her younger contemporaries, she felt that the pursuit of value was all but impossible in a commercial world and could be engaged in only by flying in the face of that world. In *A Lost Lady* the corrupting factor is money. Money, although seldom mentioned, presides over the entire action and makes its power felt upon almost every page. It is the Captain's old-fashioned notions about financial integrity that lead not only to his own downfall but to his wife's as well. His determination to remain heroically solvent and pay off all his creditors after the Denver bank failure results in Mrs. Forrester's being left destitute after he dies, and where else can she turn to for money if not to the Ivy Peterses? Willa Cather does not deal with this problem, but it is of crucial importance. If in the modern world money can be obtained— or kept—only by means of chicanery or pettifogging, what is the honorable man or woman to do?

This problem, which is also the problem of Myra Henshawe in *My Mortal Enemy,* is left unsolved by Willa Cather, probably because no satisfactory solution presented itself to her. True, in *The Professor's House* Godfrey St. Peter lives on the salary he draws from his university. This stipend is the reward for honorable work and presumably is not tainted with commercial greed. But it is hardly satisfactory to suggest that all the members of society become professors. . . . By and large, the protagonists of Willa Cather's [later works] find it increasingly difficult merely to survive in the modern world without engaging in the hectic pursuit for wealth which their society demands of them. And the pursuit of wealth runs counter to everything they hold to be most valuable and to constitute life's highest good.

Here Willa Cather joins company once more with her master, Flaubert. Like Flaubert, she instinctively recoils from the modern world of the bourgeoisie because of the inherent split it contains between what ought to be and what is, between noble aspiration and self-seeking greed. In a world devoted mainly to self-aggrandizement, the idealistic person is at a distinct disadvantage. We have seen this split in earlier stories of Willa Cather's such as "**A Sculptor's Funeral**" and "**A Wagner Matinée.**" In each case the spectator through whose eyes the story is observed would like to do something for the main character but is powerless to do so: his hands are tied and he is in no position to perform a significant action of any kind. This is equally true of Niel Herbert in *A Lost Lady*; he is unable to help the heroine in any way whatsoever or to act in accordance with the values he holds. And Marian Forrester, caught halfway between the pioneer and the commercial generations, is herself unable to act according to the values she holds. She is unable to remain faithful to her husband while he is alive or live the kind of life he stood for after he is dead.

Because Willa Cather felt frustrated and unable to express herself in the present, it was easy for her to think that the era she had grown up in was ethically superior. This attitude comes out clearly in her description of Niel Herbert's farewell to Sweet

Water. Here a panegyric on the passing heroic age is combined with criticism of Mrs. Forrester for refusing to die with that age. Although the thoughts and reflections start out as Niel Herbert's they seem gradually to pass over into comments and generalizations by the author in a way which is quite characteristic of Willa Cather's endorsements of the point of view of her major characters, especially in her later novels. . . . It is clear that the past is being glorified in . . . [*A Lost Lady*] and the present rejected. In this novel Willa Cather everywhere acquiesces in this mood and nowhere contradicts it. On the contrary, Marian Forrester is condemned precisely because she declined to reject the present. She refused to commit suttee on her husband's funeral pyre; as Willa Cather puts it, "she preferred life on any terms."

If we make the experiment of viewing Willa Cather's novels of this period in the light of the vegetation myth so important to her prairie period, we find that they are based on that part of the myth which has to do with failure of the crops to renew themselves; that is to say, on the theme of the waste land. . . . In *A Lost Lady,* the theme of the waste land becomes even more explicit than in *One of Ours.* In the original versions of the waste-land myth the land is under a blight because its king is aged, or impotent, or sick, or all three. This ailment is reflected throughout his kingdom by failure of the crops through drought and sterility in cattle and women. The blight is finally lifted when a young knight comes questing into the land, undergoes great dangers at the Castle Perilous, and as a result of triumphing over them restores the king to health, the restoration being symbolized in some versions at least by the knight's sexual union with the king's young wife. If we compare this story with *A Lost Lady,* Captain Forrester becomes a type of the Fisher-King, aged and impotent. If this is so, Marian Forrester's sexual encounters take on something of the nature of fertility rites, attempts to re-establish the bases of life. But a bitter irony has twisted the fable. Willa Cather, herself, actually shows a mingled acceptance and rejection of Marian Forrester's sexuality; she pictures it as being the source of her vitality, yet finds it degrading. In terms of the myth she is both attracted and repelled by the fertility rite, showing a mixture of affirmation of the cult of life with Christian (and perhaps spinsterish) asceticism. Mrs. Forrester is quite different in one respect from the young wife of the Fisher-King, however. No chaste questing knight comes riding to her aid; only passionless vulgarians. For Willa Cather, evidently, this is all that the modern world can provide. (pp. 198-202)

> *John H. Randall III, in his* The Landscape and the Looking Glass: Willa Cather's Search for Value *(Copyright © 1960 by John H. Randall, III. Reprinted by permission of Houghton Mifflin Company), Houghton Mifflin, 1960, 425 p.*

EDWARD A. BLOOM and LILLIAN D. BLOOM (essay date 1962)

[*The following excerpt attempts to define Cather's place in American literary history. Both Edward and Lillian Bloom consider Cather a writer in the great American tradition—a tradition given fullest expression in the works of James Fenimore Cooper, Nathaniel Hawthorne, Herman Melville, and Henry James. For these two critics, the writers in this group represent an attempt to answer those essential questions peculiar to the American phenomenon. Of all these writers, Edward and Lillian Bloom consider James the closest to Cather in moral responsibility and social concerns.*]

There is a steadiness about Willa Cather's fiction that defies the crosscurrents of the literary age in which she lived and wrote. Like many conscientious American writers, she was profoundly aware of the growing cleavage in her society between moral values and expedient action. Dislocations following the military and economic disasters she witnessed in her lifetime caused her to share a widespread fear that the future was bleakly uncertain, that a spiritual chaos threatened the central purpose of existence. More than most thoughtful Americans, perhaps, she was personally sensitive to devalued conduct and customs. Because she had consciously built her life upon a structure of traditions, and because she had preferred the solid virtues of an inspiriting past to the mercurial shifts of practical reality, she suspiciously resisted change. From time to time she protested against the violation of durable truths, although rarely in the clamorous voice used by many contemporary writers. Looking backward to the fixed values of a satisfying past, she reaffirmed the moral standards she cherished, thus ultimately denying they could be destroyed by temporary upheavals. In so doing, she committed herself to a pattern of continuity and became part of an exclusive but nevertheless great tradition of American writing.

Given fullest expression in the nineteenth century, the tradition is synthesized in the fiction of Cooper, Hawthorne, Melville, and James. Although they differed in their reactions to the convulsions afflicting an America in flux, they are unified by certain connections of personal responsibility. . . . Although all of them drew upon America as the source of their creative purpose, they resembled each other in their awareness of national exigencies rather than in any superficial resort to a common region or even set of circumstances. (pp. 237-38)

In every essential detail, Willa Cather aspired toward the ethical and creative goals of the great tradition, consequently becoming the twentieth-century successor of these four nineteenth-century novelists. Miss Cather's novels are still relatively recent, and historical perspective may not yet permit an ultimate evaluation of her literary position. We do have standards of continuity by which we may measure her achievement, however, and if these standards have any critical validity then Miss Cather is surely in the line of succession. More notably even than Cooper, and with a moral intensity comparable to that of Hawthorne, Melville, and James, Miss Cather has represented the tensions of American existence in the late nineteenth and early twentieth century. Like her predecessors—especially the last three—she is a commentator on the prevailing American condition. Sometimes urgent in her fears but always ardent in her faith, she constantly held before herself the vision of realizable ideals. Out of inspired singleness of conviction grew a distinguished art. To a greater degree than any of the four traditionalists except James, Willa Cather was absorbed in the total identification of an esthetic with moral purpose. Great achievement in the fusion of two inalienable ideals sets her apart from her own contemporaries and fixes her in a continuity of distinguished American writing whose practitioners are few. (pp. 238-39)

At first glance, Miss Cather would appear by virtue of her frequently used frontier subjects to be closest to Cooper. In fact, however, the frontier provides only a superficial resemblance, and Cooper was the writer most distant from her in temperament even as he was in time. That they were alike at all in aim is the result of the fact that they were deeply engrossed in the solution of American crises, each in his own way. Yvor Winters . . . has said of Cooper that his "concern was primarily for public morality; it was the concern of the statesman, or of the historian, first, and of the artist but secondarily.'' This statement of Cooper's literary interests, acutely defensible, it appears to us, shows the polarity between him and Willa Cather. National morality was, to be sure, intensely part of her fiction of the frontier. But in Cooper's intention we find a reversed image of Miss Cather's. She was the artist, and—more significantly—the moral artist, first. It was only after she had appeased her esthetic-moral sense that she spoke as the historian, and then but to give fuller definition to her primary intention. Dealing with ethics rather than with manners, dedicated to a personal, nondoctrinal concept of salvation, she drew her characters as moral agents, somewhat as abstractions, if more balanced in physical properties than Hawthorne's. (pp. 240-41)

In her tendency to allegorize her moral searchings, she like Hawthorne never lost sight of her function as a creative artist. Indeed, she devoted herself to the notion that only through the highest expression of art could she give worthy representation to her inner desire. More specifically than Hawthorne, she cherished people as people and incidents as incidents. She softened the lines of her figures and actions, but she never clothed them in such abstractions that they lost verisimilitude. She respected the varieties of human emotions and meant them to be credible aspects of daily, familiar experience.

She was furthermore acutely conscious of artistic techniques, giving her search for esthetic perfection equality with her yearning for inner meaning. With regard to artistic credibility, she was closer to Melville than to Hawthorne, for like the former she sought a more immediate equation between physical reality and spiritual significance. As is true of Melville, she portrayed phenomenal reality and human beings in readily identifiable proportions. She made them agents of an ultimate truth but always invested them with properties which could be accounted for immediately at the conscious level of perception as well as at the somewhat mystic level of moral insight. If she was less visionary than Hawthorne and Melville, and less profound in her moral intensity, she was the more accomplished technician and consequently the more readable novelist.

But among the major writers in the tradition, Henry James undoubtedly bears the closest creative resemblance to Miss Cather. Both as an artist and as a moral realist he was the literary personality who figured most prominently among the influences shaping her artistic development. Greatly respectful of his esthetic achievements, she was attracted to his singularity of purpose, to the manner in which he made an art form cohesive with serious thematic details. James was so evidently the novelist she herself cared to be that she imitated him unsuccessfully in *Alexander's Bridge.* Her blunder, as she realized, was the attempt to capture a style in which meaning was not appropriately related to personal experience. But if James ceased to function as her model for the execution of idea and form, he left a permanent impression upon her because of the purity of aim which she always venerated as the essence of her own practice. Although they dealt with comparable themes somewhat divergently, each drawing upon his particular genius, the subtle likenesses between them make their exterior differences relatively unimportant.

What is important, in the present connection, is the attitude which they took toward their art. It is an attitude of moral sobriety, a deeply serious concern with quintessential American problems. Basic to this commitment is an esthetic sensibility which transfigures ethical responsibility into organic narrative

situations. Both Henry James and Willa Cather believed that without appropriately conceived shape the novel fails to represent in true essence the inner experience which is the only justifiable substance of fiction. For each, therefore, a moral sense is powerfully one with an esthetic sense. Concept and form admit of no separation, the two growing simultaneously in the created work, inevitably and rightly. With respect to technical virtuosity, James and Miss Cather progressed beyond the earlier writers. In their fusion of moral idea and physical reality, they acknowledged to a remarkable degree the demands of their art, and then went on to fulfill the obligations to which they had committed themselves.

James and Miss Cather, furthermore, are related in the subjects they chose, although they attacked them from different angles. Yvor Winters . . . has pointed out that James wrote about ''the spiritual antagonism which had existed for centuries between the rising provincial civilization and the richer civilization from which it has broken away, an antagonism in which the provincial civilization met the obviously superior cultivation of the parent with a more or less typically provincial assertion of superiority.'' Whereas for James the antagonism lay between an ancient European culture and an upstart American culture, for Miss Cather the rift existed at times as an exclusively American phenomenon. That is, she focused her frontier novels on the divisions existing among native cultural forms. She may be said to have narrowed her view intensively, looking to the frontier first as a reaffirmation of traditional American values, and then to its development as a corruption of those values. As a further point of comparison, however, it must not be forgotten that even in the frontier novels, such as *O Pioneers!* and *My Ántonia,* she often considered with affection the traditions the first-generation pioneers had brought with them from Europe. But whether James and Willa Cather treated American themes as outgrowths of cultural divisions between nations or within the nation, they always did so with a moral responsiveness. Each brought to his novels a personal commitment which wedded feeling with insight, although Miss Cather's sympathies for America were the more immediate and direct.

As a traditionalist in an age which had no reverence for tradition, Miss Cather was a lonely figure. The moral integrity of the individual implied an exaltation of personality, even of egoism, which collided with the mass standardization and rapidly shifting values of mechanistic progress. To resist in a practical sense was, of course, vain. But the convictions of writers such as Miss Cather and James, as well as of Hawthorne and Melville, transcended practicality. Thus, Miss Cather, who formed very few intimate alliances in her lifetime, clung to a somewhat solitary position from which she idealized universal truth and frequently denounced temporization. Like Thoreau she challenged her own society, and like him she demanded a return to good purpose. (pp. 242-45)

Although she considered certain American writers of the 1930's— notably, Hemingway, Wilder, Fitzgerald, and Lewis—to be genuine artists, she thought the fiction of that period was largely without purpose. Yet, if she was hostile to the overt tone of pessimism and cynicism which pervaded much of contemporary fiction, she was closer in spirit to this literature of harsh reality than she herself would have cared to admit. (p. 247)

Throughout her novels . . . , Miss Cather is in the curiously ambivalent position of standing apart from her contemporaries, and yet at the same time of sharing many of the immediate moral problems which they had made their responsibility. Although she directed her vision to a traditional past, as they did not, she was nonetheless able to assess the dilemma of modern times through a conjunction of tradition with present reality. The important thing for her, of course, was that values may never be divorced from art. But it must also be acknowledged that for most serious writers of modern times moral or social responsibility must coincide with esthetic awareness. Willa Cather addresses herself most memorably to a tradition of conscience and hope; in this respect she is in the main stream of great American literary achievement. But she also addresses herself trenchantly, if in a minor key, to affairs of material reality. Eloquently joining past and present, affirmation and censure, she has memorialized herself as an American classic. (p. 250)

Edward A. Bloom and Lillian D. Bloom, in their Willa Cather's Gift of Sympathy *(copyright © 1962 by Southern Illinois University Press; reprinted by permission of Southern Illinois University Press), Southern Illinois University Press, 1962, 260 p.*

LOIS FEGER   (essay date 1970)

[*The following excerpt is taken from a close textual interpretation of Cather's* My Antonia. *In it, Feger examines three different aspects of the novel: first, the recurring imagery of darkness and evil which underscores the narrative; second, the development of the narrator Jim Burden; and third, Cather's use of internal stories and anecdotes within the novel's structure.*]

My Antonia, the most famous of Willa Cather's prairie novels, has become a classic of American literature. In my recent readings of this work, I have found it to be a deceptively simple book about pioneer family life, its roots, and its values. The fictitious narrator Jim Burden invokes the traditional pieties when, for example, he comments, "Our lives centered around warmth and food and the return of the men at nightfall. . . ." Obviously something more is meant here than physical warmth and well-being; there is the satisfaction of congenial family relations as well. The ritual of "warmth and food" finds parallels in the descriptions of the "country Christmas" . . . and in the deaconship, church suppers, and missionary societies of the elder Burdens. . . .

Operating within this ordered framework, however, is another level of meaning which I have come to see as the dark dimension of *My Antonia.* This aspect of the novel points with insistence to the violence and negation of human life and at least suggests that ultimately all may be futile. One of the early indications of this theme is Jim's "mock adventure" with the rattlesnake. The reptile becomes a symbol of "the ancient, eldest Evil" and the narrator states that "certainly his kind have left horrible unconscious memories in all warm-blooded life." . . . (p. 774)

Even before the story proper opens, though, the reader can sense the dark undertones. On the title page is a quote from Vergil, "Optima dies . . . prima fugit." Later on Jim Burden will be studying this same passage which begins: "Life's fairest days are ever the first to flee for hapless mortals. On creep diseases and sad age and suffering; and stern death's ruthlessness sweeps away its prey." This same theme is continued in the Introduction in which Willa Cather pretends to have met Jim Burden who has been writing down his impressions of Antonia, a mutual friend of their childhood. The author expresses interest but after seeing the manuscript she drops out of the story as a separate character. The book that follows

really consists of the parallel stories of Antonia and Jim. Besides establishing the plot line, the Introduction also lets us see something of the ultimate disposition of the major characters. From the very beginning the exaltation of tragedy is denied and we know that both Antonia and Jim will survive their story—although not together. The emptiness of the Antonia/Jim relationship is repeated in the Burden marriage; after a few descriptive phrases we recognize Mrs. Burden as a creature from a Gatsby world. The tonal emphasis does not change with the narrative itself; many such dark elements are present throughout the work. . . . (pp. 774-75)

A contemporary critic John H. Randall calls *My Antonia* "one long paean of praise to the joys of rural living." There *are* beautiful descriptive passages but a great deal of the imagery of the book is negative; images of darkness, death, cold, and the like are frequent and they carry thematic significance far beyond their literal function. . . .

The images of death are . . . important in the description of the suicide and funeral of Mr. Shimerda but, even apart from that, such imagery is often associated with Antonia's family: for example, the windmill frame in front of their home is called a "skeleton," and Mr. Shimerda's face is described as "ruggedly formed" but looking "like ashes."

Jim and Antonia are thrown together almost immediately and together they explore the countryside and learn to know and love the Nebraska plains. Among their initiatory experiences, however, is the killing of the snake which has already been alluded to. There are also constant references to the cold, "man's strongest antagonist," and to the wind which made the boy Jim "think of defeated armies, retreating; or of ghosts who were trying desperately to get in for shelter." . . . (p. 775)

In this novel nature passages are often a prelude to the revelation of serious, and generally pessimistic, thoughts. One of the clearest indications of this pattern occurs in the description of a Black Hawk winter. . . . Throughout *My Antonia* cold is called man's greatest enemy. Here the "pale, cold light of the winter sunset" which "did not beautify" is seen as the light of truth itself. Winter is the dark side of man: his mortality, frailty, vulnerability before the forces of nature and before himself. In this context anyway the dark dimension appears to be the only valid one: beauty, warmth, light, and loveliness are somehow lies and evil and one will be punished for loving them.

It is interesting to note that sunset scenes occur almost as regularly in *My Antonia* as the scaffold imagery does in Hawthorne's *Scarlet Letter.* As in the earlier work, the intention to create symbolism is clear. Light is important in each of these sunset descriptions. In the winter scene considered above, light has no transfiguring function, but most of the time this element is present. . . . (p. 776)

Besides being the story of Antonia, the novel also relates the education into life of its narrator Jim Burden. Jim's development goes on side by side with Antonia's: indeed, we sometimes lose sight of Antonia for long stretches at a time, while we never lose sight of the narrator. As a young boy, Jim Burden makes the symbolic journey from East to West. In the idiom of American myth, this opens him to enormous possibilities in the way of freedom and positive development. The death of his parents, the complete change of scene—all point to the fact that Jim has an opportunity to be formed as a veritable "new man." The novel follows closely the period of Jim's Nebraska development, but it does not give us many details of his life before or after that time. Son of a Blue Ridge Virginia family, Jim Burden returns to the East to a professional career and to an unfortunate and childless marriage. There is apparently little in his adult life which is meaningful, and the novel ends with only a promise of vicarious living through Antonia's family.

Although Jim understood and approved of the lessons which the West had tried to teach him, he was never able to integrate them into his own life. This failure is one of the saddest elements of the whole book but it is by no means a surprise. Even without the Introduction, there are many indications that the patterns of Burden's inherited past will continue to hold him.

In *My Antonia* the two families about whom we know the most are the Burdens and the Shimerdas: the established settlers and the new immigrants. Through the Shimerdas the young Jim comes to learn new ways and attitudes and is never attracted to them: for example, Antonia wished to give him her ring in gratitude for an English lesson and Jim comments, "I repulsed her quite sternly." Instead of finding an appeal in her instinctive generosity, he continues, "I didn't want her ring and I felt there was something reckless and extravagant about her wishing to give it away to a boy she had never seen before." . . . The boy responds in the same vein to Mr. Shimerda's promise of a gun and to that sensitive man's thoughtful greeting: after all, as Jim says, "I was used to being taken for granted by my elders." . . . (pp. 776-77)

Jim and Antonia spend a great deal of time together, and from the beginning Antonia, in spite of fragmentary English and humbler circumstances, is the dominating character. Jim often expresses his resentment by comments such as, "Much as I liked Antonia, I hated a superior tone that she sometimes took with me." . . . Less understandable is Jim's failure to respond sympathetically to Antonia's difficult position at home. Instead his dislike of Mrs. Shimerda spills over in harsh feelings towards the girl and towards people in general. It is not hard to recognize a perennial American type in the youthful Jim's "People who don't like this country ought to stay at home. We don't make them come here." . . . A passage such as that on immigrants suggests that perhaps Jim is lacking in the human dimensions which would be essential to making his "Western" education a success: Jim who *is* able to have advantages such as schooling does not seem to be able to sense Antonia's real deprivation or her own awareness of it. He can only take offense at her so-called "rough ways."

After three years on the Burden farm Jim and his grandparents move to the "clean, well-planted little prairie town" of Black Hawk. This part of the book details life in Black Hawk and is very much concerned with Jim. There is quite a bit of youthful theorizing as Jim develops his attitudes towards "hired girls," domesticity, and society in general. The town itself has a "curious social situation" which in effect places Jim and immigrant girls like Antonia on opposite ends of the social ladder. Jim, however, enjoys dancing on "popular nights" and avoids the evenings sponsored by the Progressive Euchre Club. He doesn't join the Euchre turned Owl group but does sneak off to the dances at the Firemen's Hall. As narrator he often inserts passages in favor of the "hired girls," but these easily become patronizing, "I always knew I should live long enough to see my country girls come into their own, and I have," . . . or ineffective, "He never looked at Lena again. . . . I used to glare at young Lovett from a distance and only wished I had some way of showing my contempt for him." . . . (p. 777)

At best Jim has a qualified contempt for the town girls and for Black Hawk domesticity in general. . . . This . . . is ironic when one considers the kind of adult life which Jim eventually made for himself and also when it is juxtaposed against his reaction to these same people's criticism of his social taste: "Disapprobation hurt me, I found—even that of people whom I did not admire." . . . Jim stopped dancing with the "hired girls." It is clear that Jim's intelligence guides him in his theories but as a person he will never actually make the break, and will never cross that social line which he sees so well and despises so heartily. (pp. 777-78)

In the third section of the book we lose sight of Antonia almost completely. This section deals with Jim Burden at the University of Nebraska, his mild affair with Lena Lingard, and his decision to return East to continue his studies at Harvard. Jim and his development provide the chief center of interest here; the high point is an account of a performance of *Camille,* to which Jim takes Lena. After pages of marvelous escape prose, we see that the familiar Jim has brought his umbrella to the theater and prudently "took Lena home under its shelter." Jim has a chance to marry Lena but he doesn't take it. When he decides to leave, he does so without even the appearance of a struggle, thus making him worse than the hapless Sylvester Lovett whom he so despised and castigated.

In the next section Jim, at home from Harvard in the summer vacation, learns of Antonia's fate at the hands of Larry Donovan. We are not surprised that his immediate reaction to Antonia is one of rejection as soon as the image he has of her is broken, "I tried to shut Antonia out of my mind. I was bitterly disappointed in her. I could not forgive her for becoming an object of pity." . . . Nevertheless, Jim is persuaded to visit Antonia a short time later. The pull of the land and of the past affects them both but Jim goes away again and Antonia receives his promise to return with a wise smile. Perhaps the book ought to have ended here, with Antonia left alone in the field in the gathering darkness, but after twenty years Jim *does* return to visit and he only hesitates lest he lose his illusions: "I did not want to find her aged and broken; I really dreaded it. In the course of twenty crowded years one parts with many illusions. I did not wish to lose the early ones. . . ." In the final analysis Jim Burden has been perhaps chastened by experience but he has never really learned.

In *My Antonia* a great deal of the material comes to us in the form of inserted stories or anecdotes; in other words, the reader is not once removed from the action but twice removed from it. There are at least fifteen separate instances of this in the novel and in considering them I have raised a number of questions. What, for example, is the relation between the "Pavel, Peter, and the Wolves" story and Mr. Shimerda's suicide which follows soon after the narration and in the same kind of cold, winter weather? And why are there two suicide incidents in the book: Mr. Shimerda's and that of the unknown man at the Norwegian settlement? After Antonia tells the story of the latter, she verges on serious speculation. Why does the author have Mrs. Harling change the subject so abruptly and bring the discussion into an entirely different field? . . . Perhaps most puzzling of all is why the affair of Antonia and Larry Donovan comes to us so indirectly—Antonia has told the Widow Steavens who in turn relates the story to Jim Burden. The inserts themselves are not all alike: some are anonymous references (the fellow in the Black Tiger Mine, the others who figured in the stories told by Fuchs during his work on Mr. Shimerda's coffin), some concern characters who otherwise play little or no part in the book (d'Arnault, Sylvester Lovett, Ole Benson, Old Hata), several of the narratives are more highly developed than the others (the story of Pavel, Peter, and the Wolves for one), and a few contain some of the most important information in the novel (Tony's affair is the prime example here).

These narratives certainly raise disturbing questions in terms of both theme and structure but in at least one element I have found them to be all of a piece. These are all unhappy stories whose central idea is negative; these are stories of deprivation, loss, violence, deception, death. Even the stories which do not apparently follow this pattern have a background of evil: the Mormons planted their legendary sunflowers as they were trying to escape persecution and Anton Jelinek's story of miracle and devotion takes place during a time of war and disease. In addition, some of the inserted material has apparently been manipulated in order to come across as darkly as possible: Tiny, one of the "hired girls," has managed to achieve considerable financial success but when her story is told, the emphasis is on her physical deformity and tendency towards miserliness; at another point in the book the schoolboy Jim tells his friends about Coronado and his search for the Seven Golden Cities. The mention of the explorer evokes for a moment a feeling of glory and adventure but in Willa Cather's hands Coronado becomes only another man who "died in the wilderness, of a broken heart. . . ." (pp. 778-79)

Thus, like a reversal of the beautiful image of the sunflower-bordered roads of the Mormon legend, the material of failure and disillusion underlies the whole of Willa Cather's *My Antonia*. It is ironic that this book which has become one widely read in high school should really be saying or implying such pessimistic things about life, but after reading *My Antonia* in terms of its dark dimension, it is difficult to see it in the old innocent "country-life" way. Even the so-called "happy ending" has its limitations. . . . The marriage of the Cuzaks is the idyllic highpoint of the novel but even its description closes on a note of frustration which is perhaps as inevitable on the prairie as elsewhere. (p. 779)

> Lois Feger [later Clare Louise Feger], *"The Dark Dimension of Willa Cather's 'My Antonia'"* (copyright © 1970 by the National Council of Teachers of English; reprinted by permission of the publisher and the author), in English Journal, *Vol. 59, No. 6, September, 1970, pp. 774-79.*

DAVID STOUCK   (essay date 1973)

[*In the excerpt below, Stouck argues that all of Cather's writing after* Death Comes for the Archbishop *deals specifically with the theme of regret and the problems in confronting one's past honestly. Stouck believes that after a number of personal tragedies in Cather's later years, such as the deaths of her mother and brother, the author renounced fiction as a viable means of human interaction—though paradoxically she continued writing it—and began to see life itself as the proper sphere of human relations. Stouck suggests that such works as* Obscure Destinies, Lucy Gayheart, *and* Sapphira and the Slave Girl *clearly demonstrate Cather's desire to come to terms with the past and her own personal misgivings. For other interpretations of Cather's later works see excerpts above by Clifton Fadiman, Granville Hicks, and Alfred Kazin.*]

In her major novels Willa Cather explored the archetypal dimensions of the human imagination: *O Pioneers!*, with its vision of the new land and its heroic settlers, is written in the epic mode; *My Antonia*, with its quest into the author's personal memories, is a pastoral; *The Professor's House*, which chronicles an ugly tale of human greed, is largely satiric, and *Death*

Comes for the Archbishop, with its saintly missionary priests, portrays the disciplined, timeless world of the paradisal imagination. But what of those books written after *Death Comes for the Archbishop*, particularly those last four volumes (*Obscure Destinies, Lucy Gayheart, Sapphira and the Slave Girl, The Old Beauty and Others*) which critics agree mark the decline of Miss Cather's art? Can these novels, from a writer of such depth, be as undistinguished and insignificant as has been suggested? The answer is at once affirmative and negative. With the exception of the long story, **"Old Mrs. Harris,"** the later writing lacks the imaginative energy which found consummate expression in the earlier novels. But the vision which underlies these books is precisely one which discounts the urge to expression through art; for it was the author's conviction in later years that not art but only life truly matters in the end. Consequently Willa Cather's last fictions occupy that paradoxical, but not uncommon, position of works of art pointing to their own devaluation.

As a romantic Willa Cather believed in the absoluteness of the artist's vocation. Her major novels were all written as egotistic expressions of an individual consciousness seeking to know and understand itself. Even as apparently selfless and disinterested a book as *Death Comes for the Archbishop* reflects a way of life achieved by the author after she had gone through a nadir of despair over her failure in human relationships. But the last novels and stories posit quite a different relationship between art and human consciousness. No longer driven by the Faustian urge to power through her writing, Miss Cather came to view her lifetime dedication to art as placing selfish and consequently tragic limitations on the demands of life itself. Again Miss Cather was following a path well-worn, to use one of her favorite images, by the "pilgrims" of the imagination. The futility of life's sacrifice to art had been dramatized more emphatically by artists who arrested their work in early or mid-career: by Rimbaud, for example, who went to Abyssinia to make his fortune in the slave trade; by Hardy, who ceased writing fiction after publishing his most powerful novel, *Jude the Obscure;* or by Hart Crane who, in his quest for the ideal, despaired of the mediacy of poetry and committed suicide. For Willa Cather the implications of her vision were never as wholly irrevocable or tragic, yet instinctively she moved toward that same juncture where art terminates in the mute acceptance (or, in Crane's case, hopeful transcendence) of life.

The change is first evident with the publication of *Obscure Destinies*. . . . Willa Cather's achievement of self-mastery with its fictional flowering in *Death Comes for the Archbishop* . . . , her supreme work of art, was irremediably shaken in the following years which brought the disruption of her apartment life in New York and the death of her father in Nebraska. The fictional consequence of this reversal was *Shadows on the Rock* . . . , a book set in seventeenth-century Quebec, but pervaded throughout by a very personal feeling of homesickness and the desire to retreat into a world that never changes. However, it was the illness and death in 1931 of the author's mother which determined the direction of her writing for the remaining years. . . . Where the novels of her middle years had found characters and settings in the world at large, the later fiction returns the author to her personal past once again in Nebraska and Virginia. But what is most significant is that these books are shaped throughout by a desire to see that world, at last, equably and with compassion. The imaginative tension for great art is largely gone, but in its place we have the artist's wisdom, her resolve—her testament to life which is poignantly simple and reassuring.

Miss Cather's last writings are informed throughout by a profound regret that youth in its self-absorption is so often cruel and indifferent, that greatness in any endeavor is achieved at the cost of human sympathy. The most moving expression of this final vision in her art is **"Old Mrs. Harris,"** the second story of *Obscure Destinies*. Here Willa Cather no longer attempts to prove herself in recreating the characters and incidents from her past, nor does she seek in them some way of resolving the tensions in her own private life; rather her attitude is one of remorse and humility, as though writing were a form of penance and its only objective were to win forgiveness from those remembered persons by means of their sympathetic embodiment in a work of art. In **"Old Mrs. Harris"** Willa Cather recreates the characters and a period in her life (specifically her mother and grandmother as she remembered them from adolescence) which previously she had viewed with little affection. In this story, remembering the past is not an escapist pleasure, but a confrontation with guilty memories evaded for much of a lifetime.

The art and the reprise of **"Old Mrs. Harris"** lie in the subtlety with which point of view is managed. Although the controlling perspective is ultimately the author's—the grown Vickie remembering a sequence from her childhood—the story is narrated so that the three women in the family, while not understanding each other, emerge nonetheless as sympathetic individuals. Miss Cather in effect describes the tragic undertow of this story herself in her essay on Katherine Mansfield when she singles out that author's ability to reveal the many kinds of relations which exist in a happy family: " . . . every individual in that household (even the children) is clinging passionately to his individual soul, is in terror of losing it in the general family flavour. As in most families, the mere struggle to have anything of one's own, to be one's self at all, creates an element of strain which keeps everybody almost at the breaking-point." In **"Old Mrs. Harris"** sympathy at first appears to be reserved for the grandmother alone: the story begins with Mrs. Rosen's visit to Grandma Harris, and from the neighbor's vantage point the old woman appears to be the drudge in her daughter's household and the victim of her son-in-law's ineffectuality in business. But as we are taken inside Mrs. Harris's thoughts we find that as a Southerner she accepts her role in her daughter's kitchen and is grateful to be able to follow her daughter's fortunes in this customary way. Also the picture of her daughter from the neighbor's eyes as haughty and selfish, jealous of any attention paid to her mother, begins to soften as the old woman reflects that while her daughter is indeed proud, she at the same time has a "good heart." The old woman, moreover, admits to herself that, because Victoria had been the prettiest of her children, she had spoiled her. Mrs. Harris could have been wholly idealized if the author had retained only a granddaughter's perspective, but the tension in the family is felt from the daughter Victoria's point of view as well. At the Methodist social we are given a glimpse into her motives and feelings. We see her giving money spontaneously to the children of the poor laundress and know that the gesture is not intended to be patronising; we also feel with her the intended reproach when one of the meddlesome townswomen implies that Victoria exploits her mother in the kitchen. Victoria could have been a wholly negative character, but sympathy is elicited for her in thus exposing her vulnerability.

The portrait of Vickie, however, is the most complex for hers is the "guilty" perspective; because she is a projection of the author's younger self she is viewed at once most critically and most sympathetically. Vickie's desire to go to college, to escape the cramped existence of an overcrowded family in a small midwestern town, blinds her to the feelings and needs of those around her. The measure of regret the author feels years later is suggested in the homely incident when the family cat dies. Vickie is so absorbed in her studies that she pays little attention to the death of the cat and her grandmother explains to the other children: "Vickie's got her head full of things lately; that makes people kind of heartless." It is a seemingly trivial incident, but it is steeped in the self-recrimination which underlies the story. When Vickie learns that in spite of the scholarship she has won there will not be enough money for her to go to college, she sees everyone as her enemy; she even refuses her grandmother's comfort.

The failure of sympathy and understanding in the family reaches a dramatic crescendo at the end of the story where the members of the family become so engrossed in their personal problems they do not realize the grandmother is dying. Here each of the women gives bitter expression to her frustration and despair as the grandmother looks helplessly on. Victoria asks her mother in an accusing tone if she is sick and says: "You ought to be more careful what you eat, Ma. If you're going to have another bilious spell, when everything is so upset anyhow, I don't know what I'll do." . . . When Vickie hears that her grandmother is ill and her mother lying down in her room she thinks "wasn't it just like them all to go and get sick, when she had now only two weeks to get ready for school, and no trunk and no clothes or anything?" . . . But our sympathies are never onesided: Vickie's selfish indifference is tempered by our knowledge that she is apprehensive and full of self-doubt about going away to school; and we learn that the attractive Victoria is to bring yet another child into the crowded house. The interweaving of multiple viewpoints renders movingly the imaginative tension at the heart of the story: while the memories of hidden longings and isolation are vividly recreated through Vickie's viewpoint, the narrative overview at the same time creates the mother and grandmother with sympathy and compassion. But it is a tragic ambience which surrounds the tale, for the understanding and forgiveness have come too late. The prototypes from life (and it is to life that we are directed in Miss Cather's last writings) are now gone, and compassion can only be expressed in art. The most moving image in the story is that of the poor servant woman, Mandy, washing old Mrs. Harris's feet. The power of this image derives from the Keatsian paradox that the servant's gesture of compassion is momentary but complete, while its artistic recreation must always be compensatory. The homely details of childhood are nowhere in Miss Cather's writing so lovingly described; but that affection is a quietly tragic emotion for art, though timeless, can never replenish life. (pp. 41-5)

The spirit of self-exorcism in which **"Old Mrs. Harris"** was written is pursued even more relentlessly in *Lucy Gayheart*. . . . Of all Willa Cather's novels *Lucy Gayheart* has probably received the greatest amount of negative criticism; the charge is usually that of contrivance and sentimentality. But if one perceives its design, *Lucy Gayheart* appears less contrived. The novel is built around three tales of love, three tales of remorse and reprise. In a letter to a friend Miss Cather suggested that the novel doesn't pull together until one reads the last part. It is in the final section, or Book 3, that we look at the novel through the eyes of a character who is filled with guilt and remorse over his actions in the past. Although Book 3, like the rest of the novel, is written in the third person, it is narrated from the viewpoint of Harry Gordon living on in the small Nebraska town of Haverford, twenty-five years after the heroine's death. Gordon had loved Lucy Gayheart, but he had not understood her. She had gone to Chicago to study piano and there had fallen in love with a singer, Clement Sebastian. Smitten in his pride, Gordon only thought of revenging himself on Lucy, of making her suffer. When Lucy came back to Haverford after Sebastian's death, he refused, in spite of her plea, to help or comfort her, withdrawing into the exclusive confines of his unhappy new marriage and the family bank. On the last day of her life, he had refused to give Lucy a ride in his cutter out of the cold wind. Book 3 takes place following old Mr. Gayheart's death; his winter funeral had made the townspeople feel "almost as if Lucy's grave had been opened." Harry Gordon, now fifty-five, reflects on the years that have elapsed since Lucy's death and admits to himself that he had gone to great lengths in order to make her suffer. The day on which she drowned "he refused Lucy Gayheart a courtesy he wouldn't have refused to the most worthless old loafer in town." . . . Subsequently his sense of guilt over her death has been the preoccupation of his life. He thinks of it (and his marriage) as a "life sentence" and his friendship with Lucy's father as an "act of retribution." He will never leave Haverford, for his home town is the place of his sorrow and his penance. The last section of the novel is a brief but sharply etched account of twenty-five years of remorse; but its mood creates a frame around the whole of *Lucy Gayheart,* for the book opens several years after Lucy's death, recalling the girl's vital presence in the town and mourning her loss. One of the song-cycles that Clement Sebastian performs is Schubert's *Die Winterreise,* the songs of a rejected lover who is psychically resurrected in the dead of winter to experience again and express the anguish of his loss. Although Gordon is not a singer the musical metaphor applies to him most aptly for his winter memory becomes the controlling perspective in the novel—an extension of the author's lamentation in her remorseful old age.

In "The Old Beauty," written the year after *Lucy Gayheart* was published, Willa Cather touches once again on the major preoccupation of her last writings—her theme of regret and of confronting one's past honestly. Gabrielle Longstreet, the old beauty of the title, was once the rarest flower in London's brilliant society of the nineties. Recalling his acquaintance with her in those years is a very agreeable, nostalgic experience for Seabury, the central consciousness, for those "deep, claret-coloured closing years of Victoria's reign" appear to him from the 1920's as a more noble and more gracious period in human history. But on renewing his friendship with Gabrielle Longstreet, who is living anonymously as Madame de Couçy in France, he finds that her recollections of those years are steeped in regrets. In her youth she had been surrounded by countless unsolicited admirers; they were men of achievement, but she had simply taken them for granted. Now in her old age she has come to recognize their greatness and is filled with remorse that she once held them so lightly. . . . Her chief pleasure now is to read what those men wrote and what has been written about them. In spite of his nostalgia the past has its disagreeable aspect for Seabury as well. Gabrielle recalls to him that the last time they met he had found her in the embraces of a vulgar American businessman. Seabury had gone to China after the incident and had not seen her since. This preoccupation with confronting the past brings the story to its abrupt denouement. The automobile in which Seabury and Gabrielle are riding narrowly misses colliding with a small car driven by two vulgar young American women. Gabrielle dies shortly after this incident and our sympathy for the old beauty is complete. However, that sympathy does not derive, as critics have repeatedly suggested, from a simple juxtaposition of the old order against

the new; rather it is extended to a heroine who, in the two American women, has caught a glimpse of herself in her youth. Outward appearances and life styles change but Gabrielle nonetheless marks in them her own thoughtless nature and perhaps her vulgarity too. It is a brutal confrontation, but in this moment of truth the old beauty is pardoned and redeemed.

The quest for some mode of redemption or release runs as a complementary theme throughout the last fiction to the statement of remorse. Earlier, in *The Professor's House,* Willa Cather found that the misery of failure in human relationships could only be transcended by relinquishing the desire for power and possessions in both human and material terms. In the last books the exorcism of man's lust for power still remains the antidote to the futility of ambitions and desires which leave only sorrow and regret in their wake. (pp. 45-7)

Willa Cather's preoccupation with power and possessiveness is nowhere as strikingly in the foreground as in her last novel, *Sapphira and the Slave Girl,* with its focus on the question of slavery. Dramatic conflict in this novel of pre-Civil War Virginia stems from the fact that Sapphira Colbert is a slave owner while her husband and daughter are in essence abolitionists. To Sapphira, an aristocrat, slavery is a natural part of the order to which she was raised, but for her husband and daughter the ownership of a human being is morally wrong. The attitudes to slavery are an essential expression of character in this novel; it is Sapphira, the slave owner, who experiences jealousy (the passion of possession) in relation to her husband whom she suspects of an amorous attachment to the slave girl, Nancy Till. The miller and his daughter, on the other hand, are indulgent and compassionate towards others: Henry Colbert is a gentle, understanding master and Rachel Blake is a Sister of Mercy at the bedsides of the sick. (pp. 47-8)

Much of *Sapphira and the Slave Girl,* with its evocation of a landscape and people, is still told in the loose anecdotal style, but smoldering beneath the descriptions of Virginia and the pre-Civil War way of life is a mordant drama of jealousy and revenge, the action of which is carried forward in fully dramatic scenes. The novel opens at "The Breakfast Table" when Sapphira announces to Henry her intention of sending Nancy to Winchester, and closes with Sapphira's moving repentance and her decision to invite her daughter to come and stay at her house. Such scenes in between as Martin Colbert's sexual pursuit of Nancy and Nancy's flight to Canada, which Miss Cather would formerly have avoided, are dramatized in considerable detail. As a result we see the characters as complex individuals, neither wholly good nor wholly bad, but engagingly and sympathetically human. Sapphira at first appears a malignant force; she is proud and coldly vengeful and sets out to ruin Nancy in order to punish her husband. But we are also made aware that her illness is a heavy burden and that her suspicions of her husband are not without foundation. In contrast we see the miller poring over his Bible down in the mill, striving to be a righteous man. But if Sapphira is too domineering, then her husband is too weak. He is fond of Nancy, as a father of a daughter, but does nothing to protect her from his nephew's advances; his role in helping her escape is a clandestine, non-committal gesture of leaving some money unguarded in his coat pocket. We see these two characters most equably through the eyes of Rachel Blake. She realizes that by nature she is not equipped to understand her mother, for Sapphira is indeed harsh, often cruel, with her servants and patronizing towards her husband. But she sees her mother's kindness—her indulgence with Tansy Dave and her affection for Old Jezebel—

and realizes that Sapphira genuinely likes to see her servants happy. On the other hand, while Rachel shares her father's quiet, sympathetic nature, she sees clearly his moral cowardice. The full humanity of Sapphira and the miller is disclosed in their last scene together where they recognize their mutual failings and strengths. . . . The full measure of sympathy the author feels for her characters is evident in Sapphira's penitential recognition of her shortcomings; she says contritely to the miller: "We would all do better if we had our lives to live over again." . . . (pp. 50-1)

Critics have discussed the possible directions Miss Cather's imagination would have taken in her new work, which in both time and place represented a significant departure from all her other writing. But in a letter to a friend Miss Cather clearly defines, I believe, that direction herself when she says that she has no more interest in writing since her brother's death, for she realizes nothing in life really matters but the people one loves. . . .

An artist's abandonment or renunciation of his craft, however, does not invalidate his life's work. On the contrary it places it in the more meaningful context of experience achieved, for the artist's path is a circuitous one which returns its pilgrim to life. That Willa Cather, unlike many of her American contemporaries, travelled the full road is not always recognized. But the words of Wallace Stevens are a worthy reminder: ". . . we have nothing better than she is. She takes so much pains to conceal her sophistication that it is easy to miss her quality." (p. 53)

David Stouck, "Willa Cather's Last Four Books," in Novel: A Forum on Fiction *(copyright © Novel Corp., 1973), Vol. 7, No. 1, Fall, 1973, pp. 41-53.*

EUDORA WELTY (essay date 1973)

[*Welty is a well-known Southern novelist and short story writer whose work deals specifically with life in the rural South. In the excerpt below, she pays tribute to Cather on a number of points, but most significantly praises her for the depth of her landscapes and for her "love of art." It is this last sentiment which Welty considers the most essential in Cather's work.*]

It is in looking back on Willa Cather's work that we learn how the vast exterior world she shows us novel by novel, a world ever-present and full of weight and substance and stir, visible to us along differing perspectives and in various mutations of time, has been the deliberately fitted form for each novel's own special needs. This world is here to serve her purpose by taking a fictional role, allying itself more or less openly with human destiny. It appears, according to role, a world with the power to crush and suffocate, and the power to give back life; a world to promise everything, and to deny everything; a world to open a way for living, or to close in life's face. It is all her great, expanding on-moving world; she has made it hers to take at its own beginnings and follow to its slow eclipse; and, in the full circle of it, to bring home the significance of the solitary human spirit which has elected to bring itself there, in its will and its struggle to survive.

She sought for the wholeness of the form—the roundness of the world, the full circle of life. The vital principle, this passion, has of its own a life—a seed, a birth, a growth, a maturing, a decline and sinking into death, back into the earth; it carries within it the pattern of life on earth, and is a part of the same continuity. It is "the old story writing itself over . . . .

It is we who write it, with the best we have," says Alexandra, at the conclusion of *O Pioneers!*

The emotions of Willa Cather's characters, too, have deep roots in the physical world—in that actual physical land to which they were born. In such a land, how clear it is from the start that identity—self-identity—is hard to seize, hard to claim, and hard to hold onto.

Another of the touchstones of her work, I think, is her feeling for the young. "There is no work of art so big or so beautiful," she writes, "that it was not once all contained in some youthful body, like this one [it is Thea's] which lay on the floor in the moonlight, pulsing with ardour and anticipation." The burning drive of the young, the desire to live, to do, to make, to achieve, no matter what the sacrifice, is the feeling most surpassingly alive to the author, most moving to us. Life has made her terribly certain that being young in the world is not easy. "If youth did not matter so much to itself, it would never have the heart to go on," she says, as Thea starts from home. And Doctor Archie, old friend and traveling companion, "knew that the splendid things of life are few, after all, and so very easy to miss." In *O Pioneers!* we read that "there is often a good deal of the child left in people who have had to grow up too soon." Miss Cather has a number of ways to tell us that life is most passionate in the promise, not in the fulfillment.

A strenuous physical life is lived throughout every novel, whether it is the struggle for survival or the keen experience of joy in simple physical well-being; it may reach in some characters the point of total identification with the living world around. It is a form of the passion that is all through Willa Cather's work; her work is written out of it. We see it in many modulations: desire—often exalted as ambition; devotion; loyalty; fidelity; physical nearness and kindness and comfort when it lies at rest. Love? It is affection that warms the life in her stories and hate that chills it. There is reconcilement, and there is pity. There is obsession here too, and so is the hunger for something impossible: all of these are forms of love. And there is marriage, though the marriages that occur along the way of the novels are milestones, hardly destinations; as required in the careful building of her plots, they are inclined to be unavailing. Sexual love is not often present in the here and now; we more often learn of it after it is over, or see it in its results. My own feeling is that along with her other superior gifts Willa Cather had a rare sureness as to *her* subject, the knowledge of just what to touch and what not to touch in the best interests of her story.

What her characters are mostly meant for, it seems to me, is to rebel. For her heroines in particular, rebelling is much easier than not rebelling, and we may include love, too, in not rebelling. It is the strong, clear impulse in Willa Cather's stories. It is the real springwater. It is rebelling, we should always add, not for its own sake as much as for the sake of something a great deal bigger—for the sake of integrity, of truth, of art. It is the other face of aspiration. Willa Cather used her own terms; and she left nothing out. What other honorable way is there for an artist to have her say?

The novels have the qualities and the components of love in proportions all their own, then; and I believe this may point again to the thought that they are concerned not with *two* but with *one*, in the number of human beings—not, finally, with relationships but with the desire in one heart and soul to claim what is its own, to achieve its measure of greatness, to overcome any terrible hardship, any terrible odds; and this desire is served by love, rewarded by love (but its absence or failure never compensated for by love); and most of the time, and at its highest moments, the desire is its own drive, its own gratification. One of its forms is indeed pride; and pride is not punished in Willa Cather's novels, it can be deserved. (pp. 13-15)

For this novelist, art, as she saw it and perfected it, always kept the proportions of the great world and the undeniability of the world, and it lived for her as certainly as this world lived. And the strongest *felt* relationship, a reader may come to believe, might not be any of those between the characters but the one their creator feels for them, for their developing, passionate lives.

In a landscape this wide and pulsing, it seems not at all out of keeping that the greatest passions made real to us are those *for* greatness, and for something larger than life. Men and women do of course fall in love in Willa Cather's novels and their relationship is brought into clear enough focus for us to put good reliance on; but the desire to make a work of art is a stronger one, and more lasting. In the long run, love of art—which is love accomplished without the help or need of help from another—is what is deepest and realest in her work.

There is not a trace of disparagement in her treatment of the least of her characters. The irony of her stories is grave, never belittling; it is a showing of sympathy. She *contended* for the life of the individual. Her attack was positive and vigorous and unflinching and proud of winning. This contending was the essence of her stories, formed her plots, gave her room for action. And she did it without preaching. She lacked self-righteousness, and she just as wholly lacked bitterness; what a lesson *A Lost Lady* gives us in doing without bitterness. It is impossible to think of diminishment in anything she thought or wrote. She conceived of character along heroic lines. For her, the heroic life is the artist's as it is the pioneer's. She equated the two.

Set within the land is the dwelling—made by human hands to hold human life. As we know, the intensity of desire for building the house to live in—or worship in—fills all the Cather novels. It fills the past for her, it gives the present meaning; it provides for a future: the house is the physical form, the *evidence* that we have lived, are alive now; it will be evidence some day that we were alive once, evidence against the arguments of time and the tricks of history.

In her landscape, we learn from both seeing what is there and realizing what is not there; there is always felt the *absence* of habitation. We come to know what degrees there are of the burrow and the roof. "The houses on the Divide were small and were usually tucked away in low places; you did not see them until you came directly upon them," we read of the Scandinavian settlement in *O Pioneers!* "Most of them were built of the sod itself, and were only the unescapable ground in another form." Mrs. Archie, in *The Song of the Lark*, of whom we are told "such little, mean natures are among the darkest and most baffling of created things," liked to "have her house clean, empty, dark, locked, and to be out of it—anywhere." The Professor's house, shabby and outgrown as it is, is a dated house; but the cliff house, almost older than time, is timeless. (pp. 16-17)

The Professor's House is a novel with a unique form, and to read it is to see it built before our eyes: the making of two unlike parts into a whole under a sheltering third part which defines it and is as final as that verse that comes to recite itself

to the Professor's mind. The construction is simple, forthright, and daring. By bringing the Professor's old house and the cliff dwellers' house in combination to the mind, Willa Cather gives them simultaneous existence, and with the measure of time taken away we may see, in the way of a mirage, or a vision, humanity's dwelling places all brought into one. (pp. 17-18)

Tom Outland's story, set into *The Professor's House* like the view from the casement of that Dutch interior, is the objectively told, factual-seeming counterpart of Thea's experience in the Ancient People's cliff houses in *The Song of the Lark*, which was published ten years earlier. Tom Outland's story has a further difference: the tragic view.

It is the objective chronicler for whom the story comes to a tragic end. For Thea, who has seen in her discovery of the Ancient People something totally and exclusively her own, and her own secret, it remained undamaged as a dream. She apprehended it in her own mind, and her own body, as a message for her. Tom Outland's Cliff City was there in the world, and he wanted the world to discover it as he had, to study it, venerate it, share it; and it was taken away from him, broken and desecrated; it brought about not the self-discovery of Thea, but a crisis and a lasting sorrow in human relationship. In the end, it is more of an interior story than Thea's ever was.

"Tom Outland's Story" is written with a compression and strength that the author had already showed us in *A Lost Lady*, and achieves a simplicity that, as it seems to me, nothing else she wrote ever surpassed. Such simplicity is not what a writer starts with; it is what the writer is able to end with, or hopes to be able.

The Professor's House in whole might show us that the novel, in its excellence as a work of art, stands, itself, as a house finished. In so much as it has perfection, perfection has not sealed it, but opened it to us. (pp. 18-19)

In the Cather novels, there is a setting apart of the artist in value, a setting apart of his life from that of other people. Artists, in her considered and lifelong view, are perhaps greater and more deserving to be made way for than other human beings. This could never have been a popular view, but in trying to understand it I think she extolled the artist not for what would seem vanity, or for anything less than a function he could perform—the great thing that only an artist would be able, in her eyes, to do. The artist has a role. Thea, meditating on this role, thought, of the people who cared about her singing, "Perhaps each of them concealed another person in himself, just as she did. . . . What if one's second self could somehow speak to all those second selves?" At base, I think this is an aspect of the Cather sense of obligation to give of oneself. . . . The artist is set apart the more entirely, all but symbolically, to give himself away, to fulfill the ultimate role of dedication.

Today, neither the artist nor the world holds this idea, and it has faded, along with some of her other strong beliefs (the hero and the heroine, the sanctity of the family), from our own view. Our ideas of history and art are different from hers, as tomorrow's will be different from today's. We have arrived at new places to stand to obtain our own viewpoint of history. Art, since it grows out of its times, is of itself, and by rights, a changing body. But truth?

Truth is the rock. Willa Cather saw it as unassailable. Today the question is asked if this is indeed so. Many of us align ourselves with Willa Cather—I do—in thinking the truth will hold out; but there are many who feel another way, and indeed,

I believe, many who would not feel life was over if there were no truth there.

One of the strangest things about art, nevertheless, is that the rock it is built on is not its real test. Our greatest poem made a mistake about the construction of the universe, but this will never bring the poem down.

Yet plain enough is the structure Willa Cather built on these rocks she herself believed were eternal. Her work we, today, see entirely on its own, without need of that support. It holds itself independently, as that future church appears to be doing above the dreaming head of Saint Francis of Assisi in Giotto's fresco. Her work has its own firm reason for existence. And here it stands, a monument more unshakable than she might have dreamed, to the independent human spirit she most adored.

She made this work out of her life, her perishable life, which is so much safer a material to build with than convictions, however immutable they seem to the one who so passionately holds them. It is out of our own lives that we, in turn, reach out to it. Because the house of Willa Cather contained, embodied, a spirit, it will always seem to us inhabited. There is life in that house, the spirit she made it for, made it out of; it is all one substance: it is her might and her heart and soul, all together, and it abides. (pp. 19-20)

> *Eudora Welty, "The House of Willa Cather" (reprinted by permission of Russell & Volkening, Inc., as agents for the author; copyright © 1974 by Eudora Welty; originally a paper presented at the Nebraska Center for Continuing Education, Lincoln, Nebraska on October 26, 1973), in* The Art of Willa Cather, *edited by Bernice Slote and Virginia Faulkner, University of Nebraska Press, 1974, pp. 3-20.*

DAVID STOUCK (essay date 1975)

[*Stouck interprets Cather's* O Pioneers! *as an epic novel, specifically because of its classic treatment of the individual's struggle against nature and its larger-than-life portrait of the heroine Alexandra Bergson. Though many early critics, like Frederic Taber Cooper (see excerpt above), considered Alexandra's character flat and one-dimensional, Stouck argues that this is a necessary result of the epic mode, which stresses narrative over character development.*]

In writing about the settling of the Midwest in *O Pioneers!* Willa Cather chose her subject, as Melville had earlier, from the classical matter for American epic—the struggle of man against nature. As much as from revolution and civil war, America came into being and achieved its identity from the struggle of the common man to subdue the lonely and terrifying wilderness around him. Miss Cather herself apparently referred to the novel as a "two-part pastoral" (Alexandra's story and the romance of "The White Mulberry Tree"), but doubtless she meant simply to indicate the rural subject of her book. For her novel eschews the return to childhood and self-analysis of pastoral writing; her focus is on the struggle of the earliest pioneer settlers of the prairie and on the embodiment of their most heroic gestures in the stalwart figure of Alexandra Bergson. That we respond to Alexandra as an epic heroine there can be little question. . . . Her character and her role are defined early in the novel when her dying father turns over the responsibility of the farm and the family to his daughter rather than to his two grown sons. Alexandra is not only strong in body (at one point she is described as "Amazonian"), but also her father recognizes in her a strength of will and dependability

which are wanting in his sons. That initial image of Alexandra taking up the heavy burden of a man's life does not change during the course of the novel; eventually Alexandra becomes the most successful landowner on the Divide, and in effect the leader of the Swedish pioneer community. (pp. 24-5)

While Alexandra as a woman is a particularized character, her struggle to prevail over the landscape and prepare the way for generations to come is representative of the race of early pioneers who settled the American prairie. Our attention is frequently directed in the epic manner to the activities of a whole people. In the prefatory poem, "Prairie Spring," the labors of the pioneers are described in the "miles of fresh-plowed soil," and in "The growing wheat, the growing weeds, / The toiling horses, the tired men." In the first chapter of the novel, despite its particular concerns, we are made aware from the continual reference to people in the background of the typicality of the scene and of the concerns that the people hold in common. . . . We are reminded of the movements of a whole people in those conventional set pieces (the French church fair, the grain harvesting, the great confirmation service, the mourning of the people for Amédée Chevalier), which expand the novel's focus to include those joys and sorrows which are communal. A visually striking epic sequence (the single image multiplied) describes the cavalcade of forty French boys riding across the plains to meet the bishop; it is charged with the extremes of fundamental human emotions, the ecstatic zeal of high animal spirits tempered by the somber fact of a young friend's death. But always in the foreground remains the figure of Alexandra whose valor and foresight embody the essence of the heroic spirit.

As epic heroine Alexandra's character never changes—her strength of purpose, her dependability and kindness, are constant throughout. . . . She is a woman who feels deeply (she is not without tears in her eyes at moments of crisis), but not one who can show or express her feelings very freely. Moreover, she is always able to control her emotions and proceed with the business of everyday life. . . . But consequently Alexandra is essentially a flat, one-dimensional character. While she suffers through many disappointments and losses (most agonizing is the death of Emil and Marie), there is never any question as to how she will respond; her character is constant and predictable. It is to Alexandra that everyone else turns with his or her troubles: she protects the old people like Crazy Ivar and Mrs. Lee from the indifference of youth; she advises her family and neighbors in their struggles to tame the wild land; she gives guidance and love to the younger people around her— the Swedish working girls from the old country, Emil and Marie, and her brothers' children. (pp. 25-7)

Alexandra wears a man's coat, but ultimately it is the maternal protection of a strong woman that she offers to those around her; and it is this quality—that of a larger-than-life mother figure—that is at the heart of the imaginative conception of her character. Alexandra is one-dimensional because as epic heroine she is idealized, and accordingly we can feel only a limited sense of identification with her. Her sorrows and her triumphs are those of someone stronger than we are. We hold her strength and virtue in high esteem and yet we cannot really share or emulate them. Rather our imaginative involvement is with that maternal protection she affords those around her.

In a work of the epic imagination the artist does not necessarily appear within the story. It is in the pastoral mode (in a book like *My Ántonia*) that the artist assumes the role of both creator and central figure in his art because the urge to create in pastoral is born out of a desire to understand oneself and one's past experiences more fully. That need for understanding (an understanding which ideally will lead to more satisfying forms of experience in the present) is evaded in epic by the unquestioning acceptance of other men's values and by seeing internal conflict in the form of physical or cosmic moral struggle. In becoming the spokesman for the people the epic artist eliminates his own responses and assumes a sentimental, humble point of view, one which affirms the traditional values of human experience without question. There is no pervasive humor or irony in epic because a comic response involves a critical judgment, an opposition of values which would fracture the vision of social unity. The perspective which controls the narration of *O Pioneers!* is a humble one which threatens to lapse into the maudlin, but at the same time this sentimental perspective is the source of the novel's peculiar effectiveness, for it is this point of view which bathes the humble subjects of the book and the simple facts of their lives in an enduring warmth and affection. Such a viewpoint was the means by which Miss Cather was most fully able to transmit her deep sympathy for the figures of her personal past, her almost child-like love and admiration for their humble, faithful lives.

The artist may not dramatize himself overtly in an epic, but in the manner of narration and in some of the lesser characters he invariably projects something of his intimate involvement into the story. In *O Pioneers!* the figure who most closely approximates the artist is Carl Linstrum, Alexandra's childhood neighbor and faithful admirer. Linstrum is the weak, sensitive, artistic man, ill-suited to the life of a pioneer. . . . In his failure to find a meaningful or satisfying life, he anticipates the dilemma of several of Willa Cather's disillusioned and peripatetic protagonists. . . . One cannot help but catch a glimpse here of Willa Cather herself—the writer living in eastern cities making annual pilgrimages to her home in Nebraska. The emotion out of which the novel has been created, and which is focused in Carl's point of view, stems from that desire to return "home" to the heartland of America and to those strong, heroic figures, the pioneers. (pp. 27-8)

In any work of art certain images stand out more than others and remain fixed in our memory—these images have clearly involved the imagination of the artist most deeply. In *O Pioneers!* the image of Alexandra Bergson taking up the heroic task of cultivating the stubborn soil is at the center of our response to the novel—that epic response being reinforced by the Whitman poem of the book's title, with its eulogy to those who have conquered the wild country. (p. 29)

But almost equally as engaging as Alexandra is the image of the garden, the enclosed, safe place, which is most fully dramatized in Marie Shabata's orchard with its protective mulberry hedge. The expansion of the novel by developing the love story (Miss Cather clearly felt Alexandra's story was not dramatic enough) may seem a gratuitous and unconvincing digression from the central theme of Alexandra and the land. And yet the image of the garden is as integral a part of the novel's imaginative structure as the figure of its stalwart heroine because it is that desire for an enclosed retreat, with its guarantee of maternal protection, which draws the imagination in this novel to its epic heroine. (p. 30)

The two stories woven together in *O Pioneers!* stretch back to Genesis. Alexandra's is the story of creation, the story of a human civilization being shaped out of a land as flat and formless as the sea. Emil and Marie's is the story of lovers cast from the earth's garden through sin. The timeless, ever-recurring nature of these stories is secured by literary allusion. Alexandra's heroic character and actions are enriched by her connection with the old Swedish legends. Emil and Marie's story acquires a universal pathos by its association with classical tales of lovers who die. . . . The staining of the white mulberries with the lovers' blood recalls specifically the story of Pyramus and Thisbe. While their romance is still innocent Marie tells Emil of her love for the trees in her orchard and of the old Bohemian belief in the power of the linden's virtue to purify the forest. The innocent, domestic love of Baucis and Philemon is perhaps remembered here, for those faithful lovers, wishing to die together, were changed into trees, an oak and a linden. And there is a suggestion of the Endymion story when Marie resolves in the moonlight that to dream of her love will henceforward be enough. The two stories of the novel are brought together in a nexus of creation and destruction as Ivar repeats to himself Psalm 101 from the Bible, a song of "mercy and judgment" in which the psalmist promises to remember the faithful of the land and to destroy all wicked doers.

In terms of the novel's epic theme—and it is the epic note which prevails at the end—the death of the lovers is necessary to give Alexandra's story a tragic depth and to allow her old antagonist, nature, to reassert its power. . . . Their death gives Alexandra's life a tragic quality because they represent essentially everything for which she has lived and fought. . . . However, there is a sober triumph in the novel's conclusion, for here the epic view of nature as universal foe gives way to a cyclical and reassuring vision of mutability, and here the author can express once more those feelings of love and admiration for her heroine and for her people. . . . (pp. 31-2)

> *David Stouck, "'O Pioneers!': Willa Cather and the Epic Imagination," in* Prairie Schooner *(reprinted from* Prairie Schooner *by permission of University of Nebraska Press; © 1972 by University of Nebraska Press), Vol. 46, No. 1, Spring, 1972 (and reprinted in a different form as "'O Pioneers!' and the Epic Imagination," in his* Willa Cather's Imagination, *University of Nebraska Press, 1975, pp. 23-34).*

PAUL COMEAU (essay date 1981)

[*In the following excerpt, Comeau calls* Lucy Gayheart *Cather's "most daring and certainly her most profound novel." Comeau argues that in* Lucy Gayheart *Cather was attempting to demonstrate the similarities in the processes of art and life, specifically because both have their origins in the creative process of memory. For Comeau, the novel is a moving example of the creative act itself—an act suggested in the characters' fascination with the past. Such an interpretation suggests that Cather remained committed to broadening her artistic talents throughout her career. This idea is similar to that of Merrill M. Skaggs (see excerpt below), but is opposed by Clifton Fadiman and Granville Hicks (see excerpts above).*]

In an impressive introductory essay to *The Kingdom of Art*, Bernice Slote suggests that *Lucy Gayheart* is "perhaps the most perilous voyage" in all of Willa Cather's fiction, "a Pilgrim's Progress in which no one except the book itself reaches the Celestial City." "The voyage perilous" is an early Cather phrase to describe the "mighty craft" of literature, the "awful and fearsome" journey of an idea traveling "from the brain to the hand." Most of Cather's critics have felt that it was a perilous journey as regards *Lucy Gayheart,* and that intention and execution were not matched. . . . These critics, however, have judged the novel in the light of Cather's other works rather than discussing it in its own terms. For in fact the author is attempting in this late novel something as complex and experimental as anything she had written. She is not seeking to define the artistic process as she had done previously in [*The Troll Garden, The Song of the Lark,* and *Youth and the Bright Medusa*] . . . , rather, she is reflecting on that process in the distinctly philosophical context of life, death, and immortality. More important, she was no longer making her memories the immediate and vital center of her art, but instead she was contemplating the very process by which life becomes art. *Lucy Gayheart* . . . reasserts many of Cather's former statements about life and art within a structure that reflects the artistic process as she perceived it—the strong current of personal memory shaped by a mighty craft.

Memory in one form or another is central to all of Willa Cather's major fiction, and especially to *My Ántonia* . . . , which consists mainly of Jim Burden's recollections of Ántonia Shimerda, his childhood friend and inspiration. However, where the imaginative tension in *My Ántonia,* as David Stouck has suggested, lies in "a creative opposition between the novel's content and its form," between Jim's penchant for romanticizing the past and "the tragic realization that the past can never be recaptured," in *Lucy Gayheart* this tension is wholly muted. Form and content in this later work complement rather than oppose each other, presumably because the conflict between past and present has been resolved in the author's own mind. She is now writing from the vantage point of a long perspective, a perspective colored by achieved artistic excellence, popular success, and, of course, the passing years. The result is an essentially nondramatic narrative, which accounts in part for the critics' charge of lifelessness. (pp. 199-200)

When the novel opens, Lucy has been dead for some time; what follows of her story is therefore a creation of memory. The narrator points out, in a kind of prologue, that people still talk of Lucy, but not a great deal, because "life goes on and we live in the present." . . . The emphasis falls equally on the pleasantness of Lucy's memory and on the precariousness of its survival. Similarly, as chapter 1 progresses, her youthful exuberance and the idea of mutability are held in a delicate equipoise. . . . [The] fact that photographs of Lucy are meaningless to those who knew her suggests the failure of mechanical means to depict and thereby preserve Lucy's uniqueness. But the inherent tension between life and death, between past and present, is muted, as I have indicated, because Lucy is already dead. The primary concern then is not to establish the continuing vitality of Lucy Gayheart, as Jim is concerned to do in *My Ántonia,* but to preserve and reflect on her memory. This is the particular concern of Part I of the novel.

In Part I we are shown the qualities of Lucy Gayheart that no photograph can reproduce, as well as her influence on the two major figures in her life, Harry Gordon and Clement Sebastian. In a phrase, Lucy is "a mercurial, vacillating person." . . . She embodies total emotion and gaiety of heart, as her name implies, and is the antithesis of Harry Gordon, her childhood sweetheart, who believes that "'facts are at the bottom of everything'." . . . When we first see Lucy, she is home for the Christmas holidays of 1901, skating energetically across the river that later claims her life. For Harry, who arrives at the river after work for a last "'turn with Lucy before the sun goes down'" (a brief skate which literally signifies his last turn with her before the day ends and symbolically represents his last chance with her before the sunset of their relationship), she expresses the emotional side of his nature that he feels compelled to hide. She is his romantic ideal of the perfect wife.

Unfortunately for Gordon, though, his ideal has already been touched by the power of art in the person of Clement Sebastian. (pp. 201-02)

The details of Lucy's love affair with Sebastian, like those of Harry Gordon's spiteful marriage to Harriet Arkwright and of Sebastian's unexpected death, are in themselves less important to Cather's purpose than the philosophical truths they point up. Collectively these details support the earlier "revelation of love as a tragic force," and individually they comprise the substance of those future memories that help Lucy survive Sebastian's death, thereby suggesting in both a philosophical and a concrete way that the processes of life and art are basically the same process of memory. Indeed, much of Lucy's zest for life in Part I derives from the process of memory in much the same way that Cather saw the creative process functioning. (p. 202)

In contrast, Sebastian's view of life, his pose of tragic melancholy, is the product of unhappy memories. A beautiful vase of roses sent to him from one of his old friends impresses Lucy greatly, but Clement replies pessimistically that the lady probably "'remembers things as sweeter than they were'." . . . Likewise, an obituary recalls to Sebastian his younger days and a friendship with the deceased, Larry MacGowan, but what remains now is the bitter memory of that friendship's disintegration. Sebastian sees this disintegration as an emblem of an entire life of failed relationships. (p. 203)

Sebastian's death, which concludes Part I, does not occur until, inspired by Lucy, he experiences a revival of interest in his life and art. Ironically, though, the singer's joy is equally his sorrow, as it is Lucy's, for his renewed interest in singing means long absences through extended overseas engagements. This blending of joy and sorrow seems overly sentimental, especially in the context of Sebastian's final parting from Lucy, but the union of happiness and melancholy is not foreign to great literature. It is, for instance, germane to Shakespeare's greatest plays and central to Keats's best poems, because it is the profoundest philosophical comment on life and art.

Sustaining the emotional note, Willa Cather begins the second part of her novel with an almost Keatsian ode to autumn, which has symbolic overtones in terms of winter's approach and Lucy's impending death; it is interesting to note also that in a vaguely symbolic way Lucy's story unfolds within one complete seasonal cycle. But autumn's remedial influence . . . is of first importance as Lucy, wretched and despairing after Sebastian's death, wanders the streets of Haverford in a daze. Her memories are now even more important to her than before, and her father's apple orchard becomes her refuge from the world, her place to sit and remember, and live. . . . Sebastian's tragic melancholy has been transferred to Lucy, who, in discovering firsthand the tragic nature of life and love, has lost her former zest for life.

There are other obstacles, too, that she must combat in her struggle for psychic and emotional survival. Harry Gordon's coldness is a barrier she never quite breaks through, and her sister Pauline's meddling is a constant vexation. These seemingly trivial problems are devastating for Lucy, who lives primarily through emotion, and they also develop further Cather's philosophical statement on love and human relationships. Lucy's disagreements with Pauline, in particular, shift the focus from romantic or love relationships, as detailed in Lucy's love for Sebastian, to everyday family relationships. (pp. 203-04)

Just as Part I ends with Sebastian's death by drowning, so Part II ends with Lucy's drowning, shortly after she reacquires the desire to go on living. Notwithstanding this grim duplication of events highlighting life's fragility, the emphasis remains squarely on the process of living. But whereas Lucy herself symbolizes this process in the early chapters, its chief proponent in Part II is Mrs. Ramsay, who speaks of life as Sebastian once sang his songs, from the long perspective of age and experience. (p. 205)

With Lucy's untimely death, the cycle of a single life touched by the power of art and shaped by the power of memory is completed. However, the novel's philosophical scope exceeds the limited effects of personal memories to include the broader implications of preserving an individual's memory after death. Willa Cather therefore appends an epilogue to Lucy's story, Part III, which deals directly with the survival of Lucy's memory and indirectly with the larger philosophical questions of immortality and art. Part III begins twenty-five years after Lucy's death, with old Mr. Gayheart's funeral. . . . Pauline, dead five years, is still remembered, whereas Lucy, dead twenty-five years, is almost entirely forgotten.

The effect of this deliberate emphasis on the passing years is twofold. First, it sets the stage for Harry Gordon's reminiscences, which comprise the main content of Part III. And second, it lengthens the reader's perspective in a concrete way, intimately tying the novel's content to its three-part form. In Part I, for instance, our perception of Lucy is given some immediacy by the narrator's descriptions of her relationships with Harry and Sebastian. In Part II, also, we perceive Lucy from a relatively close perspective in her dealings with Pauline, although Mrs. Ramsay's remarks help to remove us somewhat from the immediacy of Lucy's suffering. But finally, in Part III, our perception of Lucy changes markedly, as we remember her through the perspective of a middle-aged Harry Gordon. (p. 206)

Apparently . . . , *Lucy Gayheart* concludes on a pessimistic note. The sustained focus on memory has been, by definition of the human condition, a focus on mutability. And yet, another emphasis has been insistently woven into the narrative, an emphasis underlining Sebastian's interpretation and presentation of a song, the old soprano's feeling for words, and Mr. Gayheart's commitment to fine craftsmanship in his trade; in short, this other emphasis highlights the "mighty craft" that goes into creating a work of art, a craft that matures and improves long after the artist's initial youthful exuberance has given way to the long perspective of age and experience. And this mighty craft, together with the process of memory and all the feeling and emotion involved therein—the same process by which Lucy Gayheart is ultimately transformed from a sentimental, suffering young woman into a beautiful idea—represents the essence of the artistic process. Accordingly, Lucy's memory is preserved not in a photograph or in a slab of cement but in the work of art which is the novel. Perhaps this is something of what Bernice Slote means when she likens *Lucy Gayheart* to a "Pilgrim's Progress in which no one except the book itself reaches the Celestial City."

To conclude, therefore, that Lucy is lifeless and her story mawkishly sentimental is to mistake Willa Cather's purpose and accomplishment in what is possibly her most daring and certainly her most profound novel. *Lucy Gayheart* is a philosophical work in which the author reflects on the artistic process and its relationship to life, death, and immortality from a long perspective and in such a way as to effect a perfect marriage of form and content—in the final analysis, the processes of art and life are shown to be the same creative process of memory.

To be sure, the risks in terms of dramatic presentation were great. However, I believe Cather recognized and accepted the risk of sentimentality in choosing a traditional love story and a sentimental heroine, for she knew, with the aging soprano of *The Bohemian Girl*, that the foolish words of the old song could be transformed by "a sympathy, a tolerant understanding"; and her identification with the old singer may have been more personal still, for surely the author's return in *Lucy Gayheart* to her early Nebraska material was a return to an old song, which began in 1912 with the publication of a short story significantly titled "**The Bohemian Girl.**"

Similarly, I believe Cather recognized and accepted the risk of lifelessness in duplicating in her style Sebastian's manner of presentation, refusing to identify herself with her heroine or to bring Lucy too near into the present, because she did not intend Lucy to be the same kind of character as Thea Kronborg or Marian Forrester. Rather, these so-called faulty touches are at the heart of Willa Cather's determination to produce, again after the manner of Clement Sebastian, not an interpretation of the artistic process but the thing itself. For what is an artist's life work, in essence, but a love affair with "the things that haunt him," as she explains in a preface to Sarah Orne Jewett's best stories? What is Lucy Gayheart essentially but a symbol of emotion and desire, the necessary accompanists to life and art? Clearly, Willa Cather knew the perils of the voyage she was undertaking, just as she knew her limitations as an artist at age sixty-two (like the old soprano, the original physical sweetness had gone from her voice), but, as always, she was willing to risk a great deal in the name of experimentation, of artistic integrity. Moreover, the returns must have justified the risks, because *Lucy Gayheart* is an artwork that establishes finally the fundamental relationship between life and art, thus vindicating a lifetime spent in the pursuit of artistic excellence and providing legitimate hope for some measure of immortality thereafter. (pp. 207-09)

> *Paul Comeau, "Willa Cather's 'Lucy Gayheart': A Long Perspective," in* Prairie Schooner *(reprinted from* Prairie Schooner *by permission of University of Nebraska Press; © 1981 by University of Nebraska Press), Vol. 55, Nos. 1 & 2, Spring-Summer, 1981, pp. 199-209.*

MERRILL MAGUIRE SKAGGS   (essay date 1981-82)

[*Despite the general opinion among earlier critics that Cather's final works—such as* Lucy Gayheart *and* Sapphira and the Slave Girl*—demonstrate a marked decline in her artistic talents, Skaggs argues that Cather continued to experiment with her craft and to broaden her skills throughout her entire career. As an example, Skaggs cites* Sapphira *as a highly experimental novel in which Cather overturned standard literary assumptions about the antebellum South, challenged accepted stereotypes of the typical Southern lady, and, most significantly, developed a new literary structure which was based on the arousal and frustration of certain expectations within the reader's mind. For more commentary on the experimental nature of Cather's final works see the excerpt above by Paul Comeau.*]

I believe that Cather, one of our greatest sculptors of words and fictions, wrote all her novels in order to try new experiments in form. Some of her experiments concentrated on the shape of her own sentences and episodes, and on how to achieve her planned effects. Some involved testing her forms against older models, storylines, or traditions. In the latter, she set out to challenge or subvert. She never repeated herself, however, and her determination to experiment is implicit in her last works as well as in her first. In fact, experiments in both form and also subject matter, as well as challenges to older literary models, appear in her last novel, *Sapphira and the Slave Girl.* A reader's task, then, is to ask what *new* possibilities Cather was working out here. As I see it, Cather returned to the scenes of her childhood in order first to assault standard literary assumptions about antebellum Southern life, then to challenge the widely accepted stereotype of the Southern lady, and finally to try out a new and, for her, radically different, narrative form. To satisfy her, her book had to incorporate new literary strategies and fresh structural devices.

Sapphira, a Southern plantation story, continues to confuse its readers because its elements fly in the face of our social expectations, or even our "rules" about good fiction. Though we quickly recognize the traditional setting, subsequent details do not correspond to our picture of Southern life. (pp. 3-4)

Thus when Cather invokes [Southern] types only to portray them in radically "uncharacteristic" attitudes and acts, she puzzles contemporary readers. But when her choices in *Sapphira* are considered highly deliberate, and not merely the products of failing creative energies or an old woman's descent into nostalgia, the novel takes on new interest. (p. 4)

Most obviously, the novel centers around the conflict between a privileged aristocratic lady and her personal slave. As a female, Willa Cather is already exceptional in choosing an in-depth exploration of the peculiar institution. The guilts and consequences of slavery may have obsessed many Southern male writers, but unravelling its economic complexities is not an enterprise that has dominated the works of the best Southern female writers.

In any case, *Sapphira* dramatizes the evils of slavery; describes a harrowing slave escape across a threatening river (pointedly reminiscent, at first glance, of Harriet Beecher Stowe's earlier version); emphasizes the slave girl's vulnerability to sexual abuse by white males; concedes the ability of clever slaves to manipulate the system to their own advantage; acknowledges the existence of widespread miscegenation and the problems it creates; describes "good slave" internalization of the white social code; reminds us that some slaves accepted their freedom only with reluctance; includes a variety of social types from a mountaineer family through a schoolteacher and postmistress to a hard-working, self-sufficient miller; and finally stresses "typically Southern" obsessions with family backgrounds and geographic loyalties. All these elements are to be expected in Southern fiction.

Given these standard clues to Southern plots, it is no wonder that readers are sometimes brought up short by *Sapphira.* The slave girl's flight to freedom is terrifying enough to leave her hysterical; yet she is not pursued, while her escape proceeds smoothly with the help of the white mistress's daughter, who arranges a carefully planned journey. Further, here the black female sexual object does not get raped. Furthermore, her fond master does not seduce her. In fact, miscegenation arouses some disgust, but not in the person of black Till, a participant. And when beleaguered Nancy finally marries, she chooses a half-Scot, half-Indian Canadian. The Southern plantation here is ruled by an iron hand, but the hand is attached to an invalid mistress, not to her husband. Any rigid class structure based on inherited and fertile land has broken down before the novel begins, when the mistress Sapphira removes herself to the uncultivated backwoods—to Back Creek. The novel's haphazardly educated male worker is often troubled and confused

about issues like slavery which he can neither understand nor resolve; but he in fact consistently sticks to his articulated and strongly felt, if contradictory, principles. The strong-willed individual who orders others around does *not* control events or actions in the story at all. And most importantly, arrogance and sinful pride are not much punished.

With predictable irony, the story ends happily after peace and social order have been restored. But unpredictably, the greatest financial success in the novel is associated with ex-slave Nancy, who returns dressed far more opulently than her former owner's family could imagine themselves. Since Nancy is employed as a rich family's housekeeper in Canada, however, her superior wardrobe mostly indicates the present low income of one good Southern white family.

Here, then, is a book in which Cather deliberately arouses a variety of expectations, and then deliberately disappoints them. If asked why she chose to do so, she might have replied that things were not always as others had described them, at least not back in ole Virginie.

Besides the obvious and unconventional twists of plot, Cather also uses a large number of unconventional details—that is, facts or assertions that fly in the face of traditional assumptions about the Old South. For example, her first two paragraphs establish the different but familiar social types that Sapphira and Henry represent: Sapphira is a lady and Henry is a plain-folk representative. Our first indication that formulas are not to be followed here, however, is our discovery that Sapphira and Henry, exemplars of classes traditionally described as distinctly separate, are married. The first two paragraphs stress the hard physical work which this male head of the "best" family requires of himself. Further, we learn, the family has not so much inherited its position as built it up, house and rank, by hard labor, albeit on inherited but undeveloped land.

The second small shock, foretaste of things to come, registers when we realize that in this community moral leadership is not supplied by the aristocratic lady Sapphira, for Southern women have ordinarily been ceded the role of moral guardian. The major moral consciousness in this community belongs to the lady's husband, the miller. Henry, a "solid, powerful figure of a man," is known for his fair dealing. Cather compares Henry's face to "an old port" wine . . . , one of her highest accolades, connoting seasoned maturity and sweetness. Yet in this isolated and provincial community, the respected miller still talks little (always a suspicious characteristic in nineteenth-century Southern fiction), and seems rather foreign to his neighbors. (pp. 5-7)

This family, headed by an aristocrat, is clearly descending the social ladder: the "stalwart" daughter Rachel wears a sun-bonnet and a calico dress, enters by the back door, has never owned servants, and attends the Baptist church. But their decline is *not* due to the aristocrat's conventional poor head for business; Sapphira, besides being a woman, has also managed her farm as capably as she once managed her father's business affairs. The decline is directly linked to the quality and location of the land on which they have chosen to settle, and to try to farm.

A particularly interesting detail in the novel is the association of Sapphira's behavior with her Episcopal upbringing. By contrast, the Baptists here—collectively the most denigrated Protestant denomination in the Southern fiction stretching from Simon Suggs through Walker Percy's works—are much the more liberal group regarding race. The Baptists include blacks in their church services, though Baptists, as "red-necks" or physical laborers, are supposed to lack the *noblesse oblige* of the less sun-exposed and richer Episcopalians.

One of the novel's central ironies, then, is that the slaves best love their arbitrary and autocratic Ole Miss Sapphira, not her Baptist daughter Rachel. . . . Rachel believes that slavery is wrong, whether slaves like it or not. (None of the loosely supervised Dodderidge slaves has ever run away without returning eventually.) But Rachel bases her convictions on principles which are not unequivocally supported even by sacred scriptures. For nowhere in the Bible can one "find a clear condemnation of slavery". . . . Sapphira's world is based on much simpler principles of self-interest. Yet Sapphira loves, among other things, a lover, a good meal, and spunk. So she inexplicably tolerates the useless Tansy Dave, or the lazy Bluebell, or the insolent Jezebel, and therefore appears to her servants more generous and merciful than the juster Rachel or Henry. (p. 8)

If Mistress Sapphira is alternately arbitrary and implacable, quixotic and ruthless, an ineffective plotter but a harsh judge of others, she is anything but a conventional Southern lady, except in her outward manners and in the forms she insists on observing. Yet the portrait of her which emerges in this novel is one of the most daring of Cather's experiments, and Cather dramatizes in this woman a remarkably complex human mixture. For Sapphira is capable of infamous villainy, but also of extraordinary generosity. (p. 9)

[Cather] forces us to realize that Sapphira's sins and her virtues spring from the same self-confident dependence on herself, from her arrogant willfulness, and from her unfaltering courage and self-love. Though debilitated and even deformed by her illness, "She would make her death easy for everyone, because she would meet it with that composure which . . . [Henry] had sometimes called heartlessness, but which now seemed to him strength." . . . She dies in her place—in her candlelit parlor, upright in her wheel chair, looking out over the grounds she has planted, pruned, and made beautiful. She dies smiling. What Cather forces us to accept, against all our contrary inclinations, is that Sapphira deserves her beautiful death. Cather insists that we see Sapphira as a woman whose selfishness most enviably preserves and sustains her. The novel is thus as ideologically unconventional as its heroine. The main character is "typically" Southern in her willfulness and freedom from the restraints of conventional decencies. But the main character is also a widely respected and deeply loved woman. No wonder, then, that the novel continues to make us uncomfortable.

What is always interesting about Cather's work, however, is its form. In *Sapphira*, as elsewhere, Cather's most inventive experiments are with structure. Again Cather contrives a new form that is both novel and organic to her material.

Perhaps the most useful strategy in this novel is Cather's use of set-pieces or episodes which appear self-contained, like parables, and which seem to interrupt the narrative flow without contributing substantially to the main action of the plot. When something looks peculiar in Cather's purposeful work, however, it needs asking about. The apparently unrelated parables or set-pieces in *Sapphira and the Slave Girl* implicitly comment on major incidents. (pp. 10-11)

The looping backward and forward between good and bad, advance and retreat, positive and negative, in [the novel's] analogies reminds us of the splendid visual image which comes to symbolize the "truths" of this novel. The beautiful double-"S" in the road to Timber Ridge, the lovely spot surrounded by dogwood, laurel, and wild-honeysuckle in which the road seems to continue without getting anywhere, symbolizes the pace of this story (the action proper hardly begins until the half-way mark, with the arrival of Martin Colbert), the contrary directions in which the story seems to run, the confusions of debates over slavery, and the twists in each human character depicted here. Thus Henry Colbert, the community's moral pillar, still fails to act decisively when his beloved Nancy is threatened in a way he most abhors; merry Tap, who rides heroically to fetch Dr. Clavenger for the mortally ill grandchildren, is still hung by a "Yankee jury" for committing murder; and would-be rapist Martin Colbert still dies gloriously as a Confederate captain and is commemorated by a local monument. The double-"S" is one of Cather's most effective central symbols. It is first described immediately after Henry Colbert remembers the hymn "God moves in a mysterious way/His wonders to perform." . . . Importantly, the spot is one which Cather associates with beauty. But it is also one which symbolizes all human life. (pp. 12-13)

[Perhaps] the most daring experiment Cather tries in *Sapphira and the Slave Girl* involves narrative point of view. The author intrudes directly into this novel *as author*, from the beginning. She occasionally makes her own value judgments, instead of allowing characters or incidents to make them for her, or she comments directly to the reader. And in the final pages, she appears as the child she was, when she first heard this story. (p. 13)

Of course, in reminding us that the scenes she describes were those she actually observed, Cather gives credence to all the surprising details she incorporates here. Further, she pointedly reminds us that the book is a *story* which exists because she enjoys telling it, as well as because she once enjoyed hearing it. She reminds the reader to remember the personality doing the telling, as well as the mere sequence of the events. In fact, she explains the large gaps in the narrative by making the book a childhood story, subject to lapses of memory and therefore lacking all merely decorative fact. The book becomes the kind of remembered tale in which one can expect to have many realistic, scrubby, or sordid details omitted.

But ultimately, it seems to me, Willa Cather steps out of her last years' reclusiveness and consciousness of failing health, and into her book, because this novel makes a summarizing statement for its creator: life is not neatly formulaic or ideologically correct, and neither are people. Real-life characters are always more complex than merely fictional creations. Living villains can also be heroes, as well as vice versa. And sometimes offensive, isolated, and dying old women can also deserve respect. At the end of her career, near the end of her life, Cather seems to assert that something is worth remembering about even the pettiest and most difficult of women, when they have the courage to love what they are, and the stamina to remain faithful to the lives they have willfully and consciously created for themselves. (pp. 13-14)

Merrill Maguire Skaggs, "Willa Cather's Experimental Southern Novel," in The Mississippi Quarterly *(copyright 1982 Mississippi State University), Vol. XXXV, No. 1, Winter, 1981-82, pp. 3-14.*

ADDITIONAL BIBLIOGRAPHY

Bennett, Mildred R. *The World of Willa Cather.* Lincoln: University of Nebraska Press, 1961, 285 p.

Biocritical study describing the effect of the American frontier on Cather's writing, as well as the influence of a number of her friends and literary relations.

Bloom, Edward A., and Bloom, Lillian D.: "Willa Cather's Novels of the Frontier: A Study in Thematic Symbolism." *American Literature* XXI, No. 1 (March 1949): 71-93.
   Interpretive study. The critics attempt to define the "over-all pattern" of Cather's novels, arguing that the majority of criticism on her work has focused exclusively on her role as a social historian, thereby limiting her achievements.

Brown, Marion Marsh, and Crone, Ruth. *Only One Point of the Compass: Willa Cather in the Northeast*. Lynnville, Tenn.: Archer Editions Press, 1980, 136 p.
   Biography that deals exclusively with Cather's life in northeast Canada.

Gerber, Philip. *Willa Cather*. Boston: Twayne Publishers, 1975, 187 p.
   Critical study that traces the development of Cather's art by focusing on the thematic elements in her novels and stories.

Haller, Evelyn H. "The Iconography of Vice in Willa Cather's *My Ántonia*." *Colby Library Quarterly* XIV, No. 2 (June 1978): 93-102.
   Narrative examination. Haller points out the allegorical nature of Cather's *My Ántonia*.

Lewis, Edith. *Willa Cather Living: A Personal Record*. New York: Alfred A. Knopf, 1953, 197 p.
   Personal memoir of Cather's life and work.

McFarland, Dorothy Tuck. *Willa Cather*. New York: Frederick Ungar Publishing Co., 1978, 154 p.
   Biocritical study. Following a brief discussion of Cather's life, McFarland devotes the remainder of her book to a close examination of the author's major novels and stories.

Murphy, John J. "Cooper, Cather, and the Downward Path to Progress." *Prairie Schooner* 55, Nos. 1-2 (Spring-Summer 1981): 168-84.*
   Comparative study. Murphy compares Cather to James Fenimore Cooper in her reaction against the exploitation and development of the American frontier.

Murphy, John J., ed. *Five Essays on Willa Cather: The Merrimack Symposium*. North Andover, Mass.: Merrimack College, 1974, 141 p.
   Collection of five essays on Cather's art and technique by such authors as Bernice Slote, John J. Murphy, and Lillian D. Bloom.

Sergeant, Elizabeth Shepley. *Willa Cather: A Memoir*. Philadephia and New York: J. B. Lippincott Co., 1953, 288 p.
   Personal memoir of Cather's life and work.

Woodress, James. *Willa Cather: Her Life and Art*. New York: Pegasus, 1970, 288 p.
   Biocritical study of Cather's life and art which incorporates all the recent developments and findings of such prominent critics on Cather as Bernice Slote and Mildred Bennett.

Stephen Crane

1871-1900

(Also wrote under pseudonym of Johnston Smith) American novelist, short story writer, poet, and journalist.

Crane was one of America's foremost realistic writers, and his works have been credited with marking the beginning of modern American Naturalism. He is best remembered for his Civil War novel *The Red Badge of Courage*, a classic of American literature which realistically depicts the psychological complexities of fear and courage on the battlefield. Influenced by William Dean Howells's theory of Realism and by Hamlin Garland's Veritism, Crane utilized his keen observations, as well as personal experiences, to achieve a narrative vividness and sense of immediacy matched by few American writers before him. While *The Red Badge of Courage* is acknowledged as his masterpiece, Crane's novel *Maggie: A Girl of the Streets* is also acclaimed as an important work in the development of literary Naturalism, and his often-anthologized short stories "The Open Boat," "The Blue Hotel," and "The Bride Comes to Yellow Sky" are considered among the most skillfully crafted stories in American literature.

Born in Newark, New Jersey, Crane was the youngest in a family of fourteen children. His desire to write was inspired by his family: his father, a Methodist minister, and his mother, a devout woman dedicated to social concerns, were writers of religious articles, and two of his brothers were journalists. Crane began his higher education in 1888 at Hudson River Institute and Claverack College, a military school which nurtured his interest in Civil War studies and military training, knowledge of which he later used in *The Red Badge of Courage*. Thereafter, he spent two indifferent semesters at Lafayette College and Syracuse University, where he was distinguished more for his agility on the baseball diamond and the football field than for his prowess in the classroom. Throughout his college days, however, Crane was busy writing. He worked as a "stringer" for his brother's news service, and it is thought that he wrote the preliminary sketch of *Maggie* while at Syracuse. In 1891, deciding that "humanity was a more interesting study" than the college curriculum, Crane quit school to work full time as a reporter with his brother and part time for the New York *Tribune*. While in New York he became well acquainted with life in the Bowery and lived a bohemian existence among the local artists. Crane spent most of this period in poverty and so was able to convey firsthand knowledge when he wrote of tenement life. In 1893, Crane privately published his first novel, *Maggie*, under a pseudonym, knowing that his description of slum realities would shock readers. According to Crane, *Maggie* "tries to show that environment is a tremendous thing in the world and frequently shapes lives regardless." Critics suggest that the novel was a major development in American literary Naturalism and that it introduced Crane's vision of life as warfare: influenced by the Darwinism of the times, Crane viewed individuals as victims of purposeless forces, and believed that they encountered only hostility in their relationships with other individuals, with society, with nature, and with God. Also prominent in his first novel is an ironic technique that exposes the hypocrisy of moral tenets when they are set against the sordid reality of slum life. Though

it received the support of such literary figures as Garland and Howells, *Maggie* was not a success. It was not until 1896, after Crane tempered the brutalities in a second edition, that the work became widely recognized.

Crane's second novel, *The Red Badge of Courage*, won him international fame. His vision of life as warfare is uniquely rendered in this short, essentially plotless novel. Often compared to Impressionist painting, *The Red Badge of Courage* is a series of vivid episodes in which a young soldier, Henry Fleming, confronts a gamut of emotions—fear, courage, pride, and humility—in his attempt to understand his battlefield experiences; in this respect, Fleming represents the "Everyman" of war. Crane's work employs a narrative point of view which distinctively offers both an objective panorama of the war scene and the more subjective impressions of the young soldier. Since he had never been to war when he wrote *The Red Badge of Courage* Crane claimed that his source for the accurate descriptions of combat was the football field; when he finally experienced battle as a war correspondent, he said of the novel, "It was all right." Critics have long debated whether *The Red Badge of Courage* should be considered a product of any specific literary movement or method. The work has been claimed by several schools of thought and referred to as Realistic, Naturalistic, Symbolistic, and Impressionistic. Proponents of Realism view *The Red Badge of Courage* as the first unromanticized account of the Civil War and they find Fleming's maturation from an inexperienced youth to an enlightened battle-worn soldier to be truthfully depicted. Other critics indicate that the youth's actions and experiences are shaped by Naturalistic forces and that his "development" as a character is incidental to Crane's expert depiction of how these forces determine human existence. Stylistically, Crane's novel contains elements of both Impressionism and Symbolism. R. W. Stallman proposes that *The Red Badge of Courage* is a symbolic construct laden with symbols and images. However, according to some critics, his "episodic narrative structure" and his consistent use of color imagery are indicative of an Impressionistic method. Edwin H. Cady offers a succinct estimate of the novel: "The very secret of the novel's power inheres in the inviolably organic uniqueness with which Crane adapted all four methods to his need. *The Red Badge*'s method is all and none. There is no previous fiction like it."

Shortly after the publication of *The Red Badge of Courage* in 1895, Crane published *The Black Riders and Other Lines*. Though he is not widely recognized for his poetry, his volume of free verse is important because it foreshadowed the work of the Imagist poets with its concise, vivid images. During this time Crane continued to work as a journalist. He traveled throughout the American West and Mexico for a news syndicate and later used his experiences in stories. Returning to New York, Crane wrote *The Third Violet*, a story of bohemian life among the poor artists of New York. This novel is considered one of his least accomplished works and some early critics believed that it was an indication of Crane's failing talent.

In 1897 Crane met Cora Taylor, the proprietor of the dubiously named Hotel de Dream, a combination hotel, nightclub, and brothel. Together as common-law husband and wife, they moved to England where Crane formed literary friendships with Joseph Conrad, H. G. Wells, and Henry James. Shortly after this move, Crane left to report on the Spanish-American War for the New York *World;* in part, he accepted the job to escape financial debts he and Cora had accrued. Though Crane was ill when he returned to England, he resumed writing in order to satisfy his artistic needs and to earn money. With *Active Service* he produced another flawed work. This war novel, based on his experiences as a war correspondent in the Greco-Turkish War, is often described as an uneven and sprawling work. By 1900, Crane's health had rapidly deteriorated due to months spent in the Cuban jungles as a reporter and because of a general disregard for his physical well-being. After several respiratory attacks, Crane died of tuberculosis at the age of twenty-eight.

Although Crane achieved the pinnacle of his success with the novel *The Red Badge of Courage*, many critics believe that his greatest strength was in the short story. His major achievements in this genre are "The Open Boat," "The Blue Hotel," and "The Bride Comes to Yellow Sky." "The Open Boat" is based on Crane's firsthand experience as a correspondent shipwrecked on a filibustering expedition to the Cuban revolutionaries in 1897. The Naturalistic story pits a handful of men against the ruthlessness of indifferent nature. Crane's characteristic use of vivid imagery is demonstrated throughout this story to underscore the beauty and terror of natural forces. According to critics, Crane is at his best in "The Open Boat," maintaining an even tone and fluent style, while conveying a metaphysical identification between God and nature. Crane's facility with imagery is again displayed with telling effect in the tragic story "The Blue Hotel." In this deceptively simple

Western tale, "the Swede," one of Crane's most interesting characters, becomes the inevitable victim of his own preconceptions about the "Wild West"—fearing a lawless, uncivilized world, his violent reactions to Western life result in his own death. Thomas Gullason refers to Crane's depiction of "the Swede" as "almost Dostoevskyean in its psychological penetration." In another Western story, the comic "The Bride Comes to Yellow Sky," Crane parodies the "shoot 'em-up" Western myth as the characters Jack Potter and Scratchy Wilson fail to fulfill romantic illusions with a gunfight. In these short stories, as in most of his work, Crane is a consummate ironist, employing a technique which consistently suggests the disparity between an individual's idea of reality and reality as it actually exists.

Commentators generally agree that for the most part, Crane disregarded plot and character delineation in his work, and that he was unable to sustain longer works of fiction. However, with the proliferation of Crane scholarship during the last twenty years, Crane's literary reputation has grown. Critics believe that despite his minor flaws, Crane's artistry lies in his ability to convey a personal vision based on his own "quality of personal honesty." In so doing, he pioneered the way for a modern form of fiction which superceded the genteel Realism of late nineteenth-century American literature.

(See also *Dictionary of Literary Biography*, Vol. 12: *American Realists and Naturalists*.)

PRINCIPAL WORKS

Maggie: A Girl of the Streets (A Story of New York) [as Johnston Smith] (novel) 1893; also published as *Maggie: A Girl of the Streets* [revised edition], 1896
The Black Riders, and Other Lines (poetry) 1895
The Red Badge of Courage: An Episode of the American Civil War (novel) 1895
George's Mother (novel) 1896
The Little Regiment, and Other Episodes of the American Civil War (short stories) 1896
The Third Violet (novel) 1897
The Open Boat, and Other Tales of Adventure (short stories) 1898
Active Service (novel) 1899
The Monster, and Other Stories (short stories) 1899
War Is Kind (poetry) 1899
Whilomville Stories (short stories) 1900
Wounds in the Rain: A Collection of Stories Relating to the Spanish-American War of 1898 (short stories) 1900
*The O'Ruddy (novel) 1903
The Work of Stephen Crane. 12 vols. (poetry, short stories, novels, and journalism) 1925-27
The Collected Poems of Stephen Crane (poetry) 1930
**The Sullivan County Sketches of Stephen Crane (sketches) 1949
Stephen Crane: An Omnibus (poetry, short stories, and novels) 1952
Stephen Crane: Letters (letters) 1960
The Works of Stephen Crane. 10 vols. (poetry, short stories, novels, and journalism) 1969-72
The Western Writings of Stephen Crane (short stories) 1979

*This work was completed by Robert Barr.

**This work was originally published serially in the newspaper *New York Tribune* and the journal *The Cosmopolitan* in 1892.

HAMLIN GARLAND (essay date 1893)

[*Garland was a well-known author and critic whom Crane met in 1891. He became one of Crane's first mentors, encouraging him to follow his literary doctrine of Veritism, a theory similar to William Dean Howell's Realism. It was to Garland that Crane sent the manuscript of* Maggie: A Girl of the Streets *and the following essay is the earliest review of that novel.*]

['**Maggie**'] is a work of astonishingly good style. It deals with poverty and vice and crime also, but it does so, not out of curiosity, not out of salaciousness, but because of a distinct art impulse, the desire to utter in truthful phrase a certain rebellious cry. It is the voice of the slums. It is not written by a dilettante; it is written by one who has lived the life. The young author, Stephen Crane, is a native of the city, and has grown up in the very scenes he describes. His book is the most truthful and unhackneyed study of the slums I have yet read, fragment though it is. It is pictorial, graphic, terrible in its directness. It has no conventional phrases. It gives the dialect of the slums as I have never before seen it written—crisp, direct, terse. It is another locality finding voice.

It is important because it voices the blind rebellion of Rum Alley and Devil's Row. It creates the atmosphere of the jungles, where vice festers and crime passes gloomily by, where outlawed human nature rebels against God and man.

The story fails of rounded completeness. It is only a fragment. It is typical only of the worst elements of the alley. The author should delineate the families living on the next street, who live lives of heroic purity and hopeless hardship.

The dictum is amazingly simple and fine for so young a writer. Some of the works illuminate like flashes of light. Mr. Crane is only twenty-one years of age, and yet he has met and grappled with the actualities of the street in almost unequalled grace and strength. With such a *technique* already at command, with life mainly *before him*, Stephen Crane is to be henceforth reckoned with. '**Maggie**' should be put beside 'Van Bibber' to see the extremes of New York as stated by two young men. Mr. Crane need not fear comparisons so far as *technique* goes, and Mr. Davis will need to step forward right briskly or he may be overtaken by a man who impresses the reader with a sense of almost unlimited resource.

> *Hamlin Garland, in his review of "Maggie: A Girl of the Streets" (reprinted by permission of the Literary Estate of Hamlin Garland), in* The Arena, *Boston Vol. VIII, No. XLIII, June, 1893 (and reprinted in* Stephen Crane: The Critical Heritage, *edited by Richard M. Weatherford, Routledge & Kegan Paul, 1973, p. 38).*

GEORGE WYNDHAM (essay date 1896)

[*Wyndham was a member of Parliament and a literary critic for the* National Observer *and* New Review. *His laudatory critique of* The Red Badge of Courage *prompted the novel's phenomenal popularity in England and regenerated the American press's interest in Crane's work.*]

Mr. Stephen Crane, the author of *The Red Badge of Courage . . .*, is a great artist, with something new to say, and consequently, with a new way of saying it. His theme, indeed, is an old one, but old themes re-handled anew in the light of

novel experience, are the stuff out of which masterpieces are made, and in *The Red Badge of Courage* Mr. Crane has surely contrived a masterpiece. He writes of war—the ominous and alluring possibility for every man, since the heir of all the ages has won and must keep his inheritance by secular combat. . . . The sights flashed indelibly on the retina of the eye; the sounds that after long silences suddenly cypher; the stenches that sicken in after-life at any chance allusion to decay; or, stirred by these, the storms of passions that force yells of defiance out of inarticulate clowns; the winds of fear that sweep by night along prostrate ranks, with the acceleration of trains and the noise as of a whole town waking from nightmare with stertorous, indrawn grasps—these colossal facts of the senses and the soul are the only colours in which the very image of war can be painted. Mr. Crane has composed his palette with these colours, and has painted a picture that challenged comparison with the most vivid scenes of Tolstoï's *la Guerre et la Paix* or of Zola's *la Débâcle*. This is unstinted praise, but I feel bound to give it after reading the book twice and comparing it with Zola's Sédan and Tolstoï's account of Rostow's squadron for the first time under fire. Indeed, I think that Mr. Crane's picture of war is more complete than Tolstoï's, more true than Zola's. (pp. 32-3)

Mr. Crane, for his distinction, has hit on a new device, or at least on one which has never been used before with such consistency and effect. In order to show the features of modern war, he takes a subject—a youth with a peculiar temperament, capable of exaltation and yet morbidly sensitive. Then he traces the successive impressions made on such a temperament, from minute to minute, during two days of heavy fighting. He stages the drama of war, so to speak, within the mind of one man, and then admits you to the theatre. You may, if you please, object that this youth is unlike most other young men who serve in the ranks, and that the same events would have impressed the average man differently; but you are convinced that this man's soul is truly drawn, and that the impressions made in it are faithfully rendered. The youth's temperament is merely the medium which the artist has chosen: that it is exceptionally plastic makes but for the deeper incision of his work. It follows from Mr. Crane's method that he creates by his art even such a first-hand report of war as we seek in vain among the journals and letters of soldiers. But the book is not written in the form of an autobiography: the author narrates. He is therefore at liberty to give scenery and action, down to the slightest gestures and outward signs of inward elation or suffering, and he does this with the vigour and terseness of a master. Had he put his descriptions of scenery and his atmospheric effects, or his reports of overheard conversations, into the mouth of his youth, their very excellence would have belied all likelihood. Yet in all his descriptions and all his reports he confines himself only to such things as that youth heard and saw, and, of these, only to such as influenced his emotions. By this compromise he combines the strength and truth of a monodrama with the directness and colour of the best narrative prose. (pp. 33-4)

Mr. Crane discovers his youth, Henry Fleming, in a phase of disillusion. It is some monotonous months since boyish "visions of broken-bladed glory" impelled him to enlist in the Northern Army towards the middle of the American war. (p. 34)

The youth is a "mental outcast" among his comrades, "wrestling with his personal problem," and sweating as he listens to the muttered scoring of a card game, his eyes fixed on the "red, shivering reflection of a fire." Every day they drill; every night they watch the red campfires of the enemy on the far shore of a river, eating their hearts out. At last they march. . . . The book is full of such vivid impressions, half of sense and half of imagination:—The columns as they marched "were like two serpents crawling from the cavern of night." But the march, which, in his boyish imagination, should have led forthwith into melodramatic action is but the precursor of other marches. After days of weariness and nights of discomfort at last, as in life, without preface, and in a lull of the mind's anxiety, the long-dreaded and long-expected is suddenly and smoothly in process of accomplishment:—"One grey morning he was kicked on the leg by the tall soldier, and then, before he was entirely awake, he found himself running down a wood road in the midst of men who were panting with the first effects of speed. His canteen banged rhythmically upon his thigh, and his haversack bobbed softly. His musket bounced a trifle from his shoulder at each stride and made his cap feel uncertain upon his head." From this moment, reached on the thirtieth page, the drama races through another hundred and sixty pages to the end of the book, and to read those pages is in itself an experience of breathless, lambent, detonating life. So brilliant and detached are the images evoked that, like illuminated bodies actually seen, they leave their fever-bright phantasms floating before the brain. You may shut the book, but you still see the battle-flags "jerked about madly in the smoke," or sinking with "dying gestures of despair," the men "dropping here and there like bundles"; the captain shot dead with "an astonished and sorrowful look as if he thought some friend had done him an ill-turn"; and the litter of corpses, "twisted in fantastic contortions," as if "they had fallen from some great height, dumped out upon the ground from the sky." The book is full of sensuous impressions that leap out from the picture: of gestures, attitudes, grimaces, that flash into portentous definition, like faces from the climbing clouds of nightmare. It leaves the imagination bounded with a "dense wall of smoke, furiously slit and slashed by the knife-like fire from the rifles." It leaves, in short, such indelible traces as are left by the actual experience of war. The picture shows grisly shadows and vermilion splashes, but, as in the vast drama it reflects so truly, these features, though insistent, are small in size, and are lost in the immensity of the theatre. The tranquil forest stands around; the "fairy-blue of the sky" is over it all. And, as in the actual experience of war, the impressions which these startling features inflict, though acute, are localised and not too deep: are as it were mere pin-pricks, or, at worst, clean cuts from a lancet in a body thrilled with currents of physical excitement and sopped with anaesthetics of emotion. (pp. 35-6)

Mr. Crane's method, when dealing with things seen and heard, is akin to Zola's: he omits nothing and extenuates nothing, save the actual blasphemy and obscenity of a soldier's oaths. These he indicates, sufficiently for any purpose of art, by brief allusions to their vigour and variety. Even Zola has rarely surpassed the appalling realism of Jim Conklin's death in Chapter X. Indeed, there is little to criticise in Mr. Crane's observation, except an undue subordination of the shrill cry of bullets to the sharp crashing of rifles. He omits the long chromatic whine defining its invisible arc in the air, and the fretful snatch a few feet from the listener's head. In addition to this gift of observation, Mr. Crane has at command the imaginative phrase. The firing follows a retreat as with "yellings of eager metallic hounds"; the men at their mechanic loading and firing are like "fiends jigging heavily in the smoke"; in a lull before the attack "there passed slowly the intense moments that precede the tempest"; then, after single shots, "the battle roar settled to a rolling thunder, which was a single long explosion." And, as I have said, when Mr. Crane deals with things felt he gives

a truer report than Zola. He postulates his hero's temperament—a day-dreamer given over to morbid self-analysis who enlists, not from any deep-seated belief in the holiness of fighting for his country, but in hasty pursuit of a vanishing ambition. This choice enables Mr. Crane to double his picturesque advantage with an ethical advantage equally great. Not only is his youth, like the sufferer in *The Fall of the House of Usher*, super-sensitive to every pin-prick of sensation: he is also a delicate meter of emotion and fancy. In such a nature the waves of feeling take exaggerated curves, and hallucination haunts the brain. Thus, when awaiting the first attack, his mind is thronged with vivid images of a circus he had seen as a boy: it is there in definite detail, even as the Apothecary's shop usurps Romeo's mind at the crisis of his fate. And thus also, like Herodotus' Aristodemus, he vacillates between cowardice and heroism. Nothing could well be more subtile than his self-deception and that sudden enlightenment which leads him to "throw aside his mental pamphlets on the philosophy of the retreated and rules for the guidance of the damned." His soul is of that kind which, "sick with self-love," can only be saved "so as by fire"; and it is saved when the battle-bond of brotherhood is born within it, and is found plainly of deeper import than the cause for which he and his comrades fight, even as that cause is loftier than his personal ambition. By his choice of a hero Mr. Crane displays in the same work a pageant of the senses and a tragedy of the soul.

But he does not obtrude his moral. The "tall soldier" and the lieutenant are brave and content throughout, the one by custom as a veteran, the other by constitution as a hero. But the two boys, the youth and his friend, "the loud soldier," are at first querulous braggarts, but at the last they are transmuted by danger. . . . Let no man cast a stone of contempt at these two lads during their earlier weakness until he has fully gauged the jarring discordance of battle. To be jostled on a platform when you have lost your luggage and missed your train on an errand of vital importance gives a truer pre-taste of war than any field-day; yet many a well-disciplined man will denounce the universe upon slighter provocation. It is enough that these two were boys and that they became men.

Yet must it be said that this youth's emotional experience was singular. In a battle there are a few physical cowards, abjects born with defective circulations, who literally turn blue at the approach of danger, and a few on whom danger acts like the keen, rare atmosphere of snow-clad peaks. But between these extremes come many to whom danger is as strong wine, with the multitude which gladly accepts the "iron laws of tradition" and finds welcome support in "a moving box." To this youth, as the cool dawn of his first day's fighting changed by infinitesimal gradations to a feverish noon, the whole evolution pointed to "a trap"; but I have seen another youth under like circumstances toss a pumpkin into the air and spit it on his sword. To this youth the very landscape was filled with "the stealthy approach of death." You are convinced by the author's art that it was so to this man. But to others, as the clamour increases, it is as if the serenity of the morning had taken refuge in their brains. This man "stumbles over the stones as he runs breathlessly forward"; another realises for the first time how right it is to be adroit even in running. The movement of his body becomes an art, which is not self-conscious, since its whole intention is to impress others within the limits of a modest decorum. We know that both love and courage teach this mastery over the details of living. (pp. 37-9)

But had Mr. Crane taken an average man he would have written an ordinary story, whereas he has written one which is certain to last. It is glorious to see his youth discover courage in the bed-rock of primeval antagonism after the collapse of his tinsel bravado; it is something higher to see him raise upon that rock the temple of resignation. Mr. Crane, as an artist, achieves by his singleness of purpose a truer and completer picture of war than either Tolstoï, bent also upon proving the insignificance of heroes, or Zola, bent also upon prophesying the regeneration of France. That is much; but it is more than his work of art, when completed, chimes with the universal experience of mankind; that his heroes find in their extreme danger, if not confidence in their leaders and conviction in their cause, at least the conviction that most men do what they can or, at most, what they must. We have few good accounts of battles—many of shipwrecks; and we know that, just as the storm rises, so does the commonplace captain show as a god, and the hysterical passenger as a cheerful heroine.

It is but a further step to recognise all life for a battle and this earth for a vessel lost in space. We may then infer that virtues easy in moments of distress may be useful also in everyday experience. (pp. 39-40)

> *George Wyndham, "A Remarkable Book," in* The New Review *(© TNR Publications, Ltd., London), Vol. XIV, No. 80, January, 1896, pp. 30-40.*

STEPHEN CRANE   (letter date 1896)

[*Crane's letter was prompted by the editor John Northern Hilliard's request that Crane write a sketch of himself for a publication series in the* Union and Advertisor. *The letter, which is often quoted by critics, reveals Crane's artistic principles.*]

As far as myself and my own meagre success are concerned, I began the battle of life with no talent, no equipment, but with an ardent admiration and desire. I did little work at school, but confined my abilities, such as they were, to the diamond. Not that I disliked books, but the cut-and-dried curriculum of the college did not appeal to me. Humanity was a much more interesting study. When I ought to have been at recitations I was studying faces on the streets, and when I ought to have been studying my next day's lessons I was watching the trains roll in and out of the Central Station. So, you see, I had, first of all, to recover from college. I had to build up, so to speak. And my chiefest desire was to write plainly and unmistakably, so that all men (and some women) might read and understand. That to my mind is good writing. There is a great deal of labor connected with literature. I think that is the hardest thing about it. There is nothing to respect in art save one's own opinion of it. . . .

The only thing that deeply pleases me in my literary life—brief and inglorious as it is—is the fact that men of sense believe me to be sincere. **"Maggie,"** published in paper covers, made me the friendship of Hamlin Garland and W. D. Howells, and the one thing that makes my life worth living in the midst of all this abuse and ridicule is the consciousness that never for an instant have those friendships at all diminished. Personally I am aware that my work does not amount to a string of dried beans—I always calmly admit it. But I also know that I do the best that is in me, without regard to cheers or damnation. When I was the mark for every humorist in the country I went ahead, and now, when I am the mark for only 50 per cent of the humorists of the country, I go ahead, for I understand that a man is born into the world with his own pair of eyes, and he is not at all responsible for his vision—he is merely responsible for his quality of personal honesty. To keep close to this personal honesty is my supreme ambition. There is a sublime egotism in talking of honesty. I, however, do not say that I am honest. I merely say that I am as nearly honest as a weak mental machinery will allow. This aim in life struck me as being the only thing worth while. A man is sure to fail at it, but there is something in the failure. (pp. 108-10)

> *Stephen Crane, in his letter to John Northern Hilliard in January, 1896(?), in his* Stephen Crane: Letters, *edited by R. W. Stallman and Lillian Gilkes (reprinted by permission of New York University Press; copyright © 1960 by New York University), New York University Press, 1960, pp. 108-10.*

FRANK NORRIS   (essay date 1896)

[*Norris—author of* The Octopus *and* McTeague—*is often considered, with Crane, Theodore Dreiser, and Jack London, to be one of America's foremost Naturalistic writers. During the mid-1890s, Norris joined the staff of* Wave, *a San Francisco literary magazine, to which he contributed the following review of* George's Mother *and* Maggie.]

In **Maggie, a Girl of the Streets,** Stephen Crane has written a story something on the plan of the episode of Nana in *L'Assommoir,* the dialect and local color being that of the Bowery. Mr. Crane strikes no new note in his picture of the other half. Most of his characters are old acquaintances in the world of fiction and we know all about—or, at least, certain novelists have pretended to tell us all about the life of the mean streets of a great city. In ordinary hands the tale of **Maggie** would be "twice told." But Mr. Crane is, of course, out of the ordinary. I think that the charm of his style lies chiefly in his habit and aptitude for making phrases—short, terse epigrams struck off in the heat of composition, sparks merely, that cast a momentary gleam of light upon whole phases of life. There are hundreds of them throughout this tale of **Maggie.** Indeed, it is the way Mr. Crane tells his story. The picture he makes is not a single carefully composed painting, serious, finished, scrupulously studied, but rather scores and scores of tiny flashlight photographs, instantaneous, caught, as it were, on the run. Of a necessity, then, the movement of his tale must be rapid, brief, very hurried, hardly more than a glimpse.

One of the best of these "flash-lights" is that of the "truck driver." At first one is tempted to believe that it is a "long exposure," but on second thought I conclude that it is merely a great number of snap-shots taken at the same subject. (p. 164)

Good though the story is and told in Mr. Crane's catching style, the impression left with the reader is one of hurry; the downfall of Maggie, the motif of the tale, strikes one as handled in a manner almost too flippant for the seriousness of the subject.

George's Mother seems to me better than **Maggie.** For a short novel it is less pretentious, has fewer characters and more unity, conveying one distinct impression. It is the story of a "little old woman" and her boy George. The boy starts well enough, stays at home in the evening, and even goes—at least on one occasion—to prayer meeting with his mother. But he falls into bad company and becomes perverted. Incidentally the mother dies, of grief and disappointment, so Mr. Crane implies.

There is something about this death of "the little old woman" that rings surprisingly true. . . . (p. 165)

It is most remarkable in Crane's novels to observe the truly marvelous fashion in which he feels and seizes the most subtle and hardly expressed moods and emotions. This quality of his was apparent on almost every page of the *Red Badge.* We have it again in *George's Mother.* . . .

But though these stories make interesting reading, the reader is apt to feel that the author is writing, as it were, from the outside. There is a certain lack of sympathy apparent. Mr. Crane does not seem to *know* his people. You are tempted to wonder if he has ever studied them as closely as he might have done. He does not seem to me to have gotten down *into* their life and to have written from what he saw around him. His people are types, not characters; his scenes and incidents are not particularized. It is as if Mr. Crane had merely used the "machinery" and "business" of slum life to develop certain traits or to portray certain emotions and passions that might happen anywhere. With him it is the broader, vaguer, *human* interest that is the main thing, not the smaller details of a particular phase of life. (p. 166)

> Frank Norris, "Stephen Crane's Stories of Life in the Slums: 'Maggie' and 'George's Mother'" (originally published in Wave, Vol. XV, July 4, 1896), in his The Literary Criticism of Frank Norris, edited by Donald Pizer (copyright © 1964 by Donald Pizer), University of Texas Press, 1964, pp. 164-66.

RICHARD HARDING DAVIS   (essay date 1899)

[*Davis was the son of the writer Rebecca Harding Davis and perhaps the most popular reporter of his time. As a special correspondent for the New York* Sun *and for other New York and London papers, he covered numerous wars, such as the Spanish-American War, the Greco-Turkish War, and the Boer War, and travelled widely throughout the world. Davis also published a collection of short stories which are more remarkable for their craftsmanship than for their substance. Although Davis and Crane were rivals as journalists and war correspondents, Davis offers an admiring assessment of Crane's journalistic work at the Cuban front.*]

The best correspondent is probably the man who by his energy and resources sees more of the war, both afloat and ashore, than do his rivals, and who is able to make the public see what he saw. If that is a good definition, Stephen Crane would seem to have distinctly won the first place among correspondents in the late disturbance. . . .

Near the close of the war, a group of correspondents in Puerto Rico made out a list of the events which, in their opinion, were of the greatest news value during the campaign, and a list of the correspondents, with the events each had witnessed credited to his name. Judged from this basis, Mr. Crane easily led all the rest. Of his power to make the public see what he sees it would be impertinent to speak. His story of Nolan, the regular, bleeding to death on the San Juan hills, is so far as I have read, the most valuable contribution to literature that the war has produced. It is only necessary to imagine how other writers would have handled it, to appreciate that it could not have been better done. His story of the marine at Guantanamo, who stood on the crest of the hill to "wigwag" to the war-ships, and so exposed himself to the fire of the entire Spanish force, is also particularly interesting, as it illustrates that in his devotion to duty, and also in his readiness at the exciting moments of life, Crane is quite as much of a soldier as the man whose courage he described. He tells how the marine stood erect, staring through the dusk with half-closed eyes, and with his lips moving as he counted the answers from the war-ships, while innumerable bullets splashed the sand about him. But it never occurs to Crane that to sit at the man's feet, as he did, close enough to watch his lips move and to be able to make mental notes for a later tribute to the marine's scorn of fear, was equally deserving of praise. (p. 941)

> Richard Harding Davis, "Our War Correspondents in Cuba and Puerto Rico," in Harper's New Monthly Magazine (copyright © 1899 by Harper's New Monthly Magazine; all rights reserved), Vol. XCVIII, No. 588, May, 1899, pp. 938-48.*

H. G. WELLS   (essay date 1900)

[*Wells is best known today, along with Jules Verne, as the father of modern science fiction and as a utopian idealist who correctly foretold an era of chemical warfare, atomic weaponry, and world wars. His writing was shaped by the influence of Arnold Bennett, Frank Harris, Joseph Conrad, and other contemporaries with whom he exchanged criticism and opinions on the art of writing. Throughout much of his career, Wells wrote and lectured on the betterment of society through education and the advance of scientific innovation. A Fabian socialist and student of zoologist T. H. Huxley, Wells was, until his last bitter years, a believer in the gradual, inevitable moral and intellectual ascent of humanity. Much of his literary criticism was written during the 1890s at* The Saturday Review, *under the direction of Harris. A friend of Crane, Wells wrote the following essay, which is considered one of the most important early critical assessments of Crane's works.*]

[Stephen Crane's] success in England began with the *Red Badge of Courage,* which did, indeed, more completely than any other book has done for many years, take the reading public by storm. Its freshness of method, its vigor of imagination, its force of color and its essential freedom from many traditions that dominate this side of the Atlantic, came—in spite of the previous shock of Mr. Kipling—with a positive effect of impact. It was a new thing, in a new school. When one looked for sources, one thought at once of Tolstoy; but, though it was clear that Tolstoy had exerted a powerful influence upon the conception, if not the actual writing, of the book, there still remained something entirely original and novel. To a certain extent, of course, that was the new man as an individual; but, to at least an equal extent, it was the new man as a typical young American, free at last, as no generation of Americans have been free before, of any regard for English criticism, comment, or tradition, and applying to literary work the conception and theories of the cosmopolitan studio with a quite American directness and vigor. For the great influence of the studio on Crane cannot be ignored; in the persistent selection of the essential elements of an impression, in the ruthless exclusion of mere information, in the direct vigor with which the selected points are made, there is Whistler even more than there is Tolstoy in the *Red Badge of Courage.* (pp. 662-63)

I do not propose to add anything here to the mass of criticism upon this remarkable book. Like everything else which has been abundantly praised, it has occasionally been praised "all wrong"; and I suppose that it must have been said hundreds of times that this book is a subjective study of the typical soldier in war. But Mr. George Wyndham, himself a soldier of experience, has pointed out in an admirable preface to a re-issue of this and other of Crane's war studies that the hero of the *Red Badge* is, and is intended to be, altogether a more sensitive and imaginative person than the ordinary man. He is the idealist, the dreamer of boastful things brought suddenly to the test of danger and swift occasions and the presence of death. To this theme Crane returned several times, and particularly in a story called *Death and the Child* that was written after the

Greek war. That story is considered by very many of Crane's admirers as absolutely his best. I have carefully reread it in deference to opinions I am bound to respect, but I still find it inferior to the earlier work. The generalized application is, to my taste, a little too evidently underlined; there is just that touch of insistence that prevails so painfully at times in Victor Hugo's work, as of a writer not sure of his reader, not happy in his reader, and seeking to drive his implication (of which also he is not quite sure) home. The child is not a natural child; there is no happy touch to make it personally alive; it is THE CHILD, something unfalteringly big; a large, pink, generalized thing, I cannot help but see it, after the fashion of a Vatican cherub. The fugitive runs panting to where, all innocent of the battle about it, it plays; and he falls down breathless to be asked, "Are you a man?" One sees the intention clearly enough; but in the later story it seems to me there is a new ingredient that is absent from the earlier stories, an ingredient imposed on Crane's natural genius from without—a concession to the demands of a criticism it had been wiser, if less modest, in him to disregard—criticism that missed this quality of generalization and demanded it, even though it had to be artificially and deliberately introduced.

Following hard upon the appearance of the *Red Badge of Courage* in England came reprints of two books, *Maggie* and *George's Mother*. . . . Their reception gave Crane his first taste of the peculiarities of the new public he had come upon. These stories seem to me in no way inferior to the *Red Badge;* and at times there are passages, the lament of Maggie's mother at the end of *Maggie,* for example, that it would be hard to beat by any passage from the later book. But on all hands came discouragement or tepid praise. The fact of it is, there had been almost an orgy of praise—for England, that is; and ideas and adjectives and phrases were exhausted. To write further long reviews on works displaying the same qualities as had been already amply discussed in the notices of the *Red Badge* would be difficult and laborious; while to admit an equal excellence and deny an equal prominence would be absurd. But to treat these stories as early work, to find them immature, dismiss them and proceed to fresher topics, was obvious and convenient. So it was, I uncharitably imagine, that these two tales have been overshadowed and are still comparatively unknown. Yet they are absolutely essential to a just understanding of Crane. In these stories, and in these alone, he achieved tenderness and a compulsion of sympathy for other than vehement emotions, qualities that the readers of *The Third Violet* and *On Active Service,* his later love stories, might well imagine beyond his reach. (pp. 663-65)

The Open Boat is to my mind, beyond all question, the crown of all his work. It has all the stark power of the earlier stories, with a new element of restraint; the color is as full and strong as ever, fuller and stronger, indeed; but those chromatic splashes that at times deafen and confuse in the *Red Badge,* those images that astonish rather than enlighten, are disciplined and controlled. "That and *Flanagan,*" he told me, with a philosophical laugh, "was all I got out of Cuba." I cannot say whether they were worth the price, but I am convinced that these two things are as immortal as any work of any living man. (p. 666)

The Open Boat gives its title to a volume containing, in addition to that and *Flanagan,* certain short pieces. One of these others, at least, is also to my mind a perfect thing, *The Wise Men.* It tells of the race between two bartenders in the city of Mexico, and I cannot imagine how it could possibly have been better told. And in this volume, too, is that other masterpiece—the one I deny—*Death and the Child.*

Now I do not know how Crane took the reception of this book, for he was not the man to babble of his wrongs; but I cannot conceive how it could have been anything but a grave disappointment to him. To use the silly phrase of the literary shopman, "the vogue of the short story" was already over; rubbish, pure rubbish, provided only it was lengthy, had resumed its former precedence again in the reviews, in the publishers' advertisements, and on the library and booksellers' counters. The book was taken as a trivial by-product, its author was exhorted to abandon this production of "brilliant fragments"—anything less than fifty thousand words is a fragment to the writer of literary columns—and to make that "sustained effort," that architectural undertaking, that alone impresses the commercial mind. (pp. 668-69)

It was probably such influence that led him to write *The Third Violet.* I do not know certainly, but I imagine, that the book was to be a demonstration, and it is not a successful demonstration, that Crane could write a charming love story. It is the very simple affair of an art student and a summer boarder, with the more superficial incidents of their petty encounters set forth in a forcible, objective manner that is curiously hard and unsympathetic. The characters act, and on reflection one admits they act, *true,* but the play of their emotions goes on behind the curtain of the style, and all the enrichments of imaginative appeal that make love beautiful are omitted. Yet, though the story as a whole fails to satisfy, there are many isolated portions of altogether happy effectiveness, a certain ride behind an ox cart, for example. Much more surely is *On Active Service* an effort, and in places a painful effort, to fit his peculiar gift to the uncongenial conditions of popular acceptance. It is the least capable and least satisfactory of all Crane's work.

While these later books were appearing, and right up to his last fatal illness, Crane continued to produce fresh war pictures that show little or no falling off in vigor of imagination and handling; and, in addition, he was experimenting with verse. In that little stone-blue volume, *War Is Kind,* and in the earlier *Black Riders,* the reader will find a series of acute and vivid impressions and many of the finer qualities of Crane's descriptive prose, but he will not find any novel delights of melody or cadence of any fresh aspects of Crane's personality. (pp. 669-70)

In style, in method, and in all that is distinctively *not* found in his books, he is sharply defined, the expression in literary art of certain enormous repudiations. Was ever a man before who wrote of battles so abundantly as he has done, and never had a word, never a word from first to last, of the purpose and justification of the war? And of the God of Battles, no more than the battered name; "Hully Gee!"—the lingering trace of the Deity! And of the sensuousness and tenderness of love, so much as one can find in *The Third Violet!* Any richness of allusion, any melody or balance of phrase, the half quotation that refracts and softens and enriches the statement, the momentary digression that opens like a window upon beautiful or distant things, are not merely absent, but obviously and sedulously avoided. It is as if the racial thought and tradition had been razed from his mind and its site plowed and salted. He is more than himself in this; he is the first expression of the opening mind of a new period, or, at least, the early emphatic phase of a new initiative—beginning, as a growing mind must needs begin, with the record of impressions, a record of a vigor and intensity beyond all precedent. (p. 671)

H. G. Wells, "Stephen Crane from an English Standpoint" (originally published in The North American

Review, *Vol. CLXXI, No. 525, August, 1900), in* The Shock of Recognition: The Development of Literature in the United States Recorded by the Men Who Made It, *edited by Edmund Wilson (reprinted by permission of Farrar, Straus and Giroux, Inc.; copyright 1943 by Doubleday Doran & Company, Inc.; copyright 1955 by Edmund Wilson; renewed © 1970 by Edmund Wilson), Farrar, Straus and Cudahy, 1955, pp. 661-71.*

W. D. HOWELLS   (essay date 1902)

[*Howells was the chief progenitor of American realism and the most influential American literary critic during the late nineteenth century. He was the author of nearly three dozen novels, few of which are read today. Despite his eclipse, he stands as one of the major literary figures of the nineteenth century: he successfully weaned American literature away from the sentimental romanticism of its infancy, earning the popular sobriquet "the Dean of American Letters." Through realism, a theory central to his fiction and criticism, Howells sought to disperse "the conventional acceptations by which men live on easy terms with themselves" that they might "examine the grounds of their social and moral opinions." To accomplish this, according to Howells, the writer must strive to record impressions of everyday life in detail, endowing characters with true-to-life motives and avoiding authorial comment in the narrative.* Criticism and Fiction *(1891), a patchwork of essays from* Harper's Magazine, *is often considered Howells's manifesto of realism, although, as René Wellek has noted, the book is actually "only a skirmish in a long campaign for his doctrines." In addition to many notable studies of the works of his friends Mark Twain and Henry James, Howells perceptively reviewed three generations of international literature, urging Americans to read Émile Zola, Bernard Shaw, Henrik Ibsen, Emily Dickinson, and other important authors. Introduced to Crane and his work by Hamlin Garland, Howells was an early supporter of Crane's literary talent. In this excerpt, Howells, whose theories influenced Crane's art, finds the novel* Maggie: A Girl of the Streets *superior to* The Red Badge of Courage.]

The physical slightness, if I may so suggest one characteristic of Crane's vibrant achievement, reflected the delicacy of energies that could be put forth only in nervous spurts, in impulses vivid and keen, but wanting in breadth and bulk of effect. Curiously enough, on the other hand, this very lyrical spirit, whose freedom was its life, was the absolute slave of reality. It was interesting to hear him defend what he had written, in obedience to his experience of things, against any change in the interest of convention. "No," he would contend, in behalf of the profanities of his people, "that is the way they *talk*. I have thought of that, and whether I ought to leave such things out, but if I do I am not giving the thing as I *know* it." He felt the constraint of those semi-savage natures, such as he depicted in **"Maggie,"** and **"George's Mother,"** and was forced through the fealty of his own nature to report them as they spoke no less than as they looked. When it came to **"The Red Badge of Courage,"** where he took leave of these simple aesthetics, and lost himself in a whirl of wild guesses at the fact from the ground of insufficient witness, he made the failure which formed the break between his first and his second manner, though it was what the public counted a success, with every reason to do so from the report of the sales.

The true Stephen Crane was the Stephen Crane of the earlier books, the earliest book; for **"Maggie"** remains the best thing he did. All he did was lyrical, but this was the aspect and accent as well as the spirit of the tragically squalid life he sang, while **"The Red Badge of Courage,"** and the other things that followed it, were the throes of an art failing with material to

which it could not render an absolute devotion from an absolute knowledge. He sang, but his voice erred up and down the scale, with occasional flashes of brilliant melody, which could not redeem the errors. New York was essentially his inspiration, the New York of suffering and baffled and beaten life, of inarticulate or blasphemous life; and away from it he was not at home, with any theme, or any sort of character. It was the pity of his fate that he must quit New York, first as a theme, and then as a habitat; for he rested nowhere else, and wrought with nothing else as with the lurid depths which he gave proof of knowing better than any one else. (pp. 770-71)

> *W. D. Howells, "Frank Norris," in* The North American Review, *Vol. 175, No. 6, December, 1902, pp. 769-78.**

THEODORE DREISER   (letter date 1921)

[*When the Schoolmen's Club of Newark, New Jersey announced plans to unveil a bronze tablet in memory of Crane, Max J. Herzberg of the Arrangements Committee wrote to ask America's foremost literary Naturalist for "an appropriate word" to commemorate the occasion. Five days before the ceremony, Dreiser wrote the following tribute to Crane.*]

It pleases me no little to learn that the Schoolmen's Club is to honor Stephen Crane with a bronze tablet. He was among the very earliest of my purely American literary admirations and one of the the few writers who stood forward intellectually and artistically at a time when this nation was as thoroughly submerged in romance and sentimentality and business as it is today. At that time, in so far as America was concerned, there were but James and Howells and Mark Twain among the elder realists and Garland and Fuller and Crane as beginners. Of this younger group Crane was a peer. And he certainly had more of a directness and force and daring than most of his elders. **"Maggie"** and **"George's Mother,"** while little more than sketches in the best sense, bear all the marks of a keen and unblessed sympathy with life, as well as a high level of literary perception. . . .

The little that Crane did, as you will note, was done with fire and a conscious or unconscious independence of our strawy and smothering notions and theories in regard to letters. Also it boded well for American letters. He took our hampering hurdles without thought or a care. The **"Red Badge of Courage"** is a fine picture of war. And it is not pleasant. There is not much sweetness about it and very little uplift. It ends as it begins, grimly, and without any solution, moral or spiritual. This in itself is wrong, according to our moral, and hence, our spiritual standards. If you doubt it study our current books and magazines. But let that be.

> *Theodore Dreiser, in his letter to Max J. Herzberg on November 2, 1921, in* The Michigan Daily Sunday Magazine, *Vol. XXXII, No. 54, November 27, 1921, p. 1.*

EDWARD GARNETT   (essay date 1921)

[*Garnett was a prominent editor for several London publishing houses, and discovered or greatly influenced the work of many important English writers, including Joseph Conrad, John Galsworthy, and D. H. Lawrence. He also published several volumes of criticism, all of which are characterized by thorough research and sound critical judgements. The following excerpt combines Garnett's 1898 assessment of Crane's work with an emendation written almost twenty-five years later. Some current critics regard this essay as the "first real analysis" of Crane's work since the 1900 Wells essay.*]

Crane's genius, his feelings for style were wholly intuitive and no study had fostered them. On first reading **"The Red Badge of Courage,"** I concluded he had been influenced by the Russian masters, but I learned when I met him, that he had never read a line of them. Would that he had! For Crane, as Conrad reminded me, never knew how good his best work was. He simply never knew. He never recognized that in the volume **"The Open Boat,"** he had achieved the perfection of his method. If he had comprehended that in **"The Bride Comes to Yellow Sky"** and in **"Death and the Child"** he had attained then, his high water mark, he might perhaps have worked forward along the lines of patient, ascending effort; but after **"The Open Boat,"** . . . his work dropped to lower levels. He wrote too much, he wrote against time, and he wrote while dunned for money. At first sight it appears astonishing that the creator of such a miracle of style as **"The Bride Comes to Yellow Sky"** should publish in the same year so mediocre a novel as **"On Active Service."** But Crane ought never to have essayed the form of the novel. He had not handled it satisfactorily in **"The Third Violet,"** . . . a love story charming in its impressionistic lightness of touch, but lacking in force, in concentration, in characterization. My view of Crane as a born impressionist and master of the short story, I emphasized in an Appreciation in 1898, and since it is germane to my purpose here, I reprint the criticism:—

"What Mr. Crane has got to do is very simple: he must not mix reporting with his writing. To other artists the word must often be passed: rest, work at your art, live more; but Mr. Crane has no need of cultivating his technique, no need of resting, no need of searching wide for experiences. In his art he is unique. Its certainty, its justness, its peculiar perfection of power arrived at its birth, or at least at that precise moment in its life when other artists—and great artists too—were preparing themselves for the long and difficult conquest of their art. . . . To say to Mr. Crane, 'You are too much anything, or too little anything; you need concentration, or depth, subtlety, or restraint,' would be absurd; his art is just in itself, rhythmical, self-poising as is the art of a perfect dancer. There are no false steps, no excesses. And, of course, his art is strictly limited. We would define him by saying he is the perfect artist and interpreter of the surfaces of life. And that explains why he so swiftly attained his peculiar power, and what is the realm his art commands, and his limitations. "Take **'George's Mother,'** for example—a tale which I believe he wrote at the ridiculous age of twenty-one. In *method* it is a masterpiece. It is a story dealing simply with the relations between an old woman and her son, who live together in a New York tenement block. An ordinary artist would seek to dive into the mind of the old woman, to follow its workings hidden under the deceitful appearances of things, under the pressure of her surroundings. A great artist would so recreate her life that its griefs and joys became significant of the griefs and joys of all motherhood on earth. But Mr. Crane does neither. He simply reproduces the surfaces of the individual life in so marvellous a way that the manner in which the old woman washes up the crockery, for example, gives us the essentials. To dive into the hidden life is, of course, for the artist a great temptation and a great danger—the values of the picture speedily get wrong, and the artist, seeking to interpret life, departs from the truth of nature. The rare thing about Mr. Crane's art is that he keeps closer to the surface than any living writer, and, like the great portrait-painters, to a great extent makes the surface betray the depths.

But, of course, the written word in the hands of the greatest artist often deals directly with the depths, plunges us into the rich depths of consciousness that cannot be more than hinted at by the surface; and it is precisely here that Mr. Crane's natural limitation must come in. At the supreme height of art the great masters so plough up the depths of life that the astonished spectator loses sight of the individual life altogether, and has the entrancing sense that all life is really one and the same thing, and is there manifesting itself before him. . . . I do not think that Mr. Crane is ever great in the sense of so fusing all the riches of the consciousness into a whole, that the reader is struck dumb as by an inevitable revelation; but he is undoubtedly such an interpreter of the significant surface of things that in a few strokes he gives us an amazing insight into what the individual life is. And he does it all straight from the surface; a few oaths, a genius for slang, an exquisite and unique faculty of exposing an individual scene by an odd simile, a power of interpreting a face or an action, a keen realizing of the primitive emotions—that is Mr. Crane's talent. In **"The Bride Comes to Yellow Sky,'** for example, the art is simply immense. There is a page and a half of conversation at the end of this short story of seventeen pages which, as a dialogue revealing the whole inside of the situation, is a lesson to any artist living. And the last line of this story, by the gift peculiar to the author of using some odd simile which cunningly condenses the feeling of the situation, defies analysis altogether. Foolish people may call Mr. Crane a reporter of genius; but nothing could be more untrue. He is thrown away as a picturesque reporter: a secondary style of art, of which, let us say, Mr. G. W. Steevens is, perhaps, the ablest exponent of today, and which is the heavy clay of Mr. Kipling's talent. Mr. Crane's technique is far superior to Mr. Kipling's, but he does not experiment ambitiously in various styles and develop in new directions as Mr. Kipling has done. I do not think that Mr. Crane will or can develop further. Again, I do not think he has the building faculty, or that he will ever do better in constructing a perfect whole out of many parts than he has arrived at in **'The Red Badge of Courage.'** That book was a series of episodic scenes, all melting naturally into one another and forming a just whole; but it was not constructed, in any sense of the word. And further, Mr. Crane does not show any faculty of taking his characters and revealing in them deep mysterious worlds of human nature, of developing fresh riches in them, acting under the pressure of circumstance. His imaginative analysis of his own nature on a battlefield is, of course, the one exception. And similarly the great artist's arrangement of complex effects, striking contrasts, exquisite grouping of devices, is lacking in him. His art does not include the necessity for complex arrangements; his sure instinct tells him never to quit the passing moment of life, to hold fast by simple situations, to reproduce the episodic, fragmentary nature of life in such artistic sequence that it stands in place of the architectural masses and co-ordinated structures of the great artists. He is the chief impressionist of our day as Sterne was the great impressionist, in a different manner, of his day. If he fails in anything he undertakes, it will be through abandoning the style he has invented. . . . Mr. Crane's talent is unique; nobody can question that. America may well be proud of him, for he has just that perfect mastery of form which artists of the Latin races often produce, but the Teutonic and Anglo-Saxon races very rarely. And undoubtedly of the young school of American artists Mr. Crane is the genius—the others have their talents."

On the above criticism Conrad wrote me at the time, "The Crane thing is just—precisely just a ray of light flashed in and showing all there is."

But when I wrote that criticism, that journalistic novel "**On Active Service**" was yet to be published, and I did not fully comprehend Crane's training and his circumstances. I sounded a warning note against "reporting," but though he had emerged from journalism, he was still haunted by journalism and was encircled by a—well! by a crew of journalists. I remarked, "I do not think Mr. Crane can or will develop further," but pressing him were duns and debts and beckoning him was the glamour of the war-correspondent's life, and before him were editors ready for ephemeral stuff, while they shook their heads sadly over such perfect gems as "**The Pace of Youth.**" Crane had seen much for a man of his years, but he was still thirsting for adventure and the life of action, and he had no time to digest his experiences, to reflect, to incubate and fashion his work at leisure. In the two or three hurried years that remained to him after the publication of "**The Open Boat,**" he created some notable things, but the dice of fate were loaded by all his circumstances against his development as craftsman.

We must therefore be thankful that his instinct for style emerged when his psychological genius broke out and so often possessed him in the teeth of the great stucco gods and the chinking of brass in the market place. He had written his best things without advice or encouragement, urged by the demon within him, and his genius burned clear, with its passionate individuality, defying all the inhibitions and conventions of New England. . . . On re-reading "**The Red Badge of Courage**" I am more than ever struck by the genius with which Crane, in imagination, pierced to the essentials of War. Without any experience of war at the time, Crane was essentially true to the psychological core of war—if not to actualities. He naturally underestimated the checks placed by physical strain and fatigue on the faculties, as well as war's malignant, cold ironies, its prosaic dreadfulness, its dreary, deadening tedium. But as Goethe has pointed out, the artist has a license to ignore actualities, if he is obeying inner, æsthetic laws. And Crane's subject was the passions, the passions of destruction, fear, pride, rage, shame and exaltation in the heat of action. The deep artistic unity of "**The Red Badge of Courage,**" is fused in its flaming, spiritual intensity, in the fiery ardour with which the shock of the Federal and Confederate armies is imaged. The torrential force and impetus, the check, sullen recoil and reforming of shattered regiments, and the renewed onslaught and obstinate resistance of brigades and divisions are visualized with extraordinary force and colour. If the sordid grimness of carnage, is partially screened, the feeling of War's cumulative rapacity, of its breaking pressure and fluctuating tension is caught with wonderful fervour and freshness of style. . . . And his imaginative picture he supplemented, four years later, in that penetrating, sombre, realistic piece "**Memories of War**" in "**Wounds in the Rain,**" his reminiscences of the Cuban campaign that in fact had set death's secret mark already on him. I may note, too, how Crane, sitting in our garden, described that on questioning Veterans of the Civil War about their feelings when fighting, he could get nothing out of them but one thing, viz., "We just went there and did so and so." (pp. 203-13)

[Two] qualities in especial, combined to form Crane's unique quality, viz his wonderful insight into, and mastery of the primary passions, and his irony deriding the swelling emotions of the self. It is his irony that checks the emotional intensity of his delineation, and suddenly reveals passion at high tension in the clutch of the implacable tides of life. It is the perfect fusion of these two forces of passion and irony that creates Crane's spiritual background, and raises his work, at its finest, into the higher zone of man's tragic conflict with the universe.

His irony is seen in its purest form in "**Black Riders,**" . . . a tiny collection of *vers libres,* as sharp in their naked questioning as sword blades. These verses pierce with dreadful simplicity certain illusions of unregarding sages, whose earnest commentaries pour, and will continue to pour from the groaning press. In "**Maggie,**" . . . that little masterpiece which drew the highest tribute from the veteran, W. D. Howells [see excerpt above], again it is the irony that keeps in right perspective Crane's remorseless study of New York slum and Bowery morals. The code of herd law by which the inexperienced girl, Maggie, is pressed to death by her family, her lover and the neighbours, is seen working with strange finality. The Bowery inhabitants, as we, can be nothing other than what they are; their human nature responds inexorably to their brutal environment; the curious habits and code of the most primitive savage tribes could not be presented with a more impartial exactness, or with more sympathetic understanding.

"**Maggie**" is not a story *about* people; it is primitive human nature itself set down with perfect spontaneity and grace of handling. For pure æsthetic beauty and truth no Russian, not Tchehov himself, could have bettered this study, which, as Howells remarks, has the quality of Greek tragedy. The perfection of Crane's style, his unique quality, can, however, be studied best in "**The Open Boat.**" . . . Here he is again the pure artist, brilliant, remorselessly keen, delighting in life's passions and ironies, amusing, tragic or grimacing. Consider the nervous audacity, in phrasing, of the piece "**An Experiment in Misery,**" which reveals the quality of chiaroscuro of a master's etching. No wonder the New York editors looked askance at such a break with tradition. How would they welcome the mocking verve and sinister undertone of such pieces as "**A Man and Some Others,**" or the airy freshness and flying spontaneity of "**The Pace of Youth**"? In the volume "**The Open Boat**" Crane's style has a brilliancy of tone, a charming *timbre* peculiar to itself. As with Whistler, his personal note eschews everything obvious, everything inessential, as witness "**Death and the Child,**" that haunting masterpiece where a child is playing with pebbles and sticks on the great mountain-side, while the smoke and din of the battlefield, in the plain below, hide the rival armies of pigmy men busy reaping with death. It is in the calm detachment of the little child playing, by which the artist secures his poetic background; man, pigmy man, watched impassively by the vast horizons of life, is the plaything of the Fates. The irony of life is here implicit. Perfect also is that marvel of felicitous observation "**An Ominous Babe,**" where each touch is exquisitely final; a sketch in which the instincts of the babes betray the roots of all wars, past and to come. This gem ought to be in every anthology of American prose.

The descent of Crane in "**On Active Service**" . . . , to a clever, journalistic level, was strange. It was a lapse into superficiality; much stronger artistically was "**The Monster,**" . . . a book of stories of high psychological interest, which might indeed have made another man's reputation, but a book which is ordinary in atmosphere. The story "**The Blue Hotel**" is, indeed, a brilliant exploration of fear and its reactions, and "**His New Mittens**" is a delightful graphic study of boy morals, but we note that when Crane breathes an every-day, common atmosphere his æsthetic power always weakens. One would give the whole contents of "**Whilomville Stories,**" . . . for the five pages of "**An Ominous Baby**"; and the heterogeneous contents of "**Last Words,**" . . . a volume of sweepings from Crane's desk, kick the balance when weighed against the sketch "**A Tale of Mere Chance,**" the babblings of a madman, which

Dostoevsky might be proud to claim. The companion sketch **"Manacled"** (in **"The Monster"**) bears also the authentic stamp of Crane's rare vision.

To conclude, if America has forgotten or neglects Crane's achievements, above all in **"Maggie"** and **"The Open Boat,"** she does not yet deserve to produce artists of rank. Crane holds a peculiar niche in American literature. Where it is weak, viz in the æsthetic and psychological truthful delineation of passion, Stephen Crane is a master. (pp. 213-17)

> *Edward Garnett, "Stephen Crane and His Work"*
> *(1921), in his* Friday Nights: Literary Criticism and
> Appreciations *(copyright 1922 and renewed 1950 by*
> *Alfred A. Knopf, Inc.; reprinted by permission of the*
> *publisher), Knopf, 1922, pp. 201-17 [an excerpted*
> *portion of the essay used here originally appeared*
> *as "Mr. Stephen Crane: An Appreciation" (re-*
> *printed by permission of the Literary Estate of Ed-*
> *ward Garnett, in* The Academy, *Vol. 55, No. 1,*
> *December 17, 1898].*

H. L. MENCKEN (essay date 1924)

[*From the era of World War I until the early years of the Great Depression, Mencken was one of the most influential figures in American letters. His strongly individualistic, irreverent outlook on life and his vigorous, invective-charged writing style helped establish the iconoclastic spirit of the Jazz Age and significantly shaped the direction of American literature.*]

Next to Poe and Walt Whitman, Crane seems destined to go down into history as the most romantic American author of the Nineteenth Century. Even while he lived legend was busy with him (p. 496)

But Crane could write, so some of his books have outlived their time. It was his distinction that he had an eye for the cold, glittering fact in an age of romantic illusion. The dignified authors of that time were such shallow, kittenish fellows as Howells, F. Hopkinson Smith and Frank R. Stockton, with Richard Watson Gilder as their high priest. The popular authors revolved around Richard Harding Davis. Crane's first writings alarmed Howells and shocked Gilder, but gradually a gang of younger men gathered around him, and before he died he was a national celebrity—in fact, a sort of American Kipling. He was, indeed, the head and forefront of the Young America movement in the middle nineties. No man of that movement was more vastly admired, and none has survived with less damage. How far would he have got if he had lived? It is useless to speculate. He died, like Schubert, at 30. He left behind him one superlatively excellent book, four or five magnificent short stories, some indifferent poems and a great mass of journalistic trash. The Gilders of his time left only trash. (p. 497)

> *H. L. Mencken, "Stephen Crane" (originally pub-*
> *lished in the* Evening Sun, Baltimore, January 19,
> *1924), in his* A Mencken Chrestomathy *(copyright*
> *1924 by Alfred A. Knopf, Inc., and renewed 1942*
> *by H. L. Mencken; reprinted by permission of the*
> *publisher), Knopf, 1949, pp. 496-97.*

AMY LOWELL (essay date 1924)

[*Lowell was the leading proponent of Imagism in American poetry. Like the Symbolists before her, some of whom she examined in* Six French Poets, *Lowell experimented with free verse forms. Under the influence of Ezra Pound, Lowell's poetry exhibited the new style of Imagism, consisting of clear and precise rhetoric, exact rendering of images, and greater metrical freedom. Although she was popular in her time, standard evaluations of Lowell accord her more importance as a promoter of new artistic ideas than as a poet in her own right. In the following excerpt, she gives a perceptive assessment of Crane's* The Black Riders *and* War Is Kind. *Lowell finds that Crane's poetic talents waned as he matured, so that* The Black Riders *is the more substantive of his two books of poetry.*]

Crane spoke of his poems as waiting to be "drawn off." And this is an excellent expression. Once freed from the unconscious, capable of taking on words and becoming disengaged from their author, all the pent-up energies of creative thought, or rather all such pent-up energies as were ripe enough to become creative thought, came in a rush [in **The Black Riders**], and he could hardly draw them off quickly enough. Hitherto, Crane's writing had been objective. His forte was description; but along with this description went a keen, impressionistic perception of people and things. There had been no place for personal comment, no time for introspective ejaculations. Probably he was scarcely aware of the need for them. But Crane felt too vividly, he touched life too curiously and tenderly, his reactions were too bitter, his sensibility too avid, for him to remain for ever the onlooker, the recorder of other men's lives. At some time in his career, a personal speech must have forced itself upon him. The only question was when and for how long.

Crane's life was too short for the critic to hazard a positive statement, and yet I think there is strong reason to believe that, in spite of much poetry in his prose books, he was not primarily a poet. His genius lay in prose sketches, even when these expanded themselves into novels. His was not a largely imaginative talent. Even his prose tales, to be done at his best, must be solidly founded upon experience. **The Red Badge of Courage** is the one exception, and in this case he merely augmented the football games he had seen by digesting innumerable accounts of battles told by eye-witnesses. His art was tied to himself, and he was extremely dependent upon a period of gestation. Granted this period, he could produce marvellous work; without it, he was almost helpless. He was the last man in the world who should ever have attempted newspaper writing. To enable him to continue at his best, he should have been able to proceed slowly, and at every stage reached been permitted to discharge the accumulations of thought and sensation proper to that stage. Then, and then only, would he have maintained his level and advanced.

When he suddenly started writing poetry, he had in himself a full reservoir of intimate, personal experiences to tap. And he tapped them until he found that his spring had run dry. Thereafter it was necessary to wait until the energy of living had filled him up again, and this precisely because his was not a nature of inexhaustible subjective reactions. Youth is prone to express itself in verse, and, Crane being a youth of genius, and of a highly original genius, his verses were sure to be eminently worth while. But, after all, I think it cannot be gainsaid that his poetry is far more adolescent than his prose, and this leads to the obvious corollary that, as adolescence waned, so would the poetry wane. Indeed, it seems to have done so. His poetry was static. It came amply clothed, and it never improved. On the contrary, it retrograded. His second book, **War is Kind,** in spite of the fact that it contains a few pieces which surpass anything in **The Black Riders,** is as a whole less vital, less spontaneous, and less original than the earlier book.

How did Stephen Crane stumble on his form? That is really a very interesting question. It is a form with which we are all too familiar to-day. The *Vers Libre,* or Free Verse, war has rammed it down our throats in season and out of season. . . . [Crane's] contemporaries thought the form ''odd,'' but were willing to let it be. What baffled them was his use of suggestion. And here possibly lies his chief technical debt to Emily Dickinson, for she was past mistress of suggestion. This and, to a lesser degree, irony were what Crane derived from her, but his was no such light gossamer touch. Crane's irony clanks by heavily clad in steel and brandishing a molesting spear, Crane is conscious of an enemy with whom he is out to do battle—most adolescent of attitudes! Emily Dickinson's irony brushes as inconsequentially as a butterfly's wing; she is unconscious of any audience. The world exists for her solely as she sees it, and her carelessness in the matter of whether she exists for her readers or not is wholly admirable. This is maturity. This is the poet who is chiefly such and no other thing. In one poem only does Crane really remind us in the slightest of Emily Dickinson. This is it:

> A man said to the universe:
> ''Sir, I exist!''
> ''However,'' replied the universe,
> ''The fact has not created in me
> A sense of obligation.''

If Emily Dickinson cannot be made to stand for Crane's form, where did he find it? I think in the Bible. The son of a mother who was also a Methodist preacher must have been extremely familiar with the Bible. Its cadences, its images, its parable structure cannot have failed of being ground into his consciousness. When he came to expressing himself as shortly and as poignantly as his thoughts demanded to be presented, he fell back on the rhythms which were stored in his head, and these rhythms were the completely natural ones of Biblical cadence. The Old Testament is full of the most beautiful cadenced verse, if once we learn to read aside from the hampering typography of arbitrary divisions.

Crane was so steeped in the religion in which he was brought up that he could not get it out of his head. He disbelieved it and he hated it, but he could not free himself from it. A loathed and vengeful God broods over *The Black Riders.* Crane's soul was heaped with bitterness, and this bitterness he flung back at the theory of life which had betrayed him. His misery and his earnestness made the book, and the supreme irony of all is that it should have been issued as an æsthetic knick-knack and its author hailed as an ''affected ass.'' . . . Crane handed the world the acrid fumes of his heart, and they howled at him for an obscene blasphemer, or patted him on the back as a ''cracker-jack'' on whom they ''doted,'' a cranky and unexpected star beaming above the amateur magazines and proud to shed its light upon East Aurora.

Reading the book now, thirty years afterwards, one is tempted to neither reaction. What chiefly impresses is the volume's sincerity. Strangely enough, it is almost devoid of those pictorial touches which make Crane's prose so striking. Such passages, for instance, as this, of horses at a fire, kicking ''grey ice of the gutter into silvery angles that hurtled and clicked on frozen stone.'' Crane seems to have had no time for such things as these when he was writing verse. He seems concerned so greatly with *what* he has to say that embroidery of any sort is a hindrance. He speaks in symbols, far out-distancing his time, and his method is starkly epigrammatic. . . . (pp. xv-xx)

Crane's theme in *The Black Riders* is two-fold. It is at once the cruelty of universal law, and the futility of hope. It is a creed of gall and aloes, and Crane believed it. It is the key to his life. Gentle and kind, yet he was weak, a man who needed something beyond himself to bolster him up.

War is Kind adds little to our interest in Crane's poetry. The Roycroft poems [from *The Roycroft Quarterly*] were included in it, and they were the best things in the book. The first poem, **''War is Kind,''** is a satiric comment on war, in which Crane voices what so many poets of a later generation have felt and said. The poem has pathos, but the tone is subdued. The man who wrote it was profoundly weary. Occasionally Crane rises to something of his old fire in such poems as **''Have you ever made a just man?''** or **''Forth went the candid man,''** but on the whole the volume is disappointing. This man is evidently destined to abandon poetry in no long while. The last part of the book is taken up with a long love poem, **''Intrigue.''** There is no question of its sincerity, and how much Crane had ''felt'' it, but it is not memorable as poetry, however important it may be as biography. And, oddly enough, it shows Crane, as a pioneer, breaking down. His bright modernity is fading. **''Intrigue''** is full of ''thee's'' and ''thou's,'' the refrain is ''Woe is me,'' and the poet is constantly declaring ''Thou art my love.'' This will do for some men, but not for Stephen Crane. We see that he is losing his grasp, that poetry is sliding from him, that it had been no more with him than a breath of adolescence. (pp. xxvii-xxviii)

What then is Stephen Crane, in so far as his poetry is concerned? A man without a period, that is at once his plume and his forfeit. He sprang from practically nowhere, and he has left only the most isolated of descendants. There were forerunners of his type of verse, but he had never heard of them. He is that rarest of artistic phenomena, a man who creates from inner consciousness alone. The men from whom he might have learned, who spoke his speech and might have led him on, were the French *Symbolistes,* but he did not know of them; and the Chinese and Japanese poets, but he knew nothing of them either, and there were only the scattered translations of Lafcadio Hearn even if he had sought to know. The usual translations of the period would have done him no good.

Crane saw life through individual eyes, and he dared write as he pleased; therein rests his abiding merit. So short a time as twelve years after his death, a type of poetry extremely like his came suddenly into being. By all rights he should have been its direct parent, but he was not, simply because most of the practitioners of it had based themselves upon French precedent and William Blake before they knew anything of Crane. In the decade which began with 1912, Crane would have been in his element, perfectly understood, wisely praised, forced to take the position of leader. He died too soon. He did much, but the temperature of the world he lived in was unsuitable. He ranks in America somewhat as Chatterton ranks in England. A boy, spiritually killed by neglect. A marvellous boy, potentially a genius, historically an important link in the chain of American poetry. (pp. xxviii-xxix)

Amy Lowell, ''Introduction'' (1924) in The Work of Stephen Crane: ''The Black Riders and Other Lines,'' *Vol. VI by Stephen Crane, edited by Wilson Follett (copyright 1926 and renewed 1954 by Alfred A. Knopf, Inc.; reprinted by permission of the publisher), Knopf, 1926 (and reprinted by Russell & Russell, 1963, pp. ix-xxix).*

WILLIAM LYON PHELPS (essay date 1924)

[*In this favorable critique of the* Whilomville Stories, *Phelps ranks Crane with Mark Twain and Booth Tarkington as a master of childhood tales.*]

Mark Twain, Stephen Crane, Booth Tarkington are among the greatest diagnosticians of children's diseases. They not only understand children, they know what is the matter with them; and like the wisest physicians they know that the chief remedy is time. Nothing saves the world from the small boy except his lack of force; he can fortunately be outwitted by his elders, and if that method fails, they can always resort to superior brute strength.

It is illuminating to compare the *Whilomville Stories* with the Penrod books. Little children and big Africans make ideal companions, for the latter have the patience, inner sympathy, forbearance, and unfailing good humour necessary to such an association. Both Stephen Crane and Booth Tarkington have given us permanent drawings in black and white.

As a medical specialist will take the same pains with children as with adults, so in this volume we see Stephen Crane exercising the same art on boys and girls that he displayed in dealing with soldiers or with the vagabonds in city slums. There is the same remorseless and uncompromising love of truth. One feels that the novelist would rather die than write down a description, a bit of narration, or a bit of dialogue that he did not know to be verifiable. A man of the world may condescend in talking to children; but an artist will not condescend in writing about them, any more than a physician will condescend in dealing with them.

There is the same expenditure of energy that we find in Crane's other books. He is equally careful, equally meticulous. He depicts the boys as individuals and in the mass, with an analysis as profound as his humour is gay. They exhibit together the herd mind in its most unlovely aspect, a compound of cruelty and cowardice; and they have that inextinguishable love of romance that will for ever dominate the human race. Nor is he any the less relentless in the portrayl of little girls. The "angel child" is as unscrupulous a tyrant as can be found in the annals of irresponsible monarchy.

One has on every page the pleasure of recognition. We remember these scenes, these schools, these holidays, these fights, these picnics, these little people. The days of childhood return; and if they are not exactly the same in radiance as the shining dawns depicted by Wordsworth, they are as true from the standpoint of the realistic novelist as his were from that of the imaginative poet.

Stephen Crane was a curious compound of patience and impatience. As a man he was wildly impatient with hypocrisy, cant, pretence, falsehood, brutality, sentimentalism, injustice, and cruelty; as an artist, he was unendingly patient in dealing with these very things.

Even as in writing of war he wrote honestly when nearly everyone wrote sentimentally, so in writing of boys and girls he wrote sincerely. And as in reading his tales of social life in cities and of horror on the field of battle, one feels his flaming hatred of meanness and of tyranny, so in his depiction of these children at play I seem to feel, underneaath the mirth and nonsense, a terrible hatred of mass opinion, a fervent faith in the individual's right to live. (pp. xi-xiii)

> *William Lyon Phelps, "Introduction" (1924), in* The Work of Stephen Crane: "Whilomville Stories," *Vol. V by Stephen Crane, edited by Wilson Follett (copyright 1926 and renewed 1954 by Alfred A. Knopf, Inc.; reprinted by permission of the publisher), Knopf, 1926, pp. ix-xiii.*

THOMAS BEER (essay date 1925)

[*Beer is the author of* Stephen Crane, *the first Crane biography (see additional bibliography). In this excerpt, Beer presents Crane as a writer often misunderstood by critics during his lifetime, whose greatness will only be appreciated with the passage of time.*]

[Crane] was seldom a tedious writer, even in **"The Third Violet,"** where the compression is so exacting that the pretty girls and young artists of the little fable fairly sink back into the paper and the story becomes a skeleton in horrid need of rags. The compliment paid him by Frank Norris: "He knows when to shut up," is handsomely accurate. But Crane's deficiency, as a writer for general use, is simply that he didn't realize the value of stuff and nonsense. The legitimate pathos of **"Maggie"** and **"George's Mother"** lies in the understatement, as the figures of the cancerous little actress and the obsessed Bud Korpenning rise today through the rich confusion of "Manhattan Transfer" to claim the recognition of their impure, simple woe. Maggie is a stupid child; Mrs. Kelcy is what Howells called her, "a poor, inadequate woman of a commonplace religiosity"; George Kelcy is a dolt. The tramps of **"An Experiment in Misery"** and the huddled breadline of **"The Men in the Storm"** are beings dulled by their misfortune. His intense restraint served Crane badly in these sketches of the misfit and deject. His contemporaries, if you please, were snivelling on paper over Pierre Loti's "Matelot" when Crane cut under all that perfumed funereal matter and merely stated the case, and left it. His "distinguished incapacity" for the maudlin, then, was a deficiency in the early '90s. The success of **"The Red Badge of Courage"** gave him his hearing with the public and established him as an influential writer, but the rest of his story is simply that of a comedy in misunderstanding. His enemy was the tragic idea—*l'idea tragica,* true daughter of the tuberose and the obituary editorial, sister of the Queen of Spain. He had, in fact, reduced tragedy to its modern residue in 1893. (p. 426)

"The Red Badge of Courage" will probably remain his most admired affair, as the enormous effort of its production forced him into a certain elaboration of the theme. He himself thought that **"The Bride Comes to Yellow Sky"** was his best tale. Let us see. . . . The marshal of Yellow Sky, embarrassed in a new black suit, is bringing home his quite ordinary bride from San Antonio in the harassing glories of a shiny Pullman car. The marshal worries because the boys of Yellow Sky don't know that he has gone to San Antonio to be married. Meanwhile in the little town the redoubtable Scratchy Wilson has got drunk and is on the loose, shooting at things. The inhabitants simply bar their doors and crawl under tables in the saloons. None will go out to battle. Wilson meets the marshal and his bride as they round a corner, sneaking guiltily to the marshal's house. The melodrama piles itself in a direct confrontation. Wilson is the loaded truck at the fence of the playground. The stolid marshal stands with his hands thrown up and declares himself unarmed. Unarmed? Yes, he has been getting married in San Antonio and has no gun on him. Married? . . . The drunkard's mind staggers under the entry of this unknown quantity. He has been so created that his maroon sweatshop shirt and childish boots have already made him a little funny. The melodrama topples and vanishes. The truck slides away from the fence. Oh, all right! He sheaths his revolver and lurches off, his boots making holes in the sand of the street. Crane is done with the business. All the ordinary values of his situation have been thrown away; the marshal and the woman remain merely plain people. Wilson is a body containing a quart or so of rye whisky and supporting two revolvers. There is no villain and there is no hero. Anything may happen in Yellow Sky, but what does happen seems unavoidably right—and inevitably perplexing, as humanity perplexes us.

Behind these characters, so simply inarticulate, appears a chorus of idlers, frumps in kitchens, drunken stevedores, and virtuous women who fill the function of the Greek chorus by reversing its processes. They do not explain the will of the immortals; they explain nothing. They talk, chattering with the broken violence of Americans and saying something apposite only by hazard. They talk, and daze one by the perfection of their inconsequence. Henry James and Rudyard Kipling were using sensitized ladies, subalterns in the club, and writers to point up their pictures by a verbal commentary from the background. Crane used his chorus on its own merits, to display the meaninglessness of human criticism, and when he was told that his people said nothing, he drawled, "What do people usually say?" And behind the characters and the chorus appears the scene itself, so swiftly suggested, so charmingly left to speak its own part without prompting. The purple sage flows right and left of the train; the waves heave the open boat in a long, even roll and the meditative gulls sit on the tumult pensively. The signals of a warship are jewelled brooches in the tropic night. The exploding acids that wash off a man's face are elves of delicate color. The sun is glued to the sky and the unassuming moon watches us timidly as we stroll in the music of the band beside the sea's unknown emotions. So what does it matter that your own kindness will bring you into scorn and loss, or that your breath in the darkness will annoy men into wishing that the Spanish bullet had pierced your heart instead of your lungs? An eventual, dry tenderness envelops your calamities; you are no more than the light upon the leaves, a thing of transient beauty when the red fire showed you swaying above the immortal bonfire, but you are no less than the light or the piling beryl of the sea or the shark's wake circling the desperate boat or the hue of burning oil. This is no great consolation for a broken neck or a bruised self respect, but it is something. Such beauty as you had has been wrung out of you on paper, and if it isn't the pink of ribbons and best frock so admired by partisans of the Queen of Spain, it is still something that has endured for a while, and longevity is no worse a test in art than another. (pp. 426-27)

Thomas Beer, "Fire Feathers" (© 1925 Saturday Review Magazine Co.; copyright renewed © 1953 by Alice B. Beer; reprinted by permission), in The Saturday Review of Literature, *Vol. II, No. 21, December 19, 1925, pp. 425-27.*

JOSEPH CONRAD (essay date 1925)

[*Conrad and Crane admired each other's works and formed a lasting friendship during the time Crane lived in England. Though Conrad is considered the greater writer of the two, many critics point to their similar impressionistic styles, and some contend Conrad's* The Nigger of the "Narcissus" *was influenced by his reading of* The Red Badge of Courage. *The following is Conrad's assessment of Crane's Civil War novel.*]

One of the most enduring memories of my literary life is the sensation produced by the appearance in 1895 of Crane's **"Red Badge of Courage"** in a small volume belonging to Mr. Heinemann's Pioneer Series of Modern Fiction—very modern fiction at that time, and upon the whole not devoid of merit. I have an idea the series was meant to give us shocks, and as far as my recollection goes there were, to use a term made familiar to all by another war, no "duds" in that small and lively bombardment. But Crane's work detonated on the mild din of that attack on our literary sensibilities with the impact and force of a twelve-inch shell charged with a very high explosive. Unexpected it fell amongst us; and its fall was followed by a great outcry.

Not of consternation, however. The energy of that projectile hurt nothing and no one (such was its good fortune), and delighted a good many. It delighted soldiers, men of letters, men in the street; it was welcomed by all lovers of personal expression as a genuine revelation, satisfying the curiosity of a world in which war and love have been subjects of song and story ever since the beginning of articulate speech.

Here we had an artist, a man not of experience but a man inspired, a seer with a gift for rendering the significant on the surface of things and with an incomparable insight into primitive emotions, who, in order to give us the image of war, had looked profoundly into his own breast. We welcomed him. As if the whole vocabulary of praise had been blown up sky-high by this missile from across the Atlantic, a rain of words descended on our heads, words well or ill chosen, chunks of pedantic praise and warm appreciation, clever words, and words of real understanding, platitudes, and felicities of criticism, but all as sincere in their response as the striking piece of work which set so many critical pens scurrying over the paper.

One of the most interesting, if not the most valuable, of printed criticisms was perhaps that of Mr. George Wyndham, soldier, man of the world, and in a sense a man of letters [see excerpt above]. . . . He comes to the conclusion that:

"Mr. Crane has contrived a masterpiece."

"Contrived"—that word of disparaging sound is the last word I would have used in connection with any piece of work by Stephen Crane, who in his art (as indeed in his private life) was the least "contriving" of men. But as to "masterpiece," there is no doubt that **"The Red Badge of Courage"** is that, if only because of the marvellous accord of the vivid impressionistic description of action on that woodland battlefield, and the imaged style of the analysis of the emotions in the inward moral struggle going on in the breast of one individual—the Young Soldier of the book, the protagonist of the monodrama presented to us in an effortless succession of graphic and coloured phrases.

Stephen Crane places his Young Soldier in an untried regiment. And this is well contrived—if any contrivance there be in a spontaneous piece of work which seems to spurt and flow like a tapped stream from the depths of the writer's being. In order that the revelation should be complete, the Young Soldier has to be deprived of the moral support which he would have found in a tried body of men matured in achievement to the consciousness of its worth. His regiment had been tried by nothing but days of waiting for the order to move; so many days that it and the Youth within it have come to think of themselves as merely "a part of a vast blue demonstration." The army had been lying camped near a river, idle and fretting, till the moment when Stephen Crane lays hold of it at dawn with masterly simplicity: "The cold passed reluctantly from the earth. . . ." These are the first words of the war book which was to give him his crumb of fame.

The whole of that opening paragraph is wonderful in the homely dignity of the indicated lines of the landscape, and the shivering awakening of the army at the break of the day before the battle.

In the next, with a most effective change to racy colloquialism of narrative, the action which motivates, sustains and feeds the inner drama forming the subject of the book, begins with the Tall Soldier going down to the river to wash his shirt. He returns waving his garment above his head. He had heard at fifth-hand from somebody that the army is going to move to-morrow. The only immediate effect of this piece of news is that a Negro teamster, who had been dancing a jig on a wooden box in a ring of laughing soldiers, finds himself suddenly deserted. He sits down mournfully. For the rest, the Tall Soldier's excitement is met by blank disbelief, profane grumbling, an invincible incredulity. But the regiment is somehow sobered. One feels it, though no symptoms can be noticed. It does not know what a battle is, neither does the Young Soldier. He retires from the babbling throng into what seems a rather comfortable dugout and lies down with his hands over his eyes to think. Thus the drama begins.

He perceives suddenly that he had looked upon wars as historical phenomenons of the past. He had never believed in war in his own country. It had been a sort of play affair. He had been drilled, inspected, marched for months, till he has despaired "of ever seeing a Greek-like struggle. Such were no more. Men were better or more timid. Secular and religious education had effaced the throat-grappling instinct, or else firm finance held in check the passions."

Very modern this touch. We can remember thoughts like these round about the year 1914. That Young Soldier is representative of mankind in more ways than one, and first of all in his ignorance. His regiment had listened to the tales of veterans, "tales of gray bewhiskered hordes chewing tobacco with unspeakable valour and sweeping along like the Huns." Still he cannot put his faith in veterans' tales. Recruits were their prey. They talked of blood, fire, and sudden death, but much of it might have been lies. They were in no wise to be trusted. And the question arises before him whether he will or will not "run from a battle"? He does not know. He cannot know. A little panic fear enters his mind. He jumps up and asks himself aloud, "Good Lord, what's the matter with me?" This is the first time his words are quoted, on this day before the battle. He dreads not danger, but fear itself. He stands before the unknown. He would like to prove to himself by some reasoning process that he will not "run from the battle." And in his unblooded regiment he can find no help. He is alone with the problem of courage.

In this he stands for the symbol of all untried men.

Some critics have estimated him a morbid case. I cannot agree to that. The abnormal cases are of the extremes; of those who crumple up at the first sight of danger, and of those of whom their fellows say "he doesn't know what fear is." Neither will I forget the rare favourites of the gods whose fiery spirit is only soothed by the fury and clamour of a battle. Of such was General Picton of Peninsular fame. But the lot of the mass of mankind is to know fear, the decent fear of disgrace. Of such is the Young Soldier of **"The Red Badge of Courage."** He only seems exceptional because he has got inside him Stephen Crane's imagination, and is presented to us with the insight and the power of expression of an artist whom a just and severe critic, on a review of all his work, has called the foremost impressionist of his time; as Sterne was the greatest impressionist, but in a different way, of his age.

This is a generalized, fundamental judgment. More superficially both Zola's "La Débâcle" and Tolstoi's "War and Peace" were mentioned by critics in connection with Crane's war book [see George Wyndham's essay excerpted above]. But Zola's main concern was with the downfall of the imperial régime he fancied he was portraying; and in Tolstoi's book the subtle presentation of Rostov's squadron under fire for the first time is a mere episode lost in a mass of other matter, like a handful of pebbles in a heap of sand. I could not see the relevancy. Crane was concerned with elemental truth only; and in any case I think that as an artist he is non-comparable. He dealt with what is enduring, and was the most detached of men.

That is why his book is short. Not quite two hundred pages. Gems are small. (pp. 119-24)

This war book, so virile and so full of gentle sympathy, in which not a single declamatory sentiment defaces the genuine verbal felicity, welding analysis and description in a continuous fascination of individual style, had been hailed by the critics as the herald of a brilliant career. Crane himself very seldom alluded to it, and always with a wistful smile. Perhaps he was conscious that, like the mortally wounded Tall Soldier of his book, who, snatching at the air, staggers out into a field to meet his appointed death on the first day of battle—while the terrified Youth and the kind Tattered Soldier stand by silent, watching with awe "these ceremonies at the place of meeting"—it was his fate, too, to fall early in the fray. (p. 124)

> *Joseph Conrad, in his preface to* The Red Badge of Courage *by Stephen Crane, William Heinemann, 1925 (and reprinted as "His War Book," in* Last Essays *by Joseph Conrad, edited by Richard Curle, Doubleday, Page & Company, 1926, pp. 119-24).*

SHERWOOD ANDERSON   (essay date 1926)

> [*Anderson was one of the most original and influential early twentieth-century American writers. He was among the first American authors to explore the effects of the unconscious upon human life. Anderson's "hunger to see beneath the surface of lives" was best expressed in the collection of bittersweet short stories which form the classic* Winesburg, Ohio. *This, his most important book, exhibits the author's characteristically simple, unornamented prose style and his personal vision, which combined a sense of wonder at the potential beauty of life with despair over its tragic aspects. Anderson's style and outlook were influential in shaping the writings of Ernest Hemingway, William Faulkner, Thomas Wolfe, John Steinbeck, and other American authors. Much of Anderson's own writing was influenced by the work of D. H. Lawrence, Gertrude Stein, and of his close friend Theodore Dreiser. Anderson, who considered Crane an innovative craftsman in nineteenth-century literature, contributed the following appreciative introduction to* Midnight Sketches, *a collection of Crane's short stories.*]

An explosion in a city street. People in the street, thousands of them. . . .

You can imagine such an explosion. Let us say nobody has been hurt.

Stephen Crane never hurt any one. He was an explosion all right. (p. xi)

I am thinking about Stephen Crane coming along—as a writer. Writing in America must have been pretty dead then. There are signs enough of the same kind of death now.

People think they can write about people with their fingers. In Stephen Crane's day America was pretty full of individualists. Look at the pictures left of early Americans. An individualist hasn't much time to think of others. He is hot on freedom, liberty—that sort of thing. Of course he means himself, his own liberty, his own freedom. (pp. xi-xii)

You can't be an individualist and write as Stephen Crane sometimes did. You can't do it with your fingers or your arms.

You have to feel people, things. I can imagine Stephen Crane going along a street in a city and hearing a truckdriver swear at a street-car conductor. That is when the explosion occurred. Something inside a man suddenly expanding, taking in everything—self forgotten.

The real writer writes with every nerve in his body—all his nerves aroused. Clever men can write any time. They know a little bag of tricks and can just reel it off. Stevie learned to do that. I'm bound to say I think he wrote some pretty bad stories. I suppose the magazine editors of his time and the other and more successful writers told him how to do it and he listened. (p. xii)

Suppose they opened the saloons now—after this prohibition business. Cozy warm places to go on winter afternoons. Men about, telling stories, bragging, lying, laughing.

There was literary prohibition in Steve Crane's day all right. He defied them and at least partly got away with it. He sold real whisky, beer, wine, for a while anyway. What I mean is that he was a writer really writing when it wasn't being done. That is the wonder of the man. It is time he was getting a hearing. If the man wrote some bad, easy, tricky stuff, what of it?

A country gets real writers by having them. Writers who are trying to do decent work in America now do not know what they owe to Walt Whitman, Herman Melville, Steve Crane. (p. xiii)

It does not matter. What I am trying to say is that the culture of a country—a new country—builds up slowly. There is a house being built. It takes time and the labour of real craftsmen. Stephen Crane was a craftsman. The stones he put in the wall are still there.

Another thing I want to speak about. You will see I am not—in writing of Steve Crane—holding myself down to this present volume, *Midnight Sketches*. But you read it. Notice something.

Notice the colour of the prose. Something splashy—men, women, rainy nights. Colours in buildings, skies, men's faces, caught and put down.

Once long ago in Chicago I was talking with Carl Sandburg. We were walking in a city street and I was railing at American writers because their prose was so colourless. "Look at that," I said. We were walking over one of the bridges that cross the Chicago River. I pointed to the smoky skies, the buildings rearing up, the marvellous colour of the river down below the bridge.

"It's all splashy with colour, washed with colour, and none of them ever catch any of it. They make life too colourless, too eternally grey," I said. . . . "You lie," said Carl.

He referred me again to Steve Crane, sent me off to the Chicago Public Library to find a little book of Crane's early verse.

Pure colour, experiments, a man finding his way, feeling his way. What that man knew he never got said. Writers in America who do not know their Stephen Crane are missing a lot. Suppose he did put a pretty little patent-leather finish on some of

his later tales. Take him for what he was—his importance. Think of what was going on all around him then.

All the painters of that day painting in low tones—going in for facile brush work. The arts all grey. Grey cities, grey people.

A young man coming along, not too strong physically, touched with consumption, broke most of his life.

Standing up against the almost universal greyness of the art expression of his day. Putting in great splashes of colour—the tales in this volume, **"Maggie,"** *The Red Badge of Courage*—others too.

The thing to do is to have all his books on your shelves. Get him in relation to his times, the drama of the man, of his life.

He did a lot. He was an explosion all right. It's about time people began to hear the explosion. (pp. xiv-xv)

> *Sherwood Anderson, in his introduction to* The Work of Stephen Crane: "Midnight Sketches" and Other Impressions, Vol. XI *by Stephen Crane, edited by Wilson Follett (copyright 1926 and renewed 1954 by Alfred A. Knopf, Inc.; reprinted by permission of the publisher, Knopf, 1926 (and reprinted by Russell & Russell, 1963, pp. xi-xv).*

WILLA CATHER   (essay date 1926)

[*Cather is famous for her epic, yet realistic, portraits of the American frontier and the men and women who tried to settle it. In her own writing she stressed a pure, spare style and was extremely concerned with both aesthetic and moral issues. These sentiments also carried over into her critical work. In the following excerpt, Cather examines Crane's collection of short stories,* Wounds in the Rain. *Cather finds Crane to be an Impressionist who is "the best of our writers in what is called 'description' because he is the least describing."*]

The sketches in this volume are most of them low-pressure writing, done during, or soon after, Crane's illness in Cuba. He hadn't the vitality to make stories, to pull things together into a sharp design—though **"The Price of the Harness"** just misses being a fine war story. In one of them the writing is rather commonplace, the sketch **"God Rest Ye, Merry Gentlemen"**—the only story of Crane's I know which seems distinctly old-fashioned. It is done in an outworn manner that was considered smart in the days when Richard Harding Davis was young, and the war correspondent and his "kit" was a romantic figure. This sketch indulges in a curiously pompous kind of humour which seemed very swagger then. . . . (pp. 67-8)

But only this one of Crane's war sketches is much tainted by the war-correspondent idiom of the times. In the others he wrote better than the people of his day, and he wrote like himself. The fact that there is not much design, that these are for the most part collections of impressions which could be arranged as well in one way as another, gives one a chance to examine the sentences, which are part, but only part, of the material out of which stories are made.

When you examine the mere writing in this unorganized material, you see at once that Crane was one of the first post-impressionists; that he began it before the French painters began it, or at least as early as the first of them. He simply knew from the beginning how to handle detail. He estimated it at its true worth—made it serve his purpose and felt no further responsibility about it. I doubt whether he ever spent a laborious half-hour in doing his duty by detail—in enumerating, like an honest, grubby auctioneer. If he saw one thing that engaged him in a room, he mentioned it. If he saw one thing in a landscape that thrilled him, he put it on paper, but he never tried to make a faithful report of everything else within his field of vision, as if he were a conscientious salesman making out his expense-account. ("The red sun was pasted in the sky like a wafer," that careless observation which Mr. Hergesheimer admires so much, isn't exceptional with Crane. He wrote like that when he was writing well. What about the clouds, and the light on the hills, and the background, and the foreground? Well, Crane left that for his successors to write, and they have been doing it ever since: accounting for everything, as trustees of an estate are supposed to do—thoroughly good business methods applied to art; "doing" landscapes and interiors like house-decorators, putting up the curtains and tacking down the carpets.

Perhaps it was because Stephen Crane had read so little, was so slightly acquainted with the masterpieces of fiction, that he felt no responsibility to be accurate or painstaking in accounting for things and people. He is rather the best of our writers in what is called "description" because he is the least describing. Cuba didn't tempt him to transfer tropical landscapes to paper, any more than New York State had tempted him to do his duty by the countryside. (pp. 68-71)

He didn't follow the movement of troops there much more literally than he had in *The Red Badge of Courage.* He knew that the movement of troops was the officers' business, not his. He was in Cuba to write about soldiers and soldiering, and he did. . . . (p. 71)

The most interesting things in the bundle of impressions called **"War Memories"** are the death of Surgeon Gibbs, Crane's observations about the regulars, "the men," and his admiration for Admiral Sampson. Sometimes when a man is writing carelessly, without the restraint he puts upon himself when he is in good form, one can surprise some of his secrets and read rather more than he perhaps intended. He admired Sampson because he wasn't like the time-honoured conception of a bluff seaman. (p. 72)

He admired the Admiral because he wasn't theatrical, detested noise and show. (p. 73)

And that point of view caused Mr. Crane's biographer [Thomas Beer] no little trouble. He himself managed so conspicuously to elude the banquets and bouquets of his own calling that he left a very meagre tradition among "literary people." . . . His ideal, apparently, was "just plain, pure, unsauced accomplishment." (pp. 73-4)

> Willa Cather, *"Four Prefaces: Stephen Crane's 'Wounds in the Rain and Other Impressions of War'"* (copyright 1926 by Alfred A. Knopf, Inc.; reprinted by permission of the publisher; originally published as her introduction to The Work of Stephen Crane: "Wounds in the Rain and Other Impressions of War," Vol. IX by Stephen Crane, edited by Wilson Follett, Knopf, 1926), in Willa Cather On Writing: Critical Studies on Writing As an Art by Willa Cather, Knopf, 1949, pp. 67-74.

FORD MADOX FORD (essay date 1936)

[*Ford was an English man of letters who played an important role in the development of twentieth century realistic and modernist literature and art. In 1908, he founded* The English Review, *a periodical considered by some to be the finest literary journal of its day during Ford's brief tenure as editor. Founded in order to print Thomas Hardy's poem "The Sunday Morning Tragedy," which had been rejected by every other magazine in England,* The English Review *published works by such writers as T. S. Eliot, Wyndham Lewis, and Ezra Pound, whose theories of Imagism were in part derived from conversations with Ford on literature. Another contributor, Joseph Conrad, had earlier collaborated on two novels with Ford on the recommendation of William Ernest Henley, who called Ford the finest stylist then writing in English. Many years after leaving the editorship of* The English Review *and while living in Paris, Ford established the* Transatlantic Review, *to which James Joyce and Ernest Hemingway contributed. Among his own works,* The Good Soldier *and the tetralogy* Parade's End—*novels generally concerned with the social, political, and moral decline of Western civilization—are considered his most important contributions to English literature. Ford was among Crane's close literary acquaintances and frequently visited him at Crane's Brede Place Manor in England. In his high praise for the novelist, Ford refers to Crane as "the first American writer."*]

If it were desired to prove that supernatural beings pay rare visits to earth, there could be no apparition more suited to supporting the assertion than was Stephen Crane, whose eclipse is as fabulous as was his fabulous progress across this earth. . . . One awakened one morning in the nineties in England and *The Red Badge of Courage* was not; by noon of the same day it filled the universe. There was nothing you could talk of but that book. And, by teatime, as it were, this hot blast of fame had swept back across the Atlantic and there was nothing they could talk of in New York and its hinterlands but that book.

There was no doubt a non-literary reason for the phenomenon. The middle nineties and the twenty years that succeeded them formed together a period of war consciousness and war preparation such as the world has seldom seen, and it came after a quarter century of profoundly peaceful psychology. (p. 21)

[Suddenly] there was *The Red Badge of Courage* showing us, to our absolute conviction, how the normal, absolutely undistinguished, essentially civilian man from the street had behaved in a terrible and prolonged war—without distinction, without military qualities, without special courage, without even any profound apprehension of, or passion as to, the causes of the struggle in which, almost without will, he was engaged. (And is it beside the mark to note that this was exactly how we all did take it twenty years later, from the English Channel to the frontiers of Italy?) The point was that, with *The Red Badge* in the nineties, we were provided with a map showing us our own hearts. If before that date we had been asked how we should behave in a war, we should no doubt have answered that we should behave like demigods, with all the marmoreal attributes of war memorials. But, a minute after peeping into *The Red Badge,* we knew that, at best, we should behave doggedly but with weary non-comprehension, flinging away our chassepot rifles, our haversacks, and fleeing into the swamps of Shiloh. We could not have any other conviction. The idea of falling like heroes on ceremonial battle-fields was gone forever; we knew that we should fall like street-sweepers subsiding ignobly into rivers of mud. (pp. 22-3)

Crane's work is the most electric thing that ever happened in that struggle—it was and so remains. His influence on his time, and the short space of time that has succeeded his day, was so tremendous that if today you read *Maggie,* it is as if you heard a number of echoes, so many have his imitators been; and you can say as much of *The Red Badge.* That is simply because his methods have become the standard for dealing with war scenes or slum life. Until there comes a new Homer, we shall continue to see those things in that way.

His technique was amazing and extraordinarily contagious. How many stories since its day have not opened with a direct imitation of the marvellous first sentence of *The Open Boat:*

> None of them knew the colour of the sky.

Haven't a thousand stories, since then, opened with just that cadence, like a machine-gun sounding just before stand-to at dawn and calling the whole world to attention? And of course there is more to it than just the cadence of the eight monosyllables to the one dissyllable. The statement is arresting because it is mysterious and yet perfectly clear. So your attention is grasped even before you realize that the men in the boat were pulling or watching the waves so desperately that they had no time to look up. That is skill, and when it comes, as it did with Crane, intuitively, out of the very nature of the narrator, it is the pledge of genius. It is the writing of somebody who cannot go wrong . . . who is authentic.

I have spoken of Crane as the first American writer. The claim is not new, though I do not know who made it first. I dare say I did because I must certainly have been one of the first to think it. It remains perhaps a little controversial. But all American writers who preceded him had their eyes on Europe. They may have aped Anglicism in their writings, like the Concord group; or, like Mark Twain—or even if you like, O. Henry—they were chronic protesters against Europeanism. At any rate, the Old World preoccupied them.

There was nothing of this about Crane. (pp. 34-5)

No, he was the first American writer because he was the first to be passionately interested in the life that surrounded him—and the life that surrounded him was that of America. Don't believe that he was in the least changed by his residence at Brede. He paid, as it were, a courteous attention to Oxted or London or Brede, but he moved about in them an abstracted and solitary figure . . . and he footed the bills. I don't mean to say that he was homesick for a bench in Union Square. He didn't have to be; he was always there, surveying the world from that hard seat. He picked his way between dogs snarling over their bones in the rushes of the medieval hall, but he was thinking how to render the crash of dray horses' hooves and the rattle of the iron-bound wheels on the surface of Broadway where it crosses Fourteenth Street. Or he was lost in the Bowery. Or Havana. Or the Oranges. . . .

I was reading my *Congressional Record* this morning and I came upon this pious opinion in a speech of the Honorable Byron N. Scott:

> What does America stand for to the world? We have no Gothic cathedrals; no Rembrandt, no Shakespeare. We do not stand for art and culture, but we stand for the greatest experiment ever made in government. . . . If we ever have a high place along with Greece and Rome and the Italy of the Middle Ages, it will be for this contribution to history.

It won't. It will be because Crane discovered and gave a voice to America. . . . (p. 36)

Ford Madox Ford, "Stephen Crane" (originally published in The American Mercury, *Vol. XXXVII, No. 145, January, 1936), in his* Portraits from Life: Memories and Criticisms of Henry James, Joseph Conrad, Thomas Hardy, H. G. Wells, Stephen Crane, D. H. Lawrence, John Galsworthy, Ivan Turgenev, W. H. Hudson, Theodore Dreiser, Algernon Charles Swinburne (copyright, 1936 and 1937, by Ford Madox Ford; copyright renewed © 1964 by Janice Biala; reprinted by permission of Janice Biala), Houghton Mifflin Company, 1937 (and reprinted by Greenwood Press, Publishers, 1974), pp. 21-37.*

ALFRED KAZIN   (essay date 1942)

[*A highly respected American literary critic, Kazin is best known for his essay collections* The Inmost Leaf *(1955) and* Contemporaries *(1962), and particularly for* On Native Grounds *(1942), a study of American prose writing since the era of William Dean Howells. Having studied the works of "the critics who were the best writers—from Sainte-Beuve and Matthew Arnold to Edmund Wilson and Van Wyck Brooks" as an aid to his own critical understanding, Kazin has found that "criticism focussed many—if by no means all—of my own urges as a writer: to show literature as a deed in human history, and to find in each writer the uniqueness of the gift, of the essential vision, through which I hoped to penetrate into the mystery and sacredness of the individual soul." In the excerpt below, Kazin offers an estimate of Crane's unique contribution to American literature and of his limits as an artist.*]

Like every sensuous artist, [Stephen Crane] was a magnificent guesser, and nothing proved how deeply he had imagined the psychology of battle in *The Red Badge of Courage* than his experience as correspondent in the Greco-Turkish War. *"The Red Badge* is all right," he said when he came out of it.

Yet the stark greatness of the novel did grow in part out of his instinctively intimate knowledge of American manners and character. As Carl Van Doren observed, the verisimilitude of the book testified to Crane's knowledge of the popular memory and authentic legends of the war. One side of him was the local village boy who never quite lost his feeling for the small talk and the casual pleasures of the American town, and it showed not only in the campfire talk of the men in *The Red Badge,* but in the charming little-boy stories in *Whilomville Stories* and the extraordinary transcriptions of Negro speech in *The Monster.* What kept Crane alive, in one sense, was just that feeling; without it his despair might have seemed intolerable and, for an artist of his sensibility, incommunicable. He baited the universe but never those village citizens who are as benign in his work as small-town fathers in the *Saturday Evening Post.* They were his one medium of fraternity, and his strong, quiet affection for them testifies to the unconscious strength of his personal citizenship.

In this sense even the most astonishing effects in *The Red Badge of Courage* reflect Crane's background, for its soldier-hero might have been any American boy suddenly removed from the farm to fight in a war of whose issues he knew little and in which his predominating emotion was one of consummate perplexity and boredom. As a novelist of war Crane anticipated the war studies of the future; he had no palpable debt to Stendhal and Tolstoy, on whom he was supposed to have modeled his realism. Waterloo in *La Chartreuse de Parme* and Austerlitz in *War and Peace* are scenes against which the hero of sensibility enlarges his knowledge of life; but the novelists of social protest after the First World War, from Henri Barbusse to Humphrey Cobb, indicted the morality of war for its assault on the common citizen. Crane's hero is Everyman, the symbol made flesh upon which war plays its havoc; and it is the deliberation of that intention which explains why the novel is so extraordinarily lacking, as H. L. Mencken put it, in small talk.

Scene follows scene in an accelerating rhythm of excitement; the hero becomes the ubiquitous man to whom, as Wyndham Lewis once wrote of the Hemingwy hero, things happen. With that cold, stricken fury that was so characteristic of Crane—all through the self-conscious deliberation of his work one can almost hear his nerves quiver—he impaled his hero on the ultimate issue, the ultimate pain and humiliation of war, where the whole universe, leering through the blindness and smoke of battle, became the incarnation of pure agony. The foreground was a series of commonplaces; the background was cosmo-logical. Crane had driven so quickly through to the central problem that everything else seemed accessory in its effect, but he was forced to describe emotions in terms of color because the pressure behind so wholly concentrated a force drove him to seek unexpected and more plastic sources of imagery. Often he revealed himself to be a very deliberate tone-painter, as calculating and even mechanical a worker in the magnificent as Oscar Wilde or Richard Strauss. He aimed at picture qualities and he synthesized them so neatly that, like the movement of the hunters and the hunted in a tapestry of the medieval chase, they illustrated a world whose darkness was immensity. "In the Eastern sky there was a yellow patch, like a rug laid for the feet of the coming sun; and against it, black and pattern-like, loomed the gigantic figure of the colonel on a gigantic horse."

Yet for all its beauty, Crane's best work was curiously thin and, in one sense, even corrupt. His desperation exhausted him too quickly; his unique sense of tragedy was a monotone. No one in America had written like him before; but though his books precipitately gave the whole esthetic movement of the nineties a sudden direction and a fresher impulse, he could contribute no more than the intensity of his spirit. Half of him was a consummate workman; the other half was not a writer at all. In his ambitious stories of New York tenement life, **Maggie** and **George's Mother,** the violence seemed almost ce-lestial, but it was only Crane's own, and verbal; both stories suffer from excessive hardness and that strangely clumsy diction that Crane never learned to polish. In a great show piece like **The Open Boat** (drawn from an almost direct report of experiences in the Caribbean in the days when he was reporting the Cuban insurrection for New York newspapers) he proved himself the first great pyrotechnician of the contemporary novel; but the few superb stories are weighed down by hack work. The man who wrote **The Blue Hotel** also wrote more trash than any other serious novelist of his time. Even in buffooneries like his unfinished last novel, **The O'Ruddy,** there is the sense of a wasted talent flowing over the silly improvisation in silent derision. He had begun by astonishing the contemporary mind into an acceptance of new forms; he ended by parodying Rich-ard Harding Davis in **Active Service** and Stevenson in **The O'Ruddy.** Yet it was not frustration that wore him out, but his own weariness of life. His gift was a furious one, but barren; writing much, he repeated himself so joylessly that in the end he seemed to be mocking himself with the same quiet vicious-ness with which, even as a boy, he had mocked the universe. An old child, it was not merely by his somberness that he anticipated the misanthropy of the twentieth-century novel. Pride and a fiercely quaking splendor mark his first and last apotheosis: he was the first great tragic figure in the modern American generation. (pp. 69-72)

Alfred Kazin, "American Fin de Siècle," in his On Native Grounds: An Interpretation of Modern Amer-ican Prose Literature *(copyright 1942, 1970 by Alfred Kazin; reprinted by permission of Harcourt Brace Jovanovich, Inc.), Reynal & Hitchcock, 1942, pp. 51-72.**

ROBERT WOOSTER STALLMAN   (essay date 1950)

[*Stallman, author of* Stephen Crane: A Biography *(see additional bibliography), provides a Symbolistic interpretation of Crane's* The Red Badge of Courage. *This approach differs from that of critics, such as Charles Child Wallcutt (see excerpt below), who place the work in the Naturalistic school. Marston LaFrance states that Stallman's "notorious interpretation of* The Red Badge *is neither the silliest essay emanating from [the Symbolist] school nor even the most incoherent; it is merely the best known."*]

That Crane is incapable of architectonics has been the critical consensus that has prevailed for over half a century: "his work is a mass of fragments"; "he can only string together a series of loosely cohering incidents"; **The Red Badge of Courage** is not constructed. Edward Garnett, the first English critic to appraise Crane's work, aptly pointed out that Crane lacks the great artist's arrangement of complex effects, which is certainly true [see excerpt above]. We look to Conrad and Henry James for "exquisite grouping of devices"; Crane's figure in the carpet is a much simpler one. What it consists of—the very thing that Garnett failed to detect—is a structure of striking contrasts. Crane once defined a novel as a "succession of sharply-outlined pictures, which pass before the reader like a panorama, leaving each its definite impression." His own novel, nonetheless, is not simply a succession of pictures. It is a sustained structural whole. Every Crane critic concurs in this mistaken notion that **The Red Badge of Courage** is nothing more than "a series of episodic scenes," but not one critic has yet undertaken an analysis of Crane's work to see *how* the sequence of tableaux is constructed.

The form of **The Red Badge of Courage** is constructed by re-petitive alternations of contradictory moods. The opening scene establishes the same despair-hope pattern as the very last image of the book—"a golden ray of sun came through the hosts of leaden rain clouds." This sun-through-rain image, which epit-omizes the double-mood pattern dominating every tableau in the whole sequence, is a symbol of Henry Fleming's moral triumph and is an ironic commentary upon it. Crane is a master of the contradictory effect.

The narrative begins with the army immobilized—with restless men waiting for orders to move—and with Henry, because the army has done nothing, disillusioned by his first days as a recruit. In the first picture we get of Henry, he is lying on his army cot—resting on an idea. Or rather, he is wrestling with the personal problem it poses. The idea is a third-hand rumor that tomorrow, at last, the army goes into action. When the tall soldier first announced it, he waved a shirt which he had just washed in a muddy brook, waved it in bannerlike fashion to summon the men around the flag of his colorful rumor. It was a call to the colors—he shook it out and spread it about for the men to admire. But Jim Conklin's prophecy of hope meets with disbelief. . . . No disciples rally around the red and gold flag of the herald. A furious altercation ensues; the skeptics think it just another *tall* tale. Meanwhile Henry in his hut engages in a spiritual debate with himself: whether to be-lieve or disbelieve the word of his friend, the *tall* soldier. It is the gospel truth, but Henry is one of the doubting apostles.

The opening scene thus sets going the structural pattern of the whole book. Hope and faith (paragraphs 1-3) shift to despair or disbelief (4-7). The counter movement of opposition begins in paragraph 4, in the small detail of the Negro teamster who stops his dancing when the men desert him to wrangle over Jim Conklin's rumor. "He sat mournfully down." In this image of motion and change (the motion ceasing and the joy turning to gloom)', we are given the dominant leitmotif of the book and a miniature form of its structure. The opening prologue in Chapter 1 ends in a coda (paragraph 7) with theme and anti-theme here interjoined. It is the picture of the corporal, and his uncertainties (whether to repair his house) and shifting attitudes to trust and distrust (whether the army is going to move) parallel the skeptical outlook of the wrangling men. The same anti-theme of distrust is dramatized in the episode which follows this coda, and every episode throughout the remaining sequence of tableaux is designed similarly by one contrast pattern or another.

Change and motion begin the book. The army, which lies resting upon the hills, is first revealed to us by "the retiring fogs," and as the weather changes so the landscape changes, the brown hills turning into a new green. Now as nature stirs so the army stirs too. Nature and men are in psychic affinity; even the weather changes as though in sympathetic accord with man's plight. In the final scene it is raining but the leaden rain clouds shine with "a golden ray" as though to reflect Henry's own bright serenity, his own tranquility of mind. But now at the beginning, and throughout the book, Henry's mind is in a "tumult of agony and despair." This psychological tumult began when Henry heard the church bell announce the gospel truth that a great battle had been fought. Noise begins the whole mental *mêlée*. The clanging church bell and then the noise of rumors disorder his mind by stirring up legendary visions of heroic selfhood—dreams jolted by realities. The noisy world is clamoring to Henry to become absorbed into the solidarity of self-forgetful comradeship, but Henry resists this challenge of the "mysterious fraternity born of the smoke and danger of death," and withdraws again and again from the din of the affray to indulge in self-contemplative moods and magic reveries. The paradox is that when he becomes activated in the "vast blue demonstation" and is thereby reduced to anonymity he is then most a man and, conversely, when he affects self-dramatizing picture-postcard poses of himself as hero he is then least a man and not at all heroic. Withdrawals alternate with engagements, scenes of entanglement and tumult, but the same nightmarish atmosphere of upheaval and disorder pervades both the inner and the outer realms.

Henry's self-combat is symbolized by the conflict among the men and between the armies, their altercation being a duplication of his own. Henry's mind is in constant flux. Like the regiment that marches and counter-marches over the same ground, so Henry's mind traverses the same ideas over and over again. As the cheery-voiced soldier says about the battle, "It's th' most mixed up dern thing I ever see." Mental commotion, confusion, and change are externalized in the "mighty altercation" of men and guns and nature herself. Everything becomes activated, even the dead. The corpse Henry meets on the battlefield, "the invulnerable dead man," cannot stay still—he "*forced* a way for himself" through the ranks. And guns throb too, "restless guns." Back and forth the stage-scenery shifts from dream to fact, illusions pinpricked by reality. Disengaged from the external tumult, Henry's mind recollects former domestic scenes. Pictures of childhood and nursery imagery of babes recur during almost every interval of withdrawal. The nursery rhyme which the wounded soldiers sing as they retreat from the battlefront is at once a travesty of their own plight and a mockery of Henry's mythical innocence. . . .

Everything goes awry; nothing turns out as Henry had expected. The youth who had envisioned himself in Homeric poses, the legendary hero of a Greeklike struggle, has his pretty illusion shattered as soon as he announces his enlistment to his mother. "I've knet yeh eight pair of socks, Henry. . . ." His mother is busy peeling potatoes, and, madonna-like, she kneels among the parings. They are the scraps of his romantic dreams. The youthful private imagines armies to be monsters, "redoubtable dragons," but then he sees the real thing—the colonel who strokes his mustache and shouts over his shoulder, "Don't forget that box of cigars!"

The theme of *The Red Badge of Courage* is that man's salvation lies in change, in spiritual growth. It is only by immersion in the flux of experience that man becomes disciplined and develops in character, conscience or soul. The book is about a battle, but it is a symbolic battle. A battle represents life at its most intense flux, and it, therefore, exploits the greatest possible potentialities for change. To say that *The Red Badge of Courage* is a study in fear is as shallow an interpretation as to say that it is a narrative of the Civil War. It is not about the combat of armies; it is about the self-combat of a youth who fears and stubbornly resists change and spiritual growth. It probes a state of mind and analyzes the gradual transformation of this psychological state under the incessant pinpricks and bombardments of life. From the start Henry recognizes the necessity for change but wars against it. But man must lose his soul in order to save it. The youth develops into the veteran—"So it came to pass . . . his soul changed." Significantly enough, in stating what the book is about Crane intones Biblical phrasing.

Spiritual change, *that* is Henry Fleming's red badge. His red badge is his conscience reborn and purified. Whereas Jim Conklin's red badge of courage is the literal one, the wound of which he dies, Henry's is the psychological badge, the wound of conscience. Just as Jim runs into the fields to hide his wound from Henry, so Henry runs into the fields to hide his "wound" from the tattered man who asks him where he is wounded. "It might be inside mostly, an' them plays thunder. Where is it located?" The men, so Henry feels, are perpetually probing his guilt-wound, "ever upraising the ghost of shame on the stick of their curiosity." The unmistakable implication here is of a flag, and the actual flag which Henry carries in battle is the symbol of his conscience. Conscience is also symbolized by the forest, the cathedral-forest where Henry retreats to nurse his guilt-wound and be consoled by the benedictions which nature sympathetically bestows upon him. Here in this forest-chapel there is a churchlike silence as insects bow their beaks while Henry bows his head in shame; they make a "devotional pause" while the trees chant a soft hymn to comfort him. But Henry is troubled; he cannot "conciliate the forest." Nor can he conciliate the flag. The flag registers the commotion of his mind, and it registers the restless movements of the nervous regiment—it flutters when the men expect battle. And when the regiment runs from battle, the flag sinks down "as if dying. Its motion as it fell was a gesture of despair." Henry dishonors the flag not when he flees from battle but when he flees from himself and he redeems the flag when he redeems his conscience.

Redemption begins in confession and absolution—in a change of heart. Henry's wounded conscience is not healed until he confesses to himself the truth and opens his eyes to new ways; not until he strips his enemy heart of "the brass and bombast of his earlier gospels," the vainglorious illusions he had fabricated into a cloak of pride and self-vindication; not until he puts on new garments of humility and loving-kindness for his fellow men. Redemption begins in humility—Henry's example is the loud soldier who becomes the humble soldier. He admits the folly of his former ways. Henry's spiritual change is a prolonged process, but it is signalized in moments when he loses his soul in the flux of things; then he courageously deserts himself instead of his fellow men; then, fearlessly plunging into battle, charging the enemy like "a pagan who defends his religion," he becomes swept up in a delirium of selflessness and feels himself "capable of profound sacrifices." The brave new Henry, "new bearer of the colors," triumphs over the former one. The flag of the enemy is wrenched from the hands of "the rival colorbearer," the symbol of Henry's own other self, and as this rival colorbearer dies Henry is reborn.

Henry's regeneration is brought about by the death of Jim Conklin, the friend whom Henry had known since childhood. He goes under various names. He is sometimes called the spectral soldier (his face is a pasty gray) and sometimes the tall soldier (he is taller than all other men), but there are unmistakable hints—in such descriptive details about him as his wound in the side, his torn body and his gory hand, and even in the initials of his name, Jim Conklin—that he is intended to represent Jesus Christ. We are told that there is "a resemblance in him to a devotee of a mad religion," and among his followers the doomed man stirs up "thoughs of a solemn ceremony." When he dies, the heavens signify his death—the red sun bleeds with the passion of his wounds:

> The red sun was pasted in the sky like a wafer.

This grotesque image, probably the most notorious metaphor in American literature, has been much debated and roundly damned as a false, melodramatic, and non-functional figure, but it has seemed artificial and irrelevant to Crane's critics only because they have lifted it out of its context. Like any other image, it has to be related to the structure of meaning in which it functions. I do not think it can be doubted that Crane intended to suggest here the sacrificial death celebrated in communion. Henry and the tattered soldier consecrate the death of the spectral soldier in "a solemn ceremony," the wafer signifies the sacramental blood and body of Christ, and the process of his spiritual rebirth begins at this moment when the wafer-like sun appears in the sky. It is a symbol of salvation through death. Henry, we are made to feel, recognizes in the lifeless sun his own lifeless conscience, his dead and as yet unregenerated selfhood, and that is why he blasphemes against it. His moral salvation and triumph are prepared for, (1) by this ritual of purification and religious devotion and, at the very start of the book, (2) by the ritual of absolution which Jim Conklin performs in the opening scene (page 1). It was the tall soldier who first "developed virtues" and showed the boys how to cleanse a flag—wash it in the muddy river! That is the way! The way is to immerse oneself in the destructive element.

Theme and style in *The Red Badge of Courage* are organically conceived, the theme of change conjoined with the fluid style by which it is evoked. Fluidity and change characterized the whole book. Crane's style, calculated to create confused impressions of change and motion, is deliberately disconnected and disordered. He interjects disjointed details, one non sequitur melting into another. Scenes and objects are felt as blurred; everything shifts in value. Yet everything has relationship to the total structure; everything is manipulated into contrapuntal cross-references of meaning. Crane puts language to poetic uses, which, to define it, is to use language reflexively

and to use language symbolically. It is the works which employ this use of language that constitute what is permanent of Crane. Crane's language is the language of symbol and paradox. For example, the grotesque symbol and paradox of the wafer-like sun, in *The Red Badge*; or in **"The Open Boat,"** the paradox in the image of "cold comfortable sea-water," an image which calls to mind the poetry of W. B. Yeats with its fusion of contradictory emotions. This single image evokes the sensation of the whole experience of the men in their wave-tossed dinghy. But, furthermore, it suggests another telltale significance, one that is applicable to Crane himself. What is readily recognizable in this paradox of "cold comfortable sea-water" is that irony of opposites which constituted the personality of the man who wrote it. It is the subjective correlative of his own plight. It symbolizes his personal outlook on life—a life that was filled with ironic contradictions. The enigma of the man is symbolized in his enigmatic style. (pp. xxii-xxxvii)

> *Robert Wooster Stallman, "Introduction" (1950; copyright 1951 by Random House, Inc.; reprinted by permission of the publisher), in* The Red Badge of Courage: An Episode of the American Civil War *by Stephen Crane, The Modern Library, 1951, pp. v-xxxvii.*

JOHN BERRYMAN   (essay date 1950)

[Berryman is probably one of the most important, and certainly one of the most widely read, of modern American poets. His own work developed from objective, classically controlled poetry into an esoteric, eclectic, and highly emotional type of literature. In his own words, he has called poetry "the means by which the writer can shape from an experience in itself usually vague, a mere feeling or phrase, something that is coherent, directed, intelligible." Berryman's Stephen Crane, excerpted below, is a biography which amended some of the inaccuracies of the first Crane biography by Thomas Beer (see additional bibliography). The following is Berryman's critical opinion of Crane's literary style and his place in American literature.]

Crane I daresay is one of the great stylists of the language. These words "master" and "great" will trouble some readers, as they trouble me. But they seem unavoidable. The trouble we feel arises from several causes, which are worth examination. Crane's works that matter are all short. We don't see how works so little can be with any decency called great. Greatness of prose-style, however, does not require length for display. . . . Another trouble is that Crane was writing greatly, if he ever did, in his early twenties. We are told that prose-writers mature slowly; scarcely anyone writes prose worth reading under thirty. . . . A third trouble is just that he is comparatively recent; this matters less. Then there are the words themselves, grandiose. We have no objection to calling the boy Keats a master, Rimbaud a master, but the word "great" sticks a little. It looks like a catchword. Our major troubles, though, I think are two, both of them proceeding from the nature of his work and of its historical situation. There is first the relation of his style to prose style in English and American before him, and second the relation of his general art-form, the story, to Western fiction before him. (The term Western is unsatisfactory because it must include Russian fiction, but no other seems better.) Though these troubles are closely related, we must take them separately.

Nothing very like Crane's prose style is to be found earlier; so much will probably be granted at once by an experienced reader. Here I must observe that Crane wrote several styles.

He had even an epistolary style—extended, slow, uninflected, during most of his life, curter and jotty towards the end—but we are interested in his narrative styles. He began with the somber-jocular, sable, fantastic prose of the **"Sullivan County Sketches"** and the jagged, colored, awkward, brilliant *Maggie.* *Maggie* he probably revised much barbarousness out of before anyone except brothers and friends saw it, and he abandoned deliberately the method of the sketches—though fantasy, and fantasy in the quality of the prose, remained intermittently an element in his work to the end. A movement towards fluidity increases in *The Red Badge* and the **"Baby Sketches"** he was writing at the same time and produces a Crane norm: flexible, swift, abrupt, and nervous—swift, but with an unexampled capacity for stasis also. Color is high, but we observe the blank absence of the orotund, the moulded, which is Crane's most powerful response to the prose tradition he declined to inherit. In the fusion of the impassive and the intense peculiar to this author, he kept on drawing the rein. **"Horses—One Dash"** and **"The Five White Mice"** lead to the supple majesty of **"The Open Boat,"** a second norm. *The Monster,* much more closed, circumstantial, "normal" in feeling and syntax, is a third. Then he opened his style again back towards the second norm in the great Western stories, **"The Bride Comes to Yellow Sky"** and **"The Blue Hotel,"** and thereafter (for his two years) he used the second and the third styles at will, sometimes in combination, and the third usually relaxed as his health failed but peculiarly tense and astonishing in **"The Kicking Twelfth."** In certain late work also, notably in **"The Clan of No Name,"** a development toward complexity of structure is evident, which death broke off. Nevertheless we may speak of "Crane's style" so long as we have these variations in mind, and my point is that it differs *radically* both from the tradition of English prose and from its modifications in American prose. Shakespeare, Dryden, Defoe, Johnson, Dickens, Arnold, Kipling, as these develop into Edwards, Jefferson, Hawthorne, Melville, James— Crane writes on the whole, a definite and absolute *stylist,* as if none of these people had ever existed. His animation is not Kipling's, his deadpan flatness is not Mark Twain's. He is more like Tacitus, or Stendhal in his autobiography, say, than like any of the few writers of narrative English who actually affected his development. He was a rhetorician who refused to be one. In Crane for the first time the resources of American spareness, exaggeration, volcanic impatience, American humor, came into the hands of a narrative author serious and thoughtful as an artist as Hawthorne or James, and *more* serious than any others of the New England-New York hegemony. Thus he made possible—whether by way of particular influence or as a symbolic feat in the development of the language—one whole side of Twentieth Century prose. It is hard to decide that a boy, that anyone, did this, and so we feel uncomfortable about the word that characterizes the achievement with great justice.

The second difficulty with "great" is the newness of his form. I am not referring to the immense burst of talented story-writing in England and America during the 'nineties, though this is relevant; the short story had scarcely any status in English earlier, and we are less eager, naturally, to concede greatness to its artist than to crown a novelist. (pp. 283-85)

Crane's stories are as unlike earlier stories as his poems are unlike poems. He threw away, thoughtfully, plot; outlawed juggling and arrangement of material (Poe, Bierce, O. Henry); excluded the whole usual mechanism of society; banished equally sex (Maupassant) and romantic love (Chekhov—unknown to him); decided not to develop his characters; decided not to have any conflicts between them as characters; resolved not to have any characters at all in the usual sense; simplified everything that remained, and, watching intently, tenderly, and hopelessly, blew Fate through it—saying with inconceivable rapidity and an air of immense deliberation what he saw. What he saw, "apparently." The result is a series of extremely formidable, *new,* compact, finished, and distressing works of art. Mencken dated modern American literature from *The Red Badge of Courage.* The new *Literary History of the United States,* coming to hand as I write, dates it from the reissue of *Maggie* in 1896. It must come from about there, apparently.

Of course Crane did nothing such as I have just described. He was interested, only, in certain things, and kept the rest out. It is the ability to keep the rest out that is astounding. But the character of the deliberate in his prose too is conspicuous. . . . [This] was absent from his poetry, and it is time to come to the difference. The difference is that between presentation (in the poetry) and apparent presentation (in the prose); in the figure of the savage's dream that we were employing, between *rehearsal* and *investigation.* The poem can simply say what the dream (nightmare) was; at once it gets rid of the dream, and is solaced in hearing it said. An effect of style is undesirable. To *study* the dream, to embody it, as in a story—this is another matter. One needs a suit, a style, of chain armor to protect the subject from everything that would like to get into the story with it: the other impressions of life, one's private prejudices, a florid and hypocritical society, existing literature. The style of the prose aims at the same thing as the unstyle of the poetry, namely, naked presentment, but its method is ironic. Other authors are saying what things "are," with supreme falsity. Crane therefore will only say what they *seem* to be. "The youth turned, with sudden, livid rage, toward the battlefield. He shook his fist. He seemed about to deliver a philippic.

"'Hell—'

"The red sun was pasted in the sky like a wafer."

Half of Crane's celebrated "coldness" is an effect of this *refusal to guarantee.* "He seemed about to deliver a philippic." It sounds as if he weren't going to; but he is; but he isn't; but—one does not know exactly where one is. The style is merely honest, but it disturbs one, it is even menacing. If this extremely intelligent writer will not go further than that insistent "seemed," says the reader nervously to himself, should *I?* The style has the effect of obliterating with silent contempt half of what one thinks one knows. And then: a policeman begins "frenziedly to seize bridles and beat the soft noses of the responsible horses." In the next sentence the noses are forgotten. But to tell us about the horses if the author is not going to commiserate with them seems brutal. It makes the reader do the feeling if he wants to; Crane, who cared more for horses than any reader, is on his way. Again the reader is as it were rebuked, for of course he *doesn't* feel very strongly about horses—he would never have put in that "soft" himself, much less clubbed it in with "responsible." (pp. 286-88)

This is supposed, by the way, to be Realism or Naturalism. Frank Norris, who was a romantic moralist, with a style like a great wet dog, and Stephen Crane, an impressionist and a superlative style, are Naturalists. These terms are very boring, but let us agree at least to mean by them *method* (as Howells did) rather than *material* (as Norris, who called his serious works "Romance," did). "Tell your yarn and let your style go to the devil," Norris wrote to somebody. The Naturalists, if there are any, all *accumulate,* laborious, insistent, endless; Dreiser might be one. Crane selected and was gone. "He knew when to shut up," as Norris put it. "He is *the only* impressionist," said Conrad in italics to Garnett, "and *only* an impressionist." This is not quite right either: Crane's method shows realistic and also fantastic elements. But it would be better, as a label for what has after all got to be understood anyway in itself, than the categorical whim established now in the literary histories. Crane was an impressionist.

His color tells us so at once. This famous color of his plays a part in his work that has been exaggerated, but it is important. Gifted plainly with a powerful and probably very odd sense of color, fortified then by Goethe, he did not refuse to use it; sometimes he abused it, and he increasingly abandoned it. Most authors use color. "The sun emerges from behind the gray clouds that covered the sky and suddenly lights up with its bright red glow the purple clouds, the greenish sea . . . the white buildings." So Tolstoy at the end of *Sevastopol,* and it bears no relation whatever to Crane's use of color." At this time Hollanden wore an unmistakable air of having a desire to turn up his coat collar." This is more like one of Crane's colors than Tolstoy's actual colors are. Color is imposed, from an angle, like this apparently physical and actually psychological detail. Crane was interested in what Goethe called the "moral-sensual effect of color." He owes nothing whatever, apparently, to painting. The blue hotel "screaming and howling"—"some red years"—"fell with a yellow crash." The color is primitive. So with adverbs, metaphors. A man leans on a bar listening to others "terribly discuss a question that was not plain." "There was a general movement in the compact column. The long animal-like thing moved slightly. Its four hundred eyes were turned upon the figure of Collins." Here there is none of Crane's frequent, vivid condensation; and yet the eyes are not human eyes. It is primitive, an impression. A psychologist lately called red the most panicky and explosive of colors, the most primitive, as well as the most ambivalent, related equally to rage and love, battle and fire, joy and destruction. Everywhere then, in style, a mind at stretch.

We may reach toward the subject of all this remorseless animation through his characters. They are very odd. To call them types is a major critical error, long exposed, ever-recurrent. The new *Literary History* describes the hero of **The Red Badge** as "impersonal and typical," for which read: intensely personal and individual. George Wyndham (and Wells after him) fifty years ago showed the boy an idealist and dreamer brought to the test. Pete in **Maggie** is not a bartender, but Pete. Billy Higgins in **"The Open Boat"** is not an oiler, but the oiler. Crane scarcely made a type in all his work. At the same time, he scarcely made any characters. His people, *in* their stories, stay in your mind; but they have no existence outside. No life is strongly imaginable for them save what he lets you see. This seems to me to be singular, to want explanation. I think he is interested in them individually, but only as a crisis reaches them. The "shaky and quickeyed" Swede of **"The Blue Hotel"** is certainly an *individual* mad with fear, one of Crane's most memorable people, but it is as an individual *mad with fear* that he grimly matters. "Stanley pawed gently at the moss, and then thrust his head forward to see what the ants did under the circumstance." When this delightful thing happens, a love-scene is taking place two feet away, one of the most inhibited and perfunctory ever written. It is only or chiefly in animals that Crane can be interested when a *fate* is not in question. Once it is, he is acutely and utterly present with the sufferer, attending however to the fate.

"Apparently" the state of the soul in crisis: this is his subject. The society against the person will do; he uses the term "environment" in regard to **Maggie,** and this is more generally dramatized in **The Monster,** more particularly dramatized in **"The Bride Comes to Yellow Sky."** But one has less feeling in these works, and in a number of others like them, that the men are themselves against each other, than that they have been set simply facing each other—not by Crane—by a fate. War is the social situation that does this most naturally and continually, so he possesses himself of it; in imagination first, again and again, and then in fact. **"The Open Boat"** is his most perfect story partly because here for once the fate is in the open: one is *fully justified* in being afraid, one can feel with confidence that one is absolutely tested. The antagonist will not fail one, as another man might, as even society might. The extraordinary mind that *had* to feel this we shall look at in the next chapter; here we are concerned with the art. Now these states of crisis, by their nature, cannot persist; so Crane succeeded only in short work. *The Red Badge of Courage,* as most critics have noticed, is not really a novel at all, but a story, and it is a little too long, as Crane thought it was. His imagination was resolute in presenting him with conditions for fear; so that he works with equal brilliance from invention and from fact. To take **"The Open Boat,"** however, as a *report* is to misunderstand the nature of his work: it is an action of his art upon the remembered possibility of death. The death is so close that the story is warm. A coldness of which I was speaking earlier in Crane is absent here. Half of this I attributed to the stylistic refusal to guarantee. The other half is an effect from far in the mind that made the art, where there was a passion for life half-strangled by a need for death and made cold. Life thaws under the need when the death nears. In the eggshell boat, the correspondent knew even at the time, under dreadful hardship, that this was "the best experience of his life"—the comradeship, he says this is, but it was really something else: "There was a terrible grace in the move of the waves, and they came in silence, save for the snarling of the crests. . . ."

The immense power of the tacit, felt in Crane's accounts of Maggie's brother's nihilism, her mother's self-pity, Henry Fleming's self-pride, George's dreams, gives his work kinship rather with Chekhov and Maupassant than Poe. "I like my art"—said Crane—"straight"; and he misquoted Emerson, "There should be a long logic beneath the story, but it should be carefully kept out of sight." How far Crane's effect of inevitability depends upon this *silence* it would be hard to say. Nowhere in **"The Open Boat"** is it mentioned that the situation of the men is symbolic, clear and awful though it is that this story opens into the universe. Poe in several great stories opens man's soul downwards, but his work has no relation with the natural and American world at all. If Crane's has, and is irreplaceable on this score, it is for an ironic inward and tragic vision outward that we value it most, when we can bear it. At the end of the story a word occurs that will do for Crane. "When it came night, the white waves paced to and fro in the moonlight, and the wind brought the sound of the great sea's voice to the men on the shore, and they felt that they could then be interpreters." Crane does really stand between us and something that we could not otherwise understand. It is not human; it is not either the waves and mountains who are among his major characters, but it acts in them, it acts in children and sometimes even in men, upon animals, upon boys above all, and men. Crane does not understand it fully. But he has been driven and has dragged himself nearer by much to it than we have, and he interprets for us.

For this reason, as well as for his technical revolution, he is indispensable. By a margin he is probably the greatest American story-writer, he stands as an artist not far below Hawthorne and James, he is one of our few poets, and one of the few manifest geniuses the country has produced. (pp. 288-92)

John Berryman, in his Stephen Crane: A Critical Biography *(reprinted by permission of Farrar, Straus and Giroux, Inc.; copyright 1950 by Kate Berryman; renewed © 1977 by Kate Berryman), William Sloane, 1950 (and reprinted by Octagon Books, 1975), 347 p.*

JOSEPH J. KWIAT (essay date 1952)

[*Kwiat examines the demonstrable influence upon Crane's work of the artistic environment in which the author lived during the 1890s.*]

Stephen Crane, John Berryman flatly states in his recent book, "owes nothing whatever, apparently, to painting" [see excerpt above]. Berryman denies H. G. Wells's claim that the novelist was influenced by painters in his use of color, and he informs us that Crane "knew, by the way, few real painters—Linson, Jerome Myers, later Ryder; mostly illustrators." These statements may be challenged on several counts. . . .

There is evidence, however, that Crane knew graphic artists very early in his career and that this experience was reflected in his newspaper writings in two ways: in his utilization of the image of the artist as subject and in his "painterly" stylistic devices. Crane, furthermore, discussed how important it was for the writer to be "honest" and "independent," and he associated these attitudes with graphic artists and with the problems of what he considered to be a closely allied art form. Finally, Crane explicitly compared his own general literary intentions with the technical and philosophical implications of what the French Impressionists, as he conceived them, were attempting in color. (p. 331)

After his dismissal from the New York *Tribune* in 1892 and the disappointment following the publication of his novel, *Maggie*, in 1893, Crane lived and spent a great deal of time during the next two years in the old building of the Art Students League, then located on East Twenty-Third Street. Most of the inhabitants were struggling artists. These "Indians," as Crane called them, included R. G. Vosburgh, David Ericson, Nelson Greene, Frederick Gordon, W. W. Carroll, Edward S. Hamilton, and a Wolfrom. This setting and several of these men appeared in *The Third Violet* and in many of Crane's sketches. He was also associating with other cliques of artists. One of these centered around Corwin K. Linson, and another was a kind of dining-club which included Henry McBride, Gustave Verbeek, and Edward S. Hamilton.

After his dismissal from the *Tribune*, Crane contributed sketches and feature articles to various newspapers as a free-lance writer. And it was as literary-reporter on the manifold life of New York City that Crane found a rôle freer and more congenial than a city editor's insistent demands for facts rather than impressions would have permitted. Many of these sketches reveal how he was stimulated by the kind of experience which interested him intensely, namely the difficulties of the graphic artist within the city's impersonal life. There can be little doubt that Crane identified his own miserable fate as a writer during this period with the misfortunes of his artist friends.

Crane drew upon his recent experiences with the "Indians" at the old Art Students League building in **"Stories Told by an Artist in New York."** The sketch, born of its author's observation of the artistic struggle for existence within the jungle of the city, reveals a wry humor. A magazine illustrator, Pennoyer, works on a pen-and-ink drawing and hopes for payment from the *Monthly Amazement*. Corinson (Corwin K. Linson?), another artist, deserts the precarious existence of art for the relative security of turning out crayon portraits at fifteen dollars per week and is, therefore, in a position to stake his less fortunate friends to a Thanksgiving dinner. (pp. 332-33)

Because of its similarity in background, in names of characters, and in its fundamental problem, **"The Silver Pageant"** was probably written for newspaper publication at much the same time as **"Stories Told by an Artist in New York."** The situation centers upon Gaunt, a slow and absent-minded artist, who discovers that he must make drawings for book publishers in order to earn a living. When he announces to his artist friends, Grief, Pennoyer, and Wrinkles, that he intends to paint a picture, they pay him a visit and find him a suicide in his studio.

Crane's newspaper work indicated that he not only utilized the image of the artist as subject for his sketches but that he also made use, as a writer, of the techniques of the artist. Several of his early dispatches for the New York *Tribune* were characterized by an impressionistic manner which may well have been formed by his familiarity with the method of the graphic artist. For the "impressionistic" method, as Hamlin Garland pointed out in *Crumbling Idols* in 1894, was "a complete and of course momentary concept of the sense of sight" and that it should be "the stayed and reproduced effect of a single section of the world of color upon the eye." For Crane, however, the method was not only useful as a way of "seeing" the world but for "feeling" its anonymity and indifference as well. It gave, in effect, another dimension to his ironic attitude toward life. (p. 333)

Crane's final dispatch for the *Tribune* was his impressionistic account of the American Day parade of the Junior Order of United American Mechanics. "Asbury Park," he wrote, "creates nothing. It does not make; it merely amuses. . . . The throng along the line of march was composed of summer gowns, lace parasols, tennis trousers, straw hats and indifferent smiles. The procession was composed of men, bronzed, slope-shouldered, uncouth and begrimed with dust." The manner of such American impressionistic painters of the period as John Twachtman, Childe Hassam, Theodore Robinson, and J. Alden Weir as they, in turn, understood the "new disintegrations" from Monet and Sisley may possibly be seen in Crane's technical handling of the scene.

Crane later wrote a newspaper sketch, **"An Experiment in Misery,"** which was an account of the submerged and defeated lives in the midst of the impersonal life of the city. The flophouse scene, for example, is written with the feeling of a painter for the nightmarish effects of figures in shadows and gaslight upon a room. . . . (p. 334)

The beach and amusement park scene in **"The Pace of Youth"** is a brilliant illustration of Crane's affinity to the graphic artist in his skillful handling of the problems of perspective, composition, and color for the purpose of capturing a mood and an "impression." . . . And Crane's description of a picturesque section of Greenwich Village, in **"Minetta Lane, New York,"** reveals the writer striving for the pictorial effects of a painter working in chiaroscuro. . . . (pp. 334-35)

Crane's involvement in the writer's obligation to be honest, esthetically as well as in every other way, was closely linked with his feeling that the writer should maintain his individuality in thought and style. And it is important to see that Crane's attitude was identified with graphic artists and with the problems of what he considered to be an allied art. (p. 335)

[In] *The Third Violet* . . .—a story which Wilson Follett, editor of Crane's works, considers chiefly valuable as a chapter of autobiography—Crane satirized the false notion that genuine art must be divorced from the life which holds greatest significance for the artist, the life that is most immediate and intense. One of the indigent painters in the story carries on a dramatic monologue in which only "quaint" and "foreign" subject matter is interpreted as legitimate for the artist. The portrayal of American subject matter is to be shunned, he says, for two reasons: it is "hard to find" and, since it is absent from the work of previous "respectable" artists, it would damn the artist for his "originality.". . . (p. 336)

A novel, Crane explained in another place, "should be a succession of . . . clear, strong, sharply-outlined pictures, which pass before the reader like a panorama, leaving each its definite impression." He fully realized that the problem of knowing about life was accompanied by the difficulty of telling about it, and he stated that his chief desire was "to write plainly and unmistakably, so that all men (and some women) might read and understand." But he was also compelled to admit that the ability to write "plainly and unmistakably" was a difficult feat. "The complex interwoven mesh of life," Crane deplored in *The O'Ruddy*, "constantly, eternally, prevents people from giving intelligent explanation." He frankly admitted the limitations of the writer's art in **"War Memories"**: "I bring this to you," he wrote, "merely as an effect—an effect of mental light and shade, if you like; something done in thought similar to that which the French Impressionists do in colour; something meaningless and at the same time overwhelming, crushing, monstrous."

Since, as Crane indicated in **"War Memories,"** he was attempting in words what the French Impressionists were striving for in color, he prefaced his statement of his artistic intentions with his "impression" of a scene in which a church had been converted into a hospital. Underlying Crane's concern with the technical problem of presenting the qualities of his special vision, notably the mental effects of light and shade, was his deterministic attitude toward his materials. This concept of literary "impressionism" was reflected in much of his fiction.

It is almost impossible to "place" Crane as a member of a literary school. But a key to Crane's literary principles may be found in his frequently expressed admiration for Joseph Conrad's artistry. Conrad's artistic credo, as expressed in the preface to *The Nigger of the Narcissus*, was essentially a visual and pictorial approach to "life" and "truth." For the artist's task was to snatch "a passing phase of life" and, above everything else, "to make you *see*." Conrad continued: "It is to show its vibration, its colour, reveal the substance of its truth . . . the stress and passion within the core of each convincing moment." Crane, undoubtedly, would have also agreed with Henry James's assertion that the novelist had a great deal in common with the painter.

This is not to say that Crane was solely indebted to the graphic arts and artists for his literary genius. But it is equally false to say, as Mr. Berryman says, that Crane "owes nothing whatever . . . to painting.". . . It seems apparent that an understanding of the relationship between Crane's knowledge of graphic artists and his awareness of certain of the specific

problems of their art, particularly that of the "impressionists," will give valuable critical insights into the theory and practice of Crane's own literary art. (pp. 337-38)

> *Joseph J. Kwiat, "Stephen Crane and Painting," in* American Quarterly *(copyright 1952, Trustees of the University of Pennsylvania), Vol. IV, No. 4, Winter, 1952, pp. 331-38.*

ERNEST HEMINGWAY (essay date 1955)

[*The following is a brief, but often-quoted tribute by Hemingway to the artistry of Crane's* The Red Badge of Courage. *Interestingly, many critics point to similarities in the ironic style and "matter of fact war reporting" of the two authors.*]

There was no real literature of our Civil War, excepting the forgotten "Miss Ravenall's Conversion" by J. W. De Forest, until Stephen Crane wrote **"The Red Badge of Courage."** . . . Crane wrote it before he had ever seen any war. But he had read the contemporary accounts, had heard the old soldiers, they were not so old then, talk, and above all he had seen Matthew Brady's wonderful photographs. Creating his story out of this material he wrote that great boy's dream of war that was to be truer to how war is than any war the boy who wrote it would ever live to see. It is one of the finest books of our literature and I included it entire [in "Men at War: The Best War Stories of All Time"] because it is all as much of one piece as a great poem is.

If you want to find out how perfect a piece of writing is try to cut it for the purpose of making a selection for an anthology. I do not mean how good a thing is. There is no better writing on war than there is in Tolstoy but it is so huge and overwhelming that any amount of fights and battles can be chopped out of it and maintain all their truth and vigor and you feel no crime in the cutting. Actually "War and Peace" would be greatly improved by cutting; not by cutting the action, but by removing some of the parts where Tolstoy tampered with the truth to make it fit his conclusions. The Crane book, though, could not be cut at all. I am sure he cut it all himself as he wrote it to the exact measure of the poem it is. (p. xvi)

> *Ernest Hemingway, in his introduction to* Men at War: The Best War Stories of All Time, *edited by Ernest Hemingway (copyright © 1942 by Crown Publishers, Inc.; used by permission of Crown Publishers, Inc.), revised edition, Crown, 1955, pp. xi-xxvii.*

CHARLES CHILD WALCUTT (essay date 1956)

[*Walcutt is in the forefront of critics who consider Crane's work in the Naturalistic school. In the following excerpt, taken from his study of Naturalism, Walcutt discusses Crane's major works and finds evidence of the writer's Naturalism in his depiction of moral delusions, his impressionistic style, and in his "deterministic accounting for events."*]

The works of Stephen Crane . . . are an early and unique flowering of pure naturalism. It is naturalism in a restricted and special sense, and it contains many non-naturalistic elements, but it is nevertheless entirely consistent and coherent. It marks the first entry, in America, of a deterministic philosophy not confused with ethical motivation into the structure of the novel. Ethical judgment there is, in plenty. To define Crane's naturalism is to understand one of the few perfect and successful embodiments of the theory in the American novel. It illustrates the old truth that literary trends often achieve their finest expressions very early in their histories. *Mutatis mutandis,* Crane is the Christopher Marlowe of American naturalism—and we have had no Shakespeare.

Crane's naturalism is to be found, first, in his attitude toward received values, which he continually assails through his naturalistic method of showing that the traditional concepts of our social morality are shams and the motivations presumably controlled by them are pretenses; second, in his impressionism, which fractures experiences into disordered sensation in a way that shatters the old moral "order" along with the old orderly processes of reward and punishment; third, in his obvious interest in a scientific or deterministic accounting for events, although he does not pretend or attempt to be scientific in either the tone or the management of his fables. Crane's naturalism does not suffer from the problem of the divided stream because each of his works is so concretely developed that it does not have a meaning apart from what happens in it. The meaning is always the action; there is no wandering into theory that runs counter to what happens in the action; and nowhere does a character operate as a genuinely free ethical agent in defiance of the author's intentions. Crane's success is a triumph of style: manner and meaning are one.

In *Maggie: A Girl of the Streets,* . . . Crane opened fire with a loud bang. A story of the New York slums, it sounds in synopsis like a perfect bit of sordid determinism: a girl raised in violence and squalor, charmed, seduced, and abandoned by her flashy lover, rejected by her family, descends rapidly through streetwalking to suicide.

In telling this story, Crane fuses elements of poverty, ignorance, and intolerance in a context of violence and cruelty to create a nightmarish world wavering between hallucination and hysteria. The language establishes this tone through violent verbs, distorted scenes, and sensory transfer. A sampling of the first three pages discovers such terms as "howling," "circling madly about," "pelting," "writhing," "livid with the fury of battle," "furious assault," "convulsed," "cursed in shrill chorus," "tiny insane demon," "hurling," "barbaric," "smashed," "triumphant savagery," "leer gloatingly," "raving," "shrieking," "chronic sneer," "seethed," and "kicked, scratched and tore," which immediately suggest that the people are hurled through a nightmare. The device of sensory transfer appears in "lurid altercations," "red years," "dreaming blood-red dreams," and "various shades of yellow discontent." When Maggie's brother comes in bloody from fighting, "The mother's massive shoulders heaved with anger. Grasping the urchin by the neck and shoulder she shook him until he rattled. . . . The babe sat on the floor watching the scene, his face in contortions like that of a woman at a tragedy. The father . . . bellowed at his wife. 'Let the kid alone for a minute, will yeh, Mary? Yer allus poundin' 'im. When I come nights I can't get no rest 'cause yer allus poundin' a kid. Let up, d'yeh hear? Don't be allus poundin' a kid.'"

In the same vein, Maggie's parents are depicted in insanely drunken battles during which they break up whole roomfuls of furniture and crockery several times during the brief story. After one such battle, "A glow from the fire threw red hues over the bare floor, the cracked and soiled plastering, and the overturned and broken furniture. In the middle of the floor lay his mother asleep. In one corner of the room his father's limp body hung across the seat of a chair." And a bit later, Maggie's "mother drank whiskey all Friday morning. With lurid face and tossing hair she cursed and destroyed furniture all Friday

afternoon. When Maggie came home at half-past six her mother lay asleep amid the wreck of chairs and a table." Now, such people would not have more than one set of furniture, and it is improbable that they would in an ordinary drunken quarrel reduce it to matchwood, although of course one grants the likelihood of a table overturned or a chair smashed. The rather fantastic but obviously intentional exaggeration of these passages renders Crane's sense that this world is so warped as to be mad. His tone unites despair and moral outrage with the self-protection of a sort of wild humor.

A dominant idea that grows from this landscape of hysteria is that these people are victimized by their ideas of moral propriety which are so utterly inapplicable to their lives that they constitute a social insanity. Maggie is pounced upon by the first wolf in this jungle and seduced. When she is abandoned and returns home, her mother's outraged virtue is boundless. . . . (pp. 66-9)

The impressions that these people are not free agents, and that their freedom is limited as much by their conventional beliefs as by their poverty, are naturalistic concepts completely absorbed into the form of the story. One might object upon sociological grounds that Crane's ideas of the family are unsound, but his literary technique here is a triumph. It creates a coherent if terrible world, and there are no serious loose ends—no effect of tension or contradiction between abstract theory and human event. Crane's hallucinatory inferno is a gift of his style. What he says and what he renders are one. Indeed, he does not comment because the whole work is one grand roar of mockery and outrage. The hysterical distortions symbolize, image, and even dramatize the confusion of values which puts these social waifs in a moral madhouse. (p. 69)

A perennial controversy about naturalism concerns whether it is optimistic or pessimistic—whether it dwells in the horrors it portrays or believes it can correct them. The problem achieves an epitome in *Maggie:* however stark the horror, no reader can feel that Crane is scientifically disinterested or unconcerned. Where his method does, through its fascinated concern with detail, achieve a ghastly fixation, it is the quality of Goya rather than the cold form of Velasquez. The story shows that nothing can be done for Maggie and her family, for they are lost; but it presents the exact reality with an intensity that defies indifference. I say the exact reality. It seems exact, but it would be more accurate to say that Crane objectifies and renders exactly his spirited and intentional distortion of the grotesque world that he has exactly seen. (p. 72)

The Red Badge of Courage . . . , Crane's Civil War story, is the most controversial piece in his canon. It has been much discussed and most variously interpreted, and the interpretations range about as widely as they could. Is it a Christian story of redemption? Is it a demonstration that man is a beast with illusions? Or is it, between these extremes, the story of a man who goes through the fire, discovers himself, and with the self-knowledge that he is able to attain comes to terms with the problem of life insofar as an imperfect man can come to terms with an imperfect world? It is tempting to take the middle road between the intemperate extremes; but let us see what happens before we come to the paragraphs at the end that are invoked to prove each of the explanations. . . . (p. 75)

The book opens with a scene at a Union encampment in which the uninformed arguments of the soldiers are described in a manner that recalls the mockery of "infantile orations" in *Maggie.* The phrase pictures a squalling child colorfully, while it conveys the author's private amusement at the image of a shouting politician. In *The Red Badge* there is continually a tone of mockery and sardonic imitation of men who are boisterous, crafty, arrogant, resentful, or suspicious always in an excess that makes them comical, and the author seems to delight in rendering the flavor of their extravagances. An element of the fantastic is always present, the quality apparently representing the author's feeling for the war, the situations in it, the continual and enormous incongruities between intention and execution, between a man's estimate of himself and the way he appears to others, between the motivations acknowledged to the world and those which prevail in the heart. It is with these last that the book is centrally concerned—with the problem of courage—and it is here that the meaning is most confusingly entangled with the tone. (pp. 75-6)

[Henry Fleming] has "dreamed of battles all his life—of vague and bloody conflicts that had thrilled him with their sweep and fire. . . . He had imagined peoples secure in the shadow of his eagle-eyed prowess." He had burned to enlist, but had been deterred by his mother's arguments that he was more important on the farm until—the point is sardonically emphasized—the newspapers carried accounts of great battles in which the North was victor. "Almost every day the newspapers printed accounts of a decisive victory." When he enlists, his mother makes a long speech to him—which is presented by Crane with no trace of mockery—but he is impatient and irritated. (pp. 76-7)

Vanity amid dreams of Homeric glory occupy him thenceforth—until battle is imminent. Then he wonders whether he will run or stand; and he does not dare confide his fears to the other men because they all seem so sure of themselves and because both they and he are constantly diverted from the question by inferior concerns. (p. 77)

Approaching the first engagement, the youth perceives with terror that he is "in a moving box" of soldiers from which it would be impossible to escape, and "it occurred to him that he had never wished to come to the war . . . He had been dragged by the merciless government." He is further startled when the loud soldier, a braggart, announces with a sob that he is going to be killed, and gives the youth a packet of letters for his family. The engagement is described with terms of confusion: the youth feels "a red rage," and then "acute exasperation"; he "fought frantically" for air; the other men are cursing, babbling, and querulous; their equipment bobs "idiotically" on their backs, and they move like puppets. The assault is turned back, and the men leer at each other with dirty smiles; but just as the youth is responding in "an ecstasy of self-satisfaction" at having passed "the supreme trial," there comes a second charge from which he flees in blind panic: "He ran like a blind man. Two or three times he fell down. Once he knocked his shoulder so heavily against a tree that he went headlong." As he runs, his fear increases, and he rages at the suicidal folly of those who have stayed behind to be killed.

Just as he reaches the zone of safety, he learns that the line has held and the enemy's charge been repulsed. Instantly he "felt that he had been wronged," and begins to find reasons for the wisdom of his flight. "It was all plain that he had proceeded according to very correct and commendable rules. His actions had been sagacious things. They had been full of strategy. . . . He, the enlightened man who looks afar in the dark, had fled because of his superior perceptions and knowledge. He felt a great anger against his comrades. He knew it could be proved that they had been fools." He pities himself;

he feels rebellious, agonized, and despairing. It is here that he sees a squirrel and throws a pine cone at it; when it runs he finds a triumphant exhibition in nature of the law of self-preservation. "Nature had given him a sign." The irony of this sequence is abundantly apparent. It increases when, a moment later, the youth enters a place where the "arching boughs made a chapel" and finds a horrible corpse, upright against a tree, crawling with ants and staring straight at him. (pp. 77-8)

The climax of irony comes . . . , when, after a stasis of remorse in which he does indeed despise himself (albeit for the wrong reason of fearing the reproaches of those who did not flee), he sees the whole army come running past him in an utter panic of terror. He tries to stop one of them for information, and is bashed over the head by the frantic and bewildered man. And now, wounded thus, almost delirious with pain and exhaustion, he staggers back to his company—and is greeted as a hero! . . . He is now vainglorious; he thinks himself "a man of experience. . . chosen of the gods and doomed to greatness." Remembering the terror-stricken faces of the men he saw fleeing from the great battle, he now feels a scorn for them! He thinks of the tales of prowess he will tell back home to circles of adoring women.

The youth's reaction to his spurious "red badge of courage" is thus set down with close and ironical detail. Crane does not comment, but the picture of self-delusion and vainglory is meticulously drawn. In the following chapter Henry does fight furiously, but here he is in a blind rage that turns him into an animal, so that he goes on firing long after the enemy have retreated. The other soldiers regard his ferocity with wonder, and Henry has become a marvel, basking in the wondering stares of his comrades.

The order comes for a desperate charge, and the regiment responds magnificently, hurling itself into the enemy's fire regardless of the odds against it. . . . (pp. 79-80)

Heroism is "temporary but sublime," succeeded by dejection, anger, panic, indignation, despair, and renewed rage. This can hardly be called, for Henry, gaining spiritual salvation by losing his soul in the flux of things, for he is acting in harried exasperation, exhaustion, and rage. What has seemed to him an incredible charge turns out, presently, to have been a very short one—in time and distance covered—for which the regiment is bitterly criticized by the General. The facts are supplemented by the tone, which conveys through its outrageous and whimsical language that the whole business is made of pretense and delusion. . . . (p. 80)

What it all seems to come to is that the heroism is in action undeniable, but it is preceded and followed by the ignoble sentiments we have traced—and the constant tone of humor and hysteria seems to be Crane's comment on these juxtapositions of courage, ignorance, vainglory, pettiness, pompous triumph, and craven fear. The moment the men can stop and comment upon what they have been through they are presented as more or less absurd.

With all these facts in mind we can examine the Henry Fleming who emerges from the battle and sets about marshaling all his acts.

He is gleeful over his courage. Remembering his desertion of the wounded Jim Conklin, he is ashamed because of the possible disgrace, but, as Crane tells with supreme irony, "gradually he mustered force to put the sin at a distance," and to dwell upon his "quiet manhood." Coming after all these events and rationalizations, the paragraphs quoted at the beginning of this discussion are a climax of self-delusion. If there is any one point that has been made it is that Henry has never been able to evaluate his conduct. He may have been fearless for moments, but his motives were vain, selfish, ignorant, and childish. Mercifully, Crane does not follow him down through the more despicable levels of self-delusion that are sure to follow as he rewrites (as we have seen him planning to do) the story of his conduct to fit his childish specifications. He has been through some moments of hell, during which he has for moments risen above his limitations, but Crane seems plainly to be showing that he has not achieved a lasting wisdom or self-knowledge.

If *The Red Badge of Courage* were only an exposure of an ignorant farm boy's delusions, it would be a contemptible book. Crane shows that Henry's delusions image only dimly the insanely grotesque and incongruous world of battle into which he is plunged. There the movement is blind or frantic, the leaders are selfish, the goals are inhuman. One farm boy is made into a mad animal to kill another farm boy, while the great guns carry on a "grim pow-wow" or a "stupendous wrangle" described in terms that suggest a solemn farce or a cosmic and irresponsible game.

If we were to seek a geometrical shape to picture the significant form of *The Red Badge,* it would not be the circle, the L, or the straight line of oscillation between selfishness and salvation, but the equilateral triangle. Its three points are instinct, ideals, and circumstance. Henry Fleming runs along the sides like a squirrel in a track. Ideals take him along one side until circumstance confronts him with danger. Then instinct takes over and he dashes down the third side in a panic. The panic abates somewhat as he approaches the angle of ideals, and as he turns the corner (continuing his flight) he busily rationalizes to accommodate those ideals of duty and trust that recur, again and again, to harass him. Then he runs on to the line of circumstance, and he moves again toward instinct. He is always controlled on one line, along which he is both drawn and impelled by the other two forces. If this triangle is thought of as a piece of bright glass whirling in a cosmic kaleidoscope, we have an image of Crane's naturalistic and vividly impressioned Reality. (pp. 81-2)

There is an interesting connection, which scholarship has not yet traced, between what we speak of as Crane's impressionism and the "expressionism" of the modern theater. Expressionism is the theatrical mode that uses distortion, violent and intense motion, and the "yell" to convey a sense of the world as it appears to one of the characters or to the author. Usually it is the protagonist whose distorted view conveys something the author wants us to see. (p. 84)

These comments apply in almost precisely the same way to Crane's writings. What appears hysterical and twisted through the mind of the protagonist is also seen thus in the longer perspective of the author's purpose. He is showing his characters baffled and harried in a crazy world, where they do not function well enough to control their own destinies, or even to understand them very well; it is a world which the author's larger view does not make any more reasonable, for what his view particularly adds is a fuller sense of the protagonist's limitations.

Crane's writings anticipate dramatic expressionism in America by twenty years, as they do also the work of Kaiser, Toller,

and Wedekind on the Continent. Only the earliest expressionistic work of Strindberg is as early as Crane's impressionism. For its sources we might better look to the painting of the great modern impressionists—Cezanne, Matisse, van Gogh. (pp. 85-6)

Charles Child Walcutt, "Stephen Crane: Naturalist and Impressionist," in his American Literary Naturalism, a Divided Stream *(© copyright 1956 by the University of Minnesota), University of Minnesota Press, Minneapolis, 1956, pp. 66-86.*

JAMES B. COLVERT   (essay date 1959)

[*Colvert's study of the structure and theme of Crane's fiction is considered one of the best interpretations of Crane's work.*]

[In] Stephen Crane's **"The Open Boat"** the narrator describes the predicament of the men in the ten-foot dinghy as they precariously navigate the heavy seas. . . . To the men in the boat the horizon of jagged waves at which their eyes glance level marks the extreme limit of the universe. "None of them knew the colour of the sky." The waves shut all else from view, and as they sweep down upon the dinghy they seem to threaten the very nucleus of all visible creation, the men in the open boat. But suddenly the perspective changes. The narrator intrudes to suggest that the plight of the men might seem from a different point of view something less than cosmic in its significance. "Viewed from a balcony" their situation might seem simply "weirdly picturesque."

A brilliant passage in **"The Blue Hotel"** shows clearly how the distancing effect of the speaker's point of view is achieved through metaphor and imagery. The Swede, crazy with rage and terror after a ferocious fight with old Scully's son at the blue hotel, is making his way through town in a howling blizzard.

> He might have been in a deserted village. We picture the world as thick with conquering and elate humanity, but here, with the bugles of the tempest pealing, it was hard to imagine a peopled earth. One viewed the existence of man then as a marvel, and conceded a glamour of wonder to these lice which were caused to cling to a whirling, fire-smitten, ice-locked, disease-stricken, space-lost bulb.

The imagery suggests a cosmic distance between the narrator and his subject. The speaker sees the Swede as if from a balcony in space, and both the crazy Swede and his world seem indeed pathetically small and insignificant.

These passages throw light on the characteristic structural pattern of the Crane story. The narrative design of Crane's best fiction is defined by the tension between two ironically divergent points of view: the narrowing and deluding point of view of the actors and the enlarging and ruthlessly revealing point of view of the observer-narrator. To the men in the boat the universe seems to have shrunk to the horizon and to have concentrated within its narrow limits all the malignant powers of creation; but the longer view of the narrator reveals this as a delusion born in the men's egoistic assumption that they occupy a central position in Nature's hostile regard. The correspondent sees the waves as "wrongfully and barbarously abrupt," but in the very act of passing moral judgment upon Nature, he implicitly asserts his superior worth and significance. He errs in the judgment because his perspective, unlike the narrator's, is limited by his acute self-consciousness. And the Swede's point of view again in contrast to the narrator's, admits no "glamour of wonder" in his clinging to an "ice-locked . . . space-lost bulb," for in the flush of his victory over young Scully, he is "elate and conquering humanity" who can say to the bartender in the saloon, "Yes, I like this weather. I like it. It suits me."

In Crane this handling of point of view is more than a technical expediency for bringing order and clarity into the narrative structure. It is a manner of expression which grows inevitably out of his vision of the world. One sees by means of this double perspective the two polar images of the Crane man. In the narrator's view man is insignificant, blind to his human weakness and the futility of his actions, pathetically incompetent in the large scheme of things. But from the limited point of view originating in his aspiring inner-consciousness, the Crane hero creates a more flattering image of himself and the world. Trapped within the confining circle of his swelling emotions of self, he sees himself as god-like, dauntless, heroic, the master of his circumstances. The two images mark the extreme boundaries of Crane's imaginative scope—define, as it were, the limits of his vision of the world. For the Crane story again and again interprets the human situation in terms of the ironic tensions created in the contrast between man as he idealizes himself in his inner thought and emotion and man as he actualizes himself in the stress of experience. In the meaning evoked by the ironic projection of the deflated man against the inflated man lies Crane's essential theme: the consequence of false pride, vanity, and blinding delusion. The sentence which follows the passage quoted from **"The Blue Hotel"** goes to the thematic dead center of his fiction: "The conceit of man was explained by this storm to be the very engine of life."

This way of seeing the world and ordering his vision in art is evident in Crane's first fiction, the little sketches he wrote in 1892 about his youthful hunting and camping experience in the Sullivan County wilds. The hero of these stories is without even the dignity of a name; he is simply "the little man." Yet his egotism, his outrageous sense of self-importance, the heroic image of the world he creates in the ballooning illusions of his personal vision are wonderful to behold. (pp. 199-201)

But the movement of the tales is always toward the ironic deflation of "the little man." Despite his delusions of grandeur, he usually ends up in ignoble and humiliating defeat. (p. 201)

Though the 1892 Sullivan County stories are hardly more than crude groping toward a fictional subject and manner, they nevertheless throw valuable light on Crane's mature work. One is struck by the persistent recurrence of themes, motifs, and imagery which appear again and again in his later fiction—images of delusion, vanity, distorted values, of the pettiness of human pursuits. The hero of the tales is the prototype of the Crane Hero. The "very engine" of his life is the conceit which fabricates a private world of swollen heroic illusions. The motives of his every gesture are rooted in this world of perpetual falseness which his overweening ego creates out of the tag-ends of a tawdry romantic idealism; and though experience sometimes forces upon him disquieting glimpses of his inadequacy and insignificance, he is usually able to maintain his false image of the world against every assault of reality.

This same organizing vision underlies Crane's first novel, *Maggie: A Girl of the Streets,* begun perhaps as early as 1891 when Crane was a student at Syracuse University, but not finished in its final version until the winter of 1892, several months after the Sullivan County sketches were published in the *New York Tribune. Maggie,* a hard, melodramatic account of the seduction, desertion, and suicide of a New York slum girl, is chiefly responsible for Crane's reputation as a literary naturalist and is often cited as an illustration of his "cold-blooded determinism." His intention in the novel, one critic observes, "was probably to show the malevolence of all men and the indifferent and negative attitude of society to the individual, whose ruin was of no consequence to it." Crane himself wrote about the novel in similar terms: "It tries to show that environment is a tremendous thing in the world and frequently shapes lives regardless." Even so, this is only part of what Crane was saying in *Maggie.* He was aware, of course, of the role impersonal forces and the limitations of human nature play in human affairs; but he was aware, too, and more interested in, infirmities and perversities within the reach of the human will—pride and selfishness—and their effects upon moral responsibility. (p. 202)

In *George's Mother,* another novel about slum life . . . Mrs. Kelcey, through courage, humility, and self-sacrifice, makes a decent, happy home in the same tenement house the brutal Johnsons live in. She is destroyed not by her environment, but by her weak, vain, and will-less son George and her own sentimental and self-indulgent delusion that he is a paragon of virtue.

It is necessary to clear away this common misunderstanding about Crane in order to see the close thematic kinship of *Maggie* and the earlier Sullivan sketches. The basic conceptual pattern is the same. *Maggie,* like the sketches, is an ironic study of vanity and conceit, and like the *Tribune* pieces it depends for its structural coherence upon the ironic sense of situation and event. Crane brought to bear upon his slum study essentially the same attitude and the same literary idea and method he applied to his study of "the little man"; the chief difference is that in the dark and grim *Maggie* he elaborated the moral consequences of the human perversities he comically satirized in the earlier pieces.

The girl Maggie is the victim not so much of the blind impersonal force of her environment as of the inadequate morality of the unreal world view rooted in perverse pride and vanity. Like "the little man," the people in *Maggie* entertain false images of self which lead them into moral error. Pete, the villainous bartender, sees himself as a *gallant* of the most dazzling excellence; Maggie's brother, the brawling Jimmy, though he can ignobly take to his heels in a fight, is convinced that his courage is of heroic proportions; the yearning Maggie herself hopes that the poor little tinsel world of the music hall can be for her a real world; the brutal Mrs. Johnson believes that she is the most self-sacrificing of mothers. These illusions are the source of the moral outrage which drives Maggie to despair and suicide. As in the Sullivan County stories, the motif of false self-estimate emerges everywhere—in gesture, statement, act, situation—weaves into structural units, and finally fuses into an implicit statement of theme: that human incompetency—comic in the Sullivan County sketches, tragic in *Maggie*—finds its source in vanity, delusion, and ignorance of self.

This theme Crane developed more maturely and significantly in *The Red Badge of Courage,* begun in the spring of 1893 shortly after the stillbirth of *Maggie* and published in the newspaper version in December, 1894. The hero of the novel, Henry Fleming, is essentially "the little man," the deluded people of *Maggie,* and the Swede, for the "engine of his life," too, is pride, vanity, and conceit, the moral consequences of which *The Red Badge* explores. But like the correspondent in "The Open Boat" Henry is redeemed by a successful adjustment of his point of view, and for the first time Crane admits into his theme the working out of a solution to his hero's dilemma.

The novel treats four stages in Fleming's growth toward moral maturity. In the beginning he is unable to distinguish between his heroic dreams and hopes and the actual condition of war. Then follows a period of confusion and doubt as reality begins to intrude upon his dream world. Next he goes through a period of desperate but futile struggle to preserve, through deceit and rationalization, his pseudo-heroic image of himself and the world. In the end he solves his problem when he learns to see the world in its true light, when he is finally able to bring his subjectivity into harmony with the reality which his experience makes clear to him.

The structure of the novel is characteristically a series of loosely related, ironic episodes built up in the contrast between two points of view toward reality, a subjective interpretation originating in vanity, pride, and illusion juxtaposed against an "objective" reality originating in the superior long view of the narrator. So long as Henry is under the influence of his swelling vision of himself, he is incapable of acting morally and honestly. But in the end the disparate worlds of illusion and reality are brought into meaningful relationship, and in the resolution of the ironic tension between the two, the meaning of Henry's experience is made clear to him. Only then is he morally capable of facing up to war and life. (pp. 203-05)

Crane's fiction from the first progressively treats the same basic theme. One notes how closely the situation of "the little man" in "The Mesmeric Mountain," one of the early Sullivan County tales, curiously parallels Henry Fleming's in *The Red Badge.* Standing before the lowering challenge of the hill, "the little man" cowers in terror and frustration and wins its top finally in a mad, blind rush; in the face of war, Henry Fleming, too, is stricken with doubt and terror, and like "the little man" he conquers the spectre which haunts him in a wild, enraged assault. But "the little man," unlike Henry, does not change; he struts and swaggers atop the mountain, whereas Henry looks down, so to speak, with a new humility and understanding. "The little man's" world is still false. Fleming's is true.

In "The Blue Hotel" and "The Open Boat," Crane's best stories after *The Red Badge,* the fundamental thematic situation, with all its moral and ethical implication, is again defined in the tension between the world as it really is and as it is falsely perceived. Thus the men in "The Open Boat" can be interpreters only when in the trial of experience they come to realize their true relation to the universe and to their fellow men. Like Henry, the correspondent comes to know that the best experience of his life is the object lesson in humility and self-sacrifice, that in a cold and indifferent cosmos, illusions of friendly or hostile Nature notwithstanding, the best values are realized in humble human performance. In "The Blue Hotel" the Swede, like Fleming before the self-redeeming correction of his perspective, is a human failure because he is not equipped to cope with reality, even on the simplest level of behavior. Blind egotism—the "very engine of life"—distorts every manifestation of reality and creates the circumstances of his destruction.

Not many of Crane's heroes escape the predicaments their preposterous emotions of self create for them, for it is upon the absurd and sometimes pathetic world of their illusions that his vision is most narrowly focused. In the reduction of this vision to the forms of art, he was led to irony as a characteristic mode of expression. The effect of the usual Crane story is to place between the narrator and his subject a certain distance from which people and events are observed with the most ruthless detachment. At all times the observer is the master of the meanings of the enacted drama; he knows the sublime egotism and the tragic inadequacies of the actors: the prejudices of their points of view, the limitations of their wisdom, the selfish motives of their imaginations. And in narrow and brilliant ironic vision of them he recreates their shining false worlds and simultaneously destroys their illusions with laconic mockery. Only those few actors who can become interpreters survive. (pp. 207-08)

James B. Colvert, "Structure and Theme in Stephen Crane's Fiction," in Modern Fiction Studies *(© 1959 by Purdue Research Foundation, West Lafayette, Indiana 47907, U.S.A.), Vol. V, No. 3, Autumn, 1959, pp. 199-208.*

THOMAS A. GULLASON (essay date 1961)

[*Gullason examines the novels* Maggie, The Red Badge of Courage, *and* George's Mother *to illustrate Crane's consistent use of themes, characters, and images.*]

[*The Red Badge of Courage*] was part of a painstaking trilogy, which includes *Maggie* . . . and *George's Mother* . . . , wherein Crane reveals quite strikingly his own psychological involvement in his literary works, especially his earlier ones. Writing out his deep-rooted obsessions three times—seemingly to purge himself of them—he raised these personal frustrations to the level of myth and universality.

Crane was haunted by themes which are clearly demonstrated in his letters and in the biographies by Thomas Beer and Berryman. These themes include ideals versus realities; spiritual crises, where the mother image is dominant; fear, which involves courage, cowardice, and conflict or war. The leading characters in the early novels react in virtually similar ways to these themes; and though they are given names—Maggie, Henry Fleming, and George Kelcey—these vague, shadowy protagonists are all one and the same symbol.

All are young dreamers groping somewhat blindly for a way in which to make their ideals come true. They leave their own home environments hoping to find their "rightful" positions in the world. Each also has an ideal, sometimes vague love. Suddenly, they are all jolted by real-life situations and they rapidly deteriorate—except Henry Fleming, who is able to survive his ordeal.

Maggie's romantic hopes flower in the brutal slum world of Rum Alley. Faced with the prospect of a prolonged drudgery in a shirt factory or prostitution, Maggie dreams of escape from her environment and finds a "fairyland prince," Peter, who will help her find freedom as the "new" woman. Maggie magnifies, distorts Pete's charms; and after watching the action of a heroine in a play, she wonders if she too can acquire culture and refinement. She is instead acquired as Pete's mistress. Gradually she becomes aware of her false illusions: Pete is not a knight but an artful seducer; her environment, which she thought she could surmount, bewilders and traps her. Mocked and ostracized by her own degenerate society, Maggie becomes a reluctant prostitute. The ugly images just prior to her suicide effectively contrast with earlier, more fanciful scenes of the ideal life she had yearned for. Now there are only "a man with blotched features" and a "ragged being with shifting, blood-shot eyes and grimy hands."

Henry's romantic visions run an almost similar course. His monotonous farm environment, newspaper gossip, and front-line victories make him formulate ideals of Greeklike courage and yearn for battle. He wants to struggle with an enemy he has dreamed of "all his life." As he bids farewell to his schoolmates he watches the shy girl and contemplates a mysterious love pact. Nearing the front he finds an appreciative public. On the battlefield, however, he is shocked to find that his identity, his free will are gone. Then he retreats into the symbolic forest where he tries to convince himself that he is really "enlightened." Shortly he returns to the front, having recognized that public opinion is not accurate; that heroism is a sham; that his precious rationalizations are absurd. When the symbolic fog clears, Henry, now reunited with his comrades, achieves a dubious victory over his illusions.

George Kelcey's dreams, like Maggie's, evolve in the New York slums. Attracted to Bowery outcasts, he sees them as the "superior" society he always wanted to join. When he is introduced to Mr. Bleecker—who quickly becomes his ideal man—he is overjoyed by what he presumes is a show of good nature, courtesy, and warmth. He cannot see that Bleecker and his friends are weaklings, who blame their poverty on a "cruel" social order. George has other visions too—he dreams of possessing Maggie. (Both Maggie and Pete reappear in *George's Mother*.) But when he sees the aristocratic-looking Pete courting her, he becomes aware of his own lack of finery and escapes this painful truth by drinking to excess. Only the serious illness of his mother awakens him to reality. For now he must turn to his friends for monetary help and is refused by them all. As his mother dies, George is full of remorse and a deep sense of guilt for having neglected her. His own physical and mental collapse is conveyed when, in the end, he stares at the wallpaper whose patterns suddenly feel "like hideous crabs crawling upon his brain."

The religious theme is another integral part of the early novels. Each of the protagonists searches for spiritual help, which ends on a note of deception, of irony. With each novel, this religious motif gains in momentum until the entire atmosphere of *George's Mother* is pervaded with it. First Maggie, ostracized by her social group, makes a last desperate bid to save her soul by seeking the guidance of a priest: "But as the girl timidly accosted him he made a vigorous sidestep. He did not risk it to save a soul. For how was he to know that there was a soul before him that needed saving?" Not long after this rejection, Maggie commits suicide.

There are no visual priests in *The Red Badge,* but Henry Fleming's spiritual turmoil is more thoroughly treated than Maggie's. Henry's crisis occurs in chapters vii, viii, and ix of the novel, all the scenes taking place in or near the symbolic forest. He encounters a deception similar to Maggie's, for outwardly the landscape suggests a "religion of peace." Yet in this religious setting, Henry faces death, frighteningly presented by a corpse. In chapter viii, there is this same kind of incongruous juxtaposition. The celebrated wafer image in chapter ix symbolizes the culminating point of Henry's religious conflict. Here he becomes aware of the indifference of heaven to all the slaughter and bloodshed on the battlefield, and without the spiritual help he craves, Henry fights on.

George Kelcey tries to save his soul by finally accepting his prodding mother's invitation to attend church. To his surprise, he momentarily finds the clergyman not dull but glib. George seems ready to yield to spiritual guidance, which he needs in order to reform. But the church is not what he had hoped for. The speech of the clergyman proves to him "merely that he is damned." Later his mother tries to make him attend another meeting, but Geroge refuses and rejoins his hoodlum friends.

The portrayals of the mothers in the three novels are closely linked with the religious crises of the central characters and help to stress Crane's ironic attitude toward this theme. In *Maggie,* the degenerate Mary Johnson, influenced by the vocabulary of the "mission churches," wails for her dead daughter, forgetting that she is partially responsible for Maggie's suicide. Earlier in the novel she is the "righteous" Christian who shows the influence of hell-fire and Day-of-Doom Calvinism as she condemns her wayward daughter. When Maggie is abandoned by her lover, her mother denounces her: "She had a bad heart, dat girl did Jimmie." This kind of verbal ritual is summed up in the ironic last chapter which depicts Mrs. Johnson's spirit of mourning: she weeps for Maggie only after she finishes her coffee; she is swept into a religious ecstasy she does not understand by picking up the chant of a neighbor and stupidly crying: "Oh, yes. I'll fergive her [Maggie]! I'll fergive her!"

Henry Fleming's mother is a sincere religious zealot. She resigns all to God's will. Frequently she says: "The Lord's will be done"; "The Lord'll take keer of us all." When she gives Henry advice it is full of warnings not to sin. As Henry prepares to go to war, she pleads convincingly: ". . . and here's a little Bible I want yeh to take along with yeh, Henry." The young man seems to accept her pious teachings; but later, when he must rely on himself to solve his spiritual dilemma, he is unable to cope with it intelligently.

George Kelcey, on the other hand, cannot tolerate his well-meaning mother's religious fanaticism. Her every word and gesture are dedicated to the church and the possibilities of salvation. Once she prods too often and George is angered. While he resists the church, Mrs. Kelcey magnifies his faults and complains about his swearing and drinking. Finally when George agrees to attend church, it is only because he has been frightened by his hang-over at Bleecker's beer party. Ironically, his unsuspecting mother sees this as a hopeful sign of George's regeneration. But when her son renounces his short-lived affiliation with the church, the heartbroken Mrs. Kelcey becomes ill, and nearing death she sees visions of the Day of Doom. This death scene, which bewilders and frightens George, is the highest irony because a saintly woman who has tried to correct her son's behavior dies terrorized for her non-existent sins.

Crane's "mistress," fear, is also ever-present in the early novels. As a child, Maggie is terrified by her debauched parents who, after a prolonged drinking and fighting bout, finally fall asleep. A witness of this scene, the girl reacts: she "quivers," and her eyes "gleamed with fear." An older Maggie is again faced with fear, for after being deserted by her lover, she is denounced by her mother. Near the end of the novel, Maggie walks the streets a social outcast; she is more fearful than ever, for men look at her with "calculating eyes." (pp. 60-4)

Though Henry Fleming longs for the heroics of battle, he has symptoms similar to Maggie's. He fears the presence of death. One moment he is impressed by Jim Conklin's admission that he would run from battle if others ran; the next moment, listening to the loud soldier, Wilson, he develops a "thousand-tongued fear." But unlike Maggie, Henry eventually conquers his fear, which is more complex. For much of the novel, he is the mental outcast who rationalizes his fears, who fears the ridicule of his comrades. In the forest he throws a pine cone at a squirrel who scurries in fear. This "sign" makes him jubilant because Nature reaffirms his view, but only momentarily.

Henry also develops the attitude of the gang who war in *Maggie*. Like the Rum Alley boys, he displays a brief pseudo courage and a prolonged cowardice; like them, he runs from battle, magnifying the causes of his retreat. Unlike them, he studies his inner self. He even uses the pompous talk of the Rum Alley boys, for—still the unproven soldier—he assumes a courageous pose and loudly complains. When he does become "courageous," he is like Jimmie, described in animal terms: ". . . he went instantly forward, like a dog who, seeing his foes lagging, turns and insists upon being pursued."

George Kelcey discovers a less complex fear when he awakens from his drunken stupor at Bleecker's party. He learns of his mother's illness and he is full of fear and shame. As he enters his home, George "comprehended the room in a frightened glance." Even his friends are frightened. Bleecker fears the "grinding world," though earlier he and his friends were full of "valour." The hoodlums are of the same breed. Blue Billie, forced to defend his honor against George Kelcey, shows fear until his opponent has to leave because his mother is ill. Then Billie steps forward and hurls "a terrible oath."

All the protagonists—even the lesser characters—meet with fears which become more intense and more significant. In each novel at least one character acts out a problem inextricably bound up with fear and the delicate question of courage and cowardice. Continually Maggie, Henry, and George are contrasted with their larger social worlds—the slums and the regiment. Maggie's fear parallels the grotesque fear of the tenant world; Henry Fleming's inner terror parallels the external fright of Wilson and the entire regiment; and George Kelcey's fear is a symbol of a world of fear, as seen in Mr. Bleecker, his friends, and the hoodlums.

Surprisingly enough, the war motif has an important place in all the early novels. In a sense, one can see the themes already discussed (ideals versus realities, religious crises, and fear) as parts of endless conflict which are epitomized in the military language and the countless war images which are stressed mainly through the violent actions of animals and children.

Maggie depicts the unending battle of slum life. The opening scene of the novel presents a combat between two rival gangs. Maggie's home is pictured as if it were another battlefield. And in chapter xi of the novel, the tavern war between Jimmie and Pete is as vivid and intense as any individual scene in *The Red Badge*. (pp. 64-5)

Many of the combat scenes in *Maggie* refer to warlike children that Crane must have observed closely. For example: "Tattered gamins on the right made a furious assault on the gravel-heap. On their small convulsed faces shone the grins of true assassins." In *The Red Badge*, many of the combat soldiers remind one of the warlike children in *Maggie*: "A mounted officer displayed the furious anger of a spoiled child. He raged with his head, his arms, and his legs." Though they are in the heat of battle, the soldiers are continually pictured in civilian terms. They are compared to carpenters, laborers, businessmen, criminals, fishwives, drunks, blacksmiths, a detective, a parson, a shepherd, a politician, a football player, a boxer, a hunter, a deacon, and a schoolmistress.

There are other ways in which Crane makes clear that real war and civilian wars are indistinguishable and can be discussed on the same terms. Here is a typical image from *Maggie:* "In the yells of the whirling mob of Devil's Row children there were notes of joy like songs of triumphant savagery." There is the same kind of imagery in *The Red Badge:* "They danced and gyrated like tortured savages." Similar images, often pointing to some phase in conflict, can be found in *George's Mother*. There is the animal imagery: "Fidsey would turn upon him again, tears and blood upon his face, with the lashed rage of a vanquished animal." (p. 66)

All the early novels, then, show that Stephen Crane was (consciously or unconsciously) reworking and refining his themes, characters, and images. If one accepts the judgment of a few of the early critics—that *George's Mother* and not *The Red Badge* followed *Maggie*—then Crane's pattern of development becomes all the clearer. At any rate, this long, intense emotional concentration and structural focus on autobiographical themes bore excellent results: two halfway successes, *Maggie* and *George's Mother:* and one brilliant novel, *The Red Badge of Courage*. (p. 67)

Thomas A. Gullason, "Thematic Patterns in Stephen Crane's Early Novels," in Nineteenth-Century Fiction *(©1961 by The Regents of the University of California; reprinted by permission of The Regents), Vol. 16, No. 1, June, 1961, pp. 59-67.*

V. S. PRITCHETT (essay date 1964)

[*Pritchett has a high reputation for his work as a novelist, short story writer, and critic. He is considered one of the modern masters of the short story, and his work is a subtle blend of realistic detail and psychological revelation. Pritchett is also considered one of the world's most respected and well-read literary critics. He writes in the conversational tone of the familiar essay, a method by which he approaches literature from the viewpoint of a lettered but not overly scholarly reader. A twentieth-century successor to such early nineteenth century essayist-critics as William Hazlitt and Charles Lamb, Pritchett employs much the same critical method: his own experience, judgement, and sense of literary art, as opposed to a codified critical doctrine derived from a school of psychological or philosophical speculation. His criticism is often described as fair, reliable, and insightful. The first version of the following essay was written by Pritchett for* The New Statesman and Nation *during the height of World War II. In examining Walt Whitman's and Crane's realistic treatment of war, Pritchett mistakenly assumes, as had Joseph Conrad in 1925 (see excert above), that "the youth" who is the central character in* The Red Badge of Courage *remains anonymous throughout the narrative. (The youth is, in fact, identified by several fellow soldiers as Henry Fleming.) After discussing Whitman's* Drum Taps, *Pritchett addressed Crane and* The Red Badge of Courage *as follows.*]

It is worth while turning at this point to an American novelist who is the child of the Tolstoy-Whitman movement, the child of the Crimea and Bull Run. I am thinking of Stephen Crane and his book *The Red Badge of Courage* which was published in the nineties. The achievement of Crane was individual and high, but in placing it we must now confess that it came in on the Tolstoy wave; and that but for Tolstoy, it would never have been written. There is an important difference of experience between Tolstoy and Crane. In writing respectively about the Napoleonic and the American Civil Wars, both writers were reconstructing wars they had not seen; but Tolstoy *had* seen the Crimea, he had been a soldier, whereas Crane had read Tolstoy but had never seen war at all when he wrote his famous book, just as Defoe's *Journal of the Plague Year* was done by a writer who had never seen the plague: Crane became a war-correspondent after his book was written, It is in fact a romance or fable, subjective in impulse, in the tradition of Poe, Hawthorne, Melville, and James. An American critic has suggested that it was the fruit of a conflict of religious conscience and, indeed, the battle is compared with a mad religion and, at times, with a war of sectaries. The writer has been committed to "fight the good fight," is frightened at the open clash and then has to reassemble his self-respect out of fear, doubt and lies and learn to live with his experience. This may or may not be true of the origins of the book; what matters is that, Tolstoy and War Memoirs aiding, Crane has completely transposed himself into an imaginary eye-witness. One curious common emotion nevertheless unites the master and disciple. They reject the formal, the professional and rhetorical attitude to war; they reject the illusions of the profession and the traditional litanies of patriotism; but they cannot quite conceal a certain sadness at the passing of these things. (pp. 232-33)

The Red Badge of Courage is a tour de force. Crane starts a bugle call and sustains it without a falter to the end of the book. The scene is a single battlefield in the American Civil War, and the purpose of the novel is to show the phases by which a green young recruit loses his romantic illusions and his innocence in battle, and acquires a new identity, a hardened virtue. War has ceased to be a bewraying and befogging dream in his mind; it has become his world and he derives virtue from his unity with it. There is a second element in the story. To Crane a battlefield is like a wounded animal. The convulsions of its body, its shudders, its cries and its occasional repose, are the spasmodic movements and dumb respites of the groups of soldiers. There is not only the individual mind in the battlefield, but there is the mass mind also. Crane watches the merging of the individual with the herd. There is no plot in this book; it is a collection of episodes. We do not know which battle is being described or what are its objects. The rights and wrongs of the war itself are not discussed. No civilian and hardly a sight of the work of man, like a house or a cultivated field, comes into the picture. Few of the characters are named; the central figure is known simply as "the young man." The enemy are just the enemy, something fabulous and generally invisible in the blue smoke line of the engagement, terrifying and dragon-like at the worst, and at the best a singularity to be mistrusted. Who wins or loses is obscure. The whole thing is almost as anonymous as a poem or a piece of music and has the same kind of tension and suspense. For we are not specially interested in the mortal fate of the boy. We do not specially fear that he will be killed, nor do we privately hope he will cover himself with glory. Our eyes are fixed on something different in him; on each adjustment in his character as it comes along. At the end of this book, we say to ourselves, we too shall know how we shall behave when we discard out illusions about war and meet the reality. Romantically we fear or hope for battle as a way of singling ourselves out and dying; but underneath this daydream is the awe of knowing that battle is a way of living before it is a way of dying, and one in which we cannot calculate our behavior in advance. It was one of the discoveries of the unrhetorical attitude to war in literature, that even the men on the right side and in the just cause are afraid; and to Crane—an adventurous man who died young from the effects of going to see trouble all over the earth—the deep fear of fear was a personal subject.

This comes out in the first chapter of *The Red Badge of Courage*, where the young man is seen in the camp listening to the rumors and torturing himself with questions. He feels courageous but will courage stand? Will he stay or will he run in panic? These are overmastering questions. The first dead do not scare him, nor does the early uproar. He can stand the first attack and face the fear hidden in the wall of forest where the enemy lie, and after the frenzy of the first onslaught he lies for a few moments in the trench overcome by a sense of fellowship with his companions and experiencing with astonishment "the joy of a man who at last finds leisure." But, fixed on their intense personal problem, his heart and mind have not yet understood that while the imagination expects decisive and single answers, reality does not deal in such simplicities. The attack, to everyone's despair, is renewed. The second phase has begun. It is too much. The youth throws down his rifle and runs. Here Crane shows his power as a novelist, for in this part of the story he writes those dramatic scenes and draws those portraits which have given the book its place in the literature of war. This is where the dying soldier, walking white and erect like a rejected prince among his broken court, goes stiffly toward his grave. Crane was a dreamer of the ways of dying, but this death is one of the most terrible, for it is a *progress* to death. . . . If the boy's horror and quivering seem conventionally over-emphatic in that passage, the rest is not. Writers are always faced by two sets of words before they write; those which will draw a literary curtain over reality, and those which will raise the veil in our minds and lead us to see for the first time. Crane's gift for raising the veil is clear. The presence of "spectre" and "commonplace smile" in that portrait is imaginative observation at its best.

The book is filled with observation of this kind. (pp. 233-36)

[There] is this picture—how common it has become in modern realism, which Crane anticipates by thirty or forty years:

> Once the line encountered the body of a dead soldier. He lay upon his back staring at the sky. He was dressed in an awkward suit of yellowish brown. The youth could see that the soles of his shoes had been worn to the thinness of writing paper, and from a great rent in one the dead foot projected piteously. And it was as if fate had betrayed the soldier. In death it exposed to his enemies that poverty which in life he had perhaps concealed from his friends.

The only word a modern reporter would not have written in that passage is the word "piteously."

Toughness, that is to say fear of facing the whole subject, as Crane faced it, has intervened to make the modern writer's picture purely visual and inhumane—one remembers the turned-out pockets of the dead in Hemingway and his bravado about writing a natural history of the dead. The pathetic fallacy abounds in Crane's prose and we hear of "the remonstrance" and "arguments" of the guns; but for all the Whistlerian artiness—noted by H. G. Wells [see excerpt above]—there is pity, there is human feeling. There is a background of value and not a backdrop gaudy with attitudes. There is a quest for virtue—what else is the meaning of the young boy's innocent odyssey among his fears, his rages and his shames?—and not, as one sees in Kipling, the search for a gesture or some dramatic personal stand which avoids the issue and saves the face. Crane ignores the actor in human beings, the creature with the name on the personal playbill; he goes—at any rate in *The Red Badge of Courage*—for the anonymous voice in the heart. (pp. 236-37)

V. S. Pritchett," Two Writers and Modern War," in his The Living Novel & Later Appreciations (copyright ©1964, 1975 by V. S. Pritchett; reprinted by permission of Literistic, Ltd.), revised edition, Random House, 1964, pp. 225-37.*

DONALD PIZER (essay date 1965)

[*In the following study of* Maggie: A Girl of the Streets, *Pizer concludes that Crane transcends the framework of literary Naturalism through his use of irony and expressionistic Symbolism. These techniques, not usually found in a Naturalistic work, are employed by Crane to illustrate the false morality of the novel's characters, and thus their deluded sense of values become more of a deterministic force in their lives than the environment.*]

Stephen Crane's *Maggie: A Girl of the Streets* has often served as an example of naturalistic fiction in America. Crane's novel about a young girl's fall and death in the New York slums has many of the distinctive elements of naturalistic fiction, particularly a slum setting and the theme of the overpowering effect of environment. Crane himself appeared to supply a naturalistic gloss to the novel when he wrote to friends that *Maggie* was about the effect of environment on human lives. Yet the novel has characteristics which clash with its neat categorization as naturalistic fiction. For one thing, Crane's intense verbal irony is seldom found in naturalistic fiction; for another, Maggie herself, though she becomes a prostitute, is strangely untouched by her physical environment. She functions as an almost expressionistic symbol of inner purity uncorrupted by external foulness. There is nothing, of course, to prevent a naturalist from depending on irony and expressionistic symbolism, just as there is nothing to prevent him from introducing a deterministic theme into a Jamesian setting. But in practice the naturalist is usually direct. He is concerned with revealing the blunt edge of the powerful forces which condition our lives, and his fictional technique is usually correspondingly blunt and massive. . . . Crane's method, on the other hand, is that of obliqueness and indirection. Irony and expressionistic symbolism ask the reader to look beyond literal meaning, to seek beyond the immediately discernible for the underlying reality. Both are striking techniques which by their compelling tone and their distortion of the expected attempt to shock us into recognition that a conventional belief or an obvious "truth" may be false and harmful. Perhaps, then, *Maggie* can best be discussed by assuming from the first that Crane's fictional techniques imply that the theme of the novel is somewhat more complex than the truism that young girls in the slums are more apt to go bad than young girls elsewhere.

The opening sentence of *Maggie* is: "A very little boy stood upon a heap of gravel for the honor of Rum Alley." The sentence introduces both Crane's theme and his ironic technique. By juxtaposing the value of honor and the reality of a very little boy, a heap of gravel, and Rum Alley, Crane suggests that the idea of honor is inappropriate to the reality, that it serves to disguise from the participants in the fight that they are engaged in a vicious and petty scuffle. Crane's irony emerges out of the difference between a value which one imposes on experience and the nature of experience itself. His ironic method is to project into the scene the values of its participants in order to underline the difference between their values and reality. So the scene has a basic chivalric cast. The very little boy is a knight fighting on his citadel of gravel for the honor of his chivalrous pledge to Rum Alley. Crane's opening sentence sets the theme for *Maggie* because the novel is essentially about man's use of conventional but inapplicable abstract values (such as justice, honor, duty, love, and respectability) as weapons or disguises. The novel is not so much about the slums as a physical reality as about what people believe in the slums and how their beliefs are both false to their experience and yet function as operative forces in their lives.

Let me explore this idea by examining first the lives of the novel's principal characters and then the moral values which control their thinking about their lives. Crane uses two basic images to depict the Bowery. It is a battlefield and it is a prison. These images appear clearly in the novel's first three chapters, which describe an evening and night in the life of the Johnson family during Maggie's childhood. The life of the family is that of fierce battle with those around them and among themselves. . . . Crane's fundamental point in these chapters is that the home is not a sanctuary from the struggle and turmoil of the world but is rather where warfare is even more intense and where the animal qualities encouraged by a life of battle-strength, fear, and cunning-predominate. The slum and the home are not only battlefields, however, but are also enclosed arenas. Maggie's tenement is in a "dark region," and her apartment, "up dark stairways and along cold, gloomy halls," . . . is like a cave. Crane's description of the Johnson children eating combines both the warfare and cave images into one central metaphor of primitive competition for food. . . . By means of this double pattern of imagery, Crane suggests that the Johnson's world is one of fear, fury, and darkness, that it is a world in which no moral laws are applicable, since the Johnsons' fundamental guide to conduct is an instinctive amorality, a need to feed and to protect themselves.

Once introduced, this image of the Bowery as an amoral, animal world is maintained throughout *Maggie*. (pp. 121-24)

The moral values held by the Johnsons are drawn almost entirely from a middle-class ethic which stresses the home as the center of virtue, and respectability as the primary moral goal. It is a value system oriented toward approval by others, toward an audience. In the opening chapter of the novel, Jimmie hits Maggie as Mr. Johnson is taking them home. Mr. Johnson cries, "'Leave yer sister alone *on the street.*'" . . . (my italics) The Johnsons' moral vision is dominated by moral roles which they believe are expected of them. These roles bring social approbation, and they are also satisfying because the playing of them before an audience encourages a gratifying emotionalism or self-justification. The reaction to Maggie's fall is basically of this nature. She is cast out by her mother and brother for desecrating the Home, and her seducer, Pete, rejects her plea for aid because she threatens the respectability of the rough and tumble bar in which he works. The moral poses adopted by the Johnsons and by Pete have no relation to reality, however, since the home and the bar are parallel settings of warfare rather than of virtue.

The key to the morality of the Bowery is therefore its self-deceiving theatricality. Those expressing moral sentiments do so as though playing a role before a real or implied audience. Crane makes the dramatic nature of Bowery morality explicit in scenes set in dance halls and theatres. (pp. 124-25)

This . . . ability to project oneself into a virtuous role is present in most of the novel's characters. Each crisis in the Johnson family is viewed by neighbors who comprise an audience which encourages the Johnsons to adopt moral poses. In the scene in which Maggie is cast out, both Jimmie and Mrs. Johnson are aware of their need to play the roles of outraged virtue in response to the expectations of their audience. Mrs. Johnson addresses the neighbors "like a glib showman," and with a "dramatic finger" points out to them her errant daughter. . . . The novel's final scene is a parody of Bowery melodrama. Mrs. Johnson mourns over the dead Maggie's baby shoes while the neighbors cry in sympathy and the "woman in black" urges her to forgive Maggie. In the midst of her exhortaions, "The woman in black raised her face and paused. The inevitable sunlight came streaming in at the window." . . . Crane in this scene connects the sentimental morality of melodrama and the sanctimoniousness of Bowery religion. Both the theatre and the mission purvey moral attitudes which have no relation to life but which rather satisfy emotional needs or social approval. The heroes and heroines of melodrama cannot be confronted with reality, but the church is occasionally challenged. When it is, as when the mission preacher is asked why he never says "we" instead of "you," or when Maggie seeks aid from the stout clergyman, its reaction is either nonidentification with reality ("'What?'" asks the preacher) or withdrawal from it (the clergyman sidesteps Maggie). It is as though the church, too, were a sentimental theatre which encouraged moral poses but which ignored the essential nature of itself and its audience.

Both of these central characteristics of the Bowery—its core of animality and its shell of moral poses—come together strikingly in Mrs. Johnson. There is a bitter Swiftian irony in Crane's portrait of her. Her drunken rages symbolize the animal fury of a slum home, and her quickness to judge, condemn, and cast out Maggie symbolizes the entire Bowery world, both its primitive amorality and its sentimental morality. It is appropriate, then, that it is she who literally drives Maggie into prostitution and eventual death. Secure in her moral role, she refuses to allow Maggie to return home after her seduction by Pete, driving her into remaining with Pete and then into prostitution. Maggie is thus destroyed not so much by the physical reality of slum life as by a middle-class morality imposed on the slums by the missions and the melodrama, a morality which allows its users both to judge and to divorce themselves from responsibility from those they judge.

Crane's characterization of Maggie can now be examined. His description of her as having "blossomed in a mud-puddle" with "none of the dirt of Rum Alley . . . in her veins" . . . . is not "realistic," since it is difficult to accept that the slums would have no effect on her character. . . . Crane's desire, however, was to stress that the vicious deterministic force in the slums was its morality, not its poor housing or inadequate diet, and it is this emphasis which controls his characterization of Maggie. His point is that Maggie comes through the mud-puddle of her physical environment untouched. It is only when her environment becomes a moral force that she is destroyed. Maggie as an expressionistic symbol of purity in a mud-puddle is Crane's means of enforcing his large irony that purity is destroyed not by concrete evils but by the very moral codes established to safe-guard it.

But Maggie is a more complex figure than the above analysis suggests. For though her world does not affect her moral nature, it does contribute to her downfall by blurring her vision. Her primary drive in life is to escape her mud-puddle prison, and she is drawn to Pete because his strength and elegance offer a means of overcoming the brutality and ugliness of her home and work. Her mistaken conception of Pete results from her enclosed world, a world which has given her romantic illusions

just as it has supplied others with moral poses. Her mistake warrants compassion, however, rather than damnation and destruction. She is never really immoral. Throughout her fall, from her seduction by Pete to her plunge into the East River, Crane never dispels the impression that her purity and innocence remain. Her weakness is compounded out of the facts that her amoral environment has failed to arm her with moral strength (she "would have been more firmly good had she better known how" . . .), while at the same time it has blinded her with self-destructive romantic illusions ("she wondered if the culture and refinement she had seen imitated . . . by the heroine on the stage, could be acquired by a girl who lived in a tenement house and worked in a shirt factory" . . .).

There is considerable irony that in choosing Pete Maggie flees into the same world she wished to escape. Like Mrs. Johnson, Pete desires to maintain the respectability of his "home," the bar in which he works. Like her, he theatrically purifies himself of guilt and responsibility for Maggie's fall as he drunkenly sobs "'I'm good f'ler, girls'" to an audience of prostitutes. And like Maggie herself, he is eventually a victim of sexual warfare. He is used and dicarded by the "woman of brilliance and audacity" just as he had used and discarded Maggie. In short, Maggie can escape the immediate prison of her home and factory, but she cannot escape being enclosed by the combination of amoral warfare (now sexual) and moral poses which is the pervasive force in her world.

In his famous inscription to *Maggie,* Crane wrote that the novel "tries to show that environment is a tremendous thing in the world and frequently shapes lives regardless." But he went on to write that "if one proves that theory one makes room in Heaven for all sorts of souls (notably an occasional street girl) who are not confidently expected to be there by many excellent people." The second part of the inscription contains an attack on the "many excellent people" who, like Maggie's mother, immediately equate a fallen girl with evil and hell. Crane is here not so much expressing a belief in heaven as using the idea of salvation and damnation as a rhetorical device to attack smug, self-righteous moralism. The entire novel bears this critical intent. Crane's focus in *Maggie* is less on the inherent evil of slum life than on the harm done by a false moral environment imposed on the life. His irony involving Mrs. Johnson, for example, centers on the religious and moral climate which has persuaded her to adopt the moral poses of outraged Motherhood and despoiled Home.

Maggie is thus a novel primarily about the falsity and destructiveness of certain moral codes. To be sure, these codes and their analogous romantic visions of experience are present in Maggie's environment, and are in part what Crane means when he wrote that environment shapes lives regardless. But Crane's ironic technique suggests that his primary goal was not to show the effects of environment but to distinguish between moral appearance and reality, to attack the sanctimonious self-deception and sentimental emotional gratification of moral poses. He was less concerned with dramatizing a deterministic philosophy than in assailing those who apply a middle class morality to victims of amoral, uncontrollable forces in man and society. *Maggie* is therefore very much like such early Dreiser novels as *Sister Carrie* and *Jennie Gerhardt,* though Dreiser depends less on verbal irony and more on an explicit documentation and discussion of the discrepancy between an event and man's moral evaluation of an event. *Maggie* is also like *The Red Badge of Courage,* for the later novel seeks to demonstrate the falsity of a moral or romantic vision of the amorality which is war.

Crane, then, is a naturalistic writer in the sense that he believes that environment molds lives. But he is much more than this, for his primary concern is not a dispassionate, pessimistic tracing of inevitable forces but a satiric assault on weaknesses in social morality. He seems to be saying that though we may not control our destinies, we can at least destroy those systems of value which uncritically assume we can. If we do this, a Maggie (or a Jennie Gerhardt) will at least be saved from condemnation and destruction by an unjust code.

Writers who seek greater justice, who demand that men evaluate their experience with greater clarity and honesty, are not men who despair at the nature of things. They are rather critical realists. Like William Dean Howells, Crane wishes us to understand the inadequacies of our lives so that we may improve them. Although Crane stresses weaknesses in our moral vision rather than particular social abuses, these is more continuity between Howells's critical realism and Crane's naturalism than one might suspect. This continuity is not that of subject matter or even of conception of man and society. It is rather that of a belief in the social function of the novel in delineating the evils of social life. If one sees such a writer as Crane in this light, the often crude and outdated determinism of early American naturalism lessens in importance. One begins to realize that American naturalism, like most vital literary movements, comprised a body of convention and assumption about the function and nature of literature which unprescriptively allowed the writer to use this shared belief as the basis for a personally expressive work of art. Crane's fiction is therefore permanently absorbing and historically significant not because he was a determinist or fatalist writing about the slums or about the chaos of war. His fiction still excites because his ironic techique successfully involves us in the difference between moral appearance and reality in society. His fiction is historically important because his expression of this theme within the conventions of naturalistic fiction reveals the relationship between critical realism and naturalism. But his fiction is perhaps even more significant historically because he revealed the possibility of a uniquely personal style and vision within naturalistic conventions. (pp. 126-31)

> *Donald Pizer, "Stephen Crane's 'Maggie' and American Naturalism," in* Criticism *(reprinted by permission of the Wayne State University Press; copyright, 1965, Wayne State University Press), Vol. VII, No. 2, Spring, 1965 (and reprinted in his* Realism and Naturalism in Nineteenth-Century American Literature, *Southern Illinois University Press, 1966, 1976), pp. 121-31).*

ERIC SOLOMON (essay date 1966)

[*Solomon's* Stephen Crane: From Parody to Realism *is considered an important contribution to Crane studies. Solomon asserts that Crane parodied conventional nineteenth-century literature to develop his own fiction. In the excerpt below, Solomon discusses Crane's Western short stories as parodies of the Western, myth-making fiction popular during Crane's life.*]

The myth and the reality of the American West provided Stephen Crane with the setting for some of his most brutally violent and richly humorous stories. . . . Crane accepted many of the Western traditions and made them vibrant in his short fiction. Simultaneously he cast a cold eye on the myth of the Western hero. Crane laughed at this myth which had become degraded into hardened stereotypes by the 1890's. As Mark Twain in *Roughing It* was able both to parody romantic notions of gold

seekers and desperados and at the same time to create in Scotty Briggs and Jack Slade vital portraits of those types—real, humorous, generous, vernacular—so Crane undercut the myth for the sake of the imbedded reality that he had observed, then reconstructed the myth, beyond parody, into tales that approximate Western tragedies. While Crane's funniest stories are clearly anti-Westerns, employing the mode largely to reject it, his most impressive tales accept the Western ideas of individualism, violence, strength, and honor. (pp. 229-30)

Stephen Crane's early Western story "Horses—One Dash" . . . is a revealing and not wholly successful amalgam of parody and thriller. The bare plot is that of a thriller: an Easterner named Richardson, accompanied by a comic Mexican servant, José, puts up for the night in a Mexican village where a group of sinister desperadoes later arrive. These outlaws are bloodthirsty and eager to butcher the supposedly sleeping Richardson for the sake of his expensive saddle and spurs. Our hero sneaks out at dawn and rides to safety after a wild chase across the plains. Certain parodic elements are obvious in this recital of the plot. The usual Western hero is not afraid, and he almost never runs. Crane seems a bit uneasy with his attempts at comic incongruity, however. He wants something heroic for the story and settles for Richardson's horse, a tough, capable pony. Although the choice is understandable, given Crane's love for horses, it confuses the comic tone with some sentimental clichés out of *Black Beauty*. While travestying the myth of the fearless hero, Crane supports the myth of the noble horse (a naturalistic gambit, to be sure), and he fails of his desired effect. (p. 240)

The story is an interesting failure, for we see Crane experimenting with methods of enclosing the Western reality he admired—in this case, a horse's loyal courage—within an envelop of ridicule of Western myth—here the idea of the lone hero in conflict with an outlaw gang. Crane is not sure where he wants to deflate and where he wants to identify, and the story suffers. He solves the problem in his next Western tale, where wry humor and bitter cruelty, identification with and disgust for the protagonist, join in a story that is a triumph in the Western form.

"A Man and—Some Others" . . . is heroic and anti-heroic, funny and terrible, absurd and inevitable. By comprehending the pardoxes inherent in the Western setting, where freedom mixes with isolation and courage is a part of savagery, Stephen Crane uses his distortion of the traditional view of the hero to create a work of fiction that moves beyond derision to a terrible beauty.

The tale opens with a marvelously evocative panorama of isolation. Dark mesquite spreads from horizon to horizon; the world seems an unpeopled desert, and only a blue mist in the far distance reminds a sheep herder of the existence of mountains, of another world. Here following a central theme of American literature, the theme of loneliness, Stephen Crane tells his story of the lonely hero, self-dependent on a range peopled only by hostile Mexicans who insist that he leave or be killed. (pp. 242-43)

By playing off his flawed Western protagonist against a figure who comes on the scene as a surrogate for the narrator—an innocent Easterner whose stirrups do not fit—Crane complicates the characterization. True, Bill is a killer who lives by a revolver that has taken the lives of several men. Crane overwrites his hymn to the gun, comparing it to an eagle's claw, a lion's tooth, a snake's poison, but the weapon is a friend to this utterly friendless man. . . . Bill [is revealed] to be an uneasy combination of strength, amorality, vulnerability, and shame. Crane's achievement is special, for in a short story primarily dedicated to rapid action he has created an enigmatic figure who breaks down a Western stereotype and engages the reader's sympathy. (pp. 245-46)

The story comes to a swift, expected, problematic, and nearly tragic end. The reader suddenly realizes that the stranger is of some importance himself, as more than a pendant. Crane implies that increased understanding emerges from the few hours that Bill and the stranger share in the violent landscape. Thus, though the story ends as it must with Bill's death, this end is also a beginning, the real start of the stranger's story; for he too, during the Mexicans' final charge, shoots and kills. In that moment when a panther is born in his heart, understanding and perhaps manhood are also born. Whatever is born, however, comes in the blaze of Bill's last passion. Crane only impressionistically hints at the facts of the ultimate gunfight. It is a "picture half drawn" . . . that resembles a dream, so violent is the action. Forever in the young man's memory will certain lines and forms stand out from the incoherence, the author insists. The stranger learns the lessons of the West, the real West: that it is easy to kill a man; that a man who can die with dignity is a "good" man (a term that defies further definition). (pp. 248-49)

Knowledge is the key element in many of Crane's subsequent Western writings. In 1898 he wrote a pair of stories featuring two youths, the San Francisco Kid and the New York Kid. These two are audacious, bantering, and tough, and Crane might have been planning a series; the progress of the New York Kid from city streets to Mexican towns and then to gun duels, bears a superficial resemblance to the early career of Billy the Kid. While the first story, **"The Wise Men,"** is negligible, **"The Five White Mice"** utilizes the Western setting to dramatize a young man's education into the ways of fear and bluff. Like the earlier tale, much of the narrative of **"The Five White Mice"** involves an elaboration of the Kid's gambling efforts. (p. 249)

His most famous Western comedy, **"The Bride Comes to Yellow Sky,"** written that same year, combines parodic humor and chastening realism in a similar but more consistently sustained manner.

"The Bride Comes to Yellow Sky" is the triumphant example of Stephen Crane's mixture of parody and realism in his fiction. The parody of the convention is a basic part of the story's continuity, and creates, rather than comments on, the dramatic movement. The first section gently scoffs at the tradition of romance in the Western story. The newlyweds, Marshal Jack Potter of Yellow Sky and a bride who is neither pretty nor young and who has been a cook before her marriage, contribute to a travesty of the familiar Western love plot, in which marriage comes at (or after) the end and in which the couple is usually young and handsome. . . . Much of the humor derives from the behavior of Potter and his bride, who are awkward and embarrassed in the great Pullman car—an Eastern, dignified sanctum replete with Victorian ornament and Negro porters. Indeed, the act of marriage itself strikes Potter as a betrayal of the Western, Yellow Sky ethos. He is condemned in his own eyes for betraying two traditions: he has tarnished the person of Marshal, a figure fearsome and independent, and he has tampered with the custom of partnership—he has not consulted his male friends.

"The Bride Comes to Yellow Sky" is a study of identities. Although insecure in his new role as married and responsible

official, Jack Potter is conscious of his change from his former role as the lone marshal, ever ready for a fight. His opposite, Scratchy Wilson, cannot face his own two roles. For in reality Scratchy is the town bum, an aging cowboy who is an anachronism. (James Agee, in his movie version of the story, emphasized this aspect of Scratchy by making him a handyman who cleans out cesspools.) But when drunk, Scratchy reverts to his former role of tough gunfighter. In order to sustain this conception of himself, Scratchy must define it against his antagonist, Marshal Potter in his earlier guise as typical marshal of the Old West, untrammeled and quick on the draw. The serious element of this comic tale comes from Scratchy Wilson's recognition that, with Potter's shucking off his character as mythic marshal, Scratchy cannot retain his own particular dream role as mythic Western gunfighter. (pp. 251-53)

The second part of the story opens in a world of complete contrast to the Eastern Pullman: the setting is Western, the bar of the Weary Gentleman Saloon, twenty-one minutes before the train bearing the Potters is to arrive. The time shift enables Crane not only to sketch rapidly the plot situation but also to evoke the familiar Western background. Crane supplies an Easterner, a drummer, to serve as an outside observer who must learn about the local mores and the customary epic drunks of Scratchy Wilson that disturb the dozing atmosphere. Scratchy's binges are formulaic, and the formula depends upon Marshal Potter to bring the ceremony of shouting and shooting to a halt by engaging in a ritual fight with Scratchy. The bar is locked, and its inmates, supported by the two Western staples (guns and whiskey) that have turned Scratchy loose, take cover. Scratchy's position in the Yellow Sky social order becomes manifest: he is "a wonder with a gun,," "the last one of the old gang that used to hang out along the river here," and, when sober, the "nicest fellow in town." . . . That is, Scratchy is a living cliché of the Old West, a quick draw, a deadly shot, a rough with a heart of gold: in every way outdated. And the section closes on that most hackneyed of all Western dime-novel phrases, echo of a thousand descriptions of Indian or badman attacks, "Here he comes." . . . The travesty is that this attack is reduced to the singular absurdity of one old man. (pp. 253-54)

All worlds meet in the final episode when the relic of the Old West runs into the new bourgeois and his wife. The narrative brings together the modes of thriller (Scratchy's hair-trigger threats), comedy (the incongruous situation of a drunken old man confronting a blushing pair of newlyweds), and realism (the pathetic realization that age and time have triumphed). The staple of Western fiction, two strong men face to face, meets with mockery once more, just as in **"Horses—One Dash"** and **"The Five White Mice."** The tradition in this case cracks wide open because the marshal is unarmed. Marriage has removed him from the Western scene: "He was stiffening and steadying, but yet somewhere at the back of his mind a vision of the Pullman floated: the sea-green figured velvet, the shining brass, silver, and glass . . . all the glory of the marriage, the environment of the new estate." . . . Scratchy's world crumbles, the circle breaks: "There ain't a man in Texas ever seen you without no gun. Don't take me for no kid." . . . But Scratchy is a kid—in a kid's costume, playing a child's game, in the world of children's books and dime novels, in his case, sadly, in the realms of second childhood. (pp. 254-55)

The image is a particularly rich one. As in the funnel of an hourglass, the sands of Scratchy Wilson's time have run out; he leaves his footprints on these sands as his dreams end and his life closes in.

Still, the story is parody, Crane's kind of parody. All the *données* of the Western story are reversed; the empty forms are shattered. The marshal is an unarmed honeymooner; the gunman is a childish old man; the gunfight is aborted. The basic devices are comic—misunderstanding and ridicule. Yet parody need not preclude seriousness. We recall the reason given by young Ike McCaslin for killing the bear in William Faulkner's story: he does it before it will be too late, before the final day, when even the bear wouldn't want it to last any longer; for then the woods would be gone, destroyed by civilization's weapons, the sawmill and the railroad. Civilization's weapons have come to Yellow Sky, and they are stronger than Scratchy's guns. It is already too late for Scratchy Wilson. The gunfighter should have died the way he wanted, in the traditional manner—with his boots on, as the familiar phrase goes—according to the violent ritual of his calling. **"The Bride Comes to Yellow Sky"** is a beautifully balanced combination of humor and pathos, tightly, almost rigidly, organized; it is perhaps Stephen Crane's finest example of the creative uses of parody. (pp. 255-56)

Perhaps **"The Bride Comes to Yellow Sky"** is Stephen Crane's outstanding combination of parody and realism: **"The Blue Hotel,"** Crane's best-known, most anthologized and analyzed story, depends on parody less strongly but still capitalizes on the technique, and moves even closer to the stuff of tragedy.

The idea behind the story, one of the finest of all Western tales, is the search for identity and the desire of an outsider to define himself through conflict with a society. And this outsider, because of his internal contradictions, fails in Crane's world, a world once described as analogous to Hemingway's universe "of man damaged and alone in a hostile, violent world, of life as one long war which we seek out and challenge in fear and controlled panic." **"The Blue Hotel"** articulates such a conception as the battle-lustful Swede strides through the snowy winds of Fort Romper, a deserted village on an earth that one could scarcely imagine peopled. . . . (pp. 257-58)

The world that the Swede discovers in the West is dreadful and absurd, and the story chronicles the outsider's defeat, what Stephen Crane terms "a tragedy greater than the tragedy of action." . . . In simplest outline, **"The Blue Hotel"** tells of the initial victory and eventual defeat and death of an odd, disturbed stranger. The story treats, in a mixture of fantasy, realism, and parody, the fear that drives men to acts of violence. The narrative raises many questions as to the nature of fear and courage, the responsibility for a man's death, the inability of men to communicate. The questions appear throughout and not all find answers by the end of the tale, which is as problematical as most of Crane's best fiction. From the start of the long story, where no one will discuss fear or death with the Swede, to the conclusion where he has lost fear and gains death, a note of inevitability prevails. Stephen Crane once spoke of the kind of tragic event that was "not the tragedy of a street accident, but foreseen, inexorable, invincible tragedy." In this 1898 story another innocent in the long list of Crane naïfs that stretches back to Henry Fleming and Maggie must meet the test of experience. According to R.W.B. Lewis, the story of the fall of Adamic man usually appears in American writers' later works, in which they sum up their experiences of America and probe the tragedy inherent in the innocence of the new hero. In **"The Blue Hotel,"** the hero, the Swede, new to the Western world that he perceives in dime-novel commonplaces, falls victim to some of the very conventions that Stephen Crane reduces to parody throughout his Western fiction. (p. 258)

Stephen Crane's Western stories make a fitting climax to the essentially parodic approach that defines his fiction from start to finish. In his powerful and dramatic Western adventures, Crane laughs at the formulae of the Western story; without commitment he still manages to employ the traditional evocative qualities of the form while engaged in the process of criticizing the form itself.

With a style that is at once clear and ambiguous, language that is precise and evocative, settings that are immediate and impressionistic, dialogue that is lucid and vernacular, prose that is concentrated and rich, structure that is firm and flexible, Stephen Crane created an impressive body of fiction. With a philosophy of life that is bleak yet tough-minded, Crane viewed man in many situations of tense conflict—with nature, society, himself. Even in his most severe indictments of human and environmental limitations, however, Stephen Crane never lost sight of the ridiculous. Crane's major fiction most often commences in parody and concludes in creativity. He derided conventional slum sentimentality, mocked temperance fiction, glanced at certain excesses of sea tales, triumphantly made the conventions of war literature his own best medium, showed contempt for the stories of small-town America, and caricatured the narratives of the Old West. In his best work parody and realism become one. **"The Blue Hotel"** represents powerfully by the logic of the story's own action the typical development of Stephen Crane's imagination throughout his fiction. In the story he moves from an idea of stereotyped Western myth, to parody, to reality—the movement the Swede literally makes from his arrival with his head filled by mythic fears, to the absurd hotel, to the real saloon. So Crane generally views the traditional abstraction, cuts it to pieces through parody, then puts it together his way, redefining the actuality behind the abstraction. **"The Blue Hotel"** actually brings the parodic approach to its logical culmination, for the Swede is a living parody, a badly scared Don Quixote nurtured on dime-novel fiction, whose death, in the finest irony of all, is both a parody of art and the sole reality of his life. (pp. 281-82)

> *Eric Solomon, in his* Stephen Crane: From Parody to Realism *(copyright © 1966 by the President and Fellows of Harvard College; excerpted by permission), Cambridge, Mass.: Harvard University Press, 1966, 301 p.*

MARSTON LaFRANCE   (essay date 1971)

[*In his* A Reading of Stephen Crane, *LaFrance maintains that Crane's use of an ironic pattern throughout his fiction is based on his perception of reality and "shows how the values he affirmed function as the moral norm which enabled him to transcend and control his own ironic vision."*]

Crane's world is reality as he perceived it, externally amoral matter subject to chance upheavals of purposeless violence and therefore ultimately unknowable and for ever beyond man's complete control; the mere fact that human life has to be lived in such a world places full responsibility for all moral values upon man alone, and thus the separation between the physical world and man's moral world is absolute. This perception, so far as I can determine, underlies everything Crane wrote— fiction, poems, newspaper pieces—because, apparently, it had come to him 'in that vague unformulating way in which I sometimes come to know things' . . . , and he was working on the basis of it, before he examined it intellectually by sorting out its various elements and implications to form the secure, thoroughly understood philosophical position which he found tenable—an intellectual process which was well advanced before he finished work on *The Red Badge* and was completed with *The Black Riders.*

Crane's protagonists, from Uncle Jake to Timothy Lean, have freedom of the will to choose their own commitments from whatever alternatives their awareness of the particular situations they confront makes available to them: 'Free will does not mean the power to control events; it means the power to control belief and effort' . . . [according to Max R. Westbrook.] Because Crane's adult characters possess this freedom they are without exception—honest or dishonest, aware or innocent—held morally responsible for whatever choices their actions imply that they have made; and the best people in this world, those who are both honest and aware of the human situation that man has to accept, also hold themselves personally responsible for their own shortcomings even if such weaknesses are unperceived or misunderstood by other men. And because the precarious human situation in the moral desert is at best difficult, no man escapes moral responsibility by simply doing nothing: failure to act in this situation is itself an action freely chosen, and it is morally condemned. Only children are exempt from moral responsibility, and they are excused only long enough to acquire a minimal awareness of the reality with which all adults have to cope. Because the separation between man's moral world and external nature is absolute, Crane's characters are morally never subject to externality; human desires and intentions have to be carried out in the external world, and the ultimate success or failure of any human action is therefore contingent upon externals, but the moral value inherent in the choice of the action is not determined by externality. Morally, Crane's physically puny man is able to stand against the mountains and prevail. Crane's recurring pattern would not be meaningful without the morally responsible protagonist who is free to choose his own actions: he is confronted with an unknown because he has chosen to place himself in such a position that, often with the help of chance, this unknown becomes unavoidable; he suffers because of his own weaknesses; and his shamefaced deflation by the fact of experience could not occur if he did not hold himself morally responsible for his own past actions. Hence, the naturalistic frame of reference is far too narrow to contain even Crane's early Bowery writings.

Crane was aware of naturalistic doctrines and techniques and mocked them in **'Why Did the Young Clerk Swear?'** But his early development seems best described in terms of his own increasing awareness of the implications present in his own perception of reality. In the Sullivan County tales, written when he was merely 'clever', the little man's deflating experiences do not bring awareness; and in *Maggie,* where only hypocrites triumph and even existence seems to require personal dishonesty, Crane apparently wrestles with the cynicism which he later called 'uneducated' a 'little, little way' along the road to wisdom. But the little man and Maggie are different only in degree, not in kind, from the later protagonists—for example, Henry Fleming and the correspondent—who learn and succeed only because they are more completely human, not because they live in an external world which differs in any significant way from the world inhabited by the little man and Maggie. Crane wrote only one brief story, **'The Snake'** . . . , which is at least possible to read as naturalism without either distorting or ignoring anything he has to say in it; and this story is not typical because the essential action is an external fight between a man and a snake, the cause is hereditary hatred and fear, and the prose offers few indications of having been written by an

ironist. Elsewhere, truth or reality for Crane is mental and moral, even in the early work, and thus his ironic awareness is free to explore his own perceptions of man's weak and mental machinery as it struggles to carry human desire and intention into external effect. As at least one excellent scholar has perceived, 'the disappearance of irony as a prevailing tone is worth attention as a difference between Realism (Howells, Fuller) and Naturalism (Norris, Dreiser). It is a change in which the felt presence of the author's taste and reservations about human nature is succeeded, with an accompanying loss of incisiveness, by a truly faceless impersonality which is uncritical.'

If Crane's recurring psychological pattern implicitly rejects naturalism, it also militates against the attempt to explain his work by means of image clusters or interrelated symbols. If the pattern provides the essential structure of the story then Crane's powerful imagery is not primarily conceptual. The isolated image may well have stimulated Crane's imagination—the dreadful legend of the cash register must have lurked in Crane's mind before it became part of the structured whole which constitutes **'The Blue Hotel'**—but if symbols exist only in context the recurring pattern conceptually forms the structural context that determines the function of any image or symbol contained within it. . . . Crane varies his pattern conceptually and manipulates it to express his meaning from story to story; and his meaning in a particular story, once conceived in terms of structure, merely becomes intensified and enriched through his conspicuous craftsmanship with image and symbol. In short, an understanding of Crane should best be approached by way of the structural pattern itself.

Such an approach at least suggests possible explanations for some of the matters which trouble Crane's readers. For example, the recurring pattern accounts for the notable absence from Crane's work of moral commitments beyond those of the individual protagonist. *The Red Badge* gives no hint of the broad moral issues behind the Civil War, such humanistic purposes as freeing the slaves or preserving the Union as an instrument of order—purposes which Crane himself obviously would have affirmed, and which must have helped some of the soldiers in Fleming's situation to stand fast and shoulder their more immediate responsibilities. *Maggie* offers no suggestions for social reform, there is no external programme which might regenerate George Kelcey, no help for the assassin's drunkenness, no humanitarian means of relief for the suffering of Dr. Trescott—such omissions are constant in Crane's work: he, apparently, affirms an individual moral responsibility which is absolute, and simultaneously ignores the broader issues by means of which the individual translates his own efforts into specific social and political accomplishment. Crane's protagonists, however, progress to awareness of an already existing reality, and their struggle depends partly upon their lack of knowledge, partly upon their fear, and partly upon their distortions of reality because of their own weaknesses. Crane could hardly present the broad moral issues as illusions, as the unknown cause of fear, or reveal a character's lack of knowledge by means of them. More importantly, until Crane's protagonists gain an awareness of reality and suffer the chastening of ego that their experiences entail, they—like the pines to whom the shell speaks—are not morally fit to bear the responsibility of such issues. Crane's pattern, in other words, analyses the individual's progression to a moral posture which is prerequisite to a significant affirmation of moral issues beyond his own personal honesty, humility, and acceptance of the human situation. Thus, there should be nothing strange about Crane's omission of these greater responsibilities from his protagonist's progression towards the capability of assuming them.

The recurring pattern also helps to explain the scarcity of romantic love and memorable young female characters in Crane's work. Romantic love would seem difficult for anyone to portray by means of a structural pattern which acquires its aesthetic force from the impact of an ironic deflation. Joyce may have performed such a feat in 'Araby', but the best Crane could do was **'The Pace of Youth'** and **'A Grey Sleeve'**. Crane's protagonist usually makes rather an ass of himself before experience deflates his swelling illusions to an unpleasant recollection, and editors in the 1890s were not anxious to see such a thing happen to beautiful young ladies in the fiction they published. Howells conducted beautiful young Irene Lapham through an experience similar to the ones suffered by Crane's protagonists; but the misfortunes of Irene are cushioned by the rich context of an extremely well-made novel and, as Crane's trump made him primarily a writer of short stories, the well-made novel was not for him.

Much of the peculiar intensity of Crane's best work can be credited to his recurring pattern. During the greater part of the protagonist's journey to awareness he labours in an unstable nightmare-world of fear, vanity, desire, incompetence—an illusory world created from the distortion wrought by his excited imagination. Because this distortion usually increases until the deflating fact of experience, the intensity of his best portrayals of the protagonist's nightmare—perhaps *The Red Badge*, **'Death and the Child'**, **'The Blue Hotel'**, **'The Upturned Face'**—rises towards the level of hallucination as his protagonist edges closer and closer to panic. But provision for such intensity is built into the pattern itself for an author who utilizes the third-person limited narrative technique. Thus, the presence of such intensity in Crane's work need not imply the unconscious expression of hidden compulsions; it more reasonably suggests the labour of craftsmanship by an artist who was well aware of what he was pursuing—the greater the intensity of the protagonist's distortion, the greater the impact of the 'plop' when experience suddenly slams him back to reality.

Finally, a knowledge of the recurring pattern and Crane's dependence upon it should provide a viable approach to the enigma of Crane the man. Crane seems to me neither genius nor Oedipal monstrosity, but a brilliant, brutally hard-working craftsman whose powers of perception were much greater than his depth of intellect. He did not spring into life fully armed except in terms of his ironic vision—and even this had to hone its edge on experience. His writings, particularly during the first half of his career, reveal that he had to work hard to turn an angular, disjointed prose style into flexibility and smoothness; and the measure of his success can be taken by anyone who compares **'The Open Boat'** with a Sullivan County sketch, or the sustained understatement and restraint of the final section of **'The Bride Comes to Yellow Sky'** with the shrill irony of *Maggie*. Yet Crane's pattern implies that his appraoch to fiction was determined by his own acute perception, and thus at least a partial explanation of why he has proved such an uneasy subject for the literary historian is available. The structural core of Crane's work is timeless and universal, and not dependent upon whatever his literary background may have been. The realization that man's imagination is powerfully stimulated by fear is at least as old as Seneca's *dubia plus torquent mala*. (pp. 243-48)

At first glance, Crane's 'narrowness of interest'—mourned by readers from his own time to the present—seems confirmed by his dependence upon his recurring pattern. So long as he uses a structure based upon a psychological progression to awareness he is obliged to confine his subject-matter to those areas of man's inner life which his pattern can express: fear, vanity, ignorance, honesty or dishonesty, chagrin, the activity of the imagination, the necessity for self-restraint and brotherhood, the increase in awareness that results from an abrupt deflation of expectation. But such a subject-matter lies right at the foundations of man's moral life, and fashionable lamentation over the narrowness of an author intensely concerned with it therefore suggests a certain innocence. . . . The full thrust of Crane's mind cannot be measured in his fiction alone. The recurring pattern, through the consistency of Crane's attitudes towards man's moral life which it reveals, clearly implies a frame of reference greater than itself. The pattern catches the protagonist as he undergoes the crucial process of growing up psychologically to responsible manhood, and to be a man in Crane's world entails a great deal more than mere awareness that reality is after all but reality. As Crane himself suggested, the full scope of his thought is available in his poems: a mature philosophy—thoroughly examined and subjected to proof in the furnace of his irony—which has the satisfying solidity and completeness, the whole moral truth which Crane's perception allowed him to accept, and which was not to be shaken by either natural forces, the inevitability of final death, or the actions of other men. Crane's poems reveal a man who looked carefully at the realities of human life and judged wisely. The recurring pattern in his fiction concerns the most dramatic incident in the normal individual's progress towards the body of truth set forth in the poems, and thus it should point the reader towards that whole which defines the full significance of the fictional protagonists' archetypal experience.

Most interesting of all, perhaps, are a couple of loose analogies which may be drawn between the recurring pattern and Crane's stoic humanism, analogies which admittedly are more suggestive than conclusive. Crane's moral code, like the pattern itself, seems to be less an intellectual construction than a consequence of his perception. In itself, apart from the manner in which the poems and stories present it, it is neither particularly complex nor subtle, and . . . there seem to be no strong reasons for believing it derived from important sources other than Crane's own perception of the human situation. But if his stoic humanism is primarily a creation of his own perception, then the biographer who attempts to stalk Crane's mind by way of the various influences to which he was subjected is roughly in the position of the literary historian who approaches Crane's work by means of historical and literary sources. Crane did not grow up in a vacuum: he was affected by the Methodism of his parents, the American Protestant evangelical tradition, his association with painters in New York, what [Joseph J.] Kwiat calls his 'newspaper experience', the hardship of his early years, the humanity of Howells—but so far as Crane's own philosophy is concerned, such influences often seem to form part of the 'enormous repudiations' noted by H. G. Wells [see excerpt above]. Whatever contradictions exist can be attributed to Crane's ironic perception: although each of these influences helped to sharpen his vision, the vision itself would necessarily have been turned back upon the influence, and Crane—always the discriminating, organizing, repudiating ironist—in each instance must have accepted only that which his own perception told him was valuable. The result, as implied by the poems, is a common-sense moral position which Crane could continually justify on the basis of his continuing perception of the human situation, and a repudiation of whatever his perception could not affirm as acceptable. Hence, the essential Crane should continue to elude the investigator of the influences upon his life until the ironic vision is recognized as a constant factor in whatever biographical equation is used. Crane, that is, is not at all the result of influences A, B, and C: he is the result of *only* what his perception allowed him to accept from *each* of these influences at the time he was subjected to it.

Such a claim is suggested by Crane's lifelong use of his one trump in his fiction. The pattern is ultimately only a codification or organization, for artistic purposes, of the ironic vision itself. The distinctive function of an ironic perception is the same as that from which Crane's structural pattern acquires its aesthetic force: the piercing or deflation of appearance to bring about an awareness of reality. The ironist moves through the world as something of a psychological alien only because his perception makes constantly available to him precisely the bleak awareness of reality that Crane's protagonists can acquire only by passing through the unpleasant experiences of the pattern. Thus, whatever his work rejects as illusory normally figures as part of the enormous repudiations in Crane's own life. The code of values set forth in the poems and fiction, in other words, constitutes the philosophical position which Crane's perception affirmed as the one most likely to save him from suffering exactly the sort of deflation his protagonists experience. Crane the man, in brief, seems to me remarkably consistent with his work.

Crane's penetrating awareness and untiring labour were concentrated upon the moral realities of human life in this world. So long as that life continues, so long as moral values survive as realities, Crane's work will remain, as he wished, a benefit to his kind. (pp. 249-52)

> *Marston LaFrance, in his* A Reading of Stephen Crane *(© Oxford University Press 1971; reprinted by permission of Oxford University Press), Oxford University Press, Oxford, 1971, 272 p.*

JAMES DICKEY   (essay date 1972)

[*The poet Dickey, who is perhaps best known for his Naturalistic novel* Deliverance, *offers thoughts on Crane's vision and themes.*]

He had the angle. The Crane slant of vision came into a scene or onto an action or a personality with terrible ironic penetration, and it came from a direction and a distance that no one could have suspected was there, much less have predicted. He came from nowhere, and is with us, bringing his peculiar and unforgettable kind of detached animism, sometimes frightening, sometimes ludicrous, the objects and people of the world all being seen as comments on or complements or qualities of each other, and none of them safe from this. War and poverty are Crane's best themes, and the needless suffering of animals. The cosmos is filled with the most stupifying fear about which, inexplicably, there is also something funny. After reading him, we ponder the possibility that we had better use more caution before we "rush out into the red universe any more."

> *James Dickey, "Stephen Crane," in* Stephen Crane in Transition: Centenary Essays, *edited by Joseph Katz (© 1972 by Northern Illinois University Press; reprinted with permission of Northern Illinois University Press, De Kalb, IL), Northern Illinois University Press, 1972, p. vii.*

BERNARD WEINSTEIN   (essay date 1972)

[*Weinstein provides a comprehensive survey of Crane's journalism and offers critical comments which focus on similarities between Crane's newspaper work and his fiction.*]

Stephen Crane was far from an orthodox journalist. He was never completely at home in the newspaper world, although he wrote for major papers. In his early years his reporting was considered eccentric and overly subtle by editors and publishers. At the outset of his journalistic career, he had been influenced by a lecture given by Hamlin Garland on William Dean Howells in August 1891. In **"Howells Discussed at Avon-by-the-Sea"** (*New York Tribune*, 18 August) Crane reported Garland as saying that Howells "does not insist upon any special materials but only that the novelist be true to things as he sees them.". . . Crane took Howells's dictum, which was consistent with the literary doctrine of impressionism, as seriously in his journalism as he would in his fiction. (p. 6)

Crane's early journalism was almost always larger than life, and inanimate objects often took on an animate character, as if to overpower and devour man. In the *Sullivan County Sketches* Crane wrote hyperbolic descriptions of "baffled waters," "haggard tree trunks," and "vindictive weeds" (**"The Octopush"**). In **"An Experiment in Misery,"** men are anonymously clustered together (as in *The Red Badge of Courage*) in "freights," "squads" and "a blend of black figures," while streetcars rumble ominously overhead "as if going upon a carpet stretched in the aisle made by the pillars of the elevated road"; buildings "lurk" in shadows; a saloon appears "voracious," its swinging doors "like ravenous lips" making "gratified smacks as if the saloon were gorging itself with plump men.". . . Even in his later sketches [Crane] sensed the irresistable power of machines and technology, symbols of man's capitulation before forces greater than he. At the beginning of the *Commodore* sketch he describes the boarding of the boat with ammunition and rifles: "Her hatch, like the mouth of a monster engulfed them. It might have been the feeding time of some legendary creature of the sea." In sketches like **"When Everyone is Panic Stricken"** (*Press*, 25 November 1894), not machines or inanimate objects but Nature itself, in the form of fire, emphasizes man's helplessness, feebleness, and awe before overpowering forces.

In fact, Nature gradually became man's chief adversary in Crane's later journalism. In **"Nebraskans' Bitter Fight for Life,"** Nature appeared to be man's betrayer. "The imperial blue sky" of spring deceived man, leaving him helpless and unprepared for the hot wind that laid waste everything in its wake; the summer catastrophe gave over without warning to "its fierce counterpart," a winter frost that "came down like wolves of ice." If nature was not wholly malevolent, it was, as in *The Red Badge of Courage*, a symbol of a universe utterly oblivious to man's plight. Nature as a symbol dominated several of the pieces Crane wrote from Mexico and a good deal of his war journalism. One of his finest war accounts, **"A Fragment of Velestino,"** began: "The sky was of a fair and quiet blue. In the radiantly bright atmosphere of the morning the distances among the hills were puzzling in the extreme. The Westerner could reflect that after all his eye was accustomed to using a tree as a standard of measure, but here there were no trees. The great bold hills were naked. The landscape was indeed one which we would understand as being Biblical. A tall lean shepherd was necessary in it." In the **"Vivid Story of the Battle of San Juan"** he described once again the deadly opening of hostilities against the paradoxical backdrop of placid nature. (pp. 21-3)

If Nature, malevolent or merely indifferent, seemed in Crane's later journalism a more cosmic and overpowering foe, man seemed proportionately more heroic, more suited to the struggle. Crane turned from the theme of man's entrapment to that of his participation in the act of survival, and consequently, the journalism grew increasingly less dependent upon artificial literary devices—less allusive, more concerned with telling the truth of existence, simply and resolutely. Indeed, the later journalism was characterized by the kind of writing that was unmistakably Crane's. . . . In his war journalism Crane described the most harrowing of experiences with a matter-of-factness, a lean and stoic masculinity, a dearth of outward emotion suggestive of Hemingway. These qualities are demonstrated, for example, in the various interviews with Greek combat veterans that Crane wrote at the conclusion of the Greco-Turkish War. . . . (pp. 23-4)

It seems lamentable that despite the admirable restraint of Crane's war journalism, parodists should have seized upon his somewhat persistent use of the first person as an object of ridicule. . . . Still, Crane's growing objectivity and the relative unpretentiousness of his later journalism provide us with an insight into his maturation and into the salutary effects experience had upon his brilliant imagination. (pp. 25-6)

[With] the possible exception of *The Red Badge of Courage,* Crane's fiction ws grounded in personal experience as well as documentary evidence. Many similarities existed between Crane's early newspaper pieces and *Maggie, The Red Badge of Courage,* and *George's Mother:* the ironic view that deflated the illusion of romance and heroism, the symbols of entrapment and animality, the over-all sense of nihilism and despair.

But not until Crane's 1895 trip westward did the fiction grow directly out of the journalism and out of experiences he had had as a journalist. "Horses—One Dash," A Man and Some Others," and "The Five White Mice," for example, were inspired by Crane's encounter with a bandit named Ramon Colorado in a small Mexican village. "The Bride Comes to Yellow Sky," with its ritual duel and its observation of the peculiar decorum of the frontier, was suggested by his real-life attempt in Nebraska to stop a barroom fight in which a big man was pummeling a smaller one, and Crane's consequent offense to a local custom. "The Blue Hotel" seems to have grown out of an incident, possibly seen by Crane, concerning a loud-mouthed, comic gun-fighter who ranted at an unidentified opponent from inside a stationary freight-car but who was later killed in a saloon ("Caged With a Wild Man," Philadelphia *Press,* 19 April 1896). In several Western stories, the setting mirrors the central character's isolation, providing a poignant suggestion of man's insignificance in vast, alien surroundings; but, consequently, in each case the character is forced to make his own destiny. Without the conventional heroic trappings, Crane's fictional Westerners, like the Nebraskans and the Westerners whom he had met in his travels, are placed in elemental situations, frequently of life and death proportions, and are forced to act decisively, thereby gaining an heroic stature lost to such young men as Pete, Jimmie Johnson, and George Kelcey.

The experience aboard the *Commodore* provided Crane directly with two stories: "The Open Boat" and "Flanagan and His Short Filibustering Adventure." In "Stephen Crane's Own Story" he had made no mention of the ordeal in the dinghy

that followed the sinking of the filibustering boat, and one can think that the idea for "The Open Boat" was already parking in his mind at the time. Both "Flanagan" and "The Open Boat" dealt with man's struggle for survival and his capacity for heroism in a terrifying and inexplicable universe. In "Flanagan," unlike the real-life situation, the filibustering boat *Foundling* sinks in a squall after it has already accomplished its purpose of delivering arms to the Cuban insurgents; ironically, what was thought to be the chief danger was over. Flanagan, the captain, weeps and swears as he watches the boat sink, but he acts in a manly and heroic way to save his men. The short disclaimer that closes the story provides the final irony: "The expedition of the *Foundling* will never be historic." But the confrontation between man and nature and the struggle between life and death are in reality, as they were for Crane, cosmic in their implications. In "The Open Boat," as in the newspaper sketch, the chief "voice" of the story is that of the correspondent, and it is he who rails, as does Crane in the newspaper account, at the irony of fate: "If I'm going to be drowned—if I'm going to be drowned, why in the name of the seven mad gods who rule the sea, was I allowed to come thus far and contemplate sand and trees?" Finally, in both the newspaper sketch and "The Open Boat," Crane describes the sense of interdependence of men suffering a common calamity. In "Stephen Crane's Own Story" the young correspondent observes the cooperation among the bailers in the engine room, among the men atop the slippery deckhouse wrestling with lifeboats that "weighed as much as a Broadway cable car," among the men aboard the doomed *Commodore* facing a common fate, among the four in the dinghy, making their way to shore under the leadership of Captain Murphy. In "The Open Boat," the need for interdependence becomes the only "logical" explanation for the death of the oiler. When the boat turns over in the icy water, the oiler swims ahead "strongly and rapidly" but drowns within reach of land, while the others cling to some remnant of the boat: a life jacket, a piece of life belt, a section of the boat itself. At the same time that the oiler is dying in symbolic isolation, a man comes running into the water, stripping off his clothing and dragging ashore the survivors. "He was naked," Crane writes, "naked as a tree in winter; but a halo was about his head and he shone like a saint."

Finally, Crane's war journalism served as a direct antecedent for a novel and several short stories. Two fictional pieces, the story "Death and the Child" and the novel *Active Service,* came out of the Greco-Turkish War. "Death and the Child" served multiple purposes: to trace the awakening of an innocent journalist, somewhat like Crane, to the realities of battle; to demonstrate Crane's admiration for the professional soldier; to demonstrate Crane's preference for the straight-forward, unimaginative, even insensitive, attitude toward war over the reflective, intellectualized one. Unlike such earlier war fiction as *The Red Badge of Courage,* in which a thoughtful young recruit's initiation into the mysteries of warfare were treated sympathetically, "Death and the Child" ridicules the journalist Peza's illusions and leaves him not much more enlightened than it found him. *Active Service,* too, served to deflate the correspondent's overglamorized view of war and to ridicule yellow journalism. The hero, newspaperman Coleman, who becomes a war correspondent, loses his cynicism in Greece and gains a sense of involvement and concern and even thinks positively about the function of the news correspondent. He reasons that his role is to act as "a sort of cheap telescope" with which the reading public back home can view the common soldier and appreciate his efforts. (pp. 26-9)

If Crane had gone to war originally to see if *The Red Badge of Courage* ''was all right,'' to feel the bullets whistling overhead, and to know the meaning of fear, he sensed in Cuba, as he had sensed in Greece, that the intellectualization of battle was meaningless and pretentious, even an affront to the brave. In the Cuban stories, eventually collected in *Wounds in the Rain,* he saw the curious sensation-seeking correspondent as the direct antithesis of the fighting man. In stories like **''The Lone Charge of William B. Perkins,'' ''The Revenge of the Adolphus,'' ''God Rest Ye Merry Gentlemen,''** and **''Virtue in War''** he elevated and idealized the soldiers at the expense of the silly, self-important journalists. Only one correspondent is drawn completely sympathetically: Little Nell of **''God Rest Ye Merry Gentlemen,''** who resembles Crane in every attitude. Little Nell is skeptical of and bewildered by the frantic opportunism of his managing editor and fellow reporters, and he possesses ''the virtue of a correspondent to recognize the great moment in any disguise,'' seeing ''greatness'' in the commonplace and unspectacular. In **''This Majestic Lie,''** Crane comments on the strangeness that ''men of sense can go aslant at the bidding of other men of sense and combine to contribute to the general mess of exaggeration and bombast.'' Not only the journalist but even the soldiers themselves are sometimes rendered ineffectual by excessive imagination, as in **''The Sergeant's Private Madhouse,''** or by self-interested glory-seeking, as in **''The Second Generation.''**

The key to virtue, if not always to survival, in Crane's war stories as in the journalism, is the matter-of-fact performance of a singular duty. This alone was the ''mystique'' of soldiership, the strength of Private Nolan in **''The Price of the Harness''** and the professional soldier Gates in **''Virtue in War.''** The realization and affirmation of this carried Crane through the frantic and uncertain last years of his life.

Crane's journalism may be faulted for its many shortcomings: he frequently scorned the conventions of reporting; he described trivial subjects with sometimes unnecessary artistic flourishes, gaining only gradually the terseness and simplicity that gave his war dispatches their power; he wavered between the tough-minded but humanitarian realism of Howells, Garland, and Riis and the neo-romanticism of Roosevelt, Wister, and Frederick Remington which glorified courage and the strenuous life and helped to lead America into internationalism and world power; his political views were frequently simplistic and self-righteous—though, in justice, one might say that he had to accommodate himself to yellow journalism in order to earn a living, and that he nevertheless tried, whenever possible, to speak for responsible journalism.

But the strengths of Crane's journalism far overshadow its weaknesses: highly personalized observation and selectivity of detail; concern and compassion that embraced both the poor and the weak and that, in war time, enabled him to sacrifice views of major strategies in order to write personal observations of soldiers in the field—a characteristic of such a celebrated World War II correspondent as Ernie Pyle; most importantly, a pattern of thought, moving from despair about man's helplessness to an existential view that all men are to a degree responsible for themselves and their fellows and that the tests of life are courage and endurance. And, of course, Crane's journalism helps to trace the patterns of his thought and to throw new light on his literary work. (pp. 29-31)

> *Bernard Weinstein, ''Stephen Crane: Journalist,'' in* Stephen Crane in Transition: Centenary Essays, *edited by Joseph Katz (© 1972 by Northern Illinois University Press; reprinted with permission of Northern Illinois University Press, De Kalb, IL), Northern Illinois University Press, 1972, pp. 3-34.*

FRANK BERGON　(essay date 1975)

[*The following excerpt from* Stephen Crane's Artistry *is a balanced assessment of Crane's writing ability and what Bergon refers to as Crane's unique ''habit of imagination.''*]

Crane's art is admittedly of narrow range. There is nothing of Melville's expansiveness in it, nor of James' ramifications of social encounter, nor of Whitman's multitudes. Yet such Sunday-book-review comparisons of range and bulk can do little justice to the startlingly intensive performance of a brief career. Conrad's cautious lament remains a more fitting consideration: ''His grip is strong but while you feel the pressure on your flesh you slip out from his hand—much to your own surprise.'' . . . We are surprised because Crane, as his friend says in the same letter, has strength, rapidity of action, an amazing faculty of vision, outline, color, movement—everything, in short, that an artist of staying power might have. . . . Certainly Crane's characters, even Maggie or Fleming, do not invade our memories as does an Ahab, a Gatsby, or even a Wakefield or Rappaccini. And with a few possible exceptions, such as Jim Conklin's dance of death, what events in Crane's fiction return with the weight of historic development or dramatic vividness? Four men adrift at sea in an open boat is potentially a situation of high drama, but in terms of remembered particulars, nothing much happens. We do remember pictures: Potter staring down Wilson, the Kid from New York staring down the Mexican posed as a Spanish grandee, Fleming staring at a corpse, the Swede at a cash register, Judge Hagenthorpe at a monster's unwinking eye, and Timothy Lean at an upturned face. Even if specifics of character and event cannot be recalled (and generally they can't—at least not commonly agreed-on specifics, for at their most reductive they are only a bunch of words), from fiction that retains its grip there always remains a memory that the arrangement of characters and events somehow formed a design that made sense, that in a world without shape an order was realized. (pp. 133-34)

As old-fashioned as these characteristics might appear now, they are discoverable in most nineteenth-century fiction that has endured through a renewable appeal to ''the common reader,'' and may indeed be part of what Conrad found wanting in Crane's work. Yet these are the very virtues Crane rejected. Only when pressed did he give the fictional figures in *Maggie* any names at all. Reviewers criticized his lack of interest in events, but he continued to write stories in which nothing happened. Unwilling to see relations between events as they were presumed by the fictional structures of his contemporaries, he became one of the early innovators of the plotless story. While these self-imposed limitations insured a loss to literature as readers generally knew it, they freed experience, as Crane knew it, from the shackles of structural formulas. There was a price to be paid, and according to the larger measures of Conrad's judgment, Crane still disappoints. But these sacrifices enabled him to dramatize how fatuous is the immediate linkage of identity to a name, social position, or action, allowing him to examine how a man first defines himself by a point of view. In Crane's fiction a shift in point of view can be as important as a rifle bullet through the thorax. Whether or not a situation evolves into an identifiable action is less crucial than are all the normally unseen components of potential action. Despite contrary appearances, Crane shows that nothing is static; and human acts are never truly apprehended until they are broken into their components, and labels disappear. An urgent assertion of usable patterns and forms in literature too eagerly diminishes to human terms a world that is limitlessly dynamic and random. Conclusions are not to be toyed with, and even those Crane stories which masterfully employ accepted narrative techniques, like "**The Blue Hotel,**" finally elude normal schematization through their emphasis upon the inconclusive. (pp. 134-35)

Crane's rejection of traditional techniques finds modern echoes in "the tension or dissonance between paradigmatic form and contingent reality" that troubled Sartre, Musil, and other authors discussed by Frank Kermode in *The Sense of an Ending*. These writers maintain there is an inherent simplicity in narrative order that is not shared by reality, and any easy adaptation of patterns, myths, or philosophies that blinds us to the pure contingency of modern reality is dishonest. The similarity to Crane's aesthetic attitude is not surprising—H. G. Wells is not alone in dating Crane's work as the beginning of modern American literature [see excerpt above]—but it is not necessary to propel Crane into the mid-twentieth century. The modern call of "existential" artists for immediacy and sincerity, a call shared by Crane as a "romantic" artist, and the modern rejection of "old solemn art as being in *mauvaise foi*" substantiate Iris Murdoch's contention that existentialism is really "the last fling of liberal Romanticism in philosophy." The contemporary "happening," she says, shares these values and is therefore "the proper child of existentialism." However, though they try to be sincere and immediate, true to a changed sense of reality, the works of Crane, Sartre, and Musil are not happenings. Crane, who shared Poe's stern sense of craft, was too aware of the chaos around him to let his work contribute to that chaos by duplicating pure contingency. Art is ceremony. Necessarily arbitrary, though not absolutely fraudulent, his art is a stay against the horror of the nothingness it delineates. . . . Crane most successfully walks that thin line between the fraudulent and the meaningless in those short stories, such as "**The Open Boat,**" whose open form least falsifies contingent reality.

It is in the organization of his longer, more episodic works that Crane seems to cause profoundest disappointment and most often loses his grip on the reader after the book is closed. Torn between a sense of the inconclusiveness of individual reflection and a desire for some realization of manhood on his character's part, Crane seems to have opted for neither in *The Red Badge*. The reader knows that somehow Fleming has become a member of his regiment, he is a veteran of sorts, but the statement "He was a man" (with Crane's special implications of that word) has never been substantiated to everyone's satisfaction in terms of the dramatic events of the novel. The reflective conclusions of the last chapter are too similar to those of chapter 15 for the former to be trustworthy. Whatever Crane's intentions, the unstated implications of the drama are not sufficiently precise for the reader to know whether Henry really is what he seems to be at the end of the novel. *Maggie* also is the product of an artistic sensibility not yet strong enough to accept the contradictions within itself and within its subject. Missing is the particular power of the artist, as opposed to that of the craftsman, the power to transcend conscience and to comprehend a fictional world as a whole, despite all its possible irregularities. The result is confusion rather than the clear ambivalence found in "**The Open Boat**" and "**The Blue Hotel.**" Although an artist's ultimate subject may be mystery, he must not obscure that mystery through mystifications of his own. When Crane gave up the struggle of giving form to his uncommon percep-

tions, the results were *The Third Violet, Active Service*, and *The O'Ruddy*. Each has Crane's imprint; each—especially remarkably energetic portions of *The O'Ruddy*—entertains and excites our imaginations in flashes. But unlike the other novels, and even unlike *George's Mother* (which is half novel and half personal essay), none fundamentally affects our way of seeing the world around us.

The technical refusals and innovations Crane perpetrated in the name of sincerity bear the seeds of further artistic limitations that have become self-willed in the kind of "modern" novel that is "developing within itself those elements which will show how it is related to the rest of reality." Despite Michel Butor's claims for this contemporary activity, there is really nothing astonishingly new about it. Crane's realization that there remains a gap between his own artifice and experience is commonly shared by earlier nineteenth-century romancers. (pp. 135-37)

There is a distracting self-consciousness in his fiction, other than that written when he was merely being clever. "**One Dash—Horses**" is only one example. And his transfigurations of reality put him dangerously close to those nineteenth-century artists who, as Auerbach says, "consistently value life only as literary subject." . . . Crane, who already considered himself stigmatized as a preacher's son was also that late nineteenth-century American phenomenon, the Writer. Never a surveyor in a customhouse, a sailor, or a minister before or while he wrote, he was without any other trade. Understandably he bears some of the impoverishing marks of the alienated aesthete as described by Auden and Auerbach, but ultimately . . . Crane escapes megalomania and exact categorization through his humor and irony.

Mordant as it may be at times, a comic sense suffuses his work. "Your little brother is neither braggart or a silent egotist," he wrote to William Crane . . . , and he was right, for he did not spare even himself from that wit that razed everything within its ken. Equally important, as Ralph Ellison has shown, is the range of keen historical awareness informing all Crane's best work. The Western tales bring this awareness to the surface in their astute observations of social and historical process. Finally, Crane's conviction that "art is man's substitute for nature" . . . is not an endorsement of withdrawal. Crane enters into direct competition with reality, an act, he knew, of folly and conceit, but also an expression of human vitality, for in flinging these ceremonial acts of fiction into timeless disorder, he momentarily "destroys the disorder and the dead time of the world." The purpose of these substitutes is not to replace reality but to provide the means of getting "the nearest to nature and truth." Only by transforming nature, by making it strange, can we illuminate what is ordinarily imperceptible. At this point, Crane the romantic joins hands with the existentialists of Kermode's study, for who is this illuminator, this transformer, this true hero, but the artist himself? Crane, as the seer, the man aware of his special sensibility, the man courageous enough to accept the oddity of his position outside of normal society, the man who implies that the kind of sensibility registered in writing is the same sensibility necessary to savor experience, the man who can remain the "isolato" true to his perceptions and even his hallucinations without joining the Swede on a barroom floor—even when invisible, that man is the true hero at the core of all Crane's art. When he did make himself highly visible, in his dispatches from Greece, Crane opened himself to . . . the many and often superficial parodies of his work. (pp. 138-39)

[The] "I" is Crane's two-edged sword. Consistently present in even his most "objective" works, it is the source of his art's integrity. It is also most likely the first reason Conrad felt Crane's pressure, just as it is probably the reason he slipped from Crane's grasp, for that "I" is governed by the perceptions and voice of a poet. Not only are the techniques of **"The Open Boat,"** as Daniel Hoffman contends, "essentially the techniques of poetry," but the concentrated language of that story is the natural expression of an intensely subjective emotional response. Interest in human relations pales before Crane's interest in the individual's relationship to the universe; or rather, the point of view and voice in his work are those of a man acutely aware of that relationship, almost as if he himself were stationed in some sidereal void. The current running through his work is the lyric cry, and the reader is forced to speak of it metaphorically, as Mailer does in commenting on that "sense of a fire on the horizon which comes back always from *The Red Badge of Courage,*" or as Pritchett does when he says, "Crane starts a bugle call and sustains it without falter to the end of the book." Whether in verse or prose, the virtue of Crane's art is found less in a work's structure than in the individual phrases that make up what is normally called its texture, and it is to texture that Conrad referred when he talked about "ideas" in Crane's fiction: "yours come out sharp cut as cameos—they come all living out of your brain and bring images—and bring light." . . . With all Crane's best work, the reader must return to his exact phrasing. Memorable "characters" and "events," the creations of narrative or dramatic sequences, at times can maintain in our minds a reasonable though, perhaps, distorted life apart from their contexts. Like a lyric poem, a Crane story works in smaller units, and one must constantly return to the words and individual sentences that trace those elusive shiftings and turnings of consciousness, feeling, and sensibility.

The poetic impulse, as Crane's longer pieces show, does not easily adapt to the humdrum busywork of constructing houses of fiction. H. L. Mencken noted that Crane was weak in passage work—"he lacked the pedestrian talent for linking one thing to another"—but Crane wasn't concerned with these novelistic contrivances. As in **"An Eloquence of Grief,"** he wanted to get on to that girl's scream that "disclosed the gloom-shrouded spectre . . . in so universal a tone of the mind." There is something of the expressionist behind this impulse; the world of measurement often gets shoved aside in favor of some emotion-ridden realm that functions according to its own principles and ignores all common sense. . . . Emotions become larger and more real than characters or events. Although such creative projections may take their shape from an author's feelings, they may also float in a void when they fail to call enough attention to the causes of those feelings, or at least the amount of attention that fictional models of the world usually require. This limited specialness of vision and fictional invention seems to be the second fundamental reason Crane slips from our grasp; the realms he enters often bear only minimal relation to familiar experience.

If Crane was a poet, he was anything but a poet of the familiar. One must return to the phrasing of details not only for their qualification of incident, but for the quality of the details themselves. The distortions and transfigurations they effect will not adjust to a common-sense and a conventionally moral framework. In the world of **"A Mystery of Heroism,"** a wounded horse turns its nose "with mystic and profound eloquence toward the sky," while an officer's eyes, resembling beads, sparkle "like those of an insane man." Collins finds his initial action "supernaturally strange." He "appeared as a man dreaming," and he "suddenly felt that two demon fingers were pressed into his ears. . . . The sky was full of fiends." Reaching the well, the expected source of relief from his heat and thirst, he discovers a "pink reflection" from "Crimson light" shining through "swift-boiling smoke," and jerks away from this "furnace." In this demonic realm there "screamed practical angels of death." Still, Collins ran away like a "farmer chased out of a dairy by a bull." Few novelists, Mailer claims, can move with ease "from mystical to practical reactions with [their] characters. . . . It's the hint of greatness." (pp. 139-41)

It is somewhat surprising to discover a writer as unique as Crane to be in league with many other American authors. But the Swede of **"The Blue Hotel"** is almost an archetypal American character in his loneliness, isolation, and madness ("Yes, I'm crazy"). As an artist Crane found himself in a position of isolation, a state American writers have been inclined to cultivate. What results is the writer's habit of falling back on himself and the indulgence of going, as Thoreau claimed, only far enough to please his own imagination. The style that evolves from this habit closely resembles one predicted by Tocqueville, and attributed by him to the effects of democracy:

> Style will frequently be fantastic, incorrect, overburdened, and loose—almost always vehement and bold. . . . Small productions will be more common than bulky books: there will be more wit than erudition, more imagination than profundity; and literary performances will bear marks of an untutored and rude vigor of thought. . . . The object of authors will be to astonish rather than to please, and to stir the passions more than to charm the taste.

Probably no other American writer could surpass Crane in fulfilling this prediction. (p. 143)

> *Frank Bergon, in his* Stephen Crane's Artistry *(copyright © 1975 Columbia University Press; reprinted by permission of the publisher), Columbia University Press, 1975, 174 p.*

EDWIN H. CADY   (essay date 1980)

[Cady is the author of Stephen Crane, *a balanced biocritical study of Crane from which the following survey is taken.]*

Crane who learned what he had to know before he could write *The Red Badge* was multivalent. He had an ideal of realism which had supplanted but not suppressed a boyish ideal of romance. And he had a self which could not be contained in either camp, which has always successfully eluded categorization, and which broke out in unpremeditated, startling verse at the first peak of his creative powers.

Multivalence accounts for his ability to produce *Sullivan County Sketches* at the same time as he was struggling toward the first printed *Maggie* and the half-realized **"Midnight Sketches."** (p. 100)

[*Sullivan County Sketches*] foreshadowed greatness. Perhaps the most wholly successful is the one without slapstick: **"Killing His Bear, a Winter Tragedy with Three Actors"**—the bear, a hound, and "the little man." (p. 101)

The largest significance of *The Sullivan County Sketches* may be, however, their recording so early and purely the meaning and weight to Crane the artist of the experience of Crane the sportsman. . . . Crane from boyhood joined the sporting fraternity with "fiendish glee." He rode, hiked, hunted and camped, played baseball with a sacrifical passion, coached and played a bantam quarterback on a Jersey town football team in the fearsome days of massed interference and helping the runner. He pursued the mystery of manliness into the West as far as Mexico, on the filibuster *Commodore,* to Greece, and at last to Cuba.

It might be arguable that the trope basic to Crane's vision was that of the game. But the complexities of that vision to which he wished so desperately to be faithful were, to use one of his favorite words, immense. The trope is pervasive. He begins his serious efforts at fiction with hunting and camping sketches. The opening scene—and a governing symbol—of *Maggie* shows slum children viciously playing a favorite game: "King of the Hill." No few poems suggest that the procession of life is a game God plays with man, keeping the rules to Himself. The psychology, the whole essence of *The Red Badge of Courage,* Crane said he learned on the football field. (p. 103)

His experience of sports brought Crane knowledge, and attitudes consequent on that knowledge, important to his point of view. It gave him the experience of testing his courage and thence his personal knowledge of pain and fear, victory and defeat. From that vantage point he commanded the cosmic gambler's stoic outlook: despising the petty, safe, and comfortable; prizing the chance-taking, the enterprising, the seeking, aggressive and tough. In this respect he was at one with the prophets of the strenuous life. But he went beyond them in the depth of his forceful but ambivalent compassion for losers. He was anxious that their courage or at least their agony be defended against and registered upon the smug and ignorant. But he would not defend them against the law, against the rules of the game of life. It is because they express that compassion so magnificently, each differently from the other, that **"The Open Boat"** and **"The Blue Hotel"** are superior to, for instance, **"Five White Mice," "A Man and Some Others,"** or **"Horses—One Dash."**

Whatever else it may be in actuality, *Maggie: A Girl of the Streets,* was intended to be—and was understood by Crane to be—a work of realism. "I had no other purpose in writing 'Maggie' than to show people to people as they seem to me," he wrote in his oft-quoted letter to Miss Catherine Harris. "If that be evil, make the most of it." (p. 104)

Supposing, as there is fair warrant for doing, that *Maggie* went through several drafts (Stallman guessed at four), it is clear that the turn toward realism is what differentiates it from *The Sullivan County Sketches* both in style and "perspective." (p. 105)

Maggie: A Girl of the Streets is . . . a Bowery "perspective made for the benefit of people who have no true use of their eyes." And that seems the key to settling the problem of its "form." Formally Crane's problem was a characteristically realistic or, indeed, Jamesian problem of perspective and proportion, of vision; and he solved it as well as he was able by the characteristic technique James called "scenes" and "pictures," habitually setting the action within the picture. Crane's numbered sections are significant of this technique, each having a kind of unity of its own. With his characteristic intensity, indeed, Crane may have scored an advance on realistic painterlike technique. (pp. 105-06)

Crane's *donnée* . . . was that Maggie "blossomed in a mud puddle." That central metaphor raises the question whether the story is about the flower or the puddle, from which every frog tells Maggie, "Go teh hell." Certainly the reader comes to know more about the puddle than about its impossible flower. The story tells, as Crane said variously in various inscriptions upon the original printing, that "environment may be a tremendous thing in life" and that therefore there may be "room in heaven even for an occasional street-girl." Nevertheless the book establishes unmistakably the point that his environmental concern, common to the realistic tradition at least since Flaubert and Turgenev, by no means prepared him or his work to abandon the idea of personal moral responsibility and guilt. On the contrary, in the tension lay much of the essential irony.

The right question becomes whether the motif of the tale is not actually perception of the ironies upon which the dynamics of the work climax with fearful emphasis. Though they are indeed the old tragic ironies of the clash between illusion and reality, Crane's art, especially in his portrait of Mary Johnson, her character and behavior as mother and moralist, suggests that *Maggie*'s motif is at last the shame, sin, and horror of conventional condemnations of the prostitute, the "wicked" or "fallen" woman. (p. 111)

With our present revival (after a fleeting illusion that it was withering away) of the American slum in more ominous, less tractable forms, *Maggie* has become more contemporary to us, speaks more immediately to our condition, than many a book written on like themes during the current century and thought somehow "more modern." (pp. 112-13)

[*The Black Riders*] was wholly other than realistic, and the poems set Howells to grumbling about a waste of Crane's time and talents. It was free verse, strikingly imagistic, and masculine in a total rejection of Tennysonian euphonies. Perhaps it was symbolistic, perhaps not—it was hard to tell. Any reader could tell that the poet was earnestly engaged with ideas even if he did not know that the poet had insisted to the publisher that he not "cut all the ethical sense out of the book. All the anarchy, perhaps. It is the anarchy which I particularly insist upon. . . . The ones which refer to God . . . I am obliged to have. . . ." (pp. 113-14)

Though there was much in *The Black Riders* not dreamt of in the philosophy of *Le Roman expérimental,* or of *Criticism and Fiction,* that says nothing of the quality as poetry of these and the rest of Crane's "lines," "pills," or what not, as he called them to evade the sissy soubriquet of "poet." They constitute a perfectly personal expression, defying categorization; they are much more difficult to paraphrase than they seem until one tries; at their best, they are extraordinarily subtle in phonetic effect. One can find analogues, but no true sources for them as poems. To be sure they are "biblical" and have predecessors in the wisdom literature of the ages—or the pseudowisdom literature of Crane's age. But there are no poems like these: Crane, by not trying to be a poet, achieved a genuinely organic expression of the religious, moral, amatory, the nature-loving, and particularly the ironic experiences rioting through his head.

The result was above all intense. Taking the best of Crane's poetry from all volumes (and one judges poets first and last by their best), the imagery is unforgettable. The power of definition is as illuminating as Emily Dickinson's. (pp. 115-16)

In a way one could say that *The Red Badge of Courage,* Crane's masterpiece, was built of the romantic irony of the sketches, plus the complicit irony of *Maggie,* plus the imagistic fire of the poems, plus Crane's unexpectedly gifted historical imagination, plus his life-long intimations of war, plus a new heightening of his artistic powers and perceptions. But saying so, one would not have covered the ground—only have suggested some of the approaches to a work which has "made" all sorts of lists of "classics," sold fabulously (to whose enrichment?). It has engendered a body of criticism curiously inconsistent and stubborn, tending evermore (ignoring the merely eccentric) to repetition or, at best, to small variations on themes by somebody else. When was the last time anybody said anything both fresh and reasonably applicable about *The Red Badge of Courage?* (p. 117)

One does not read far into *The Red Badge of Courage* . . . without discovering that it is different from the traditional realistic novel. The extended and massive specification of detail with which the realist seems to impose upon one an illusion of the world of the common vision is wholly missing. Equally absent is the tremendous procession of natural and social "forces" characteristic of naturalism—of Frank Norris or Dreiser trying to be Zola. Detail is not absent, but it is comparatively sparingly deployed on a light, mobile structure; and it is used for intensive, not extensive effects. Reference to "forces" is there, but no effort at all to show them streaming in their mighty currents, floating the characters as tracers, as chips on the stream whose significance is to reveal the trending of the currents. (p. 123)

The Red Badge of Courage is a unique work of psychological realism deeply affected in style by the fact that the author was an ironic, imagistic, metaphysical poet. (p. 132)

Except for a few poems, his future greatness was all to come in the short story. The one possible exception to that generalization would be *George's Mother.* In length it is a *nouvelle,* as Henry James called the form, at the most. But then, *The Red Badge* is hardly more; and one apologizes, if apology is ever needed, for the lack of complexity, of rich social involvement, which is the penalty *The Red Badge* pays for its superb compression, by noting that it too is perhaps a *nouvelle.* One does not expect of it what *Tom Jones* or *The Portrait of a Lady* offer.

With *George's Mother* Crane returns to the slums to tell the story of George's mother's losing fight to keep her boy uncorrupted in the Rum Alley neighborhood of *Maggie.* As she loses George to drink, delinquency, and a sure future as a Bowery bum, the mother loses her grip on life and slides away into death. The accent falls on George's confusion of values between home, mother, and church on one hand and street gang and saloon on the other. A more careful and mature study than *Maggie,* it lacks the dramatic intensity and compassion of Crane's first slum book. Brief, cold, and disillusioned, it focuses as much on George's cowardice as his bewilderment. It makes an interesting forerunner, Protestant and Old New York in viewpoint, of James T. Farrell's *Studs Lonigan.*

As this and all Crane's subsequent flights at the novel show, he did not live to grow into a mastery of manners which might have permitted the traditional novel, though he showed signs, especially in "The Monster," of growing that way. There is no surprise, given the circumstances of his last five years, in the fact that his three other efforts at the novel failed. The surprise lies in the greatness of the tales. (p. 145)

The Third Violet has by far the most charm. It came from a relatively happy and strong period of Crane's life, written in the midst of his perturbations over the success of *The Red Badge* and done because he wanted to do it—with some misgivings but *con amore.* It attempted to make use of Crane's

experiences with painters and "Indians," and its hero, Hawker, was apparently more or less modeled on Linson. Crane had disclosed glimmers of capacity to dramatize manners in moments of *Maggie* and in incidental writings like "Mr. Binks' Day Off" and "An Experiment in Luxury." There is no doubt that maturity and adult experience would have ripened his powers to true mastery of the great tradition in the novel. But *The Third Violet* tends to show why novelists are seldom great before the age of forty. By contrast, it shows how youthful yet unique, how experimental yet inherently brilliant, Crane's best writing is.

The Third Violet, though exploiting autobiography, was a fascinating attempt to imitate W. D. Howells. The first part takes place in a resort like Hartwood, where Hawker has returned to his farm home to paint and where he sees and falls in love with Miss Fanhall at the summer hotel and courts her on the tennis court, on picnics, and on walks, with the help of his friend Hollanden, a cool Craneian writer. Howells, of course, had virtually invented the summer-vacation novel, had turned it into a *genre* convertible to all sorts of purposes, and had made its exploitation a steady part of his career. The other half of Crane's book was placed among the "Indians" of the Art Students' League Building. (p. 146)

Crane of course knew and could do things Howells couldn't. Widely acquainted with painters, sculptors, architects of his own day, Howells knew Crane's generation best through his son, John Mead, and his daughter, Mildred. The impecunious "Comanches" of *The Third Violet,* fine portraits, and the model, Florinda "Splutter" O'Connor, a Maggie competent for survival, were as beyond Howells as the wonderful sketches of "Stanley"—a "large, orange and white setter." There are many fine touches in *The Third Violet* to prove that it was written by Stephen Crane: Hawker's perceptively studied farm folks; the Hartwood scenery; the Bohemians at home—"Wrinkle," "Great Grief" Warwickson, "Penny" Pennoyer, "Purple" Sanderson; and of course Splutter and Stanley. Those characters were all minor, however. It was in the perceptions of the real situations of the major characters and in the clarification of ideas to which those perceptions should have led that Crane fell down.

Probably it did not occur to Crane that Howells had spent thirty years learning how. Of course Howells, disillusioned of egalitarian myth, had discovered the broad drama involved in a situation like Crane's confrontation of poor, farmerish, gifted, artistic, personally superior Hawker with rich, urban, cultivated, sensitive but snobbish Miss Fanhall. It confronted two basic, fascinating American types, as Howells saw early: the "Social" and the common, the "conventional" and "unconventional," Society's lady and nature's gentleman. Over many years, with deepening perception and disillusion, Howells had studied the implications of all this until it had made an independent, semi-religious and democratic socialist of him. In *The Third Violet* Crane saw only personal injustice and amatory affront. Similarly, Crane wholly failed to dramatize the point Howells was making about the artist in a world of chance: that the combat conditions of a competitive, acquisitive society stifled art. Having the Bohemians just talk about it was not enough. (pp. 146-47)

The failure to face and develop the conflicts of class and convention, of sex and of art against society, destroys the novel and strips its deficiencies of all concealment. Its fragmentary brevity, its lack of competence to carry off scenes requiring the full development of conversation, its confusion of ideas and missed opportunities of a dozen sorts, and its ultimate lack of achieved, over-all form protrude like the skeleton of a half-built house. And the key to all this failure may easily be seen on consideration to be Crane's entire inability to comprehend women, especially Miss Fanhall.

The real trouble with *The Third Violet* and *Active Service* is that in dealing with women in fiction, Crane's irony deserted him. He did not have a clear single view of them, much less a double or triple vision. One of the difficulties, in fact, of accepting the recurrently popular notion that Crane's early "affairs" were more than the passion of the moth for the star, that he was a roistering whore-chaser, an experienced lover before Cora, a trapped exemplar of Freud's case of "A Special Type of Choice of Object Made by Men," is that none of this experience did anything for his imagination. (p. 148)

For the rest, it seems impossible to improve on Van Doren's criticism of *Active Service* as far as it goes. Beyond Van Doren, the significance of *Active Service* and Crane's part of *The O'Ruddy* lies in their revelation of the late, desperate, and pathetic struggle of Crane's integrity with bestsellerism. In the age of *Trilby*, *Graustark*, and *When Knighthood Was in Flower*, inferior literary talents coined money in such golden floods as had never before been won by authors. Cuban glory, an exasperated consciousness that his superior talent still earned far too little, haste, and that pressure of money for "Brede" which Ford and Liebling believed killed Crane, all tempted him to cash in on the fad. In pieces like **"The Private's Story"** and **"The Clan of No-Name"** he gave in occasionally to embarrassingly Kiplingesque ideas and mannerisms. (p. 149)

Crane's historical imagination was keen, but he never had confused things either by supposing that he could seriously re-enter the past or by lacking respect for the sense of the past because it was imaginary. Therefore to him the irresponsible historical romance was fair game. In *The O'Ruddy* he tried to write a sword-clashing, picaresque, true-love-laden, coincidence-packed romance *and* make fun of the silly, golden *genre* by burlesquing it with the best sustained humor he had yet achieved. All the life goes out of style and characterization when Robert Barr takes over. Barr's troubles were not, as he supposed, with plot so much as with focus of character, tone, atmosphere, and dialogue. If Crane had lived, *The O'Ruddy* might have been a brilliant *tour de force* on themes by the ghostly Stevenson.

After *The Red Badge*, then, Crane's aspiring novels are about what one would expect of a novelist his age: essentially autobiographical, occasionally intense, sporadically gifted, weak in characterization, fragmentary in form. A number of the short stories on the other hand, are absolutely first-class; some of them are of definitive, classic stature. (p. 150)

I, for one, think that Crane's gifts ranged widely beyond and above those of Dreiser. The tragedy of Crane's early silencing, quite apart from any element in it personal to Crane, is that of the death of any gifted young person. It is the tragedy of the unperformed, the unrealized, the never to be known.

In the end the real power of Stephen Crane is in awareness, the power to register and to make the reader see what he saw. Regardless of qualifiers, of what the vision saw, he is supremely a visionist. The one greatest unfairness dealt him has been the repeated implication that it was romantically himself he was trying to make the reader see. On the contrary, the essence of his art was to give, in his characters, persons with eyes and to set them in turn within perspectives which would let readers see both very sharply and complexly around them and so to feel life as Crane felt it. That is true of every great artist. It is equally true of them all that, having felt their power, one must decide for himself how far to accept it. Crane's vision was preternaturally "modern" in its progression to irony. Accept it or not, no honestly hospitable reader can deny either the power of its artistic transmission or, therefore, the youthful yet permanent greatness of Stephen Crane. (p. 160)

Edwin H. Cady, in his Stephen Crane *(copyright © 1980 by Twayne Publishers; reprinted with the permission of Twayne Publishers, a Division of G. K. Hall & Co., Boston), revised edition, Twayne, 1980, 171 p.*

JAMES NAGEL (essay date 1980)

[*In his* Stephen Crane and Literary Impressionism, *Nagel defines the parameters which place Crane's fiction in the realm of Impressionism. Differing from those critics who label Crane a Naturalistic writer, Nagel maintains that "it is precisely Crane's Impressionistic tendencies which form his most significant influence on the twentieth-century and which evoke the Modernistic tone of his fiction."*]

Literary Impressionism is more than an occasional tendency in Crane's fiction; it is the continuing and informing concept of both art and theme throughout his works. It has a direct bearing on his central themes and methods from his earliest stories through his major works to his final novel. The norms of Impressionism provide a context in which his narrative methods, themes, characterizations, images, and structural devices can be perceived as part of a holistic aesthetic behind nearly everything he wrote.

But Impressionism is not the only impulse visible in Crane's fiction. His work embraces a wide range of literary tendencies. The occasional use of personification as a device of characterization, and of zeugma as figure, reveal studied Classical tendencies. The suggestion of spiritualism in nature implies Romanticism and Transcendentalism, although Crane's use of this idea is decidedly limited. There are Genteel elements in the romance plots of *Active Service* and *The Third Violet* and some of the short stories, such as **"The Grey Sleeve."** Indeed, as Daniel G. Hoffman has said, "Crane was a literary chameleon, writing in almost every fashion then prevailing: naturalism, impressionism, psychological realism, local color, native humor." But the only two movements, other than Impressionism, that have played a significant role in his fiction are Naturalism and Realism.

The extent to which Naturalism can be perceived as having influenced Crane's work depends on definition. If Naturalism is described as an historical period, as is sometimes the case, then Crane may be considered part of it, perhaps even the originator of it in American literature with the publication of *Maggie* in 1893. But pure historicism is surely not adequate to the task, for it fails to discriminate among concurrent movements and does not specify what aspects of Crane's works justify this classification. Nor do broad assumptions about an author's "vision" or "intentions" serve this matter well, operating, as they do, on uncontrollable and nondiscursive methodologies. Ultimately, some comprehensive model must be constructed which embraces specific and fundamental themes and artistic devices. If Naturalism consists of themes involving pessimistic determinism, atavism, and evolutionary concepts with both genetic and socio-economic implications, if omniscient narrative methods help generate these themes, as do re-lated and dominant symbols, then Naturalism played a minor but undeniable role in Crane's fiction. (pp. 163-64)

Crane can be considered a Realist in only a qualified sense. His work shares with the norms of American Realism a rejection of many of the tendencies of Romanticism, including stylistic elevation, transcendental metaphysics and pantheism, symbolization, allegorical plots and characters, and a general inclination to represent people and events as emblematic of a significance beyond themselves. As did most realists, Crane portrayed ordinary people who spoke in the vernacular and confronted situations drawn from within a common range. But unlike the Realists, Crane depicted an unstable, changing world in the process of being perceived. Things "seem" to be a certain way in Crane; they "are" in Realism.

Viewed in totality, and with regard for both craft and meaning, Crane's fiction exceeds the limits of both Realism and Naturalism and ultimately must be described and interpreted as being essentially Impressionistic. When seen from this perspective, the Crane canon, and the major phases within his work, reveal a rather different writer, and a rather different contribution, than has generally been recorded in modern scholarship.

The Impressionistic tendencies in Crane's fiction are evident from the first of his artistic efforts to his last, with some indications of a growing dominance. Even the early stories such as **"Uncle Jake and the Bell-Handle"** and **"The King's Favor"** develop their force from a multiplicity of views of life, from a protagonist's uncertainty of what is truth and what is illusion, and from a pervasive irony. Sensory imagery, sensational descriptions of landscape, the stress on epistemological process, plots that culminate in an altered consciousness or perception of reality, all adumbrate the ideas and devices Crane would develop in his mature fiction. Similarly, the sketches in the Sullivan County tales are more valuable for what they predict than for what they accomplish. (pp. 169-70)

At about the same period in his life when he was writing his Sullivan County sketches, Crane was also at work on what would become a more important and complex body of fiction, his tales of the Bowery. The most substantial of these works, *Maggie: A Girl of the Streets*, represents a significant advance beyond the earlier tales, but it also shares many of the same thematic and artistic traits that link Crane's fiction to Impressionism. The narrative is composed of abbreviated episodic units filled with sensory imagery. Although the threatening natural world of Sullivan County has become the abusive urban environment of New York, the ultimate human dilemma is much the same: uncertainty about reality, deflation of a tenuous pride, distorted views of life. (p. 170)

Crane embraces Impressionistic methods and ideas throughout the Bowery tales, intertwined, at times, with other tendencies. But to overlook the Impressionistic nature of these works is to ignore not only the artistry of the stories but the underlying perceptual and interpretive difficulties as well. Maggie's death comes not of economic or social necessity but of her delimited ability to see and comprehend herself and the world around her. A similar conceptual malaise invests the themes of *George's Mother*, especially in the emphasis on the destructive capabilities of gratifying illusions. The other major stories of the Bowery, **"An Experiment in Misery"** and **"The Men in the Storm,"** contain some aspects of Naturalistic social degradation and characterization, but they also employ fundamentally

Impressionistic artistic devices in narration, imagery, and structure, as do the several score of lesser works.

The Red Badge of Courage is Crane's major work and the first monumental Impressionistic novel in American literature. It is the finest piece of extended fiction that Crane ever wrote and it depicts a far more significant series of experiences than anything he had previously written, but it is very much of the same impulse as the Sullivan County sketches and the Bowery tales. It represents the artistic fruition of his earlier work, not a distinct inspiration. Here his typical narrative strategy, imagery, structure, characterization coalesce into a richly satisfying aesthetic whole. The primary focus is still on epistemology; the conflicts are psychological; their resolution comes in a more balanced integration of thought and feeling. Crane's sensory emphasis makes reading the novel seem more a visual than a verbal experience, one recorded as a series of related yet distinct episodes of intense perceptual acuity. Throughout, in addition to Henry's continuing experience, the artistic components of the novel, the carefully controlled patterns of images, juxtaposed scenes, and tightly restricted experiential data, give these isolated scenes a sense of wholeness, of aesthetic completion, that Henry's brief story does not of itself possess.

These traits are shared by nearly everything Crane wrote after *The Red Badge,* although there are some variations. Certainly *The Third Violet* and *Active Service* were influenced by the popularity of Genteel novels of the trials of young love, which reveal their influence in artistry as well as in subject and plot. Crane's two novels are longer, less tightly controlled, inclined more toward an omniscient narrative stance than his characteristic, more serious, work. *The O'Ruddy* shares many of these tendencies while affecting the norms of the picaresque in a manner perhaps influenced by Crane's trip to Ireland with Harold Frederic and by Frederic's own *The Return of the O'Mahony*. But even in these works there are Crane's habitual irony, disparities among interpretations of reality, episodic development of plot, deflations of pride, and other traits consistent throughout Crane's work.

But beyond these aberrations, Crane's fiction continued to utilize the fundamental devices and themes of Impressionism to the end of his career, from his tales of Whilomville, to those of the American west, to his dramatic stories of war. The struggle for new realizations in **"The Bride Comes to Yellow Sky"** and **"The Little Regiment,"** the parallactic interplay of points of view in **"Death and the Child"** and **"A Man and Some Others,"** the extraordinarily restrictive data of **"Three Miraculous Soldiers,"** the epiphanies of **"The Open Boat"** and **"The Blue Hotel,"** the structural organization of **"The Monster"** and **"The Clan of No-Name,"** the sensory imagery of **"The Veteran,"** and the dramatically revealed characterizations, irony, restriction, and truth-illusion disparity of nearly all of his fiction identify his work as Impressionistic. Crane's world is remarkably unsettled, tentative, inscrutable for his time, and his characters display the uncertainty, anguish, and sense of isolation more common to the Modern sensibility than that of the late nineteenth century.

Indeed, it is precisely Crane's Impressionistic tendencies which form his most significant influence on the twentieth century and which evoke the Modernistic tone of his fiction. His objective mode of presentation and ability to portray tragedy with understated emotion are a dramatic foreshadowing of what would become hallmarks of the style of Ernest Hemingway. (pp. 171-72)

Crane wrote out of the Flaubertian style, not the Balzacian. His work is sparse, crisp, sensory; there is no authorial presence, little unobserved description and even less judgment, and few wasted words. The ultimate impact of his work is aesthetic. There is little call to social action, no program of economic reform, and rarely a word of popular social theory. Those scholars who would place him on the Naturalistic shelf with Frank Norris, Jack London, Theodore Dreiser, John O'Hara, and others, respond only to the surface of his work, to the environment of the Bowery tales. But Crane's fiction shares almost nothing with such writers and their expository novels. Rather, his line of influence leads to the economy of Imagist poetry, as Carl Sandburg acknowledged in his "Letters to Dead Imagists":

Stevie Crane:

War is kind and we never knew the kindness of war till you came;
Nor the black riders and clashes of spear and shield out of the sea,
Nor the mumblings and shots that rise from dreams on call.

It also points to the brevity and sharpness of Hemingway, Sherwood Anderson, F. Scott Fitzgerald, Caroline Gordon, and to parts of John Steinbeck, William Faulkner, John Dos Passos, and a host of other writers who used Impressionistic themes and devices in their work. Crane is thus an important figure in the line of development of Impressionistic tendencies from Flaubert's fiction through the sensory images of the French Symbolist poets to such writers as George Moore and Virginia Woolf, the Norwegian Jacob Lie, and other writers in the decades around the turn of the century. The relativistic realities of Crane's Impressionism play a key role in the development of what came to be known as Modernism, especially in its sense of an indifferent and undefinable universe and a lack of individual significance. His evocative and surrealistic imagery predicts similar strategies in Expressionism. In his Impressionism, in its empirical isolation, are the seeds of Existential alienation and resultant despair and anguish; the interpretive uncertainties of his Impressionism foreshadow the absurdity of the French New Novel and much of Post-Modernism. The aesthetics of Crane's Impressionism, especially its anti-didacticism and art-for-art's sake implications, bear some similarities to such recent developments as Sur-Fiction in the United States. The recognition of Crane's role as an Impressionist is thus a crucial determinant of his place in cultural history. (pp. 174-75)

> *James Nagel, in his* Stephen Crane and Literary Impressionism *(copyright © 1980 by The Pennsylvania State University), The Pennsylvania State University Press, University Park, 1980, 190 p. [the excerpt of Carl Sandburg's work used here was originally published in "Letters to Dead Imagists" (copyright 1916 by Holt, Rinehart and Winston, Inc.; copyright 1944 by Carl Sandburg; reprinted by permission of Harcourt Brace Jovanovich, Inc.), in his* Chicago Poems, *Henry Holt and Company, 1916].*

ADDITIONAL BIBLIOGRAPHY

Beer, Thomas. *Stephen Crane: A Study in American Letters.* 1923. Reprint. New York: Octagon Books, 1972, 248 p.
First Crane biography. Beer's biographical work was enthusiastically accepted when it was first published, for it closed many of the curious biographical gaps in Crane's life. Though more recent biographers and critics point out factual errors in the book, it is still generally regarded as an important contribution to Crane studies.

Berryman, John. "Stephen Crane: *The Red Badge of Courage.* In his *The Freedom of the Poet,* pp. 168-75. New York: Farrar, Straus & Giroux, 1976.
Stylistic consideration of *The Red Badge of Courage.* Berryman is the author of the biography *Stephen Crane* (see excerpted entry above).

Brooks, Van Wyck. "The New Cosmopolis." In his *The Confident Years: 1885-1915,* pp. 137-62. New York: E. P. Dutton & Co., 1952.*
Explains the appeal of Crane's *The Red Badge of Courage* and discusses several of his other works.

Conrad, Joseph. "Stephen Crane." In his *Last Essays,* pp. 93-118. New York: Doubleday, Page & Co., 1926.
Fond reminiscence of Conrad's friendship with Crane. Conrad recalls his visits to Brede Place, his literary discussions with Crane, and the mutual admiration they had for each other's work.

Cooley, John R. "Stephen Crane." In his *Savages and Naturals: Black Portraits by White Writers in Modern American Literature,* pp. 38-49. Newark, N.J.: University of Delaware Press, 1982.
Considers Crane's use of the savage mode (that is, his use of a "disguised presentation of many racially pejorative statements and stereotypes") in "The Monster," especially in his depiction of the black coachman, Henry Johnson.

Cox, James Trammell. "Stephen Crane As Symbolist Naturalist: An Analysis of 'The Blue Hotel'." *Modern Fiction Studies* III, No. 2 (Summer 1957): 147-58.
Detailed analysis of "The Blue Hotel" which determines that Crane's "fictional method is that of the symbolist rather than the naturalist." Cox regards the "stove" as the central symbol of this short story.

Ellison, Ralph. "Stephen Crane and the Mainstream of American Fiction." In his *Shadow and Act,* pp. 60-76. New York: Random House, 1964.
Examines *The Red Badge of Courage* and several Crane short stories as an expression of Crane's moral struggle and his depiction of social reality.

Garland, Hamlin. "Stephen Crane As I Knew Him." *Yale Review* III, No. 3 (April 1914): 494-506.
Anecdotal reminiscence of Garland's literary friendship with Crane.

Geismar, Maxwell. "Stephen Crane: Halfway House." In his *Rebels and Ancestors: The American Novel, 1890-1915,* pp. 69-138. New York: Hill and Wang, 1935.
Offers a Freudian interpretation by indicating Oedipal symbols throughout Crane's works.

Gibson, Donald B. *The Fiction of Stephen Crane.* Carbondale and Edwardsville: Southern Illinois University Press, 1968, 169 p.
Thorough and balanced interpretive study of Crane's fiction.

Griffith, Clark. "Stephen Crane and the Ironic Last Word." *Philological Quarterly* XLVII, No. 1 (January 1968): 83-91.
Explains the ambiguities which many critics find at the close of Crane's works as the novelist's "strategy of the ironic last word." Griffith maintains that Crane's use of ironic twists undermines the learning experiences of his characters and ultimately reveals their helpless fate in a naturalistic universe.

Gullason, Thomas A., ed. *Stephen Crane's Career: Perspectives and Evaluations.* New York: New York University Press, 1972, 532 p.
Valuable and comprehensive collection of essays which includes reminiscences, early criticism of Crane's works, and a wide range of more recent interpretive studies. Also included in this book are four Sunday school stories by Crane's father, Reverend Jonathan Townley Crane.

Hafley, James. "'The Monster' and the Art of Stephen Crane." *Accent* XIX, No. 3 (Summer 1959): 159-65.

Sees Crane's "The Monster" as an examination of moral values. In this regard Hafley finds the short story similar to "The Open Boat" and "The Blue Hotel."

Hoffman, Daniel G. *The Poetry of Stephen Crane*. New York: Columbia University Press, 1957, 304 p.

Discusses Crane's prose as an extension of his poetry and notes the similarities between these two modes of Crane's expression.

Holton, Milne. *Cylinder of Vision: The Fiction and Journalistic Writing of Stephen Crane*. Baton Rouge: Louisiana State University Press, 1972, 353 p.

Discusses Crane's concern with the perception of reality throughout his work.

Katz, Joseph. "The Maggie Nobody Knows." *Modern Fiction Studies* XII, No. 2 (Summer 1966): 200-12.

Compares the 1893 edition of *Maggie: A Girl of the Streets* with the 1896 revised edition of the book. Katz's essay notes several of the changes Crane and his editors made to alleviate some of the novel's brutalities thus rendering it more acceptable to nineteenth-century readers.

Kwiat, Joseph J. "Stephen Crane, Literary-Reporter: Commonplace Experience and Artistic Transcendence." *Journal of Modern Literature* 8, No. 1 (1980): 129-38.

Discusses Crane's newspaper reporting as experience critical to his literary development and his insistence on truth and sincerity in his fictional works.

McFarland, Ronald E. "The Hospitality Code and Crane's 'The Blue Hotel'." *Studies in Short Fiction* 18, No. 4 (Fall 1981): 447-51.

Thorough study of the hospitality motif in Crane's short story "The Blue Hotel."

Modern Fiction Studies, Stephen Crane Number V, No. 3 (Autumn: 1959): 195-291.

Issue devoted to Crane studies by notable Crane critics such as Eric Solomon, Thomas Gullason, and R. W. Stallman. This special issue includes interpretive essays on *The Red Badge of Courage*, *Maggie: A Girl of the Streets*, and "The Blue Hotel," among others.

Øverland, Orm. "The Impressionism of Stephen Crane: A Study of Style and Technique." In *Americana Norvegica: Norwegian Contributions to American Studies*, Vol. 1, edited by Sigmund Skard and Henry H. Wasser, pp. 239-85. Philadelphia: University of Pennsylvania Press, 1966.

Studies Impressionistic aspects of Crane's style and techniques and offers a general discussion of Impressionism. Øverland, in part, supports his thesis that Crane is an Impressionist with several of Crane's own critical comments on his craft.

Solomon, Eric. *Stephen Crane in England: A Portrait of the Artist*. Columbus: Ohio State University Press, 1964, 136 p.

Recounts the time Crane spent in England, his literary associations with H. G. Wells, Joseph Conrad, Ford Madox Ford, and Henry James, as well as the English critical response to Crane's work.

Stallman, R. W. "Stephen Crane." In his *The Houses that James Built and Other Literary Studies*, pp. 63-110. Athens: Ohio University Press, 1961.

Collection of critical essays on diverse authors by an author who has written extensively on Crane's work.

Stallman, R. W. *Stephen Crane: A Biography*. New York: George Braziller, 1968, 664 p.

Comprehensive biography which updates the earlier Crane biographies of Thomas Beer and John Berryman. Stallman's book includes a helpful bibliography and checklist of Crane's work.

Studies in the Novel, Special Number on Stephen Crane X, No. 1 (Spring 1978): 6-182.

Special issue on Crane which offers some of the most current criticism on Crane's work and a useful bibliography of Crane scholarship since 1969.

Van Doren, Carl. "Stephen Crane." *The American Mercury* I, No. 1 (January 1924): 11-14.

Perceptive assessment of Crane's literary contribution. Van Doren maintains that Crane's literary canon was the beginning of modern American literature.

Vanouse, Donald. "Women in the Writings of Stephen Crane: Madonnas of the Decadence." *Southern Humanities Review* XII, No. 2 (Spring 1978): 141-48.

Proposes that Crane's literary treatment of women deviates from that of the traditionally suppressed women in nineteenth-century literature.

Weinstein, Bernard. "*George's Mother* and the Bowery of Experience." *The Markham Review* 9 (Spring 1980): 45-9.

Posits that *George's Mother* is more of a psychological study than the earlier work *Maggie*. Weinstein believes *George's Mother* represents a more mature vision of the Bowery life based on Crane's actual experiences which he also recorded in "The Men in the Storm" and "An Experiment in Misery."

Westbrook, Max. "Stephen Crane's Social Ethic." *American Quarterly* 14, No. 4 (Winter 1962): 587-96.

Maintains that Crane's work reflects his belief in social determinism "based on a universal principle which holds all men responsible for doing the best they can with what they have been given."

Wilson, Edmund. "A Vortex in the Nineties: Stephen Crane." In his *The Shores of Light: A Literary Chronicle of the Twenties and Thirties*, pp. 109-14. New York: Farrar, Straus and Young, 1952.

Praises Thomas Beer's biography *Stephen Crane: A Study of American Letters* and calls attention to Crane's importance as a nineteenth-century literary figure.

Ziff, Larzer. "Outstripping the Event: Stephen Crane." In his *The American 1890s: Life and Times of a Lost Generation*, pp. 185-205. New York: The Viking Press, 1966.

Biocritical overview of Crane's literary career.

Dazai Osamu

1909-1948

(Pseudonym of Tshushima Shūji) Japanese novelist, short story writer, and essayist.

Dazai is one of the most important novelists of postwar Japan. His principal English translator, Donald Keene, has described him as the Japanese novelist "who emerged at the end of World War II as the literary voice of his time." *Shayō (The Setting Sun)* and *Ningen skikkaku (No Longer Human)* are Dazai's best known novels outside Japan. Both convey a sense of moral and philosophical disorientation in a world where traditional values have been undermined by the pressures of modern existence and, in a deeper sense, where every value is negated by the strain of life itself. The title of the first book was quickly adapted into a term in the Japanese lexicon: *shayozoku* or "declining aristocracy," a phrase which opposed the familiar epithet "land of the rising sun" with the somber designation "people of the setting sun." The title of the second book, which has been more literally translated by Keene as "disqualified as a human being," expresses Dazai's lifelong frustration with, and estrangement from, the world around him. This state of mind was alternately relieved and aggravated throughout the author's life, until eventually he drowned himself on his thirty-ninth birthday. Although Dazai is principally recalled for his postwar novels of personal and cultural disenchantment, he is also the author of a varied body of works dating back to the early 1930s; and while he attracts readers because of the strongly autobiographical elements of his work, he is also distinguished as one of the most adept storytellers in modern Japanese literature.

The youngest of ten children, Dazai was born in Kanagi, a town in northern Japan. His family was wealthy, owning land worked by tenant farmers, and Dazai grew up a physically and emotionally sensitive child in a comfortable home. Later in his life, self-consciousness about his prosperous background contributed to his sense of isolation, as did a deeply ingrained image of himself as that freakish creature—the artist. "The true artist," he wrote, "is an ugly man." By the time he attended Hirosaki Higher School, enrolled in the literature department, Dazai had begun living in the unconventional, hectic style for which he became famed through his autobiographical fiction. Alcoholism, drug addiction, affairs with geishas, suicide attempts alone or with another, and frequent psychological traumas of various sorts were situations integral to Dazai's existence. In 1930 he entered the department of French literature at Tokyo University. Though academic success had always come easily to Dazai, he was not particularly intent on benefiting from his university courses, and later claimed never to have set foot in a college classroom. Instead he became involved in left-wing politics, caroused, and renewed his relationship with Koyama Hatsuyo, a geisha he had known while he was at Hirosaki Higher School. His family's disapproval of this relationship led him to attempt suicide by drowning with a woman who was a hostess in a bar. Though his companion died, Dazai survived and was saved from being charged as an accomplice to suicide by the intervention of his older brother. This episode, among several instances of double suicide in Dazai's fiction, is retold in *No Longer Human*. On

at least three other occasions, Dazai attempted to take his life. Although his family later granted him permission to marry Hatsuyo, the couple eventually separated, and Dazai went on to a second marriage and numerous other romantic affairs, finally succeeding in a double suicide with a young war widow in 1948.

Dazai believed that "the writer should voice his intent in his story until his voice becomes hoarse and his strength expires." Dazai's intent, according to most critics, was the fictional recreation and dissection of the crises that made up his life. For example, his first publication, a collection of short stories entitled *Bannen*, contains the directly autobiographical "Remembrances." It also offers such pieces as "Ha" ("Leaves") and "Sarugashima" ("Monkey Island"), which succeed in displaying the author's attainment of an artistic imagination and a skillful narrative technique. *Bannen* was fairly well received by both critics and the reading public, allowing Dazai to pursue a literary career. In his next major work, the novel *Dōke no hana*, Dazai began the story with an account of his first double suicide attempt. The narrator, Yozo, is the namesake of the narrator in *No Longer Human*, who also recalls this episode in the author's life. Both narratives disqualify themselves from the scrupulous truth-telling of Japanese autobiographical literature, the *shishosetsu* or "I-novel," by Dazai's ironic treatment of his fictional personas. Throughout

Dōke no hana, whose title has been translated as "The Flower of Buffoonery," Dazai suggested the complex and perhaps ridiculous nature of autobiographical fiction, rather than indulging in this narrative form as a means of redemption or self-advertisement. For many critics this playful self-mockery exonerates the often despairing tone of Dazai's works, while also making them more effective as autobiography. Dazai also used retellings of well-known works to examine himself. For example, in the novel *Shin Hamuretto* the "new Hamlet" of the title serves as another of Dazai's literary selves. Among his most successful reworkings of stories by other authors are *Shinshaku shokoku banashi* and *Otogi zoshi,* adaptations of classic Japanese fiction and fairy tales. As critics have remarked, the stories of these collections are among the few works of artistic value produced by a Japanese author under the strict government censorship during World War II. It was after the war that Dazai wrote his most popular and highly regarded works, *The Setting Sun* and *No Longer Human.*

In *The Setting Sun,* the narrator Kazuko writes to the man who will father her child: "Victims. Victims of a transitional period of morality. That is what we both certainly are." Among the other victims in the novel are Kazuko's mother, the last representative of a gracious and defunct aristocracy, and Kazuko's brother, whose desperation for an ideal results in suicide. Kazuko's gesture of bringing a child into a precarious society in transition is often seen by critics as a sign of faith in a better, if radically different, future society. Described by Makoto Ueda as "an elegy mourning the death of the nobility in twentieth-century Japan," *The Setting Sun* has been called a record of its time in the form of a consummate work of art. Like Dazai's other works, it is also discussed as an autobiographical record of the author himself, whose personality traits are distributed among the various characters in the story. More directly autobiographical is *No Longer Human,* the novel most often considered Dazai's greatest work. Told in the form of three notebooks by a narrator who is described in the epilogue as a "madman," this story outwardly parallels the author's own life—one characterized by the use of alcohol and drugs, confinement in a mental institution, disastrous romantic affairs, and a failed double suicide attempt. The dominant mood of the narrator's world is one of alienation and fear. Unable to lie with "righteousness" like others he encounters, Yozo disguises his alien nature by acts of clowning, and lives in terror of being exposed as a fraud and an outsider. But having become a source of amusement, Yozo manages to integrate himself with the world around him, allowing a third party at the end of the novel to call this self-described outcast "an angel." This epithet, critics observe, calls into question Yozo's view of himself and ironically suggests the complicated, unreliable nature of autobiography in fiction. As always, Dazai's own view of his tormented life is alleviated by an ironic perspective and the distractions of an artistically structured narrative.

As well as representing some of the best examples of modern Japanese literature, Dazai's works compare favorably with those of Western literary modernism. The social and psychological upheavals of his novels parallel those of his contemporaries in Europe and America, especially his combining a strong need for personal expression with a fine sense of artistic construction. His volatile life and violent death are told and foretold throughout a body of works in which, as a consensus of his critics indicates, confessions of disaster and hopelessness are examined from the elevating viewpoints of humor and nobility.

(See also *Contemporary Authors,* Vol. 107.)

PRINCIPAL WORKS

Bannen   (short stories)   1937
Dōke no hana   (novel)   1937
Hashire merosu   (short story)   1940
Kakekomi uttae   (short story)   1941
   ["*I Accuse*" published in journal *The Reeds,* 1958]
Kojiki gakusei   (short story)   1941
Shin Hamuretto   (novel)   1941
Tsugaru   (nonfiction)   1944
Otogi zōshi   (short stories)   1945
Shinshaku shokoku banashi   (short stories)   1945
Buiyon no tsuma   (short story)   1947
   ["*Villon's Wife*" published in *Modern Japanese Literature,* 1956]
Shayō   (novel)   1947
   [*The Setting Sun,* 1956]
Ningen shikkaku   (novel)   1948
   [*No Longer Human,* 1958]
"Cherries"   (short story)   1953; published in journal *Encounter*
"Of Women"   (short story)   1953; published in journal *Encounter*
"Osan"   (short story)   1958; published in journal *Japan Quarterly*
"The Courtesy Call"   (short story)   1961; published in *Modern Japanese Stories*
Dazai Osamu zenshu. 13 vols.   (novels, short stories, and essays)   1962-63
"Romanesque"   (short story)   1965; published in journal *Japan Quarterly*
"Leaves"   (short story)   1968; published in journal *Monumenta Nipponica*
"The Father"   (short story)   1969; published in journal *Monumenta Nipponica*
"Morning"   (short story)   1969; published in journal *Monumenta Nipponica*
"Mother"   (short story)   1969; published in journal *Monumenta Nipponica*
"Metamorphosis"   (short story)   1970; published in journal *Japan Quarterly*
"Monkey Island"   (short story)   1971; published in journal *Voices*

EDWARD G. SEIDENSTICKER   (essay date 1953)

[*Seidensticker has translated several of Dazai's stories.*]

Weak physically and unstable psychologically, [Dazai] indulged in a flamboyant bohemianism that has made him a legend and the idol of a cult, a sort of Japanese Rimbaud. He was on occasion a drug-addict and an alcoholic, and he tried suicide at least three times before he succeeded in drowning himself in June, 1948, a month after ["**Cherries**"] was published.

His writings are largely autobiographical, falling in the personal, subjective tradition that has dominated 20th century Japanese fiction. Naturalism, introduced from France around 1900, took a strange turn in Japan; the Japanese writer, converted by

Zola and convinced of the need to report on contemporary Japanese society, looked about him and found that Japanese society, changing rapidly and very possibly disintegrating, quite refused to reveal itself; hence he concluded that the only thing he could write about truthfully was himself, and the "I-novel" became the standard vehicle for Japanese "naturalism." Today the movement shows signs of bankruptcy, and Dazai's extraordinary post-war novel *No Longer Human* has perhaps brought it as far as it can go.

Dazai would have been unhappy and uncertain in the most conservative and stable Japanese environment. His psychological troubles, one would judge from his writings and especially from *No Longer Human,* had their origins in his position as the youngest child of a large family with a strong and dominant father—in the traditional Japanese family system. His final collapse, however, clearly resulted from his confrontation with Tokyo and its chaos of clashing cultural influences. The passages in *No Longer Human* in which he describes his early terror at the city are as effective as anything he wrote, and the brief sections of the same novel in which he tells of his longing and inability to go back to the provinces are symptomatic of a nostalgia very basic to the modern Japanese mind.

> *Edward G. Seidensticker, in his extract from "Two Stories by Osamu Dazai," in* Encounter *(© 1953 by Encounter Ltd.), Vol. 1, No. 1, October, 1953, p. 23.*

DOROTHY VAN GHENT (essay date 1956)

[*In their early reviews of the English translations of* The Setting Sun, *both Van Ghent and Earl Miner (see excerpt below) find that Dazai's fiction lends itself to comparisons with Western literature, while at the same time serving as exemplary works of Japanese literature.*]

The characters in **"The Setting Sun"**—the girl Kazuku, her brother Naoji, the degenerate novelist Uehara by whom Kazuku, in a pathetic attempt to create life out of sterility, gets herself with child—. . . have their spiritual counterparts . . . in the Paris of Rainer Maria Rilke's "Notebook of Malte Laurids Brigge," around 1905. Naoji could be that haunted student who occupied the room next to Malte (actually the student was Rilke's own neighbor), who had contracted a nervous weakness which caused one of his eyelids to close, "like a blind snapping down," and who in his nervous misery walked up and down all night, throwing things onto the floor and picking them up again—round, metallic objects that rolled for a while—while Malte (Rilke) felt his own strength sapped through the dividing wall. "I wonder if there is anyone who is not depraved," Naoji wrote in his notebook, and his sister's comment—"Those words made me feel depraved myself, and my uncle and even Mother somehow then seemed depraved. *Perhaps by depravity he actually meant tenderness"*—expresses a sensibility so close to that pervading Rilke's "Notebook" that the words might have appeared there. (p. 282)

[Dazai's] background has its similarities with that of Rilke's Malte, or with that of Rilke himself; but Rilke, by some saving miracle, "pushed through" (the words are his own) Malte and beyond him to powerful and beautiful assertion, while Osamu Dazai committed suicide in 1948 when he was thirty-nine, condemned to the destiny of the character Naoji in his novel.

It is very infrequently that a book can sustain itself as achieved form when dominated so nearly exclusively by expression of sensibility as this one is, with so little narrative movement; yet

"The Setting Sun" is achieved form. The characters are curiously inarticulate, as if inhibited by a felt doom. "It's as though an unseasonable frost had fallen all over the whole world," the girl Kazuku says. Naoji writes in his diary that he has "a sensation of burning to death," and "excruciating though it is, I cannot pronounce even the simple words 'it hurts.'" The mother says, "Even when I want to cry, the tears don't come any more." They communicate by glances, small gestures, facial expressions, single words or phrases. Hence the chief modes of meaning which the novel uses are minor symbolic happenings that suggest larger situations—the mother's swollen hand, the mother's sore tongue that prevents her from speaking, the snakes that, on the evening of the father's death, are seen twisted around the azaleas, the wistaria, and the cherry trees. Kazuku destroys some snake eggs that she thinks are viper's, then sees the mother-snake wandering around the garden, seeming to be searching for the eggs, and it occurs to her that her mother's face "rather resembled that of the unfortunate snake" and that something dwelling in her own breast might one day end "by devouring this beautiful, grief-stricken mother snake." In this method, too, the book resembles Rilke's "Notebook," although the editors point out justly that it is here indebted to Japanese poetry, particularly the miniature seventeen-syllable haiku, where each word is the distillation of a world. Despite the novel's intense inwardness, one is constantly aware of natural scene—the garden, the stars, the rice fields—but it is as if the characters moved in a scene that was without density, that was only two-dimensional, as if limned on silk. The effect is not only a poetry of a delicate and foreign quality, but an expression of the spiritual dislocation which is the condition of the characters. (p. 283)

> *Dorothy Van Ghent, "The Race, the Moment, and the Milieu," in* The Yale Review *(© 1956 by Yale University; reprinted by permission of the editors), Vol. XLVI, No. 2, December, 1956, pp. 274-88.**

EARL MINER (essay date 1957)

[*Like Dorothy Van Ghent (see excerpt above), Miner attests to the comparability of* The Setting Sun *with the best of Western literature.*]

[In *The Setting Sun*] Dazai successfully merged two Western traditions in a work dealing with postwar Japanese social and moral dislocations—the French tradition of Flaubert and Mallarmé with the English late Romantic tradition of D. H. Lawrence. The nonchalance with which he borrowed situations, character, and theme from *Lady Chatterley's Lover* is remarkable. Kazuko, a girl from the postwar, impoverished nobility finds no way to achieve individuality or even live in a society which is "rotten"—Lawrence's very word. Like Lady Chatterley, she ends by taking a lover from the lower classes in order to have a child by him. There are further resemblances between the two novels, but *The Setting Sun* is more remarkable for its differences in handling the materials. Lawrence ends, as a proper romantic novelist ought, with marriage. Dazai does not. Lawrence's most powerful and most credible "character" is sexual passion, the Life Force. Dazai's human characters and theme both excite belief—or at least a willing suspension of doubt.

A willing suspension of hostility is perhaps more like it. Kazuku's brother Naoji is far gone in decadence, like her stolid but nonetheless un-Laurentian lover, Uehara, who is a fake besides. With such characters, the theme of the novel must lie in Dazai's resolution of Kazuko's motives in having such an affair. Essentially, her act is what she calls a "private revolution" in which the rebels become willing victims who create standards of love in the face of a hostile world. She writes Uehara:

> Victims. Victims of a transitional period of morality. That is what we both certainly are.
>
> The revolution must be taking place somewhere, but the old morality persists unchanged in the world around us and lies athwart our way. However much the waves on the surface of the sea may rage, the water at the bottom, far from experiencing a revolution, lies motionless, awake but feigning sleep.

But the resolution of the theme also entails a French artistic cleanness, a complete lack of sentimentality reflected in Kazuko's remark about herself and her unborn child—"A bastard and its mother." This unblinking realism is an older wisdom than Lawrence's romantic vision, just as the form of the novel is superior to his meandering plot. The denouement reveals that, unknown to either of them, the fine Kazuko has had her affair with the worthless husband of the good woman whom the decadent Naoji had idealized in frustration. These and many other parallel lines meet at the end when Kazuko realizes that an anguished love can bring beauty into the inimical world. Her love is depraved by social standards which themselves are corrupt, but Kazuko learns that depravity may mean tenderness in a world where it is the only avenue to love. The addition of French honesty to Lawrence's Life Force of mystic regeneration turns his abstract Passion into the more fully human motivation of love. The result is a splendid artistic whole and a new formal perfection in Western-inspired Japanese fiction. (pp. 305-06)

> *Earl Miner, "Traditions and Individual Talents in Recent Japanese Fiction," in* The Hudson Review *(copyright © 1957 by The Hudson Review, Inc.; reprinted by permission), Vol. X, No. 2, Summer, 1957, pp. 302-08.* *

DONALD KEENE (essay date 1964)

[*Unlike critics who read Dazai's work strictly in terms of Western literary traditions, Keene—Dazai's foremost English translator—places his novels and short stories in a context of Japanese traditions and literary conventions.*]

The *Times Literary Supplement*, a notoriously severe journal, said of *No Longer Human* [*Ningen Shikkaku*] that "it achieves in a high degree the ironical poignancy of Dazai's model, Dostoevsky. It is, in fact, a consummate work of art."

I cannot recall ever having read a Japanese criticism of Dazai which either likened him to Dostoevsky or claimed that one of his novels was a "consummate work of art." Perhaps the English reviewer was foolishly enthusiastic, but I think it likely that the Japanese reluctance to employ such superlatives stems not only from oriental modesty but from the different meaning Dazai's work possesses when read in the original language. It is impossible when confronted with Dazai in Japanese not to be aware of his profound connections with the autobiographical fiction which has such a long history in Japan. The tendency among Japanese, then, has been to consider Dazai's fiction as one might consider his letters or diary, as somehow supplying evidence about the personality or beliefs of the author, or demonstrating the relationship of the author to his themes. The artistry of the writer has consequently tended to be overlooked or subordinated to other considerations. It gives the Japanese reader pleasure when he feels he can detect Dazai Osamu's deepest emotions emerging through the characters in the novels; this, of course, is not the manner in which one appreciates, say, characters in a Dostoevsky novel who possess a life quite apart from the author's. The Japanese reader may even feel a sense of betrayal if he discovers that the "I" of a Dazai novel is actually quite unlike the author. It is rather like discovering that a man has lied in his diary. One remembers the consternation when new evidence revealed that *The Narrow Road of Oku* by the revered "saint of poetry" Bashō departed at times from the truth in the interests of artistic excellence.

Dazai complicated the distinctions between autobiography and fiction by including in most of his writings an important character who *might* be considered the author himself. In the case of *The Setting Sun (Shayō* . . .) we may even obtain the impression that all three main characters—the girl Kazuko, her dissolute brother Naoji, and the novelist Uehara—represent no more than different aspects of the author; the reader who can identify himself with any one of the three may therefore feel a special affinity for Dazai himself. (pp. 186-87)

The Western reader receives a different impression from, say, *No Longer Human* because, not knowing as much about Dazai's life as a Japanese, he may imagine that the work is entirely fictional, though he will surely sense that Dazai is personally involved. But even if all the facts were known, the tendency among Western critics would probably be to evaluate Dazai's writings in terms of his success in making his personal experiences meaningful to all readers, and not in terms of his success in revealing himself. A reviewer in India, comparing the character Yōzō in *No Longer Human* with the salesman Gregor Samsa in Kafka's *Metamorphosis*, found that Yōzō's discovery that he had lost his human qualifications resembled the metamorphosis of Gregor Samsa into a cockroach. He continued, "But as in the case of Kafka's eerie tales, there is far more in Dazai's story than can be summed up in a neat moral. It brings us face to face with the formless, nameless, terror of life. Dazai gives it a form and a name. We cannot expect more from any writer." This comparison between Dazai and Kafka certainly seems to me more rewarding than attempts to contrast the actual details of Dazai's childhood with their fictional versions.

It is obvious, of course, that some aspect of Dazai himself is present in all works from the earliest. This fact can be interpreted unfavorably, as meaning that he failed to create a fictional, objective world in the manner of the great nineteenth-century novelists, but Dazai shares this failing with many of the best twentieth-century authors, and it is absurd to insist that all writers conform to a single standard. Even if Dazai had not invented one incident in his novels—of course, this is not the case—his method of treating existing material and, above all, his literary style would have made him a creative artist.

Dazai had a remarkably precocious awareness of his particular domain as a writer, as we can tell from one of his first stories, *Gyofukuki* ["Metamorphosis"] The untranslatable title was borrowed from a Chinese story known to Dazai only by name, but the direct inspiration came from the adaptation of this story by the eighteenth-century Japanese novelist Ueda Akinari, a tale called *Muō no Rigyo* ("The Dream Carp," 1768). Akinari's story is about a priest living by Lake Biwa who loves to paint pictures of carp. He dreams that, being very ill, he wanders in delirium to the edge of the lake and plunges in. He swims about happily as a carp, only to be caught by a fisherman. Just at the moment when he is about to be cut up into *sashimi*, he awakens from the dream, only to discover that all the events have actually occurred, leaving the reader to wonder where to draw the line between fantasy and reality. In Dazai's story an unhappy girl, living with her brutish father in a remote place, is driven by wretched circumstances to commit suicide by throwing herself into a deep pool. Transformed after death into a fish, for a while she enjoys the sensation of swimming about freely, but at the conclusion of the story the fish, still under the spell of the terrible gloom which had afflicted the girl, swims deliberately into a whirlpool, there to commit a second suicide. In this story Dazai not only twists the original material in a highly original manner, but gives expression to his own morbid fascination for suicide. Suicide was to figure so prominently as a theme of Dazai's writings that we may find it strange that he managed to stay alive so long. But despite the persistent darkness of mood in his stories, one is led in the end to the judgment that the personality of the author was not interchangeable with that of the characters in his fiction. Dazai, knowing in which moods he was most effective, generally clung to them, but this was a deliberate posture; he did not merely pour out his thoughts as they welled up. He was, above all, an artist.

Dazai's concern for style is revealed in the almost obsessive interest he displayed in words and their implications. . . . (pp. 187-89)

The most extreme example of Dazai's preoccupation with language is found in the scene in *No Longer Human* where Yōzō and Horiki play their game of tragic and comic nouns, followed by a game of antonyms. A novelist with so hypersensitive an interest in words suggests a poet, and indeed, much of Dazai's writing is close to poetry. (p. 189)

The conscious artistry of Dazai reveals itself also in the construction of his writings. Surely no modern Japanese novel has a superior beginning and ending to *No Longer Human*. The device he employs in the prologue, the three photographs of the subject at different stages of his life, has since been imitated by other writers, but still has overpowering impact. It does not matter whether or not the photographs described are related to actual photographs of Dazai; the prologue sets the mood of the novel flawlessly with a poetic economy of words. And there is something peculiarly appropriate in a novel about Japan, the country of photographers, that the hero be introduced in this manner. The photographs are the sad proof of the existence of a person who, in his own words, was never a human being.

The epilogue to the same novel is perhaps even more remarkable. Many Japanese novelists seem to encounter difficulty in ending their works, leaving the reader to feel that the book is still incomplete, or that it might have ended earlier, but *No Longer Human* acquires its full intensity only with the last words. Dazai employs the frequently used convention of the writer who has been entrusted with the notebooks of a deceased person, and in the epilogue, where we leave the notebooks for the world of the objective outsider, we are suddenly made to see that the picture Yōzō has painted of himself in the notebooks, for all its unspeakable honesty, is grossly inaccurate. The madam of the Kyōbashi bar tells us, "The Yōzō we knew was so easy-going and amusing, and if only he hadn't drunk—no, even though he did drink—he was a good boy, an angel." This would hardly occur to the reader as the proper description of the Yōzō *we* have known, but with these words we sense the turning of a kaleidoscope: just as most people, incapable

of perceiving their own faults, tend to justify their every action, so Yōzō has only been able to interpret his actions, however welcome to others, in the most distorted terms. What he has reported may be factually correct, but it is essentially wrong. The reversal of our ideas comes as a shock. Yōzō has insisted that he is not even a human being, but the final judgment is that he is superior to other human beings—"an angel"—and we suddenly realize that, paradoxically, this is true. Yōzō, despite his self-proclaimed loss of human character, has acted throughout in an almost excessively human manner, if to be human means to be aware of oneself and one's condition. The author with this final touch has transformed the novel from a confession into a complex work of art.

Dazai's most perfect artistic creation may be *Otogi Zōshi (Bedtime Stories)*. He managed in his adaptation of these fairy tales, known in general outline to every Japanese child, to impart the characteristic Dazai flavor, normally associated with an extremely dark outlook on the world, without violating in any way the lighthearted spirit of the originals. Dazai's mordant humor was a well-established part of his style from *Dōke no Hana* ("Flowers of Buffoonery" . . .) onwards, and numerous anecdotes in his autobiogrqphical writings indicate how often Dazai was given to clowning, even as a child. Even in his last bitter works there always remains a thread of humor: at the end of *No Longer Human*, Yōzō, afflicted by depression and illness, takes a large does of sleeping pills, only to discover that he has been provided with the wrong medicine, and has actually taken a powerful laxative instead. There is nothing appealing about Dazai's portrayal of himself as a clown: "I was fascinated by my own face. Whenever I got tired of reading I would take out a mirror and practice smiling, frowning, or meditating chin in hand, and stare without tiring at my reflected expression. I mastered a whole repertory of expressions guaranteed to make people laugh." *(Omoide)* The kind of humor found in such late works as "Cherries" *(Ōtō . . .)* is harrowing. But in *Otogi Zōshi* the humor is real and brings genuine laughter. One of the delights of the collection, moreover, is to find here familiar figures from other Dazai stories—the heartless man who passes for a saint, the impractical artist, the scheming woman, and so on—drawn with even greater perception than in the stories involving Dazai more personally. The deceitfulness of society, a fact which never ceased to trouble Dazai, is perfectly evoked in the tale of *Urashima-san*, more effectively even than in *No Longer Human*. Freed of the self-imposed necessity of writing about his own experiences, Dazai could express his views easily and gracefully within the framework of an existing story. His humor here was the more brilliant because untouched by self-pity or self-hatred. The stories of *Otogi Zōshi* are virtuoso examples of Dazai's style divorced from the mood which it generally served to create.

Another purely literary feature of Dazai's writings that strikes anyone reading the collected works is his genius for the short, effective scene. (pp. 190-92)

[*Ha* ("Leaves")] though not a successful work as a whole, contains many brilliant flashes, including the unforgettable vignette of the little Russian girl who sells flowers at Nihonbashi, or such statements as: "He spent three full years of his life educating his wife. By the time her education was more or less completed, he began to wish he were dead." We can imagine this single line of print being developed by another author into hundreds of pages. (p. 193)

Dazai is able in the same manner to evoke a place or person with a remarkable economy of language. His recollections of scenes known from childhood in Tusgaru, or the views of Mount Fuji, or of different corners of Tokyo where he has known misery, are generally achieved with a few telling details. One never has the impression that Dazai has carefully filled notebooks with observations so that he will be able to provide local color when needed. Instead, the reader senses that each scene has been distilled through Dazai's poetic imagination into its essential ingredients. The reader is often surprised on returning to a favorite passage to discover how short it is; it has grown within our imagination because the essentials were all present. The same is true of Dazai's characters. He rarely mentions details of physical appearance except when absolutely necessary to our understanding of the character. . . . Dazai never tells us, where the information is not vital, that a character had a round face or broad shoulders or any other conventional descriptive matter. His characters tend to be fixed in our minds as the result of one utterance or gesture, rather than through exhaustive description. "Flatfish" in *No Longer Human* is forever epitomized in one paragraph:

> I can never forget the indescribably crafty shadow that passed over Flatfish's face as he laughed at me, his neck drawn in. It resembled contempt, yet it was different: if the world, like the sea, had depths of a thousand fathoms, this was the kind of weird shadow which might be found hovering here and there at the bottom.
>
> (pp. 193-94)

I have thus far been discussing Dazai in terms of his purely literary skills. This approach may seem almost paradoxical in view of the intensely personal nature of his writings, the subject of so much criticism by Japanese, but I have been anxious to insist on his excellence as a craftsman because it tends to be obscured by his repuration as a writer of autobiographical fiction. But of course it is impossible to deny the unmistakably autobiographical impulse which charges Dazai's work, and a comparison between the early *Omoide* and *No Longer Human* affords absorbing insights into Dazai both as a chronicler of his own life and as an artist. The personality of the speaker is clearly the same in both works, and certain incidents recur almost unchanged in the later book. The chief difference is that the "I" of *Omoide* is still a human being with recognizable bursts of affection for his family and other people. Although he dislikes his elder brother, he by no means considers him a total stranger:

> My brother knew I had been collecting unusual insects. The paper bag he offered me rustled with the clawing of insect-legs inside. The faint sound told me of a brother's love.

What a contrast with the cold, utterly unsympathetic elder brother described in *No Longer Human*! Dazai's affection for his younger brother is another endearing element in *Omoide*, but had to be suppressed in *No Longer Human*, where no suggestion of human ties would be possible for the non-human Yōzō. At the end of *Omoide* the younger brother shows the narrator the picture of a servant-girl with whom he imagined himself to be in love, a scene possessing a warmth that is not merely the product of artistic skill. But if our impressions of Dazai as a person are more favorable in *Omoide* than in *No Longer Human*, we cannot help noticing the superior literary quality of the latter. The author has stripped away everything not essential to his theme, and at the same time given maximum importance to each incident. Undoubtedly *Omoide* depicts the boy Dazai much more faithfully, and this autobiographical

quality has its own interest, but the way in which the mature artist has transformed the material is a tribute to Dazai the artist.

Gyakkō ("**Against the Stream**" . . .) carries forward the story, at once more impressionistically and more urgently. The first of its four episodes opens in a manner suggesting *No Longer Human*:

> He was not an old man. He had barely passed his twenty-fifth birthday. Yet "old man" might be the best designation for him, after all. He had lived each year that an ordinary man lives, three or four times over. Twice he had unsuccessfully attempted suicide.

Here, obviously, we have a description of Dazai during the period of *Bannen*. The next episode, "The Thief," tells of Dazai's actual experiences at Tokyo University, where he pretended for years to be studying French literature without attending a class or learning anything of the French language. This period in his life, marked by attempts at suicide, addiction to liquor and drugs, an abortive interest in Communism, and his unsuccessful love-suicide, would later be chronicled in *No Longer Human* with greater mastery than Dazai was capable of when so close to the events, but the reader cannot help share emotions so intensely stated:

> I am a thief. A notorious subversive. Artists never used to kill people. Artists never used to steal. Swine! You and your paltry, smart-alecky friends.

The unsuccessful love-suicide was the most traumatic of his experiences and marked the depth of his depression. He refers to this event again and again in his writings, sometimes, as in *Dōke no Hana*, with brutal realism; sometimes as in "**Of Women**" (*Mesu ni tsuite* . . .), in analytical terms; sometimes, as in *Obasute* . . . with an awareness of the almost farcical aspects; sometimes, as in *Tokyo Hakkei* ("**Eight Sights of Tokyo**" . . .) with terrible bitterness; and finally in *No Longer Human*, in the final development of the theme, as an expression of the essential nature of the character Yōzō.

In his revelations of the love-suicide and other sordid episodes of his youth Dazai does not hesitate to disclose the worst about himself. He is so ready to impute to himself the basest motives that we may feel in reading the chain of autobiographical stories something akin to masochism. At the same time, however, we must bear in mind that the story is incomplete in one fundamental respect: during this period of violent emotion and despair Dazai was desperately intent on becoming an author. Already in *Omoide* he had expressed this determination. . . . (pp. 194-96)

There is little, however, in the autobiographical stories to suggest the seriousness with which Dazai applied himself to his self-appointed task, or that creative efforts gave him any satisfaction. When Yōzō tells Flatfish that he would like to become a painter (Dazai sometimes disguised his writers as painters), Flatfish merely laughs. Yōzō himself admits that except for a few terrifyingly self-revealing portraits painted as a boy, he never painted anything of consequence. In the novel, art occupies Yōzō very little, and his work quickly degenerates into foolish cartoons or pornography; in reality, Dazai was deeply committed to his work. . . . (p. 196)

Not until *Fugaku Hyakkei* ("**The Hundred Views of Fuji**" . . .) did Dazai choose to portray himself as an author who had won recognition (particularly among young people). This story is conspicuously more cheerful that those in which the "I" is a person without fixed occupation, and at the same time is the closest to autobiographical writing of anything in Dazai's works. Instead of the self-destroying monster who normally frequented Dazai's pages, we have a recognizable human being, friendly to the young people who gather around him, appreciative of the kindness of the maid at his inn, sensitive to the beauty of Fuji, and capable too of a marriage quite dissimilar to the acts of desperation described in the other stories. This relatively happy period, which includes the delightful short *Mangan* ("A Vow Fulfilled" . . .), shows Dazai at his most attractive, but he must have sensed that his forte lay elsewhere. The character of the devoted, attentive husband and father would not suit the Dazai of fiction.

It is true that at the end of **"Villon's Wife"** (*Buiyon no Tsuma* . . .) the dissolute poet (often assumed by readers to represent Dazai himself) discloses that he stole in order to provide his wife and child with money for New Year, but we remember this less than the indifference he most often displayed. The hero of most Dazai stories is dissolute; he even suggests in *The Setting Sun* that this is desirable, when Kazuko writes to Uehara: "For all I know, you may earn the gratitude of people in years to come by recklessly pursuing your life of vice rather than by your 'splendid career.'" In *Kirigirisu* (**"Grasshoppers"** . . .) the paradox is even greater: the wife, who has loved her husband as long as he was dissolute and irresponsible, abandons him when he turns respectable and achieves social prestige. In *Katei no Kōfuku* (**"The Happiness of the Family"** . . .) the leading character is a model husband and father, but a heartless monster in the office where he works; the conclusion is that "The happiness of the family is the root of all evil."

Dazai thus not only portrayed himself in terms of dissolution and despair, but often approved of these qualities, at least in his fiction. He decided that having once established the dark atmosphere of *Bannen,* this would be his characteristic milieu, as a painter might choose a palette of sombre colors. The small group of cheerful stories clustered around *Fugaku Hyakkei* is so winning that we may regret Dazai's decision, but it was justified when viewed in terms of the artistic successes of later years. At the same time, Dazai may thereby have prevented himself from developing into a novelist of even greater range and power.

One way in which Dazai attempted to enlarge his scope was by adapting stories derived from Western sources, including *Kakekomi Uttae* [**"Direct Appeal,"** or **"I Accuse"**] . . . on the betrayal of Christ by Judas, *Hashire Merosu* (**"Run, Melos!"** . . .) about a young Greek who proves to a wicked king his loyalty to a friend, and *Onna no Kettō* (**"Duel of Women"** . . .), based on a German story originally translated by Mori Ogai. These works were followed . . . by his long novel in the form of a play, *Shin Hamuretto,* or the new Hamlet. These are the most difficult of Dazai's works for a Western reader to appreciate. Dazai's characteristic skill is evident in the breathless narration of *Kakekomi Uttae,* and the reader welcomes the sunny tale of Melos, after so many cynical accounts of human nature, but I for one find something peculiarly unconvincing in Dazai's handling of foreign themes. He could transform with brilliance the characters in the original *Otogi Zōshi* or in Saikaku's *Tales from the Provinces* (*Shokoku-banashi,* 1685) into lively, modern Japanese, but his foreign characters seem uneasily poised between two worlds, as if Dazai

were unwilling to make them completely Japanese and yet incapable of creating believable non-Japanese. My opinion, I must state, is not shared by most Japanese readers. *Hashire Merosu* is not only frequently acclaimed as one of Dazai's best short stories, but it has been widely adopted for use in school textbooks. But just as a novel written about Japanese people by a non-Japanese novelist would undoubtedly seem false to a Japanese audience, so these new versions of European stories are likely to puzzle a European reader. Perhaps the best is *Kakekomi Uttae,* if only for its vivid narration and powerful ending, and for its indication of one aspect of Dazai's interest in Christianity.

The innumerable references to Christianity in Dazai's works are another source of difficulty for a Western reader. Christianity seems at times to have filled a spiritual vacuum in Dazai's life, and some think that at the end he genuinely considered himself to be a Christian. But the mentions of Christianity are hardly more convincing than an American beatnik's references to Zen. In *The Setting Sun* especially there is such excessive quotation of the Bible that this was the one place where I felt it necessary to abridge in making a translation. The quotations and frequent references to Christianity at no point suggest sincere belief or even the desire to believe. Dazai is intrigued by Christianity, and he is delighted to discover appropriate passages to insert in his books, but whatever degree of faith he may have attained in private life, in his writings Christiantiy is a disconcerting and not very important factor. It failed to give his works the additional depth he sought.

The basic lack of depth in the writers of the time, Dazai among them, may be attributed to the times. *Bannen* was written as the militarists were taking control of Japanese life; the works of Dazai's middle period were all subjected to wartime censorship; and the works of his last period were published amidst the confusion of post-war days. If Dazai had been writing ten years earlier or later his works might, under more favorable conditions, have acquired the broadness of scope they lack. But this is mere conjecture. The reader must be grateful that Dazai was able to grasp the nature of the society in which he lived and to describe it magnificently. (pp. 197-99)

It is true that even Dazai on occasion seems to have followed the tide of militarism during the war. His short story *Jūnigatsu Yōka* (**"December Eighth"** . . .), describing the outbreak of the war, has been cited by some critics to prove that Dazai acquiesced before the trend of the times, but the same story has also been included in collections of "resistance literature." Whichever view is correct, the lighthearted, objective tone of the story distinguishes it from the mass of works composed under the emotional impact of the declaration of war. A few of Dazai's wartime stories were banned in entirety by the government and could be printed only after the end of the war, but his chief works of the wartime period—[*Udaijin Sanetomo* (**"The Minister of the Right Sanetomo"**), *Shokoku-banashi* (**"Tales of the Provinces"**), *Tsugaru,* and *Otogi Zōshi*] . . .— appeared like shining stars over the sunken horizon of literature. As the titles of the works indicate, Dazai, in common with most other writers during the war, avoided insofar as possible treating contemporary subjects in his fiction.

The life of the thirteenth-century ruler and poet Sanetomo was a particularly popular subject during the war. Probably this was because Sanetomo's dual career suggested the proper path for all writers in war-time Japan. Dazai was provided in *Udaijin Sanetomo* with the opportunity to relate in a highly moving fashion his conceptions of aristocratic truth; he appears to have found in Sanetomo the embodiment of all he most respected in human beings.

Shokoku-banashi is a collection of short stories derived from Saikaku's work. Nothing is harder in Japanese than successfully rewriting in the modern language a work of the classical tongue, but Dazai, thanks to his fluent style, was triumphant. *Tsugaru* tells in curiously moving terms of Dazai's journey during the war to his birthplace in northern Japan, a work of non-fiction which contains some of his finest pages.

Otogi Zōshi, mentioned above, is one of the masterpieces of Dazai's art. These tales, originally related to his daughter during the fierce wartime bombings of Tokyo, form a central part of Dazai's literary patrimony. (pp. 199-200)

The immediate postwar days were chronicled by Dazai in many short stories including the wryly humorous **"A Visitor"** [or **"The Courtesy Call"**] (*Shinyū Kōkan, . . .*) with its savage portrait of a boorish acquaintance in the country. The atmosphere of Tokyo at the time is best suggested by **"Villon's Wife,"** though *The Setting Sun* seemed to its first readers the literary embodiment of the changing society. (pp. 200-01)

No Longer Human is set in the Japan of the 1930's, and conveys fairly accurately the general mood of the times, but Dazai was not especially interested in creating a period piece. It was the one book he had to write, his final attempt to elucidate himself and his unhappiness. (p. 201)

It is inevitable that people who experience less trouble than Dazai in accommodating themselves to the world and its ways should feel impatience or even active dislike for his writings. The note of self-pity which is sounded often, though generally with ironic overtones, offends those who either have never been afflicted by Dazai's doubts or else have overcome them. But it is meaningless to reproach Dazai for having revealed himself so brutally. He *had* to write *No Longer Human* in order to purge himself for once and for all of the devils which had long beset him. The book is not literally true, as we have seen, but it is sometimes embarrassingly close to what we suppose is the truth about Dazai. The language is occasionally exaggerated, and we may be revolted when Yōzō admits that he cannot even recall the name of the woman with whom he attempted to commit suicide. Such a self-centered attitude is so repelling that we may decide that Yōzō's problem was simply that he never loved anyone more than himself. The surprising statement at the end of the book, "It was his father's fault," seems to suggest that if Yōzō's father had been more understanding the boy would never have grown up to be such a failure. But the novel itself offers little evidence to support this belief. Yōzō was disqualified as a human being because, unlike his brothers, he was sensitive to insincerity, to the conflicting motives of others, to the insipidity of the world. This awareness made for Yōzō's unhappiness, but it was a virtue and not a vice. The terrible strength of the awareness inevitably drove him to excesses of self-pity and even to cruelty. Yōzō, far from being non-human, carries certain human virtues to such excess that we may agree with the madam of the Kyōbashi bar who tells us at the end, "When human beings get that way, they're no good for anything."

What was Dazai to write after *No Longer Human?* Having at last spewed out the poison which had accumulated within his system from childhood, he could not write still further versions of the same autobiographical data. He would have to start anew. It was possible now even for him to write a book without bitter, sardonic overtones. *Goodbye,* left unfinished at the time of his death in June, 1948, might have developed into a genuinely comic novel. It approaches farce in its account of how the hero ingeniously rids himself of a series of women in his life, and the brilliance of its colloquial dialogue is remarkable even for Dazai. It is impossible to tell, of course, how the novel would have developed. Perhaps Dazai, fearing that he could not complete *Goodbye* or any other book, now that *No Longer Human* was written, was driven closer to suicide, but *Goodbye* seems to me rather the work of a man who has made a fresh start. I should prefer to believe the theory that his suicide was not premeditated. Probably we shall never know, but the last tantalizing fragment of Dazai's writing indicates that a new writer was emerging. (pp. 202-03)

[It] seems safe to assume that Dazai's writings will remain as powerful evidence not only of the author's artistic excellence but of the Japanese acquisition of a modern literary sensibility. (p. 203)

> *Donald Keene, "Three Modern Novelists: Dazai Osamu" (originally published as "Dazai Osamu," in* Chūōkōron, *1964), in his* Landscapes and Portraits: Appreciations of Japanese Culture *(copyright, 1971, by Kodansha International Ltd.), Kodansha, 1971, pp. 186-203.*

MASAO MIYOSHI (essay date 1974)

[*Miyoshi considers one of the central characteristics of Dazai's stories—their autobiographical content and first-person viewpoint—along with the value and shortcomings of the confessional style of writing, finding that Dazai's narrative versatility saves his work from being "the redundant self-analysis of a seedy self-indulgent individual."*]

Dazai lovers look for the man in his works. . . . There is a monomaniacal "first-person" quality about everything he wrote. No matter what mask he assumed, it is always his own, very personal self who is speaking. He wrote everything furthermore with the expectation that his reader would recognize and enjoy *his* words, *his* thoughts, *his* feelings. For him a novel was a personal record, and its fictionality consisted in its tonal manipulations, the various ways he looked at himself. The seer was Dazai, and the landscape Dazai, and despite the high degree of tonal variation, Dazai always believed he was being absolutely honest. Fiction was the "truth" for him, that is, non-fiction—a paradox that shows itself whenever a Dazai is read. (p. 123)

The earliest collection of his stories . . . was called *The Declining Years (Bannen).* Dazai apparently meant by the title that his end was already present at the beginning, which is true: the book's most conspicuous features precisely forecast those of his later works. First, there is the absence of a coherent unity. Even as short stories, the items in the volume are fragmentary. There are a few meant to be collections in turn of shorter units, these having, however, no evident common denominator among them. For instance, the very first item, called **"Leaves"** (*Ha)*, is no more than a few dozen aphorisms and paragraphs which at times string out to something of a story. Second, the "first-person" quality of Dazai's work is fully present in his first book. I do not necessarily mean here the use of the pronoun "I" specifically, although it is indeed prominent. Rather, the first person is implicit even in stories employing dramatic personae. [In a footnote, the critic explains: "Autobiographical" is the word I am deliberately avoiding here. *David Copperfield, The Mill on the Floss, Sons and*

Lovers, and *A Portrait of the Artist* are all usually called "autobiographical," but the difference is that in these books the authors have managed to provide their surrogate characters with emotions and thoughts to some extent independent of the authors' own by taking a more or less clearly discernible stance vis-à-vis the characters. The fact that "events" in their works often derive from their own experience is, finally, not very important when considered in the context of the works themselves. Dazai's "first person" is in a sense *meta*-autobiographical: the "I" is insufficiently filled out to constitute a truly independent character in the book, and thus so much is left to the reader's assumed knowledge of the writer himself. This is true even of a work written and read during his relative obscurity. Although many Japanese writers and critics tend to identify this type of first-person work or I-novel *(shi-shōsetsu)* with the post-Renaissance individualism of the West, the two traditions are really quite different.] **"The Monkey-Masked Clown"** *(Sarumen Kanja),* for one, maintains an ostensible third-person framework, insisting on the presence of a would-be writer distinct from Dazai Osamu. But the mask is admittedly transparent. In the first paragraph, "this man" is said to have a "habit of thinking of himself as a 'he'"—as though the "he-ness" had no "reality." Dazai soon seems uneasy with even this thinnest of masks, and before long he abandons it by turning the story of "this man" into a series of letters which are not only first person, but no longer pretend to be "in character." The requisites for a complex narrative manipulation are all there. With Dazai, however, his apparent preference for vocal complexity derives less from his overall artistic plan than from his serious unease in the discipline of maintaining an even fictional distance from his work.

Concomitant with this is the author's preoccupation with the "truth" of his life which is boldly evident in **"Recollections"** *(Omoide)* describing the childhood of an "I" identical with Dazai. But the almost compulsive confessionalism is prominent even in supposedly fictional pieces like **"The Paper Crane"** *(Kami no Tsuru),* which describes the "I's" extortion from his wife of a confession about her premarital experiences, and his reaction to the revelation. The whole story enclosed in quotation marks, **"The Paper Crane"** is to be taken as a letter addressed to a "you" who is a fellow writer. More concerned with the speaker's own reaction than with either the wife's act of confession or her premarital life itself, the story quickly becomes the speaker's confession, and it is *his* urge to confess and show himself that energizes the work. Clearly, the confessor's presence is vital, but the story also maintains the structure of a double listener: the "I" who receives his wife's "truth" and the "you" (or reader) to whom his own confession is addressed. The final effect of the story thus very much depends on the reader's willingness to accept the intimate role of "you" who is a kind of father-confessor for the speaker. If he is inclined to feel friendly toward the "I," he will like the story; if not, he will be bored by it.

Dazai's movement in **"The Paper Crane"** from the relatively simple form of a confession to that of a confession about a confession is part of the larger pattern of involution in his writing. The "I" in **"The Paper Crane"** is a writer who writes about himself as a writer. He also writes to a writer. Such an imaginative realm is bound to be self-enclosed. Where unable to penetrate the boundary of the self even a little, Dazai's imagination must forever turn back on itself. His self-consciousness is a series of Chinese boxes, endlessly reduplicating themselves. His work talks about his work, which talks about his work, which . . . Formally, we can see how this is related

both to confessionalism and to the tendency toward division and subdivision in his work. The involutionary substance of his work is also inseparable from his habit of authorial intrusion. Dazai is not interested in sustaining a certain level of fictionality in his work, which would mean wrenching himself away from the self and constructing a separate world. That would be a lie. Fiction is a lie, and he must be honest at all costs. So he breaks in at points with a new intimate revelation, disrupting whatever fictional order exists. He is a cannibal, his compulsion to nullify the distance from his work—and from his reader—amounting to eating them up and eating himself up. Fiction is after all a trivial matter, while his hold on himself is of vital importance to him. But if his self-digestion must stop somewhere, it should be at the innermost core of the self, where there is possibly some resistive substance that will stand revealed in art, in spite of art.

If Dazai's art were no more than a cloak of rags to be torn away to disclose the truth, his work would prove quite tedious at the end, being merely the redundant self-analysis of a seedy self-indulgent individual. Such, fortunately, is not the case. Unlike the run of the mill "I-novelists," Dazai is remarkably versatile in varying his tones. The subject may be the self-same "I," but he is looked at variously from a wide range of angles including a self-ironic braggadocio, a sly mischievousness, and an immovable depression. . . . Thus we are invited to join the author on bright days and dark nights along the wayward progress of the work. And since the characters in his work, being essentially inseparable from the author himself, grow up and age along with the author, over the years we get to know him as though he were an old friend whose whole past is continually open before us. Rather than being confined to any specific work, Dazai's art transpires over the long period of time and the numerous works shared by author and reader. (pp. 125-28)

The diary form comes to Dazai almost effortlessly. **"Human Lost,"** written in November 1936, covers the "I's" life in October and November of that year, referring at one point to his stay at a mental hospital very much like the one Dazai himself retired to at this time for treatment of his drug dependency, and, at another, to his relationship with his wife, identical to Dazai's and Hatsuyo's. As with all diaries, this one begins and ends with the start and finish of the duration of time covered, and there is little organizing impulse arising out of the work itself. Its "fictionality" depends almost entirely on the degree of one's ignorance about the author: a reader who knows nothing about the author's life might be impressed by the "inventiveness" of the situation and the "imaginative" arrangement of the characters, and respond positively to its various verbal and stylistic features such as the recurring waves of pathos, the *haiku*-like disjunction, the rhythm of involvement and detachment, and indeed the aura of confidentiality inherent in the form itself. Of course the better-informed reader will tend to consider first the generic aspect of the diary form and make some comparisons between the real or imagined private "truth" of the author and the public "fiction" of his work. Such a reader will be prepared to admire—or not—the author's insight into a situation in which he, the author, was in fact involved. A human being's life experience and his response to it are what constitute the work, not some severed self-enclosed imaginary experience. Among Dazai's diary-form works, even the more fictional ones like *Justice and Smile (Seigi to Bishō)* arouse similar reactions, depending on the reader's information.

The letter form occasionally poses similar problems, when as in *Pandora's Box (Pandora no Hako)* at least some of the letters composing the work are slightly altered versions of the author's actual correspondence. When these personal letters are addressed to the generic "you," as they often are, the reader's role as confessor is quite explicitly set. Of course, there are letter stories with distinct personae for both writer and addressee, and in these works Dazai can be quite successful in striking a balance between truth and fiction. After all, the epistolary form permits the author to invest his thought and feeling in the letter-writer, while enabling him to stand at the critical distance implied by the identified addressee. **"The Sound of the Hammer,"** for instance, describes the writer's recurrent hearing of a hammer striking, which inexplicably drums down whatever energy and interest he might feel at crucial moments of his life. All the defeated man's gloom and despair is gathered into the dry, hollow sound of the hammer, while Dazai's self-ironic awareness is expressed in the comment on the letter attached at the end.

For this reason, too, the dramatic monologue is Dazai's most natural métier. While it allows him to commit his ideas and emotions to the assumed persona, it also leaves room for critical irony. Unlike Browning, Dazai always treats his speaker gently, never stooping to undercut him with too poisonous an irony (as can be found in "My Last Duchess" or "The Bishop Orders His Tomb"). Humor and mischievousness best fit a sensibility like Dazai's; he can straddle the fence, lampooning and pleading at the same time. **"Villon's Wife"** *(Viron no Tsuma),* for instance, is a woman's apology for her abusive writer-husband. By creating a speaker who is a sympathetic victim of his surrogate, Dazai can simultaneously plead for understanding from his reader and project a fair degree of ironic judgment on the whole matter. Thus by balancing his distress and his critical intelligence, he can go as far out of the self as he ever can for an outside view.

To be sure, Dazai's works are not all "first person." There are some that try to be "third person." Among the most conspicuous are his renderings of old well-known works. Dazai's fictional imagination, seldom sustained enough to fabricate a whole tale, requires some ready-made lifelike material if his own life is not to be used. So he reinterprets and reevaluates *Hamlet,* the life of a samurai hero, an obscure German play (translated by Mori Ōgai), various pieces from folklore and fairy tales. But even here, the plays and tales he whimsically remodels are fascinating—we see *his* imprint everywhere—while the works he took seriously, like *The New Hamlet (Shin Hamuretto)* and *Lord Sanetomo (Udaijin Sanetomo),* are almost unreadable. The reason is obvious: works having their own existence forced an examination on their own terms before they would submit to a rewriting. Clearly Dazai was a thoroughly first-person writer.

Dazai's first-person techniques are best utilized in three of his last and best works, **"Villon's Wife,"** *The Setting Sun,* and *No Longer Human (Ningen Shikkaku),* which are the climax, and the conclusion, of his writing career. Since Dazai himself, as I read the modern Japanese novel, constitutes both climax and conclusion of the I-novel tradition, a closer examination of the best known of these novels is in order.

The Setting Sun (Shayō) was completed in June 1947 and serialized in a monthly magazine from July to October of that year. Dazai thus had no numerous deadlines to fight, and this novel is consequently somewhat more of a piece than his other long works. But fragmentation, of course, is the inescapable

shape of his vision, and this work, too, inevitably breaks up into diaries, letters, and confessions, with all that such first-person forms imply. (pp. 129-31)

The characters and many episodes of *The Setting Sun* undoubtedly have their sources in Dazai's personal life. The two writers, the aspirant Naoji and the fast deteriorating Uehara, are impersonations of Dazai himself. The central event, Uehara's fathering a baby for Kazuko, is of course Dazai's experience. Dazai's family, if not precisely "aristocratic," was old enough and once rich enough to make many people attribute that status to it. Narcotics usage played a considerable role in the author's life, and the depression permeating the novel closely resembles Dazai's. To the extent that Kazuko makes excuses for both Naoji and Uehara (as Villon's wife does for her husband), the novel becomes Dazai's self-apology. Thus, what we have here in *The Setting Sun* is the *Shi-Shōsetsu* par excellence—in its imaginative energy, as well as the events, characters, setting, and tonality.

The one element of the novel which does not entirely succumb to the prevailing death-wish is the heroine Kazuko herself. But even at that, she is scarcely brought to life in the novel, being little more than a half-hearted rekindling of the author's by then almost smothered life-force. Indeed, her quasi-immaculate conception, like so many Biblical references in Dazai, sits there rather isolated, without significant integration with the rest of the work. And there are other elements of the novel deriving from extra-personal sources that also fail to cohere with the rest. One is the running reference to *The Cherry Orchard.* Thematically, Chekhov's play of course treats the decline of the aristocracy, but beyond this thin resemblance, there is no reasonable basis of comparison between the play and the novel. Another is the snake imagery that appears at the death of both parents. Regardless of the reptiles' possible psychogenetic origin, they are not adequately shaped into a significant artistic role in the book. For instance, there is Kazuko's disposal of the snake eggs, a snake's appearance at her father's deathbed, the snakes' "mourning" in the garden at his death, the "delicate, graceful" mother snake's search for her lost eggs, and then the by-then expected appearance of a snake at the mother's deathbed—all these episodes seem to carry some elaborate symbolic significance, but they fall far short of making it clear and become merely props for the scenery of impending death.

If there is one "idea" dominating the novel, it is Dazai's notion of "aristocracy." (pp. 132-33)

[There] is a confusion inherent in the notion of "aristocracy" in *The Setting Sun* which I see as inseparable from Dazai's childlike uncertainty about the whole social milieu and how to relate to it. He defied authorities all his life, but he was also invariably in awe of them. There are many stories about his hankering for acceptance, of which his desperate wish for the Akutagawa prize, a kind of Japanese Pulitzer prize, is only one example. And he was never able to resolve conflicting impulses in relating to others. He fared better with those socially beneath him, but even then he was no Whitmanesque prophet of the streets. Only with his youthful admirers does he seem to have felt truly at ease.

In a vertical society, a person with no developed sense of his own place, one who cannot "size up" at once his relative position of superiority or inferiority with anyone he comes into contact with, is lost. He will not even be able to conduct a comfortable conversation with anyone except a close friend. If he happens to be a writer, the results might very well be disastrous. For the novel, unlike poetry, must define a character within an actual society; the writer must locate his sympathy or hostility on the social map so that he may set out the novel's scenes, shape its plot, and populate its world. And this is exactly what Dazai was unable to do. Those early radical activities of his notwithstanding, he soon became wholly indifferent to political problems; despite his frequent references to Marxism and the Revolution, his social and political understanding did not go beyond the level of the average high-school student. True, Dazai was an uncomfortable person, and he felt vague sentiments for social justice. But he possessed neither an analytic mind nor adequate knowledge of his society to do anything about it. *The Setting Sun* is not only vague in its notion of aristocracy; it also lacks sufficient scale and the sort of developed attitude toward its society that would provide a powerful and comprehensive vision of postwar Japan.

And yet we recall that the book was wildly popular around 1950, contributing the word *shayō-zoku* (the people of the setting sun) to the nation's vocabulary. Besides, Dazai accomplished something no other writer could do in recent Japan— he brought colloquialism back to the written language.

In the multiple-leveled Japanese language, Dazai's awkwardness in finding the correct social position for himself in the pyramid parallels his inability to find the correct level of reverence in speech. . . . Use of a formal and correct Japanese employing subtle gradations of hierarchy would place him as a member of the fold, which he is not; a rough and slangy Japanese overriding precise gradations would make him a churlish schoolboy, which he also is not—besides, even the most vulgar speech is never free from implied caste. Thus, as in social intercourse, Dazai is always slightly bewildered, slightly fidgety where Japanese is concerned. And this speech embarrassment, part and parcel of his social awkwardness, is powerfully operative in the making of his style. For instance, no one is more sensitive than Dazai to the possibility that any mode of speech may turn absurd. Whenever his writing turns a bit too ponderous, or affected, or cumbersome, or rigid, or just too formal, he shifts into reverse and writes with humor, or a meticulously measured colloquialism, or vulgarisms, or babyish onomatopoeia, or a sprinkling of learned diction and foreign words, here and there a grotesque word, an archaism or two, or he omits a pronoun or a postposition, or he staccatos a passage with overpunctuation. Occasionally, especially in the aphoristic diary pieces, he can somehow manage to stay neutral, but even there his remarkable awareness of the ever-possible absurdity keeps his style clear of the turgid and the affected alike.

Those who know Japanese sense this at once, although I am aware of how hard it is to convey the sense of it to those who don't know the language. What Edward Seidensticker meant when he called Dazai a "poet" is at least partly this quality, I believe. And I regret that discussion of the precise dynamics of one language is extremely difficult to conduct in another. The translations of the works are of little help sometimes in getting across this "poetic" quality. Donald Keene's version of *The Setting Sun,* for example, though generally excellent, fails at times to transmit the nuances of the rude and the polite in Dazai's writing that makes his style dance with such rare grace. I can only point to the drunken chant at Uehara's party, "Guillotine, Guillotine, shooshooshoo" . . . , or the old mother's use of the word *oshikko* (wee-wee) as bringing in just the right touch of absurdity to the respective passages which, by a sort of juxtaposition and reversal, set in motion waves of rich connotation. Probably Dazai's most notable stylistic accomplishment lies in his creation of that pervasive feeling of shyness and embarrassment in his work, reflecting the overwhelming absurdity he so purely perceived all around him. The gap between the spoken and the written language is still a very serious problem for the Japanese writer, and Dazai managed to show at least one direction for a possible coming together of the two. (pp. 136-39)

Masao Miyoshi, "Till Death Do Us Part," in his Accomplices of Silence: The Modern Japanese Novel *(copyright © 1974 by The Regents of the University of California; reprinted by permission of the University of California Press), University of California Press, 1974, pp. 122-40.*

JAMES O'BRIEN (essay date 1975)

[*In his* Dazai Osamu, *from which the following excerpt was taken, O'Brien offers the most comprehensive study in English of the author's life and work.*]

Dazai's skill as a creative writer manifests itself principally in his style; his talents for organizing plot or creating a fictional world are relatively meager. To study Dazai means to study the way in which he uses language to tell and retell the story of his own life.

But Dazai is not merely a skillful autobiographer. He takes himself as his principal subject, yet composes a series of works far more diverse and varied than a conventional autobiography. He sees himself in many ways and in many guises. That he can even see himself in a monkey or a badger will suggest the distance between his kind of writing and autobiography. (p. viii)

Dazai Osamu does not fit easily into the history of modern Japanese literature. Certain literary currents, the I-novel, for example, must be brought into any discussion of Dazai's place in modern Japanese fiction; but almost any subject other than Dazai—be it a school, a doctrine, a style, or whatever—can only be used as a contrast, that is to say, as a definition of what Dazai is not. . . . Dazai, as a Japanese literary phenomenon, is truly sui generis. Possibly no writer even in world literature has pursued his self-image in such various ways as Dazai. (pp. 14-15)

In **"Landlord for a Generation"** Dazai wrote for the first time an extended story told in full from the first-person point of view. Curiously, the character he created as his initial first-person narrator appears to a considerable extent beyond the favor and sympathy of the author. (p. 28)

Dazai's use of first-person narration raises several questions. Admittedly the landlord shows himself a "reliable narrator" in Wayne Booth's sense of the term [in *The Rhetoric of Fiction*]. (p. 29)

The question naturally arises: to whom is he addressing himself? The text of his account contains few clues. Since the landlord is at first concerned with rectifiying distorted accounts circulated by rumor and the newspapers, it would seem that he intends his account for the public at large, or perhaps for the educated public.

I suspect, however, that Dazai, at this state of his development, was not concerned with such technical matters as the implied audience of his first-person narrations. It would be difficult even to argue that he is concerned with the quality of mind inherent in the manner in which the landlord spins his tale.

The manner in which Dazai chanced to unfold "**Landlord for a Generation**" opened the way for interesting literary effects. The landlord is recalling the past, and describing that past to an unspecified audience, in order to justify his own position and behavior. Reviewing the past, he tends to dramatize his own role and relive the emotions he once felt. Yet Dazai seems far more interested in providing the reader with the comedy of the landlord figure than in probing the psychological truth of a character caught in such a peculiar situation. (p. 30)

In his next lengthy story, **Student Comrades,** Dazai again took up the theme of rebellion. The rebellion in **Student Comrades** is based in the main on an episode that occurred at the Hirosaki Higher School while Dazai was a student there. When the principal was accused of embezzling from a student fund, a large part of the student body clamored for a strike; another group of students counseled moderation, while the faculty found itself, as usual, caught between the conflicting demands of conservative administrators and radical, voluble students. In an attempt to reveal various aspects of the disturbance, Dazai found himself dealing with a larger group of characters and a more complex set of personal relationships than in any earlier work. With the rebellion and movements of student factions in the forefront, there is little room in **Student Comrades** for scenes of private brooding. (p. 33)

Presumably Dazai was open to the influence of various writing styles during [his] period of apprenticeship. Although Japanese critics and scholars are not agreed on specific influences, it seems that apparently detectable influences are really just temporarily "borrowed styles," which, being in some way unsuitable, did not become a permanent part of Dazai's style, already basically formed as humorous self-caricature. However, this is to jump to a conclusion. A reader going through Dazai's works chronologically will recognize the humor; but at this point he does not know Dazai well enough to realize that such humor is meant as self-caricature. That realization comes only with reading the later, more mature works. (p. 37)

[From] 1933 to 1936, Dazai gave his manuscripts one by one, as the need for money arose, to friends in a position to have them published. Later they were collected and published as **Final Years,** a title reflecting Dazai's intention at the time of writing to take his life. (p. 40)

[Among the stories in **Final Years**], "**Leaves,**" the earliest work by Dazai available in English translation, is a montage of comment, anecdote, and incident. Certain sections, notably the description of the lascivious grandmother of "**Landlord for a Generation,**" quote passages from earlier published works; other parts are purportedly taken from the stories Dazai abandoned.

Although he retouched certain passages quoted from earlier works, Dazai did not attempt, in the manner of Raymond Queneau, to create different versions of the same incident. Indeed, "**Leaves**" is the sort of work that tempts one to agree with Edward Seidensticker's complaint about Dazai's morbid preoccupation with what he had already written. (p. 41)

Dazai . . . began writing "**Remembrances**" as a testament to his own life. Reading the work, one can readily discern the pessimism incessantly turning the author's thoughts toward suicide; at the same time one can also detect the creative energy that impelled Dazai to go on composing, after he finished "**Remembrances,**" the remaining works in **Final Years.**

"**Remembrances**" displays the swift turns of event and quick surprises evident in the earlier works. At the same time it reveals an author more attentive than before to problems of organization and transition. Composed of two contrasting parts, the memoir treats first Dazai's infancy and childhood and then his adolescence. The author's entry into middle school at the age of fourteen divides the two periods chronologically. In thematic terms, infancy and childhood are characterized by affection and contentment while adolescence is a time of trouble and anxious searching for friendship. (p. 42)

The first of several Dazai stories concerning monkeys, . . . ["**Monkey Island**"] is narrated in the first person by a monkey newly arrived on an unidentified island. The tale is brief, well-knit, and extremely provocative. In the monkey Dazai hit upon a perfect vehicle for rendering his ironic view of reality. (p. 47)

In "**Monkey Island**" Dazai constructed a narrative more integrated than most of his other early works, but he stopped short of writing a full allegory. Within a loosely allegorical frame the actors of "**Monkey Island**" assume varying symbolic values. Once the story ends these actors are free to continue a half life within the mind of a reader confronting the final puzzle of "**Monkey Island.**"

Is the island simply a thinly disguised version of modern society, whose members enjoy a degree of security and comfort but only enough freedom to make playful gestures and sounds? . . . Finally, if one finds such conditions of society unendurable and elects to escape, where does flight take him? Further, are questions of this type too conventional an approach to a writer like Dazai? Perhaps, as he claimed in "**Remembrances,**" you escape by writing. The only response to society is to compose a beguiling tale like "**Monkey Island.**"

Part of the satisfaction in reading "**Monkey Island**" comes from seeing one's suspicions confirmed. But the finest pleasures of the tale are less tangible. The reader's curiosity is aroused on a number of points and then left unsatisfied. But Dazai works this effect in a manner that leaves the reader to muse instead of feeling cheated. On the simplest level, the question of whether the island represents Japan or England remains moot. The two monkeys seem to have been raised in Japan and to have come across the sea to another island. Their escape at the end of the story from a London zoo would answer the question of the identity of this second island for a literal-minded reader. Yet, the other monkeys on the island are described in ways which conceivably suggest Japanese behavior. And the narrator monkey once remarks that one of the trees growing on the island seems very like an oak common to the Kiso region of central Japan. (pp. 48-9)

The Flower of Buffoonery . . . was initially intended to form part of **Final Years.** Based on Dazai's double suicide attempt at Kamakura and the succeeding days spent in recuperation at a nearby hospital, **The Flower of Buffoonery** is intimately connected with the despair that motivated the entire writing project and suggested the title **Final Years.** (p. 55)

The Flower of Buffoonery begins in the following manner:

> "Beyond here, a place of sorrows." My friends all gaze mournfully at me from a distance. Speak to me, friends, laugh at me. They simply turn away. Question me, friends. I'll tell everything. I shoved Sono under the waves with this hand. In demonic pride I wished death for her and survival for myself. Shall I go on? My friends merely gaze mournfully at me.

Oba Yozo sat up in bed and looked out at the sea. The offing was dim in the rain.

Waking from a dream, I read over these lines. I felt like disappearing into shame and loathing. Well, the exaggeration's reached a limit; now, to get on with it, just who is this Oba Yozo?

Even for Dazai, this is an extreme manipulation of the "I." Yozo begins the narration as a first-person observer undergoing a reverie. But, in a moment he is interrupted by the author, who breaks into the narration as a second "I". The opening passage sets a pattern for the whole of *The Flower of Buffoonery*. On the one hand there is Oba Yozo, the protagonist struggling with a crucial personal problem; and, on the other hand, there is Dazai Osamu struggling to tell Yozo's story. Doubtless a biographical-minded critic would regard these two figures as identical.

In a sense Yozo and Dazai are identical. The manner in which Dazai intrudes to comment within the narrative, however, tends on occasion to emphasize his function as author separate from the work. For example, pretending to an exasperation at his inability to properly develop the plot, Dazai calls *The Flower of Buffoonery* "senile" and himself a "third-rate author." In another passage he conceives of his novel becoming a classic, then labels himself crazy for entertaining such a thought. (p. 57)

Dazai feigns an uncertainty as to how to relate his story until the very end. Recall the final line, which follows immediately Yozo's contemplation of the sea below: "Then . . . no . . . that's all there is to it." Dazai, it would appear, is not suggesting that Yozo has transcended his fears. The author, to put it baldly, is unable himself to continue narrating. For he *is* Yozo, not simply in the sense that he is writing an autobiography of past experience but, more significantly, in the sense that he as well as Yozo does not know what step to take next. (p. 58)

[Dazai] conceived of a novel or story in a manner similar to that of the Japanese proletarian writer: a straightforward narrative embodying the relatively definite and unitary views of the author. . . . He began writing a few relatively overt autobiographical pieces, along with anecdotal and fabliaulike tales exemplifying various notions about society. Such works freed Dazai to insert authorial comment and to manipulate the steps of his plot with great boldness.

Already by this period Dazai had developed the knack of *fixing* a character in a scene with a few brief words, rather than rendering character with an accumulation of detail. The reader remembers a few telling details—the behavior of Ryuji's mother on the train for Tokyo or the sudden plunge of the carp in **"Metamorphosis."** As Donald Keene has perceptively written [see excerpt above] "One never has the impression that Dazai has carefully filled notebooks with observations so that he will be able to provide local color when needed. Instead the reader senses that each scene has been distilled through Dazai's poetic imagination into its essential ingredients." For precisely this reason a reader familiar with Dazai can readily accept the patchwork construction of such a work as **"Leaves."**

These sudden perceptions in Dazai's works often seem to relate to the author's life. When Dazai does not compose straight autobiography, he is often writing disguised autobiography. He may be speaking merely of a monkey or a boy; but the reader who goes through his work chronologically senses in a certain gesture or remark that Dazai is present in the boy or the monkey. Once initiated into the Dazai manner, a reader can easily begin to take the works as clever exercises in covert autobiography.

Yet, Dazai is not pinned down so readily. For one thing, he is exceedingly elusive at the game of hide-and-seek. (pp. 58-9)

Clearly, Dazai wants his readers to see *him*. He is neither wearing a mask, in the manner of a Mishima, nor entering into a persona, in the manner of a Yeats or a Pound. He is not much concerned with creating a social self distinct from the person, nor with extending the range of his experience through imagining characters beyond his experience. Dazai's mask is like the Halloween kind; he wears it in fun, to give his friends a momentary thrill. And there is seldom any doubt as to who is actually wearing the mask.

It is tempting, then, to see in Dazai an entrepreneur of comedy. But the presence of such a work as *The Flower of Buffoonery* gives one pause. Dazai sees the pathos and potential self-destruction in the kind of comedy he practiced both in life and in writing. Any full account of his career must, above all, come to grips with the tragicomedy of Dazai Osamu. (p. 59)

In choosing the title **"Das Gemeine,"** Dazai seems to have had in mind more than the meaning of the word itself. The final three syllables would be pronounced "ma-i-ne" in Japanese and thus mark the negative imperative form of the verb in the author's Tsugaru dialect. However, the story does not appear to be predicted on a relation between the terms "vulgar" and "must not."

Indeed, **"Das Gemeine"** bristles with problems for the reader seeking to analyze it. Dazai seems even less bound by literary convention than was usual for him. A character named Sano Jiro is the first-person narrator until nearly the end of the story, when he is struck by a train and killed. Sano confesses to an overwhelming love for a mystery women at the beginning of the story, but his beloved turns out to be a prostitute who is shown to the reader only as she sits at the window of a brothel attracting customers. In addition to specific oddities of this kind, the general plot, consisting of conversations almost unrelated to each other, seems uncommonly bizarre. (p. 70)

In the main, though, **"Das Gemeine"** seems a deliberate attempt by Dazai to create a feeling of disorientation toward life. It is occasionally said that Dazai fashioned a style for **"Das Gemeine"** under the influence of Dadaism and Surrealism which had begun to make their way into Japanese literature in the late 1920's.

Precisely because the story is disjointed, **"Das Gemeine"** presents certain of Dazai's characteristic methods of style in high relief. (p. 71)

> The guy's got a face smooth as an egg—no eyes, no mouth, no eyebrows. At least, what eyebrows are there seem painted on, and the eyes and nose glued on. And the *art* he makes of showing you this nonchalance. Christ! The first time I looked at him, I felt like a tongue of gluten paste was wiping across my face.

Thus does the author allow one of his characters to describe the oddest figure of all in **"Das Gemeine,"** writer Dazai Osamu. (p. 72)

When Japanese critics accuse Dazai of "striking a pose," they seem to be claiming that he deliberately contrived his life to enable himself to write autobiographical pieces consonant with his particular stylistic skills. The idiosyncratic nature of Dazai's life and certain of his works lends credence to this explanation. Yet, if one is tempted to accept such an extreme claim, he ought to probe for the motives that drove Dazai to put his life to such an unconventional use. (p. 74)

"**The Indictment**" [is a] rapid monologue by Judas Iscariot explaining before the high priest his motives for betraying Christ.

In essence, Judas's monologue is a resentful tirade against Christ. Scornful of supernatural claims, Judas regards Christ's references to the Heavenly Kingdom and Son of God as pure nonsense. Drawn to Christ physically, Judas pays homage to the beauty of his lord and vents his strongest resentments against those for whom Christ expresses affection. (p. 77)

One cannot read "**The Indictment**" without realizing on occasion that Judas has a good case against Christ. Judas recalls for the reader of Dazai the protagonist of "**Landlord for a Generation**," a narrator so prejudiced he does not feel the need to doctor the facts as he understands them. Like this earlier narrator, Judas assures his credibility by the contradictory nature of his speech; unlike the landlord, however, Judas does not expose himself as a fool. At first glance, one aspect of the first-person narration of "**The Indictment**" seems unusual for Dazai. Judas indicates, by his repeated use of the word *danna*, or "master," that the high priest is listening to his account. Some might argue, on the basis of this awareness, that Dazai was examining the way in which Judas would try to justify himself in a public forum. Nevertheless, the more plausible argument is that Dazai has not changed one whit from his earlier method of allowing his first-person narrators to blurt out their feelings directly. The rhythms of Judas's speech suggest a man driven to the breaking point, a man desperate to salve his wounded pride by angrily abusing the one who has rejected him. To attribute craft, guile, or even presence of mind to Dazai's Judas seems utterly unwarranted.

Maintaining a steady pace, Dazai published what many Japanese regard as one of his greatest short stories," "**Run Melos**." This judgment is surprising in view of the general tendency in Japan to value the author's more somber works, whose dark mood is relieved only on occasion by flashes of mordant, sarcastic humor. Dazai's best lengthy works in a lighter vein, *A Collection of Fairy Tales* and *A Retelling of the Tales from the Provinces*, are among those least known to the Japanese reading public. "**Run Melos**," though, is possibly the brightest, most optimistic work in the entire Dazai canon.

In "**Run Melos**" Dazai set out to write a tale exemplifying the highest kind of fidelity. Seemingly unable to use his own experience in pursuing such a theme and chronically plagued (so he claimed) by a weak imagination for the creation of plot, Dazai chose as his source a work by Schiller entitled "Die Burgschaft" (The Hostage).

Dazai's version is essentially a retelling of the Schiller work, with certain additions characteristic of Dazai. In Dazai's version the young shepherd Melos, accompanied by a lifelong friend, goes to Syracuse to make some purchases in preparation for the wedding of his younger sister. Informed that the local king is a tyrant, the valiant Melos enters the palace to save the city from this scourge. Apprehended and brought before the king, Melos unabashedly proclaims his rebellion, whereupon the king sentences him to death by crucifixion. Recalling that he must return home for his sister's wedding, Melos offers his

friend as a hostage, promising to return for his punishment in three days.

After the wedding Melos braves such obstacles as a flooding river and a host of mountain bandits while hurrying back to Syracuse to keep his promise. Exhausted, he once falls down by the roadside exclaiming: "Virtue, fidelity, love! When you think about it, they're nonsense. Kill your opponent and protect yourself. Isn't that the way of the world?" Awakened by the sound of running water, he changes his mind: "I gave my word. That's the only consideration. Run, Melos!"

Predictably, he arrives to find his friend hoisted aloft, but still alive. He immediately tells the friend of his momentary loss of faith. Then he asks the friend to strike him hard on both cheeks so he, Melos, can feel free to embrace him before going to his death. After doing as instructed, the friend asks for the same treatment from Melos. The friend, it turns out, had himself momentarily lost faith in Melos's word that he would return to redeem the hostage. The king is so impressed by the friendship and loyalty of Melos and his friend that he not only reprieves Melos but asks both of the friends to take him into their friendship.

Stylistically, "**Run Melos**" is pure Dazai. Probably such passages as the description of Melos frantically running toward Syracuse account in large part for the tale's reputation in Japan: "Pushing aside and leaping over the people on the road, Melos ran like the wind. Cutting across a field he raced directly through a drinking party, upending all guests. Then he kicked aside a dog and leapt into a river, fleeing ten times as fast as the slowly sinking sun."

The student of Dazai also recognizes his author's hand in the additions Dazai makes to Schiller's original tale. In Schiller there is no doubting by either party of his friend's fidelity and hence no confessions of such doubt. Again, Dazai has his Melos preach to his sister that, once a person begins distrusting others, he will soon begin to tell lies. Finally, in an episode which catches the reader by surprise, the king declares that Melos and his friend could never understand the loneliness of a king. It was characteristic of Dazai to have the villain in a story make a direct, moving appeal for sympathy. (pp. 78-80)

Like most of Dazai's adaptations from Western sources, *The New Hamlet* resembles its prototype only on the surface. Inside, as Dazai proudly declared in the preface, much is different, most notably, the "new Hamlet" himself.

One need only read the first act to see why Dazai, with some reason, chose his subject. Without a great deal of juggling, Hamlet and certain of his actions take on a resemblance to Dazai and his experience. Hamlet's very ambiguity, permitting great leeway for specifying certain actions, was a boon to Dazai. There is no need, for instance, to probe the new Hamlet's feelings toward his mother. He is, for Dazai, precisely what Joseph Anderson and Donald Richie [in *The Japanese Film*] have claimed he is for the educated Japanese: "little more than a faithful son avenging his father's death; one who loves his mother not in Olivier's Oedipus-like fashion but merely as every good boy should."

Hamlet is Dazai-like in numerous ways. "Since his infancy," Gertrude declares, "he has been a clever cry-baby." When King Claudius remarks much more concretely than in Shakespeare on Hamlet's height, thinness, and poor facial color, the image is clearly that of Dazai. When Claudius refuses to permit Hamlet to go to Wittenberg for fear he will merely dissipate, one is almost forcibly reminded of Dazai's profligate ways in Tokyo. Again, Hamlet's ancestry is mediocre—inferior perhaps to what Dazai imagined his own to be. (pp. 82-3)

Dazai's attitude toward Hamlet, like his attitude toward himself, is deliberately ironical. Other characters give free rein to their criticisms of Hamlet. To Claudius he is inflexible and hypocritical. To Gertrude he is foppish, reckless, tied to the past, and—of course—a cry-baby. Laertes and Polonius accuse him of affectation, and even Ophelia, pregnant with Hamlet's child, delivers a long tirade at one point summing up just about all these criticisms. (p. 83)

[Hamlet] simply tries to outdo the criticisms others direct at him: "I suppose I'm an indulgent drunkard. A disgusting, affected creature. I don't mind. If that's the way things are, it can't be helped." These very remarks, though, set the stage for a series of self-compliments—although backhanded ones— a few lines later in the same speech: "I know my own shortcomings and vices, know them with almost unbearable clarity. I'm no sophist, nor am I a social climber. I'm simply a realist. I'm aware of everything—just as it is."

Readers with some experience of Japanese fiction, classical as well as modern, realize they are expected to accept the self-valuation of main characters much more readily than in reading Western fiction. Dazai wants his readers to accept the "new Hamlet" at face value rather than to ask what sort of neurosis prompts him to make such a declaration. (pp. 83-4)

In the end the "new Hamlet" is more a buffoon than a tragic hero. Claudius has admitted that he planned to kill Hamlet's father, but claims the latter died before he could accomplish his purpose. Hamlet pulls out his sword, readies himself to avenge his father on Claudius, then slashes himself superficially across the cheek. Thereupon Horatio reports that Gertrude has committed suicide. The play ends with Hamlet and Claudius in an unseemly spat over which one of them has suffered more. (p. 84)

The range of Dazai's experimentation [during the second half of the 1930s] reveals itself in the vastly different works of this period. Some, like **"Das Gemeine"** and **"Human Lost,"** seem eccentric and pointless; others, like . . . **"One Hundred Views of Mount Fuji"** and **"Run Melos,"** are optimistic and light; finally, works like **"The Indictment"** contain a message of desperation expressed with great clarity and craft. (p. 85)

[In] these works Dazai turned from his own experience to well-known books for his basic story situation or even for the details of his plot. And, with this dependence on other sources, Dazai's outlook took on a moral tone more definite than that in any earlier works. Despite the ironies and ambiguities, these works readily yield fairly definite notions on such matters as money, friendship, and honesty in speech. Although I would not wish to push the correlation too far, it is almost as if Dazai, relieved of the bother of working out the basic plot structure, found the freedom to insert certain of his own moral ideas. The temptation to see Dazai's evolution in these terms becomes stronger during the next period of his career, the years of World War II. Dazai's important works during those years derive their plots even more closely than **"Run Melos"** or *The New Hamlet* from other literary works. And Dazai's major genre of writing during these war years might properly be called the "moral fable." (pp. 86-7)

A study of Japanese sources on Dazai's life yields little detailed information on the author's activities during these war years.

No doubt the limitations on Japanese life imposed by the government and by the necessities of the war itself prevented Dazai from fully indulging himself in his habitual activities. And lacking recent experience in attempted suicide and drug addiction, he wrote nothing significant on his own initiative in his customary "autobiographical" manner. The critic of Dazai is strongly tempted to see in this negative evidence for the proposition that the autobiographical subject most appealing to Dazai was himself in extreme difficulty.

Unable perhaps to make himself such an interesting subject during the war, Dazai turned by and large for his writing inspiration to [such sources as Ihara Saikaku's *Tales From the Provinces, The Eternal Storehouse of Japan,* and *Tales of Warriors and Duty* and the thirteenth-century collection *Tales from Uji*]. Though he used such sources, Dazai remained himself; the style of the work is one in which only Dazai could have written. In examining these works, the student of Dazai constantly discovers expressions and gestures characteristic of the author.

The works of this period [*A Retelling of Tales from the Provinces; Sanetomo, Minister of the Right; Tsugaru;* and *A Collection of Fairy Tales*] differ from the early, more autobiographical pieces in their relatively more precise moral commentary. Given, for example, a samurai from Saikaku or a badger and a hare from a Japanese fairy tale, Dazai's sense of irony usually went to work trying to find the real (as opposed to the traditional) moral quality of these actors. The reader senses even in the animal legends the same quality of ironic distance between author and character as he found between the author and his Dazai-like protagonists in the early works. (p. 118)

Dazai's return to autobiographical modes of writing in the postwar years reflects to some extent the fact that he was once again leading a frenzied existence. Perhaps he deliberately chose such a life—as a protest against the times or as a way of reviving the urge to turn his life into literature. . . . Regardless of the reasons for his dissipation, the fact that he chose to make use of his postwar life in his writing supports the contention that Dazai found in the unsavory aspects of his character his best subject for autobiographical writing.

The final autobiographical works show, in some ways, a complexity well beyond that of the earlier works. Even with such a relatively subtle work as *The Flower of Buffoonery* the reader contends with just one Dazai Osamu (in a thinly fictional guise). And, reading a series of autobiographical works from the early periods, he sees through just a single character in each work the developing image of Dazai.

The postwar works add significant complications to the role of this autobiographical figure. There are more kinds of first-person narrators, both men and women of various ages. In addition, particularly in *The Setting Sun,* Dazai appears to be "dividing" himself among a number of characters, allowing each of them to represent limited aspects of himself. The drama worked out in the novel might then be taken as representative of conflicts within Dazai's own self.

Many of the similarities and differences between the Dazai of the postwar years and the Dazai of *A Retelling of the Tales from the Provinces* and *A Collection of Fairy Tales* will be apparent to the reader. One of the most intriguing similarities is the author's refusal to permit his own ego to dominate the bulk of his works in these two periods. In retelling both the animal and human tales from earlier Japanese sources, Dazai must have examined the action through the eyes of the participating characters in order to determine his own attitude toward the characters and the manner in which he would unveil this attitude in the details of his retelling.

A reader of the postwar novels and stories suspects a similar method. Dazai confronted the need to work out more of the plot in his postwar works than in *A Retelling of the Tales from the Provinces* or *A Collection of Fairy Tales;* yet he seems to have examined with care the diverse ways in which different characters would view and react to a given set of facts and circumstances. The results of this process are quite striking. While the typical prewar "fiction" usually portrays a single character as he sees himself, the postwar fiction transcends this fixed viewpoint to describe several individuals of a social group diversely viewing one another. A reader of the postwar stories learns, for example, the viewpoint both of a husband like Dazai and of a woman married to the likes of him; the reader of *No Longer Human* must come to terms with two conceptions of Yozo, the negative figure of the notebooks and the "angel" envisioned by the madame of the Kyobashi bar. (pp. 148-49)

Japanese readers—and to a lesser extent critics also—tend to identify the author with his life and works of the three postwar years before his death. This is an understandable tendency. Critics who regard *No Longer Human* and *The Setting Sun* as Dazai's best novels naturally emphasize the last years of Dazai's career. Readers familiar with Dazai's degenerate life following the war find in him a perfect expression of the bewilderment and nihilism often said to characterize the times.

Dazai's reputation since the time of his death has dimmed to some extent. With his life a part of history, he is safe from the sort of attack Kawabata Yasunari once made in arguing against a literary prize for Dazai on the basis of the author's immorality. At the same time, Dazai's works do not have the emotional hold on certain kinds of people they once had, and some critics such as Eto Jun have come forward to declare him a second-rate writer.

Regardless of his fortunes on the critical market, Dazai continues to be read with enthusiasm. (p. 150)

> *James O'Brien, in his* Dazai Osamu *(copyright © 1975 by Twayne Publishers; reprinted with the permission of Twayne Publishers, a Division of G. K. Hall & Co., Boston), Twayne, 1975, 179 p.*

MAKOTO UEDA   (essay date 1976)

[*Ueda examines in detail Dazai's concern with human weakness throughout his fiction, noting the characteristic sympathy and understanding with which Dazai portrayed those whom others would consider evil or monstrous.*]

Of all Dazai's works, the one that most directly reveals his ideas on the art of writing is a relatively unknown novel called *A Women's Duel.* It is based on a short story of the same name, "Ein Frauenzweikampf" by Herbert Eulenberg (1876-1949). Dazai read this German work in Japanese translation, and was so dissatisfied with it that he was moved to rewrite it in his own way. By examining why he was dissatisfied and how he went about rewriting it, we can learn much about Dazai's attitude toward literary realism, as well as toward the relationship between art and objective external reality.

"Ein Frauenzweikampf" is a story only a few pages long. Its main character is a Russian woman named Constance, who has just discovered her husband's infidelity. She wants to dissolve the love triangle by a duel between herself and her husband's young mistress, a medical student. They duel in a field at the edge of town, and Constance, who has never handled a revolver before, somehow manages to shoot her opponent to death. Immediately, she gives herself up to the authorities and enters a jail, where, before anyone notices, she starves herself to death. In a letter left behind she testifies that she is killing herself as a martyr of love; she lost all purpose in living, she says, when she discovered that her victory at the duel saved her honor, but not her love.

Why was Dazai dissatisfied with the story? Because, he said, the author was too realistic in describing the incidents. . . . Dazai compares Eulenberg to a camera; in his judgment, Eulenberg's story is just a police photograph of the scene of a crime. From all this he concludes that "when a story describes a scene with outrageous frankness, the reader, though impressed, will come to hold serious misgivings." (pp. 145-46)

If a novelist should not portray reality as it is, how should he portray it? Dazai's answer is revealed in the way in which he rewrote Eulenberg's story. The greatest difference between Eulenberg's original and Dazai's adaptation is that the latter tells us far more about what is going on in the minds of the story's three main characters. The German writer says almost nothing about the medical student's feelings when she received Constance's challenge to a duel. Dazai, on the other hand, delves deep into her mind and makes clear the psychic process through which she reaches the decision to accept the challenge. As he tells us, she has already become disillusioned with her lover, whom she finds ugly, weak-willed, and snobbish. (p. 147)

The difference between the original story and its adaptation is even more noticeable in the treatment of Constance's husband, for, whereas he makes no appearance in the former, he plays a major role in the latter. As might be expected, in Dazai's version he is Eulenberg himself. According to Dazai, the husband was an indecisive intellectual who had two vices characteristic of the artist: amorousness and curiosity. He remained indecisive even when he knew that his wife and his mistress were to fight a duel on account of him; not knowing what to do, he timidly watched the duel from behind a tree. When he saw his mistress shot to death, he hurried back home and sank back in his sofa. At the police interrogation he answered that he knew nothing about the duel, that he wished both women were alive. He was deeply moved, however, when he learned of his wife's suicide and her motive for it as revealed in her letter. He was touched by the "violent seriousness" with which human life could be lived—so touched that he even thought of killing himself to join his wife. Real life, however, was not so romantic, and he did not commit suicide. Instead, he became a writer of popular fiction and lived a long, comfortable life. He never married again.

The portraits of the medical student and her lover, thus drastically modified by Dazai, change the entire story and affect the image of its heroine, Constance, too. In the Eulenberg story she is depicted with a detachment that prompted Dazai to imagine that the author had harbored personal hostility toward her. In contrast, Dazai's adaptation presents her as an intense, pure-hearted woman who thinks life is not worth living if it is bereft of love. The proud, almost arrogant woman who feared neither God nor man in the original story turns into a young idealist who lives for love and dies for love. Although Dazai does not delve into her psychology, he contrasts her both with the medical student and with the artist-husband. Out of the contrast she emerges as a person of heartfelt sincerity.

The reason why Dazai was tempted to change the story and its three main characters is now clear: he wanted to make every one of the characters a person worthy of the reader's sympathy. Constance, her husband, and his mistress, being human, are all potentially "cold and heartless"—as Eulenberg seemed to imply in his original story. Dazai did not deny this, but he also felt that they were redeemed from complete egotism by a degree of insight into their own emotions. The medical student found herself sympathizing with her rival in love, the wife who shot the student felt obliged to commit suicide, and the husband who learned of the suicide gave up his ambition to be a respectable writer. The situation was an ugly one, but the characters in the story were painfully aware of this. To depict them as if they were not aware of it, or as if no one ever had a decent thought or feeling, was to distort reality, not copy it. (pp. 147-49)

The same idea is suggested elsewhere in Dazai's writings. *A Women's Duel* was not the only story by another author that he reworked. In every case, he made his characters more sympathetic figures than they had been in the original. By and large, these characters were well aware of their own depravity. In *The New Hamlet*, Claudius, Gertrude, and Polonius are far more sympathetic characters than in Shakespeare's play, because they are more aware of their own weaknesses. Similar traits can be found in the stories collected as *Nursery Tales*. The Bad Old Man in **"The Old Man with a Wen"** is pitiably obsessed with a large wen on his cheek. The Bad Badger in **"The Rabbit's Revenge"** is a clumsy, ugly-looking animal who is hopelessly in love with the Good Rabbit and is cruelly victimized by her. The Bad Old Woman in **"The Tongue-Cut Sparrow"** is a former maid who for many years looked after her frail, impractical husband, the Good Old Man in the original tale. In *Sanetomo the Minister of the Right,* the assassin Kugyō is described as a nobleman who, "despite his carefree appearance, had something timid and subservient in his smile, the kind of smile one would expect to see in someone whose life since childhood had been wracked with care." In **"Appeal to the Authorities,"** the "bad" man is no less than Judas Iscariot. He emerges as a sympathetic character who is trying to protect the charismatic but naïve Jesus from the pressures of the practical world. In order to keep his master pure amid the impurities of daily life, Judas himself sinks deeper into the mire. His struggle is threefold, for her has to fight with the ill will of the Pharisees, with the whims of his unpredictable master Jesus, and with his own introspective, and hence indecisive, mind. All those characters, as they appear in the stories rewritten by Dazai, have personalities that appear weak rather than evil. Indeed, it is because of their weakness that they have won Dazai's sympathy and are held up by him for the reader's sympathy as well.

For Dazai, then, weakness is a sign of goodness, not of evil. In his view, an evil person is a man who has no understanding of, and therefore no sympathy for, human weakness. (pp. 149-50)

The same point is made in a short story by Dazai entitled **"Seagulls."** It includes a scene in which the hero, whose name is Dazai, is asked what he thinks is most important in literature. Is it love, humanism, beauty, social justice, or something else? His answer is instantaneous: he says it is regret. "A literary work devoid of regret is nothing," he says. "Modern literature—the very spirit of the modern age—was born of regrets,

confessions, reflections, and things like that." He goes on to explain that all these self-incriminating thoughts are derived from one's "awareness that one is a dirty fellow." Dazai was nothing if not faithful to this principle. His very first work of creative writing, entitled **"Recollections,"** resulted from his wish to "bare a record of my sins since childhood." In his last complete novel, *No Longer Human,* the hero's opening words are those of regret: "My past life is filled with shame." Other works by Dazai show the same characteristic. In **"Villon's Wife,"** both husband and wife are aware that all men are criminals; the difference between them is that he always thinks of suicide, whereas she wants to live on even as a criminal. Naoji, a leading character in *The Setting Sun,* who eventually commits suicide, also suffers from the painful knowledge that there could be no man who is not depraved, while his sister Kazuko, who shares this belief, decides she can live with it. The reason why the heroes choose death over life and the heroines do the reverse (though both suffer equally from the knowledge of man's basic depravity) is related to Dazai's belief that women are more capable of withstanding the world's evil. Young, innocent women are an exception, however. In **"Metamorphosis,"** for instance, the young daughter of a woodcutter flings herself over a waterfall when she is raped by her drunken father. Constance, in *A Women's Duel,* wants to die when she discovers her husband's infidelity; failing to die in a duel, she starves herself to death.

Dazai's ideas concerning the relationship betwen life and art can be summed up as follows. In his view, human reality was ultimately filthy and ugly, and human nature inherently depraved. He maintained, however, that literature should not concern itself wholly with that fact. The reason he gave was that it might be fact, but it was not truth. Truth, according to Dazai, lay with the "weak" people who were painfully aware that human reality is ugly and human nature foul. Their sufferings, their regrets, their remorseful reflections, their desperate attempts to ward off the ugliness and filth of life—all these were beautiful. The prime concern of literature was to depict that beauty. (pp. 150-52)

If the function of a novel is to depict a man painfully aware of his innate depravity, a novelist's prime qualification is to have a thorough and sympathetic understanding of basic human weakness. Dazai repeatedly emphasized this. On one occasion he remarked: "Artists have always been friends of the weak," and on another: "To be a friend of the weak—that is the artist's point of departure as well as his ultimate goal." (p. 152)

All through his writings Dazai can be seen elaborating on this concept of human weakness. "Agony of a fugitive. Weakness. The Bible. Fear of life. Prayer of a loser." Such are the associations that it had for him. "A fugitive"—the word occurs frequently in Dazai's writings—is defined as "a wretched loser, a delinquent," in *No Longer Human.* The term evidently refers to a person like Ōba Yōzō, who, because of his awareness of "a lump of evil" lying deep within him, cannot be aggressive, and therefore cannot win a victory in the struggle for survival that is life. "Fear of life" is another favorite term of Dazai's; it denotes the fear of a man who lives a fugitive's life. For instance, the poet Ōtani in **"Villon's Wife"** says he is "always fighting with fear": he is afraid of God, who has seen through the "lump of evil" within him and who might punish him for it at any time. Dazai's reference to the Bible should be taken in the same context. In Christian terminology, all men are guilty of original sin; they are all depraved. The "prayer of a loser" is a prayer to Jesus, who was crucified to redeem humanity from original sin. Kazuko in *The Setting Sun,* when she realizes that becoming a sinner is the condition of being alive in this world, says: "Labeled a delinquent. That's the only kind of label I want to be crucified under." In **"Appeal to the Authorities,"** Judas cannot convince himself of his absolute innocence, and he suffers painfully from it. "A leading characteristic of geniuses," says one of the letter-writers in **"Letters in the Wind,"** "is that they are one and all convinced of their own sinfulness." In Dazai's opinion, this applies with peculiar force to geniuses who write novels.

But if a novelist is firmly convinced of his own depravity, will he not become a kind of holy man, and turn from literature to seek God and redemption? Dazai's answer is in the negative, unless "holy man" is interpreted in the broadest sense. Indeed, Yōzō in *No Longer Human* is "a good boy, like an angel"; Uehara in *The Setting Sun* is "a noble martyr"; and Ōtani in **"Villon's Wife"** is a poet who lives in fear of God. Yet they are all far from being saints or sages of any religion, Eastern or Western. In fact, they resemble Judas Iscariot more than the rest of the apostles. Dazai was too conscious of his own shortcomings to create a character in search of redemption. He was so sensitive on this score that it was difficult for him not to see a touch of pride (and hypocrisy) in the image projected by any religious leader. Convinced of basic human depravity, and moved by the nobility of men suffering from their awareness of it, he was too introverted, too self-conscious, and too timid to take any positive action. "A road leading to construction is a false road," he once wrote in a letter. "For today's young men, the only right road is the road to despair." (pp. 153-54)

To Dazai's way of thinking, the heroes of autobiographical novels must be self-appointed pseudo-villains. They must be thieves, libertines, prodigals, and scoundrels who have consciously become what they are. They must refuse to become happy, because it is wrong to want happiness in this world of men who, they know, are all depraved.

There is some question, however, as to whether Dazai's own heroes are cast exactly in this mold. The protagonists of **"Villon's Wife,"** *The Setting Sun,* and *No Longer Human*—perhaps his three best works—are still "good boys" in some respects, and not without the author's knowledge. *No Longer Human* ends with the comment that its alcoholic hero, Yōzō, was "a good boy, like an angel." Uehara, in *The Setting Sun,* is a "noble Martyr." Otani, in **"Villon's Wife,"** is compared to the famous French poet. Dazai has often been criticized for being too indulgent toward his heroes, despite his promise to make them "most ill-natured and monstrous." His critics have a point. It should be remembered, however, that the characters Dazai attempted to create were pseudo-villains, not just plain villains. His heroes were ill-natured and monstrous, but they knew it—and suffered. If Dazai was overlenient toward them, it was because of his own good nature. (pp. 156-57)

Dazai's views on how a literary work should affect the reader have already been touched on. In a word, he liked the beauty of weakness. To him, this was the beauty that emerges from a confession by a sensitive person who knows the sinful nature of man, is pained by the knowledge, and refuses to be happy. . . . "What else does it [a novel] need," wrote Dazai in his comment on *The Declining Years,* "if it is tender, sorrowful, humorous, and noble?" The qualities imparted by a successful work of literature are tenderness, sorrow, humor, and nobility.

Of these four, sorrow is the one most closely connected with human weakness. The reader feels sorrow when he reads a novel describing human weakness, or when he reads about a man who suffers from his knowledge of the weakness that is in him. (pp. 157-58)

[Dazai's] main characters may be weaklings in the conventional sense, but they are drawn in such a way as to inspire the reader's deepest sympathy. Here, for instance, is Uehara talking to Kazuko in *The Setting Sun:*

> I don't care if I do drink myself to death. Life's too sad—I can't stand it. It's worse than just feeling lonely or depressed. I'm sad, I tell you. How can you be happy when the very walls are sighing all around you? How would you feel if you discovered there was no way you could find happiness or fame during your lifetime? Work harder? Hungry beasts will eat it up, that's all. There are too many wretched people. Is that a snobbish thing to say?

Kazuko, herself a child of misfortune, allows him to make love to her. Uehara, as Kazuko has just realized, is dying of tuberculosis. And yet he apologizes for being too snobbish, and indulges in a great deal of amusing intellectual banter. With touches like these, Dazai evokes real sympathy not only for his characters but for all people caught in a situation they cannot control. This, he seems to say, is the fate of all of us, and we should pardon each other's weaknesses.

Hence the "tenderness" that Dazai spoke of as another important literary effect. Dazai defined it as "sensitivity to the loneliness, melancholy, and misery of others." . . . A number of characters in Dazai's stories display this quality of tenderness. The hero of **"Osan"** is a married man who dies in a suicide pact with his mistress. Yet his widow remembers him as "a tender husband" and counts herself a happy woman to have loved such a man. The poet in **"Villon's Wife"** is a thief, drunkard, and libertine, yet his poor wife comes to conclude, toward the end of the story, that he is "more tenderhearted than most men around." (pp. 158-59)

We can see now why Dazai disapproved so much of "Ein Frauenzweikampf": its author was entirely lacking in tenderness toward its three main characters. (p. 160)

"Nobility," the third of Dazai's array of desirable literary effects, is also related to tenderness. To be sympathetic and kind toward others presupposes a capacity for self-sacrifice, a capacity to keep selfish thoughts in check. An egotist can never be noble, because he is not sensitive to the suffering of others. A work of art, Dazai thought, should create an impression of nobility by describing sensitive, tenderhearted people. . . . [He] declared: "Literature is always a *Tale of the Heike.*" This rather eccentric definition of literature makes sense when *The Tale of the Heike* is understood as an epic eulogizing the fall of good but weak people, cultured to a fault, nobly meeting a tragic fate at the hands of their inferiors.

Many of Dazai's own works can be considered tales of this sort. The most obvious example, of course, is *The Setting Sun,* which may be considered an elegy mourning the death of the nobility in twentieth-century Japan. Kazuko's mother, with her extreme refinement and gentleness, best represents that nobility; she is "the last noblewoman in Japan." But Naoji also prides himself on his noble birth and concludes his suicide note by saying "I am a nobleman." The word "noble," in these instances, has at once social and moral implications, suggesting that a member of the nobility is likely to have a noble character, too. The commoners, on the other hand, are physically energetic, mentally robust, and aesthetically crude. They are the rough warriors who destroy the refined, gentlehearted courtiers. The sad inevitability of this outcome is narrated in a tone of Buddhist resignation in *The Tale of the Heike,* but Dazai preferred to see it in the context of a Marxist view of history. He seems to have thought that the people of noble birth, including himself, would have no place in the utopian society that would emerge after the forthcoming proletarian revolution. His pessimism is shared by Naoji, Yōzō, Ōtani, and other Dazai heroes, many of whom are of aristocratic birth. They are of "the perishing class," as Dazai called them. "They get beaten, they perish, and their mutterings become our literature," he explained; and elsewhere: "Despair begets elegance." Presumably this "elegance" in literary form is what Dazai meant by nobility.

There are occasions, however, when despair begets humor rather than elegance. It is, of course, humor with a difference, a kind of gallows humor. No doubt it is to humor of this kind that Ōtani, in **"Villon's Wife,"** is referring when he writes of "a great big laugh at the end of the world." His wife uses these words to describe the unexpected laughter that grips her when she learns that her husband is not only a thief but hopelessly in debt. Her laughter is directed at herself and her husband, who have long found life without meaning but have nevertheless gone on living it. When Dazai speaks of humor, then, it is of this kind of existentialist laughter. In the very last line of *The Setting Sun,* Kazuko calls Uehara "My Comedian." Kazuko herself, who was an elegant lady of the nobility at the story's beginning, ends up as a comic rather than a tragic figure, since she outlives both her mother and brother and is determined to make some sort of life for herself and her illegitimate child. The main character of *No Longer Human* is a conscious comedian: Yōzō has always tried hard to make other people laugh. When he is small his audience is his parents, brothers, and sisters; when at school, his teachers and classmates; as a grown-up, his friends and acquaintances. Appropriately, he becomes a professional cartoonist.

Despair can be overcome by laughter. As Dazai observed: "Pain, when there is too much of it, seems to transcend itself and turn into humor." Ōtani's wife, who turns her plight into a transcendental joke, and Kazuko, who willingly makes a fool of herself, both overcome pain and decide to live on. Yōzō becomes a mental patient, but he is not the "I" of the novel; there is a distance between him and the writer. In a postscript to his stories Dazai observed that he had written some of them out of pain and indignation, but that as he read them again he felt humor instead. That humor had arisen from the distance between Dazai the writer and Dazai the reader: the latter could look at the former with detachment and laugh at him. The haiku poet Bashō had a similar notion of humor; in order to distinguish it from the ordinary kind, he called it "lightness" (*karumi*). Apparently Dazai shared Bashō's view. In *Pandora's Box,* he wrote:

> The spirit of the new age is certainly here with us. It is as light as a robe of feathers, as clean as the water of a shallow brook flowing over white sand. . . . "Lightness" does not mean levity. No one will understand that frame of mind until he reaches a point at which he is able to see his desires, his life itself, as nothing. It is a gentle breeze that comes after long hours of hard, agonizing labor. . . . The peace and

calm of a person who has lost everything; that is "lightness."

Pandora's Box was the first novel Dazai wrote after the Second World War. "The new age," therefore, refers to the chaotic period immediately following the war, when many Japanese felt as if they had lost everything that was dear to them. In Dazai's view, it was this sense of utter loss that led to the lightness of which he spoke. Lightness, then, comes very close to what he elsewhere called humor.

Dazai, however, was perhaps a bit too exuberant in *Pandora's Box.* His own works in the postwar period do not really express this "spirit of the new age." There is far more to *The Setting Sun* than lightness: it also has tenderness, sorrow, and nobility. The same can be said of *No Longer Human,* except, perhaps, that there is more sorrow and less nobility. If Dazai had come close to achieving lightness in his last years, this would surely be evident in his last novel, *Good-bye.* Indeed, this unfinished work, to judge from what there is of it, has more humor than any of Dazai's other desired effects. Its prose style is also more even than that of most other Dazai stories. Unfortunately, the novel is unfinished because Dazai killed himself. The reader is left wondering whether its hero, Tajima, will be able to say good-bye to the "tense air amid the great chaos of the world." But Dazai's suicide was probably his answer to that question. In the end he found himself unable to transcend the world's chaos. He chose to hurl himself into the muddy turbulence of the Tama River rather than to patiently seek out a shallow brook flowing over white sand. (pp. 161-64)

In Dazai's view . . . literature is basically of little practical use and the novelist is a good-for-nothing. And yet it may be helpful to people with serious problems. But it is clear that the circumstances under which it is helpful are always exceptional ones. Dazai repeatedly stressed the uselessness of both art and artist in the practical domain. . . . In a postscript to *The Declining Years* he warns his readers: "Reading my stories would not help you earn your living, nor would it help you rise in the world. It wouldn't help you in anything. Therefore, I can't much recommend these stories to you." (p. 171)

Can a literary work provide consolation to a despairing mind when its implications are nihilistic, or, at best, existentialist? For some it can, and for others it cannot; it all depends on the reader's age, temperament, and philosophy of life (Dazai would have wanted to add sex, too). For that reason, Dazai's works are balm for some and poison for others. All literature is like that to a certain extent; Dazai's case is an extreme. (p. 172)

> *Makoto Ueda, "Dazai Osamu," in his* Modern Japanese Writers and the Nature of Literature *(with the permission of the publishers, Stanford University Press; © 1976 by the Board of Trustees of the Leland Stanford Junior University), Stanford University Press, 1976, pp. 145-72.*

J. THOMAS RIMER   (essay date 1978)

[*Rimer discusses* The Setting Sun *as an intense portrayal of moral and philosophical alienation from a world where traditional values have been undermined by the pressures of modern existence.*]

The existential anguish Dazai portrays gains spiritual depth from the fact that, for many Japanese of his generation, even the best in the values of the past remained impotent in the face of militarism. (p. 184)

Dazai's cry echoes from his own heart; its genuineness has never been in dispute. Indeed many Japanese readers assume that his characters are merely ill-disguised manifestations of his own personality. In terms of the author's entire *oeuvre*, perhaps the charge can be sustained. But in *The Setting Sun*, at least, Kazuko, Naoji, and their mother present themselves as distinct figures who complement each other in producing a cumulative poignancy central to Dazai's concerns.

The contemporary quality of the anguish expressed in the novel is reinforced by certain techniques used by Dazai in the construction of his text. It is doubtless natural that this should be so—how difficult it would be to mirror such anxieties using only traditional aesthetic means. Dazai's literary strategies grow naturally out of his concerns. Many of them will put a Western reader at ease immediately. The narrative has been assembled with enormous care, its shifting moods rigorously arranged to build toward the climax sought. Dazai has unified the atmosphere of the novel in a manner familiar to contemporary readers everywhere. In particular, his use of repeated symbolic images adds an enormously resonant layer to the text; even when the meaning of the images remains obscure, their unconscious, Jungian significance is real, their presence authentic. There are, for example, repeated references to flowers, and constant allusions to death in summer. Most powerful are the images of snakes. Early in the novel, Kazuko sees a snake in the garden; she feels nervous but nevertheless finds the snake somehow beautiful. She makes the association between the snake and her mother; suddenly she has the feeling that "the ugly snake dwelling in my breast might one day end by devouring this beautiful, grief-stricken mother snake." She then tries to burn the eggs the snake has laid. Later, as her mother grows more ill, Kazuko reflects that ". . . Mother pretends to be happy, but she grows thinner by the day. And in my breast a viper lodges which fattens by sacrificing Mother, which fattens however much I try to suppress it." (pp. 186-87)

Whatever the meaning of the snakes (death and renewal have been suggested as one possibility), they represent a set of troubling images that evoke a strange beauty whenever they appear in the narrative. The emotional states they suggest are more powerful than the images themselves. On this level, Dazai's appeal touches a Western reader with as much force as it does a Japanese one. We all share a culture that recognizes the symbolic significance of the unconscious. Dazai too inhabits that shared present. In many ways, he . . . can be said to share fully in the painful world we have all made together.

Yet *The Setting Sun,* even while chronicling the death of the past, remains impregnated with it. Indeed, neither the structure nor the theme of the novel could find adequate expression without constant reference to the culture and literature of the past. The presence of such traditions pervades the text, giving the novel a peculiar power to move even those who do not share those inherited ideas or attitudes.

The Setting Sun . . . is comprised of a series of documents juxtaposed together. Like the Heian diaries and the Bashō travel diaries, these documents are written in the first person. The bulk of the narrative, through the sixth chapter, is in the form of a memoir written by Kazuko herself, who recalls the various experiences that have led her to her present state. The final two chapters provide the most penetrating glimpses of the two young people given the reader. Chapter Seven is the suicide letter written by Naoji to Kazuko. Chapter Eight is a final letter written by Kazuko to Uehara. These two sections in many ways form the kernel of the novel. The sections preceding them

prepare the reader to understand the nuances and implications of the statements that the two young people make about themselves and about each other. Interspersed with Kazuko's memoir are other documents as well. In Chapter Three, for example, sections of a diary kept by Naoji, the "Moonflower Journal," are inserted as a means to illustrate the growing apprehensions of Kazuko concerning the family's desperate situation. Chapter Four gives the text of three letters written by Kazuko to Uehara in her attempt to help her brother and, even more importantly, as a means of making her own appeal to him. The reader is always given narrative information by means of a document, never directly. The various sources of information provided tend to reinforce each other; the same truths come from different angles, and the truth becomes that much more inexorable. Use of the letters and the journal helps to pace the flow of the narrative and gives a satisfying rhythm to the whole. . . . Dazai makes no use of speculation, preferring to reinforce his central theme from several directions.

The use of the first person narration . . . has a heritage in Japanese literature going back to the early diary writers and essayists. Like many of these writers, Dazai can, through the economy possible in such a restricted narrative environment, quickly sketch a mood or render an emotional attitude. In particular, he has in Kazuko created a character of such sensitivity that the briefest of her observations manages to remain both precise and evocative at the same time. (pp. 188-90)

In terms of the three major characters in the novel, Dazai's use of the diary form permits him to stress the reticence that all show concerning any direct and human contact. Faced with others, they are mute. The briefest examination of the text reveals how little the characters actually say to each other and how little their conversations suggest of the larger emotional significance of the moment portrayed. (p. 191)

Dazai can so create a reticence in his characters and overcome that same reticence through his use of the diary form. Such a narrative structure thus serves a double purpose.

The diaries and letters of Kazuko and Naoji reveal with great force the torment of their inner worlds. No such direct exposure toward the inner life of their mother is given the reader. She is portrayed through the responses of her children; and as she represents the last manifestation of a dying culture, her slight air of remoteness is altogether appropriate. Her own reticence and her own patience sustain both young people. Without her, and the values she stands for, the two feel abandoned. No matter that her world remains at too great a distance from the children, beyond the range of efficacy—her effect on them remains powerful. (p. 192)

The stress on the private layers of anguish in the minds and souls of [Dazai's] characters suggests an atmosphere of emotional intimacy redolent of that found in many Heian works of literature, notably in *The Tale of Genji,* where the social and political life outside the secluded women's quarters is seldom mentioned. In the Heian diaries too, the exterior lives of the figures portrayed are seldom sketched in any detail. We know much about how they responded to the circumstances of their lives, but little about what they actually did. Our knowledge concerning Naoji and Kazuko is often of the same order. None of the political turmoil of the early postwar period finds mention in the text, Kazuko's rebellion remains throughout an intense interior state of mind.

Overt references to such diary literature in *The Setting Sun* indicates that Dazai sensed the importance of the parallels between such atmospheres and made good use of them. In many ways, Kazuko herself seems a Heian sensibility transplanted, or rather thrust, into the contemporary world. In this regard, Dazai's references to the Heian period *Sarashina Diary* are particularly significant. That diary chronicles certain responses and attitudes of a delicate and reticent woman from a minor branch of the Fujiwara family who finds difficulties in adapting to her life in court. She shows as well a certain spiritual restlessness that gives her diary continuing significance as a psychological document. Indeed, Lady Sarashina, as she has come to be known, serves as an appropriate model for Kazuko. (pp. 193-94)

For Kazuko, to be a "Lady Sarashina" is to be a victim. Nevertheless for Dazai, and for his readers, the passing of that which is beautiful is profoundly moving. (pp. 194-95)

The corrosive pressures of contemporary society on these retiring aristocrats provide a major source of creative tension in the novel. The reader is continuously forced to witness their anguish and they are obliged to take cognizance of the world around them. Dazai is careful to show not only their malaise and their gaucheness in facing that society. By his use of the diary form, he can show their self-consciousness of that awkwardness, which in turn gives both Kazuko and Naoji a certain peculiar strength. Both can sense falsehood in others. Naoji harbors a particular disdain for those of Marxist persuasion who have not thought through the implications of their doctrines; Kazuko sees through the postures struck by the novelist Uehara and can cut him down with a single remark.

In emphasizing the interior world of his characters, Dazai insists that such a world be complete: thus he records all the pressures from the relentless, alien world in a fashion quite unnecessary for those characters created by Lady Murasaki. The harmony between the interior and the exterior world has been broken decisively. In one compelling incident, Kazuko records her own shock of awareness at her own otherworldliness. Early in the novel, through inadvertence, she neglects to put out a fire. Sparks set the woodshed afire, and only a great deal of hard work on the part of the villagers prevents the destruction of her home. Kazuko is ashamed of her carelessness and makes her apologies to various people who live nearby:

> Wherever I went the people sympathized and attempted to console me. Mr. Nishiyama's young wife—I say young but she's already about forty—was the only one who rebuked me. "Please be careful in the future. You may belong to the nobility, for all I know, but I've been watching with my heart in my mouth the way you two have been living, like children playing house. It's only a miracle you haven't had a fire before, considering the reckless way you live. Please be sure to take the utmost care from now on. If there had been a strong wind last night, the whole village would have gone up in flames."

Through Kazuko's own words the reader is jolted, like her, into an awareness of how dangerous such otherworldliness can be. By the occasional insertion of such scenes, Dazai "objectifies" the emotional world inhabited by his characters, making their plight all the more poignant. Society now penetrates into the most sensitive layers of the human soul. Kazuko has the will to take new strength from the intrusion. Naoji her brother does not.

For this reader at least, the compelling power of *The Setting Sun* derives from the relentless will shown by Naoji and Kazuko in confronting their own realities, their own destinies. Kazuko feels able to proceed because, in her own terms, she possesses what she calls "a clear conscience." On this emphasis on triumphant sincerity, Dazai pays a profound homage to the Japanese traditional literary virtue of *maketo*, the same trait that made Ariwara no Narihira such an appealing figure in *Tales of Ise*. Now, however, that search for sincerity perforce takes on a restless, nervous quality that marks contemporary life. Still, the traditional concept remains flexible enough to persist as a virtue in a novel of contemporary concerns. Naoji and her sister both exhibit this quality. Kazuko searches for a new order. Naoji has searched but has found nothing. . . . (pp. 196-98)

Looking at the world he terms "out of joint," Naoji finds his self-realization must end in self-destruction. . . . (p. 198)

In his suicide note, Naoji examines his own weaknesses, his social insecurity, and his own consciousness of the failure of any political philosophy or system to fully sustain him in his understanding of life. . . . (pp. 198-99)

Naoji, knowing his own weaknesses, is powerless before them. He searches for answers to his terrible questions, and his relentlessness cannot fail to leave a profound impression on a sympathetic reader. In "Burnt Norton" of his *Four Quartets*, T. S. Eliot has reminded several generations that "Human kind / Cannot bear very much reality." Naoji and Kazuko, in the view of Dazai at least, must be seen as sympathetic because they are trying to find, and bear, as much of their reality as possible. In describing their search, Dazai does not hesitate to make use of the past even as he shows us its dissolution. (p. 199)

> *J. Thomas Rimer, "Dazai Osamu: The Death of the Past," in his* Modern Japanese Fiction and Its Traditions: An Introduction *(copyright © 1978 by Princeton University Press; excerpts reprinted by permission of Princeton University Press), Princeton University Press, 1978, pp. 182-99.*

PHYLLIS I. LYONS (essay date 1981)

[Lyons examines the subtlety of Dazai's first-person narrative strategy and its effect on readers.]

In modern Japanese literature as in Western, the question of the individual "self" of the characters inhabiting the created world of the novel is a central issue. In the case of Dazai Osamu (1909-1948), whose writing was almost entirely in the autobiographical-fictional mode known in Japan as the *watakushi shosetsu* ("I-novel"), the matter of the "self" of characters in the novel is intimately tied in with the issue of narrative voice. . . . In such a special kind of fiction, there is the additional problem of the relation of the author to the multitude of novelistic selves, and of the relation of all of them to the reader. Since much modern Japanese fiction has a recognizably personal tone, these relationships are important even in writing that is not obviously autobiographical. . . . The "self" of the author and his personal style (in the sense intended by Peter Gay in *Style in History*) is in this genre of personal fiction a major part of the effect of the work. . . . I characterize the personal style of the writer Dazai, the persona of the artist Osamu through whom he speaks in his stories, as that of the "observant scapegoat." A scapegoat is one who is expelled from the group, one who takes on the role of symbolic outsider; and I would argue that a set of special disqualifications, which he characterized in the titles of two of his stories as being *Human Lost (sic)* and *Ningen shikkaku* . . . (literally, "disqualified as a human being"), kept him from full participation in the largely homogeneous central cultural tradition while at the same time—and this is most important—he fully accepted its values; and it was this special perspective that made him "best equipped" to communicate the naked interpersonal truths he was "uniquely capable of grasping." It was a consciousness of not belonging—because of social class, geographical origin, psychological orientation—to any of the collectivities of the central culture, that made it possible for him to dissect the rituals of social expression, and create of his own mind a stage where others could act out emotion felt but perhaps unacknowledged. . . . (p. 102)

Dazai "opens" himself, and pulls his audience in (for the process of reading him is never a passive one) typically by fracturing narrative stream, by demanding active participation of the reader, not just as "hypocrite lecteur, mon frère," but as fully implicated co-conspirator, judge, confessor, tormentor, sympathetic fellow-traveler, and a dozen other roles by turns. Three works from the autobiographical cycle of stories I have elsewhere called the "Osamu Saga" will serve to illustrate this "passionate" involving style in its most obvious form. These are, by type, a "chronicle tale" and two "real-name" stories.

Tōkyō hakkei (Eight Views of Tokyo) is both a story about writing a story and a chronicle of the author's first ten years in Tokyo. The image the narrator uses to describe the structure of the story is that of "the full moon of a drawn bow"; it begins and ends with the narrator at an inn where he has gone to write his story. At the end, the narrator tells us that ten days have passed, the time required to tell the story within-the-story that is the ostensible reason for *Tōkyō hakkei*. Within the frame, there is yet another narrative dislocation, about two-thirds of the way through, when the narrator tells how he got the idea for *Tōkyō hakkei* in the first place and how he developed it; before this break we get the actual narrative of the events of the previous ten years, and after it we get two vignettes from the immediate past, covering the days just before the narrator left on his trip. The reader thus is required to make some rather athletic shifts in following the focus of attention; but the performance is so carefully orchestrated that he never loses track of the parallel progress of the stories, although he will find himself pulled as a very different participant into each of the worlds of the stories; and in fact, the "full moon" also enfolds the reader. For the narrative voice speaks in several modes: he is a harried writer organizing his professional life and dealing with maids at the inn in present time; he is a less intrusive narrator telling a story about the past; within the narrated past he is a young and anguished prodigal son, directly upbraiding the woman he loves (and, simultaneously, implicating the reader in her crimes of omission), yet cataloguing his own misdeeds with both self-loathing and the defensiveness of outraged innocence. There is further dialogue within the "told" story and in the frame for this story; there is discourse directed simultaneously at the woman and at the reader. (pp. 102-03)

It is through this manipulation of the relative distance between and direction of writer and reader, that the teller of the tale comes to the conclusion that art does not exist in some world of ideal forms, and has not just possessed him, but is paradoxically himself; and his active accomplice, the reader, who

has similarly become part of the tale, is forced to agree. By the end of the story, even the "told self" has made himself into an art object, one of the "eight views of Tokyo." . . . Along the way, the reader too has slipped into so many personae that he has become a part of this artwork, an accomplice of its style.

Kikyōrai . . . (Going Home) and *Kokyō . . . (Hometown)* have a further kind of "worlds-within-real-worlds" structure. (p. 104)

The argument of *Kikyōrai* looks quite straightforward: I, the narrator (named Shūji, Dazai's real name), have caused a great deal of trouble to many people; here are some of them; in the past, I caused them the following kinds of trouble, and this is how they reacted, so you will know what kind of people they are; and recently, on the basis of our history, the following situations arose. Two of Dazai's long sufferers, Mr. Nakabata and Mr. Kita, are referred to by their real-life names, as is the author-narrator. But [Prof.——] is called "a certain *sempai* [mentor]" because, Shūji tells us, as awkward as that literary device may be, it is necessary since the real-life man in question hates to see his name appear in *shōsetsu* [stories] and *zuihitsu* [essays].

Thus, the question of "history as a novel" and "the novel as history," to use Norman Mailer's distinctions, is addressed directly, and is in fact a major preoccupation of Dazai's "story." (pp. 104-05)

Kokyō . . . shows another variant of joint participation in emotional experience by narrator, reader, and author. Here, in the course of a "normal" narrative account, Shūji has just left the bedside of his dying mother, to seek refuge alone in a distant, unheated room of the house:

> I paced around the room, struggling to control my tears, telling myself over and over again, if *you* cry now, you're a fake, one tear and you're a fake. Ah, what a wonderful, gentle son *he* is, brimming over with love for his mother, stealing away to weep by himself. Pretentious! Isn't that just too sweet? Here you are, like some cheap movie. Thirty-four now, *our* dear, gentle Shūji. You're not likely to become a good son at this late date. Enough of this self-indulgence. Cut it out! If *you* cry now, you're a fake. . . .

The "I" gives way to a "you" who is not the reader-audience, but rather has appropriated the audience's place. Then Shūji becomes neither "I" nor "you," but a jointly observed "he." Suddenly, the narrator is sitting beside the reader, as we jointly comment on "our" Shūji. Finally, the direction of address settles down with ourselves, the readers, subliminally the target of the self-encouragement. The fact that the Japanese does not specify these pronouns but calls for the reader to supply them— by implication in Japanese, directly in translation—enhances the transitions.

The affective results are as multiple as the persons "involved" in this scene: Shūji, the narrator, gets to indulge in self-pity and self-contempt while genuinely grieving for his mother. Dazai (if we assume that this story is "genuinely" autobiographical) gets to maintain self-control through art while achieving emotional release. And the *reader*—we who have surely had experience ourselves of having to suffer bravely in silence, unbeknownst to the rest of the world—gets the satisfaction of public recognition of that suffering, with both the embarrassment of having been discovered and the comfort of sympathetic acknowledgement of the pain. The text mocks you, forgives you, and invites you at the same time.

I shall conclude with a few corollaries. I would suggest that this subversive narrative program accounts for the polarity of reactions Dazai elicits from readers: either a popularity bordering on adolescent idolatry, or an exquisite embarrassment that "I was once interested in those things, but I'm older now and much better, thank you," a reaction which may then mellow to boredom. Mishima Yukio, who wrote of his own strongly ambivalent feelings toward Dazai's writing, suggested simply that he was "a writer who worked deliberately to expose what I most wanted to hide." It is the degree of untidy, uncontrollable participation that Dazai elicits from his readers that can explain, I think, why many people continue to read about Dazai's brushes almost fifty years ago with suicide, alcoholism, drug addiction, and political radicalism, or his run-ins with his elder brother, his disinheritance and his reunions and reconciliations with his family. Again and again, Dazai advances irresistibly innocent presumptions of intimacy with his reader; and the reader experiences, or experiences anew, feelings he usually keeps under wraps even from himself. (pp. 106-07)

Phyllis I. Lyons, " 'Art "Is" Me': Dazai Osamu's Narrative Voice As a Permeable Self," in The Harvard Journal of Asiatic Studies, *Vol. 41, No. 1, 1981, pp. 93-110.*

ADDITIONAL BIBLIOGRAPHY

Baird, James. "Contemporary Japanese Fiction." *The Sewanee Review* LXVII, No. 3 (Summer 1959): 477-96.*

Survey of themes, trends, and authors of postwar Japanese literature. Sections of this essay consider various themes in Dazai's two translated novels, including the influence of French Impressionist painting, while discussing these works in the context of their literary times.

Brudnoy, David. "The Immutable Despair of Dazai Osamu." *Monumenta Nipponica* XXIII, Nos. 3-4 (1968): 457-74.

Reads the whole of Dazai's work as "a portrait of his own tortured consciousness," a nihilistic and highly personal vision of reality.

Keene, Donald. "Translator's Introduction." In *The Setting Sun*, by Osamu Dazai, translated by Donald Keene, pp. ix-xvii. Norfolk, Conn.: New Directions, 1956.

Describes the cultural background of Japan during the period depicted in *The Setting Sun*, and also discusses the thematic and stylistic traits of this novel.

Keene, Donald. "Translator's Introduction." In *No Longer Human*, by Osamu Dazai, translated by Donald Keene, pp. 3-10. Norfolk, Conn.: New Directions, 1958.

Discusses this novel as representative of Western influence in modern Japanese literature.

"Dazai Osamu, 1909-1948." *Modern Japanese Literature in Translation: A Bibliography*, pp. 38-40. Tokyo, New York, and San Francisco: Kodansha International, 1979.

A bibliography, with complete bibliographic references, of translations of Dazai's works into English and other languages.

Rexroth, Kenneth. "World Ills in the Far East." *The Nation* 183, No. 13 (29 September 1956): 271-72.*

Descriptive review of *The Setting Sun*.

Sakai, Robert K. "Japanese Moderns." *Prairie Schooner* XXXI, No. 2 (Summer 1957): 99-102.*

Informative short essay on modern Japanese literature, reviewing *The Setting Sun* as "an especially moving novel."

Léon-Paul Fargue

1876-1947

French poet, essayist, and memoirist.

Fargue's works are among the earliest and best examples of avant-garde writing in twentieth-century French literature. Both his subjects and his poetic forms share the preoccupations of the nineteenth-century Symbolist poets. Like Charles Baudelaire, Fargue devoted much of his imagination to Paris, where he lived his entire life. The unearthly charm and pathos contributed to the Symbolist mystique by Paul Verlaine, whom Fargue knew during the older poet's last years, are also essential qualities of Fargue's poems, as are the bizarre and shattering visions characteristic of Arthur Rimbaud and another "deranged" poet who had a similar impact on Surrealism—Lautréamont (Isidore Ducasse), author of the hallucinatory *Chants de Maldoror*. While Fargue was only briefly and marginally involved with Surrealism, his poems helped form the artistic climate in which it flourished, and they share with this movement a preoccupation with striking, dream-like imagery. But more than bridging two centuries and two artistic movements, Fargue's writing successfully displays the extent to which the obsessions of modern French literature—death, absurdity, and nostalgia for an unknown realm—were his own.

Fargue was born in Paris, and during his childhood his family often relocated within the city. His parents were unmarried, and the state of illegitimacy, along with frequent dislocations, contributed to Fargue's sense of himself as a rootless outsider. Nonetheless, Fargue had a deep love for his parents, who eventually married when he was thirty years old. The death of his father in 1909 was a profound experience of grief and loss which later was reflected in much of his writing and was commemorated in the poem "Depuis il y a longtemps." At the Lycée Henri IV, Fargue was a classmate and friend of Alfred Jarry, whose impulsive nature and haphazard way of life have their parallel in Fargue's lifelong bohemian wanderings around Paris. With Jarry, he founded the journal *L'Art littéraire,* in which his earliest writings appeared.

Throughout his life Fargue was associated with the most elite literary circles in Paris, and with their publications: he helped supply the *Nouvelle Revue Française* with its initial literary momentum, and coedited the periodical *Commerce* with Valéry Larbaud and Paul Valéry. But while Fargue was on intimate terms with the most distinguished artistic figures of the time—among them André Gide, Paul Claudel, Jean Giradoux, and Maurice Ravel—his own pursuit of public distinction was at best unmethodical. Not until 1912 did he compile a major collection of his work; and although he twice stood for election to the French Academy, his politicking for this honor was rather indifferent, and he failed to secure it on both occasions. In any case, Fargue's personal milieu was not centered on literary officialdom but extended into the streets, the cafés, the oldest and the most modern districts of the city, the humblest and the highest circles of Parisian life. He was renowned as an habitué of both salon and café society, and everywhere was prized for his imaginative, energetic, and intelligent conversation. Fargue's intimate acquaintance with many aspects of Parisian life and history led to his being called the "Poet of Paris." In 1943 Fargue's activities were severely curtailed

when he was stricken with hemiplegia following a stroke. In his last years he continued to support himself by writing numerous newspaper and magazine articles, many of which found their subjects in his encyclopedic knowledge of Paris.

Fargue's earliest work, *Tancrède,* was written in the 1890s and most directly establishes his link with the Symbolists, particularly Arthur Rimbaud. Composed of lyrics in both poetry and prose, *Tancrède* is a youthful testament of dreams and despair, a sensuous vision of an aesthetic world transcending the mundane. In this respect it resembles the author's later and most characteristic work, beginning with *Poèmes*. Many of these pieces are in the form of prose poems, the medium through which Fargue's peculiar talents and temperament were best conveyed. Rich in haunting visual images, musical language, and occult conjunctions of objects and ideas, these poems make up what has been called a "literature of enchantment." In his daily life Fargue went out of his way to remain acutely alert to the world around him and to note with an exacting sensibility the impressions he received from even the dullest scenes. Transmuted by his imagination, outer worlds become inner "landscapes where things remembered come to sight like the perspectives of roofs seen by lightning." Nostalgia and melancholy are the predominant moods of Fargue's poems, which convey a vision of solitude, bereavement, the inanity of human existence, and the richness of the imagination in a spiritually barren universe. Although much of Fargue's writing has qualities in common with Surrealism, including a predilection for the prose poem and free verse forms, it is not the result of the same process of automatic writing. Fargue stated in an interview that automatic writing "is an illusion. . . . To write automatically, is to give voice to one's habits, education, social experience, in short to all the conventional and superficial 'first aid to living' that civilization has imposed upon us. It is to allow the part of ourselves that most readily flows from our being to speak first." Fargue outlined his own contrasting poetic method: "It is only by the application of one's conscious will that one can succeed in discarding whatever in one's creative production belongs to the artificial and conventional in us."

Among Fargue's most valued and deeply felt writings, comprising about half of his output, are those which take Parisian scenes as their subject. The literary outcome of this approach is an amalgam of the poet's personal devotions and a document of a highly alluring era of French cultural history. In prose both conversational and poetic, Fargue pays tribute in "Mon quartier" ("My Quarter") to his "neighborhood of poets and locomotives"; while in "Saint-Germain-des-Prés" he captures a time and a place where "American women, almost wealthy, almost beautiful . . . come to swing their hips in front of the last Surrealists whose names are known on the other side of the ocean even if they haven't crossed the boulevard." Although Fargue is not as visible a literary figure as some of his contemporaries—Gide, Valéry, the Surrealists André Breton and Paul Eluard—his work exemplifies many of the most valuable traits that emerged during the first half-century of literary modernism: the revitalizing power of experimentalism, the devaluation of previous social and psychological conventions, and, perhaps above all, the utilization of newly discovered poetic modes to examine the artist's encounter with pain, alienation, and death. These, for Fargue, were realities which provided the substance of his art and which he felt were obscured by a complex world of social conventions. "The true poet," Fargue contended, "struggles unto death to free himself from these earthly illusions and delusions in order to reach what is deepest and truest in him."

PRINCIPAL WORKS

Tancrède (poetry) 1911
Poèmes (poetry) 1912
Pour la musique (poetry) 1912
Banalité (poetry) 1928
Épaisseurs (poetry) 1928
Espaces (poetry) 1929
Sous la lampe (poetry) 1929
Les ludions (poetry) 1930
D'après Paris (poetry) 1932
Le piéton de Paris (memoirs, interviews, and essays) 1939
Haute solitude (poetry) 1941
Déjeuners de soleil (essays) 1942
Refuges (poetry) 1942
La lanterne magique (essays) 1944
    [*The Magic Lantern*, 1948]
Méandres (poetry) 1946
Correspondance Larbaud-Fargue (letters) 1971

*This work was originally published in the journal *Pan* in 1895.

Selections of Fargue's poetry have appeared in the following publications: *Mid-Century French Poets. The Penguin Book of French Verse 4*, and *The Random House Book of Twentieth-Century French Poetry*.

RÉGIS MICHAUD   (essay date 1934)

A musician, a craftsman, an essayist and a poet, Fargue made his début in the Symbolist circles and attended Mallarmé's receptions. One of his first poems, *Tancrède* . . . , was a characteristic Symbolist confession and dramatized the plight of the young man as an artist: "He thinks of dying prematurely. He will retreat into silence, wishing to write no longer, and he will write a book to notify people of his decision." A pathetic strain has run, since then, through Fargue's books. Solitude, death, and tragic inanity of life, the swarms of countless human beings in the huge modern ant-hills, darkness and its nightmares, the plight of soul and body make the major themes of Fargue's verbal symphonies in prose and verse, collected in *Poèmes* (1902-1919), *Sous la Lampe* and *Espace*. *Under the Lamp* includes under the title of *Suite familière* suggestive reflections on art and poetry, and in the other volume we have the fantastic visions of *Vulturne* and *De Stade en Stade*. A great experimenter in words, images and sounds, Fargue makes a link between Symbolism and Surrealism. (pp. 170-71)

> *Régis Michaud, "A Pageant of Poets," in his* Modern Thought and Literature in France *(copyright, 1934, by Funk & Wagnalls Company; reprinted by permission of Harper & Row, Publishers, Inc.), Funk & Wagnalls, 1934, pp. 166-78.**

S. A. RHODES   (essay date 1935)

[*Rhodes elaborates on the visionary quality of Fargue's poetry, viewing it as an exercise in mysticism.*]

The poetry of Léon-Paul Fargue is the expression of a state of grace. It is a virtue the poet derives from the things his spirit deifies; the reward of that "politeness rendered unto God," of which he speaks, and which comes from the heart. He possesses certain human faculties common to the rest of us. But he is a poet only in proportion as he rises above them, in proportion as he reveals by his poetry that his kingdom is not earthly, though of this earth. To one who can be touched by it is given that sixth sense which is the key that opens the gate of heavens to the blessed. (p. 26)

Fargue was a mere adolescent—his pocket allowance was "ten cents a day"—when he published . . . *Tancrède,* that "poor prelude." . . . *Tancrède* was a faint star in a crepuscular sky where shone, with kindred light, the *Voyage d'Urien* and *Paludes* of André Gide, Henry Bataille's *Chambre Blanche, De l'Angélus de l'Aube a l'Angélus du Soir* by Francis Jammes, *Le Livre de Monelle* of Marcel Schwob. It was also the era of *Le Rat noir* and *Le Chat noir*, of the *Café Cyrano* and the *Café Nouvelle-Athènes*, the era when women of the night were stylized not "Les Cydalises," as in the time of Nerval and Gautier, but "Les Chimères."

The Paris of the fabulous Nineties was full of chimeras. This "low-Empire of the Decadent era," as Valéry Larbaud calls it, filled the poets with what the aesthetes of the preceeding symbolist generation had not felt, ''the immense diversity of living.'' The diversity extended to both confines of reality and dream. ''We were,'' says Fargue, ''enamoured of spiritual refinement, and, at the same time, tormented by a kind of anarchical aestheticism in the manner of Paul Adam, a childish desire to flaunt bombs with white gloves . . . —but we loved the poems of Wilde, the English Preraphaelites, the Yellow Book, the drawings of Beardsley, the books of Marcel Schwob, the pictures of Whistler, of Lautrec, of Van Gogh and of Gaugin . . .''

There is something of all this luster and twilight in Tancrède, that epitome a twentieth century Chatterton. He thinks of dying prematurely, of spending his life in silence, and writes a book to proclaim it, exactly as the hero of Valery's *La Soiree avec M. Teste* will do. But Tancrède is a poet. He does not know the intellectual frustration of M. Teste. His vision of the world is as yet evanescent. His expression is chaste, made up of equal parts of sentimental pessimism and poetic persiflage.

The chaste Tancrède ''dies well'' in the mauve decade. But the poet in him lived on into the crimson twenties. The frail aesthete was metamorphosed into a strangely magnetic poet, with the physical appearance of Harum-al-Rashid, Nero and Lohengrin reincarnated all three in one human being. Fargue is more fabulous in his ways than was the first in his; he is more artistic than the second, and more mystic than the last; and he is, moreover, more real than all three.

The Fargue of the mature years loves the earth with a love equal to that he has for the heavens; his intoxication with the wine of life equals his hallucination with the vision of after-life. His poetry smells of sunshine upon the prairies, and of dark shadows in modern cities. It is redolent with the fragrance of rain and mist in parks and streets; the circumambience of bent silhouettes concealing in tortuous alleys their poverty and poetry, of gray, ragged walls barring the horizons to gargoyles and men, and of sudden, deep-blue clearings in the jumble of reality through which all the earth, gathering its strength, seems to want to make off, and to climb to the heavens.

The poetry of Fargue is essentially two-toned. On the one hand it expresses the tyranny of whatever holds man by his senses, and on the other, the ecstasy of whatever pulls him by his spirit. In one case as in the other, for the senses as for the spirit of Fargue, the pain and nostalgia is always the same, intense and infinite. So the two tones of his poetry are heard, intermittently at times, the earthly often in **Poèmes,** and the unearthly often in **Espaces.** But at no time is one ever drowned out by the other, or silenced by it. More often they are heard simultaneously, one carrying the melody to the accompaniment of the other.

The lyricism of Fargue is the expression of an harmony achieved by the inner liberation of living experience. Music sounds in the labyrinth of reality like a bird's call in the night. In Fargue, it echoes his tuition and intuition of existence with mixed flutter and pathos. It is, in effect his poetic transcription of the burden of his sensibilities freed of both encumbrances of reality and dream. (pp. 27-9)

Fargue is allied to both spirit and matter in a common fight against their decay and death. His poetic thought takes root in concrete, earthly actuality, which he colors and illumines, however, to the potentialities of allusion and vision. So it reads like a message from ''the strangely Real.''

But Fargue never poses as the messenger of anything poetical or metaphysical. He is like a somnambulist upon the surface of the earth, and yet he is thoroughly awake to every action and word in it. No mirage or nightmare can confound him. Shrieking cities in the valleys, sorrows ascending to the heavens, memories descending to the grave, these things are the dramatic personae of his tone poems, and love, desire, pain, are the emotional expression of their word-music. (p. 30)

The world Fargue projects upon the canvas is real and unknowable. It teems with living phantoms limping upon the cobblestones of life with love and pain. We see old, wrinkled women parading along dark streets the last tatters of their earthly gowns; young women clutching with gasping desire to their bosoms the deflowered thorns of their discarded passions; withered men panting with their sorrows in and out of wretched hovels; the specter of buried hopes and loves shadowing the living remnants of unburied souls. We see the evening twilight inflaming the crumbling walls and roofs of the poor with the hectic glow of tearful faces; the public square enfolding within the gusts of its whirlwinds women and children huddled together against fear and grief; dark shadows creeping over the fences of ageless cemeteries, and phantasmagoria extending its *ignis fatuus* and mystery over man and beast.

But let us turn the page, and the succeeding poem, like a magic lantern, unfolds refreshing and winning aspects of the same world. For Fargue is more than man and beast. He is a satyr, a gnome, a jinn, a spirit, Oberon, Ariel astray in the twentieth century.

Fargue is very close to nature, as he is to man. He dispells the artifice that accumulates between man and nature, man and man, and senses both as artist and as man. He feels the ''esprit naturel, avec ses mysteres.'' He knows the art of charming birds and snakes. ''If you wish to,'' he confides, ''you can walk upon the waves, climb up very high into the sky by stamping secretly upon the earth, at the proper place, in a state of trance . . .'' The world he unveils at this stage seems also in a state of trance. His poetry takes on the delicacy of fine lace, the fragrant frailty of dowers in a crystal vase. Pictures of remembered yesterdays are painted against faint, blue skies. The dust of memory emulates the semblance of eternal things. The past is resuscitated with the exquisite tenderness of unforgotten springs.

So Fargue shifts his poetic gaze from the mournful observation of suffering humanity benumbed by misery to the enchanted contemplation of beauty that will not be dimmed. He descends and condescends to the nethermost orders of the earth, where nature lies still in plasmatic confusion, where good and evil remain unformed, and from where they may rise to the level of consciousness, to form and deform life. And he ascends to the uppermost orders of heavens, where nature becomes divinity, and man spirit.

Fargue loves nature especially in its imaginative and fanciful moods, when it exchanges its dazzling dress of sunlight for the mystic veil of moonlight. He shows the earth lying a-dreaming at the edge of an inviting abyss; the sky swaying low over sleeping waters; insects intoning in the night an air familiar for once to both men and beasts; the dance of nymphs peopling again the depths of wood and valley; the ghosts of Faust and Marguerite, Orpheus and Verlaine playing a tune the poet understands; the whispering shadow of an undying youth returning to love. . . . (pp. 31-2)

But despite his intimacy with the physical universe, the soul of the poet is never tangled within its wiles. He abandons to all winds fragments of his desire, and all winds leave their desired fragrance in his being. Withal, he remains unintoxicated and conscious of his experience as of its poetry; and in the presence of nature, alive to her hidden essence as sensible to her actuality. By virtue of this pervading poetic sympathy, Fargue commutes the external, moral insensibility of nature towards man into spiritual communion with his spirit. What nature shapes, dresses and veils, the poet reshapes, undresses and unveils. By an act of his poetic clairvoyance, he succeeds in breaking up her outer exclusiveness and frigidity. The way is open then to her inner unity, to the entrance of man into her sanctuary. Poetic creation becomes thus a thaumaturgic function. It breaks down the external order of things and brings them together again in a new and miraculous relationship. A landscape takes on then the beauty of a moral percept, a natural phenomenon bespeaks a human emotion, a bit of sky mirrors a soul.

Poetry is an act of living. Like music, it does not observe reality, it discovers it. It rolls back the cloak fashion and convention weave daily for it, and exposes it in its naked freshness to our jaded and sophisticated senses. Poetry expresses in this respect the highest order of activity in life. It simulates an evasion from actuality only in order to recapture it more completely. For poetry is, as Fargue observes, the only dream during which dreaming is forbidden. So the poet dwells in the realm of the commonplace with wonderment. He perceives things and beings with eyes that see in the darkness, hands that feel the void, ears that hear the silence. And he renders them in his poetry as they appear to him, freed from all subterfuge—limpid and pure. (pp. 32-3)

The poetry of Fargue does not lead to the confessional or the altar. He never sentimentalizes himself or the world. One may question the validity of his earthly exploration, but not its genuineness. The image of it he exhibits may seem hazy or blurred. But it is our eyes that are not properly focussed upon it. He transposes the order of things. He transfuses the rhythm of living and dreaming. The materials he uses are alike in both realms. But he transmutes and reintegrates them. The objects of his daily, social perspective become the incredible ingredients of his credible, though strange, reality. The astral and the subastral intermingle their glittering and variegated aspects within the framework of his universe. Hence our "provisional senses" are of no immediate assistance within it. For Fargue, as for Rimbaud, they must be "deranged," cast and recast into the poetic mould, which alone seizes the shape of life in its absolute aspect, *sub specie aeternitatis.*

Fargue is never more himself as when his very entrails seem to lend violence to his revolt against and execration of all social, literary and artistic pontificates. He would tear apart the cloud that screens human callousness. "I call bourgeois," he says, "whoever turns his back to himself, to strife and love, for the sake of his security. Whoever can breathe only the exhalations of others. Whoever is held up by his clothes, and not they by him." (pp. 33-4)

* * * * *

Fargue is a poet of the night. He is a Bohemian wandering from light into night, and from the shadows of the night into those of death. The dark radiance of death overcasts the sharp joys and soothing pains his poems suggest. All the earthly motives he sings form a procession Love leads and Death closes. . . .

Fargue experiences insufferable pain at the thought of death in its physical aspects, however. It is an unendurable agony to him to imagine himself deprived of the delight of sensing the form, color and fragrance of things. . . . All the roads in the fabled heavens of human desire, all the turbid and tortuous ways of men in the "city of gall," in the "hive of bitter honey," lead to the "station of all sorrow," to death, mourns the poet. . . . (p. 127)

But the poet attempts to frustrate the immanence of physical death. He constructs for his earthly grief a mnemonic bark capable of ferrying him back across the dark waters of his imaginary Styx. New loves on earth, he hopes, will illumine the darkened highways, fresh tears will revive drooping memories. (pp. 127-28)

A wind from another world fans the poetry of Fargue then, a melody from another reality sings in it, a dream from another existence is mirrored in it. He moves on a plane that draws away from the terrestrial. (p. 128)

"Remember!" The poetry of Fargue echoes throughout this nostalgic admonition: "remember." It is impregnated with the fragrance, the music, the color of lost things, the whiffs of memories wafting before his inner eyes, the signs seen once in the sky, in a woman's eyes, in a field speckled with flowers. His memory is a searchlight playing over the pastures of his yesterdays, and every spot is dotted with a forget-me-not.

Léon-Paul Fargue sits alone in his inner cell, and aspires through the windows of his senses the scents and sounds that mount to him from the past. They reach him with the plaint of things that fear to die. And he re-echoes their pain with moving tenderness. He communes with their soul in a realm which his soul alone can revisit. The communion leaves an unearthly light in his eyes. That light serves him as a beacon to illumine his way through the invisible. He makes no attempt to coordinate the rhythm of his conscious perception of life with that of his imaginary conception of it, however. He does not yield his spiritual prerogatives to any mortal necessities, nor, on the other hand, does he lead the earth astray in the sway of a poetic whim. (pp. 128-29)

Fargue's love of man is in direct ratio to his disgust with him. Having lived too long and too constantly face to face with him, he ends by seeking escape from him. He attempts to break the enchantment that holds captive the senses, and through evasion from the human condition, to ascend to spiritual resurrection. He follows in a fury of aspiration the oracles of undeciphered paradises. Having uttered all the tragic cries he is capable of in the whirlwinds of life, he casts off his earthly cargo, in the end, and takes off. A passage from the *Apocalypse* becomes his chart: "Then I saw a new heaven and a new earth." . . . The poet ascends through this extraordinary maze freed from earthly cavil and reason, knowledge and doubt, cognizant of its mystic significance. . . . He permits nothing reasonable to obscure his instinct of God. For that is the object of his pursuit: the recapture of life, the rediscovery of God.

In his poem **Vulturne** Fargue ranges through all the planes of creative evolution, all the way from its lowest physical stratum to its most mystical expression. He undertakes a journey through the nether and upper spheres of reality accompanied by two fabulous personages: Pierre Pellegrin and Joseph Ausaudre, as was Dante by Vergil. But they disclose, fortunately, no nightmare of hell here, no purgatorio, both of which they leave behind. They are intent only upon the abode called paradise their minds had elaborated on earth. For if the twentieth century does not believe anymore in hell, it still dreams of paradise. The celestial spaces succeed to the terrestrial, and the trio of spirits reach finally the goal of their ascension, the city of God and pure eternity.

So physical matter, the reality of what is finite, leads them, athwart death, athwart the proof of life, to the surreality of what is infinite. Freed from the spell of earthly attributes, it becomes pure again, and is spiritually reintegrated. "What does it serve a man to have been, for a day, for a moment, conscious of the life of the world, a moment the soul of matter, if he forget his eternal life.

—You are too indulgent of your earthly life. Forget yourself! . . . Let your little stone sleep in the immense stoneyard of death." Thus echo the voices of the three disincarnated souls in quest of their Author. The visible universe, they see, is composed of invisible bodies. Matter is an illusion, and so is the earth.

And yet Fargue does not renounce the earth. But he regards it as only a momentary lapse in the mystery of life, as a field from where to take off for the unknown. "Life was not good, but it was beautiful. Your youth. The street. Your room in the attic. The sounds of a piano . . ." Fargue remembers the earth the better to forget it, and so the better to find God. Only one thing is worth seeking, winning, losing again, forgetting, finding again in this precious dust. That is what I seek through my tears. I ask permission to begin anew. I ask of God . . ." Human storms and pains seem to be pathways to the ultimate Being. "But when shall we come to him?" the poet asks on the threshold of the mystic citadel. And a voice from within replies, "I have often been among you."

Fargue conceives God in the spirit of the old Vedas. God, he thinks, ceased to be at one time in order to see. He fell from heaven into the heart of man. His singleness turned to complexity and penetrated all things. But ultimately God returns to his unity, and enfolds man within it. The old shepherd gathers his flock unto himself.

The essence of every living thing is constituted by this divine presence, the poet believes. It may be experienced in the labor and pain of our hands and eyes, in the joys and frustrations of our minds and hearts. One thing only the poet excepts: man's logic. He sees in it a distortion of the divine will to be, a toxin of the intelligence that limits man to the stature of man, and represses his inner urge towards identity with the deity. Instead of seeking to discover the why and wherefore of created things, man should love them for what they are, he reflects. From human ideas, doubts, desires and vain cries, he should turn to communion with God, and bury his ignorance in His omniscience. "Nothingness. . . . Omnipresence! Nothingness. . . . Peace. Return to the luminous ignorance."

The last word in the mystery of life and death, Fargue concludes, is ignorance, and that is the same as knowledge. "Since you are going to know all, without learning, unlearn everything which taught you nothing." The answer to the enigma of destiny is silence. (pp. 130-32)

He is moved by a deep sense of the magnitude of our human loneliness and unhappiness. But he does not fight windmill battles in the metaphysical emptiness. He is dearly attached to the material world, which is the only anchor the gods vouchsafe man in a shifting universe. He senses the abyss the spirit digs around all matter of course. But he does not let go the hand of God. His poetic ecstasy illumines his way. His Spinozism remains active, buoyant. "I am an Occidental, active shadow," he says, "Saki-Mouni cannot do anything for me."

In the end, the poet resumes his place among men. His journey through the heavens ends upon the earth, and the image of God re-enters its human abode in him. . . . (pp. 132-33)

There is no ostentatious rhetoric in the art of Fargue. His expression is straightforward and simplified, immediate and symbolic. He rejects both the philosophy and practice of traditional prosodies. To dress modern poetry in the rigid forms of yesterday seems to him either a disrespectful or ridiculous performance. For it is, on the one hand, he thinks, like dressing one's mistress in the outworn garments of one's grandmother and, on the other, it is equivalent to making a drill-sergeant of the poet. A poem consisting of well-regimented, well-drummed verses may please the eye and ear. But there are moments when the soul is atuned to subtler music. It is for those moments that Léon-Paul Fargue writes. His rhythm is free and dictated from within. His language is so uniquely his own, that one must carefully pitch one's sensibility to it in order to appreciate fully its melody and harmony. He introduces words in the orchestration that no French dictionary lists, words dug out of old glossaries, from which he extracts fresh sounds; words built out of the wreckage of old syllables, which he carves again into new music-boxes. But no matter what their origin, these words acquire distinction and letters of nobility the moment they take their place in his writings. A pompous phrase, he had said, sounds like a shriek from a courtesan. In his books there are only Vestals, whose words and signs are ideographic symbols of the spiritual fire they keep alive in his poetry. (pp. 133-34)

Fargue objects to works of art that represent only the art of work. All human reason and rhyme are feeble and fallible, he holds. Life alone is indestructible. But art must sift and choose. Or rather the artist must. Hence the dilemma: to be or to live. The artist obviates the alternative, however. He chooses both to live and to survive, thus emulating nature in life as well as in art.

This is why the poetry of Fargue is so little tainted with philosophical pretentions. For ideas, he has an instinctive distrust. Ideas are parasites on life. An idea is a beautiful but lost chance for silence, he believes. They are the corpses of emotions that have ceased to be. And poetry feeds on living emotions, not on corpses. Poetry is symnonymous with love, in life and beyond life. That of Fargue is free from the impersonal quality which is characteristic of pure reason. It is a cup brimming with the ecstasy of love, both earthly and spiritual. (p. 135)

Poetry becomes in his hands an instrument of redemption, a lyre with which to play an accompaniment to the passionate pilgrimage of the poet in the universe. It serves, in the twentieth century, for the few who can be atuned to it, as a rallying-cry through its confusion, as an angelus to their souls homeward bound. (p. 136)

S. A. Rhodes, "The Poetry of Léon-Paul Fargue," in The French Review *(copyright 1935 by the American Association of Teachers of French), Vol. IX, Nos. 1 and 2, November and December, 1935, pp. 26-35; 127-36.*

ALLANAH HARPER   (essay date 1949)

[Harper describes Fargue as an interpreter of the Paris of his day and the poet of its moods and locales.]

Léon-Paul Fargue was Paris and Paris was his, and he re-created it for us. In a sense, he was the poet of Paris even more than Baudelaire, his verse is more intimate than those overwhelming masterpieces that take us beyond the particular into the universal. Fargue's vision was so personal, his relations with his surroundings so intimate that he pierced through objects; mute things spoke to him, animals and human beings communicated with him in their private, their secret voices. Fargue's poetry and prose poetry are composed of a fusion of the colloquial and the mysterious; his language is accessible to all the senses like the language of the great symbolists. Fargue was more completely aware than most poets of the relation of musical notes to word sounds. He heard the music inherent in things and he found or created words which conveyed that music, those particular sounds. Remembering the past, which was so important to him, he remembers the music of a house or a person or an object; he is attracted back to the place or the time by the music playing in his memory. (p. 355)

Léon-Paul Fargue was a most accurate interpreter of his own period, he is also the link between the delicacy of Verlaine and the robustness of Villon. He combines these two qualities. Fargue is, I think, the most original French poet since Rimbaud. As great an innovator as Apollinaire who owed him much—in the same manner as Fargue himself was indebted to Mallarmé, the master of the Symbolists, the alchemist of hermetic art. But Fargue was not an imitator of anyone. Perhaps the greatest living French poet, Paul Claudel, a poet whose spiritual experience is deeper and whose work is of vaster dimensions than Fargue's, said that Fargue was a poet born. 'That is, not a spectator, but a maker of life; not a copyist, but an associate and collaborator of creation, one to whom the Fairy had given a grain of salt and a spark of fire. . . . When one reads a page of Fargue, the lines do not remain still like an inanimate passementerie, but the whole rectangle of the page starts to walk and to boil, agitated by a kind of colloidal movement like a market place on a Saturday or the street in front of the Town Hall the day of the drawing of the lottery! One sees dancing, turning, pushing, taking arms, taking off hats, pinching in their gussets with an imperceptible hand a microscopic watch, a crowd of tiny beings prodigiously active and alive, made of a name, a noun, an adjective, a verb and an adverb, a comma and an exclamation mark' Claudel said. . . . (pp. 356-57)

[Fargue's] creation of new words, and the new associations he made between words, his prodigious analogies and metaphors, his creation of phonetic caricature, give fresh life to the French language. He was doing in his manner what Joyce was doing for the English language. (p. 358)

Fargue is the poet of the melancholy of cities. I can think of no other writer who gives the local tone, the particular atmosphere of the place and the thing described with such precise analogy. He wrote much about barrel-organs in sad streets. The barrel-organ in his own street facing the Gare de l'Est, had a monkey on its carpet and smelled of petrol, it played a tune that accompanied the trains into the station. He wrote of 'the sad street like a discharged baker's boy, and all the houses have on their grey aprons . . . ' (p. 359)

Fargue composed his work with the precision of an artisan selecting and examining each piece before constructing a mosaic; or a naturalist dissecting the minute mechanism of an insect. Minuteness was visible to his microscopic eye.

Flies also write everywhere with a small noise.

A patrol of mosquitoes dances sometimes around our heads, like a sad little head of hair, like

St. Elmo's fire at the peak of some midnight spar.

(p. 360)

In Fargue, poetry and life were consubstantial; writing poetry was the crystallization of memory, in fact the only manner by which those precious memories were made eternal, were turned into black diamonds that gave off sparks of fire and lit up the darkness of his night. He was so much a poet in his living that had he not written a line he would have lived his poetry, would have illuminated the lives of his friends by the fantastic imagery of his conversation. He juggled with words as he spoke. . . .

I write to put order in my sensuality. It is not necessary to blacken paper in order to be a poet. Poetry expresses a psycho-physiological state, to put it simply, one lives or one does not live in a state of poetry. Everything in life that has no material interest for its object gives you the right to the good road and can lead to the poetic condition. As for the poet-writer, well, he is a hunter. His mission is to bring back beauty for everyone. . . .

Fortunately for posterity, Léon-Paul Fargue was a hunter who brought back all kinds of fabulous creatures both beautiful and strange. He was the most human of writers. He used to say that he had long made his choice—he preferred men to works. 'Do not specialize. Beware of Orthopaedia. Remain a distinguished amateur.' (p. 361)

What matter whether you dream the world or the world dreams you, what matter whether we are electric pencils, a kind of bat, the sparks of an overwhelming association, a divine catalyst, a growth of the cosmic dust, the error of a vortex swinging the master loops of a lassoo, or whether I empty myself out vertiginously with my chair. All we can say, find or do, after all! is of man, and the Unknown plays with us as the cat plays with the mouse.

But Fargue also wrote, 'It is not necessary to write to be a poet. One must be in a state of grace and contemplation, and that is enough.' (p. 362)

Allanah Harper, "Recollections of Léon-Paul Fargue," in Horizon, *Vol. XIX, No. 113, May, 1949, pp. 354-67.*

ANDRÉ BEUCLER   (essay date 1952)

[*In his memoir of his long friendship with Fargue, Beucler provides a character sketch of the poet.*]

It was his ubiquitousness and versatility that led some to see two Fargues and to dissociate the one from the other. On the one hand, they saw the charming schemer, the diner-out (who, incidentally, always came late), the 'Wandering Jew of the outer boulevards, adored by duchesses, petted by girls'. On the other, the man of letters, hardworking, cultured, and conscientious, who, laying his legendary personality aside, got quietly on with his job. (p. 40)

In this they were wrong. Fargue lived as he spoke, spoke as he felt, and wrote of what he saw. He would begin one of his works in a friend's house and carry on with it in a café. He would spend an hour at a station, as others in a reference library, and correct his proofs at the bank. Wherever he went, whatever he did, it was all of equal importance. You can see it in his work: the romance of man and artist inextricably intertwined. (pp. 40-1)

Turn this way or that way as he might, in one respect he never deviated. He was a poet everywhere; he was a poet all day long. Naturally, without effort, and whether he was discussing great things or small. It might be a journey from Paris to Lyons or a ride up to the fourth floor in a lift. Critics might have their reservations; and some did in 1924, for he didn't fit in with their theories. He mistrusted them. He was in revolt against intellectualism, which he didn't regard as one of the essentials. In those days we were still in the literature of limited liability. More tolerant than it is today, society didn't force those who held a pen to take sides. We were still a long way from 'the absurd', from blind alleys and flagrant social injustice. The 'complete uselessness of art to the masses' had not forced itself on people's attention. Power, wealth, and luxury belonged to the elegance of the age; they didn't stigmatise a camp. The class struggle had not yet engulfed the sensibilities, and the free man did not yet need to feel ashamed of devoting himself to a life of the senses, to loneliness, and dreams. . . .

Rooted in a still more tolerant age, Fargue could give himself to himself without wondering whether he oughtn't to be taking up the cudgels against exploitation. He was a soldier all right, but of no army, the champion of everyday life. (p. 41)

> *André Beucler, in his* Poet of Paris: Twenty Years with Léon-Paul Fargue, *translated by Geoffrey Sainsbury (reprinted by permission of the author and Chatto & Windus; originally published as* Vingt ans avec Fargue, Milieu du monde, 1952), *Chatto & Windus, 1955, 248 p.*

LÉON-PAUL FARGUE (essay date 1952)

[*In a conversation recorded in André Beucler's* Poet of Paris: Twenty Years with Léon-Paul Fargue, *Fargue discusses some of his attitudes toward life and literature.*]

We have all of us, tucked away in our innocence, a little nest of sincerity, a nodule, a kernel, and we say to ourselves—and this is true of all the arts—that it might be amusing to the spectator or the reader to see it more closely, to discover what we think of human beings and their passions, their landscapes, the condition of their souls. Literature is a continuation of conversation. You're expected in a drawing-room, you're watched at a dinner, you're tracked down on a first night to be asked 'what do you think of it?'. . . . (p. 27)

I only write for my own pleasure. When I experience sensations, I note them; I promptly begin chewing them. Certainly I try to give them a form, and do my best to convey them to others. I think we have all of us, deep down, an instinct to do that. It's natural. . . .

That is to say, you are concerned to let others know your sentiments and through them to know you yourself. That implies a career, then fame, then glory.

I'll confess something. The mere fact of wanting to be read contains already the idea of glory, in its embryonic or magic state. It's the desire for complicity between the bird and the fowler, the charmer and the charmed. For the last fifty years men of letters have been pestered with the question, whether, absolutely alone in the world or marooned on a desert island, they would still write. Of course they wouldn't. For one thing, how could one be all alone in the world and yet be in possession

of a language, of paper, of pen and ink? . . . We write because we are many. . . . Yet I still maintain that I write for my own personal delectation. If I think of the public—and I certainly do—it's without being conscious of it. Feelings—that's what I put first, the gathering together of friends, the interactions of people who have hearts, a home, and memories. I love life, even when I don't like it, even when it strews my path with banana skins. I have a taste for everything. The least little thing, the humblest, reflects the light. It has its own little story, its own little smell, which it may be amusing or pathetic to discover and then to reveal. . . .

I come and go; I feel myself to be on high land in the same sense as sailors are on the high seas. All that I see, all that is done in the round of the clock, is to me intoxicating—every sound, the clatter of saucepans in the kitchen, the rumbling of the *Métro,* the turmoil of faces and the flow of traffic, music, card games, children streaming out of school, hospitals, circuses, night, clouds—all the richness and variety of each instant, the little instant in the middle of which we stand, helplessly, porous while life flows through us, resonant while it echoes within us. . . . Intoxicating, yes, to me, to everyone, and we finish up all of us trembling with poetry, trembling with love, till we can neither see nor understand, as though some malignant pest was eating out our brains. . . . (pp. 28-9)

I like cats and ears and courtyards and chimneys. I like nice warm cafés and rainy days. I like handicrafts and quays, cheeses and pianos, grazing deer, blind alleys, and frogs. Those are my guiding principles! . . . For the rest—opinions are for the mediocre. . . . (p. 30)

So far as I'm concerned, everything that comes to us through any other channel than feeling is false. And by false I mean just that. I use the word in its everyday sense. In a work of art, ideas and intentions leave me cold. But the least hint of real tenderness—and it may be simply a gramophone blaring away through a window—goes straight down my spine. (p. 58)

> *Léon-Paul Fargue, in extracts from conversations recorded by André Beucler (reprinted by permission of the author and Chatto & Windus), in* Poet of Paris: Twenty Years with Léon-Paul Fargue *by André Beucler, translated by Geoffrey Sainsbury (originally published as* Vingt ans avec Fargue, Milieu du monde, 1952), *Chatto & Windus, 1955, pp. 9-45, 46-66.*

THE TIMES LITERARY SUPPLEMENT (essay date 1955)

[*Excerpted below is a brief summary of Fargue's poetic identity and importance.*]

There is little to recommend it now, but *Tancrède* takes its place with *Les Cahiers d'André Walter* and the first poems of Paul Valéry, "où s'irise une faible lune"; it has the illogical style, the wryness, the *appel à l'inconnu* that characterize "advanced" works from the end of the century.

By 1912, when his *Poèmes* were published, Fargue was perhaps at his poetical height. . . . **"Aeternae Memoriae Patris,"** quick with grief, the first and longest of his collected poems, is most poignant in its expression of memory and solitude. . . . This was a distinct advance beyond the early ironic lyrics collected under the title *Ludions,* and the poetry in *Tancrède* and the rest of *Poèmes,* arranged as prose, maintain a grave emotion that defines love and regret, the twilight, the region between dream and pain, the nostalgia that the simple process of life engenders.

After the First World War Fargue published little, and the next event of consequence was Princess Bassiano's founding of the excellent periodical *Commerce* in 1924. Co-editor with Larbaud and Valéry, Fargue worked frenziedly to achieve a renovation of the spirit, and in this sane and adventurous review a new stage in his development is apparent. It was towards a richness of imagery, rhythm and texture. The books *Banalité*, *Epaisseurs*, and *Suite Familière* belong to this period of full recognition and success. . . .

The stroke [which Fargue suffered in 1943] removed no essential quality from his work, but intensified his journey into the interior; immobility caused him to call upon the reserves of memory and dream, on a generous, active past that shimmered in the white light of remembrance, the days of the *belle époque*. Memories crowded into his solitude, crackling under his pillow, he says, like insects of glass.

But there was an irreparable change in the legend of Fargue the *vieux garçon*, trailing around Paris for hours on end in his own faithful taxi; a change from the noctambulant, irresponsible poet, the idler on the alert, the gourmand, always turning in the enchanted circle of Paris, "ce bon géant plein de finesse." Fargue, as he amply demonstrates, had a tutored heart for places, a sharp sense of mobility, a feeling for departures totally different from the urbanities of the *wagon-lit* school of writing. He had contrived to make Paris a fertile country, yielding in a hundred aspects.

He could justly claim, then, to be the poet of Paris. From his recreative solitude he rebuilt a Grandville-like setting of metamorphosis, where bicycles are water-spiders, the *fiacres* are prehistoric survivals that almost speak, where the streets are filled with ghosts. His hotels, *chambres meublées*, taxis, concierges, and cigarette-ends become alive and familiar through sharp metaphors and a style that combines the Mother Goose tales of Perrault with the zoologist's laboratory, or that echoes the bituminous mysteries of Rabelais's scholar who deambulated "by the compites and quadrives of the Urb." Fargue found the Museum of Natural History a fecund starting-point, and prehistory and anatomy provide him with words and ideas for what is essentially a cosmic view of life. He sees not only the skeleton beneath the flesh, but the diplodocus not far under the subsoil; like T. E. Hulme, he hears men laughing at a bar, but cautions himself to wait for the fundamental chaos to reveal itself. The rather medieval, cataclysmic view is typical of Fargue's awareness of disorder. . . .

A collection of short pieces, half essay and half prose-poem, published under the title *Haute Solitude* in 1941, is perhaps the best expression of every attitude that had developed in Fargue. Heaven and Hell, the Deadly Sins, the virtues, the Music of the Spheres and the Dance of Death, the Feast of Fools and the Chain of Being are his skeletal beliefs; his preoccupations are chimera and mutability, his own sensibility and vulnerable heart, and the hazards of the brittle mould of flesh. His method was to write a *littérature d'enchantement*; he expressed a horror of style "qui ne pique pas le nez," for style, he claimed, should be a Twelfth-tide cake with a hidden reward for the good reader. In practice, this brought certain difficulties in its wake; in fact, the reader suffers occasional indigestion from too rich a material and too liberal a love of such devices as telescoped metaphor, puns, conceits, Spoonerisms ("Batiplantes—Jardins des Gnolles"), inversions, and categories of things to all appearance unrelated but whose clandestine marriage he loved to make public—although it must be said that Fargue is masterly in the quick discernment of "occult resemblances," the *discordia concors* that is part of the substance of poetry.

"*Léon-Paul Fargue*," *in* The Times Literary Supplement (© *Times Newspapers Ltd. (London) 1955; reproduced from* The Times Literary Supplement *by permission), No. 2786, July 22, 1955, p. 410.*

WALLACE FOWLIE (essay date 1955)

[*Fowlie is among the most respected and comprehensive scholars of French literature. His work includes translations of major poets and dramatists of France (Molière, Charles Baudelaire, Arthur Rimbaud, Paul Claudel, Saint-John Perse) and critical studies of the major figures and movements in modern French letters (Isidore Ducasse, Stéphane Mallarmé, Marcel Proust, André Gide, and the Surrealists, among many others). Broad intellectual and artistic sympathies, along with an acute sensitivity for French writing and a first-hand understanding of literary creativity (he is the author of a novel and poetry collections in both French and English), are among the qualities that make Fowlie an indispensible guide for the student of French literature.*]

With exceptional precociousness Fargue wrote his first poems between the ages of ten and fourteen. Some of these he preserved and published in the collection *Ludions*. His father and uncle ran a factory of ceramics and glass-work, and the poet all his life cherished the concept of the craftsman or the artisan, a love of objects, a respect for the precision of technical terms. His visits as a child to the Natural Museum explain to some degree the fabulous world he created in *Vulturne* and *Visitation Préhistorique*, with their petrified flora and fauna. (p. 48)

Tancrède was the title of [Fargue's] first volume and was the name given to a school mate who had inspired Fargue by his elegance and grace. Fargue himself has acknowledged the influence on his work of such poets as Laforgue, Corbière and Lautréamont. There is also visible an influence of Rimbaud in the rhythm of the sentences and in the condensation of the images. His form of writing is markedly independent, an intermediary form between narrative prose and rigorously composed verse. The writing of Fargue is distinguished by its musical effects, by its purely verbal virtuosity. . . .

[In *Poèmes, suivis de Pour la Musique*] and in all the subsequent volumes of Fargue, there are examples of that art of the genius whose sensibility closely resembles the child's. Everything is an image or a metaphor. Everything is evocative of an earlier period, of a reality which most men lose sight of. The Poet willingly turns toward the past and even a very distant past, as that in *Vulturne*, and questions all that is perpetually mysterious for man. He can see back to the creation of the world, and ahead to its dissolution. Throughout this vast space of time he claims the age-old privilege of the poet to explore and to exploit the secret forces of the universe. He wonders about the centuries that have passed and about the last scenes of the world's destruction. But he is also a man of science who knows the precise terms of his subject, who knows the popular songs of his age and the slang of his contemporaries. The ease with which Léon-Paul Fargue evokes the past and the present, and the vigor of his style remind one of Rabelais, that other student of the past, whose imagination was unruly. (p. 49)

Fully half of [Fargue's] writings are devoted to Paris. His pieces on St. Germain, on the Ile Saint-Louis, on the railroad stations and the faubourgs are lyric-realistic prose poems where, underneath comic metaphors and concetti, one can sense a deep sadness. His language at all times is musical and supple. His use of enumeration and analogy is reserved but always exhilarating. Fargue's poetic style is comparable to that developed by Michaux and Audiberti, and, to some extent, to the style of Giraudoux. The delicate tenderness of these four writers never exists without some element of anguish, some degree of distrust. The poets dream turns ironical, as it once did with Laforgue. (p. 51)

> *Wallace Fowlie, "Léon-Paul Fargue: Introduction and Bibliography," in Mid-Century French Poets, edited by Wallace Fowlie (reprinted by permission of Grove Press, Inc.; copyright © 1955 by Wallace Fowlie), Grove Press, 1955, pp. 48-51.*

H. P. BOUCHÉ (essay date 1979)

[*Excerpted below is Bouché's introduction to a section translated from* Haute solitude. *Bouché is allied with the worldwide College of Pataphysicians. Based on the writings of French author Alfred Jarry, Pataphysics is the "science of imaginary solutions," a casual ideological doctrine which takes an absurdist view of all aspects of existence.*]

The most sedentary poet of the century was its most untiring explorer of the imagination. . . . An individual with "twelve thousand senses, wharves of ideas, colonies of feeling, and a memory of three million acres" (**Haute Solitude**) could easily consider the travels and experiences of a tourist vain and valueless. (p. 302)

[Fargue] couples a bent for discovery with a flair for creating a style suited to these astonishing circumnavigations, with their uncertain, hilarious or deceptive endings, to these ambiguous "dead ends cluttered with butterflies" where we observe the pataphysical creation of imaginary memories. The **Ludions** . . . , set to music by Erik Satie, whose childlike "counting" style matches Fargue's taste for mystification, re-create with frequently invented and distorted words an eerie and vital world, more immediate than the present. The past disappears—and with it, once and for all, every type of poetry which concerns itself with the past.

Fargue was as little inclined to follow a literary school (he quickly dissociated himself from the surrealist poets, whom he referred to as "false witnesses") as to seek out the public, and it was often necessary to take his manuscripts away from him.

[*Sous la lampe*, Le Piéton de Paris and especially *Haute Solitude*] . . . stake out his tireless and solitary prospecting of the imaginary.

At the end of his voyaging, like Jules Verne's polar captain, he arrives finally at "**Destiny**" [*Saison en Astrologie* and *Les Quat' Saisons*]. . . : in his role as director of the obsequies of the universe—to the tune of his "**Danse Mabraque**" (*Haute Solitude*)—Fargue unveils his mystification; everything has been foreseen in the ineluctable, delectable disorder of that grandiose and final voyage. At the crossroads of the breakdown of twenty centuries of civilizations, Fargue calmly watches the universal chaos roll by. (pp. 302-03)

> *H. P. Bouché, "Léon-Paul Fargue," in Evergreen Review Reader: 1957-1961, edited by Barney Rosset (reprinted by permission of Grove Press, Inc.; copyright © 1979 by Grove Press, Inc.), Grove Press, 1979, pp. 302-03.*

ADDITIONAL BIBLIOGRAPHY

Auster, Paul. Introduction to *The Random House Book of Twentieth-Century French Poetry*, edited by Paul Auster, pp. xxvii-xlix. New York: Random House, 1982.*

> Brief commentary in which Auster states that Fargue's poetry of Paris "transforms the city into an immense interior landscape. The poem of witness is at the same time a poem of remembrance, as if, in the solitary act of seeing, the world were reflected back to its solitary source and then, once more, reflected outward as vision." This anthology includes translations by various hands of several of Fargue's prose poems with the French originals on facing pages.

Hartley, Anthony. Introduction to *The Penguin Book of French Verse 4: The Twentieth Century*, edited by Anthony Hartley, pp. xx-lii. Baltimore: Penguin Books, 1959.*

> Passing comment on Fargue which observes that "his dominant emotion is nostalgia and he adds to it a capacity for conveying blank unhappiness which is all his own." This anthology includes prose translations by the editor of a poem and a prose poem by Fargue.

Rhodes, S. A. "Candles for Isis: A Symposium of Poetic Ideas among French Writers." *The Sewanee Review* XLI, No. 2 (April-June 1933): 212-24.

> Includes a three and a half page transcription of a conversation with Fargue.

Rudolph Fisher

1897-1934

American short story writer, novelist, dramatist, critic, and essayist.

In his brief career, Fisher distinguished himself among Harlem Renaissance authors with novels and short stories noted for their narrative ingenuity and satirical objectivity. With masterful attention to detail, he captured the gradations of Harlem speech patterns and lifestyles during the 1920s and early 1930s. Fisher was one of the first "New Negro" writers to satirize both black and white society as he explored the serious problems of the newly-migrated black southerner in Harlem, examining interracial and intraracial prejudices and the conflict between traditional and modern mores.

Born in Washington, D.C., to middle-class parents, Fisher attended primary and secondary schools in New York and Providence, Rhode Island. A Phi Beta Kappa at Brown University, where he earned his B.A. and M.A. degrees, Fisher went on to graduate with honors from Howard University Medical School and continued his education at Columbia University. Not a professional writer, Fisher published his first short fiction while still a medical student. He continued to write fiction and literary criticism, as well as scholarly articles for medical journals, throughout his medical career. He died at the age of thirty-seven from a chronic intestinal ailment.

In the early years of the Harlem Renaissance, writers like Claude McKay and Jean Toomer accepted the "primitive" treatment of black characters popularized by white writers, including Eugene O'Neill in his *The Emperor Jones* and Carl Van Vechten in *Nigger Heaven*. Reacting against this stereotyping, black novelists such as Jessie Fauset and Nella Larsen tried to present respectable black characters while still appealing to white readers. Embracing neither the primitivism nor the self-conscious pleading that dominated the fictional treatment of black Americans, Fisher portrayed his characters with an unbiased, though sympathetic detachment. He maintained a tone of impartiality in stories like "The City of Refuge" and "Miss Cynthie," leaving moral judgments about the city and its people to the reader.

The examination of class, color, and cultural distinctions recurs throughout Fisher's short stories: in "Blades of Steel," the low class "rats" and rich "dicties" are pitted against one another; in "High Yaller" a "white" black girl, taunted when she appears in public with her boyfriend, crosses the color line to escape both black and white prejudice. While white prejudice is a secondary issue in Fisher's works, of primary concern are the divisive influences of money and skin color within Harlem, as well as the negative reaction of black Americans to "outsiders" like Africans and West Indians. In "Common Meter," as in several other stories, music symbolizes the common bond among black people. Using a dance to bring together otherwise nonsocializing factions of the community, Fisher vividly illustrated class conflicts and the potential for resolution of conflict within Harlem society.

Often considered his best story, "Miss Cynthie" combines two of Fisher's recurring concerns—the contrasting value systems of traditional southerners and modern northerners, and the

value of music as a form of cross-cultural communication and reconciliation. Cynthie, initially disappointed to find that her grandson's success is achieved as a disreputable, "sinful" cabaret performer and not as a doctor, or "at least" as an undertaker, gradually changes her opinion of his profession. Reconciliation results when the grandson reminds Cynthie that it was she who first taught him the joy and self-expression possible through music.

Aside from his short stories, Fisher wrote two novels. *The Walls of Jericho*, written after his short stories had met with some success, brings together Harlem insiders and outsiders at a General Improvement Association dance. The angry new negro, professional uplifters, thrillseekers from downtown, and organizations like the NAACP are satirized in a dramatic comedy of manners. *The Conjure Man Dies*, written two years before Fisher's death, is distinguished for being the first detective novel written by a black author. Critics consider it typical of the genre in style and quality. Like his short stories, Fisher's novels display strong characterizations. Old time preachers, newly-migrated black southerners, West Indians, and city-slick Harlemites are vividly portrayed through their personal and cultural dialects. Sensitive to the subtle gradations of slang and dialect, Fisher has been compared to American humorist Ring Lardner for his manipulation of spoken idioms. Informed with puns and inventive personifications which animate the Harlem cityscape, the novels and short stories sustain subtle humor even when they treat serious themes. Descriptively vivid and detailed, Fisher's works faithfully render their Harlem setting—from the Sugar Hill bourgeosie "dictidom" to the "rats" below—complete with schools, hospitals, night clubs, and barber shops on streets which correspond to distinct class associations.

Langston Hughes called Fisher the "wittiest of these New Negroes of Harlem, whose tongue was flavored with the sharpest and saltiest humor." While other Harlem Renaissance writers used satire directed at whites, Fisher's satire was directed at the black community, which critics considered a skillful and sophisticated innovation. Fisher took a stand for neither the "common" individual, as did Claude McKay, nor the "respectable," often servile, middle class depicted by such writers as Jessie Fauset. This detachment, which some attribute to Fisher's distance from the masses of black people because of his social class and education, contributes to the quality of documentary realism in his fiction. Because of this realism, some commentators find his works to be important historical documents as well as accomplished literary creations. While most praised Fisher for writing about aspects of Harlem other writers neglected, some critics, notably W.E.B. Du Bois, objected to his treatment of low-life blacks. In his review of *The Walls of Jericho*, Du Bois criticized Fisher for presenting the "low class" Linda and Shine as detailed, well-developed characters, while leaving his "own kind," the "better class negroes," sketchy in their development. Du Bois nonetheless considered the novel "a strong, long, interesting" step up from the works of Claude McKay and Carl Van Vechten.

Though some critics view stories such as "Blades of Steel" and "Dust" as contrived and constructed solely to reveal surprise endings reminiscent of O. Henry, many others agree with Robert Bone that, at their best, Fisher's "stories contain isolated passages that are unexcelled in their depictions" of Harlem life. Fisher wrote: "Outsiders know nothing of Harlem life as it really is. What one sees in a night club or a dance hall is nothing, doesn't scratch the surface—is in fact, presented solely for the eyes of the outsider." Many feel that Fisher had not reached his full potential as a writer when he died at age thirty-seven. Yet he stands as one of the few Harlem Renaissance writers who emphasized intraracial conflict without bitterness or blame, and who sought to emphasize the common experiences of black people.

(See also *Contemporary Authors*, Vol. 107.)

PRINCIPAL WORKS

"The City of Refuge" (short story) 1925; published in journal *Atlantic Monthly*
"High Yaller" (short story) 1925; published in journal *The Crisis*
"Ringtail" (short story) 1925; published in journal *Atlantic Monthly*
"The South Lingers On" (short story) 1925; published in journal *The Survey Graphic Number;* also published as "Vestiges: Harlem Sketches" [revised edition] in *The New Negro*, 1925
"The Backslider" (short story) 1927; published in journal *McClure's Magazine*
"Blades of Steel" (short story) 1927; published in journal *Atlantic Monthly*

"The Caucasian Storms Harlem" (essay) 1927; published in journal *American Mercury*
"Fire by Night" (short story) 1927; published in journal *McClure's Magazine*
"The Promised Land" (short story) 1927; published in journal *Atlantic Monthly*
The Walls of Jericho (novel) 1928
"Common Meter" (short story) 1930; published in journal *Baltimore Afro-American*
"Dust" (short story) 1931; published in journal *Opportunity*
The Conjure Man Dies (novel) 1932
"Ezekiel" (short story) 1932; published in journal *Junior Red Cross News*
"Ezekiel Learns" (short story) 1933; published in journal *Junior Red Cross News*
"Guardian of the Law" (short story) 1933; published in journal *Opportunity*
"Miss Cynthie" (short story) 1933; published in journal *Story 3*
"John Archer's Nose" (short story) 1935; published in journal *The Metropolitan*
Conjur Man Dies (drama) 1936

*This drama is an adaptation of the novel *The Conjure Man Dies*.

THE TIMES LITERARY SUPPLEMENT (essay date 1928)

Mr. Rudolph Fisher, one of the most interesting of contemporary negro writers, has given in *The Walls of Jericho* . . . a sympathetic and extraordinarily impressive account of negro thought and habit. As a storyteller he holds the reader's attention from first to last; his story has vigour and naturalness, and it is told with unfailing and pungent humour. But it is hard to dissociate the literary virtues of the narrative from its merit as a piece of evidence touching social and racial psychology in the United States. Mr. Fisher has no point of view to labour; on the contrary, he is impatient of systematic efforts to solve the negro "problem" and rather scornful of those people who look for a solution in endless discussion and futile organization. His concern is rather with the everyday characteristics of the negro temperament and with their impact on the development of negro society. The unusual thing about his novel is that its modes of thought and feeling, patiently spontaneous, are such as no "white" man could achieve; their truth to life is never in doubt, but it is quite plain that they are characteristic of the negro consciousness. The language of the story is the language of Harlem (the "expurgated and abridged" glossary of terms at the end of the book is fascinating reading), but every idea or sentiment it conveys is just as obviously "Harlemese."

At either end of the social scale the negro's tastes and experience, it seems, are in flat opposition to custom and privilege. Fred Merrit, the wealthy lawyer, bought a house in a street in one of the residential quarters in New York in which no negro had as yet dared to plant himself. Joshua Jones, known to his fellows as Shine, helped to move Merrit's furniture into the house, and in so doing observed a negro housemaid entering a house a few doors away. Neither fact may appear particularly significant, but together they provide Mr. Fisher with the means of illustrating the entire outlook of the negro on his ambitions and personal behaviour, and on his place in American society.

Merrit's house is duly burned down, not by his neighbours, however, but by another negro who bears him a grudge. And Shine proceeds to become better acquainted with the housemaid. Into this seemingly ordinary narrative pattern Mr. Fisher has contrived to set a brilliant and cunningly diversified picture of negro character. Merrit, confessedly rabid on the subject of race, whose chief joy is in making white people uncomfortable, presents an illuminating contrast with Jinx and Bubber, Shine's fellow-workers, who have not a thought about the negro question between them, and whose racy, colloquial humour forms a pleasant feature of the novel. But it is Shine himself, a massive giant of a man, distrustful of people, white or black, resolved to keep every act "sentimentally air-tight," who best brings out the potential strength and philosophy of character the author has discovered in the inhabitants of Harlem.

> *A review of "The Walls of Jericho," in* The Times Literary Supplement *(© Times Newspapers Ltd. (London) 1928; reproduced from* The Times Literary Supplement *by permission), No. 1388, September 6, 1928, p. 630.*

NEW STATESMAN   (essay date 1928)

It is evident that, following the success of [Carl Van Vechten's] *Nigger Heaven*, we are to be given a number of novels celebrating the migration of literary New York from Greenwich Village to Harlem. Some may be very good indeed; the majority are likely to be, like [*The Walls of Jericho*], mediocre. *The Walls of Jericho* is not a bad book, but it seems continually to be drawing back from the problems it suggests. Defying popular prejudice, a "white" Negro buys a house in "a snob of a street," hitherto wholly "Nordic." He makes the acquaintance of a fellow-resident, who discovers his black blood only after having asked him to call. He never does call, and when his house is burned down it is not by his neighbours but by another Negro who seeks revenge for purely private and personal reasons. The major part of the story concerns the quite simple love-affair of two other Negroes, a furniture mover and a servant girl, the determination of the former to be a "hard guy"—his delusion that he *is* a "hard guy"—being the barrier referred to in the title. The book as a whole is somewhat fragmentary, and there is perhaps a little too much back-chat of a music-hall type between the furniture movers. (pp. 704, 706)

> *A review of "The Walls of Jericho," in* New Statesman *(© 1928 The Statesman Publishing Co. Ltd.), Vol. 31, No. 803, September 15, 1928, pp. 704, 706.*

[W.E.B. Du BOIS]   (essay date 1928)

[*DuBois was one of the most prominent black authors in American literature. In addition to writing novels, poetry, and sociological studies, he also edited the magazine* Crisis, *in which the following review of* The Walls of Jericho *originally appeared.*]

["**The Walls of Jericho**"] is another story of Harlem, following the footsteps of "Nigger Heaven" and [Claude McKay's] "Home to Harlem." The casual reader wading through the first third of the book might think it nothing else but a following of these pathfinders into the half-world north of 125th Street. But a little persistence and a knowledge of what Rudolph Fisher has already accomplished in his remarkable short stories, will bring reward. For the main story of a piano mover and a housemaid is a well done and sincere bit of psychology. It is finely worked

out with a delicate knowledge of human reactions. If the background were as sincere as the main picture, the novel would be a masterpiece. But the background is a shade too sophisticated and unreal. Mr. Fisher likes his two characters, Jinx and Bubber, and lingers over them; but somehow, to the ordinary reader, they are only moderately funny, a little smutty and certainly not humanly convincing. Their conversation has some undoubted marks of authenticity, for this kind of keen repartee is often heard among Negro laborers. But neither of these characters seems human like Shine.

Mr. Fisher does not yet venture to write of himself and his own people; of Negroes like his mother, his sister and his wife. His real Harlem friends and his own soul nowhere yet appear in his pages, and nothing that can be mistaken for them. The glimpses of better class Negroes which he gives us are poor, ineffective make-believes. One wonders why? Why does Mr. Fisher fear to use his genius to paint his own kind, as he has painted Shine and Linda? Perhaps he doubts the taste of his white audience although he tries it severely with Miss Cramp. Perhaps he feels too close to his own to trust his artistic detachment in limning them. Perhaps he really laughs at all life and believes nothing. At any rate, here is a step upward from Van Vechten and McKay—a strong, long, interesting step.

> [*W.E.B. DuBois], in his review of "The Walls of Jericho," in* The Crisis *(copyright 1928 by The Crisis Publishing Company, Inc.), Vol. 35, No. 1, November, 1928, p. 374.*

ISAAC ANDERSON   (essay date 1932)

The "conjure-man" in Dr. Fisher's first mystery novel ["**The Conjure-Man Dies**"] is a native African, a King in his own right, who has come to America, and after taking a degree at Harvard has settled in Harlem, where, for a consideration, he is prepared to reveal the past and foretell the future of those who wish to consult him. When he interviews his clients he sits in the dark back of a bright light which shines in the face of the seeker after hidden truth. One of his clients, so seated, suddenly discovers that he is talking to a dead man. This is the beginning of a mystery which takes on such varied aspects as time goes on that the reader is kept busy wondering who, if anybody, has been murdered—to say nothing of the how and the why. The characters are all Negroes, and almost the entire action of the story takes place in the conjure-man's apartment in Harlem. The author, who is a Negro physician, has one excellent earlier novel, "**The Walls of Jericho**," to his credit. In the present book he presents a puzzling mystery yarn which is at the same time a lively picture of Harlem and its various types of Negroes. He does not make the mistake, so common with Caucasian authors, of making all his Negroes comic; but those who are intended to be funny are very funny indeed, and their comedy has a legitimate place in the story.

> *Isaac Anderson, in his review of "The Conjure-Man Dies," in* The New York Times Book Review *(© 1932 by The New York Times Company; reprinted by permission), July 31, 1932, p. 13.*

BROOKS ATKINSON   (essay date 1936)

[*As drama critic for the* New York Times *from 1925 to 1960, Atkinson was one of the most influential reviewers in America.*]

To a paleface, fresh from Broadway, ["Conjur' Man Dies"] seems like a verbose and amateur charade, none too clearly written and soggily acted. . . .

When the play bursts into an undertaking parlor, Frimbo, the conjure man, is apparently murdered, and the police start tracking down the criminal. But before the play is half over Frimbo returns, apparently from the dead, although that part of the question is open to doubt. Not to draw too fine a point on this free-hand sketch in mumbo-jumbo, "Conjur' Man Dies" is stuffed full of clues, terrified and superstitious suspects, a comic detective, a devil's chamber of weird lights, a doctor's laboratory, some gift furniture and a regal robe for the black man of baleful magic. Mr. Fisher wrote out of a reliable box of theatre tricks.

With considerable judicious cutting and after a few ruthless rehearsals, "Conjur' Man Dies" will doubtless improve and become a routine mystery show. Obviously, the Harlem audiences love a buffoon with a brown derby and a stutter, and they are right.

> *Brooks Atkinson, "Harlem Mumbo-Jumbo," in* The New York Times *(© 1936 by The New York Times Company; reprinted by permission), March 12, 1936, p. 18.*

STERLING BROWN (essay date 1937)

[*Brown was a poet, folklorist, educator and critic of Harlem Renaissance writers. His criticism and anthologies are among the most important contributions to the field of black literature. In the following excerpt from his* The Negro in American Fiction, *Brown sees traces of mystery writer Octavus Cohen's burlesque character Florian Slappey in Fisher's slapstick characterizations of Jinx and Bubber. The wise-cracking duo appears in both of Fisher's novels,* The Walls of Jericho *and* The Conjure Man Dies.]

Rudolph Fisher portrays Harlem with a jaunty realism. *The Walls of Jericho* deals with types as different as piano-movers and "race-leaders." The antics of Jinx and Bubber are first-rate slapstick, and though traces of Octavus Roy Cohen appear, most of the comedy is close to Harlem side-walks. Fisher is likewise master of irony. Miss Cramp, the philanthropist, who believes that mulattoes are the result of the American climate, is caricatured, but the picture of the Annual Costume Ball of the G.I.A. (General Improvement Association) is rich comedy of manners. He deftly ridicules the thrill-seekers from downtown who find everything in Harlem "simply marvelous." Satiric toward professional uplifters, *The Walls of Jericho* still has the New Negro militancy. Merrit is an embittered "New Negro"; he believes that the Negro should let the Nordic do the serious things, and spend his time in "tropic nonchalance, developing nothing but his capacity for enjoyment," and then take complete possession through force of numbers. Fisher likewise shows the spirit of racial unity between the "dicties" and the masses—"'Fays don' see no difference 'tween dicky shines and any other kind o' shines. One jig in danger is ev'y jig in danger." It is significant, however, that the wrecking of a Negro's house in a white neighborhood is the work of a disgruntled Negro, the villain of the book.

But Fisher was less interested in the "problem" than in the life and language of Harlem's poolrooms, cafes, and barber shops. *The Conjure Man Dies* . . . , the first detective novel by a Negro, brings Jinx and Bubber back to the scene to help solve one of Harlem's grisliest murders. A high-brow detective, an efficient Negro police sergeant and an erudite doctor

of voodoo are interesting new characters. The novel is above the average in its popular field and was followed by a Harlem tenement murder mystery solved by the same detective.

Before his untimely death, Fisher became one of the best short story writers of the New Negro movement. "The City of Refuge," containing a good description of the southern migrant's happy amazement at Harlem, and "Blades of Steel" are first-rate local color of the barber shops, dance-halls and cafes. "Vestiges" and "Miss Cynthie," for all of their light touch, have an unusual tenderness and fidelity to middle class experience. Fisher was an observer with a quick eye and a keen ear, and a witty commentator. At times his plots are too neat, with something of O. Henry's trickery. His Harlem is less bitter than McKay's, but it exists; and his realism, as far as it goes, is as definite as that of any of the numerous writers who took Harlem for their province. (pp. 135-36)

> *Sterling Brown, "The Urban Scene," in his* The Negro in American Fiction *(copyright, 1937 by The Associates in Negro Folk Education; reprinted by permission of the author), Associates in Negro Folk Education, 1937 (and reprinted as his* The Negro in American Fiction. Negro Poetry and Drama, *Arno Press, 1969, pp. 131-50).* *

HUGH M. GLOSTER (essay date 1948)

In his treatment of Harlem in *The Walls of Jericho* . . . Rudolph Fisher, concentrating upon the everyday life of the Negro metropolis, describes the relations of representative Harlemites with each other as well as with their white associates. The main thread of the story recounts the wooing of Linda Young, a respectable housemaid, by Joshua "Shine" Jones, a piano mover. (p. 174)

The Walls of Jericho successfully interweaves life in at least three separate levels of Harlem society. One of the social strata is that represented at Patmore's Pool Parlor, a drinking and gambling center where lower classes vent their spleen for "dickties." . . . In striking contrast to the group at Patmore's place is the respectable domestic class, exemplified by Linda and Merrit's housekeeper, Arabella Fuller. Linda does not easily submit to male conquest, avoiding the blandishments of Patmore and not yielding to "Shine" until sure of his honorable intentions. The third Harlem group portrayed in *The Walls of Jericho* is the sophisticated coterie that mingles freely with white people. The leader of this set, "superiorly self-named the Litter Rats," is J. Pennington Potter, a proud, loquacious, and pompous person who believes that amalgamation is the only key to interracial harmony. On the other hand, Merrit, also a member of the set, is vigorously anti-Nordic. . . . (pp. 174-75)

Fisher's descriptions of the general social life of Harlem are realistic. We catch glimpses of church life, the Sunday promenade on Seventh Avenue, the coarse fun of pool room patrons, and the General Improvement Association Annual Costume Ball at Manhattan Casino. (p. 175)

In his treatment of the General Improvement Association Fisher satirizes the National Association for the Advancement of Colored People. J. Pennington Potter, for example, wisecracks that Negro agencies seek to furnish "delineation, history and prophecy in a single title." Again, Linda, in a conversation with Miss Cramp, gives the following unwittingly derogatory account of the work of the organization:

Well, they collect a dollar a year from everybody that joins, and whenever there's a lynch-
ing down South they take the dollar and send
somebody to go look at it.

(p. 176)

The Walls of Jericho, resorting neither to debunking nor to
glorification, handles racial issues with independence and objectivity. This novel reveals the first Negro author skilled in
comic realism and able to use irony and satire not only upon
whites but also upon various classes of his own people. Fisher's
preoccupation with humanity, rather than with race, enables
him to tell a dispassionate story. *The Walls of Jericho,* in brief,
shows that Fisher has an intimate understanding of the Harlem
scene as well as the ability to treat this setting with frankness
and detachment. Much of Fisher's success in depicting the
Negro in New York City is traceable to his mastery of Harlem
speech. . . . (pp. 176-77)

Further evidence of Fisher's knowledge of Harlem and its inhabitants is revealed in his short stories and in his second novel,
The Conjure-Man Dies. . . . *The Conjure-Man Dies,* in which
all of the characters are colored, is the first full-length detective
novel written by an American Negro. Turning from controversial racial issues, the book is a refreshing creation that compares favorably with other works of its type. In establishing
the guilt of a paranoiac murderer, Fisher not only makes use
of his own medical and psychiatric training but also introduces
interesting sidelights on the Harlem policy racket and African
sex ritual. "Jinx" Jenkins and "Bubber" Brown, brought over
from *The Walls of Jericho,* furnish spicy comic relief; and Dr.
John Archer, who has the leading male role in the novel,
deserves a place in the gallery with Van Dine's Philo Vance
and other well-delineated heroes of detective fiction. The most
original creation in the book, however, is N'Gana Frimbo, an
African prince educated at Harvard and practising as a psychiatrist in Harlem. (p. 177)

> *Hugh M. Gloster, "Fiction of the Negro Rena-*
> *scence," in his* Negro Voices in American Fiction
> *(copyright, 1948, by The University of North Car-*
> *olina Press), University of North Carolina Press,*
> *1948, pp. 116-95.**

WATERS E. TURPIN (essay date 1967)

Rudolph Fisher in his **"Miss Cynthie"** shares with Toomer
[the] ability to evoke the atmosphere of a locale and at the
same time limn a character so sharply that the reader feels he
is observing a living, breathing person, one whom he has met
before and delights in meeting again.

On the surface, **"Miss Cynthie"** is a deceptively simple tale
of a proud, elderly but sprightly grandmother's visit to Harlem
at the behest of her grandson, David, who is obviously prosperous—"Mus' be at least a undertaker," Miss Cynthie speculates to a friendly Red Cap who is working summers to pay
his way in medical school, "'cause he started sendin' the
homefolks money, and he come home las' year dressed like
Judge Pettiford's boy what went off to school in Virginia. . . ." But the story is more than that, for Fisher manages
through his portrait of this little old lady from the South to
voice the hopes, higher aspirations and values of a minority
group seeking to enter the mainstream of American life. Her
grandson, motherless almost from birth, carries for her the
banner of fulfillment which she in her lifetime had not been
able to hold high. When the Red Cap tells her that he is studying

medicine, her response reveals this: "'You is?' She beamed.
'Aimin' to be a doctor, huh? Thank the Lord for that. That's
what I always wanted my David to be. . . .'" . . . Here is
not just a Negro grandmother speaking; here is an archetypal
figure, voicing the spirit of all grandmothers in all times and
places. (p. 62)

The discovery that her grandson is a famous song-and-dance
man, teamed with his wife Ruth, comes as a shock to Miss
Cynthie when they take her to the old Lafayette theater to
witness a Broadway-bound revue in which they are the stars.
At first to the religious old lady Ruth and David are sinful
nymph and satyr backed by a chorus of lascivious other nymphs
and satyrs. But Fisher skillfully brings about the reconciliation
between the grandma's "old-time religion" and the superb art
of the stars and the ensemble. (p. 63)

In **"Miss Cynthie,"** then, Rudolph Fisher has created a living
portrait of an archetypal grandmother whose high aspirations
for her grandson clash with his real calling in terms of his
particular talent. Within the logic of his story, Fisher has brought
about a believable reconciliation between the old lady's values
and those of her grandson. (p. 64)

> *Waters E. Turpin, "Four Short Fiction Writers of*
> *the Harlem Renaissance—Their Legacy of Achieve-*
> *ment," in* CLA Journal *(copyright, 1967 by the Col-*
> *lege Language Association; used by permission of*
> *the College Language Assocation), Vol. XI, No. 1,*
> *September, 1967, pp. 59-72.**

WILLIAM H. ROBINSON, JR. (essay date 1969)

Rudolph Fisher chose to depict the Harlem "black folk" character. (p. ii)

Always a realistic satirist, Fisher was very much aware of the
pseudo-modishness, the cruel hypocrisy of much of the Harlem
Renaissance—for instance, the average Harlem resident of the
time was not allowed into the fashionable, white-owned and
white-attended nightclubs in his own community. Fisher's fictional themes are varied, but he seems to be most concerned
with the outcome of confrontations between big city corro-
siveness and newly urbanized "rural" Negroes. He may have
indulged some romantic primitivism in *The Conjure Man Dies,*
but generally, as in **"The South Lingers On,"** a sensitive five-
part sketch, he is sincere in reflecting the folk life around him.

While color-consciousness destroys a romance in **"High Yaller,"**
color does not seem pivotally important in most of his other,
uncollected, short stories. Written on a bet that no one short
novel could blend the extremes of Harlem society into a single
cohesive story successfully, *The Walls of Jericho* is an especially comprehensive display of the themes that are common
in American Negro literature and Fisher's own brilliantly satirical treatment of such themes. Thus, color (with the lawyer,
Merit), the well-intentioned but hopelessly uncomprehending
white philanthropist (Mrs. Agatha Cramp), the antics of the
conveniently paired stock "folk" characters (Jinx and Bubber),
the ultimate triumph of the put upon, honest and simple Negro
(Shine), the pretensions of the educated avant garde Negro
(The Litter Rats) and other literary ploys are all presented here
for inspection and enjoyment. (pp. iv-v)

> *William H. Robinson, Jr., "Introduction" (copy-*
> *right ©1969 by Arno Press, Inc.; reprinted by per-*
> *mission of the author), in* The Walls of Jericho *by*
> *Rudolph Fisher, Arno Press, 1969, pp. i-v.*

DORIS E. ABRAMSON (essay date 1969)

[Rudolph Fisher's] short stories and novels exhibited animated wit and humor abundantly, but his play [*Conjur Man Dies*] failed to be anything more than an evening's light entertainment, with some suspense of the "whodunit" variety. (p. 60)

The novel *The Conjure-Man Dies* became the play *Conjur Man Dies,* but by the time it was on stage at the Lafayette Theatre . . . , Rudolph Fisher had been dead for over a year. . . . One cannot help thinking that *Conjur Man Dies* needed cutting and rewriting during the rehearsal period, and that no one but the author could have done these things to make it a better play.

Although *Conjur Man Dies* was very popular with Federal Theatre audiences and was toured by traveling WPA outdoor players as part of New York's recreation program, the script is far from satisfactory. The structure of the play is clumsy, a three-act play in fifteen scenes (five, four, and six), with none of the rich language and subtle characterization for which Dr. Fisher's short stories are famous. (pp. 60-1)

N'Gana Frimbo, for all his bizarre qualities, is the most interesting and believable character in the play. He is on the stage, unfortunately, only a short time. . . . This man, with his Harvard degree, who had been a king in Africa, who dealt in dark chambers and disguises, is not a new phenomenon in our society. His existence suggests the only Negro problem in the play—and one that is not a strictly Negro concern—a tendency to superstition.

Rudolph Fisher's *Conjur Man Dies* only touched on the whole problem of superstition and its role in the lives of Negroes. (pp. 62-3)

Rudolph Fisher can scarcely be held to account for the flaws in his play, *Conjur Man Dies.* With more experience in the theatre, this brilliant young man who wrote such dramatic stories might have written a good play, but he died before he had a chance to do so. The one play that we have is an awkward first attempt. (pp. 86-7)

> *Doris E. Abramson, "The Thirties," in her* Negro Playwrights in the American Theatre, 1925-1959 *(copyright © 1967, 1969 Columbia University Press; reprinted by permission of the publisher), Columbia University Press, 1969, pp. 44-88.**

STANLEY ELLIN (essay date 1971)

[*Ellin, an award-winning mystery writer, evaluates Fisher's mystery novel,* The Conjure Man Dies, *in the following excerpt.*]

The Conjure-Man Dies is, first and foremost, highly readable, wholly entertaining.

This should go without saying, since the book is a mystery novel of merit, and the sole function of any mystery story is to entertain. (p. iii)

But it is a fact that a writer of authentic talent can and will create within the genre a novel which, while staying in bounds, offers a good example of that talent. Rudolph Fisher was such a writer, and the one mystery novel he wrote, *The Conjure-Man Dies,* originally published in 1932, offers striking evidence of it, especially when viewed in the light of its times. Its success on publication was great enough to carry it into production as a play by the Federal Theater Project. Its rediscovery, and appearance in [a 1971] edition, are no more than proper tributes

to both its readability and its merits as a record of its period. (pp. iii-iv)

His authorship of *The Conjure-Man Dies* gave Fisher a lonely distinction. Since the 1860's, when Metta Victor in America and Wilkie Collins in England produced the first formal mystery novels, there had been no Negro writer who utilized this technique as a means of literary expression until Fisher came along. (p. iv)

It is highly probable that Rudolph Fisher, intrigued by the idea of presenting Harlem, from top to bottom, in a mystery novel that could reach a larger audience than a straight novel, devoted himself to some serious study of what made the books of both Hammett and S. S. Van Dine tick, since both their approaches are clearly evident in *The Conjure-Man Dies.* Fisher's extremely complex plotting and his occasionally too-pedantic writing of descriptive and expository passages is in the classical mode. But the characters, their broad range of background, and the handling of dialogue are wholly of Hammett's realistic school.

Overall, it is clear that Fisher's own sympathies and interests lie with Hammett, much as he deferred to traditional techniques. Stylistically, if one judges by the descriptive and expository writing in his novel, *The Walls of Jericho,* it is possible that he was not so much deferring to what he thought the mystery reader demanded as reflecting a background of pre-World War I reading. Every writer is strongly influenced by the reading he most enjoyed in his teens. It is the exceptional writer who, like Fisher, can dispense with its influence even in part.

In either case, there is no question that it is Fisher's adherence to the new realism which, as in Hammett's works, invests *The Conjure-Man Dies* with the qualities of a social document recording a time and a place without seeming to. One is drawn through the book by its story, but emerges at last with much more than that story in mind. (pp. vi-viii)

> *Stanley Ellin, "Introduction" (reprinted by permission of Curtis Brown, Ltd.; copyright © 1971 by Stanley Ellin), in* The Conjure-Man Dies: A Mystery Tale of Dark Harlem *by Rudolph Fisher, Arno Press, 1971, pp. iii-viii.*

ARTHUR P. DAVIS (essay date 1974)

Rudolph Fisher, a Harlem physician and roentgenologist, viewed the black community with an understanding and amused eye. To him, it was a place where all kinds of Negroes—good, bad, and indifferent—from several areas—the South, the West Indies, and Africa—found a haven from the hostile white world. Fisher knew Harlem intimately—its con men, its numbers barons, its church goers, its night-life people, its visitors from the outside white world, and, above all else, the new migrants from the South, who found Harlem a miraculous city of refuge. His short stories and novels belong, with Cullen's *One Way to Heaven* and McKay's *Home to Harlem,* to the literature of the black ghetto; but his picture of Harlem is fuller than that of either McKay or Cullen. A comic realist, he laughed at the foibles of all classes of Harlemites from the "rats" (ordinary Harlem folk) to the "dickies"; but his laughter is healthy and therapeutic. It comes from a deeper-than-surface knowledge of and a fondness for the inhabitants of the black city. (p. 98)

Fisher's first Harlem short story ["**City of Refuge**"] was written while he was in medical school. . . . The story deals with a theme expressed in its title—a theme which appears often in Fisher's work—the wonder, pleasure, protection, and pride the black newcomer finds in Harlem. (p. 99)

["**The South Lingers On**"], republished in [Alain Locke's] *The New Negro* as "**Vestiges**," consists of five sketches or vignettes showing the impact of Harlem on the Southern Negro. The first of the five deals with a Negro preacher whose flock has left one by one for Harlem. He finds them again, by accident, and reclaims them from a charlatan. The second sketch (which does not appear in *The New Negro*) concerns the faith which an unskilled Negro worker, in spite of disappointments and rebuffs, still has in the promise of Harlem. The third vignette deals with that much-used character, the Negro grandmother, who is the family anchor. Unsuccessfully trying to keep her granddaughter from the sinful ways of the city, the old lady in her defeat has only one recourse left—prayer. The next deals with the ambitions of a Negro girl who wants to go to college but whose Southern-born father feels that graduation from high school is enough. "Too much learnin' ain' good f' nobody." Pride causes him to change his mind when his daughter wins a scholarship to Columbia Teachers' College. The last story concerns two Harlem men about town who drop in on a tent revival just for kicks. The preaching and the praying are too much for one of the young men. He has not lost as much of his Southern upbringing as he had thought. In these sketches Fisher gives a nonsensational look at the deep imprint which the South has left on its sons and daughters who made their way North. In these simple and uncontrived vignettes he has shown Harlem to be, not the fun city of downtown white thrill seekers, but, actually, a transplanted Southern community, bigger and brassier, of course, but still essentially a slice of the South.

The best of Fisher's transplanted-Southerners stories is "**Miss Cynthie**." . . . It, too, has one of those strong, colorful grandmothers, in this case a spry and positive old lady known in her native town by black and white alike simply as Miss Cynthie. (p. 100)

In several of Dr. Fisher's stories, color prejudice within the Negro group plays a significant part. Fisher, unlike McKay, does not overplay the issue, but he does not ignore or sidestep it. Moreover, he shows that all of the bias is not on one side. One of the most revealing stories of this type is "**High Yaller**." . . . It concerns the hard road a light-colored Negro girl has to travel in a community of dark-skinned persons. Trying to make an adjustment, she dates a black boy and gets into trouble with her dark-skinned Negro "friends" on the one hand and white people on the other. Discouraged and disgusted, she gives up the battle for acceptance and crosses over the line. . . .

Although both Claude McKay and Langston Hughes have written a larger amount of short fiction than Fisher, their works lack the controlled intensity, the suggestiveness, the subtlety, and the overall artistry that his short stories have. (p. 101)

Fisher's style in [his novels *Walls of Jericho* and *The Conjure-Man Dies: A Mystery Tale of Dark Harlem*] is clear and uncomplicated. If there is a weakness, it is a tendency to write like a professor on occasion; but he does not have any trouble in making his characters talk convincingly and naturally. One notes that in both these novels, large segments of each dealing with lower-class life, there is absolutely no use of four-letter words and no sex. Fisher, like Du Bois and other New Negro authors, believed in putting one's best foot forward. There were

some things that one just did not parade for the white folks to see. McKay had shown the "debauched Tenth" and was condemned for it—by Negroes. Although Dr. Fisher could easily have played *up* the primitive side of Harlem life, he preferred to play it *down*. It was part of the price one's dual-inheritance demanded. (pp. 102-03)

Arthur P. Davis, "Rudolph Fisher," in his From the Dark Tower: Afro-American Writers, 1900 to 1960 *(copyright ©1974 by Arthur P. Davis; reprinted by permission of Howard University Press), Howard University Press, 1974, pp. 98-103.*

ROBERT BONE   (essay date 1975)

[*Bone has stated that as "a white man and critic of black literature, I try to demonstrate by the quality of my work that scholarship is not the same thing as identity." The following excerpt is taken from his* The Negro Novel in America.]

The best of local-color fiction strives to transcend the merely picturesque, and when it succeeds, it moves in the direction of pastoral. . . .

Fisher's most mature stories, "**Common Meter**" and "**Miss Cynthie**," are concerned with reconciliation, within a pastoral framework, of the classes or the generations which divide the black community. (p. 141)

In a story called "**High Yaller**," Rudolph Fisher gives us a brief glimpse of his Harlem boyhood: "Over One Hundred and Thirty-fourth Street's sidewalks between Fifth and Lenox Avenues Jay Martin's roller-skates had rattled and whirred in the days when that was the northern boundary of Negro Harlem. He had grown as the colony grew, and now he could just recall the time when his father, a pioneer preacher, had been forever warning him never to cross Lenox Avenue and never to go beyond One Hundred and Thirty-fifth Street; a time when no Negroes lived on or near Seventh Avenue and when it would have been almost suicidal for one to appear unarmed on Irish Eighth."

This fictional account of Fisher's boyhood encompasses the chief ingredients of his imagination. The notion of a *boundary*, an artificial barrier creating a forbidden territory, and thereby denying access to experience, is basic to the impulse of the picaresque. The taboo, moreover, is enforced by the boy's father, whose paternal authority is associated with the Negro church. Several of Fisher's stories are concerned thematically with the crossing of forbidden boundaries, or in theological terms, with snatching Experience from the jaws of Sin. Their rogue-heroes bear witness to the fact that they derive from the tradition of the picaresque.

At the same time, the passage has profound historical reverberations. All the tensions and hostilities of the Great Migration are embodied in the clash between the Negroes and their Irish neighbors. The exposed position of the blacks, making racial solidarity imperative, is the source of Fisher's pastoral romances. Throughout his work, divisive tendencies within the black community are mollified and harmonized. His primary effort is to bridge the gap between the classes, but differences arising out of regional, generational, or (in the case of West Indians) former national affiliation are likewise subject to the healing qualities of pastoral. (pp. 150-51)

Harlem is the stamping ground of Fisher's imagination; without exception it provides the setting of his tales. (p. 152)

Fisher's intimate knowledge of the Harlem scene led him to exploit its possibilities as local color. His stories contain isolated passages that are unexcelled in their depiction of the Harlem cabaret, the rent party, the barbershop, the dance casino, and the Sunday promenade on Seventh Avenue. Good social history, however, is not necessarily good literature. If presented for its own sake, such material may detract from the author's larger purposes. In the end Fisher pays a heavy price for his reliance on local color. As the novelty of his Harlem settings wears thin, his imagination falters, and he tends to repeat himself.

Two metaphors convey Fisher's essential relation to the Harlem scene. In several of his stories the protagonist looks down upon the spectacle of Harlem life from an upper box, upper window, or upper balcony. This spatial metaphor embodies the social perspective of the black bourgeoisie, which overlooks the Harlem scene from the lofty eminence of Sugar Hill. In other stories Fisher seems to be conducting a guided tour of Harlem for a party of visitors from downtown. The name of the tour is "Adventures in Exotic Harlem," and it includes observations on the quaint customs of the country, helpful hints for fraternizing with the natives, and a Berlitz phrase-book for the comprehension of contemporary Harlemese.

The psychological setting of Fisher's stories—the interior landscape to which he compulsively returns—is a state of intolerable estrangement from his father. Several of his tales are concerned with dramatizing this estrangement, and effecting a symbolic reconciliation. **"The Backslider"** and **"Fire by Night"** . . . , for example, are variations on the theme of the Prodigal Son. In these stories a backsliding, ne'er-do-well, and potentially criminal youth is rescued from his self-destructive impulses and restored to middle-class respectability.

In essence there are two Rudolph Fishers: a conforming and rebelling self. The conformist is the middle-class child who obeys his parents when they warn him not to play with roughnecks. He is the brilliant student who is Class Day Orator at Brown, who graduates *summa cum laude* from Howard, and establishes his professional identity as Dr. Fisher. The rebel is Bud Fisher, frequenter of speakeasies and cabarets, who has always envied the bad kids on the block and who writes about them in his fiction. The rebel self, however, is more mischievous than dangerous, and after a period of bohemian adventures settles into middle-class routine. Such is the psychodrama at the heart of Fisher's cruder tales.

In a second group of Fisher tales, the theme of breach and reconciliation is projected outward on the social plane. Here the author strives to repair various divisions that threaten to destroy the black community. Thus **"Ringtail"** is concerned with the enmity between West Indian and native-born American; **"High, Yaller,"** with the potentially disruptive force of a light complexion; **"Blades of Steel"** and **"Common Meter"** with the social class division that separates the "rat" from the "dicty." In each of these contexts, Fisher's aim is to exorcise the demons of disruption and cement the ties of racial solidarity. (pp. 152-54)

The object of his fiction is precisely to provide a common ground, to bind the social classes in a racial confraternity, and thus to rescue union from diversity. A favorite setting for his fiction is the ballroom scene, where all of Harlem gathers for the communal rite of the Saturday night dance. The action of **"Common Meter,"** for example, takes place in a dance casino symbolically denominated "The Arcadia." For the ballroom

and its ethnic music qualify as common ground, where the mediating force of pastoral can work its magic spell.

Fisher's "Arcadia" is modeled on the old Savoy, where two jazz bands played nightly for the Harlem throng. A lusty paganism fills the hall: the Pipes of Pan are jazz trumpets, at whose prompting nymphs and satyrs cavort across the floor. Metaphorically at least, it is a sylvan scene: "a brace of young wild birds double-timed through the forest, miraculously avoiding the trees." . . . Against this background a rivalry develops between two band leaders for the favors of a lovely girl. As appropriate to pastoral romance, however, the contest is contained within a ritual frame. The two musicians and their bands will compete for "the jazz championship of the world," with the tacit understanding that the victor wins the girl.

Two styles of musical performance thus provide the main dramatic contrast of the tale. Fess Baxter's work is flashy but inauthentic; his music is full of tonal tricks and false resolutions. Bus Williams' stuff, on the other hand, is the genuine down-home blues. Threatened with defeat in honest competition, Baxter slits his rival's trapdrum with a knife. Our heroine, however, saves the day, by instructing Williams' band to beat time with their feet, thus converting the blues performance to a shout. This ancestral form, handed down through generations from the tribal past, so stirs the crowd that opposition fades, abandoning the field to love.

At the center of the story is a pastoral inversion. The smart money hits the canvas; the city slicker is confounded; country music and elemental honesty combine to win the girl. The superiority of blackness is the point: to be possessed of soul is precisely to be capable of improvising, of winning the contest *without* your drums. At bottom, Fisher is warning the black community to guard itself against a certain kind of spiritual loss. Don't abandon your ancestral ways when you move to the big city; don't discard the authentic blues idiom for the shallow, trivial, flashy, meretricious values of the urban world.

A third group of Fisher stories is explicitly concerned with the Great Migration. As the author's imagination reaches out to embrace the historical experience of millions, his art assumes a greater density of texture and complexity of vision. On the plane of history, moreover, Fisher's divided self proves to be an asset: it enables him to project and then to mediate the central value conflict of his age. For the split personality of the Baptist preacher's son mirrors the divided soul of the Southern migrant. Both are torn between a set of standards that are traditional, religious, and puritanical, and a series of temptations that are novel, secular, and hedonistic.

Fisher's strength lies in the fact that he is genuinely torn between these value systems. His very ambivalence allows him to achieve a delicate balance of rural and urban, traditional and modern values. His divided psyche generates a powerful desire to mediate, or reconcile, or find a middle ground, which is the source of pastoral. He is therefore able to encompass the paradoxes of change and continuity, of spiritual loss and gain, which are the essence of the Great Migration. He is able to record the disappointments and defeats of the Southern migrants, and yet to celebrate the hope which survives their disillusionment.

"The City of Refuge" . . . is Fisher's first attempt to treat the paradoxes of the Great Migration. King Solomon Gillis, a greenhorn from the South, is bamboozled by a Harlem gangster and left to face a twenty-year sentence for peddling dope. His arrest by a black policeman, however, reconciles him to his fate, for he perceives that Harlem, while it may betray the Southern migrant, also offers him the possibility of manhood. The final scene where Gillis stands erect, exulting in his new-born sense of dignity and racial pride, is a powerful epiphany of the New Negro. Unhappily the story as a whole, which is riddled with bad writing, does not match the brilliance of its dénouement.

"The Promised Land" . . . is a more successful treatment of the migratory theme. As the story opens, a spiritual and a blues are contending for supremacy from opposite sides of an air-shaft. The words of the spiritual ask, "How low mus' I bow / To enter in de promis' land?" Fisher's subject, then, is the social cost of the Great Migration. Divisiveness is the price the black community must pay to enter in the promised land. Urbanization brings division between the generations; between skilled and unskilled black workers; between established and more recent immigrants; between the partisans of gospel music and the blues.

These divisions are dramatized by the conflicts between Mammy and her grandsons; between the cousins, Sam and Wesley; and between the country cousins and Ellie, the city girl. Mammy is the first of several matriarchal figures who embody the old-fashioned virtues in Fisher's tales. In a memorable scene, she tosses the family Bible through a window of the opposite apart-ment to restrain her grandsons from fighting over Ellie. She represents the unifying, mediating force of pastoral, and she supplies whatever of cohesiveness and continuity the migratory family is able to achieve. Yet in the end she fails, and one of her grandsons is a sacrifical victim to the gods of racial prog-ress.

"Miss Cynthie" . . . is the best of Fisher's stories, by virtue of a crucial technical advance. Having given us a gallery of static characters, he suddenly discovers how to *interiorize* his dramatic conflicts, so that his protagonists have an opportunity to grow. The title character, Miss Cynthie, is thereby able to embody in her own person the spiritual agony of the Great Migration. Painfully, reluctantly, and only after a sharp internal struggle, her old-fashioned morality bends and stretches to accommodate the new. Fisher's theme is the emergence of new moral codes, appropriate to new historical conditions. (pp. 155-58)

The aim of pastoral is reconciliation. In this instance it is not so much a matter of reconciling rural and urban values, or of mediating a conflict between the generations, as of bridging a gap between the black artist and the black middle class. The secret theme of "Miss Cynthie" is the reconciliation of bour-geois success norms with the unconventional and slightly sus-pect enterprise of art. David is a projection of Fisher's artist-self. The folk material that each employs as the basis of his art is suspect in the eyes of the black elite. To reconcile Miss Cynthie to her grandson's métier is thus to reconcile the black bourgeoisie to a certain kind of "lowlife" art.

Beyond these public meanings, the story serves a private end. The symbolic action indicates that Fisher has resolved the basic conflict of his adolescence and achieved the integration of a perilously fractured self. In the love and mutual respect of David and Miss Cynthie, his rebelling and conforming selves are harmonized. The result is an impressive gain in poise and equilibrium. "Miss Cynthie" constitutes, in short, a psycho-logical as well as an artistic triumph. Published in the shadow of impending death, it testifies to Fisher's inner growth and aggravates our loss of his maturing powers. (pp. 158-59)

Robert Bone, "Three Versions of Pastoral," in his Down Home: A History of Afro-American Short Fic-tion from Its Beginnings to the End of the Harlem Renaissance (copyright © 1975 by Robert Bone; re-printed by permission of the author), G. P. Putnam's Sons, 1975, pp. 139-70.*

THOMAS FRIEDMANN (essay date 1976)

[*Friedmann views Fisher's short story "Common Meter" as ex-hibiting a prescient "consciousness of blackness," stating: "By fully fifty years, Fisher anticipates the notions of 'Black is beau-tiful'."*]

Although its appearance in Abraham Chapman's *Black Voices . . .* , does not represent the first printing of **"Common Meter,"** the story is still not well known. Neither is its author, Rudolf Fisher, prominent in the gallery of Black writers, al-though he published two novels and many short stories during his lifetime. Perhaps this neglect is due to the fact that he has been dead for more than forty years and that younger writers are addressing themselves to contemporary issues in language more familiar to today's generation. Be that as it may, one reads this half century old story with a shock of recognition. Hardly could one find issues more contemporary than those examined in this story. More important, the terminology used to discuss those issues is up to date as well. By fully fifty years, Fisher anticipates the notions of "Black is beautiful," and uses the blackness of a man's skin to indicate his goodness much the same way that the vintage Western informed us of the hero's sterling character through the glaring whiteness of his hat. As such, **"Common Meter"** is a valuable source for those who look for early indications of the change in Black consciousness and for those who search literature for positive uses of the color black. As one goes about trying to reverse "the bigotry of language" which associates white with good and black with bad, scarcely a better source for examples is available than **"Common Meter."**

Set in a dance hall, "The Arcadia," on Harlem's Lenox Av-enue, **"Common Meter"** is the story of two men, leaders of jazz bands, who compete for supremacy in music and in love. The object of their affection is Jean, one of the dance hall hostesses. The essence of their musical contention is the proper place of rhythm in jazz. To the cynical modern reader, the outcome is possible only in a fairy tale. The winner is the most noble and upright character, the jazz musician who prizes rhythm above all else and the man whose skin is darkest. The less cynical reader can appreciate the prophetic vision of the author who acknowledges and even encourages the fairy tale quality but is realistic enough to be ironic and optimistic enough to believe in the triumph of a black consciousness.

Our first sight of Bus Williams, leader of the "Blue Devils," presents the criteria for his ethical and amatory standing. His face is "jolly" and "round," and it "beamed" down on the crowd. The description is clearly positive, particularly in con-trast to the one applied to Fessenden Baxter. The leader of the "Firemen" has an impersonal "countenance," unlike Bus's human "face." His features are presented as being much harsher as well. They are "blunt," where Bus's were round; glaringly "bright," where Bus was softly beaming.

More important, however, in our search for "color-coded" identification, Bus is a brown man while Fess is the "cheese colored," specifically "Swiss-cheese." The yellowish-white skin color thus ascribed to Fess places him at the far end of the spectrum. The middle ranges of this dark to light spectrum are occupied by Jean, a girl literally and figuratively "in the middle," whose skin is amber—brownish yellow—and by Curry, the manager of the dance hall, who is "yellow." Just as the skin color of these people ranges from dark to light, so does their moral character. Where the traditional association would have been from low to high moral standing, in **"Common Meter"** a new tradition is begun. In this story the lighter the skin color the lower the moral character of the individual.

Fessenden Baxter is guilty, of course, of sins and errors that bear no connection to his color. He tries to seduce Jean, for example, "talking her up" during their dance together with only dishonorable intentions in mind. Then he brags of conquering her, crudely announcing, "Yea. And I says, 'I'm a cash customer, baby. Just name your price.'" Threatened by Bus to declare which girl it was that he claims "fell," to him, the cowardly Fess retracts his claim. He is also vain, "surreptitiously adjusting his ruffled plumage," a thief, rearranging other people's music and claiming it as his own, and a cheat, sabotaging the musical instruments of the rival band in his attempts to win the "battle of the bands." Those shortcomings of character do not, however, relate to the author's color scheme.

Fisher uses color to denote character when Fessenden's crimes are committed against color itself. He declares Fess guilty of rejecting his blackness. His indictment is thorough. Fess has "straightened brown hair," he tells us, stressing the fact that his hair, as his attire and music, are not natural. Consistent with his rejection of blackness of feature, Fess avoids the black elements in his jazz. Denying the association of blackness and rhythm, Fess Baxter "considered rhythm a mere rack upon which to hang his tonal tricks." Fisher's description of the Baxter style stresses the deliberately non-rhythmic aspect of his jazz. The price he plays during the contest is "dizzy with sudden disharmonies," is filled with "dissonances," contains "twists" and "false resolutions."

What is wrong with this philosophy, explains Fisher, is that it is a false representation of the race. Where Bus's rendition of the blues is genuine, "the nakedest of jazz," interpreting for his people "like leaden strokes of fate," their dissatisfaction with their lot, Baxter's music attempts to mislead and misdirect them, not merely helping them forget their existence but insisting their perceptions of it to be incorrect. His music exhausts his listeners, "distorting" and "etheralizing" their emotions. Fisher declares his contempt through Bus, stressing Fess Baxter's lack of black consciousness. "The cream-colored son of a buzzard!" Bus exclaims, bleaching that Swiss-cheese colored, yellowish-white skin into still a lighter shade.

In contrast to Fess Baxter's whiteness is Bus William's blackness, in color, music, and identity. As with Baxter, Bus's character is established with no reference to color. He displays his forthrightness and honesty by honorably proposing to marry Jean, by defending her reputation and by creating his own music, unlike Baxter, who often makes use of some "re-arrangement." This behavior makes Bus a good man. His sense of being a black, on the other hand, also gives him nobility.

It is in his philosophy and interpretation of music that Bus displays his black consciousness. In theory, he values rhythm, holding tone to be "merely the vehicle" for rhythmic patterns. For Fisher, the black musician as the black man, yearns for harmony, for "unfaltering common rhythm." And as Bus begins to play, Fisher makes clear that the harmony Bus achieves is the harmony with the self. His music enables his listeners

to forget, just as Fess Baxter's playing did. But where Baxter's jazz put his listeners out of touch with their emotions, Bus's enables them to get in tune with their feelings. When Baxter plays, the dancers sweat against one another. When Bus Williams plays jazz, the dancers "forget their jostling neighbors" and become aware instead "that some quality hitherto lost had at last been found."

What the listeners find in true black jazz, argues Fisher, is their origin. "Two hundred years ago they had swayed to that same slow fateful measure," Fisher tells us, then lets the music lead us further back, "They had rocked so a thousand years ago in a city whose walls were jungle." Bus Williams plays a music that was "not a sound but an emotion that laid hold on their bodies and swung them into the past."

Fisher is not, however, simply a nostalgiac, reaching into the past for sentimental memories. The virtue of this swing into the past is that it refreshes. More, returning, the "blueness itself, the sorrow, the despair, began to give way to hope," until the transformation into genuine human feeling is complete. Filled with a sense of possibility by the sound of the jazz, the black men and women in the Arcadia dance hall, "A restless multitude of empty, romance-hungry lives," do so by dipping deep into their racial consciousness, for a moment, while the spell of the music remains, it creates "an all-pervading atmosphere through which seared wild-winged birds." The illusion of freedom suggested by the ironic "Arcadia," becomes real; the dance hall is that pastoral place where people can soar as freely as wild birds.

And the way, declares Fisher, is clear. It is the way of blackness, in physical, historical and spiritual acceptance of blackness.

The story ends with Bus Williams being declared winner by Jean's spontaneous gift to him of her love and loving cup. The message is thus underlined once more by this prophetic writer. In the battle between Bus, the black man who accepts color and Fess, the black man who rejects it, the winner is Bus, his genuineness irresistable to Jean, the amber colored girl "in between." In the fight to vibrate "like nearing thunder," the source of the power is consciousness of blackness. That this was how the story would end was made clear of course from our very first glimpse of the "color-coded" antagonists, a color scheme that shows goodness in blackness. How truly Rudolf Fisher, in **"Common Meter,"** was a man of clear and far-seeing vision. (pp. 8-9)

> *Thomas Friedmann, "The Good Guys in the Black Hats: Color Coding in Rudolph Fisher's 'Common Meter',"* in Studies in Black Literature *(copyright 1976 by Raman K. Singh), Vol. 7, No. 2, Spring, 1976, pp. 8-9.*

LEONARD J. DEUTSCH (essay date 1979)

> [*Deutsch discusses Fisher's short stories as literary documents of the geography and history, as well as the "morals and manners," of Harlem in the 1920s.*]

The argument can be made that more fully than any other chronicler of the manners and morals of Harlem in the 1920s, Fisher captures the breadth of black experience—and American and universal human experience—during a spectacularly dynamic era.

The Harlem Renaissance was occasioned, as observers have remarked, by a "demographic shift of the Black population that is perhaps the most crucial fact of Afro-American history in the twentieth century." Fisher took a lively look at this "crucial fact" and explored many of its consequences and manifestations in his short stories.

By his own admission, he saw himself as an interpreter of Harlem. Just as F. Scott Fitzgerald took "East and West Egg" for his milieu, so Fisher took Harlem for his. He succeeded in charting the physical and moral topography of Harlem during the Renaissance period as no writer has ever done. (p. 159)

In terms of physical topography, Fisher reconstructs the black community block by block. Practically every story is set on a specific street or cluster of streets. And when those streets are revealed to the reader, they are presented in both graphically realistic and metaphorically imaginative terms.

Fisher's favorite figurative device is personification and his personified analogies imbue each street with a precise and appropriate life of its own, ranging from glamorous to sordid. In **"Ringtail,"** for example, "Harlem's Seventh Avenue was dressed in its Sunday clothes," for this is where the dicties paraded themselves; but Lenox Avenue, in **"Fire by Night,"** is like a corpse divested of its fine clothes. The sights and smells of each street are there: 133rd Street in **"Guardian of the Law"**; 135th Street in **"Blades of Steel"**; "a wide open lot, extending along One Hundred and Thirty-Eighth Street almost from Lenox to Seventh Avenue, sharing the mangy backs of a long row of One Hundred and Thirty-Ninth Street houses" in **"The South Lingers On."** **"Miss Cynthie"** provides a tour of the ritzier sections of the city-within-a-city; and so on.

Fisher virtually creates a verbal map of Harlem containing a great many of its hospitals, schools, cabarets, and apartment buildings. He even delineates the neighborhoods in **"Fire by Night"** and indicates the territorial disposition of the various classes—that "dictydom," for example, was located "west of Seventh Avenue" in the 1920s, and Harlem's middle class lived between Lenox and Seventh Avenues.

But most of all, Fisher presents Harlem's people.

His first story, **"The City of Refuge,"** . . . was chosen for inclusion in Edward J. O'Brien's *The Best Short Stories of 1925*. It establishes the literary mode most characteristic of Fisher's work: irony. King Solomon Gillis is neither powerful nor rich nor wise; he is simply green around the gills and easily gulled. . . . Gillis falls victim to the myth of Harlem. It may seem to be a city of and for blacks, a place where "you had rights that could not be denied you; you had privileges protected by law. And you had money. Everybody in Harlem had money. It was a land of plenty." But Harlem is the locus of intraracial exploitation (a black operator named Uggam muses, "Guess you're the shine I been waitin' for"); it is a battlefield of intraracial hostility (Gillis, hardened by his exposure to city values, derisively yells "Monkey-chaser!" at a West Indian); and it is the stalking ground of undiminished interracial enmity ("They's a thousand shines in Harlem would change places with you in a minute jess f' the honor of killin' a cracker"). Harlem is a place where one can become rich quickly, if like Tom Edwards, he becomes a drug pusher and pays off the police. Finally, the land of plenty offers Gillis a room "half the size of his hencoop back home," replete with all the sights, sounds, and smells of a sewer. More a city of refuse than refuge. (pp. 160-61)

In March of 1925 Fisher's second story appeared, **"The South Lingers On,"** reappearing later that year under the title **"Vestiges: Harlem Sketches,"** in Alain Locke's famous volume, *The New Negro*. Just as his first story depicts a newcomer's evolving response to Harlem—his naivete, his disillusionment, his gradual hardening—here, too, Fisher presents vignettes indicating the ways "the South lingers on" in Harlem for those who have recently arrived. The South lingers on in terms of attitudes toward religion, education, and morality. (p. 161)

[**"Ringtail"**] returns to the theme of intraracial conflict announced in **"The City of Refuge."** Cyril Sebastian Best, a dandified black from the British West Indies, is called a "ringtail monkey-chaser" by some black Harlemites; Best, in turn, holds Negro Americans in contempt. Although a character named Eight-Ball may complain: "You jigs are worse 'n ofays. . . . You raise hell about prejudice, and look at you—doin' just what you're raisin' hell over yourselves," even Eight-Ball seems to be won over by his cronies who believe a West Indian is naturally inclined to maniacal revenge. The resolution of Fisher's story—Cyril Sebastian Best kills the Harlemite who insulted him—seems to demonstrate the veracity of the conventional saying. The plot of **"Ringtail"** represents a rare instance when Fisher countenanced stereotyping. Despite some fine writing and a number of interesting passages, the story is further weakened by Fisher's use of the romantic triangle; here it is simply too contrived.

"High Yaller," awarded the Spingarn Prize of 1925, is a more complicated tale. It tackles the dual themes of intraracial and interracial enmity. Evelyn Brown's problem is that she is colored but looks white—there is "nothing brown about her but her name." At first she is accused of having "yellow-fever," that is, favoring fair skinned individuals and choosing her friends on that basis. The charge rankles and she laments that she is not darker (an inversion of Emma Lou's obsessive desire to become white in *The Blacker the Berry* by Wallace Thurman). Her response is to throw herself more fully into the black community by dating a black youth, Jay Martin. . . . When her dark-skinned mother dies, Evelyn decides to pass for white. Fisher shows with trenchant candor the vicious pressures that drive Evelyn to her decision to pass. It was undoubtedly this candor that led an early black critic to condemn the story for its "sensationalism." For Fisher, it is an uncharacteristically sardonic story. (p. 162)

[**"The Promised Land"**] demonstrates that terrestial Harlem is as far from the celestial heaven as death is from life. Interwoven in the texture of the tale are the blues and the melody of a spiritual: "one was a prayer for the love of man, the other a prayer for the love of God." In the city, with its philosophy of "ruthless opportunism," the secular blues take dominance over the otherworldly hymns. Harlem is no more a promised land than it is a city of refuge; it makes promises that it does not keep. And so Mammy, a living symbol of the generation gap, succeeds in stopping one fight involving her two grandsons by flinging a Bible between them, but must watch one kill the other over a girl (who is every bit as shallow and unworthy as Fitzgerald's Daisy Buchanan). The migrants have evaded misery in the South only to find tragedy in the North. But some become so callous that they fail to recognize the tragic dimensions of their behavior. . . .

"Blades of Steel" is a brutal story which pits gambling-man Eight-Ball against knife-wielding Dirty Cozzens; Eight-Ball wins after his girlfriend, Effie, teaches him a trick with a "safety" razor blade. Despite the violence and occasional gore of the action, the story contains Fisher's full quota of puns and Harlemese. In a tale which plays upon the "blades of steel" motif we learn that "whoever whittles [Dirty Cozzens] down will be a hero," and that "Effie's tongue had cut like steel." The locale shifts from a barber shop to a dance hall, to a bar-and-grill, and in so doing Fisher utilizes music (jazz from a "low-down" orchestra at the dance hall, Tessie Smith's blues from a phonograph at the bar-and-grill) both as background and as commentary upon the story's action. (p. 163)

["**Fire by Night**"] sets elements from Harlem's three social classes against each other. Rusty Pride, the son of a beloved and upstanding preacher, is born a member of the temperate, respectable middle class but, made "swaggering, regardless, and worldly-wise" by the first World War, he returns from the service and rejects his middle class values; he rebelliously submerges himself in the life of the lower class (the so-called rats). It is not an attractive picture that Fisher presents of this class or its milieu—the "tameless corner of Harlem." These are the tough men and their heirs who "protected the colony in its infancy by their skill with pistols and knives and fists." . . . (pp. 163-64)

The so-called So-and-Sos tend to be snobbish and are not treated very sympathetically by Fisher either. They are comparable to the Blue Vein Society in Charles Chesnutt's "The Wife of his Youth," and Fisher satirizes the type again in *The Walls of Jericho*. Attending the dance at the *New Casino* thrown by the So-and-Sos—but standing apart from their aristocratic pretensions—is Roma Lee, the patient girlfriend of Rusty, who rescues her when he appears on the scene. Together they seek refuge in a dwelling which, all too patly, turns out to be Reverend Pride's parsonage. Symbolically, the two youths are saved when they come home to the safety and sanity of the God-fearing middle class (as Turpin's Club burns like a Satanic inferno in the background). The conclusion of the story suggests that Rusty is no longer going to wander around like a billiard ball, aimlessly ricochetting from one meaningless experience to another. Perhaps his father's prayers have been answered; perhaps Rusty has found God. At least he has found himself. . . .

[In 1927, Dr. Fisher wrote] an essay for *American Mercury* entitled "**The Caucasian Storms Harlem**." Fisher's major point in this historical guide through Harlem is that the formerly black cabarets have begun catering to whites—almost to the exclusion of blacks. "Why, I am actually stared at, I frequently feel uncomfortable and out of place" in these cabarets, he confesses. He not only explores the phenomenon by contrasting the way cabarets used to be when he first came to Harlem with the way they were becoming later in the decade; he also tries to account for this change, this new "active and participating interest" in Negroes. While not a story itself, "**The Caucasian Storms Harlem**" serves as a useful companion piece to the fiction providing, as it does, factual background on famous clubs in Harlem and sketches of such black stars as Ethel Waters, Florence Mills, and the comedy team of Miller and Lyles (possible prototypes of Bubber and Jinx—two characters in both of Fisher's novels). (p. 164)

Fisher explored the ways of love and the techniques of jazz in "**Common Meter**." At the Arcadia Ballroom Fess Baxter's Firemen and Bus William's Blue Devils vie with each other for the jazz championship and for Jean Ambrose, the contested girl. The story centers on their conflicting philosophies of jazz and sportsmanship. . . . To the delight of his readers, Fisher includes a great deal of winning badinage and felicitous phras-

ing—such as when Bus Williams's endeavor "to drain the girl's beauty with his eyes" is described as "a useless effort since it lessened neither her loveliness nor his thirst." In addition, Fisher makes thematic use of bird imagery. For example, Williams's baton droops "like the crest of a proud bird, beaten"; when Baxter faces defeat he must adjust "his ruffled plumage"; and when the men fight it out through their music, they look like "two roosters bearin' down on the jazz." But Williams finally beats the "buzzard" when "the unfaltering common meter of [his] blues" takes off and soars like "wild-winged birds." With this last metaphor, Fisher neatly merges his bird imagery and his allusions to music. It might be added that his motif of interwoven blues lyrics to comment on the action reminds one of the poems of Langston Hughes. (p. 165)

["**Dust**"] is the single story by Fisher not set in Harlem. Pard and his girl Billie are driving along in the Connecticut countryside; when Pard's black-and-white roadster is passed by a spunky yellow sport coupe with a Georgia license plate, Pard curses the unseen "cracker" and makes it a point of honor to overtake him. In so doing he almost wrecks both cars only to discover—to his utter astonishment—that the other driver is a black man too. Here misplaced racial animosity produces comical results (by contrast, in *The Walls of Jericho* the results are tragic for Fred Merrit). Still, Billie's observation that prejudice is a horrible thing makes the serious point of the story. "**Dust**" is very short but it offers an exciting chase, inventive metaphors, and a concluding sentence which in itself would have made the rest of the story worthwhile: "A far hill covered the face of the sun, like a hand concealing a grin." (pp. 165-66)

"**Ezekiel**" is a psychological study of a Southern boy's first day in "the Negro colony of New York City"; the story charts his inner struggle from self-doubt to growing self-assurance. . . . Having been sent North "so that he might attend the excellent New York schools," his education in self-knowledge has begun on the streets of Harlem. "**Ezekiel**" is a slight but pleasant performance by Fisher.

So is "**Ezekiel Learns**," which appeared the following year, 1933. Ezekiel, by this time, has acclimated himself to all the wonders of Harlem, including the "proud parade of uniformed societies" which had been Marcus Garvey's legacy, as well as the "occasional riots between oddly excited mobs and grimly determined policemen." He has also witnessed the incredible sights of the rest of the city. But the one enduring memory is of an experience which gave him a glimpse into the enigma of his own personality. Fisher proceeds to tell the story of Ezekiel's clever and judicious response to the spiteful vengefulness of a mischievous playmate. Except for a relatively few word-plays, such as "the vendor disgustedly turned from a *fruitless* search of Sam," a suspect in the theft of a plum—except for this, "**Ezekiel Learns**" presents its anecdotal tale in a straightforward manner. Thematically it is similar to the poem, "Incident," written by Fisher's friend, Countee Cullen; in both, one seemingly little incident leaves a deeper impression on the sensibility of a young boy than all of his other experiences put together. (p. 166)

"**Guardian of the Law**" is notable for its humorous badinage; for its wry descriptions (as Sam and his adversary, Grip Beasley, fight they are described as "embracing each other with enthusiasm"); also notable is the story's use of personification ("a battered piano whose key-board grinned evilly at her"); and the characterization of Grip Beasley as a hoodlum who had "too much Harlem in him." Also of interest is the skillful use Fisher makes near the beginning of the story of a quasi-stream-of-consciousness technique ("comment pursued comment" across Grammie's mind "like successive windflaws sweeping the surface of a pool"). In addition, there is the fascination of the recent migrants with the idea that blacks could become symbols of authority—police officers. Gillis in **"The City of Refuge"** thinks with awe of becoming a policeman, a position never open to a black "down home"; Sam simply becomes one. (p. 167)

The image Fisher creates of Harlem [in **"Miss Cynthie"**] is closer to Claude McKay's lusty Harlem in *Home to Harlem* than Gillis's meretricious Harlem in **"The City of Refuge."** Here the black colony is a colorful and "tireless carnival." The very atmosphere exudes "laughter, abandoned strong Negro laughter." It was a Harlem which, historically, it would seem, had passed from the scene by Depression-haunted 1933, and a Harlem which, even in the twenties, had been able to offer such ostentatious luxury to very few (Dave's car is "a robin's egg blue open Packard with scarlet wheels"; his apartment is stunningly furnished). Also pre-Depression in spirit is Dave Tappen, an unself-conscious and uninhibited man like Jake in McKay's novel (and wealthy besides) who seems to be one of those exceptional cases. His lifestyle certainly was not typical of Harlem's life in general.

Still, the change from life in the South to life in Harlem had appeared dramatic. When the female dancers in **"Miss Cynthie"** return to the stage of the Lafayette Theater after their cotton-fields number, they wear "scant travesties on their earlier voluminous costumes—tiny sun-bonnets perched jauntily on one side of their glistening bobs, bandanas reduced to scarlet neck-ribbons, waists mere braissieres, skirts mere gingham sashes." . . . (p. 168)

A genre that Fisher introduced to Black Literature and perfected all in one stroke is the detective novel. An unusual and ingenious work, *The Conjure Man Dies,* appearing in 1932 to solid critical applause, is a classic with all the standard ingredients and complications of the suspenseful novel of detection. It holds up remarkably well and seems not at all dated. In this novel Fisher introduces Sergeant Perry Dart, the professional detective, and his associate, Dr. John Archer, an amateur sleuth, who is the more sagacious of the two. Fisher enjoyed writing about these two characters so much that he intended "to use them in at least two more mystery novels—we'll call it the Dart-Archer series," he said. Fisher did not live to realize this goal but he did dramatize *The Conjure Man Dies* (which was produced posthumously) and he did finish a fine story featuring Dart and Archer [**"John Archer's Nose,"** the author's longest story]. . . . It is practically as good as the novel and it illustrates Fisher's inexhaustible fascination with policework. In it Dr. Archer denounces the kind of superstition and backwardness which resists the benefits of modern medical technology. A father, he tells Dart, has refused X-ray treatment for his sick baby, relying instead on a charm consisting of human hair fried in snake oil supplied by a conjure woman. The baby had worn the charm but, of course, he had died—the victim of superstition. . . . In a supremely clever and witty story, Fisher shows how "superstition killed Sonny." (pp. 168-69)

Just as William Faulkner, in his saga of Yoknapatawpha, creates an interrelating matrix of characters and places, so too does Fisher people his literary landscape with characters who recur in different stories. Spider Webb, for example, appears in both **"The Backslider"** and *The Conjure Man Dies.* Jinx and Bubber (based upon popular vaudeville teams of the twenties) appear in both novels. (p. 169)

There are undeniable lapses into stock types—matriarchal grandmothers, awed country bumpkins, and Jinx and Bubber in his novels—but they never remain one-dimensional stereotypes. It is also true that some of Fisher's characters are cartoons. But in most cases his caricaturing serves the aims of penetrating satire.

If there is comic exaggeration of character in Fisher's stories, there is rigorous realism of place. As has already been noted, Fisher delineates Harlem—lovingly and accurately—street by street. **"Miss Cynthie"** presents one perspective on Harlem—Harlem as race capital and mecca. Most of the other stories, however, present a less sanguine perspective. In **"The South Lingers On,"** Majutah's grandmother sees Harlem as a "great, noisy, heartless, crowded place where you lived under the same roof with a hundred people you never knew." Much like Gillis's room in **"The City of Refuge,"** Mammy's apartment in **"The Promised Land"** is compared to "a fifth-story roost on the airshaft of a seven-story hencoop," and Lil in **"The Backslider"** likens her room to a clothespress. As people move into the flats of Harlem their prospects—at least for some of them—turn flat too, even if the pace of their lives speeds up.

The citizens of Harlem certainly have not left all of their old problems behind. In **"High Yaller,"** school for Jay "had been a succession of fistfights with white boys who called him nigger," and he must remember never to cross Lenox Avenue or go beyond 135th Street or venture on or near Seventh Avenue because "it would have been almost suicidal for [a Negro] to appear unarmed on Irish Eighth." And where old problems have been left behind, they have often been replaced by new ones; for Harlem was a place "where there was so much more for one to quarrel about and resent"—as Sam and Wesley (who have such disparate salaries in **"The Promised Land"**) discover. If Fitzgerald's geography of East and West symbolically represents corruption and hope, respectively, Fisher's geography of North and South, more often than not, has the North representing disappointed hopes and expanding anxieties. And yet there is always the pulse of excitement and the counterbalance of new hopes and opportunities in Harlem.

Fisher's language is the medium of a rich style which informs while it entertains and elates. The author had appended a glossary of Harlemese to *The Walls of Jericho* but the stories burst with definitions too—some serious and helpful, others wry and ironic. If the reader does not know what a *dicty,* the *dozens,* a *rent party,* the *camel walk,* and other artifacts of black culture are, he will be enlightened by reading the stories in which they are explicitly defined. (pp. 169-70)

Always—whether he is being informative or entertaining—Fisher's language sings. His stories are filled with imaginative puns, inventive personifications, and other playful twists of language (as when he paradoxically describes Harlem apartment buildings as "mountains of flats"). In addition, the stories are a gold-mine of lines and stanzas from old hymns, blues, and popular songs. The collection, moreover, offers a compendium of Harlem idioms and dialects, the old-time preacher's sermons; the West Indian speech pattern; the people of Harlem bantering in Harlemese. It is no wonder that Langston Hughes considered Fisher "the wittiest of [the] New Negroes of Harlem." Hughes asserted that Fisher "could think of the most incisively clever things to say," and confessed, "I used to wish I could talk like Rudolph Fisher."

In 1933 Fisher averred: "Outsiders know nothing of Harlem life as it really is. What one sees in a night club or a dance hall is nothing, doesn't scratch the surface—is in fact presented solely for the eyes of outsiders. . . . But what goes on behind the scenes and beneath the dark skins of Harlem folk—fiction has not found much of that yet." Fisher was an insider who scratched deeply. The stories reveal his love for the people of Harlem and the diversity of talents they represent. They also help us to understand the quality of life of Harlem during the Renaissance period. (pp. 170-71)

> *Leonard J. Deutsch, '' 'The Streets of Harlem': The Short Stories of Rudolph Fisher,'' in PHYLON: The Atlanta University Review of Race and Culture, 40 (copyright, 1979, by Atlanta University; reprinted by permission of PHYLON), Vol. XL, No. 2, Second Quarter (June, 1979), pp. 159-71.*

ADDITIONAL BIBLIOGRAPHY

Bone, Robert. "The Harlem School." In his *The Negro Novel in America*, rev. ed., pp. 65-108. New Haven: Yale University Press, 1965.*
  Brief discussion of Fisher as the forerunner of black self-satirists.

Brawley, Benjamin. "The New Realists." In his *The Negro Genius: A New Appraisal of the Achievement of the American Negro in Literature and the Fine Arts*, pp. 231-68. New York: Biblo and Tannen, 1937.*

Summarizes Fisher's novels and stories, commenting that "with keen perception and a fine sense of irony he had also the detachment of the artist, and could employ humor when he pleased or be serious without being heavy."

Chamberlain, John. "The Negro As Writer." *The Bookman*, New York, LXX, No. 6 (February 1930): 603-11.*
  Compares Fisher to Ring Lardner "as a manipulator of native idiom," and remarks that each of the stories "The City of Refuge" and "Blades of Steel" "turns on a trick, but the tricks depend on character for their effectiveness."

Emanuel, James A., and Gross, Theodore L., eds. "Rudolph Fisher, 1897-1934." In their *Dark Symphony: Negro Literature in America*, pp. 110-11. New York: The Free Press, 1968.
  Introduction to a reprinting of "Miss Cynthie," pp. 112-23 of this anthology. This brief biocritical sketch states that "Fisher is particularly effective in evoking the saturnalian quality of Harlem life, but he attempts more than mere local color; he humanizes the corrupt as well as the innocent figures in his stories, and he suggests the great influence of place in the morality of his characters."

Henry, Oliver Louis. "Rudolph Fisher: An Evaluation." *The Crisis* 78, No. 5 (July 1971): 149-54.
  Summarizes Fisher's novels and short stories, with commentary and brief biography.

Kent, George E. "Patterns of the Harlem Renaissance." In *The Harlem Renaissance Remembered*, edited by Arna Bontemps, pp. 27-50. New York: Dodd, Mead & Co., 1972.*
  Brief critical sketch of the novels and short stories, stating that Fisher "gave us pictures of the ordinary workaday black who was largely neglected by other Renaissance writers."

Douglas Southall Freeman

1886-1953

American biographer, historian, editor, journalist, and essayist.

Freeman was one of America's most distinguished biographers and historians. His massive, Pulitzer Prize-winning biographies *R. E. Lee* and *George Washington* are considered the definitive works on two of the greatest figures in the history of the United States. These multivolume studies, along with the author's other major work, *Lee's Lieutenants: A Study in Command,* evidence what Virginius Dabney described as Freeman's "well-nigh unparalleled military understanding, plus enormous industry and capacity for research."

Throughout his career, Freeman was noted for his extensive knowledge of the history of Virginia and of the Confederate South, interests inherited from his parents. Born in Lynchburg, Virginia, Freeman was the son of Bettie and Walker Burford Freeman, the latter a former soldier in General Robert E. Lee's Army of Northern Virginia. Freeman frequently accompanied his father to reunions of the United Confederate Veterans, where he listened to eyewitness stories of the War between the States. Lee, masterful in battle, gracious in defeat, and an outspoken proponent of forgiveness and reconciliation during the South's hate-filled Reconstruction, was soon established as young Freeman's ideal of noble character and spiritual fortitude. After graduating from the University of Richmond in 1904, Freeman entered the doctoral program at Johns Hopkins University with the intent of preparing himself to write a history of the Civil War. He received his Ph.D. in 1908 at the age of twenty-two, and during the same year he published his first book, *A Calendar of Confederate Papers,* which was compiled of Confederate war records. The following year Freeman began writing for the jointly owned *Richmond Times-Dispatch* and *Richmond News Leader,* assuming in 1915 the editorship of the evening *News Leader,* a position he held for thirty-four years. In 1915, Freeman also signed a contract with Charles Scribner's Sons to write a short biography of Lee. But after beginning his research for the work, he realized that his intended biography would merely cover material hitherto available to and presented by all other chroniclers of the general's life. Under an agreement with editor Maxwell E. Perkins of Scribner's, Freeman was given as much time as needed to write the definitive biography. Waiting until a crucial collection of Lee's correspondence was released by his estate for public scrutiny, Freeman spent nearly twenty years researching and writing *R. E. Lee.* The four-volume work received nearly unanimous critical praise, won the 1935 Pulitzer Prize in biography, and established Freeman as America's foremost military biographer. Despite his very evident high esteem for Lee, Freeman stripped away many of the South's long-cherished myths about the man and demonstrated that Lee's gentlemanly hesitancy to criticize the actions of his corps commanders was a key factor in the Confederacy's military downfall. Nevertheless, in revealing that much of the high admiration accorded Lee is well warranted, the author vindicated, to a great extent, Viscount Garnet Wolseley's appraisal of Lee as "a man who was cast in a grander mold and made of different and finer metal than all other men."

Using notes left over from his research for *R. E. Lee,* Freeman worked for several years on what he considered his best and most difficult work, *Lee's Lieutenants: A Study in Command.* This biographical and historical study exhaustively traces the wartime careers of Lee's subordinate generals and field commanders. Freeman's balanced treatment of the legendary Thomas J. "Stonewall" Jackson—a general whose story has led lesser writers into sentimentality and near-worship—was the subject of particular praise by critics. After *Lee's Lieutenants,* Freeman devoted his skill to his most ambitious project, the definitive biography of Washington. He had been researching his subject since the mid-1930s, and the ensuing volumes of *George Washington,* like his earlier works, were critically praised for their detail, documentation, and broad scope. The acclaimed biographer of Thomas Jefferson, Dumas Malone, wrote, "If Freeman did not know precisely where Washington was and what Washington was doing every day of his adult life, as he did in the case of Lee, he came as near to it as is humanly possible and he carefully reconstructed every important scene." Because of his age and the need to relax his busy schedule, Freeman retired from newspaper work in 1949 to give his full attention to *George Washington;* but he died shortly before finishing the sixth volume. The seventh was completed by Freeman's research assistants, and the complete series was awarded the 1958 Pulitzer Prize in biography.

"When a thing is done," wrote Freeman in 1905 of the historian's role, "at least when you have done it, let it be indeed done, so that not a new word can be said." The nearness to which Freeman approached his stated goal is explained, in part, by the nearly unvarying daily work schedule he devised for himself. Each day, he arose at 2:30 A.M., travelled to the *News Leader* offices, and worked at his various editorial duties until late morning. Returning home, he lunched, rested, gardened for a short while, and then spent the afternoon meticulously researching, compiling notes, and writing his books. After dinner and a period of relaxation, he retired early. In addition to writing, Freeman delivered daily newscasts over Richmond radio, reaching a wide audience with these and with his weekly Sunday morning radio program, "Lessons in Living." Freeman also found time to serve as visiting professor of journalism at Columbia University during the late 1930s, and to counsel numerous younger journalists, historians, and biographers who sought his direction. Malone wrote that Freeman "was a living illustration of certain truths that Thomas Jefferson proclaimed to his young daughter: 'No person will have occasion to complain of the want of time who never loses any.'"

During World War II, Generals Douglas MacArthur, Dwight Eisenhower, and Omar Bradley recognized Freeman's tremendous military knowledge and read his books for the strategic advice contained therein. Instructive to the military mind and of interest to the common reader is Freeman's "fog of war" approach to history and biography, a technique used in his three multi-volume studies. With the knowledge that the eighteenth and nineteenth-century field general did not, like the historian, know precisely the troop strength and location of the enemy nor the exact terrain of the battlefield, Freeman sought to recreate the conditions and confusions faced by Lee, his lieutenants, and Washington. Only those facts are presented which were perceived by these commanders before and during their battles, amid the "fog of war." This method of writing history is the fulcrum of much of the criticism of Freeman's works. While some critics praise the tension, authenticity, and high drama which result from Freeman's technique, others claim that the method is overly subjective; all credit for victory, or blame for defeat, falls solely upon the subject's army, with no reference made to the actions and movements of the enemy forces. Another point of critical contention is Freeman's attitude toward the Confederacy and particularly toward Lee. Although some critics have found the author to be overly defensive of his hero's every decision, most have found that Freeman was thorough enough in his research and objective enough in his writing to create the definitive biography of Lee and the "final word" on the Army of Northern Virginia. The attitude apparent in Freeman's Civil War books is not that of a bitter, racist, "unreconstructed" Southerner, but that of a man keenly interested in the history of his home state. A devout Christian, Freeman did not regret the end of slavery and the South's loss of the Civil War, but believed that out of America's four years of struggle and bloodshed a stronger nation was formed, according to the permissive will of God.

To understand Freeman's mind more completely, it is necessary to understand a fairly common attitude among Virginia citizens, who revere their state's distinguished history and often consider themselves the heirs and trustees of the legacy of Washington, Jefferson, Lee, and other notable Virginians of the past. Freeman saw himself as the humble chronicler of the greatest armies that ever fought in America and as the biographer of two of Virginia's most famous citizens. "The creators of noble books about noble men are public benefactors," wrote Malone, "and such a creator was Douglas Southall Freeman."

(See also *Dictionary of Literary Biography*, Vol. 17: *Twentieth-Century American Historians*.)

PRINCIPAL WORKS

A Calendar of Confederate Papers [editor]   (history)   1908
Lee's Dispatches [editor]   (letters)   1915
R. E. Lee. 4 vols.   (biography)   1934-35
The South to Posterity: An Introduction to the Writing of Confederate History   (essays)   1939
Lee's Lieutenants: A Study in Command. 3 vols.   (history) 1942-44
George Washington. 7 vols.   (biography)   1948-57

THE VIRGINIA MAGAZINE OF HISTORY AND BIOGRAPHY (essay date 1909)

[*A critic for* The Virginia Magazine of History and Biography *provided perhaps the only review of Freeman's first work,* A Calendar of Confederate Papers.]

The Southern Historical Manuscripts Commission, a branch or close ally of the Confederate Memorial Literary Society, has made an admirable beginning in its work of making the records relating to the Confederate States known to students. The selection of an editor and compiler has provided to be very wise and in this pioneer work Dr. Freeman has shown that the right man is in the place. (p. 332)

The editor has, in the introduction, given a useful account of Confederate sources of material, of their value, and the pressing necessity for steps being at once taken to preserve them.

The entries in the Calendar are very clear and intelligible, the notes are numerous and carefully studied and there is a complete index.

In every way the volume is creditable to the Society and the editor, and is a most important contribution to the literature of Confederate history.

The bibliography of Confederate publications now a part of the noble collection in the Museum is excellently done. (p. 333)

> *A review of "A Calendar of Confederate Papers, with a Bibliography of Some Confederate Publications," in* The Virginia Magazine of History and Biography, *Vol. XVII, No. 3, July, 1909, pp. 332-33.*

STEPHEN VINCENT BENÉT (essay date 1934)

[*Benét was an American man of letters whose poetry and fiction is often concerned with examining, understanding, and celebrating American history and culture. The comic short story* "The Devil and Daniel Webster" *and the Pulitzer Prize-winning Civil War epic* John Brown's Body *are his best-known works.*]

Literary genius in the biographer is not, by itself, enough—as witness Charles Dickens and the "Life of Our Lord."

For true biography is a very difficult art. And it is curious that, in our short history as a nation, two of our greatest figures—Washington and Lee—should have been such difficult subjects for true biography. . . .

Dr. Freeman, fortunately for us all, is a true biographer. . . .

In the first place, he shows us from the very first lines of his foreword [to **"R. E. Lee"**] the thoroughness, the patience, the honesty and the true gift for research which are the rare marks of the real biographer.

He has winnowed, and winnowed away an enormous mass of legend. He has collected and set down for the first time in print a vast number of new, precise and salient facts. He has woven together a thousand strands of testimony from the words of forgotten reports to the words on the lips of old men remembering their great youth. In Dr. Freeman's two volumes we get for the first time the complete, slow growth of a man. The unregarded years—the years of youth and early manhood, the years before the Mexican War and after it, are filled in with completeness and patience for the first time. (p. 1)

But thoroughness and patience are not enough. A scholar may be very thorough and very patient and yet remain a scholar read only by scholars. There must be proportion, balance, composition; most of all, vitality in the work itself. Dr. Freeman's style is not a showy one, and he does not go in for purple passages. But every one of his 1,200 pages is intensely readable from the first page to the last. He is readable when he describes the Battle of Chancellorsville; he is readable when he describes the education of a West Point cadet in the 1820s or the technical details of the building of an obscure fort by an Army engineer. He has a positive genius for quotation—it is always the live quotation, not the dead one, that appears on his pages—and always at the point where it simplifies, explains, elucidates, gives life and color to the whole. He never points out the obvious; he never grows windy or pedantic. When he gives you an opinion on a disputed point he gives you his reasons as well. "There they are," he seems to say, "to the best of my judgment. My conclusion is this—you may draw another if you disagree with me. But here are the facts, as far as they can be known."

If I had sufficient space I should very much like to quote his brief sketch of Anne Carter Lee, Lee's mother. . . . It consists of a short appraisal and the only two known surviving letters of Mrs. Lee. The appraisal is short enough. It tells what is known of Anne Carter Lee; it does not tell what is not known. And it is a model to biographers. There is no one fact and twenty barrels of conjecture. There is no "As she did this, she must have done that." There is a human being there, faintly outlined, because the written evidence is slight; but the outlines, though faint, are definite. There is a real and living woman, not a fictional character or a reverential image. I, for one, never knew her before.

As it is with Anne Carter Lee, so it is with the whole of the story. Slowly, on the firmest of foundations, there builds up the full picture of the man. (pp. 1-2)

All through the life, the threads in the web are mixed ones. When Lee married Mary Custis [George Washington's granddaughter] he married a delightful woman but a temperamental one—and a woman who was to become an invalid, needing an invalid's care. And, when he married her, as Dr. Freeman points out, he married Arlington as well—Arlington with its name, its heavy responsibilities and the great shadow of Wash-

ington brooding over it. Dr. Freeman's analysis of the influence of the Washington tradition on the character of Lee is subtle, convincing and profound. Throughout the book, indeed, his study of the gradual development of Lee's character is masterly. It has the fascination of a detective story and the inevitability of the growth of a tree. . . .

I have stressed Dr. Freeman's dealings with Lee's early years because they are the essential foundation on which all true knowledge of Lee must be built. When Lee assumed command of the forces of Virginia he was fifty-four and the main lines of his character were formed. He grew after that, but he grew along those lines, not contrary to them. Where many biographers are content to show effects, Dr. Freeman shows us the causes of those effects—and he does it so well and so thoroughly that by the time we come to the Civil War we have a real knowledge of Lee, not a set of phrases about him, and a real ability to know what Lee may do in a given circumstance. Dr. Freeman shows also—and this is invaluable—on the military side, exactly what experience of war and the conduct of war Lee had had, the sort of strategy and tactics that were likely to appeal to him, both his practical knowledge and the bent of his mind. I have never seen this done so clearly and so well.

There were weaknesses as well as strengths in both Lee's temperament and Lee's training—Dr. Freeman shows them both unfalteringly. The first untrained Virginia volunteers were a very different proposition from Scott's Mexican army—and Lee made mistakes in the West Virginia campaign. Dr. Freeman shows us what the mistakes were and what Lee learned from them. A courteous amiability, in dealing with subordinates, was likely to develop, with an obstinate subordinate, into failure of execution at a crucial moment—as it did with Longstreet at Gettysburg—Dr. Freeman shows us the cloud at its beginning, no bigger than a man's hand. Indeed, for all Dr. Freeman's practical delineation of the campaigns up to and through Chancellorsville (with which these two volumes end) I can only have the most unstinted praise. With their excellent, clear and numerous maps, they should prove invaluable to all students of military history. And to the average reader they are perfectly fascinating.

For Dr. Freeman, in describing them, has taken a novel point of view. The reader is always with Lee, at Confederate headquarters, in possession of such knowledge as Lee had but no more. In other words, the battles develop before us as battles do to a general who is fighting one, with all their momentary chances. Excellent schemes go astray because of unknown factors—the "fog of war" is over the field, not swept away by after-knowledge. And the battles and campaigns are real. Behind the charges and the yells there is always the constant, wearing question of food and shoes and horses, of men who come down with measles and men who cannot march on the hard roads of Maryland because their feet are sore. All this is a constant reminder of warfare, but it does not always get into the histories. It is continually present in Dr. Freeman's. And we know not only Lee, by the time we have reached Chancellorsville—we know the Army of Northern Virginia as well.

In any account of events in the Civil War, the historian or biographer must strike upon a number of moot points. Dr. Freeman, as Lee's biographer, inclines, very naturally, to cast his vote for Lee, on most of these points. But he never does so without giving full reasons for his statements. His explanation of Jackson's lethargy during the Seven Days is clear, well reasoned and convincing—and his account of the genesis of the turning-movement at Chancellorsville seems to me a little miracle of reconstruction. On the other hand, for the average reader, I think he might have stressed, even more than he does, Jackson's personal brilliance in the Valley Campaign. It is one thing to tell a general you would like a certain enemy beaten, if possible, and quite another to have the general do it—as Lincoln, to his sorrow, very often found. Nor is it my opinion that the reader who is unversed in the Civil War will form an utterly correct estimate of the miliary abilities of Joe Johnston, from Dr. Freeman's account of him in these two volumes. Johnston was an unlucky general, in many ways, but the most competent testimony, including that of great adversaries, pronounced him a master of craft.

These are small criticisms on a monumental work, but, while I am about it, I will make one or two more. Dr. Freeman deals with John Brown and Harper's Ferry entirely from the viewpoint of Lee and he is perfectly justified in doing so. But John Brown was not exactly an ordinary disturber of the peace nor was the raid on Harper's Ferry precisely a riot. And the actual confrontation of Robert E. Lee and John Brown happens to be one of the great dramatic coincidences of history. I think Dr. Freeman could have made more of this than he has done without sacrificing truth to false picturesqueness. . . .

Jackson, Stuart, Longstreet, Magruder, Hood are vividly portrayed, but one might wish for a little fuller physical description of the two Hills, Ewell, Alexander and some of the other Southern leaders. They appear in their words and actions—and admirably—but the readers of an Iliad like to know the faces and armor of all the chiefs. The same might be said of the Northern commanders opposed to Lee. It does not fall directly within Dr. Freeman's province to describe them, except as they showed themselves in action—but a brief, well-placed footnote on each, showing what sort of man he was, would assist the casual reader. Another, and somewhat vaguer criticism, is this. The heart of the Northern resistance was a man named Abraham Lincoln. Dr. Freeman is writing a life of Lee, not a life of Lincoln. Nevertheless, it seems to me that Lincoln's presence should somewhere, somehow be felt by the reader—not as the amateur strategist recalling troops for the safety of Washington but as the soul of the other Cause. However, there is room for all this, and more, in the next two volumes.

Dr. Freeman is kinder to Davis than some Southern historians have been, and, I think, juster. In his dealing with Northern "atrocities" (the term is not his) he seems to me, now and then, a trifle biased. War is a dirty game, no matter how played. I remember an old man, with passion and indignation in his voice, showing me the marks of Confederate shell on the walls of my mother's town. And he was as right—and as partisan—as Dr. Freeman. There is little of this in the book, very little, but as it struck me, I mention it. On the larger issues, he states his own feelings admirably in his Foreword—and they are without illusion.

The present two volumes begin with Stratford and end just after Chancellorsville. There are two more to come. One can ask no more of them than that they should equal the two already in print. For those two already comprise by far the best biography of Lee of which I have any knowledge. . . . Dr. Freeman has worked nearly twenty years on these volumes. And for those years, we are all of us in his debt. For he has revivified for us, lastingly and surely, one of the largest figures of our national past. It is a superb achievement. I do not know how Pulitzer prizes are awarded but I should be in favor of giving at least ten of them to Dr. Freeman. And then, if I were dictator, I would have him chained to a desk and make him spend his next twenty years writing a life of Washington, whether he wants to or not. (p. 2)

> *Stephen Vincent Benét, "Robert E. Lee, a Great American Biography: The Whole Man—Boyhood, West Point, Mexico, and the Civil War," in* New York Herald Tribune Books *(©I.H.T. Corporation; reprinted by permission), October 14, 1934, pp. 1-2.*

MAXWELL E. PERKINS   (letter date 1935)

[*According to Perkins's biographer, A. Scott Berg, by the time the final two volumes of* R. E. Lee *were published, "Freeman was already considering subjects to which he might devote the next ten years of his life." Although Freeman's next major projects were* The South to Posterity *and the three-volume* Lee's Lieutenants, *by January 1935 he was discussing with his editor the possibilities of writing the definitive biography of George Washington.*]

[Whatever] else may be said about Lee, the accounts of the campaigns, and battles, are I believe, excelled by no other writer on military matters. I thought this when I first read the ms., and now we know that authorities think it. The clarity and intensity with which these campaigns are described makes most fascinating reading, and most enlightening. Of course in Washington's case, the military strategy would be much less complicated, but I do not think that the Revolutionary campaigns are even as well understood as the Civil War ones, and I think you would handle them magnificently, and that all your study of war for the *Lee* and previous to that, would be of great advantage to you. (pp. 228-29)

> *Maxwell E. Perkins, in an extract from his letter to Douglas Southall Freeman on January 11, 1935 (copyright © 1978 by A. Scott Berg; reprinted with the permission of Charles Scribner's Sons), in* Max Perkins: Editor of Genius *by A. Scott Berg, Pocket Books, 1979, pp. 228-29.*

CARL SANDBURG   (letter date 1935)

[*Sandburg was one of the central figures in the "Chicago Renaissance," an early twentieth-century flowering of the arts in the Midwest. A lifelong believer in the worth of the common, unsung individual, Sandburg expressed his populist beliefs in poetry and songs, and in his Pulitzer Prize-winning biography of Abraham Lincoln. Writing three years before the publication of his Lincoln biography, Sandburg states his critical approval of* R. E. Lee *in the following letter. Lloyd Lewis, to whom Sandburg is writing, was a Chicago newspaperman and author of the definitive biography of General William Tecumseh Sherman.*]

Dear Lloyd

Long before I reached the comradely finish of your *Lee*-Freeman review I said it was the keenest of the nine or ten reviews I have read of that work. In justice you could have handed Freeman much more on his workmanship and his rich depth of sentiment always under nice control. I cried with his last chapter as I did with yours on Sherman. Then on rereading and considering I felt nearly all of the old mystery of Lee was there for me. When I see Freeman sometime I shall tell him his grand book lacked a chapter on what Lee's men from their hells and golgothas did to him; what poverty, shabbiness, rain, mud, rats, vermin, the scurvy, endured in comradeship by that final remnant which stuck to the last, did to the aristocrat in Lee. Also I would like to know if so good a fighter did not enjoy fighting, and when he did what became of the christian gentleman? It is either paradox or mystery. Where Freeman wins is that he can answer that he put all the essential facts in his book, loved his man as a man, and the reader can make his own derivations. . . . What happened to Lee from Gettysburg on was a slow, titanic, merciless series of operations which brought him thoughts, writhings, outlooks he had never known before. What they did to him, whether he changed slightly or deeply, is the mystery. And part of the mystery maybe only the familiar one of the front line fighting man who comes back from the human slaughter-house and has nothing to say because he knows it can't be told. "How did you lose your leg, grandpa?" "A bear bit it off." (pp. 314-15)

> *Carl Sandburg, in his letter to Lloyd Lewis on March 9, 1935, in his* The Letters of Carl Sandburg, *edited by Herbert Mitgang (copyright © 1968 by Lilian Steichen Sandburg, Trustee; reprinted by permission of Harcourt Brace Jovanovich, Inc.), Harcourt Brace Jovanovich, 1968, pp. 314-15.*

H. L. MENCKEN   (essay date 1935)

[*From the era of World War I until the early years of the Great Depression, Mencken was one of the most influential figures in American letters. His strongly individualistic, irreverent outlook on life and his vigorous, invective-charged writing style helped establish the iconclastic spirit of the Jazz Age and significantly shaped the direction of American literature. As a social and literary critic—the roles for which he is best known—Mencken was the scourge of evangelical Christianity, public service organizations, literary censorship, provincialism, democracy, all advocates of personal or social improvement, and every other facet of American life that he perceived as humbug. In his literary criticism, Mencken encouraged American writers to shun the anglophilic, moralistic bent of the nineteenth century and to practice realism, an artistic call-to-arms which is most fully developed in his essay "Puritanism as a Literary Force," one of the seminal essays in modern literary criticism. Another important polemic, "The Sahara of the Bozart"—considered a powerful catalyst in spurring realism in Southern literature—attacked the paucity of fine arts in Southern culture as well as the tendency in the region's literature toward romanticizing the Old South as a land of latter-day knights and fair ladies. Mencken's essay on R. E. Lee reveals that Freeman met his strict standards of scholarship and antisentimentalism.*]

The award of a Pulitzer Prize to Dr. Douglas Southall Freeman's **"R. E. Lee"** can add nothing to the renown of that remarkable work. The Pulitzer Prizes, in fact, have been given to so much trash that it is now an insult rather than an honor for an author of any dignity to receive one. Dr. Freeman surely needs no such pat on the head from his inferiors. His four volumes represent twenty years of extraordinarily diligent and fruitful labor. From end to end they show a complete knowledge of the matters discussed, covering the whole field and bulging out on all sides. The author never gets lost in his materials. The stream of his narrative is always a clear one, and in scores of places it washes out old obscurities and dubieties, and converts romantic legend into sober history.

The work, of course, is very long, and hence puts a considerable strain upon the reader's patience. It is not to be read idly, but must be given, at least in parts, something resembling deliberate study. Dr. Freeman describes the battles of Lee with magnificent clarity, but battles, after all, are complicated affairs, and grasping them is sometimes not easy. Here they are

not only described precisely but also given the colors of drama. There is never any resort to mere rhetoric, but when he is stirred, as he often is, Dr. Freeman manages to communicate his emotion to the reader. He writes first and always as a scientific historian, but he also makes it plain, and pleasantly, that he is a Southerner.

Now and then he pauses in his story to formulate judgments of Lee. They are always shrewd, and sometimes full of new illumination. The tinsel saint of Southern tradition is slowly converted into a veritable man. . . .

It will be Dr. Freeman's unhappy fate, I suspect, to serve as authority for a radical reconsideration of his hero. His own veneration seems to be unshaken, but his candor supplies a large amount of ammunition for any skeptic who chooses to explode it. His account of the Gettysburg campaign offers a case in point. He describes that sorry misadventure in terms of Lee's own view of it, setting forth the situation exactly as it appeared through the "fog of battle," and avoiding all easy moralizing in the light of events then unforeseen. But he simply can't get rid of the massive fact that the whole thing was horribly botched—that its tactics were almost as insane as its strategy, and that Lee, and Lee alone, was responsible for the bloody débâcle of July 3. . . .

Thus Dr. Freeman leaves him—still a great gentleman, still an astonishingly bold and resourceful commander in the field, calm in victory and unshaken in defeat, but hardly the stupendous paragon that Southerners have been taught to revere. He is not deflated; he is simply restored to reality.

> *H. L. Mencken, "Twilight of a God" (used by permission of The Enoch Pratt Free Library of Baltimore in accordance with the terms of the will of H. L. Mencken), in* The Evening Sun, *Baltimore, May 13, 1935, p. 17.*

STEPHEN VINCENT BENÉT   (essay date 1939)

[**"The South to Posterity"**] is not, nor does it pretend to be, a complete history of Confederate literature—but, for either layman or scholar who is interested in the subject, it offers a remarkably engaging and readable introduction to the field.

In the first place, Dr. Freeman can write—a little detail too often neglected by historians. It is worthy and admirable to assemble facts, to put truth in the place of legend, to investigate impartially, to throw new light on an old problem. But, when this has been done, the words still have to be put down on the page in such a way that a human being of average intelligence can read them without going to sleep. For, if you don't tell the truth so people will believe it, they are going to believe the first highly-colored lie that comes along. Dr. Freeman can tell the truth so you keep on wanting more of it. He does so here. Anybody who reads the chapter called "The War through Women's Eyes" is going to want to go to some of its sources, to "A Southern Woman's Story" and the diary of Mrs. Chesnut, to the two Louisiana diaries and the magnificent account of the doughty Mrs. McDonald. For Dr. Freeman quotes so skillfully that he always leaves you hungry for more. . . .

Familiar letters, memoirs, official records, biographies—Dr. Freeman touches upon them all. He has some shrewd comments to make on the controversy and apologia indulged in by certain figures after Appomattox, a good chapter on the various foreign historians and biorAphers who dealt with the Confederate side. He shows the later gathering of glamor on the Lost Cause—

and why it happened. And in the chapter, "Yet to be Written," he mentions half a dozen or a dozen books still to be written that leave me licking my lips and wishing I had them right now. . . .

Meanwhile, we not only have this book, and the able Confederate Book Shelf in the appendix (though, surely, the "Diary of a Georgia Girl" should be included in any collection of reminiscences by Southern ladies) but a sentence that is almost a promise. Dr. Freeman remarks, with truth, "Even the fame of George Washington would be enhanced if, among the hundreds of books written of him, there were one first-class biography." There is just one man to do that, and I will not embarrass Dr. Freeman by mentioning his name.

> *Stephen Vincent Benét, "The Lost Cause in Literature," in* The Saturday Review of Literature *(© 1939, renewed © 1966, by Saturday Review Magazine Co.; reprinted by permission), Vol. XXI, No. 5, November 25, 1939, p. 6.*

C. G. WOODSON   (essay date 1940)

[*A noted historian of black American history, Woodson assumes— in the following blistering review of* The South to Posterity—*that the chronicler of the Confederate South is necessarily a defender of slavery and of other antebellum institutions. At the time he wrote this review, Woodson was influenced by Dr. Charles Wesley's* The Collapse of the Confederacy, *a work which holds that the Confederacy "was a backward step toward medievalism which the southerners themselves did not wholeheartedly support."*]

[*The South to Posterity*] is a production of the well known defender of the Confederacy and the advocate of the perpetuation of its philosophy of inequality and injustice to the man far down. From the author's point of view the South has left to posterity not only an unexampled record of military genius and gallantry on the field of honor but also an unexampled morale, something which he believes was inherent in the Southerners. This tradition he would make appear as the American tradition itself. In other words, the only real American was the backward, medieval Southerner. He believes that this contribution of the South will be all but eternal in America.

The book, however, does not conform to the rules of scientific research and independent treatment. Others have said in another way what Freeman expresses herein in *ex parte* fashion. He admits that there was not exactly a united South, but he discounts the discordant elements as "The coward, the self-seeker, the glutton, the sentimentalist." No historian will agree with such a characterization of the large number of Southerners who failed to show that morale spoken of by the author as the real American tradition. In that number would be distinguished statesmen, high public functionaries like governors of States, and generals who, although born in the South, chose to stand by the Union. The fact is that what Freeman praises as most desirable in the make-up of the Confederate was merely blind ignorance before the bugbear of social equality and the socalled menace of white supremacy—the slogan by which the small number of actual slaveholders brought to their rescue in a terrible extremity, the poor whites who had been all but starved out by the institution which they tried to save.

Books like this under review have no historical value; but, on the contrary, they do the cause of modern historiography much harm among persons who learn history only from biased newspapers. Such works serve also to feed the vanity of the descendants of the Lost Cause. These volumes are being written

not from all sources of Southern history, but from such documents as support a certain point of view and produce the desired effect to which this propaganda is directed. (pp. 385-86)

> *C. G. Woodson, in a review of "The South to Posterity," in* The Journal of Negro History *(reprinted by permission of The Association for the Study of Afro-American Life and History, Inc. (ASALH)), Vol. XXV, No. 3, July, 1940, pp. 385-86.*

BERNARD DeVOTO   (essay date 1942)

[*An editor of* The Saturday Review of Literature *and longtime contributor to* Harper's Magazine, *DeVoto was a highly controversial literary critic and historian. A man whose thought enraged much of America's literary establishment during the 1930s and 1940s, he was frequently motivated by anger at authors he considered ignorant of American life and history. As a critic, he admired mastery of form and psychological subtlety in literature. His own work is characterized by its scholarly thoroughness and by its vigorous, infectious style. DeVoto was "profoundly interested" in American history and authored several historical works, notably the Pulitzer Prize-winning* Across the Wide Missouri *(1947). In the following review of* Lee's Lieutenants, *he praises the work but takes issue with Freeman's method.*]

Mr. Freeman's subtitle [to **"Lee's Lieutenants"**], **"A Study in Command,"** is something of an understatement. His book, the first of three projected volumes, is indeed a study of the training, testing, fitness, and unfitness of the principal Confederate commanders in Virginia (and many lesser ones brilliantly and briefly characterized) from Bull Run to Malvern Hill. But it is also a detailed history of the campaigns they fought, sometimes perhaps a little too detailed for his purpose. Mr. Freeman is the most objective as well as the most distinguished of contemporary Southern students of the Civil War but vestiges of the tradition he has broken through cling to him, and one of them is a willingness to trace small movements in battle of regiments which are remembered more personally in Southern emotion than they are in military history.

As both a history and a critique of the war, the book is a new and independent study, usually based on wider investigation than anything that has preceded it, dispassionate in judgment, obviously authoritative, alive and enthusiastic. Sometimes, as in the study of the much-studied Jackson, it amends the accepted views fundamentally. (Jackson gets more space than anyone else. The Valley Campaigns are superbly done and in Jackson's movement toward and share in the Seven Days, Mr. Freeman displaces Henderson.) And some of the chips that fall from its hewing to the line are no less than iconoclastic. We have come a long way when it can be calmly shown that the Southern soldier had no marked natural ability as a cavalryman, and that the Southern cavalry sometimes fought badly and was sometimes managed stupidly. . . .

The book is a landmark in the study of the Civil War. It would be presumptuous to question its page by page authority. Nevertheless, in breaking through the convention of Southern military studies, Mr. Freeman has not altogether freed himself from it. Just as vestiges of its rhetoric remain in his inversions, his "ere's" and "social glasses," his ready use of "gallant" and the number of Southern generals who look like eagles, so he cannot really bring himself to believe that there were armies and generals on the other side. Thus he comments on the comparative ineffectiveness of Confederate artillery in the Peninsula but he treats that ineffectiveness as purely a failure of Confederate organization and management, ignoring the equally portentous facts that Northern industry was supplying cannons in quantity and Federal generals had learned how to use them. He only occasionally takes into account the fact that there was going on in the Union armies the same testing, rejection, and development that he is studying on the Southern side—that such men as Reynolds, Hancock, Buford, Howard, and Meade were coming on, just as Early and Ewell were, that field and company officers and private soldiers who wore blue were learning their job.

The Civil War, that is, remains for Mr. Freeman primarily a process of Southern development, Southern management or mismanagement, Southern achievement or failure, and only in the second remove a contest. In his **"Lee"** he devoted a whole chapter to exploring the reasons why Gettysburg was lost, found his answers exclusively in Southern errors and failures, and never once took into account the rather important fact that the Army of the Potomac, with its generals, was also fighting on that field. . . . One gets from this book little sense that the Confederates' enemy made trouble or even that the enemy existed—little sense that battles imply an enemy or that an enemy can make trouble. This inability is something of a limitation in this book; it may well become a weakness when we have got past Chancellorsville to Gettysburg and move on from there to the Wilderness.

> Bernard DeVoto, *"The Confederate Military System," in* The Saturday Review of Literature *(© 1942, copyright renewed © 1969, by Saturday Review Magazine Co.; reprinted by permission), Vol. XXV, No. 43, October 24, 1942, p. 15.*

ALLEN TATE   (essay date 1943)

[*Tate's criticism is closely associated with two American critical movements, the Agrarians and the New Critics. The Agrarians were concerned with political and social issues as well as literature, and were dedicated to preserving the Southern way of life and traditional Southern values. In particular, they attacked Northern industrialism as they sought to preserve the Southern farming economy. The New Critics, a group which included Cleanth Brooks and Robert Penn Warren, among others, comprised one of the most influential critical movements of the mid-twentieth century. Although the various New Critics did not subscribe to a single set of principles, all believed that a work of literature had to be examined as an object in itself through a process of close analysis of symbol, image, and metaphor. Tate's most important critical essays are on modern poetry, and on Southern traditions and the legacy of the Civil War. In the following excerpt, he offers a reserved review of the first two volumes of* Lee's Lieutenants.]

The third and concluding volume of [**"Lee's Lieutenants"**], not yet published, might make a great difference in our judgment of the whole; yet even in these two volumes Mr. Freeman has achieved what nobody could have predicted and what I for one did not believe possible. He has gone again over the ground of his **"R. E. Lee,"** given us the same campaigns and battles, the same scenes and leaders (only more of them), and has succeeded in writing a different book. In what ways it is different is what interests me here. It is, of course, in itself a magnificent story: I am perhaps not a trustworthy witness to the value of Mr. Freeman's treatment, since I can read the story even when it is badly told; and I am not a military critic, who, I suppose, is alone competent to pass final judgment upon this moving story of Lee's subordinates.

But the story of Lee's subordinates is only a part of it, only the overt pretext for telling the greater story again. And there are interesting and even curious features discernible in the tone, style, detail and organization of this work that anybody concerned with the art of narration is entitled to have an opinion of, apart from the military judgment. Why is Mr. Freeman retelling this story? Surely not, as he hints, to give illuminating examples of success and failure to future commanders. His subtitle is **"A Study in Command."** If it is mainly that, why are we also given a vast amount of rich and hitherto unknown detail about the backgrounds, personal lives and friends of minor officers, and the sights, sounds and smells of battle and camp? These are not the necessary qualities of a technical "study in command." I am not reproaching Mr. Freeman for including all this contingent detail; I am praising him for it; for this is the real substance of his work. The work is not a study in command; it is the complete image of Lee's Army of Northern Virginia projected through the historical imagination.

We have here, I think, in the case of Mr. Freeman, a mind which is not very interesting or resourceful apart from this historical scene; but a mind which is so perfectly saturated with this scene and so perfectly in command of all its minute and shifting detail that even in his digressions he never loses the main thread, because he himself is always holding it, letting it out or drawing it in. But this, indispensable as it is to the structure of his book, is not what makes it go. Nor does the "tone" explain the flow of the narrative: it is the lecturer's tone. Nor is it the style, which is never distinguished and at times is even a little clumsy (Mr. Freeman always puts his adverbs before the auxiliary verbs). But this work, like the **"R. E. Lee,"** has a powerful and convincing movement, and I am somewhat at a loss to understand the power and to know of what I am being convinced.

Is there not something of capital significance in Mr. Freeman's persistent neglect of two great historical factors that most historians would feel compelled to deal with? First, there is the opponent of Lee and his lieutenants, the Federal Army of the Potomac; second, there is the South, a people or even a nation at war. The curious thing in Mr. Freeman's two great works is that Lee's army is not fighting another army, for that army only occasionally appears in an incidental reference or in a footnote: we seldom know, unless we already know, who its commander is, and we almost never know its position and formidable numbers as Lee's men advance to the attack. Moreover, if Lee and his subordinates are not fighting anybody, they are equally not fighting for anybody: the South scarcely exists in Mr. Freeman's War Between the States—only Virginia, and Virginia not very distinctly. What then is all this war about? There is no war in Mr. Freeman's magnificent reconstructions of this ragged gray army of the Golden Age.

It seems to me that the secret of Mr. Freeman's great success as an historian is not his overwhelming documentation, his mastery of historical method; it lies quite simply in his own peculiar romanticism. Lee's army is here cut off forever in a kind of "cold pastoral" not only from the time of its action but from all history: it has become assimilated to a very great poetic convention, that of the Golden Age, in which we may all, North and South, and men everywhere, participate, a Platonic world in which historical men achieve a Homeric stature. . . .

I am suggesting that in addition to the solid knowledge of his period that Mr. Freeman gives us, he has something of the sensibility of a poet; but of this I suspect that he must be wholly unaware; and I am not sure that he ought to be aware of it. Never mind; he will not be. Too many people have told him that he is a historian—which, of course, he is.

Allen Tate, "Cold Pastoral," in The New Republic *(© 1943 The New Republic, Inc.), Vol. 108, No. 19, May 10, 1943, p. 644.*

PERRY MILLER (essay date 1949)

[*An American historian, Miller served for over thirty years as an instructor and professor at Harvard. The principal concern of his several published studies is America's Puritan heritage. He is considered a pioneer in recording and interpreting the literature and culture of seventeenth-century New England. In the following review, he offers high—if guarded—praise for the first two volumes of* George Washington.]

The only question that existed in anticipation of Mr. Freeman's *George Washington* was whether it would or could match his *Lee.* The first two volumes, subtitled *Young Washington,* prove that it can and does. Here is the same broad canvas, the meticulous piecing together of detail, the full documentation, the leisurely pace, the relish for drama and for human personality, and especially the elevated, even Jovian, tone. These volumes have already been so extensively praised, and their major achievement—their dignified and yet realistic humanizing of Washington—has been so frequently underscored that in a belated notice there is need only for again saluting a great performance. These volumes displace all previous studies, as the completed work will undoubtedly become at once the standard treatment.

Amid so unanimous a chorus of praise it becomes difficult, or rather futile, to express the slightest dissent. But there is even greater hazard in attempting to formulate certain reflections that are not so much criticisms of the book as it stands, but lamentations that precisely because it is what it is, and as splendid, it will unfortunately complicate the problem of other historians. I mean, because Freeman tells the biography with such overwhelming amplitude, the rest of us will be virtually compelled henceforth to see Virginia cultural history through the eyes of his *Washington.* Yet it is precisely at this point I locate the only area of any importance where Mr. Freeman's portrait appears at all deficient. He has, as far as was humanely feasible, brought back the man in his habit as he lived, and he has sketched in the background of the times and the manners. Yet he has not made quite evident, or even plausible, the respects in which this man was the product of—or the representative embodiment of—this peculiar and perplexing culture.

Perhaps the book illustrates the old adage that when Virginians confront the writing of their own history, they above all others experience the difficulty of seeing the forest for the trees. (Possibly because they above all others must thread the labyrinths of so confounded much genealogy!) Yet Mr. Freeman can assuredly not be accused of failing to put young Washington squarely into a social setting. The first chapter, indeed, announces the intention unmistakably in its title, "An Ambitious Landed Society." It makes abundantly clear that the story of the Northern Neck for a century can be told with only one verb: "it was grab, grab, grab." Of course, the revolution that has been wrought in modern historiography becomes apparent if we compare this judgment of Virginia's greatest historian of today with those of Brown or of Bruce a generation ago. Mr. Freeman's fourth chapter is a masterful résumé of the conditions that shaped young Washington, and demonstrates that

they, like their offspring, were complex, but that the spirit of grab, grab was pervasive. No poor man could any longer stand the competition, and Washington himself later expounded the clue to the social pattern when he said that the great estates had been accumulated "by taking up and purchasing at very low rates the rich back lands which were thought nothing of in those days."

Hence, one cannot charge that Mr. Freeman lacks a realistic appreciation of the society where "George might be King but tobacco was master," and in which young men of enterprise and courage would infallibly grow up with the conviction that the promise of a fortune lay in "the great, open, unclaimed Valley of the Ohio." Since he makes the drive to wealth so comprehensible, one cannot complain because Mr. Freeman refrains from committing himself to labels and does not quite say that this order was an imperialistic agrarian capitalism. However, the fascination (and the complexity) of his Washington begins to impress itself upon us if we, accepting provisionally some such label, then find that this child of the grabbing society was indeed economically ambitious, even to a demonic degree, but that at the same time he exhibited in his behavior a code which we customarily associate with the medieval knight or the Spanish grandee, or with the hero of a Scott novel, rather than with the modern capitalist. In brief, Mr. Freeman's Washington is, in the terms of social history, a contradiction in terms. Filled with a consuming ambition for wealth, he is punctilious to the point of downright pedantry on the subject of "honor." He is the scion of a society in which the economic fact was capitalism, but for which the ethic was still status. Hence his problem—one as nerve-wracking as the modern era can lay upon a man—was to become wealthy not only without sacrifice of honor but through being conspicuously honorable. (pp. 253-55)

It is possibly an irrelevance in the presence of so monumental a work to demand that it pronounce upon what is not its concern. After all, its subject is Washington, not Virginia. Yet when Mr. Freeman gallantly faces up to the sordid realities, when he, speaking as a Virginian, does not hesitate to give full play in Virginia history to the spirit of grab, though we must admire his candor and compliment him upon a patriotism that cannot be tarnished by a hundred such admissions, still we are obliged to note that Mr. Freeman speaks thus as a moralist and not as an economist, or even (in that sense) as a historian. The nobility, the forthrightness of Mr. Freeman's frame of reference gives him freedom to do complete justice to the deficiencies as well as to the merits of his hero. His last chapter is an impressive summing up of a man's qualities, but it is, like his chapter on Virginia society, an array of particulars, not a definition. It is fundamentally a moral analysis, not a cultural. The only question, thereupon, is whether a discussion so oriented, although it never shrinks from the utmost candor, is the best way, or the only way, to gain an understanding of economic and social patterns, or to comprehend fully how the particular patterns of Virginia culture were translated into the conduct and code of one George Washington. (pp. 256-57)

Perry Miller, in his review of "George Washington, a Biography: Young Washington, Vols. 1 and 2," in The New England Quarterly *(copyright 1949 by The New England Quarterly), Vol. XXII, No. 2, June, 1949, pp. 253-57.*

DUMAS MALONE (essay date 1951)

[*Malone is the author of* Jefferson and His Time, *a massive six-volume biography which, in research and scholarship, rivals*

Freeman's R. E. Lee *and* George Washington. *Malone reviewed nearly all of Freeman's books upon publication and was highly impressed with each of them. Below, he reviews volumes III and IV of* George Washington.]

With the publication of these handsome volumes [*George Washington,* Vols. III and IV] Dr. Freeman's monumental biography of Washington reaches the halfway point. The two previous volumes carried the story through his participation in the French and Indian War, ending with his resignation of his commission late in 1758 in his twenty-seventh year. The present story covers a score of years. It begins with his marriage to the rich young widow, Martha Dandridge Custis, and his assumption of the life of a great planter—which absorbed him for some fifteen years, until the struggle with the Mother Country caused him to unsheathe his sword. It ends, in the spring of 1778, with the receipt by him, as Commander in Chief, of the news of the French Alliance—which ushered the Revolution into a fresh phase.

Equally significant with the scope and thoroughness of this treatment is its spirit. Not only is Dr. Freeman giving us a biography of unexampled fullness, with ample annotations and an abundance of good maps. He has approached his gigantic task without preconceptions, and has refused to let the legend obscure the man. Step by step and stroke by stroke he is showing Washington as the abundant sources (inadequately exploited hitherto) reveal him. In his earlier volumes, his candor may have seemed devastating to some readers who were disposed to indulge in hero worship. The Young Washington whom he depicted was brave and dashing enough for any taste, and was notable for his justness, but he was too ambitious, too calculating, too sensitive to personal affront, to be thoroughly likable. Many may have wondered just when the wise, patient, and heroically self-sacrificing Washington would appear. He appears in the present volumes, especially in Number IV. The author does not re-create and embroider a legend, however, any more than he indulges in debunking for its own sake: he traces the development of a character. Even at Valley Forge, Washington appears as neither a perfect man nor a perfect soldier, but he has become the worthy embodiment of a cause greater than himself.

> Dumas Malone, "The Making of a Great Man: George Washington, 1758-1778," *in* New York Herald Tribune Book Review (© *I. H. T. Corporation*), October 14, 1951, p. 3.

[VIRGINIUS DABNEY] (essay date 1953)

[*Early in his newspaper career, Dabney worked under Freeman at the* Richmond News Leader. *Many years later, Dabney—the Pulitzer Prize-winning editor of the* Richmond Times-Dispatch—*wrote the following elegaic tribute to his former editor.*]

Dr. Freeman was so many-sided, his capacity for work was so prodigious, and his ability to parcel out his time on a precise schedule for 24 hours of each day so amazing, that he accomplished more in one lifetime than three men could normally do. . . .

Undoubtedly Dr. Freeman's greatest and most permanent single contribution lies in his four-volume *R. E. Lee,* and his three-volume study, *Lee's Lieutenants.* These books have come to be regarded as classics, and rightly so. They are based on superb scholarship, they reveal a balanced point of view, and they are written with deep feeling for the subject. The cause for which the South fought, and the character of the leadership

it enjoyed in the Civil War are here set forth in words that will live. . . .

These books are far from being unrestrained eulogies of the Southern leaders. Dr. Freeman seeks at all times to give the actual facts, and to let those facts speak for themselves. Take, for example, his analysis of "Stonewall" Jackson's personality, and his Valley Campaign of 1862 in *Lee's Lieutenants.* He does not soft-pedal Jackson's peculiarities or deny that some of Jackson's men, early in the war, thought their general might be insane. In appraising the infantry tactics employed by Jackson in his stunning succession of victories over the Federals in 1862, despite their marked numerical superiority, Freeman pronounces those tactics "commonplace." Yet he finds much to commend in the campaign as a whole.

Dr. Freeman's nonpartisan approach to the controversial aspects of the war remind one of the similarly dispassionate attitude of Benjamin P. Thomas in his recently published one-volume biography, *Abraham Lincoln,* one of the finest biographical studies in years. Both Freeman and Thomas display an admirable detachment, while at the same time revealing great literary gifts.

Dr. Freeman's literary capacities were nowhere more effectively displayed than in his description of the final events in the Civil War's tremendous drama at Appomattox. This poignant chapter of *R. E. Lee* is written with a fine Americanism, in that it gives General Grant full credit for his magnanimous treatment of his beaten adversary, while at the same time doing full justice to the grandeur of Lee's character in defeat, and to the overwhelming admiration and devotion which the Confederate commander's men felt for him. No one, whether Northerner or Southerner, can read Chapter IX, "The Ninth of April," in Volume IV of *R. E. Lee* without being a better American. . . .

Now that Dr. Freeman is gone, it is more than ever apparent how large a place he occupied in the civic, social and scholarly life of Richmond and Virginia. No man of his generation, it seems safe to say, touched the Commonwealth at so many points, or influenced it in so many directions. His was, indeed, a many-sided genius.

> [*Virginius Dabney*], "Douglas S. Freeman—1886-1953," *in* Richmond Times-Dispatch (*reprinted by permission of the publisher*), June 15, 1953, p. 14.

MICHAEL KRAUS (essay date 1953)

[*Kraus provides a survey of the major works in Freeman's career and briefly discusses Freeman's technique of limiting the reader of* Lee *and* Washington *"to the knowledge possessed by the commander at the moment of decision."*]

In 1934, Douglas Southall Freeman brought out the first two volumes of his long-awaited biography of Robert E. Lee, and the final two volumes came soon after. Many years of devotion to his task lay behind the biographer, who said that he was "privileged to live, as it were, for more than a decade in the company of a great gentleman. . . . What he seemed, he was— a wholly human gentleman, the essential elements of whose positive character were two and only two, simplicity and spirituality." Freeman unearthed a vast fund of material dealing with Lee's strategy, and he adopted the unusual device of allowing the reader no more knowledge than Lee possessed at the time of any particular battle or campaign. (pp. 338-39)

It is hard to believe that we shall ever need another biography of Lee, for Freeman's work has no superior in the whole range of American biographical literature.

So deeply was Freeman immersed in study of the Civil War that his vast knowledge of the Confederate side of the struggle overflowed into three more volumes, *Lee's Lieutenants: A Study in Command*. . . . The massive work was an analysis of the command of the Army of Northern Virginia. As in the biography of Lee, great stress was placed on the disaster for the South which lay in Stonewall Jackson's death. (p. 340)

The laurels of some Southern leaders looked somewhat worn under Freeman's critical exposure, but Lee and Jackson emerged still the great figures of the lost cause.

Freeman next turned his superb powers as a biographer to the study of Washington, whose personality was still veiled despite investigations by countless students; the mystery was a challenge to the artist in Freeman. Long ago Hawthorne had ridiculed biographers of the first President: "Did anybody ever see Washington nude? It is inconceivable. He had no nakedness, but I imagine he was born with his clothes on and his hair powdered, and made a stately bow on his first appearance in the world.". . .

Freeman's large-scale biography of Washington went far beyond all previous works in the thoroughness of its research and in the amplitude of its canvas. Indeed, if there is any serious criticism to be made of it, it is that much is included with which Washington did not have close association. The first two volumes . . . brought Washington only to the age of twenty-seven. His early career was told against a detailed portrayal of the Virginia society in which he matured. (Freeman's description is the best yet made of that society.) (p. 341)

The third, fourth, and fifth volumes . . . narrated the undramatic years of 1759-73, and then the tempo was speeded up with the oncoming Revolution. . . .

The planter and the patriot had become the leader of the Revolution. Freeman's unrivaled skill in military history carried the narrative along at a rapid rate. . . . The end of battle came at Yorktown, and the eloquence of Freeman reaches its height in describing the climax of surrender.

The technique that Freeman used in his *Lee* (in the sections on war) was repeated in the *Washington;* the biographer limited himself to the knowledge possessed by the commander at the moment of decision. Clearly this device recreated the hesitancy which hampered action and added suspense to a tale that seemed new-told. Therein lies the secret of Freeman's art—what seemed a trite and threadbare tale through uninspired retellings lives again in the freshness of its first wonder. (p. 342)

> *Michael Kraus, "Biography," in his* The Writing of American History *(copyright 1953 by the University of Oklahoma Press), University of Oklahoma Press, 1953, pp. 315-44.**

DUMAS MALONE   (essay date 1954)

[*Malone's "The Pen of Douglas Southall Freeman" is the most extensive biographical work yet published on Freeman.*]

While an undergraduate [Douglas Southall Freeman] began to be a newspaper correspondent, besides contributing to [his] college literary magazine, and once having got printer's ink into his veins he never could get it out. For the moment,

however, history had the priority. He gained a fellowship at the Johns Hopkins University, where he studied history and economics, and at the unusually early age of twenty-two received the Ph.D. degree. . . . The only copy of the young graduate student's dissertation—on the Virginia Secession Convention—was destroyed by fire before ever it was published, but his *Calendar of Confederate Papers* appeared in the same year that he took his degree.

Leaving Baltimore, where the atmosphere may have seemed Southern but was not quite Confederate, he returned to Richmond. There, before embarking irrevocably upon a newspaper career, he served as secretary of the Tax Commission of the state and drafted its report. For a time he was on the staff of the *Times-Dispatch,* but his enduring connection was with the afternoon paper, the *News Leader*. This began when he was twenty-five. At the age of twenty-nine (1915) he became the editor, and he held this post until he was sixty-three. It was also when he was twenty-nine that his edition of *Lee's Dispatches* appeared in print and that he signed a contract for a biography of the great Captain, but nearly a score of years were to pass before he could publish that.

Of Dr. Freeman's journalistic career I can speak with no special competence and I make no pretense of describing it with any adequacy. Being the editor of a paper with a small staff was no sinecure. One of his associates on the *News Leader* estimated at the time of his death that during his service of more than a third of a century he wrote at least 600,000 words every year—that is, the equivalent of about three books the size of this one and perhaps a hundred altogether. Yet his associates remembered him as one who always emphasized the virtue of brevity in a newspaperman. With this went an emphasis on restraint. "Don't gush, and don't twitter," he told his juniors. "Play it straight." In the course of his career he championed many changes which may be described as "reforms" while opposing others which he regarded as backward steps, but the predominant impression he gave was not that of a crusading editor. He was too judicious for that, and, while liberal in spirit, he could hardly have embodied the Lee tradition without being conservative in the true sense of that much abused term. He sought to safeguard old and enduring values and was wholly unsympathetic with demagoguery of any brand. (pp. xiv-xv)

The local celebrity became a national literary figure and gained a sure place in American historiography with the publication of *R. E. Lee* in 1934-1935, when he was forty-eight. The one-volume work he had contracted for in 1915 had grown to four large volumes, and the calendar showed that it had been a score of years in preparation. (p. xvii)

I shall never forget the impression his *R. E. Lee* made on me at the very first reading. By that time, although I had no such acquaintance with the man as I gained later, I had first-hand knowledge of his scholarship, for I had seen the articles on Lee, Stonewall Jackson, and others that he had prepared for the *Dictionary of American Biography*. He afterwards told me that he found the writing of these sketches, under sharp restrictions of space, a cruel task. These were miniatures, and to paint them he had to turn aside from the vast canvas on which he was then working and to which he had become accustomed. But they left no doubt of his historical craftsmanship and his skill in portraiture, whatever the scale might be, and I awaited with confidence the appearance of his long-heralded life of Lee. Great as my personal expectations were, the realization far surpassed them, and never did I devour a major historical work with such insatiable appetite and more unalloyed satisfaction. (pp. xviii-xix)

This work, like all the major works of Freeman, is a blend of biography and military history, and it has the qualities of exhaustiveness and judiciousness which became his hallmark. . . . Recognizing that Lee, like every other leader, must be judged "by what he accomplished, where he was, with what he had at his command," he indulged in no extravagant utterance and purposely avoided historical controversy. He gave the record of deeds and events with unexampled fulness and can be safely controverted only by students of comparable diligence, of whom there never can be many. Some have objected to his story on the ground that he always viewed the scene through the eyes of Lee and kept the reader at Confederate G.H.Q. That, however, was a matter of method, and a wise method it was, for this was intended as no history of the War Between the States. It is a biography of the Confederate Commander and a story of the war as he waged it. Gettysburg was a Federal victory as well as a Confederate defeat, but Freeman sought to show, in terms of military circumstances and personalities, why Lee lost it, leaving to others the task of describing it from Meade's headquarters.

As military history this story requires supplementation, and nobody realized that more than its author, but as the biography of a great soldier it approximated completeness so nearly as to be virtually unchallengeable. By comparison, other accounts of Lee—neglecting important phases of his earlier and later life, and emphasizing battles to the exclusion of problems of management and supply—seem pale and meagre. There is vast leisureliness in this narrative and at times its flow is impeded by detail which may seem unnecessary, but trivial items may assume crucial importance in battle and the texture of this tapestry is provided by its richness of detail. From this carefully wrought and slow-moving story Lee emerges in full glory. This is not to say that he was impeccable in judgment; Freeman describes his mistakes with complete candor at the times he made them and sums them up in a final critique—the chapter entitled "The Sword of Robert E. Lee." Also, he underlines the General's chief temperamental flaw, his excessive amiability at times in dealing with his commanders. But the balance is heavily on the credit side, and fresh and needed emphasis is laid on the intellectual quality of Lee's generalship. In his great ability as an administrator and his genius as a commander there was more of the infinite capacity for taking pains, more of the clear thought of an orderly and penetrating mind, than had been previously supposed. It took the orderly and penetrating mind of a Freeman to discern this.

The man who is shown is essentially the Lee of legend, far more fully pictured and far better explained. He is made more real by being made more human, but in life as in legend he was heroic—a knight *sans peur et sans reproche* and the *beau idéal* of the Christian gentleman. If there be those among us who have repudiated this ideal, or those whose vanity is flattered when human idols are shown to have feet of clay, they will find scant comfort in this book. But as most Americans rejoiced a score of years ago they can still rejoice that the painstaking labors and fair judgment of scholarship served to provide a firm foundation for one of the noblest of our symbols. (pp. xix-xxi)

[Freeman] did not enter upon another major historical undertaking for two or three years, but given the necessary health and strength, he was for sure to do so, for he had not yet completed the task he set himself in his youth. This was "to preserve the record of our fathers of the Army of Northern Virginia." In a real sense his *R. E. Lee* told the story of that army, but in that military biography he had wisely adopted the device of viewing the field from headquarters and thus had been unable to give a full account of the actions of Lee's officers. Fearing that unwittingly he had done them an injustice, he wanted to redress the balance and fill out the story. The result was a second major work, *Lee's Lieutenants,* which may be regarded as a supplement to its predecessor but turned out to be even more popular. (p. xxi)

Before finishing the first volume of *Lee's Lieutenants,* he turned aside to do a little book which grew out of a series of lectures he delivered in 1939 at Alabama College for Women. This was *The South to Posterity,* and he described it in a subtitle as **"An Introduction to the Writing of Confederate History."** This readable volume, which he insisted was merely an introduction to a vast body of writing, has proved useful to professional historians and laymen as he hoped it would. It unmistakably reveals his understanding of his Confederate compatriots and his sympathy with them, but it shows him as no special pleader. One of his conclusions was that "Confederate history was most persuasive where authors had the least intention of making it so." Friends were not won to the Lost Cause by "mustered argument and paraded declamation" but by simple tales of actual events and experiences. It was in the spirit of truth-seeking and fair play that he wrote his own books, and that is a major reason why they gained a national and international audience.

The popularity of *Lee's Lieutenants* was partly owing to the author's established reputation, partly to the fact that these volumes came out while the world was at war and that his findings were very pertinent. More even than *R. E. Lee,* this work is required reading in military circles. Freeman himself regarded it as the best of his books—chiefly because it imposed on him the most difficult problems of organization. No book plans itself, but there is a degree of simplicity in a biography, for it centers in a single figure and events can be grouped around him. In his desire to do justice to Lee's officers, Freeman began a series of sketches, but he soon saw that these would involve too much repetition in the accounts of battles. He got his clue at length from a letter of Lee to Hood (1863) in which Lee agreed that the Army would be invincible if properly organized and officered. "There never were such men in an Army before," he said. "They will go anywhere and do anything if properly led. But there is the difficulty—proper commanders—where can they be obtained?" Lee's biographer decided, therefore, to write a book about the Command of the Army, the connecting thread of which would be the effort to create and maintain proper senior officers. This is the story of a shifting group of leaders—shown in action. The point of view is not that of headquarters but of these commanders. This is again a combination of biography and military history, but it is group biography, and that is exceedingly difficuly to write. The scene has to shift to bring in commander after commander, as it did from Jackson to Early to Wilcox at Chancellorsville, and the sense of unity is sometimes lost. But the plan of organization is admirable and the results received plaudits enough to satisfy anybody. Probably this is the most colorful of all Freeman's works; it has been accepted as a classic in the field of tactics; and it will long live as a penetrating study of military personalities.

Two weeks after his fifty-eighth birthday, Freeman finished *Lee's Lieutenants,* and he began outlining the first chapter of another major work six months later—on January 7, 1945, to be precise. This was his biography of George Washington, and he was engaged on it the rest of his life, spending 15,693 hours on it according to his own records. (pp. xxi-xxiii)

It is an extraordinarily full story of a man of affairs and action, set on an immediate background which is always meticulously drawn and often elaborately detailed. If Freeman did not know precisely where Washington was and what Washington was doing every day of his adult life, as he did in the case of Lee, he came as near to it as is humanly possible and he carefully reconstructed every important scene. He rode and fought alongside of Washington, maintaining an Olympian detachment all the while and afterwards summing up these actions and operations with unerring skill. Also, he viewed with penetrating eye the man's personality and character as these developed, analyzing them stage by stage as no other writer had ever done. This is biography in the grand manner which gains its texture and color from exact detail but which is unmarred by special pleading. It is as full a story of a planter's life as anybody is likely ever to write, and it is military biography *par excellence*. It is the full record of a public man, and in its portrayal of Washington's relations with the civil authorities, from Governor Dinwiddie to the Continental Congress, the author is an irreproachable narrator and commentator. Finally, it is a thoroughgoing examination and judicious appraisal of a legend.

Yet, while it is all of this, it is not everything; it is not the history of an age and, despite its extraordinary richness of detail, it requires supplementation. The author explored with zest the society of Virginia in the hero's youth and turned up and organized a mass of fresh descriptive material, but he did not write social history in the full sense. He focused attention on the immediate scene rather than the larger setting, and he did not have time to attain the degree of familiarity with the eighteenth-century world that he had gained with the times of Lee and Jackson. For all Washington's nobility of spirit and high intelligence he was not a man of thought in the sense that Franklin, Jefferson, and John Adams were, and his biographer did not venture far into the history of ideas. He did not even write political history in the usual meaning of the term. He did not essay a fresh interpretation of the causes of the American Revolution or of the movement for the Constitution, and in his account of Washington's first term he kept out of the partisan struggle, just as the President himself tried to keep above it. At this point the biographer's unwillingness to accept secondary authority and his determination to hew his own path did him some disservice. He may be criticized for his rather external treatment of Hamilton, Jefferson, and Madison—about all of whom, apparently, he was reserving judgment until he should come to the time when Washington himself was unable to remain above the combat. He stuck to Washington, saw the scene through his eyes, and raised no question which was not voiced by the President himself. In this work as a whole he did not adhere to the formula he had used in his biography of Lee, but he seems to have recurred to it at the last. The result is that his account of Washington as President is only part of the story, just as his account of the battle of Gettysburg is. He speaks with the voice of unimpeachable authority, however, when he describes the President's specific actions and movements and his assumption of his historic role as the Father of a united people.

It will appear, I think, that Douglas Southall Freeman rendered the same sort of service to his countrymen in the case of George Washington that he did in that of Lee. By the slow and pain-staking processes of scholarship he examined, verified, and preserved a major legend. With a wave of the hand he dismissed the trivial and false story of the cherry tree, but he placed on a new pedestal of truth the legendary figure of a national hero whose greatness lay chiefly in his unselfish patriotism and unassailable character. The portrait is convincing because it is utterly candid, and the character assumes reality in the mind of the observer because it is shown not as something static but as something that develops. At the end of the first two volumes of this work, when the character of a bold and dashing but ambitious and calculating young man was analyzed with devastating candor, no reader could help wondering if the legend of Washington was not something of a hoax. But as the man and patriot grew before the discerning eye in the successive volumes, as his portrait was painted by a thousand deft but scrupulously honest strokes, he emerged in the lineaments that his countrymen have so long recognized and so long honored. By and large, his latest and greatest biographer enhances his military stature, showing him not as a military genius but as a great commander, within the sharp limits that were set by circumstance. . . . The verdict of the scrupulous historian after years of unremitting inquiry is that, as nearly as can be in human life, the legend and the man were identical.

To say that the biographer merely gave us in elaborate form what we already had is, however, to do much less than justice to the invaluable work of historical conservation. Legends grow shadowy with the passing years and need to be buttressed by freshly established truth; and the finest traditions of a free people, like their liberties, can be maintained only by eternal vigilance and incessant labors. National heroes can be cast from their pedestals by unholy hands and the ideals that patriots lived by can be dishonored. Unlike stones, literary monuments have life within them and they often prove more enduring. The creators of noble books about noble men are public benefactors, and such a creator was Douglas Southall Freeman. (pp. xxix-xxxi)

> *Dumas Malone, "The Pen of Douglas Southall Freeman," in* George Washington, a Biography: Patriot and President, Vol. 6 *by Douglas Southall Freeman (copyright, 1954, by Charles Scribner's Sons; copyright renewed, 1982 by Anne Freeman Adler, Mary Freeman Clarke, James D. Freeman; reprinted with permission of Charles Scribner's Sons), Charles Scribner's Sons, 1954, pp. xi-xxxi.*

T. HARRY WILLIAMS (essay date 1955)

[*A recognized authority on the Civil War, Williams provides a lengthy critical analysis of Freeman's strengths, weaknesses, and characteristics as revealed in* R. E. Lee *and* Lee's Lieutenants.]

Long before his life had ended, Douglas Freeman had become a name and a legend. To him was accorded the rare honor of being accepted, while still alive, as a great historian, as *the* authority in his field and of having his works acclaimed as classics that would endure permanently. (p. 91)

Now, before his myth hardens into an unchangeable mold, seems an appropriate time to evaluate him and his work. I will discuss his books about Lee and Lee's lieutenants under three headings: the case for Freeman, the weaknesses of Freeman, and finally what might be termed the basis of Freeman or the basic quality of his work.

First in any listing of Freeman's virtues must be his literary style. Here was a historian who knew how to write. His pages are marked by grace, clarity, and eloquence. There are passages of vivid, moving action (Pickett's charge at Gettysburg in *R. E. Lee*) and others of haunting, moving beauty (the surrender at Appomattox in the same work). Freeman employed devices that only a literary master knows when and how to use. He had a talent for ending a chapter with a sentence that not only provided a transition to the next but also sustained the mood of the whole work. An example is the manner in which he concluded the chapter dealing with operations in 1864: " . . . surely, when the last December sun of 1864 set over the Petersburg defenses it brought the twilight of the Confederacy." It may be conceded that his subject lent itself to, even demanded, the use of techniques that evoked a mood of sadness and impending doom. He was writing about that most appealing of tragic themes, the man who goes down to defeat battling against great odds. (Interestingly enough, his favorite adjective to describe the condition of the Southern cause at a given moment, repeated over and over in every volume, is "dark.") He rose to the requirements of his subject. Some of his chapters, such as "The Sword of Robert E. Lee" and "The Pattern of a Life," meet the standards of history as a form of literature.

A second strong point of Freeman's was his great sense of fairness and honesty. He tried to be objective and usually was. He did not, however, write without feeling. The Civil War was fought by passionate men. The historian of the war, to really tell the story, has to catch some of their passion. Freeman could feel as they felt. One gets the impression that Freeman said to himself: "I am going to be impartial. I will tell the truth, even about Lee." But he tried to tell the truth without wounding anybody. Here there is a curious parallel between Freeman and his hero. Lee was notoriously humble in dealing with other people whether they were his superiors or his subordinates. With the latter he was particularly tender. When he criticized a subordinate in a report, he usually did so with a vagueness that makes it difficult to determine what he was getting at. That is he tried to tell the truth without hurting. Freeman, in discussing Lee's relations with his colleagues, remarks that the general was "a gentleman in every impulse." Was this habit of consideration a weakness? asks Freeman. He answers that it was "a positive weakness." It is evident, however, that he considers it a proper kind of weakness for a man like Lee to have had; more iron in Lee would have been unfitting. Likewise there is no dash and slash in Freeman. Several times he says that it is beyond the function of a Lee biographer to criticize the skill of Lee's opponents or to compare Lee with other generals. Why should he not have done so? Such comparisons would seem necessary in order to understand Lee and his war. But a gentleman historian speaks the hard truth no more than a gentleman general.

The quality of Freeman's which has been most censured is his attention to detail. Readers complain that they get lost in the rich abundance of his items; critics ask why he saw fit to record the state of the weather on a night when Lee did something. The answer to these complaints is that Freeman decided to tell the complete story of Lee. Unless the validity of his decision is open to question, the detail has to be accepted. Considering Lee's stature as an historical figure, Freeman seems to have decided correctly. There is much to be said for having the full record of Lee set down where the patient reader can work it out for himself. It has been conjectured that Freeman knew much more than he told. Probably so. At least he did not get lost in the detail which he presented. He could rise above it to grasp and describe the bigger picture: the growth of Lee as

a general or the developing strategic features of a particular campaign.

Much of the criticism of Freeman's detail is really criticism of a kind of detail that is unfamiliar to many readers. Americans have been strangely reluctant to study seriously the history of war. Most reluctant have been the academicians. I have heard professors complain that they cannot understand Freeman and other military writers because they get confused by the multiplicity of names: Smith's division moved upon the right, Brown's regiment moved to the left, and so forth. The same professors will run riot in their own writings about elections, minor politicians, caucuses, factions, and subfactions. Their detail is as massive as Freeman's, but it seems less monolithic because it is familiar and couched in a familiar jargon. The reader who knows something about the war to begin with will not find that Freeman's volumes are overloaded with facts. In *Lee's Lieutenants* the detail is kept to a minimum. Some people have been turned away from Freeman because they tried to read a volume or two at a stretch. The cumulative effect of the detail in such, is, of course, appalling. The best way to take military history is, like any other kind, in small, well-chewed bites.

Lastly, any table of Freeman's credits must include a tribute to his scholarship, which was of a high order. He used and mastered a tremendous number and variety of sources. The military documents of the Civil War are as difficult a set of sources as any historian ever had to use: incomplete, contradictory, and frequently inaccurate. From a number of conflicting accounts the historian has to try to reconstruct an approximately truthful story of *what* actually happened. Frequently he has to solve the problem of *when* something happened: At what time was an important order sent or received? The documents disagree or do not say at all. The historian has to deduce the time from other events mentioned by the generals in the case or by their subordinates. Freeman excelled in this type of reconstruction. Anyone who wishes to realize the appalling confusion in the documents has only to turn to the pages in *Lee's Lieutenants,* 1, where Freeman examines such controversies as whether Beauregard's battle order before First Manassas was distributed to the regimental commanders and whether Ewell received Beauregard's order to cross Bull Run in the same battle. Freeman's analyses of these disputed points and of others are models of historical criticism and of historical detective work. Every historian of the war who has to describe a battle will find his task immeasurably easier if Freeman has worked it over first.

One quality of Freeman's that I think is a weakness is considered by his admirers to be one of his strong points. This is his "fog of war" theory. In a battle a general knows only a part of what is happening. He may not know where the enemy is or what he is planning; he may not know completely even the movements of his own forces. He operates in a fog of the unknown. This fog is a reality, said Freeman, and therefore the most scientific method is to write from the viewpoint of the general. That is, you tell the reader only what the general knew at a particular moment. In *R. E. Lee,* the reader, with a few exceptions, stays with Lee; he sees what Lee saw and no more. Curiously enough, in view of the criticism of his detail, Freeman says that one reason he adopted the fog theory was to avoid confusing detail; by restricting the story to Lee he hoped to simplify it.

Freeman's bold decision to describe battles as they appeared to Lee has been compared to Lee's own audacity. Freeman's admirers claim that his technique produces a powerful dramatic impact and a story of superior literary artistry. Their argument can be illustrated by a hypothetical incident. Let us say that in a battle Lee saw an enemy force approaching on his right. Not knowing its size, he took vigorous measures to meet it. Now, say Freeman's defenders, if at any point in his narrative the historian lets the reader know that the enemy force was small, he ruins the effect of the whole episode. The reader must not know until Lee knows. To all of which, the answer is that drama and artistry are not necessarily the most important things in a description of a battle. The military biographer is depicting a scene in which his subject plays a dominating role. He has to tell enough of the scene to make the role intelligible. If he has to sacrifice drama in the process, so be it. After all, he is recounting an historical episode, not writing a story for the *Saturday Evening Post*. (pp. 91-5)

Freeman's "fog of war" device is likely to confuse even a fairly well-informed reader. As an illustration, take his application of it to Lee's pursuit of the Union army as it retreated from the York to the James in the Seven Days. Here is a vast, chaotic operation, puzzling to all but the specialists. Probably nine out of ten people cannot understand it unless they are told something about the general movements. Freeman almost ignores the Federals and does not even relate fully what all the units in Lee's command were doing. His whole account tends to break apart in his hands. By insisting on remaining at headquarters with Lee, he fails to give a clear and complete picture of Lee's campaign and hence of Lee himself. It is probable that many people who complain that they get lost in Freeman's detail are really lost in the fog of his presentation.

A second weakness of Freeman's is that he was a little too worshipful of Lee. Somebody has said that he always approached Lee on his knees. This is an exaggeration. He was more like the little girl in Richmond who came home from Sunday School and said, "Mama, I can never remember. Was General Lee in the Old Testament or the New Testament?" Although on occasion Freeman was capable of pointing out Lee's mistakes and deficiencies, he was more likely to concern himself with making excuses for his hero. Thus, in analyzing the reasons why Lee failed to destroy the Union army in the Seven Days, Freeman emphasized the lack of good maps, inadequate artillery, and a poor staff. It comes as something of a shock to hear Freeman say blandly that in the reorganization after the Seven Days Lee did nothing to remedy these shortcomings. Freeman speculates that Lee did not act because he realized Confederate success depended on utilizing the resources at hand without waiting to perfect them and that much had to be left to chance. Freeman's guess may be correct, of course, but it is just as possible that Lee did not understand the importance of certain branches of a modern army.

Freeman's tendency to worship Lee resulted in several chapters in the *R. E. Lee* that are open to serious question. In the section on Chancellorsville he stated that Lee had it within his power to destroy Hooker's army and was prevented from doing so only by the threat of the Federals at Fredericksburg to his right rear. His conclusion was based almost entirely on Confederate sources and seems to me to be at complete variance with the facts. Certainly the Union corps commanders never dreamed that their 70,000 massed men were in danger of destruction from 43,000 Confederates.

Perhaps the chapters that have been most criticized are those on Gettysburg. Here Freeman contended that Lee could have carried Cemetery Ridge on July 2 because the Federal army was not as yet concentrated and that Longstreet's pigheaded slowness was largely responsible for the Confederate failure. In *Lee's Lieutenants,* after more study and reflection, he retracted these statements. In discussing the causes of Confederate defeat at Gettysburg in *R. E. Lee,* he listed such factors as the absence of Stuart, Longstreet's delays, and the failure of Ewell to move. Here he exhibited a too common characteristic of Southern historians—that of assuming that the Confederates possessed the complete power to determine the outcome of a battle. This weakness too he corrected in *Lee's Lieutenants.* He named what he considered to be the mistakes of the Confederates and then added: There were 90,000 Yankees on Cemetery Ridge. Of course, it is to Freeman's credit that he could admit errors and modify earlier beliefs.

The weakest section in *R. E. Lee* is, in my opinion, chapter twenty-four in Volume III. Freeman has just finished describing the maneuvering after Cold Harbor in which Grant disappeared from Lee's front and eventually turned up at Petersburg. Freeman then writes a chapter that is almost pure special pleading to prove that Lee was at no time deceived as to Grant's intentions. . . . This chapter lowers the quality of the entire volume, which is in other respects one of the finest in the set. Freeman came close to arguing that whatever Lee did was right because he was Lee.

A third weakness of Freeman's is that he did not realize that the Civil War was the first of the modern wars. It marked a transition from the older, leisurely, limited-objective kind of war to the all-out for keeps, ruthless, total war of modern times. In this respect Freeman was as unmodern-minded as Lee. Both abhorred economic warfare as needless cruelty. In discussing Lee's reception of the news that McClellan had been removed as commander of the Army of the Potomac, Freeman quotes Lee as saying that he was sorry because he and McClellan understood each other so well. Freeman then adds: "He was sorry too that a man who had always conducted operations with science and humanity was supplanted by one whose respect for principle he had no means of determining until Burnside should begin field operations." This is the old tournament notion of war. Did Freeman expect Burnside to send Lee a brochure announcing how he was going to fight? (pp. 95-8)

A final weakness of Freeman's is that he does not relate Lee's military thought and actions to military developments before and after the war. He does not place Lee, a great general, in the nexus of American military history. His treatment of Lee lacks perspective. As an example, increased firepower was changing the nature of war. A strong force protected by field fortifications or trenches was almost impregnable against frontal assault by attacking infantry. The old style of advancing in regular lines was becoming suicidal. New and more flexible tactical formations were called for. There is hardly a hint of any of this in Freeman's accounts of Lee's attacks at Malvern Hill and Gettysburg. Surely the revolutionary military changes in which Lee was an actor are a part of the Lee story. In Freeman's volumes it is as though Lee and the Army of Northern Virginia are wrenched out of the context of military history to be presented brilliantly in a kind of historical void.

Perhaps the best way to summarize Freeman as a historian is to say that he was a Virginia gentleman writing about a Virginia gentleman. He could understand Lee because he was like Lee. The limitations of Lee are also the limitations of Freeman. As Lee's military genius was restricted because he was a Virginia gentleman, so are Freeman's historical talents. The problem of Freeman cannot be separated from the problem of Lee.

Lee persisted always in viewing the war as primarily an affair of Virginia. Operations in other theaters were almost a kind of side show. Freeman saw the war in the same way. In discussing the favorable situation Lee has created in Virginia as a result of Second Manassas, Freeman writes that this had been achieved when the Confederates on other fronts "had been able to do nothing to relieve the pressure on Virginia." Needless to say, the commanders in Tennessee, Arkansas, Texas, South Carolina, Louisiana, and other places were not charged with the mission of lightening the pressure on Virginia. (pp. 98-9)

Because Freeman is like Lee, he did not quite see the tremendous importance of Lee's motivation in joining the Confederacy. Nor was he quite able to explain why Lee did so. In discussing Lee's decision to go with the South, he speaks about Lee's faith, about something deep in his heart, about the spirit of Virgina: "He did not stop . . . to reason out the nature of his feeling, which was instinctive." Lee was a strange, almost a baffling creature. He did not believe in slavery and he did not believe in secession, yet he elected to fight to defend both because his state seceded. He went into the war and waged war in almost an unthinking way. The pull of his home state—its houses, its soil, its rivers, its people—overpowered his mental or rational nature. He could not analyze this pull, nor could he resist it. Freeman understood Lee's feeling, but he did not realize that it constituted a tragic limitation in the man. The emotion that impelled Lee into the war also influenced the way he fought. He fought for Virginia. Freeman did not recognize Lee's limitation because to him too the war is in Virginia. It did not occur to him to examine the effects of Lee's preoccupation with Virginia on total Confederate strategy. Nor did he see the tragic result of Lee's limitation. In the end, all the brilliance and fortitude of the greatest Confederate general availed little to save his country. It fell to pieces behind his back, and most of his efforts in Virginia went for nothing. (pp. 99-100)

T. Harry Williams, "Freeman, Historian of the Civil War: An Appraisal," in The Journal of Southern History *(copyright 1955 by the Southern Historical Association; reprinted by permission of the Managing Editor), Vol. XXI, No. 1, February, 1955 (and reprinted in his* The Selected Essays of T. Harry Williams, *Louisiana State University Press, 1983, pp. 185-94).*

RICHARD HARWELL   (essay date 1961)

[*A personal friend of Freeman, Harwell was the editor of a 1961 one-volume abridgment of* R. E. Lee.]

Dr. Freeman was able to make Lee a real presence to the readers of history because Lee was a very real presence to Dr. Freeman. And he believed that something of the greatness of Lee could be transmitted to a later generation by a thorough knowledge of the man and his times. In an informal address to members of the Chicago and Richmond Civil War Round Tables Dr. Freeman said, just a few weeks before his death June 13, 1953:

> There, gentlemen, is where we get the great reward of our study of this period. We are dealing four times in five, aye, nine times in ten, with men of character, and the great delight we have is that we can keep the company of truthful gentlemen. No honor that ever comes to a man in life is greater than the honor that may be

yours by learning thoroughly the life of one of the great men of that era.

He spoke feelingly on that occasion, for he knew from experience whereof he spoke. In a day when history was emerging from its chastening period of muckraking that had been popular in the early 1900's into its "revisionist" approach of the 1920's and '30's and in a decade when the debunking biography, the subjective approach of Gamaliel Bradford or Lytton Strachey, was at the height of historiographical fashion, Dr. Freeman eschewed the tricks of the word-monger (though as a veteran newspaper editor he certainly knew them well) in favor of straightforward history. Concerning Lee, he wrote in 1934, that there was no occasion "to attempt an 'interpretation' of a man who was his own clear interpreter." He emphasized this respect for facts in his address to his fellow Civil War Round Tablers:

> I have often looked at Lytton Strachey's five-page account of what was happening in the mind of Essex after a famous interview with Queen Elizabeth. Five pages he devotes in his "psychography," so-called, to the thoughts of Essex at that particular time. Although I lived twenty years with General Lee and have lived for ten years with General Washington, I am prepared humbly to submit to you that I do not know what either of them ever was thinking at a given moment unless he happened to have written it down himself. We cannot be too sure. Of all the frauds that ever have been perpetrated on our generation, this "psychography" is, in my opinion, the worst. How dare a man say what another man is thinking when he may not know what he himself is thinking! That is the fate of a good many of us.

(pp. xi-xii)

Dr. Freeman's whole life was preparation for his achievements as biographer of Virginia's two greatest heroes and as chronicler of the army which defended the state throughout the Civil War. . . .

He completed in 1908, while still at the Hopkins, his *A Calendar of Confederate Papers* describing in detail the collections at Richmond's Confederate Museum and pleading for further collection and use of manuscripts relating to the Confederacy. His expressions in that book on the care with which materials concerning all aspects of history must be collected and studied as a prerequisite for the writing of adequate, truthful history are of significance in light of his later career. (p. xiv)

Dr. Freeman's first large work with Lee was *Lee's Dispatches*, a compilation published in 1915 of the until then unpublished military messages sent by the General to President Jefferson Davis. His editing of the dispatches (then owned by Wymberley Jones DeRenne of Wormsloe, Georgia; later presented to the Virginia State Library by Bernard Baruch) led to his choice by Scribner's as the author of an authoritative biography of Lee. . . .

[The] years 1915-1934 were the Lee years. No effort was spared to complete fully and well the task the biographer had undertaken. It was this effort and care and ability as an author that produced at last one of the great biographies of our time, a biography that is the ultimate answer to the question that Dr. Freeman posed (and briefly answered) in his pamphlet *The Lengthening Shadow of Lee* in 1936: "How is it," he asked, "that his shadow lengthens daily? The answer is to the honor of mankind. A generation sometimes mistakes the theatrical for the dramatic, the specious for the serious, the pretender for the defender. . . . The 'hero of the hour' may not have deserved his place even for that hour; he who is a hero when his century is done has qualities that are timeless." (p. xv)

> *Richard Harwell, "Introduction," in* Lee *by Douglas Southall Freeman, edited by Richard Harwell (copyright ©1961 Estate of Douglas Southall Freeman; reprinted with permission of Charles Scribner's Sons), Charles Scribner's Sons, 1961, pp. xi-xvii.*

JOHN L. GIGNILLIAT　(essay date 1977)

[*Gignilliat examines the controversy surrounding a little-known incident in the life of Lee. In question is Freeman's interpretation of a letter written in jest by Lee a quarter century before the Civil War.*]

Less than a year after the publication of Douglas Southall Freeman's monumental *R. E. Lee* the biographer acquired documentary evidence that presented him with a difficult dilemma: a newly discovered letter written by Lee seemed to him to conflict with his published interpretation of Lee's character. Freeman's handling of this document, published here for the first time with an explanation of its contents, constitutes an informative new footnote for *R. E. Lee* today, over forty years after its initial publication. (p. 217)

Freeman fully understood the appeal that the figure of Lee had for the American public in the 1930s. He found it natural that the best-selling biographies in the years of the Great Depression were "longer studies of the truly great," for, as he expressed it," in these turbulent times we bewildered mortals find strength in the company of those strong men who met tests more severe than our own and kept the captaincy of their souls." Freeman's persistence brought *R. E. Lee* to completion at a time propitious for its popular acceptance.

All his persistence, nevertheless, afforded insufficient protection against the perverse elusiveness of historical fact. Freeman was soon to obtain a document hitherto unknown to him that seemed to offer very human exception to his portrait. His personal correspondence reveals the salient facts concerning his acquisition and historical treatment of this document, as it also reveals his uncertainty in dealing with the dilemma it posed for him.

In November 1935, less than a year after the publication of the final volumes of *R. E. Lee*, Freeman bought a letter written by Lee from Thomas F. Madigan, an autograph dealer in New York. (pp. 219-20)

The letter in question was written in the summer of 1835 on Turtle Island in Lake Erie near Toledo, Ohio, while Lieutenant Lee, age twenty-eight, was engaged in a surveying mission to determine the disputed boundary between Ohio and the territory of Michigan. It was directed to Lieutenant George Washington Cullum, a young assistant in the chief engineer's office in Washington, where Lee was also attached, and was apparently sent by army couriers. Much of the letter, bantering in tone, deals with personal matters such as the prospect of Lee's return to Washington, when Cullum hoped to secure a leave, evidently to go courting. . . . The "subject matter" that assured the document's value, in the judgment of Thomas Madigan, is a passage in the second half of the letter, an account of events that had recently involved Lee and some other members of the party on Canada's Pelee Island, located near the western end of Lake Erie. Lee wished Cullum to tell Brigadier General Charles Gratiot, the chief engineer, the "Genl." mentioned several times in the letter, of the incident on Pelee Island. The text of the letter follows in [part] . . . :

> Tell the Genl. that in my last communication I forgot to confess an act of indiscretion which I now beg leave to do through you—viz. While at Pt. Pelè [*sic*], Hood & myself were Sent over to Pt. Pelè [*sic*] Island to make a Survey of the Point on which the Light House Stands—& that it was very necessary to ascend to the Top, to descern [*sic*] our station at the Pt. The door was locked & we could not gain admittance, but after Some time Succeeded i[n] getting through the window i[n] rear when we discovered the keeper at the door. We were warm & excited, he irascible & full of venom. An altercation ensued which resulted in his death. We put him in charge of the men, gained the Top, attained our object, & in descending I discovered Some glass lamp shades, which we stood much i[n] need of as all ours were broken. I therefore made bold to *borrow* two of his Majesty's, for which liberty, as well as for that previously taken, I hope he will make our Apology to his Minister at W. We have nothing to offer in our behalf, but *necessity* and as we found the Lt. House in a most neglected condition & shockingly dirty, & were told by the Capt. of the Cutter that there had been no Light in it for more than a year, I hope it will not be considered that we have lopped from the Government a useful member, but on the contrary—to have done it some service, as the situation may now be more efficiently filled & we would advise the New Minister to make choice of a better Subject than a d———d Canadian *Snake*. . . . Remember me to the Genl & all in the office—direct to Detroit—our Boys are all well & send much love & 100 kisses. Yrs truly—
>
> R. E. Lee

Though minor corrections were made intermittently in the text of *R. E. Lee* over the next decade, there was no new edition. Nor does mention of this particular letter recur in the Freeman correspondence until February 1945, when the biographer received the first of a series of communications from Milo Milton Quaife, secretary and editor of the Burton Historical Collection of the Detroit Public Library. Quaife had secured an excerpt from Lee's letter to Cullum. . . . Quaife could assign a general time and location for the writing of the document, if indeed it were bona fide, but he doubted its authenticity. (pp. 220-23)

Freeman immediately acknowledged the existence of the letter and his ownership of it and explained to Quaife his intention "to use it in the final edition of '*R. E. Lee.*'" He had made "every effort . . . to ascertain all the circumstances attending this affair," he wrote, "but no record has been unearthed in Canada." If there had ever been any reports about lighthouses and their personnel, he believed that they must have been destroyed. He wanted to give Quaife and the person from whom he received the excerpt his "assurance that the letter will, in due time, be printed." He concluded, "Naturally, I wish to reserve so sensational an item for a new edition of my book." (p. 224)

Freeman evidently took no action about inserting the letter in *R. E. Lee* until the summer of 1946. Then, after receiving complaints about indistinct printing, he wrote an editor at Scribner's to ask if there were any chance of resetting the book in the immediate future. He would want to make some changes in the text. . . . In February 1949, for a new printing of *Lee,* Freeman submitted an insertion covering the incident in a footnote to the text. The insertion gave the date and recipient of the letter and summarized its meaning as Freeman saw it but did little else:

> An unhappy incident of Lee's experience on this survey was the accidental death of a Canadian lighthouse keeper "in a scuffle" over the use of his tower for running one of the survey lines. The only reference to this, so far as is known, is in Lee to G. W. Cullum, July 31, 1835 (Freeman MSS). A search of Canadian records yields no details.

Freeman's protectiveness toward Lee is apparent in his handling of this matter. Despite his statement that historical truth indicated publication of the letter, he clearly hesitated at the prospect. His intention had been to include "every known, important fact" about Lee in his biography. By that standard Lee's involvement in the death of a Canadian lighthouse keeper, whatever the attendant factual uncertainty, surely merited a fuller description than it finally received. The tone of the letter must have posed a particular problem for the biographer. His interpretation of the incident as expressed to Milo Quaife absolved Lee from responsibility for the death itself, but it could hardly have reconciled Lee's epistolary lightness in describing the death with his own previously published interpretation. Faced with this dilemma, Freeman compromised He told part of the story as he saw it in a revised footnote for *R. E. Lee,* preserved the letter—and left the rest to time.

The irony of this situation is that Freeman apparently allowed his protectiveness to lead by some curious reflex to a historical misjudgment of Lee's letter. The letter is unquestionably bona fide, and the trip to Pelee Island did occur, but Freeman almost certainly misinterpreted the description of the incident at the lighthouse and thereby vastly inflated its significance. (pp. 225-26)

External evidence . . . yields no clues to the circumstances of the death at the Pelee lighthouse and in fact by its negative nature tends to deepen the mystery—until considered in conjunction with internal literary evidence. Then the lack of the former adds to the persuasive force of the latter. It is precisely the levity of Lee's account that provides an explanation. His letter opens on a facetious note with his reference to the sex of his newborn child and his joshing of Cullum's projected courting. It later sends courtly greetings to Mrs. Gratiot and her young daughters, sustains the joking with an amused description of speculation in Detroit, and concluded by sending "much love & 100 kisses" from "our Boys." Even the reference to establishing a camp "*among Enemies*" is probably humorous hyperbole. Close examination of the passage describing the episode at the lighthouse suggests compellingly that it too is facetious, that what the Americans killed there was quite literally "a d———d Canadian *Snake*." Earlier in the letter Lee has mentioned the prevalence of "*Moscitoes & Snakes*" in the area. His account of the adventure on Pelee Island is in fact a sustained mock-heroic conceit that he thought would amuse Lieutenant Cullum and General Gratiot. "The keeper at the door" suggests a guardian dragon of the castle.

(Considering the small compass of the ground floor of the lighthouse, it would seem logistically improbable that the American party could have "discovered" a human being "at the door" *after* entering "the window in rear only a few feet away.) The "keeper" is depicted as "irascible & full of venom." His death, Lee trusts, will not "have lopped from the Government a useful member." Only in conclusion is he named, specifically, as "a d———d Canadian *Snake*." Lee's description does employ the very slight "shadow of an oath," but the only actual "indiscretion" to which the lieutenant confesses is the lighthearted "*borrow*[*ing*]" of some lampshades from a lighthouse he believed to be nonfunctioning. It was the kind of joke that would have been immediately perceived as such by certain intimates of Lee's with whom he frequently indulged his humorous propensities.

George Washington Cullum, Lee's junior by two years, was definitely such an intimate in 1835. The two men shared duties as General Gratiot's assistants from 1834 to 1836. Extant letters from Lee to Cullum during the next few years offer further examples of mock-serious jesting. (pp. 228-29)

Examples of humor are abundant in the correspondence of Lee. Though his jests occur more frequently in letters he wrote as a young man, he persisted throughout his life in sending facetious messages to members of his own family. (p. 229)

Freeman certainly recognized the existence of Lee's sense of humor, for he quoted numerous examples of epistolary jest in *R. E. Lee.* Even clearer proof of the biographer's awareness rests in his articles on **"Lee and the Ladies"** published some ten years before the completion of the biography itself. The two essays, which appeared in successive issues of *Scribner's Magazine* in 1925, rely heavily on Lee's humorous correspondence. (p. 231)

That he recognized the existence of Lee's genial humor did not guarantee that Freeman would accurately identify every instance of it. Humor was not in fact the biographer's forte. A determined man whose disciplined use of time allowed him several careers simultaneously, Freeman specialized more in purpose and system than in humor. Practically every moment of his life was planned and scheduled. The scope of his activities, added to the cast of his own mind, may have contributed to an occasional misreading of Lee's humorous subtleties. At least one misreading other than that of the letter to Cullum did occur. It involved a quotation from a letter to Talcott written in October 1834, in which Lee referred to the infant Charles Gratiot Talcott, the namesake of the general: "As to Genl. *Charles,* it is useless to waste a man's good wishes on him, in as much as he never requires them, & will serenely knock his way through life as he has so far done through the hands of the d[octo]rs." In *R. E. Lee* Freeman acknowledged that the remark was made "half in jest," but he mistakenly applied it to General Gratiot himself, rather than to his seven-month-old namesake. (pp. 231-32)

The final element in Freeman's misjudgment of the incident at Pelee Island would seem to be his protectiveness toward Lee, a matter as complex as the ancestral roots of the biographer's historical orientation. By his own constantly reiterated admission the strongest influence in Douglas Freeman's early life came from his father, Walker Burford Freeman, a veteran of four years in the Army of Northern Virginia. The elder Freeman revered his commander-in-chief and viewed his own experiences in the war with a stoicism drawn from a deeply religious nature. A devout and life-long Baptist, Walker Freeman regarded struggle and suffering as an unavoidable concomitant of life. . . . Young Douglas absorbed his father's religious views along with his reverence for General Lee and his enthusiasm for the history of the war. (p. 233)

There can be no doubt that Lee was Freeman's highest personal exemplar, the greatest hero of his life.

Nor can there be any doubt about Lee's significance in the biographer's privately held interpretation of the war: he represented quite simply the personification of the best in the Confederacy's cause. Surely the commander's reaction to the war did coincide remarkably with Freeman's ideal of human fortitude. He could have found no better exemplar than Lee, a man who accepted his role as the best available to him in an imperfect world and performed it with brilliant devotion. In the mind of the biographer the moral hero described in *R. E. Lee* could not be separated from the military hero. Freeman was equally jealous of both the moral and military components in his hero.

Of course, there is nothing in Lieutenant Lee's letter to Lieutenant Collum damaging to either component. Freeman's mistaken reading of the letter, like his protective treatment of it, would seem to be the reflexive product of his intense regard for Lee. The biographer was apparently caught off guard, after the successful publication of *R. E. Lee*, by a somewhat ambiguous letter to a correspondent not well known to him. His own seriousness of mind contributed to his mistake. And the final jest of a letter written in 1835 was the failure to perceive the joke exactly a century later by a biographer who had every reason to wish to give the document the most favorable interpretation possible. (pp. 235-36)

The biographer apparently left no instructions concerning the incident at Pelee Island when he died in 1953. He had preserved the letter, and he asked that his personal papers, which included the correspondence with Madigan and Quaife, be made available to scholars, actions that suggest he deliberately left to a later time and agent a more complete explanation of this posthumous footnote. That he would have been delighted to have the explanation pronounce his own interpretation mistaken is the supreme irony of the historian's dilemma. (p. 236)

> *John L. Gignilliat, "A Historian's Dilemma: A Posthumous Footnote for Freeman's 'R. E. Lee'," in The Journal of Southern History (copyright 1977 by the Southern Historical Association; reprinted by permission of the Managing Editor), Vol. XLIII, No. 2, May, 1977, pp. 217-36.*

ADDITIONAL BIBLIOGRAPHY

Benét, Stephen Vincent. "Generals in Action and under the Stress of Action." *The New York Times Book Review* (25 October 1942): 5.
> A review of *Lee's Lieutenants*. Benét concludes his enthusiastic appraisal with the sentence: "As vivid and fascinating narrative, as a study of men in action and under the stress of action, it will keep any reader enthralled."

Cheek, Mary Tyler Freeman. "Douglas Southall Freeman: My Father As a Writer." *Richmond Literature and History Quarterly* 1 (Spring 1979): 33-41.
> Interesting reminiscences by Freeman's daughter.

Commager, Henry Steele. "The Life of Lee." *The Yale Review* XXIV, No. 3 (Spring 1935): 594-97.
> An insightful, laudatory review of *R. E. Lee*. Commager finds Freeman's "fog of war" technique to be "disappointing."

Commager, Henry Steele. "The Generals Who Fought with R. E. Lee: A Masterly Analysis of the Work of Beauregard, Johnston, Stonewall Jackson and Others." *New York Herald Tribune Books* (18 October 1942): 3.
> A glowing review of the first volume of *Lee's Lieutenants*.

DeVoto, Bernard. "Mr. Freeman's Continuing Study." *The Saturday Review of Literature* XXVI, No. 22 (29 May 1943): 16.
> High praise for volume II of *Lee's Lieutenants*. DeVoto writes of Freeman: "Students will be in his debt indefinitely: no action is too slight, no organization too small, for him to follow exhaustively."

Glasgow, Ellen. *Letters of Ellen Glasgow*. Edited by Blair Rouse. New York: Harcourt, Brace and Co., 1958, 384 p.*
> Contains several letters written to Freeman, expressing Glasgow's friendship and her admiration for Freeman's works.

Harrison, Joseph H., Jr. "Harry Williams, Critic of Freeman: A Demurrer." *The Virginia Magazine of History and Biography* 64, No. 1 (January 1956): 70-7.
> A systematic rebuttal of T. Harry Williams's "Freeman, Historian of the Civil War: An Appraisal" (see excerpt above). Harrison claims that Williams understands neither the mind of Robert E. Lee nor that of Freeman.

Henrickson, W. B. "A Review of Reviews of Douglas S. Freeman's *Young Washington*." *The Library Quarterly* XXI, No. 3 (July 1951): 173-82.
> Summarizes favorable and unfavorable reviews of the first two volumes of *George Washington*.

Lytle, Andrew Nelson. "*R. E. Lee*." *The Southern Review* I, No. 2 (Autumn 1935): 411-22.
> A review of *R. E. Lee* that explains why the critic does not believe the biography to be definitive.

Lytle, Andrew [Nelson]. "*Lee's Lieutenants: A Study in Command*." *The Sewanee Review* 51, No. 1 (January-March 1943): 177-79.
> A review which finds *Lee's Lieutenants* to be markedly inferior to *R. E. Lee*. Lytle believes that the work's failure is grounded in Freeman's excessive detail, his "stubborn enthusiasms," and in the lack of overall perspective afforded by his "fog of war" technique.

Malone, Dumas. "Freeman on the First of the Great Virginians: Quenchless Ambition of an Ordered Mind in *Young Washington*." *New York Herald Tribune Weekly Book Review* (17 October 1948): 1-2.
> An enthusiastic review of *Young Washington*.

Malone, Dumas. "Washington as Leader and Man, When Victory Hung in the Balance." *New York Herald Tribune Book Review* (19 October 1952): 1, 22.
> Finds *Victory with the Help of the French* to be the most interesting volume written to-date in the Washington biography.

Sandburg, Carl. *The Letters of Carl Sandburg*. Edited by Herbert Mitgang. New York: Harcourt, Brace & World, 1968, 577 p.
> Contains two admiring letters to Freeman. The first, of 21 September 1938, discusses the depth of *R. E. Lee;* Sandburg states that "with but few reservations I accept your portrait. And those reservations are in a realm where no one can prove anything." The second letter, dated 5 November 1945, was written to encourage Freeman in his work on *George Washington*.

Sheldon, Richard N. "Editing a Historical Manuscript: Jared Sparks, Douglas Southall Freeman, and the Battle of Brandywine." *William & Mary Quarterly* 36, No. 10 (April 1979): 255-63.*
> A defense of the nineteenth-century historian Jared Sparks, whose editing of Washington's papers was attacked by Freeman in *Leader of the Revolution*. The interpretation by one of Freeman's research assistants of a military dispatch is brought into serious question.

Tate, Allen. "The Definitive Lee." *The New Republic* LXXI, No. 1046 (19 December 1934): 171-72.

> A review of praise for the first two volumes of *R. E. Lee*. Tate finds fault, however, with what he sees as Freeman's vague depiction of Lee's milieu. Because of the demands thrust upon the reader by Freeman's "fog of war" technique, Tate believes the book will never reach a wide audience.

Tate, Allen. *"R. E. Lee* Complete." *The New Republic* LXXXI, No. 1062 (10 April 1935): 255.

> A review which reveals Tate's mixed reactions to the completed *R. E. Lee*. Tate believed that Freeman did not delve deeply enough into Lee's psyche, and that the biographer created a "Victorian" character who is, in some respects, incomprehensible to the modern reader.

(Sir) H(enry) Rider Haggard

1856-1923

English novelist, nonfiction and short story writer, historian, and autobiographer.

A renowned author of adventure novels, Haggard was second only to Robert Louis Stevenson in popularity during the late nineteenth and early twentieth centuries, and for a time he was critically regarded as the equal of Rudyard Kipling. He produced over fifty novels set in exotic places, with most featuring intrepid heroes, beautiful heroines, and nonstop action. Among his works, *King Solomon's Mines* and *She* are today considered classics in the field of fantasy and adventure writing.

Haggard was the eighth of ten children born to a Norfolk country squire and his wife. Considered a slow child, Haggard was not granted the more extensive education that some of his older brothers received. His education ended shortly before he turned seventeen, when he moved to London to study for entrance into the Foreign Office. During this time he experimented briefly with spiritualism, attending séances which he frequently disrupted by faking "manifestations." He was never wholly convinced, however, that he had not occasionally witnessed genuine supernatural occurrences. At nineteen, his father obtained for him a post on the staff of Sir Henry Bulwer, the newly appointed lieutenant-governor of Natal, Africa. For over a year Haggard dispatched clerical and social duties, and explored the African countryside, listening to stories told by early settlers and members of local Zulu tribes. He acquired enough fluency in the Zulu language to travel extensively alone, and met with several important Zulu chieftains, taking copious notes during his talks with them. He realized that the Zulu nation faced certain disintegration and he wanted to preserve something of the heritage of a people he had come to admire. During this time he anonymously published several vividly descriptive accounts of African ceremonies in London magazines. In 1879 Haggard decided to leave government service, purchased an African farm in the Transvaal, and started the first commercial ostrich-raising venture. He vacationed briefly in England and married, returning with his wife to Africa, where their experiences on the farm later provided material for the novel *Jess*. When in 1881 the Transvaal was receded to the Dutch, Haggard and his family returned to England. There he began a law practice which occupied little of his time and which he abandoned in 1885 with the success of the novel *King Solomon's Mines*.

Popular legend holds that Haggard wrote *King Solomon's Mines* in six weeks after betting that he could produce a boys' adventure story to rival *Treasure Island*. He frankly admitted that his novel was inspired by Stevenson's, and borrowed such elements as the dying explorer passing on a tattered treasure map to an ill-assorted band of adventurers. Instead of the sea, however, Haggard set his story in Africa, an exotic and little-known region to most of his readers, and he peopled his novel with characters familiar to him from his years there. Most critics note the similarities between Haggard's and Stevenson's works immediately, and the name of Stevenson is frequently mentioned in critical discussion of Haggard. While most critics regard Stevenson as the superior craftsman, they grant Hag-

gard far more imaginative power. *King Solomon's Mines* was an enormous critical and popular success, having been written to a ready-made audience which had enthusiastically received Stevenson's adventures and was eager to read more of the same. Haggard followed *King Solomon's Mines* with *She*, which also enjoyed immediate success. In writing *She*, Haggard borrowed freely from his own earlier successful novel. Instead of a treasure map, his little band of explorers is guided by ancient writing upon a broken fragment of pottery; and the party is led by Ludwig Horace Holly, a character very similar to Allan Quatermain, the hero and narrator of *King Solomon's Mines*. *She* contains elements of the supernatural, and while there do exist legends of isolated African tribes ruled by immortal white queens, Haggard maintained that his creation of Ayesha was original. The immortal Ayesha, "She-who-must-be-obeyed," has captured the imaginations of three generations of readers and has become familiar to many people through the several films based on the novel. Carl Jung has interpreted her compelling character as a classic fictional example of his concept of the anima.

Haggard made repeated use of the familiar setting of Africa for many subsequent novels and continued to feature his popular hero Allan Quatermain in new novels. The mysterious figure of Ayesha also reappears in *Ayesha: The Return of She*, *Wisdom's Daughter*, and in *She and Allan*, which united Haggard's two most famous characters. Haggard also travelled widely to gather firsthand impressions of settings for new novels: to Egypt before writing *Cleopatra,* and to Iceland for *Eric Brighteyes.* He and his wife were in Mexico researching the background for the novel *Montezuma's Daughter* when they received word that their eldest child and only son had died at the age of nine. Haggard sank into a deep depression from which he never fully recovered. For several years he lived in semiretirement at his wife's ancestral estate, Ditchingham. He became an orchid-breeding enthusiast, established a thriving orchard, and sought new land to supplement his wife's inherited property. Rudyard Kipling, his close friend, was in the process of building up his own estate, and the two writers often conferred on matters both agricultural and literary. Kipling was instrumental in helping Haggard develop the plots and characterizations of many of his later novels. Haggard also wrote several books examining agricultural techniques, including *Rural England* and *A Farmer's Year,* and proposed a new method of draining marshes to recover more arable land. A trip to Denmark yielded material for a book about Danish farming practices, *Rural Denmark and Its Lessons,* in much the same way that earlier trips abroad had given Haggard the authentic local color for his adventure novels. It was for his agricultural work that Haggard was knighted in 1912. For the rest of his life he continued to write novels, producing at least one annually, with several published posthumously. Despite the never-ending enthusiasm with which readers received each new Haggard novel, none of the later works ever garnered the critical acclaim which had greeted *King Solomon's Mines* and *She.* It was generally thought by critics that in these novels Haggard had hit upon a winning formula of fast-paced action touched with the supernatural, and had consequently never varied or attempted new themes.

Haggard's greatest flaw as a writer was noted by one of his first editors, John Cordy Jeaffreson: he never got over the idea "that novels are dashed off." He wrote quickly and almost never revised anything once set down. His slapdash method of writing is at contrast with the painstaking research which preceded each novel. He would not give a novel a setting with which he was not familiar; and he began *King Solomon's Mines* only after he and a sister-in-law had carefully produced a prototype of the treasure map, executed in blood upon a torn scrap of shirt. Similarly, they created the potsherd that contains the inscribed history of Kallikrates which figures prominently in the plot of *She.* Their "antique" was so well constructed that a noted Egyptologist, unaware of its origins, said that it was possibly a genuine artifact.

With the exception of *King Solomon's Mines,* all of Haggard's novels were written for adults, but provided some of the favorite reading for children in the late 1800s and early 1900s. From the time of their publication until today, they have given pleasure to readers of all ages who enjoy a fast-paced adventure. While Haggard occupies a minor place in the larger context of world literature, within the smaller genre of the adventure romance his novels are considered among the best of their kind.

(See also *Contemporary Authors,* Vol. 108 and *Something About the Author,* Vol. 16.)

PRINCIPAL WORKS

Cetywayo and His White Neighbours   (history)   1882
Dawn   (novel)   1884

The Witch's Head   (novel)   1884
King Solomon's Mines   (novel)   1885
Allan Quatermain   (novel)   1887
Jess   (novel)   1887
She   (novel)   1887
Allan's Wife   (short stories)   1889
Cleopatra   (novel)   1889
The World's Desire [with Andrew Lang]   (novel)   1890
Eric Brighteyes   (novel)   1891
Nada the Lily   (novel)   1892
Montezuma's Daughter   (novel)   1893
A Farmer's Year   (nonfiction)   1899
Rural England   (nonfiction)   1902
Ayesha: The Return of She   (novel)   1905
The Ghost Kings   (novel)   1908
Queen Sheba's Ring   (novel)   1910
Marie   (novel)   1912
Child of Storm   (novel)   1913
Rural Denmark and Its Lessons   (nonfiction)   1913
Allan and the Holy Flower   (novel)   1915
The Ivory Child   (novel)   1916
The Ancient Allan   (novel)   1920
She and Allan   (novel)   1921
Wisdom's Daughter: The Life and Love Story of She-Who-Must-Be-Obeyed   (novel)   1923
The Days of My Life   (autobiography)   1926
Belshazzar   (novel)   1930

THE SPECTATOR   (essay date 1882)

Two books concerning Zululand, very different in character, but each the result of considerable personal experience, come not inopportunely to contribute their quota towards determining the vexed questions what is the character of Cetywayo, and whether, even if his restoration to power be an act of justice, it will be acceptable or odious to English settlers. The first of these books, that of Mr. Haggard [*Cetywayo and his White Neighbours*], may be described as historico-political, dealing as much, or more, with the affairs of Natal and the Transvaal than with those of Zululand. . . .

While professing a certain sympathy with the dethroned King, Mr. Haggard contends that we have no right, for the sake of one man, to destroy the happiness and security of thousands of Zulus and colonists, by whom the settlement of Zululand under English government is ardently desired. . . . Mr. Haggard's contention is that having conquered the Zulus and removed Cetywayo, we are morally bound to follow up our work by governing the country ourselves, in other words, by annexing it. That is to say, that having committed an act of injustice, and made a political mistake, our present duty is to persist in the same course.

This writer casts a good deal of ridicule upon the feminine admirers of the model of injured innocence and virtue, "so good, so big, and so beautiful," whose taste for massacre is so pronounced, and whose word is so little to be depended upon; although this, as he confesses, is beside the mark, except in so far as such exaggerated partisanship is calculated to mislead the ignorant. That Cetywayo, however, even if inclined to be peaceable, had no choice but to engage in war, is quite clear from Mr. Haggard's own showing. (p. 1089)

[Though he] absolutely disclaims the writing for any party purpose, professing to set forth nothing but the naked truth, and probably believing that he does so, Mr. Haggard expresses himself towards those in power in a manner that shews all too plainly the strong animus by which he is influenced,—an animus that should set the reader on his guard, and prevent him from being too ready to accept a foregone conclusion. (pp. 1089-90)

> *"Our Sable Visitor," in* The Spectator *(© 1882 by The Spectator), Vol. 55, No. 2825, August 19, 1882, pp. 1089-90.**

GEORGE SAINTSBURY   (essay date 1884)

[Saintsbury has been called the most influential English literary historian and critic of the early twentieth century. His studies on French literature, particularly his History of the French Novel, *have established him as a leading authority on such writers as Guy de Maupassant and Honoré de Balzac. Saintsbury held to two distinct sets of critical standards: one for the novel and the other for poetry and drama. As a critic of novels, he believed that "the novel has nothing to do with any beliefs, with any convictions, with any thoughts in the strict sense, except as mere garnishings. Its substance must always be life not thought, conduct not belief, the passions not the intellect, manners and morals not creeds and theories. . . . The novel is . . . mainly and firstly a criticism of life." As a critic of poetry and drama, Saintsbury was a radical formalist, who frequently asserted that subject is of little importance and that "the so-called 'formal' part is of the essence." René Wellek has praised Saintsbury's critical qualities: his "enormous reading, the almost universal scope of his subject matter, the zest and zeal of his exposition" and "the audacity with which he handles the most ambitious and unattempted arguments." Below, he offers an unfavorable review of Haggard's first novel.]*

We have, we think, seen the name of Mr. Rider Haggard on the title-page of books, but not of novels; and *Dawn* (a somewhat obscure title) bears many of the familiar marks of inexperience in novel-writing. It is well written, it has considerable interest of plot, and the characters are not borrowed, and show not a little ability in character-drawing. But there is altogether too much of it. It is too long—too long by at least two hundred pages of its thousand. It covers too great a stretch of time. There are too many heroines, and they are too beautiful. There are too many minor characters, and they have too much to do. The wicked people (of whom there are several) are too elaborately wicked; and, lastly, not content with an immense amount of legitimate business, Mr. Haggard has infused a strong element of occult arts and astral spirits, and other devices after the manner of the late Lord Lytton, which are perilous stuff to handle. All this not merely interferes somewhat with the merit of the book, but makes it very difficult to give any idea of it in small space. Generally speaking, it may be said to deal successively with the schemes of one George Caresfoot to step into the shoes of his cousin Philip Caresfoot, and his partial success; with the schemes of Philip Caresfoot to get the shoes back, and of *his* partial success; with the intrigues of George with a certain Mrs. (afterwards Lady) Bellamy, and her machinations, under pressure, to secure him the hand of Angela Caresfoot, his second cousin and Philip's daughter; with the more honest loves of Angela and a certain Arthur Heigham, who in his turn is beloved by a certain Mildred Carr. All this, with two excellent dog-fights (in one of which a dog is killed, and in the other a man) and some other rarities, enables Mr. Haggard to fill his thousand pages full enough—indeed, as we

have said, too full for any but a somewhat voracious appetite. He must "train down" if he is to write a really good novel.

> *George Saintsbury, in his review of "Dawn" (reprinted by permission of the Literary Estate of George Saintsbury), in* The Academy, *Vol. 25, No. 620, March 22, 1884, p. 200.*

[ANDREW LANG]   (essay date 1885)

[Lang was one of England's most important nineteenth-century literary critics. He contributed greatly to the career of Robert Louis Stevenson through his largely favorable reviews; here he does the same for Haggard, even comparing King Solomon's Mines *with* Treasure Island. *Lang later collaborated with Haggard on the novel* The World's Desire.]*

After Mr. Rider Haggard's description of African adventure in **The Witch's Head,** it must have been plain to every reasonable critic that he was the very man to write a boy's book. He has written it, and we congratulate the boys. Since *Treasure Island* we have seen no such healthily exciting volume. It would be hard to say whether the piratical John Silver or the mysteriously aged witch Gagool (of **King Solomon's Mines**) strikes to the youthful heart the more delightful terror and apprehension. Sometimes we are inclined to give Mr. Stevenson's invention the palm for the wonderful astuteness and versatility of his villanous hero; sometimes we think that Mr. Haggard's African witchwoman (possessing a touch of supernatural dread) is, on the whole, the more successfully appalling of the two. Comparisons of this kind are sure to be drawn by people who have read the two books, and retain enough of Plato's "immortal child" to have been heartily frightened and happily agitated by both. Like *Treasure Island,* **King Solomon's Mines** deals with the quest for hidden wealth. But in the latter volume it is not the gold of buccaneers which is sought, in the last century, by a crew of pirates captained by a confiding squire, and rescued in the last peril by a boy of miraculous courage and resource. The treasure in Mr. Haggard's book is nothing less than the diamond mines whence the Sidonian galleons brought King Solomon his jewels. The scene is the centre of Southern Africa, Kukuanaland, a region unexplored. The time is the present day, and the seekers are Allan Quatermain, an old elephant-hunter, in whose mouth the narrative is put, Sir Henry Curtis, an Englishman in quest of a lost brother, Captain Good, his friend, and Umbopa, a mysterious Zulu recruit who is not all a Zulu. Quatermain meets Curtis and Good, the naval officer, on board a steamer. Curtis is a man with a giant's strength, and a hero, withal, of the noblest daring and equanimity. Good, his friend, adds the comic element, and, if we had a fault to find with this enthralling tale, it is that Mr. Haggard gives us too good measure of comedy. . . . [Quatermain] has a trick of constantly quoting the *Ingoldsby Legends,* and of attributing to Barham the lines of other poets; and this trick (like Betteredge's references to *Robinson Crusoe* in the *Moonstone*) waxes a little tedious. Mr. Haggard makes Quatermain tell his tale very much as such a man would have told it, with flashes of boisterous humour; and, dramatically, this is all very well. But for the manner of the telling we decidedly prefer Mr. Stevenson's boy narrator in *Treasure Island.* Good, as we have said, is also partly comic. He wears an eyeglass constantly fixed in his eye, and he possesses a moveable set of false teeth. These properties come in wonderfully handy when certain savages are to be impressed with the idea that Good and his friends are supernatural beings. But perhaps we hear too frequently about the resources of civilization possessed by Captain Good.

With this carping our fault-finding ends; and we have only praise for the very remarkable and uncommon powers of invention and gift of "vision" which Mr. Haggard displays. . . . He is intimately acquainted with the wild borders of Zululand, Bechuana, and the Transvaal, and he has a most sympathetic knowledge of the Zulu. The Kukuanas of the tale are, in fact, Zulus, long isolated, wholly ignorant of European ways, and better organized, on the whole, than the tribesmen of Chaka and Mpanda. (p. 485)

Mr. Haggard is so correct in his descriptive touches and pictures of African life, that one is constantly tempted into discussion too grave for the task in hand. To be brief, Curtis and the rest reach the Kukuanas, and persuade them (by various civilized dodges) that they are children of the Stars. But if Twala, the Kukuana king, a desperate tyrant, is half-deceived, Gagool is not deceived at all. Gagool is the master stroke of Mr. Haggard's invention. She is a witch-finder (Twala, like Cetywayo and Saul, "smells out witches"), a malignant being of unknown and almost supernatural antiquity. She has been the evil genius of many Kukuana kings, and the scene in which she "smells out" every suspected Kukuana chief, and ends by trying to give Umbopa over to death, is most terrible, and, unhappily, not more terrible than true. By a wonderfully ingenious stroke of wit, which it would be unfair to reveal, the white men baffle Gagool and Twala. Umbopa is proved to be the true heir of Kukuanaland; Twala is a mere usurper. The Kukuanas take sides, and there is a splendid savage battle-piece. . . . The slaying is Homeric. Naturally the white men, with Umbopa, win, and then we have a duel, as good as the greater combat, between Sir Henry and Twala, the gigantic one-eyed king. Twala is slain. Umbopa is accepted as king, and he makes Gagool, the impish witch-finder, guide the Englishmen to Solomon's Mines. But, first, they must look on the White Death and the White Dead, a scene of high and even poetical imagination, of which we shall not spoil the interest by any explanation or analysis. What chanced in the awful treasure cave, what was the last dread trump in the hand of the undefeated Gagool, how Good's lover, the Kukuana Pocahontas, fared (for this amount of "feminine interest" Mr. Haggard offers), and the conclusion of the whole matter, we leave the reader to discover. His curiosity will not be disappointed, if he be a reader of the right sort, who is capable of being carried beyond the commonplace by a peculiarly thrilling and vigorous tale of adventure. After the scene in the Treasure Chamber (when Gagool plays her trump), excitement seems exhausted, but it is not. There remains another surprise. We have found Solomon's Mines—we have still to find Sir Henry's brother.

In this narrative Mr. Haggard seems, as the French say, to have "found himself." He has added a new book to a scanty list, the list of good, manly, and stirring fictions of pure adventure. The sentiment of his regular novels, *Dawn* and *The Witch's Head,* is absent, of course, but perhaps, at least in the former of these, sentiment was unduly to the fore. No one can call Allan Quatermain sentimental. And, to tell the truth, we would give many novels, say eight hundred (that is about the yearly harvest) for such a book as *King Solomon's Mines.* (pp. 485-86)

[*Andrew Lang*], in his review of "King Solomon's Mines," in The Saturday Review, London, Vol. 60, No. 1563, October 10, 1885, pp. 485-86.

H. B. [pseudonym of WILLIAM ERNEST HENLEY] (essay date 1887)

[*Henley was an important figure in the counter-decadent movement in English literature during the late nineteenth century. A writer who, like Rudyard Kipling and Robert Louis Stevenson, propounded virility and inner strength over the alienation and despair of the decadents, Henley welcomed the resurgence of the adventure novel during the 1880s and saw Haggard as one of the key figures in the resurrection of romance. In the following review, Henley offers enthusiastic—though by no means, uncritical—praise for* She.]

Mr. Rider Haggard has the gift of invention to such a point as to be practically a man of genius. But he is not an artist; and the consequence is that when you read him you grudge him his genius, and wish (for art's sake) that he was only a man of talent. In '**She**,' his new romance, the invention is, to my thinking, admirable; but the writing, the taste, the treatment, are often beneath criticism. And the worst is, there is no hope of better. Mr. Haggard went out to Africa when he was very young; he returned to achieve success, almost at once, with '**King Solomon's Mines**.' He had far rather act his works than write them; and it is hardly to be doubted that he will go on writing ill and inventing well until he is exhausted. Of course you have read '**She**,' and of course you read it at a gasp. For my part, I couldn't put it down until I had finished it, and Ayesha, by the operation of the Rolling Pillar of Life, had been turned into a reminiscence of the Gagool of '**King Solomon's Mines**.' But I have it on my conscience to say, that I blessed and banned alternately, and in proportions very nearly equal, all through the book. I couldn't help wishing that Mr. Stevenson had invented it; I couldn't help regretting that Mr. Rider Haggard is not Mr. Stevenson, and has never taken seriously to heart the difficulties of his profession. When I came to the Fight in the Cave, and to the Vision of Ayesha cursing Amenartas (with that inspiration of the fire that follows her hands as they rise and fall in imprecation!), I could have hurrahed in my enthusiasm; and when I came to Ayesha coquetting with Holly, and making puns on his name, exactly as if she had read the works of the late H. J. Byron, I stopped short as before an open drain. I reflected that God sends meat and the devil cooks. That is incontrovertible, but that it should be so as regards the art of literature is a shame as well as a misfortune. Walter Scott wrote ill enough sometimes; but he wrote ill in another way than Mr. Haggard's; and, moreover, he picked himself up in his dialogue, and towered, and was Walter Scott; whereas Mr. Haggard—unless he is dealing with a noble savage like Ustane—is only Mr. Haggard, and deforms his situations with facetiousness, or flatulence, in a way that is really heartbreaking to witness.

All the same, invention is a mighty good thing; and Mr. Haggard has so much of it that to refuse him countenance is impossible. Who is there, for instance, that would not rather read '**She**' than the third and last instalment of the 'Greville Memoirs?' . . . In Kôr, among the Amahagger, one can live with a certain pleasure, and be sure of excitement and romance. In the England of Charles Greville there is neither one nor other; there is not much besides pettiness and jealousy and intelligence which is mistaken quite as often as not. And I, for one, vote for the Impossible, and put away the Real as it deserves. (p. 78)

H. B. [*pseudonym of William Ernest Henley*], "London Letter," in The Critic, New York, n.s. Vol. VII, No. 163, February 12, 1887, pp. 78-9.*

JAMES RUNCIMAN (essay date 1890)

[*Runciman provides convincing documentation to prove his contention that Haggard plagiarized a scene included in the novel* Allan Quatermain *from a work entitled* The Cruise of the Falcon, *by E. F. Knight. Runciman, further, cites an article of his own which appeared in the* Pall Mall Gazette—*and which reappears, with minor changes, in a scene from Haggard's* Mr. Meeson's Will.*]*

Now this business [of plagiarism] has become a serious scandal; and to many of us it is the more serious for this very weighty reason—if one author plagiarises from another, it always happens that the wrong man gets into trouble with the journals and the public. What is more, the one who has suffered can rarely manage to clear himself; if his work has been appropriated by a popular writer he may go on telling the truth till he is black in the face, but the original charge of plagiarism brought against him sticks quite fast in the memories of thousands who do not see the disclaimer. As I mean to put down some very straight talk, I shall illustrate this point carefully. Mr. Rider Haggard, who has developed into the most cool and audacious individual known in literary history, has contrived to get a close friend of mine into a mess, and my friend, though he is one of the most calm and daring of modern explorers, was unwise enough to let himself be driven half mad by the results of Mr. Haggard's amiable eccentricity. Before I go on with the story, I will say that there must be no nonsense about "spite" and "jealousy," so far as I am concerned. I should never dream of saying that the Last Stand of the Greys is not a thrilling chapter, and the whole story of the Mines is real romance—good for boys and good for men. Moreover, I pursued *Jess* with a running chorus of praise as it appeared, and I still regard it as mainly a noble book. Some of the writing is so vivid and fine that the author's later stuff baffles me, and I am half inclined to wonder how the same man could have written both *Jess,* and that shocking lump of incompetency, *Allan's Wife,* the formless baboon epic. Furthermore, I may say that I was almost the only reviewer who boldly praised *The Witch's Head* when it first came out, and I gratified myself by doing so more than once. The famous fight between Jerry Jones and the Boer is classed by literary authorities with the greatest battles in descriptive literature, and there are newspapers worked by well-known hands in which this pleasing combat is mentioned about once a month all the year round. I did not learn to spar in a literary club, and I cannot therefore admire the pugilistic masterpiece, because in the first place it is evidently done by a man who never put up his hands to fight in his life, nor saw two good boxers. . . . The amateurish errors apart, the novel had strong points, and I freely said so. I repeat that there must be no talk of "envy" to me. It is a luxury to praise good work; it is a luxury to find it out, and if I can only get my eye on a capable man, I shall throw up my hat and cheer him, maybe a long time before the mob give tongue. . . . Besides—envy of *Allan's Wife* and *Mr. Meeson's Will!* Come, come! These odious preliminaries have been made necessary by Mr. Haggard's more infatuated friends, so I do not apologise for them.

And now to the plain story. Mr. E. F. Knight is an amateur sailor who has been born just three centuries after his proper time. To call him daring would be no compliment, because he has no physical fear to resist. He is one of the finest seamen in the world, and he took a little eighteen-ton boat over twenty-two thousand miles of dangerous waters; he sailed her twenty-five hundred miles into the interior of South America; he had so many narrow escapes that they are not easy to count, and

he told all about his voyagings in *The Cruise of the Falcon.* . . . Well, Knight explored the lonely volcanic island of Trinidad, and a most moving account he gives; in all fiction there is not anything so appalling as the demure, modest description of that actual exploration. The three men who went on shore had to slide down a crumbling precipice, which sloped sharply into a gulf so deep and narrow that no light of day could pierce the gloom; they lay on their backs, and made their desperate bid for life; they jobbed their heels into the rolling pumice, and the least mistake in pressure would have sent them to death. After reading that tremendous scene again and again, I still want to shut my eyes when I realize it.

Then the adventurers finally landed in a dread gorge haunted by foul birds, and they rested one night there. Rested! Huge land crabs made a dead set at them, and millions—millions, mark you!—seemed to be coming upon them. For sheer horror I know nothing like that night in the gorge. . . . At any rate, the whole chapter is instinct with a gruesome, yet artistic, terror, and it is a masterpiece.

Now Mr. Rider Haggard saw this book, and he thought some of it might suit him, so he helped himself to the description of the gorge and the terrible denizens, and he stuck it into *Allan Quatermain.* Of course, we must have some comedy, so one of the land crabs "nipped Good behind, and he jumped up with a howl which set the wild echoes flying with a vengeance." That sort of wit is inevitable in Mr. Haggard's work, and some people enjoy it. The dreadfulness of Knight's chapter is perhaps a little vulgarised by Mr. Haggard, but the essence is cleverly kept. (pp. 423-25)

Mr. Knight stepped into a trap. The editor of *Cassell's Saturday Journal* was much struck with the *Falcon* book, so he asked the author for a story of adventure, and he received one in which Knight embodied some of his more creepy experiences. . . . He paid dearly for thinking that a man can do as he likes with his own, for the "London Correspondent" soon came out with this:

> Mr. Rider Haggard is beginning to pay the penalties imposed on genius. Last week a story by E. F. Knight appeared in *Cassell's Saturday Journal,* which story is mainly abstracted from Mr. Haggard's *Allan Quatermain;* that fascinating work which we have all been reading. Anyone who looks at Chapter X. of Mr. Haggard's story will at once see that Mr. Knight has transferred, without acknowledgment, a large portion of perhaps the most striking pages in Allan's adventures. This certainly shows some audacity, and an even stronger word might be used.

The rumour thus gracefully published travelled far and wide, for it was excellently spiteful, and Knight was quite distracted. Mr. Haggard was asked to clear the reputation of the gentleman on whom he had brought this grievous worry, and he might have done it with consummate ease. . . . Mr. Haggard took the plagiarist's usual imperial way, and this is how he set about it. In a little flyleaf to a new edition of *Allan Quatermain*—a flyleaf stuck at the end of the volume—he presumes to make game of the clever gentleman whom he had exposed to ridicule. Look at this:—

> I acknowledge my indebtedness to an extract in a review from some book of travel of which I cannot recollect the name, to which I owe the

idea of the great crabs in the valley of the sub-terranean river. But if I remember right, the crabs in the book when irritated projected their eyes quite out of their heads. I regret that I was not able to 'plagiarise' this effect, but I felt that, although crabs may, and doubtless do, behave thus in real life, in romance 'they will not do so.'

Then in a most royal foot-note this veritable champion of coolness observes:—

It is suggested to me that this is the *Cruise of the Falcon,* with which work I am personally unacquainted.

One learns to be composed under stress of circumstances, but I confess that when I read that note I gasped. . . . Observe, he durst not say anything definite: he only "suggests." An ordinary man—not a plagiarist—would have sent to Mudie's or the London Library, and, after making sure of his ground, would have told the blunt truth, but it is a symptom of a subtle demoralisation that Mr. Haggard could not take a plain, direct road, and he edges himself away with a sneer at a splendid writer who is certainly a better workman than the author of **Allan Quatermain.** Then look at the eccentricities of memory. First it is "a review" that supplies the useful literary patch. In taking his notes from the "review," Mr. Haggard could not take the trouble to look at the name of the book which was quoted, though some people would have thought that a very natural step. But we must be royal and easily impertinent, or we cannot hold place among the successful "conveyers." Again, Mr. Haggard could not plagiarise the truth—at least so he says. The land crabs of real life have outstanding eyes, but in fiction they "will not do so." That is Mr. Haggard's petty little sneer, that is his petty little evasion. (pp. 426-27)

Mr. Haggard denies also having taken his description of the underground river from *Peter Wilkins.* He did not need to read *Peter Wilkins* because he got the notion of the river from the Trinidad ravine in Mr. Knight's book. That was a wonderfully long "review" that Mr. Haggard studied. (p. 427)

And now, . . . I must drive home an accusation which I laughingly brought against him before I saw the full scope of trouble which his amiable ways may open up for other people. I say that when he wrote **Mr. Meeson's Will,** he could not find a story for himself, and so, to supply a summer number for *The Illustrated London News,* he boldly took a sketch of my invention and made it the central idea of his tale. This he did without writing to me or saying a word. I will now tell how my sketch came to be written.

One bad, dark night, I was among the steerage folks on a rather ricketty steamer, and we were doing fourteen knots. I was just thinking that our boats would be of no use if we got into collision, for I had climbed up and counted the carrying capacity of each one; then I became uneasy because the chant of the look-out men ceased; then I went on deck, and amid a hurricane roar of curses, a big barque sprawled away from the bluff of our port bow to our very stern, and his spanker-boom scraped us all the way. . . . In the morning, when all our nerves were right, I borrowed some invoice forms from the purser and a bake-board from the cook, and I wrote an article in which I tried to let the public know what *might* happen if a big liner hit another vessel in mid-ocean. (p. 428)

Turn to **Mr. Meeson** and you find the thing taken bodily, but adulterated in places with some of the most silly, woolly,

ineffective English that ever aroused a shopgirl's wonder or made her say, "He *do* have language." Mr. Haggard leads off by taking liberties with something which may be regarded as even more important than my writings. In a really royal burst he explains that "a mighty vessel was steaming majestically out of the mouth of the Thames, and shaping her imposing course straight at the ball of the setting sun." It is bad enough for Mr. Haggard to re-arrange the English language, but I think he might leave the Solar System alone. Here is the Orb of Day changing sides like a party politician!

But that is nothing to what takes place when the collision business begins. In the series of articles called *The Amateur Emigrant* I described the lightless ship, and Mr. Haggard studied that carefully, for he gives my own words. But alas! for the rest of the poor article. I spoke of the stokers coming up like rabbits from a burrow, and I described the rush of passengers. Here is the tail end of Mr. Haggard's most foolish paraphrase:—"Up they came, pouring aft like terrified spirits flying from the mouth of hell, and from them arose a hideous clamour," &c. This is a penny-a-liner's work, and the ineptitude vexes me. I know if I were a spirit and got out of the mouth of hell I should not be "terrified;" I should be very glad. Then my English gentleman becomes Lord Holmhurst, and my figures are altered so that one thousand people are on board the colliding steamer, while the boats can take three hundred; and my navvy becomes "a big Irishman." The scene at the boats is repeated with flattering fidelity, and the whole annexation is a masterpiece of pettifogging acuteness.

So cleverly is the thing twisted about; so obtrusively are fragments of padding stuffed in here and there, while the original notion is still kept in view, that our old friend, "I have never seen the work in question," might be easily brought in. But there are certain peculiar coincidences which no mathematical reasoning can explain, excepting in one way, and that way precludes the use of the imperial formula. (pp. 432-33)

It may be said that Mr. Haggard improves on his annexed fragments as Shakspere did. That will not hold; Shakspere was a man who could write very good English, whereas Mr. Haggard is a man that cannot write English at all; and in his later books he makes one's ears turn hot when he tries to be fine. I only want him to let my writing and other folks' alone. (p. 435)

James Runciman, "King Plagiarism and His Court," in The Fortnightly Review, Vol. 53, March 1, 1890, pp. 421-39.

JAMES KENNETH STEPHEN   (poem date 1891)

[*In perhaps his most famous light poem, Stephen decries what he considers the sorry state of late nineteenth-century English letters and reveals, at the end, two of the writers he believes to be chiefly responsible.*]

Will there never come a season
Which shall rid us from the curse
Of a prose which knows no reason
And an unmelodious verse:
When the world shall cease to wonder
At the genius of an Ass,
And a boy's eccentric blunder
Shall not bring success to pass:

When mankind shall be delivered
From the clash of magazines,
And the inkstand shall be shivered
Into countless smithereens:
When there stands a muzzled stripling,
Mute, beside a muzzled bore:
When the Rudyards cease from kipling
And the Haggards Ride no more.

> *James Kenneth Stephen, "To R. K." (originally published in* The Cambridge Review, *February, 1891), in his* Lapsus Calami and Other Verses, *edited by Herbert Stephen, sixth edition, Macmillan and Bowes, 1896, p. 3.*

RUDYARD KIPLING   (letter date 1899)

[*A close friend of Haggard, with whom he was pilloried in Stephen's famous derisive poem (see excerpt above), Kipling praises Haggard's first agricultural book in the following letter. (Gilbert White, mentioned at the end of the letter, was an eighteenth-century English naturalist and the author of* Natural History and Antiquities of Selborne.*)*]

I wish you knew how much the wife and I have enjoyed your **"Farmer's Year."** In our tiny way we also have made experiments with land: and your figures made us groan sympathetically over and above the cruel facts. I don't think there has ever been a better book of the sane, common (which is uncommon) quiet humourous real country life of England. I've been going back and rereading it slowly and leisurely: for the mere taste of it—same as Gilbert White. (pp. 41-2)

> *Rudyard Kipling, in his letter to Rider Haggard on November 12, 1899, in* Rudyard Kipling to Rider Haggard: The Record of a Friendship, *edited by Morton Cohen (reprinted by permission of the National Trust), Hutchinson & Co (Publishers) Ltd, 1965, pp. 41-2.*

H. L. MENCKEN   (essay date 1910)

[*From the era of World War I until the early years of the Great Depression, Mencken was one of the most influential figures in American letters. His strongly individualistic, irreverent outlook on life and his vigorous, invective-charged writing style helped establish the iconoclastic spirit of the Jazz Age and significantly shaped the direction of American literature. A well-read critic who, as a boy, had enjoyed Haggard's romances, Mencken expresses a mixed opinion of* Queen Sheba's Ring, *revealing his doubts about the response of more cultivated twentieth-century readers to Haggard's writing.*]

Rider Haggard . . .—a voice from the literary tomb! Do you remember how eagerly you read **"King Solomon's Mines"** when the world was younger—and **"Allan Quatermain"** and **"Nada the Lily"** and **"She"**? And you remember how keenly you felt the outrage when Mr. Haggard took to writing political tracts and books of travel and novels with commonplace human beings in them! Well, in **"Queen Sheba's Ring"** . . . there is a happy return to first principles. Once more we are in the heart of Africa, among its ancient and forgotten races; once more we deal with stupendous riches and a queen of ravishing beauty; once more we meet Quatermain in the flesh, though now his name is Richard Adams. This book is a second **"She,"** and if you still like that sort of thing, despite the spread of free education and the progress of civilization, you will fairly wallow in it. (p. 166)

> *H. L. Mencken, "Mainly about Novels" (used by permission of The Enoch Pratt Free Library of Baltimore in accordance with the terms of the will of H. L. Mencken), in* The Smart Set, *Vol. XXXII, No. 4, December, 1910, pp. 163-68.**

THEODORE ROOSEVELT   (essay date 1911)

[*Shortly after his Presidential inauguration, Roosevelt met Haggard during the latter's two-month visit to the United States in 1905. The two quickly became close friends, with Roosevelt remarking, "It is an odd thing that you and I, brought up in different countries and following such different pursuits, should have identical ideas and aims." After his term-of-office ended, Roosevelt—then an editor of* The Outlook—*wrote the following ringing review of Haggard's* Regeneration, *a portrait of the Salvation Army and of grim social conditions in England's cities.*]

Mr. Rider Haggard, in his book called **"Regeneration"** which he has dedicated to the men of the Salvation Army in token of his admiration of their self-sacrificing work for the poor and wretched throughout the world, has written an absorbingly interesting account of the social work of the Army in Great Britain. Mr. Rider Haggard is probably most widely known as a novelist, but, as a matter of fact, there are few men now writing English whose books on vital sociological questions are of such value as his, and hardly one among this small number who has grasped as he has grasped the dangers that beset the future of the English-speaking people, and the way these dangers can best be met. Mr. Haggard, for example, is one of the men most thoroughly alive to the dangers that threaten not only England and the older portions of the United States, but the newer portions of the United States and Canada and Australia, from the drift of country people toward the city, and the unhealthy development of city at the expense of country life, and naturally he has felt a peculiarly keen sympathy with the Salvation Army's efforts to aid in bringing the people back to the land. (pp. 476-77)

One very interesting feature brought out by Mr. Haggard incidentally is that, in a sense which is more literal than figurative, the work of regeneration often means such a complete change in a man's nature as is equivalent to the casting out of devils. Few people who read his book can fail to be almost as much impressed as Mr. Haggard acknowledges himself to have been by what he witnessed of this kind. Mr. Haggard's accounts of the land and industrial colonies, small-holding settlements, and similar works give an almost startling inside view of the extraordinary combination of lofty disinterestedness, intense zeal and understanding, and first-rate business ability, which have enabled General Booth and those associated with him to accomplish so much in directing what otherwise would be the waste forces of benevolence to national ends.

I wish it were in my power to convey to others the vivid impression which this book on the Salvation Army has made on me; and perhaps I may be allowed to add that my own limited experience with the Salvation Army has in every respect borne out what Mr. Haggard writes of it. (p. 477)

> *Theodore Roosevelt, "Rider Haggard and the Salvation Army," in* The Outlook, *July 1, 1911, pp. 476-77.*

RUDYARD KIPLING   (letter date 1912)

[*Kipling, originator of the expression "the white man's burden," offers a nearly self-parodic appraisal of* Child of Storm, *one of Haggard's African novels which he had proofread.*]

Dear Haggard,

The proofs of **"Child of Storm"** go to you today. I've read it; re-read it and re-reread it and I don't think you're wrong when you say it's the best you've done. *I* can't see where it needs anything being done to it. It marches straight off from the first and holds like a drug! I'm especially pleased with the characterisation of Mameena, who is a nice little bitch though dusky. (p. 75)

> *Rudyard Kipling, in his letter to Rider Haggard on November 9, 1912, in* Rudyard Kipling to Rider Haggard: The Record of a Friendship, *edited by Morton Cohen (reprinted by permission of the National Trust), Hutchinson & Co (Publishers) Ltd, 1965, pp. 74-5.*

KATHERINE MANSFIELD (essay date 1920)

[*Mansfield was an important pioneer in stream-of-consciousness literature and among the first English authors whose fiction depends upon incident rather than plot, thereby significantly influencing the modern short story form. Throughout 1919 and 1920, Mansfield conducted a weekly book-review column in* The Athenaeum, *a magazine edited at the time by her husband, John Middleton Murry. Below, she reveals her indifference to Haggard's most recent adventure thriller.*]

[**'The Ancient Allan'**, Sir Rider Haggard's new novel,] opens on a familiar note:

> Now, I, Allan Quatermain, come to the weirdest (with one or two exceptions perhaps) of all the experiences which it has amused me to employ my idle hours in recording here in a strange land, for after all England is strange to me.

This is the kind of thing to settle down to when the destination is Devonshire, if it is not Cornwall; but, alas! it needs—it dreadfully needs—the flying interruptions outside the carriage window—the mysterious interruptions of people's sandwiches—the indignant emotion aroused by the tea-basket, and the blissful sight of the train making a great scallop round the blue edge of the sea—to enable us to swallow such a very dusty dose of ancient Egypt.

Here is battle, murder and sudden death, wheels within chariot wheels, villains and heroes and black slaves, who in their land were kings; here is the mighty battle with the crocodile, the torture of the boat—all the ingredients that once upon a time, only to get a whiff of, knew us hungry. But nowadays, to read of how one was placed in an open boat and another boat put on top, so that only the head and hands remained outside—to be launched on a river and allowed to linger—awakes no response in us at all. (pp. 167-68)

> *Katherine Mansfield, "Mystery and Adventure" (originally published in* The Athenaeum, *No. 4687, February 27, 1920), in her* Novels and Novelists, *edited by J. Middleton Murry (copyright 1930, copyright renewed © 1958, by Alfred A. Knopf, Inc.; reprinted by permission of The Society of Authors as the literary representative of the Estate of Katherine Mansfield), Knopf, 1930, pp. 166-68.**

H. RIDER HAGGARD (essay date 1925)

[*In his autobiography, Haggard reprinted several undated letters he received from Robert Louis Stevenson. They appear below, interspersed with Haggard's comments and his views on style.*]

Among the many letters that I received about **'King Solomon's Mines'** perhaps the most interesting that I can find were from Robert Louis Stevenson. The first of these, undated, as they all are, is written from Skerryvore, Bournemouth, where he was living at the time. Here I should state that to my sorrow I never met Stevenson face to face: always we just missed each other.

> Dear Sir,—Some kind hand has sent me your tale of **'Solomon's Mines'**; I know not who did this good thing to me; and so I send my gratitude to headquarters and the fountainhead. You should be more careful; you do quite well enough to take more trouble, and some parts of your book are infinitely beneath you. But I find there flashes of a fine weird imagination and a fine poetic use and command of the savage way of talking: things which both thrilled me. The reflections of your hero before the battle are singularly fine; the King's song of victory a very noble imitation. But how, in the name of literature, could you mistake some lines from Scott's 'Marmion'—ay, and some of the best—for the slack-sided clerical-cob effusions of the Rev. Ingoldsby? Barham is very good, but Walter Scott is vastly better. I am, dear sir,
>
> Your obliged reader,
>
> Robert Louis Stevenson.

Of course I answered Stevenson's letter—by the way, I have not the least idea who sent him the book—thanking him and pointing out that he had overlooked the fact that Allan Quatermain's habit of attributing sundry quotations to the Old Testament and the Ingoldsby Legends, the only books with which he was familiar, was a literary joke.

Stevenson wrote back, again in an undated letter from Bournemouth and on a piece of manuscript paper:

> Dear Mr. Haggard,—Well, yes, I have sinned against you; that was the part of a bad reader. But it inclines me the more to explain my dark saying. As thus:
>
> You rise in the course of your book to pages of eloquence and poetry; and it is quite true that you must rise from something lower; and that the beginning must infallibly (?) be pitched low and kept quiet. But you began (pardon me the word) slipshod. If you are to rise, you must prepare the mind in the quiet parts, with at least an accomplished neatness. To this you could easily attain. In other words, what you have still to learn is to take trouble with those parts which do not excite you.
>
> Excuse the tone of a damned schoolmaster, and believe me,
>
> Yours truly,
>
> Robert Louis Stevenson.

The next letter, also from Skerryvore, Bournemouth, which, because of its allusions to **'King Solomon's Mines,'** although undated, must have been written at this time [contained the following postscript]: (pp. 235-36)

P.S.—Further reflection on '**K.S.M.**' makes me think you are one who gets up steam slowly. In that case, when you have your book finished, go back and rewrite the beginning up to the mark.

My case is the reverse: I always begin well, and often finish languidly or hurriedly.

P.P.S.—How about a deed of partnership?

(pp. 236-37)

Stevenson's remark as to his finishing languidly is interesting, and, so far as my judgment goes, his romantic work shows its truth. . . . In an adventure story what is called style, however brilliant, is not enough: the living interest must be kept up to the last page; it should increase to the very end. Of course I know that many of our critics, like those of Alexandria in the first centuries of our era, think and preach that style is the really important thing, much more important than the substance of the story. I cannot believe that they are right. The substance is, as it were, the soul of the matter; the style is its outward and visible body. I prefer a creation with a great soul, even if its form is somewhat marred, to one with a beautifully finished form and very little soul. Of course when the two are found together, a rare event, there is perfection. Also people differ in their ideas of what style really is. . . . I am not an authority, but my own view is that above all things the written word should be clear and absolutely readable, and that work which does not fulfil these conditions can scarcely be expected to endure. It runs a grave risk of passing with the fashion of the hour. (pp. 237-38)

> *H. Rider Haggard, in his* The Days of My Life: An Autobiography, Vol. I, *(1925), edited by C. J. Longman, Longmans, Green and Co. Ltd., 1926, 294 p.*

STELLA GIBBONS (essay date 1945)

[*Gibbons offers a short, favorable overview of Haggard's works.*]

Rider Haggard wrote at least one minor classic, *King Solomon's Mines,* and I would put *She* not far below it. He was a writer in the pure romantic tradition, possessing a marvellous creative imagination peopled by heroic Zulus, noble white hunters, faithful servants, animals that are half-gods and beautiful stately women who are half-goddesses.

He was deeply filled with a sense of the mystery of life and of the historic past. He wrote in a simple style, with Biblical echoes and turns of phrase which surely owe something to his love for, and interest in, the African savages; in his pages they talk like poets and their poetry, simple and a little monotonous, seems to have crept into his style. He is a wizard among storytellers, with an unending flow of incident most deftly woven with conversation and character-drawing, a strong and severe sense of right and wrong, and a rather dry masculine sense of humour which is never petty or cruel.

I was fortunate enough to discover Rider Haggard's books in my early teens, which is the right age at which to enjoy them most. It is perhaps impertinent and ungrateful to say that he is not a writer to give great pleasure to adults, but it is true that his characters have an Homeric simplicity and that his view of life is sharply black and white. He is a writer for simple and whole-hearted readers, who do not suffer from a split personality. One puts down a book by Haggard with the sigh: "Ah, if only life were like that!" and then one suspects

that somewhere, for some people, it may be. It may be like that for the people who have kept the sharply-defined values of extreme youth, unblurred by the necessity to temporize and make allowances which comes with maturity. His values are those of the Old Testament, awesome in their rectitude and purity. His books are permeated by the sense of a just God and an ordered universe. It is instructive to compare Rider Haggard's sense of the mystery in all things with the same sense as it appears in pages written by Marcel Proust; the latter has an even deeper sense of mystery but is content to wonder and admire. Haggard feels the mystery but has all the spiritual sense that Proust seemingly lacked.

There is a wonderfully good book about the Crusades called *The Brethren*; one about the siege of Leyden called *Lysbeth*; another about the siege of Jerusalem called *Pearl Maiden*; one about the Black Death called *Red Eve.* All these are, of course, historical in theme, and excellent and exciting as they are, I prefer the African ones, *Child of Storm, Marie, The People of the Mist, The Ghost Kings,* and many others. His descriptions are never lush, and those of places are usually put in because the hero is telling us, like Hemingway, about the precise position of some large animal (it may even be a man) which he is hunting, but they convey a feeling of the open air, of mountains and rivers and stars, which is like a breath of wind blowing off the page scented by unfamiliar African flowers. One of the unpleasant qualities in the contemporary novel is the way it creeps about in streets and factories and night clubs and bedrooms and brothels and bars, making them all sound and smell and look alike. Rider Haggard's novels seem to ride through their large landscapes as if he were on horseback, and when I think of his books I recall Keats' line—"The large utterance of the early gods". (pp. 404-05)

> *Stella Gibbons, "A Voyage of Rediscovery," in* The Fortnightly (*reprinted by permission of Contemporary Review Company Limited*), *n.s. Vol. CLVIII, No. 948, December, 1945, pp. 401-06.**

MORTON COHEN (essay date 1960)

[*Haggard's biographer Cohen surveys his subject's literary career.*]

Cetywayo and His White Neighbours, Haggard's initial literary effort of sizeable proportions and probably his least professional book—a collection of fact, impression, and opinion—is all the same one of his most important works and a singular contribution to the annals of Empire. It is read today primarily by the specialist—but here precisely is its merit: no scholar writing about South African history can afford to pass by *Cetywayo.* The book itself is really more than a history; it is a historical document, and as such is extremely valuable. It is a lively chronicle that reconstructs for the reader clearly and with considerable detail the events that occurred in Natal, Zululand, and the Transvaal during the crucial years between 1875 and 1881. Haggard's official relationship with British headquarters, the information that his position provided, his knowledge of the people of South Africa and the geography of the country, and his ability to see into the political motives and judge the behaviour of the interested parties—all contribute to the worth of *Cetywayo.* (p. 68)

'You lie; you always were a liar, and you always will be a liar,' is the opening sentence of the novel [*Dawn*]. It strikes the shrill tone that dominates the thousand or so pages of the book. Deception, as a matter of fact, is a mild vice compared to the parade of cardinal sins to follow. For *Dawn* is packed with a series of intrigues, treacheries, knaveries, and collusions, and with few exceptions its characters are villains. It is in fact a shapeless anthology of two-dimensional actors, vague symbolism, stringy plots, and blood-curdling horror stories. In its manifold pages, it seeks to engage every human emotion. As a novel it raises technical barriers which would be formidable for the modern reader to hurdle in a book half its length. The tale's greatest difficulty is that its author seems to know nothing about character motivation; as often as not, the people in *Dawn* seem to have no reason for behaving as they do, particularly when their deeds are overwhelmingly diabolical. Never does Haggard seek to understand his characters, nor does he seem aware of the influence they might have on one another. As a result they seldom come alive. (p. 79)

Because *Dawn* was Haggard's first attempt at fiction, it was yet too early for the author to realize where his strengths and weaknesses lay. For that reason the book is an encyclopedia of Haggard's incidental observations, small philosophical comments, and a sounding board for his likes and hatreds, many of which are grafted upon the tale. But Haggard was hearing the sound of every note on a new instrument he had taken up for the first time—and it was not to take him long to decide which tunes he could play best. (p. 81)

Within a year after *Dawn* was published, Haggard's second piece of fiction . . . was on sale in the bookshops. This one was called *The Witch's Head,* a title that, in its obvious sensationalism, embodies again Haggard's love of the grotesque.

The Witch's Head is another three-volume tale of country life, much like *Dawn.* But it differs from *Dawn* in two significant ways, one in a sense an outgrowth of the other. First, although *Dawn* had all the outer fittings of an autobiographical novel— Norfolk squirearchy, frustrated lovers, Madeira (where the Haggards had stopped on their way back from Africa), and so on—*The Witch's Head* is a much more personal book; in fact, it becomes for Haggard a device by which he can compensate psychologically for the blows he had to suffer in earlier years. Noteworthy is the change in character emphasis. In this story, we have a more fully developed hero, Ernest Kershaw—the story is about him, and, by and large, he lives the life Haggard had lived in his earlier years. . . .

The other difference between *Dawn* and *The Witch's Head* is that part of the story is laid in Africa. Here the grotesqueries vanish, and Haggard writes from the heart, with fresh strokes, about excitements he knows well. He no longer has to rely on the worn-out novelist's tricks—here he needs only remember and write. From the moment the reader sets foot on African soil until he leaves it, he is gripped by a new kind of story, one filled with three-dimensional pictures of a strange but real world; he becomes a tourist in a far-off land. He feels the hot sun and sees the strange people—and he is exhilarated by the new experience. The African interlude places *The Witch's Head* far above *Dawn* on the critical scale. (p. 82)

The Haggard family recalls how on a day early in 1885, Rider and one of his brothers were discussing *Treasure Island* on a London train. When Rider suggested that Stevenson's book was perhaps not so remarkable as many seemed to think, his brother offered to bet him that he could not do anything half so good himself. Rider took the wager. . . . In six weeks he finished his first tale of African adventure, *King Solomon's Mines.* (p. 85)

Only one African novel of note had appeared in London before *King Solomon's Mines,* Olive Schreiner's *The Story of an Af-* rican Farm (1883), a remarkable tale of Boer life in the back country. But London did not take to Miss Schreiner's work at first, perhaps because, in its descriptions of spiritual struggles, its focus on family relationships, and its strong feminist theme, it resembled too closely the usual domestic novel. *King Solomon's Mines* was different. It appealed to all readers, critics, schoolboys, housewives, and working men alike, who found in it a story that was swift, terse, packed with thrills. It was a tale of adventure and heroic deeds, and its hero was a well-adjusted Englishman, competent, strong, sensible, in whom they could believe. There was no heroine, nor should there have been. Penetrating Africa was strictly a man's job. The adventure was the thing, and there was plenty of it. *King Solomon's Mines* was just what readers wanted. (p. 90)

For too long the reader's attention had been trained on London slums, prison houses, artists' attics, Manchester mills, and village vicarages, and *King Solomon's Mines* was one of the books that offered a 'way out.' It let the reader turn his back on the troublesome, the small, the sordid; and it took him on a journey to the Empire's frontier to perform mighty deeds he could believe in. If nothing more, *King Solomon's Mines* helped bring the story of adventure up to date.

For Haggard the story-teller, *King Solomon's Mines* stands as a milestone. There he eliminates many of the false elements that crowd his earlier work. Wild, warm, vivid landscapes supplant cold, gaunt Tudor country houses; realistic, hair-breadth escapes replace Gothic nightmares; a brave and confident hero unseats fainting damsels and male manikins; the memoir replaces the third-person narrative; and a crisp, taut, thrilling tale of deeds takes the place of a formless melodrama. At this point in Haggard's career, some observers saw in him the promise of an artist. But for Haggard himself, *King Solomon's Mines* stood rather as a landmark of financial success than literary accomplishment, and too soon he would come to see in it the formula for many of his later works. (pp. 96-7)

He wrote *Allan Quatermain,* a sequel to *King Solomon's Mines,* and *Jess,* his first African 'novel,' before the end of 1885, and these were both taken up for serial publication. . . . But the first tale to emerge in book form after *King Solomon's Mines* was *She.*

Haggard wrote *She* . . . in a little over six weeks. It virtually flowed from his pen of its own accord. 'The fact is,' he tells us, 'that it was written at white heat, almost without rest. . . . I remember that when I sat down to the task my ideas as to its development were of the vaguest. The only clear notion that I had in my head was that of an immortal woman inspired by an immortal love. All the rest shaped itself round this figure. And it came—it came faster than my poor aching hand could set it down.' When he had finished the story . . . , he sagely proclaimed, 'There is what I shall be remembered by.'

And he was right. For *She,* in spite of its weaknesses, has enjoyed a persistent popularity since it first appeared, more than seventy years ago. It was a best-seller from the first. (p. 97)

[Haggard's] strange blending of narrative elements; the anthropological, cultural, and ethnic ingredients; and the psychological symbols present a challenging puzzle to the specialist as well as the casual reader. The story, furthermore, has a bewildering power, the sort one is accustomed to meet only in superior works of art such as 'Christabel' and some of Poe's masterpieces, a power that grips the reader so fiercely that he brushes aside Haggard's errors in taste, his occasional grammatical lapses, his imperfect character portrayal and lack of emotional unity. The power of his imagination is far stronger than the obstacles his writing puts in our way. (pp. 102-03)

The appeal of *King Solomon's Mines* and *She* turned their author's name into a household word. By 1890, three years after *She* appeared, Haggard, at thirty-four, had already fashioned for himself a literary reputation and was well on his way to earning a fortune. (p. 118)

He took four months to write *Eric Brighteyes*, and though it is one of his least read books, it is one of his best. . . .

Eric Brighteyes, despite its unfortunate title, is a thoroughly successful Anglicized saga that deserves a place alongside Scott's *The Pirate* and Kingsley's *Hereward the Wake*. It is an Icelandic love story of broad dimensions filled with heroic vikings and a long succession of bold actions thwarted by witchery and vengeance. The saga is so convincing that Haggard here seems to write instinctively, as though his notion that in some previous incarnation he himself had been a viking were true. Again he displays his own peculiar creative force, but this time he is on new ground and brings forth a fresh and powerful story. Nor was the time he spent polishing the work wasted. There is less to offend the reader here, and the language rises to artistic heights more often than in his other tales. Students of Icelandic literature say, furthermore, that Haggard's dialogue reminds them of the original sagas, and one commentator goes so far as to place *Eric Brighteyes* ahead of all English novels written in the saga style. . . . Of all Haggard's neglected stories, *Eric Brighteyes* deserves most to be read. (p. 130)

Haggard, though an impatient wanderer, was also irrevocably tied to the soil. Always drawn to the beauty and mystery of nature, he was a sharp observer of everything that grew. . . . [He] devised a plan for a book he 'enjoyed' writing and consequently could write from the heart, a book which better than anything else offers a picture of Rider Haggard the Norfolk squire, the 'maister' of Ditchingham, and captures the flavour of a way of life that has fairly vanished. (p. 161)

A Farmer's Year was a very informative handbook. The advice Haggard gave was sound (some of it still is), the instructions and descriptions for performing various farming tasks clear and detailed. An ample supply of illustrative material accompanies the prose, and the writing is never overtly technical. A long table of contents, a comprehensive index, and a chronological arrangement allow the reader to find advice readily on any subject. How does Haggard shed barley in dry seasons, what price does he get for his beans, which method of lifting beets does he prefer, what does he have to say about pond water for drinking purposes, or what and how to feed toads? It is all there, and can be found in a jiffy.

But before Haggard is finished, *A Farmer's Year* becomes something more than a delightful excursion into the country and a practical handbook for farmers. In his effort to write a useful book for the 'reader of utilitarian mind,' he sought to record as accurate a picture of rural life as he could. His 'research' threw him into closer acquaintance than ever before with his neighbours, his tenants, and Ditchingham labourers. He learned at first hand about the state of English agriculture and about the people who tried to make a living on the land in the days of agricultural depression. What he learned was even more appalling than he had imagined, and he had not been unacquainted with the difficulties of the English farmer. He was stunned by what he saw at first hand, by what, he was forced to conclude, was the ruinous decay of a treasured part

of English life; and immediately his shock and concern were reflected in his chronicle. . . . Not that Haggard becomes a reformer—he merely sets down the facts which so astonish him and which he is sure will astonish his reader. As a result of his experiences on the land while he writes the book, the end product becomes something different from what Haggard originally intended. But it is more valuable than it might otherwise have been. For the reader gets more than the aura of country life, more than a quiet ramble through a wooded grove; he also gets an interesting picture of what agricultural life is like in England in 1898—the practical side, the financing of the farm, the prices of the produce, the hopes and disappointments of the farmer. The record of Haggard's experience as farmer for a year is also a picture of English farming for a year, a morose picture of a way of life deteriorating before the onslaught of 'progress.' *A Farmer's Year*, intended to be a congenial conversation about farming, turned out to be a plea for the English farmer. (pp. 163-64)

When in late spring [of 1900] he returned to England from [a] sojourn in the Near East, Haggard made immediate plans for what he later called 'the heaviest labour of all my laborious life,' an investigation of the English countryside and the state of English farming. For large parts of 1901 and 1902, Haggard, accompanied by the indomitable Arthur Cochrane, travelled up and down England, from county to county, village to village, by train, horse, and ship, gathering data. (p. 168)

[He] spent the early months of 1902 assembling and arranging the material and writing introductory and explanatory paragraphs and a concluding chapter for it. Finally, in November 1902, the heavy two-volume tome appeared as *Rural England, Being an Account of Agricultural and Social Researches Carried out in the Years 1901 & 1902.*

Some minor flaws exist in *Rural England*, and we must acknowledge them. There is nothing wrong with Haggard's journalistic style, but the way he reports material as he finds it leads him into some difficulty. The arrangement of the counties follows Haggard's itinerary rather than any geographical plan, and that makes for some rather abrupt and unreasonable jolts. At one point, for instance, he jumps from Kent to Devonshire, and later from Yorkshire to Suffolk. Treating counties individually creates unnecessary repetition, also, as Haggard records similar circumstances in different parts of the land. Nor does Haggard's thoroughness extend to the index as it ought to, where cross-references are noticeably lacking.

In spite of the faults, however, the reader cannot but stand in awe of the display of energy, the magnitude of the task, the endurance and devotion the two volumes attest. Haggard completed the survey in something more than a year, and the volumes appeared hardly two years after he started his study—formidable evidence of his capacity for hard and close work. For *Rural England* is an immense document, a permanent reference book for historians, economists, agricultural specialists. A detailed survey of agrarian conditions in England at the turn of the century, it is invaluable to the student of rural life. Its thoroughness sets it apart from most surveys before and since, and its value is increased by Haggard's stern objectivity. (pp. 169-70)

Haggard's activities in agriculture, politics, finance, and travel did not reduce the steady flow of his fiction through the years. The quantity and variety of his output are another index of the man's vigorous energy and imagination. He wrote a total of fifty-eight volumes of fiction. (p. 219)

Of the fifty-eight volumes, forty-seven are conventional Rider Haggard adventure romances, and twelve are novels of contemporary life. One is a propagandist novel. Of the romances, almost a dozen can be called historical novels, and four comprise a loosely knit story of the rise and fall of the Zulu dynasty in South Africa. Allan Quatermain appears in eighteen adventures (four of them short stories), Ayesha in four romances, in one of which they appear together. Haggard's romances are not restricted to Africa and England; he also wrote about other lands, Iceland, Mexico, Peru, Denmark, Spain, the Holy Land among them. Yet, even though the landscape changes, the quality differs, the subject matter varies, and theme and texture alter as Haggard ages, there is in almost all his work a fixed combination of basic ingredients.

The world that Haggard creates is new in the geographical sense, but it is actually the old, conventional world of the medieval romance adapted to modern tastes and contemporary attitudes. (pp. 219-20)

Haggard's work is uneven and many of his stories are undistinguished. A few, however, deserve particular mention. Of his early works, those he took pains with have literary merit. The best of these is his Icelandic saga, *Eric Brighteyes,* and his first Egyptian tale, *Cleopatra,* is still worth reading. Though Haggard did not really grow in artistic stature with the passing years, his later work does become more fluent and taut, as narrative kinks and some of the stylistic faults disappear. Of the later tales, [*Lysbeth, Ayesha, Queen Sheba's Ring, Red Eve, The Holy Flower, The Ivory Child, When the World Shook,* and *The Virgin of the Sun*] . . . at least, are outstanding. And in a series of African tales, he also achieves a high level of storytelling.

These are his Zulu stories, his saga of the black nation, *Nada the Lily* . . . (Lang called it an 'epic of a dying people' and Besant thought it 'splendid, the best thing . . . since "She"'), and [*Marie, Child of Storm,* and *Finished*], . . . which he wrote as a trilogy. . . . Free of conventional moral limitations and British restraint, remembering the simple, dignified savages he knew as a young man in South Africa, he reconstructs the rise and fall of the Zulu dynasty. He writes of giants and their deeds in the deep African wilderness. He works on a broad scale, spanning almost a hundred years, centring his tales on the royal house of Chaka, the black Alexander. He tells of the Zulu people's unification under the military leadership of the great warrior-king and how the nation fell into oblivion under the sons' divisive jealousies and the white man's advance. Much of the material is factual, much based on oral legend which Haggard himself heard in South and Central Africa, and much is Haggard working most creatively. Chaka emerges a classic figure, a medley of militaristic greatness and primitive brutality, a man whose personal force enabled him to unite the Zulu tribes into a single nation, organize their finest youth into mighty battalions and lead them with a military perfection and crusading determination rarely excelled in history. Chaka and his armies took a million lives, and Haggard makes us feel the meaning of that statistic, gives us the emotion to accompany the fact.

In these tales Haggard does for the Zulus what Cooper does in his Leatherstocking tales for the American Indian. But there is a difference. Cooper tells of a people now so thoroughly subjugated that they can no longer hope to emerge as a cultural entity or national unit, whereas Haggard writes of a people with a future. In Africa the overpowering majority of black people are restless and eager to assert the authority of their numbers; they still aspire to national unity and cultural recognition. When they assert their independence and rule once more in their native lands, Haggard's Zulu saga may come into its own. For he captures in it a clear, engaging picture of Zulu life and comes to terms with the turbulent Zulu spirit. As the African nations continue to take their place in the modern world of states, during the late twentieth century and in the twenty-first, their writers will, if they follow the pattern of those in other new or reborn nations, try to portray the glories of their people's past. Among their sources will most likely be found Haggard's works.

But there is more in these four volumes than the raw material for a later writer to use. Haggard himself, when writing of Zulu life, achieves some distinction. There is little on the Haggard shelf more convincing than these tales. The people, the language, the landscape—they all ring true. Zulus could not be otherwise than Haggard pictures them; Africa must have been exactly as he paints it. Out of these pages come his ostrich-plumed warriors. They stamp their salute to Chaka on the ground and then, assegais raised on high, sweep over the crest of a mountain and with a shriek rush down upon their enemy. Haggard had known the black man, and his knowledge combined with his imagination to give rise to an eloquence he seldom reached in his other work.

But the tales that display Haggard at his most original are, after all, *King Solomon's Mines* and *She.* Their unchanging freshness has commanded a reading audience for seventy years now and will continue to do so. In them Haggard has come closest to capturing universal elements and satisfying an essential need in mankind. The imaginative quality of these two stories makes them classics of a kind, and many readers feel, as Stuart Cloete does, that it is 'amazing to read *She* again at the age of sixty and recapture the charm and excitement I felt at fourteen,' or as the reviewer who recently wrote in the *Times Literary Supplement* that 'on the strength of *King Solomon's Mines* alone . . . [Haggard] deserves a place higher than is generally reserved for him.' (pp. 228-30)

> *Morton Cohen, in his* Rider Haggard: His Life and Works *(Morton Cohen 1958; reprinted by permission of the author), Hutchinson & Co (Publishers) Ltd, 1960, 327 p.*

C. S. LEWIS   (essay date 1960)

[*Lewis is considered one of the foremost Christian and mythopoeic authors of the twentieth century. Indebted principally to George MacDonald, G. K. Chesterton, Charles Williams, and the writers of ancient Norse myths, he is regarded as a formidable logician and Christian polemicist, a perceptive literary critic, and—most highly—as a writer of fantasy literature. A traditionalist in his approach to life and art, he opposed the modern movement in literary criticism toward biographical and psychological interpretation. In place of this, Lewis practiced and propounded a theory of criticism which stresses the importance of presuppositions and prejudices. Lewis examines Haggard as a mythmaker, in the following review of Morton Cohen's* Rider Haggard: His Life and Works.]

I hope Mr Morton Cohen's excellent *Rider Haggard: His Life and Works* [see excerpt above] will move people to reconsider the whole Haggard question. For there really is a problem here. The vices of his style are inexcusable; the vapidity (and frequency) of his reflections, hard to bear. But it is no longer any good pretending that his best work was merely an ephemeral and commercial success. It has not passed away like the works of Ouida, Mrs Oliphant, Stanley Weyman, or Max Pemberton. It has survived the whole climate of opinion which once made its imperialism and vague pieties acceptable. The promised time 'when the Rudyards cease from Kipling and the Haggards ride no more' [see excerpt above, 1891] has failed to arrive. Obstinately, scandalously, Haggard continues to be read and reread. Why?

The significant fact for me is the feeling we have as we close *King Solomon's Mines,* or, still more, *She,* 'If only . . . ' are the words that rise to our lips. If only we could have had this very same story told by a Stevenson, a Tolkien, or a William Golding. If only, *faute de mieux,* we were even allowed to re-write it ourselves!

Note, the very same story. It is not the construction that is faulty. From the move of his first pawn to the final checkmate, Haggard usually plays like a master. His openings—what story in the world opens better than *She*?—are full of alluring promise, and his catastrophes triumphantly keep it.

The lack of detailed character-study is not a fault at all. An adventure story neither needs nor admits it. Even in real life adventures tend to obliterate fine shades. Hardship and danger strip us down to the bare moral essentials. The distinction between shirker and helper, brave and cowardly, trusty and treacherous, overrides everything else. 'Character' in the novelist's sense is a flower that expands fully where people are safe, fed, dry and warmed. That adventure stories remind us of this is one of their merits.

The real defects of Haggard are two. First, he can't write. Or rather (I learn from Mr Cohen) won't. Won't be bothered. Hence the *clichés,* jocosities, frothy eloquence. When he speaks through the mouth of Quatermain he makes some play with the unliterary character of the simple hunter. It never dawned on him that what he wrote in his own person was a great deal worse—'literary' in the most damning sense of the word.

Secondly, the intellectual defects. No one after reading Mr Cohen can believe that Haggard was out of touch with reality. Apparently his agricultural and sociological works are a solid meal of hard-won facts and of conclusions firmly drawn. When he decided that the only hope for the land lay in a scheme which flouted all his political preferences and shattered all his treasured hopes for his own class and his own family, he recommended that scheme without flinching.

Here lies the true greatness of the man; what Mr Cohen calls his 'overall sturdiness'. Even as an author he can sometimes be shrewd—as when in *She* Allan Quatermain neither succumbs to the charms of Ayesha nor believes her 'tall' autobiographical stories. By making Quatermain keep his head Haggard shows that he can keep his own.

But though Haggard had sense, he was ludicrously unaware of his limitations. He attempts to philosophise. Again and again in his stories we see a commonplace intelligence, armed (or hampered) with an eclectic outfit of vaguely Christian, theosophical and spiritualistic notions, trying to say something profound about that fatal subject, 'Life'. This is seen at its embarrassing worst whenever Ayesha speaks. If she was really Wisdom's daughter, she did not take after her parent. (pp. 128-30)

What keeps us reading in spite of all these defects is of course the story itself, the myth. Haggard is the text-book case of the mythopoeic gift pure and simple—isolated, as if for inspection, from nearly all those more specifically literary powers with

which it so fortunately co-exists in, say, *The Ancient Mariner, Dr Jekyll and Mr Hyde,* or *The Lord of the Rings.* To make matters even clearer, in Haggard himself the mythopoeic power seems to have grown less as the literary art improved. *Ayesha* is not such good myth as *She,* but it is better written.

This gift, when it exists in full measure, is irresistible. . . . It was silly of Haggard to treasure a belief that there was, in a factual sense, 'something in' his myths. But we, as readers, need not concern ourselves with that at all.

The mythical status of *She* is indisputable. As we all know, Jung went to it for the embodiment of an archetype. But even Jung did not, I think, get to the centre. If his view were right, the myth ought to function only for those to whom Ayesha is a powerfully erotic image. And she is not so for all who love *She.* To myself, for example, Ayesha or any other tragedy Queen—any tall, crowned, stormy, deep-breasted contralto with thunder in her brow and lightnings in her eye—is one of the most effective anti-aphrodisiacs in the world. Ultimately the life of the myth is elsewhere.

The story of Ayesha is not an escape, but it is about escape; about an attempt at the great escape, daringly made and terribly frustrated. Its closest relative, perhaps its child, is Morris's *Well at the World's End,* which came ten years later. Both stories externalise the same psychological forces; our irreconcilable reluctance to die, our craving for an immortality in the flesh, our empirical knowledge that this is impossible, our intermittent awareness that it is not even really desirable, and (octaves deeper than all these) a very primitive feeling that the attempt, if it could be made, would be unlawful and would call down the vengeance of the gods. In both books the wild, transporting, and (we feel) forbidden hope is aroused. When fruition seems almost in sight, horrifying disaster shatters our dream. Haggard's version is better than Morris's. Morris makes his heroine too human, too wholesome. Haggard, truer to our feeling, surrounds the lonely she-Prometheus with terror and misery.

Haggard's best work will survive because it is based on an appeal well above high-water mark. The fullest tides of fashion cannot demolish it. A great myth is relevant as long as the predicament of humanity lasts; as long as humanity lasts. It will always work, on those who can receive it, the same catharsis.

Haggard will last, but so will the hatred of Haggard. The vindictiveness with which adverse critics attacked him in his own day had, no doubt, some local and temporary causes. His own truculence was one. Another was the natural jealousy of the Gigadibs who can produce only a *succès d'estime* for the writer who produces 'popular'—but also living and viable—work. . . . But there was, and there always will be, a deeper cause. No one is indifferent to the mythopoeic. You either love it or else hate it 'with a perfect hatred'.

This hatred comes in part from a reluctance to meet Archetypes; it is an involuntary witness to their disquieting vitality. Partly, it springs from an uneasy awareness that the most 'popular' fiction, if only it embodies a real myth, is so very much more serious than what is generally called 'serious' literature. For it deals with the permanent and inevitable, whereas an hour's shelling, or perhaps a ten-mile walk, or even a dose of salts, might annihilate many of the problems in which the characters of a refined and subtle novel are entangled. (pp. 130-32)

C. S. Lewis, "The Mythopoeic Gift of Rider Haggard" (originally published as "Haggard Rides

Again,'' in Time and Tide, *Vol. 41, No. 36, September 3, 1960), in his* On Stories and Other Essays
on Literature, *edited by Walter Hooper (copyright ©
1982 by the Trustees of the Estate of C. S. Lewis;
reprinted by permission of Harcourt Brace Jovanovich, Inc.; in Canada by William Collins Sons & Co
Ltd), Harcourt Brace Jovanovich, 1982 (also published in England as* Of This and Other Worlds *by
C. S. Lewis, edited by Walter Hooper, Collins, 1982,
pp. 128-32).*

ALAN SANDISON   (essay date 1972)

[*Sandison compares Haggard's and Kipling's visions of empire
and heroism as reflected in their works.*]

Empire for both Kipling and Haggard [was] a milieu where
young men could perform outsize tasks in outsize circumstances, with life constantly in hazard. To function in such an
environment was to have one's existence imbued with an epic
quality. Courage and loyalty were demanded of these youths
in sacrificial measure, and an appropriate *mise en scène* was
furnished for their translation. Life in the active service of the
imperial idea was rendered more intense, noble and simple: so
much so, that it was an encouragement never to grow up and
very many of those who participated in it bore to the end of
their days the indelible, Empire-made mark of arrested adolescence.

Into this elemental scale Haggard's quasi-mythical heroes—so
much in contact with a Homeric and a Norse past—fit easily
and naturally. The epic scale of empire readily accommo-
dates—if it does not, indeed, inspire—a moral and spiritual
vision of proportional simplicity and grandeur, and human activity is prompt to identify itself with eternal verities. Man is
more starkly presentable in permanent confrontation with the
Lords of Life and Death, to use Kipling's phrase, and the Great
End becomes a question of perpetual moment.

Kipling and Haggard had, then, the Empire in common; but
there was little real identity in the deeper *moral* significance
it had for the two men. The picture of Haggard and Kipling
sitting opposite each other in the quiet of the latter's study
companionably occupied with their gloomy speculations on
human destiny, or, alternatively, overcoming together some
knotty problem of composition, while it says a lot about the
closeness of their personal friendship, does not signify a unity
of vision.

Haggard's favoured world is one of heroic men and deeds, a
world full of 'the din / Of victories; gods revealed; supernal
calls' as Ronald Ross put it. But the world he creates is simultaneously vanishing—and he with it, for he is intimately
involved in this 'fictional' universe. In fact, by associating his
own life-cycle with the decline of the Zulus, which he does
continually, Haggard very successfully blends the individual
with the cultural cycle, postulating in the process the notion
that if any meaning is to be discovered in existence, it must
be sought in time.

This brings us to the heart of Haggard's moral vision and also
to the heart of what distinguishes him fundamentally from
Kipling. His consuming preoccupation is with time: the words
of the burial service 'Man that is born of woman hath but a
short time to live, and is full of misery. He cometh up and is
cut down like a flower; he fleeth as it were a shadow and never
continueth in one stay', are directly quoted at least once in his

work, but, paraphrased, they are the verbal stock-in-trade of
his characters, in particular of his sententious Zulus.

Implicit in such reflections—and very often explicit too—is a
continual questioning of purpose. His characters find it very
difficult to square the notion of a beneficent providence with
the amount of human suffering they see around them; the only
hope lies in the possibility that the pattern may be too big for
man's strictly limited perspective. Again it is his Zulus who
seem best able to express this with the desired rhetorical sonority which is the only way Haggard knows of achieving emphasis: 'All things are a great pattern, my father, . . . and our
lives, and what we do, and what we do not do, are but a little
bit of the pattern, which is so big that only the eye of Him
who is above, the Unkulunkulu, can see it all.'

Haggard was deeply influenced by the evolutionary argument
but it is clearly his own mystical bent that impelled him to find
solace in reflections upon the vast process of time. And most
of what is characteristically the Haggard 'voice' has its source
in this preoccupation: such as his fatalism, or his cultural relativism which saved him from his contemporaries' racial exclusiveness and condescension. As an instance of the latter,
one thinks of his regard for 'black' culture in all his African
books, or of his contemptuous dismissal of those who see the
native African as 'just a native, a person from whom land may
be filched upon one pretext or another, or labour or taxes
extracted and who if he resists the process and makes himself
a nuisance must be suppressed'. But there are plenty of other
examples. In the introduction to *Allan Quatermain* we find this:

> Civilisation is only savagery silver-gilt. A vain
> glory is it, and like a northern light, comes but
> to fade and leave the sky more dark. Out of the
> soil of barbarism it has grown like a tree, and
> as I believe, into the soil like a tree it will once
> more, sooner or later, fall again, as the Egyp-
> tian civilisation fell, as the Hellenic civilisation
> fell, and as the Roman civilisation fell . . .

Given this cyclical view of history, Haggard's instincts constantly urged him to pierce the veil that drops between one
cycle and another. Ayesha is perhaps the most conspicuous—
even blatant—example of this, but nearly all his major characters at one time or another teeter on the brink of their own
apotheosis: conversely, goddesses appear and divulge secrets
of past and future with a garrulous disregard for the professional
inscrutability of the divine.

The ready resort to allegory is further testimony to the strength
of his desire to find a greater reality beyond the finite human
vision. As Kipling wrote to him after reading *Wisdom's Daughter:* 'You are a whale at parables and allegories and one thing
reflecting another'; and for once his schoolboy colloquialism
is quite appropriate. One immediately thinks of the 'celestial
barmaid' Ayesha, though in *She* Ayesha is not wholly allegorical—that is clear from the discovery of the real thing in
the Moneta-like sculpture in the ruined city of Kôr, 'perhaps
the grandest allegorical work of Art that the genius of her
children has ever given to the world'. The figure is Truth,
beseeching mankind to draw the veil from her face but carrying
etched on the base a tart rebuke from an anonymous authority
to the effect that by death alone can the veil be drawn. There
is, of course, a teasing similarity between Ayesha and Truth,
but she has to be individualized, temperamental Ayesha as
well, since Haggard was thoroughly convinced that sanctified
or not—and Ayesha is often a thorough-going no-nonsense

sceptic—human nature is eternal: '. . . it is the one fixed unchangeable thing, fixed as the stars, more enduring than the mountains'. 'Time hath no power against Identity' says Ayesha grandly, expressing Haggard's own view that individual personality was immeasurably ancient, capable of being born again and again.

No other aspect of Haggard's vision so completely differentiates him from Kipling, one of the two men with whom he found himself to be 'in supreme sympathy'. Such an extraordinary stability of identity was not only what Kipling lacked even in ordinary measure; its absence and his consciousness of it is precisely what distinguishes his own creative vision. (pp. 129-31)

Practising . . . a careful economy of self he offers the sharpest contrast with Haggard: in fact, someone who sought to find his answer in the fluidity of time could never be at one with Kipling *au fond*.

It is no mere playing with words to suggest that where Haggard is preoccupied with time, Kipling is preoccupied with space. (p. 131)

Where Haggard at most rises to a gloomy pathos Kipling comes near achieving a truly tragic vision. Moreover, at some point the former's heroes are always to be found on tip-toe aching with aspiration, whereas Kipling's never are: they *know* they are doomed. For them the struggle is to secure a space, an identity, for the brief moment of their problematic existence. These men are persecuted by the gods almost in the classical manner, unlike Haggard's characters who tend to make chums of their divinities. . . .

Thus while space for Haggard rolls outwards and upwards towards the infinite, for Kipling, in his scheme of things, it must necessarily remain altogether finite. This is what makes his literary use of the imperial idea so much more subtle and interesting than Haggard's, furnishing as it does such an apt metaphor for the tensions of his own moral universe. (p. 132)

Truth for Kipling was not a veiled and alluring enigma to whose seduction he was only too willing to submit: he knew too much for that: '. . . Truth is a naked lady, and if by accident she is drawn up from the bottom of the sea, it behoves a gentleman either to give her a print petticoat or to turn his face to the wall and vow that he did not see'. Unlike Haggard, who was for ever nipping behind the Veil to catch the Animating Spirit at a disadvantage, Kipling prayed for

> A veil 'twixt us and thee, dread Lord. . . .
>
> (p. 133)

'Even your imagination is out of the fifth form,' Andrew Lang once wrote to Haggard with unusual bluntness. Kipling's is certainly not, though for purposes of camouflage he often made it sound as though it were. It is a tactic he uses even in his letters to Haggard, which are full of slang and schoolboy persiflage reflecting his essential closeness and reserve and inability to give freely of himself.

Haggard, on the other hand, despite his recurrent pessimism, could be described as spiritually expansive. It is significant that it was not the man for whom service and discipline were concepts *necessary as concepts* to his imaginative and moral life who involved himself in actual service to his country. It was Haggard, the writer with the strong inclination to mysticism, who, in addition to writing over fifty novels, a massive and highly-regarded study of the state of English agriculture,

and a number of other substantial works, served on several important commissions, touring the Dominions at least twice in a semi-official capacity and eventually getting his knighthood for public services—something which pleased him greatly.

There can, of course, be no doubt about Haggard's inferiority to Kipling as a writer: despite his ability to work on us through a vividly deployed image of archetypal force, he continually fails to provide a full literary communication with the primitive and elemental. Yet he, too, had vision of a sort—a sympathy, a largeness of soul which raised him above the materialism, the complacency and the shallow-minded paternalism of many of his contemporaries. And it was this quality of soul which—in contrast to Kipling—he sought to communicate, ultimately allowing the end to take precedence over the means. With a revealing, if typical, choice of vocabulary he frankly states his position: 'In an adventure story . . . the substance is, as it were, the soul of the matter; the style is its outward and visible body. I prefer a creation with a great soul even if its form is somewhat marred, to one with a beautifully finished form and very little soul.' He himself was aware of the difficulty. Some five years before he died he wrote: 'In these latter days—thank Heaven I do seem to be grasping the skirts of vision—though they slip from the hand like water. But to describe—to set down!—There's the rub!—'

Both Kipling and Haggard cared intensely about what can only be called the human condition, and for both it was acutely focused in the death of a beloved son from which neither fully recovered. 'A long talk with Kipling is now one of the greatest pleasures I have left in life,' Haggard wrote in 1918, and the two imperialists remained the staunchest of friends until Haggard's death in 1925, linked by the largeness of their view and their consequent pessimism and suffering. (pp. 133-34)

Alan Sandison, "A Matter of Vision: Rudyard Kipling and Rider Haggard," in The Age of Kipling, *edited by John Gross (copyright © 1972 by George Weidenfeld and Nicolson Ltd.; reprinted by permission of Simon and Schuster, Inc.; in Canada by Weidenfeld (Publishers) Limited), Simon & Schuster, 1972 (also published in England as* Rudyard Kipling: The Man, His Work and His World, *Weidenfeld and Nicolson, 1972), pp. 127-34.**

RICHARD F. PATTESON (essay date 1978)

[*Patteson examines* King Solomon's Mines *as a typical example of the "imperial romance," a term which is explained and applied to others of Haggard's books, as well.*]

In the mid-1880's, with the publication of **King Solomon's Mines** and **She,** a type of novel that might be called the imperialist romance first began to reach a wide audience. The reason for its sudden popularity at this particular juncture is not difficult to guess. In its purest form, the imperialist romance chronicles the adventures of European explorers who travel into previously uncharted territory and establish their benevolent influence among the dark-skinned natives. The late Victorians must have found in this basic plot an immensely flattering image of their own imperial situation. Other common structural features of the genre tend to reflect related cultural attitudes. For instance, in many imperialist romances the explorers discover the ruins of an ancient white civilization—proof positive that even in the distant past, something approximating a colonial condition prevailed. Seen in this light, European penetration merely constitutes restoration of the old (and correct) order. Similarly, natives encountered by the adventurers are often divided into two warring factions, one more susceptible to westernization than the other. The ''good'' faction (almost always led by the tribe's secular chief rather than by the high priest or witch doctor) usually wins the struggle, but only with the active intervention of the European visitors.

A list of the twelve most frequently recurring plot functions of the imperialist romance reveals the genre's overall shape:

> 1. European or American adventurers plan a journey into unexplored regions. Their goals are usually clearly defined and more often than not are both idealistic and materialistic.

> 2. A series of preliminary adventures takes place, during which the heroes triumph over numerous adversities (typically involving the elements, dangerous animals, and human enemies).

> 3. At some point during the journey they descend into caves. Language describing this descent combines traditional allusions to Hades with the notion of envelopment by the female body.

> 4. At or near their destination, the heroes encounter evidence of previous or current rule by a relatively advanced—and always white or partly white—civilization.

> 5. At or near their destination, the heroes meet a native people (or peoples) divided into two political factions—one more receptive than the other to European culture.

> 6. Frequently the heroes establish their influence over the natives through a technological device (a gun, a match) or through some special scientific knowledge (such as the ability to predict an eclipse). As a result, the whites are held in awe by the natives—at least temporarily—and may even be worshipped as gods.

> 7. Native religious beliefs are often divided along these same factional lines, with the more ''humane'' sect corresponding to the more nearly European faction.

> 8. If a division between priests and secular leadership exists, the European visitors always take the side of the secular chief or monarch.

> 9. If any women are encountered, they are either treacherous villains or beautiful but helpless nonentities.

> 10. If one of the Europeans falls in love with a native woman, the woman usually dies. Generally speaking, the lighter her skin, the greater her chances of survival in the novel.

> 11. The more civilized faction of the tribe usually emerges victorious, but only with the aid of the Europeans.

> 12. The Europeans, having established order in most cases, get what they came for and depart.

King Solomon's Mines, as I shall demonstrate, is a nearly ''pure'' example, but these plot elements have been collected from more than fifty other imperialist romances as well. It is un-

deniable that the popularity of *King Solomon's Mines* helped solidify the genre in its standard mold, but Haggard was not the first to write such books; and the survival of this narrative pattern over a period of many years cannot, it seems to me, be attributed exclusively to the appeal of one writer. Before turning to a close look at *King Solomon's Mines,* therefore, it might be well to survey the broader contours of the imperialist romance as a whole.

Implicit in the first important plot function of the imperialist romance—preparations and goals—is an ambivalence that runs throughout the genre. This ambivalence can be traced directly to the dual role of the nineteenth-century imperialist as both missionary and merchant. Europeans saw themselves as ambassadors of an enlightened civilization, but they also realized that they came to the unchartered regions of the earth to acquire wealth. Their very motives were schizophrenic. Consequently, although whites always appear as heroes in the imperialist romance, they often appear as villains, too—a narrow-minded Boer, for example, or a Portuguese slave trader. Nowhere in the plot structure of the imperialist romance can this duality be more clearly seen than in the goals defined at the beginning of each tale. In most cases, the object of the anticipated quest is both altruistic and materialistic. Haggard's *Allan and the Holy Flower* involves the rescue of two white women held captive by savages as well as the acquisition of a rare orchid worth twenty thousand pounds. (pp. 112-14)

Most imperialist romances include the discovery either of an advanced white civilization or of ruins indicating white rule at some time in the past. This particular narrative feature may well have its origin in certain anthropological notions current in the nineteenth century. The Zimbabwe ruins were found by Europeans in 1868, and it was widely thought until comparatively recent times that they could not have been built by black Africans. According to his daughter, Rider Haggard himself believed that Phoenicians mined gold in the vicinity of Zimbabwe until they were massacred by ''the subject tribes, having learned their wisdom.'' Haggard's fictional histories parallel his view of actual history: whites were in Africa in ancient times; whites ruled over native blacks; blacks could defeat or outlast their white masters only by ''learning their wisdom.'' In various Haggard novels the ruins are traced back to Phoenicians, Hebrews, Egyptians, Persians, and so on, but never to the native Bantu themselves. (p. 114)

The classic example of native factionalization is the one tribe divided into ''savage'' and ''civilized'' groups. . . . Sometimes the division pits a white tribe against a darker one, as in Haggard's *The Ivory Child* or *Queen Sheba's Ring.* (p. 115)

Before we leave the plot functions relating to racial and political divisions, we should take special note of the frequency with which animals are placed in the structural position of natives. That is, they function within the plot as human natives do in other tales. Doyle's *Lost World* is populated by the usual two native factions—but the barbarian faction is composed of half human ape-men. Similarly, in Haggard's *Allan's Wife,* the ''hostile natives'' are a pack of baboons led by a demented white woman, and in his *Heu-Heu, or The Monster,* they are the not-quite-human ''Hairy Folk.'' The good faction in each case is human. A number of scholars have pointed out the late Victorian's obsession with what Jonah Raskin calls ''the border country between civilization and savagery.'' The barbarian, A. P. Thornton argues, is feared to be a part of ourselves. The native is Hyde to the European's Jekyll. . . . There seems to be a suggestion in the imperialist romance of a desire—perhaps subconscious—to get back to the animal or savage within, face and conquer it. But beneath this pattern lies a strangely ambivalent attitude toward the bestial element itself: the wish to repress or defeat it is mixed with admiration for its strength and virility.

Plot functions relating to sex reveal that the imperialist romance is primarily a male-oriented genre. The exploration of hostile territory is often described in terms of sexual conquest. Women are consistently identified with the earth, while men are closely linked to various heavenly bodies. The descent into caves—an important feature in many types of romance narratives—is especially frightening in the imperialist romance precisely because it does represent envelopment by the female. The hero always emerges from the caves, but he often finds there the bones of men who were not so lucky. The words "womb" and "tomb" occur with remarkable frequency in these episodes. To all this must be added the rather restricted roles female characters play in the imperialist romance. They are either villains (the sinister, seductive queen, the evil hag, the Mediterranean adulteress) or roughly corresponding ciphers (the fair queen in need of male assistance, the maiden held captive by savages, the loyal girl back home in England). When a native girl happens to fall in love with a white man, she almost always dies. The reason for her death is not merely racial; marriage is unmistakably presented as a betrayal of masculine camaraderie. "No more dreadful fate can befall a man than to become the tool of an unscrupulous woman, or indeed of any woman," Allan Quatermain remarks. Within this overwhelmingly sexist framework, the occasional appearance of a white jungle queen or goddess must be seen as the ultimate literary emasculation of native peoples.

The narrative framework of *King Solomon's Mines* is more complex than that of many imperialist romances, but the essential features are all there. The story begins when Allan Quatermain meets Sir Henry Curtis and Captain John Good on board a ship bound from Capetown to Durban. Sir Henry is in Africa to search for his brother George, who disappeared several years earlier while looking for the mines of Solomon. Quatermain has heard of Sir Henry's brother, and he has, in addition, heard of the mines. As luck would have it (and so often does in romance), Quatermain has in his possession a map procured from an old Portuguese adventurer, José Silvestre, whose remote ancestor first attempted the journey. The three agree to trek northward in search of both George Curtis and the mines. Here, as in other imperialist romances, altruistic motives are tightly intertwined with materialistic ones.

One characteristic element of the imperialist romance is the fantastic but intriguing yarn that fires the hero's imagination and prompts him to set out on his quest. This is not an absolutely necessary function, and many imperialist romances do quite well without it, but many others, particularly Haggard's, include it almost as a matter of course. In *The Ivory Child* two light-skinned Africans appear in England and tell a strange tale. Soa, an African woman in *The People of the Mist,* spins a similar yarn of a lost civilization. Occasionally, instead of being transmitted orally, the yarn will take the form of old papers discovered after many years, as in *She. King Solomon's Mines,* the richest imperialist romance in virtually every way, employs both devices. During the first several chapters there are Sir Henry's yarn about his brother, Allan Quatermain's yarn about the mines (which contains José Silvestre's own yarn), and the map itself, along with a note from José's ancestor—in Portuguese. These personal histories and recollections,

maps, and documents lend verisimilitude to what would otherwise be a highly implausible story, and they are all the more effective because maps and memoirs are just the types of communication one associates with actual explorations. The imperialist romance, to a certain extent, used the tools of history in the craft of fiction.

The preliminary adventures in *King Solomon's Mines*—the journey to Kukuanaland, the region where the mines are believed to be located—serve primarily to introduce minor characters and to increase suspense. The most important non-white character is Umbopa, who later proves to be Ignosi, the long-lost heir to the Kukuana throne. (pp. 115-17)

Almost as soon as the adventurers set foot in Kukuanaland, they fall into the hands of hostile natives led by Infadoos, who later turns out to be Umbopa's uncle. Umbopa's history—the novel's third major yarn—is rather complicated. . . . The restoration of the legitimate heir to the Kukuana throne may seem to have little to do with King Solomon's mines, and still less with the search for George Curtis, but the effort to establish order is perhaps the *sine qua non* of the imperialist romance—whether or not that effort succeeds.

The political situation in Kukuanaland has deteriorated under Twala. His rule is cruel, bloodthirsty, and highly arbitrary. . . . On Twala's side in the ensuing struggle are his son Scragga, old Gagool, and all the Kukuanas too terrified to oppose the king. On Umbopa/Ignosi's side are his uncle Infadoos, a number of brave Kukuanas, and of course the Englishmen.

The Twala faction represents not only cruelty but also disorder, barbarism, and ignorance. . . . In most imperialist romances, the witch doctor or high priest is the villain, while some secular leader (in this case Ignosi) who wants to establish a more "enlightened" regime is the native hero. Gagool represents the old pagan ways, and she is Twala's chief counselor. Scragga is hardly any less cruel. . . . In sharp contrast to Scragga's disrespect for his uncle are the attitudes of Allan Quatermain and Sir Henry Curtis, both of whom have a strong sense of family ties, and Ignosi, who has lived close to Europeans all his life and has absorbed many of their ideas and values. Scragga's action signals just how serious the breakdown of order in Kukuanaland is. Nothing in *King Solomon's Mines* is more calculated to stir the passions of the British reading public than the spectacle of a family divided against itself.

After a bloody armed conflict, Twala is defeated, Ignosi is proclaimed king, and the three Englishmen are free to proceed to King Solomon's mines. Haggard has made it quite clear that the mines, and the ruins in their vicinity, were constructed not by the Kukuanas but by a superior white people who preceded them. . . . This particular function of the imperialist romance—white rule either in the present or in the distant past—is so prevalent that it is hard to accept Alan Sandison's contention that Haggard was a cultural relativist [see excerpt above]. Sandison maintains that Haggard shows us not just the imperial triumph over native peoples, but "humanity absorbed with its squalid vices and petty aspirations in its honeycomb of racial compartments, struggling blindly with the incomprehensible and inexorable movement of which it is an unwilling part." This may be true enough, but the fact remains, I have not been able to find a single imperialist romance (by Haggard or anyone else) in which a superior civilization—past or present—did not result from the infusion of at least *some* white blood. It is also true that the native life described in *King Solomon's Mines* is not just colorful background material. The Kukuanas do, as Sandison argues, "hold their own with the white man who has strayed into their world." Nevertheless, the Englishmen's intrusion is more than just a method of introducing European readers to native life. When Allan Quatermain and his friends leave Kukuanaland, that region, in Brian Street's words, "has become in spirit, if not in fact, a colony of the British Empire." Whatever Haggard's intention, his plot structure—ruins built by whites, order finally established by whites—spoke directly to Victorian society in a language that society understood and appreciated.

When the Englishmen descend into Solomon's mines, certain racial and sexual attitudes are incorporated into the plot. But before we look at that plot function, we need to retrace our steps and fill in some important background information. There is never any doubt that the imperialist mission is a man's prerogative. *King Solomon's Mines* is dedicated "to all the big and little boys who read it." . . . And when Khiva dies, Umbopa remarks that "he died like a man." . . . Allan himself observes, not without a trace of disdain, "Women are women, all the world over, whatever their colour." . . . Color is important, too, however. When Ignosi offers him the fairest Kukuana maiden, Captain Good replies, "'Thanks, O king, but we white men wed only with white women like ourselves. Your maidens are fair, but they are not for us!'." . . . And finally, when Foulata, the native girl who loves Good, realizes that she is about to die, she pleads, "'Say to my lord, Bougwan, that—I love him, and that I am glad to die because I know that he cannot cumber his life with such as me, for the sun cannot mate with the darkness, nor the white with the black'." . . .

In the imperialist romance the feminine is consistently identified with the earth, while the masculine is linked to the sun, the moon, the stars—anything *high*, anything *above*. At several points in *King Solomon's Mines* the moon plays a key role (as when the Englishmen win a temporary reprieve by predicting a lunar eclipse). (pp. 117-20)

For the imperialist romancers, the earth is the eternal feminine—the body to be conquered, penetration followed by possession. Haggard is no exception. His intrepid adventurers move up the torso of Africa, from the lush vegetation of the south, across a flat, burning desert and past a navel-like, life-giving well, to a pair of mountains called Sheba's Breasts, which are, on occasion, "modestly veiled in diaphanous wreaths of mist." . . . But when Allan and his party descend into caves, they are, in effect, being enveloped by the female body. . . . When Gagool traps the Englishmen in the mines, Allan says, "We were buried in the bowels of a huge snow-clad peak." . . . The caves in *She* are described as the womb of the world, and here, too, they are womb-like. It is a woman, moreover, who traps them there. The men, through perseverance and ingenuity, escape the womb-tomb, but both Gagool and Foulata are killed.

The Englishmen fill their pockets with diamonds before they make their way to the surface, and they eventually locate Sir Henry's brother in a desert oasis; but the most important part of their mission is neither the treasure nor the rescue. As they are preparing to return to Durban, Sir Henry asks his friend Ignosi to promise him "'that the killing of men without trial shall not take place in the land.'" . . . In effect, white influence over Kukuanaland has been re-established after a lapse of many centuries.

The restoration of order and legitimacy in Kukuanaland can be seen as part of a larger salvation myth that is crucial to the expression of the imperial idea in *King Solomon's Mines*. Haggard's novel is really two narratives in one. The embedded plot is the story of Ignosi, the native hero who returns (ostensibly from the dead) to conquer the evil Twala. But surrounding that plot is the story of Allan Quatermain and his companions, in which white heroes arrive to free the entire kingdom (and implicitly, all of Africa) from superstition and barbarism. The Quatermain story contains the Ignosi story; the book begins in white-ruled South Africa and returns to it at the close; the Quatermain plot frames the native plot. . . . If Ignosi is Christ-like, a savior who finally defeats a Satanic usurper, he succeeds in his redemptive mission only with the aid of the Englishmen. The quasi-theological implications of the Englishmen's role should not be underestimated; the imperialist romance is the canonical literary form for the fantasy religion of white male hegemony. When Foulata, earlier in the novel, is threatened by Gagool, she cries out to Good, "'O white father from the stars! . . . throw over me the mantle of thy protection; let me creep into the shadow of thy strength, that I may be saved'." . . . This is literally a prayer; it is the prayer that, were all native peoples to utter it, would be the imperial dream come true. (pp. 121-22)

Richard F. Patteson, "'King Solomon's Mines': Imperialism and Narrative Structure," in The Journal of Narrative Technique *(copyright © 1978 by* The Journal of Narrative Technique*), Vol. 8, No. 2, Spring, 1978, pp. 112-23.*

GLEN ST. JOHN BARCLAY   (essay date 1978)

[*An Australian historian and a political scientist who has written extensively on Australian-American relations, Barclay is also a scholar of occult practices and fiction. Having traced his own interest in the supernatural to a strong interest in the martial arts, Barclay has authored two books on occult concerns:* Mind over Matter *(1973) and* Anatomy of Horror *(1978), the latter a literary, philosophical, and psychological study of several influential occult writers, including Bram Stoker, Haggard, and H. P. Lovecraft. Below, he examines Haggard's fiction, paying particular attention to the character Ayesha of* She *and its sequels.*]

The most impressive of all English writers of occult fiction must on all counts be Henry Rider Haggard. In the first place there is the simple aspect of quantity: the greater part of his enormous literary output, including some thirty-four novels, is composed of stories which either deal directly with the occult, or in which occult interventions play a fundamental part in the evolution of the plot. Moreover the assorted occult aspects can be related to one another as integral parts of a generally consistent if not always coherent philosophy which provided the inspiration for Haggard's own life. He differs in this respect from Stoker, who had no philosophy but was merely haunted by erotic fantasies; from Lovecraft, who never believed in his own myths; and from Dennis Wheatley, who indeed expresses a completely coherent philosophy in his novels, but one which appears to be totally unrelated to everything else in them, and even to everything else about Mr Wheatley himself.

Haggard's incoherence is indeed virtually a source of strength, in the sense that it reflects an attitude to human experience apparently completely free from any kind of dogmatic constraint or preconception. His total relativism is indicated by an entry in his diary made a few months before his death, with reference to the ancient Egyptians:

It is terrific to think that all these hordes were deluded by a faith which we know to be false, as are the multitudes of India and China, by other faiths which we know to be false. . . . If this inference were true, their lot was terrible indeed. But I for one do not believe it to be true. I look upon religion (from that of the lowest savage up to that of the most advanced Christian) as a ladder stretching from earth to heaven. . . . In that ladder the faith of the old Egyptians was a single rung, that which we follow is another rung, and perhaps there are many more, out of our sight and knowledge, for God's skies are far away.

Anyone who holds such a viewpoint is of course free from the inhibitions involved in the orthodox Christian concept that supernatural interventions within the framework of any other religious system were necessarily the work of the Devil, whatever they might seem to be from an objective analysis. . . . The truth seems rather that Haggard was simply refusing to let his observation abdicate to the constraints of dogma. It was in any case evident that the whole basis of Haggard's approach to the occult was that precise statements were necessarily inappropriate in an area not subject to the limitations of the physical universe.

This was not the only regard in which Haggard displayed a freedom of approach remarkable in any generation, and exceptionally uncommon in his own. His sympathy for the religious beliefs of other peoples was rendered peculiarly complete and uncomplicated by an almost total absence of any kind of ethnic or racial prejudice. He argues seriously in *Child of Storm* that the civilization of the Zulus is in many ways actually superior in human terms to that of contemporary Europe, which he identifies elsewhere with 'gunpowder, telegraphs, steam, daily newspapers, universal suffrage', which he believes have not only made people not a whit happier but have cursed them with the evils of 'greed, drunkenness, new diseases, gunpowder and general demoralization'. Haggard does indeed tend to dislike the Boers, but this is essentially because of what he regards as their own indefensible attitude towards the blacks. This freedom from prejudice even extends to sexual matters. Haggard appears to accept that miscegenation is impracticable in the white man's world, and the dying black girl Foulata in *King Solomon's Mines* laments that 'the sun may not mate with darkness nor the white the black', but she nonetheless looks forward to finding her lover, John Good RN, eventually in the stars, after death. Good himself complains after his return to England that he 'hadn't seen a woman to touch her, either as regards her figure or the sweetness of her expression'.

Love after death is in fact the continuing theme of Haggard's stories. It is indeed his conviction that love can be found satisfactorily nowhere else. There can be no doubt that at least one motivation for Haggard's concern with the occult was his dissatisfaction with the known world. Young, handsome, physically powerful, popular, intelligent, genial, brilliantly successful, he appears to have accepted by his twenties that the appropriate response to human life was one of despair. He never changed that view. . . . It is what happens to human relations in the physical universe that makes it, as Haggard assured Kipling, 'one of the hells'. The good always suffer at the hands of the worldly-wise. Love itself may be more of a curse than a blessing: Haggard noted in his diary that sex was, 'at any rate in highly civilized conditions, the source of our

worst woes'; and Ayesha explains to Allan Quatermain that friendship between men and women is at once a higher and more serviceable relationship than love, because nothing could be worse than for couples who had nothing in common except their physical relationship, and were therefore condemned to be bored with each other's company throughout eternity. (pp. 58-61)

In Haggard's vision, it is the world of physical reality, not that of the occult, in which one encounters true horror. The only hope of human happiness is to be sought in worlds beyond this one, and the first problem is of course to be at all sure that they exist. Haggard in fact did experience a few encounters with the occult in the course of an incredibly busy life, as well as a number of frightening or disturbing experiences which may well have rendered him unusually susceptible in that area. (p. 62)

There are also references in his memoirs to his possession of a faculty for precognition, though without any corroborating data. However, two experiences later in life undoubtedly justified his belief in precognition itself and also in the reality of the curse he felt himself doomed to bear. In his novel *The Way of the Spirit,* written in 1906, he depicts the hero, Rupert, hearing nomad musicians, known as The Wandering Players, who are said by the Arabs to be ghosts who bring misfortune to all who hear them, and appear to Rupert before events causing him great personal suffering. The Egyptian antiquarian, Sir Gaston Maspero, wrote to Haggard after reading the book, asking him how he had learned of a legend which as far as he knew had never been written down before, but which Haggard had described almost exactly in *The Way of the Spirit.* Haggard himself was convinced that he had invented the episode entirely from his imagination. Far more disturbing was the appalling irony of the opening paragraph of *Allan Quatermain:* 'I have just buried my boy, my poor handsome boy of whom I was so proud, and my heart is broken. It is very hard having only one son to lose like this, but God's will be done.' The novel was dedicated to Haggard's own son, Jock. Six years later Jock was dead, and Haggard was haunted for the rest of his life by the emotions which he had attributed to Allan Quatermain, as well as by the reflection that by thus killing off the son of his fictional alter ego, he might somehow have psychically contrived the death of his own son. (pp. 63-4)

These experiences certainly helped to confirm Haggard's ideas about the occult, and to inspire episodes in some of his fiction. His basic concerns and beliefs seem however to have been formed in his youth, without the aid of any psychic encounters, at a time when he was living the life of a John Buchan hero. Haggard's despair over the tragedy of human existence was certainly not derived from any personal inability to enjoy life. . . . [He] wrote *Cetywayo and His White Neighbours,* an indispensable introduction to the history of South Africa, scrupulously researched and documented but distinctly coloured by Haggard's admiration for the Zulus and dislike for the Boers. It was most unsuccessful. So he turned to fiction, publishing his first novel, *Dawn,* a few months later. The heroine was interestingly inspired by the sight of another dazzlingly beautiful girl in the village church. This effort also failed totally. A second novel, *The Witch's Head,* was more encouraging in that its sales reimbursed Haggard for the fifty pounds he had lost in publishing *Cetywayo* and *Dawn.* A few months later he wrote *King Solomon's Mines* and became the most popular living English author, whose books still outsell those of any of his contemporaries with the exception of Kipling. (pp. 64-6)

Haggard's occult novels can be conveniently grouped into three categories. There are those which introduce supernatural interventions into tales of high adventure; those which are explicitly moralistic in purpose, serving essentially as vehicles for the expression of Haggard's opinions about life and death; and those in which he develops the enormous symbolic figure of Ayesha, or 'She-Who-Must-Be-Obeyed'.

The first group would include for example *King Solomon's Mines* itself, in which the supernatural element is provided by the demon-witch Gagool, although typically Haggard makes it possible for the reader to believe that Gagool was merely a wicked and deceitful human being; *The Holy Flower,* perfect in construction, suspense and unfailing good humour and incorporating on the occult side precognition and witchcraft; and *The Ivory Child,* possibly Haggard's most successful work in literary terms, rivalling Wilkie Collins' *The Moonstone* for plot, atmosphere, balance and style, but including as an additional bonus hypnotism, telepathy, precognitive dreams, reincarnation, apparitions and a demon elephant. On a marginally lower level of quality if not necessarily of entertainment is *The Treasure of the Lake;* in which the adventure is complicated by the presence of the beautiful 'White Mouse', who loves and rescues Allan Quatermain, without ever leaving him entirely clear as to whether she is black or white, or even whether she is human or a spirit; and *The Ancient Allan,* in which the adventure is presented as an occult exploration by Quatermain and Lady Luna Ragnall, the heroine of *The Ivory Child.* Ironically, the one novel in the Allan Quatermain series, *Allan Quatermain* itself, which has really no occult aspects at all, is the one which has the most significant occult implications for Haggard's own life, in that it contains the reference to the death of Quatermain's son, which anticipated so tragically Haggard's reaction to the death of his own child.

There is perhaps little of an extraordinary nature about these stories, apart from their tremendous if uneven literary skill, and their lack of any of the psychotic undertones of Le Fanu's or Stoker's tales. Haggard indeed never attains the cool perfection of Le Fanu's style, and is often mechanical, repetitious and sloppy. However, he is normally nothing less than a perfect storyteller, with brilliant imagination, an excellent sense of plot, splendid narrative and expository vigour, remarkable humour, effective characterization and a gift for dramatic dialogue which can seriously be compared only with that of Sir Walter Scott at his best. In other words Haggard does not need the assistance of the occult to make his stories interesting.

What adds immensely to the effect of the occult aspects is indeed the cool scepticism with which they are presented, and the manner in which they are almost but not quite explained away. Thus in *The Holy Flower* Quatermain can dismiss his Zulu witchdoctor's forecast of the time at which the mad white man Dogeetah will arrive as merely a guess; but he cannot explain what it was that impelled him to add half an hour to the witchdoctor's estimated time of arrival, and thereby save everybody's lives. Similarly, in *The Ivory Child* the powers of the conjurers Harut and Meerut are dismissed as merely stagecraft, even though nobody is able to explain how the powers of telepathy and hypnotism they possess actually work; but Quatermain is unable even to guess how it was that he and that other infallible shot, Lord Ragnall, could not hit the demon-elephant Jana even at point-blank range, while his Hottentot servant Hans could not miss it.

This is indeed basically technique, although it does in fact correspond to what might be termed the normal run of occult experiences: the occult commonly presents itself as that aspect of an otherwise explicable happening, for which in fact an explanation cannot now be found. Far more important however is what may be termed the atmosphere of Haggard's descriptions of the occult. The events beyond the limits of the physical universe are not presented as symbols of desires either unadmitted or inadmissible, but as simple human experiences on another level of existence. Haggard does not need symbols for his repressions or those of his characters, because he seems to have been incredibly free from the need to repress anything.

It was not only in his attitudes to race that he was singularly immune from the preconceptions which distorted the vision of his contemporaries. His freedom and honesty in sexual matters are also literally unique. For example he does not seem to have been bothered by three issues unmentioned elsewhere in respectable Victorian or Edwardian fiction: pornography, lesbianism and female nudity. Quatermain observes in *Finished* that Dr Rodd's library contains 'novels, mostly French, and other volumes of a sort that I imagine are generally kept under lock and key.' In the same novel, the European heroine Heda asks Quatermain: 'Tell me, Mr Quatermain, is it possible for one woman to be in love with another?' Quatermain replies with what he calls the 'cheap joke' that 'women, as far as I had observed them, were generally in love either with a man or with themselves, perhaps more often with the latter than the former'. However, he questions the female witchdoctor Nombe, and learns that all men are hateful to her and that she will never be parted from Heda as long as she lives. Quatermain describes her feelings at the time as abnormal and unnatural. He nonetheless describes as 'splendid' and 'triumphant' the death in which Nombe gives her life for Heda. . . . (pp. 66-9)

In *Allan's Wife,* Quatermain's own wife Stella is the object of passionate love by the baboon-woman Hendrijka, who tells Quatermain that 'they say in the kralls that men love women better than women love women. But it is a lie.' Quatermain does not condemn her attitude, commenting merely that it 'is generally supposed that this passion only exists in strength when the object is of another sex from the lover, but I confess that, both in this instance and in some others which I have met with, this has not been my experience'. The statement is hardly revolutionary or even very well expressed, but it stands alone in the popular fiction of its time.

Haggard's success in creating female archetypes is certainly consistent with his unfailing capacity to confront the supreme physical fact of female nudity without the complications of prudery or prurience. Nudity occurs in his stories probably more often than it does in those of Dennis Wheatley, for example. Mameena is normally naked, except for her apron of blue beads, and she is even divested of that in *Child of Storm;* Ayesha, who dresses in transparent robes when she is dressed, strips before Kallikrates and Amentares in *Wisdom's Daughter;* and the two queens in *Allan Quatermain* are specifically described in the narrative as wearing robes that left their breasts uncovered. This was too much for Haggard's illustrators, who invariably felt compelled to cover the ladies up. However, the only emotions ever attributed to the observers of any of these displays are wonder and admiration. . . . Haggard presents his women as objects of literally unbounded love, but never as sex objects.

While Haggard did not find it necessary to transform his women into vampires in order to convey the fact that they loved and even desired each other, he did portray them as essentially spirits. There is no doubt that Haggard's heroines play far more important and active roles when they are out of their bodies than when they are in them. White Mouse in *The Treasure of the Lake,* for example, can only be assumed to be a spirit, even though she never admits this directly to Quatermain, whom she loves, telling him that there is really no important difference between women and spirits anyway. Lady Luna Ragnall and Quatermain console themselves for their inability to marry in their present existence by reliving previous existences in which they had been lovers. (pp. 69-70)

But the spiritual activities of all these ladies are limited and sedate compared with those of Haggard's archetypal creation, the beautiful Mameena, who quite literally haunts his three other great adventure stories, *Marie, Child of Storm* and *Finished,* and plays while still dead a decisive role in *The Ivory Child.* Her earthly life is indeed sufficiently energetic: she pretends to royal blood to which she has no claim; she seduces Saduko, chief of the Amangwane, into massacring another tribe to acquire the bride-price to marry her, but actually marries the objectionable and repulsive Masupo, chief of the Amansomi. She then establishes an adulterous relationship with Saduko, who has in the meantime married the good and noble Nandie, princess of the Zulu house of Senzagakona; she poisons their child in order to have Masupo executed for the murder, and becomes Saduko's second wife, only to betray him for Umbelazi, the crown prince of the Senzagakonas, whom Saduko in revenge leaves to be killed by Cetywayo. (pp. 70-1)

However, her career is even more dramatic after death. Her spirit appears repeatedly to Quatermain, although he is at the time unsure whether it is actually her or the almost equally beautiful Nombe. She embraces him at least once, although he is not wholly sure at the time whether he actually felt her or not; she protects him from a demon-elephant; she rides before him to frighten off the Zulus while he escapes from the field of Isandlhwana. (p. 71)

It is certainly remarkable that there is no suggestion at all that Mameena has undergone any punishment or even any remorse for actions which would entitle her to rank among the most formidable villainesses of fiction. It is of course possible that Haggard, as a believer in reincarnation, assumes that our crimes and follies are expiated in subsequent existences on an earth which he regards as a hell. It is at least evident that he never bothered to formulate a rigid system of moral values. His attitude remained that of Allan Quatermain in *Finished:*

> Our lives cannot be judged by our deeds; they must be judged by our desires or rather by our moral attitude . . . those who seek to climb out of the pit, those who strive, however vainly, to fashion failure to success, are, by comparison, the righteous, while those who are content to wallow in our native mire and to glut themselves with the daily bread of vice, are the unrighteous.

It leaves a great deal of room for interpretation, which is no doubt exactly what Haggard intended. His position remained flexible to the end. (pp. 72-3)

One of the things which he continued to think about all his life was the presentation in fiction of perhaps the ultimate female archetype, the Queen of the Heavens, whose cult had existed throughout the Middle Ages, among the Egyptians, the modern African tribes, the ancient Germans, the Celts and the Ainu of Japan. The 'She-Who-Must-Be-Obeyed' quartet, *She, Ayesha,*

She and Allan and *Wisdom's Daughter* constitute Haggard's quite deliberate though distinctly tentative foray into genuine myth-making and the world of symbolism. The occult elements in his other books are presented as aspects of reality, as has been said; Luna Ragnall, White Mouse and even Mameena are all mortal in some respects, even though, especially in the case of Mameena, possessed of literally immortal beauty, passion and will; She or Ayesha, to use her more euphonious alternative name, is not mortal and presumably never has been. In terms of Haggard's own thinking, of course, this may not really matter: if we all are, even when physically existent, merely embodied spirits, the distinction between the mortal and the immortal becomes very tenuous indeed. This is indeed one of the numerous problems with which Haggard found himself compelled to grapple when composing his giant myth. They were never resolved satisfactorily. If they could have been, there would have been no need of a myth. (pp. 73-4)

Haggard had many reasons for feeling less than satisfied with his first venture into myth-making. In the first place, it is much less successful as a story than the Quatermain tales, because the characters of Vincy and Holly are quite uninteresting and unconvincing. Ayesha herself is abundantly interesting and even convincing, but also baffling. She is in fact a superbly comprehensive evocation of the Eternal Feminine, but she is utterly elusive both as a personality and even as a being. She is ruthless, fascinating, incomparably beautiful, capricious and omnipotent in her dealing with mortals of the human species. However, her own immortality is in some sense conditional since it was necessary for her to bathe in the Pillar of Fire to acquire her first two thousand years of existence in the physical world, and her second attempt causes her own physical destruction. She is therefore something less than a goddess in the usual sense, and indeed refers to herself as being bound by the Eternal Law. She might well stand for a symbol of ideal beauty, which can neither exist permanently in the physical universe nor be united with humanity there, were it not for the fact that her own personality seems somewhat less than ideal. On the other hand, she is not simply a siren, destroying herself rather than luring mortals to destruction.

Haggard was himself fully aware of the fact that his treatment of the Ayesha myth had not been wholly satisfactory. . . . The only real surprise is that Haggard waited some eighteen years before buckling to the task again. *Ayesha* returned in the book of that name. (pp. 75-6)

Haggard's literary technique is perhaps hardly more successful in *Ayesha* than it had been in *She,* because of the intrinsic impossibility of making Vincy and Holly convincing or even interesting. The myth however gains tremendously in its second instalment. The transformation of Ayesha's destroyed body symbolizes the recreative powers of love and truth, and the death of Vincy reminds us that complete union with ideal beauty cannot be attained within the limits of the physical universe. It is necessary that time and space should be transcended, and this can be accomplished only by the act of dying. There are on the other hand some aspects which do not resolve themselves so effectively. The conflict between Ayesha and Atene is presented as a version of the duel between sacred and profane love. However, Ayesha's love is not simply spiritual, since it involves physical union with Vincy; and Atene's love is not simply physical, since she looks forward to reunion with Vincy in a world beyond death. There is also a clear implication that Ayesha herself regards her relationship with Holly as being more important and more permanent than her love for Vincy.

In any case, the distinction between Ayesha and Atene is not even that between beauty which uplifts and beauty which degrades: if Atene is disloyal, Ayesha is a murderess; both are liars; and Ayesha's love has the effect of destroying Vincy, physically at least, while Atene's love destroys herself. Moreover, if Ayesha can look forward to recovering Vincy after death, so apparently can Atene.

Least of all does Ayesha solve the basic problem of who or what she actually is. A priest at the end of the book refers to her as 'the woman—or the sorceress—or the mighty evil spirit . . .' all of which descriptions are in fact evidently inadequate. It does however seem inherent in Haggard's conception that Ayesha should in fact remain equivocal and ill-defined: the most authentic aspect of Haggard's whole attitude towards the occult is that there is no point in trying to be precise when dealing with matters which by their nature cannot be fully comprehended by the denizens of a physical universe. It is in any case not inappropriate that a symbol of the Eternal Feminine should be all things to all men, and different things to the same man.

This quality of infinite variety is indeed emphasized in the third volume of the Ayesha quartet, *She and Allan,* published sixteen years after *Ayesha,* but in fact presented as an introduction to *She,* which precedes it by thirty-four years. Like all the Quatermain stories, the book is first of all a superb adventure story of Africa, written with all the skill of a man who would certainly appear to be the best writer of adventure stories in the language. It is also at least a partially successful attempt by Haggard to bring together his three great archetypes, Ayesha, Mameena and Quatermain himself. (pp. 77-8)

Ayesha does at least make some reasonably definite statements about her own nature to Quatermain. She is the Eternal Feminine; she is a goddess, albeit with limited powers, subject to the Law of Nature; she is Woman Incarnate; she is also Nature Incarnate, revealed in the feminine form of humanity, which means that she is either the Goddess Isis or spiritually linked with her. It is however still fundamental to the validity of the myth that its nature should never be wholly clarified, and Ayesha is left endowed with some traits which seem to be inconsistent with spiritual perfection. For a start, she gets on Quatermain's nerves: he is convinced that two thousand years of immortality would have no attractions for him if it meant that he had to listen to Ayesha rating him for much of the time. He indeed generally regards her, as does his ferocious Zulu companion Unslopogaas, as a witch deceitful and capricious. The old Zulu witchdoctor Zikali, who himself is more than human, sees her also as a witch, but a witch whose function is to reveal truth to mankind. There is no final answer.

Nor is there a satisfactory final answer in the last of the Ayesha stories, Ayesha's own memoir of her birth and her first incarnation, *Wisdom's Daughter.* Ayesha tells us that she is the daughter of Isis, who is Nature, and whose powers she shares to some extent. . . . Her purpose on earth is apparently to struggle with Aphrodite, who symbolizes Life, but whose effect on humanity is to render it forgetful of the things of the spirit. Again, the issue would seem to be one of sacred and profane love, were it not for the fact that some of Ayesha's own activities are more than somewhat profane. (p. 79)

These are massive problems to encounter in what are presented as basically tales of adventure. They are certainly dealt with by Haggard far more acceptably in the medium of the adventure yarn, however, than in his explicitly moral stories, *The Way*

of the Spirit, Love Eternal, Beatrice and *Barbara Who Came Back,* which are interesting only to the extent that they express Haggard views of the occult. Apart from that, they are in general mawkish, uninspired, contrived and profoundly unentertaining. The fact is that Haggard found an ideal form of expression in the story of African adventure, and in six or seven novels of this genre he stands supreme both as storyteller and myth-maker. Nor are his myths simply symbols of sexual variations. He is concerned with the same order of human problems as Plato was, with the issues of immortality, the varying roles of flesh and spirit, expiation, retribution and love. (p. 80)

Glen St. John Barclay, "Love after Death: Henry Rider Haggard," in his Anatomy of Horror: The Masters of Occult Fiction *(copyright © 1978 by Glen St. J. Barclay: reprinted by permission of St. Martin's Press, Inc.; in Canada by Weidenfeld (Publishers) Limited), Weidenfeld and Nicholson, 1978 (and reprinted by St. Martin's Press, 1979), pp. 58-80.*

V. S. PRITCHETT   (essay date 1980)

[*Pritchett has a high reputation for his work as a novelist, short story writer, and critic. He is considered one of the modern masters of the short story whose work is a subtle blend of realistic detail and psychological revelation. Pritchett is also considered one of the world's most respected and well-read literary critics. He writes in the conversational tone of the familiar essay, a method by which he approaches literature from the viewpoint of a lettered but not overly scholarly reader. A twentieth-century successor to such early nineteenth century essayist-critics as William Hazlitt and Charles Lamb, Pritchett employs much the same critical method: his own experience, judgement, and sense of literary art, as opposed to a codified critical doctrine derived from a school of psychological or philosophical speculation. His criticism is often described as fair, reliable, and insightful. In an essay originally written in review of Morton Cohen's biography of Haggard (see excerpt above), Pritchett provides a general discussion of Haggard's works and their characteristics.*]

It is only this week, when my duties have obliged me to read Mr Morton Cohen's careful and sympathetic life of Rider Haggard, that I have taken my first plunge into the choking verbiage of *King Solomon's Mines* and *She,* and I am past the age when I can bring to works of this kind the elation of a chaste and hero-worshipping sensibility. What ought to scare me simply makes me laugh. How can people who admire Stevenson, as I do, think anything of *King Solomon's Mines?*

An initiator of the revival of Romance in late Victorian times, his work deliriously received, Rider Haggard never understood why he did not rank with Stevenson, Meredith, Henry James and, shall we add?, Falkner, the author of *Moonfleet,* Kipling, who was his great friend, or Joseph Conrad. Today he would find his place among the gaudier historical or horror films or among the new school of science fiction writers. Like many popular best-sellers, he was a very sad and solemn man who took himself too seriously and his art not seriously enough. The fact is that he was a phenomenon before he was a novelist: other novelists are content to be simply themselves, Rider Haggard was his public.

To be identified with the public is the divine gift of the best-sellers in popular Romance and, no doubt, in popular realism. E. M. Forster once spoke of the novelist sending down a bucket into the unconscious; the author of *She* installed a suction pump. He drained the whole reservoir of the public's secret desires. Critics speak of the reader suspending unbelief; the best-seller knows better; man is a believing animal. So, in the age of religious doubt, Rider Haggard tapped the mystical hankerings after reincarnation, immortality, eternal youth, psychic phenomena. He tracked down priestesses and gods. So, in a peaceful age, he drew on preoccupations with slaughter; and, in an empire-building age, on fantasies of absolute, spiritual rule in secret cities. His triumph—though it baffled him—was in the creation of *She*. The journey into mysterious Kor comes flawlessly out of the agonies of sexual anxiety; Ayesha herself is an identifiable myth or rather a clutter of myths: everything from Jung's Anima, the White Goddess, *la belle dame sans merci,* down to the New Woman or, as Henley said, 'the heroic Barmaid, the Waitress in Apotheosis'.

But the remarkable visions of Rider Haggard would have got him nowhere without three other qualities. One of these cannot be praised enough: he is a constantly inventive storyteller. The other two, paradoxically, support it: his stories are so tall that only bad grammar and slipshod and even vulgar writing can get him round the difficulty; and he dare not go in for more than pasteboard character. Anything in the nature of a human being would stand in the way. Look at Stevenson and one sees the enormous difference. Finally, Haggard has the enviable gift (common to many writers of popular Romance) of pouring it all out in a great gush in a few weeks. He has the confessional form of genius. He never corrected a line. (pp. 25-6)

Haggard's mind was almost totally serious. His humour, always uncertain, is clumsy and vulgar. . . . The Haggards had loud voices; they were said in Norfolk to be able to 'chat across a field'. It is not a bad description of his manner as a novelist. He wrote to be heard a long way off. (pp. 27-8)

The blood lust and the moralizings are the worst things in the Haggard novels; the dramatic invention—the old witch crushed by the closing stone door in the cave, the sight of the mummified explorer in *King Solomon's Mines*—is marvellous and so also is the first vision of the mountains, although in description he is usually better in local detail than in the set-piece. The sunbeam that lights the plank when Ayesha, Leo and the narrator are crossing the precipice in *She* is a brilliant stroke; and the account of the sinking of the dhow and the ride through the breakers in the same book is admirable. A collector in everything, Haggard had the art of piling it on. It is an art. His flow is molten, burning from one event to the next. And although we have to stress the triumphantly naïve part played by his unconscious we have to repeat that he was a voracious and intelligent observer. His two serious works, on English farming and the political issues in Africa, show him to be capable of the serious historical document. On one plane, the very great writers and the popular romancers of the lower order always meet. They use all of themselves, helplessly, unselectively. They are above the primness and good taste of declining to give themselves away. (pp. 28-9)

Ayesha is undoubtedly a disturbing figure and, I think, because she is a compendium. . . . It is his misfortune that his compelling imagination could create a creature of primitive and over-mastering passion and savage jealousy and yet, at the same time, apply the most trite Victorian moralizations to her case:

> I saw him struggle—I saw him even turn to fly:
> but her eyes drew him more strongly than iron
> bands, and the magic of her beauty and con-
> centrated will and passion entered into him and
> overpowered him—ay, even there in the pres-
> ence of the body of the woman who had loved

him well enough to die for him. It sounds horrible and wicked enough, but he should not be too greatly blamed, and be sure his sins will find him out.

And there is a curious suggestion, somewhat coarsely made, that if the love of the temptress is evil, many men have found respectable marriage to be hell. Haggard's rhetoric sounds like the kind that is clumsily covering up.

One is led to speculate on the inner life of a generation that responded eagerly to his allegory, to the fantasies of masochistic travel, to those precipitous mountain walls, those caverns, tunnels, caves and tombs, and all the bloodshed. And who liked to have it all dressed up in prose that is at one moment all baccy and Norfolk tweed and, the next, Liberace's trousers. Yet his African books represent a real response by a most suggestible man to African legend, which—as we have seen recently in the works of Amos Tutuola—is far bloodier than anything Haggard put down.

Mr Morton Cohen indeed argues that his books may find a place in an African, as distinct from an English, tradition. He compares Haggard with Fennimore Cooper, pointing out the distinction that Haggard was writing for a people with a future. 'When they assert their independence and rule once more in their native lands Haggard's Zulu saga may come into its own. For he captures in it a clear, engaging picture of Zulu life and comes to terms with the turbulent Zulu spirit.' He is writing especially of *Nada the Lily.* I have not read it but if in that work he completely freed himself of Norfolk, then I can see that the speculation is an interesting one. He had in his impure imagination something powerfully accessible. (pp. 29-30)

> *V. S. Pritchett, "Rider Haggard: Still Riding" (orig-*
> *inally published in a slightly different form in* New
> Statesman, *Vol. LX, No. 1537, August 27, 1960), in*
> *his* The Tale Bearers: Literary Essays *(copyright ©*
> *1980 by V. S. Pritchett; reprinted by permission of*
> *Random House, Inc.; in Canada by Literistic, Ltd.),*
> *Random House, 1980, pp. 25-30.*

ADDITIONAL BIBLIOGRAPHY

Cohen, Morton N. "Rudyard Kipling and Rider Haggard." *The Dal-housie Review* 40, No. 3 (Fall 1960): 297-322.
> Account of the close friendship between the two authors, which began in the early 1890s and continued until Haggard's death in 1925.

Ellis, H. F. "The Niceties of Plagiarism." *The Atlantic Monthly* 203, No. 1 (January 1959): 76, 78.
> Apologia for the "borrowed" elements in Haggard's fiction, touching on one of the instances labelled plagiarism by James Runciman (see 1890 excerpt above). Ellis mentions several occurrences in Haggard's fiction that closely resemble incidents in other author's earlier works; he suggests "there is no copyright" on specific fictional incidents.

Ellis, Peter Beresford. *H. Rider Haggard: A Voice from the Infinite.* London: Routledge & Kegan Paul, 1978, 291 p.
> Extensive, thoroughly researched biography. Ellis quotes many reviews by other critics but makes few critical statements of his own regarding Haggard's works. The book contains an extensive bibliography of Haggard's works, giving complete British and U.S. publication information, as well as a bibliography of criticism about Haggard's works.

Elwin, Malcolm "Our Boyhood's Favorite: Rider Haggard." In his *Old Gods Falling*, pp. 218-63. New York: The Macmillan Co., 1939.
    Lengthy biocritical examination of Haggard's life and works. Elwin provides a largely negative critical evaluation of Haggard's works, and expresses his wish that Haggard had written more slowly and revised more of what he wrote.

Greene, Graham. "Rider Haggard's Secret." In his *Collected Essays*, pp. 209-14. New York: The Viking Press, 1969.
    Characterizes Haggard as "perhaps the greatest of all who enchanted us when we were young." Greene notes an occasional poetic element in Haggard's writing.

Haggard, Lilian Rider. *The Cloak that I Left: A Biography of the Author Henry Rider Haggard K.B.E.* London: Hodder and Stoughton, 1951, 287 p.
    Anecdotal biography by Haggard's youngest daughter, compiled with the aid of Haggard's letters, notebooks, and diaries.

Higgins, D. S. *Rider Haggard: A Biography*. New York: Stein and Day, 1983, 266 p.
    Biography that makes use of many previously unpublished letters.

Jung, Carl. "The Meaning of Individuation." In his *The Integration of the Personality*, pp. 3-29. New York: Farrar & Rinehart, 1939.*
    Briefly mentions the character of Ayesha from Haggard's novel *She* as a classic representation of the concept of anima: man's feminine aspect which is often projected by him onto a real woman. Jung finds Ayesha to be among other literary "natural archetypes, primordial figures of the unconscious."

Kipling, Rudyard. *Something of Myself: For My Friends Known and Unknown*. Doubleday, Doran & Co., 1937, 252 p.
    Recurring mention by Kipling of his close friendship with Haggard, one of his first acquaintances in London literary circles "to whom I took at once."

Kraus, René. "Problem Child." In his *Winston Churchill: A Biography*, rev. ed., pp. 24-38. Philadelphia: J. B. Lippincott Co., 1924.
    Recounts Haggard's meeting with the very young Churchill, who later sent him a letter praising *Allan Quatermain* as a better novel than *King Solomon's Mines*.

Mullen, Richard Dale. "The Prudish Prurience of H. Rider Haggard and Edgar Rice Burroughs." *Riverside Quarterly* 6 (August 1973, April 1974): 4-19, 134-46.*
    Examination of instances of nudity, rape, seduction, pre and post-marital sex, and various character reactions and author approaches to these occurrences, in the works of Haggard and Burroughs.

[Oliphant, Margaret]. "The Old Saloon: *She: A History of Adventure*." *Blackwood's Edinburgh Magazine* CXLI, No. DCCCLVI (February 1887): 101-05.
    Rare negative review of *She*. The critic finds that Haggard, though "a strong and daring inventor," lacks the poetic imagination necessary to sustain the fantastic elements of the plot. Oliphant praises, however, his depiction of the shipwreck and several other more realistic events.

Prescott, Orville. Introduction to *"She" and "King Solomon's Mines,"* by H. Rider Haggard, pp. v-ix. New York: The Modern Library, 1957.
    Brief introduction to Haggard's two best-known novels. Prescott recounts the popular story that Haggard wrote *King Solomon's Mines* on a wager that he could produce a better boy's adventure story than *Treasure Island*. He finds *King Solomon's Mines* to be "the best introduction to Haggard," and *She* to be "similar to *King Solomon's Mines*, but more extravagent in its imaginative fantasies."

Shanks, Edward. "Sir Rider Haggard and the Novel of Adventure." *The London Mercury* II, No. 61 (November 1924): 71-9.
    A discussion of Haggard's novels, paying particular attention to *King Solomon's Mines* and *She*.

Joseph Hergesheimer

1880-1954

American novelist, short story writer, autobiographer, biographer, essayist, and critic.

Among the most popular and critically acclaimed American authors of the 1920s, today Hergesheimer is primarily of interest as a period figure. Writing during a literary era which stressed realism and social iconoclasm, he was a conservative aesthete whose fiction became famous for its lavish, accurately detailed settings. In *Java Head* and *The Three Black Pennys*, the novels for which he is best known, Hergesheimer looked to the American past for the artistic excellence and human integrity he admired. While longing for the past, Hergesheimer viewed the emptiness of contemporary life with bitter disgust. This attitude is most successfully expressed in *Cytherea*, a novel set in the disillusioned, affluent America of the Jazz Age.

Hergesheimer was born in Philadelphia and raised in the home of his maternal grandfather, a typefounder and hymn writer. A sickly boy, Hergesheimer spent a great deal of time at home surrounded by material comforts and the traditional formality of aged relatives. His formal education was limited to a few undistinguished years at the orthodox Quaker school in Germantown, followed by two years of study at the Philadelphia Art Academy. A chance meeting with a popular novelist, who asked him to proofread her manuscript, led Hergesheimer to believe that he too could become a novelist. Fourteen years later, after countless rejections, he published his first piece of short fiction at age thirty-three. As *The Saturday Evening Post* and other popular magazines began to buy his material, Hergesheimer's popularity and critical acclaim grew, and he was well paid for short stories which exhibited his highly wrought style. His first novel, *The Lay Anthony*, published in 1914, established the exotic subject matter which would characterize the works that followed during his twenty-year career. By 1934, Hergesheimer's growing disdain for contemporary values and aesthetics, and an unwillingness to yield his style to the angry Naturalism and realism that had grown popular, led him to abandon fiction writing. During the remainder of his life, he devoted himself to historical study, essay writing, and travel.

Like James Branch Cabell, with whom he shares many artistic affinities, Hergesheimer rejected the modern world and set his works in a mythical past of sensual beauty and aristocratic privilege. Raised amid wealth and tradition, Hergesheimer idealized the independence, solitude, and personal integrity which he associated with early America and which he found lacking in contemporary society. *The Three Black Pennys*, his first successful novel, illustrates the luxury and privilege Hergesheimer felt was the proper domain of the aristocrat. *Java Head*, considered Hergesheimer's best novel, compares the effects of changing mores on several generations of a family; traditional values decline as the family's patriarch loses control over his sons. Set in maritime Salem, Massachusetts, of the 1840s, this novel was paramount in spreading Hergesheimer's influence and fame; it combined a complex, interesting plot and structure, colorful details and characters, and a wistful sense of nostalgia for a vanished era. In *Java Head* and other

Culver Pictures

novels, characterization is overshadowed by the author's close attention to setting and decor. Clothing, furnishings, and the various possessions of his characters are lingered over in lengthy passages of detailed description. Hergesheimer once stated that he was more interested in the homes and possessions of people than in the people themselves. Women, whom Hergesheimer believed epitomized natural beauty, appear in the novels as ornate prizes who inspire or destroy the men who would possess them. *Linda Condon*, one of his strongest novels and one which many critics feel was written to refute the claim that Hergesheimer's female characters were not "alive," explores the background of a beautiful, wealthy woman devoid of deep emotional feeling beyond that which she attaches to her own physical beauty. A sculptor, who loves her but cannot have her, preserves her beauty in bronze, creating one of the century's artistic masterpieces. Such romantic plots and characters placed within a realistically detailed setting result in a type of fiction that is called impressionistic and dreamlike.

Hergesheimer's stories and novels set in contemporary America treat the "smart set" of the Jazz Age. The settings are still lavishly described, but there is a tone of contempt rather than aesthetic appreciation underlying the descriptions. Likewise, the beguiling female, still unsurpassed in her seductive powers, no longer inspires, but simply destroys. Erotic love and exotic locales lure the dissatisfied modern man and woman to their fate. In *Cytherea,* for example, the object of a respectable family man's uncontrollable desire, Savina Grove, dies in the heat of exotic Cuba, symbolizing her "burning" passion and its consequences.

Hergesheimer's luxurious lifestyle and literary preoccupation with decor have drawn both praise and contempt from his critics. Clifton Fadiman, in a bitter essay, contends that Hergesheimer's work is "dependent on the theology of money," and argues that the author's attachment to the past has little to do with moral or religious ideals, but rather exposes a desire to return to the social stratification and servitude of the period. Cabell and Hugh Walpole—themselves the authors of ornate period fiction—have, on the other hand, praised Hergesheimer's elaborate descriptions. Many critics, however, have faulted his prose for its poor grammar and punctuation, a consequence of the author's scanty education. These critics also claim that Hergesheimer's highly recognizable writing style became a pretentious affectation in his later works. The "literary" tone, particularly in the works set in contemporary times, gives the language an artificial effect. While H. L. Mencken largely agreed with this charge, he discounts its importance when set beside Hergesheimer's other accomplishments; he, like Cabell, believed that the musicality of the language and the beauty it depicts through imagery more than compensate for Hergesheimer's technical shortcomings.

During most of his career, Hergesheimer enjoyed popular and critical success. The escapist quality of his fiction, accentuated by romance and beauty, offered readers an alternative to the frequent pessimism of the Naturalists and realists, while adding a European aestheticism to American regionalism. But as American literature continued to examine the effects of modern society upon the individual, Hergesheimer's works were judged to be superficial and his characterizations shallow and unsatisfactory. Today, Hergesheimer is studied as a transitional writer, falling between the genteel authors of the Victorian era and the radical young realists of the early twentieth century.

(See also *Dictionary of Literary Biography,* Vol. 9: *American Novelists, 1910-1945.*)

PRINCIPAL WORKS

The Lay Anthony (novel) 1914
Mountain Blood (novel) 1915
The Three Black Pennys (novel) 1917
Gold and Iron (short stories) 1918
Java Head (novel) 1919
Linda Condon (novel) 1919
San Cristóbal de la Habana (travel essay) 1920
The Bright Shawl (novel) 1922
Cytherea (novel) 1922
The Presbyterian Child (autobiography) 1923
Balisand (novel) 1924
From an Old House (autobiography) 1925
Tampico (novel) 1926
Swords and Roses (essays) 1929
The Party Dress (novel) 1930
The Limestone Tree (novel) 1931
Sheridan: A Military Narrative (biography) 1931
Berlin (travel sketches) 1932
Biography and Bibliographies (essay) 1932
The Foolscap Rose (novel) 1934

LUCIAN CARY (essay date 1914)

The first chapters of "The Lay Anthony" are surprisingly good. Mr. Hergesheimer has evidently taken great pains to select the precise details which would suggest his young hero and the American town in which he lives. I thought as I read these pages that I had discovered a writer who knew American life and had both the courage and the skill to record it. But Mr. Hergesheimer is bound to move his readers at any cost. He is not satisfied with the stuff he has in his head; he must dress it up with the stuff that he has found in yellow newspapers and in the speeches of romantic social workers. "The Lay Anthony" ends with one of the situations made so familiar by the "white slave" literature of the past two or three years. It is a pity, because Mr. Hergesheimer undoubtedly knows a number of things that his readers would have been glad to learn, in place of this clap-trap. (pp. 204-05)

> *Lucian Cary, in his review of "The Lay Anthony,"* in The Dial *(copyright, 1914, by The Dial Publishing Company, Inc.), Vol. LVII, No. 678, September 16, 1914, pp. 204-05.*

SINCLAIR LEWIS (essay date 1917)

[Between 1915 and 1922, the realist Lewis wrote letters of high praise and admiration to Hergesheimer, whom he believed used words to evoke beauty in an increasingly cynical age. There were several points about which the two writers did not agree, as is evident from the letter reprinted below.]

Yes! I like [*The Three Black Pennys*] enormously! A score of scenes in it stick in my mind, and I know the characters are real because they come back to me constantly, as living beings. I [*sic*] fact I'm going to give you the compliment of being influences [*sic*] by the Pennys in the serial I hope shortly to commit—the life and empire of Jim Hill, builder of Minnesota and the northwest. I see better from reading it how to handle the railroading and daily life of the Hill of 1860 to 1890.

Most of all I like the last Howat and his friends. Not only is he most real to me, but most sympathetic, and Mariana—is that her name? the book is downstairs—is so vividly the young woman of today and of that environment. The dinner of the lamentable fish and the uneasy plodders who knew darn well they'd oughta put on Dress Suits is glorious—not to be beaten.

Of course I have criticisms. I think that all thru Part I there is too much likeness to Pepys Diary—too much He arose, went to the office, came home, dressed in so and so, came down, found Ludowica (glorious woman! glorious!) dressed in so and so, and Caroline in so and so, and Myrtle as follows, they sat down in such and such an order, ate these various details—and then next evening the same exact schedule all over again. So, too, Jasper too definitely takes the train each time he goes to Philadelphia.

Eh? Go to hell then. But it's true. I feel you had too much "material" (hear the man curse!) on your hands, and couldn't—in this day of Hoover—abear to throw any of the beautiful drapery away. Whereas in the past part, viewing the stuff not as material but as life, you don't try to get it all in—you dress Marriannnnaa or whatever her name is, but don't insist on not leaving out one single camisole. (p. 240)

Sinclair Lewis, in an extract from his letter to Joseph Hergesheimer on November 3, 1917 reprinted by permission of the Executors of the Estate of Sinclair Lewis), in American Literature, *Vol. XXXVIII, No. 2, May, 1966, pp. 239-41.*

JOSEPH HERGESHEIMER   (essay date 1918)

[*Hergesheimer flippantly recalls his early career and indicates pride in commercial success acquired by pandering to popular literary tastes.*]

The students of the earnest school of American "literary" autobiography can have but an overwhelming condemnation for the course which led me to the publication of my books and stories. I am certain that, in addition, they would be affronted. The actual facts are rather an amazing refutation of a number of celebrated "moral truths". Men with a nice sense of performing long-drawn and disagreeable duties will find nothing here to reassure them that virtue is its own reward, or rather that such virtue only is rewarded. (p. 8)

Asked for explanations by a large class for the study of story writing, I sat in a silent quandary. . . . The instructor gently prodded me: they want to know about the tricks by which you get effects, he put in. This was not helpful. In self-defense I repeated the history of my first two published novels. One, of which a thousand copies were exempt from royalties, sold nearly nine hundred; the single financial activity connected with the other was the privilege of later buying the copyright and plates.

I was . . . opposed to both providence and propriety, for the subject of one novel was a boy's purity   in a world where that quality is a cause for excruciating jest—and the second the failure of an aging man to repair a spiritual wrong with gold. People, I learned, preferred to read of immaculate young women and be reassured concerning the money to the obtaining of which they sacrificed so much. The earlier indifference gave place to a prodigious amount of advice.

It was continued by the editors who wrote me after a story or so appeared in a highly reputable place. Enthusiastic letters arrived and I answered enthusiastically with manuscripts. The admonitions: our readers demand more optimistic and vital stuff. More action! Mary, the daughter of the wealthy manufacturer, must marry Alfred, the laborer, who at imminent peril bursts open the fire-escape doors locked by the villain and releases the panic-stricken girls in the loft. Still more action, if Alfred is equally the child of a wealthy manufacturer in disguise.

I was, in addition, condemned for dealing with a love slightly different from the eugenic legend of the stork, and for deducing from the movement of women's skirts that they were propelled by legs. Or else I was metaphorically pounded on the back and invited to write, for disturbing sums, gingery serials. Without conviction in either direction, I fell between. It was then discovered by the erudite that my books held actual grammatical errors—infinitives were severed, adjectives crowded in unauthorized procession. These criminal facts were exposed; yet, in spite of them, I saw a novel of mine being read in a Pullman car. In spite of them other publishers appeared and other readers.

Almost nothing can be said in defense of such a career, a composition of wilful idleness and labor, unsupported by any vision of success. It is obviously a provocation to virtue that,

as a result, I should be able to smoke very long and very pale brown cigars with an import stamp on the box. (p. 11)

If my first novel had been of the "vital" sort people prefer, it might have sold half a million copies instead of nearly nine hundred. That is a consideration; but grass can be only so green, a terrier no more than faithful. . . .

There is brandy on the sideboard, . . . and cigarettes before breakfast, and shelves of books largely condemned or ignored. . . . The breeze—so finely ruffling the maples—continues to blow on the just and unjust. Babylon stands. I have written the last word of another novel preposterous now in time and setting. It will be published while countless other books written by the most exemplary will be refused, and justly annoyed superiority will endure the strain of again seeing my self-indulgent countenance looking out at them from the pages of their favorite reliable journals. . . . Tough! (p. 12)

Joseph Hergesheimer, "Some Veracious Paragraphs" (reprinted by permission of the Literary Estate of Joseph Hergesheimer), in The Bookman, *New York, Vol. XLVIII, No. 1, September, 1918, pp. 8-12.*

M[AXWELL] A[NDERSON]   (essay date 1919)

[*One of America's leading dramatists during the 1930s Anderson is noteworthy for his successful reintroduction of verse drama to the stage and for his adherence to Aristotelian concepts of dramatic content. Anderson's artistic and critical theories were closely concerned with the need for individual integrity, bravery, and other high values. Writing early in his career, Anderson offers a generally favorable review of* Java Head *and discusses Hergesheimer's handling of the novel's dramatic elements.*]

A rosy, normal girl, waking to the morning of her eleventh birthday and banishing by taking thought the childish fancy of personality in chairs; an ancient, plethoric sea-captain, angered with the commercial generation of clipper-ships that gather meagrely enough at this failing port of Salem; a trader who has lived too long in China, burned hollow with strange hectic pleasures; the Manchu wife of an American sea-captain, poised and astute is an insoluble situation among the élite of a provincial harbor city; and over these the dimness of dark old weary ways and days—shadowed with obsolete prejudices, and the clouds of settling age—drugged with the stench of forsaken wharves. . . . Such is the air of Java Head, and such are its people. No other city would have served so well as Salem for the setting were it not that we remember it has served the purpose before. Is it Salem or the tradition about Salem that remains as Hawthorne left it?

But these things are not all of ***Java Head,*** nor half its virtues. Hergesheimer has an immense capacity for putting himself in the other fellow's place. Even the task, difficult to the verge of impossibility, of following Taou Yuen through the nuances of aristocratic Chinese reflection that follow her arrival in dowdy, churchly Salem is carried off with a show of likelihood, though this is the weakest twist in the slight history. It is the author's method to tell the story mainly from within the minds of his protagonists, shifting his vantage ground from psyche to psyche as the action calls him. He reveals a virtuosity in human experience quite amazing to the student of narrative method. The happenings are dated in history by the California gold rush and Polk's administration, and about these outstanding facts contributive evidence of the epoch is piled in convincing confusion. It is no easy matter to assume an age so near as 1848, and vastly difficult to work out the inter-relations of character that made up two households in that day. All this is well done in *Java Head*. It is done by means of half-lights and suggestion. Boldness of execution is entirely foreign to the fabric. Though the plot is coherent and clear it is woven of beginnings and endings, hints and asides. It avoids forthright situations and conclusive struggle, evading you as your own life evades you, even at the end. For the crisis is the almost casual death of Taou Yuen, a tragedy which we understand only by implication, and imperfectly. Our knowledge of the people and events that lead up to it is built of such wavering material that we find ourselves a little at a loss in regard to motives. Let us admit that this too is much like life. The police court may make out clear records, and the jury come to crystal conclusions, yet there has been no perfectly explicable murder for the reason that we have only tag-ends of exterior evidence from which to judge. Hergesheimer constructs his world deliberately and artfully of tag-ends. He puts so much attention on details that we find it necessary to invent a whole to fit the parts vouchsafed us, much as a scientist recovers the mastodon from a tangle of wasted bones.

Readers of *The Three Black Pennys* will find in *Java Head* an increasing tendency to dodge crucial scenes. And since our beliefs go back so commonly to our capacities it is probably fair to say that the author of *Java Head* has less dramatic talent than is common in a good novelist, less than he could use to the advantage of his popularity. The interest he rouses in these people of a former time is only faintly personal. There is certainly nothing gripping in a story that progresses by successive pastels, however much we may admire them. It is as if the author rebuked us for demanding drama with the remark that "there is no drama in life. The most momentous things happen merely by the way. Even death is a mild disturbance, like a pebble tossed to sea. The only tragedy is our eternal futility." . . . But we must admit that it is after all a stage of well calculated illusions, of true though faded, disintegrating beauty. It is content to suggest rather than simulate reality. It never affects the pulse nor moves to more than mild sympathy, but it is sincere and adequate in an age that has borne with much bumping and squeaking of pulleys behind the curtain as a prelude to moral rhetoric interspersed with true love and tears. (pp. 123-24)

> M[axwell] A[nderson], "Salem Revisited," in The New Republic (*reprinted by permission of* The New Republic; © *1919 The New Republic, Inc.), Vol. XVIII, No. 225, February 22, 1919, pp. 123-24.*

CONRAD AIKEN (essay date 1919)

[*An American man of letters best known as a poet, Aiken was deeply influenced by the psychological and literary theories of Sigmund Freud, Havelock Ellis, Edgar Allan Poe, and Henri Bergson, among others, and is considered a master of literary stream of consciousness. In reviews noted for their perceptiveness and barbed wit, Aiken exercised his theory that "criticism is really a branch of psychology." His critical position, according to Rufus A. Blanshard, "insists that the traditional notions of 'beauty' stand corrected by what we now know about the psychology of creation and consumption. Since a work of art is rooted in the personality, conscious and unconscious, of its creator, criticism should deal as much with those roots as with the finished flower." Below, Aiken praises* Linda Condon, *comparing the book to* Java Head.]

Mr. Hergesheimer is already known in England through the publication of *The Three Black Pennys* and *Java Head*. Mr.

Cabell has had, I believe, no books published there, and has therefore probably not been heard of. Both authors have just brought out new novels—Mr. Hergesheimer his *Linda Condon*, and Mr. Cabell his *Jurgen*. And of both authors it is beginning to be said, as is customary here of an author who has reached a certain point, that "he is the great American novelist."

It is permissible, on this point, to remain skeptical. Yet these two novels are of great interest, and one of them at least, Mr. Hergesheimer's *Linda Condon*, is delightful. . . . I should like to be a little rash and say, with such reservations, that *Linda Condon* is one of the most vivid and charming portraits of women which we have had—lyric, colorful, accomplished in a minimum of space. As a study in the coefficient of the forces of heredity and environment it is, in fact, brilliant; and it is also, in a sense, amazingly a complement to *What Maisie Knew*, by Henry James—with the difference that the inheritance is not, in the case of Linda, vicious on both sides, nor even where vicious, unmitigatedly vicious; and that Mr. Hergesheimer does not concern himself solely with the childhood of Linda, as James did with Maisie, but in Linda's later life unfolds gradually, with a fine contrapuntal sense of inevitability, the many deep implications of the prelude. Mr. Hergesheimer's analysis of character is acute. Linda, by a kind of miracle, like an exotic flower, grows before our eyes, grows and yet seems not to change, retains even after many disenchantments a singular, remote, cool, childlikeness of mind. The conception is a finer one than anything in *Java Head*, though it will be obvious that the *milieu* is less charmingly ready to Mr. Hergesheimer's hand than, in that book, Salem was. Perhaps it is this that gives one a recurring sense of disappointment—one misses in *Linda Condon* the tranquillity, the slow grave beauty of style, for which Salem gave, in the first fifty pages of *Java Head*, so happy an opportunity. May one suspect also that the touch is not always quite so sure? Mr. Hergesheimer is not, for example, at his best when he describes the talk of artists. Or does he not take them quite so seriously as he seems to? A minor point, no doubt, and more than offset by the many occasions on which he reminds one richly that the novel is lineally descended from the narrative poem.

I have not dwelt further, in the case of Mr. Hergesheimer, on the presence in his work of what I defined earlier as the "emotional sterility" which blights so much contemporary American work; if one feels this at all in *Java Head* and *Linda Condon*, one feels it only a little, in retrospect, and less as if it were something *in* these novels than as if it were something which in the most impalpable of ways hung over them. It is a suspicion rather than a charge. (pp. 144-45)

> Conrad Aiken, "James Branch Cabell" (*originally published as "Letters from America, II: Two American Novelists," in* The Athenaeum, *No. 4676, December 12, 1919), in his* Collected Criticism (*copyright © 1935, 1939, 1940, 1942, 1951, 1958 by Conrad Aiken; reprinted by permission of Brandt & Brandt Literary Agents, Inc.), Oxford University Press, New York, 1968, pp. 143-48.**

KATHERINE MANSFIELD (essay date 1920)

[*Mansfield was an important pioneer in stream-of-consciousness literature and among the first English authors whose fiction depended upon incident rather than plot, thereby significantly influencing the modern short story form. Throughout 1919 and 1920, Mansfield conducted a weekly book-review column in* The

Athenaeum, a magazine edited at the time by her husband, John Middleton Murry. In the following review, she assesses Hergesheimer's collection of short fiction—Gold and Iron—to be a work of promise, though not of maturity.]

Mr. Joseph Hergesheimer is a writer whose few books have been hailed by the generous critic as masterpieces of their kind. Perhaps it is owing to the fact that he comes from America that their praise has been more formal, less familiar, less—may we say?—avuncular than that which they are accustomed to bestow upon our very own young men. In the latter case, it is their habit upon the appearance of a first novel, however superb they may consider it, to acknowledge the fact that the writer is a young writer. 'These young men have grown up in our midst. They have attended our schools, they have been to our universities and come down. While we do not dispute their genius for one moment, we question whether the finest flower, the ripest fruit is yet within our hands.' But Mr. Hergesheimer has been allowed no youth. They have been to the woods for him already; they have returned with an armful of those strange branches that look and smell like laurel, and there is nothing more to be said except to say it over again.

Nevertheless it is just this quality of 'promise' which we venture to think he possesses. It is more noticeable than ever in the stories collected under the title **'Gold and Iron.'** These three stories are all most obviously the work of a writer who feels a great deal more than he can at present express. They are in form very similar. In the long, slow approach to the 'crisis,' he writes well and freely; he takes his time, one has the impression that he feels, here, at this point he is safe, and can afford to let himself go. But when the heart of the story is reached, when there is nothing left to depend upon—to cling to—then he is like a young swimmer who can even swim very well, disport himself unafraid and at ease as long as he knows that the water is not out of his depth. When he discovers that it is—he disappears. So does Mr. Hergesheimer. But watching sympathetically from the bank, we hope the disappearance is only temporary. (pp. 157-58)

> *Katherine Mansfield, "Promise" (originally published in* The Athenaeum, *No. 4684, February 6, 1920), in her* Novels and Novelists, *edited by J. Middleton Murry (copyright 1930, copyright renewed © 1958, by Alfred A. Knopf, Inc.; reprinted by permission of The Society of Authors as the literary representative of the Estate of Katherine Mansfield), Knopf, 1930, pp. 157-58.*

CARL VAN DOREN (essay date 1921)

[Van Doren is considered one of the most perceptive critics of the first half of the twentieth century. He worked for many years as a professor of English at Columbia University and served as literary editor and critic of The Nation *and* The Century *during the 1920s. A founder of the Literary Guild and author or editor of several American literary histories, Van Doren was also a critically acclaimed historian and biographer. Howard Moss wrote of him: "His virtues, honesty, clarity and tolerance are rare. His vices, occasional dullness and a somewhat monotonous rhetoric, are merely, in most places, the reverse coin of his excellence." In the following review, Van Doren offers a critical overview of Hergesheimer's work, and finds* Linda Condon *to be the author's masterpiece.]*

Joseph Hergesheimer employs his creative strategy over the precarious terrain of the decorative arts, some of his work lying on each side of the dim line which separates the most consum-mate artifice of which the hands of talent are capable from the essential art which springs naturally from the instincts of genius. On the side of artifice, certainly, lie several of the shorter stories in **Gold and Iron** and **The Happy End,** for which, he declares, his grocer is as responsible as any one; and on the side of art, no less certainly, lie at least **Java Head,** in which artifice, though apparent now and then, repeatedly surrenders the field to an art which is admirably authentic, and **Linda Condon,** nearly the most beautiful American novel since Hawthorne and Henry James.

Standing thus in a middle ground between art and artifice Mr. Hergesheimer stands also in a middle ground between the unrelieved realism of the newer school of American fiction and the genteel moralism of the older. (p. 122)

Mr. Hergesheimer does not, of course, merely blunder into beauty; his methods are far from being accidental; by deliberate aims and principles he holds himself close to the regions of the decorative. He likes the rococo and the Victorian, ornament without any obvious utility, grace without any busy function. He refuses to feel confident that the passing of elegant privilege need be a benefit. . . . For himself he clings sturdily, ardently, to loveliness wherever he finds it—preferring, however, its richer, its elaborated forms.

To borrow an antithesis remarked by a brilliant critic in the work of Amy Lowell, Mr. Hergesheimer seems at times as much concerned with the stuffs as with the stuff of life. His landscapes, his interiors, his costumes he sets forth with a profusion of exquisite details which gives his texture the semblance of brocade—always gorgeous but now and then a little stiff with its splendors of silk and gold. An admitted personal inclination to "the extremes of luxury" struggles in Mr. Hergesheimer with an artistic passion for "words as disarmingly simple as the leaves of spring—as simple and as lovely in pure color—about the common experience of life and death"; and more than anything else this conflict explains the presence in all but his finest work of occasional heavy elements which weight it down and the presence in his most popular narratives of a constant lift of beauty and lucidity which will not let them sag into the average.

One comes tolerably close to the secret of Mr. Hergesheimer's career by perceiving that, with an admirable style of which he is both conscious and—very properly—proud, he has looked luxuriously through the world for subjects which his style will fit. Particularly has he emancipated himself from bondage to nook and corner. The small inland towns of **The Lay Anthony,** the blue Virginia valleys of **Mountain Blood,** the evolving Pennsylvania iron districts of **The Three Black Pennys,** the antique Massachusetts of **Java Head,** the fashionable hotels and houses of **Linda Condon,** the scattered exotic localities of the short stories—in all these Mr. Hergesheimer is at home with the cool insouciance of genius, at home as he could not be without an erudition founded in the keenest observation and research.

At the same time, he has not satisfied himself with the bursting catalogues of some types of naturalism. . . . He has loved the scenes wherein his events are transacted; he has brooded over their moods, their significances. Neither pantheistic, however, nor very speculative, Mr. Hergesheimer does not endow places with a half-divine, a half-satanic sentience; instead he works more nearly in the fashion of his master Turgenev, or of Flaubert, scrutinizing the surfaces of landscapes and cities and human habitations until they gradually reveal what—for the particular observer—is the essence of their charm or horror, and come, obedient to the evoking imagination, into the picture.

Substantial as Mr. Hergesheimer makes his scene by a masterful handling of locality, he goes still further, adds still another dimension, by his equally masterful handling of the past as an element in his microcosm. . . . Readers in general hardly notice how large a use of history appears in, for instance, *The Three Black Pennys* and *Java Head*. The one goes as far back as to colonial Pennsylvania for the beginning of its chronicle and the other as far as to Salem in the days of the first clipper ship; and yet by no paraphernalia of languid airs or archaic idioms or strutting heroics does either of the novels fall into the orthodox historical tradition. They have the vivid, multiplied detail of a contemporary record. And this is the more notable for the reason that the characters in each of them stand against the background of a highly technical profession—that of iron-making through three generations, that of shipping under sail to all the quarters of the earth. The wharves of Mr. Hergesheimer's Salem, the furnaces of his Myrtle Forge, are thick with accurate, pungent, delightful facts.

If he has explored the past in a deliberate hunt for picturesque images of actuality with which to incrust his narrative, and has at times—particularly in *The Three Black Pennys*—given it an exaggerated patina, nevertheless he has refused to yield himself to the mere spell of the past and has regularly subdued its "colors and scents and emotions" to his own purposes. His materials may be rococo, but not his use of them. The conflict between his personal preference for luxury and his artistic passion for austerity shows itself in his methods with history: though the historical periods which interest him are bounded, one may say, by the minuet and the music-box, he permits the least possible contagion of prettiness to invade his plots. They are fresh and passionate, simple and real, however elaborate their trappings. With the fullest intellectual sophistication, Mr. Hergesheimer has artistically the courage of naïveté. He subtracts nothing from the common realities of human character when he displays it in some past age, but preserves it intact. The charming erudition of his surfaces is added to reality, not substituted for it.

Without question the particular triumph of these novels is the women who appear in them. Decorative art in fiction has perhaps never gone farther than with Taou Yuen, the marvelous Manchu woman brought home from Shanghai to Salem as wife of a Yankee skipper in *Java Head*. She may be taken as focus and symbol of Mr. Hergesheimer's luxurious inclinations. By her bewildering complexity of costume, by her intricate ceremonial observances, by the impenetrability of her outward demeanor, she belongs rather to art than to life—an Oriental Galatea radiantly adorned but not wholly metamorphosed from her native marble. Only at intervals does some glimpse or other come of the tender flesh shut up in her magnificent garments or of the tender spirit schooled by flawless, immemorial discipline to an absolute decorum. That such glimpses come just preserves her from appearing a mere figure of tapestry, a fine mechanical toy. The Salem which before her arrival seems quaintly formal enough immediately thereafter seems by contrast raw and new, and her beauty glitters like a precious gem in some plain man's house.

Much the same effect, on a less vivid scale, is produced in *The Three Black Pennys* by the presence on the Pennsylvania frontier—it is almost that—of Ludowika Winscombe, who has always lived at Court and who brings new fragrances, new dainty rites, into the forest; and in *Mountain Blood* by the presence among the Appalachian highlands of that ivory, icy meretrix Meta Beggs who plans to drive the best possible bar-

gain for her virgin favors. Meta carries the decorative traits of Mr. Hergesheimer's women to the point at which they suggest the marionette too much; by his methods, of course, he habitually runs the risk of leaving the flesh and blood out of his women. He leaves out, at least, with no fluttering compunctions, any special concern for the simpler biological aspects of the sex. . . . (pp. 123-28)

Such robust doctrine is a long way from the customary sentimentalism of novelists about maids, wives, mothers, and widows. Indeed, Mr. Hergesheimer, like Poe before him, inclines very definitely toward beauty rather than toward humanity, where distinctions may be drawn between them. In Linda Condon, however, his most remarkable creation, he has brought humanity and beauty together in an intimate fusion. Less exotic than Taou Yuen, Linda, with her straight black bang and her extravagant simplicity of taste, is no less exquisite. . . . It is as the poet musing upon the fleet passage of beauty rather than as the satirist mocking at the vanity of human wishes that Mr. Hergesheimer traces the career of Linda Condon; but both poet and satirist meet in his masterpiece.

A woman as lovely as a lyric, she is almost as insensible as a steel blade or a bright star. The true marvel is that beauty so cold can provoke such conflagrations. Granted—and certain subtle women decline to grant it—that Linda with her shining emptiness could have kindled the passion she kindles in the story, what must be the blackness of her discovery that when her beauty goes she will have left none of the generous affection which, had she herself given it through life, she might by this time have earned in quantities sufficient to endow and compensate for her old age! Mr. Hergesheimer does not soften the blow when it comes—he even adds to her agony the clear consciousness that she cannot feel her plight as more passionate natures might. But he allows her, at the last, an intimation of immortality. From her unresponding beauty, she sees, her sculptor lover has caught a madness eventually sublimated to a Platonic vision which, partially forgetful of her as an individual, has made him and his works great. Without, in the common way, modeling her at all, he has snared the essence of her spirit and has set it—as such mortal things go—everlastingly in bronze.

If Mr. Hergesheimer offers Linda in the end only the hard comfort of a perception come at largely through her intellect, still as far as the art of his novel is concerned he has immensely gained by his refusal to make any trivial concession to natural weaknesses. His latest conclusion is his best. *The Lay Anthony* ends in accident, *Mountain Blood* in melodrama; *The Three Black Pennys,* more successful than its predecessors, fades out like the Penny line; *Java Head* turns sharply away from its central theme, almost as if *Hamlet* should concern itself during a final scene with Horatio's personal perplexities. Now the conclusions of a novelist are on the whole the test of his judgment and his honesty; and it promises much for fiction that Mr. Hergesheimer has advanced so steadily in this respect through his seven books.

He has advanced, too, in his use of decoration, which reached its most sumptuous in *Java Head* and which in *Linda Condon* happily began to show a more austere control. The question which criticism asks is whether Mr. Hergesheimer has not gone as far as a practitioner of the decorative arts can go, and whether he ought not, during the remainder of the eminent career which awaits him, to work rather in the direction marked by *Linda Condon* than in that marked by *Java Head*. The rumor that his friends advise him to become a "period novelist" must disquiet his admirers—even those among them who cannot think him likely to act upon advice so dangerous to his art. Doubtless he could go on and write another *Salammbô*, but he does not need to: he has already written *Java Head*. When a novelist has reached the limits of decoration there still stretches out before him the endless road—which Mr. Hergesheimer has given evidence that he can travel—of the interpretation and elucidation of human character and its devious fortunes in the world. (pp. 128-31)

> Carl Van Doren, ''Art: Joseph Hergesheimer,'' in The Nation *(copyright 1921* The Nation *magazine, The Nation Associates, Inc.), Vol. CXII, No. 2916, May 25, 1921 (and reprinted in his* Contemporary American Novelists: 1900-1920, *The Macmillan Company, 1922, pp. 122-31).*

JÁMES BRANCH CABELL   (essay date 1921)

[*Combining extremes of lavish romance and degraded reality, idealistic fantasy and jaded disillusionment, Cabell was one of the outstanding oddities in American fiction. His most enduring achievement,* The Biography of Manuel *(1904-29), belongs to a tradition of fantasy literature that includes Edmund Spenser's* The Faerie Queene *and Jonathan Swift's* Gulliver's Travels. Beyond Life *(1919), an important collection of literary criticism which was written to introduce the* Biography, *outlines the literary and philosophic concepts which serve as its foundation. Cabell adhered to a special definition of fiction which allowed him to portray glorified adventures beyond mundane reality without falsifying what he saw as the harsh truths of existence: the suffering of life, the emptiness of death, and a permanent alienation at the core of even the most intimate human relations. Cabell's most important later criticism appears in* Some of Us *(1930), a defense of several contemporary writers—including Elinor Wylie, Ellen Glasgow, and Hergesheimer—against the trend of New Humanist criticism, which demanded the subservience of art to moral and social issues. In an essay which, in part, parodies Hergesheimer's style, Cabell finds that Hergesheimer is not a technically ''correct'' writer, but that ultimately he is a great writer whose works evoke dream-like beauty.*]

So say they, speak they, and tell they the tale, in ''literary gossip,'' that Joseph Hergesheimer ''wrote'' for a long while before an iota of his typing was transmuted into ''author's proof.'' And the tale tells how for fourteen years he could find nowhere any magazine editor to whose present needs a Hergesheimer story was quite suited. (p. 7)

So Joseph Hergesheimer kept on with his foolishness, without any gleam of success, or even (they report) any word of encouragement. (pp. 7-8)

This Joseph Hergesheimer did: and that is the fable's significant point. (p. 8)

Yes, it is the boy's illogical pertinacity that is the fable's point, because it so plausibly explains why nearly all the men in Mr. Hergesheimer's books are hag-ridden by one or another sole desire which spurs them toward a definite goal at every instant of their mimic lives. These men but variously reflect, I take it, that younger Hergesheimer's ''will to write,'' that unconquerable will. (p. 9)

It explains to me the Hergesheimer women, too, those troublingly ornamental odalisques. They are fine costly toys, tricked out in curious tissues: and, waiting for the strong male's leisure, they smile cryptically. They will divert him by and by, when the day's work is dispatched, maintaining their own thoughts inviolate, even in the instant of comminglement wherein the strongest man abates reserve: but their moment is not daylit, for the Hergesheimer women are all-incongruous with what is done during office hours, nor are they to be valued then. Sometimes they are embodied ideals, to be sure, remotely prized as symbols or else grasped as trophies to commemorate the nearing of the goal: but for the most part they rank candidly as avocational interests. I find nowhere in Joseph Hergesheimer's stories any record of intimacy and confidence between a man and a woman. . . . And this too, I think, reflects that all-important formative fourteen years wherein, whatever may have been Mr. Hergesheimer's conduct of his relatively unimportant physical life, his fundamental concernments were pursued in a realm, of necessity, uninhabited by women. (pp. 9-10)

[In] all that is to-day accessible of Mr. Hergesheimer's creative feats—with one exception duly noted hereinafter—there is a patent negligence, and indeed an ostentatious avoidance, of any aiming toward popularity. That during the fourteen years young Hergesheimer labored toward the applause and cheques of a ''best seller,'' is to the considerate inconceivable. . . .

No, Mr. Hergesheimer's monomania, one estimates, was then, just as it seems to be to-day, to write for his own delectation—in large part because he could not help it, and in part with the hope of, somehow and some day, obtaining an audience with the same or, at any rate, a kindred sense of beauty. . . . This, to be sure, is always a vain aspiration. (p. 11)

''Beauty'' . . . is by the judicious conceded to be an unembodiable thought, not even quite to be grasped by the mind; and certainly never nicely nor with any self-content to be communicated via the pages of a book, wherein are preserved, at best, the faded petals and the flattened crumbling stalks of what seemed lovely once to somebody who is as dead as are these desiccated relics of his ardor and of his disputable taste.

In brief, it may be granted—and by Mr. Hergesheimer most cheerfully of all persons—that during these fourteen years Mr. Hergesheimer was attempting the preposterously impossible. (pp. 11-12)

Now, to my thinking, there is something curiously similar to that unreasonable endeavor to be found in all the Hergesheimer novels. Here always I find portrayed, with an insistency and a reiteration to which I seem to detect a queer analogue in the writings of Christopher Marlowe, men laboring toward the unattainable, and a high questing foiled. No one of the five novels varies from this formula.

Anthony Ball, of *The Lay Anthony,* strives toward the beauty of chastity—not morally concerned one way or the other, but resolute to preserve his physical purity for the sake of a girl whose body, he finds at last, has long ago been ravished by worms. Again there is in *Mountain Blood* no hint of moral-mongering—for Mr. Hergesheimer is no more concerned with moral values than is the Decalogue—when Gordon Makimmon toils toward the beauty of atonement, to die in all a broken man, with his high goal yet gleaming on the horizon untouched. The three black Pennys flounder toward the beauty of a defiant carnal passion, which through the generations scorches and defiles, and burns out futilely by and by, leaving only slag where the aspiring lovely fire was. And through the formal garden ways of *Java Head* pass feverishly at least five persons who struggle (and fretfully know their failure to be fore-doomed) toward the capturing of one or another evincement of beauty, with the resultant bodily demolishment of three of them and the spiritual maiming of the others.

That which one, for whatever reason, finds most beautiful must be sought; it is a goal which one seeks futilely, and with discomfort and peril, but which one seeks inevitably: such is the "plot" of these four novels. Such is also, as I need hardly say, the "plot" of the aforementioned fourteen years wherein not anything tangible was achieved except the consuming of youth and postage. . . .

Nor does the dénouement differ, either, in any of these novels: the postman comes with the plethoric envelope which signals from afar that the result of much high-hearted striving is not quite suited to the present needs of this world's editor; and sometimes the postman is Age, but more often he is Death. (pp. 13-14)

Now the fifth, and incomparably the finest and loveliest, of the Hergesheimer novels is *Linda Condon,* which renders self-confessedly a story of "the old service of beauty, of the old gesture toward the stars"—"here never to be won, never to be realized"—of the service which "only beauty knows and possesses". . . . For *Linda Condon* is to be valued less as the life-history of a woman than as the depiction—curt, incisive, and yet pitying—of a shrine that, however transiently, was hallowed.

At the exacting workaday pursuit of being a human being this Linda fails, fails chilled and wistful. She has, like more of us than dare proclaim the defect, no talent whatever for heart-felt living, so that most persons seem but to pass grayly upon the horizon of her consciousness, like unintelligible wraiths gesticulating,—and always remaining somehow disjunct and not gravely important,—the while that all the needs and obligations of one's corporal life must be discharged with an ever-present sense of their queer triviality. Toward nobody, neither toward Linda Condon's mother nor lover, nor husband, nor children, may she, the real Linda, quite entertain any sense of actual attachment, far less of intimacy. . . .

Meanwhile she has her loveliness, not of character or mind, but a loan of surpassing physical beauty. And to Linda Condon her own bright moving carcass becomes a thing to be tended and preserved religiously, because beauty is divine, and she herself is estimable, if at all, as the fane which beauty briefly inhabits. . . . And by and by, under time's handling, her comeliness is shriveled, and her lovers are turned to valueless dust: but first, has Linda's lost young beauty been the buried sculptor's inspiration, and it has been perpetuated in everlasting bronze. The perfection of Linda Condon's youth is never to perish, and is not ever to be dulled by old age or corrupted in death. She comprehends this as she passes out of the story, a faded, desolate and insignificant bit of rubbish, contented to know that the one thing which really meant much to her is, as if by a miracle, preserved inviolate. The statue remains, the immutable child of Linda's comeliness and Pleydon's genius, the deathless offspring of transitory things.

Beauty is divine; a power superior and even elfinly inimical to all human moralities and rules of thumb, and a divinity which must unflinchingly be served: that, in this book as always, is Mr. Hergesheimer's text. For this is the divinity which he, too, serves unflinchingly, with strangely cadenced evocations, in striving to write perfectly of beautiful happenings.

It is an ideal here approached even more nobly than in the preceding Hergesheimer books. Nowhere has Joseph Hergesheimer found an arena more nicely suited to the excercise of his most exquisite powers than in this modern tale of *domnei,*—of the worship of woman's beauty as, upon the whole, Heav-

en's finest sample of artistic self-expression, and as, in consequence, the most adequate revelation of God; and as such a symbol, therefore, a thing to be revered above all else that visibly exists, even by its temporary possessor. That last is Mr. Hergesheimer's especial refinement upon a tenet sufficiently venerable to have been nodded over by Troy's gray-gearded councillors when Helen's skirts were rustling by. . . . (pp. 15-16)

[Dismissing] *Gold and Iron* (after some reflection) with unqualified applause, I take up *The Happy End;* and of the seven stories contained therein six seem to me to display a cornerstone of eminently "popular" psychology, ranging from the as yet sacrosanct belief that all Germans are perfectly horrid people, to the axiom that the quiet and unrespected youngest brother is invariably the one to exterminate the family enemies, and duly including the sentiment that noble hearts very often beat under ragged shirts. And I am made uneasy to see these uplifting faiths—these literary baking-powders more properly adapted to the Horrible Trites and the Gluepot Stews among reading-matter confectioners—thus utilized by a Joseph Hergesheimer.

I am made uneasy because I reason in this way: when Mr. Hergesheimer consciously is writing a short story to be printed next to advertising matter in some justly popular periodical, Mr. Hergesheimer, being rational and human, cannot but think of the subscribers to that popular periodical. . . . [Certainly] not many thousands of our fellow citizens can regard Mr. Hergesheimer at his best and purest with anything save bewildered abhorrence. So he must compromise,—subconsciously, I believe,—and must adapt his methods to the idiosyncrasies and limitations of his audience, very much as he probably refrains from addressing his cook in the heightened and consummated English of *San Cristóbal de la Habana.*

The danger is not that Joseph Hergesheimer will lower his ideals, nor in anything alter what he wishes to communicate; but is the fact that he must attempt to transmit these things into the vernacular and into the orbits of thought of his enormous audience, with the immaculate motive of making his ideas comprehensible. He cannot, being rational and human, but by and by be tempted yet further to endeavor—as he has flagrantly endeavored in the tale called *Tol'able David*—to convey his wayside apprehensions of life via some such always acceptable vehicle as the prehistoric fairy-tale cliché of the scorned and ultimately victorious third champion. This is with a vengeance the pouring of new wine into a usage-battered and always brazen cup which spoils the brew. . . .

Six of these stories, then, are beautifully written moral tales: although, to be sure, there is an alleviating seventh, in The Flower of Spain, which is a well-night perfect and a profoundly immoral work of art. (pp. 18-19)

Mr. Hergesheimer, even in the least worthy of his magazine stories, writes really well. . . .

But Mr. Hergesheimer always writes really well, once you have licensed his queer (and quite inexcusable) habit of so constantly interjecting proper names to explain to whom his, Hergesheimer's, pronoun refers. . . . I cannot but note in this place how discriminatingly Mr. Hergesheimer avoids the hurdles most commonly taken with strained leaps by the "stylist," through Mr. Hergesheimer's parsimony in the employment of similes; and how inexplicably he renders "anything from a chimneypot to the shoulders of a duchess' by—somehow—communicating the exact appearance of the thing described without evading the whole issue by telling you it is like something else. (p. 21)

Now this non-employment of time-approved devices seems even the more remarkable when you consider how intensely Joseph Hergesheimer realizes the sensuous world of his characters and, in particular, the optic world. He is the most insistently superficial of all writers known to me, in his emphasis upon shapes and textures and pigments.

His people are rendered from complexion to coat-tail buttons, and the reader is given precisely the creasing of each forehead and the pleating of their under-linen. Mr. Hergesheimer's books contain whole warehousefuls of the most carefully finished furniture in literature; and at quaint bric-à-brac he has no English equal. It is all visioned, moreover, very minutely. Joseph Hergesheimer makes you observe his chairs and panelings and wall-papers and window-curtains with an abnormal scrutiny. The scenery and the weather, too, are "done" quite as painstakingly, but these are indigenous to ordinary novels.

Now of course, like virtually every other practise of "realism," this is untrue to life: nobody does in living regard adjacent objects as attentively as the reader of a Hergesheimer story is compelled to note them. For one, I cannot quite ignore this fact, even when I read with most delight: and I sometimes wonder if Mr. Hergesheimer premeditatedly sits down to study an andiron or a fan for literary use, or whether his personal existence is actually given over to this concentration upon externals and inanimate things. But he was once a painter; and large residuals of the put-by art survive.

All this results, of course, in a "style" to which the reader is never quite oblivious. The Hergesheimer dramas—dramas wherein each of the players has a slight touch of fever—are enacted, with a refining hint of remoteness, behind the pellucid crystal of this "style," which sharpens outlines, and makes colors more telling than they appear to everyday observation, and brings out unsuspected details (seen now for the first time by the reader, with a pleasurable shock of delight), and just noticeably glazes all.

The Hergesheimerian panorama is, if I may plagiarize, a little truer than truth: and to turn from actual life to Joseph Hergesheimer's pages arouses a sensation somewhat akin to that sustained by a myopic person when he puts on spectacles. . . . (pp. 22-3)

Such, then, are this artist's materials: in a world of extraordinary vividness a drama of high questing foiled, a tragedy of beauty sought, with many blunders but singlemindedly, by monomaniacs,—in fine, a performance suggestively allied, in its essentials, to the smaller-scaled and unaudienced drama of the young man with the percipient eyes of a painter. . . .

These things are but the raw materials, . . .—the bricks and mortar and the scantlings,—for, of course, there is in Joseph Hergesheimer's books far more than plot or thought, or even "style": there is that indescribable transfiguring element which is magic.

When Linda Condon came to look closely at Pleydon's statue, you may remember, she noted in chief the statue's haunting eyes, and marveled to find them "nothing but shadows over two depressions." Very much the equivalent of that is the utmost to which one can lay a crude finger in appraising Mr. Hergesheimer's books. They are like other books in that they contain nothing more prodigious than words from the nearest dictionary put together upon quite ordinary paper. . . . But the eyes of Pleydon's statue—you may remember, too—for all that they were only indentations in wet clay, "gazed fixed and aspiring into a hidden dream perfectly created by his desire." (p. 24)

Now, at its purest, the art of the real Hergesheimer, the fundamental and essential thing about Joseph Hergesheimer, is just that intangible magic which he ascribes to his fictitious Pleydon. And the dream that Joseph Hergesheimer, too, has perfectly created by his desire, and seeks to communicate in wellnigh every line he has thus far published, I take to be "the old gesture toward the stars . . . a faith spiritual, because, here, it is never to be won, never to be realized."

It is, I think, the "gesture" of the materially unproductive fourteen years: and its logic, either then or now, is clearly indefensible. . . . [One] is conscious of "a warm indiscriminate thrill about the heart" and of a treacherous sympathy, which abhors reason. . . . Yes, one is conscious of a most beguiling sympathy, that urges one already to invest blind. Faith in what is to come very soon, but stays as yet unrevealed,—in *The Bright Shawl,* and in the retempered *Steel,* and in *Cytherea,* and even more particularly in *The Meeker Ritual,* which promises, to me at least, to reveal upon completion an especial prodigality of perturbing magics. (p. 25)

It is through distrust of this beguiling sympathy that I have spoken throughout with self-restraint, and have hedged so often with "I think" and "I believe" and "it seems to me," and have niggled over Hergesheimerian faults that are certainly tiny and possibly non-existent: because of my private suspicion that all my private notions about Joseph Hergesheimer are probably incorrect. To me, I confess, he appears a phenomenon a little too soul-satisfying to be entirely credible.

Pure reason does not brevet it as humanly possible that the Hergesheimer I privately find in the pages of the Hergesheimer books should flourish in any land wherein the self-respecting author is usually restricted to choose between becoming the butt or the buttress of mediocrity: so that I cautiously refrain from quite believing in this Joseph Hergesheimer as a physical manifestation in actual trousers . . . Indeed, his corporeal existence cannot well be conceded except upon the hypothesis that America has produced, and is even nourishing, a literary artist who may endure in the first rank. Which is absurd, of course, and a contention not to be supported this side of Bedlam, and, none the less, is my firm private belief to-day. (p. 26)

James Branch Cabell, in his Joseph Hergesheimer: An Essay in Interpretation *(copyright 1921 by James Branch Cabell; reprinted by permission of First & Merchants National Bank, Executor of the Estate of Margaret F. Cabell; originally published in a different version in* The Bookman, *New York, Vol. L, Nos. 3 & 4, November-December, 1919),* The Bookfellows, *1921, 27 p.*

HENRY SEIDEL CANBY (essay date 1922)

[*Canby was a professor of English at Yale and one of the founders of* The Saturday Review of Literature, *where he served as editor in chief from 1924-36. He was the author of many books, including* The Short Story in English *(1909), a history of that genre which was long considered the standard text for college students. Despite the high acclaim his writings received, Canby always considered himself primarily a teacher, whose declared aim was "to pass on sound values to the reading public." In the excerpt below, Canby concludes that Hergesheimer, writing in* Cytherea *about love in the decadent 1920s, does not achieve the necessary de-*

tachment that Edith Wharton shows in The Age of Innocence, *which was published shortly before Hergesheimer's novel. The two works are compared throughout Canby's essay.*]

Mrs. Wharton found the age of innocence in the 1870's; Mr. Hergesheimer discovers an age of no innocence in the 1920's. In "The Age of Innocence," the lovely May, a creature of society's conventions, loses her husband and then regains the dulled personality left from the fire of passion. In "Cytherea" the less lovely, but equally moral Fanny loses her Lee because she cannot satisfy his longings and nags when she fails. But she does not regain him when his love chase is over, because he is burned out. Athene and Aphrodite, the graces of the mind, the seductions of the person of the Countess Olenska, together draw Newland Archer, husband of May; but it is Aphrodite only, Cytherean Aphrodite, who, being sex incarnate, is more than mere temptations of the flesh, that wrecks Fanny's home.

In the '70's the poor innocents of society believed their code of honor impregnable against sex. They dressed against sex, talked against sex, kept sex below the surface. The suppression froze some of them into rigidity and stiffened all. But they had their compensations. By sacrificing freedom for personal desire they gained much security. Good husbands required more than a lure of the body to take them off. And when they gave up a great romance for respectability, like Newland Archer, at least they remained gentlemen. There was a tragedy of thwarted development, of martyred love, of waste; but at least self-respect, however misguided, remained.

Not so with this trivial, lawless country club set of the 1920's, drunk part of the time and reckless all of it, codeless, dutiless, restless. For the virtuous among them Aphrodite, a vulgar, shameless Aphrodite, was a nightly menace; for the weak among them (such as Peyton Morris), a passion to be resisted only by fear; for the wayward, like Lee, she was the only illusion worth pursuing. To resist for a woman was to become "blasted and twisted out of her purpose," to be "steeped in vinegar or filled with tallow"; to resist for a man was to lose the integrity of his personality. There were no moral compensations, for there is no morality but self-development, at least in Mr. Hergesheimer's town of Eastlake. There is no god for a man in love but Cytherea.

And this is one way of describing Mr. Hergesheimer's study of love in idleness in the 1920's. Another way would be to call it an essay upon insecurity, although the word essay is too dry to use in a story which is fairly awash with alcohol. The war, the story seems to say, sapped our security of property and comfort and life. But insecurity is an insidious disease that spreads, like bacteria, where strength is relaxed. It infects the lives of those who have lost their certainties and become doubtful of their wills. In this relaxed society of the 1920's, where nothing seemed certain but the need of money and a drink, insecurity spread into married life. Not even the well-mated were secure in the general decline of use and wont. A home wrecked by vague desires running wild—that is the theme of "Cytherea."

Or take a third view of this provocative book. The triangle we have had tiresomely with us, but it is woman's love that is, perversely, always the hero. Hergesheimer studies the man, studies him not as will, or energy, or desire a-struggle with duty or morality, but merely as sex. Man's sex in love, man's sex dominated by Cytherea, is his theme. This is new, at least in fiction, for there man is often swept away, but seldom dominated by sex. And indeed Hergesheimer has to find his man in the relaxed society to which I have referred, a society

wearied by unchartered freedom, where business is profitable but trivial, where duty and religion exist only as a convention, disregarded by the honest, upheld by the hypocritical, a society where Cytherea marks and grips her own. Even so, it is an achievement.

Cytherea in the story is a doll with a glamorous countenance, bought and cherished by Lee Randon as a symbol of what he did not find in his married life, what no man finds and keeps, because it is an illusion. Cytherea is Lee Randon's longing for emotional satisfaction, a satisfaction that is not to be of the body merely. And when he meets Savina Grove, a pathological case, whose violent sex emotions have been inhibited to the bursting point, he thinks (and fears) that he has found his heart's desire. In the old, old stories their elopement would have been their grand, their tragic romance. In this cruel novel it is tragic, for she dies of it; but she is not Cytherea; she is earthly merely; it is felt that she is better dead.

It is a cruel story, cruel in its depiction of an almost worthless society with just enough of the charm of the Restoration to save it from beastliness; cruel in its unsparing analyses of man's sex impulses (by all odds the most valuable part of the story); cruel particularly because the ruined Lee Randon is a good fellow, honester than most, kinder than he knows to individuals, although certain that there is no principle but selfishness, and that it is folly to limit desire for the sake of absolutes, like righteousness, or generalities, like the human race. It is a cruel study of women, for Fanny, the model of the domestic virtues, has lost her innocent certainties of the triumph of the right and at the first conflict with Cytherea becomes a common scold; cruel to Savina Grove, who, in spite of her exquisiteness, is only a psychoanalyst's problem; cruel to us all in exposing so ruthlessly how distressing it is to live by stale morality, yet how devastating to act with no guide but illusory desire.

All this is not new in outline. One can find the essence of this story in monkish manuals. There the menace of Cytherea was not evaded. There the weaknesses of man's sex were categoried with less psychology but more force. What is new in Hergesheimer's book is merely the environment in which his characters so disastrously move and an insight into the mechanism of their psychology which earlier writers lacked. I have called it a story of the age of no innocence, but that would be the author's term, not mine; for indeed his characters seem to display as naïve an innocence as Mrs. Wharton's of the laws of blood and will, and they know far less of practical morality. (pp. 217-21)

Critics will raise, and properly, a question as to the worth of his materials. He is not studying a "ripe" society, as was Mrs. Wharton, but the froth of the war, the spume of country clubs, the trivialities of the strenuous but unproductive rich. This is a just criticism as far as it goes, and it lessens the solidity, the enduring interest, of his achievement. True, it was in such a society that he could best pursue the wiles of Cytherea. He has a right to pitch his laboratory where he pleases, and out of some very sordid earth he has contrived some beauty. Nevertheless, you cannot make a silk purse out of a sow's ear, skilled though you may be.

I should be more inclined, however, in a comparison with Mrs. Wharton, to criticize his lack of detachment. That able novelist, who is bounded so exclusively in her little social world, nevertheless stands apart from it and sees it whole. Mr. Hergesheimer has his feet still deep in the soil. He is too much a part of his country club life. He means, perhaps, to be ironical, but in truth he is too sympathetic with the desires, emotional and esthetic, that he expresses to be ironical until the close. There is a surprise, too sharp a surprise, at the end of his novel, when one discovers that the moral is not "do and dare," but "all is vanity." He is so much and so lusciously at home with cock-tails, legs, limousine parties, stair-sittings, intra-matrimonial kissings (I mention the most frequent references) that one dis-trusts the sudden sarcasm of his finale. It would have been better almost if he had been a Count de Gramont throughout, for he has a *flair* for the surroundings of amorous adventure and is seldom gross; better still to have seen, as Mrs. Wharton saw, the picture in perspective from the first. His book will disgust some and annoy others because its art is muddied by a lingering naturalism and too highly colored by the predilec-tions of the artist.

It is a skilful art, nevertheless, and "Cytherea" confirms a judgment long held that Mr. Hergesheimer is one of the most skilful craftsmen in English in our day. And this I say in spite of his obvious failure to grasp inevitably the structure of the English sentence. He is one of the most honest analysts of a situation, also; one of the most fearless seekers of motives; one of the ablest practisers of that transmutation of obscure emotion into visible detail of dress, habit, expression, which is the real technique of the novelist. His fault is a defect in sympathy, a lack of spiritual appreciation, if I may use and leave undefined so old-fashioned a term. His virtue lies in the rich garment of experience which careful observation and skil-ful writing enable him to wrap about his imaginative concep-tions. It is this which makes his novels so readable for the discriminating at present, and will make them useful historical records in the future. One aspect of a troublesome period when the middle generation achieved the irresponsibility without the earnestness of youth he has caught in "Cytherea." It is un-fortunate that it is a partial portrait of important motives in people who themselves are of little importance; and it is doubly unfortunate that he has been too much a part of his muddy world to be as good an interpreter as he is a witness of its life. (pp. 221-23)

> *Henry Seidel Canby, "Mr. Hergesheimer's 'Cy-therea'," in* The Literary Review *(copyright, 1922, by N.Y. Evening Post, Inc.; reprinted from* The New York Post*), January 21, 1922 (and reprinted in his* Definitions: Essays in Contemporary Criticism, *Har-court, Brace and Company, 1922, pp. 217-23).*

HUGH WALPOLE (essay date 1922)

[*Walpole, a friend of Hergesheimer and himself a popular author of period fiction, glowingly reviews* The Bright Shawl.]

The only thing that is quite certain about Joseph Hergesheimer in this stage of his literary life is that he is an artist, and by artist I mean some one who loves both truth and beauty, who cares enough to work desperately hard to make that truth and that beauty clear, who has succeeded in making his revelation with a fashion different from any other artist. Because he cares for truth he is a realist, and because he cares for beauty he is a poet. The combination today is rare.

Every book that he has written has had moments of the com-pletest success, and every book that he has written has been a little short of its promise. This is because Hergesheimer is a man of infinite courage. His courage is the greatest of all his qualities, greater than his fine prose, greater than his unique gift for the visualization of beautiful things, greater than his power of creating character. Every book that he has written has been the result of this courage.

After "Java Head" it would have been easy enough for him to take the line of least resistance. Instead of doing so he wrote "Linda Condon," one of the most difficult attempts of our time. And after "Linda Condon" he wrote "Cytherea." He is himself absolutely. He writes with eyes fixed intensely on the flying form of beauty that he is pursuing, never on his public, never on his sales, never on his critics. . . .

Once again, in his new book, "The Bright Shawl," he takes the hardest way. This book would have been in the hands of almost any other writer a story of sensation. It offers for a writer of Mr. Hergesheimer's peculiar gifts almost extravagant temptations toward glittering color. Concerned with the Cuban struggle against Spanish domination, it has for its incident spies, sudden death, betrayals, torture, mystery. . . .

There is a wonderful scene in this book, the best scene that Mr. Hergesheimer has yet given us, the scene in the fencing school between Charles Abbott, the hero, and Gaspur de Vaca, the Spaniard. It is a scene that lends itself to melodrama. Hence it covers six short pages. There is no extraneous detail at all and there is a physical horror there that will never be forgotten by any spectator. The new restraint shown by the narration of this episode marks a fresh advance in Mr. Hergesheimer's artistic history.

But there is restraint also in all the underlying passion of the book. The two themes of Abbott's friendship and his patriotism are felt behind every line and are almost never brought to the surface. The business of the friendship between Charles Abbott and the young Cuban Andrea might have wallowed in senti-ment, and on the other hand it might have been conducted with so stern a hand that it failed to move.

It is here deeply moving and never for a moment sentimental.

The book, being by whom it is, is of course soaked in atmo-sphere, but it is an atmosphere of the soul as well as of physical life. It is an atmosphere quite peculiar to Mr. Hergesheimer's art. There was a time when he seemed to owe something to George Moore, something to Henry James, much to Joseph Conrad. He is now quite his own master. The last struggle between La Clavel and Santacilla is all this author's own, his own in its reality, its pathos, and a strange, symbolic effect which no other novelist now writing in English is able to secure.

We offer no suggestions as to whether "The Bright Shawl" is better or worse than "The Pennys," "Java Head" or "Cy-therea." It weaves quite definitely a new strand of color into the Hergesheimer pattern; it is a book of which America should be quietly but surely proud.

> *Hugh Walpole, "The New Hergesheimer Entry," in* The New York Times Book Review *(© 1922 by The New York Times Company; reprinted by permission), October 15, 1922, p. 1.*

ELLEN GLASGOW (essay date 1924)

[*Glasgow was one of America's foremost regional writers, and her work is often considered the first example of the powerful new Southern literature which dominated the American literary scene during the early twentieth century. Glasgow began her career at a time when most Southern fictions were romanticized portraits of the ideals and institutions lost during the Civil War. A native of Richmond, Virginia, she drew upon her rich knowledge of Virginia social life and manners as well as her deep under-*

standing of the South's complex history to rebel against the re-
gion's unrealistic tradition; she depicted the South's social and
moral code as restrictive and false, and satirized its idealization
of the past. In the following essay, she reviews Balisand, *a novel*
set in Virginia.]

In this frugal literary era, when "economy of material" is preached as sedulously as if economy were a virtue and not a necessity, it is encouraging to find a novelist who is not afraid of the great tradition. Whatever attributes of fashion Mr. Hergesheimer may possess, thinness of texture and brevity of style are not among them. His resources are apparently inexhaustible; and since he is gifted with discrimination, he adroitly weaves his abundance into a pattern of subdued richness and variety. Notwithstanding his fondness for ornamental detail, he is one of the few American novelists whose interpretations of life have depth as well as surface, though the depth is of intuition rather than intellect. With morality he is as little concerned as with decorum. Happily for him and for us he is untroubled by convictions; and except in **"Cytherea"** (where he is more of Puck and less of Ariel) "an ayrie spirit" inhabits the body of the Presbyterian Child.

In **"Balisand,"** Mr. Hergesheimer has again written the "novel of manner" as distinguished from the novel of manners. The place is picturesque Gloucester County in Virginia; the time is the age of Washington and Jefferson, an age of clipped box and wild roses. True to his temperament, Mr. Hergesheimer has selected a period when people who could afford it still wore what is known among historical novelists as costume; and the advantage of costume over clothes, any one who has ever worn costume, if only for a single evening, is obliged to acknowledge.

One is obliged to acknowledge, also, that, though **"Balisand"** reproduces a period, the value of the narrative depends less upon decoration than it does upon a precise analysis of human motive. In this book Mr. Hergesheimer uses historic occasion as a setting for a drama of the inner realities. Against a vivid tapestry of events he has projected a crowd of robust figures, in the midst of the turbulent politics of the time; yet one never forgets that the closely woven scene was created not as an end in itself, but as a background for the subjective processes of Richard Bale of Balisand. There are passages, doubtless, where the tumultuous politics seem to threaten the vitality of the characters; but this, as every one who has witnessed an election in Virginia must admit, is the usual procedure of politics. The clash of ideas and temperaments is admirably portrayed. On one side we find a privileged minority of Federalists, and on the other side Jefferson, the idol of the people, defying the minority, as idols of the people always have done and always will continue to do.

From this struggle and against this background the figures of the book emerge, dissolve, and emerge again more clearly. Now and then, Mr. Hergesheimer may have generalized too widely from a particular instance; here and there, he may have magnified a casual episode into a custom. He has shifted his lights and shadows at his discretion, intensifying or subduing the values of his perspective; but this subtle treatment of illusion is permissible in an artist whose aim it is to create character, not to copy a scene. Though the author's sympathy inclines toward the pictorial rather than the practical, the sum of his argument for the Bales of Balisand is not entirely convincing. The breed would have been improved by a dash of that "humility amounting almost to self-forgetfulness," which the "old gentleman of Maryland" found so impressive in the "Virginia gentlemen he met at the Springs."

But the imperishable legend which embalms, like a preserving fluid, the sacred mummy of the old Virginia gentleman, is honored chiefly by its absence in Mr. Hergesheimer's Gloucester. One imagines that the old Virginia gentleman must have been drunk indeed before he stooped to such sports in the servants' quarters as the author describes; and that he must have imbibed again when he dismissed so lightly the rigid obligations due from a guest to a hostess. It is not easy to believe that any race of men could have drunk so deeply and so frequently all other human activities or approaches to experience, until, in the end, she becomes as dry and as inadequate in flavor as a painted apricot. Even when, as in **"Balisand,"** we are introduced to a formal society, where women were confirmed in reticence and were taught from their cradles up that she who hesitates is loved, these blooming creatures are incapable of either coyness or coldness. Lucia Mathews is brilliantly drawn. Every Virginian will recognize her as a familiar part of the social structure; yet she also, beneath her hard, smooth surface, is too tropical at the core for the temperate climate in which she has ripened; and accustomed to Mr. Hergesheimer's more dilatory masculine protagonists, we read, without surprise, that Richard Bale, who was damaged beyond repair and nearly twenty years too old, was at last, "swept into the deep reality of Lucia's passionate feeling." In this basket of nectarines how refreshingly piquant would be the tartness of an occasional apple.

But when the last word is said, one returns to the essential charm of the narrative. The years have perfected Mr. Hergesheimer's art while they have disciplined his exuberant imagination. Always interesting, always sincere in his treatment of life, he has written nothing more impressive than this realistic novel of the romantic past in Virginia. **"Balisand"** is a rich, a rare, a beautiful book.

Ellen Glasgow, "Old Virginia," in The Saturday
Review of Literature *(© 1924 Saturday Review Magazine Co.), Vol. I, No. 8, September 20, 1924, p. 123.*

JOSEPH WOOD KRUTCH   (essay date 1926)

[*Krutch is widely regarded as one of America's most respected literary and drama critics. Noteworthy among his works are* The American Drama since 1918 *(1939), which analyzes the most important dramas of the 1920s and 1930s, and "Modernism" in* Modern Drama *(1953), in which he stressed the need for twentieth-century playwrights to infuse their works with traditional humanistic values. A conservative and idealistic thinker, he was a consistent proponent of human dignity and the preeminence of literary art. In the following discussion of Hergesheimer's early works and review of* Tampico, *Krutch examines what he considers both the major strength and weakness of Hergesheimer's style: his preoccupation with glamorous and colorful detail.*]

In the days when Hergesheimer was first attracting critical attention his books refused to fit very well into the pattern of contemporary interests. . . . He could not be discussed in relation to the social and intellectual movements from which he seemed completely aloof and there was nothing in the way of classification to be done beyond linking him (rather strangely) with Miss Cather and saying of both of them that they were exclusively concerned with "Art."

Now "Art" is a vague term. Perhaps in the present instance it would be better to discard it entirely and to say instead that Mr. Hergesheimer is concerned most of all with appearances. Each of his most popular novels serves chiefly as the occasion for the creation of a colorful scene. **"The Three Black Pennys"** is a study in heredity, tracing the gradual modification of a family trait as it descends from one generation to another; **"Java Head"** delves a little into the American past; and **"Cytherea"** reveals Mr. Hergesheimer, for once, on the point of interesting himself in our changing morals. But in none does the chief interest arise out of the theme; it comes instead from the picturesqueness of the scene and, especially, from the contrasting colors. In the first two the same device is employed— the device of contrasting an exotic woman, brought from a far and highly civilized society, with the primitive American background—and in the third a somewhat similar effect is obtained by having the hero flee from his familiar surroundings in New York to a richly colorful background in Cuba. None is psychologically very penetrating, all are pictorially striking.

If in **"Linda Condon,"** with its study of a cold woman incapable of understanding either the passion or the idealism of which her beauty is the cause, Mr. Hergesheimer came nearer than in any other novel to transcending his limitation, **"The Bright Shawl"** represents his most complete and undisguised indulgence of all his tendencies. In **"Java Head"** and **"The Three Black Pennys"** he had not only endeavored to introduce non-pictorial elements, but he had, besides, followed the method of the greatest colorists and merely touched a somber background with vivid fragments. But in **"The Bright Shawl"** he abandoned himself to indulgence. Of character drawing or of psychology there is extremely little and we are asked to accept wholly upon faith both the young American who is seized by a romantic passion for Cuban liberty and the gorgeous Spanish dancer with whom he becomes involved. Nothing would be less likely to interest Mr. Hergesheimer than an abstract passion for political independence, but he is fascinated by the gesture which it can occasion, especially if these gestures can be performed by men and women versed in the elaborate ritual of aristocratic Spanish life. It is the spectacle of these men of the world, of the flashing figures of the half world with whom they consort, and of Havana rotting physically and spiritually in the blaze of the tropic sun, that fires his imagination. The shawl itself, symbol of his hero's memory, moves him to one of his most glowing passages:

> Such heat and such golden roses, all had been his against that background of perilous endeavor. . . . Its flowers took root, casting about splendor and perfume; the blue widened into the sky, the tenderness of the clasping sea; the dark greens were the shadows of the ceiba trees, the gloom of the jungles, the massed royal palms of the plains. And not only was it the setting, the country; its violent dissonances became cries, victorious or helpless, the sweep of reddened swords, the explosion of muskets. There was the blood that had welled into the laurel ditch of Cabanas; and, as well, the mysterious presence of Africa in the West.

Surely this Andalusian shawl is a symbol of more than the memory of the hero. It is a symbol of Mr. Hergesheimer's artistic ideal as well.

The cult of the picturesque has, however, its dangers. Outsides grow monotonous and if the devotion to the sensuous is not controlled by an exquisite taste it is likely to lapse into vulgarity. From this danger Mr. Hergesheimer has not been entirely free. At his best he is colorful; at his worst merely gaudy. Before now critics have noted in him a Corinthian tendency;

a willingness to depend more than an artist should upon crude colors and obvious appeals. On the side of plot this tendency reveals itself in not infrequent touches of mere melodrama, on the side of character in a fondness for types whose psychology is more striking than convincing. Violent action moves against a background too obviously exotic and involves characters too immediately striking to remain profoundly interesting. It is, then, no accident that the "movies" have called him. It is not merely because he is picturesquely rich, but because even his situations and characters can often be translated into gestures and subtitles without great loss.

Nor is it unfair to say that his more recent books have not been without touches of a rather cheap knowingness, the intellectual gestures of the globe-trotting smart-set. Prosperity, one may guess, opened for him the door to the world of smart bohemianism and he took to it with zest. From the time of his travel book **"San Cristobal de la Habana"** . . . on, each of his novels, with the exception of **"Balisand,"** has been rather obtrusively marked by the air of a man of the world. The flash of expensive silks draped upon the bodies of expensive women and the tinkle of ice in silver cocktail shakers have been too complacently detailed by an author too obviously impressed by what he has been privileged to see. There has been an irritating amount of "flash" and of "side," a touch of the "high hat." There has been, in a word, a smartness which suggests the pages of "Vanity Fair" and a knowingness not always very far above the knowingness of "Snappy Stories."

This touch of vulgarity—and vulgarity is not too strong a word— is nowhere so strongly marked as in the women about whom as a center he has contrived what I am afraid the "movies" would call "an exotic lure." No one—not even George Moore— evokes an atmosphere in which the thought of "girls" is so nearly all-pervasive, and these girls are generally conceived in a mood of extravagantly decadent romanticism. They are fascinating, exotic, and unaccountable to the very last degree. They are generally unbelievably close to nature or unbelievably sophisticated. They are primitive, fierce, passionate and treacherous; either they wear shawls on their shoulders and knives in their garters or they have been raised like orchids under glass. Moreover, they are invariably intoxicating or "dangerous" and in this last attribute is the most important key to the temperament of their creator. After all, there is no such thing as a "dangerous" woman; there are only susceptible men. And it is impossible not to conclude that Mr. Hergesheimer's imagination is of the sort which corresponds to such a man. His male characters are desperately anxious to be intoxicated and seduced. They go poking about the world in search of more potent cocktails or more "dangerous" women and they are ready to project their rather heated imaginations upon any odd looking female who happens to come their way.

"Tampico" must be regarded as one of its author's major works, since it displays at full length both his virtues and his vices. Never has he told a story which is, superficially at least, more interesting, and never has his story been more skillfully told. Beginning with a psychological analysis of a man returning after an attack of tropical malaria to the scene of his former adventures as the agent of an oil company in Mexico, it proceeds to unfold a complicated melodrama so artfully managed as to have always a surprise in reserve. From the beginning, for example, one knows that a fatal love affair is impending; one is even reasonably sure that it is going to involve the wife of the manager of the company's sea terminal, but it is not until the hero and the heroine meet suddenly in a passionate embrace that one realizes that the preliminaries have been accomplished before the book opens. As a result the story leaps forward at a speed double the speed one had expected, and the same thing happens again and again. Whatever its defects, **"Tampico"** is a novel which one reads with haste and persistence, if only to see "how it is going to turn out."

For the moment it makes but little difference that the melodrama is sometimes incredible and that the color is most intemperately laid on. There are bandits and spies, plots and hairbreadth escapes in plenty, and there are besides innumerable scenes in a Mexican café, where the men break brandy bottles over one another's heads and the girls stab at their erstwhile lovers in a pause between grenadines. (pp. 1-2)

Frank melodrama is in itself legitimate enough, but in the conception of this heroine is most plainly evident that streak of vulgarity of which I have complained. She is the typical Hergesheimer woman at her worst—a creature created half out of lingerie and perfume, half out of the sensational imaginations of the men who are supposed to love her. She is seductive as seductiveness is conceived in advertisements of stockings and underwear; she has the langorous body and the heart of steel beloved of the "movies." Men grow weak when they gaze upon her, and she is capable, between puffs upon a cigarette, of murmuring coldly to the man who is about to take her from her husband: "Of course, kill people who are in your way if you can; but what good would it do to kill a man I wanted to leave you for? I'd be gone already." "Dangerous," she is called; but "dangerous," one asks, "to whom?" (p. 2)

It is no small triumph to have made such melodrama even temporarily credible and to have disguised even partially the vulgarity with which it is streaked. Nor is this, indeed, all. **"Tampico"** has pages which are more than skilfully meretricious. The atmosphere of the oil station, even if unnecessarily heavy, is created out of a familiarity with details which appears amazingly thorough; there are passages of vivid narrative and there are moments when the author's feeling for romantic adventure reaches a genuinely imaginative level, suggesting at instants the most admired of Conrad's effects. And yet the book as a whole is spoiled by Mr. Hergesheimer's inability to exercise any sort of restraint, by a certain continuous floridity. Upon almost every page it crossed the line which separates the genuinely interesting from the merely sensational.

Certainly the characteristics here described have tended to become increasingly accentuated as Mr. Hergesheimer's career has developed. They are, in general, the defects of his qualities, the result of a process in the course of which his love of sensuous color and romantic adventure were not, as they might well have been, still further chastened by restraint and enriched by reflection, but were, instead, encouraged to grow into rank excess. Why this development, rather than a more happy one, should have taken place I cannot pretend to know. Perhaps there was something incurably florid in Mr. Hergesheimer's temperament which time inevitably allowed to grow or perhaps it was merely the result of a widening audience which, as it becomes more numerous, demands for its satisfaction cruder and more obvious appeals. But whatever the cause, the result is highly unfortunate, since it is scarcely less than the transformation of a significant novelist into a merely popular one. The Hergesheimer revealed in **"Tampico"** is an author who, in spite of all his talents, either cannot or does not dare do without an element of the sensational in every incident and his "dangerous" women are merely the most obvious embodiments of the most obvious sort of appeal. The "movies" have got to the point where they must call the history of Henry the Eighth "Passion" and advertise the story of the Prodigal Son as "glorifying the Babylonian girl." Mr. Hergesheimer is not so very far behind. He has apparently lost the power to think in other than melodramatic terms and he has lost, too, the power to have confidence in the interest of any situation which does not have a woman, exotic, mysterious and "dangerous," somewhere in the background at least. He has not yet, I believe, got to the point of labeling her, after the fashion of the "movies" and by the way of complete characterization, merely "vampire." But perhaps he will. (pp. 2-3)

> *Joseph Wood Krutch, "Glorifying the 'Dangerous' Woman," in* New York Herald Tribune Books *(© I. H. T. Corporation; reprinted by permission), September 19, 1926, pp. 1-3.*

UPTON SINCLAIR   (essay date 1927)

[*An American novelist, dramatist, journalist, and essayist, Sinclair was a prolific writer who is most famous for* The Jungle *(1906), a novel which portrays the unjust labor practices, filth, and horrifying conditions of Chicago's meat-processing industry, and which prompted passage of the Pure Food and Drug Act of 1906. A lifelong, outspoken socialist, Sinclair addressed the excesses of capitalist society in most of his works and demanded, in his critical theory, the subservience of art to social change. Although most of his fiction is dismissed in the United States for its obtrusive didacticism, Sinclair is one of America's most-read authors outside of North America, his works being particularly popular in the Soviet Union. Sinclair scorns Hergesheimer, his wife Dorothy, and his books, in the following critical attack. ("Colonel" George Horace Lorimer, mentioned near the end of the excerpt, was the highly successful editor of* The Saturday Evening Post*).*]

The tallest ivory tower in the United States is known as "Dower House," and is located near the town of West Chester, Pennsylvania, an ultra-fashionable suburb of the opulent city of Philadelphia. And if I take you inside this "Dower House," and introduce you to the master and mistress and the servants, and tell you what they do and what they say and what they eat and what they wear, do not suspect me of violating the laws of hospitality, or of spying upon a fellow-craftsman: no, the owner of the tower has invited the public inside, and what I tell you is what Joseph Hergesheimer consents for you to know. It is a book called "From an Old House," advertised by the publishers as a work upon American colonial furniture and landscape gardening, but in reality the spiritual confession of an ivory tower artist. (pp. 92-3)

What stories come from such a source? **"The Three Black Pennys"**—a novel about three generations of Pennsylvania ironmasters, and how they loved ladies of that charm which ivory tower artists require in ladies, and how their line thinned out into elegant sterility. Here, at the beginning of his writing career, we discover Joseph Hergesheimer as a "real" artist; he is going to bring his lovely characters to ruin—or, as he himself phrases it, be "a merchant in unhappy endings." He doesn't believe in the power of the human will to master circumstance, and he doesn't think it matters much anyway. "I didn't much believe in the triumph or importance of the individual." What is the origin of this curse laid upon the leisure class, an evil spell binding them, so that they can do nothing but go down with mournful dignity to their ruin?

And then **"Cytherea,"** a picture of the fashionable free-spending set, moved from West Chester to Long Island as a matter of courtesy to Dorothy's folks. These people live, not by producing wealth, but by speculating in paper titles to wealth; therefore they have no creative purpose, and no moral resistance, and corruption gnaws in their bones. A young stock-gambler bored with his own wife, conceives a passion for his friend's wife, and runs away to Cuba with her and sees her die amid tropical horrors, corresponding to those in her own soul. A familiar enough theme, but with a new feature derived from Mr. Hergesheimer's custom of gazing at articles of furniture and objets d'art, and writing his stories around them. Perhaps it was Christmas time, and one of Dorothy's friends had sent her a "kewpie" doll, one of those comic figures that are set up on mantles in the nursery; anyhow, the hero of this novel brings home a painted doll and gazes at it until the creature becomes Cytherea, the ancient Paphian goddess of sex license, and he falls under her spell. This is what is called "high art" in the present-day high art world. (pp. 95-6)

And then **"Balisand,"** the story of a landed gentleman of Maryland during the revolutionary war; here again is "stateliness" to the nth power, and as usual written around an article of furniture. Under an illustration in the "Dower House" book you find this caption: "The walnut sideboard, inlaid with long conch-shells in apple-wood, had rare brasses stamped with an Ionic temple. It bore Philadelphia and Georgian silver and a shameless cocktail shaker." It was gazing at this last objet de joie that generated the story of Richard Bale of Balisand. We see him in the opening chapter getting elaborately drunk; he is drunk in gentlemanly and aristocratic fashion most of the way through, until he is killed in gentlemanly and aristocratic fashion in a duel over a woman. When I read this novel, I said to a friend, "This Hergesheimer is an eighteenth century Tory." My friend, a victim of the "art for art's sake" bunk, insisted that the book might be a literary exercise. But now we don't have to dispute any more, Mr. Hergesheimer has settled the matter in his spiritual confession. "Politically, I discovered, writing **'Balisand,'** I was a Federalist; a party soon discredited, and—or for this era—completely lost."

He goes on to tell us what he likes in life: "privilege and the exercise of privilege;" "pleasantness and security;" "time to choose neckties;" "a room with a graceful Hepplewhite table, and on it a box of Cabañas cigars—Tabacos Del Almurezo—and Balkan cigarettes"; "a measure of dry gin in a glass with British ginger beer, and ice, and a few drops of the juice of a lime." Such are the tastes of a gentleman of letters. (p. 97)

But these joys cost real money, and so Mr. Hergesheimer takes a trip to the fountain-head of real money in the arts, and writes a series of articles for Colonel Lorimer, describing life among the movie stars in language of the most top-lofty stateliness. All in the sacred cause of high art we learn how Mr. Lasky ties his necktie, and how Mr. Goldwyn's car is upholstered, and how the valet at the Ambassador looks at the red suspenders which Mr. Knopf gave to Mr. Hergesheimer; we are taken the round of luncheons and dinners, and meet the exquisite young "shapes in light" in their homes, and gossip with them and play cribbage, and in all my reading of the literatures of seven languages and four thousand years, I cannot recall any artist lending his fancy language to the glorifying of more empty vanity and pretense. The climax comes in the home of one of these money-stuffed dolls; the spell of Cytherea begins to steal over us, and we sit lost in it, until the beautiful "shape in light" asks what is the matter, and we reply, "I was just thinking what in the name of God I'd say if I happened to be in love with you." To this the "shape" replies, "Don't be silly," and we agree with all our heart. (p. 98)

Upton Sinclair, "The Ivory Tower," in his Money Writes! *(copyright, 1927 by Upton Sinclair; reprinted by permission of the Literary Estate of Upton Sinclair), Albert & Charles Boni, 1927, pp. 92-9.*

EMILY CLARK   (essay date 1929)

[*Clark was a founding editor of* The Reviewer *(1921-1936), a literary journal devoted to realistic Southern literature. She was a friend of Hergesheimer, who contributed several sketches to* The Reviewer *and tried to attract other major writers to the fledgling journal. Below, Clark enthusiastically reviews her friend's* Swords and Roses, *a collection of biographical essays on figures of the Civil War.*]

The mood and manner of this Civil War record ["**Swords and Roses**"] is one of romantic simplicity, as different as possible from the mood and manner of Mr. Hergesheimer's last long work, "**Tampico.**" Indeed, his style here departs from any of his former books, since its simple forthrightness is in direct contrast with the mannered prose which has given him his place among the foremost contemporary stylists. Whether this is a permanent departure or merely a temporary method for the writing of history cannot yet be known, since a new field perhaps requires new treatment. History, concerned in its accepted definition only with war and politics, is an indubitably new field for Mr. Hergesheimer, whose period novels have never been, in the old sense, historical, but rather novels of personal emotions, of manners, costume and exquisitely detailed setting.

In this latest book, also, emotions are always partly personal, for, since the Roman Republic, politics has probably never been so intensely an affair of the heart as in the American South. The important fact, however, is that the Hergesheimer style has lost none of its beauty in its fresh incarnation, since it is as sure a medium for the sharply defined lights and shadows of the War Between the States, and the years preceding it among the high and the low of the South, as his more complex manner for that highly finished elaboration of surfaces, both human and inanimate, which often engages him. For Mr. Hergesheimer an earlier America has been always the land of escape which Poictesme has been for Mr. Cabell, and if it share Poictesme's detachment from actuality that is unimportant. These two authors, of practically the same age, have been perpetual refugees from a present which is, to both of them, apparently unendurable. On Mr. Hergesheimer's infrequent returns to the present, as in "**Cytherea**" and "**Tampico,**" he finds it unlovely and without dignity. In "**Linda Condon**" the present is made possible for Pleydon only when he turns his back upon it, lost in contemplation of a feminine beauty as cool and remote, as ageless and unattainable as the Parthenon frieze. And for Mr. Hergesheimer women gain as immeasurably by a crinoline as for Mr. Cabell they gain by medieval robes.

So, in "**Swords and Roses,**" Mr. Hergesheimer's most inspired title, he is once more at home in a world which he loves, a world of simple formalities, of hot, clear, uncomplicated passions, of a code of living which admits only black and white, with no infusion of gray, a code expressed in such unarguable terms for both men and women as honor, courage, fidelity, chastity and loyalty. . . .

In his story of the war which on both sides was surely, of all wars, most decent and legitimate, Mr. Hergesheimer is sufficiently the novelist to offer no argument, to hold no brief.

But his aesthetic and emotional responses belong to the South, before and during the war, and these responses are beautifully stated.

If this sheaf of swords and roses is presented with a deeper bow, a graver dignity and a trifle more of romantic respect than most Southerners, cowed by the critical clamor of the last decade against the South's irrational attitude to its past, would dare present such a bouquet, it is unlikely that there will be serious objections. At a moment when the science of de-bunking may shortly succeed in creating an attitude to history nearly as false as the old sentimental one, these brave, gay and courteous figures out of a past more remote in its standards than in years are to be made peculiarly welcome.

> *Emily Clark, "Lost Loveliness," in* New York Herald Tribune Books *(© I.H.T. Corporation; reprinted by permission), April 7, 1929, p. 5.*

ST. JOHN ADCOCK   (essay date 1930)

[*An English author of numerous works, many of which concern the City of London, Adcock served as editor of the London* Bookman *from 1923 until his death in 1930. Below, he considers Hergesheimer a gifted artist who writes beautifully, but finds* The Party Dress *a trivial story about the futile, dissipated people of the "smart set."*]

That it is beautifully written . . . is about all you can say of Mr. Joseph Hergesheimer's **"The Party Dress."** You would have to be as simple as Powys's Rev. Silas Dottery to believe that Nina Henry, turned forty and with grown-up children, developed a fatal sex complex and went wrong because, for the first time in her life, she wore a marvellous party dress made in Paris, which fitted her too tightly, showed too much of her figure and made her look and feel younger than she was. She would have gone wrong in any dress. She is tired of her husband; he is devoting himself to another lady; Nina is kissed fiercely by Francis Ambler, but though he stirs her she decides at length that she does not love him; she is kissed also by Roderick Wade, who smells strongly of gin and cigarettes, but she does not love him either. She moves in a smart set that is not troubled with any morals, and drinks more frequently and copiously than you would think possible under Prohibition. . . . With about two exceptions, her crowd of friends in the American smart set are as futile and dissipated as herself. Were such people worth studying and such a story of them worth telling? Not, I think, by an artist so greatly gifted as Mr. Hergesheimer. (pp. 121-22)

> *St. John Adcock, "What Is Wrong with the Novel?" in* The Bookman, *London, Vol. LXXVIII, No. 464, May, 1930, pp. 121-24.**

LLEWELLYN JONES   (essay date 1931)

[*Jones classifies Hergesheimer as a Platonist in whose stories love transcends sex, and as a writer of valuable historical novels which are untainted by propagandistic philosophy.*]

Perhaps the one American author who has been least swerved by prior philosophical considerations is Joseph Hergesheimer. Really, however, in this instance, there is a philosophic prejudice, as we may call it, but it happens to be one which for a complex of reasons, historical and psychological, seems to help the artist oftener than it hinders him. That prejudice is the Platonic conception of love as something that may begin in the sexual realm but transcends it, that, through the loved one, leads the lover to a love of divinity. It will be remembered that in Mr. Hergesheimer's first book, **The Lay Anthony,** Tony Ball, the young, mechanically-minded, ill-educated youth, whose love story is there told, is unknowingly a Platonist in his love. And this Platonic idea of a purity, an excellence that is superior to circumstance and exists in its own right, is to be met with all through Mr. Hergesheimer's works. As applied to the love of women, the idea is sometimes given us "straight" as in **The Lay Anthony,** sometimes as a divine accident which may manifest itself through a very unknowing instrument, as in **Linda Condon,** and once Mr. Hergesheimer, through a hero who has worldly irons in the fire, expresses a worldly man's irritation at the idea. That is in **Balisand,** where the ghost of the woman whom he had loved and who had been killed before he could marry her, haunts Balisand until, wishing to be psychically free so that he may marry happily—as a good Federalist, he wishes to found a family—he exorcises the disturbing ghost.

On a lower level Mr. Hergesheimer's prejudice in favor of Platonic eternals expresses itself in a liking for the Federalists and a dislike of the Jeffersonian tradition in our history. In **Balisand** and in **The Limestone Tree** the Federalists as representing not so much sound currency as the sense of honor which is offended by inflated currency, not so much wealth as the stability and family and State pride which wealth makes possible, is the burden of his song. It is a beautiful song, but some of its beauty, of course, is owing to the fact that its choice automatically releases one from the dangers of certain discords—while **"Swords and Roses,"** to borrow a title of Mr. Hergesheimer's, are handed one, so to speak, immediately one anticipates the choice of theme. And yet one feels that the tune is a little restricted in its range. After all, destiny voted for something different.

Mr. Hergesheimer's novels which deal with American history, however, are not sentimental nor are they merely costume novels. Even when most costumed, his books have a core of the sort of thing I have just talked about, and such books as **The Three Black Pennys** and **The Limestone Tree** are permanent additions to American literature and really do illuminate our past for us—vivify those years which our history text books only desiccate. (pp. 501-02)

> *Llewellyn Jones, "Contemporary Fiction," in* American Writers on American Literature, *edited by John Macy (reprinted by permission of Liveright Publishing Corporation; copyright 1931 by Horace Liveright, Inc.; copyright renewed 1959 by Liveright Publishing Corporation), Liveright, 1931, pp. 488-502.**

H. L. MENCKEN   (essay date 1932)

[*From the era of World War I until the early years of the Great Depression, Mencken was one of the most influential figures in American letters. His strongly individualistic, irreverent outlook on life and his vigorous, invective-charged writing style helped establish the iconoclastic spirit of the Jazz Age and significantly shaped the direction of American literature. As a social and literary critic—the roles for which he is best known—Mencken was the scourge of evangelical Christianity, public service organizations, literary censorship, boosterism, provincialism, democracy, all advocates of personal or social improvement, and every other facet of American life that he perceived as humbug. A man who was widely renowned or feared during his lifetime as a would-be destroyer of established American values, Mencken once wrote: "All of my work, barring a few obvious burlesques, is based upon*

*three fundamental ideas. 1. That knowledge is better than igno-
rance; 2. That it is better to tell the truth than to lie; and 3. That
it is better to be free than to be a slave." Below, Mencken reviews*
Berlin, Biography and Bibliographies, *and* Sheridan.]

[Of late Mr. Hergesheimer] has shown a new impatience with
the somewhat onerous bounds of the novel, and in **"Biography
and Bibliographies"** he dismisses it cavalierly as "a dying
form", and hints plainly that he longs to be shet of it. His
rebellion, it appears, is quite devoid of that facile iconoclasm
which animates such fellows as James Joyce and John Dos
Passos. He has no yearning to generate a new and shocking
kind of novel, with a red flag in its hand and tinsel in its hair.
The old model, such as it is, seems to him to be sufficient to
its ends. What upsets him, apparently, is the inescapable flavor
of unreality that must get into all fiction, whatever its form—
its inevitable dependence upon imagination rather than fact.
He longs to come to grips with a world that is in veritable and
lusty being, and to set down some of his reflections upon it
before the lightnings begin to blaze along the skyline, and the
heavens open, and the Second Coming is upon us.

Of the three books under review, **"Biography and Bibliographies"** seems to me to be the best, and **"Sheridan"** the worst.
The former is a sort of gloss upon the latter, and, as has
happened so often before, the gloss is far more amusing and
illuminating than the parent text. The essential trouble with the
Sheridan lies in the fact that its author approached it under a
thumping misapprehension. Fresh from the Confederate hooches
of **"Swords and Roses,"** he sought something out of the same
bottle from the Union side, and what seems to have been a
memory of his school-books led him toward Sheridan, the
romantic galloper of Winchester. The book, I gather, was commissioned by the publisher before any fresh reading for it had
been done. When that reading was begun it appeared at once
that the immortal Phil was almost as imaginary as the hero of
a novel—that the actual man was a shanty Irishman who was
far more gifted as a victualler than as a strategist—in brief,
that here was a hero who refused absolutely to fit into either
bronze or stained-glass. So the historian was thrown back upon
the record, and found himself doomed to do a volume that was
as dispiriting to him as a treatise on conic sections.

I offer a specimen of the result:

> . . . The enemy left advanced in a species of
> right wheel; the Southern batteries poured a
> concentrated fire on the Ridge; the infantry
> charged with a fearful roll of musketry from
> both sides. Deas and Manigault reached the
> Union position, assailing Brannan; Johnson,
> Gregg, and McNair, on the right, toiled on up
> in a smoke so dense that only the flashes from
> the guns could be seen. The Confederates gained
> ground.

To me, at least, the news that the Confederates gained ground
is pleasant: I only regret that they did not continue all the way
to Boston. But what actually happened during the battle remains as dark to me as if the story were written in Choctaw
or the horrible jargon of Lord Hoover's press agent: the whole
thing is enshrouded in smoke. I suspect, indeed, that the writing
of scientific military memoirs is very far from Hergesheimer's
Fach, and I get a malicious kind of consolation when the author
himself denounces this one as "the cursed book, the bitch of
a book." It is, he adds gloomily, "a book empty of ornament
and of supporting, reassuring illusion." But there, perhaps, he
goes a shade too far. Not *all* of it is straight military reporting;

there are also some interludes of the authentic Hergesheimer.
One comes at the very start: General Sheridan's visit to the
camp of Bismarck during the Franco-Prussian War. It provides
pleasant writing, indeed—smooth, colorful, and properly ironical. One learns more about the hero than by suffering a score
of his complicated and uninteresting battles. (pp. 251-52)

I was in hopes, having got so far, that the whole book would
be the same. But most of it, I found, was more like the sample
I have offered—true and perhaps important, but somehow extremely sad. (p. 252)

"Biography and Bibliographies" [was] "written in West Chester for Part VIII of the *Colophon.*" My fraternal obeisance to
the editor of the *Colophon.* From the wreckage of Hergesheimer's hopes he salvaged one of the frankest, most rambunctious and most amusing self-vivisections I have ever encountered. It is the distilled essence of the authentic Hergesheimer.
Into it went all of the savors that were driven out of **"Sheridan"**
by the unseemly sweating of a short, dumpy, highly alcoholized
military union man in red sanitary underwear. (pp. 252-53)

"Berlin" is something else again. There are six chapters, only
two of which actually deal with the gaudy Hoboken on the
Spree. The others have to do with Munich, Vienna, Budapest
and a little town in the Bavarian Oberland. The book had its
first incarnation as a series of travel articles in the eminent
Saturday Evening Post, and the excessive discretion which goes
with writing for a magazine of immense circulation is still
visible in it. One meets many ladies who appear to be very
interesting, and then parts from them without learning much
about them. During his second invasion of Berlin the traveler
drinks "perhaps nineteen" cocktails at a party, but neglects to
describe with any particularity the engineering devices used to
get him back to his hotel, and to bed. But these omissions,
after all, are not many, nor are they important. One can read
between the lines. Those lines are always charming, and often
brilliant. There is an easy competence about the writing that
makes excellent reading. The thing is done simply, without
any display of literary virtuosity, but it is done nevertheless
with sound cunning. Here Hergesheimer is on his own ground,
and makes capital practise. No other American author can
describe more vividly a thing seen; none is more adept at
conveying to the reader a sense of the movement and color of
a spectacle.

The thing, of course, does not go much below the surface, but
that is no argument against it, for the surface is precisely what
Hergesheimer is trying to deal with. The politics of the countries he visits does not interest him: in fact, he seldom so much
as mentions the subject. Nor is he visibly taken by what they
regard as the ponderable and imponderable halves of their cultural heritage: he never enters an art gallery, he hears no music
save dance tunes, and he is humanely silent about historical
monuments. What interests him is simply the life of the people,
and especially their life in their leisure. He doesn't inquire into
the ways they earn their livings, or into their views about the
war debts, or into their speculations about the hereafter: he is
content to examine them when they stretch (or shake) their
legs, and are pleasantly loose, and not thinking much about
anything. He watches them as they dance, drink, eat, bathe
and lie in the sun, and tries to formulate some notion of the
kind of men and women they are. It seems to me that it is
proof sufficient of his skill that, in spite of the apparent superficiality of his observations, there is a plentiful soundness
in his conclusions. He watched Berlin at play, but the Germany

that finally emerges from his impressions is a Germany hard at work. (p. 253)

The world, to Hergesheimer, is predominantly a thing for the eye. It was not by mere chance that he began life as a painter. His books are still, in their fashion, paintings—even his novels. His aesthetic is an aesthetic, not of form and organization, but of surfaces—textures, colors, all kinds of pleasant and instructive externals. It has been said against him that the women in his novels are sometimes mere functions of their clothes. Well, why not? It is so in real life, and in **"The Party Dress"** he has certainly demonstrated that it can be made so very plausibly in a theorem. The surface, I often think, tends to be neglected unduly. There is probably just as much authentic news about people in the way they look as there is in what they say. Hergesheimer, sticking to the surface, has here achieved a picture of Berlin that is curiously lifelike and plausible. I believe that it gets much closer to the reality than all the solemn ponderosities of the current publicists. (p. 254)

> *H. L. Mencken, "A Novelist on Furlough" (used by permission of The Enoch Pratt Free Library of Baltimore in accordance with the terms of the will of H. L. Mencken), in* American Mercury, *Vol. XXVII, No. 106, October, 1932, pp. 251-54.*

CLIFTON FADIMAN (essay date 1933)

[*Fadiman became one of the most prominent American literary critics during the 1930s with his often caustic and insightful book reviews for the* Nation *and the* New Yorker *magazines. He also managed to reach a sizeable audience through his work as a radio talk-show host from 1938 to 1948. Writing during the nadir of the Great Depression, Fadiman characterizes Hergesheimer as a money worshipper and interprets the author's obsession with the past as a Tory's desire for a return to strict social stratification.*]

For twenty years Mr. Hergesheimer has written novels, short stories, and even autobiographies about people who do not work for a living. In the mucilage of his style he catches every detail of the life of the leisure class, omitting, indeed, only the comparatively minor matter of the effect this class has had upon the negligible rest of us. It is no mean achievement: to have been the Sargent of the modern American novel. And now history comes to lend even greater point to his work. The class to which for twenty years he has dedicated himself with almost fanatical devotion—even to the martyr's gesture of binding himself to the *Post*—is apparently disappearing or changing into a quite different thing. He is the chronicler of a disappearing Atlantis—and therefore a writer of great historical interest. As the only contemporary romancer whose relevance ceased with the stock crash of November, 1929, he will be to the literary paleontologist of the future a figure of primary importance.

What gives Mr. Hergesheimer his supreme position as a predepression novelist is not merely the completeness of his survey of the aristocracy but its rigorous unity. Just as the Greek drama depends upon a particular theology, so Mr. Hergesheimer's work is, in every slightest detail, dependent upon still another theology—that of money. His masterpiece, **"Cytherea,"** contains a chiseled phrase referring to "the undistinguished evils of improvidence"; but aside from this slight lapse, there is never any vulgar relaxation of Mr. Hergesheimer's social sympathies. Money polarizes every one of his characters; they are free to act and feel only in accordance with the liberty with which their bank balances endow them. Mr. Hergesheimer's

most glamorous heroine, Linda Condon, trades herself in (though still-unused) for fifty thousand a year; the flight of Lee Randon and Savina depends for its effect on the money they are able to spend while making their escape from the vulgarities of the upper middle class. It is a measure of her exquisiteness that the slightest discomfort destroys completely Savina's equilibrium. "Savina's bottles on a dressing-table were engraved crystal with gold stoppers: it was all as it should be."

Mr. Hergesheimer's world of gold stoppers is a world of complete logic and exclusiveness, an architecture erected upon the excellent foundation of stocks and bonds. Of all the writers of his time Mr. Hergesheimer has the clearest and most consistent view of the presuppositions of life. He knows on what terms life must be met—profitable terms only. Thus after the uncertainties of Dreiser or Anderson it is sheer relief to fall back on Mr. Hergesheimer's gold stoppers and feel that all is as it should be.

However, even the best of all possible worlds may have to yield to a new one. Mr. Hergesheimer's closely knit universe is passing. And because it is passing, Mr. Hergesheimer's pages become of greater and greater value. For these pages are unstirred by the foul intrusion of any breath save the wind blowing through the musical colossus of Mammon. They distil the pure essence of conspicuous waste. . . .

[While] Mr. Hergesheimer has no false vanity about his art, he is justly proud of the feudally aristocratic position his art enables him to maintain. He is beyond any doubt our best gentleman writer, the one with the clearest apprehension of what it is that differentiates him from vassal and serf. (p. 175)

It is extremely important for us to understand this feudal viewpoint, for otherwise Mr. Hergesheimer's work cannot be fully appreciated. Of late, for example, he has [shown] a tendency to satirize his own class. But we must remember that Mr. Hergesheimer is more royalist than the king. Today's aristocrats do not come up to snuff. That is because they have relinquished their snuff-boxes. They have been spoiled by a democratic association with the lower classes. Accordingly, in his endeavor to express the true gentlemanly ideal, Mr. Hergesheimer is frequently forced to return to the past, to feudal or semi-feudal states of society. Hence, in his stories of the past—**"The Three Black Pennys," "Java Head," "The Bright Shawl," "Balisand," "Quiet Cities"**—he condenses his most telling criticism of the shortcomings of the present. The structure of modern capitalism is too shifting: where are the fixed classes and positions, for example, of pre-Civil War days? For real breeding one must go back to pre-Revolutionary times, to duels and to knee breeches. (Does this, by the way, account for Mr. Hergesheimer's own pure passion for plus-fours?) His feeling for the days when the bearing of arms was a mark of honor is not that of a romantic antiquarian, as some critics have basely asserted. For Mr. Hergesheimer the duello is a very real thing; it is not mere romance, but the true sign of a gentleman. In **"Balisand"** the duel is taken, as it should be, with the greatest gravity, not at all as a mere convention of the costume novel. In **"Balisand,"** too, the politics of federalism are not exhumed for the purposes of historical coloring, but because Mr. Hergesheimer is a genuine, perhaps the only living, Federalist.

And more than that: he is a dependable pro-slavery man. Contemplating one of the stories in **"Quiet Cities,"** he writes:

> As I considered Natchez and Sylvester Dering and his momentary friend Damaris Vaun, I was

conscious of a certain sympathy for the institution of slavery. It seemed to me to be neither inhuman nor inappropriate. I wasn't convinced of the existence of the brutalities asserted to belong to it by the different North.

(pp. 175-76)

He ends on that delicately philosophical note which really underlies everything he has written: "Most men, anyhow, were slaves." All this is no idle gesture on Mr. Hergesheimer's part; he is far too honest to indulge in mere rhetoric.

Mr. Hergesheimer is not the man to evade the logic of his own position. His finely phrased disdain for the generality of people leads him inevitably to the high worship of things. Among all the writers of our time he is the only one who may be said really to have put things in their proper place. And to his love of things we, his readers, owe our own insight into Mr. Hergesheimer's character. In **"From an Old House"** we follow his furniture-collecting career more and more breathlessly until at last we reach the almost unbearable triumphant climax: "I had what I was convinced was the only very early high-posted walnut bed in existence." A sentence like this is as revealing as anything in the "Confessions" of Rousseau.

Mr. Hergesheimer's high regard for beautiful things runs through every one of his books. Two of his most characteristic novels are, indeed, hardly concerned with people at all, except indirectly. One of them revolves about a doll (expensive); the other about an evening dress (from Paris). His ability to deal with the inanimate is so masterful that frequently the characters recede into complete banality as compared with the rooms they inhabit, the jewels they wear, the chairs they sit upon. Let us take a typical Hergesheimer passage:

> They were at lunch in the Feldt dining-room, an interior of heavy, ornately carved black wood, panels of Chinese embroidery in imperial yellow, and a neutral mauve carpet. The effect, with glittering iridescent pyramids of glass, massive frosted repoussé silver, burnished gold-plate, and a wide table decoration of orchids and fern, was tropical and intense.

After this description of the Feldt dining-room, who could care about the Feldts themselves? . . .

Mr. Hergesheimer's technical resources have never received adequate tribute. He can arrange and serve a dinner with more aplomb than the suavest captain at the Colony. No one can do a better genre picture of an attractive lady slowly dismembering an artichoke; describe a hotel lobby with greater fire and enthusiasm. . . . (p. 176)

Mr. Hergesheimer's novels show his mastery of one of the major principles of salesmanship—the appeal to the gentler but more prodigal sex. . . . Again and again he creates, as in Linda Condon, women single-minded in their desire to give little and get much—and any advertising executive will tell you that this sound American upper-class female trait is responsible, to a very respectable degree, for keeping the wheels of industry turning. (pp. 176-77)

His women, of course, represent Mr. Hergesheimer's major claim to immortality. If his works are ever collected as a set, I should suggest as a general, if somewhat clumsy, title: "A Chronicle of the Omnipotence of Really Glamorous Women." For, when you get right down to it, his books *are* his women, enigmatic creatures always on the lookout for something be-yond passion. (On the other hand, one must not forget the flaming insight which gave us the memorable cries of Savina Grove: "I want to be outraged!" and "I want to burn up with a red flower in my hair and not cool into stagnation.") Mr. Hergesheimer himself has uttered the last word on all his heroines, whether they be Manchu princesses or ladies-in-waiting from the English court:

> They were created delicate and charming, impracticable in cambric and chiffon, for my personal reassurance and pleasure. I wanted them that way and there they were. Later, when I met delightful women, I discovered a secret they shared with each other and with me: what I had always wanted them to be they wanted to be—delicate and charming in cambric and chiffon, tender and faithful and passionate.

To expect these creatures, impracticable in cambric and chiffon, to be subject to the emotions of ordinary women would be a social error of the most heinous variety. It is true that a sentence such as "Every little while a specially insinuating melody became apparently entangled in the women's breathing, and their breasts, cunningly traced and caressed in tulle, would be disturbed" would seem to indicate the contrary. Yet, one realizes at once that a single magical touch, the tulle, immediately lifts the scene above the level of ordinary sensuality into the more refined domain of lingerie.

We have mentioned previously the necessity Mr. Hergesheimer has been under, in his endeavor to depict an ideal aristocracy, of relying upon the past. Particularly of late he has shown a certain lack of confidence in the society he ornaments. This is not to be attributed to any lack of esprit de corps. With all Society's faults he loves it still. Yet his misgivings make for a kind of ambiguity in his approach to his material which lovers of his fine consistency will be the first to deplore. In **"Cytherea,"** for example, he devotes four lapidary pages to the description of a fox hunt—and at the end the reader is troubled with some slight doubt as to the seriousness with which Mr. Hergesheimer takes this high ritual. The novel itself, it will be remembered, deals with the revolt of Lee Randon against the comforts of country-club life and the endearments of a good woman. For a moment it would seem that this revolt might be part and parcel of a deeper rebellion against what wild young radicals would call the System; but this is a superficial judgment. At bottom, it is clear, Lee Randon is fleeing his forty-seven years. His virility, urged into activity by the doll Cytherea, makes its last stand with Savina Grove. Together they float into a travel-bureau paradise of special compartments, luxury liners, Daiquiri cocktails, and gold stoppers. Still even this *voyage en Cythère* betrays a kind of failure of nerve, a hint that all is not right with the best people. . . .

"Tropical Winter," a super-epic of Palm Beach, serves to emphasize this impression. Here Hergesheimer turns Cassandra. The real Palm Beach aristocrats were stricken by the market crash and only the dross, the *nouveaux riches,* remain. The wealthy are faced with Æschylean tragedy (one poor lady is left with a mere $3,000 a year for life), and the only humor to be extracted from the whole deplorable situation lies in the amused contemplation of those vulgarians who either have not enough money really to get by or who, even if rich, cannot possibly know the ropes. In this saddening book Hergesheimer's chosen people have succumbed to boredom; some are even homicidal; all appear to be dipsomaniacs. These stories are Mr. Hergesheimer's contribution to the literature of the depression: meeting his artistic responsibilities nobly, he offers this ten-act Palm Beach tragedy as his reaction to the social crisis which confronts the world. (p. 177)

> *Clifton Fadiman, "The Best People's Best Novelist," in* The Nation *(copyright 1933 The Nation magazine, The Nation Associates, Inc.), Vol. CXXXVI, No. 3528, February 15, 1933, pp. 175-77.*

ALFRED KAZIN   (essay date 1942)

[*A highly respected American literary critic, Kazin is best known for his essay collections* The Inmost Leaf *(1955) and* Contemporaries *(1962), and particularly for* On Native Grounds *(1942), a study of American prose writing since the era of William Dean Howells. Having studied the works of "the critics who were the best writers—from Sainte-Beuve and Matthew Arnold to Edmund Wilson and Van Wyck Brooks" as an aid to his own critical understanding, Kazin has found that "criticism focussed many—if by no means all—of my own urges as a writer: to show literature as a deed in human history, and to find in each writer the uniqueness of the gift, of the essential vision, through which I hoped to penetrate into the mystery and sacredness of the individual soul." In the following essay, Kazin offers a balanced overview of Hergesheimer's career.*]

Hergesheimer . . . always had much to say; he was even a born storyteller. He had zeal, a definite talent, and a purpose in life. He composed, over a period of twenty years, an elaborate series of novels in which he detailed with relish the appetites, the dinners, the adulteries, the manners, the fleeting passions, and the clothing of the rich. In a drawling and lacquered prose that was obviously a work of art, he dedicated himself, with a patience that once seemed as inexhaustible as his capacity for affectation, to the pleasures and opinions of the international leisure class. It was no mean achievement, as Clifton Fadiman once said, to have been the Sargent of the modern American novel [see excerpt above]. Hergesheimer's vision may have been narrow, his scale of values limited; but he had taken his subject for his very own, and one could hardly call him pretentious. He had no society of his own; but he was a court painter to the rich, and the rich were everywhere.

It did not matter where a Hergesheimer character had gained his wealth, or how; he needed only to occupy one of those lush, tropical interiors that marked the true aristocracy of eighteenth-century Richmond or Washington Square or Cuba. Even the Black Pennys, growing poorer despite three centuries of middle-class expansion, preserved their fastidious aloofness to the end. Richard Bale of Balisand had that most signal of virtues in early nineteenth-century America, he loathed Thomas Jefferson. Linda Condon, who would not sell herself in marriage for less than fifty thousand a year, was still the perfect symbol of the perfect lady. (pp. 235-36)

Yet it has to be said that Hergesheimer's passion for the rich was not a vulgar passion. Above all things in this mortal life he loved beauty; the rich had access to it. It was a beauty that flourished in splendor on the faces of their women, the clothes they wore, the silken pursuits of their play; it grew heavily like tropical plants through rooms riotous with color and massive with Hergesheimer furniture. His novels were like a museum devoted to the households of the past. Like Thackeray, he had been a painter before turning to the novel, and he never relinquished a taste for the decorative. The ultimate beauty, however, was the beauty of women, particularly those upper-class women who reflected the chromium-and-gold interiors in which they seemed always to live. He knew them well and

celebrated them passionately; to no other American novelist had been divulged in equal measure the secret of their charm. His was frankly a feudal world, and women ruled in it with a fine medieval grace. (p. 236)

Yet if Hergesheimer was, as even his friend Cabell was once moved to confess, the most insistently superficial of writers, his books were weighed down by a curious melancholy. He sought not merely to pay tributes to beauty, but to imprison it like a genie in his books; and he built so well that his characters suffocated. Everything yielded at some point in every Hergesheimer novel to his passion for decoration, and it was a passion often indistinguishable from snobbery. Even the exquisite and authentic tragedy of **Cytherea** became faintly ridiculous when Hergesheimer wrote sentences like . . . "the ice was frozen into precisely the right size; and the cigars before him, a special Corona, the Shepheard's Hotel cigarettes, carried the luxury of comfort to its last perfection. Mrs. Grove smoked in an abstracted long-accustomed manner." His characters all became dolls led up a graveled path by footmen; and the synthetic majesty of the scenes amid which they lived steadily crowded them out of view. The fancy prose, lost in its winding epithets, made movement impossible. (p. 237)

"Always the Court," cries Ludowika Winscombe in **The Three Black Pennys,** "do you know what that means? It's a place where women are pretty pink and white candies that men are always picking over. It's a great bed with a rose silk counterpane and closed draperies. Champagne and music and scent and masques." It might have been the world of Hergesheimer's novels itself. (pp. 237-38)

> *Alfred Kazin, "The Exquisites," in his* On Native Grounds: An Interpretation of Modern American Prose Literature *(copyright 1942, 1970 by Alfred Kazin; reprinted by permission of Harcourt Brace Jovanovich, Inc.), Reynal & Hitchcock, 1942 (and reprinted by Harcourt Brace Jovanovich, 1963), pp. 227-46.**

JOHN TYREE FAIN   (essay date 1952)

[*Fain provides strong evidence that two sections of Hergesheimer's* Swords and Roses *are close paraphrases of the works of two other authors.*]

Commentators often rank Joseph Hergesheimer high among writers of popular historical works. In one such opinion the late Sarah Haardt (Mrs. H. L. Mencken) gives an account of the author's method of composition [see additional bibliography], an account which is interesting when considering two of the sources of **Swords and Roses.** She says, "Always in his period works, Joseph Hergesheimer has begun by having a vital interest in a particular person and in all the people surrounding him." Next comes the visualizing process; he must actually see some vivid, characterizing detail in the life of the person he has chosen. Then comes the research. . . . (p. 497)

Of the nine sketches in **Swords and Roses,** a group of portraits of the Old South, the present notes treat of only two: **"The Pillar of Words"** (William Lowndes Yancey) and **"The Lonely Star"** (Albert Sidney Johnston). Hergesheimer's method in his sketches is to give a series of important scenes from the lives of his subjects and to summarize briefly in between when necessary. As far as I can tell, all of the summarized material in **"The Pillar of Words"** comes from J. W. Dubose's biography of Yancey. The treatment of Dubose's material in the scenes themselves can be observed in the following comparison:

HERGESHEIMER His first oration was delivered at Lodi, where there was a celebration of the Declaration of Independence. He was constantly interrupted with the question, "Will you not fight for the land of your birth?" and he continually replied, "Where liberty is there is my country." If South Carolina became the advocate of anarchy, William Lowndes Yancey proceeded, he would not follow. He gazed at his audience, assembled in a meadow, and remarked the men around him, scarred and broken with age, who had been soldiers in the old war for independence. There was a prodigious supper spread under the trees, toasts were proposed and drained; Yancey rose and, in place of a conventional period, he begged to read a sentiment handed him by a lady.

DUBOSE The first speech of Yancey's in the campaign, of which there remains any report, was an oration delivered at Lodi, Abbeville District, on the occasion of the celebration there of the anniversary of the Declaration of Independence. . . . The orator said the Nullifiers continually brought up one question: "Will you not fight for the land of your birth?" To this he would make answer: "Where liberty is, there is my country." If South Carolina became the advocate of anarchy he, for one, would not follow her lead. Looking around him, he saw men bent with age and marked with scars . . . they were old soldiers of the war for liberty. . . . A great feast was spread under the trees and at the conclusion toasts were called . . . he rose and begged to read a sentiment which had just been handed to him by a lady, in lieu of anything less expressive which he might say for himself.

(pp. 498-99)

The treatment of source material is similar in **"The Lonely Star,"** which forms the fifth section of *Swords and Roses.* Here the source book is Johnston's life by his son. (p. 501)

In speaking of Hergesheimer's process of imaginative visualization of his material, Miss Haardt says, "He had a clear picture of General Johnston as he rode down the line on the field at Shiloh." The following comparison avouches the truth of Miss Haardt's observation:

HERGESHEIMER General Johnston rode slowly along the line, his hat was off and his sword was in its scabbard. In his right hand he held a little tin cup. . . .

JOHNSTON General Johnston rode out in front, and slowly down the line. His hat was off. His sword rested in its scabbard. In his right hand he held a little tin cup. . . .

The battle begins:

HERGESHEIMER He rode easily, on a thoroughbred horse named Fire-eater. His voice was compelling. "Men," he cried, "they are stubborn. I must lead you." A sheet of fire burst from the Federal position along the crest of a ridge; the Confederate line sank in death through the dark valley; the Confederates went up to the crest of the hill; the Union troops fell back. Johnston's horse was shot in four places, his uniform was cut by bullets, his boot sole was torn by a minié ball. . . .

JOHNSTON He sat his beautiful thoroughbred bay, "Fire-eater," with easy command. . . . His voice was persuasive, encouraging, and compelling. . . . "Men! they are stubborn. . . . I will lead you!" he cried. . . . A sheet of flame burst from the Federal stronghold, and blazed along the crest of the ridge. . . . The Confederate line withered, and the dead and dying strewed the dark valley. . . . Right up the steep they went. The crest was gained. The enemy were in flight. . . . His noble horse was shot in four places; his clothes were pierced by missiles, his boot-sole was cut and torn by a Minié. . . .

This seems sufficient to indicate Hergesheimer's method. Although I have not checked every fact, allusion, and figure of speech against the source material, the check was dishearteningly successful as far as I went. The evidence shows that in the two sketches under consideration Hergesheimer is not synthesizing masses of material, using hundreds of records, steeping himself in the period. It shows instead that he is using two source books—and probably nothing else. It also raises incidentally the question as to how closely a writer of popular period works may legitimately follow his sources. The main purpose is somehow to get the flavor of the period, and a writer may be able to get it only by quoting old records. Hergesheimer may justify in this way his use of source material. Howerver, I believe that for the type of work he is doing in *Swords and Roses,* which purports to be actual history in a popular form, Hergesheimer is closer to his originals than a first-class man of letters should be. At any rate, if his use of sources in the other parts of *Swords and Roses* and in the other historical works is similar to that here indicated, his method of composition is not at all like the somewhat romantic account given by Miss Haardt, and we can agree without qualification with the statement which she attributes to the author himself: "There is nothing in his method of marshaling his material, he insists, that has the slightest thing to do with scholarship." (pp. 503-04)

John Tyree Fain, "Hergesheimer's Use of Historical Sources," in The Journal of Southern History *(copyright 1952 by the Southern Historical Association; reprinted by permission of the Managing Editor), Vol. XVIII, No. 4, November, 1952, pp. 497-504.*

RONALD E. MARTIN (essay date 1965)

[*In* The Fiction of Joseph Hergesheimer, *Martin provides lengthy examinations of all of Hergesheimer's major works and discusses the author's themes and techniques. In the following excerpt from that book, Martin analyzes three of Hergesheimer's most significant novels:* The Three Black Pennys, Java Head, *and* Cytherea.]

The Three Black Pennys . . . was the third novel published by Hergesheimer, but it was his first substantial achievement in the art of fiction. His earlier novels, *The Lay Anthony* . . . and *Mountain Blood* . . . , had many of the characteristics of the apprentice works of a good writer. They both had highly dramatic materials, a youthful intensity, and an extremely idealistic morality; lacking was a mature insight into experience and a convincing control over the structure, speed, and rhythm of the narrative. In all, they can be regarded as "promising" but incompletely realized novels, and they were so regarded by many of their reviewers. With *The Three Black Pennys,* however, Hergesheimer achieved a fuller understanding of the materials with which he was working and displayed a fuller technical competence for developing them, so that the novel quite deservedly brought him much more recognition as a writer than he had previously enjoyed.

One of the technical factors which made this novel more successful than his earlier works was a device by which Hergesheimer was able to master the problem of structure. His earlier two efforts had been diffuse and uneven in their narrative movement, primarily because their structural pattern—of continuous action viewed from a single point of view—put too many demands on the relatively inexperienced writer for him to be able to maintain both interest and continuity. In *The Three Black Pennys* he solved this problem with something of a structural innovation in the American novel: a discontinuous novel of three separate, self-contained (although interrelated) long stories, with different characters and different actions but related themes. (pp. 50-1)

The basic motif here is the familiar one of a sophisticated, haughty, beautiful woman being won by an individualistic and willful young man. It differs from the ordinary success-story, however, both in its treatment of motivation and in the wider implications suggested by the forces which Howat and Ludowika represent. Howat strives to possess her not for the purpose of proving himself or of attaining some flattering goal. Rather he is responding to an irresistible instinctual force which he tries to fight against, regarding it as "tyranny" and "entanglement," an unthinkable abridgement of his individuality. His actions when controlled by this force are as merciless as the force itself: Howat cares nothing for his family (even his mother), Ludowika's husband, or even Ludowika herself, but only for the satisfaction of his dominating impulse. Ludowika's own motivation is postulated on the hot-bloodedness and clear-sightedness she shares with Howat, but it is developed in terms of her romantic distortion of primitive life in America. . . . She continually misrepresents to herself the nature of the life around her, viewing it as an Arcadian escape when in fact it is more ruthless and passionate than anything she had known in Europe. Her disillusionment comes after her seduction when she realizes the universality of evil:

> "How detestable men are!" . . . "Arcadia,"
> she laughed. "I thought it was different here,
> that you were different; that feeling in my heart—
> but it's gone now, dead."
>
> (pp. 54-5)

The larger implications of the conflict of Howat and Ludowika grow out of the imagery and characterization primarily; these elements clearly suggest that this conflict involves more than just two personalities. Howat and Ludowika are identified with forces which make up their personalities and environments in such a way that the conflict between the characters also becomes, on the level of theme, a conflict between opposing principles. The opposition of wilderness and civilization is one such fundamental theme: Howat's kinship with the unsettled territories, "the still immensity of a land unguessed, mythical" . . . is brought into conflict with Ludowika's background of courtly manners and aristocratic leisure. Nature versus artificiality is a closely related theme, with Howat's untamed

woods contrasting with the formal gardens Ludowika had known on the continent. Concomitant with these themes is that of purity versus decadence. Ultimately the antithesis includes ruthlessness, directness, naturalness, and purity as a constellation around Howat, and sophistication, deviousness, artificiality, and depravity around Ludowika. This opposition is reinforced by such symbols as the relentless pulse beat of the forgehammer and Ludowika's sly and obsequious Italian servant. In its opposition of a pure, strong-willed America facing a corrupt Europe the story even attempts to foreshadow the Revolution. Certainly an appreciation of this story might be firmly based on the insight contained in the motivation of the characters and the thematic overtones of the situation. (pp. 55-6)

Hergesheimer is able to maintain an intensity and a coherence which result from his focussing on a single affair. In the story of Howat I every element serves the purpose of depicting or developing the central conflict; thus all characters, events, and even things exist in the story only insofar as they serve the main purpose. If a story benefits esthetically from such complete coordination it also suffers somewhat in the breadth of its depiction of life; the focus is clear and the subject stands out, but the depth of field is quite shallow.

Even with the intensity Hergesheimer strives for in the story of Howat I, he still must cover a variety of incidents and a little over a month's time, and it is in this aspect that his earlier fiction was weakest. The representation of time and change is uneven in this story and the development seems sometimes too precipitous, sometimes too leisurely. Similarly casual events are often made to carry the weight of important background or preparations for climaxes in such a way as they sometimes have no probability in themselves. Such are the conversations frequently held in the Penny household during or after dinner, which have little coherence or plausibility but do a great deal to prepare, explain, and fill in the background of the central dramatic situation.

Hergesheimer shows in this story an interest in exactness of expression which hinders him almost as much as it aids him. By showing us as often as he does the actual groping for exactness he detracts somewhat from the bluntness and provinciality which are supposed to be the dominant characteristics of Howat, the central consciousness. (pp. 56-7)

In [the second] story the crisis the hero must face is that of moving out of the past and into the future. Jasper must cut away his passionate, rebellious, and selfish youth and establish a new identity more in accord with the spiritual needs he had earlier left unfulfilled. But try as he might to expiate his former acts, he is unable to erase the taint fully enough so that Susan will accept him; she is the ultimate voice of the puritanical morality which informs the story as she refuses his advances. . . . Once Jasper commits himself and his awakened spiritual outlook to Susan's standards, there is no escaping the tyranny of his past acts. Without the possibility of expiation there can be no resolution to the situation, and generations later when Howat II ponders over the bare fact that Susan did eventually marry Jasper after Essie died, such a fate seems out of keeping with the inevitability of the forces in the story itself.

The story might be criticized on a far more basic level than this, however; one might object to Hergesheimer's projection of this sort of conversion in a mature and sensitive man wholly in terms of a love story. The whole of Jasper Penny's life is summed up in this polarity of two women, Essie and Susan. Also, many of the trappings of popular romantic fiction surround Jasper's aspiration toward Susan: Hergesheimer must assume a sort of mutual love-at first-sight attraction between the two, and especially a rather girlish romanticism beneath Susan's exacting idealism which accounts for her motivation in being attracted to Jasper. In addition, Hergesheimer, in projecting a spiritual quest in terms of a love affair, wasn't always sure which level was fundamental. . . . In his later works Hergesheimer often treats the man who founded his spiritual quest on a woman but always with the intent that the quest prove illusory. Thus the difficulties he had with characterization, motivation, and action in trying to identify a woman with a spiritual ideal were obviated by his evolving cynicism.

In this second part of *The Three Black Pennys* Hergesheimer is focussing on the middle-aged hero with an intent . . . to develop the themes which relate to the question of what in the life of a man or a family remains constant and what changes with the passage of time. Especially highlighted are Jasper's discontent and eventual sublimation of passion (represented by his movement from Essie to Susan), his turning more toward the past to get confidence and support from remembering his heritage, and his feelings of doubt and weakness prompted by age and complication. (pp. 61-3)

[The] last of the Pennys, his rebellious youth devoted to polite society instead of the wilderness, became an esthete, and for the second time decadence had come to the family from Europe. Howat discovers, however, that the life he had elected (or had been fated to) had lacked something very important:

> Yes, it had been a mistake. He had missed the greatest pleasure of all, that of accumulating power and influence, of virile achievement. . . .

Howat lives in the past, by standards formed in the past, and he can no more reconcile himself to the new age than he can reconcile himself to its unmelodious music. He can only disparage the modern age for its failure to measure up to the old standards.

Appropriately enough, Howat can be quite fully characterized by the things around him and the details of his life. . . . [His] sense of "the right things" is projected by his dress, his taste in *objets d'art* and his surroundings. This character's tastes and mental processes are far more convincingly depicted by Hergesheimer's prose style than were those of Howat I. Here the qualifications and nice distinctions which seem to be part of Hergesheimer's natural prose style, but which seemed so out of accord in Howat I, can serve to depict the fastidiousness of Howat II's style of life. (pp. 64-5)

In view of the role the past plays in each of the stories, the unifying theme of the novel seems to be this: as the generations progress, certain finer traits are continuous but faults tend to magnify and increase in range at the same time that the basic vitality declines, the final result being increasing weakness and eventual extinction. (pp. 69-70)

Hergesheimer's best-known novel, *Java Head*, was published in 1919. Built around a suspenseful plot and rife with the color of its locale—Salem in the 1840's with its obsessions with shipping and puritanical morality—this book perhaps more than any other helped spread Hergesheimer's fame and influence to the extent that he came to be regarded one of America's leading literary figures.

Java Head is an unusual combination of a relatively simple central plot and a highly complicated means of development. (p. 86)

The novel is divided into ten chapters, each written from a different point of view, so that Hergesheimer achieves a somewhat greater breadth of situation and characterization in this book than in some of his others: more aspects of any given situation can be considered and more characters can be developed according to their own perceptions and responses than would otherwise be possible. Also, the succession of points of view has been arranged by Hergesheimer so that it reinforces the natural climax of events. Beginning by viewing the situation through characters who are on the periphery of the main action, characters who had a natural concern with the recent past, he was able to supply background and description without impeding the action. By progressing to characters more centrally concerned with the action he was able to increase the reader's involvement until, after the climax, he was able again to place the point of view in a relative outsider in order to achieve the esthetic distance necessary for a satisfactory denouement.

Hergesheimer's commitment to the points of view of his characters is not complete, however. Writing in the third person he is willing to rely on their perceptions and their scale of values, but he retains his own diction rather than using that of the characters. (p. 87)

The underlying movement in the novel is a movement of time—from Laurel Ammidon's spring morning in the garden at Java Head to Roger Brevard's autumnal reflections as he watches the Nautilus slowly leaving Salem behind. And in this movement from youth and vitality to a peculiar type of withdrawn, middle-aged stagnation, time and change have been the abiding concerns of most of the characters. (pp. 98-9)

The ultimate effect of the novel's preoccupation with time and change is the sense of loss, transience, and nostalgia which it produces in the reader, a regret at the passing of the times and the dispersal of the characters. And it is within this framework of feeling that the dramatic conflicts are enacted. (p. 99)

Gerrit has a wife whom he admires and respects and toward whom he feels a powerful (though not all-transcending) obligation; he also has another woman whom he loves and admires, and who needs him almost as much as his wife does. Possessing either one means sacrificing the other; unable to decide and at the same time unable not to decide, Gerrit can only vacillate and despair, doubting himself (which might have done him some good in time) and imprecating against fate, society, and morality. Up to this point Hergesheimer has dealt realistically with the problem and seems to have been leading up to a tragic resolution embodying some moral insight. But then Dunsack threatens Taou Yuen, she commits suicide, and Gerrit is saved from having to make an unpleasant decision by fate (or, more disturbingly, by the author, who by this act seems to have been interested only in rigging a happy ending for his hero).

The solution really is not worthy of the problem: the moral question is not solved or even illuminated but rather ignored. Gerrit is absolved of all human responsibility; he got exactly what he wanted simply by doing whatever he felt like doing at each stage in his life. Likewise, the moral for Nettie is questionable. After years of stubborn independence she finally acquiesced in hopelessness, and immediately chance brought her the fulfillment of her dreams. The lesson we seem to learn from the resolution of the Gerrit-Nettie plot is that things take care of themselves.

This flaw then pervades *Java Head:* the resolution of the main plot seems inconsistent both with the forces within that plot and with the general emotional tenor of the novel as a whole.

The book is still an admirable novel with its vivid characters and setting, its genuine sentiment of nostalgia, and its complex and interesting structure and succession of points of view, but it rings false in its plot resolution. (pp. 102-03)

Hergesheimer's first and best full-length treatment of contemporary life was *Cytherea*. . . . In *Cytherea*, . . . he attempted to depict his own times and to record his opinions about its shortcomings and vagaries. He put in the mouth of his protagonist many of his own characteristic judgments about society, morals, religion, law, sex, and love; consequently the novel has a superstructure of idea which is absent in his earlier work.

The ideas Hergesheimer expresses in *Cytherea* are polarized around a preoccupation of his at that time, which he characterized as:

> an endless interest in the destructive qualities of the passion of love operating in a society not quite designed for it.

This preoccupation determines the main interest in the novel, and Hergesheimer uses as its vehicle the motif of marriage and adultery in which a sensitive and courageous man is placed between a conventional wife and an exciting mistress and forced to choose between them. In this novel the hero chooses the romantic alternative and escapes with his mistress, only to find his decision nullified and mocked by her death, a result, the doctor says, of "excesses." The drama is enacted against a background of postwar suburban restlessness and infidelity, and constructed in such a way that the hero's predicament and that of the society compliment and comment on each other. (pp. 111-12)

In the way that Hergesheimer, in the mind of Lee Randon, pits passion against civilization and against Lee's "continence," "restraint," and "decency," it is quite clear that the phenomenon of Cuba stands as a symbolical moral commentary on the actions of Lee and Savina. Seemingly the forces they have set loose within themselves, the passion and the anarchy, have a close kinship with the debased primitivism of their surroundings. (p. 124)

The world depicted in *Cytherea* is an exceedingly depressing one. In it failure is inevitable and individual effort futile. All one can hope for in life is either a temporary and sterile escape or an unqualified surrender to the inanities which rule so absolutely the everyday life of respectability. (p. 126)

Hergesheimer seems to be narrowing the dimension of the moral world in his book, just as he narrowed the dimension of his characters in this and other books, for the purpose of dramatic effect. And the dramatic effect in this novel seems to depend on dilemma—a situation in which his hero is forced to choose between black-and-white alternatives, both ultimately hopeless. The end result is the one so diligently sought by Hergesheimer: a hero facing impossible odds and going down to his failure in a magnificent gesture of self-assertion.

Dilemma produces Hergesheimer's desired esthetic effect, and dilemma is produced by the high degree of selectivity with which he chooses and develops his materials. . . . Characters and their attributes, situations and their complications, events and their implications all appear in the novel solely for their erotic meaning or potency. And even love has only two possible aspects, adulterous or connubial, "the defilement of a pandering to the flesh" or "the waste of a negation with neither courage nor rapture," Cobra or Eastlake.

The effect of this extreme selectivity on the value of the novel is both positive and negative. It certainly provides the author with a tractable piece of experience which he can develop with clarity, cogency, and intensity. Our total absorption in the love-quest of Lee Randon accounts for both the sense of unity and completeness we get from *Cytherea* as well as the economy with which the author can introduce characters (such as Savina) and themes (such as the conflict of civilization and anarchy). Once we grant Hergesheimer the premises implicit in his selectivity, the reading of *Cytherea* can be a movingly dramatic experience.

If, on the other hand, we ask of a novel that it represent life to us in such a way as to add something to our sensitivity or insight, we must admit that such extreme selectivity puts severe qualifications on the kind of life that can exist in a novel. If we fail to grant the premises of *Cytherea,* if we fail to allow that Lee Randon's world is the real world, Hergesheimer's characters will seem to us to be monomaniacal, arbitrary, and oversexed. (pp. 127-29)

Cytherea is probably the best case in point to illustrate the war between the individual and contemporary society; one of the book's prime values is that it is one of the earliest critiques of what we now refer to as suburbia. The characters who have sensitivity and perceptiveness all find their longings unsatisfied by conventional society. (p. 135)

The struggle between the individual man and society is especially despressing because it is inevitable, following from the natures of man and society, and because man can only lose. Nowhere in Hergesheimer's writings is there any suggestion of social reform or humane dedication; the hero's aspirations are always purely aspirations of self.

Hergesheimer's pessimism seems even more pervasive when, from the vantage point of *Cytherea,* we see that not only society is set against individuality, but the universe seems to be so too. Lee Randon escaped being stifled by Eastlake only to be defeated by the sterility of the Cytherean alternative. (p. 138)

> *Ronald E. Martin, in his* The Fiction of Joseph Hergesheimer *(© 1965 by the Trustees of the University of Pennsylvania), University of Pennsylvania Press, 1965, 288 p.*

JAMES H. JUSTUS (essay date 1973)

> [*Justus considers* Berlin *a superficial look at Germany which neglects the political mood, the historic sights, and the people in favor of beergartens, hotel restaurants, and a romantic longing for the past.*]

[*Berlin*] is surely one of the most curious volumes of a literary type which, for all its vigorous and perceptive judgements, is itself something of a curiosity. By now, I suppose, it is a commonplace that the travel book, the elegant bastard of genres, invariably reveals more about the traveller than about the geography he supposedly describes. . . . And whatever other defects mar, say, Truman Capote's *Local Color* (1950) or John Knowles's *Double Vision* (1964), the failure to impose personality on the scene—to let voice and stance, even with their inadequacies, shape and experience—is in large measure the source of our disappointment in those books. Hergesheimer's *Berlin* does not fail for this reason. Like *Local Color,* it is mannered, and like *Double Vision,* it is thin; but it is not merely mannered and thin.

To those few readers still familiar with his upholstered historical novels (*Java Head*, *The Three Black Pennys*) or his chic contemporary novels (*Cytherea*, *The Party Dress*), the personality-dominated scenes in *Berlin* clearly mark it as a brother to other Hergesheimer works. Indeed, in many ways it simply continues the leisurely indulgent exercises in observation and evaluation which we first see in *San Cristóbal de la Habana* . . . , and the detached, orchestrated identity we find in the two volumes of autobiography, *The Presbyterian Child* . . . and *From an Old House*. . . . Throughout his twenty productive years, Hergesheimer recorded a progressively deteriorating modern America, both in the muted melodrama of his fiction and in the lectures and interviews that grew increasingly testy. (pp. 47-8)

The image of Hergesheimer in Germany . . . is of a piece with his fiction and his other occasional prose. Permeating *Berlin* is the sense of the practitioner at work; and its author is an appropriate embodiment of old-fashioned *belles-lettres*, with its use of the disinterested but accurate eye, the educated ear, the aristocratic tone, the reflexive imagination. What impresses us about this book is its author's sense of himself in a series of sketches: Hergesheimer musing on a park bench, Hergesheimer dressing with discrimination, Hergesheimer admiring but hardly touching the brunhilde flesh that always seems empty of passion. These vignettes, and a hundred more, are dominated by a figure untouched—by choice—by the vigour and genuine life, tawdry and otherwise, surrounding him. He is a figure who seems strangely anachronistic to the Germany between the wars that we have come to know from Auden, Isherwood, Brecht, Weill, Grosz, Kessler, and others. Rhetorically, he is almost self-created, almost fictional, a figure skimming quietly, precisely, through well-thought-out itineraries like certain minor characters in the fiction of Henry James. As the early reviewers pointed out, *Berlin* is a guidebook more to a private Hergesheimer than to a public Mitteleuropa. What marks this writer's particular imagination is the sense of honesty in not only what the selective eye sees but also in what the mind makes of the perception; the sense of a consistency even in the faithful recording of tensions and their non-resolutions; and most important, the sense of an intensely personal voice and stance which artistically mirror the raw experience itself. (pp. 49-50)

How tolerant . . . need we be of an apolitical writer doing a book on Germany in 1932, a man of animal appetite and selective receptivity who never records the stirrings of the Third Reich? We look in vain for a consciousness of Germany's slow drift into nationalism. The name of Hitler never appears in *Berlin,* although, by the time of Hergesheimer's visit, he had already organized his party, gathered about him Hess, Goering, Rosenberg, Streicher and others, fomented rebellion against the central government from his power base in Bavaria, almost succeeded in his premature putsch at the Buergerbrau, gained his expected headlines in harangues during a treason trial, published both volumes of *Mein Kampf,* and was already intriguing his way to the chancellorship by 'constitutional' means. The Brownshirts were a common sight in Berlin as well as in other German cities, but in Hergesheimer's passing mention they resemble lapsed Boy Scouts. (p. 50)

He sees poverty and its resultant attitudes: bitterness and cynicism in some, spartan self-control in others, cheerful indifference in still others. But that any combination of these attitudes could eventually be useful in the shaping of political power does not occur to him. . . . Hergesheimer had no ideologies. He was indeed apolitical, which is to say that his politics had reference only to vaguely defined but history-sanctioned general categories, such as Aristocracy, Democracy, Class Responsibilities, Individuality. And in *Berlin* even his characteristic responses to such categories in social or ethical judgements are like second thoughts; they grow out of a more immediate, a more personal experience—the aesthetic impact of new Germany on his sensibilities.

Admiration for and reservations about Germans both young and old mingle without much order in *Berlin,* and this mingling stems not so much from a desire to report accurately on what Germany is like in 1931, though that is certainly part of it. Hergesheimer's overt habit of seeing art as an aristocratic enterprise constantly places an Olympian distance between the eye and the object and, more covertly, fashions that distance into a calculus of value. Politics, social activities, manners, ethnic variations—all are submitted to the uses of Hergesheimer's particular art. We should not be surprised, then, that political realities, *per se,* are less important in *Berlin* than the search for and commentary on aesthetic pleasure, a search that is, in varying ways, an exploration of himself. An all-encompassing self-absorption, itself coolly distanced, occupies most of this book on Germany, where Hergesheimer notes approvingly the residual respect for class and professional differences. Elderly shoeshine men, manservants, chambermaids, waiters, policemen, even women, still do in Germany what they were intended to do—serve, being 'simple, voluble, and concerned' with a patron's satisfaction. (p. 51)

There is something of both the Romantic Aesthete (in both its Wordsworthian and Gauginesque aspects) and the Presbyterian Child throughout *Berlin,* mutually exclusive postures that rather cheerfully co-exist without the metaphysical dissonance we have come to admire in more serious writers. The sometimes dizzying alternation of postures can be seen, in fact, as a literary enactment of the authorial self, making the travel books more revealingly autobiographical than the autobiographical volumes themselves. Hergesheimer says he 'envied' the healthy people of Tegernsee:

> I would have gladly surrendered everyone I knew, the books I had written, the fine old simplicity of the Dower House, to live on the high, flowery meadows above the Tegernsee. An Alpine dwelling with a painted gable, a Bavarian wife, sturdy Bavarian children. . . . Yes, it would be far better to have only a little, a precious moderation of material benefits, to inhabit a mountain between the sky and a lake. . . .

And fifty pages later:

> I had no inclination to make a moral pronouncement upon the deadening influence of absolutism, no need to repeat the truth that tyrannies, empires, came like republics to nothing, fell, before the law of ceaseless change, at the end. I was delighted to reflect that the Viennese, once, had had such an excess of good times. I even envied them the Hapsburgs—the best, in an imperial sense, of all emperors. It was needful, now, for them to become mature, to substitute thought for evasions and an irresponsible happiness. I did not wholly envy them their necessity. I would rather, by far, have

been an archduke than become an enlightened democrat. . . .

(p. 56)

In envy begins imagination. It is not surprising that Hergesheimer in each case envies the lots of those furthest removed from his. Envy may produce discord and violence, estrangement both earthly and supernal, but in the service of aesthetic impulse, it is here transposed, harmlessly, into the scale of daydream, which nevertheless in the recording becomes a moment of remarkable self-judgment. There are certainly here a radical want of modesty, a hectoring of archdukes after proclaiming no interest in such matters, perhaps even an arch whimsicality. But what there is not is more to be remarked: no doctrinal bluster, no ideological tantrums, no spiritual malaise masquerading as social criticism; in short, no exacerbated imagination. Even envy can be subverted by conscious artifice. Such passages project a temperament that asserts a most unfashionable notion: the possibility that selves may unagonizingly dwell within the self.

Temperamentally, Hergesheimer revels in this willed nostalgia. And though for him it is nostalgia without a referent, the very act of conjuring a vanished past is our clue to a complex aesthetic sensibility. The experiences themselves, not only the literary articulation of them, are the stuff of artifice. Hergesheimer's highly wrought style, which pushes the tactile and visual senses to such limits that they have more explicable reference to themselves than they do to the objects which they invoke, is such that it permits few of the distinctions we customarily make between the event and the event rendered, between the author and the author's account of himself. The *I* who steps his way through the pages of *Berlin* has cultivated a way of seeing, of experiencing, just as rigorously as he has a way of literarily recreating what he sees and experiences. This remarkable confluence of act and art accounts, I think, for the complaint of one of Hergesheimer's contemporaries— and it can stand for most of them—that the style 'postures at times so consciously that it drops over into the obviously insincere'. Posturing it may be, but the posturing of experience is anterior to, and of a piece with, the style. Hergesheimer does not possess —because of a long apprenticeship in both painting and writing before he published a word—what someone has called 'the innocent eye'. His practised eye cannot avoid, of course, the contingencies of experience, those unlooked for, unwanted things; but it can go far—and quickly— in shaping those things according to long-settled convictions.

Further, Hergesheimer's aesthetic sensibility is complex because it is double-faceted. This modern American can, with the greatest facility, identify with the grace, culture, taste, and beauty of an order of society erased by war and the democratization of the twentieth century. But he can also admit the shallowness, rigidity, and absurdity of that very aristocracy— a world well lost—when faced with the simplicity and naturalness of peasant or mountain people. It is not a simple matter of being emotionally responsive to one impossible extreme and of intellectually willing a response to another, equally impossible, extreme. Both responses are willed.

It is perhaps natural that we should expect of Hergesheimer a deeper perception than he obviously possessed of political conditions in Germany in 1931. Our impatience with his minute concerns of sartorial and gustatory pleasures and his diffident observations of what we now so easily refer to as the 'spirit' of Germany between the wars is of a piece with our present lack of interest in his fiction, where the same sensuous (and obliquely sensual) temperament suggests the same effortless pronouncements on the values of conservatism and the decay of values in the American 1920s. (pp. 56-8)

It is easy to disparage Hergesheimer and his all-too-selective eye. If foresight is not his strong point, it is in part his deliberate choice not to predict the nature of the new German order. Nor should we stand appalled at the misreading of clues that he brushed against lightly wherever he went in Germany. As we depressingly discovered in the early 1940s, more perceptive men than Hergesheimer turned out to be myopic. (p. 63)

Within his own terms, Hergesheimer refashions the cities he visits into constructs of *his* space. Berlin, Munich, Egern, Vienna are curiously stripped, partly because he shuns museums, cathedrals and opera houses and cultivates instead the present pleasures: mingling with the street life, walking in the park, luxuriating in his hotel room, and eating and drinking at gasthaus, wine restaurant and club. But these cities also appear stripped because from them Hergesheimer arbitrarily chooses only those moments in their presentness that are required for his self-absorbing imagination to distil, ready-made, as artifice. What lingers are the vignettes of people he comes to know only casually, and even these are tentative, more than half-shaded by Hergesheimer's own presence. But in these momentary glimpses, a few caught phrases, a lightly sketched scene, Hergesheimer manages to show us something of the value of an art of surfaces.

The nature of the Nazi threat is never actualized in *Berlin*, even in the most sinister or bizarre episodes. But a troubled feeling is released by Hergesheimer's controlled artifice. The texture of this account—what is both pertinently seen and extravagantly imagined—is for at least once in his career a mirror of something more than his competing psychological impulses. But precisely because there are contrarieties in Hergesheimer himself we find a reflexion of the contrarieties which he describes (and does not resolve), perhaps better than he knew, in Germany. (p. .66)

James H. Justus, "Joseph Hergesheimer's Germany: A Radical Art of Surfaces," in Journal of American Studies *(© Cambridge University Press 1973), Vol. 7, No. 1, April, 1973, pp. 47-66.*

INGEBORG KEJZLAROVÁ (essay date 1976)

[*Kejzlarová, a Czech critic, surveys Hergesheimer's career, and contends that shallow protagonists and the failure to develop full dramatic action account for Hergesheimer's loss of appeal. In spite of this criticism, Kejzlarová believes that Hergesheimer's novels and short stories are an important link between the first generation of American Realists, and the postwar realists.*]

[Joseph Hergesheimer] tried to combine . . . realism and romanticism, and to arrive at a synthesis. (p. 73)

The Lay Anthony . . . , Hergesheimer's first novel, is a romantic story about a young man in search of his ideal of love and beauty. (p. 75)

The basic tone of this novel is much the same as that of many European decadent novels and there are also affinities with Latin American modernist novels of that time. The descriptions of the milieu are realistic and convincing as are the portraits of the episodic characters, for example, the intellectual Annot Hardinge and her fanatical, mentally deranged father, the two Jewish passengers who draw the hero into their sordid adventure, Anthony's parents and his sister, the old woman who leaves Anthony all her money. On the other hand the protagonist, though most of his experiences and adventures seem probable enough, is rather shallow and anemic, and sometimes almost stupid. But this is what the author wanted him to be to make the contrast between him and Eliza more effective. (pp. 75-6)

Eliza remains vague, ethereal, the ideal of beautiful and fragile womanhood Hergesheimer greatly admired in the works of the English Pre-Raphaelites and esthetes. Eliza is the first of Hergesheimer's decorative woman characters. Decorativeness is also one of the characteristics of his style, the more so when he describes out-door scenery. He wants to express the impressions he has as a painter of varying and fading colours and shades in nature. . . .

Before the publication of his first novel Hergesheimer had written only short stories and sketches. No wonder he was not able at once to develop a full dramatic action in *The Lay Anthony*. Each of the episodes in the book is better worked out than the whole, which lacks dramatic tension. *The Lay Anthony* is in all respects a work of apprenticeship. The author was in search of his way in literature, as his hero was in life. Anthony's search for his romantic ideal had to end tragically. Hergesheimer took a more straightforward road in his next novel.

One year after *The Lay Anthony* Hergesheimer published *Mountain Blood* . . . , a regional novel with its scene in the Highland country of Virginia where Hergesheimer had lived for about two years. . . . (p. 76)

The basic idea of this book is the impact of money and new business relations on the lives of the Highland people. (p. 77)

Mountain Blood is a much better novel than *The Lay Anthony* and one of Hergesheimer's best achievements in American-bred realism. Hergesheimer made good use of his own experiences and observations during his stay in the Highland County of Virginia. This is evident in the structure as well as in the style of the novel, which are both adapted to the needs of the story. The narrative is condensed and carried directly to the climax. The main characters and also most of the secondary ones are well outlined. There is hardly any ornateness or exuberance in his style. Still there is some amount of romanticism and late nineteenth-century sentimentalism left in the conception of the story. A poor man at the end of his youth with no career or any prospects for the future suddenly marries a rich girl whose sympathy (more than her love) he happens to arouse by defending her. Then the newly rich shows off to the man who once impoverished him. In the clash of passions the enemy's son is crippled and there comes still another melodramatic scene at the end of which the hero's wife dies. The protagonist's insolence is now broken by fate and redemption awaits him in death after an exhausting effort to save his rival's life. But even with this outpouring of romantic sentiment, realism prevails and determines the story and the narrative method of this novel. . . .

The Three Black Pennys is the history of a Pennsylvanian iron and steel manufacturing family from the middle of the eighteenth century to the very end of the nineteenth century. The book consists of three independent parts, each having its respective protagonist and each reflecting an important phase in the rise of the family business and in human life in general. Against the background of the development of iron mills into large iron and steel works, the story of three members of the Penny clan is told. The three characters have one common trait:

a strong passion for independence linked with a strain of Welsh blood, black hair and a rebellious nature. (p. 78)

The Three Black Pennys is doubtlessly Hergesheimer's masterpiece. Though, with the material he had at hand, he could have used the conventional narrative technique of a family saga, Hergesheimer chose the constrictive form of short stories linking them together with one aspect in characterization and in social development. The three parts, or stories, have been symbolically called "The Furnace", "The Forge" and "The Metal" and they correspond also to three important stages in human life: youth, middle age and old age. The youth of the first Howat Penny and of his violent passion which dominates and overwhelms him, equals in the social sphere the economic rise of the family in the iron and steel industry. This social ascent culminates in the second part, where Jasper Penny is the master and the head of large and prospering steel works. This fact and his life experience give him more balance to enable him to submit to the trial the puritanism of his beloved schoolmistress imposes on him. The third protagonist has given up economic activity. Though trained in law he never practices it. The social position and wealth he has inherited from his hard-working ancestors insures him the kind of freedom and independence his predecessors had much longed for. He makes use of them not only to cultivate his aristocratic tastes, but also to reconcile the social iniquities in his own family.

The main point of the novel is the revolt carried out by the three "black" Pennys. In the first two parts Howat and Jasper are restrained in their revolt by women, the first by a rather passive and decorative type, the latter by the moral chastity of an upright puritan. In the third part the revolt is taken over by a young lady whom the author provided with much common sense and it was more to her than to her detached and aging uncle that he assigned the role of adjusting the already weakened "black" strain of Penny blood in her veins, and in those of her proletarian husband, to the requirements of the coming twentieth century.

In this concise novel in which Joseph Hergesheimer successfully joined a historical and a contemporary social theme, he also succeeded in combining his aesthetic predilections in style and character-drawing with the realistic description of background and events. [When] . . . *The Three Black Pennys* was published, the tradition of the historical novel about the American past was still greatly flourishing and the social novel was gaining more and more popularity. Hergesheimer rendered skillfully the development of the Pennsylvanian iron industry and the people engaged in it. His aesthetic view, i.e. his painter's vision, shows itself only here and there in style (in some decorative expressions) and in descriptions of interiors and dressing. This is what Sinclair Lewis [see excerpt above], who was very enthusiastic about the novel and its characters, pointed out to his friend Hergesheimer in a letter. . . . (pp. 79-80)

Hergesheimer had always been an admirer of Conrad's exotic vision of the Far East and the picturesqueness of Conrad's settings. And it was in his next novel *Java Head* . . . that Hergesheimer also chose an exotic element in his theme. (p. 80)

In this book Hergesheimer already mixes realism and historical authenticity with cheap and fantastic effects to heighten the dramatic tension of the plot. There is Nettie's debility due to her accident, Edward Dunsack's sensual stupor and intoxication and Taou Yuen's momentary loss of control over her feelings. The novel is divided into ten chapters, each of which is narrated by another character, with the exception of the protagonist Gerrit Ammidon, who is given two chapters. In this way Hergesheimer tried to introduce his characters to the reader and join their particular individual stories with the main stream of the narrative. In some disproportion to other chapters are those narrated by episodic characters such as Rhoda Ammidon and her daughters Sidsall and Laurel. To Laurel, the youngest member of the family, the introductory chapter is allotted.

Some of the book's critics have pointed out that the novel lacks real dramatic power, due to the author's inability to develop a "logical sequence of events", that the author planned his story for effect and relied upon the unexpected and even gave way to the popular demand for a happy ending. Through the sudden outbreak of her subdued passion the Manchu, who up to this moment had only dazzled the other characters with her exotic beauty, becomes the center of the story. And it is not the pressure of a foreign culture on her, as one would have imagined, but the moral deterioration and irresponsibility of one of this culture's degenerated members that drive the Eastern woman into her desperate act of self-sacrifice.

In *Java Head* Hergesheimer abandoned the realistic novel pursued in *Mountain Blood* and *The Three Black Pennys*. The aesthetic decorativeness which in these novels has been fruitfully counterbalanced by good stories and authentic settings, emerges in *Java Head* not only in style, but also in characterization and in the development of action. (Like the one in which Taou Yuen is involved and which leads to the climax of the novel.)

Though Hergesheimer's fame as a novelist will grow yet, his artistic achievement seems to be at a loose end, showing no signs of further development.

The next novel, *Linda Condon*, . . . subtitled "a romantic character study", made Hergesheimer's deviation from the American realistic tradition more obvious.

Linda Condon tells the life-story of a girl whose childhood and youth at the side of a frivolous mother is marked by loneliness, dreams, introspection and absence of deep feeling. The girl has been led to admire her mother's good looks and to value physical beauty as her greatest possession. (pp. 81-2)

Dodge Pleydon, the sculptor, is a much livelier figure. He is a man of action and courage, a strong individuality, an artist, who turned away from Linda's cold beauty to build his own passionate image of her. The sculptor is the most real character of the book. Unreal and improbable is Linda's beauty as a permanent source of Pleydon's artistic inspiration. The line the author drew from Pleydon's passion for the woman he never possessed to his sculptures is rather vague and unconvincing. Convincing are once again most of the episodic characters of the novel, because with them it has not been necessary to give reasons for their actions. . . .

As a whole the novel is an interesting piece of a "romantic character study". Dramatic action and tensions are softened. There is no apparent climax. The story goes on in the same subdued tone as it started. Descriptions of interiors and settings predominate, very little dialogue is used. Hergesheimer's style is more ornamental and elaborated than ever before. (p. 83)

With the novels *Java Head* and *Linda Condon* published in the same year Hergesheimer easily abandoned the promising line of straight realism of his regional novel *Mountain Blood* and even made less of the synthesis of realism and his aesthetic ideals attained in *The Three Black Pennys*. Some critics imputed

this to his talent and training as a painter and his adherence—dating from his youth—to the aesthetic ideals of European symbolists; others attributed it to his life of comfort (Hergesheimer never had any financial troubles) and to the growing popularity of his books and short stories. The contemporary social problems of his country and of the world after World War I seem to have touched him only slightly. (pp. 83-4)

When on the advice of friends Hergesheimer chose a modern story for his novel *Cytherea* . . . , the number of his readers still increased but his artistic reputation lost ground he never regained. (p. 84)

Hergesheimer attempted to criticize the superficiality and aimlessness of American postwar society in this novel. If he had carried out this criticism through irony, he might have succeeded. But as he considered mainly the impact of exotic beauty on a dissatisfied and aging man, and narrated the flight of Random and his mistress to Cuba simply as a physical adventure in passion, the result was a conventional piece of society prose fiction much read at its time but without any artistic value.

The only value of this novel . . . is that it reflects American middle-class and upper middle-class society at the beginnings of the twenties, its restlessness and discontent with the past and unwillingness to face the future. Youth is considered the summit of life. Those who are over forty feel old and sterile and to regain youth and vigor they often change their conventional wife for an unconventional mistress. In 1922 this had been a quite new attitude to life, but very soon it was overcome by other standpoints going more to the core of the problems in American society at that time: poverty, unemployment, social and racial discrimination, the disintegration of old values and the impact of industrialization and civilization on the old patriarch way of life. But Hergesheimer sought no new attitudes. He preferred to return to the romanticism and the aesthetic ideals and historical settings of his beginnings, and to describe beauty in nature and in man. And it was an external, seizable beauty he looked for. (Hergesheimer's conception of beauty even differed from that of other American and English novelists of his time, e.g. James B. Cabell or John Galsworthy, the latter making use of the impact of beauty on the declining world of property to serve his critical purpose.) (pp. 84-5)

Joseph Hergesheimer seems to be quite forgotten, though from 1914 to 1922 (and even later) he was one of the most popular and widely read authors and also played an important part in the American literary development leading from the first generation of American realists and naturalists to the postwar young radicals.

Joseph Hergesheimer filled a gap in the evolution of American prose fiction in the years of World War I enriching American regionalism with European aestheticism. And that is why this author, and at least two or three of his early novels . . . should not fall into complete oblivion. (p. 86)

Ingeborg Kejzlarová, "Joseph Hergesheimer: A Lost Writer of American Twentieth Century Fiction?" in Philologica Pragensia (© Academia, Praha 1976), *Vol. 19, No. 2, 1976, pp. 73-86.*

ADDITIONAL BIBLIOGRAPHY

Adcock, St. John. "Joseph Hergesheimer." In his *The Glory That Was Grub Street: Impressions of Contemporary Authors*, pp. 89-93. New York: Frederick A. Stokes Co., 1928.

A general discussion of Hergesheimer's life and work.

Angott, Charles. "Recollections of Elinor Wylie, Thomas Mann, Joseph Hergesheimer, James Stevens, Logan Clendining." *The Literary Review* 10, No. 2 (Winter 1966-67): 169-70.*

Reminiscences by the man who succeeded Mencken as editor of *The American Mercury*. Angoff recounts several interesting conversations between Hergesheimer and Mencken in the *Mercury*'s offices.

Beach, Joseph Warren. "Incoherence in the Aesthete: Mr. Joseph Hergesheimer." In his *The Outlook for American Prose*, pp. 137-41. 1926. Reprint. Port Washington, N.Y.: Kennikat Press, 1968.

A critical attack on Hergesheimer as a "fussy and often unintelligible" writer.

Clark, Emily. *Ingénue among the Lions: The Letters of Emily Clark to Joseph Hergesheimer.* Edited by Gerald Langford. Austin: University of Texas Press, 1965, 221 p.

Reprints the correspondence of Clark, founding editor of *The Reviewer,* to Hergesheimer, who contributed material to the journal and aided Clark in other professional capacities.

Colum, Padraic, and Cabell, Margaret Freeman, eds. *Between Friends: Letters of James Branch Cabell and Others.* Harcourt Brace & World, 1962, 304 p.*

Reprints critical letters from Cabell and Burton Rascoe to Hergesheimer.

Follett, Wilson. "Joseph Hergesheimer." In *The Borzoi 1920: Being a Sort of Record of Five Years Publishing,* pp. 15-19. New York: Alfred A. Knopf, 1920.

A defensive overview of Hergesheimer's career.

Haardt, Sara. "Joseph Hergesheimer's Methods." *The Bookman,* New York LXIX, No. 4 (June 1929): 398-403.

A biographical essay, describing memories of Hergesheimer and praising his methods of research for *Swords and Roses.*

Hicks, Granville. "Two Roads." In his *The Great Tradition: An Interpretation of American Literature since the Civil War,* pp. 206-56. New York: The Macmillan Co., 1933.*

Finds that Hergesheimer's promising early romantic works gradually wore into a formula in which pessimism became a pose and the author's "passion for physical luxury nakedly revealed itself as simply the vulgar longings of the idle rich."

Mencken, H. L. "Four Makers of Tales." In his *Prejudices, fifth series,* pp. 34-63. New York: Alfred A. Knopf, 1926.*

Reprints an approving appraisal of Hergesheimer's skill and a review of *Cytherea,* in an essay originally written for the April 1922 issue of *The Smart Set.*

Napier, James. "Conrad's Praise of Joseph Hergesheimer." *Notes and Queries* n.s. 6, No. 6 (June 1959): 210.

Reprints a short letter from Joseph Conrad to Alfred A. Knopf, commending Hergesheimer's "vital work" "Wild Oranges," a story which Conrad believes combines "strength of vision with delicate perception and masterly expression."

Priestley, J. B. "Joseph Hergesheimer: An English View." *The Bookman,* New York LXIII, No. 3 (May 1926): 272-80.

Finds that, at its best, Hergesheimer's literature creates "fictional worlds from intriguing surfaces that appeal to the visual senses," and blends this with the romance of a "dreamlike inner light." But in other instances, Priestley judges Hergesheimer guilty of merely "cataloguing fussy objects and lacy underwear."

Van Vechten, Carl. "How I Remember Joseph Hergesheimer." *The Yale University Library Gazette* 22, No. 3 (January 1948): 87-93.

A memoir which fondly recalls travels with Hergesheimer.

West, Geoffrey. "Joseph Hergesheimer." *The Virginia Quarterly Review* 8, No. 1 (January 1932): 95-108.

A contemporary discussion of Hergesheimer's work. West judges Hergesheimer to be "the most considerable artist writing in America today."

Hugo (Laurenz August Hofmann Edler) von Hofmannsthal
1874-1929

(Also wrote under pseudonyms of Loris, Loris Melikow, Theophil Morren, and Archibald O'Hagan) Austrian dramatist, librettist, poet, essayist, short story writer, critic, and editor.

Hofmannsthal is considered the preeminent Symbolist writer of German literature. Although he is often identified with the German fin de siècle "art for art's sake" movement, his work is distinguished by a rare combination of the aesthete's view of art with that of the artist who is morally committed to life. Hofmannsthal's international reputation rests on his libretti for several of Richard Strauss's operas and on his role as one of the originators of the Salzburg Festival, where his symbolic dramas, most notably *Jedermann (The Play of Everyman)* and *Das Salzburger grosse Welttheater (The Salzburg Great Theatre of the World)*, are still performed.

Born and raised in Vienna, Hofmannsthal was the only child of a prominent family who encouraged their son's studies in the arts. While still in school, he wrote lyric poetry under the pseudonym of "Loris," critical essays on contemporary authors, and, at seventeen, published his first lyric drama, *Gestern*. Hofmannsthal's precocious literary activity brought him to the attention of such prominent German and Austrian men of letters as Stefan George and Arthur Schnitzler, who were astounded by the display of mature thought and form in the young Austrian's work. For a short time Hofmannsthal contributed literary works to George's periodical, *Die Blätter fur die Kunst*. Directed at the intellectual community, the journal promoted George's idea of a new German spirit based on a glorification of youth and leadership. Hofmannsthal eventually grew uncomfortable with George's elitist view of art, and though he maintained an aloof friendship with the German poet, he ended the master/disciple relationship George had tried to nurture. Along with other writers of his own generation, including Hermann Bahr and Richard Beer-Hofmann, Hofmannsthal formed the *Jung Wien* (Young Vienna), a coterie of writers who rejected the trend of naturalism in literature and who artistically allied themselves to the French Symbolist tradition. In 1899, he graduated from the University of Vienna with a doctorate in Romance philology but chose to continue his writing career rather than to teach at a university. Thereafter, with the exception of travelling to Italy and France, and service as a translator and courier during World War I, Hofmannsthal remained in his homeland, living a quiet, genteel life until his death in 1929.

Critics of Hofmannsthal's works usually divide his literary development into three overlapping phases. The early phase began when he was sixteen and lasted through the turn-of-the-century. The poetry and lyric dramas of this period, such as *Gestern*, *Der Tod des Tizian (The Death of Titian)*, and *Der Tor und der Tod (Death and the Fool)*, brought him attention as an aesthete associated with the "art for art's sake" movement. These works, which are usually set in the baroque era, are commonly concerned with cultivated men who reject society for a life devoted to art, arriving at a social consciousness only when they are confronted with death. Characterized by an egocentric aestheticism, the works in this early phase convey a dream-like detachment from life—a mystical state Hof-

mannsthal later called "pre-existence." According to Hofmannsthal, in this contemplative condition the writer is in harmony with the universe and intuitively understands life with a wisdom that exceeds his experiences. He attributed to "pre-existence" his ability to compose works seemingly beyond the artistic and spiritual range of his seventeen years.

The middle phase of Hofmannsthal's career began around 1900 and lasted to World War I. It was a transitional period in which he focused more on human concerns and less on the artistic preoccupation of his earlier "pre-existence" stage. He now emphasized the need to accept the responsibilities of life. During this time Hofmannsthal despaired over the insufficiency of language to express a world view. This crisis is artfully expressed in his *Ein Brief (The Letter of Lord Chandos)*, a fictional letter written by an Elizabethan gentleman to Francis Bacon, the sixteenth-century essayist and philosopher. *The Letter of Lord Chandos* is important not only as a description of Hofmannsthal's personal doubts about his creative abilities, but also, as recent criticism reveals, as an indication of his belief that art should not supplant life; therefore, *The Letter of Lord Chandos* warned his contemporaries of the dangers of aestheticism. Hofmannsthal's aesthetic crisis precipitated his abandonment of lyric poetry and lyric drama for the more straightforward expression of prose drama. In 1903, he staged a successful adaptation of the Greek tragedy, *Elektra (Electra)*.

Throughout the drama, Hofmannsthal maintained morbid imagery which helped transform the title character from her traditional role as a woman who methodically seeks justice into a vengeful psychotic. His association with the composer Strauss began shortly after this production of *Electra*. Strauss regarded Hofmannsthal as a "born librettist" and together they created several classic operas. *Der Rosenkavalier (The Rose-Bearer*, also known as *The Cavalier of the Rose)* endures as the most popular of their creations. As a librettist, Hofmannsthal found that operatic expression often transcended the inadequacy of language through its music and grand theatrical staging. In 1911, he wrote an adaptation of the English morality play *Everyman*. The drama represents the apex of Hofmannsthal's middle phase and indicates the dominant concern of his later period—suppression of "self" and cultivation of a Christian spirit.

Hofmannsthal's last period of literary development produced several social comedies and the morality plays written for the Salzburg Festival. *Der Schwierige (The Difficult Man)*, which is often praised for its subtle craftsmanship, is his best comedy in this post-war period. The protagonist of the drama, Hans Karl Bühl, is one of Hofmannsthal's most interesting characters, an aristocrat with a social conscience. Unlike the characters in Hofmannsthal's earlier works, Hans Karl is given the opportunity to develop fully his awareness of the world around him, realizing both the benefits and responsibilities of social relationships. With the establishment of the Salzburg Festival, Hofmannsthal hoped to restore Austrian culture, which was devastated by war. This contemporary theater advocated a Christian ethic and appealed to the common audience through its use of simple peasant speech. Hofmannsthal's *Everyman* was the first festival production, followed by *The Salzburg Great Theatre of the World*, a spiritual drama based on the seventeenth-century Spanish play *The Great Theatre of the World* by Calderón. In this religious allegory, Hofmannsthal successfully rendered the metaphor of "the world as a stage" and created a timeless universal plane on which the play is acted. His third drama written for the festival theater, *Der Turm (The Tower)*, is also an adaptation of a Calderón play, *Life Is a Dream*. As one of his most symbolic works, *The Tower* expresses the hopeless fate of human existence ravaged by the brutal forces of a modern world devoid of a Christian mission.

Critics generally regard Hofmannsthal as a proficient writer in several genres. Though his works are usually discussed as if they formed discrete phases of his career, most critics agree that they possess consistent themes which demand that they be considered as a unified body of work. According to Lowell Bangerter, the dominant concern of Hofmannsthal's canon is "that of synthesis, of bringing all things harmoniously together—people, nations, art forms, traditions, ideas, past, present, future." His works insist upon social consciousness and moral commitment to life, qualities which can be awakened by art. Thus, while the expressed purpose of his contemporaries was "art for art's sake," Hofmannsthal's literary doctrine was "art for life's sake." Hofmannsthal's commitment to life mirrored his commitment to art and the preservation of European culture; for this reason, he is considered among the most important contributors to Austrian literature in the twentieth century.

(See also *Contemporary Authors*, Vol. 106.)

PRINCIPAL WORKS

Gestern [as Theophil Morren] [first publication]   (drama)
   1891

Der Tor und der Tod   (drama)   1898
   [*Death and the Fool*, 1913]
Der Tod des Tizian   (drama)   1901
   [*The Death of Titian*, 1914]
Ein Brief   (fictional letter)   1902; published in newspaper
   Der Tag
   [*The Letter of Lord Chandos* published in *Selected Prose*,
   1952]
Ausgewählte Gedichte   (poetry)   1903
Elektra   (drama)   1903
   [*Electra*, 1908]
Das kleine Welttheater [first publication]   (drama)   1903
   [*The Little Theater of the World; or, The Fortunate Ones*
   published in *Poems and Verse Plays*, 1961]
Das gerettete Venedig   (drama)   1905
   [*Venice Preserved*, 1915]
Das Märchen der 672. Nacht, und andere Erzahlungen
   (short stories)   1905
Ödipus und die Sphinx   (drama)   1906
   [*Oedipus and the Sphinx*, 1968]
Die Gesammelten Gedichte   (poetry)   1907
Elektra   (libretto)   1909
   [*Electra*, 1930]
Christinas Heimreise   (drama)   1910
   [*Christina's Journey Home*, 1916]
Jedermann   (drama)   1911
   [*The Play of Everyman*, 1917]
Der Rosenkavalier   (libretto)   1911
   [*The Rose-Bearer*, 1912]
Ariadne auf Naxos   (libretto)   1912
   [*Ariadne auf Naxos*, 1912]
The Lyrical Poems of Hugo von Hufmannshtal   (poetry)
   1918
Der Schweirige   (drama)   1921
   [*The Difficult Man* published in *Selected Plays and
   Libretti*, 1963]
Buch der Freunde   (aphorisms)   1922
Das Salzburger grosse Welttheater   (drama)   1922
   [*The Salzburg Great Theatre of the World*, 1958]
Der Turm   (drama)   1928
   [*The Tower* published in *Selected Plays and Libretti*,
   1963]
Andreas oder Die Vereinigten   (unfinished novel)   1932
   [*Andreas, or The United*, 1936]
Briefe: 1890-1901   (letters)   1935
Briefe: 1900-1909   (letters)   1937
Gesammelte Werk in Einzelausgaben. 15 Vols.   (poetry,
   dramas, libretti, and essays)   1946-59
Das Bergwerk zu Falun   (drama)   1949
   [*The Mine at Falun* published in *Poems and Verse Plays*,
   1961]
Richard Strauss und Hugo von Hofmannsthal: Breifwechsel
   (letters)   1952
   [*The Correspondence between Richard Strauss and Hugo
   von Hofmannsthal*, 1961]
Selected Prose   (essays, short stories, unfinished novel, and
   aphorisms)   1952
Poems and Verse Plays   (poetry and dramas)   1961
Selected Plays and Libretti   (dramas and libretti)   1963
Three Plays   (dramas)   1966

*This work was written in 1899.

HUGO von HOFMANNSTHAL   (essay date 1902)

[*The following is an excerpt from* The Letter of Lord Chandos. *In this work—written as a letter from an Elizabethan author to Francis Bacon—Hofmannsthal explains the nature of his own crisis during this period, a crisis which caused him to view language as an insufficient vehicle for recording and understanding human experience. Afterward Hofmannsthal turned to literary forms, such as dramas and librettos, which included non-verbal means of expression to augment and enrich language. For commentary on the Chandos letter, see David G. Daviau's and Egon Schwarz's essays excerpted below.*]

[It] is my inner self that I feel bound to reveal to you—a peculiarity, a vice, a disease of my mind, if you like—if you are to understand that an abyss equally unbridgeable separates me from the literary works lying seemingly ahead of me as from those behind me: the latter having become so strange to me that I hesitate to call them my property. (p. 130)

I wanted to decipher the fables, the mythical tales bequeathed to us by the Ancients, in which painters and sculptors found an endless and thoughtless pleasure—decipher them as the hieroglyphs of a secret, inexhaustible wisdom whose breath I sometimes seemed to feel as though from behind a veil.

I well remember this plan. It was founded on I know not what sensual and spiritual desire: as the hunted hart craves water, so I craved to enter these naked, glistening bodies, these sirens and dryads, this Narcissus and Proteus, Perseus and Actaeon. I longed to disappear in them and talk out of them with tongues. (p. 131)

To sum up: In those days I, in a state of continuous intoxication, conceived the whole of existence as one great unit: the spiritual and physical worlds seemed to form no contrast, as little as did courtly and bestial conduct, art and barbarism, solitude and society; in everything I felt the presence of Nature, in the aberrations of insanity as much as in the utmost refinement of the Spanish ceremonial; in the boorishness of young peasants no less than in the most delicate of allegories; and in all expressions of Nature I felt myself. When in my hunting lodge I drank the warm foaming milk which an unkempt wench had drained into a wooden pail from the udder of a beautiful gentle-eyed cow, the sensation was no different from that which I experienced when, seated on a bench built into the window of my study, my mind absorbed the sweet and foaming nourishment from a book. The one was like the other: neither was superior to the other, whether in dreamlike celestial quality or in physical intensity—and thus it prevailed through the whole expanse of life in all directions; everywhere I was in the centre of it, never suspecting mere appearance: at other times I divined that all was allegory and that each creature was a key to all the others; and I felt myself the one capable of seizing each by the handle and unlocking as many of the others as were ready to yield. (pp. 132-33)

To a person susceptible to such ideas, it might appear a well-designed plan of divine Providence that my mind should fall from such a state of inflated arrogance into this extreme of despondency and feebleness which is now the permanent condition of my inner self. (p. 133)

My case, in short, is this: I have lost completely the ability to think or to speak of anything coherently.

At first I grew by degrees incapable of discussing a loftier or more general subject in terms of which everyone, fluently and without hesitation, is wont to avail himself. I experienced an inexplicable distaste for so much as uttering the words *spirit,*

soul, or *body*. I found it impossible to express an opinion on the affairs at Court, the events in Parliament, or whatever you wish. This was not motivated by any form of personal deference (for you know that my candour borders on imprudence), but because the abstract terms of which the tongue must avail itself as a matter of course in order to voice a judgment—these terms crumbled in my mouth like mouldy fungi. (pp. 133-34)

Even in familiar and humdrum conversation all the opinions which are generally expressed with ease and sleep-walking assurance became so doubtful that I had to cease altogether taking part in such talk. It filled me with an inexplicable anger, which I could conceal only with effort, to hear such things as: This affair has turned out well or ill for this or that person; Sheriff N. is a bad, Parson T. a good man; Farmer M. is to be pitied, his sons are wasters; another is to be envied because his daughters are thrifty; one family is rising in the world, another is on the downward path. All this seemed as indemonstrable, as mendacious and hollow as could be. My mind compelled me to view all things occurring in such conversations from an uncanny closeness. As once, through a magnifying glass, I had seen a piece of skin on my little finger look like a field full of holes and furrows, so I now perceived human beings and their actions. I no longer succeeded in comprehending them with the simplifying eye of habit. For me everything disintegrated into parts, those parts again into parts; no longer would anything let itself be encompassed by one idea. Single words floated round me; they congealed into eyes which stared at me and into which I was forced to stare back—whirlpools which gave me vertigo and, reeling incessantly, led into the void.

I tried to rescue myself from this plight by seeking refuge in the spiritual world of the Ancients. Plato I avoided, for I dreaded the perilousness of his imagination. Of them all, I intended to concentrate on Seneca and Cicero. Through the harmony of their clearly defined and orderly ideas I hoped to regain my health. But I was unable to find my way to them. These ideas, I understood them well: I saw their wonderful interplay rise before me like magnificent fountains upon which played golden balls. I could hover around them and watch how they played, one with the other; but they were concerned only with each other, and the most profound, most personal quality of my thinking remained excluded from this magic circle. In their company I was overcome by a terrible sense of loneliness; I felt like someone locked in a garden surrounded by eyeless statues. (pp. 134-35)

Since that time I have been leading an existence which I fear you can hardly imagine, so lacking in spirit and thought is its flow: an existence which, it is true, differs little from that of my neighbours, my relations, and most of the land-owning nobility of this kingdom, and which is not utterly bereft of gay and stimulating moments. It is not easy for me to indicate wherein these good moments subsist; once again words desert me. For it is, indeed, something entirely unnamed, even barely nameable which, at such moments, reveals itself to me, filling like a vessel any casual object of my daily surroundings with an overflowing flood of higher life. I cannot expect you to understand me without examples, and I must plead your indulgence for their absurdity. A pitcher, a harrow abandoned in a field, a dog in the sun, a neglected cemetery, a cripple, a peasant's hut—all these can become the vessel of my revelation. Each of these objects and a thousand others similar, over which the eye usually glides with a natural indifference, can suddenly, at any moment (which I am utterly powerless to evoke), assume for me a character so exalted and moving that words seem too poor to describe it. Even the distinct image of an absent object, in fact, can acquire the mysterious function of being filled to the brim with this silent but suddenly rising flood of divine sensation. Recently, for instance, I had given the order for a copious supply of rat-poison to be scattered in the milk-cellars of one of my dairy-farms. Towards evening I had gone off for a ride and, as you can imagine, thought no more about it. As I was trotting along over the freshly-ploughed land, nothing more alarming in sight than a scared covey of quail and, in the distance, the great sun sinking over the undulating fields, there suddenly loomed up before me the vision of that cellar, resounding with the death-struggle of a mob of rats. I felt everything within me: the cool, musty air of the cellar filled with the sweet and pungent reek of poison, and the yelling of the death-cries breaking against the mouldering walls; the vain convulsions of those convoluted bodies as they tear about in confusion and despair; their frenzied search for escape, and the grimace of icy rage when a couple collide with one another at a blocked-up crevice. But why seek again for words which I have foresworn! You remember, my friend, the wonderful description in Livy of the hours preceding the destruction of Alba Longa: when the crowds stray aimlessly through the streets which they are to see no more . . . when they bid farewell to the stones beneath their feet. I assure you, my friend, I carried this vision within me, and the vision of burning Carthage, too; but there was more, something more divine, more bestial; and it was the Present, the fullest, most exalted Present. There was a mother, surrounded by her young in their agony of death; but her gaze was cast neither toward the dying nor upon the merciless walls of stone, but into the void, or through the void into Infinity, accompanying this gaze with a gnashing of teeth!—A slave struck with helpless terror standing near the petrifying Niobe must have experienced what I experienced when, within me, the soul of this animal bared its teeth to its monstrous fate.

Forgive this description, but do not think that it was pity I felt. For if you did, my example would have been poorly chosen. It was far more and far less than pity: an immense sympathy, a flowing over into these creatures, or a feeling that an aura of life and death, of dream and wakefulness, had flowed for a moment into them—but whence?. . . .To me, then, it is as though my body consists of nought but ciphers which give me the key to everything; or as if we could enter into a new and hopeful relationship with the whole of existence if only we begin to think with the heart. As soon, however, as this strange enchantment falls from me, I find myself confused; wherein this harmony transcending me and the entire world consisted, and how it made itself known to me, I could present in sensible words as little as I could say anything precise about the inner movements of my intestines or a congestion of my blood. (pp. 135-38)

I have troubled you excessively, my dear friend, with this extended description of an inexplicable condition which is wont, as a rule, to remain locked up in me.

You were kind enough to express your dissatisfaction that no book written by me reaches you any more, "to compensate for the loss of our relationship." Reading that, I felt, with a certainty not entirely bereft of a feeling of sorrow, that neither in the coming year nor in the following nor in all the years of this my life shall I write a book, whether in English or in Latin: and this for an odd and embarrassing reason which I must leave to the boundless superiority of your mind to place in the realm of physical and spiritual values spread out harmoniously before your unprejudiced eye: to wit, because the language in which I might be able not only to write but to think is neither Latin nor English, neither Italian nor Spanish, but a language none of whose words is known to me, a language in which inanimate things speak to me and wherein I may one day have to justify myself before an unknown judge. (pp. 140-41)

> *Hugo von Hofmannsthal, "The Letter of Lord Chandos" (1902), in his* Selected Writings of Hugo von Hofmannsthal: Selected Prose, Vol. 1, *translated by Mary Hottinger, Tania Stern and James Stern, Bollingen Series XXXIII (copyright 1952 by Princeton University Press, © renewed 1980 by Princeton University Press; reprinted by permission of Princeton University Press), Pantheon Books, 1952, pp. 129-41.*

ASHLEY DUKES   (essay date 1911)

[*Dukes was an important English dramatist and drama critic during the first half of the twentieth century. He is most noted for his writings on modern European theater, particularly poetic drama. He had a broad knowledge of continental drama and, both as a translator and as the manager of his own theater, introduced English audiences to the work of several important French and German dramatists, including Ernst Toller, Georg Kaiser, and Lion Feuchtwanger. In the following survey, Dukes praises the artistry of Hofmannsthal's verse-dramas.*]

[Hofmannsthal] published his first work in 1891—at the period, that is to say, of the Freie Bühne in Berlin and the independent Ibsenite theatres in the rest of Europe. He had nothing to do with Ibsenism or "movements," however, and very little to do with the theatre. He was only seventeen years of age, and the influence under which he had come was not that of the new *bourgeois* drama (the term is used in no sense of abuse) of Ibsen and Hauptmann, but that of Italian art. . . . In addition to many poems and essays, he had [at nineteen] already published two complete verse-dramas, **"Gestern,"** the scene of which is laid "in the time of the great painters," and **"Der Tod des Tizian."** Hofmannsthal's reaction against modern realism, then, although an unconscious reaction, dates from even earlier than the symbolism of Maeterlinck and the Théâtre de l'Oeuvre. He turned deliberately to a more heroic age in search of beauty. (pp. 160-61)

Both melody and image [in **"Gestern"**] show an extraordinarily fastidious choice of words; and that is the most distinctive gift of this poet-prodigy, who at seventeen could absorb the art of centuries and realise the emotions of a lifetime. There is little dramatic power in **"Gestern,"** and hardly more in **"Der Tod des Tizian."** Both are records of the first impressions of an artist—first love, the first creative impulse and the first glimpse of Italy. Even in the very names of their characters—Desiderio, Fortunio, Vespasiano, Fantasio, Tizianello and the rest—they are musical.

Hofmannsthal's next play was **"Der Tor und der Tod."** . . . The speeches here are measured; there is no overflow of rhetoric, and the verse, in its form, its substance and even its rhythm of sound, moves into step with drama. (pp. 163-64)

It is a little play of rare beauty. Written before he was twenty years of age, it marks the close of what for Hofmannsthal must be called his youthful period. The treatment alone distinguishes him very clearly both from Wilde and from the French symbolists.

A number of short dramatic poems followed between 1895 and 1899, among them **"Die Frau im Fenster," "Der Kaiser und die Hexe," "Das Kleine Welttheater"** and **"Das Bergwerk in Falun."** Longer pieces are **"Die Hochzeit der Sobeïde"** and **"Der Abenteurer und die Sängerin."** For the most part these are only exercises in drama, some of them effective, all of them exquisitely written. They are still inspired by Italy, but a gradual change of tone is noticeable which seems to show that Hofmannsthal's later choice of Greek tragedy in **"Elektra"** and **"Oedipus"** was no haphazard choice of a poet at a loss for subject-matter. What is most important, however, in these earlier works is not their plot (always of the slightest), nor even the decorative beauty of their language (as well suited, in itself, to a volume of poems as to drama), but their constant striving after new verse-forms for the theatre. All writers of verse-drama have made use of a change of rhyme or metre in order to obtain a certain dramatic effect. Among the most familiar examples are the rhymed couplet of the Shakespearean plays, used to round off a speech or to add an air of finality at the close of a scene, and the change from verse to prose in certain passages. Hofmannsthal uses both devices freely, but in other respects he goes much further than any poet before him. His verse changes its form continually. It is like a mountain lake upon an April day, sensitive to the shadow of every passing cloud and rippled afresh by every gust of wind. Perhaps it would be too much to say that his verse has a new metrical lilt for every emotion, but in many passages of the later plays even this is true. The Venetian play **"Der Abenteurer und die Sängerin"** shows the adaptation of rhythm to the passing mood of drama. (pp. 165-67)

Apart altogether from subject-matter, Hofmannsthal must be credited with having given new life to verse-drama. In **"Oedipus und die Sphinx"** the method is perfected. The tragedy begins with the ordinary iambic. Musically speaking, this metre is Hofmannsthal's recitative. As the drama develops, the verse breaks into other forms. . . . (p. 170)

[The] play runs on, passing from blank verse to rhyme, from rhyme to irregular metre, or again to prose.

Drama cannot live, however, by new forms alone; and I turn now to Hofmannsthal's work as playwright. He has become most widely known through his modernisations of Greek legend in **"Elektra"** and **"Oedipus."** The **"Elektra"** has acquired a certain vogue as the libretto of Strauss's opera, but **"Oedipus"** is unquestionably the greater play. Both are described as free adaptations of Sophocles. The title-page of **"Oedipus und die Sphinx"** bears the quotation from Hölderlin: "The surging waves of the heart would never foam into the heights of the soul, were it not that they break upon the ancient, immovable rock of Fate." There is the spirit of tragedy summed up in a single sentence. The same inscription might have been written upon the plays of Sophocles. Hofmannsthal has followed him; the only question is whether his newer treatment can be fruitful—whether it can have any meaning for our time. (pp. 172-73)

When we say that "Oedipus Rex" is an immortal tragedy, we mean that it is an immortal work of art written by a man individually great, and not that its superstition, its morality, its motive and its setting are immortal. If the work of art is great enough, it will inevitably stereotype and perpetuate the legend or the personages of which it treats in a certain form; that is all. The form does not necessarily bear any relation to historical truth or fact; it becomes a tradition. Sophocles created such a tradition for his characters; Hofmannsthal seeks to create another.

But here the difficulty arises. The setting of the Sophoclean tragedies was an Attic setting. Their morality of revenge was an Attic morality. Their Fate was an Attic Fate. The Oracle, the Sphinx, the gods—all of these may be the determinant forces of Attic tragedy, but for us they have no literal meaning. They were stereotyped as ideas by Sophocles as inevitably as the legends in which they played a part were stereotyped. A Viennese poet comes, fresh from rhymings of renaissant Italy, and seeks to galvanise them all into life—adulterous kings, incestuous queens, seers and oracles and bloody myths. They move as sleep-walkers move, in a black mist. They scream of passion; they dance "nameless dances"; but they have no being. Hofmannsthal has attempted the impossible.

I take the **"Elektra"** first. The verse is perhaps the most beautiful that he has written. It is worthy of more than recitation by these blood-bespattered ghosts, whose pallor is not hidden by all the coloured veils of metaphor. The "modernisation" of Elektra herself consists chiefly in endowing her with a certain wild-cat animalism. She "crouches like a beast in its lair." She paces upon a fixed course "like a captive creature in a cage." The change from Sophocles to Hofmannsthal is the change from a morality of revenge to a thirst for revenge. With the one, the murder of the guilty mother satisfies the honour of a nation; with the other, it gratifies the sadistic lust of a madwoman. This modern Elektra is pathological to her fingertips. She belongs to the pages of Krafft-Ebing; never to the Attic landscape. Even the pathology is artificial and "literary" rather than dramatic. Hofmannsthal has never entered into the emotions of his tragedy; he has only painted them in words. He proves himself a great—artificer.

There is no academic question here of the historical form of the legend, nor of any defence of Sophocles against perversion. The characters must be taken upon their merits. They never live.

"Oedipus und die Sphinx" . . . is a completer, as well as a more ambitious, work. I have referred already to its originality of form. There is less "modernisation" in the play than in **"Elektra,"** less oppressiveness in its atmosphere; but the figures have the same inevitable unreality. They are no more than pegs upon which is hung the fabric of verse, and they remain as unreal in the hour of triumph as Elektra in the hour of approaching death. Oedipus returns from the mountain cave, where the Sphinx, instead of dragging him down into the depths, has greeted him by name as the deliverer. Jokaste sinks upon his arm "like a broken flower," crying, "Ah, what is it that we do?" and he replies "The blind deed of the gods." The people greet him with shouts of "Hail to the King, the unknown King!", Kreon spreads his cloak upon the ground, and Oedipus and Jokaste pass triumphantly toward the city. There is artifice here again, but little drama or conviction. It is all "a blind deed of the gods"; and already modern Germany is returning to Sophocles, preferring to study its determinism at first hand.

One other play by Hofmannsthal must be mentioned; the prose drama **"Christinas Heimreise."** . . . It is altogether uninspired, and must rank with Hauptmann's "Griselda" as a profoundly disappointing piece which would never have found its way on to any stage but for the reputation of its author. It has no more dramatic power than the early dramatic fragments I have already mentioned; and without verse it lacks their charm. The failure, in Hofmannsthal's case, need not be taken very seriously, for he is still many years younger than Hauptmann, and he has proved himself to be a greater artist. So far his completest work lies in a little volume of collected poems

(Gesammelte Gedichte . . .), which contains the now famous "**Ballade des äusseren Lebens**" and also "**Der Tod des Tizian.**" His future lies beyond a doubt in the writing of verse-drama. As to the quality of the verse there can be no fear; there is every hope for the greatness of the drama.

It is not easy to form any definite judgment of a poet-dramatist of thirty-five, not yet at the height of his powers. A contemporary Bavarian critic, Josef Hofmiller, has perhaps summed up Hofmannsthal's present achievement most clearly, and I quote one passage from his essay on the collected poems:—"Hofmannsthal's chief danger lies in virtuosity. He is a philologist in the highest sense, and his peril is the peril of the philologist—that of becoming stiff and mannered through the beauty of his inheritance of language, and of seeking his own tone of expression in the union of other tones, in themselves noble, but together jarring and incongruous. His works are perhaps the most aristocratic of our time. Other literature appears crude and clamorous beside them. Their artistic austerity is such that other literature seems mere babbling, devoid of, style. There are some poems one can no longer read, where one has read his. They have timbre, rhythm, colour, light. . . . The verbal perfection of his youthful dramas gave rise to the fear that he might be a poetic phenomenon, like the pianist-prodigies; early ripe, early played out; flashing for a time and then forgotten. Time has proved this fear to be groundless. . . . Of all our German authors to-day, he is the most distinctively European." (pp. 173-79)

Ashley Dukes, "Austria," in his Modern Dramatists *(reprinted by permission of the Estate of Ashley Dukes), Frank Palmer, 1911, Charles H. Sergel and Company, 1911, pp. 151-80.**

ELISABETH WALTER   (essay date 1915)

[*Walter's essay is a favorable critique of Hofmannsthal's early lyric dramas.*]

To the aesthete beauty of form must necessarily be of paramount importance, but unlike other neo-romanticists, [Hofmannsthal] is never a blind worshipper at beauty's shrine, never surrenders idea or feeling to mere perfection of form. Though he sets art above life, his work is never merely artificial. On the contrary, he is fully conscious of the danger that lurks in subservience to mere artificiality, and voices this danger in his exquisite dramatic poem, "**Death and the Fool,**" the tragedy of an aesthete who in his delectation of art has completely lost all enjoyment of life:

"The artificial so completely bound me,
That dead mine eyes looked on the golden sun,
And deaf mine ears were to the world around me."

Hofmannsthal is a born lyricist in whom thought, emotion, and word ever sound in perfect harmony. His poems are spoken pictures, that entrance through depth of thought and soulful verse. When first taking up his work, we cannot help but marvel at his seeming magic. Through rich melodious verses we glimpse an indescribable loveliness, from rarely, delicately chosen phrases a spirit, perfectly formed smiles to us. Freed from the dark chaos of life, we see the world full of a perfect harmony, beauty, and vastness. Warmth caresses us and as from a dream we waken to a perfect unification of the simplicity of the remote and fulness of the immediate. Hofmannsthal himself is full of learning, and his works are all in perfect taste and unalloyed beauty.

Over the pseudonym, Theophil Morren, he published his first work, "**Yesterday,**" "A Study in One Act, in Rhymes". This poem, rare flower in the garden of lyrical didacticism, is full of a strangely beautiful philosophy steeped in the fragrance of personal feeling. The hero is a sickly Don Juan of moral and sensual pleasure, to whom life is but a vessel ever to be filled with powerful impressions. Desirous of tasting every moment of life in all its completeness, to him all serves only his insatiable craving for sensation. . . . The whole poem reveals so perfect ripeness and clearness of vision, so complete mastery of the intricacies of life, that one can hardly conceive of an eighteen year old boy as its creator.

A marvelous pageant is presented in the one act drama, "**Titian's Death,**" in which the poet sings the decease of the artist Boecklin. Against the background of the city of Venice, we see the garden of Titian; from its terraces his pupils look down through the gathering twilight upon the slumbering city, while in the lighted studio within, the artist is at work on his last picture. This is the setting of the poem in which more than in any other of his works, Hofmannsthal sings of the painter's art with glowing and ecstatic fervency. He draws a sharp line between the sensuous persons of pale material enjoyments, the dull, stupid mob, and the sensuous beings of creative art. He hails the artist as alone capable of interpreting nature, as the only teacher of life truly worthy to bear the name. (pp. 645-47)

The dreaminess and fairytale atmosphere of Venice must prove an irresistible attraction to a poet of Hofmannsthal's temperament. On three occasions he has made use of the Queen of the Lagunes in his dramatic works. One of these, "**Venice Preserved**" bears upon its title page the information that it was built upon the work of same name by Thomas Otway. In the main ideas of the plot it is the same, but taken as a whole it is an entirely new, entirely different creation. A puny weakling who only through love is carried beyond his narrow self, is driven through the accumulation of misfortune into a treacherous plot concerned with the overthrow of the government. Through cowardice and perhaps also through his love for his wife, he betrays the plot and his friends. Such is the main idea of Otway's drama and also of Hofmannsthal's. But Hofmannsthal's characters are living creatures, pulsating with life, love, hate, and friendship. The accumulation of events produces emotions in them, which, whether we sympathize or not, we too are compelled to feel. Even as "**Elektra**" is a tragedy of hate, so Hofmannsthal's "**Venice Preserved**" is a tragedy of treachery, but through it all runs a sweetly beautiful refrain of friendship ideal.

It is not possible to discuss here all the works of this prolific author of barely forty years, but of his drama "**Elektra**" a few words must be said. When first produced in 1903 it was received with a storm of disapproval: brutal! unnatural! inhuman! not the historical person of Electra! No, Hofmannsthal's Electra is not Sophocles' Electra, but has not an author the right to depict his heroine as he sees her? Hofmannsthal's Electra was seen with Hofmannsthal's eyes, lived with Hofmannsthal's life, conceived in Hofmannsthal's soul. And though the critics cry, "this is not Electra!" Hofmannsthal answers, "she is as I see her!", and the creator's positive production remains in the right against the critics' negative censorship. To some this conception of Electra may appear brutal and inhuman but to all the drama must give alike the impression of living life, of passion and emotion vivified, and that is the highest attainable pinnacle of art. A drama of hate, but hate raised to the highest power of dramatic conception, "**Electra**" is the ripest production of Hofmannsthal's pen and to all must bear promise of still greater things to come. Its still youthful creator has proved himself master of word, color, and melody. . . . (pp. 647-48)

Elisabeth Walter, "*Hugo von Hofmannsthal: Neo-Romanticist*," in Poet Lore (*copyright, 1915, by Poet Lore, Inc.; reprinted by permission of Heldref Publications*), Vol. XXVI, No. 4, September, 1915, pp. 644-48.

CHARLES WHARTON STORK   (essay date 1918)

[*Stork was one of the first to translate Hofmannsthal's lyric poetry into English. In the following excerpt, Stork discusses Hofmannsthal's poetry, which he believes to possess a greater poetic vision than that found in the works of his Austrian contemporaries.*]

[Hofmannsthal] may be called an extremist of his kind: an extreme lover of rich and remote beauty, an artist unusually detached from everyday existence, a genius of oppressive melancholy, a magician of startling power in the revelation of human consciousness, an unequaled exponent of style. (p. 5)

Although Hofmannsthal was a product of his environment and was even part of a literary tendency, the forcefulness of his genius was sufficient to raise him far above his possible rivals. Neither the vaguely mystical lyrics of Stefan George nor the wistful reveries of Rilke can compare in ultimate importance with the work of their associate. The intellect of Hofmannsthal dominates the school to which he belongs and has already called forth many followers. He is the one symbolist writing in German who has an absolutely sure touch, a perfect sense of balance in all that he does. In this respect also his plays seem to me to excel those of Maeterlinck.

The English poets who most resemble Hofmannsthal are Vaughan, Blake, Rossetti and Francis Thompson. Vaughan's ability to soar into a world of spiritual exaltation is not unlike what we find in *A Dream of the Higher Magic*. Vaughan, however, takes his moral sense and his human feelings with him, whereas the daemon of Hofmannsthal surveys all things impersonally. The splendor of their language and imagery is very similar, except that the brilliance of the English poet shows in flashes, that of the Austrian in a deep and constant glow. Blake is like Hofmannsthal in the abstractness of his poetic world, and his doctrine that the imagination is God comes very near that pictured in *A Dream of the Higher Magic*. But Blake's expression is simple and intuitive; his is altogether a more aërial spirit.

In their combination of somewhat heavily decorative style with mystic thought, Rossetti and Thompson stand much nearer to Hofmannsthal than do the earlier poets. "Fundamental brain-work," to quote Rossetti's famous phrase, is almost equally evident in the three; the underlying plan of their poems is laid with a similar definiteness. Hofmannsthal differs from Rossetti in that he gives more general pictures, producing effects more purely like those of music; whereas the pre-Raphaelite revels in sharply drawn detail. Both Rossetti and Thompson seem much more passionate; Hofmannsthal's emotion is always subdued and even in texture. The quaint, rather self-conscious style of the two modern English poets contrasts with the smooth diction of Hofmannsthal, whose mind moves in its dim spiritual world with the seemingly unconscious grace of a golden fish in shadowy depths.

Because the quality of Hofmannsthal's mood is so all-pervasive, we have spoken much of the effects which his poetry produces, without giving more than a hint of its actual content. This content might be defined as impersonally subjective, if the phrase does not seem to be an oxymoron. What is meant is that Hofmannsthal writes of his own consciousness, or that of others with whom he for the moment identifies himself, in a manner which shows great power of divination but only the most remote shade of sympathy. He does not wish human emotion to disturb him in his attempt to contemplate reality. For instance, in *The Two* he symbolizes admirably the mysterious relation of sex to sex, but we who read, instead of being stirred to a poignant feeling of pity, are only impelled to murmur: "How strange is truth!" Similarly in the poem *Of Mutability*, when he says it is

A thing too dreadful for the trivial tear:
That all things glide away from out our clasp,

we are in no real danger of a tear or even of a shudder. This impassive attitude toward the facts of life gives a tone of fatalism to nearly every poem in [*The Lyrical Poems of Hugo von Hofmannsthal*]. The interest shown in nature and humanity is exclusively artistic and speculative.

The earlier poems of this volume are purely philosophical or symbolic of the poet's own sensations. The *Three Little Songs* are somewhat more personal than the pieces which precede them; but even the third, a most delicate bit of lyricism, has not the ring of ordinary human feeling. In the remarkable group of *Figures* the poet identifies his soul with those of such various persons as the Emperor of China, a child, a captive ship's cook, and the collective personality of several interacting characters at a social entertainment. Into each of these minds in turn we are made to enter by the same exquisite art which, in the earlier lyrics, enables us to examine the intimacies of the poet's own consciousness. The *Idyll* at the end is a neo-classic study of the same kind, except that, instead of being static, it has dramatic motion, thus pointing the reader on to Hofmannsthal's plays.

We have still to mention the *Prologues and Addresses-of-Mourning*. These, though in a somewhat different vein, are wonderfully fascinating poems. The prologue to *Anatol* is a delicious piece of atmosphere. With the following prologue it constitutes, as we have indicated, a good exposition of the author's artistic purpose: namely, to present the truth, but only under the mask of beauty. In this point Hofmannsthal differs from Arthur Schnitzler, author of the short realistic plays grouped under the title *Anatol*. Schnitzler, though he is what we might call a selective realist, lets us at times see the ugliness of life pretty clearly.

Tributes to the two actors, Mitterwurzer and Müller [in *In Memory of the Actor, Mitlerwurzer* and *On the Death of the Actor, Hermann Müller*] show how intensely Hofmannsthal feels the identity of soul and body. He is, to be sure, thinking only of the soul of the given actor, but this soul has the gift of so informing and transforming the body it inhabits that the two cannot be thought of as separate, but only as mingled in varying proportions. The poem on Böcklin [*For a Commemoration on the Death of Arnold Böcklin*] is of course the finest of the five, showing as it does how the spirit of a true artist can "adorn the image of the world" for us and can thus live in the added charm which it flings over the visible forms of nature. (pp. 10-14)

Though some of Hofmannsthal's plays have been very successful on the stage and have run to from ten to thirty editions, the fact remains that his best work is for the few. He does not picture life as the ordinary man sees it or can see it. He generalizes what he sees in nature and eliminates the detail, like the designer of a stained-glass window. His interest in a given idea, scene or personality is only for the purpose of arriving at some philosophical conclusion. The result in his art is arresting, both intellectually and aesthetically, but cannot be dissociated in the reader's mind from a feeling of monotony and oppression, as if one were shut up in the darkly beautiful temple to which Hofmannsthal compares the poetry of Stefan George. There is a lack of free air and natural light. His thought has, far more than Matthew Arnold's, the melancholy of the pantheist. (pp. 17-18)

> *Charles Wharton Stork, "Hofmannsthal As a Lyric Poet," in* The Lyrical Poems of Hugo von Hofmannsthal *by Hugo von Hofmannsthal, translated by Charles Wharton Stork & others (translation copyright, 1918, by Yale University Press), Yale University Press, 1918, pp. 1-20.*

EDWIN MUIR   (essay date 1923)

[*Muir was a distinguished Scottish novelist, poet, critic, and translator. With his wife Willa, he translated works by various German authors unfamiliar to the English-speaking world, including Gerhart Hauptmann, Hermann Broch, and, most notably, Franz Kafka. Throughout his career, Muir was intrigued by psychoanalytic theory, particularly Freud's analyses of dreams and Jung's theories of archetypal imagery, both of which he often utilized in his work. In his critical writings, Muir was more concerned with the general philosophical issues raised by works of art—such as the nature of time or society—than with the particulars of the work itself, such as style or characterization. In the following discussion of Hofmannsthal as poet, Muir maintains that the author's early poetry displays a clearer and broader vision of life than any of his later works.*]

In writing of Hofmannsthal one can not avoid making an attempt to discover why the genius which burned so purely, so entirely by its own light, in his youth, should later have become more and more overlaid with talent, and almost negated by it. A nemesis has sometimes followed precocity of genius, and sometimes not; but in reading Hofmannsthal's early poems, one feels that it was bound to follow his. The astonishing thing in the early poems of Hofmannsthal, is that nothing is expressed there tentatively. Everything is complete with a formidable artistic ripeness, as if in reaching youth the poet had attained maturity; a lovely maturity derived not from experience, as maturity so almost invariably is, but from a clear and beautiful imagination whose power laid a chill upon him when he was in the first freshness of his life. This is the unique quality of these poems: an objectivity sad and resigned which is like the objectivity of no other poet, because it is that not of manhood, but of boyhood and youth. Hofmannsthal's *Sturm und Drang* ["Storm and Stress"] was frozen immediately into calm form and objective vision; he passed over without touching it the phase which most of the poets of his race have experienced before they gained a clear vision of life. (p. 152)

Hofmannsthal's early lyrics were inspired not by a knowledge of life as it is experienced by men, but by the spectacle of life's processes, by the perception that so and so things happen, that children grow up, become something different, and die, that some men are born to glory and others to poverty; above all, that all things pass, and having passed, can never be recaptured; and in these poems he was without a trace of uncertainty. They were evoked almost entirely by the unaccount-able and dreadful development of life, its apparently unjust diversity of fortunes, its end in death and its incomprehensibility while it lasts; and this process, seen so entirely from the outside, and before he was surprised by it into the normal acceptance of adult life, was set down with a clearness which experience would have confused. Rarely has life been seen so purely from the outside, and at the same time with such passion. The "**Ballade des Ausseren Lebens,**" Hofmannsthal's greatest short poem, and one of the greatest in the German language, expresses all the emotion which the incomprehensibility of life awoke in him. . . . It has the naïve accent of childhood and at the same time a steadfastness of vision which we are accustomed to regard as the fruit of a long and strict literary discipline. The form is so beautiful, so capable of giving pleasure in itself, that the poem will delight even those who can not enter into its mood, that mood which nevertheless gives it tis originality and poignancy. . . . There are poems, too, in which the poet wavers on the edge of manhood, and feels the visions of his childhood slipping away from him and behind him, never to be recaptured except in those moments which seem to come by a chance of some other world. . . . (pp. 153-54)

Hofmannsthal is not a major German poet; he did not write enough poetry of the first rank. But he has written some of the finest lyrics in the German language, lyrics to which men will return as long as poetry is read. His later works show talent of a high order, and they are always distinguished by that beauty of form which is part of his genius; but they have not the fullness of vision which glorified his earlier work, and it is hard to believe that they will be read in another fifty years. His aphorisms on life, art and literature are profound and full of finesse, and his literary criticiam is probably better than that of any other living writer. But all these one would gladly resign for another volume of poetry equal to his first. Still, it was not altogether a loss that his genius reached so soon the balance of qualities which constituted its perfection; for that genius, grasped in all its power before the preoccupations of existence had had time to condition it, to change it to something less beautiful than itself, has expressed itself in poetry which in a profound sense is unlike any other poetry, and in being strange remains in the grand tradition of the German spirit. (p. 154)

> *Edwin Muir, "Hugo von Hofmannsthal," in* The Freeman *(copyright, 1923 by The Freeman Corporation), Vol. VIII, No. 189, October 24, 1923, pp. 152-54.*

RONALD PEACOCK   (essay date 1946)

[*Peacock attributes Hofmannsthal's change in literary modes to his search for the perfect form to adequately express the "elements of his imagination and emotional life." The critic discounts the idea that Hofmannsthal turned to the theater because of a loss of poetic inspiration.*]

Hofmannsthal's work offers peculiar difficulties to criticism, because he developed neither as a lyric poet nor as a straightforward dramatic poet, but instead devoted his main energies to writing works which strike one at first as curiously if not bewilderingly dissimilar in subject and manner: opera-texts, some serious, some comic, some a mixture of both; the two religious plays *Jedermann* and *Das Grosse Welttheater;* and comedies of a very delicate poetic quality but rather too slender for successful stage performance, and written, moreover, in prose.

Here are indications enough of an intellectual life and an artistic sensibility that were extremely complex. The salient feature is that all these three kinds of writing, together with the lyric dramas, are founded in the theatre, and yet none of them is orthodox dramatic poetry like Shakespeare's or Grillparzer's or Racine's. They seem to constitute an exploration of possible forms for the theatre.

The clue to this phenomenon lies principally in a peculiar relationship between diverse elements of Hofmannsthal's artistic personality. There was in him first a poet of extreme esthetic impressionability, seen most clearly in the lyric dramas, seen also in a certain disguise in many of his prose essays on general and artistic subjects. The early pieces show a virtuosity in which it is difficult to separate sensuous responsiveness from technical facility, and which is to the last degree astonishing. Jumping any apprenticeship, he is from the start a master of mellifluous language, poetic phrase and apt imagery, of a readiness and fluency and movment that never falter; but these qualities are the sign, not of the true technical self-possession of the mature artist, but of the utmost vivacity of response to impressions and poetic thoughts of all kinds. It is a virtuosity of sensuousness that is without backbone, and it ends with the poet being controlled by, instead of controlling, memory and associative fancy; inundated by impressions and swept along by his own facility, he finds himself a prisoner in an autonomous verbal world, cut off from life and truth by the gift that should reveal them. It is the quality in Hofmannsthal most closely related to "estheticism."

But there was also in him a writer distinguished by intellectual coolness and lucidity, by a disposition to philosophical irony that is more at home in comedy and prose than in poetry. It is an aspect that is already apparent in the lyric dramas, in most of which there is often a curious contrast between the poetic texture and an insistent precocious knowledge of life expressed in the dramatic point of the whole. This side of Hofmannsthal presents a moralist with a didactic interest in general truths, an interest that persists throughout his work. Quite early he speaks of what seems to him to be "a favourite form": to take a character with a given set of ideas and put him in a situation that forces him to revise them. Such ironical awareness determines the conception of some of the lyric dramas and leads to the later comedies, *Cristina's Heimreise* and *Der Schwierige.* His didacticism and preoccupation with general truths appear also in the moral and metaphysical atmosphere of *Jedermann* and *Das Grosse Welttheater.* It has been insufficiently appreciated that Hofmannsthal's originality in subject-matter derives mainly from this source.

There was thirdly in Hofmannsthal a mystic who faced him with his greatest problem of form, because he led him away from words which were the immediate medium of his genius; but took him towards theatre and music where he was forced to collaborate. The mystic in him—the *Letter of Lord Chandos* is the document of this artistic crisis, and perhaps also the mysteriously symbolic *Das Bergwerk zu Falun*—felt that there was a world of spirituality higher and deeper and freer than words allow for. Language is not only insufficient to communicate this world but it is a barrier to it, a turbid medium that distorts and obfuscates. The fictive Lord Chandos takes the logical step and declares his intention of writing no more poetry; and it would be simple indeed, though less interesting, if Hofmannsthal had done the same. But the finality of this step is part of the intense expression of the letter, it gives completeness to a mood, making for what is really a poem in

prose without involving Hofmannsthal himself in such an extreme practical decision.

This brief analysis of dominating tendencies helps us to understand how Hofmannsthal came to use such varied methods, as lyric drama, morality play, allegory, comedy, and opera texts, the latter again highly coloured and dramatic like *Elektra,* or delicately sentimental and comic like *Der Rosenkavalier;* and a certain unity of effort begins to appear amidst the differing inspiration. All these works are essentially poetic conceptions, they rely on the collaboration of various arts, and the medium of collaboration is theatre. There is no name for this composite and elastic form that Hofmannsthal developed for his complex inspiration, and the only way to indicate it briefly would be to call it a poetry of theatre, borrowing a phrase from Cocteau. (pp. 134-36)

Behind all this is Hofmannsthal's passion for the metaphysical. The attraction of allegory for him was that whilst using the language and images of life it deliberately repudiates their face-value and uses them freely as signs. *Faust Part Two* and the *Märchen* are allegorical; so are his own *Jedermann* and *Das Grosse Welttheater.* The attraction of music and dance and mime for him is that they have a more intense sensuousness than words have, a more direct appeal to feeling, but at the same time touch deeper levels of life, stirring primeval fears and reverences, expressing more mysteriously the emotions of religion and a life that is unseen and unspoken. Hofmannsthal was aware of the various contributions the different arts could make, as a matter of esthetic discrimination. He felt that words generalize best; that music gives the greatest emotional intensity; whilst a single gesture of mime or dancer can express a state of mind and dramatic relations with unequalled vividness and particularity. . . . But his sense of the collaboration of the arts in the theatre is more than esthetic discrimination. It is a profound sense of ritual, cult, liturgy, and festival, which have always, both in primitive and enlightened religions, used the various arts in combination to one end. The unity of his whole conception of a composite art depends on his consciousness of the ritualistic foundations of theatre, of the festivals of popular and religious life, of the theatre as the conscious stylization of the natural dramas of life lived between the human and the divine. The discovery of theatre is the discovery of the deepest continuities in human life, the discovery of symbols that express total human community. Such a conception is no mere artificial resuscitation of something dead and gone, no mere nostalgia. It is vital and creative because it springs from Hofmannsthal's own metaphysical passion. His work lives on this twofold force, however obvious or obscured it may be in any single piece: on the one hand the ceremony, the festive occasion, the celebration in community life, rooted in the primary needs and joys of the race; and on the other his mystic feeling for the eternal in the repetition, for the typical structure of life, for the primeval and divine that links the generations of humanity. His opera-text *Elektra,* enveloped in an atmosphere of pagan religion, working up to a culmination in Elektra's frenzied dance when her revenge is accomplished, and marred not in its conception but only in its execution by a certain hysteria, is the obvious stark illustration of where the origins of Hofmannsthal's conception of theatre are to be found. *Das Grosse Welttheater* is of course the summit of his achievement in this respect. (pp. 137-38)

Hofmannsthals's religious plays *Jedermann* and *Das Grosse Welttheater* are his weightiest achievements as an independent poet, in the sense that they show the greatest degree of interfusion of his creative qualities: the poetic, the dramatic, the metaphysical, the didactic, the ritualistic. To see in them a skilful adaptation of an old morality play and an old allegorical idea, the one most famous in the English version, the other in Calderon's treatment, is a superficial reading. They have the force of original poetic creations because their subject and theme are essentially Hofmannsthal's own, expressing his spirituality, and because their form suited his particular powers. The dramatic poet, moreover, has achieved here a greater independence by dispensing with the collaboration of music, whilst absorbing its qualities into the symbols, the rhythmic formalization of persons and action, and the evocations of ritual. The dramatic scene is on the edge of life, from which it borrows vividness and particularity whilst pointing all the time to another world of meaning. The method is moral analysis by illustration; the object is the theatre as a vehicle of religious emotion.

The interest in generalized truths that is observable in the didacticism of the early lyric dramas reappears in its mature phase; and because it is mature it is assured and forceful. Hofmannsthal's abnormality as a young poet was of an unusual kind, because he was so knowing in a worldly sense. He was precocious in his perceptions; but his precocity is in fact the sign of his immaturity, being knowledge without experience. Expressions of general truth in poetry rely for their power and effectiveness not simply on their accuracy but on the authority with which they are put forward, and that is only conferred by a gravity of experience acquired in sufficient extent and variety and deepened by repetition. To reach this stage was for Hofmannsthal, to whom generalization was natural, to find the moment of great opportunity. The instinct that took him to the allegorical morality play is one that confirms genius. For moral generalization, religious simplification, the barest, austerest analysis of life's typical features, are of the essence of the form. In these plays the force of appropriate generalization can be traced everywhere: in the detail of the characters and speeches as well as in the conception and construction. . . . It is true, of course, that Hofmannsthal's subjects, themes, and interpretations of truth are the common property of Christian Europe. But that is their strength; any great human truth makes originality superfluous. It can never be commonplace in itself, but only when it is inadequately grasped or insincerely stated. The power of "sentences," the epigrammatic pointing of common experience, which dramatists used to be very fond of and which is now out of fashion, lies in this adequacy of statement that renews the truth they contain. Hofmannsthal's handling of general truth, determined by a perfectly responsive mind, is adequate and has produced genuine poetry. In these circumstances, its conformity—with the most comprehensive religious wisdom of modern times—is its power. The test is whether Hofmannsthal as dramatic poet can rise to the height of the Christian theme. The climax of *Das Grosse Welttheater* leaves no doubt about it; the scene in which the Beggar, roused by suffering and the sense of social iniquity, is impelled by his resentment to use violence against the privileged. . . . [This scene] contains the essentials: the pathos of the human situation at its most dramatic, moral illumination and spiritual victory, the transcendent continuity of the power of the Christian God. (pp. 142-47)

I have tried to treat the case of Hofmannsthal as a problem of form rather than as one of decadence, which is the line taken by hostile critics. What emerges from such a treatment is a consistent artistic ideal and a continuous development, which contrasts with the notion that his inspiration was dependent on

the *décadence* and dried up with the "lyric dramas." Each of Hofmannsthal's forms is a different attempt to find an adequate expression for elements of his imaginative and emotional life that were diverse and difficult to reconcile; to find different forms for the demands of a complex sensibility. Only an analysis that appreciates his problem as that of finding the right form—simple and compound—for a genuine but unusual inspiration can do justice to his originality and his achievement. Hofmannsthal was creative, but he needed a complex medium. The composition of creative artists being as infinitely varied as that of men's characters, those whose assortment of talents and sensibility does not fit into standard forms have to look for other forms that enable them to say what they have to say. From such circumstances arise the deviations and combinations of the various arts that add to the richness of art as a whole. Hofmannsthal came to create not a dramatic poetry in the orthodox sense, but a poetry of theatre in a special sense. If he had to rely for realizing his conception on musicians and dancers and actors—he was fortunate in meeting a composer and a producer of genius, Strauss and Reinhardt—that does not detract from his creativeness but emphasizes its originality. We are reminded of Yeats's *Plays for Dancers* and his description of them as "a different art-form." To recall in addition Cocteau's search for a *poésie du théâtre* is to see that Hofmannsthal, like these two artists, was in fact contributing largely to a particular need of the time felt all over Europe, the renewal of the theatre's poetic vitality, and doing so not by merely superimposing an art of "production" on an indifferent text, but by starting with a total poetic conception and realizing it in a complex form.

Not the least remarkable thing about Hofmannsthal's work, however, is that in solving his private problems of form, he finds at the same time a solution of two general problems of poetry in his generation and ours; poetry in relation to the social theme in drama, and to the theatre audience in the twentieth century. *Das Grosse Welttheater* is a treatment of the social theme on a metaphysical plane; and whether you agree with the religion or not, it is poetry, and stands in strong contrast to the failure of "social problem plays" to achieve poetry. . . . Hofmannsthal deliberately attempted to rediscover the cultic power of the theatre, and he achieved it with the festival play that has its roots deep in the religious and ethical consciousness of society, and in a spontaneous popular impulse towards the theatre. Most of the attempts at a poetic drama in this century have sprung from minority interests and have found only an exclusive audience; and we recall how Yeats in working out his ideals accepted this peculiarly modern condition. But Hofmannsthal, with *Jedermann* and *Das Grosse Welt-theater*, succeeded in the broader aim. He created a dramatic symbol that united a whole society and enveloped it in a poetic situation. (pp. 147-50)

> *Ronald Peacock, "Hugo von Hofmannsthal," in his* The Poet in the Theatre, *Routledge & Kegan Paul Ltd, 1946 (and reprinted by Hill and Wang, 1960, pp. 129-50).*

VICTOR A. OSWALD, JR.   (essay date 1952)

[In this appraisal of Hofmannsthal's last three dramas, Oswald discusses them as the unique dramatic expressions of a mature artist.]

As a young man, [Hofmannsthal's] writing of plays was marked by a striving toward what he rather pathetically called "dramatic drama.'' His last works both overtake and surpass his youthful goal. *Der Schwierige* is a perfect pure comedy, unique in modern German letters; *Das Salzburger Grobe Welttheater* is a milestone in the march of the modern theater away from make-believe reality towards spirituality and surrealism; and *Der Turm* marks the conquest by symbolism of the domain of grand tragedy.

Hofmannsthal's frequent recourse to the classics of all times and countries, both for plots and for models of dramatic technique, has provoked the criticism that he was incapable of originality; but all the plays that he claims as his own—all those not plainly labeled translations or adaptations—are radically different from their original sources.

Calderon's *El gran teatro del mundo,* for instance, gave him the start for his *Welttheater,* but it would be a naïve critic who could see nothing in Hofmannsthal's play but a revival of the Spanish Baroque theater. Calderon's play on the stage of the world is static, his ''characters'' are traditionally allegorical representations of the diverse conditions of men. Hofmannsthal's central play is the imitation of an action, and two of its figures, the Rich Man and the Beggar, have strikingly modern attributes. The Rich Man is a tycoon, a capitalist who uses money as the tool to make himself the power behind the throne. The Beggar is the outcast of the system, the proletarian; not very long ago we should have called him the Forgotten Man. The clash between the Beggar and the other five figures is built up to a pitch of dramatic intensity that is resolved only when Divine Grace intervenes to prevent the symbolic destruction of the world by revolution.

Hofmannsthal's elaboration of the external setting proceeds from the Baroque tradition to break deliberately with modern theatrical convention. The casting, in the prologue, of six unborn souls in the roles of the six central figures, with the Begger-to-be obstinately refusing his part until an angel compels him to accept it; the visible staging of the main action, with casual interruptions by the World, by Impudence, and by the Devil—the last costumed, by the way, as a colleague of ours—all this suggests not Calderon but Pirandello. It is, of course, a coincidence that there are the same number of central figures in Hofmannsthal's *Welttheater* and in Pirandello's *Six Characters in Search of an Author,* but there is an unmistakable kinship between them, and we could readily subtitle Hofmannsthal's play ''The Author in Search of Six Characters.'' The two plays are, moreover, of equal importance to the growth of anti-realism in the theater. The extravagances of German Expressionism caricatured but left intact the pretension that the theater is make-believe-reality. Hofmannsthal and Pirandello move beyond Expressionistic masks and grotesques toward the surrealistic treatment of the theater as an undisguised fiction. I suppose we cannot speak of pure surrealism in the theater until we get to the *bizarreries* of Cocteau, but the fundamental assumptions of his stage are complete in the *Welttheater.*

Finally, the play's frank acceptance of dogma and its adaptability to playing in a church or cathedral . . . contribute to the rebirth of cordial relations between church and theater in a quite different way from *Jedermann,* which *was* purely a revival. The acceptance by the Catholic Church of so sophisticated a play as the *Welttheater* points the way toward the Anglican acceptance of Eliot's *Murder in the Cathedral* and of Fry's *A Sleep of Prisoners.* The order of the day makes it imperative to view *Welttheater* as a thoroughly modern play.

Der Schwierige is one work of Hofmannsthal's of which the plot is incontestably original. It is, moreover, unique among his writings in that it is unequivocally set in the time and place of its composition: Vienna after World War I. Is it not, therefore, curious that both public and critics have had difficulty in arriving at the pathetic distance appropriate to it? It has never had more than a *succès d'estime* in the theater, and it has been discussed critically as a drawing-room comedy, as an ironic self-portrait, as a tribute to the vanishing Austrian aristocracy, as a comedy of errors, and as a social satire. There has been no lack of praise for its flawless structure, its witty dialogue, its precisely sketched galaxy of characters. No one doubts that it represents Hofmannsthal's conquest of ''dramatic drama.'' But the commendation has been cool, the criticism somewhat bemused. Perhaps we can see why this has been so, from the vantage point of our transatlantic perspective, and especially since the calamitous march of history in our times has made a museum piece of this play of our own era.

Should not its very title have told us all along that it is a comedy of character, in the tradition of Molière's *Misanthrope* and Terence's *Self-Tormentor?* And can we not now plainly see that it also is a modern comedy of manners? Both the eccentricities of its protagonist and the very thinness of the plot are hallmarks of the genre. That Kari Bühl is self-absorbed and shy to the point of distraction, eager for solitude, wary of the social entertainments of the gregarious, incapable of making decision, skeptical even of the efficacy of speech as a medium of communication—does not this mark him as the modern self-tormentor, the troubled introvert? And is it not in the best tradition that the misfit is to be seen in the social setting of his opposites, happy extroverts who quite unself-consciously thrust their personalities into the foreground and treat life as a game with fixed rules in which everyone pursues his personal goal? Of the lot, only Helene Altenwyl, whom Kari loves but has never ventured to approach, has the sort of delicate balance that enables one to live both within himself and for the outer world. She can thus provide the solution for Kari's dilemma by maneuvering him into proposing to her when he makes a pathetically ludicrous attempt to ''play the game,'' that is, at his sister's request goes to a soiree with the fixed purpose of persuading Helene to marry his nephew.

It is really not difficult to determine why *Der Schwierige* has never met with adequate appreciation. It never had a chance to live, so to speak, its natural life as a comedy of manners. That would have required the survival of the aristocracy it portrays and of an audience that could understand the play's intent with instant sympathy. As a closet drama it bemuses its German readers simply because there is no tradition of pure comedy in German literature, which upholds as its finest exemplars of the comic species the half-tragic sobriety of *Minna von Barnhelm,* the rowdy humor of *Der zerbrochne Krug,* and the broad satire of *Der Biberpelz. Der Schwierige* with its intent to provoke thoughtful laughter by sympathetic ridicule, is an alien intruder. It is the sole high comedy in modern German literature that is born of what Meredith calls ''the Comic Spirit.''

We overlook the significance of *Welttheater* to the modern theater unless we look forward from its time of writing to Cocteau and Eliot. We fail to catch the subtle charm of *Der Schwierige* unless we look back to the classic comedy of manners and character. To read *Der Turm* rightly we must look both to the past and to the present: to the past to see how the play is related to tragedy of the great tradition, to the present to understand its symbolism.

Its myth is derived from Calderon's *La vida es sueño,* but its denouement is the dramatic opposite of the Spanish play's happy ending: apocalyptic terror. Its trappings are those of the Kingdom of Poland in the seventeenth century, but its atmosphere is the air we breathe and its theme is the theme of our times: mankind brutalized by the worship of power, humanity crushed by naked force.

These definitives apply, of course, only to *Der Turm's* stage version, not to that fascinating grotesque, the book version. Upon the Calderonian fable of the prince brought up in a dungeon in order to avert the prophecy that he will cast his father down, the book superimposes a symbolically charged tragedy of flaw of character. The welter of its plot and the clutter of its symbolic effects, matched by an excrescence of dialogue, almost overwhelm its design, which is by no means untraditionally patterned. (pp. 192-95)

The book version of *Der Turm* has indeed much of the mysteriousness and some of the allure of *Hamlet,* but the ultimate impression it leaves upon the reader is that of a turgid *Haupt- und Staatsaktion* whose figures are oddly blurred. . . . What Hofmannsthal was aiming at, in his own words, was "a palpable foreground, a concrete and specific action, behind which there was gradually to be revealed something higher, something spiritual, universal, difficult to express, not rationally perceptible, but perceptible only through intuition." What he actually brought forth in the book version was a heavily overcharged canvas, most of whose figures appear in double exposure.

For the stage version Hofmannsthal pruned the dialogue, precised the lineaments of all the principal characters, condensed the action to the point of Sigismund's scene with Basilius, and radically altered the rest of the plot, so that a quite different play emerges: a classical tragic agon, its protagonist overwhelmed by forces with which he cannot cope; and, at the same time, a symbolic depiction of Hofmannsthal's concept of the *condition humaine* in the twentieth century. (pp. 195-96)

The fact that the stage version of *Der Turm* was published in 1927 lends it the effect of prophecy. Certainly it is much more readily intelligible now than it was before Hitler's rise to power and before the Dictatorship of the Proletariat had discarded the cloak of benevolence. Our critical attention, however, should be focused on its contribution to the heritage of symbolism. Hofmannsthal has done for tragedy on the heroic scale what Thomas Mann has done for the novel: maintained the tradition, but quickened it by adding a latent content to the manifest fable. There is an obvious analogy between the stage version of *Der Turm* and Mann's *Doktor Faustus.* Indeed, the parallel is so striking that the principal line of divergence is salient. Mann's allegory of human damnation leaves one faint ray of hope for redemption; Hofmannsthal's is a total disavowal of faith in mankind. (p. 197)

> *Victor A. Oswald, Jr., "The Old Age of Young Vienna," in* The Germanic Review *(reprinted by permission of Joseph P. Bauke), Vol. XXVII, No. 3, October, 1952, pp. 188-99.**

H. A. HAMMELMANN   (essay date 1954)

[*In his* Hugo von Hofmannsthal, *written in 1954 and published in 1957, Hammelmann offers an overview of Hofmannsthal's creative transition: from the isolation of youthful lyric poetry to the social orientation of mature stage dramas which culminated in the tragedy* Der Turm.]

The little work which gave so overwhelming a proof of Hofmannsthal's prodigious early maturity, indeed completeness as a poet, and placed him, in the enthusiasm of his generation, at once almost with the immortals, with Keats and Rimbaud, with Novalis and Leopardi, was the 'lyrical drama' *Gestern.* *Gestern* is among the very earliest of Hofmannsthal's surviving poems and, I believe, the very first in point of time which he was willing to include in his own final collection of his poetry. The subject of this short verse play is the sad and tender bitterness of adolescence, its diffident shrinking from all ties and commitments. Only complete surrender to the mood of the moment, to the to-day, seems to promise enjoyment of all the beauty which life offers and of its pleasures, yet the young hero must learn, in disenchantment, that the yesterdays are ever with us. . . . If the story, Andrea's betrayal by his mistress, is commonplace and trivial, it is rendered poignant by the dignity with which the characters accept the inevitable dénouement. In any case, however, Hofmannsthal is not concerned with a sequence of events, but with a mood out of which he weaves the pattern of his poem. It is the mood of his time. Here is the fastidious search for exquisite personal pleasures, but also, coupled with it, nameless misgivings, *Weltangst,* the fear that, in all this refinement of pleasure, the essence of life, so desirable and so elusive, may pass the poet and his generation by. . . . It is fear—the young poet's insight is intuitive rather than experienced—which makes man a slave of time, as the materialism from which he seeks to escape would prove him a slave of his body.

Together with this high degree of consciousness we find in *Gestern* another of the young Hofmannsthal's outstanding characteristics, his faculty so to saturate his sensibility with other lives and forms of existence as to achieve a kind of self-identification. (pp. 9-10)

Almost all the poems which Hofmannsthal himself cared to publish and to preserve were written between his seventeenth and his twenty-third year of age, a period which he himself described as the 'most lonely' of his life. During these years, in an adolescent stage to which he later gave the term 'pre-existence', he was able to see order and coherence where we commonly perceive only the individual concrete personal experience. An understanding with inanimate objects, which opened a vision transcending all experience of the senses, might be kindled suddenly by a breath of wind, by the sight of a tree or a Greek vase, even (as in the **'Chandos Letter'**) by a battered watering can. In this semi-mystical state the limitations of time, place and consciousness, the force of gravity to which man is subject, seemed to be overcome; the borderline between the finite and the infinite was temporarily suspended and he felt himself freed from the burden of the here and now. This momentary suspension appears in Hofmannsthal's poetry frequently as a dream. (p. 12)

Nowhere did Hofmannsthal realise and express [the] immanent awareness of the essence of existence more perfectly than in his famous poem, **'Ein Traum von grosser Magie',** where rhythm and diction move with an airy, gliding, evanescent lightness which leads almost imperceptibly to a splendid, magic vision of a higher, timeless reality. . . . Poems such as this cannot be interpreted by setting one symbol for another. They must be experienced; but if they meet the reader at a receptive moment, they achieve what Hofmannsthal believed to be the function of true poetry: 'to touch strings and strike harmonies which have been asleep in us without our knowledge, so that we look into the depths of wondrous mysteries as if a new meaning of life were opened to us'.

Inevitably perhaps, the early super-sensitivity which enabled, indeed impelled the young Hofmannsthal at times to immerse himself so completely in a world outside his own existence appears to be accompanied by a sense of aloofness and detachment, amounting almost to passivity. The gift, as he himself recognised when he spoke at one stage deprecatingly of his 'chameleon-like attitude', of his 'lack of character' even, is a great, but dangerous one; it is the one which, above all others, has caused him to be dubbed an aesthete, a 'pure' poet concerned only with aesthetic effects. Only later did Hofmannsthal himself fully understand his position when, in his essay **'Der Dichter und diese Zeit'**, he called the poet, by one of his happiest images, 'the silent brother of all things'. For, from the very outset, the detachment was not by any means the detachment of unconcern, but evidence, on the contrary, of a desire, and the ability, to step back at times, or upwards out of a bewildering world to a point of vantage from where the eye, surveying the human scene, commands a comprehensive view. (pp. 14-15)

Hofmannsthal was barely in his middle twenties when he became aware of a drying up, perhaps an exhaustion of that abundant lyric gift which during his adolescent years had poured itself into the world 'like a gushing mountain stream'. It was a cessation no less over-powering than the splendid, precipitate effusion of his early genius. (p. 16)

It was when he had reached this point that Hofmannsthal was able, in writing his famous imaginary **'Chandos Letter'** . . . to face and state, and in this way to overcome, his experience. Lord Chandos, a young Elizabethan nobleman of great intellectual attainments and exactly the author's own age, in an imaginary letter to Lord Chancellor Bacon, explains to his paternal friend the reasons for his complete abandonment of all literary pursuits. He describes a most terrifying crisis, one taken from Hofmannsthal's own inner life, a vital experience: the complete loss of the ability to think or speak coherently on any general subject and to utter even casual opinions and judgments because he has been seized by a paralysing doubt about the adequacy of the language he must use: how, at first, he began to feel an inexplicable distaste for abstract terms and generalizations until he found himself unable any longer to comprehend human beings and their actions with the simplifying eye of habit; everything disintegrated into parts and words 'congealed into eyes staring at me and forcing me to stare back, whirlpools leading into the void which made me reel'.

The predicament of Lord Chandos is told by Hofmannsthal with great force in a succession of immediate and startling pictures and with unrelenting sharpness of focus; the haunting conviction carried by this important small prose piece brings out in strong relief the closeness of the experience to the poet himself, which had been, and obviously still was, almost an obsession. For all that, the situation of Chandos is not wholly his own: the very writing of this imaginary letter shows that it was rather an imagined extreme possibility of a state of mind recognised as temporary. Here the problem of communication crystallises itself. The inexplicable distaste, even 'hatred', is the product of a double scruple, a two-fold pressure unrelieved: on the one hand moral disgust, a strong sense of intellectual honesty outraged by the misuse of words and unconsidered judgments on the part of others; but also, no less grave, mistrust, nagging, crippling mistrust in the adequacy of words, his own words even, to convey to others the meaning they are intended to communicate. It is a problem which was to recur again and again in Hofmannsthal's later work, not least in his comedy **Der Schwierige**. (pp. 17-18)

The exhaustion of Hofmannsthal's early lyrical gift . . . coincided with a growing recognition that for an artist isolation, however splendid, must inevitably lead to sterility. He began to realise that the loneliness and the pessimism, no less than the *Weltangst* of his adolescence were all one, and had their roots in tragic non-attachment to that which was close at hand. In his **Buch der Freunde,** a collection of aphorisms and short, carefully formulated observations rather similar to Novalis, we find this sentence: 'German intellectuals are born to real life late and with heavy labour; that is when they undergo a second birth during which many die'; a remark whose autobiographical nature is made fully explicit in the private meditation on his own development as an artist which he jotted down under the title *Ad Me Ipsum*. Hofmannsthal knew that man can find himself only in seeking others.

In a two-fold sense, this knowledge is already inherent in Hofmannsthal's early lyrical dramas, especially in **Der Tor und der Tod**. . . . This is the tale of the fool who only learns that he has wasted his life in eternal toying and trifling when death comes to fetch him—the first reality he has encountered. (p. 20)

The closing lines of **Der Tor und der Tod,** which celebrate death as a mystical experience, are taken up again in the last of Hofmannsthal's lyrical dramas, **Das Bergwerk zu Falun,** which he never published as a whole and probably never considered finished. The theme is the search for greater awareness, symbolised in a miner who abandons action, power and human love, and chooses the uncertain way into the dark shaft whose end is unknown: death and what may be beyond. . . .

Das Bergwerk zu Falun is interesting chiefly as marking the furthest point to which the poet went in the attempt to find an answer in direct mysticism. The shaft into which he descended proved a *cul-de-sac* not so much perhaps because he was incapable of the self-abandonment, the self-immolation which is required, but because he was too honest to pretend, even to himself, that he had found at the bottom of the pit anything but the silence of withdrawal. This is the turning point at which Hofmannsthal appears to have finally abandoned the isolation of mysticism and to have recognised that man needs the world in order to understand what he is, to realise himself in action and suffering. With the knowledge that action within the social context is for the non-mystic the most immediate way to the 'higher self' which he sought, he stepped out of the aloofness and seclusion of his adolescence and found his true road in acceptance of his commitment to the community and to tradition. (p. 21)

During the first decade of the new century, dramatic production gained such a hold on the poet as to become an all-absorbing preoccupation; so much so that, with a charming sense of humour, he could poke fun at his apparently haphazard choice of themes and materials when he wrote to Schnitzler: 'I want to dramatize everything that falls into my hand, even the correspondence between Schiller and Goethe, or the *Linzer Tagespost'*, the dullest of provincial newspapers. Greek tragedy, adaptations of plays by Molière and Calderon, and of Otways' *Venice Preserved,* ballets, even a pantomime or two—all these were in a way essential steps on Hofmannsthal's road to the theatre. (p. 26)

With his eyes always open for that which can draw present strength from tradition, Hofmannsthal came to consider the stage as 'the only one among the great secular institutions that had retained universal validity' and one still capable of being a true centre of festive social occasion, bringing 'art' and 'life' together. (p. 27)

Out of this conception grew Hofmannsthal's hope for a renaissance of the German theatre on the foundation of a living Austrian and Bavarian baroque tradition which eventually led to the idea of the Salzburg Festival and to his own ambitious allegorical spectacles *Jedermann* and *Das grosse Salzburger Welttheater*. But the same premise, that in the theatre a state of spontaneous receptivity and participation can be created by an author who succeeds in amusing, entertaining and thus 'holding' an audience, led Hofmannsthal also in quite a different direction, to his comedies for stage and opera, especially to his social comedy *Der Schwierige*.

Hofmannsthal's comedy was not a mere funny play; his was the old conception of the term: a serious play dealing in an amusing way with a serious question. He possessed, as it proved, a very fertile dramatic imagination and often, though not invariably, succeeded in fitting his comedies, both for the dramatic and the operatic stage, with good acting plots and situations. For all that it was rarely the story which had his first concern; the true purpose of all his comedies, as indeed of all his dramatic work and of his novel, was not so much to convince the audience of the reality of the action as to open their minds to the symbolic content of the inter-relation between the figures, to that which is universally significant in individual destiny. Thus the theatre's power of magical make-believe and realisation is always directed to something which transcends the action on the stage: in *Cristinas Heimreise, Der Rosenkavalier, Arabella* to the beauty and ultimate sadness of love, resignation and acceptance; in *Ariadne auf Naxos* and *Der Schwierige* to man's isolation and to his need for loyalty and union. (pp. 27-8)

The Strauss-Hofmannsthal operas (with the exception perhaps of *Die Frau ohne Schatten,* where the poet moved in a rarified atmosphere to which the composer could not follow him) in performance unfold quite unmistakeably, each in its own way, through a direct appeal to the emotions, the significant meaning and intent which Hofmannsthal wished them to carry. It is neither the words nor the music alone but an idiom gained out of the conjunction of the two which lends them conviction. No less than *Der Rosenkavalier, Ariadne auf Naxos* and *Die ägyptische Helena* reveal Hofmannsthal's preoccupation with time and its passing. Both operas may be said to centre on the antithesis between transience and eternity, between being and becoming, between permanence and mutation. In *Die ägyptische Helena* the music helps to express, and distinguish, the two-level structure of the libretto, the subjective spiritual action which develops parallel with the outward events. Thus the opera suggests the working of conflicting symbolic forces greater than the characters themselves: the daemonic element in Helena and the human, moral one of Menelaos. In *Ariadne auf Naxos,* the attempt to open up the circumscribed stage to the world at large and 'to extend it into the infinite' led Hofmannsthal, as elsewhere on occasion, to mythology and the supernatural. Here the main action is raised out of the realm of ordinary existence into the sphere of the gods, and since the music helps further to suspend the critical faculties, the audience is led immediately into a world of the imagination where spiritual experience of a higher order becomes communicable, and its universal validity acceptable.

In this way *Ariadne auf Naxos,* prepared, as the author himself chose to pretend, 'merely as a wire frame on which to hang the music prettily', is in fact perhaps the most delicately wrought of the six operas for, behind the gay fable of the old story, attention is focussed on a deeper meaning: the glory of the steadfast heart. (pp. 33-4)

In *Jedermann* and *Das grosse Salzburger Welttheater,* still trying to base himself on a form of dramatic representation earlier than the modern 'literary' theatre, he turned with far greater success to the medieval western tradition of the allegorical religious spectacle. *Jedermann* . . . is derived from the English morality *Everyman*. Sir George Franckenstein, after seeing a performance in London, had drawn Hofmannsthal's attention to the old play, and the poet himself likens his own work to a mere 'cleaning off the cobwebs from an old clockwork so that with the chiming of the hours the old figures will appear again'. . . . The essay **'Das alte Spiel vom Jedermann'** . . . shows that Hofmannsthal was above all concerned that his play be taken by a simple, naive audience as an unfolding of essential Christian truths and moral attitudes, and—whether he succeeded as fully as he believed, and whether or not the magnificent setting on the Salzburg Domplatz, where *Jedermann* is usually performed, actually gave him, as he believed, 'a crowd of spectators where the gap between the educated and the people has disappeared'—it is perhaps not permissible to judge such an attempt by literary standards alone. Impressive though the spectacle is, it makes one wonder whether it might not have gained if performed as a dumb show. To some extent this may be due to the language of the play; all the figures speak in exactly the same rather self-conscious idiom which is largely modelled on the homely *Knüppelreim* of Hans Sachs, the Nuremberg shoemaker-cum-poet, but strikes one in fact as 'antique', a second-hand language with a period flavour not very happily resurrected. The figures, moreover, declaim each for himself, not so much addressing each other as the spectator—a feature no doubt to some extent inherent in a representation in which we are all on the stage, but one which tends to give the later part of this 'human fairy tale in Christian dress' more and more the aspect of a sermon.

The message of *Jedermann* is that this life is part of a greater life; that the world is but a passing stage, and that, for our actions on it, we shall all be called to account on the Day of Judgement. When Hofmannsthal returned to allegory some ten years later with *Das grosse Salzburger Welttheater* . . . , God, 'the Master', actually tells a personified World to stage this life as a play. This metaphor of human life as a spectacle played out before the eyes of God is taken from Calderon's *Great Theatre of the World*. Here and elsewhere, the great Catholic playwright's baroque drama, centred not on human beings and psychological conflicts but on the relation between man and God, between divine grace and human freedom, offered the Austrian poet a model and inspiration for his own endeavour to encompass in one personal vision the whole of the universe, the 'imperishable timeless root of things'. . . . Yet, for all this affinity with Calderon, Hofmannsthal claimed *Das grosse Salzburger Welttheater* as his own, and rightly so, because the powerful *active* figure of the beggar here gives the play an entirely new dramatic meaning and climax.

The beggar, who stands for the have-nots who demand to have, for the lawless as well as those who enjoy no rights, for the oppressed as well as those who are in constant revolt, this beggar is yet a highly individualised figure, facing, for one dramatic moment, the whole world. When, in his wrath, he raises the axe to strike and bring down not merely established order, King, Rich Man, Peasant, but also Beauty and Wisdom and Piety, we know that this is the threat of chaos against the very idea of order; we realise at once that if the beggar does strike he will destroy all. Yet by a lightning illumination he is inspired to lay the axe aside, and the play can go on.

The figure of the beggar points, in a manner perhaps more powerful than the profane theatre can often achieve, the antithesis between man's destructive instinct and the creative power of moral decision. (pp. 35-7)

Hofmannsthal's work in narrative prose in not voluminous. Apart from fragments which may still be in the hands of his literary executors awaiting publication, all we have are three 'Novellen': [*Reitergeschichte, Bassompierre* and *Lucidor*]; and four other stories, best described as fairy tales, of which two, *Märchen der 672. Nacht* and *Die Frau ohne Schatten* were completed. Hofmannsthal made only one attempt in the direction of the novel, to which he gave the provisional title *Andreas oder Die Vereinigten.* Its abandonment after about one quarter of the projected length was written implied that no more was to be done in this genre.

As it is, the *Andreas* fragment, just over one hundred pages, contains some of Hofmannsthal's finest prose, pure, crystal clear classic German, the language of Goethe and Stifter, unequalled and even unapproached by any of his contemporaries. Here the poet succeeded in combining great depth of thought and rich imagery with complete simplicity of language, and the effortlessness of the whole makes this, even in its fragmentary state, one of the most enchanting things he has written.

The subject of the novel was described by Hofmannsthal himself in a letter to Richard Strauss . . . as 'die Entwicklung eines jungen Wieners zum Menschen'—how a young Viennese comes to reach manhood. It is the story of a young Viennese gentleman of good family, named Andreas von Ferschengelder, who is sent by his parents to Venice to finish and broaden his education, and of his adventures on this journey into life. The conception was that of the great *Bildungsroman,* of which the outstanding example in German literature is Goethe's *Wilhelm Meister,* and, when one remembers the fate of Novalis' *Ofterdingen,* it is perhaps not altogether surprising that it failed to reach completion. (p. 38)

In *Andreas,* Hofmannsthal was chiefly preoccupied with the individual and his growth toward maturity, although a passing, almost contemporary comment . . . on this work suggests that the story was perhaps also to be read on another level as a discussion of the German character in a more general way: 'If one regards the eighteenth century as the adolescence of the modern German', the poet wrote, 'it must be said that it was a dangerous adolescence: narrow, vapid, and calculated to undermine self-assurance, to create a gap between spirit and life'. It is certain that, as he grew older, and especially after the world war, Hofmannsthal was more and more driven towards an examination of the social position of man in the community, until, in his final work, *Der Turm,* the individual . . . is placed almost exclusively, if in a highly individual way, in the hub of public life.

Die Frau ohne Schatten . . . may be regarded as the connecting link between *Andreas* and *Der Turm.* The story, in its oriental fairyland setting, turns once more on the search for the road to true humanity, but the test of human action appears firmly focussed on (if not yet, as in *Der Turm,* actually subordinated to) the needs and purposes of society as a whole. As in the comedies which the poet wrote at about this time, marriage and parenthood are conceived as the mainstay of social existence. Central to the whole fable (though by no means easy to fathom) is Hofmannsthal's interpretation of the meaning of conjugal love and of the child to be born as representing continuity. (p. 45)

Die Frau ohne Schatten as a poetic fairy tale, the only major prose work which Hofmannsthal completed, was intended to exemplify the Novalis epigram he was fond of quoting: 'The impossible is the true realm of poetry.' There are indeed passages of great beauty in this ambitious long story where Hofmannsthal does succeed, as in *Andreas,* in divesting the magic of its improbability, and reaches solidity and relief of action which might arouse the envy of any writer of realistic prose. (p. 47)

Under the impression of the upheavals which shook Central Europe in the years immediately after the 1914-1918 war, as he witnessed the downfall of the established civil order and with it the progressive disintegration of the spiritual structure, Hofmannsthal, in *Das grosse Salzburger Welttheater* . . . , had undertaken once again to evoke and display, in the theatre, a larger view of the essence of humanity above the confusion of contemporary experience. In his final great tragedy, *Der Turm,* he returned, with ever greater anxiety and insight, to the search for a solution of the power struggle raging at all levels of the human community, a society rapidly losing its coherence, a common faith in common values. In fact, almost every scene of this historical play can be projected into political reality, and the picture of a world in which 'Power and Justice, the two mainstays of our social existence, are locked in gigantic battle' reveals a terrible and terrifying, sometimes even prophetic, likeness with our most recent past. (pp. 53-4)

Petrified and fascinated at the same time by the terrible task of representing in *Der Turm* 'the irruption of the forces of chaos into an order no longer upheld and supported by the power of the spirit', Hofmannsthal allowed this tragedy (on which he was at work, at intervals, for almost a quarter-century) to become the dominating and often torturing preoccupation of his closing years.

What was at stake here for him was . . . far more than the success or failure of a work of art; it was an attempt not to escape from reality, however brutal it may be, but, on the contrary, intellectually and spiritually to master the intolerable and apparently inexorable unfolding of events. Once he had set out on this task, Hofmannsthal, being the man he was, had to go all the way. It is not only the testimony of his friends that bears witness to the poet's heroic struggle with his subject; the tragedy itself is proof enough: the sentences of immense weight, desperately, often labouriously wrought; the heavy atmosphere of corroding evil which pervades the work, the ambivalence of the two alternative closing acts with their contrasting solutions. 'The walls are shaken in their foundations and our way is lost in impassable terrain', says one of the characters in *Der Turm.* Hofmannsthal had long ago learnt that in order to understand the calamity and the suffering of the world in which he lived he had to be fully involved in it, but he also knew that in order to give it shape and form he would have to lift himself out of this involvement and to rise above it. (pp. 59-60)

[Hofmannsthal's] work after the first world war shows a gradual steady assimilation of ideals and conceptions of the Christian religion, indeed of the Christian Church. To that end his work converged; from the immanent mystical experience of his pagan adolescence he arrived, in ripe manhood, at a conscious re-conquest of comparable assurance through an active faith. It is reported by those who were close to Hofmannsthal in the last years of his life that he confessed that he was, on occasion, experiencing moments of 'total apprehension of God'. With this knowledge of the immanent presence of the divine he represented in his final great work that which, in the last resort, can never be understood except in the certainty of visionary knowledge. Even to the poet himself this was only granted at rare moments of elevation. At other times Hofmannsthal was alternately tortured and spurred on by the intellectual inadequacy (for so they must seem) of the solutions he had found to the questions raised in his tragedy. (pp. 60-1)

H. A. Hammelmann, in his Hugo von Hofmannsthal, *Bowes & Bowes, 1957, 64 p.*

MARY E. GILBERT   (essay date 1957-58)

[*Gilbert is the author of several critical essays on Hofmannsthal. In the following excerpt, she examines Hofmannsthal's two short stories as important works in the author's artistic development.*]

It may be said that the interest in Hofmannsthal is waxing. What is, however, only slowly beginning to be appreciated is his epic work. Yet he has written ten narrative works all told; works which are without question of great interest for the understanding of the poet's personality. Indeed his whole development—both in its technical and intellectual aspects—can be seen from a comparison of his first and last narrative work, *Das Märchen der 672ten Nacht* . . . , and *Die Frau ohne Schatten.* . . . Of the remaining narratives two compel our attention in that they are neither fragmentary nor a first version for later use as a libretto; they are the *Reitergeschichte* . . . and *Das Erlebnis des Marschalls von Bassompierre.* . . . They belong to the last years of the productive phase preceding the Lord Chandos crisis; and there is no doubt that these two stories are typical of the works of these last three years of early productivity, that there are close parallels in respect of plot, thought content, characters and imagery with other works of the same period, such as [*Die Frau im Fenster, Der Abenteurer und die Sängerin, Die Hochzeit der Sobeide* and *Der weisse Fächer*]. On the other hand, they are something quite apart: they are 'Novellen'.

These two stories, then, are an experiment in form on Hofmannsthal's part, and this fact, at this juncture, i.e. just before his lyric productivity came to a stop, seems sufficiently interesting. . . .

Hofmannsthal's letters of this period provide ample confirmation that he was consciously experimenting in what to him was a new genre: the form of narrative prose. (p. 102)

The 'thought content' of both 'Novellen' is admittedly slight; and the popular criticism comes to mind which has so often been levelled against Hofmannsthal's work—against *Elektra, Jedermann, Das Gerettete Venedig, Der Turm*—the reproach that the poet is a 'Nachempfindler', an imitator or, at best, a recreator of already existing works of art. For is not his *Bassompierre* a descendant of Goethe's Bassompierre in *Die Unterhaltungen deutscher Ausgewanderten*? But may it not be this very fact that attracted Hofmannsthal? In the days when he so obviously experimented with forms and tried his tools, genre and language, he felt it a challenge to use the same material that the originator of the 'Novellenform' in Germany had used a hundred years earlier. At first sight it may seem strange for one who can claim as his immediate predecessors the great German Novellen-writers, Storm and Meyer, who is a contemporary of Schnitzler and Thomas Mann, to disregard their achievements as he did and to turn for his model so far back

into the past, to the Romance form of the 'Novelle'; for, indeed, we hear that besides Goethe he read Boccaccio at this time.

Why this excursion into the literary past? Hofmannsthal's reversion to the original form of the 'Novelle', far from being an isolated and accidental event, seems quite on the contrary to exemplify a trend that is characteristic of this whole period of his productivity. For this phase, the years of the crisis and the first decade of the new century, saw experiments with a variety of art forms all along the line; and in each case the poet returned to the very fountain-head of his chosen literary genre: to the Greek drama, the Elizabethan tragedy, to the medieval mystery play and to Calderón. This trend on the practical poetic plane has its parallel and finds its explanation in his theoretical preoccupations during this period of crisis; the great essays after all represent a sustained attempt at a fundamental aesthetic self-clarification. These are surely not unrelated activities, the descending to the sources of his creativity on the one hand, and on the other to the archetypes of the forms in which he sought to create.

The fact, then, that Hofmannsthal chose Goethe's Bassompierre as his model is significant in itself; and no less significant are the points of divergence from his chosen model. A comparison of the two texts has been undertaken before and reveals to a nicety the poetic temper and intellectual attitudes of Hofmannsthal in his youthful period, as well as the fact that each writer is a child of his time. (p. 103)

[Images] of fire and light pervade the whole fabric of [*Bassompierre*]. Everywhere the contrast between light and darkness is brought out by Hofmannsthal. The darkness in which the events unfold is a foil for the light that breaks it: the open fire, the light of a lantern shining through the shutter, a streak of light beneath the door, a candle and finally the light of the dawn creeping in—how intense every ray of brightness becomes in such dark. Moreover, Bassompierre, the narrator, must rely on sound and touch more than on perceptions of sight. In fact, the only colour in the whole story is the green of the woman's petticoat and this Hofmannsthal found in the source. It is a world of light and darkness, then, of flickering flames and shadows. This is well suited to the tenor of the story with its 'demiclair'. The fire motif in its structural function, the prevalence of oral and tactile images, these are some of the means that impart form to the story.

That Hofmannsthal seized upon this symbol as the organizing principle of his Novelle is a creative triumph. A passage in his *Der Abenteurer und die Sängerin* of the year before shows a striking similarity in the use of the fire image and throws light on the poetic meaning of *Bassompierre*. . . . (p. 104)

Is there also a central image in the *Reitergeschichte*? For if so, it would suggest that Hofmannsthal considers the poetic symbol to be one of the structural features of this type of epic prose. And indeed there is.

The story is called *Reitergeschichte* and a 'Reitergeschichte' it is in more than one sense. Hofmannsthal narrates the ordinary fighting day of a cavalry squadron in the Italian war of liberation, complete with reconnaissance, hand-to-hand fighting, attack, victory, triumphant entry into Milan and recall. It is a soldier's story. More than that, it is the story of a horseman, because the rider and his horse—'ein Brauner mit gefleckten Beinen'—form an indissoluble unity. Horse and rider become ever more fused as we experience the scene through their joint consciousness. The poet describes the city of Milan as it appears from horseback, the streets and houses flying past the rider and his horse, and he does so in cadences which by their syntax as well as by their rhythm evoke the swiftness of the horse's canter. Never throughout the story is Anton Lerch, the hero, seen without his horse. Only once does he dismount and that is, very characteristically, when he begins to emerge as an individual, at the moment when meeting a woman he once knew he pledges himself to return to her and his thoughts turn to the charms of a private existence. At this moment the horse tries to pull at the reins and neighs, as if to remind him that the war is still on. Lerch follows his squadron. From this moment onwards what is going on in the hero is related by the poet through the reactions of his horse in a variety of situations. Lerch ventures into a deserted village in search of booty—an episode like any other of that exciting and busy day of war, it seems, distinguished only by the deliberate coarseness and stark ugliness of the description. But closer inspection reveals other features which show that this is more than an ordinary adventure. . . . The dreamlike intensity of all the events leaves no doubt of the inward nature of what passes. . . . By what means has the poet established the hero's deep estrangement from his self? The horse (symbol of his 'persona', as we may call it) shies and baulks, and it is not until Lerch, on leaving the village, meets his double, his old self, that horse and rider are at one again. The ensuing battle scene is significantly related by the same stylistic device the poet had used before: the world is once more seen from horseback. We feel the horse's movement through the rhythm and syntax of the sentences; and by experiencing the scene through their joint consciousness the renewed oneness of horse and rider is brought home to us. . . . This horse becomes the embodiment of all his hopes and dreams; from the moment of possession the Wachtmeister ['sargeant-major'] cannot think of giving it up any longer. When the Rittmeister gives the order to let go of the booty, the grey horse, snorting and prancing, gives vent to the silent insubordination he senses in his master. The Rittmeister shoots and Lerch falls to the ground between the two horses.

A dreamlike intensity, a sense of not being quite real, clings to the story as a whole, and this impression is enhanced by the queer absence of spoken words. As in *Bassompierre* we become doubly aware of the light through the contrasting darkness, so here we realize how quiet this world is, when we read of the horses' hoofs, their neighing, the hissing of the cannon balls, the church bells, trumpets, banging of doors, suppressed laughter, the death shriek of a rat in the deathly silence of the village, the fateful report of the gun in the deathly silence. Only twice in the whole 'Novelle' are any words spoken. On the first occasion Lerch utters his sudden desire for a more private life in one sentence which touches off all the tumult in his soul. The second time it is the Rittmeister's command that cuts short this wish-dream. Each time these words are, as it were, announcements of a decision made in silence. They are not part of a dialogue, nor do they establish a verbal communication between the characters. Perhaps more significantly still, there is no reported speech whatsoever in this 'Novelle'. Thus Hofmannsthal creates the impression of a dreamlike isolation of his Wachtmeister. The conflict between Wachtmeister and Rittmeister, revealed as it is only through looks and glances, is a more direct thing than words could be, but also less tangible and less accessible to reason.

Looking back on the two works under discussion, then, it would appear that the leading poetic image, absent in both Goethe's story and his French source, and so central in Hofmannsthal's, is a crucial element in the poet's narrative technique.

Another striking feature of Hofmannsthal's narrative technique is his handling of character and situation. . . . In *Bassompierre* Hofmannsthal has retained the 'Ichform' ["I-Form"] both of the French original and Goethe's translation. But contrary to what they do, the identity of his Bassompierre is not revealed until the story and its central relationship are well under way. This namelessness has a double effect. By not confining the narrator within the limitations of a definite historical personality, the poet has gained some considerable freedom. His nameless 'I' gains a certain ubiquity, an agility of being which fits it to be the 'point of view' of the story. On the other hand, this anonymity of the character ensures unobtrusiveness. He does not loom too large in the reader's vision. Both these features help the poet to achieve the shift of emphasis which, more than anything else, distinguishes his story from its French model. For the central figure of his 'Novelle' is no longer Bassompierre but the woman that loves him. It is her character and her behaviour in an extraordinary situation which the sensitivity of the narrating 'I' is called upon to record. This narration is entirely objective. This does not mean that the narrator does not reveal a great deal about himself that is highly subjective in nature—his moods and his reflections. It is objective in the sense that nowhere does the story-teller exceed the limitations of his knowledge as an outsider, nowhere does the omniscient poet interfere.

The woman is seen entirely from the outside; what we know of her character and motivation—and it is very little indeed—we must gather from her physical demeanour, from the expressions, gestures and movements as they are recorded by Bassompierre. . . . The significant thing is that Hofmannsthal does *not* go beyond the visible evidence. The meaning of her gesture remains a mystery; and evidently it is intended to remain one, for he has specifically drawn our attention to it. That his description by physiognomy and gesture is a deliberate technique of Hofmannsthal's becomes clear from a comparison of the original text with his 'Novelle'. (pp. 105-07)

The poetic emphasis, then, has been shifted from Bassompierre to the young woman. But can she really be called the centre of the story? Significantly, she, too, remains nameless and she remains without name throughout. Her past and her future remain a closed book to us. Whether she falls a victim to the plague we are not told. And even the being before us is realized only to the limit of the poet's chosen technique, i.e. fragmentarily—only as far as she responds to the situation in which she has her being and which informs her mood. Such powerful glimpses are all we know. The rest of her being is not filled in.

Exactly the same is true of the *Reitergeschichte*. Here too we do not know the kind of person the hero is, and of the other two characters that affect his fate we know practically nothing. We share one day with him, and all we know of him is his reaction to the extraordinary situation he encounters. There is no explanation of the past, no motivation of the present. What is presented to us is not so much an individual personality, but a state of mind and feeling translated into action, as it unfolds in a given situation.

And indeed it is this given poetic situation, on which the poet has lavished a wealth of detailed invention. . . . All the individualization which is absent from the characters seems to have gone into the depiction of the situation. There is a host of names to compare with the namelessness of the protagonists in *Bassompierre*: names of minor characters, names of places and buildings evoking a picture of sixteenth-century Paris. Customs and idiosyncrasies of simple people as well as of court society help to create the atmosphere of the period.

And so too in the *Reitergeschichte*, starting as it does with the words 'Den 22ten Juli 1848 vor sechs Uhr morgens', the eve of the battles of Somma Campagna and Custozza and abounding in names of places, technical terms relating to war in general and life in a cavalry regiment in particular; most surprising perhaps are the most exact particulars of that very heterogeneous thing, the Italian army of the war of liberation. But it is not surprising to find the historical setting given in considerable detail in what are after all historical 'Novellen'. The poet has chosen periods to which he felt drawn by his own predilection and of which he knew a good deal—both the wars of the Austrian Empire and the French Renaissance were such periods. What is more, and only too often forgotten: the aesthetic youth of the Café Griensteidl himself knew a good deal about military life . . . and in the letters written between 1894-98 many an eager account of riding, manoeuvres and horses is to be found. But when we examine the detail of the stories more closely it becomes obvious that truth to the facts—historical and otherwise—can hardly have been the poet's purpose, i.e. Milan was in fact evacuated by Radetzky, but much earlier in the year; the Duc de Nemours is a well-known figure; but who is the Kanonikus von Chandieu? Hofmannsthal deals with these facts with sublime disregard for their correctness, concerned as he is to create the mood and atmosphere that will offset most effectively the 'besondere Situation' that is his concern.

That 'besondere Situation' then is not, in essence, a particularized specific situation. It is, rather, an extraordinary situation . . . which, since Goethe, we have come to associate with the form of the Novelle as such. And in both stories this situation is remarkably similar. Both times it is an insignificant incident that results in the most far-reaching and utterly unforeseeable consequences, out of all proportion to the act that set them off. Both times it is an apparently slight amorous advance which turns out to contain the seed of death. (pp. 108-09)

The Wachtmeister's downfall is compressed into one day; Bassompierre's ill luck into three. And when the final catastrophe does come, it comes with lightning speed; literally from one moment to the next. Neither Lerch nor his comrades, drunk with victory, suspect what is about to happen until the fatal shot rings out. And Bassompierre still dreams of love and beauty as he opens the door upon the gruesome scene.

These novels derive much of their poignancy from Hofmannsthal's treatment of the moment. Each moment is capable of transforming a life in its entirety; each moment is, quintessentially, a 'wendepunkt' ['turning-point']. . . . The 'Novelle' could not but gain in the hands of one who experienced time as a configuration of turning points. (p. 109)

When we survey the results of this short investigation, three principal features would seem to stand out: that conspicuous use is made of a dominant poetic symbol; that the characterization is slight; and that decisive emphasis is assigned to the 'unerhörte Begebenheit' ['shocking event']. . . .

The connection in these stories between character and events is not easy to discern. First, there is so little of the characters; we do not know in a single instance what lies 'behind' their actions. And then the connection between these actions and the fantastic events that ensue is equally difficult to discover. Lerch's advance to the woman Vuic and his death seem completely disproportionate, and so does the provocative behaviour of his horse which immediately precedes his execution. Similarly, the nameless woman's death by plague seems unmotivated by anything she is or does. The missing link between the world of character and the objective sphere of events is to be found in the poetic symbol. Hofmannsthal has confined himself to the depiction of the visible surface of his characters; of the elemental forces buried in the reaches below consciousness he has remained silent. Only the imagery, which in both cases is taken from the elemental sphere, tells us of the existence of these forces and of their secret effects on the outward events. Fire and horse, symbols of passion in these 'Novellen', are also the agents that bring about the final destruction. This formal link is all the poet will reveal about the connection between character and catastrophe. For the rest, the projection of the forces of the unconscious into the outward world is complete; and the external situation becomes imbued with a mysterious logic of its own. (p. 110)

What was it, in the last resort, that bade the poet shun the exploration of character and motive and instead express his sense of destiny in terms of the fatal configuration of events? It was, I think, a genuinely epic impulse as well as his basic experience of the transforming power of the moment: it is this integration of the structure of his experience and the structure of the narrative form in which he worked which is the secret of his genius as a 'Novellist'. (pp. 110-11)

Mary E. Gilbert, ''Some Observations on Hofmannsthal's Two Novellen 'Reitergeschichte' and 'Das Erlebnis des Marschalls von Bassompierre','' in German Life & Letters, *n.s., Vol. XI, October-July, 1957-58, pp. 102-11.*

MICHAEL HAMBURGER (essay date 1961)

[*An accomplished lyric poet in his own right, Hamburger has been widely praised for his translations of several German poets unfamiliar to English readers, including Friedrich Hölderlin, Georg Trakl, and Hofmannsthal. He has also written extensively on modern German literature. In the following excerpt, Hamburger proposes that Hofmannsthal's works are interrelated and that in order to understand this author, who would not ''draw a categorical line between 'art' and 'life','' they must be studied as a whole.*]

Hofmannsthal's precocity was a real one. In reading his letters of the early period one is struck by his astonishing capacity for receiving and absorbing disparate experience, so that his attitudes never remain fixed for long, but are perpetually modified, corrected, and strengthened by self-criticism. His openness to external influences of every order—including the aura of persons, things, and places, of institutions, ways of life, ways of thinking and feeling—was such as to amount to a danger. To take only the most obvious of relationships, the personal, he was always in danger of being fascinated, overwhelmed, and abused by those whose strength lay in their monomania, the one kind of strength opposed to his own. This danger was inseparable from his strength; and the ''magical'' inspiration of his early work was nothing other than the presentiment or intuition of a multiplicity and underlying unity which his later work could only embody in a corresponding multiplicity of media, themes, and forms. The difference, as he said, lay between ''pre-existence'' and ''existence,'' between potentiality and realization, between the homunculus in his bottle—endowed with prophetic and magical faculties as in Goethe's *Faust*—and the mature man's need to particularize, to separate, and to distinguish, a need inseparable from involvement in active life. Where Hofmannsthal's later works remain fragmentary or imperfectly realized, it is nearly always because the conception is too complex to be subordinated to the demands of the particular medium chosen, to be absorbed into the surface. So in the cases of his first prose comedy, *Silvia im Stern,* abandoned because too crowded with diverse characters and their intricate interactions, of the novel *Andreas,* the most tantalizingly enthralling of his many unfinished works, and, to a lesser extent, of his last tragedy, *Der Turm.*

All the hostility and misunderstandings to which Hofmannsthal's later work and person were subject arose from the prejudice that a writer so protean, so receptive, and so many-sided must be lacking in individuality and integrity. Yet even in the early poems and playlets Hofmannsthal's individuality had been nourished by his uncommon capacity for identification with what was not himself, whether experienced directly in his environment or indirectly in paintings, in the theatre, or in books. Unlike Yeats or Stefan George, he assumed no mask or anti-self, but relied on the social conventions to protect his privacy. "Manners," he noted, "are walls, disguised with mirrors"; and "manners are based on a profound conception of the necessity of isolation, while upholding—deliberately upholding—the illusion of contact." In the same way, Hofmannsthal could at once project and conceal his individuality by borrowing the artistic conventions of past ages; his refusal to draw a categorical line between "art" and "life," past and present, not only absolved him from the false dichotomies of his time but gave him a scope and a freedom that far exceeded the resources of direct self-expression. Needless to say, it also exposed him to the charge that he was a mere imitator of obsolete conventions, a receiver and renovator of stolen goods. Only the most minute attention reveals how much of himself he put even into adaptations of other men's works. His so-called translation of Molière's little comedy *Les Fâcheux* is a good instance; it is nothing less than a preliminary sketch for Hofmannsthal's own comic masterpiece, *Der Schwierige.* (pp. xviii-xx)

The totality of Hofmannsthal's work is as open to misunderstandings as Goethe's. Like Goethe, and unlike most of his contemporaries, he attempted that most difficult thing—difficult enough in Goethe's time, much more in Hofmannsthal's—to extend an essentially personal and esoteric vision to the most diverse spheres, to cut across established divisions and specializations, to make connections everywhere, and produce not only works, but a literature. That Hofmannsthal, as an Austrian, inherited a different culture did not make his task basically different from Goethe's; in trying to produce a literature, "a whole repertory," as he said, he drew not only on a national heritage, but on whatever seemed most congenial to him in ancient, mediaeval, and modern, European and Oriental tradition—Goethe's *Weltliteratur.* Goethe, too, "dabbled" in every branch of literature, including the writing of librettos; nothing was too small for him to attempt, nothing too great. Both denied an ultimate significance to transitory phenomena and institutions, yet applied themselves with intense devotion to their study and service. A century and a half of critical and scholarly industry has not exhausted Goethe's work, or made it widely accessible as a whole, because its diversity is more palpable than its unity. *Mutatis mutandis*—and it is their kind, not their stature, that makes the two writers comparable—the sum is likely to be true of Hofmannsthal's work. Every new reading of any one of his works in the light of another reveals new inter-relations, new intricacies of texture and allusion, new seeming contradictions and paradoxes. "Man is a manifold

person," Hofmannsthal wrote, and few men were more manifold than he. Because of his unceasing endeavour to grasp and shape this multiplicity, rather than to suppress it for the sake of an easy victory, even his failures remain interesting and admirable. (pp. lxii-lxiii)

> *Michael Hamburger, in his introduction to* Selected Writings of Hugo von Hofmannsthal: Poems and Verse Plays, Vol. 2 *by Hugo von Hofmannsthal, edited by Michael Hamburger, translated by John Bednall & others, Bollingen Series XXXIII (copyright © 1961 by Princeton University Press; reprinted by permission of Princeton University Press), Pantheon Books, 1961, pp. xiii-lxiii.*

EGON SCHWARZ (essay date 1970)

[*In the following excerpt, Schwarz maintains that Hofmannsthal's critical essays, which he wrote throughout his career, not only provide an essential key to understanding the Austrian's departure from aestheticism, but also reflect the sociopolitical concerns of the times.*]

From 1891, when he was seventeen, till 1929, the year of his death, Hofmannsthal wrote critical essays dealing with French, English, German, Italian, Slavic, and even ancient letters. They range from poetry to biography, from the epic to the theatre, from literature to linguistics, as well as from books to such non-verbal arts as music and pantomime, dance and painting. His gallery of portraits includes not only Goethe and Balzac, Ibsen and Swinburne, Stefan George and d'Annunzio, Shakespeare and Calderón, Oscar Wilde and St.-John Perse, but also Beethoven, Gustav Mahler, Eleonora Duse, Ruth St. Denis, and so many others that they cannot be enumerated. Yet he is also willing, and in his mature years increasingly so, to abandon the world of art and books altogether and to describe places he visited or to address himself to problems of civilization touching upon the political questions of his day. His characterizations of Greece or Sicily, his distinction between Prussians and Austrians, his observations about language, his visions of Europe, and his warnings of the future belong to the most illuminating and often moving utterances of that period of history. And all of this is done with style and charm, humility and wisdom, an endless supply of information, and an inexhaustible wealth of humanity. Hugo von Hofmannsthal is a great European critic and a thorough acquaintance with his essayistic work is a complete education in itself. (pp. 12-13)

Almost eight decades have elapsed since the publication of Hofmannsthal's first one-act play, *Gestern,* and the case for his early insistence on the immorality of an ivory-tower art has long since been vigorously made. Had his contemporaries paid more heed to his essays and their unequivocal language, instead of misinterpreting the more ambiguous imagery of his poems and short lyrical plays, the question could have been settled right at the beginning. Years of controversy could have been avoided. No matter what subject he chose to dissect critically, be it d'Annunzio's last novel or Oscar Wilde's humiliating fate, in his essays Hofmannsthal never tired of preaching the supremacy of life over art and the artist's obligation towards this life in all its manifestations, the humbler the better. (pp. 15-16)

Many of Hofmannsthal's essays are astutely penetrating, critical scrutinies of writers, dancers, and painters from all countries, but they are also self-revelatory. Much of this criticism is self-criticism. Once the principle has been recognized, it is easy to uncover the pattern even in unexpected places. Take the progression one can observe in the essays on Gabriele d'Annunzio ["**Gabriele d'Annunzio I**," "**Gabriele d'Annunzio II**," "**Der neue Roman von d'Annunzio**," and "**Die Rede Gabriele d'Annunzios**"], the darling of the *fin de siècle*. In the first one, written in 1893 at the age of nineteen, Hofmannsthal once more laments the emptiness of the elite of aesthetes to which he pretends to belong: "We have nothing but a sentimental memory, a paralyzed will and the uncanny gift of self-duplication. We watch our own life; we empty the goblet prematurely and yet remain interminably thirsty. . . . We have no roots in life, as it were, and move about the children of life like clairvoyant and yet blinded shadows." The rest of the essay is devoted to showing how representative the Italian writer was of this generation. If there is any disharmony, it is not between Hofmannsthal and d'Annunzio but between their generation of artists and life.

The second essay, published only a little later, shows the first signs of critical detachment. D'Annunzio is still praised for having lived by the aesthetic prescription of the age. He is acknowledged as a poet whom "the words with which we designate the joys and pains of life have made tremble, earlier, more strongly and more deeply than life itself." But this artificial anticipation of experience is a deception which cannot be carried on indefinitely. . . . The conclusion is inevitable: "There is indeed something rigid and something artificial in Signor d'Annunzio's philosophy of life, and his books are still lacking the ultimate: revelation." The only saving grace is: "But he is still young."

Hofmannsthal returns to d'Annunzio again and again, as if driven by a compulsion. In his third essay, "Der neue Roman von d'Annunzio, *Le vergini delle rocce*" of 1896, the reason for his revisitation becomes clear. Evidently he has not yet said everything that was on his mind, or rather his development has now reached a point where he can demonstrate with deadly outspokenness the sources of his earlier vague malaise: "At that time I found only uncertain and not very precise words for an enormous phenomenon which it will not be easy to ignore when the attempt is made to write the moral and aesthetic history of the present age. . . . The strange, or if you will, the horrible and dreadful thing about d'Annunzio's books was that they were written by one who did not *stand in life*. They were throughout the experiences of a man whose only connection with life had been through watching it. For every creative writer fashions incessantly but one basic experience of his life; and in the case of d'Annunzio this basic relationship to things had been *that he was watching them*." These are portentous sentences. Hofmannsthal has found his own basic experience: that his era was divorced from life. His attempts to remedy this absurdity and to enter life will dominate his intellectual and artistic endeavors henceforth. The pampered *Wunderkind*, the aesthetic darling of the *fin de siècle* in Vienna, professes an ethical rigorism incompatible with the atmosphere in the "Capua of the spirits." [In a footnote Schwarz explains this phrase: This is Franz Grillparzer's expression to signify the effeminating influence of Vienna's intellectual atmosphere with its surfeit of stimuli.] A crisis seems inevitable. (pp. 17-20)

[It] was not until 1902 that it broke out with savage virulence and found inimitable expression in a brilliant and moving piece, half fiction, half essay, entitled "**Ein Brief**," which has since attained fame in the intellectual world. This outbreak of despair had grave consequences for Hofmannsthal himself. Not only did he cease to write poetry, the poetry to which he owed his

privileged position among the men of letters in his time, he turned to other genres, notably drama, as his principal modes of expression. More significantly, Hofmannsthal also changed his artistic style and basic outlook upon life, with the result that most of his earlier devotees no longer understood him and regretfully parted company with their erstwhile idol.

Hofmannsthal's crisis was not merely a private affair. It was part of a much wider intellectual crisis in Europe which left its imprint on the writings of Joyce and Maeterlinck, Kafka and Musil, Rilke, Valéry, and T. S. Eliot. The fourteen pages of '**Ein Brief**" are merely the most striking statement and the most penetrating analysis of a widespread upheaval in the intellectual sensibility of Europe at the turn of the century. This is Hofmannsthal's historical merit, and as a "confrontation with a phenomenon in his culture" one of his most notable critical achievements.

The essay—best known as "**The Letter of Lord Chandos**" because it poses (with subtle hints at Hofmannsthal's own relationship with Stefan George) as a fictitious communication directed by an Elizabethan gentleman to Francis Bacon—is more than the lament of a gifted writer who feels the sources of poetry, his very medium, language, drying up in his mind. It is a full account of the writer's development in which we readily recognize Hofmannsthal's intellectual career, and it aroused such resonance only because it was paradigmatic for the development of the European mind as a whole. (pp. 20-2)

After the "Chandos crisis" Hofmannsthal repeatedly returned to religious topics and left behind a precious heritage of modern morality plays. In them there can be no doubt that Christianity plays the metaphorical role of Western tradition in conflict with the pagan non-values of the industrial age, just as there can be little doubt that the author searched for more than the allegorical meaning in Catholicism. Whether he as an individual reached such firmness of faith must and ought to remain an open question. Rather than joining a fruitless controversy, one should listen to the words he puts into the mouth of his double, the younger son of the Earl of Bath, Philipp Lord Chandos: "For me the mysteries of faith are condensed into a lofty allegory which hovers over the fields of my life like a luminous rainbow, invariably distant, always ready to recede if it occurred to me to approach it and to wrap myself in the hem of its cloak." This points to a quest much larger than that of overcoming mere poetic sterility. "**The Letter of Lord Chandos**" marks the end of the first stage in Hofmannsthal's *oeuvre*. The crisis was not new nor is it over now. It never will be. But from this point on his work is characterized by an unceasing endeavor to subordinate its aesthetic values to an ethical philosophy, by entering the very premises of life, and to place art in the service of life. (pp. 24-5)

Egon Schwarz, "Hugo von Hofmannsthal As a Critic," in On Four Modern Humanists: Hofmannsthal, Gundolf, Curtius, Kantorowicz, *edited by Arthur R. Evans, Jr. (copyright © 1970 by Princeton University Press; excerpts reprinted by permission of Princeton University Press), Princeton University Press, 1970, pp. 3-53.*

DAVID G. DAVIAU (essay date 1971)

[*Daviau's detailed analysis of Hofmannsthal's* The Letter of Lord Chandos *is considered the standard interpretation. Daviau regards the fictional letter as a warning by Hofmannsthal to his contemporaries of the "dangers of aestheticism." Daviau departs from earlier critics who believed that the Chandos letter repre-*

sented a personal language crisis in Hofmannsthal's creative development.]

Hofmannsthal's *Ein Brief,* more popularly known as the **Chandos letter,** has occasioned more discussion by scholars than almost any other of his works. In addition to approximately twenty substantial articles and separate chapters in books, that have been devoted exclusively to this essay, virtually every work on Hofmannsthal regardless of specialized topic generally makes mention of the **Chandos letter,** or the Chandos crises, as it is often called.

Out of this considerable body of material a more or less standardized interpretation of the work's significance has gained acceptance along the following lines: that after a richly productive decade as a lyric poet and lyric dramatist, Hofmannsthal experienced a crisis in his productivity around 1900 which caused him to renounce the writing of poetry in order to devote himself to the new goal of achieving more popular success in the theater; that the decision of Lord Chandos to renounce all further writing, because of the inadequacy of language to express his total view of the world, represents Hofmannsthal's personal language crisis or language scepticism; that by turning to the theater and later to opera Hofmannsthal moved toward forms that were capable of expanding the communicative power of words by supplementing them with gestures, mimicry, stage techniques, painting, and music; finally, that the Chandos letter marked the end, the "death" of the introverted, introspective, aesthetically oriented poet and the beginnings of the mature, socially-directed Hofmannsthal.

Naturally, not all critics espouse all of these points, but when they are viewed collectively, the above generalized account of the position of the Chandos letter in Hofmannsthal's development results. Since this more or less standard version does seem to correspond on the surface with the factual details of Hofmannsthal's career, it appears convincing and hence easy to accept. Hofmannsthal did in fact experience some kind of crisis between 1900 and 1903. He did cease writing lyric poetry about 1900 to dedicate himself thereafter to creating predominantly for the theater and the opera. He did express doubts about the communicative power of language, at least regarding its capacity to render the visionary, multi-dimensional view of the world—an aspect that was his special domain and concern. In a sense, then, he did change his artistic focus.

However, a re-evaluation of *Ein Brief* and the complex personal and artistic circumstances surrounding it suggests the possibility of an alternative interpretation of the Chandos letter and its significance within Hofmannsthal's evolution as a writer. By redefining several of the generally accepted premises in a more precise manner, that is, by shifting some of the accents normally applied to the available evidence, a new perspective on the Chandos letter and its position within the framework of Hofmannsthal's development emerges.

[By] concentrating on six of the generally accepted premises found in the research devoted to this work, it will be possible to demonstrate the major lines along which the new interpretation is developing and to indicate two conclusions: 1. That Hofmannsthal's work is an integral, progressive unity from beginning to end. and 2. that the Chandos crisis, particularly as a language crisis, has been misunderstood and greatly exaggerated in its application to Hofmannsthal. These two points actually stand in a cause and effect relationship: Because the Chandos crisis has been disproportionately emphasized, the overall unity of Hofmannsthal's work has been distorted and generally overlooked.

The first major premise encountered in the criticism of *Ein Brief* is the widespread acceptance of the date 1901, which was established by Herbert Steiner in *Prosa II* of his edition of the *Gesammelte Werke.* However, on the basis of Hofmannsthal's own comment, it is certain that *Ein Brief,* which was published in the newspaper *Der Tag* in Berlin in October, 1902, was written in August of 1902. Thus, the work was not written, as has been assumed, during the height of Hofmannsthal's personal crisis in 1901 but instead was produced at the conclusion of that crisis, which by the fall of 1902 was fairly well resolved.

Proper dating of the letter solves one of the major enigmas concerning this work, specifically, how a man supposedly experiencing the language crisis that Hofmannsthal has mirrored in Chandos could describe his inability to use words so beautifully and articulately. Since the work was written after the crisis had passed, it is plausible that Hofmannsthal was able to describe a situation that he had experienced but that no longer prevailed. The final proof of Hofmannsthal's "cure" was the very fact that he could write *Ein Brief.*

The second basic premise encountered in the criticism of *Ein Brief* is that Lord Chandos represents Hofmannsthal. Critics have proceeded on the assumption that is permissible and possible to interpret Hofmannsthal literally on the basis of the attitudes and views of Chandos.

Hofmannsthal in a letter to his close personal friend Leopold von Andrian states clearly and unambiguously that the Chandos letter is based on personal experience. . . . (pp. 28-9)

Despite this personal element, which Hofmannsthal reemphasizes in a second lengthy explanatory letter to Andrian, he defends his presentation in masked form. Almost as if to preempt Andrian, who then did criticize this feature of the work, Hofmannsthal argued that he has no other possibility of expressing himself except through the medium of fantasy. *Ein Brief* is clearly a poetic work even though Steiner included it among the essays. The fact that the Chandos letter along with outher works of this type was originally intended for a volume entitled *Erfundene Gespräche und Briefe* further shows Hofmannsthal's poetic intent here.

The Chandos letter, taken literally, rests on the impossible condition, the absurdity, in fact, that a man in Chandos' condition could write any letter, not to mention one involving such complexity of thought. When Chandos states that he has completely lost the ability to think or speak coherently, he precludes the possibility of writing anything, including the letter in which he makes such a statement. The point is that Chandos, who is an invented figure, did not write the letter, Hofmannsthal did. Hofmannsthal, who does not have Chandos' problem of disorientation, is able to compose the letter that he imagines Chandos would have written had he been able to write.

Ein Brief carries to its logical, theoretical extreme the imagined fate of a young writer with some features of the youthful Hofmannsthal. Hofmannsthal is warning himself, the poet Stefan George, and his contemporaries in general that unless their approach to art and life changes, the dilemma of Chandos is a possibility that awaits them. However, it must be emphasized that the fate of Chandos was never a genuine possibility for Hofmannsthal. Chandos' fundamental withdrawal from life must be viewed as a negative conclusion, while Hofmannsthal was positively life-oriented throughout his entire career. However, the personal characteristics of Chandos that made possible his fate were latent in Hofmannsthal and were more prominent in his early period. Yet, from his beginnings in *Gestern* and throughout the series of dramas in the 1890's such as *Der Tod des Tizian, Der Tor und der Tod* and up to and including *Das Bergwerk zu Falun,* Hofmannsthal consistently repudiated the aesthete and advocated life over aesthetic preoccupation.

The conclusion then to be drawn concerning this premise of equating Chandos and Hofmannsthal is that it is an error to interpret Hofmannsthal on the basis of what Chandos says and does without careful qualification. Such qualifications have often been absent in the criticism to date which as tended to consider the two men interchangeable.

The third premise considers that the writing of *Ein Brief* marks the end of Hofmannsthal's lyric production. Actually Hofmannsthal's main poems, as he himself stated, were written between 1892 and 1896, the period which he called the loneliest of his life. The few poems written after 1896 are not included among his best. Thus, Hofmannsthal's essential lyric production ended approximately six years before he wrote the Chandos letter. In December 1901 he confessed to Richard Dehmel that he could no longer write a single poem. However, lyricism *per se* remained an essential ingredient of his poetic style throughout his entire career.

The fourth premise, a corollary of the previous point, states that just as Candos renounced writing until he could discover the new universal language that he needed, Hofmannsthal similarly repudiated the writing of lyric poetry in favor of writing in the more universal forms of drama and opera, forms which supplemented language with music, gestures, and staging. There are two points here that require separation and clarification: 1. Hofmannsthal did not renounce lyric poetry and 2. the loss of his lyric gift and his interest in drama do not stand in a cause and effect relationship.

Looking first at *Ein Brief,* it is evident that Chandos does not renounce writing; it renounces him. Similarly, Hofmannsthal did not voluntarily give up writing lyric poetry. His talent for lyric poetry simply disappeared, without his knowing why or how any more than his friend Leopold von Andrian could explain the loss of his literary talent after completing one book, *Der Garten der Erkenntnis* in 1895.

One of the difficulties in analysing *Ein Brief* results from an inner contradiction in the work itself, which has caused much of the difficulty in interpreting the attitude of Hofmannsthal toward Chandos. Hofmannsthal's changes in the original manuscript make evident how this situation arose. (pp. 30-1)

Comparison with the manuscript version reveals that Hofmannsthal was initially undecided about the proper word he wished to use at the point where he employed the word *Verzichtes* ["renunciation"]. His original choice was *Aufhörens* ["cessation"]. This was crossed out and in its place he put *Unterlassens* ["discontinue"] over the line. He then crossed this out and wrote *Aufhörens* again under the line. Finally, he decided upon *Verzichtes* which he inserted over the line and to the right of the word *Unterlassens* that he had rejected earlier.

This single alteration becomes a great importance in showing that the conception of the Chandos situation changed in Hofmannsthal's mind during the writing of the work. Knowing the earlier choices enables one to speculate on the process of its development. Ultimately, it shows a vacillation on the part of Hofmannsthal about the intention and meaning of his own work.

In the original instance, the word *Aufhören* denotes a relatively neutral statement that Chandos has ceased literary activity without specifying any cause. Thus, the cessation could be the result of his own volition but it also could stem from some other force of necessity beyond his own will. The same interpretation would be true of *Unterlassens,* although this already implies greater personal choice than *Aufhören* and shows Chandos moving in the direction of independent resignation. The final choice of *Verzicht* clearly implies voluntary renunciation.

By this shift Hofmannsthal actually has brought the beginning of the work into harmony with the end, but in doing so he has created a contradiction with the middle. For Chandos states that he has ceased writing because he has lost the ability to think or to speak about anything in a connected way. . . . (pp. 31-2)

It would seem that Hofmannsthal began the Chandos letter with the idea of depicting the fate of a man who was suffering from an inability to write, and then changed the focus of the argument to make it appear as if the renunciation stemmed from the inadequacy of language rather than from some psychological disability. . . . The introductory passage which originally permitted both interpretations was then amended to coincide with the new ending. However, Hofmannsthal failed to change the middle paragraph which now stands in contradiction to the beginning and the end.

One can see the differing possibilities now implicit in the essay as a result of Hofmannsthal's altered view. If one accepts the idea that Chandos renounces writing because of the inadequacy of language to express his view of the world, one can see the reason for the prevailing interpretation of the Chandos letter, as indicating a language crisis in Hofmannsthal, and motivating his turning to drama and opera, that is, forms that supplement language with additional means of communication. However, if one considers Hofmannsthal's original intention, as indicated by the wording that he changed, then it is possible to read the Chandos letter as a much more personal document, reflecting the difficulties that Hofmannsthal experienced with writing during the years 1900-1903. Possibly to mask somewhat the highly personal nature of his work, Hofmannsthal changed the emphasis during the writing and either overlooked or ignored the resulting ambiguity.

By adopting this latter view as best fitting the overall context of the Chandos episode in Hofmannsthal's life, it follows, returning to the second point mentioned above, that since Hofmannsthal did not renounce his lyric production, he did not turn to the theater and opera as a direct result of such renunciation. In actuality, Hofmannsthal's interest in the theater stems from his beginnings as a writer, and his desire to excel in drama as the form best suited to his ability and outlook on life was already adumbrated in 1896. In the letter to Andrian in which Hofmannsthal repudiates aestheticism as impoverishing life, he describes the theater as the vantage point which permits one to join life and at the same time maintain the distance from it that he required in order to maintain his personal balance.

The fifth premise is that the language problem of Chandos represents Hofmannsthal's personal language crisis. Again, there are several ideas here that require separation. For example, Chandos is not suffering from a language problem but from a life problem which has its major symptom in the inability to think or speak coherently. Hofmannsthal carefully refrains from specifically labelling the cause of the Chandos problem. Most likely he does not know himself. But he can describe the effects even without specifying the cause. However, it does seem clear that Chandos, who finds it impossible even to talk to his four year old daughter, is the victim of a neurotic condition that goes far deeper than merely a surface distrust of words. (pp. 32-3)

The sixth and final premise to be discussed is the view that the Chandos letter reflects Hofmannsthal's sceptical, if not negative attitude toward language. Shifting the emphasis, as has been attempted in this essay, from a language to a personal crisis resolves the apparent paradox of why Hofmannsthal, supposedly mistrustful of words, would turn to drama and to opera, which are still basically word-oriented forms. The consideration that opera and drama supplement words with other art forms only begs the question but does not answer the problem of language. Hofmannsthal's decision to devote himself to drama and particularly to comedy after 1900 is not rooted in language scepticism, but in a broadening of his social outlook. If Hofmannsthal had any doubts about the value of words, they were certainly dispelled by his experiments in pantomime and ballet during the years 1900 and 1901, which proved to him the severe limitations of wordless forms. (p. 35)

In conclusion, *Ein Brief* is not an attack on language nor an indication of scepticism about language but, like *Der Tor und der Tod* and most of his early works, is a warning by Hofmannsthal to his contemporaries of the dangers of aestheticism. (pp. 37-8)

> Donald G. Daviau, "Hugo von Hofmannsthal and the Chandos Letter," in Modern Austrian Literature (© copyright International Arthur Schnitzler Research Association 1971), Vol. 4, No. 2, Summer, 1971, pp. 28-44.

DAVID H. MILES   (essay date 1972)

[*The following comments are excerpted from Miles's book-length study of Hofmannsthal's unfinished novel,* Andreas. *Here, Miles speculates about why Hofmannsthal never finished the novel.*]

Over the years countless theories have been advanced as to why Hofmannsthal was never able to complete his novel. Having begun the work when he was thirty-three, he had completed only eighty pages of it when he died almost a quarter of a century later. Jakob Wasserman, in his postscript to the novel's first edition in 1932, implies that it was the tragic collapse of the Austro-Hungarian monarchy, the Habsburg world of Hofmannsthal's youth and early manhood, that finally brought this particular project of the poet to a standstill. C. J. Burckhardt, on the other hand, feels that it was due to Hofmannsthal's long and frustrated attempt to complete *Der Turm,* the magnum opus of his later years. Karl Gautschi, approaching the question from a more psychological viewpoint, finds, like Hermann Broch before him, that it was the highly self-confessional nature of *Andreas* that ultimately rendered it impossible for Hofmannsthal to finish; the poet was, as Broch had put it, too strongly oriented toward an aesthetic of absolute objectivity to be able to cope effectively with the extremely autobiographical themes in the novel.

There is, however, at least one more reason why Hofmannsthal did not complete, and perhaps never could have completed, *Andreas.* This was, briefly, the innate difficulty of portraying Andreas' ideal love for Romana in such a realistic form as that of the novel. Indeed, we need only recall the examples of

Hyperion and *Heinrich von Ofterdingen,* two earlier Bildungsromane with no definite ending, to realize the immense difficulty of depicting in the medium of prose the fulfillment of an ideal love. For without the aid of a formal framework of poetic meter or a thematic one of transcendence (as in Dante's case), the prophecy of paradise regained through love tends to remain a mere prophecy, an unrealized ideal. Moreover, the conclusion of the Bildungsroman is obviously more problematic than that of most novels. For if the plot closes with the classic "comic" ending of the hero's marriage, as in *Wilhelm Meister* and *Nachsommer,* this not only tends to devalue the Bildung by setting it a mundane goal, but also creates the illusion that the hero has achieved some form of permanent plateau in his development. The open ending, on the other hand (as in *Hyperion* or *Malte*), although it adheres more closely to the openness of the life-process itself, must sacrifice formal and symbolic completeness. It is impossible, in other words, for the Bildungsroman to be mimetically true to both life *and* art—to be true to the reality of unending change and growth *and* to the Aristotelian ideal of a fixed beginning, middle, and end.

However, no matter which reason or reasons lay behind Hofmannsthal's inability to finish the novel, he did provide us with a possible conclusion to it, in an entirely different art-form. For in his opera collaborations with Richard Strauss he produced libretti in which all of the major themes of *Andreas* reappear and are carried to their symbolic conclusions. With the aid of music and the operatic stage, it seems—a world where the willing suspension of disbelief was more easily achieved than in the realistic novel—Hofmannsthal was finally able to give expression to his complex ideas of an immanent-transcendent, ideal love and an allomatic constancy within change. (pp. 202-03)

> David H. Miles, in his Hofmannsthal's Novel "Andreas": Memory and Self (copyright © 1972 by Princeton University Press; excerpts reprinted by permission of Princeton University Press), Princeton University Press, 1972, 226 p.

W. H. AUDEN   (essay date 1973)

[*Often considered the poetic successor of W. B. Yeats and T. S. Eliot, Auden is also highly regarded for his literary criticism. As a member of a generation of British writers strongly influenced by the ideas of Karl Marx and Sigmund Freud, Auden considered social and psychological commentary important functions of literary criticism. As a committed follower of Christianity, he considered it necessary to view art in the context of moral and theological absolutes. Thus, he regarded art as a "secondary world" which should serve a definite purpose within the "primary world" of human history. This purpose is the creation of aesthetic beauty and moral order, qualities that exist only in imperfect form in the primary world but are intrinsic to the secondary world of art. Consequently, it is both morally and aesthetically wrong for an artist to employ evil and suffering as subject matter. Auden concluded that "to write a play, that is to construct a secondary world, about Auschwitz, for example, is wicked: author and audience may try to pretend that they are morally horrified, but in fact they are passing an evening together, in the aesthetic enjoyment of horrors." While he has been criticized for significant inconsistencies in his thought throughout his career, Auden is generally regarded as a fair and perceptive critic. The following excerpt considers the successful collaboration of Hofmannsthal and Richard Straus. As librettist and composer, the two contributed equally in their joint creative efforts, according to Auden,*] *who himself was involved in numerous artistic collaborations throughout his career.*]

The mating of minds is, surely, quite as fascinating a relationship as the mating of the sexes, yet how little attention novelists have paid to it. . . . The normal intellectual marriage produces one child, e.g., Liddell and Scott, Russell and Whitehead for example, but occasionally (more commonly, I suspect among scientists than among artists) a union is formed which begets a succession of works; the collaboration of Hofmannsthal and Strauss is a striking example and the only one of which, thanks to their correspondence [*Richard Strauss und Hugo von Hofmannsthal: Breifwechsel*], we possess a detailed record. One rather suspects that we should not have been so fortunate if they had liked each other more as persons or, at least, if Hofmannsthal had liked Strauss more. It seems evident that Hofmannsthal did not care to see Strauss more often than was absolutely necessary, and he made it quite clear on what plane their relationship was to be. . . . Even after collaborating for twenty-three years, they were still not on first-names terms—Strauss will write *Lieber Freund* but Hofmannsthal sticks to *Leiber Doktor Strauss.* (pp. 345-46)

In their collaboration, that is to say, the choice of dramatic subject and its sytle of treatment was to be the librettist's business, not the composer's who must wait patiently till the librettist finds a subject which excites his imagination. As in a marriage, for a collaboration to endure and be successful, each partner must have something valuable to give and to receive. Strauss received from Hofmannsthal a succession of libretti which, while being admirably settable, are a pleasure to read by themselves. The poetry is often beautiful, the characters and situations are interesting. Furthermore, each is unique and sets the composer a new musical and stylistic challenge.

Hofmannsthal also did a great deal, not only for Strauss, but also for the general cause of opera by insisting that, in the production of their works, as much attention be paid to their visual aspects as to their musical. At the time when they began collaborating, the decor, costumes and stage direction of most productions in most opera houses were appallingly bad—heavy, crude, huggermugger. Strauss, who was not very visually minded, was used to this and expected no better, but Hofmannsthal belonged to a group, led by [Max] Reinhardt, who were determined to revolutionize stage production and succeeded. (Only too well, alas: today most operas suffer from being over-produced.) Strauss had the good sense to realize that in such matters Hofmannsthal had better taste than himself and gave him complete authority. If Hofmannsthal was sometimes excessive in his demands and unnecessarily rude when they were not met—he could not understand why a composer should prefer a plain singer with a great voice to a beautiful singer with a second-rate one—it was probably necessarily to bully Strauss a bit or he would have let things slide.

In return, Strauss gave Hofmannsthal much. In the first place, he gave him the opportunity to write libretti at all, which had always fascinated him. . . . And in the second place he taught him a lot about how to write a good one. As Hofmannsthal himself admitted, Strauss had the better theatrical sense, at least for opera in which the action must be much more immediately intelligible than it need be in a spoken play. If the alterations which Strauss suggested sometimes offended Hofmannsthal's artistic conscience and set him into fits, there was always some flaw which prompted them, and often, as in the second acts of *Rosenkavalier* and *Arabella,* they were brilliantly right.

Again like marriage, any artistic collaboration must have its ups and downs: there are factors, some personal, some external, which cause friction and even a threat of divorce. If most of the irritation was on Hofmannsthal's part, there were more reasons for this than his touchy temperament. Before Berlioz, Wagner, and Verdi in his middle years, no composer worried much about the libretto; he took what he was given and did the best he could with it. This was possible because a satisfactory convention had been established as to how libretti should be written, the forms for arias and ensembles, the style for *opera buffa,* the style for *opera seria,* etc., which any competent versifier could master. This meant, however, that while a composer could be assured of getting a settable text, one libretto was remarkably like another, all originality and interest had to come from the music. Some librettists might be better than others and enjoy a reputation among composers, but to the public all were anonymous and content to remain so. Aside from Goethe, who never found a good enough composer, Hofmannsthal was the first poet with an established public literary reputation to write libretti, and in his day this was a daring thing to do. In the literary circle to which he belonged, opera was not highly regarded as an art form and it may well have been that Strauss' music was not much admired either. Certainly, most of his friends thought that he was wasting his time and talents writing libretti of which few words would be heard in performance, and, of course, the managers of opera houses and his musical friends, accustomed to the conventional libretto, thought Strauss was wasting *his* time and talents trying to set such dense and incomprehensible texts.

A librettist is always at a disadvantage because operas are reviewed, not by literary or dramatic critics, but by music critics whose taste and understanding of poetry may be very limited. What is worse, a music critic who wishes to attack the music but is afraid to do so directly, can always attack it indirectly by condemning the libretto. A librettist is at a further disadvantage because music is an international language and poetry a local one. Wherever an opera is performed, audiences hear the same music but, outside the country of its origin, either they hear alien words which are meaningless to them or a translation which, however good—and most translations are very bad—are not what the librettist wrote. To know that however valuable your contribution, your public fame will always be less than that of your collaborator is not an easy position for anyone, and for Hofmannsthal, to whom fame mattered a great deal, it must often have been a torture. (pp. 347-49)

[*W. H. Auden,*] *"A Marriage of True Minds," in* The Times Literary Supplement (© *Times Newspapers Ltd. (London) 1961; reproduced from* The Times Literary Supplement *by permission), No. 3,115, November 10, 1961 (and reprinted in a different form in his* Forewords and Afterwords, *edited by Edward Mendelson, Random House, Inc., 1973, pp. 345-50).*

LOWELL A. BANGERTER   (essay date 1977)

[*Bangerter's* Hugo von Hofmannsthal, *from which the following excerpt is taken, provides a comprehensive survey of Hofmannsthal's works.*]

In 1907, Hofmannsthal published an essay entitled **"The Poet and This Time."** It was based in part on ideas taken from Schiller's *Über die ästhetische Erzilung des Menschen.*

Hofmannsthal's main purpose in writing **"The Poet and this Time"** was to compare the respective social roles of modern and earlier writers. Using Schiller's time-citizen concept as a point of departure, Hofmannsthal attempted to demonstrate that the role the poet plays depends upon the time in which he lives. He argued that because a poet must be a "living" force to be relevant, the poet must use his genius to convey to the reader the essence of the times. The role of the poet is thus inseparable from the age in which he lives.

It is extremely difficult to assess what the modern poet should be doing. Hofmannsthal argues that since ethical constants are absent, it is impossible to define the poet's role in terms of such constants. Therefore the public fails—whether the poet or his influence is actually in evidence or not—to accord the poet his rightful status of leadership. Indeed, the modern poet has become the antithesis of the leader. (p. 103)

Hofmannsthal attributes the modern public's failure to accept the poet to its inability to distinguish between the poet's role in the present and that of the past. In order to place the poet of the twentieth century in his proper perspective. Hoffmannsthal devotes the rest of his essay to reorienting the public toward a realistic view of contemporary poesy.

For Hofmannsthal, the main task of the poet was to provide the reader with an access to the whole of human experience. In speaking of the poet, Hofmannsthal wrote: "In him everything must and will come together. It is he, who within himself binds together the elements of the times. Either the present is within him or it is nowhere." Yet the poet also unites the present with the past to make elements of the past a living and relevant part of the present. He records, preserves, and analyzes everything that moves his time, whether from the present, past, or future. Hofmannsthal refers to him metaphorically as a seismograph vibrating with every tremor. It is not that the poet thinks unceasingly about everything in the world, but rather that everything in the world acts upon him. For him, everything is living reality that affects the present.

The public, however, desires to enjoy the fruits of the poet's intimacy with the times. It therefore expects of the poet a synthesis of the "content" of the times. When this synthesis is not in evidence, the poet loses his leadership. Herein lies the necessity to awaken the public to the difference in the product of the contemporary poet as compared to that of his predecessors.

Hofmannsthal asserted that the works of earlier poets yield the type of synthesis for which the present-day public is searching. The modern poet, however, does not create such a synthesis. That does not mean that the poet has not fulfilled his responsibilities to the present era. Both the times and the poet's relationship to them have changed. The events of the preceding century have emphasized individual experience so strongly that the focus of interest has shifted away from the composite. The demand for a synthesis no longer fits reality. The world of the new generation is within the self. The responsible poet of the present era must therefore use what he experiences of the times to awaken the reader to the inner world of his own experience.

The poet of the twentieth century, according to Hofmannsthal, has an even greater responsibility than those before him. The former duty to synthesize has been replaced by the duty to awaken the reader to himself, thus enabling the latter to create his own internal synthesis and thereby establish his own "time citizenship."

Hofmannsthal's works as a whole document his lifelong attempt to satisfy the stringent demands set forth in **"The Poet and this Time."** The views expressed in this essay, concerning what literature should be and do, explain in part the immense diversity of Hofmannsthal's creations, and even why he extended his creative efforts into the realm of the opera. A single genre, even a combination of genres, could not by itself convey the essence of Hofmannsthal's era as he felt it should be conveyed. He saw each individual work as exposing the reader to only a small part of human experience and existence. It took many works of many different kinds to even suggest a degree of appreciation for the whole.

In his essays, Hofmannsthal tried to meet his own demand that the poet record, preserve, and analyze everything that moves his time. Among the things that he considered most important in that regard were art, music, literature, theater, architecture, history, politics, religion, philosophy, people, places, cultural institutions, and language. He wrote penetrating, colorful, provocative essays about all of these and more.

Hofmannsthal's poetry represents a very special attempt to give the reader a meaningful sampling of the myriad of possibilities for self-interpretation, to acquaint him with just a few of the things that can be found or created within the individual's internal world. Although the poems too are diverse, they all offer answers to two basic questions: What is man? How can man perceive and thus create himself and that which comprises his personal world?

The prose narratives stress the fact that life is the experience of the individual. Again and again the stories point out the fallacy in being passive, in waiting for others to make life meaningful. No person in Hofmannsthal's literary world can find or establish his personal identity without actively working to create it. In Hofmannsthal's terms, the failure to act is the failure to live.

Hofmannsthal came closest to achieving the personal artistic synthesis that he sought for himself, in his dramas and operas. In writing them he utilized elements from personal experience, history, fantasy, and the writings of others, to create literary works that would have the power to touch the lives of actors and spectators alike. Moreover, through his works for the stage as nowhere else he realized the goal of reawakening the public to the whole of European cultural heritage.

The goal of Hofmannsthal's literary work, then, was to provide the tools, the stimulus, the raw materials that the author deemed necessary for an individual to create, awaken, or expand his internal world and achieve his own personal artistic synthesis. (pp. 104-06)

Lowell A. Bangerter, in his Hugo von Hofmannsthal *(copyright © 1977 by Frederick Ungar Publishing Co., Inc.), Ungar, 1977, 134 p.*

ADDITIONAL BIBLIOGRAPHY

Barker, Andrew W. "The Triumph of Life in Hofmannsthal's *Das Märchen der 672. Nacht.*" *The Modern Language Review* 74, No. 2 (April 1979): 341-48.
> Analysis of *Das Märchen der 672. Nacht* which emphasizes Hofmannsthal's concern for all manifestations of life.

Bergstraesser, Arnold. "The Holy Beggar: Religion and Society in Hugo von Hofmannsthal's *Great World Theatre of Salzburg.*" *The Germanic Review* XX, No. 4 (December 1945): 261-86.

Philosophical study which examines the Holy Beggar, one of Hofmannsthal's most interesting characters, in a religious and social context.

Braun, Felix. "Encounters with Hofmannsthal." *German Life and Letters* n.s. II, No. 1 (October 1948): 1-12.
Reminiscences by Braun, an Austrian writer, who served as Hofmannsthal's personal secretary for a short time.

Broch, Hermann. Introduction to *Selected Prose,* by Hugo von Hofmannsthal, translated by Mary Hottinger, Tania Stern, and James Stern, pp. ix-xlvii. New York: Pantheon Books, 1952.
Discusses Hofmannsthal's prose works as indicative of his striving to unify human existence with the universe.

Carter, T. E. "Structure in Hofmannsthal's *Der Schwierige.*" *Life and Letters* XVIII, No. 3 (October 1964): 15-24.
Structural analysis of *Der Schwierige* as a comedy.

Coghlan, Brian. *Hofmannsthal's Festival Dramas: "Jedermann, Das Salzburger Grosse Welttheater, Der Turm."* Cambridge: Cambridge University Press, 1964, 397 p.
Thorough critical analysis of Hofmannsthal's festival dramas. Coghlan's study focuses on the development of these important dramas and maintains that they "demonstrate a certain continuity and progress in thought and technique."

Corrigan, Robert W. "Character As Destiny in Hofmannsthal's *Electra.*" *Modern Drama* 2, No. 1 (May 1959): 17-28.
Character analysis of Hofmannsthal's tragic figure, Electra. Corrigan states that Hofmannsthal uses the Electra theme in a new way "to express the tortured reality of human existence" and ultimately its destiny.

Daviau, Donald G., and Buelow, Georg J. *The "Ariadne auf Naxos" of Hugo von Hofmannsthal and Richard Strauss.* Chapel Hill: University of North Carolina Press, 1975, 269 p.*
Detailed examination of the opera *Ariadne auf Naxos.* This collaborative work by Hofmannsthal and Strauss is approached in this study as a unique blend of "musical and poetic forces."

Gilbert, Mary E. "Recent Trends in the Criticism of Hofmannsthal." *German Life and Letters* V (1951-52): 255-68.
Overview of Hofmannsthal criticism from 1940-50. Gilbert discusses critical works by Richard Alewyn, Hermann Broch, Frank Wood, and others.

Goff, Penrith B. "Poetry and Life in the Early Criticism of Hugo von Hofmannsthal." In *Literature and Society by Germaine Brée and Others: A Selection of Papers Delivered at the Joint Meeting of the Midwest Modern Language Association and the Central Renaissance Conference, 1963,* edited by Bernice Slote, pp. 213-26. Lincoln: University of Nebraska Press, 1964.

Discussion of Hofmannsthal's early critical essays which set forth his ideas on art and life. Goff concludes that Hofmannsthal believed "the best art is born of those who have truly lived and have been able to live and write with perspective."

Norman, F., ed. *Hofmannsthal: Studies in Commemoration.* London: University of London, 1963, 147 p.
Contains six lectures that were presented during a Hofmannsthal exhibition at the University of London in 1961.

Porter, Michael. "Hugo von Hofmannsthal's *Der Tor und der Tod:* The Poet As Fool." *Modern Austrian Literature* 5, Nos. 1-2 (1972): 14-29.
Critical study of *Der Tor und der Tod.* Like many later critics of Hofmannsthal's works, Porter finds that this early play actually represents a reproval of aestheticism and calls for a greater awareness of life.

Schultz, H. Stefan. "Hofmannsthal and Bacon: The Sources of the Chandos Letter." *Comparative Literature* XIII, No. 1 (Winter 1961): 1-15.
Examines *Ein Brief,* the fictitious letter from Lord Chandos to Francis Bacon, as a "reshaping of traditional material" to present a seemingly historical account of sixteenth-century England.

Schwarz, Alfred. "The Purgation of the Will: Tragic Theater in the Christian Tradition." In his *From Buchner to Beckett: Dramatic Theory and the Modes of Tragic Drama,* pp. 223-59. Athens: Ohio University Press, 1978.*
Comparative study of Hofmannsthal, Paul Claudel, and T. S. Eliot. Schwarz examines the Christian theater of these three dramatists who share the idea that the world is a stage on which humankind performs and who "approach the drama as a re-enactment of the tragic moments in the life of the Christian hero."

Schwarz, Egon. "Hofmannsthal and the Problem of Reality." *Wisconsin Studies in Contemporary Literature* 8, No. 4 (1967): 484-504.
Analysis and clarification of Hofmannsthal's aesthetic crisis and transition from elitist poet to socially committed dramatist.

Sondrup, Steven P. *Hofmannsthal and the French Symbolist Tradition.* Edited by Gerhard P. Knapp. Bern: Herbert Lang, 1976, 147 p.
Thorough study of Hofmannsthal's orientation to French Symbolism. Sondrup's examination clarifies Hofmannsthal's position as a writer who used Symbolist technique in his works, yet who did not totally submit to the ethical tenets of the Symbolist tradition.

Wood, Frank. "Hugo von Hofmannsthal's Aesthetics: A Survey Based on the Prose Works." *PMLA* LV, No. 1 (March 1940): 253-65.
Asserts that Hofmannsthal's prose works were influenced by both the relativistic and senseistic philosophies of Ernst Mach and Henri Bergson, as well as the ethics of religious doctrine.

Henry James (Jr.)

1843-1916

American novelist, short story and novella writer, essayist, critic, biographer, autobiographer, and dramatist.

James is considered one of the greatest novelists in the English language. From the very beginning he placed his individual stamp on the art of fiction: he enlarged the scope of the novel, introduced dramatic elements to the narrative tale, and developed the point of view technique to a level unknown before his time. His highly self-conscious narrators prepared the way for the interior monologues of such later writers as James Joyce and Virginia Woolf. Most importantly, James led the revolt for more realism in American literature, particularly with his criticism and essays on the art of fiction. Besides matters of technical innovation, he brought to his native literature a number of original themes. Perhaps the most obvious is the myth of the American abroad—the encounter of the New World with the Old. James incorporated this myth in the "international novel" of which he was both the originator and master. But he also dealt with other social and psychological concerns, such as the artist's role in society, the need for both the aesthetic and the moral life, and the benefits of a developed consciousness receptive to the thoughts and feelings of others. According to Van Wyck Brooks, James was most of all a "historian" of his age—an author who interpreted a generation of people on both sides of the Atlantic.

James was born in New York City, the second son of well-to-do, liberal parents. Because of his grandfather's enormous wealth, a fortune he divided equally among his children, James's father never had to work for his income. Henry James, Sr. was an intellectual man of his day: a devotee of the philosopher Emanuel Swedenborg and an occasional theorist on religion and philosophy. His wife was a more practical person, a quality she was forced to develop in order to compensate for her husband's erratic behavior. James himself was a shy, bookish boy who assumed the role of a quiet observer beside his active elder brother William, who later became the founder of psychological study in America and the prominent philosopher of pragmatism. Both Henry and William spent much of their youth traveling between the United States and Europe. They were schooled by tutors and governesses in such diverse environments as Manhattan, Geneva, Paris, and London. Both developed a skill in foreign languages and an awareness of Europe rare among Americans in their time. This constant oscillation between two worlds had a profound effect on James: it became the major theme of his fiction and an attraction throughout his life.

At the age of nineteen James enrolled at Harvard Law School, briefly entertaining thoughts of a professional career. However, this ambition soon changed and he began devoting his study time to reading literature, particularly the works of Honoré de Balzac and Nathaniel Hawthorne. Inspired by the literary atmosphere of Cambridge and Boston, James wrote his first fiction and criticism, his earliest works appearing in the *Continental Monthly, The Atlantic Monthly,* and *The North American Review.* He met and formed lifelong friendships with William Dean Howells—then assistant editor at *The Atlantic*—Charles Eliot Norton, and James Russell Lowell. Howells was

to become James's editor and literary agent, and together the two could be said to have inaugurated the era of realism in American literature. In 1869 James went abroad for his first adult encounter with Europe. While in London he was taken by the Nortons to meet some of England's greatest writers, including George Eliot, John Ruskin, Dante Gabriel Rossetti, and Alfred Lord Tennyson. The year 1869 also marked the death of James's beloved cousin Minny Temple, for whom he had formed a deep emotional attachment. This shock, and the intensity of his experiences in Europe, provided much of the material that would figure in such later works as *The Portrait of a Lady* and *The Wings of the Dove.*

James returned to the United States in 1870 determined to discover whether he could live and write in his native country. During this time he wrote his first novel, *Watch and Ward* (unpublished until 1878), and his first significant American-European tale, "A Passionate Pilgrim." However, after a winter of unremitting hackwork in New York, James became convinced that he could write better and live more cheaply abroad. In 1875 he moved permanently to Europe, settling first in Rome, then in Paris, and eventually in London, where he found the people and conditions best suited to his imagination. He wasted no time in producing the early novels which would establish his reputation—*Roderick Hudson, The American,* and *The Europeans.* While in Paris, James was admitted into the renowned circle of Gustave Flaubert, Émile Zola, Guy de Maupassant, Alphonse Daudet, and Ivan Turgenev. He greatly admired the French writers, but felt closest to Turgenev, who confirmed his own view that a novelist need not worry about "story," but should focus exclusively on character. Though James earned recognition with his first European novels, it was not until the publications of *Daisy Miller* and *The Portrait of a Lady* that he gained popular success. The latter marked the end of what critics consider the first period in his career. Throughout the following decades and into the twentieth century he progressed toward more complex effects in his novels and stories. Because of his experiments he eventually lost the popularity that he had achieved with *Daisy Miller* and *The Portrait of a Lady*. Many critics suggest that it was his growing neglect by the public which induced him to try his hand as a playwright. However, after several attempts at drama—most notably his dramatization of *The American*, and his new productions, *Guy Domville* and *The High Bid*, all of which failed at the box office—James gave up the theater.

The years 1898 to 1904 were the most productive of James's literary career. During this period he brought out several volumes of stories as well as the consummate novels of his late maturity—*The Wings of the Dove, The Ambassadors*, and *The Golden Bowl*. After 1904 James's health and creativity began to decline. Though he still produced a sizeable amount of work, consisting mainly of his autobiographies, essays, and criticism, he finished only one novel, *The Outcry*. With the outbreak of the First World War, James became particularly distressed. He devoted much of his remaining energy to serving the Allied cause, and when the United States did not immediately back the Allies he assumed British citizenship in protest against his native land. On his deathbed the following year he received the British Order of Merit.

Most critics divide James's career into three periods. In the first, from 1876 to the mid-1880s, he established himself as the originator of the international novel and a masterful portrayer of the American character. In such early works as *Roderick Hudson, The American*, and *The Europeans*, James explored the effects of European civilization—with its rich mixture of history and art, sophistication and corruption—on the naive American. The tragedy, as well as the humor, in this situation—as James fully discovered—consists in the protagonists' insistence on partaking of the European experience without sacrificing their New World innocence. Numerous critics have interpreted the story of James's protagonists as a quest for identity, or, more specifically, as a deep passion to enter into the history of civilization. In all meanings of the word, his heroes and heroines become "civilized"—both morally and aesthetically fulfilled. It was also in *Roderick Hudson*, perhaps the best of these three novels, that James first developed his concern with the artist's role in society, a theme which pervades much of his middle and late fiction. Here the European experience is merged with the story of a young American sculptor who struggles between his art and his passions. It was in effect James's version of "the portrait of the artist as a young man." James ended this first phase of his career by producing what many critics consider the most balanced of all his novels, *The Portrait of a Lady*. As a picture of Americans living in the expatriate society of England and Italy this novel has rarely been equaled. It is a profound study of a young woman from upstate New York; she brings to Europe her provincialism and moral pretensions, but she also demonstrates a sense of sovereignty and a "free spirit" capable of living greatly at odds with the Victorian world. *The Portrait of a Lady* is a convincing

demonstration of James's shrewd insight into American character and his understanding of the role power plays in personal relations.

The second period, from the mid-1880s to 1897, is often considered the transitional phase in James's career. Many of the novels and stories written during this time show a marked advance in form and narrative technique. James began experimenting with the point of view narration and with elements from poetry, such as symbolism and recurring motifs. He also abandoned his "international" theme and began focusing on the clash between art and life, aesthetics and social morality—particularly in such short stories and novellas as "The Lesson of the Master," "The Real Thing," "The Beast in the Jungle," and *The Aspern Papers*. The 1880s also saw the publication of two novels dealing specifically with contemporary social issues: *The Bostonians*, which depicts the struggle between a conservative Southerner living in New England and a man-hating suffragette, and *The Princess Casamassima*, in which James portrayed the downward path of a young man who toys with revolution and is eventually destroyed by it. Perhaps the most significant work of this period is *The Tragic Muse*, not because of its treatment of the artist in philistine London, which critics consider rather poorly presented, but because it signified James's growing interest in the world of drama. Stung over the neglect of his once-large reading public, he turned to the theater during the 1890s in hope of regaining his popularity. His dramatization of *The American* was a modest success, but his attempts at comedy, and his one historical play—*Guy Domville*—proved that James lacked the qualities to become a successful dramatist. However, from his experience he brought back to his novels a new commitment to economy in writing and an extraordinary aptitude for framing fictional situations in a scenic and dramatic manner.

The third and final period of James's career, from 1897 to his death, saw the full development of techniques he had begun using during the 1880s. With the publication of such works as *The Spoils of Poynton, What Maisie Knew, The Turn of the Screw*, and *The Awkward Age*, he refined the methods of "scenic" progression, the point of view narration—which he narrowed to a single angle of vision—and the art of "indirect suggestion." The subjects of this period are the expanding consciousness of the individual, the moral education of children, and the clash between subjective and external realities. James even experimented with psychic phenomena—such as projected fantasies and repressed hysteria—and the reliability of language itself in *The Turn of the Screw*. However, the most important works of this final period are the three novels written at the beginning of the century: *The Wings of the Dove, The Ambassadors*, and *The Golden Bowl*. The first of these is the story of a dying American heiress, and, more specifically, of those characters who seek to inherit her millions. Though the subject borders on the melodramatic, James managed to create a moving study of a well-intentioned individual who becomes the victim of her own graces. Most critics view the character of Milly Theale as the apogee of James's American innocent, a figure so weak and pure that she suggests the Christ-like heroines in Fedor Dostoevski's stories. *The Ambassadors* again shows James's talent for investing a limited plot with grandeur and elegance. The novel is essentially a high comedy of American and European manners, as a middle-aged, self-satisfied American named Lambert Strether undertakes a mission to Paris to bring back the son of a wealthy provincial family. The irony of the story turns on Strether's accomplishing his mission against his will, for the young man agrees to return home even though Strether, now captivated by Parisian life, urges him to stay. *The Ambassadors* is often considered the most finely wrought of James's novels; the narration as well as the blossoming of Strether's consciousness are handled with the utmost skill, and the climax and conclusion are the most satisfying of anything he wrote. *The Golden Bowl* is James's final novel of any significance. It is also regarded as the most symbolic and richest in poetic imagery of all his works. Perhaps the most complex of James's novels, next to *The Sacred Fount, The Golden Bowl* again incorporates a number of Jamesian themes: the marriage of American and European cultures, the conflict of innocence and experience, the "knowledge" of sin, and the redemption—specifically through the character of Maggie Verver—of a world of moral order.

Critial interest in James's work has risen steadily since the centennial of his birth in 1943. Throughout much of his career he was regarded as a "writer's writer," particularly during his middle and mature years. The average reader was, and often still is, apt to find him verbose, excrutiatingly complex, often times awkward, and overly concerned with matters of social propriety. Many early critics accused him of indulging his talents for his own pleasure. The most common attacks held that his stories lacked the necessary amount of action to sustain interest and, more seriously, that they had no relation to events in the real world. The two novels in which James awkwardly tried to deal with social issues—*The Bostonians* and *The Princess Casamassima*—were proof to these critics that he lacked the imagination to produce anything but romantic portraits. This attitude resulted in the author's near obscurity following the First World War, a period when his novels and stories seemed particularly trite. There was also the problem in the United States of his expatriation and abandoned citizenship. However, through the work of such critics as F. O. Matthiessen, F. W. Dupee, and Leon Edel, a revival of interest in James's work took place in the 1940s and 1950s. Those who approached his work unburdened with stereotypes and prejudices found a skilled technician and a master at presenting the subtleties of human character. By the 1960s most critics realized the depth of James's fiction. No longer were his plots considered mere contests between innocent Americans and corrupt Europe; discerning readers deciphered his symbols and found a broad philosophical and psychological interest. Many critics began interpeting James's novels and stories according to previously established myths, such as the Fall of Man, the figure of Christ, the Nietzschean notion of the "created self," and the famous battleground of the conscious ego and subconscious alter ego. Quentin Anderson has even posited that James's fiction incorporated a detailed exposition of his father's Swedenborgian philosophy.

Today the critical furor over James's work has subsided, though most scholars believe this is because his position in English literature is firmly established. There now exists a unanimity in both the United States and Europe that he is one of the most imposing figures in twentieth-century literature, influencing such diverse writers as James Joyce and Graham Greene, Virginia Woolf and Joseph Conrad. His originality, his stylistic distinction, and the psychological complexity of his characters have led many critics to regard him as the subtlest craftsman who ever practised the art of fiction.

(See also *TCLC*, Vol. 2; *Contemporary Authors*, Vol. 104; and *Dictionary of Literary Biography*, Vol. 12: *American Realists and Naturalists*.)

PRINCIPAL WORKS

A Passionate Pilgrim, and Other Tales   (short stories) 1875
Roderick Hudson   (novel)   1876
The American   (novel)   1877
The Europeans   (novel)   1878
French Poets and Novelists   (criticism)   1878
Watch and Ward   (novel)   1878
Daisy Miller   (novel)   1879
Hawthorne   (criticism)   1879
The Madonna of the Future, and Other Tales   (short stories)   1879
Confidence   (novel)   1880
The Portrait of a Lady   (novel)   1881
Washington Square   (novel)   1881
*Daisy Miller [first publication]   (drama)   1883
The Siege of London. Madame de Mauves   (novellas) 1883
A Little Tour in France   (travel essays)   1885
The Bostonians   (novel)   1886
The Princess Casamassima   (novel)   1886
The Aspern Papers. Louisa Pallant. The Modern Warning (novellas)   1888
Partial Portraits   (criticism)   1888
A London Life   (short stories)   1889
The Tragic Muse   (novel)   1890
**The American   (drama)   1891
The Real Thing, and Other Tales   (short stories)   1893
Theatricals. Two Comedies: Tenants, Disengaged [first publication]   (dramas)   1894
Guy Domville   (drama)   1895
Theatricals, second series: The Album, The Reprobate [first publication]   (dramas)   1895
The Other House   (novel)   1896
The Spoils of Poynton   (novel)   1897
What Maisie Knew   (novel)   1897
The Two Magics: The Turn of the Screw, Covering End (novellas)   1898
The Awkward Age   (novel)   1899
The Sacred Fount   (novel)   1901
The Wings of the Dove   (novel)   1902
The Ambassadors   (novel)   1903
The Golden Bowl   (novel)   1904
English Hours   (travel essays)   1905
The American Scene   (travel essays)   1907
The Novels and Tales of Henry James. 24 vols.   (novels, novellas, and short stories)   1907-09
The High Bid   (drama)   1908
Views and Reviews   (criticism)   1908
Italian Hours   (travel essays)   1909
The Outcry   (novel)   1911
A Small Boy and Others   (autobiography)   1913
Notes of a Son and Brother   (autobiography)   1914
Notes on Novelists, with Some Other Notes   (criticism) 1914
The Ivory Tower   (unfinished novel)   1917
The Middle Years   (unfinished autobiography)   1917
The Sense of the Past   (unfinished novel)   1917
Within the Rim, and Other Essays   (essays)   1918
The Letters of Henry James. 2 vols.   (letters)   1920
Notes and Reviews   (criticism)   1921
The Art of the Novel   (criticism)   1934
The Notebooks of Henry James   (notebooks)   1947
The Complete Plays of Henry James   (dramas)   1949

*This drama is an adaptation of the novel *Daisy Miller*.

**This drama is an adaptation of the novel *The American*.

THE NORTH AMERICAN REVIEW (essay date 1876)

[*In the excerpt below, taken from an anonymously written review of* Roderick Hudson, *the critic voices a number of concerns which were frequently expressed during James's early career, namely that he spends an extraordinary amount of time on unnecessary information and on minor characters, that his stories lack sufficient action, and that his style often falters—particularly in developing individual characters. For a twentieth-century view of James's shortcomings see the essays by Pelham Edgar and Maxwell Geismar excerpted below.*]

If the authorship of **"Roderick Hudson"** were a secret, we think few people would guess it to be a first novel. It has little of the freshness and none of the crudeness of most such attempts. Its merits and its interest are not such as usually gush from a new-found spring of talent, while its faults are not those of youth and inexperience. Yet the reading public would be puzzled on whom to fix it. Anonymous productions of so much ability are immediately assigned to half a dozen well-known writers, with more or less plausibility; the book in question reminds us of no other; Mr. James has imitated nobody; the only novelist to whose temper of mind there is the least affinity is Thackeray, and few writers resemble one another less. Therefore, to begin with, if **"Roderick Hudson"** is not what can be called an original work of genius, it is entirely peculiar. As far as one can describe a book in a single phrase, this one is a study of character. There is no plot, strictly speaking; the slight framework which supports the personages being the career of a young village genius who is taken by a munificent acquaintance from the purgatory of a law-office in his native Northampton to study sculpture in Rome. The story follows him, and three or four others whose common tie is in him, through the hopes and fears, the promise and disappointment, of his course. These three or four are, first, Rowland Mallet, the hero's friend and patron; Mary Garland, his cousin and betrothed; Christina Light, his fate: there are several other characters of less importance who are quite as carefully and minutely drawn. There is too much of this minuteness, too much detail. It was not necessary to our comprehension of Rowland Mallet that we should be told all about his father and mother, his grandfather and grandmother, as he inherited nothing from them, except, perhaps, from the last his Dutch coloring and phlegm. . . . And why, as the cousin Cecilia had no part to play in the book, is she so conspicuous a figure; and why, since she is so nice a woman, does the author of her being like her and let us like her so little? With her, the Cavaliere Giacosa, and one or two more, it looks as if Mr. James had had these admirable studies in his sketch-book and could not resist transferring them to his canvas, although they have as little to do as lay-figures, or at best the *deus ex machina*. There are no lay-figures in Mr. James's compositions; the perfect finish of each part is like nothing but some performances we once saw given by the leading actors of the Théâtre Français in London. . . . There is in this elaboration a trace of the influence of M. Tourguénieff, of whom Mr. James is an admirer and student, but the effect is very different from that of M. Tourguénieff's simply grouped supernumeraries.

The central figure, of course, is Roderick Hudson, and we foresee that the undiscriminating will fancy a resemblance between him and Hawthorne's Donatello, but it is scarcely skin-deep. The irresponsibility of the Faun is his greatest attraction, it is Roderick Hudson's most intolerable vice. The character of the hero strikes us as the great failure of the book; the conception is capital and is consistently carried out; but in working it up there occur traits of selfishness and shamelessness which, although natural in themselves, make the relations of others to him unnatural. His personal charm is not felt by us, while his detestable egotism is; we are repelled, and the friendship of Rowland, the constancy of Mary, and even the idolatry of his mother, seem like infatuation. This is a cardinal error, for it leaves the reader outside the sympathies of the whole circle; he has no hold on the electric chain which binds them together. It is due in great part to this, no doubt, that their wonderfully told vicissitudes of feeling leave us cold; it is not that they are unlike real people; they are most real and living, but we do not identify ourselves with them; we never for a moment cease to be spectators; we are intellectually interested, but as unmoved as one may suppose the medical class of a modern master of vivisection to be. Rowland is not meant for the hero, and, like him as we must, we cannot concentrate our sympathies on the second fiddle; at the same time we are very grateful for such a delightful, possible character, if he be not impossibly good; one almost loses patience sometimes with his patience. The heroine is a very fine outline, defined like all the rest with extreme distinctness, but there is a plainness about her which unfits her for her position; it is improbable that a woman so devoid of all but moral grace, and with less of that than positive loftiness, should attract a man of Rowland's cultivation and civilization; there is a similar improbability in Hannah Thurston, which takes the lifelikeness out of that sober picture of American local manners. (pp. 420-21)

[What] do all these animated varieties of men and women do? They do nothing but talk. There is as great a want of incident as of plot. Their conversations are amazingly clever, and bring out the dispositions of the speakers with consummate skill. (p. 423)

But the conversations are often too prolonged, and the author endows all his personages with his own turn for analyzing, in consequence of which they all occasionally talk alike, blurring for the moment their individuality. The effect of this perpetual analysis is fatiguing; the book never ceases to interest, but it taxes the attention like metaphysics. There are signs that it occasionally wearied the author; while such pains and care are bestowed upon his characters, his style is sometimes slipshod. . . . This is curious carelessness in a writer of such remarkable flexibility of thought and plastic power of expression. His control of language is like the facility of a great pianist; there is no turn or running accompaniment of thought, no cadence, no modulation, that is not executed with the easiest precision. His language owes something of its malleability to his command of French; but this sometimes carries him too far into constructions that are not idiomatic, and a use of words which is not in the genius of the mother tongue, as, for instance, his favorite "supreme," which he sometimes takes in its English significance of highest, and sometimes in its French meaning of final.

It was to be expected that more would be made of the background and side-scenes in a story whose action goes on chiefly in Rome and Florence, but Mr. James has refrained with almost stoical firmness from the opportunities and temptations which they offered. Readers of his tales and sketches of travel will find but few of those incomparable passages, half descriptive, half suggestive, in which the psychological bearings of outward things are so delicately hinted; he has done wisely, no doubt, in using his exquisite gift sparingly, and wherever these bits occur they greatly enhance the situation.

Looking at the book as a whole, it is like a marvellous mosaic, whose countless minute pieces are fitted with so much skill and ingenuity that a real picture is presented, but with an absence of richness and relief, of all that is vivid and salient; there is a pervading lowness of tone, and flatness of tint. This should not be the impression left by a novel of remarkable talent; we think, however, that it is not the result of a failure to produce the desired effect, but of a mistaken aim. The method, too, is a mistaken one; no aggregate of small particles, however cunningly put together, will produce the effect of honest cutting and shaping from the piece; it may be *marqueterie*, or a Chinese puzzle, but it will not be art. Moreover, such work has the disagreeable property of making criticism seem like picking to pieces. (pp. 424-25)

The story has the immense merit of rising to a climax at the end; there is more breadth and movement in the final twenty-five pages than in all the rest of the book. . . . [The] close of **"Roderick Hudson"** is beautiful, powerful, tragical; it is intense, yet not overstrained; all it lacks is to have been told with more human feeling. (p. 425)

> *"James's 'Roderick Hudson'," in* The North American Review, *Vol. CXXII, No. CCLI, April, 1876, pp. 420-25.*

BERNARD SHAW (essay date 1895)

[*Shaw is generally considered the greatest and best-known dramatist to write in the English language since Shakespeare. Following the example of Henrik Ibsen, he succeeded in revolutionizing the English stage, disposing of the romantic conventions and devices of the "well-made play," and instituting the theater of ideas, grounded in realism. During the late nineteenth century, Shaw was also a prominent literary, art, and music critic. In 1895, he became the drama critic for* The Saturday Review, *and his reviews therein became known for their biting wit and brilliance. During his three years at* The Saturday Review, *Shaw determined that the theater was meant to be a "moral institution" and an "elucidator of social conduct." The standards he applied to drama were quite simple: Is the play like real life? Does it convey sensible, socially progressive ideas? Because most of the drama produced during the 1890s failed to approach these ideals, Shaw usually assumed a severely critical and satirical attitude toward his subjects. As Samuel Hynes has noted, Shaw was driven by a rage to better the world. A Fabian socialist, he wrote criticism which is often concerned with the humanitarian and political intent of the work under discussion. The following excerpt is taken from Shaw's review of* Guy Domville *after its premier in London. The "handful of rowdies" Shaw criticizes refers to those in the audience who jeered the actors and actresses following the performance. Though Shaw disagrees with James's dramatic method, he considers* Guy Domville *a play worthy of the modern theater. For other comments on James's dramas see the Rudolf R. Kossmann essay excerpted below.*]

The truth about Mr. James's play ["**Guy Domville**"] is no worse than that it is out of fashion. Any dramatically disposed young gentleman who, cultivating sentiment on a little alcohol, and gaining an insight to the mysteries of the eternal feminine by a couple of squalid intrigues, meanwhile keeps well aloof from art and philosophy, and thus preserves his innocence of

the higher life of the senses and of the intellect, can patch up a play to-morrow which will pass as real drama with the gentlemen who deny that distinction to the work of Mr. Henry James. No doubt, if the literary world were as completely dominated by the admirers of Mr. Rider Haggard as the dramatic world is by their first cousins, we should be told that Mr. James cannot write a novel. That is not criticism; it is a mere begging of the question. There is no reason why life as we find it in Mr. James's novels—life, that is, in which passion is subordinate to intellect and to fastidious artistic taste—should not be represented on the stage. If it is real to Mr. James, it must be real to others; and why should not these others have their drama instead of being banished from the theatre (to the theatre's great loss) by the monotony and vulgarity of drama in which passion is everything, intellect nothing, and art only brought in by the incidental outrages upon it? As it happens, I am not myself in Mr. James's camp: in all the life that has energy enough to be interesting to me, subjective volition, passion, will, make intellect the merest tool. But there is in the centre of that cyclone a certain calm spot where cultivated ladies and gentlemen live on independent incomes or by pleasant artistic occupations. It is there that Mr. James's art touches life, selecting whatever is graceful, exquisite, or dignified in its serenity. It is not life as imagined by the pit or gallery, or even by the stalls; it is, let us say, the ideal of the balcony; but that is no reason why the pit and gallery should excommunicate it on the ground that it has no blood and entrails in it, and have its sentence formulated for it by the fiercely ambitious and wilful professional man in the stalls. The whole case against its adequacy really rests on its violation of the cardinal stage convention that love is the most irresistible of all the passions. Since most people go to the theatre to escape from reality, this convention is naturally dear to a world in which love, all powerful in the secret, unreal, day-dreaming life of the imagination, is in the real active life the abject slave of every trifling habit, prejudice, and cowardice, easily stifled by shyness, class feeling, and pecuniary prudence, or diverted from what is theatrically assumed to be its hurricane course by such obstacles as a thick ankle, a cockney accent, or an unfashionable hat. In the face of this, is it good sense to accuse Mr. Henry James of a want of grip of the realities of life because he gives us a hero who sacrifices his love to a strong and noble vocation for the Church? And yet when some unmannerly playgoer, untouched by either love or religion, chooses to send a derisive howl from the gallery at such a situation, we are to sorrowfully admit, if you please, that Mr. James is no dramatist, on the general ground that "the drama's laws the drama's patrons give." Pray which of its patrons?—the cultivated majority who, like myself and all the ablest of my colleagues, applauded Mr. James on Saturday, or the handful of rowdies who brawled at him? It is the business of the dramatic critic to educate these dunces, not to echo them.

Admitting, then, that Mr. James's dramatic authorship is valid, and that his plays are *du théâtre* when the right people are in the theatre, what are the qualities and faults of "**Guy Domville**"? First among the qualities, a rare charm of speech. Line after line comes with such a delicate turn and fall that I unhesitatingly challenge any of our popular dramatists to write a scene in verse with half the beauty of Mr. James's prose. I am not now speaking of the verbal fitness, which is a matter of careful workmanship merely. I am speaking of the delicate inflexions of feeling conveyed by the cadences of the line, inflexions and cadences which, after so long a course of the ordinary theatrical splashes and daubs of passion and emphasis, are as grateful to my ear as the music of Mozart's "Entführung aus dem Serail'' would be after a year of ''Ernani'' and ''Il Trovatore.'' Second, **''Guy Domville''** is a story, and not a mere situation hung out on a gallows of plot. And it is a story of fine sentiment and delicate manners, with an entirely worthy and touching ending. Third, it relies on the performers, not for the brute force of their personalities and popularities, but for their finest accomplishments in grace of manner, delicacy of diction, and dignity of style. . . . In fact, had the second act been equal to the first and third . . . the result would have been less doubtful. (pp. 7-10)

Unfortunately, the second act dissolved the charm rather badly. . . . Little of this act can be remembered with pleasure except . . . a few cognate scraps of dialogue. It had better have been left out, and the wanderings of the prodigal taken for granted. (pp. 10-11)

> Bernard Shaw, ''Two New Plays'' (originally published as ''The Drama's Laws'' in The Saturday Review, London, January 12, 1895), in his Dramatic Opinions and Essays with an Apology by Bernard Shaw, Vol. I (copyright by Brentano's 1906, 1907), Brentano's, 1907, pp. 7-14.*

WILLIAM DEAN HOWELLS (essay date 1903)

[*Howells, the most important American literary critic at the turn-of-the-century, was also James's editor and literary agent for much of the author's early career. In the excerpt below, he argues against the common assumption that James's later fiction was unintentionally ambiguous and obtuse. Instead, he concludes that James wanted to express life in all its complexity and ambiguity, and that such works as* The Sacred Fount *resist definitive interpretations because they are so much like life itself. For further discussion of this point see the essay by Frederick C. Crews excerpted below.*]

It has been the curious fortune of [Mr. James], so supremely gifted in divining women and portraying them, that beyond any other great novelist (or little, for that matter) he has imagined few heroines acceptable to women. Even those martyr-women who have stood by him in the long course of his transgressions, and maintained through thick and thin, that he is by all odds the novelist whom they could best trust with the cause of woman in fiction, have liked his anti-heroines more,—I mean, found them realer,—than his heroines. I am not sure but I have liked them more myself, but that is because I always find larger play for my sympathies in the character which needs the reader's help than in that which is so perfect as to get on without it. . . . I find myself diffident of heroines in fiction because I have never known one in life, of the real faultless kind; and heaven forbid I should ever yet know one. In Mr. James's novels I always feel safe from that sort, and it may be for this reason, among others, that I like to read his novels when they are new, and read them over and over again when they are old, or when they are no longer recent.

At this point I hear from far within a voice bringing me to . . . Milly Theale in *The Wings of a Dove*, asking me, if *there* is not a heroine of the ideal make, and demanding what fault there is in her that renders her lovable. Lovable, I allow she is, dearly, tenderly, reverently lovable, but she has enough to make her so, besides being too good, too pure, too generous, too magnificently unselfish. It is not imaginable that her author should have been conscious of offering in her anything like an atonement to the offended divinity of American womanhood for Daisy Miller. But if it were imaginable the offended divinity ought to be sumptuously appeased, appeased to tears of grateful

pardon such as I have not yet seen in its eyes. Milly Theale is as entirely American in the qualities which you can and cannot touch as Daisy Miller herself; and (I find myself urged to the risk of noting it) she is largely American in the same things. There is the same self-regardlessness, the same beauteous insubordination, the same mortal solution of the problem. Of course, it is all in another region, and the social levels are immensely parted. Yet Milly Theale is the superior of Daisy Miller less in her nature than in her conditions.

There is, in both, the same sublime unconsciousness of the material environment, the same sovereign indifference to the fiscal means of their emancipation to a more than masculine independence. The sense of what money can do for an American girl without her knowing it, is a ''blind sense'' in the character of Daisy, but in the character of Milly it has its eyes wide open. In that wonderful way of Mr. James's by which he imparts a fact without stating it, approaching it again and again, without actually coming in contact with it, we are made aware of the vast background of wealth from which Milly is projected upon our acquaintance. She is shown in a kind of breathless impatience with it, except as it is the stuff of doing wilfully magnificent things, and committing colossal expenses without more anxiety than a prince might feel with the revenues of a kingdom behind him. The ideal American rich girl has never really been done before, and it is safe to say that she will never again be done with such exquisite appreciation. She is not of the new rich; an extinct New York ancestry darkles in the retrospect: something vaguely bourgeois, and yet with presences and with lineaments of aristocratic distinction. They have made her masses of money for her, those intangible fathers, uncles and grandfathers, and then, with her brothers and sisters, have all perished away from her, and left her alone in the world with nothing else. She is as convincingly imagined in her relation to them, as the daughter of an old New York family, as she is in her inherited riches. It is not the old New York family of the unfounded Knickerbocker tradition, but something as fully patrician, with a nimbus of social importance as unquestioned as its money. Milly is not so much the flower of this local root as something finer yet: the perfume of it, the distilled and wandering fragrance. It would be hard to say in what her New Yorkishness lies, and Mr. James himself by no means says; only if you know New York at all, you have the unmistakable sense of it. She is New Yorkish in the very essences that are least associable with the superficial notion of New York: the intellectual refinement that comes of being born and bred in conditions of illimitable ease, of having had everything that one could wish to have, and the cultivation that seems to come of the mere ability to command it. If one will have an illustration of the final effect in Milly Theale, it may be that it can be suggested as a sort of a Bostonian quality, with the element of *conscious* worth eliminated, and purified as essentially of pedantry as of commerciality. The wonder is that Mr. James in his prolonged expatriation has been able to seize this lovely impalpability, and to impart the sense of it; and perhaps the true reading of the riddle is that such a nature, such a character is most appreciable in that relief from the background which Europe gives all American character. (pp. 126-28)

Never, in my ignorance, have I had a vivider sense of London, in my knowledge a stronger sense of Venice, than in *The Wings of a Dove*. More miraculous still, as I have tried to express, was the sense he gave me of the anterior New York where the life flowered which breathed out the odor called Milly Theale— a heartbreaking fragrance as of funeral violets—and of the anterior New England sub-acidly fruiting in Mrs. Stringham. As for social conditions, predicaments, orders of things, where shall we find the like of the wonders wrought in *The Awkward Age*? I have been trying to get phrases which should convey the effect of that psychomancy from me to my reader, and I find none so apt as some phrase that should suggest the convincingly incredible. Here is something that the reason can as little refuse as it can accept. Into quite such particles as the various characters of this story would the disintegration of the old, rich, demoralized society of an ancient capital fall so probably that each of the kaleidoscopic fragments, dropping into irrelevant radiance around Mrs. Brookenham, would have its fatally appointed tone in the "scheme of color." Here is that inevitable, which Mr. Brander Matthews has noted as the right and infallible token of the real. It does not matter, after that, how the people talk,—or in what labyrinthine parentheses they let their unarriving language wander. They strongly and vividly exist, and they construct not a drama, perhaps, but a world, floating indeed in an obscure where it seems to have its solitary orbit, but to be as solidly palpable as any of the planets of the more familiar systems, and wrapt in the aura of its peculiar corruption. How bad the bad people on it may be, one does not know, and is not intended to know, perhaps; that would be like being told the gross facts of some scandal which, so long as it was untouched, supported itself not unamusingly in air; but of the goodness of the good people one is not left in doubt; and it is a goodness which consoles and sustains the virtue apt to droop in the presence of neighborly remissness.

I might easily attribute to the goodness a higher office than this; but if I did I might be trenching upon that ethical delicacy of the author which seems to claim so little for itself. Mr. James is, above any other, the master of the difficult art of never doing more than to "hint a fault, or hesitate dislike," and I am not going to try committing him to conclusions he would shrink from. There is nothing of the clumsiness of the "satirist" in his design, and if he notes the absolute commerciality of the modern London world, it is with a reserve clothing itself in frankness which is infinitely, as he would say, "detached." But somehow, he lets you know how horribly *business* fashionable English life is; he lets Lord Mark let Milly Theale know, at their first meeting, when he tells her she is with people who never do anything for nothing, and when, with all her money, and perhaps because of it, she is still so trammelled in the ideal that she cannot take his meaning. Money, and money bluntly; gate-money of all kinds; money the means, is the tune to which that old world turns in a way which we scarcely imagine in this crude new world where it is still so largely less the means than the end.

But the general is lost in the personal, as it should be in Mr. James's books, earlier as well as later, and the allegory is so faint that it cannot always be traced. He does not say that the limitless liberty allowed Nanda Brookenham by her mother in *The Awkward Age* is better than the silken bondage in which the Duchess keeps her niece Aggie, though Nanda is admirably lovable, and little Aggie is a little cat. . . . What he does is simply to show you those people mainly on the outside, as you mainly see people in the world, and to let you divine them and their ends from what they do and say. They are presented with infinite pains; as far as their appearance (though they are very little described) goes, you are not suffered to make a mistake. But he does not analyze them for you; rather he synthetizes them, and carefully hands them over to you in a sort of integrity very uncommon in the characters of fiction. One might infer from this that his method was dramatic, something like Tour-

guénieff's, say; but I do not know that his method is dramatic. I do not recall from the book more than one passage of dramatic intensity, but that was for me of very great intensity; I mean the passage where old Mr. Longdon lets Vanderbank understand that he will provide for him if he will offer himself to Nanda, whom he knows to be in love with Vanderbank, and where Vanderbank will not promise. That is a great moment, where everything is most openly said, most brutally said, to American thinking; and yet said with a restraint of feeling that somehow redeems it all. . . . (pp. 132-34)

The Awkward Age is mostly expressed in dialogue; *The Wings of a Dove* is mostly in the narration and the synthesis of emotions. Not the synthesis of the motives, please; these in both books are left to the reader, almost as much as they are in *The Sacred Fount*. That troubled source, I will own, "is of a profundity," and in its depths darkles the solution which the author makes it no part of his business to pull to the top; if the reader wants it, let him dive. But why should not a novel be written so like to life, in which most of the events remain the meaningless, that we shall never quite know what the author meant? Why, in fact, should not people come and go, and love and hate, and hurt and help one another as they do in reality, without rendering the reader a reason for their behavior, or offering an explanation at the end with which he can light himself back over the way he has come, and see what they meant? Who knows, what any one means here below, or what he means himself, that is, precisely stands for? Most people mean nothing, except from moment to moment, if they indeed mean anything so long as that, and life which is full of propensities is almost without motives. In the scribles which we suppose to be imitations of life, we hold the unhappy author to a logical consistency which we find so rarely in the original; but ought not we rather to praise him where his work confesses itself, as life confesses itself, without a plan? Why should we demand more of the imitator than we get from the creator?

Of course, it can be answered that we are *in* creation like characters in fiction, while we are outside of the imitation and spectators instead of characters; but that does not wholly cover the point. Perhaps, however, I am asking more for Mr. James than he would have me. In that case I am willing to offer him the reparation of a little detraction. I wish he would leave his people more, not less, to me when I read him. I have tried following their speeches without taking in his comment, delightfully pictorial as that always is, and it seems to me that I make rather more of their meaning, that way. I reserve the pleasure and privilege of going back and reading his comment in the light of my conclusions. This is the method I have largely pursued with the people of *The Sacred Fount*, of which I do not hesitate to say that I have mastered the secret, though, for the present I am not going to divulge it. Those who cannot wait may try the key which I have given.

But do not, I should urge them, expect too much of it; I do not promise it will unlock everything. If you find yourself, at the end, with nothing in your hand but the postulate with which the supposed narrator fantastically started, namely, that people may involuntarily and unconsciously prey upon one another, and mentally and psychically enrich themselves at one another's expense, still you may console yourself, if you do not think this enough, with the fact that you have passed the time in the company of men and women freshly and truly seen, amusingly shown, and abidingly left with your imagination. (pp. 134-36)

William Dean Howells, "Mr. Henry James's Later Work," in The North American Review, *Vol. 176, No. 1, January, 1903, pp. 125-37.*

EDMUND GOSSE (essay date 1920)

[*Gosse's importance as a critic lies mainly in his introduction of Henrik Ibsen's "new drama" to an English audience. He was among the chief translators and critics of Scandinavian literature and was decorated by the Norwegian, Swedish, and Danish governments. Among his other works are studies of John Donne, Thomas Gray, Sir Thomas Browne, and important early articles on French authors of the late nineteenth century. Although Gosse's works are varied and voluminous, his intellectual style is somewhat casual, with the consequence that his commentary lacks depth and is not considered to be in the first rank of modern critical thought. However, his broad interests and knowledge of foreign literatures lend his works much more than a documentary value.*]

Voluminous as had been the writings of Henry James since 1875, it was not until he approached the end of his career that he began to throw any light on the practical events and social adventures of his own career. He had occasionally shown that he could turn from the psychology of imaginary characters to the record of real lives without losing any part of his delicate penetration or his charm of portraiture. He had, in particular, written the *Life of Hawthorne* in 1879, between *Daisy Miller* and *An International Episode*; and again in 1903, at the height of his latest period, he had produced a specimen of that period in his elusive and parenthetical but very beautiful so-called *Life of W. W. Story.* But these biographies threw no more light upon his own adventures than did his successive volumes of critical and topographical essays, in which the reader may seek long before he detects the sparkle of a crumb of personal fact. Henry James, at the age of seventy, had not begun to reveal himself behind the mask which spoke in the tones of a world of imaginary characters.

So saying, I do not forget that in the general edition of his collected, or rather selected, novels and tales, published from 1908 onwards, Henry James prefixed to each volume an introduction which assumed to be wholly biographical. He yielded, he said, "to the pleasure of placing on record the circumstances" in which each successive tale was written. I well recollect the terms in which he spoke of these prefaces before he began to write them. They were to be full and confidential, they were to throw to the winds all restraints of conventional reticence, they were to take us, with eyes unbandaged, into the inmost sanctum of his soul. They appeared at last, in small print, and they were extremely extensive, but truth obliges me to say that I found them highly disappointing. Constitutionally fitted to take pleasure in the accent of almost everything that Henry James ever wrote, I have to confess that these prefaces constantly baffle my eagerness. Not for a moment would I deny that they throw interesting light on the technical craft of a self-respecting novelist, but they are dry, remote, and impersonal to a strange degree. It is as though the author felt a burning desire to confide in the reader, whom he positively button-holes in the endeavour, but that the experience itself evades him, fails to find expression, and falls stillborn, while other matters, less personal and less important, press in and take their place against the author's wish. Henry James proposed, in each instance, to disclose "the contributive value of the accessory facts in a given artistic case." This is, indeed, what we require in the history or the autobiography of an artist, whether painter or musician or man of letters. But this includes the production of anecdotes, of salient facts, of direct historical statements, which Henry James seemed in 1908 to be completely incapacitated from giving, so that really, in the introductions to some of these novels in the Collected Edition, it is difficult to know what the beloved novelist is endeavouring to divulge. He becomes almost chimaera bombinating in a vacuum.

Had we lost him soon after the appearance of the latest of these prefaces—that prefixed to *The Golden Bowl,* in which the effort to reveal something which is not revealed amounts almost to an agony—it would have been impossible to reconstruct the life of Henry James by the closest examination of his published writings. Ingenious commentators would have pieced together conjectures from such tales as *The Altar of the Dead* and *The Lesson of the Master,* and have insisted, more or less plausibly, on their accordance with what the author *must* have thought or done, endured or attempted. But, after all, these would have been "conjectures," not more definitely based than what bold spirits use when they construct lives of Shakespeare, or, for that matter, of Homer. Fortunately, in 1913, the desire to place some particulars of the career of his marvellous brother William in the setting of his "immediate native and domestic air," led Henry James to contemplate, with minuteness, the fading memories of his own childhood. Starting with a biographical study of William James, he found it impossible to treat the family development at all adequately without extending the survey to his own growth as well, and thus, at the age of seventy, Henry became for the first time, and almost unconsciously, an autobiographer.

He had completed two large volumes of memories, and was deep in a third, when death took him from us. *A Small Boy and Others* deals with such extreme discursiveness as is suitable in a collection of the fleeting impressions of infancy, from his birth in 1843 to his all but fatal attack of typhus fever at Boulogne-sur-Mer in (perhaps) 1857. I say "perhaps" because the wanton evasion of any sort of help in the way of dates is characteristic of the narrative, as it would be of childish memories. The next instalment was *Notes of a Son and Brother,* which opens in 1860, a doubtful period of three years being leaped over lightly, and closes—as I guess from an allusion to George Eliot's *Spanish Gypsy*—in 1868. The third instalment, dictated in the autumn of 1914 and laid aside unfinished, is the posthumous *The Middle Years,* faultlessly edited by the piety of Mr. Percy Lubbock in 1917. Here the tale is taken up in 1869, and is occupied, without much attempt at chronological order, with memories of two years in London. As Henry James did not revise, or perhaps even re-read, these pages, we are free to form our conclusion as to whether he would or would not have vouchsafed to put their disjected parts into some more anatomical order.

Probably he would not have done so. The tendency of his genius had never been, and at the end was less than ever, in the direction of concinnity. He repudiated arrangement, he wilfully neglected the precise adjustment of parts. The three autobiographical volumes will always be documents precious in the eyes of his admirers. They are full of beauty and nobility, they exhibit with delicacy, and sometimes even with splendour, the qualities of his character. But it would be absurd to speak of them as easy to read, or as fulfilling what is demanded from an ordinary biographer. They have the tone of Veronese, but nothing of his definition. A broad canvas is spread before us, containing many figures in social conjuncture. But the plot, the single "story" which is being told, is drowned in misty radiance. Out of this *chiaroscuro* there leap suddenly to our vision a sumptuous head and throat, a handful of roses, the glitter of a satin sleeve, but it is only when we shut our eyes and think over what we have looked at that any coherent plan is revealed to us, or that we detect any species of composition. It is a case which calls for editorial help, and I hope that when the three fragments of autobiography are reprinted as a single composition, no prudery of hesitation to touch the sacred ark will prevent the editor from prefixing a skeleton chronicle of actual dates and facts. It will take nothing from the dignity of the luminous reveries in their original shape. (pp. 17-20)

> Edmund Gosse, "Henry James," in Scribner's Magazine (copyright, 1920, by Charles Scribner's Sons; copyright renewed 1948; reprinted with permission of Charles Scribner's Sons), Vol. LXVII, Nos. 4 & 5, April & May, 1920 (and reprinted in a slightly different form in his Aspects and Impressions, Charles Scribner's Sons, 1922, pp. 17-53).

PERCY LUBBOCK (essay date 1921)

[*Lubbock's literary criticism was greatly influenced by Henry James. Like James, he believed that the novel was meant to be, above all else, a realistic portrait of a portion of life. Also like James, Lubbock considered dramatic presentation, rather than authorial narration and description, as the best of all means of narrative expression. However, Lubbock disagreed with his mentor on a number of points, most significantly the correspondence of form and content. In this matter he considered the "sense of life" presented more important than formal symmetry, though when combined with the latter the former becomes much more effective. In general, Lubbock saw the history of the novel as a matter of evolution. Fiction progressed from the mere telling of tales to the intricate use of dramatic presentation and irony evidenced best in the work of James. In his essay on* The Ambassadors, *Lubbock shows how James gradually altered his narrative position during the course of the novel in order to present a more objective rendering of Strether's consciousness—an adjustment he had to make if he was to realistically depict the development of Strether's personality. This objectification produced what Lubbock considers the dramatic quality of the novel.*]

[*The Ambassadors*] is entirely concerned with Strether's experience of his peculiar mission to Europe, and never passes outside the circle of his thought. Strether is despatched, it will be remembered, by a resolute New England widow, whose son is living lightly in Paris instead of attending to business at home. To win the hand of the widow, Strether must succeed in snatching the young man from the siren who is believed to have beguiled him. The mission is undertaken in all good faith, Strether descends upon Paris with a mind properly disposed and resolved. He comes as an ambassador representing principle and duty, to treat with the young man, appeal to him convincingly and bear him off. The task before him may be difficult, but his purpose is simple. Strether has reckoned, however, without his imagination; he had scarcely been aware of possessing one before, but everything grows complicated as it is touched and awakened on the new scene. By degrees and degrees he changes his opinion of the life of freedom; it is most unlike his prevision of it, and at last his purpose is actually inverted. He no longer sees a misguided young man to be saved from disaster, he sees an exquisite, bountiful world laid at a young man's feet; and now the only question is whether the young man is capable of meeting and grasping his opportunity. He is incapable, as it turns out; when the story ends he is on the verge of rejecting his freedom and going back to the world of commonplace; Strether's mission has ended success-

fully. But in Strether's mind the revolution is complete; there is nothing left for him, no reward and no future. The world of commonplace is no longer *his* world, and he is too late to seize the other; he is old, he has missed the opportunity of youth.

This is a story which must obviously be told from Strether's point of view, in the first place. The change in his purpose is due to a change in his vision, and the long slow process could not be followed unless his vision were shared by the reader. Strether's predicament, that is to say, could not be placed upon the stage; his outward behavior, his conduct, his talk, do not express a tithe of it. Only the brain behind his eyes can be aware of the color of his experience, as it passes through its innumerable gradations; and all understanding of his case depends upon seeing these. The way of the author, therefore, who takes this subject in hand, is clear enough at the outset. It is a purely pictorial subject, covering Strether's field of vision and bounded by its limits; it consists entirely on an impression received by a certain man. There can accordingly be no thought of rendering him as a figure seen from without; nothing that any one else could discern, looking at him and listening to his conversation, would give the full sense of the eventful life he is leading within. The dramatic method, as we ordinarily understand it, is ruled out at once. Neither as an action set before the reader without interpretation from within, nor yet as an action pictured for the reader by some other onlooker in the book, can this story possibly be told.

Strether's real situation, in fact, is not his open and visible situation, between the lady in New England and the young man in Paris; his grand adventure is not expressed in its incidents. These, as they are devised by the author, are secondary, they are the extension of the moral event that takes place in the breast of the ambassador, his change of mind. That is the very middle of the subject; it is a matter that lies solely between Strether himself and his vision of the free world. It is a delightful effect of irony, indeed, that he should have accomplished his errand after all, in spite of himself; but the point of the book is not there, the ironic climax only serves to bring out the point more sharply. The reversal of his own idea is underlined and enhanced by the reversal of the young man's idea in the opposite sense; but essentially the subject of the book would be unchanged if the story ended differently, if the young man held to his freedom and refused to go home. Strether would still have passed through the same cycle of unexpected experience; his errand might have failed, but still it would not have been any the more impossible for him to claim his reward, for his part, than it is impossible as things are, with the quest achieved and the young man ready to hasten back to duty of his own accord. And so the subject can only be reached through Strether's consciousness, it is plain; that way alone will command the impression that the scene makes on him. Nothing in the scene has any importance, any value in itself; what Strether sees in it—that is the whole of its meaning.

But though in *The Ambassadors* the point of view is primarily Strether's, and though it *appears* to be his throughout the book, there is in fact an insidious shifting of it, so artfully contrived that the reader may arrive at the end without suspecting the trick. The reader, all unawares, is placed in a better position for an understanding of Strether's history, better than the position of Strether himself. Using his eyes, we see what *he* sees, we are possessed of the material on which his patient thought sets to work; and that is so far well enough, and plainly necessary. All the other people in the book face toward him, and it is that aspect of them, and that only, which is shown to the reader; still more important, the beautiful picture of Paris and springtime, the stir and shimmer of life in the Rue de Rivoli and the gardens of the Tuileries, is Strether's picture, *his* vision, rendered as the time and the place strike upon his senses. All this on which his thought ruminates, the stuff that occupies it, is represented from his point of view. To see it, even for a moment, from some different angle—if, for example, the author interposed with a vision of his own—would patently disturb the right impression. The author does no such thing, it need hardly be said.

When it comes to Strether's treatment of this material, however, when it is time to learn what he makes of it, turning his experience over and over in his mind, then his own point of view no longer serves. How is anybody, even Strether, to *see* the working of his own mind? A mere account of its working, after the fact, has already been barred; we have found that this of necessity is lacking in force, it is statement where we look for demonstration. And so we must see for ourselves, the author must so arrange matters that Strether's thought will all be made intelligible by a direct view of its surface. The immediate flaw or ripple of the moment, and the next and the next, will then take up the tale, like the speakers in a dialogue which gradually unfolds the subject of the play. Below the surface, behind the outer aspect of his mind, we do not penetrate; this is drama, and in drama the spectator must judge by appearances. When Strether's mind is dramatized, nothing is shown but the passing images that anybody might detect, looking down upon a mind grown visible. There is no drawing upon extraneous sources of information; Henry James knows all there is to know of Strether, but he most carefully refrains from using his knowledge. He wishes us to accept nothing from him, on authority—only to watch and learn. (pp. 158-63)

It is necessary to show that in his attitude toward his European errand Strether is slowly turning upon himself and looking in another direction. To announce the fact, with a tabulation of his reasons, would be the historic, retrospective, undramatic way of dealing with the matter. To bring his mind into view at the different moments, one after another, when it is brushed by new experience—to make a little scene of it, without breaking into hidden depths where the change of purpose is proceeding—to multiply these glimpses until the silent change is apparent, though no word has actually been said of it: this is Henry James's way, and though the *method* could scarcely be more devious and roundabout, always refusing the short cut, yet by these very qualities and precautions it finally produces the most direct impression, for the reader has *seen*. That is why the method is adopted. The author has so fashioned his book that his own part in the narration is now unobtrusive to the last degree; he, the author, could not imaginably figure there more discreetly. His part in the effect is no more than that of the playwright, who vanishes and leaves his people to act the story; only instead of men and women talking together, in Strether's case there are innumerable images of thought crowding across the stage, expressing the story in their behavior.

But there is more in the book, as I suggested just now, than Strether's vision and the play of his mind. In the *scenic* episodes, the colloquies that Strether holds, for example, with his sympathetic friend Maria Gostrey, another turn appears in the author's procedure. Throughout these clear-cut dialogues Strether's point of view still reigns; the only eyes in the matter are still his, there is no sight of the man himself as his companion sees him. Miss Gostrey is clearly visible, and Madame de Vionnet and little Bilham, or whoever it may be; the face of Strether himself is never turned to the reader. On the evening of the first encounter between the elderly ambassador and the young man, they sat together in a café of the boulevards and walked away at midnight through quiet streets; and all through their interview the fact of the young man's appearance is strongly dominant, for it is this that first reveals to Strether how the young man has been transformed by his commerce with the free world; and so his figure is sharply before the reader as they talk. How Strether seemed to Chad—this, too, is represented, but only by implication, through Chad's speech and manner. It is essential, of course, that it should be so, the one-sided vision is strictly enjoined by the method of the whole book. But though the seeing eye is still with Strether, there is a noticeable change in the author's way with him.

In these scenic dialogues, on the whole, we seem to have edged away from Strether's consciousness. He sees, and we with him; but when he *talks* it is almost as though we were outside him and away from him altogether. Not always, indeed; for in many of the scenes he is busily brooding and thinking throughout, and we share his mind while he joins in the talk. But still, on the whole, the author is inclined to leave Strether alone when the scene is set. He talks the matter out with Maria, he sits and talks with Madame de Vionnet, he strolls along the boulevards with Chad, he lounges on a chair in the Champs Elysées with someone else—we know the kind of scene that is set for Strether, know how very few accessories he requires, and know that the scene marks a certain definite climax, wherever it occurs, for all its everyday look. The occasion is important, there is no doubt about that; its importance is in the air. And Strether takes his part in it as though he had almost become what he cannot be, an objective figure for the reader. Evidently he cannot be that, since the center of vision is still within him; but by an easy sleight of hand the author gives him almost the value of an independent person, a man to whose words we may listen expectantly, a man whose mind is screened from us. Again and again the stroke is accomplished, and indeed there is nothing mysterious about it. Simply it consists in treating the scene as dramatically as possible—keeping it framed in Strether's vision, certainly, but keeping his consciousness out of sight, his thought unexplored. (pp. 164-67)

The Ambassadors is without doubt a book that deals with an entirely non-dramatic subject; it is the picture of an *état d'âme*. But just as the chapters that are concerned with Strether's soul are in the key of drama, after the fashion I have described, so too the episode, the occasion, the scene that crowns the impression, is always more dramatic in its method than it apparently has the means to be. Here, for instance, is the central scene of the whole story, the scene in the old Parisian garden, where Strether, finally filled to the brim with the sensation of all the life for which his own opportunity has passed, overflows with his passionate exhortation to little Bilham—warning him, adjuring him not to make *his* mistake, not to let life slide away ungrasped. It is the hour in which Strether touches his crisis, and the first necessity of the chapter is to show the sudden lift and heave of his mood within; the voices and admonitions of the hour, that is to say, must be heard and felt as he hears and feels them himself. The scene, then, will be given as Strether's impression, clearly, and so it is; the old garden and the evening light and the shifting company of people appear as their reflection in his thought. But the scene is *also* a piece of drama, it strikes out of the book with the strong relief of dramatic action; which is evidently an advantage gained, seeing the importance of the hour in the story, but which is an advantage that it could not enjoy, one might have said.

The quality of the scene becomes clear if we imagine the story to be told by Strether himself, narrating in the first person. . . . [Is] it not clear how the incident would be weakened, so rendered? That speech, word for word as we have it, would lose its unexpected and dramatic quality, because Strether, arriving at it by narration, could not suddenly spring away from himself and give the impression of the worn, intelligent, clear-sighted man sitting there in the evening sun, strangely moved to unwonted eloquence. His narration must have discounted the effect of his outburst, leading us up to the very edge of it, describing how it arose, explaining where it came from. He would be *subjective*, and committed to remain so all the time. (pp. 167-69)

The Ambassadors, then, is a story which is seen from one man's point of view, and yet a story in which that point of view is itself a matter for the reader to confront and to watch constructively. Everything in the novel is now dramatically rendered, whether it is a page of dialogue or a page of description, because even in the page of description nobody is addressing us, nobody is reporting his impression to the reader. The impression is enacting itself in the endless series of images that play over the outspread expanse of the man's mind and memory. When the story passes from these to the scenes of dialogue—from the silent drama of Strether's meditation to the spoken drama of the men and women—there is thus no break in the method. The same law rules everywhere—that Strether's changing sense of his situation shall appeal directly to the onlooker, and not by way of any summarizing picture-maker. And yet *as a whole* the book is all pictorial, an indirect impression received through Strether's intervening consciousness, beyond which the story never strays. I conclude that on this paradox the art of dramatizing the picture of somebody's experience . . . touches its limit. There is indeed no further for it to go. (pp. 170-71)

> Percy Lubbock, in a chapter in his The Craft of Fiction *(reprinted by permission of Jonathan Cape Ltd, on behalf of the Estate of Percy Lubbock), Cape, 1921 (and reprinted by Charles Scribner's Sons, 1955), pp. 156-71.*

VAN WYCK BROOKS   (essay date 1925)

[*Brooks is noted chiefly for his biocritical studies of such writers as Mark Twain, Henry James, and Ralph Waldo Emerson, and for his influential commentary on the history of American literature. His career can be neatly divided into two distinct periods: the first, from 1908 to 1925, dealt primarily with the negative impact of European Puritanism on the development of artistic genius in America. Brooks argued that the puritan conscience in the United States, carried over from Europe, produced an unhealthy dichotomy in American writers and resulted in a literature split between stark realism and what he called "vaporous idealism." During this early period, Brooks believed that in reality America had no culture of its own, and that American literature relied almost exclusively on its European heritage. After 1925, and his study on Emerson, Brooks radically altered his view of American literary history. He began to see much in America's past as unique and artistically valuable, and he called for a return in literary endeavors to the positive values of Emerson, as opposed to the modern pessimism of such writers as T. S. Eliot and James Joyce. Despite the radical difference in these two critical approaches, one element remains constant throughout Brook's career, namely his concern with the reciprocal relationship between writer and society. In the excerpt below, Brooks discusses perhaps* the central theme in James's fiction, and one which he credits James with introducing to American literature, namely the fascination of Americans with Europe, and, in particular, the fascination of American artists who have developed beyond the "general development of the civilization to which they belong." Brooks calls James a "historian of manners," for it is individual manners and social relations he seeks to explore within this theme. For a discussion of other themes in James's fiction see the essays by Osborn Andreas and Daniel J. Schneider excerpted below.]

[James] is a historian, a historian of manners. He is never to relinquish this rôle which is that of all the novelists he admires; he is never to relinquish his belief that "the novel is history" and that "the air of reality (solidity of specification) is the merit on which all its other merits helplessly and submissively depend." The fact obsesses him: it has called into play all his knowledge of form. With what grace, what lightness and purity he has learned to transmit his impressions! Turgenev has shown him how to deal with small groups of characters, isolated and analyzed; Flaubert has taught him the art of achieving a certain unity of tone; Daudet has helped him to render the most delicate shades of the actual. But behind these secrets of the trade there is always life; and he regards it as the task of the novelist to find out, to know, to see. He has himself found out, he has known, he has seen: but what does he know? He knows as no one else has known it one of the two or three capital phases of the civilization of his country. Do not ask him if he knows the America that is rooted in the soil, the sober, laborious America of the pioneers, the dim, unconscious, Titanic America that is taking shape in the darkness of the hinterland. His America, no less real, is that of the great towns of the Atlantic seaboard; it is, in particular, the America that lives in the thought, the memory, the expectation of the European world from which it has sprung. The nostalgia for the home of his ancestors of the American who has been liberated from the bondage of necessity, the romantic vision of the Old World that exists in the American heart, the drama of the *émigré* in search of the arts of life—this is his natural domain. He possesses it as truly as Balzac possessed the Paris of the Restoration.

He invented it—he discovered it, that is, for literature. He was the first to become conscious of an actual historic drama that has played its part in countless lives on the stage of two continents. He seized upon this drama, traversed and penetrated it in all its aspects; he distinguished the principal types that were involved in it; he found in it themes for tragedy, comedy, satire. The American business man who, having made his fortune, sets out in quest of the fortune he has missed; the village artist for whom his own country is too immature to provide a school; the ambitious wife of the captain of industry who is so anxious to discover "the best"; the schoolmistress whose parched imagination has been nourished on photographs of castles and cathedrals; the young girl for whom the idea of Europe is interchangeable with the idea of culture; the colonists, the wanderers, the dilettanti, the lovers of the past—such are these beguiled, unsatisfied, imaginative, aspiring, or merely avid souls whose individual development has outshot in some fashion or other the general development of the civilization to which they belong. (pp. 92-4)

These crusaders are, in our author's phrase, "almost incredibly unaware of life, as the European order expresses life." They are themselves the creatures of another order; they know nothing of the traditions of the Old World, they are unconscious of the fund of evil that runs in the blood of ancient societies, and they take it for granted that the Europeans among whom they are thrown are as ingenuous as themselves. Thus they expose themselves to the direst misunderstandings or they fall into traps and are victimized. To the end of his life, in various forms, James is to repeat this story: for Isabel Archer is only a lovelier Daisy Miller, and Milly Theale is the shadow of Isabel Archer. (p. 95)

A historian of manners, a critic of manners, a mind at home with itself, alert, witty, instructed, in its own familiar domain. Yes, and in the foreground of life, the ground of the typical, the general. Turgenev said of Flaubert's Monsieur Homais that the great strength of such a portrait consisted in its being at once an individual, of the most concrete sort, and a type. James creates these types again and again: they are not universal but they are national—there are scarcely half a dozen figures in American fiction to be placed beside them. Christopher Newman remains for all time the wistful American business man who spends his life hankering after the fine things he has missed. Daisy Miller's character, predicament, life, and death are the story of a whole phase of the social history of America. Dr. Sloper, that perfect embodiment of the respectability of old New York; Miss Birdseye, the symbol of the aftermath of the heroic age of New England; Mrs. Burrage, the eternal New York hostess; Gilbert Osmond, the Italianate American—these are all veritable creations: indeed one has only to recall Winterbourne, in *Daisy Miller,* the American who has lived abroad so long that he has ceased to understand the behavior of his fellow-countrywoman, to perceive with what an unfailing resourcefulness James infuses into the least of his characters the element of the typical. It goes without saying that all this, together with the tenderness and the benevolent humor that bathe the primitive Jamesian scene, indicates the sort of understanding that is born only of race. These novels are the work of a man who was so sure of his world that he could play with it as all the great novelists have played with their worlds. The significant theme came to him with a natural inevitability, for he shared some of the deepest and most characteristic desires of his compatriots. And this relation, as long as he maintained it, endowed him with the notes of the great tellers of tales, the note of the satirist, the note of the idyllist, the note of the tragedian. (pp. 102-03)

> *Van Wyck Brooks, in his* The Pilgrimage of Henry James *(copyright, 1925 by E. P. Dutton & Company; copyright renewal 1952 by Van Wyck Brooks; reprinted by permission of the publisher, E. P. Dutton, Inc.), Dutton, 1925, 170 p.*

PELHAM EDGAR (essay date 1927)

[*The following survey of James's early novels is taken from Edgar's* Henry James: Man and Author, *an important, comprehensive study of James's work as a novelist, short story writer, critic, and dramatist. In that work, Edgar adopts a generally negative view of James's early novels, attacking the author for his implausible development of character, his inability to effectively handle much of his material, and his failure to control his indirect method of narration.*]

Like many another first novel, *Roderick Hudson* . . . is too ambitiously planned, but its author has more art than the ordinary beginner to make a failure interesting, and to beguile his readers with a fallacious sense of effortless ease when he was really floundering through difficulties and labouring for breath. [James's] design was to portray a man of genius, and to reveal him to us in his formative period, in the moment of his success and in the decline of his intellectual and moral

nature. Fiction shows few examples of artistic or literary genius convincingly displayed, and for a young writer to attempt the task and complicate it by a representation of the decay of these abnormal powers was to invite almost inevitable failure.

The peculiar distinction of James in his maturer work is his competence to occupy the whole scope of his design. His books are so planned that his intentions are amply fulfilled; and though he may drive his road through hazardous country, he never advances without a preliminary survey and measures taken for the surmounting of all engineering difficulties. In *Roderick Hudson,* by throwing pontoon bridges across the rivers and rope ladders across the gorges, he gets us precariously to the end of our journey; but lest these metaphors should mislead us into the assumption that the book is complicated by dangers of flood and fire and sword, I hasten to add that the processes of Roderick's decay are attended with singularly few incidents of an adventurous kind. He escapes from Rowland Mallet's oppressive company, but his borrowing of a few hundred pounds is our only indication that he has enjoyed himself in Baden-Baden. There he meets the balefully beautiful Christina Light, who completes what Rome had already begun—his alienation from his native country, and his abnegation of all the sentimental ties that bind the ordinary man to his home. (pp. 232-33)

[James] felt that he had failed in vividness on the American side of the picture, but, after all, the volubly vulgar Mr Striker and Mary Garland hemming her coarse kitchen towel sufficiently meet the realistic demands of the reader. More important is the failure of perspective he notes in the abruptly foreshortened account of Roderick's moral collapse. Revolutions of character are not often so catastrophic as James has made this particular one appear, and the author further involved himself in the equally difficult task, which confronted him later in Miriam Rooth, of accounting also for the sudden development of power that preceded the decay. Genius is a word to conjure with, but even genius requires some preparation, and must use ladders like the humblest talent. If, for Roderick's development, we are willing to accept mere affirmations for demonstration, the process of sudden decay is still to be accounted for. James has recourse in his dilemma to the old convention of the wild irregularity of genius, its inborn contempt of prescription, its rudderless reliance on impulse. Artistic conscience is allowed also to exercise its pressure, and Roderick is given us as an example of a creative genius whose technique, however wonderful, is incompetent to register his dreams of ideal perfection. But the great instrument of his moral decay was a woman of devastating beauty and diabolic charm, and James exerts himself to the utmost to represent the personality and influence of the enigmatic Christina Light. It was reserved for a later book [*The Princess Casamassima*] to reveal her more completely. In the early novel, not only was his knowledge of the sex less profound, but his hands were tied by his method, since we are dependent for our knowledge of her complexity on Rowland Mallet's unsupported testimony, and Rowland does not impress us as possessed of he requisite subtlety or depth for his task. (pp. 234-35)

The American, like *Roderick Hudson,* was subjected by James to a rigorous verbal revision before being admitted into the New York edition of his works. . . . There is hardly, I imagine, a page in either book that was allowed to remain precisely as it was written. (p. 237)

The situation that our author works out in this book he carried in his mind for years before he had the courage to attack it.

In so far as the surmounting of difficulties is concerned he might as well have tackled the theme in the first flush of his invention, or have given himself the luxury of a longer incubation. He admits the falseness of the central conception—that is, the ascription of a dastardly and motiveless crime to Madame de Bellegarde and her eldest son; but he flatters himself that he has made a merit of his defect by creating for his book an atmosphere of romantic mystery and suspense. Now James, and to his ultimate advantage, was very imperfectly endowed to explore the possibilities of adventurous romance—the romance of the dagger and the cowl, of dark, mysterious chambers and subterranean caves. His earliest efforts, and weak and groping they were, abound in melodramatic situations and overflow with effusive descriptions; but a chastening process gradually mitigated this exuberance, and by the time *The American* was written he had already achieved his emancipation from romantic extravagance. Christopher Newman has no impulse, for example, to scale the walls of the convent of the Rue d'Enfer, but paces the streets instead like an ordinarily disappointed man. The virtues or demerits, therefore, that attach to romanticism are not in question here, and we accept the crime as a somewhat clumsy expedient for precipitating the crisis that his plot demanded. (pp. 241-42)

[*The American*] is sufficiently commonplace, and is only inadequately relieved by the subordinate episode of the Nioches, which has the slenderest connection with the main story. The saving element that . . . enters is Claire's younger brother, the superlatively attractive Valentine, in whose life the book lives, and in whose death it dies. And truly the book was in full need of enlivenment, for Christopher was not born under the planet Mercury, and tradition and authority have set their killing weight on any natural spirits that Claire might normally have had. (p. 244)

With Valentine out of the story, James falls back for the sustainment of interest upon the elaboration of his original first conception—a guileless yet strong-willed American, the suitor of a woman of high birth, infamously rejected by the family that has accepted him, and presently possessed of information that would utterly discredit them. The theme is not adapted to his genius, yet working with alien material he does not wholly fail of his effects. A dozen contemporary writers could have manipulated more skilfully the element of suspense, but we cannot be certain that they would have divined the quite special value that might be elicited from the ultimate renunciation of revenge. This and the Valentine portrait are the redeeming features of a faulty book. I rank it for importance not above *The Bostonians,* and its reperusal satisfies me that the alteration of manner and method that begins to be so marked towards 1890 was prompted by an instinct wholly sound. James was not completely himself until he discovered that he was totally unlike everybody else. It has happened before in literary history that sincerity and naturalness have suffered rebuke as pose and affectation. The truth about James is that his particular form of sincerity and naturalness has never formed a working alliance with simplicity.

We now arrive at *The Portrait of a Lady* . . . , which is a book fortunate amongst its fellows in having enough of the obvious to recommend it to the casual reader, and enough subtlety to recompense attentive perusal. (p. 245)

The theme of the book is clearly enough the career of an attractive girl who fronts life confidently, gains a few small triumphs, inspires a few loyal affections, yields to the weakness of a momentary infatuation, is miserable, escapes, and returns under compulsion of her sense of duty to the life of torture, for which there seems now no alleviation, and from which only the accident of death may set her free. (p. 249)

There is not much to be gained by portraying a woman with a mind, if that mind is ultimately to be cramped in its opportunity for growth, nor in emphasising the value of experience, if experience is to lead in the end to a spiritual prison in which the natural impulses of the heart must suffer an inevitable decay. We do not exact from a great artist a comfortable ending. It is not customary to approve Dr Johnson's reproach to Shakespeare for his disregard of poetic justice, and James has high enough sanction for his neglect of that same principle. But the ends of art might have been served, and one's sense of inevitable sequence might have suffered no injury, if some more immediate vista of escape had been granted to Isabel Osmond. This, after all, is not a Hardyesque tragedy, where everything co-operates to precipitate the impending doom, and where the gateless, unscalable wall of circumstance hems us in. It is the story of a girl of quick and eager mind, of affections and impulses equally quick and eager; and if I read the author's intention aright, he desired to illustrate the growth and not the paralysis of all these bounding energies. If there is one lesson that James, ordinarily so little dogmatic, is still inclined to emphasise, it is the value of abundant living. "Live as you like best," Ralph Touchett once told Isabel, "and your character will take care of itself." We know that there is nothing Rabelaisian involved in this prescription of conduct. There is always for James the check of moral decency, and to live abundantly implies with him always to live beautifully as well. But here is a character for whom fullness of life spells disaster, and whose determination to live beautifully seems to lead to no serener fate. Our difficulties in Isabel's case are not to supply explanations for her ultimate decision. These James marks out for us with sufficient clearness. . . . She had wilfully followed her unsupported judgment in choosing her husband, and she is equally wilful now in her determination to accept the consequences. All this I say is clearly enough expressed, but the flaw in the conclusion still remains. We are cheated of our desire to see an abundant nature expand, and we are not permitted to witness in exchange for this extinguished hope her recovery of strength through suffering. James wrote a later book, *The Golden Bowl,* to prove how a wife, by the exercise of no gross efforts, may redeem a situation that a husband has put in jeopardy. But Amerigo was amenable and affection had not died. Neither condition exists in our present book, where we do not experience the justifiable satisfaction of seeing an impossible situation adjusted, nor entertain even the remote hope of its amelioration. We readily grant the effective manner in which James has represented the actual suffering. The art he displays in the whole second part of the story marks a distinct advance on anything he had hitherto done and points in the direction of his later subtlety and power. (pp. 249-51)

It is quite possible . . . to read *The Portrait of a Lady* with no consciousness of innovation; but we are not doing the book full justice until we realise that the author is tentatively striving after a new method of romantic expression. If, as our self-complacency assures us, we belong to the class of readers who, as James says, insist on shaking his tree for him, and are therefore as much interested in the way situations are presented as in the story itself, *The Portrait* will have merits, and imperfections even, that will reward our closer attention.

I have quarrelled with the book perhaps quite irrationally for what it does not contain, and have recorded a disappointment that is possibly only personal at the abortive ending. Coming to the actual substance of the story, we realise that it has all the elements of a transitional work, and if we rank it only short of James's best efforts in fiction, it is because we feel that the old and the new methods of composition are not perfectly fused. James thought it the most symmetrical of all his productions except *The Ambassadors,* but for many readers the combination of two compositional styles will have the effect of roughening the surface, so to speak, and the book as a result will seem to lack the smoothness of finish and harmony of tone that characterise perhaps even to excess the novels of his full maturity. (p. 252)

The Bostonians is of the year 1885, and we gather from several references in the letters that only exigencies of space induced James to omit it from the New York edition of his works. He considered the book to possess merely a secondary value, but he was willing to let it stand for the best sort of thing he could produce in the old-fashioned manner. . . . The processes of its design are so clear as to seem almost mechanical in their artifice. The author's intention is evident in every line. Everything that has happened is carefully explained, and we are as carefully prepared for everything that is about to happen. When a new character appears he is neatly labelled and docketed. A few pages suffice to put us in complete relation with Olive, with Mrs Luna, Miss Birdseye, the Tarrants, the Burbages and Basil Ransom. Verena is the only character who is not fully revealed to us from the outset, but in her case the mystery is legitimately due to the fact that hers is the only character that has not taken its mould. She is obviously in process of transformation, and we are permitted to gain our estimate of her from a series of anticipatory hints which, but for their inferior subtlety, suggest the art of preparation and gradual revelation that is to signal a virtue in his later work. (pp. 256-57)

In the work of his later prime [James] was never in doubt as to what his principal theme might be. Here there is some confusion of background and foreground, for even in his own mind he was not clear whether his main purpose was to give a fantastic account of the feminist movement at a time when it was more comical than effective, or to tell the love story of Verena and Basil Ransom. He solved his doubts by blending the two themes, and thus gave himself the licence to wander to the prejudice of unity and concentration. (p. 265)

Reading this novel, where all the old devices abound, we find it difficult to realise that he was so soon and so radically to change his methods of expression, and even, so it would seem, the very texture of his thought. Between *The Bostonians* and *The Ambassadors* there is a wider gulf than is indicated by the space of years.

The Princess Casamassima . . . , which was concurrently written, is separated by a notably narrower margin. It was an audacious thing for James to attempt a novel treating of social conditions with which he was incompetent to cope, and we are uneasily aware that in *The Princess Casamassima* he is conscious of his difficulties, and is seeking to avoid them by the evasion of the central issues. If this were a book purporting to reveal the acute distress of a great city like London, and the revolutionary activities that misery engenders, it would be a patent and palpable fraud upon our intelligence. If, on the other hand, the amenities of life and the aesthetic conquests of civilisation may be shown to rest inevitably upon a *vague* basis of wretchedness, the author then will be under no constraint to establish a clear case for human misery, and so far as the artistic purposes of his book are concerned these evils may remain inferential and undetermined. There are writers of course for whom the social problem imposes more exacting conditions. Mr Galsworthy, for example, would have felt himself compelled to a much more exact notation of the facts, and we should have had a realistic novel in which the artistic and propagandist intention would have striven, perhaps in vain, for reconciliation. James was saved from this dilemma both by the absence in him of all dogmatic tendencies and by his defective knowledge of the actual facts. The reasons, however, that he advances for dodging these latter will not satisfy the most indulgent reader. We might have been contented had he said that he wished to relieve his book as far as possible of controversial matter, or had he confessed frankly his inability to cope with subterranean conditions. It was somewhat disingenuous of him to say: "I felt in full *personal* possession of my matter; this really seemed the fruit of direct experience. . . ." (pp. 268-70)

The Lomax Place life is observed and rendered so vividly as to suggest the results of "direct experience," which in the case of an author so fastidious is the equivalent merely of imaginative contact. But in the later foreground of the picture, where we are entitled to expect a definite delineation of revolutionary figures, we are fobbed off with "loose appearances—just perceptible presences and general looming possibilities." We cannot take the fastidious slumming of the Princess very seriously; Hyacinth recoils from the besotted intelligence of the submerged masses; and only Lady Aurora would be competent to speak from actual experience of the horrors of the pit, which, for her gentle nature, are an opportunity for hard sacrificial work rather than an occasion for theorising. It is this failure on the author's part to face ultimate facts that accounts for our incomplete sympathy with his hero, and robs his tragedy of its full appeal to our imagination. If a tragedy misses poignancy it misses everything; and when we come to examine into the motives that precipitate Hyacinth into his fatal revolutionary activity, we shall realise why he succeeds in being futile and fails to be impressive. His early history is admirably conveyed, and so successfully is the boy of ten launched that we are keyed up to a high pitch of expectation for the incidents of his subsequent career. The prison scene is one that Dickens or Gissing would have seized upon with avidity, and it is not certain that either of them would have produced a more impressive result. The episode is at least as tender and penetrating as anything that James has given us, and it is a scene that will project its lurid light through all the years of the boy's growing consciousness—the puzzled, shrinking child himself, the timid Pinnie, the inexorable Mrs Bowerbank, and the fevered, yearning mother babbling French phrases. The pity of it is that the author does not carry to its logical conclusion this rankling sense of the world's injustice that had been so powerfully stimulated in the child. Pinnie is for ever there to remind him that he is a little aristocrat; and what ultimately moves him to act is less sympathy for the downtrodden poor than annoyance at being debarred from access to the fuller life to which his father's blood flowing in his veins impelled, if not entitled, him. (pp. 270-71)

James has told us that the history of little Hyacinth sprang up for him out of the London pavements. Many and fine though the passages are that render the life of the teeming city, we yet do not obtain from his pages the acrid savour of reality that we taste in Dickens or Wells. He is not willing to sacrifice an orotund fullness for the sake of vividness, and the art of representation is better served—the confession must be made—by their coarser, staccato methods. The passion that actually propelled the story was the sense, so pre-potent in our author's mind, of the accumulated values which the past has stored up for our present use, and he merely amused himself with the palpable fiction of an aesthetic anarchist and a revolutionary princess, the one halted on the frontiers of the world of beauty and the other free of that region, yet wantonly forsaking it. (p. 280)

The Princess Casamassima . . . appeared concurrently with *The Bostonians* and five years later than *The Portrait of a Lady*. James's art was obviously in these years in a state of transition, when he was tentatively feeling his way, and was not yet certain which devices of the older method to reject and which to retain. *The Portrait of a Lady* is almost as advanced in its manner as *The Princess,* whereas *The Bostonians* is puzzlingly retrogressive, which means nothing more than to say that it is a plain straightforward romance of the traditional English type, with all the characters honestly labelled and classified on their first appearance. In the comparatively early *Roderick Hudson* James had adopted somewhat cautiously the more artistic device of presenting his personages by a process of gradual revelation. *The Portrait* utilises the same method with greater success, but the book is weighed down with a great amount of preliminary biographical material that his maturer art would have absorbed into the narrative. Then five years later comes *The Bostonians,* with a return to the older treatment, and simultaneously *The Princess Casamassima,* which, though a less attractive book than *The Portrait of a Lady,* for reasons that I have endeavoured to make clear, possesses certain formal advantages. The biographical antecedents of Hyacinth are not more suppressed than they were with Isabel Archer, and if it is a fault to supply such a background, which James asserts and many readers deny it to be, then both books stand upon a level, and from the standpoint of construction are equally defective. But the innovation making for advance in the later book is the Princess herself, whose qualities are never categorically presented to us, and who is studied by the method not only of gradual but also of indirect revelation. . . . [James] admits that he "goes behind" right and left in *The Princess Casamassima,* but the Princess herself he never goes behind, and what we learn of her is never gained from her own reflections upon her case. The pity of it is that we learn nothing definite of her from any other source, unless to be enigmatic is to be definite, and consequently for this negative result the method is not to be blamed. There would seem to be a certain degree of indecision even with James, who pondered these questions more deeply than other haphazard writers, as to when he shall have recourse to the direct and when to the indirect process. Minor characters of course must not be given the privilege of self-analysis, but with the major ones also there seems to be no settled law. And we must further note that even when James had obtained a greater mastery of the method of indirection than he was possessed of in our present novel, the zest of experimentation was so strong in him that he occasionally flung his system overboard and produced a novel like *The Awkward Age,* in which everybody "goes behind" everybody else and no one behind himself. *The Princess Casamassima,* we conclude, was a sort of *ballon d'essai* to test the upper rarer air in which its author was ambitious to spread his wings. Without denying the validity of his theories one must permit oneself the ironical observation that his successes in this book lie with characters and situations delineated and described after the old fashion, with Miss Pynsent and Mr Vetch rather than with Hyacinth and the Princess; and that even when he was borrowing a leaf from the book of Dickens or Daudet, as witness the descriptions of Mrs Bowerbank and Rose Muniment, his success is not inconsiderable. I am not sure that his most delicate triumph of observation was not achieved in the diffident, dowdy, and wholly delightful Lady Aurora. (pp. 281-83)

> *Pelham Edgar, in his* Henry James: Man and Author *(Reprinted by permission of Houghton Mifflin Company), Houghton Mifflin, 1927 (and reprinted by Russell & Russell, Inc., 1964), 351 p.*

ANDRÉ GIDE   (essay date 1930)

[*Many critics consider Gide as one of France's most influential thinkers and writers of the twentieth century. In his fiction, as well as his criticism, Gide stressed autobiographical honesty, unity of subject and style, modern experimental techniques, and the author's sincere confrontation with moral issues. In the following excerpt, Gide voices a common criticism of James's art, namely that the author failed to "commit" himself to the lives of his characters. This failure, for many critics, has resulted in an appearance of "detachment" and "insensitivity" on James's part in a number of his novels. Gide's comment that James "dominates his narrative from too great a height" is similar to the remarks of Maxwell Geismar in his discussion of* The Wings of the Dove *(see excerpt below).*]

[James] lets only just enough steam escape to run his engine ahead, from page to page: and I do not believe that economy, that reserve, has ever sagaciously been carried further. The proportion remains perfect between the propulsive force and the drawing out of the narrative. No wonder, since nothing really alive nourishes him, and James only extracts from his brain what he knows to be there, and what his intelligence alone has put there. The interest is never in the outpouring, but is solely in the conduit. His work is like that of the spider, who ceaselessly widens her web by hanging new threads from one chosen support to another. Doubtless I shall praise him for taking his stand always on the same data of a problem. The skilfully made network spun out by his intelligence captivates only the intelligence: the intelligence of the reader, the intelligence of the heroes of his books. The latter seem never to exist except in the functioning of their intellects, they are only winged busts; all the weight of the flesh is absent, and all the shaggy, tangled undergrowth, all the wild darkness. . . .

Another thing: these characters never live except in relation to each other, in the functioning of these relations: they are desperately mundane; I mean by this that there is nothing of the divine in them, and that intelligence always explains what makes them act or vibrate. I do not feel so much that the author is snobbish as *profane:* yes profane, incurably so. To tell the truth, he does not interest me at all; or rather, it is his *métier* that interests me, his *métier* only, the prodigious virtuosity. But here also, there would be a great deal to say, and say again: this need of delineating everything, this conscience even, this scruple against leaving anything in the shadow, this minuteness of information, all this fatigues me, wears me out; his narratives are without color, without flavor; I hardly ever feel behind his figures, which are lighted from every side, that cone of unexplorable shadow where the suffering soul lies hidden, but his characters have no need of shelter—they have no souls. And I have not succeeded in persuading myself that this patience, this meticulousness . . . no, that is not great art; his strokes are too fine; he is afraid of the robust touches; he proceeds through subtleties.

And, again, this distresses me: he dominates his narrative from too great a height; he does not commit himself to it, nor compromise himself; it is as if he himself had perhaps nothing to confess to us. I notice incidentally that a character never interests me so greatly as when it is created—like Eve—from the very flesh of the author; when it is not so much observed as invented—and there indeed is the secret of the profoundest "analysts." . . . James, in himself, is not interesting; he is only intelligent; he has no mystery in him, no secret; no "Figure in the Carpet." At the most, he does at moments hoodwink us, as happens with the author hero of that specious narrative. Yes, this is exactly what distresses me—and what distresses me also in Meredith—to feel the author dominate, glide above the conflict that he invents, pull from too great a height the wires that make the actors move. (It seems to me that the value of Fielding, of Defoe, of Dickens, of George Eliot, of Hardy, comes from the fact that they never believe themselves, never show themselves, superior.)

Never do I feel that James is "in" with any one of them—and I am most certainly grateful to him for being impartial: but Dostoievsky, for example, finds a way of being impartial and committing himself at the same time to the most contrary, the most contradictory characters, who make him enter the heart of life, and us after him. Yes, it is just that; the secret of the great novelist is not in the domination of situations, but rather in the multiplicity of his intimate connivances. Undoubtedly these novels of James are marvels of composition; but one might say as well that the qualities of his narratives are always, are never anything but, the qualities of composition. We can marvel at the delicacy, at the subtlety of the gear wheels, but all his characters are like the figures of a clock, and the story is finished when they have struck the curfew; of themselves they return to the clock-case and to the night of our forgetting.

It goes without saying, nevertheless, that I am aware of all the importance of H. James; but I believe him more important for England than for France. England has never sinned up to the present by too much good cooking; James is a master-cook. But, as for me, I like precisely those great untrimmed chunks that Fielding or Defoe serves us, barely cooked, but keeping all the "blood-taste" of the meat. So much dressing and distinction, I am satiated with it in advance; he surpasses us in our own faults. (pp. 641-43)

> *André Gide, "Henry James," in* The Yale Review
> *(©1930 by Yale University; reprinted by permission
> of the editors), Vol. XIX, No. 3, March, 1930, pp.
> 641-43.*

CONRAD AIKEN (essay date 1935)

[*An American man of letters best known for his poetry, Aiken was deeply influenced by the psychological and literary theories of Sigmund Freud, Havelock Ellis, Edgar Allan Poe, and Henri Bergson, among others, and is considered a master of literary stream of consciousness. In reviews noted for their perceptiveness and barbed wit, Aiken exercised his theory that "criticism is really a branch of psychology." His critical position, according to Rufus A. Blanshard, "insists that the traditional notions of 'beauty' stand corrected by what we now know about the psychology of creation and consumption. Since a work of art is rooted in the personality, conscious and unconscious, of its creator, criticism should deal as much with those roots as with the finished flower."*]

Mr. Blackmur and Messrs. Charles Scribner's Sons, between them, in making the James critical prefaces available in a single volume [*The Art of the Novel*], have performed a service to English letters which it is difficult to overstate. The result is in some respects the most important single book of English

criticism—*practical* criticism—since the time of Arnold: even some might say, since the time of Coleridge and Hazlitt. James was not a "great" critic in the sense of being a wide one: the range of his natural sympathies was too narrow for that, and too idiosyncratically refined; he had as little eye as ear for poetry (as one may see by looking at his early review of Swinburne's *Chastelard,* his essay on Baudelaire), and his feelings about the "slice of life" sort of fiction, or fiction as "revelation," are well known. But that he was a great *specialist* in criticism this collection of prefaces makes admirably clear. Never has there been, never perhaps can there be again, such a taking to pieces and such a putting together again of the whole idea and craft of the fictive art. As James was the most completely "formal" novelist who has ever written, everywhere and always passionately conscious of the smallest items of design, sequence, mass, picture, and scene, so in a sense it was inevitable that it should be he who would first think of taking himself as a critical *corpus vile* and making of his own practice a theory. Implicit in even the earliest of his work, almost glaringly explicit in the latest, the theory was the thing that was dearest to him; and that he should end his days by going through those extraordinary novels for a last loving analysis of his own devotion to form was the most natural thing in the world.

Of course, James loads the dice, unconsciously, in his own favor: he is concerned entirely with that sort of pure fiction, that abstract "other world" creation, of which he himself became the first practitioner and the consummate master. The novel as a mere representation of life, or as mystic penetration into it, doesn't interest him. Of those, he merely says: "These are the circumstances of the interest—we see, we see; but where is the interest itself, where and what is its center, and how are we to measure it in relation to *that?*" What he wants, above all, is organization, and it is wholly characteristic that we find him saying in one of these prefaces that he sees it as impossible to make any real distinction between theme and form. Verisimilitude, if it threatened to get in the way, was ruthlessly sacrificed, or at any rate compromised. . . . James was aware of what he was doing in pushing the novel into a logical world of form in which the probabilities must often be sustained by form alone. . . . [Consider] his remarks in the preface to the **Princess Casamassima,** where, confronted with the problem of rendering the unknown London underworld of anarchy and conspiracy, he ingeniously discovered that to be *vague,* to use hints and notes, "not of sharp particulars but of loose appearances . . . just perceptible presences and general looming possibilities," was precisely to achieve an effect of reality. The reality, for us, may not be quite convincing, and obviously, for James, it was of secondary importance—*enough* of it must be there, but it need not be dominant. But one wonders a little, also, whether he was not a trifle self-deceived in this, the method ancillary to the nature, and that superb aesthetic economy precisely compelled by the comparative poverty of experience?

And to wonder this is also to wonder whether those miraculous last novels, which so triumphantly take possession of the "other world" (a possession as complete, in a diametrically opposite way, as Dostoevsky's), were not in *some* degree a queerly uncalculated by-product of the theory and the nature, their precise beautiful quality of *logical unreality* not wholly seen by James himself . . . . Impossible to speak with any certainty, of course, one can only guess; and at all events it *is* certain that the novels are the kind of thing which James, the critic, makes enticingly clear, in these brilliant and copious prefaces, as desirable. The prefaces are not easy reading, they are often diffuse and repetitious, the late vice of the dragged-in and obligatory metaphor, for the sake of "brightness," is tiresomely overdone; but for all that they are the most fascinating critical adventure of our time, and the profoundest. Granted the aim, the theory, there is not an aspect of the fictive art which is not here dealt with brilliantly and subtly and—one is tempted to add—forever. (pp. 236-38)

Conrad Aiken, "Henry James" (originally published as his review of "The Art of the Novel: Critical Prefaces," in The Criterion, Vol. XIV, No. 57, July, 1935), in his Collected Criticism (copyright © 1935, 1939, 1940, 1942, 1951, 1958 by Conrad Aiken; reprinted by permission of Brandt & Brandt Literary Agents, Inc.), Oxford University Press, New York, 1968, pp. 236-38.

OSBORN ANDREAS (essay date 1948)

[The following excerpt is taken from Andreas's Henry James and the Expanding Horizon, a study of the fundamental themes in James's fiction. In this book Andreas concludes that the single, most prominent concern in James's work is the expansion of the individual's consciousness. It is toward this increase in awareness that, for Andreas, all James's protagonists strive. This point is also made by Dorothy Van Ghent (see excerpt below). Other critics, including Van Wyck Brooks (see excerpt above), consider the exploration of the "international episode" as James's most important theme.]

The uniqueness of James, the single new thought in the world to which his fiction gives expression, consists in his recognition that sensitivity to other persons expands the consciousness. James's greatness as man and artist, all the edifices of his thought and the very texture of his sentences, grew from the fertile soil of this idea. It not only impregnates the thought content of his themes but also directs the turn of phrase and gives strength and grace and movement to his prose rhythms. The man and his art are so completely identified with the idea that they seem to be three incarnations of one essence.

James's work does not intellectually or philosophically expound the idea; it embodies the idea in an art form. The characters in his novels do not even discuss the idea or elucidate it in any way except by their characteristic action. It is so implicit in their nature that only an outside observer can make the abstraction and define their personal timbre.

The thematic synthesis which is here presented as the purport—the figure in the carpet—of James's fiction is derived from and built upon an analytic inspection of the text of James's fiction. The idea is discoverable in the fiction itself and is the natural product of an inspection, free from preconceived notions, of the entire range of James's writings. With the completion of James's final work in fiction, the idea stands revealed as the Jamesian canon, the law by which he tests not only the individual nature but entire civilizations.

This pivotal center of James's thought—that the quality of one's sensitivity to other persons determines the growth of one's greatest possession, consciousness—radiates a conditioning influence on all other aspects of his world view. By locating the source of value in the relations man conducts with his fellow men, rather than in economic goods or in supernatural considerations or in scientific knowledge, it stamps him as a humanist; by resolutely confining his attention and the scope of his study to the contemporary grain of the world's

human product, man, rather than to his economic, supernatural, or scientific history and destiny, it identifies him as an artist; and by asserting the universal applicability, not only to the artist but to all mankind, of the principle that growth of consciousness is the foremost boon in life, it supplies him with the essential elements of a world view.

The pressure, never weak and never violent, of a James sentence on the mind of a reader is similar in character to the kind of pressure which, in a Jamesian world, would hold between people. That resilience which is the dominant quality of a James sentence, that scrupulous renouncing of shock and sudden assault while at the same time remitting no jot of its demand on a reader's attentiveness and intelligence, illustrates the attribute which James would require of all human intercourse. For the want of that attribute, much of the life which James observed in the world about him—and which he then imaginatively reproduced in his fiction—fell for him into patterns of emotional cannibalism: arrogant moral opinion, meddling, parasitism, coercion, exploitation, revenge.

These modes of behavior correspond to flaws in the personal grain of representative human beings, persons qualitatively representative of the human race during James's historical period. James's apprehension of the world was neither intellectual nor philosophic nor scientific but aesthetic, in the sense that the main object of his examination was to determine an individual's fineness or coarseness of texture. James did not deal in causes or in historical analysis; he dealt with the end product only—which is man as he is today. And this man—the composite man of his time—James found unsatisfactory, for definite reasons fully elaborated in his fiction. (pp. 153-55)

I advocate the reading of James, not only because I believe his idea to be true and important and an encounter with his mode of sensibility to be in itself a prepotent imaginative stimulus, but also because the sound and movement of his sentences—aside from their prose sense—are fully consonant with his meanings. James succeeded in achieving what all artists attempt: complete transference of the self to an external medium. The qualities of his mind, the characteristic physical motion of his body, the kind of ideas he espoused, the flavor of his personality—all are reproduced in the carriage and demeanor of his language. . . . We are as astonished at what a page of James's later, and especially his latest, writing does with language, with our old familiar words, as at what a new composer for piano, such as Prokofiev, does with the old and familiar twelve tones of the musical scale. James gained such mastery of his medium that his use of language is as unlike any one else's, either before or after him, as one man's face is unlike another's. His peculiar fragrance, inimitable and rare, emanates from his idea, so that we sense his meaning as much from the contour of his language as from the content. (p. 170)

The characters in some Jamesian scenes communicate to us so articulate and intense a sense of their individual and separate awarenesses—moving on swiftly in time—that we begin to know in a new way how it feels to be alive. The unspoken and unwritten thoughts between the lines of a characteristic Jamesian page outnumber the ones actually printed there. The tenor of each remark indicates that certain thoughts had occurred, sometimes to the character and sometimes to the author, between that remark and the one previous to it. These thoughts, although unspoken and unwritten, must nevertheless be retrieved and lived through by the reader if he is to get the full meaning of the printed words. This kind of writing makes such great demands on a reader's attention that it in reality amounts to a new mode of sensibility. The sheer measureable quantity of charged consciousness, of conscious mental life, in his fiction challenges the intellectual capacity and persistence of readers who are habituated to more conventional writing.

The reward which accrues to a reader who accepts and undergoes the Jamesian discipline is, however, immediate. The very next conversation he overhears or engages in will be more alive for him with unspoken meanings, because he will be awake to the thinking which is going on in the minds and between the remarks of the discoursers. Such unspoken thinking constantly occurs, even in the mind of a six-year-old child, but seldom do we consider—or are we even conscious of—anything but the audible spoken words. In consequence, we but partially understand the meaning of the words we hear. By putting us in possession of this inaudible conscious world, James makes a luminous addition to our powers of awareness. To have been able to convey mental life to such a charged degree, he himself must have been a completely conscious man. (pp. 171-72)

> *Osborn Andreas, in his* Henry James and the Expanding Horizon: A Study of the Meaning and Basic Themes of James's Fiction *(copyright 1948, by The President and Regents of the University of Washington), University of Washington Press, 1948, 179 p.*

DOROTHY VAN GHENT   (essay date 1953)

[*In the excerpt below, Van Ghent touches on a number of interesting themes in James's* The Portrait of a Lady. *First, she determines the important role money, specifically wealth, plays in the novel—its means of providing the heroine with the freedom necessary in a drama of moral responsibility; second, she suggests the major difference between America and Europe, the cultural impoverishment of the former and the immense history of the latter. For Van Ghent,* The Portrait *evolves in a movement towards historical experience and an "investment" in the "binding past." This idea suggests Van Wyck Brooks's interpretation of James's American protagonists as individuals in search of a historical identity (see excerpt above). Van Ghent also echoes the point made by Osborn Andreas (see excerpt above) when she concludes that* The Portrait *deals specifically with the heroine's ability to "see" things as they really are, to experience a "growth of consciousness."*]

[*The Portrait of a Lady*] is not . . . a tragedy, but it is . . . deeply informed with the tragic view of life: that tragic view whose essence is contained in the words, "He who loses his life shall find it," and "Except a corn of wheat fall into the ground and die, it abideth alone: but if it die, it bringeth forth much fruit." We associate tragic seriousness of import in a character's destiny with tension between the power of willing (which is "free") and the power of circumstances ("necessity") binding and limiting the will; and if either term of the tension seems lacking, seriousness of import fails. . . . In James's *Portrait,* and in his other novels as well, the protagonist appears to have an extraordinarily unhampered play of volition. This appearance of extraordinary freedom from the pressure of circumstances is largely due to the "immense deal of money" (the phrase is taken from an early page of *The Portrait*) with which James endows his world—for, in an acquisitive culture, money is the chief symbol of freedom. The vague rich gleams of money are on every cornice and sift through every vista of the world of *The Portrait,* like the muted gold backgrounds of old Persian illuminations; and the human correlative of the money is a type of character fully privileged with easy mobility upon the face of the earth and with magnificent opportunities for the cultivation of aesthetic and intellectual refinements. It

is by visualizing with the greatest clarity the lustrously moneyed tones of the James universe that we make ourselves able to see the more clearly what grave, somber shapes of illusion and guilt he organizes in this novel. The tension between circumstances and volition, "necessity" and "freedom," is demonstrated at the uppermost levels of material opportunity where, presumably, there is most freedom and where therefore freedom becomes most threatening—and where necessity wears its most insidious disguise, the disguise of freedom. (p. 212)

The "international myth" that operates broadly in James's work, and that appears, in this novel, in the typical confrontation of American innocence and moral rigor with the tortuosities of an older civilization, gives its own and special dimension to the moneyed prospect. . . . If the shadows of the physically dispossessed—the sweat and the bone-weariness and the manifold anonymous deprivation in which this culture-buying power had its source—are excluded from James's money-gilded canvas, the shadow of spiritual dispossession is the somber shape under the money outline. We are not allowed to forget the aesthetic and moral impoverishment that spread its gross vacuum at the core of the American acquisitive dream—the greed, the obtuse or rapacious presumption, the disvaluation of values that kept pace to pace with material expansion. James's characteristic thematic contrasts, here as in other novels, are those of surface against depth, inspection against experience, buying power against living power, the American tourist's cultural balcony against the European abyss of history and memory and involved motive where he perilously or callously teeters. In *The Portrait,* the American heroine's pilgrimage in Europe becomes a fatally serious spiritual investment, an investment of the "free" self in and with the circumstantial and binding past, a discovery of the relations of the self with history, and a moral renovation of history in the freedom of the individual conscience. It is a growing of more delicate and deeper-reaching roots and a nourishment of a more complex, more troubled, more creative personal humanity. It is, in short, what is ideally meant by "civilization," as that word refers to a process that can take place in an individual.

The postulate of wealth and privilege is, in revised terms, that of the second chapter of Genesis (the story of Adam in the garden)—that of the optimum conditions which will leave the innocent soul at liberty to develop its potentialities—and, as in the archetype of the Fall of Man, the postulate is significant not as excluding knowledge of good and evil, but as presenting a rare opportunity for such knowledge. It is the bounty poured on Isabel Archer (significantly, the man who gives her the symbolical investiture of money is a man who is fatally ill; significantly, also, she is under an illusion as to the giver) that makes her "free" to determine her choice of action, and thus morally most responsible for her choice; but it is the very bounty of her fortune, also, that activates at once, as if chemically, the proclivity to evil in the world of privilege that her wealth allows her to enter—it is her money that draws Madame Merle and Osmond to her; so that her "freedom" is actualized as imprisonment, in a peculiarly ashen and claustral, because peculiarly refined, suburb of hell. Isabel's quest had, at the earliest, been a quest for happiness—the naïvely egoistic American quest; it converts into a problem of spiritual salvation, that is, into a quest of "life"; and again the Biblical archetype shadows forth the problem. After eating of the fruit of the tree of knowledge of good and evil, how is one to regain access to the tree of life? (pp. 213-14)

The Portrait identifies life with the most probing, dangerous, responsible awareness—identifies, as it were, the two "trees," the tree of the Fall and the tree of the Resurrection. The heroine's voluntary search for fuller consciousness leads her, in an illusion of perfect freedom to choose only "the best" in experience, to choose an evil; but it is this that, by providing insight through suffering and guilt, provides also access to life—to the fructification of consciousness that is a knowledge of human bondedness. (p. 215)

The title, *The Portrait,* asks the eye to see. And the handling of the book is in terms of seeing. The informing and strengthening of the eye of the mind is the theme—the ultimate knowledge, the thing finally "seen," having only the contingent importance of stimulating a more subtle and various activity of perception. The dramatization is deliberately "scenic," moving in a series of recognition scenes that are slight and low-keyed at first, or blurred and erroneous, in proportion both to the innocence of the heroine and others' skill in refined disguises and obliquities; then, toward the end, proceeding in swift and livid flashes. For in adopting as his compositional center the growth of a consciousness, James was able to use the bafflements and illusions of ignorance for his "complications," as he was able to use, more consistently than any other novelist, "recognitions" for his crises. Further, this action, moving through errors and illuminations of the inward eye, is set in a symbolic construct of things to be seen by the physical eye—paintings and sculptures, old coins and porcelain and lace and tapestries, most of all buildings: the aesthetic riches of Europe, pregnant with memory, with "histories within histories" of skills and motivations, temptations and suffering. The context of particulars offered to physical sight (and these may be settings, like English country houses or Roman ruins, or objects in the setting, like a porcelain cup or a piece of old lace draped on a mantel, or a person's face or a group of people—and the emphasis on the visual is most constant and notable not in these particulars, extensive as they are, but in the figurative language of the book, in metaphors using visual images as their vehicle) intensifies the meaning of "recognition" in those scenes where *sight* is *insight,* and provides a concrete embodiment of the ambiguities of "seeing." (pp. 215-16)

Much of James's work is an exploration of the profound identity of the aesthetic and the moral. . . . Aesthetic experience proper, since it is acquired through the senses, is an experience of *feeling.* But so also moral experience, when it is not sheerly nominal and ritualistic, is an experience of *feeling.* Neither one has reality—has psychological depth—unless it is "felt" (hence James's so frequent use of phrases such as "felt life" and "the very *taste* of life," phrases that insist on the feeling-base of complete and integrated living). Furthermore, both aesthetic and moral experience are nonutilitarian. The first distinction that aestheticians usually make, in defining the aesthetic, is its distinction from the useful; when the aesthetic is converted to utility, it becomes something else, its value designation is different—as when a beautiful bowl becomes valuable not for its beauty but for its capacity to hold soup. So also the moral, when it is converted to utility, becomes something else than the moral—becomes even immoral, a parody of or a blasphemy against the moral life. . . . Moral and aesthetic experience have then in common their foundation in feeling and their distinction from the useful. The identity that James explores [in *The Portrait*] is their identity in the most capacious and most integrated—the most "civilized"—consciousness, whose sense relationships (aesthetic relationships) with the external world of scenes and objects have the same quality and the same spiritual determination as its relationships

with people (moral relationships). But his exploration of that ideal identity involves cognizance of failed integration, cognizance of the many varieties of one-sidedness or one-eyedness or blindness that go by the name of the moral or the aesthetic, and of the destructive potentialities of the human consciousness when it is one-sided either way. His ironies revolve on the ideal concept of a spacious integrity of feeling: feeling, ideally, is *one*—and there is ironic situation when feeling is split into the "moral" and the "aesthetic," each denying the other and each posing as *all.* (pp. 217-18)

The moral question that is raised by every character in the book is a question of the "amount of felt life" that each is able to experience, a question of how many and how various are the relationships each can, with integrity, enter into. Or, to put the matter in its basic metaphor, it is a question of how much each person is able to "see," and not only to see but to compose into creative order. (p. 222)

> Dorothy Van Ghent, "On 'The Portrait of a Lady'," in her *The English Novel: Form and Function (copyright © 1953 by Dorothy Van Ghent; reprinted by permission of Holt, Rinehart and Winston, CBS College Publishing),* Holt, Rinehart and Winston, 1953 *(and reprinted by Harper & Row, Publishers, 1961, pp. 211-28).*

FREDERICK C. CREWS (essay date 1957)

[*In the excerpt below, taken from his* The Tragedy of Manners: Moral Drama in the Later Novels of Henry James, *Crews analyzes the moral awareness of the main characters in* The Golden Bowl. *Like William Dean Howells (see excerpt above), Crews concludes that James purposely made his later novels morally ambiguous in order to approximate "'real life' in its broadest aspect."*]

Few novels resist clear analysis more stubbornly than *The Golden Bowl.* No novel in my acquaintance poses so many questions while providing so few definite answers, and none contains so many careful ambiguities of ultimate meaning. Ambiguity, indeed, could be called one of the book's major themes; all the action depends on the preservation of colossal misunderstandings among the four principal characters. "Hard facts," the real basis for the drama, never rise to the surface at all. They do come close enough for the characters and ourselves to form working hypotheses and to stumble toward general conclusions, but they are never so near that we can positively identify them, or deny the presence of other, less visible circumstances. James will place several conflicting explanations before us in equal relief, and then let the matter drop. No one is entirely sure of what has just happened, to say nothing of what will happen next. (p. 81)

[In *The Golden Bowl,* no] absolute, "real" point of perspective recommends itself to us. There is no Hyacinth or Strether or Densher to whom we can turn for James's own judgment of the action. The four "heroes" of *The Golden Bowl* are seen by the reader only as they are seen, alternately and in different lights, by each other, and James refuses to imply that one point of view is more valid than the others. In order to arrive conclusively at one set of moral insights we must therefore deny three other sets. James is scrupulous to divert us from such rashness. Any critic who has found one point of view completely vindicated is guilty of carelessness, for *The Golden Bowl* simply does not lend itself to [this] type of unilateral interpretation. . . . (pp. 81-2)

The Golden Bowl is perhaps an attempt at juxtaposing—not identifying—the two parts of James's moral awareness, his intuitive inclusiveness and his social conscience. Neither of them can be expected to disgrace the other in the novel's final meaning.

Some such explanation, at any rate, is necessary to an understanding of this novel. The only alternative would be to conclude that James did try to "say things" through its action but that he lost interest, or failed through an overcomplication of poetic effects. This view finds James guilty of sacrificing his moral incisiveness to his love of vagueness and ornamentation. Certainly *The Golden Bowl* exhibits the height of his interest in mystery, innuendo, and elaborate dramatic dialogue, and its characters seem to speak for themselves rather than for their social histories. They are all perceptive and generous, and they appear to act in accordance with their roles in the immediate situation rather than with national or class-ingrained traits. However, these traits have been named and minutely described, and when the action is finished we realize that no other circumstances can explain the radical differences in behavior that the various characters have shown. It is true that by taking all these social factors into account we must see the moral issue as complicated almost to the point of self-contradiction, but perhaps this, again, is an accurate account of "real life" in its broadest aspect. It is certain at any rate that each of the characters in *The Golden Bowl* is allowed to think of his social background so ambiguously that in any given crisis he is "free" of it—i.e. he may choose to obey any one of his numerous, conflicting impulses.

This subtlety of method need not be set down to preciousness on James's part. . . . Characters who are not dominated by personal or social idiosyncracies of feeling, but who are able instead to confront their problems with a large measure of detachment, will necessarily tell us more about the real nature of those problems than more predictable characters could. In *The Ambassadors* . . . the absence of absolute, unqualified villains made the social issues clearer rather than less so; Strether was finally able to see the merits and drawbacks of the opposing values without committing himself entirely to one set of characters or another. . . . This kind of situation has been further intensified in *The Golden Bowl.* Each of the principal characters admires the other three sufficiently for us to be sure that any clash of personality will be determined only by the problem at hand, and everyone regards his social background—the usual basis for motivation in James—with a significant critical reserve. We can no longer predict the behavior of any character. Instead of beginning with the fact of socially determined motivation, as in *The Ambassadors,* and then observing actions which are explainable in those terms, we begin only with the actions, committed by ostensibly free characters, and in retrospect we see their true motivation. If James's immediate reason for this refinement was a desire to escape once and for all from the use of stereotypes, on our own part it should justify a closer attention than ever to the problem of social causality. (pp. 83-4)

The subject of [*The Golden Bowl*], in my opinion, is power. What is its nature? Who possesses it? What are its moral implications? These, I think, are the questions posed with the deepest urgency. Each of the characters is seeking control over the others, or resisting their control, or deliberately acquiescing in it. Each has the matter of social dominance in the front of his consciousness. The four main characters represent four distinct kinds of power, and the motion of the book is a gradual shift in emphasis from the power of one character to that of another. We come to recognize the power of each, but realize with every change of focus that the person now under observation is stronger than his predecessor. At the end of the novel we have made out fairly well who is the most powerful character and why. The final and greatest exercise of power dissolves the situation which called for a test in the first place.

The person who seems at once to be most powerful is Adam Verver, for he has amassed the greatest wealth. However, we are prevented from contemplating the size and nature of his influence, in the early books, by James's refusal to bring him into the foreground; the first object of our attention is Prince Amerigo, Maggie's husband. The Prince enjoys power of a peculiar and seemingly limited nature. He enters the story with only his pedigree as a social asset; the hard cash which should ideally accompany it is lacking. Furthermore, his noble birth stands for certain dangerous restrictions in his adaptability. . . . His consciousness of his value as an object of curiosity interferes with his ability to deal with people on any other basis. He cannot maneuver freely.

However, the Prince's attraction as a museum piece ought not to be underestimated, for it gains him an access to the very type of power he has lacked. If he enters the story only with an inherited charm, he quickly turns it into a large monetary capital. Adam Verver, wealthy as he is, feels incomplete without the polish and leisure that Amerigo represents, and his "collection" of Amerigo gives the Prince a unique freedom. . . . Thus his real power consists in his invulnerability to the destructive influence of others. In addition, he has the valuable art of making himself liked by men and, even better, loved by women. (pp. 85-6)

Charlotte Stant also comes to life early in the novel, but we are not impressed with her power until the third of the six books into which *The Golden Bowl* is divided. This is because she remains financially poor, and hence an object of pity, until that time. But our interest in power gradually leads us from Amerigo to her, for she proves herself clearly superior to him. She too acquires some of Adam's wealth by being "collected," although her appeal is more fortuitous than the Prince's. She luckily answers the description of a wife for Adam who will be able to get along with all three parties and avoid the vulgar appearance of fortune hunting. Once she is accepted in this role she displays a versatility and courage that Amerigo cannot match. Whereas Amerigo's power is all for resistance, Charlotte is capable of swift and positive action. (p. 87)

Before Part IV is quite over, however, we are subjected to another and more sudden shift in focus. Maggie has stumbled upon Charlotte's and Amerigo's secret, and with the aid of the repentant Fanny Assingham she brings herself to face the conclusion that things have turned out badly. Now Maggie steps into the spotlight, and remains there permanently. Her power, which is radically different from that of either Charlotte or Amerigo, gradually makes itself felt as greater than either of theirs. Like Amerigo's it is a capacity chiefly for preserving rather than acquiring, yet it has no basis in any venerable tradition. . . . Like Milly Theale's, her strength is her ability to love and forgive. But it differs from Milly's in two essential respects. First, it is a power for self-redemption as well as for the redemption of others. . . . Secondly, and similarly, Maggie's power is much more tangible than Milly's. Although she too appears as a figure of generous innocence—hence gaining Amerigo's firm loyalty in the two final sections of the book—she also exercises direct social power on Charlotte's level. Her discretion and patience are apparently limitless, and she has a sure feeling for the proper moment to make herself felt. She can be ruthless when necessary. Furthermore, her general aspect of innocence and good will is an element of power. Because she appears to be naïve on a colossal scale and is willing to maintain this appearance even after she has discovered the truth, she can prevent her opponents from dealing with her on the basis of accepted knowledge. In fact, the other characters are unanimous in feeling that it would be criminal to disenchant so innocent a girl. . . . In addition to the power of Adam's wealth, which stands squarely if unobtrusively behind every step that she takes, she has the double weapon of social presence and spiritual inaccessibility. Charlotte turns out to be no match for her.

Power, then, is seen to consist in several virtues, both Christian and Machiavellian, but above all in the virtue of not letting one's antagonists know what is on one's mind. Maggie is superior to both Charlotte and Amerigo in this respect. But if inscrutability is the key to power, no one can deny that Adam Verver holds that key. This is the truth that becomes increasingly plain as the novel unfolds, until at the finish everyone has discovered for himself that Adam is supreme. He not only is the chief source of their own power, but has a great amount of it reserved to himself—more than anyone is capable of guessing. His success depends on just this ability to mask his strength. (pp. 88-9)

One of the central facts about power in *The Golden Bowl* is that a pose of utter unconcern for one's self is the surest means of getting what one wants. Actual unconcern, which Adam is far from possessing, is not so efficacious. Adam has disciplined himself to behave as if nothing mattered to him, with the consequence that one can neither "talk him up" when selling to him nor question the fairness of his price when buying. For himself, emotion is systematically banished from his mind. His every effort is toward cultivating the appearance of perfect ambiguity. (p. 90)

From the deterministic point of view *The Golden Bowl* ends in moral neutrality. Yet we have . . . seen that each character manages to transcend or contradict any single trait of country or class that we might choose to emphasize. The Americans are not satisfied—but for typically American reasons—with being merely American, and the same holds true for the Italian Prince. Although none of the action is "out of character," James has made character itself ambiguous, so that at any given point we cannot say for sure that the motive for an act is selfish or altruistic. Everyone can look back and say with honesty that he has done something constructive about his social limitations.

It is therefore a significant fact that each character admits to a basic sense of guilt. Fanny Assingham is uneasy from the first about having promoted Maggie's marriage to a man whom she knew to be in love with another woman, and in concealing her knowledge of Charlotte's all too adequate credentials for getting along with her prospective son-in-law. She fears that in both cases her motive will be seen as partiality to Amerigo, with whom she is infatuated. Charlotte too is upset about allowing her childhood friend to marry a man whom she knows to be still completely in love with herself. The particular importance she places on the expiatory wedding gift stresses this fact. Amerigo also feels guilty, not about marrying for money but rather for leaving his penniless mistress out of the picture. Maggie feels guilty about having upset her old relationship with Adam, and Adam in return is sorry that he has allowed

Maggie to fret over this essentially trivial but disturbing impression.

All this penitence at the outset, in a situation which seems to fall barely short of being ideal for everyone, must strike the reader as evidence of a great and perhaps even excessive moral delicacy. Each character feels it his duty to atone for some oversight, mistake, or coincidence for which he is careful to accept the blame. However, is it true that this constitutes genuine moral insight? Fanny's sin lies not in allowing her motives to be suspected, but in meddling in the first place. She tries to redeem herself only through further meddling. . . . Amerigo's conscience does not prevent him from capitalizing on every possible opportunity to deceive the Ververs. And if Maggie and Adam should do penance, surely it is not for any harm they have inflicted on each other. Each character is concerned with preserving the innocence—that is to say the ignorance—of some other character, but none is really interested in his own guilt. The issues are not being faced.

Doesn't this constitute a preliminary judgment on the social microcosm we are asked to enter? Fanny, Charlotte, the Prince, Adam, and Maggie are all guilty of various failings, but each is enabled to sidestep his true responsibility. "Society" itself—the contrived double marriage—is the field in which each is encouraged to ease his conscience falsely. Instead of exposing moral errors, society assimilates them and thrives on them. Everything is converted, hypocritically, into "service for others," while the real truth is hushed and sanctified in accepted social forms. (pp. 96-8)

In the central drama of the book there are really two moral camps, not four; Adam and Charlotte are the leaders of two opposing attitudes which are merely defended, not formulated or understood, by Maggie and Amerigo respectively. It is to Adam and Charlotte that we must turn for the true sources of action.

This brings us to the most difficult aspect of a moral reading of *The Golden Bowl,* namely the fact that the two major philosophies never come to a direct comparison of worth. Adam's guilt lies entirely in his original creation of a hypocritical, self-satisfied world, whereas Charlotte's lies entirely in her exploitation of that world. Adam's guilt is thus completed, or nearly so, at the beginning of the novel, while Charlotte's develops during the observed action. Unless we are unusually careful we may be likely to evaluate Charlotte and Adam according to only one of two valid perspectives. If we concentrate chiefly on the action at hand Charlotte will appear guiltier, but if we ask only why such action was made necessary in the first place, we shall blame Adam. There is sufficient evidence that James expected us to see the problem from both points of view, but unfortunately there is no accurate means of subtracting one set of results from the other. The reader is left to decide for himself whether Charlotte or Adam is more to blame.

Charlotte's guilt is difficult to explain away under any deterministic theory, for although she is the character who is most aware of the moral oddity of the quadrangular marriage, she is also the most eager to exploit it. Her professed philosophy is a sort of enlightened fatalism. . . . For Charlotte everyone is a victim of his circumstances, and freedom consists only in putting one's self in the way of the most advantageous conditions. . . . Charlotte's supposed fatalism is contradicted at every point by her shrewd, deceitful, and altogether opportunistic manipulation of the Ververs' society. Like Kate Croy she makes her own luck, and she no less than Kate must be held responsible for the low ethics that she uses.

Nevertheless, Adam strikes me as sharing this responsibility. As he admits to himself, he has deliberately used Charlotte as a means of improving his relationship with Maggie. . . . Although he feels morally obliged to render Maggie's life as happy and innocent as possible, this very obligation as he conceives it makes him see his other friends only in terms of their usefulness to his plan. This error of vision—the development of the novel demonstrates that it *is* an error—brought Charlotte to his attention in the first place, and is at least partly the cause of her deceiving him. He *wants* to be deceived. He implicitly strikes the bargain of exchanging a share of his wealth for the privilege of not being told that his pampering of Maggie is unrealistic. . . . [Adam] is capable of enormous good, but by the same token he can inspire the lowest kind of hypocrisy. Although we see his power for goodness at work in the second half of the novel, I think that some of the opposite force is responsible for the initial confusion. Adam's power is amoral in itself . . . ; its use depends more on Maggie than on himself. But certainly we cannot pass over the fact that if he had not entered the book with a lack of respect for everyone but Maggie, the whole fantastic game of deception could never have been started. (pp. 99-101)

> *Frederick C. Crews, in his* The Tragedy of Manners: Moral Drama in the Later Novels of Henry James *(© 1957 by Yale University Press, Inc.), Yale University Press, 1957, 114 p.*

MAXWELL GEISMAR   (essay date 1963)

[*Geismars criticism is generally concerned with the historical and social aspects of a work of literature. Though he often openly confessed that literature is more than historical documentation, Geismar's own critical method suggests that social patterns and the weight of history, more than any other phenomenon, affect the shape and content of all art. Geismar's major enterprise—a multi-volume history of the American novel from 1860 to 1940—clearly demonstrates his fascination with the impact of external forces on literature. His praise of such writers as Ernest Hemingway, John Dos Passos, and John Steinbeck, and his criticism of others, such as Henry James and the post World War II writers, depends almost exclusively on how these artists were affected by and responded to the conditions in their particular societies. Many of Geismar's contemporaries, and many scholars today, have criticized his inability to see art as anything beyond social documentation. The following essay on James's* The Wings of the Dove *is drawn from Geismar's* Henry James and the Jacobites, *an important, highly critical study of James's imagination and creative method. In it Geismar argues that* The Wings of the Dove *clearly illustrates this author's narrow, romanticized vision of life. For Geismar, the novel fails to meet the criteria of "serious literature" because its characters are never allowed to explore their true natures. For an opposing interpretation of* The Wings of the Dove *see the excerpt below by Joyce Carol Oates.*]

[*The Wings of the Dove*] is, to begin with, another old-fashioned "romance" of Europe, a sequel to or a revision of *The Portrait of a Lady,* often rather glamorous and touching, if at times tedious; but refinished with a new technique (the late James), and refurbished with a subplot that is in essence a melodrama of lust and greed; while all this is viewed through the particular focus of the later Jamesian sensibility. (p. 226)

[The] story's opening, up through the Fourth Book, is slow, heavy, verbose, extended, magnified, both in style and in structure. What James called his "misplaced centre" really described his elaborate, portentous, elongated openings, where there was no middle to the narrative at all: but only the sudden gripping of the melodrama for which he had set the scene. The formal structure of the *Dove* is really that of "pre-analysis," in which the characters reveal themselves and their past while they reflect upon each other and speculate, sometimes coyly, about the impending event. Then there is the "big scene" itself, in which we see them all functioning; or that is to say, talking. And then there is the "post-analysis," where the characters, reverting to their reveries, examine the event which has happened, both in their own minds and in further conversations with each other. And this baroque, complex structure which James had evolved for his drama of consciousness—the multi-circle or con-circular narrative of "analysis"—had even more elaborate developments. (p. 229)

[With] Milly Theale's confrontation of English society towards the close of the first volume of the *Dove,* we have reached the point of impending melodrama and of the novel's real theme. Is it the familiar conflict of "appearance and reality?" . . . At Matcham, the great English country house where Lord Mark takes over Milly's education, where she has never felt life and civilization at so high a peak, where her vibrations, her sensibilities, are almost too tense and sharp for comfort, the Jamesian heroine feels that her quest has been achieved. But in James's own mind, of course, this modern English "society" of Mrs. Lowder and Lord Mark is no real social set at all; and moreover they are all conspiring to entrap the innocent, beautiful and wealthy American princess. The real conflict is that of illusion and illusion; or illusion upon illusion.

The American princess is false, or at least a romantic, improbable and rather thin embodiment of James's own pubescent concept of a heroine; without apparently any social, economic, or domestic reference at all. Her vision of English culture is false, since it represents James's own earlier (and now disenchanted) dream of the Old World. And the actual appearance, or materialization, of this dream in the smart British circle of *The Wings of the Dove* is not only false, but designed to be false—a deliberate lure and snare. In the novel's ever-widening and deepening circles of ambiguity, which are all constrained into a rigid pattern of deception by the plot line, there can be no sense of reality anywhere.

That was the central flaw of the "plotted novel," which, despite all the elaborate involutions of technique to hide, as it were, rather than to reveal the central action, James now clung to rigidly, and at the expense of any genuine literary realism. This was the novel of manipulation, rather than the novel of experience or revelation. Milly must become the pawn of all these glittering (and deceitful) English society figures; just as they in turn are the pawns of the plot, or of James himself. Moreover, while Milly possesses the early Jamesian vision of "Europe" almost intact—and how this vision, this obsession, or this fixed compulsion still haunted the Jamesian mind—so the "reality" of English society which is portrayed so glamorously and so villainously in the novel was simply his later disenchantment with "Europe." It is the obverse of the fairy tale, or the nightmare extreme of the artist's disillusionment; where the daylight world of solid, material factuality hardly can be represented. Thus the Jamesian manipulation of all these Jamesian characters (or embodied fantasies) is at the core of the novel; it is the real secret, and perhaps the real fascination of *The Wings of the Dove.* The plot action has completely superseded any chance of genuine character development, or of true human relations in the later narratives; but what they *do* reveal is what Henry James was thinking about Henry James.

These Jamesian "themes" (fantasies, illusions, notions, conceits) were, to be sure, dramatized with great skill. Under the spell of this magician's dusky enchantment, the characters, motives, relations are *almost* convincing—until you look at them in the cold light of day. . . . What one really becomes most conscious of at the middle point of this novel (or at the close of the first volume) is simply the high degree in which this whole cast of literary characters—who, except for the two women, are a rather mediocre lot—are "handling" and manipulating each other for their own purposes; or, more accurately, how James himself is handling and manipulating every one of them for the purposes of his own highly plotted melodrama. How, in short, this supposedly great novel, interesting as it is to read and speculate about, is centered around a series of tricks, angles and twists in the narrative.

What a curious middle-climax exists in *The Wings of the Dove,* where each character is plotting against almost every other character: where Kate is hiding her real relationship with Densher, even while she is planning to offer Densher to Milly. Where Milly, in turn, is concealing her own "secret" earlier relation with Densher, even while she may vaguely suspect, or may not suspect, the secret relationship (though how could it be?) of Kate and Densher. Where these leading characters, and the supporting cast of minor characters, snoop and spy continually upon each other's behavior, and "doings," from those hidden balconies or windows which are, as well as old-world decoration, the theatrical stage props of James's voyeurism. Or where these baroque literary figures actually *catch* each other walking with each other down the—it would seem quite public—aisles of the great British art museums! (pp. 230-32)

Surely, among the supposedly great novels of world literature, this one is the most singular, fantastic, baroque and byzantine in its values and in its form alike. The calculated, contrived, altogether esoteric literary method merely reflects the artificial and fabricated human values—which, in part at least, as I say, this method was also designed to conceal from us.

This is a novel which proceeds from false premises to false conclusions; which constrains all of its character development to its own rigid, tricky form; which is based on a completely idiosyncratic vision of life always alternating between the make-believe extremes of the fairy tale and the nightmare; which is compounded of illusion upon illusion, with no possible sense of human reality or of true human experience in its increasingly complex, convoluted and, above all, numerous and abundant pages, chapters and books.

But then, can *The Wings of the Dove* really be classified among the great novels of world literature? No; of course not; naturally not—since the major novels always do bear on human destiny, while this one concerns itself with human daydreams of a very special order. The "noble end" which James proscribed for Densher destroys the possibility, even, that James was aware, conscious, or ironic about his own daydreaming fantasy life; on the contrary, he was completely immersed in it, to the extent that he saw no other reality except his own. Quite similarly, his Kate Croy, starting out as an interesting portrait of a powerful, ambitious and passionate woman, is also subordinated to the Jamesian notion of romance melodrama, rather than to life itself, and ends on an ignominious rather than a tragic note. Here, more clearly than in all his previous work, the deep repressions of James, acting upon the writer's natural flow of unconscious material, produce a curious kind of "psycho-morality" . . . where the "noble," the sentimental, the romantic, the theatrical emotions preclude any chance of depth psychology, or any true view of human nature.

The Wings of the Dove is high and unusual entertainment, if you like, rather than serious literature. Perhaps the real question is how James himself—working in such an artificial sphere of literature; using such elaborately contrived methods of art; giving us finally not a picture of any recognizable side of life but of a special and unique *fantasy* of society, civilization and "culture": how this Gothic Romancer (who looked down upon Hawthorne) can yet hold our interest to the degree that he does, and stimulate our imagination to the point, at least, of trying to understand what *his* literary illusion really means. That is the true Jamesian spell; the enchantment of an extraordinary magician of art, whose bag of literary tricks contains ever more astounding surprises. Very likely the *Dove* is an example of just that "magic hope" and "magic faith" which Ernest Schachtel has described in his study of early childhood called *Metamorphosis*—or of that period in infantile development when the child imagines that his wants, needs and fears really *do* dominate and control the outside world.

Yes, I suspect that the final "secret" of the *Dove,* a novel based on such spurious secrets, is just there: that it draws us back to that childlike fantasy world of how things "might have been," although we realize they never were, and never could be like that. Most artists, just like most people, draw their primary inspiration, it is true, from this buried, but never altogether abandoned, core of human illusion. But the great writers confront the infantine dreams of life with the hard reality of things as they are. The revelations of art all too often consist precisely in this stripping away of such primary illusions. By contrast the art of Henry James is not only magic hope or magic faith, or magic fear, or magic craft. It is, at its real center, a kind of magic-magic. What a series of pure, entrancing, inviolate visions this writer presents to us! And what an extraordinary kind of elite vision—or visions for the elite—he propounded at a certain period in the climax and flowering of the great American fortunes; in their transient heyday of golden munificence—and in the face of the whole hitherto accepted literary record of common human aspiration and of general human suffering.

Thus *The Wings of the Dove* brings us a step closer to the true nature of America's first leisure-class novelist, who saw all history, all culture, all life within the rarefied and narrow confines of his own completely fabricated "aristocratic" values. This was a class-view of civilization so powerful, so intense, so absolute, and so confined as to make a Marxist blush. (pp. 243-45)

> *Maxwell Geismar, in his* Henry James and the Jacobites *(Copyright © 1962, 1963 by Maxwell D. Geismar. Reprinted by permission of Houghton Mifflin Company), Houghton Mifflin, 1963, 463 p.*

J. A. WARD   (essay date 1967)

[*The following excerpt is drawn from Ward's* The Search for Form: Studies in the Structure of James's Fiction. *In it he interprets* The Princess Casamassima *not as a political novel, despite its political subject, but as a broad social portrait of the city of London. Ward argues that in* The Princess *James tried to fuse the social world of London with the private consciousness of his hero, Hyacinth, but failed becuse his hero is unable to assimilate and reinterpret for the reader the novel's massive detail.*]

It is a common assumption that the main, perhaps the exclusive, theme of *The Princess Casamassima* is politics. The assumption is understandable for *The Princess* is James's only novel with a political subject. Furthermore the politics are of some obvious importance in themselves (unlike the remote parliamentary activities of Lord Warburton in *The Portrait of a Lady* and Nick Dormer in *The Tragic Muse*). . . . (p. 114)

It would be rash to argue that *The Princess Casamassima* (in which several characters are anarchists) is no more a political novel than, say, *The Golden Bowl* (in which several characters are millionaires) is an economic novel. Still one suspects that such a category fails to define *The Princess;* it is not an irrelevance, but it is needlessly confining and slightly arbitrary. . . . *The Princess* is "about" politics, but it is also about other things; and, as I shall try to argue, its theme is not political at all.

Following the lead of James's preface (and of certain letters and essays he wrote around the time of the publication of *The Princess*), we infer that he wanted to do something on the order of the social novels of the French naturalists and the English Victorians, especially the former. Such an intention accounts for the often observed similarities between *The Princess* and the other two novels of the same period, *The Bostonians* and *The Tragic Muse*. In these three novels James most nearly matches Balzac, Zola, Dickens, and Thackeray in his representation of a dense, sprawling "world." James, it would appear, sought a kind of reconciliation between the scope, solidity, and variousness of these French and English authors and the craftsmanship of such precisionists as Daudet, Flaubert, and Maupassant. His overriding structural problem was to do justice to the vastness and multiplicity of his subject without modifying his regular passion for tightness and coherence. (pp. 115-16)

The preface makes clear that the subject of *The Princess* is London, a city overwhelming in its variety, immensity, and seeming impenetrability. . . . London is a constant and forceful presence throughout the book, represented both as the sum total of its multitudinous details and as a massive absorbent unity. The sense of London is realized less in passages of description than in action, dialogue, and streams of consciousness. The force of the city is felt in everything that engages its occupants. (pp. 116-17)

It is also significant that Hyacinth does not dominate the novel, as James's centers of consciousness commonly do. To be sure, it is his "passion of intelligence" . . . that brings the other characters into focus; but, as the preface implies, he is as much a vehicle for revealing them as they are for revealing him. There are lapses in consistency of point of view in *The Portrait of a Lady* and other James novels that employ the central consciousness, but in none are the lapses so frequent and so undisguised as in *The Princess*. In the preface to *The Tragic Muse* James says that *The Princess* makes no claim to consistency of point of view. . . . *The Princess* is not a portrait of its major character but of his city. London is more than a setting, more even than a Zolaesque environment; it is a Balzacian society, and thus a kind of character in its own right. (p. 117)

In James's London nearly everyone is in motion, both horizontally and vertically. The horizontal movement is the general drifting away from national, cultural, and social ties. Hyacinth is the offspring of a marriage that is not only socially mixed, but also nationally mixed, his father being English and his mother French. The Poupins are French exiles, Schinkel and Hoffendahl are German, the Muniments are from a family of miners from the north of England, Madame Grandoni is a German whose husband is Italian, and Captain Sholto is a rootless sybarite who returns to his English home from a Monte Carlo casino or an African safari only to pursue the Princess. Of course, the Princess, the American wife of an Italian prince, is the major illustration of the general denationalized condition. James thus gives us a London that is a polyglot world of aliens, exiles, and adventurers. The odd and fluid internationalism is even illuminated by the title of the novel, which gives an old world Italian name to a story about modern London.

The international types of *The Princess,* unlike those of *The Portrait of a Lady* and *The Golden Bowl,* are deracinated; they are not so much shaped by a foreign culture as they are cultureless. So the forefront of the novel dramatizes their various vertical movements—that is, their efforts to find an identity within different social classes. They demonstrate not only envy but also instability in their pursuits of their opposites. The novel is full of occasions in which someone sets out to discover, possess, or be absorbed into an alien class. (pp. 118-19)

Characteristically James suggests countless parallels between apparent opposites: the Prince and Hyacinth secretly observe the Princess betraying them; proletariat Rosie receives her callers in a manner as grand as that of the Princess; a stroll with the Princess reminds Hyacinth of a stroll with Millicent; Muniment, like Sholto, introduces Hyacinth to a new life. . . . [The] purpose of the ironic parallels is not simply to achieve intensity, but to define the quality of human existence in London. It is a society in which class distinctions are of little account; more accurately, no one gains any security from social rank and everyone imitates—intentionally or otherwise—those of his opposite class. Everyone acts in much the same way. The most prominent details of the novel—details of character, situation, and incident—all reveal a society in flux. (pp. 119-20)

The plot [of *The Princess Casamassima*] has a typically Jamesian structure. As in *The Portrait of a Lady,* the first half is centered on the hero's initiation into a society and the second half exposes the insufficiency of that society; the first half creates the illusions, the second half demolishes them. *The Princess Casamassima* differs from the pattern only in that Hyacinth's enchantment and subsequent disenchantment are not with one but with (apparently) two societies. Yet there is a sense of simultaneity in his being introduced by the Princess to the world of aesthetic elegance and by Muniment to the world of political revolution; there is also a sense of simultaneity in his betrayals by both sides. The effect is that of a single society, but one that is most complex, even contradictory. The effect is heightened when the Princess becomes Muniment's lover; then the distinct acts of betrayal merge in a tacit conspiracy.

But it is questionable whether James succeeds completely in unifying all the sprawling diffuse materials. Probably the fault lies in the major strategy. Clearly this strategy is to use Hyacinth Robinson not simply as a means of bringing together many characters and social viewpoints, but as a character whose private crisis is intended to crystallize the themes of the book. Hyacinth's crisis, originating in his dual identity as aristocrat and working man, operates as a paradigm of the London world, a shapeless, fluid world in which everyone is in motion. It may be that James's predilection for symmetrical coherence proves inappropriate for *The Princess*. To represent the quality of life in a society in upheaval James places great symbolic weight upon the opposite social stations of Hyacinth's parents. James's scheme requires that the bastard son of a French prostitute and an English nobleman be drawn in equal measure to a pity for the suffering poor and a reverence for aristocratic culture. His personal life follows the same pattern, as he is alternately fond of an elegant Princess and a Cockney working girl. On this contrivance James insistently builds the novel. The very rigidity of the design seems especially out of place in a novel whose subject is social flexibility. The effect is not to recover order from disorder; it is to impose order on disorder. Actually the dualities that so disturb Hyacinth cut out too much of the experience in the novel. The quality of London life is pictured in images of density and obscurity and dramatized by social interpenetration. It resists James's dichotomous formula. (pp. 121-22)

James's controlling vision of London is of a city anything but formless, but its form is not the stratified class structure that most of the characters assume it to be. Its form is organic, not mechanical: not only is it marked by a self-generated fluidity, but its members are all expressions of the whole. However, James seems to require for his novel a more emphatic kind of unity and coherence. Thus he severely patterns Hyacinth's social initiation and requires his hero to view his experience as a set of balanced alternatives. True, all this is sadly ironic: for example, . . . Millicent turns out to be not very different from the Princess. James yet exploits Hyacinth's misconceptions to his own literary advantages, constructing his novel in accordance with his hero's false judgments. The resultant symmetry is not much more forced than in some other James novels, but it is quite obtrusive here. . . . [The] symmetrical form of *The Princess Casamassima* rather clashes with the steady emphasis given to the massive impenetrability of the social scene the novel seems intended to represent.

One of James's intentions is to equate revolution and betrayal, and Hyacinth's tragic situation is his principal means of doing so. Finally the treachery is directed not against the social system, but against Hyacinth. Not merely the plots of the anarchists, but the various aggressions of the Princess, Millicent, Lady Aurora, and Sholto have as their most immediate and extreme result the betrayal of Hyacinth's friendship. . . . The final hundred pages of the novel dramatize Hyacinth's growing estrangement from his friends. In a succession of valedictory meetings with Millicent, Poupin, Vetch, and the Princess, he discovers the unwillingness or inability of each to save him. Four times he receives a Judas-like kiss as he is sent away to face his crisis alone.

The flaw in this final turn of the novel is that the public theme and the private theme do not quite coalesce. Before the novel is two-thirds complete, it is perfectly clear to Hyacinth that political insurrection necessitates a betrayal of art and culture; or, as Hyacinth interprets the situation, assassination of the duke would amount to a *"repetition"* . . . of the murder of his aristocratic father. . . . Thus the general moral terms of the crisis are firmly established well before the end of the novel. James must hold them in abeyance throughout the final chapters that are given over to Hyacinth's private betrayals. The effect is not so much to extend the implications of the conflict between aesthetics and reform, but rather to make the social subject much less pervasive than it had been before. In effect the novel changes directions in its final movement. The great "political" issue that has troubled Hyacinth and engaged nearly everyone is certainly redefined and perhaps even transcended. The social question counts far less than the question of whether Hyacinth's few friends will offer him the loyalty and compassion that he is shown to require. Revolution implies infidelity all through the novel, but toward the end the scope is narrowed; the dra-

matic context is Hyacinth's private circle and not "the great grey Babylon" . . . of London. True, James continues to place his characters against detailed London settings, ever evoking the sense of the city, but this alone fails to compensate for the structural flaw: Hyacinth's tragic dilemma has been too soon formed. (pp. 122-24)

It seems clear that James's effort in *The Princess* is not simply to match Zola's bulk, solidity, and accumulation of detail, but to effect some fusion of this "totally *represented* world" with "the private world"—in other words, to create a private consciousness that is also a public consciousness, so that the two become one. To an extent the fusion is gained simply by a reduction of Zola's (or Balzac's) scale: excessive facts, relevant to the texture of society but not to the moral and emotional lives of the characters, are ruled out. More positively, all the persons whose lives touch Hyacinth's are made to lead public lives. Economically, politically, or culturally, they speak for some part of London society; the intelligent Hyacinth clearly sees them as such, just as he sees them as part of the buildings, streets, and general density of the city. Of course, his own insignificance—like his self-consciousness, his seriousness, his naïve gentility—also has a representative value. So the question of James's achievement with Hyacinth comes down to the issue raised in the preface: is James's sense of London credibly transferred to Hyacinth, and is the restricted mind of Hyacinth capable of possessing such a complete awareness? The imperfections that I have suggested may well be implicit in the scheme of the novel, since Hyacinth is required not just to possess a consciousness of London, but ever to be organizing the materials of that consciousness—to be, in fact, both actor and artist. In any case, the aesthetic requirements that James makes of his protagonist add up to his most penetrating critique of the naturalist novel. Hyacinth is the absorbent moral intelligence who gives unity and significance to "the thick undergrowth" of Balzac and Zola. (pp. 127-28)

[If] *The Princess Casamassima* is looked upon as an experiment in the French naturalist or the English social novel—or both—it can hardly be concluded that James has sacrificed unity to multiplicity. If anything, James has sacrificed multiplicity to unity, especially in his tactic of making Hyacinth's involvement with London follow so schematic a pattern, though he otherwise represents a London resistant to such imposed designs. Though his accomplishment is not flawless, James' rich dramatization of the relations of his protagonist to his crowded and diversified London environment is a literary achievement very nearly unique. (p. 140)

> *J. A. Ward, in his* The Search for Form: Studies in the Structure of James's Fiction *(copyright © 1967 by The University of North Carolina Press), University of North Carolina Press, 1967, 228 p.*

RUDOLF R. KOSSMANN   (essay date 1969)

[*The following excerpt is drawn from Kossmann's* Henry James: Dramatist, *one of the most comprehensive studies of James's brief career as a dramatist.*]

After the provincial success and London failure of *The American,* Henry James published late in 1894 *Theatricals: Two Comedies* containing *Tenants* and *Disengaged,* which he had written at the beginning of the dramatic years, 1890-1895. (p. 51)

Tenants was based on *Flavien: Scènes de la vie contemporaine,* a story by Henri Rivière. . . . The play, which had first tentatively been called *Mrs. Vibert,* has little merit and is another example of James's adherence to the tenets of what G. Bernard Shaw once called "Sardoodledum". It shows all the signs of the fussiness attending the well-made play, and it only distinguishes itself by being singularly insignificant. (pp. 51-2)

James had written *Tenants* originally for John Hare who was unsuccessful in his attempts to produce the play because of difficulties in casting. . . . The play as a whole is decidedly not a success, however, and it is not surprising that it was never acted. If anything, the play proves the shallowness of the well-made play in general. Technically it is rather well constructed: there are no loose ends; scenes dovetail neatly; suspense is maintained, be it often in ways which violate the credibility of events; and in general the various characters are easily recognizable and unambiguous in what they are or stand for. But these things are also the very weaknesses of the play as there is nothing else we find in it, except for plain melodrama. (We have all the stock situations and characters of melodrama: a woman with a past; an illegitimate son who discovers his real father; rivals in love who turn out to be brothers; a villain who blackmails a widow; and so on.) The characters do not become personalities from whom the actions flow naturally, nor are they really characterized by the action, so that no one becomes recognizable as an individual with a voice, mind or character particular to that specific person. They never spring to life in their own right: all they do is further the progress of events. The solidity of structure and neatness of plot development show excellent carpentering work but at the same time workmanship without originality or imagination. Characters are type-cast; exits and entrances so neatly constructed that they attract attention to themselves and become annoying; and so many characters keep flitting on and off stage that one cannot help wondering if all this fussy busyness is really needed. The answer unfortunately is that it is not necessary at all, and that all it does is display clever joinership.

Tenants is a poor play in virtually all respects, but it does show that James had learned much from what he saw in the Théâtre Français. If artifice is its strong point, it is also its main weakness as the play never for a moment raises itself above the purely artificial.

The second play, *Disengaged,* deals with suspected unfaithfulness and an engagement brought about by trickery. In the prefatory "Note" to *Theatricals: Two Comedies* James stated: "The idea on which *Disengaged* mainly reposes was supplied by a little story of his own." The story he referred to is *The Solution.* . . . From it James took two basic ideas on which he built most of his play: the idea of a man tricked into getting engaged to a girl by his friends who convince him that he has compromised her, and the idea of a lovely young widow who saves the victim of the joke and marries him herself. For the rest the play is different from the story. (pp. 53-4)

Disengaged is a highly artificial, not to say impossible, comedy. Up to this point in his career as a playwright James had not produced a better example of the sterility of the kind of playwriting he admired in a Scribe or Sardou. All of *Disengaged* is froth, madly whipped up not to collapse before the required playtime of three acts has passed. James's intent was obviously to write a comedy in the Restoration tradition, but his play misses entirely the kind of polished wit and *brille* we find in the plays of a Congreve. Neither does it have the humour (sophisticated or bawdy) that makes many Restoration come-

dies so entertaining. (Of course, the Victorian theatre for which James wrote would not have allowed any bawdy or lusty humour, even if James had been inclined so, which he obviously was not.) Neither subtle, nor bawdy then, the humour in *Disengaged,* what little there is of it, is purely flat stuff taken straight from the clichés of farce and vaudeville. The most glaring weakness of the play is the overly complicated, and therefore confusing, plot structure. If one looks at *Disengaged* without considering it as a theatre piece, one can admire the dexterity and almost acrobatic skill with which Henry James handles all the plot-lines criss-crossing each other. It is indeed a *tour de force* of sorts, although one is tempted to call the result a *tour forcé.* The speed with which situations develop and change, the never ending flitting in and out of characters, and the sudden turn-abouts made by them, bewilder the observer or reader. It is like watching a scene in an old Chaplin film with a revolving door madly spinning and stopping, and people going in and out at a dizzying pace.

It is difficult to understand how a seasoned theatre-goer like James could assume that an audience would be able to keep up with all that happens without getting hopelessly confused after five minutes. As a comedy the play is a failure also, because there is nothing inherently serious about what happens on stage, and one of the criteria of good comedy is that it be in essence serious—be it a comment on the *mores* of a society or on man's frequent flaws in character. It would be more accurate to classify *Disengaged* as a farce but as such it is not a success either, because it is clearly meant to be a comedy of manners. As a result the farcical elements one would enjoy in straight farce become poor comedy because they are out of step with what the playwright is so obviously trying to achieve in the rest of the play. (pp. 54-5)

Early in 1895 Henry James published *Theatricals: Second Series* containing two plays, *The Album* and *The Reprobate. The Album* is a comedy which relates how Mark Bernal is cheated out of an inheritance by his cousin Sir Ralph Damant who fails to inform his uncle that Bernal is still alive (he was thought to have died in America). So Sir Ralph inherits everything but he finds he has lost his peace of mind because he is relentlessly pursued by Maud Vanneck and Lady Basset who are out to marry him for his money. . . . The title of the play refers to Mark Bernal's sketching album which plays a central part in the plot. The first part of the play deals with the attempts of various people to get the inheritance or to marry the heir, and the second part focusses on the efforts made by Grace Jesmond to obtain a rightful share of the money for Mark Bernal.

The Album starts off as good comedy: the scenes between the two predatory females are well done, and we enjoy their catty exchanges and little fights when they are vying for Sir Ralph's hand. What makes this chase even funnier is that they are after the wrong man in the beginning because they take Bernal for Sir Ralph. When they discover their error, they do not stop the chase for one moment but immediately turn around and now set upon the real Sir Ralph who happens to be afraid of women and detests the idea of ever having to get married. The humour in the play is often farcical in nature and is based on well-known character types and plot developments: the aggressive women (Lady Basset) pursuing the bashful, unwilling man (Sir Ralph); the poor but happy artist (Mark Bernal) who enjoys life and does not care about money; the rich heir whom money does not make happy (Sir Ralph); the poor but honest girl who unselfishly works for others and is rewarded by finding true love (Grace Jesmond); and of course the fool (Teddy Ashton) who suffers from unrequited love for one of the predatory females (Maud Vanneck) and who can be trusted always to do the wrong thing at the right moment. Although characters and situations are not original, James handles them very well, and as a result we have a fastmoving and amusing first act.

Unfortunately, the play starts to deteriorate after Act I. No longer is Act II good comedy but rather a combination of melodrama and farce without the light touch necessary to carry it off. Coincidence reigns supreme: it just so happens that *all* the characters in the play come to Bernal's studio at the same time. Bernal's poverty is sketched in obviously sentimental terms—his studio is a shambles, he has no money whatsoever, no commission now or in the near future to earn something with his painting, yet he is quite cheerful and confident, we are asked to believe. . . . When we find that Teddy Ashton is there (he is taking painting lessons), that the undefatigable pursuers of Sir Ralph are also there (they want to take lessons so they can be present when Sir Ralph will come to sit for his portrait), and that a little later Sir Ralph himself arrives as well, we may agree that we have too much of a good thing. (pp. 58-9)

In Act III we find again that everyone just happens to meet each other at Sir Ralph's house. Sir Ralph proposes to Grace but finds she did not want to marry him at all: her only concern was that Bernal would receive his fair share of the inheritance. Then in true farce tradition Sir Ralph suddenly has a change of heart: now that she does not want him, he suddenly wants her very much. He proposes to her again, this time sincerely, but Grace refuses again. After a long, artificially protracted dialogue between Bernal and Grace, they finally admit their love to each other and the happy ending is assured. . . . In short, everything comes out fine in the end, but it means that most of the charm and credibility James had achieved in Act I has been destroyed by all these incredible developments and coincidences. The main trouble with this comedy is that James is half-serious most of the time; as a result the lightness of tone is missing which is necessary to carry off all the complications and sudden developments of the plot.

Quite different in this respect is the second play in *Theatricals: Second Series,* entitled *The Reprobate.* Here Henry James avoided almost completely the pitfalls of sentimentalism and half-seriousness in which he had fallen with *The Album. The Reprobate* is a delightful light comedy, parts of which are frankly and boisterously farcical. The characters are without exception caricatures but the humour is sustained and the fast pace of the action never flags. The plot is undoubtedly intricate and full of the classic misunderstandings, unexpected developments and complete reversals characteristic of light comedy and farce at their best. But James handles everything very well. The instances in which the pace slackens or the tone of the dialogue sounds false are few, and are invariably found in love scenes where Henry James shows again how uncomfortable he was whenever he had to deal directly with the emotions of people, while he was such an expert in dealing indirectly with them. As soon as we come to a love scene the characters become wooden and speak in insufferably stiff lines. (pp. 59-60)

The play contains the intricately worked out plot of the well-made play but James manages to avoid most of the drawbacks of this dramatic genre. *The Reprobate* succeeds because of its consistency in presenting characters as caricatures and in having them behave and speak in the exaggerated larger-than-life way we expect and enjoy when watching caricatures. Only in two love scenes, between Blanche and Paul, do we find the

pace slackening and the dialogue sounding false. Both characters are serious in these scenes and there is no attempt to be funny. . . .

But these are about the only instances of wooden, clumsy dialogue one can find in the play; for the rest the dialogue is exactly tuned to the situation and the characters involved. On the whole the play is decidedly a success as light comedy or farce, and the actors romp across the stage in a continuous confusion of delightful nonsense. (p. 61)

> *Rudolf R. Kossmann, in his* Henry James: Dramatist *(© 1969 Wolters-Noordhoff n.v., Groningen, The Netherlands; reprinted by permission of the author), Wolters-Noordhoff, 1969, 136 p.*

JOYCE CAROL OATES (essay date 1974)

[*In the excerpt below, Oates delivers perhaps the harshest criticism of James's fiction: that James failed to present the "real" world with all its richness and vulgarity. Comparing James to Virginia Woolf on this point, Oates argues that both these artists opted instead for a dramatic picture of reality as a "subjective phenomenon." For Oates, James's reality, as well as Woolf's, is a world defined by human relationships, rather than by the psychological dynamics of individual character. Oates also echoes a point made by Dorothy Van Ghent (see excerpt above) when she considers James's "great myth" as the "myth of the Fall." In her interpretation of* The Wings of the Dove, *Oates significantly opposes Maxwell Geismar's reading of the novel (see excerpt above), concluding that it is a story of important character revelations, specifically in Milly's movement from "innocent" to "savior," and in Merton's and Kate's eventual moral development. Oates also interprets* The Golden Bowl *not as a novel concerned primarily with power, as Frederick C. Crews believes (see excerpt above), but as a "story of an education."*]

It is felt generally, even by admirers, that in the novels of James and Woolf the aesthetic sensibility has so constricted life as to distort or pervert it, taking into account little of the richness and the vulgarity of the real world. It is not my suggestion that James and Woolf are similar in many important aspects; surprisingly enough, they seem quite clearly unrelated in matters of form, since James prepares forms quite as rigorous, though not as visible, as the plots of the traditional novel, and Woolf seeks to discover, along with her characters, design in the free flux of life; thematically, James is obsessed with the moral education of pastoral creatures—whether princesses or hardy Adamic voyagers from America—while Woolf is concerned with the necessary though doomed attempt to forge out of daily life a meaning that will somehow transcend it.

They are related, however, in their creation of subjective worlds that seek to define themselves in relationship to the larger, "real" world, the process often bringing with it annihilation, as in *The Voyage Out* and *The Wings of the Dove.* They are related most clearly in their use of minute psychological observations, Woolf casting about much more freely and inventively than James; and in their deliberate, unhurried, at times relentless faithfulness to these observations. What is most interesting about their art, however, is that it seems dehumanized to the ordinary intelligent reader. One cannot abstract from their worlds characters who are able to survive in an alien environment, as it would seem one might with other novelists—Dickens, Austen, Twain, Joyce. But this apparent weakness, however, may be seen as a necessary part of their literature.

One need only think of representative novelists—Thackeray and Conrad, for instance—to see that the vision of reality accepted by James and Woolf is severely different. For Thackerary and Conrad, unrelated though they are in most respects, reality is set and may be defined objectively, as history; for James and Woolf reality is a subjective phenomenon—more accurately, an endless series of subjective phenomena that may or may not be related. The secret lives of other people remain secret; one cannot penetrate into them, and the few flashes of rapport between people are perishable and cannot be trusted. Even the dead are mysterious. Milly Theale and Mrs. Ramsay influence "reality" after their deaths, but their effect on others does not bring with it any sudden understanding on the part of their survivors. Human essences, shrouded in mystery, are forever one with the single existing moment in which they are expressed—they cannot be abstracted out of it; they cannot be summed up, understood, even forgotten. If, in modern art, it is a truism that things do not exist and relationships alone exist, this observation will work well in explaining the literature of James and Woolf. Their concern is primarily with the mystery and beauty and tragedy of human relationships, not with the depths of reality that constitute individual "personality." The creation of characters as ends in themselves, complete without functioning in a social or psychological equation with other characters, implies a metaphysical basis that is apparently not available to, or not chosen by, James and Woolf. Their metaphysics has in common the suggestion that man gains his identity, experiences his "life," in terms only of other people—other intelligent consciousnesses with whom he can communicate. Moreover, an individual's "reality" as an individual is determined by these relationships, which are entirely temporal and, especially in Woolf, undependable. The older sense of man defining himself in terms of God or of country or of family "history" has been replaced in James and Woolf by the sensitivity of the modern secular intellectual who admits of no reality beyond that experienced by the mind.

James's great myth is essentially the myth of the Fall: to James, heir of his Puritan ancestors as were Hawthorne and Melville, the fall is unfortunate in that it brings with it the mortal taint of decay as well as the "education" that is supposed to constitute a kind of minor, compensatory victory. One needs, then, to define James's world as essentially pastoral: an extension, into a more recognizable social *donnée,* of the blighted Eden of *The Turn of the Screw.* The paradise of innocence is carried precariously within a series of virginal heroines who are rounded, humanized descendants of Hawthorne's Hilda rather than Richardson's Clarissa—American purity typifying a spiritual purity that extends to mythic proportions, rather than being a reality, an end in itself as it is in the English novel. So we have Isabel Archer, the betrayed child Maisie, the children Miles and Flora, Maggie Verver, Milly Theale, and Fleda, who loses the spoils of Poynton because she is "too good" to compete for them. We also have Lambert Strether, the ambassador from Woollett, Massachusetts (innocence hardened into sterility, banality), to Paris (intuitive life hardened into sordidness), who is a widower, has experienced his only child's death, yet is seen to be unfulfilled until he comes to terms not simply with the richness of life Europe appears to offer but with the devastating underlying suggestion of evil this "real" life hides. In *The Ambassdors* . . . James refines experience so that it takes on the quality of thought rather than life. . . . [At] the same time, James develops to perfection the art of narrative by point of view, third-person restrictive, telling the story only through Strether's limited, though expanding, consciousness. The novel may be defined as a minute recording of an education into the reality of the self and the world entirely through the hero's deciphering of his relationships to other people and their re-

lationships with one another. One is reminded of music cast into visible forms: of the dance, the changing and rechanging of partners, not, as in Austen, the gravitational pull toward "truth" and the "good," which are one, but the relentless pull toward knowledge. One cannot feel that Strether can be imagined apart from the novel; his psychic environment defines him, becomes him. For a man of Strether's sensitivity, by no means rare in our time, it is the consideration of what is not immediate that blights or undermines the present: "The obsession of the other thing is the terror," he says. Is the reality of this world of endless qualifications less legitimate than the reality of violence in the American novel, the one so committed to the mind, the other so committed to the body? James was surely influenced by the transcendentalists in his understanding of and insistence upon the legitimacy of psychic experience as total reality in the face of opposition by such critics as H. G. Wells. In an important sense all art is pastoral, its exclusions being at least as significant as its inclusions. For James the technique necessary to investigate reality to its depths is so precise, so fine, that the range investigated must be limited. The Jamesian technique cannot effectively be fused with the novel of action, nor is there any reason why it should be or why, failing its involvement in "total life," it should be considered somehow incomplete. . . . (pp. 12-16)

In James as well as in Woolf there is the suggestion that art controls life, that the demands of the "architecturally competent" novel must alter the free flow of life and that, in Woolf especially, the exquisite epiphany becomes an end in itself rather than a means of illuminating character: as if the novel were a novel only of "character" in the old-fashioned sense. If James's most satisfactory and perhaps most Jamesian work, *The Wings of the Dove* . . . , is considered in some detail, however, it will be seen to give us what must surely be the most exhaustive attempt ever made of rendering the sensitivity or reflection of a tragic experience. It is the experience that matters; the aesthetic achievement is secondary. The plot of the novel sounds legendary: a dying American heiress, Milly Theale, is betrayed by her "lover," Merton Densher, who is in love with another woman. This woman, the beautiful and powerful Kate Croy, has directed the love affair in the hopes that with the marriage of Milly and Densher, and Milly's expected death, Milly's fortune will come to them and complete their lives. Milly learns of the plot, her death is hastened, but she wills her money to the young man just the same: by this act forcing in her betrayers a moral sense so violent as to change their lives. Milly reminds us of the passive victims in Dostoyevsky—the saintly, the weak, the helpless, who possess paradoxically, as Dostoyevsky thought, the greatest power in the world. It is Milly's submission to her "fate" that secures her power; but it is not a perverse masochistic submission as Dostoyevsky's women sometimes exhibit—for instance, the suicidal Nastasia Philipovna of *The Idiot*—so much as a Christlike surrender of the self to the sins of others, in this way bringing about a moral transformation in the sinners. Not that James was Christian, or even ostensibly concerned with religious problems. But the movement of the novel, its very rhythm of sacrifice and moral self-realization, the theme of the power of selfless love—all are unmistakable parallels with the religious experience, whether Christian or tragic in the Greek sense. Milly embodies the symbolic roles of the Adamic innocent and the savior, the transition from the one to the other being precipitated by her encounter with evil; she is the dove whose wings spread to enclose the soiled, to carry her innocence away into the safety of death. (pp. 16-17)

It is not, crudely synopsized, a working out of the conventional fear Milly has at the beginning of Book Three when we first meet her—the fear that the two lone women, touring Europe together, "were apt to be beguiled and overcome"? Precisely: but the brute experience itself is not what is important. It is Milly's consciousness of her experience, and the consciousness of sin on the part of Kate and Densher, that make the novel great. It is an education, a growth of the moral sense in all involved, that is the "reality" of the novel. Milly is the instrument by which we are shown the tragic knowledge of the relationship between life and death, life being fulfilled only through death (knowledge), the dove becoming the symbol—and James makes us see the rather trite image in the actual process of *becoming* symbol—of death-in-life, life-in-death. The Greek *ate* is here defeated, for the assimilation of evil by the innocent, the refusal to continue the power of evil by passing its suffering along to others, are affected by Milly's silence: in the clichéd sorrow of Mrs. Stringham's remark, "She has turned her face to the wall." The beauty of the spirit overshadows the "talent for life" of Kate Croy, Milly's opposite; the power of the dove overshadows that of the panther. (pp. 18-19)

The Golden Bowl . . . continues the theme of innocence accosted by evil, or the world, the essential—and rather surprising—difference here being that where the earlier heroines were defeated because of their innocence, the young heroine Maggie Verver is able to achieve a victory by way of her innocence. It is most clearly the story of an education, more faithful to life perhaps in its refusal to surrender life along with "innocence," less effective as art than **The Wings of the Dove**, which tends to equate (one is reminded of *Billy Budd*) purity and life itself. It involves the awakening of a "moral sense" adumbrated in the earlier **What Maisie Knew** and, though the parallel is rather sinister, in **The Turn of the Screw**. (pp. 19-20)

Essentially the story of a family, the novel's movement is determined by the changing of individuals into roles, the discovery of individuals that they are participants in a drama that has rich and threatening implications for them all. . . . The conclusion of the novel involves, depends upon, a re-establishment of *order* not on a moral level but on a social level, a preservation of something rather like an institution—the institution of marriage, of "love," of civilization—not of the individual. If James's work contains any single great irony, it is the irony of the imprisonment of the individual in relationships and forms precisely at the moment of his "illumination." James's people are usually wealthy, bathed in riches as the lambs and children of Blake's pastoral are bathed in sunshine, and they are wealthy for the same reason that Shakespeare's tragic figures are kingly: their economic freedom assures them moral freedom. (pp. 20-1)

The reader feels constantly the mercenary shallowness of both the Prince and Charlotte, so that James's refusal to concern himself with the morality—and good taste—of the transaction is puzzling. That he does not do so seems clear by his complete absorption in the character of Maggie, who begins as a shadow, a pronouncer of the customary, proper remarks, and who ends as the "creator" of her world—she has nearly acquired omnipotence by the end of the novel. That her fight for her husband must be waged behind social forms makes the struggle more difficult and, for the loser, Charlotte, who never learns how much anyone knows about her adultery, more cruel. Neither Maggie nor James shows any remorse. Maggie is the victor,

having surrendered a father and chosen a husband; she enters history; it seems perhaps a regrettable flaw that the man for whom she sacrifices her innocence is not worth her sacrifice, since a better man would not have betrayed her—would not have necessitated her education. The novel ends with Maggie's father taking Charlotte to America, leaving Maggie with her husband, whom she both pities and dreads. She has learned to deceive in order to impose her will upon the world. . . . (pp. 22-3)

James must be understood . . . , in his later novels especially, as a creator of relationships; the actors—the fictional "characters"—come second. Though we may agree in part with his brother, William, when he criticized what he saw to be a "method of narration by interminable elaboration" . . . we must see that his apparent sacrifice of life to art is necessary for his vision of character *as* art. Like the medieval alchemists, whom he may resemble in other ways also, James transformed himself into a lifework, and each of his characters carries the transformation further. His main characters are artists, and the art they create is their own lives. (pp. 23-4)

> *Joyce Carol Oates, "The Art of Relationships: Henry James and Virginia Woolf" (originally published in a different form in* Twentieth Century Literature, Vol. 10, No. 3, October, 1964), in her New Heaven, New Earth: The Visionary Experience in Literature *(reprinted by permission of the publisher, Vanguard Press, Inc.; copyright © 1974 by Joyce Carol Oates), Vanguard Press, 1974, pp. 9-35.**

KENNETH GRAHAM (essay date 1975)

[*The following excerpt is taken from Graham's* Henry James, the Drama of Fulfilment: An Approach to the Novels, *which examines a selection of James's major work. In this excerpt he discusses the narrative method James utilized in* The Aspern Papers, *particularly the creation of a narrator who is both "reliable and unreliable, objective and subjective."*]

Henry James in the 1880s means James the realist—the mature creator of **Portrait of a Lady, The Bostonians, The Princess Casamassima,** and **The Tragic Muse.** That is our usual emphasis, and a perfectly proper one. But James had many styles in each period of his writing, and it is important to take a reminder from **The Aspern Papers** . . . that James was also a master of the grotesque fable, and could use it, characteristically, to parody the theme he treated elsewhere with more obvious gravity. It is a very modified grotesque, of course, and an essentially positive form of parody. A note of the bizarre and even of the playful is always compatible with the most serious activity of James's imagination: the slightly rococo can quickly pass without incongruity into effects that are, as it were, fully human, fully implicative, and even tragic. . . . The successful fusion of modes in **The Aspern Papers** is clearly achieved by James using a first-person narrator who is himself something of a wit and something of a grotesque. The question of the author's attitude to this narrator is one that has long vexed critics. . . . Some of the difficulties, one suspects, have been created by the critics themselves. Having failed to be drawn into the deeper feelings and poetry of a tale, they have been left to look with too scrupulous an eye on a narrating figure who is not meant to bear continual judicial scrutiny from outside, or to be 'placed' definitively in any fixed category of value, and certainly not meant to offer an individual 'psychology' as the tale's main purport. There is an important duality in James's use of him, but a duality that is not the same as a 'blur'. This is a narrator who is at once reliable and unreliable, objective and subjective. We can stand outside him with one part of our minds, judging his selfishness and irresponsibility, aided by moments of obviously 'loaded' irony against him and also by moments where the narrator expressly judges himself. This allows us to resist full illusion and to see around the dangerous subjectivity of his narrative. It also helps us to read a meaning into his motives and his experience that goes far beyond his conscious understanding of them. And yet in another respect we are identified with the narrator—drawn into illusion by the traditional persuasions of literary rhetoric, and made to experience directly that which we will subsequently interpret. The narrator's words become an immediate means of entry into certain 'truths': truths of our own experience which we are now 'tricked' into re-creating in our imaginations. There may be a strictly logical contradiction between these two aspects of the narrator, but there is no contradiction in terms of how we actually experience his story. What we experience is a perpetually dual and moving thing: we are always moving into the narrator, and moving out of him. At moments his 'character' is individualized and judgeable. At other moments it is not important—we accept it and pass on into what he is undergoing. This kind of interplay between distance and identification is absolutely intrinsic to the nature of art—and it is perhaps intrinsic to human perception outside the aesthetic field, too, one's whole perceptional apparatus being surely the most devious (and Jamesian) of narrators. To suggest, as a general preliminary to reading *The Aspern Papers,* that any aesthetic experience is a fluid thing, yet can come with a self-authenticating authority and coherence; that we experience illusion and forgetfulness, yet watch ourselves as we do so; that we can participate imaginatively in a narrator's life, yet see the meaning of that life in a wider context; that we lose ourselves in art in order to rediscover ourselves—to suggest these things in only to restate a set of paradoxes that have determined much of the history and the energy of aesthetic theorizing, and will continue to do so.

A further paradox that emerges from asking where the reader stands in relation to this narrative is that we are drawn closer to the narrator's experience by features in his portrayal that can only be seen as non-realistic. He is too obsessive to be 'natural', too feverish, too mannered in his expression; too literary by half. And yet the result is that this Nabokovian figure draws us straight into his fantasy-realm, where 'reality' unexpectedly seizes us in the form of powerful and almost hallucinatory images, which lose nothing of seriousness for their comicality. By refinement, artifice, and caricature, James is always able to touch on the actual at least as intimately and revealingly as can a more naturalistic art. His fictional characters—even in works much less distorted than this one—are often not quite human, and yet are utterly full of life. . . . A modicum of distortion in literature, such as we have in the action and the language of *The Aspern Papers,* is only another means of implicating the reader's imagination—exciting it to participation and entry into the work by reminding it directly of its own transformative powers. An image of life that a creative mind has twisted a little, to please itself, is always a challenge to an audience. The result can be that experience of intensity—sparked off by the meeting of two minds, the author's and the reader's—which is the prerequisite of all 'truth' of effect in literature. Thus the convincing 'reality' of *The Aspern Papers* is partly brought about by its elements of unlikeness and exaggeration (and partly, of course, on another level, by its elements of mimetic accuracy). The reader, for all his intervals of detachment and disapproval, is enticed into the editor's self-conscious style (let us call him the editor now,

since that is how he regards himself): the deliberate ponderousness, the strangely attractive self-parodying wit, the over-ripe hyperboles and mock-epic extravagances. We will surmise certain things about the kind of man who would use such a style; but more importantly, at first, we join in the actual *play* of the story's surface—so often a vital factor in our approach to James. This is a sophisticated game of style that contains its seriousness of import, and leads gradually towards revelation as the end of the game. The hyperboles are affected and infectious in themselves, and they are also, at a deeper level, sincere: sparks from a distant fire. (pp. 58-61)

The very movement and arrangement of the plot—like the style—is a subtle vehicle for . . . suggested meanings. Above all, I think, its movement combines the excitement of pursuit with the stress of frustration. The story progresses, like a siege, through stages of approach—some lingering and gradual, some directly aggressive—towards a dimly seen centre of alluring and menacing power. The stages are physical, room by room, box by box, as well as figurative. And repelling the approach, creating the pressure of the narrative, are the many obstacles: walls, veils, masks, locked doors, locked cabinets, tests and trials, a silent statue, a mocking picture. Mrs. Prest, who belongs to the outside world of factuality and scepticism, serves as the initial and most external stage, and her gondola, in which the editor comes to the Bordereaus' *palazzo,* marks the first reconnoitering. Then comes an entry—as far as the *sala,* as far as Juliana's niece, Miss Tita. Then an inner room, where Juliana herself receives the editor. The editor takes up residence, and prowls through the *sala* and the garden, staring up at the blank wall that conceals the *palazzo's* treasures. He confesses his intentions to Tita in the garden at midnight, worms himself closer to her private feelings and therefore to the forbidden Papers—and so on, around and around, closer or further, until at last he is defeated and expelled. The baroque style, the comically or disturbingly overdrawn images, add to our sense of incipient violence. . . . It creates an extreme narrative tension, in which the climaxes of plot come with a release of bottled-up feeling—a sense of strain, obsession, and claustrophobia that reminds one . . . of Poe, and of his whole Gothic-psychological tradition. The tension, just as in Poe, moves towards a crisis where something is disclosed or triumphantly possessed. What is desired is to possess the past, to achieve 'esoteric knowledge', and to defeat time. . . . (pp. 63-4)

[*The Aspern Papers*] is the story not only of the editor and the Papers, but of the editor and Tita Bordereau, with Juliana as the guardian of both niece and Papers manipulating and watching them all (just as her chief adversary in his turn manipulates and watches). Tita is caught up in this machinery of their personal contest, and our awakening to the reality of her own frustrated nature is vital if we are to grasp the full meaning of the story and the firmness of its basis in character and feeling. She is created for the reader by the merest wisps of suggestion. And what James suggests, as he can always do so well, with a delicate blend of laughter and sympathy, is a woman with a spiritual self, and with the potentialities of an emotional life: an *animula vagula blandula,* feeble, mild, faded, totally innocent and transparent, awkward and shy, but on the brink of discovering and declaring herself. She has much to undergo in this small space: the growth of her first and misplaced affection; the first flurry of a vital self-seeking; then shame, and forgiveness. And in the end she discovers, for the briefest flash, a luminosity of spirit that shines straight through the intrigues of Juliana and the editor and is a hint to us that the Aspern power itself, so aggressively profane, may be neither comprehensive nor ultimate in itself. But this flash comes only once. . . . And for most of the story Tita is clearly before us as an oppressed and dingy spinster, clenched in the 'strange, soft coldness' of her aunt, and only beginning to learn (as Catherine Sloper learned, in **Washington Square**) that the authority even of well-intentioned guardians can be resented and resisted. (pp. 66-7)

The editor forces Tita, whose affections he only just suspects, to be his accomplice against the ailing Juliana. Juliana in turn tries to force Tita into the editor's arms—into the financial security which she knows her niece will need before long. It is revealing to watch how James, as always, uses money as one of the central principles of power, both for itself and for what it can represent. Tita is one of the impoverished and the meek. But Juliana makes the world pay, with a vengeance. The extortionate rent she charges the puzzled editor is an indicator of her price in ways that are also non-pecuniary. He finds such greed embarrassing in a woman of heroic associations, but it does suggest the way in which so many other sources and ends of human energy are concentrated in the Papers. Money becomes, as it were, the residue of passion and poetry for Juliana, and it, at least, can still trickle into her hoard. Her cupidity is a love of power and an appetite for survival, and it turns the superbly dramatic scene where she and the editor haggle over a 'price' for Aspern's portrait into a real battle to the death. Here is a desperate power game between them, full of bitter duplicity, gibes, and *doubles entendres*, and it is being played, figuratively speaking, for the highest possible stakes. Of course the money question is not all figurative—it is based very realistically on the uncomfortable facts of Tita's need for provision in the outside world. And Juliana's malevolent covetousness is not all a symbol of that ravening quality that so clearly attaches to the power of the Papers—she is also a merely stubborn and greedy old American expatriate, playing a bizarre game of hide-and-seek. Nevertheless, such an encounter cannot fail to touch on the important concept of paying and spending in wider terms. The story of the editor is the story of a man prepared to 'pay' so much, and no more; a man who expects sacrifices of others but who cannot expend himself. And he is a man, somewhere in his nature, who wishes to spend: who can at least invoke a world where great poets, lovers, and warriors spend greatly and dangerously, and had, in consequence, a great return. Juliana's greed is not only a vestige of the vitality that still flickers behind her mask; it is also, in the way she applies it, an instrument and a judgement against her enemy, the editor. The high 'price' she sets is to show her withering contempt for this unheroic and contemporary man, whom she sends scurrying to his bankers in a vain attempt to find a cash value equivalent to her life and her memories of Aspern. And the 'price' is so high for Juliana herself, and calls for such expenditure of emotional force in the defence of it, that it drives her into her last illness. (pp. 69-70)

[At the end of **The Aspern Papers**, there] are for us two measures of what the editor lost: one is moral, one in the widest sense aesthetic. One is expressed by Tita's forgiving 'soul' and his own not quite defunct conscience; the other by the power of poetry and love and Venice. The two worlds of value, though perennially different, have almost come together to offer the fullest of all fulfilments to this half-conscious Jamesian quester— Tita representing the chance of goodness, gentleness, affection, and marriage; *and* the quite other tradition of the Papers which she alone, symbolically at least, can transmit. To have suggested issues of such amplitude, and to have touched on the

sense of a larger existence towards which all separate insufficient people are impelled—this is the achievement and final justification of that witty grotesqueness of method which we began by considering. The method has been only another way of catching normal life off balance, through comedy, stylization, and exaggeration. . . . The editor, absurd and bungling human being that he is, is left with these two different but complementary glimpses of the power of this greater life that he has failed to purchase. One lies in his memory of Tita's long look of beatific farewell. And another view of it, we imagine, will continue to stare down at him from the worldly derisive eyes in the one thing he *has* purchased—the portrait above his desk of that latter-day *condottiere*, creator, and man of passion, Jeffrey Aspern. (p. 78)

> *Kenneth Graham, in his* Henry James, the Drama of Fulfilment: An Approach to the Novels *(© Oxford University Press and Kenneth Graham 1975; reprinted by permission of the author), Oxford at the Clarendon Press, Oxford, 1975, 234 p.*

DANIEL J. SCHNEIDER (essay date 1978)

[*Schneider's* The Crystal Cage: Adventures of the Imagination in the Fiction of Henry James *is an important study which attempts to determine the "single imaginative center" from which James's art unfolds. In the following excerpt, Schneider argues that James's fiction, at its very center, expresses his knowledge of the polarities of his own psyche, namely his "passive" ego and his "aggressive" alter ego. For Schneider, this dichotomy works itself out in James's fiction in a number of different forms, such as the innocent versus the experienced, the free spirit versus the established individual, or the spiritual versus the material. For other discussions of the major themes in James's work see the essays by Van Wyck Brooks and Andreas Osborn excerpted above.*]

If, as Willa Cather once remarked, all of a writer's most valuable material is acquired before he reaches the age of fifteen, Henry James's *A Small Boy and Others* might be expected to contain the richest material available both for shedding light on the personal problems with which James was concerned when he composed his fiction and for illuminating our understanding of the basic themes of his work. When we find, moreover, that his memoir tends to sound, in the most disparate contexts, a single note and to sound it emphatically, we may feel sure that our examination of the reverberations of that note is bound to yield immense insight into the manifest and latent content of his work. The note that hums most persistently through the pages of *A Small Boy and Others* is one of envy; and it is so far from being an unconscious motif of the memoir that James felt it necessary to devote two pages to an explicit analysis of his state of mind. (p. 18)

The inferiority complex is as common as grass, and there is no question that James was its victim. Nor was it the simple outgrowth of his sense that he was hopelessly behind his brother William, that he could not possibly catch up. That is a part of the story, and by no means . . . the least significant part; but what is equally plain, for James as well as for the reader of his memoir, is that he felt himself temperamentally debarred from "life," from action, from "going in" for things, from the "displeasing ferocity" of competition. There was, he tells us—in a phrase so pertinent to his case that he repeats it twice . . . : his "foreseen and foredoomed detachment"—his temperamental incapacity to give himself to anything, any cause, any person. Always he was to be the onlooker, "taking in" but, unlike his brother Wilky, incapable of "going in" for things and people. . . . (pp. 19-20)

[It] is when we turn to James's fiction that we see most strikingly the incorporation of the passivity-aggression equations of *A Small Boy and Others*. Merely to line up these equations is to see how directly and unvaryingly they are made to inform the fiction. The untyped and unformed observer versus his alter ego, the typed and formed man, the doer, the aggressor; the inconsistent, free, and rootless versus the consistent, fixed, established, or "placed"; the detached versus the attached; the impractical versus the practical; ineffectuality versus shrewdness, know-how, worldly acumen; stillness and passivity versus power, action, energy; tameness versus wildness and passion; the spiritual and inward versus the worldly and external or the hard and functional view of life; the tendency to give up or relinquish versus the tendency to take, seize, get: these are the very terms of conflict in James's fiction. And James's handling of these polarities is marked by a constant ambivalence—as we might well expect, based on the hypothesis that his fiction is the expression of his self-knowledge. For if he accepts that he is what he is and can be nothing else, and if, as artist, he feels proudly that he does "live" in his own way—and live intensely—that acceptance does not preclude his yearning to overcome his temperamental limitations and to give over the reins to his alter ego. More exactly, if he is inclined to side with the ego because of its superior breadth, detachment, openness, and freedom, he is also acutely aware that its passivity and tameness, its inclination to shrink from direct contact, constitute a terrible and dangerous limitation and that (as he remarks in his Preface to the New York edition of *The Spoils of Poynton*) the free spirit is all too often " 'successful' only through having remained free." In a world in which the fittest survive, the alter ego obviously has awesome advantages

What is most pertinent to our understanding of James's fiction is that the relationship between the two selves is almost invariably seen as that of the hunter and his prey, the trapper and the trapped; and what is equally important is that James presses, whenever the normal probabilities of the situation permit—and increasingly in his later fiction—to effect a reversal of positions, so that the hunter becomes the hunted and vice versa. Much of his later fiction may in fact be viewed as an elaborate paradigm of the situation in **"The Jolly Corner,"** that remarkable story which has inevitably engaged the attention of biographers and critics. The hero in that tale, Spencer Brydon, returns to America to put his property in order and discovers, to his surprise, that he has a "real gift" for practical affairs . . .—a mastery so great, in fact, that he falls to wondering what might have been had he remained in America and chosen business as a career. . . . [Seized] by his fascination with his alter ego, he begins to revisit the old house in which he had lived in order to track down his fiercer self. But is he the hunter or the hunted? James plays with the question, and if Brydon at first feels himself to be "some monstrous stealthy cat" prowling after "the poor hard-pressed *alter ego*" . . . , the tables are presently turned; and it is he who becomes the prey stalked by his alter ego. (pp. 32-3)

In discussing . . . the problem of the confrontation with the alter ego, most critics have so far focused on a few of James's stories, those in which the alter ego is unmistakably identified by James as alter ego. Yet it requires very little extrapolating, I think, to see that virtually all of his fiction is concerned with just that confrontation. The conflict is developed, in the main, between those worldly people who "know how"—the manip-

ulators, the arrangers, the enslavers, who seek to seize and appropriate everything for themselves—and those innocent and unhardened souls who, unable to operate effectively in the world, can counter the assault of their enemies, their enslavers, only by learning a strange method of resistance: the renunciation and sacrifice of their material interests. James's typical hero is, as we might expect, almost invariably the victim: he is acted upon, he does not himself act until he is driven to the wall by an evil, predacious worldliness. He gives, they take; he renounces, they make the most of their opportunities. Yet again and again the mild, "feminine," helpless victim displays an unexpected strength, and the aggressors, far from looking formidable, are exposed in the end as "small," "sterile," "dead," "old," or cowardly. The victim, neither weak nor enslaved, is revealed as large, virile, youthful, and free. And if, at the end, the hero comes away empty-handed, it is clear that he might have triumphed on his own terms. What prevents him from doing so is both his refusal or inability to accept the world's premises and a moral strength so abundant that generosity is its spontaneous issue.

The permutations of the conflict are, of course, often very subtle, and as I have indicated, the ego is by no means regarded with total sympathy, nor the alter ego with a total lack of sympathy. . . . But the essential pattern perdures in tale after tale, from the beginning to the end of James's career. There are, however, some interesting developments in the way James handles the hero's response to aggression. In the early tales the characteristic response tends to be the renunciation of the hero and his removal from the world of action: a sort of symbolic recognition that functioning in such a world, on the terms established by the grasping, active people of the earth, is simply impossible. After 1890, however, the hero's response increasingly exhibits a determination to fight for whatever is at stake in the action—to employ, indeed, all the tactics of the aggressors and to turn the tables whenever the normal probabilities of the story permit. And this shift from renunciation and retirement from life to active fighting testifies eloquently to the change in James's state of mind during these years.

To trace these transformations of plot-structure and symbolism in his fiction is to trace, at one remove, the darkening of James's vision of life, the progressive deepening of his "imagination of disaster." One witnesses his growing conviction that all of life is a fight and that evil arises even in conduct apparently innocent or noble. Behind apparently benign and unselfish conduct James discerns the shadow of rapacious egotism, a will to power, an instinct of territoriality. But as he penetrates into this heart of darkness, he continues to work with the passivity-aggression equations of his earliest work; his evaluation of passivity, however, is subtly altered.

In the first place, an apparently innocent and passive victim may be seen to be, in his own way, quite as capable of exemplifying "ferocious and sinister" qualities as are aggressive and active people. Indeed, James discovers that the victim's passivity in the face of aggression, his renunciation or retirement from the battle of life, is also a great evil—a monstrous beast in the jungle. To shrink from the battle, to retreat into some sanctuary of peace and safety, even as the artist retreats into his world of fictions—is this not in truth a desire to regress to Nirvana, to the paradisaical state of the infant, to seek omnipotence in a self-created world, free from all the "responsibility of freedom"? Passivity, then, so far from eliciting sympathy, becomes the strategy of egotists, queer monsters who wish to live effortlessly in the perfect safety of their self-created world, imposing their wills on a static world that offers no threat whatsoever.

In the second place, James develops his imagery and symbolism in such a way as to reveal that the active, aggressive people are really even more "passive" than the inactive. Despite all the ferocity and bullying of the "great active ones of earth—active for evil," their very acceptance of the ways of the world, their surrender to the world, "ferocious and sinister" as it is, is a form of passivity and marks them as stamped-out products of the time-machine of the world or as caged beasts in the great trap of life—the great round material earth, the circus, the show, the *bousculade*. Thus the villains are exposed as helpless in their passivity. And passivity, whether in the victimized ego or in the aggressive alter ego, becomes, I believe, the greatest of evils in James's work, especially in his last novels. (pp. 34-6)

> *Daniel J. Schneider, in his* The Crystal Cage: Adventures of the Imagination in the Fiction of Henry James *(copyright © 1978 The Regents Press of Kansas), Regents Press of Kansas, 1978, 189 p.*

EDWARD WAGENKNECHT   (essay date 1983)

[*The following survey of James's middle or "transitional" novels is drawn from Wagenknecht's* The Novels of Henry James, *a comprehensive study of James's entire career as a novelist.*]

Compared to the three great monuments of James's "later manner"—*The Ambassadors, The Wings of the Dove,* and *The Golden Bowl—What Maisie Knew* is still a "short" novel (361 pages of the New York Edition . . .), but although it was written not long after its predecessor [*The Spoils of Poynton*], it is considerably more "advanced." It is also more difficult. Thus while there is no excuse whatever for the eccentric readings of *Poynton* with which we have been blessed of late, it is only fair to say that James must bear some share of responsibility for the less extensive mauling to which *Maisie* has been subjected, for he has left in shadow a number of matters about which he might, without injury to his story or his method, have been more explicit. As with *Hamlet,* so with *Maisie;* one may find a sentence somewhere to bolster almost any misreading, however obtuse, and James is without Shakespeare's excuse that we have three texts of his play but no authorized text. (p. 152)

In *What Maisie Knew* James attempted to paint a picture of a corrupt society as seen by a child and at the same time to trace the child's own development toward spiritual maturity. His original idea was to limit his presentation to what Maisie "might be conceived to have *understood,*" but he soon realized that she was too young for that; consequently, although his "*line*" remained her "dim, sweet, sacred, wondering, clinging perception," he included also what she *saw* without understanding and employed a variety of devices to supplement and interpret her perceptions. Although there are still a few glaring instances of old-fashioned direct authorial comment ("Oh, decidedly I shall never get you to believe the number of things she saw and the number of secrets she discovered!"), such passages stand in the sharpest possible contrast to his highly sophisticated employment of "suppressed scenes and indirect discourse" to achieve "variety in his handling of scenes."

One asks oneself whether all the relationships portrayed in this novel, all the minute reactions of the characters, and all their kaleidoscopic regroupings are convincing. Personally I do not

believe they are, but I am not sure the question is relevant. James admits in his preface that it was in the interest of symmetry that he had *both* Maisie's parents remarry. We are, I think, never made to feel what it was in Ida that attracted so many lovers nor how she could have enthralled such decent men as Sir Claude and the unnamed Captain, and it is equally hard to believe that both she and Sir Claude and Beale and Miss Overman should begin to be estranged from each other almost as soon as they are married. If we must have literary analogues for the kind of pattern James seems to be working out, let them be sought not in the realistic novel but in Restoration comedy or French classical tragedy or, better still, in the formations and figurations of classical ballet.

The attempts which F. R. Leavis and others have made to interpret *Maisie* as essentially comic are hopelessly one-sided; a book which eventuates in spiritual victory for the heroine and spiritual failure for almost everybody else can amuse neither God nor the devil. Nevertheless, the author has made abundant use of subordinate comic devices, sometimes embracing broad caricature. . . . Aside from one of Ida's lovers, Mr. Perriam, whom we glimpse only in passing, the most daring caricature is that of the "brown" countess whom Beale has descended to living upon at the end. . . . But caricature appears also in the description of Maisie's parents. (pp. 154-56)

Maisie's governess, Mrs. Wix, is, however, in this novel, James's greatest grotesque. . . . James uses every device Dickens would have used in describing Mrs. Wix except one; he does not invent a distinctive speech for her. . . . Mrs. Wix has her limitations as both an intellectual and a moral guide, but when the chips are down, she stands with the sheep, not the goats; it is all the more interesting, then, that James should not have refused to see the comic side of either her much-vaunted "moral sense" or her devotion to the memory of her daughter, Clara Matilda, who had been killed in traffic and for whom Maisie must in a measure act as surrogate. (pp. 156-57)

But what, then, *did* Maisie know? James plays a cat-and-mouse game with the idea, comparable to that of Henry Adams with education. And this not only makes for the difficulty of the book but determines its method. From first to last, the pages of the novel are studded with passages reflecting childish innocence. (p. 158)

On the other hand, she sometimes shows an insight and even prescience that reveals her as being in unconscious possession of a wisdom as old as the everlasting hills. The most touching example is in the great, powerfully underplayed scene in Chapter 17 in which she has her only encounter with the Captain, who seems to have been the most decent and deluded of her mother's many lovers. Having learned that he thinks Ida an angel and likes her better than any other woman, Maisie begs him not to love her "only for just a little," like "all the others," but to "do it always." This wonderful hit seems to have killed two birds with one stone, for when Maisie innocently mentions the Captain to Ida in Chapter 21 and Ida must make an effort to recall him as "the biggest cad in London," the reader understands that the girl has done both his and her mother's business for them. (p. 159)

What Maisie Knew ends when Sir Claude asks Maisie whether she would give up Mrs. Wix to live with him and Mrs. Beale. Being afraid of herself, she first asks time to consider and then declares that she will not go with him unless he gives up Mrs. Beale. (p. 160)

If the illicit nature of the tie between Sir Claude and Mrs. Beale has created the problem Maisie faces at the end, it must be understood both that she is not yet fully aware of all the implications of this and that her judgments, unlike those of Mrs. Wix, do not rest upon a strictly legalistic basis. By this time her "moral sense" has developed beyond that of her preceptress, whom she now needs only for mothering. James says that at last she knew what she wanted; I should say rather that she knows what she *needs*. There is more intuition than reason in her judgments, and being still a child, she could not be expected to explain them fully. But she *has* learned that people go together in twos, not threes, and (as her conversation with the Captain shows) that a dignifying and satisfactory relationship can exist only on a basis of permanency and fidelity. These qualities may be lacking, of course, in legalized as well as unlegalized relationships, as, notably, in those which Maisie has known thus far. She has already been disillusioned about Mrs. Beale, and she is in the process of being disillusioned about her erstwhile knight in shining armor, Sir Claude. In a sense, the proposition she places before him, is, whether she realizes it or not, part of a testing process. She has no desire to become part of a setup which would share the characteristics of those of which she has already seen far too much. (pp. 161-62)

Like its two immediate predecessors, [*The Awkward Age*] was conceived as a short story, but this time the beginning was not an anecdote or a situation but merely an idea and what must strike us today as a trifling, snobbish, and hypocritical idea at that. What happens to the "good talk" in the fashionable drawing room when the adolescent daughter, having outgrown the nursery, begins to "sit downstairs" but being still unmarried, is not supposed to know what her elders are talking about? Must the good talk be so expurgated to avoid bringing what Mr. Podsnap called the blush to the cheek of the young person? If so, what becomes of the level of sophistication? And if not, what becomes of her innocence? In France the problem could not arise, for the girl would be in a convent school until she was married and so passed at a bound from knowing nothing to knowing everything, nor yet in America, where talk was never "good" in the sophisticated English fashion. (pp. 162-63)

The Awkward Age represents the height of James's interest in "method," and his satisfaction in it seems to have derived from the conviction that he had so triumphantly brought it off. It is divided into what [Oscar] Cargill calls "ten books or acts and thirty-eight scenes" (James planned it all out almost mathematically), and there is no central reflective consciousness. Instead each book is named for one of the characters, intended to furnish what James calls a "lamp" to illuminate the action. (pp. 164-65)

In the predecessor of this novel, James had tormented his readers with the riddle of what Maisie *knew*. Here we are not so much concerned with that (Nanda obviously knows everything) as with whether she has been corrupted by what she knows and her contacts with immoral people, and even more with what must be the effect of all this upon her eligibility as a *parti* in the marriage market. Since nobody has ever suggested that she is either dishonest or unchaste, this may well strike modern readers as even more much ado about nothing than the basic problem or situation with which James began. The only thing Nanda is ever convicted of in the course of the action comes when her mother forces her to admit that she had read what was considered an indecent French novel, and since she did

that only to find out whether it was fit to be read by her friend Tishy Grendon, who certainly needed no protection from her, this act shows her up as rather naive than corrupted. (pp. 166-67)

James deliberately deglamourizes Nanda. She has "no features" unless she has "two or three too many," and it is a question whether she is pretty at all. She lacks not only her mother's grace but humor and brightness also; at one point Mrs. Brook calls her "as bleak as a chimney-top when the fire's out." But her loyalties are absolute; degradation in others does not repel her; neither does she resent slights that have been shown to herself. Nanda does not love sinners for their sins but because they need loving. Her plea to Van not to desert her mother because "she's so lovely" and "so fearfully young" is even more touching because she is more fully aware of what she is saying than Maisie in her plea to the Captain. . . . She even begs Mr. Longdon to see to it that Van shall not lose financially by having turned down the endowment Mr. Longdon proposed to supply him with because he could not bring himself to take her along with the money! And it is quite clear that young as she is, she is going to be a mother to Mr. Longdon quite as much as he will be a father to her.

Mitchy's marrying Little Aggie to please Nanda would be more at home in a book like *Wuthering Heights,* where Cathy marries Linton to help Heathcliff, than in the at least outwardly realistic *Awkward Age,* but although Mitchy is not so "pure" as Nanda, he does share her charity. . . . Van is another story; for all his charm, his behavior at the end leaves room for nothing but contempt. . . . Although he quite lacks Gilbert Osmond's capacity for deliberate cruelty, he is like him in his hopeless conventionality and his inability to distinguish between the real and the apparent, and Dorothea Krook may well be right when she suggests that he would not be capable of living with a woman whose judgment and sense of values were superior to his own. What he really likes is the old-fashioned girl, but it is his pride, not purity, that causes Nanda to repel him; he could not bear to mate with a girl coming out of her environment so precious a creature as himself.

One of James's most surprising self-judgments is his special enthusiasm over Mrs. Brook, whom he . . . considered the best thing he had ever done, and some of the critics have been eager to outdo him on this score, comparing her to the great ladies of Restoration comedy and seeing her as an artist molding her environment into a work of art. It is true that Mrs. Brook is not the worst member of her circle; I agree that she is almost certainly not an adulteress (most of the adultery in this novel is committed by characters on the border of the circle); neither is she personally unsympathetic or cruel. But the higher one rates her potentialities, the deeper must be the condemnation she incurs for her useless life; indeed, as she herself perceives at one point, the fact that passion is absent even deprives her of an excuse she might otherwise have had. Surely those who have praised the intellectuality of her circle are easily impressed in this area. The only justification for such a judgment is that these people are all immensely preoccupied with analyzing each other's motives and reactions, often in disreputable situations. There is never the slightest suggestion that any of them ever had what could be called an idea in their lives or that they had ever manifested any interest in anything affecting the vital interest or general welfare of mankind. Mrs. Brook is greedy and morally indifferent (she even wants her daughter's life "to be as much as possible like my own") and her only real concern is to keep intact a circle of friends, if you can call them that, most of whom are even more useless than herself.

The basic idea for *The Sacred Fount* . . . posited a marriage between a young man and older woman, after which she bloomed and he languished, growing progressively older and weaker as she grew younger, stronger, and prettier. James promptly considered combining this with the experience of a second pair of this time unmarried lovers, exhibiting a once dull man who has drained the wit from a clever woman, the transformation in both persons being the means through which the liaison comes to light. (pp. 167-70)

The Sacred Fount resembles *The Awkward Age* in being developed largely in terms of a series of dialogues but differs from it in that these interchanges are both linked and interpreted by the unnamed narrator (it is the only novel by James, as distinguished from many short stories, written in the first person). This aids our understanding if we are willing to be guided by him but increases our difficulty if, with his antagonist Mrs. Brissenden (generally called Mrs. Briss), we think or pretend to think him crazy or, with some of the critics, envisage James as a concocter of puzzles who entrusted his readers only to guides who might lead them astray. Although J. A. Ward goes entirely too far when he tells us that we cannot even be sure whether the narrator is a man or a woman, it is true that we receive no information that has not been filtered through his consciousness; we have only his word not only for what the others do but for much of what they say, for he tells his story in retrospect and, as he informs us, sometimes paraphrases. (p. 172)

The Sacred Fount is generally regarded as James's most difficult novel, and even some of his admirers have called it unreadable. . . . The difficulty has been much exaggerated, however. It arises not from the style, which is clear enough, but from the intense concentration demanded and from James's insistence that readers interpret for themselves phenomena which admit of more than one interpretation instead of depending upon the author to do it for them. Consequently, the novel has been read as a vampire story . . . a spiritual detective story, and a study of how fiction is created, this last sometimes running over into the absurd notion that the author is burlesquing himself. (p. 174)

If there is any one thing in the novel that is more obscure than everything else, it is the haunting, sinister picture of "The Man with the Mask." . . . (p. 175)

This surely is an impressive use of symbolism which might well hold the key to the meaning of the book, but if so, neither the characters nor the critics have been able to turn the lock. The people looking at the picture seem agreed at least that the man looks like "poor Briss" and the mask like May Server, but there is no agreement as to whether the man is life and the mask death, if that is what they mean, or vice versa; Mrs. Server takes the first view, and the narrator the second. In any case the scene has a strange and eerie power. It seems odd that the reader should be so much affected by something so opaque—unless indeed that is the very reason.

The unnamed narrator is by all means the most important character, and since we know about the others only through him, perhaps it is not surprising either that there should be such a wide range of opinion about him or that so many should have made a pretty good job out of judging themselves through attempting to judge him. The range is indeed extraordinary, stretching all the way from the notion of a sneaking, sniveling Paul Pry or voyeur, through a deluded, pride-blinded fool attempting to play providence, or even, as Mrs. Briss, almost certainly insincerely, puts it at last, a lunatic, to an embodiment of the creative spirit of the artist. (pp. 175-76)

Our attitude toward the narrator necessarily determines what we believe about his antagonist, Mrs. Briss, and our interpretation of the interview between them which fills the last three of the book's fourteen chapters. To me nothing is clearer than that Mrs. Briss is another of James's great evil women and that in this scene she is completely mendacious and insincere. She denies everything she had previously affirmed and affirms everything she had previously denied. She now describes Gilbert Long as the same "poor fool" he had always been, although she had remarked the change in him even before the narrator noticed it, and denies that May Server had ever had any connection with him. (p. 179)

If the narrator is right in his hypothesis that May Server has been used as badly by Long as "poor Briss" has been used by his wife, that the two victims have now turned to each other for comfort while the two victimizers have embarked upon a fresh liaison with each other (which would be as neat a piece of Jamesian symmetry as anything in *What Maisie Knew*), and if Mrs. Briss now feels reasonably certain that the narrator is in the process of figuring all this out (he has certainly been giving her daring though ambiguous hints in this direction for some time), she has abundant reason for seeking the midnight interview with her antagonist, for her complete change of front when she encounters him, and for her bad manners toward him. Otherwise the whole situation is inexplicable.

But why, then, it may be asked, the contrived ambiguity of the ending? Why especially the last two sentences: "I *should* certainly never again, on the spot, quite hang together, even though it wasn't really that I hadn't three times her method. What I fatally lacked was her tone." This need not necessarily mean anything more than, as Ora Segal suggests, that "all the narrator admits is that he cannot match her brashness, insolence, and effrontery." Joan of Arc, I suppose, lacked the "tone" of the tribunal that sent her to the stake, but that did not prove them right nor her wrong. We must face the fact that there are many circumstances under which the children of light cannot look for anything but defeat by the children of darkness, simply because there are weapons that the children of light cannot use without undoing themselves. (pp. 180-81)

Edward Wagenknecht, in his The Novels of Henry James *(copyright © 1983 by Edward Wagenknecht), Frederick Ungar Publishing Co., 1983, 329 p.*

ADDITIONAL BIBLIOGRAPHY

Anderson, Quentin. *The American Henry James.* New Brunswick, N.J.: Rutgers University Press, 1957, 369 p.
   Biocritical examination which attempts to show that James's work was greatly influenced by his father's philosophical thought.

Beach, Joseph Warren. *The Method of Henry James.* Philadelphia: Albert Saifer, 1954, 289 p.
   One of the earliest full-length critiques of the narrative technique of James's major novels.

Bowden, Edwin T. *The Themes of Henry James: A System of Observation through the Visual Arts.* New Haven: Yale University Press, 1956, 115 p.
   Thematic study that interprets the central themes in James's fiction through a "system of observation" based on the novelist's use of the visual arts.

Brooks, Cleanth. "The American 'Innocence' in James, Fitzgerald, and Faulkner." In his *A Shaping Joy: Studies in the Writer's Craft*, pp. 181-97. London: Methuen & Co., 1971.*
Thematic examination of the "American innocent" as developed by James in *The American*, by F. Scott Fitzgerald in *The Great Gatsby*, and by William Faulkner in *Absalom! Absalom!*

Brownell, W. C. "Henry James." In his *American Prose Masters: Cooper, Hawthorne, Emerson, Poe, Lowell, Henry James*, pp. 280-332. New York: Charles Scribner's Sons, 1923.
Concise examination of James's method, his philosophy, his influence, as well as a discussion of many of his novels.

Canby, Henry Seidel. *Turn West, Turn East: Mark Twain and Henry James*. Boston: Houghton Mifflin Co., 1951, 318 p.*
Biocritical and comparative study of the personalities and the art of James and Mark Twain, specifically with respect to their American heritage.

Cary, Elisabeth Luther. *The Novels of Henry James: A Study*. New York: Haskell House, 1964, 215 p.
Critical study detailing a number of different aspects of James's fiction, including his characterization, his imagination, and his philosophy.

Cook, David A., and Corrigan, Timothy J. "Narrative Structure in *The Turn of the Screw*: A New Approach to Meaning." *Studies in Short Fiction* 17, No. 1 (Winter 1980): 55-65.
A structuralist interpretation of *The Turn of the Screw*.

Donadio, Stephen. *Nietzsche, Henry James, and the Artistic Will*. New York: Oxford University Press, 1978, 347 p.*
Comparative discussion of the aesthetics of both James and Friedrich Neitzsche, focusing on the similarities in their vision of art "as the only activity capable of creating values and raising experience from insignificance."

Edel, Leon. *Henry James*. 5 vols. Philadelphia and New York: J. B. Lippincott Co., 1953-72.
Definitive biography. Edel's five-volume biography, for which he was awarded the Pulitzer Prize, traces James's life and career as a writer in five separate stages: 1843 to 1870, 1870 to 1881, 1882 to 1895, 1895 to 1901, and 1901 to 1916.

Falk, Robert. "The Tragic Muse: Henry James's Loosest, Baggiest Novel?" In *Themes and Directions in American Literature: Essays in Honor of Leon Howard*, edited by Ray B. Browne and Donald Pizer, pp. 148-62. Lafayette, Ind.: Purdue University Studies, 1969.
Structural examination arguing that *The Tragic Muse*—despite the opinion of such critics as Edmund Wilson, Leon Edel, and F. W. Dupee—is not a sprawling or uneven novel, but a structurally cohesive work.

Goode, John, ed. *The Air of Reality: New Essays on Henry James*. London: Methuen & Co., 1972, 368 p.
Collection of nine critical essays on those novels by James which the editor believes have been seriously neglected or poorly interpreted in recent years.

Holland, Laurence Bedwell. *The Expense of Vision: Essays on the Craft of Henry James*. Princeton: Princeton University Press, 1964, 414 p.
Interpretive study. Holland treats a number of James's novels and examines the manner in which his imagery, his plots, his symbolism—in short his imagination—defines the structure and development of his stories.

Jefferson, D. W. *Henry James and the Modern Reader*. New York: St. Martin's Press, 1964, 240 p.
Critical study that focuses on James's later novels, suggesting ways of reading the novelist which will help eliminate many of the problems associated with these works.

Kappeler, Susanne. *Writing and Reading in Henry James*. New York: Columbia University Press, 1980, 242 p.
Critical and theoretical study that offers a "creative reading" of two of James's most unusual works: *The Aspern Papers* and *The Sacred Fount*.

Poirier, Richard. *The Comic Sense of Henry James: A Study of the Early Novels*. New York: Columbia University Press, 1960, 260 p.
Study that focuses on James's dependence on "melodrama" and "comic extravagance" in such early works as *Roderick Hudson*, *The Americans*, *Washington Square*, and *The Portrait of a Lady*.

Seltzer, Mark. "*The Princess Casamassima*: Realism and the Fantasy of Surveillance." *Nineteenth-Century Fiction* 35, No. 4 (March 1981): 506-34.
Interpretive study of covert activities in *The Princess Casamassima*.

Tompkins, Jane P., ed. *Twentieth-Century Interpretations of "The Turn of the Screw" and Other Tales*. Englewood Cliffs, N.J.: Prentice-Hall, 1970, 115 p.
Collection of critical essays on *The Turn of the Screw* and a number of James's other popular short tales, such as "The Real Thing" and "The Figure in the Carpet."

Veeder, William. *Henry James—the Lessons of the Master: Popular Fiction and Personal Style in the Nineteenth Century*. Chicago and London: The University of Chicago Press, 1975, 287 p.
Critical study that discusses the different literary traditions which influenced James and analyzes the manner in which "he transformed those materials into great art."

Pierre Loti

1850-1923

(Pseudonym of Louis Marie Julien Viaud) French novelist, short story writer, essayist, diarist, dramatist, and autobiographer.

Described by Lafcadio Hearn as "the most romantic of the romantics," Loti was one of the foremost impressionistic writers in nineteenth-century French literature. A prolific writer of exotic romance literature, seafaring adventures, and travel essays, he is most often praised for sensuous descriptions of foreign lands and cultures. Although Loti earned an international reputation with such melancholic idylls of exotic love as *Aziyade* and *Le mariage de Loti (Rarahu; or, The Marriage of Loti)*, it is his unromanticized novel about Breton fishermen, *Pêcheur d'Islande (An Iceland Fisherman)*, that is considered his masterpiece.

Born in Rochefort, France, Loti was raised in a pious household dominated by an over-protective mother. His autobiographical work *Le roman d'un enfant (A Child's Romance)* nostalgically recounts his family life and expresses his longing to return to the innocence and security of childhood, a common motif found throughout his work. For the most part, his early education consisted of private tutelage in the classics and Bible readings. In 1866, following the tradition of his family, Loti entered the French naval academy at Brest; two years later he embarked on his first voyage around the world. Inspired by the exotic environments and experiences of his travels, Loti recorded his impressions in diaries and letters that were to become the basis for his early novels. In 1879, while he continued his naval career, he published his first novel, *Aziyadé*. A lightly disguised account of his love affair with a woman of a Turkish harem, the work conveys dream-like impressions of their romance. In addition, *Aziyadé* calls attention to Loti's propensity for assimilating himself into a foreign culture; as he did in real life for a short time, he assumes the identity of a Turk in the novel. His most popular early work, *The Marriage of Loti*, is an exotic and imaginative rendition of his sojourn on the island of Tahiti and the erotic love he encounters there. This sentimental work depicts the deterioration of the primal Polynesian culture after its exposure to Western civilization. On another level, *The Marriage of Loti* symbolizes Loti's concern with life's disillusionments after childhood innocence is lost. Similarly, *Le roman d'un Spahi (The Romance of a Spahi)* continues Loti's exoticism as it describes his intense liaison with a Creole girl and his painful love affair with a married woman. While his personal experiences shape *The Romance of a Spahi*, it is the first novel in which he is not clearly the protagonist—an important stage in Loti's artistic development.

According to critics, Loti's maturity as a writer is represented by his stories of Breton fishermen. The first of these, *Mon frère Yves (My Brother Yves)*, is less melodramatic and more realistic than his earlier works and describes a drunken sailor's battle with alcoholism. Loti's next novel, *An Iceland Fisherman*, is considered his most masterful work. With characters modeled on people he knew, the novel describes the hardships endured by sailors and the families who wait for their return. In this work, there are no exotic settings to provide escape,

only the harsh realities of life at sea and the simplistic tenets of life in Brittany. In addition it contains evocative descriptions of the sea which, according to some critics, often surpass the seascapes of Joseph Conrad. The novel realistically depicts the struggle of a small group of Bretons against the sea, while symbolically it evokes every individual's psychological and spiritual struggles.

Loti's travel essays form a substantial part of his works. The essays offered turn-of-the-century readers the opportunity to experience the mystique of foreign lands as Loti had encountered them. His impressions, recorded in such works as *Au Maroc (Morocco)* and *L'Inde (sans les Anglais) (India)*, imparted not only colorful visual descriptions, but conveyed emotional sentiments stirred by strange lands and a desire to preserve their cultures. Some critics have noted that many of the essays recounting Loti's global wanderings, such as *Le désert (The Sahara)*, *Jérusalem (Jerusalem)*, and *La Galilée*, indicate the Frenchman's search to regain a meaningful religious ethic and the security he knew as a child.

Loti enjoyed both popular and critical acclaim during his career, and was elected to the French Academy in 1892 as a man of letters. The popularity of his novels and essays in his lifetime is attributed to the receptiveness of his readers to explore new environments and escape the dissonance inherent in a changing world. Though Loti is often unfavorably criticized for the lack of characterization and plot in his works, most commentators regard him as a master of impressionism whose voluptuous prose artfully depicts the exotic settings of his works. Loti's biographer Edmund D'Auvergne echoes the critical consensus: "He imparts to everything, men and things, such an intensity to life, such relief, so much movement and so much colour, that we do not read them, we see them." While Loti's reputation has diminished through the years, his works stand as the embodiment of a spirit that longed to escape to a simpler, more primitive time. For this reason, and for his sensuous blend of the romantic and the exotic to create his artful impressions, Loti remains a significant anomaly in French literature.

(See also *Contemporary Authors*, Vol. 107.)

PRINCIPAL WORKS

Aziyadé (novel) 1879

Le mariage de Loti (novel) 1880
　[*Rarahu, or, The Marriage of Loti*, 1882]

Le roman d'un Spahi (novel) 1881
　[*The Romance of a Spahi*, 1890]

Fleurs d'ennui (novel) 1883

Mon frère Yves (novel) 1883
　[*My Brother Yves*, 1887]

Pêcheur d'Islande (novel) 1886
　[*An Iceland Fisherman*, 1888]

Madame Chrysanthème (novel) 1887
　[*Madame Chrysanthème*, 1892]

Au Maroc (travel essay) 1890
　[*Morocco*, 1914]

Le roman d'un enfant (autobiography) 1890
　[*A Child's Romance*, 1891]

Le livre de la pitié et de la mort (essays) 1891
　[*The Book of Pity and Death*, 1892]

Matelot (novel) 1893

Oeuvre complètes. 11 vols. (novels and travel essays)
　1893-1911

Le désert (travel essay) 1895
　[*The Sahara*, 1921]

Jérusalem (travel essay) 1895
　[*Jerusalem*, 1916]

La Galilée (travel essay) 1896

Ramuntcho (novel) 1897
　[*Ramuntcho*, 1897]

Les derniers jours de Pékin (travel essay) 1902
　[*The Last Days of Pekin*, 1902]

L'Inde (sans les Anglais) (travel essay) 1903
　[*India*, 1907]

*Les désenchantees: Roman des Harems Turcs
　Contemporains* (novel) 1906
　[*Disenchanted*, 1906]

Un Pèlerin d'Angkor (travel essay) 1912

L'horreur Allemande (essays) 1918

Un jeune officier pauvre (autobiography) 1923
　[*Pierre Loti: Notes of My Youth*, 1924]

Journal intime 1878-1881, Vol. 1 (diary) 1925

Journal intime 1882-1885, Vol. 2 (diary) 1929

Stories from Pierre Loti (travel essays) 1933

LAFCADIO HEARN　(essay date 1883)

[*An American journalist, author, and critic, Hearn was one of the first to translate and introduce to American readers many of the rising French writers of the time, such as Émile Zola, Guy de Maupassant, Paul Bourget, and Loti. Especially enthusiastic about Loti's works, Hearn shared a common artistic bond with him: both writers employed impressionistic techniques in their works and familiarized readers with the exotic cultures of other lands. Of Loti, he stated:* "I hold him the greatest of living writers of the Impressionist School. . . ."]

[To] those who know [Pierre Loti's] books, it is almost exasperating to find in every fresh review of recent French literature, the most elaborate notices of fourth-rate *feuilletonistes*, and not a syllable about one who ranks in some respects higher than Gustave Flaubert, and whose work contains beauties of color comparable to the rich word-painting of Gautier. No other writer has really trodden upon his domain; he has cultivated a virgin soil, and invented for its cultivation a style so peculiarly his own, that it is only susceptible of comparison with other styles according to the force of the impression it produces. (p. 126)

Aziyadé [Loti's first romance] was the history of an amour between a European officer and the inmate of a Constantinople harem,—a theme that might not seem particularly novel. But the whole treatment of the episode was supremely original, and the vividness of the Oriental pictures surprising. There were evidences of remarkable personal research in almost every page—delightful sketches of Turkish interiors,—curious notes of Oriental superstition and customs,—microscopic details concerning things no other European had mentioned,—portraits of *hamals*, interpreters, dervishes, boatmen of the Golden Horn,—singular conversations in Turkish and French,—above all such painting of skies and clouds and shadows and colors as revealed the feeling of a master-artist. Much pathos and passion also—perhaps too much, enough to reveal the heart of a very young man, urged rather by an irresistible desire of self-expansion than by the desire to become known. (pp. 127-28)

The charm of [*Le Mariage de Loti*] is simply inexpressible; its beauty is as essentially exotic as the scenes which it paints,—but its fancies are replete with that inimitable, unutterable weirdness which characterizes the Breton mind; and Lucien Viaud [Pierre Loti] is of Brittany! Only Doré could have illustrated the strange lights and shadows of the narrative. The scenes are laid in Polynesia—"latitude 16° south, longitude 154° west"; and the perusal of all accounts of voyages made to such regions could not give so vivid an idea of those landscapes "never created for European eyes to see, for European imagination to dwell upon." The romance is rich in linguistic curiosities also; Loti has chosen with admirable art the most singular words in the language of the islands, and expounded their astonishing meanings; he has published also a collection of pathetic and beautiful letters in the dialect of Tahiti. These letters seem authentic; and indeed the whole story has a verisimilitude which is nothing short of painful. The last chapter is not only an agony of pathos, but an agony made awful by contrasts so weird and supernatural fancies so ghostly that no idea could be formed of it by those who have not read the book. It creates an impression not to be forgotten in a lifetime:—nothing like it has been written by any other. The vision of the shadowy island with its phantom-palms,—the spectral ship bearing the dreamer noiselessly over a silent sea,—the ghostly sun,—the dead face that laughs with the laugh of a skull,—would form of themselves one of the most eldritch pictures conceived by a modern brain; but all this anguish of the fancy is suddenly intensified almost to the point of torture by the memory of the letter:—*O my dear little friend, O my perfumed flower of evening, great is the pain in my heart because I cannot see thee!—O my star of the morning, mine eyes melt in tears at the thought thou will never return. . . .*

This exquisite romance succeeded, created a well deserved artistic sensation, sold largely in spite of the rage then prevailing for naturalistic literature. And Loti is the most romantic of Romantics; he has shown that true art can prevail in despite of naturalistic innovations.

Not less remarkable was his next effort [*Le Roman d'un Spahi*]. . . . Such luminous pictures of Africa,—such strange and startling colors, as of desert sunsets,—such monstrous landscapes and fantastic incidents as he paints in this book must have been studied on the spot. In fact, Viaud was not only long in Senegal, but accompanied military expeditions against the negro kings of the unknown interior. He again displays in this sinister romance his capacity for curious linguistic study; and exhibits with not less surprising power the same old Breton weirdness of fancy, the same magic of pathos. (pp. 128-30)

Probably [Viaud] will have no successor in his special quality of exotic novelist; for such experiences as he describes are possible only to those who lead a seafaring life. But his style will certainly be studied and imitated by a new school of romantic writers, and will endure when the works of the Naturalists will survive only as morbid curiosities. . . . [For] he is certainly destined to shine as a great light in the modern world of fiction, unless carried off prematurely by some marine disaster or mishap of war. In his last book a certain strange horror of death is manifested—such a horror as only those can know the fullness of who have beheld the wonders of the most wonderful lands, the most marvelous miracles of nature. To the deep thinker, so intimately and awfully are Life and Death connected, that where he beholds the mightiest manifestations of the evolution of being, there also is he most poignantly reminded of the inevitable and universal law of ultimate dissolution. (pp. 131-32)

> Lafcadio Hearn, "*A New Romantic*" (*originally published in the* New Orleans Times-Democrat, *September 23, 1883*), *in his* Essays in European and Oriental Literature, *edited by Albert Mordell* (*copyright, 1923, by Dodd, Mead and Company, Inc.*), *Dodd, Mead, 1923, pp. 125-32.*

HENRY JAMES   (essay date 1888)

[*As a novelist James is valued for psychological acuity and a complex sense of artistic form. Throughout his career, James also wrote literary criticism in which he developed his artistic ideals and applied them to the works of others. Among the numerous conceptualizations he formed to clarify the nature of fiction, he defined the novel as "a direct impression of life." The quality of this impression—the degree of moral and intellectual development—and the author's ability to communicate this impression in an effective and artistic manner were the two principal criteria by which James estimated the worth of a literary work. James admired the self-consciously formalistic approach of contemporary French writers, particularly Gustave Flaubert, an approach which contrasted with the loose, less formulated standards of the English novel. On the other hand, he favored the moral concerns of English writing over the often amoral and cynical vision which characterized much of French literature in the second half of the nineteenth century. His literary aim was to combine the qualities of each country's literature that most appealed to his tempera-*]

ment. After considering various fictional strategies, James arrived at what he thought the most desirable form for the novel to take. Basically objective in presentation—that is, without the intrusion of an authorial voice—the novel should be a well-integrated formal scheme of dialogue, description, and narrative action, all of which should be received from the viewpoint of a single consciousness or "receptor." In James's novels this receptor is usually a principal character who is more an observer than a participant in the plot. Equal in importance to the artistic plan of a novel is the type of receptor a novelist chooses to use. The type demanded by James's theory is a consciousness that will convey a high moral vision, humanistic worldview, and a generally uplifting sense of life. James's criteria were accepted as standards by a generation of novelists that included Ford Madox Ford, Joseph Conrad, and Virginia Woolf. The following early survey by James is a balanced treatment of the subjective impressionism in Loti's works.]

[When] a new French talent mounts above the horizon we watch with a kind of anxiety to see whether it will present itself in a subversive and unaccommodating manner. M. Pierre Loti is a new enough talent for us still to feel something of the glow of exultation at his having not contradicted us. He has in fact done exactly the opposite. . . . At the moment we are under the spell of such a talent as Alphonse Daudet's or Emile Zola's or Guy de Maupassant's or (to give variety to the question) that of so rare and individual a genius as this exquisite Loti, it takes not great sophistry to convince us of the indelicacy, of the ingratitude even, of turning an invidious eye on anything so irrelevant as deficiencies. But the spell is foredoomed to fluctuations, to lapses, and we end by seeming to perceive with perplexity that even literary figures so brillant as these may have too happy, too insolent a lot. Are they after all to enjoy their honors without paying for them? How *we* should have to pay for them if *we* were to succeed in plucking them and wearing them! The fortunate Frenchmen give us the sense of a kind of fatuity in impunity, a kind of superficiality in distinction, a kind of irritating mastery of the trick of eating your cake and having it. Such is one of the reflections to which Pierre Loti eventually leads us. In common with his companions he performs so beautifully as to kick up a fine golden dust over the question of what he contains—or of what he doesn't. The agility of all their movements makes up for the thinness of so much of their inspiration. To be so constituted as to expose one's self to the charge of vulgarity of spirit and yet to have a charm that successfully snaps its fingers at all "charges," is to be so lucky that those who work in harder conditions surely may allow themselves the solace of small criticisms. It may be said that if we indulge in small criticisms we resist our author's charm after all; but the answer to this is that the effort to throw off our enthralment even for an hour is an almost heroic struggle with a sweet superstition. The whole second-rate element in Loti, for instance, becomes an absolute stain if we think much about it. But practically (and this is his first-rate triumph) we *don't* think much about it, so unreserved is our surrender to irresistible illusion and contagious life.

To be so rare that you can be common, so good that you can be bad without loss of caste, be a mere sponge for sensations and yet not forfeit your human character—secure, on the contrary, sympathy and interest for it whenever you flash *that* facet into the sun—and then on top of all write, as Goldsmith wrote, like an angel—that surely is to wear the amulet to some purpose, the literary feather with a swagger that becomes pardonable. This rarity of the mixture, which makes such a literary unity of such a personal duality, is altogether in Pierre Loti a source of fascination. He combines aptitudes which seldom sit down to the same table, and combines them with singular facility and naturalness, an air of not caring whether he combines them or not. He may not be as ignorant of literature as he pretends (he protests perhaps a little too much that he never opens a book), but it is very clear that what is at the bottom of his effect is not (in a degree comparable at least to the intensity of the effect) the study of how to produce it. What he studies is a very different matter, and I know no case in which literature, left to come off as it can, comes off so beautifully. To be such a rover of the deep, such a dabbler in adventure as would delight the soul of Mr. Robert Louis Stevenson, and yet to have at one's command a sensitive and expressive apparatus separated by the whole scale from that of Jim Hawkins and John Silver, is to have little need of "cultivating" originality, as M. Guy de Maupassant the other day recommended us to do. (pp. 159-62)

The literature of our day contains nothing more beautiful than the Breton passages, as they may be called, of *"Mon Frère Yves"* and *"Pêcheur d'Islande."* There is a sentence in the former of these tales, in reference to the indefinable sweetness of the short-lived Breton summer, which constitutes a sort of image of the attraction of his style. "A compound of a hundred things; the charm of the long, mild days, rarer than elsewhere and sooner gone; the deep, fresh grasses, with their extreme profusion of pink flowers; and then the sense of other years which sleeps there, spread through everything." All this is in Pierre Loti, the mildness and sadness, the profusion of pink flowers, and that implication of *other* conditions at any moment, which is the innermost note of the voice of the sea. (p. 166)

"Madame Chrysanthème," the history of a summer spent in very curious conditions at Nagasaki, the latest of the author's productions and the most distinctively amusing, has less spontaneity than its predecessors, and seems more calculated, more made to order; but it abounds in unsurpassable little vignettes, of which the portrait of certain Japanese ladies of quality whom he met at the photographer's is a specimen. . . . (pp. 167-68)

It may be that many an English reader will not recognize Pierre Loti as a man of action who happens to have a genius for literary expression, the account he himself gives of his exploits not being such as we associate with that character. The term action has a wide signification, but there are some kinds of life which it represents to us certainly much less than others. The exploits of the author of *"Madame Chrysanthème,"* of *"Aziuydè,"* of *"Rarahu,"* of *"Le Roman d'un Spahi,"* and *"Pasquala Ivanovitch,"* are—I hardly know what to call them, for we scarcely mention achievements of this order in English—more relaxing on the whole than tonic. An author less tonic than Pierre Loti can indeed not well be imagined, and the English reader ought already to have been notified (the plainest good faith requires it and I have delayed much too long) that a good deal of what he has to tell us relates mainly to his successes among the ladies. We have a great and I think a just dislike to the egotistic-erotic, to literary confidences on such points, and when a gentleman abounds in them the last thing we take him for is a real man of action. It must be confessed that Pierre Loti abounds, though his two best books are not autobiographical, and there is simply nothing to reply to any English reader who on ascertaining this circumstance may declare that he desires to hold no commerce with him; nothing, that is, but the simple remark that such a reader will lose a precious pleasure. This warning, however, is a trifle to the really scandalized. I maintain my epithet, at any rate, and

I should desire no better justification for it than such an admirable piece as the *"Corvèe Matinale,"* in the volume entitled *"Propos d'Exil,"* which describes how the author put off at dawn from a French ship of war, in a small boat with a handful of men, to row up a river on the coast of Anam and confer, with a view of bringing them promptly to terms, with the authorities of the queerest of little Asiatic towns. A writer is to my sense quite man of action enough when he has episodes like that to relate; they give a sufficient perfection to the conjunction of the "chance" and the pictorial view. Danger has nothing to do with it; the manner in which M. Loti gives us on this occasion the impression of an almost grotesque absence of danger, of ugly mandarins superfluously frightened as well as of the color and temperature of the whole scene, the steaming banks of the river, with flat Asiatic faces peeping out of the rushes, the squalid, fetid crowds, the shabby, contorted pagodas, with precious little objects glimmering in the shade of their open fronts—the vividness of all these suggestions is the particular sign of this short masterpiece. The same remark applies to the *"Pagodes Souterraines,"* in the same volume— the story, told with admirable art, of an excursion, while the ship lingers exasperatingly on the same hot, insufferable coast, to visit certain marvellous old tombs and temples, hewn out of a mountain of pink marble, filled with horrible monstrous effigies and guarded by bonzes almost as uncanny. The appreciation of the exotic, which M. Jules Lemaître marks as Loti's distinguishing sign, finds perfect expression in such pages as these.

There are many others of the same sort in the *"Propos d'Exil,"* which is a chaplet of pearls; but perhaps the book is above all valuable for the sketch entitled *"Un Viex"*—the picture of the old age, dreary and lamentable, of a worn-out mariner who has retired on his pension to a cottage in the suburbs of Brest. It has delicate sentiment as well as an extraordinary objective reality; but it is not sentimental, for it is characterized by an ineffable pessimism and a close, fascinated notation of the inexorable stages by which lonely and vacant old age moulders away, with its passions dying, dying very hard. *"Un Vieux"* is singularly ugly, and *"Pêcheur d'Islande"* is singularly beautiful; but I should be tempted to say that in Pierre Loti's work *"Un Vieux"* is the next finest thing to *"Pêcheur d'Islande. "Mon Frère Yves"* is full of beauty, but it carries almost to a maximum the author's characteristic defect, the absence of composition, the *décousu* quality which makes each of his productions appear at first a handful of flying leaves. *"Un Vieux"* has a form as a whole, though it occurs to me that, perhaps, it is surpassed in this respect by another gem of narration or description, the best pages of the *"Fleurs d'Ennui."* (We hesitate for a word when it is a question mainly of rendering, as Loti renders it, the impression, of giving the material illusion, of a strange place and strange manners.) I leave to the impartial reader to judge whether *"Les Trois Dames de la Kasbah,"* the gem in question (it has been extracted from the *"Fleurs d'Ennui"* and published in a pretty little volume by itself), is more or only is less ugly than *"Un Vieux."* That will depend a good deal on whether he be shocked by the cynicism of the most veracious of all possible representations of the adventures of a band of drunken sailors during a stuffy night at Algiers. Such, and nothing more (the adventures are of the least edifying, and the *dénoûment* is not even mentionable to ears polite), is the subject of *"Les Trois Dames de la Kasbah, Conte Oriental";* and yet the life, the spirit, the color, the communicative tone, the truth and poetry of this little production are such that one cannot conscientiously relegate it (one wishes one could) to a place even of comparative obscurity.

If our author's ruling passion is the appreciation of the exotic, it is not in his first works that he confines his quest to funny calls on nervous mandarins, to the twilight gloom of rheumatic old sailors or the vulgar pranks of reckless young ones. *"Le Roman d'un Spahi," "Aziyadé,* and *"Rarahu"* each contain the history of a love-affair with a primitive woman or a combination of primitive women. There is a kind of complacent animalism in them which makes it difficult to speak of them as the perfection of taste, and I profess to be able to defend them on the ground of taste only so long as they are not attacked. The great point is that they will not be attacked by any one who is capable of feeling the extraordinary power of evocation of (for instance) *"Le Mariage de Loti"* (another name for *"Rarahu"),* at the same time that he recognizes the abnormal character of such a performance, a character the more marked as the feeling of youth is strong in these early volumes, and the young person has rarely M. Loti's assurance as a *viveur.* He betrays a precocity of depravity which is disconcerting. I write the gross word depravity because we must put the case against him (so many English readers would feel it that way) as strongly as it can be put. It doesn't put it strongly enough to say that the serene surrender to polygamous practices among coral-reefs and in tepid seas is a sign much rather of primitive innocence, for there is an element in the affair that vitiates the argument. This is simply that the serenity (which, I take it, most makes the innocence) cannot under the circumstances be adequate. The pen, the talent, the phrase, the style, the note-book take care of that and change the whole situation; they invalidate the plea of the primitive. They introduce the conscious element, and that is the weak side of Loti's spontaneities and pastorals. What saves him is that his talent never falters, and this is but another illustration of his interesting double nature. (pp. 168-73)

> Henry James, "Pierre Loti" (originally published in The Fortnightly Review, n.s., Vol. XLIII, No. CCLVII, May, 1888), in his Essays in London and Elsewhere (copyright, 1893, by Harper & Brothers), Harper & Row, 1893, pp. 151-85.

ANATOLE FRANCE (essay date 1892)

[*France is one of the most conspicuous examples of an author who epitomized every facet of literary greatness to his own time but who lost much of his eminence to the shifting values of posterity. He embodied what are traditionally regarded as the intellectual and artistic virtues of French writing; clarity, control, perceptive judgment of worldly matters, and the Enlightenment virtues of tolerance and justice. His novels gained an intensely devoted following for their lucid appreciation of the pleasures and pains of human existence and for the tenderly ironic vantage from which it was viewed. A persistent tone of irony, varying in degrees of subtlety, is often considered the dominant trait of France's writing. In his critical works this device of ironic expression becomes an effective tool of literary analysis. In the following excerpt France considers Loti's thematic use of "exotic love" in his works.*]

It was reserved for Pierre Loti to make us taste to intoxication, to delirium, even to stupor, the acrid savour of exotic loves.

It is a lucky thing for him and for us that M. Pierre Loti entered the navy and that he has travelled a great deal, for nature gave him that eager and fickle temperament which requires a crowd of images. She gave him, moreover, exquisite senses to feel the beauty of this amorous universe, a simple and comprehensive intelligence, and that rare artist's faculty which sees, hears, observes, and crystallises its memories. He was expressly fitted

to bring to us fantastic beauty and strange delights. And beyond question he has not proved false to his destiny.

Pierre Loti's women—Azyadé, Rarahu, Fatou-Gaye—are indeed true savages, redolent of the brute animal. We approach them as if they were an unknown fruit. Loti loves them, he loves them with a childish and perverse love that is infinitely gentle and infinitely cruel.

Those unions of the daughters of men with the sons of God which were overwhelmed by the waters of the deluge, were neither so impious nor so full of anguish. To marry Loti to Rarahu, the spahi to Fatou-Gaye, to unite white men and little yellow or black animals, this is a thing which Chateau-briand did not fully imagine, when, in his melancholy flirtations, he loosened the dark tresses of the two Floridans who had three parts Spanish blood in their veins. (pp. 315-16)

[In] Loti's exotic marriages, hearts never, never beat in unison. Rarahu and Loti feel and understand nothing in the same way. Hence an infinite melancholy.

I am speaking here only of Loti and of his black or yellow women; I say nothing of his two great masterpieces, *"Mon frère Yves"* and *"Pêcheur d'Islande,"* which carry us into another world of feeling and sensation. And there is hardly time even to come to the latest marriage of Rarahu's fugitive spouse. You know that M. Pierre Loti married Mademoiselle Chrysanthème for the length of a spring, before the authorities at Nagasaki, and that forthwith out of that marriage he made a capital volume [*"Madame Chrysanthème"*] (p. 318)

What give its special character and charm to M. Pierre Loti's [*"Madame Chrysanthème"*] are its short, living, and moving descriptions: its animated picture of Japanese life, so tiny, so quaint, and so artificial. Lastly, there are the landscapes. They are divine, the landscapes Loti draws in a few mysterious touches. How deeply does nature impress him! How lovingly he enjoys her, and with what sadness he comprehends her! He is able to see thousands and thousands of images of trees and flowers, of sparkling waters and of clouds. He is acquainted with the multiform figures which the universe shows us, and he knows that these figures, innumerable in appearance, really reduce themselves to two—the figure of love and that of death. (pp. 319-20)

> Anatole France, "Exotic Love," in his On Life & Letters, fourth series, edited by Frederic Chapman, translated by Bernard Miall (reprinted by permission of Dodd, Mead & Company, Inc.; originally published as La vie littéraire, Vol. IV, Calmann Lévy, 1892), Dodd, Mead, 1924, pp. 314-20.

EDMUND GOSSE (essay date 1902)

[*Gosse's importance as a critic lies mainly in his introduction of Henrik Ibsen's "new drama" to an English audience. He was among the chief translators and critics of Scandinavian literature and was decorated by the Norwegian, Swedish, and Danish governments. Among his other works are studies of John Donne, Thomas Gray, Sir Thomas Browne, and important early articles on French authors of the late nineteenth century. Although Gosse's works are varied and voluminous, his intellectual style is somewhat casual, with the consequence that his commentary lacks depth and is not considered to be in the first rank of modern critical thought. However, his broad interests and knowledge of foreign literatures lend his works much more than a documentary value. In the excerpt below, Gosse discusses several of Loti's well-known travel essays.*]

There is no more curious phenomenon in the existing world of letters than the fascination of Loti. Here is a man and a writer of a thousand faults, and we forgive them all. He is a gallant sailor, and he recounts to us his timidities and his effeminacies; we do not care. He is absolutely without what we call "taste"; he exploits the weakness of his mother and the death-bed of his aunt; it makes no difference to us. Irritated travellers of the precise cast say that he is inaccurate; no matter. Moralists throw up their hands and their eyes at Aziyadë and Chrysanthème and Suleima; well, for the moment, we are tired of being moral. The fact is, that for those who have passed under the spell of Loti, he is irresistible. He wields the authority of the charmer, of the magician, and he leads us whither he chooses. The critical spirit is powerless against a pen so delicately sensitive, so capable of playing with masterly effect on all the finer stops of our emotions.

Even the semipiternal youth of Loti, however, is waning away, and we are sensible in *Le Désert* that the vitality of the writer is not what it was when he made his first escapades in Senegambia, in Montenegro, in Tahiti. Doubtless, the austerity of the theme excludes indiscretion; there is little room for scandal in the monastery of Mount Sinai or in the desert of Tih. But the secret of the sovereign charm of Loti has always been the exactitude with which his writing has transcribed his finest and most fleeting emotions. He has held up his pages like wax tablets and has pressed them to his heart. This deep sincerity, not really obscured to any degree by his transparent affectations, has given his successive books their poignancy. And he has always known how to combine this sincerity with tact, no living writer understanding more artfully how to arrange and to suggest to heighten mystery or to arrest an indolent attention. Hence it would not be like him to conceal the advances of middle age, or to attempt to deceive us. We find in *Le Désert* a Loti who is as faithful to his forty-five years as the author of *Le Roman d'un Spahi* was to his five-and-twenty. The curiosity in mankind, and in particular in himself, seems to have grown less acute; the outlook on the world is clearer and firmer, less agitated and less hysterical. The central charm, the exquisite manner of expressing perfectly lucid impressions, remains absolutely unmodified.(pp. 202-03)

The peculiar sentiment of Zion is well expressed for us in the volume which Pierre Loti has dedicated to it, a book [*Jérusalem*] which none of those who propose to visit the Holy Land should fail to pack away in their trunks. M. Loti is the charmer *par excellence* among living writers. To him in higher degree than to any one else is given the power of making us see the object he describes, and of flooding the vision in the true, or at all events the effective, emotional atmosphere. He has no humour, or at least he does not allow it to intrude into his work. To take up a book on the Holy Land, and to find it jocose—what an appalling thing that would be! We fancy that Jerusalem is one of the few cities which Mark Twain has never described. May he long be prevented from visiting it! A sense of humour is an excellent thing in its place; but the ancient and mysterious cradles of religion are not its proper fields of exercise. Mr. Jerome's Three Men do very well in a Boat; but it would require the temper of an archimandrite to sojourn with them in Jerusalem. M. Loti is never funny; but he is preeminently sensitive, acute, and sympathetic. (pp. 208-09)

The trilogy of travel is now concluded with *La Galilée*. The completed work certainly forms the most picturesque description of the Holy Land and its surroundings which has yet been given to the world. We close this third volume with a sense of having really seen the places which had been a sort of sacred mystery to us from earliest childhood. Loti is a master of enchantment, and so cunningly combines the arts of harmony and colour in writing that he carries us, as though we were St. Thomas, whither we would not. In other words, by the strange and scarcely analyzable charm of his style, he bewitches us beyond our better judgment. But a reaction comes, and we are obliged to admit that in the case of *La Galilée* it has come somewhat soon.

It was only while reading this third volume that we became conscious that Pierre Loti was doing rather a mechanical thing. In *Le Désert* we were ready to believe that nothing but the fascination of wild places took him across the wilderness and up into that grotesque shrine of Christianity that lurks among the fierce pinnacles of Mount Sinai. In *Jérusalem,* led away by the pathos of the scene and the poignant grace of the pilgrim's reflections, we still persuaded ourselves to see in him one who withdrew from the turmoil of the West that he might worship among the dead upon Mount Moriah. But in *La Galilée* the illusion disappears. Loti crosses Palestine, embarks upon the Sea of Gennesaret, ascends Mount Hermon, winds down into the rose-oasis of Damascus, no longer as the insouciant and aristocratic wanderer, "le Byron de nos jours," but as a tourist like ourselves, wrapped in a burnous, it is true, and not personally conducted by Messrs. Cook & Sons, yet not the less surely an alien, manufacturing copy for the press. He is revealed as the "special correspondent," bound, every night, however weary he may be, to "pan out" sufficient description to fill a certain space on the third page of the "Figaro."

There is nothing dishonourable in being a special correspondent, nor is there is a journalist living who might not envy Pierre Loti the suppleness and fluid felicity of his paragraphs. But this is not the light in which we have learned to know him. He has very carefully taught us to regard him as one to whom literature is indifferent, who never looks at a newspaper, whose impressions of men and manners are formed in lands whither his duties as a sailor have casually brought him, who writes of them out of the fullness of his heart, in easy exquisite numbers cast forth as the bird casts its song. We have had an idea that Loti never looks at a proof, that some comrade picks up the loose leaves as they flutter in the forecastle, and sends them surreptitiously to kind M. Calmann Lévy. When he is elected to the French Academy, he is the last to know it, and wonders, as he is rowed back from some Algerian harbour, what his men are shouting about on board his ship. All this is the legend of Loti, and we have nourished and cherished it, but it will not bear the fierce light that beats upon *La Galilée*. We cannot pretend any longer; we cannot force ourselves to think of a romantic pilgrim of the sea, flung ashore at Aleppo and wandering vaguely up into the spurs of Carmel. Certainly not! This is a Monsieur Loti who is travelling in the pay of an enterprising Parisian newspaper, who does his work very conscientiously, but who is sometimes not a little bored with it. (pp. 213-15)

It has long been the custom of Pierre Loti to gather together at intervals those short pieces of his prose which have not found their place in any consecutive fiction or record of travel. In the case of most authors, even of the better class, such chips from the workshop would excite but a very languid interest, or might be judged wholly impertinent. All that Loti does, however, on whatever scale, is done with so much care and is so characteristic of him, that his admirers find some of their richest feasts in these his baskets of broken meat. (p. 217)

The convinced Lotist, then, will not be discouraged to hear that *Figures et Choses qui passaient,* which is the twentieth tune (or volume) which this piper has played to us, is made up entirely of bits and airs that seem to have lost their way from other works. On the contrary, it will amuse and stimulate him to notice that *Passage d'Enfant* suggests a lost chapter of *Le Livre de la Pitié et de la Mort;* that *Instant de Recueillement* reads like a rejected preface to the novel called *Ramuntcho;* that *Passage de Sultan* is a sort of appendix to *Fantôme d'O-rient'* and that *Passage de Carmencita* forms a quite unexpected prelude to *Le Mariage de Loti.* (pp. 217-18)

A large section of [*Les Derniers Jours de Pékin*] deals with the customs and landscape of that extreme corner of southwestern France which the author has made his own during the years in which he has been stationed at the mouth of the Bidassoa. All these studies of the "Euskal-Erria," the primitive Basque Country, are instinct with the most graceful qualities of Pierre Loti's spirit. He has an exquisite instinct for the preservation of whatever is antique and beautiful, a superstitious conservatism pushed almost to an affectation. As he grows older, this characteristic increases with him. He has become an impassioned admirer of cathedrals; he is moved, almost to an act of worship, by sumptuous and complicated churches; he bows a dubiously adoring knee at Loyola and at Burgos. He is very eager to take part in processions, he is active among crowds of penitents, he omits no item in the sensual parts of ritual, and is swayed almost to intoxication on the ebb and flood of mysterious and archaic incantations. The reader of his *Jéru-salem* will recall how earnestly and how vainly Pierre Loti sought for a religious idea, or a genuine inspiration of any spiritual kind, among the shrines and waters of Palestine. Once more this unction is denied him. Doomed for ever to deal with the external side of things, the exquisite envelope of life, Loti, as time goes by, seems knocking with a more and more hopeless agitation at the door of the mystical world. But that which is revealed to children will never be exposed to him. It ought to be enough for Loti that he surpasses all the rest of his fellow-men in the perfection of his tactile apparatus. That which is neither to be seen, nor touched, nor smelled, nor heard, lies outside his province. (pp. 219-20)

It was a fortunate chance which sent to China, in the late autumn of 1900, the man in whom, perhaps more delicately than in any other living person, are combined the gifts of the seeing eye and the expressive pen. The result is a book [*Les Derniers Jours de Pékin*], which, so far as mere visual presentment goes, may safely be said to outweigh the whole bulk of what else was sent home from the extreme East, in letters and articles to every part of the world, during that terrible period of storm and stress. Pierre Loti arrived when the fighting was over, when the Imperial family had fled, and when the mysteries of the hitherto inviolable capital of China had just first been opened to the Powers. He reaped the earliest harvest of strange and magnificent impressions, and he saw, with that incomparably clear vision of his, what no European had seen till then, and much that no human being will ever see again. Moreover, the great artist, who had seemed in *Jérusalem,* and still more in *La Galilée,* to have tired his pen a little, and to have lost something of his firm clairvoyance, has enjoyed a rest of several years. His style proclaims the advantage of this reserve of vigour. Loti is entirely himself again; never before, not even in the matchless *Fleurs d'Exil,* has he presented his talent in a form more evenly brilliant, more splendidly characteristic in its rich simplicity, than in *Les Derniers Jours de Pékin.* (pp. 228-29)

Edmund Gosse, "Pierre Loti" (1902) in his French Profiles, *revised edition, William Heinemann, 1913, pp. 199-232.*

BENJAMIN De CASSERES   (essay date 1912)

[De Casseres was an American poet and critic whose writings militantly celebrated individualism and derided any political or philosophic system that suppressed the individual. He considered critical writing an art, and his work is characterized by a verbally lush rhetorical style. De Casseres held "logic to be one of the lowest forms of mental activity and imagination the highest"; hence, his critical judgements are usually founded on spontaneous intuition. "I think in images, flashes, epigrams. Creators should spurn Reason as an eagle would spurn a ladder."]

It may be said of Pierre Loti, as of Lafcadio Hearn, that he phantomized a universe. He is the Prospero of Impressionism. His world is the baseless fabric of a vision and his adventures nothing but the insubstantial pageant of his own mind. His books are an aromatic hasheesh. His creations—*Aziyadé, Ma-dame Chrysanthème, Ramuncho*—file by like wraiths who have a swift passion to be buried.

The difference between Pierre Loti and the modern world is the difference between the Orient and the Occident, a difference fundamental and eternal, and one that can only be settled at the Armageddon of races. The Impressionist is Oriental. The soul of Loti has its roots in India, where life is a mirage invented by Maya, the Evil One. Impressionism cages the world in the brain. Only images and sensations are real. Matter is a myth. Resistance is a legend of touch. The external universe is a superstition of the senses.

Guy de Maupassant invented a being called Horla, a creature of some unimaginable world. It absorbed into itself whatever it touched. In all of Loti's works there is a Horla. Phantas-magoria and Terror are the protagonists of all his books—and Mystery, that sense of mystery that overcomes one in Gothic glooms and tropic distances.

Read *Fantôme d'Orient.* There is no book just like it in existence. It is nightmare; it is life; it is the psychology of illusion. Loti seeks the tomb of his sweetheart in Constantinople. That is the theme, as simple as a fairy story, and as true. It is all atmosphere built up of pity, tenderness and the unreal.

Flaubert has been called the "Colossus of Ennui." Pierre Loti is Ennui itself. Like the Proserpina of Swinburne, Loti has gathered "all things mortal with cold, immortal hands." An unconquerable nostalgia for the *Néant* wells from every page he has written. For him to discover the spectre Ennui it is only necessary to rend a shadow—that is, act. He yawns behind each gesture. Pleasure is, to Loti, only the glittering scabbard of Ennui. His thoughts are the sad, ironic dreams of the demon Ennui. All gods and demigods and humans will gray and pass through the twilight of senescence into the Nothing—except one, that reigns from everlasting to everlasting. It is Ennui.

The incurable melancholy of Pierre Loti is the purple mantle that robes his genius. He has fallen in love with the reflection of his own nothingness in the monstrous mirror of Time. The black Cup of Despair from which he has drunk has become his Holy Grail.

But it is as the supreme literary Impressionist of his time that Pierre Loti will be known to the future. He never comes into contact with things. He has never seen the real, only effigies of the real. He has not pursued "subjects," only the reflection of subjects. He does not possess things, but only the sentiment that things inspire. Images and thoughts being the very pulp of his consciousness, it follows that Loti's impressionism is Impressionism itself. The universe of sense-contact has passed through the spectrum of his mind and only color and vibration remain.

Loti's hatred of the practical and his bitter antagonism to the most practical people in the world, the English, is rooted in his metaphysical romanticism. He is the enemy of the Ugly— that is, of the real, the practical. There is a kind of mind that grows more beautiful and more delicate the closer it comes into contact with the ugly and the mean. It is the kind of mind that grows in direct contrast with its physical and economic environment. It becomes stronger through an unkernelled principle of revolt and dissent as it comes into contact with the things that tend to weaken it. In Pierre Loti there has been since his birth a continuous reaction of his personality against the age and the world he lives in. Hence, in his literary life there has been no "evolution." There is no "early Loti," no "later Loti." From his first book to *The Daughter of Heaven* the style and the implied dissent are the same. Loti cannot change. His is the Eternal Vision. Only the beautiful and the transitory have value. All else is a lie.

"Spectators of life" are in reality spectators of their own emotions. Amiel—who was the Loti of philosophy—cried that he was doomed forever to stand motionless on the bank of Time and watch the triremes, the vikings and the galleons go by. But Amiel did not see the stream, but millions of shadows which he projected on the stream. It is so with Loti. he has foisted himself upon things. It is Loti's desert; Loti's Stamboul; Loti's Japan; Loti's Roumania; Loti's sunset; Loti's Egypt; Loti's China; Loti's Pyrenees. And they are immortal because no other being has ever seen those things in that way before. It is the miracle of isolation; a miracle worked by Théophile Gautier and Lafcadio Hearn and "faked" by the Goncourt brothers.

Pierre Loti is the Spirit of the Exotic. Whatever is foreign is poetic. Whatever is near is ugly. It is a beautiful illusion— those Blessed Isles that we call Abroad. The hunger for Elsewhere has driven Loti all over the world. To be in the place where one is not, if not physically, then mentally, that is the psychic base of the love for the exotic. Add to this the "call of the wild," the beckoning of a perpetually retreating Unknown, the perfume of impossible paradises that haunts the nostrils, and the love of adventure.

When Loti describes a "bock" that he is sipping he gives us the impression that the "bock" is ten thousand miles away. His passion for the exotic caused him to change his European attire for that of a Moslem and espouse the cause of the Crescent. All of us, some in lesser, some in greater ways, have this passion for the exotic. Some feed the craving with alcohol, others with the blasting dreams of religious mysticism. The pirate of the South Seas and the hermit of the Thebaid, Balzac dressed as a monk, Tolstoy masquerading as a moujik, Loti in Moslem attire—all are moved by the same impulse, love of the novel, the strange, the exotic, the Elsewhere. In Loti and Poe the exotic is a life-principle. In Wilde and the Goncourt brothers it is pure attitude.

The passion of distance is the original sin. Distance, psychological or real, is the mother of desire, and its unattainable horizons the cause of all pessimism. Loti is a distance-drunkard. He invents distances that were never in air or sea or firmament. He is distance-mad. The Hindu seer travelling his upward Path rises from Prospect to Prospect with a rapt joy blazoned on his soul, indulging that passion of distance, the frenetic desire to be lost in the Infinite, to be the hub of a million perspectives. It is something of this divine intoxication which has taken possession of Loti of late years. The Infinite has petrified him and he creates like a man in a dream.

Loti is the enemy of the familiar. The average person holds fast to the limited; the boundaries of the territory in which he strolls are as clearly marked for him as the streets of his native place. He ambles through life the smiling prisoner of use and wont, chilled by the unfamiliar, a scarcely manumitted automaton of instinct. He feels well housed, safe in the concrete, in the very real walls of his mental abode, surrounded by his lares and penates, his unchanging God of Sundries back of it all.

To Loti only the spectral is real. He bears about him the air of one sent on a strange, perplexing errand, and his life, as much as his books, has been a Search. Whatever he has touched he has transfigured. He has put the glamour of dream and mystery on the most commonplace objects. Like Blake and Whitman, like every artist of the first rank, he has restored the world to the magic and wonder of the First Morning. Nautch girl or Sphinx, Jerusalem or the sea, catacomb or sunset, desert or hovel—all dissolve and become fugacious and inexplicable as they pass through the spectrum of that strange temperament. (pp. 369-72)

Benjamin De Casseres, "Pierre Loti," in Forum (copyright, 1912, by Events Publishing Company, Inc.; reprinted by permission of Current History, Inc.), Vol. 48, September, 1912, pp. 369-72.

JULES LEMAÎTRE (essay date 1921)

[*As Loti was a practitioner of impressionistic fiction, Lemaître, a leading French critic of the nineteenth century, is known for his impressionistic criticism. The following is an excerpt from his laudatory consideration of his fellow impressionist.*]

I have just read over again, almost without pause, in the country, huddled close to mother earth, beneath an enervating thunder-laden sky, Pierre Loti's six volumes. Now, as I turn over the last page, I feel a sense of complete intoxication. I am full of the sad and delicious memory of a prodigious quantity of most profound sensations, and my heart is filled with a vague and universal tenderness. To speak, if I can, with more precision, those two thousand pages have suggested to me, have made me imagine too great a number of unexpected perceptions, and those perceptions were accompanied by too much pleasure and, at the same time, by too much pain, too much pity, too many indefinite and unrealizable desires. My soul is like an instrument that has vibrated overmuch, and to which the mute prolongation of past vibrations is painful. I would like to enjoy and suffer the entire earth, the totality of life, and, like St. Anthony at the end of his temptation, to embrace the world.

You can, if you like, regard this impression which those novels leave upon me as excessive. I myself confess that my critical conscience is perturbed. The greatest masterpieces of literature have never troubled me thus. What is there then in those stories of Loti? For they are composed with extreme negligence, written in a restricted vocabulary, in little, closely-constructed phrases. You will find in them neither extraordinary or powerful dramas, nor subtle analyses of character, for everything is reduced to love affairs followed by separations, the characters in which have very simple souls. Many books, both old and recent, presuppose a far higher effort of thought, invention, and execution. But, in spite of this, Loti's novels take possession of me and oppress me more than a drama of Shakespere, a tragedy of Racine, or a novel of Balzac. And it is for this reason that I am perturbed. Have they some witchcraft in them, some sorcery, some charm which is inexplicable or only explicable by something other than their literary merits?

For these novels move the soul at once in all in it that is most refined and in all in it that is most elementary. They strike, if I may use the phrase, both extremes of the key-board of sentiment. For, on the one hand, you have under your eyes the most singular objects, you receive from them the newest, the rarest, and the sharpest impressions; and, on the other hand, you have experienced the most natural feelings, those most completely human, those accessible to all. You, with your eyes of a Western dilettante in love with the picturesque, have seen the *upa-upa* danced in Tahiti; you have seen Burmese dancers who look like bats . . . ; and you have wept for old women, dying children, or parting lovers with the best part of your soul, the part of you that is simplest and healthiest, with the same heart as that with which you love your mother or your country. You have known the agitations of the most inquisitive and most experienced sensuality—and the emotions of the purest sympathy and the chastest pity.

Thus you enjoy in those books the limpid charm of ingenuous poems and the perverse charm of the last investigations of contemporary æstheticism—that which is at the beginning of literatures and that which is at their end. A page communicates to you two distinct impressions between which there are thousands of years—and between which there is sometimes also 'the frightful thickness of the world.' And little by little the poet insinuates within you his own soul, a soul that seems contemporary with humanity at its birth and in its old age, that seems to have traversed the entire surface of the terrestrial globe; a soul amorous and sad, always restless and always quivering. And it is this soul that gives Loti's little phrases their immense power to make you tremble.

One can see from Loti's example how it is, and by what path, old literatures sometimes return to absolute simplicity. An extreme artistic sensibility employed upon the most extraordinary objects and finally resting in the translation of the simplest feelings; what is called 'impressionism' resulting in a purely natural poetry—such is almost the case of the author of *Aziyadé* and *Pêcheur d'Islande*. Now, on looking a little more closely, we think we see that it is the 'exoticism' of the objects which first occupied it that has sharpened his sensibility to this point, and that it is certain feelings engendered by this exoticism which have led it back to the fine simplicity of the idylls or the familiar tragedies. (pp. 187-91)

I do not believe that it is much more than a hundred years since exoticism made its entrance into our literature. It presupposes a gift which is not entirely developed until very late in blind and routine-ridden humanity—the gift of *seeing* and loving the physical universe in all its details. . . . [However] interesting descriptions of reality close to us may be, exoticism, when it is sincere, preserves a special charm, at once penetrating and saddening. For proof I only require some pages of *Salammbô*, Fromentin's two volumes *Sahel* and *Sahara*, and the novels of Pierre Loti, that king of exoticism.

Everything, as I have said, seems to have conspired to secure this sovereignty to the author of *Azaiyadé*. At least three con-

ditions were necessary. It was a good thing, in the first place, that the writer should see the entire world, not only the Pacific but the Polar Seas, not only America but China, not only Tahiti but Senegal. For if he had only known one or two regions, he would run the risk of confining himself to describing only them, and of repeating continually with artifice what he would have done at first with sincerity. His sensibility should, moreover, in order to become more sharpened and rejuvenated, employ itself upon objects as diverse as possible. Now the complete inspection of this immense universe was hardly permissible and easy except to a man of the end of this century. Pierre Loti has had the good sense to be born in it—and to be a naval officer, that is to say, condemned by his profession to endless wanderings. It was necessary, in the second place, that the writer should know how to see. That is not so common, at least in the degree in which this gift was needed in the case we are discussing. I have said that it is only a century since the superior section of humanity began properly to grasp the marvellous diversity of its habitation. . . . Now, Pierre Loti has in an eminent degree the gift of seeing and feeling. He accounts for it in *Aziyadé* with a little effort and some pedantry; but this very effort of expression is an assurance that he knows the inestimable rarity of the gift that is in him. . . . (pp. 196-200)

Lastly, it is necessary that the writer should be able to express what he has seen and felt. How many men have had rare impressions and original visions, of whom we shall never know anything because they were powerless to translate them into words! Pierre Loti has found himself in possession of this supreme gift of expression. And, as he has grown freely, outside of all literary schools, it has been given him to have at once the sharpness of perception of the subtlest of his contemporaries and something of the simplicity of form of the primitive writers. (p. 202)

How am I to get close enough to this wizard, Pierre Loti, and define him with any precision? He is first of all in the very things that the writer places under our eyes. We very easily allow ourselves to be captured by exoticism. It was by exoticism that *Paul et Virginie* a century ago, and *Atala* since then, seized so powerfully upon the public imagination. Men of the people and simple-minded folk adore romances that speak to them of things they have not seen, of lagoons and gondolas, or that present them with vignettes of the East, with caravans, minarets, and yataghans. For us there is a less vulgar charm, but one of the same species, in Pierre Loti's descriptions. In the first place, they flatter the desire for novelty that we have within us. And these evocations of objects to which our senses are not accustomed move us all the more keenly. Then, those unknown things, those combinations hitherto unexperienced of lines, colours, sounds, and perfumes, give us the impression of something distant and fugitive, remind us that the world is large, and that we never grasp more than tiny portions of it at the same time. And, finally, while we imagine new aspects of the universe, it happens that as soon as we have well entered into these visions, we find ourselves ill at ease and vaguely anxious among them, we feel a homesick regret for known and familiar visions whose familiarity has rendered them reassuring to us.

Thus there is something delicious and melancholy in exoticism. It enchants us like a Paradise and depresses us like exile. But this melancholy and this delight are of a peculiar intensity in Pierre Loti. Why? Quite simply (it is always necessary to return to this point), because he feels more profoundly than we do, and because he represents his sensations with more sincerity or more directly, or arranges them less. He fears neither disorder nor repetitions; there are only primitive methods and no 'manner' in his style. Continually, when he despairs of being able to render an impression in its entirety, he ingeniously employs the words 'strange,' 'inexpressible,' 'indefinable.' But these words with him are never empty of meaning; his pictures are so precise that these vague words, so far from weakening them, finish them, and carry them on in a dreamy prolongation. And I need not say that his descriptions are never purely external, that he habitually notes down at the same time the sensation and the feeling which it excites in him, and that this feeling is always very strong and very sad. But what is peculiar to him is that sensations and feelings usually resolve themselves into a sort of languor of voluptuousness and desire, as if the trouble that the face of the Earth awakens within him were similar to another trouble, to that which comes from woman, and fills the whole soul and body.

All this is very difficult to say clearly. What is certain is that a mortal languor exhales from every page of the *Mariage de Loti*. Tahiti, so far away, has the sorrowful attraction of a sensual, inaccessible Paradise to which we shall never go. (pp. 203-05)

Aziyadé troubles you in another way. In the first place by the impression of strange voluptuousness that proceeds from it, profound and absorbed voluptuousness, without thought or speech. That bed of love, at night, on a boat, in the Gulf of Salonica; then that life of silence and solitude, for a year, in an old house in the oldest quarter of Constantinople—I know no sweeter or more enervating dream, nor one in which the conscience and the will are more lulled to sleep. (pp. 208-09)

In the *Roman d'un Spahi* the general impression is cruel. Pierre Loti shows us this time the unfriendly aspects of the earth. The landscape in that book is, of all landscapes, the most sterile, the most hostile to man, the most desolate, beneath its blinding sun the most lugubrious. There are tawny, boundless sands, stained with frightful negro villages like leprous sores, or marshes full of poisons which ooze horribly at sunset. And humanity is at its most wretched, most brutal, closest to the beasts. (p. 210)

From this voluptuous and sad exoticism there issue certain very great, very simple, and eternal feelings which prolong and deepen the sensations noted down. There is, in the first place, the ever-present feeling of the immensity of the world. One can say that the total image of the earth is obscurely evoked by each of Loti's landscapes; for each landscape holds us only because it is new to us, and because we feel that it is separated from us by unmeasured spaces. Now this feeling brings with it a certain melancholy: through it we clearly know our own littleness, and that we shall never be able to enjoy all the universe at once. And this idea of the size of the earth is still more increased by that of its duration. Into Pierre Loti's descriptions there often slip geological visions, recollections of the history of the globe. (p. 211)

[It] is the very exoticism of his romances that guided Pierre Loti to simple subjects and elementary dramas, and imposed them upon him. The subjects could hardly be other than stories of love with the women of the different countries which the poet has traversed—a sensual and dreamy love, an absolute love in the woman; a curious, proud, and sometimes cruel love in the man. The drama is the simplest and most painful of all— the unique, eternal drama of the separation of beings who love

one another. Thus exoticism explains, in Pierre Loti's novels, alike the novelty and intensity of the sensations, and the universal and largely human character of the feelings. (p. 213)

Pêcheur d'Islande is also, like *Loti*, like the *Spahi*, like *Aziyadé*, the story of a love and a separation; the story of the fisherman Yann and of the good and serious Gaud who love one another and marry, of Yann who goes away and does not return, and of an old woman whose grandson is going to die away 'on the other side of the earth.' *Mon Frère Yves* is the story of a sailor who gets drunk whenever he goes on land, who marries and becomes a father, and who will reform perhaps; and it is the story of the strange and touching friendship between this sailor and Pierre Loti. And I have nothing to say of these two narratives except that they are marvelously picturesque, that their emotion is penetrating, and their simplicity absolute. (p. 215)

I am afraid that I have not been able to convey the impression that these books make upon me, and I am also afraid that I may be blamed for having tried to convey that impression. I shall be told: 'All these novels of Loti's are very negligently composed.' Is it my fault if that does not affect me? Or: 'Do you not find too many curios and trinkets in this exoticism, too much day-dreaming, too much about coral necklaces, mangroves, cholas, and diguhelas? We cannot verify the accuracy of these paintings; this abundance of details is comparable with nothing that we know.' Shall I say that I am childish enough to find a charm in mysterious words? Moreover there are not so very many of them. Or: 'Does not nature rather overwhelm man in those novels? That would have been M. Saint-Marc Girardin's opinion. Would you not like there to be a little more psychology?' Why? I find in them quite as much as I need, and I find it of the sort that it ought to be. 'But why do you not say, for instance, that Pierre Loti proceeds from Musset and from Flaubert? And why do you not attempt to assign him his rank in contemporary literature?' Alas! I am so little of a critic that when a writer takes hold of me I am entirely his; and as another will perhaps take quite as great a hold of me, even to the extent of almost effacing my former impressions, and as those various impressions are never of the same sort, I can neither compare them nor state that the latter writer is superior to the former. 'But we do not want to know the emotions that books give you; it is upon their value that we desire to be instructed.' I am here all the more incapable of rising above feeling, as Pierre Loti is, I think, the most delicate machine for giving sensations that I have ever met. He gives me too much pleasure and too acute a pleasure, and one which is too deeply sunken in my flesh for me to be in a condition to judge him. I am scarcely able to say that I love him. (pp. 216-18)

> *Jules Lemaître, "Pierre Loti" (originally published in his* Les contemporains: études et portraits littéraires, *Vol. 3, Societé française d'imprimerie et de librairie, 1898), in his* Literary Impressions, *translated by A. W. Evans, Daniel O'Connor, 1921, pp. 187-218.*

STUART SHERMAN (essay date 1925)

[*Sherman was, for many years, considered one of America's most conservative literary critics. During the early twentieth century, he was influenced by the New Humanism, a literary movement which maintained that the aesthetic quality of any literary work must be subordinate to its support of traditional moral values. During ten years of service as a literary critic at* The Nation, *Sherman established himself as a champion of the long-entrenched*

Anglo-Saxon, genteel tradition in American letters and as a bitter enemy of literary Naturalism and its proponents. Theodore Dreiser and his chief defender, H. L. Mencken, were Sherman's special targets during the World War I era, as Sherman perceived the Naturalism they espoused to be a life-denying cultural product of America's enemy, Germany. During the 1920s, Sherman became the editor of the New York Herald Tribune *book review section, a move that coincided with a distinct liberalization of his hitherto staunch critical tastes; in the last years of his life, he even praised his old enemies Dreiser and Mencken. In the following excerpt from his* Critical Woodcuts, *Sherman praises Loti's works for their romantic exoticism.*]

Pierre Loti is not the first but only the most proficient of the long line of French prose masters who offer travel as something better than hashish or absinthe as an exit from the cul-de-sac of civilization. (p. 202)

A totally flippant person might summarize his work as thirty-five volumes about the good fortunes of a French Academician who was a larking midshipman before he was a captain, and had a sweetheart in every port. And I suppose that Loti, if asked to speak of love, might have replied like Socrates, "I certainly cannot refuse to speak on the only subject of which I profess to have any knowledge." But Loti, it should be said emphatically, is something infinitely more complex than a mere sailor-love. His vague rich passion invades and envelops him with a ravishing melancholy, like the music of Chopin and the poetry of Musset, in which his adolescence reveled. It has overtones of almost mystical rapture and undertones of philosophical despair. It is begotten of life poignantly conscious of itself and shuddering wide-eyed before the black gulf of annihilation. (pp. 203-04)

Loti is no simple-hearted sensualist. The specific "carnal sting" is sharply indicated where it is patently present, as in the vernal orgies of the *"Roman d'un Spahi"*; but it is the least of his preoccupations. Loti is a romanticist and an imperfect lover. He doesn't keep his mind on the object or the subject; it wanders into the moonlight and among flowers and plays with the amulets and the ancestors and the gods of his mistress. The merely fleshly relation between him and Mme. Chrysanthème he does not present as even interesting. That relation, he declares outright, was detestable. He tolerates her only when he regards her as a bit of art in amber-colored flesh, as a translation from a painted fan or a piece of porcelain. Emotionally, they have less in common than a child and a doll. She has not even the heart to be heartbroken when, having paid her wages, he departs for his ship. Returning unexpectedly, he finds her busy with a little hammer testing the lapful of coins he has left.

"An impious hymen," says Antatole France, and suggests that the sadness of Loti is due to his perpetual quest of little thrills and to the impassable racial and cultural abyss which yawns between the Parisian and the Japanese. Yes, Père Anatole, perhaps. A more or less flattering unction to the Occidental soul. But is this spectacle quite so inhuman after all? What about the unfathomable abyss between any two wedded mortals, surveying each other across the coffee cups—between Mr. and Mrs. Jones, who have washed their faces and brushed their hair in considerable intimacy these many years? Have Mr. and Mrs. Jones many more words than Loti and Mme. Chrysanthème, which really pass from heart to heart and make their spirits one? Suppose Jones departs for *his* ship—dies—to-morrow, as he may, easily enough. Won't there be three good days of mixed grief and mourning show—till Jones is safely out of sight? And then, even in this Western world, won't they pretty calmly go over the will, with the relict, and open the

lockbox and tap the securities with their "little hammer" to see if they are sound, and say cheerfully enough, if all is as it should be: "Well, Jones didn't do badly by her." And life will go on much as before, and all the more tolerably because Jones and Mrs. Jones were never so close together as they pretended to be. Loti is sad because he knows that human life is like that, and he can't forget it, even in Nagasaki. (pp. 204-05)

> *Stuart Sherman, "Pierre Loti and Exotic Love" (originally published in a slightly different form as "Pierre Loti," in* New York Herald Tribune Books, *January 18, 1925), in his* Critical Woodcuts *(copyright, 1924, 1925 by New York Tribune, Inc.; copyright, 1926, by Charles Scribner's Sons; reprinted with permission of Charles Scribner's Sons), Charles Scribner's Sons, 1926, pp. 200-08.*

DENIS SAURAT   (essay date 1947)

[*In this essay, Saurat concludes that the romantic quality of Loti's language compensates for his literary flaws.*]

Loti gives perhaps least rise to controversy among the tale-tellers of his period; he is not even a novelist, he tells tales. Or rather he tells one tale, which he transports, being a sailor by profession, to all quarters of the globe: Iceland, Tonkin, Tahiti, Turkey, Japan, the Basque country, anywhere. His first book on Turkey, *Aziyadé*, in 1879, tells all that Loti has to say, and truly it is rather silly. A young man, a sailor of course as a rule, in a far and very foreign land, meets an unknown, but no doubt beautiful girl; they have a love affair, a wonderful love affair, and then the young man's ship goes (or some such thing happens); the girl dies—how, does not matter—and years after the former young man, now become a mature sentimental philosopher, comes back to visit her grave, and, if occasion offers, her relatives. Thus *Aziyadé, Barabu, Le Mariage de Loti, Les Désenchantées.* (p. 35)

Loti's faults are so obvious as to be amusing: he has nothing whatever to say outside the description of people and landscape; no politics for him, no philosophy, no religion. Life is a very sad thing, because people die; especially the people one loves die; but there is nothing to be done about it. Meanwhile how beautiful the world is, how varied, how terrible, how tender, how changeful; how beautiful people are, physically, and morally, or rather immorally, which is the same thing. How divine the creation is; there may not be a God—though who knows—but there is this Earth and the many various people on it: more than our hearts can cope with, really.

The great pity of the world; the heart-break. *Pécheur d'Islande* is perhaps unequalled in sentimentality; but the sentimentality is so pure, so true, so eternal, so simple that the book has an everlasting quality. The simple hearts of Breton peasants and fishermen; and their hard lives, which to them are quite acceptable if their family affections, their friendships, and their most moderate ambitions are left them. In a more sophisticated stage of society, all this would be pretence: at this stage where the human beings are only more beautiful, more pathetic animals, the unavoidable truth in the presentation of the elementary but fundamental feelings of human nature makes the book a masterpiece. Yann, the Breton sailor who dies in an Iceland wreck, has lived a greater and a fuller life than any character in Marcel Proust or André Gide; and Gaud his widow can fill the rest of her life with the kind of suffering that leads to eternity: she has lived. As for the young boy killed in the Indo-

Chinese wars, as for his grandmother in Brittany when she hears of his death—these are of the eternal French people, and if any one wants to know what the French are at bottom, behind the scum of towns and the rotten politics, let this grandmother of a dead little peasant sailor tell them.

Mon frère Yves is a curious counterpicture: the presentation of a drunken sailor to whom drink is life; but what a good sailor, what a good drunkard, what a good Breton! what a man, what a sea, what a ship! Conrad has never been so good, perhaps because he writes of people not his own; whereas Loti writes of his own people, of himself. Yves is truly Loti's brother.

But chiefly, what writing, what French! The critic can do no justice to Loti; quotation can only mangle him. As a landscape painter he is unequalled. Whether he describes the port at Constantinople, the mountains of the Basque country, the terrible cliffs of the French Pacific islands, he has a range and a power of language, a force of conveying his impressions such that many of his readers must have been disappointed when seeing the actual landscapes, Loti being truly better than the facts; and the sea in all its moods belongs to him: the great northern waves that wrap up Yann into eternal peace, so that his death is hymeneal to him, or the full flat sea of the becalmed tropics, and the fogs and the winds and the sun—they are his.

A curious result of the Romantic period. The seventeenth century did not appreciate landscape. Then Rousseau discovered the hills; then Chateaubriand discovered the sea; and the more we discovered the more bored we became. Romantic landscapes are deadly. Still, literature had discovered nature, and it became everybody's duty—Hugo's, Flaubert's, even Zola's—to put in a little description of a landscape whenever it could be done. But all but the most conscientious readers skipped those bits, which were inserted to prove that literature had progressed since the seventeenth century (whereas, of course, it had not)—a sort of trade mark.

And then suddenly, a century later (*Pêcheur d'Islande* is in 1886), here it is: Loti's landscapes are not boring, they are exciting; nature has come alive at last in literature, in sympathy with simple human feelings that must not be called romantic, but which the Romantics had also, mostly in vain, tried to describe.

But no one but Loti has ever done it, and therefore no one should try again. Once a thing is done, let it alone. A work of art cannot be repeated; it can only be looked at again and again. (pp. 36-8)

> *Denis Saurat, "Loti: 1850-1923," in his* Modern French Literature: 1870-1940 *(copyright, 1946, Denis Saurat), J M Dent & Sons Limited, London, 1946 (and reprinted by Kennikat Press, 1971, pp. 35-8).*

PIERRE BRODIN   (essay date 1962)

[*Brodin's essay is an assessment of Loti as an author who should be valued for his impressionistic travel works and for his melancholy, autobiographical works which reveal the spirit of a romantic era.*]

Some critics frankly state their belief that Loti is not only "out of fashion" but that he will and should be forgotten by posterity. Does he deserve this treatment? . . .

First of all, may I say that much of Loti's work had only an ephemeral value and was not designed for posterity. Such pieces of writing as *Japoneries d'Automne* or *l'Inde sans les Anglais* were more in the line of journalistic impressions than of durable art. (p. 97)

I believe, however, that even these books—at least some of them, have still much to offer to the reader. One may disagree with enthusiasts of *Madame Chrysanthème*: present-day Japanese certainly do. But we might read Van Gogh on the subject and wonder whether Loti, the painter, did not help other painters to find themselves. As a matter of fact, the *Journals* and letters of Gauguin and Van Gogh let us know how much they felt they owed Loti.

Au Maroc, another of the author's impressionistic works, is an admirable *documentary* (like today's documentary motion pictures) on Morocco as it was just before the European penetration—a land of medieval mores and atmosphere—and as it was seen by a very keen-eyed painter. *Rarahu* or *Le Mariage de Loti* is also a documentary, dealing with a Tahiti as it will never be again, that magic island which inspired Gauguin and others.

A second group of books continues to be of interest to us, because of the quality of the fiction or of the artistic description. *Pêcheur d'Islande* is still a good, simple and deeply moving tale, which appeals to primitive but powerful feelings. It has some enchanting pages. In his pictures of Brittany, in his vision of the sea, Loti shows himself an unequaled painter. . . . (pp. 97-8)

Even *Ramuntcho,* which is too sentimental and perhaps presents too much of a clear-cut conflict between divine and human love, contains some beautiful, unforgettable pictures of the Pays Basque.

The greatness of Loti, however, does not seem to me to reside in his novels as such, but in the books where we can see more directly Loti the man, paradoxical, contradictory, unique, perhaps impossible to explain—a bit like Lawrence of Arabia.

Like T. E. Lawrence, Loti appears, in his writings, as deeply lonely. Unable to find happiness, he suffers constantly from his surroundings and seeks simultaneously an escape from reality, the full enjoyment of the present, and the illusion of eternity. Religious, but in a way quite different from that of his time and his church, he sometimes gives the impression or being a dreamer thirsting for sanctity; he pursues, without knowing it, the dream of medieval hermits. Preoccupied with moral values, but constantly assailed by primitive, pagan forces, he seems to be a perpetual internal battlefield. Although fundamentally hostile to colonial conquests, he makes a career as an officer of a great colonialist power. Upset by the spectacle and the horrors of war, he does not shirk his duty and shows himself a courageous and patriotic warrior. While driven by a migratory instinct which makes of him the greatest *écrivain-voyageur* of his time, he constantly feels nostalgic about his native land. He believes himself to be romantic, but he aspires to order and to the classical tradition. For a long time, he exercises a great influence on youth, drawing towards the sea, by his vivid writings, many a future Navy officer. But he cannot reach them to convey his moral message, and he suffers from being deprived of any contact with youth and immediate posterity.

It seems to me, however, that Loti, after a long absence, is drawing a little nearer to us.

For a long time circumstances and the prevailing state of mind were not favourable to a just comprehension of Loti. The youth of the twenties were neither contemplative nor inclined to daydream. They loved pleasure, but refused to associate with it the idea of death, as had Ronsard and Baudelaire, d'Annunzio and Loti. Some were turned away from the author of *Jerusalem* by the *proustian*, intellectual type of analysis. Others deliberately looked towards progress, realities, action, towards the ideal of Anglo-Saxon civilizations. Gide and Bergson drove their disciples towards the joy of living, towards an optimistic sympathy with the universe. At the opposite pole, Loti's melancholy and powdered face represented a kind of dream, contemplation, artifice, a return to apparently outdated forms of life, a mixture of voluptuousness and preciosity which were very *fin de siècle*.

Later, the problems of the period between the two World Wars were to claim the undivided attention of the French, at the expense of the qualities of reverie, poetry and music illustrated by Loti. After 1930, youth turned to a renewed and active faith, towards heroism, towards a more positive Christianity. It could not appreciate Loti who was, apparently, amoral, negative and pessimistic. Could one simultaneously adore Péguy and Loti? Loti, less understood than ever, certainly could not unite the young Frenchman of 1930-1940.

During the forties and, even more clearly, during the fifties, posterity begins to take a new view of Loti. His life is beginning to be appraised in the light of those of a few great writers whom we know a little better—Rousseau and Gide, for instance. (pp. 99-101)

Like Gide, Julien Viaud found himself, in his childhood, surrounded by women, old people, descended from a long line of Huguenots. A protestant education stamped his soul with indelible impressions. Like Gide, he became a dreamy, solitary young man, strongly attracted by music. Even more than Gide, he was nurtured on the Bible, the images and deep poetry of which are reflected in his style. Like many other young men brought up by women, he was spoiled and sheltered, and he grew up in an atmosphere at once sensual and religious. Women taught him to pray, but they developed in him a jealous independence; they gave him a taste for melancholy voluptuousness.

Thus grew Loti, tender, *sensitive as a raw wound*, unable to suffer pain—that of others as well as his own. As an adult, he will still be a spoiled child, who cannot accept the fate of mortal creatures. He will remain the child who is afraid of death, who unceasingly renews his religious puberty crises—the crisis which strikes the young Protestant catechumen faced with death and its terrors at the age of the awakening of the senses. At that age, too, the contemplative young man is filled with an unconscious pantheism at the sight of a long familiar nature. It seems that Loti always remained under the power of that childhood atmosphere with its soon defeated aspirations toward faith, its moments of pagan fever, its burning, eager communion with nature.

Critics have often noticed in Loti a substitution of the poetic ideal for the Christian ideal. But have these two ideals necessarily to be dissociated? Sensual in his religious nostalgia, Loti aspires toward the absolute, but seeks sensual pleasure. This unbalance or, on the contrary, this oscillation between two poles, seems to have constituted the rhythm of Loti's inner life.

Like Rousseau's personality, Loti's ego is proud, unique, solitary, and he cannot submit, kneel before a priest. But he confesses himself to the passer-by, just as Gide, later on, a jealously independent Gide, will make the public his confident,

his *total* confident. These effusions will sometimes startle the reader by their uncontrolled nature. Like Gide, although more moderate, more puritanically reserved, Loti turned to the reader as to a confessor. He revealed to him his doubts, his struggles, his distress. He cries to him for help. He does not hide his conceit, which, more than once, makes us smile. One must see there an effort towards total, absolute sincerity.

But was Loti sincere in those intimate Journals from which he drew his entire work?

A few years ago, the author of this article and Professor Maurice Coindreau, of Princeton University, engaged in a friendly controversy on this subject. Professor Coindreau felt that Loti lacked true sincerity. He called to our attention the fact that, from childhood, Loti had an instinct for *camouflage* and *dissimulation*. Young Julien Viaud wrote a diary, but kept it hidden, wanted it to be burned, unread, should he not come back from his travels. He always liked disguises and mascarades. He wore women's shoes, with high heels. He used powder and make-up. He presented Pierre Le Cor, his sailor friend *(Mon Frère Yves)*, as just a brother, whereas his ardent, jealous feelings toward this friend probably arose from a deeply troubled subconscious.

Sincerity, of course, is a relative notion. Professor Coindreau's facts are quite exact, but one can also find dissimulation, coquetry and half-truths in André Gide's *Journals*, which M. Coundreau and other would be tempted to call sincere. I have had no reason to change my opinion that Loti's work, almost entirely autobiographical, is almost entirely sincere.

Today, Loti the man, as much is not more than the writer, appears as eminently worthy of being known and again stimulates the curiosity of a new generation.

The beauty of his work should be interpreted in the light of his nostalgia for his childhood, for his country, for his faith. In the many countries he visited, Loti sought the faith of his ancestors, the exotic visions of his childhood (nourished by the letters of his brother and of his friend Lucette, who both had left for the colonies) and the magic of his native land.

Like Marcel Proust, Loti revived and transmuted his childhood. The difference between the author of *Le Roman d'un Enfant* and the author of *A la Recherche du Temps Perdu* resides in Proust's discovery that it is through art, and art alone that one can think, i.e. bring out of the shadows what one had felt, and transmute it into the spiritual. In other words, Proust's discovery goes to the universal; Loti's remains always on a personal plane.

Loti owes very little, if anything, to books (his famous quip: ''je ne lis jamais'' [''I never read''] is fundamentally true) and nearly everything to his soul and to nature. (pp. 101-04)

The sentimental generation has disappeared, which liked in Loti the magnificent echo of its melancholy and doubts. But other generations have learned to recognize that the author of *Pêcheur d'Islande* possessed eminent and definitive merits which *la belle époque* only suspected.

These are the reasons why Loti, I believe, will not be forgotten by posterity. (p. 104)

*Pierre Brodin, ''Should We Forget Pierre Loti?''
(reprinted by permission of the author), in* The American Society Legion of Honor Magazine *(© copyright by The American Society of the French Legion of Honor Magazine 1962), Vol. 33, No. 1, 1962, pp. 97-104.*

ROLAND BARTHES (essay date 1971)

[Barthes was among the most influential and revolutionary writers in modern critical thought. His importance derives less from persuasive illumination of his themes or from his introduction of certain nonliterary perspectives into his writing (he has at various times employed viewpoints adopted from Marxism, psychoanalysis, and structuralism), than it does from a dominant method of critical analysis which Barthes applied to both literary and worldly subjects. This method is based on the insight that language—or any other medium of communication: painting, fashion, advertising—is a "system of signs." No given system is either natural, reflecting some necessary condition of physical reality, or transcendent, enjoying the authority of eternal spiritual laws: it is purely the artificial construction of a particular society at a particular point in history. The aim of Barthes's method is to expose the "myths" of a specific sign system, revealing their origins in custom and convention, in order to practice what Barthes views as the only valid purpose of criticism. This purpose is the observation of the inner workings and interrelationships governing a sign system, to define the symbolic elements that constitute everything from a work of literature to an advertising billboard to a striptease act. The value of Barthes's critical method, however, is not centered on the strictly intellectual pleasures of perceiving symbolic abstractions at work, but rather on the insight that what seems to be fundamental—the norms of middle-class society, the techniques of conveying "reality" in realistic fiction—is in fact accidental and artificial, supported only by the internal structure of a closed system. In reference to literary systems of signs, Barthes wrote in the preface to his Critical Essays: *"writing is never anything but language, a formal system." Not essentially a means for revealing "truths" about the human condition or expressing the writer's emotional state, writing is only indirectly and superficially concerned with these subjects, while its direct and exclusive meaning lies in its own nature and functions. In his essay on* Aziyadé, *excerpted below, Barthes offers a more subtle and complex consideration than is common in criticism on Loti's fiction. He explores, among other topics, the relationship between Louis Viaud the man, Pierre Loti the author, and Pierre Loti the protagonist of* Aziyadé. *Barthes also discusses the role that homosexuality plays in this work.]*

Loti is [*Aziyadé*'s] hero (even if he has other names and even if this novel presents itself as the narrative of a reality, not of a fiction): Loti is *in* the novel (the fictive creature, Aziyadé, constantly calls her lover *Loti: "Look, Loti, and tell me. . ."*); but he is also outside it, since the Loti who has written the book in no way coincides with the hero Loti: they do not have the same identity: the first Loti is British and dies young; the second Loti, whose first name is Pierre, is a member of the Académie Française, and he has written many other books besides the account of his Turkish *amours.* Nor does the game of identities stop there: this second Loti, so well established in the world of literary commerce and honors, is not the actual, civilian author of *Aziyadé:* the latter was named Julien Viaud and happened to be a little gentleman who toward the end of his life had himself photographed in his house at Hendaye, dressed *à l'orientale* and surrounded by a whole bazaar of exotic objects (and had at least one taste in common with his hero: transvestism). It is not the pseudonym who is interesting (in literature, that is banal), but the other Loti, the one who is and is not his character, the one who is and is not the book's author: I don't think there exists one like him in literature, and his invention (by the third man, Viaud) is quite a bold stroke: for if it is a commonplace to sign the narrative of what happens to you and thereby to give your name to one of your characters (this is what occurs in any private diary), it is not one to invert the bestowal of the proper name; yet this is what Viaud has done: he has given to himself, the author, the name of his hero. So that, caught up in a network of three terms, the man who signs the book is false twice over: the Pierre Loti who guarantees *Aziyadé* is not at all the Loti who is its hero; and this guarantor *(auctor,* author) is himself fabricated, the author is not Loti but Viaud: it is all played out between a homonym and a pseudonym; what is missing, what is passed over in silence, what is wide open, is the proper name, the propriety of the name (the name which specifies and the name which appropriates). Where is the scriptor?

Monsieur Viaud is in his house at Hendaye, surrounded by his Moroccan and Japanese trash; Pierre Loti is in the Académie Française; Loti the British lieutenant died in Turkey in 1877 (at which time the other Loti was twenty-seven years old, so that he has survived the first one by sixty-six years). Of whom is this the story? Of which *subject?* In the very signature of the book, by the adjunction of this second Loti, of this third scriptor, a hole is made, a person is lost, by means much more cunning than mere pseudonomy. (pp. 106-07)

In his adventure with Aziyadé, Lieutenant Loti is helped by two servants, by two friends, Samuel and Achmet. Between these two affections, *"there is an abyss."*

Achmet has tiny eyes; Samuel's are very gentle. Achmet is original, generous, he is the friend of hearth and home, the intimate; Samuel is the boat boy, the attendant of the floating bed, he is the messenger, friend of the waves. Achmet is the man of Islamic fixity; Samuel is a mixture of Jew, Italian, Greek, and Turk; he is the man of mixed language, of the Sabir, the *lingua franca.* Achmet is Aziyadé's knight and espouses her cause; Samuel is her jealous rival. Achmet is on the side of virility (*"built like Hercules"*); Samuel is feminine, he casts wheedling glances and is clean as a tabby cat. Samuel is infatuated with Loti; this is not articulated, of course, though it is signified (*"His hand trembled in mine and squeezed it more than would have been necessary. 'Che volete,' he said in a dark and troubled voice, 'che volete mi?' What do you want with me?. . . Something unheard-of and shadowy had flashed through poor Samuel's mind—in the East, anything is possible!—and then he buried his face in his arms and stood there, terrified of himself, motionless and trembling. . ."*). A motif appears here—which is visible in other places as well: no, *Aziyadé* is not altogether a novel for well-brought-up girls, it is also a minor Sodomite epic, studded with allusions to *something unheard-of and shadowy.*

The paradigm of the two friends is therefore clearly formulated (the friend/the lover), but it has no consequence: it is not *transformed* (into action, into plot, into drama): the meaning remains somehow indifferent. This novel is an almost motionless discourse, which posits meanings but does not resolve them.

Strolling through Constantinople, Lieutenant Loti passes along endless walls, linked high above him by a little gray marble bridge. It is the same with the Forbidden: it is not only what we follow endlessly but also what communicates above us: an enclosure from which we are excluded. Another time, Loti makes his way, in a venture of immense daring, into the second interior courtyard of the holy mosque of Eyoub, fiercely forbidden to Christians; he raises the leather curtain which closes off the sanctuary, but we know that inside mosques there is nothing at all: all this trouble, all this transgression in order to verify a void. Here again, perhaps, the same is true of the Forbidden: a heavily proscribed space whose heart is nonetheless *aseptic.*

Loti I (the book's hero) confronts many forbidden things: the harem, adultery, the Turkish language, the Islamic religion,

Oriental dress; how many enclosures he must find the password into, imitating those who are permitted to enter them! The difficlties of the enterprise are often emphasized, but curiously enough, how they are surmounted is scarcely mentioned. If we imagine what a seraglio might have been (and so many stories exist to tell us of their fierce closure), if we recall for a moment how difficult it is to speak a foreign language such as Turkish without betraying one's character as a foreigner, if we consider how rare it is to dress exotically without seeming to be in disguise, how can we admit that Loti could have lived for months with a woman of the harem, spoken Turkish in a few weeks, etc.? We are told nothing about the concrete means of the enterprise—which would elsewhere have constituted the essentials of the novel (of the plot).

This is, no doubt, because for Loti II (the book's author) the Forbidden is an idea; it matters little, in short, if the Forbidden is violated; the important thing, endlessly expressed, is to posit it, and to posit oneself in relation to it. *Aziyadé* is the necessary name of the Forbidden, the pure form under which a thousand social transgressions can be accounted for, from adultery to pederasty, from irreligion to grammatical errors.

The pale debauch is that of the earliest hours of the morning, when a whole night of erotic dawdling comes to an end (*"The pale debauch often kept me out in the streets well into the daylight hours"*). Waiting for Aziyadé, Lieutenant Loti knows many such nights, filled by *"strange things,"* *"a strange prostitution,"* *"some imprudent adventure,"* all experiences which certainly include *"the vices of Sodom"* for whose satisfaction appear Samuel or Izeddin-Ali, the guide, the initiator, the accomplice, the organizer of saturnalia from which women are excluded; these refined or low-class revels, to which several allusions are made, always end in the same way: Loti condemns them disdainfully, claims, but a little too late, to have no part in them (as in the case of the cemetery guard, whose advances he accepts before pitching him over a precipice; as in the case of old Kairoullah, whom he provokes into offering his twelve-year-old son, "handsome as an angel," and whom he ignominiously dismisses at dawn): a familiar stratagem of bad faith, this discourse serving retrospectively to annul the preceding orgy, which nonetheless constitutes the essential element of the message; for ultimately *Aziyadé* is *also* the story of a debauch. Constantinople and Salonika (their poetical descriptions) cover for encounters hypocritically called untoward, and for persistent cruising of young Asiatic boys; the seraglio covers for the ban on homosexuality; the young lieutenant's blasé skepticism, which he works up into theories for his Western friends, covers for the spirit of the hunt, the insatiability—or the systematic satisfaction—of desire, which permits it to sprout all over again; and Aziyadé, so gentle and pure, covers for the sublimation of these pleasures: which explains why she is so nimbly dispatched, like a moral couplet, at the end of a night, of a paragraph of "debauch": *"Then I remembered that I was in Constantinople—and the she had promised to come there."*

"Debauch": that is the strong term of our story. The other term, the one to which this one must be in opposition, is not, I believe, Aziyadé. Counter-debauch is not purity (love, sentiment, fidelity, conjugality) but constraint, i.e., the Occident represented twice over in the form of the police commissioner. By sinking deliciously into Asiatic debauchery, Lieutenant Loti is fleeing the *moral* institutions of his country, of his culture, of his civilization; whence the intermittent dialogue with the tiresome sister and the British friends Plumkett and Brown, both so menacingly sprightly: you can skip these letters: their

function is purely structural: it is a matter of assuring desire its repellent term. But, then, Aziyadé? Aziyadé is the neutral term, the zero term of this major paradigm: discursively, she occupies the front rank; structurally, she is absent, she is the place of an absence, she is a fact of discourse, not a fact of desire. Is it really she, is it not rather Constantinople (i.e., the "pale debauch"), which Loti finally wants to choose against the *Deerhound*, against England and the politics of the great powers, the sister, the friends, the old mother, the lord and lady playing Beethoven in the salon of a *pension de famille*? Loti I seems to die of Aziyadé's death, but Loti II carries on: the lieutenant nobly dispatched, the author will go on describing cities, in Japan, in Persia, in Morocco, i.e., will go on designating and searchlighting (by emblems of discourse) the space of his desire. (pp. 110-14)

> *Roland Barthes, "Pierre Loti: 'Aziyadé'" (1971) in his* New Critical Essays, *translated by Richard Howard (reprinted by permission of Hill and Wang, a division of Farrar, Straus and Giroux, Inc.; translation copyright © 1980 by Farrar, Straus and Giroux, Inc.; originally published as* Le degré zéro de l'écriture suivi de Nouveaux essais Critiques *(copyright © 1972 by Editions du Seuil), Editions du Seuil, 1972), Hill and Wang, 1980, pp. 105-21.*

CLIVE WAKE   (essay date 1974)

[*The following excerpt from Wake's* The Novels of Pierre Loti *is a critical survey of Loti's novels.*]

Most general studies of Pierre Loti's work emphasize the tension between escape and reality. They show him as the restless escapist who is constantly aware of the destructive power of time. This approach inevitably means that his themes are treated as static and unchanging, with the result that they can be placed into fairly definite categories, such as death, childhood, exoticism, the sea, and so on. The approach is, of course, perfectly acceptable and it teaches us a great deal about the composition of Loti's personality and the world he creates in his books. (pp. 10-11)

The basic, underlying tension in Loti's life and work between escape and responsibility evolved with the modification of his attitudes and his personality as he grew older. The struggle between the conflicting tendencies of his personality expressed itself with greater passion and violence in the young man than it did in the older. The violence and passion of youth is most apparent in Loti's early novels, up to and including **Mon Frère Yves**, and is followed by the final defeat of the will to accept the responsibility of facing up to life in **Pêcheur d'Islande**, written in his mid-thirties. In his middle years, the emphasis is on passive acceptance of escape (with an awareness, nevertheless, of its opposite) in **Matelot**, and a probing of the lost dream-world of childhood both in **Matelot** and, especially, **Ramuntcho**. In **Les Désenchantées**, his last novel, written in his early fifties, we are confronted with a novelist whose emotions themselves have become a part of the past, leaving him with nothing but empty memories. (pp. 11-12)

[Symbolism] is one of the structural features of [*Aziyadé*]. Because of it, this first novel, in spite of a certain thinness of structure, and even of narrative, does have an internal framework. It is not, moreover, always a literary, or contrived symbolism, for it grows out of the subconscious preoccupations of the author, who is probably not really aware of what he is doing. The two most striking symbols in the novel—the love of secluded places and the constant recurrence of tombs and cemeteries—reflect his two chief obsessions: the longing for the comfortable security of the dream and the knowledge that death lies beneath it. . . . (p. 63)

In [Loti's] later work, the symbolism inherent in the Romantic view of nature is much more developed and plays a more significant role. The descriptions in *Aziyadé* are rather cursory, but already they reflect the hero's moods. The sea, the sun, the light, the stars and the bright colours of nature are an image of the hero's joy. He is fascinated by the beauty of the Corne d'Or, but it is only much later, in *Les Désenchantées,* that he found he possessed the technical ability to describe it in all its splendour. In *Aziyadé,* the reader has to be content with brief, almost incidental descriptions which seem to have a stereotyped simplicity. . . . The novel is also held together by two sets of contrasts. There is, first of all, the contrast between traditional Turkey and the threat of Turkey's corruption through contact with Europe. Loti was aware of the political events that took place during his stay largely because he had been commissioned to provide drawings for *Le Monde Illustré.* But in the novel, these political events, starting with the blockade, culminating in the adoption of a new, modern constitution, and ending with the war that finally destroys the old Turkey, are worked into the thematic fabric of the novel. The death of the old Turkey and of Loti coincide, and the final fanfare heralds the end of an outmoded civilization as well as the end of a personal dream. (pp. 63-4)

Azivadé was an attempt to create a dream-world in the present in order to escape from the anxieties of the present. *Le Mariage de Loti,* on the other hand, tells of Loti's desire to realize a childhood dream and at the same time to renew his lost links with that period of his life through the memory of his dead brother, Gustave. As with *Aziyadé,* the writing of the novel, and possibly the experience itself, is a form of exorcism, the realization of an obsession in order to free himself from its continuous and urgent presence. (p. 67)

Le Mariage de Loti is an Orphic descent into the past in order to renew his links with Gustave by attempting to trace his dead brother's presence and descendence on the island. Like Orpheus, he failed because, after leaving this island he could not prevent himself from continuing to look over his shoulder at the past. The theme is presented in the novel on three levels: the island itself is synonymous with paradise, owing its existence as such in Loti's imagination to the dreams, affections, and ambitions of his childhood; Rarahu, the heroine of the novel, is a narcissistic, symbolic reflection of the hero's lost childhood itself; indeed, she emerges as the image of the hero as a child. The hero's dead brother, Georges (that is, Gustave), is the focal point of the quest, for it is his memory, and in particular the hero's recollection of their affection for one another, which provides the impetus for the quest. (pp. 67-8)

The novel has its weaknesses. It seems at times to have been stifled by the same immobility that is characteristic of the world it evokes. There are several chapters, as in *Aziyadé,* which are simply examples of gratuitous exoticism and which, even less than similar passages in *Aziyadé,* have no relation, either direct or indirect, with the main theme. Loti describes two voyages of exploration undertaken by the hero in the novel—the first is pure tourism and the second constitutes his search for his brother's children. Unless the first is intended as a contrast with the second, so as to highlight its significance, it is wholly irrelevant. Literary influences are, however, much less obvious than in *Aziyadé,* in spite of passing references to Faust . . . ,

to the Natchez . . . and to Thomas' *Mignon.* . . . Like the first, this novel reveals his strong sense of thematic structure through the combination of realism and symbolism. The style has an unaffected and spontaneous simplicity which was lacking in *Aziyadé* and, as brief as they are, the descriptive passages begin to reveal some of the power they are to have in later novels. They are much less sketchy than in *Aziyadé* and are more intimately identified with the themes. They are beginning to show that peculiar intensity of what one might call "symbolic emotion" which, along with his very limited range of vocabulary, is so typical of Pierre Loti's descriptions. Loti's descriptions usually contain two basic ingredients—a vivid visual quality which establishes the uniqueness of the scene, as if it were being viewed with all the amazement of the child's sense of wonder, and the inclusion, here and there, of vague but emotive words which indicate the author's subjective reaction to the scene, and involve the reader at the same time. (pp. 75-6)

The most typical characteristics of the descriptions in this novel are their evocation of the 'apocalyptical' or 'antediluvian' nature of Tahiti, and an almost overpowering sense of the vastness of the universe—of the island lost in the middle of the ocean and of the world lost in the immensity of the sky. (p. 77)

The most significant innovation in *Le Roman d'un Spahi* is Loti's use, for the first time, of a hero who is not strictly speaking himself, however much he may endow him with his personal anxieties. It is also the first time that a handsome hero holds the centre of the stage. . . .

The novel tells the story of Jean Peyral, born and bred in an isolated village in the Cévennes, who is called up to do his military service and is sent to join the Spahis in Senegal. . . . Throughout the novel, Loti contrasts the honesty and simplicity of Peyral's parents, along with the purity and beauty of his fiancée, Jeanne Méry, with the Spahi's debauchery and gradual moral decline. (p. 83)

Initiation into sensuality is the cause of the Spahi's corruption. Sexuality is a leitmotif of the novel, and it is seen against a background of primitive, violent human and natural sexuality. Sex is portrayed as something belonging primarily to nature and therefore it cannot be warded off or controlled. The African environment and climate provide Loti with what he needs to present this theme with great intensity. In the African rainy season, nature is engaged in a monstrous, violent, and ravenous sexual act which produces equally monstrous birth and is inevitably followed by the sterility and the overpowering heat of the dry season. The sexual awakening of nature is accompanied by that of men. It is as violent and sensual as that of the plant and animal life. (pp. 84-5)

As usual in Loti, evil is presented as an external force over which the individual has little or no control. The Spahi is the innocent victim of his senses, and the circumstances of his life, which have brought him into this dangerous African environment, are to blame. This enables Loti to vindicate his hero. The Spahi himself does not sin, and the more he is dragged down into the mire of evil, the more he increases in beauty. He is ennobled by his suffering. Although he has lost the innocence of ignorance, his body and soul still retain the innocence of the spotless victim. . . . This highlights a contradiction in Loti's argument. The Spahi remains fundamentally innocent, but at the same time he suffers from a sense of guilt. His decision, for example, not to accept transfer to Algeria is his own choice, and it is this choice which initiates the final stages of his decline. The contradiction is, however, psychologically valid and is at the heart of Loti's *drame intérieur*, for it reflects the double presence of a sense of personal guilt and a desire to cancel out this guilt by means of a philosophy of fatalism. Caught by this contradiction, the Spahi evades it by falling into a sate of moral torpor, what Loti calls an "atonie morale". (p. 87)

From the outset, Loti's fatalistic outlook makes salvation for the Spahi improbable. . . . Whatever attempts he makes to reform, Africa's hold on him is too strong for him to succeed. Initiation into sexuality is an irreversible act. Related to this theme is the fact that, because he does not really want to reform, when he does eventually try to do so, it is too late. This is a crucial theme in three of Loti's subsequent novels—*Mon Frère Yves, Pêcheur d'Islande,* and *Matelot.* At what point, though, does it become too late? Loti's fatalism would seem to suggest that from the very beginning it is too late because of the pull of fate. . . . The fatalism suggests a fundamental desire not to succeed, or at least a deep-seated lack of will-power to do so, whereas the retention of the idea that there is a choice comes from the fear of complete surrender and the sense of guilt Loti cannot overcome. In the conclusion that it is too late, the two apparently incompatible principles come together: the hero can make the gesture of withdrawal from hell, but he will not succeed. Thus it is that the campaign which is to vindicate him takes him into the interior which had always fascinated him. (p. 89)

The concluding scenes, in their realism as well as their symbolism, have all the elements of tragedy on a grand scale, but they are perhaps too melodramatic to succeed. . . . The conclusions of *Le Roman d'un Spahi* and of *Aziyadé* resemble one another in that in both cases the hero dies violently because of his dream. But there is an important difference in the effects they have. In *Aziyadé*, Loti's death has a romantic, almost idyllic quality about it, because in this novel the dream had been portrayed as something delightful and worthwhile. In *Le Roman d'un Spahi,* the exact opposite is the case. The Spahi's death is meant to underline the appalling horror and sterility of his failure. (p. 90)

The transition from *Le Roman d'un Spahi,* the last of the three early novels, to the first novel of Loti's mature period, *Mon Frère Yves,* is very striking. To begin with, *Mon Frère Yves* has a much greater technical assurance. The early novels are the work of a young man and their themes are presented in the more aggressive manner of a young man. There is a vitality and a superficial self-assurance which come from his frustration and impatience with life. Having exorcized his early youth through these first three novels, he is left with a more clear-cut picture of his *drame intérieur.* The basic trends of his inner life and his novels are now more or less established, the outcome is a foregone conclusion, but it is still a question of how long and through what process he will get there. *Aziyadé* and *Le Roman d'un Spahi,* even *Le Mariage de Loti,* conclude with the failure and moral death of the hero, but they are only hypothetical. Loti has yet himself to experience to its full extent the failure he portrays, by way of experiment, in these early novels. Their conclusions are melodramatic because they are not really authentic; they portray what might have happened. The novels of Loti's 'maturity' tell us what actually did happen. It is interesting to pair off and compare *Aziyadé* and *Madame Chrysanthème; Le Mariage de Loti* and *Ramuntcho; Le Roman d'un Spahi* and *Matelot,* with the two major novels, *Mon Frère Yves* and *Pêcheur d'Island* holding the balance between them. (p. 94)

Mon Frère Yves is ostensibly the life story of Loti's friend, Pierre Le Cor. Yet the book is not really a biography. Loti presents the facts, and alters and modifies them as well, in such a way that the life story becomes a novel which is a projection of Loti's personal pre-occupations during the period of its composition. (p. 96)

An important feature of *Mon Frère Yves* is Yves' dependence on Loti for moral support in fighting against his weakness. . . . Loti's emphasis on this factor in his novel reveals an insight which can only come from personal experience. It is probably an indication of the way in which the novel is a projection of Loti's own difficulties. (p. 99)

In *Mon Frère Yves,* Loti shows his hero's exclusion in terms of a tangible social stigma. Yves' alcoholism is in the same category as the Spahi's cohabitation with a black mistress. Loti still sees the problem in terms of a violent, open conflict with society, and, although *Mon Frère Yves* is in many ways a much 'calmer' book, there is something of the 'angry young man' attitude which is carried across from the early to the mature period. Loti is still concerned with his conflict with society because this is uppermost in his mind, as one would expect it to be in the younger man. . . . [The] next novel, *Pêcheur d'Islande,* marks an almost radical change in attitude. The conflict has withdrawn inside the hero, so to speak, and it expresses itself externally on the level of more normal, if tense, personal relationships. At the same time, the novel's symbolism places the theme on a more universal, even metaphysical level. Where Yves is a rebel, Yann takes his attitude to life for granted. Where Yves is violent, Yann is largely passive. This is because a profound change has taken place in Loti himself during the period which separates the writing of *Mon Frère Yves* from the writing of *Pêcheur d'Islande.* He, too, is more resigned, more inclined to take himself and his weaknesses for granted, and to abandon the role of a Sysiphus. (p. 100)

It is quite evident when one compares *Pêcheur d'Islande* with Loti's other novels that it is a much more conscious work of art. In its symbolism and structure it strikes the reader as being more literary, not necessarily in any pejorative sense, although one may be conscious of the absence of the spontaneity which is so typical of Loti's other novels. It is a conscious work of art not only because Loti perhaps sensed that he had reached the height of his career as a novelist. It is more conscious because he was putting into this novel the climax that his life itself had reached, and the attempt to be more objective (which fails), along with a more conscious use of symbolism, is intended to justify himself by universalizing his experience. More than he had done in the case of Yves, Loti projects Yann as Everyman engaged in a tragic conflict with the fatalistic forces that cause his defeat. (p. 119)

Pêcheur d'Islande has its weaknesses, which in the final analysis prevent the novel from attaining true greatness. The author's sentimentality is still too much in evidence, and as irritating as ever. Perhaps, too, we are repelled by his characters because their qualities are exaggerated. They somehow belie the realism upon which the book is based. Yet, on the other hand, the novel has enough striking qualities to give it the right to be called Loti's most successful book and to make it worthy of the regard that has almost made it a classic. Its chief virtue is that, more than anything else Loti wrote, *Pêcheur d'Islande* can stand on its own feet as a novel. As much as it is a projection of Loti's subjective preoccupations, the world and the characters of *Pêcheur d'Islande* enjoy a large measure of independence. Moreover, and partly for this same reason, the novel's theme takes on an obvious universality. The symbolism makes the novel an expression of man's struggle with himself, while its realism provides a picture of Breton life in the late nineteenth century which is vivid partly because of the author's obsessions and partly because of his economy of detail and style. But far above any other reason for the novel's success, is the fact that Loti portrays the full extent of his hero's conflict and does not attempt, as he usually does, to justify it. Yann's fate is not really tragic, because he got what he asked for, but nor is it merely pathetic, like the fate of Aziyadé, Rarahu, the Spahi and Loti the hero. . . .

Yet the novel remains a parable: a parable of Loti's last real confrontation with himself. Perhaps this is the real reason why he found it so difficult to write. It has the impressiveness of any honest recognition of personal failure, in spite of its fatalism. (p. 142)

Madame Chrysanthème . . . is less a novel than an interlude. Loti takes little or no care to give it the appearance of one. In some respects it resembles *Aziyadé* and *Le Mariage de Loti,* in that it is the account of a temporary liaison with a woman of another race in an exotic environment. But whereas in the two earlier works, the author tried to turn his experiences into a novel by disguising the real names of the characters and even sometimes inventing some of the things that happen to them, in this work he does not even do this. The book gives an account of Loti's temporary 'marriage' to a Japanese girl when his ship, *La Triomphante,* was based in Nagasaki harbour in the summer of 1885. The ship's name is not even changed. Only Yves and Loti retain their literary names since it is by them that they are better known to Loti's reading public. . . . Disguised or not, most of Loti's novels are to a very large extent extensions of his autobiography. They are novels insofar as they present, in a form dramatized by Loti's imaginative insight into himself and his relations with the world around him, the crucial elements of his confrontation with reality. This imaginative transformation is produced by the author's identification of himself with the world around him, so as to heighten his experience of love and suffering and to universalize it through the resulting symbolism. . . .

Madame Chrysanthème tells us something about Pierre Loti that we rarely, if ever, see in his other novels: his sense of humour. There were glimpses of it in *Aziyadé,* and in the account of his stay at Joinville in the first volume of the *Journal Intime.* Loti enjoyed practical jokes, what he called clowning, because the resulting moment of *désinvolture* meant a temporary release from the tensions of his life. *Madame Chrysanthème* is therefore, a brief release from the intensely subjective world of *Pêcheur d'Islande,* which he was still writing during his stay in Japan and which immediately preceded *Madame Chrysanthème* in order of publication. *Madame Chrysanthème* is a very personal book, but it reflects the exterior of Loti's personality—the social figure, the famous writer. It is almost as if, in *Madame Chrysanthème,* Loti is drawing attention away from his real self, so deeply portrayed in *Pêcheur d'Islande,* in a kind of pastiche of his own work. . . . (p. 145)

[*Matelot*] is a complex meditation on Loti's own childhood and youth, and Jean Berny the hero is, in fact, a composite character based on [Loti's friend] Léo Thémèze, Gustave Viaud, Joseph Bernard and Loti himself. From what Loti has written about his relationship with Thémèze, it is clear that it was not only the realization of his ideal of friendship, and as such akin to the relationship he dreamed of achieving with Gustave and

Joseph Bernard; it was also a rediscovery of his childhood and youth through the almost complete identification of personality that he achieved with Léo Thémèze. . . . (p. 149)

Matelot lacks the vitality of Loti's previous novels. In it, Loti tries to justify failure, and in doing so overdoes the element of pity to the point of unbearable sentimentality. . . . The novel ends with an invocation to the Virgin on the part of the author which indicates how much the book reflects his own preoccupations, but it is unacceptably sentimental. Yet, in spite of these objective weaknesses, the novel remains a very revealing representation of Loti's obsession at the time with his lost childhood and the roots of his own failure. (p. 160)

Like *Matelot,* [*Ramuntcho*] was written in the shadow of the middle-aged writer's memories of childhood, begun with the publication of *Le Roman d'un Enfant* in 1890. *Matelot* tells primarily of the young hero's expulsion from childhood and the effects this event has on his personality. It ends with the hero's failure to adjust, symbolized by his death. *Ramuntcho* deals with a similar theme, but the emphasis is different, and the conclusion almost totally unexpected. It portrays the tension between the desire to retain the world of childhood and the desire to break out of it. This is a theme that runs throughout *Le Roman d'un Enfant,* where it is symbolized by the call of the sound of sailors singing in the distance. . . . (p. 163)

Loti's last novel ought to have been *Ramuntcho,* for with it he comes to the end of the interior self-searching begun in his youth. Some thirteen years later, however, he published a further novel entitled *Les Désenchantées.* . . .

The novel is based on a practical joke played on Loti by three women. From October 1903 until March 1905, Loti was commander of *Le Vautour* based at Constantinople. Three women, pretending to be Turks, arranged a series of clandestine meetings with him in order to persuade him to write a novel about the status of Turkish women. Although Loti suspected a hoax, he never really learnt the full truth. The scheme was dreamt up by the French writer Marc Hélys (the pseudonym of Mme Léra), assisted by two young half-French, half-Turkish women. Loti agreed, against his will, to write the novel, which amounts in fact to an account of their meetings and the publication of the edited versions of their correspondence. (p. 173)

Les Désenchantées is, therefore, a novel within a novel, or rather, it tells how the novel came to be written. It is by far Loti's longest novel, and also his most tedious. In the absence of any really personal involvement on Loti's part in the emotional situation, the book seems almost lifeless. It has a three-pronged theme: recollections of Aziyadé (referred to as Nedjibé), with an account of Loti's restoration of her tomb; the various encounters with Djénane and her cousins, Zeyneb and Mélek; and, finally, a great deal of totally unrelated description of Constantinople, mainly to enable Loti to indulge in his love for the city and its people. The second theme is ostensibly the purpose of the book, but it consists almost solely of an account of clandestine meetings and discussions about the status of women in Islamic countries. The chief dramatic content of these meetings is the tremendous dangers the hero and the women are incurring, and the chief outcome of it all is the impression that the hero enjoyed a rather puerile pride in his escapades.

The central plot and the two themes relating to his earlier visits and his love of Turkey are logically in conflict. While, on the one hand, the young women are trying to interest him in the reform of Islamic society, the hero, on the other hand, reminisces about the past as he had known it and deplores the changes that have taken place in Turkey as the result of Western influence. . . . For the first time in Loti's novels, we come away with the impression that this is a book by and about a man who has well and truly reached middle-age. The secret of the book's meaning lies perhaps in the irony of its title. The hero suggests to his young lady friends that his novel ought to be called *Les Désenchantées,* that is, women who are no longer held by the spell of outmoded tradition. But, ironically, it can be applied to Loti as well, and to the way the magic has gone out of his own life. (p. 174)

All of Loti's previous novels were the product of his own most intimate preoccupations. . . . Loti likes to be in the position of the producer, as it were, of the drama he is creating. In the case of *Les Désenchantées,* Lot was himself 'produced' and manipulated by others. His attitude to his subject is, as a result, somewhat uneasy. Anxious to overcome this feeling of uneasiness, he tries to take control of at least a part of the situation by fancying that Djénane is in love with him, and that here is a possibility of reviving the past in a more convincing manner.

But this attempt to resuscitate the grand lover of the past shows the novel's real flaw. The opening pages introduce us to the hero, the famous novelist, André Lhéry, as he reads his enormous fan-mail, significantly, mostly from women. The hero of the novel is not Pierre Loti the man who has delved deep into his complex and troubled personality for the material of his novels, but Pierre Loti the famous, lionized society author, the public image of the real man. Just as he had found it neccessary to change his name from Julien Viaud to Pierre Loti in order to give himself a three-dimensional view of his personality and to be able to convert it into literary terms, so he now gives himself a new name which crystallizes his public image.

Perhaps it would have been better for his reputation as a novelist if *Les Désenchantées* had not been written. Yet, it is not without interest for what it tells us about Loti and his relations with his (mostly feminine) admirers. Moreover, by being so different from everything that he had written before, it throws the earlier novels into relief. It is, in a way, a fitting conclusion to his career as a novelist. (pp. 174-75)

> *Clive Wake, in his* The Novels of Pierre Loti *(©copyright 1974 Mouton & Co. N. V., Publishers), Mouton, 1974, 182 p.*

MICHAEL G. LERNER   (essay date 1974)

[*A specialist in late nineteenth and twentieth-century French authors, Lerner has stated that "as a great globetrotter—having visited most countries including China and worked in Europe, the United Kingdom, Australia, and Canada—I enjoyed writing on Pierre Loti who was a naval officer by profession." Lerner's* Pierre Loti, *from which the following excerpt is taken, provides a comprehensive biocritical study of Loti's works.*]

There is [the] same mixture of the real and the realistic, the personal and the artificial, truth and illusion, in the style of Loti's work as in his personality. It is evident in his contrived use of the diary form and letters as well as in the way he disguises and distorts names and situations in his plots. It is clear, too, that his claim that he had read hardly any literature was completely misleading; for he had a good knowledge of the Bible, some classics, the Romantics, and some current writers, and although he asserts in *Fleurs d'Ennui* that his work was composed from an indiscriminate accumulation of his over-

all impressions on his travels, his style is, despite its appearance of being "simple, fluent, almost commonplace," as complex and rhetorical as that of any of his literary contemporaries and not just a felicitous combination of the right evocative words used with subtle discretion. . . . For his aim is to convey to his readers with what one critic has seen as "sentimental immodesty" his highly personal impressions of an exotic situation—impressions which, as has been explained above, he did not always experience in the way or place he describes. Just as in his sketches of Easter Island and Tahiti he occasionally distorts the scene or subject before him to heighten the impression of mysteriousness and idyllicism he wishes to convey— he reconstructs the monoliths and idealizes the natives so he carefully arranges his novels to evoke the sensations and thoughts he desires to communicate. In short, he uses an accurate and discriminating realism to render with greater conviction a romanticized exoticism behind which he often hid rather than reveal his true feelings and the real situation.

The simple but evocative realism of Loti's narrative derives both from the representative selection of typical incidents he describes and from his impressionistic use of vocabulary, syntax and sentence structure, and the point of view to convey them. He uses simple words for easy understanding, often repeating them in slightly different terms or setting them in apposition for emphasis and greater continuity: occasionally, he contrasts them with exotic words or uses an indefinite adjective or phrase in order to achieve a greater impressionistic effect of strangeness; or includes an abstract noun instead of an adjective for more emphatic effects of color. Furthermore, the fact that Loti describes only definite colors, sounds, and scents means that he only requires simple vocabulary. The apparent simplicity of his sentences also contributes to his prose's dynamism; this he creates by the usual means of present and past participles and present and imperfect tenses for effects of immediacy and action; and of questions, exclamations, short sentences, and indirect free speech or interior monologue to give his prose the fluent realism of dialogue. More specifically, Loti's artifices for instilling dynamism and immediacy are the infinitive, imperative, apostrophe, and verb-form at the beginning of sentences; the series of short sentences to convey quick impressions of a place or itinerary: and the economical use of dots and dashes in the text to qualify what precedes with implied comment and separate details or themes without starting fresh sentences.

Finally, Loti achieves a lifelike realism in his exotic settings by not merely juxtaposing such contrasting facets of life as the exotic events he describes and the universal sentiments they provoke, as the critic Jules Lemaître suggested to explain somehow the strange appeal of Loti's novels, but by maintaining a constantly changing point of view in his narration and often setting several points of view in apposition or using them as antitheses within a paragraph. . . . In short, while apparently detaching himself from the narrative by switching the viewpoint and giving the appearance of casual realism thereby, Loti remains in firm control of the impression given since all the views relate to him, his actions, or reactions in some way; this allows the reader, as Mme [Juliette] Adam remarked, to view the scene as if through his own eyes and at the next through Loti's while it is in fact always seen through the narrator's.

This technique is not only underlined by the discriminatory economy of the retrospective diary form Loti uses to show a representative collection of realistic scenes, but also by the contrived yet imperceptible manner he builds up a descriptive passage, using a similar series of switching shots to impose his views of the world he is describing. Whether it is Aziyadé's face, the fishermen of Papara, the ball at Pomaré's palace, or Peyral's night at sea near the Equator, Loti constructs his description by first stating the facts of the situation—the weather, time of year, location, hour of the day, or statement of an object or circumstance—and then concentrating like an artist making a draft sketch on the shape or layout of what he is describing; next, he adds some details such as the color or dress or other minor fact to qualify what precedes and gives some impressions of the sounds, smells, and shades of color of the scene and, finally, links these with his imagined themes and mood; thus, gradually, Aziyadé's eyes are related by the green of their pupils to the sea-green praised by Oriental poets; the return of the Tahitian fishermen merges into a scene from prehistoric times through the shells they blow into; the outline of the mountains, banana clumps, and groups of people against the starry sky in Pomaré's gardens is related to the perfume and silence of Tahitian nights, which dispose one to be enchanted by music and by Meyerbeer's *Africaine* in particular; and the warmth and stillness of the equatorial night on board the silent ship makes Peyral think of the geological creation of the earth. In each case, realistic detail—as intricate as the bejeweled coffee cups pointed out on Loti's visit to the Sultan or the crabs' claws noted by Peyral on the riverbank in Guinea—and impressionistic relief, like the ecstatic sensations felt by the Fataoua stream or the grating sound of the hanged men's nails on the ground at Salonica, contribute to the final impression associated with the narrator's thought or person that Loti wishes to convey in the novel: the romantic exoticism of Aziyadé, the fatal idyllicism of Tahiti, and the fossilized primitiveness of Senegal. These total impressions are as authentically romanticized by a sort of poetic inflation as his descriptions of the Tahitian streams and Guinean jungle are in their exaggeratedly realistic representativeness of the oceanic paradise and the African wild. They are, nevertheless, contrasted with European values and customs by the narrator's frequent comparison of the two; this in turn provides Loti's views on life in France.

His realism becomes thus a mere stepping-stone for the impressionistic communication of his moral ideas; the external world becomes, as Paul Bourget pointed out, a passive recipient of Loti's ideas and sensations; the countries he describes become largely realistic representations in romanticized exotic terms of his ideal and anguished thoughts on life; and his characters become functional representatives of his impressions of their country and implicit criticisms of Europe and only exist through these, without any individual psychology and development; they are merely there to epitomize Loti's impressionistic, implicitly critical evocation of their exotic settings and yet to conceal the omnipresent imposition on his reader of the particular sentiments and moral inferences which the author contrives by his style to convey. Despite the emphasis on the personal and authentic, there is thus as much complex detachment in the contrivances of Loti's style as there was in his exoticism and the egocentric cults that composed it; the refinement of his style does not lie in the preciosity of the Goncourts' impressionism or the complexity of Gide's kaleidoscopic approach, with both of which it has close affinities, but in the deliberate concision of his apparent simplicity for evocative and moral effect. Just as years earlier he, like his mother

and sister, had been able to evoke life overseas or [his brother] Gustave's memory by their sentimental, imaginative attachment to certain objects and places and to letters received, so in his novels he not only drew on his travels to romantically recreate his version of life overseas, disguising the names of his characters for his plot—as his sister did in her draft novel *Autour de Paulette* and Loti did in real life in referring to close friends—but used the dynamic intimacy and detail of their exotic realism in order to convey his moral ideas on life and the personality, which he wished his readers to recognize as his. (pp. 41-5)

Michael G. Lerner, in his Pierre Loti *(copyright © 1974 by Twayne Publishers; reprinted with the permission of Twayne Publishers, a Division of G. K. Hall & Co., Boston), Twayne, 1974, 172 p.*

ADDITIONAL BIBLIOGRAPHY

D'Auvergne, Edmund B. *Pierre Loti: The Romance of a Great Writer.* New York: Frederick A. Stokes Co., 1926, 253 p.
　　Informative biography.

France, Anatole. "Why Are We Sad?" In his *On Life and Letters,* third series, translated by D. B. Stewart, pp. 3-10. New York: John Lane Co., 1922.*
　　Discusses melancholy in Loti's essay *Japoneries d'automne.*

Harris, Frank. "Pierre Loti: A Lord of Language." In his *Contemporary Portraits,* second series, pp. 192-200. New York: Frank Harris, 1919.
　　Remembrances of Loti's early popularity; also critical comments which praise Loti's descriptive prose, but find the Frenchman's works too pessimistic to achieve lasting importance.

Hearn, Lafcadio. "The New Romantic" and "The Most Original of Modern Novelists: Pierre Loti." In his *Essays in European and Oriental Literature,* pp. 125-32, pp. 133-40. New York: Dodd, Mead and Co., 1923.
　　Reprints of two early laudatory reviews of Loti's works by one of his first English translators. Hearn is responsible for introducing Loti's works to American readers.

Henry, Stuart. "Pierre Loti." In his *French Essays and Profiles,* pp. 287-96. New York: E. P. Dutton & Co., 1921.
　　Early reminiscence by Loti's friend.

Lerner, Michael G. "Pierre Loti As Dramatist: 'Judith Renaudin'." *Nottingham French Studies* XIII, No. 2 (October 1974): 61-72.
　　Thorough discussion of Loti's drama *Judith Renaudin.* According to Lerner, the drama is an attempt by Loti to return to the security of his childhood and to regain belief in a religious ethic.

Mauriac, François. "Loti." In his *Men I Hold Great,* translated by Elsie Pell, pp. 105-08. New York: Philosophical Library, 1951.
　　Discusses the unyielding pessimism in Loti's works. According to Mauriac, Loti's continual "howling at death" in his works reflects the author's non-religious ethic which is a belief in only what "the hands and lips" can touch," including pain and, ultimately, death.

Mordell, Albert. "Hearn's Translations from Pierre Loti." In his *Discoveries: Essays on Lafcadio Hearn,* pp. 104-08. Tokyo: Orient/West, 1964.
　　Interesting essay which gives an account of Lafcadio Hearn's relationship with Loti, as well as several critical comments by Mordell on Loti's works.

Margaret (Munnerlyn) Mitchell (Marsh)

1900-1949

(Also wrote under the name Peggy Mitchell) American novelist and journalist.

Mitchell is the author of *Gone with the Wind*, the most popular novel in American fiction. From the time of its publication in 1936 to the present day, this historical romance of the Civil War era has outsold any other hardcover book with the exception of the Bible. Praised as the first Civil War novel to be told from a Southern woman's point of view, *Gone with the Wind* won the 1937 Pulitzer Prize in fiction. Three years after its first publication, Mitchell's novel was adapted into a lavish film that has also become a popular classic.

Mitchell was born into an upper middle-class family and raised in Atlanta, Georgia. Her father was an attorney and her mother was an activist for women's suffrage. Throughout her childhood, Mitchell was captivated by her parents' and grandmother's stories of Atlanta and tales of heroic efforts during the Civil War; these stories eventually served as material for her famous literary work. Mitchell attended Smith College for one year, leaving school to manage her father's household after her mother's death. In 1922, following a brief marriage that ended in divorce, she became a journalist for the *Atlanta Journal* and rose in status from a fledgling reporter to one of the newspaper's best feature writers. However, Mitchell's journalistic career lasted only four years, ending when an ankle injury confined her to her home. During convalescence, at the suggestion and with the editorial assistance of her second husband, Mitchell began to write a novel with the working title "Tomorrow Is Another Day." For her story, she drew upon her knowledge of Atlanta and the South, and created fictional characters that were composites of people she knew. Although Mitchell finished most of the work by 1929, she researched historical facts and rewrote sections of the novel for nearly seven more years. In 1935, the manuscript was brought to the attention of Harold S. Latham, editor for Macmillan, who was in Atlanta on a trip to find publishable manuscripts. Never expecting her work to be published, Mitchell reluctantly allowed Latham to read the imposing manuscript, which was over one thousand pages long. He immediately accepted the novel, and after one year of exhaustive revisions, Mitchell's book was published as *Gone with the Wind*—retitled from a line in Ernest Dowson's poem "Non sum qualis eram bonae sub regno Cynarae." Upon its entry into the literary market, *Gone with the Wind* not only broke all publishing records, but also dramatically altered the life of its author. Mitchell spent the remaining years of her life trying to maintain a modicum of privacy for herself and her husband. In 1949 she was struck and killed by a taxicab near her home in Atlanta.

Gone with the Wind is in the tradition of the historical novel. In her work, Mitchell employed a simple narrative style to combine a sentimental account of the "Old South" with the historical facts of an era that experienced immense social and economic change. From the threat of war between the states to General Sherman's fiery march on Atlanta, and through the Reconstruction period, *Gone with the Wind* depicts the tribulations of Scarlett O'Hara, Rhett Butler, Ashley Wilkes, and Melanie Hamilton—four of the best-known fictional char-

acters in American literature—as they attempt to adapt to the changing circumstances of their homeland. However, only the willful heroine Scarlett and the roguish Rhett emerge as survivors in the "New South," while the ineffectual dreamer Ashley is defeated in spirit and the docile "Southern woman" Melanie dies. Both Melanie and Ashley are viewed by critics as representatives of the antebellum South—a way of life that was destroyed by war. Most critics indicate that Scarlett O'Hara is Mitchell's most interesting character, and she is frequently compared to Becky Sharp in William Thackeray's *Vanity Fair*. Similar to Becky's determination, Scarlett's will to survive dictates her actions throughout the novel; thus, she appears coquettish, clever, selfish, amoral, and even loving to suit her needs. Although Mitchell is praised for the clarity, vitality, and sheer readability of her story, most critics agree that *Gone with the Wind* suffers in comparison to other works of American Civil War literature. W. J. Stuckey offers a somewhat harsh but representative opinion of the novel, when he states: that "while one can hear distant echoes of Fielding, Thackeray (especially), and Emily Brontë in *Gone with the Wind*, Miss Mitchell's art most noisily proclaims its indebtedness to the literature of wish fulfillment—the bosomy and sub-pornographic historical romance, the sentimental novel, and the Hollywood extravaganza." Similarly, Floyd C. Watkins comments that "*Gone with the Wind* is narrowly patriotic, prudish, melodramatic, and sentimental."

Critics often express bewilderment at the continued appeal of *Gone with the Wind* and, generally, their discussions focus on the novel's popularity and on its characters and concerns as a reflection of mass consciousness. Mitchell's work has been both praised and mocked for its romantic portrayal of the South. Some critics have defined the novel's initial popularity in terms of its value as escapist literature during the troubled times of the 1930s, while others remark that readers simply admired the "gumption" of Scarlett O'Hara. Mitchell herself was perplexed by the success of her novel, describing the work as "just a simple story of some people who went up and some who went down, those who could take it and those who couldn't." In her 1983 biography of Mitchell, Anne Edwards offers a recent opinion of *Gone with the Wind*'s mass appeal and comments that "it contains something for everyone." Edwards explains that the novel has a "lurking sensuality" and provides the reader with romance, adventure, war, and history. Regardless of its artistic weaknesses, *Gone with the Wind* has proven itself an alluring epic which has unceasingly held the public's attention.

(See also *Dictionary of Literary Biography*, Vol. 9: *American Novelists, 1910-1945*.)

PRINCIPAL WORKS

Gone with the Wind (novel) 1936
Margaret Mitchell's "Gone with the Wind" Letters: 1936-1949 (letters) 1976

STEPHEN VINCENT BENÉT (essay date 1936)

[*Benét was an American man of letters whose poetry and fiction is often concerned with examining, understanding, and celebrating American history and culture. The comic short story "The Devil and Daniel Webster" and the Pulitzer Prize-winning Civil War epic* John Brown's Body *are his best-known works. According to Mitchell's biographers,* John Brown's Body *was one of her favorite works of poetry and the novelist was appreciative of Benét's review of* Gone with the Wind.]

We have had other novels about the Civil War by women. . . . But I don't know of any other in which the interest is so consistently centered, not upon the armies and the battles, the flags and the famous names, but upon that other world of women who heard the storm, waited it out, succumbed to it or rebuilt after it, according to their natures. It is in the diaries and the memoirs—in Letitia Macdonald and Mrs. Roger A. Pryor and a dozen more. But it has never been put so completely in fiction before. And it is that which gives **"Gone With the Wind"** its originality and its individual impact.

It is a long book and a copious one, crowded with character and incident, and bound together with one consistent thread, the strong greediness of Scarlett O'Hara who was bound to get her way, in spite of the hampering ideal of the Perfect Southern Gentlewomen and the ruin that follows men's wars. She didn't, quite, in the end, though she got a great many other things, including money and power—but the tale of her adventures and her struggles makes as readable, full-bodied, and consistent a historical novel as we have had in some time—a novel which, in certain passages, as in the flight from burning Atlanta, rises to genuine heights. Miss Mitchell knows her period, her people, and the red hill country of North Georgia—she knows the

clothes and the codes and the little distinctions that make for authenticity. Tara is a working plantation, not a white-porched movie-set—and Atlanta is itself and an individual city, not a fabulous combination of all the first-family features of Richmond, Charleston, and New Orleans. The civilization of the antebellum South was something a little more than a picturesque gesture in gentility—and to a public a little surfeited with wistful reminiscence of the cape-jessamine side of it, Miss Mitchell's rather more realistic treatment should come as a decided relief. . . .

As background and accompaniment, there is the breakdown of a civilization and the first tentative steps at its rebuilding. Miss Mitchell, as I have said, attempts no battle-pieces, but the grind of the war is there, the patriotic fairs and the slow killing of friend and acquaintance, the false news and the true, the hope deferred and the end and the strangeness after the end. When Scarlett and Melanie, fleeing from Atlanta before the approach of Sherman's army, return to the O'Hara plantation, they return, quite literally, to a ruined world. That was the way it was, and Miss Mitchell's description of Scarlett's frenzied, tireless attempt to rebuild some semblance of life and vigor into Tara is one of the most fascinating sections of her novel. . . .

How [Scarlett] made her determination good and what paths her determination led her through form the theme of the last sections of the book. I shall not spoil Miss Mitchell's plot by recounting it in detail, for it is a good one. But her picture of the early days of Reconstruction and the tainted society of scalawags and carpetbaggers through which Scarlett moved with Rhett Butler is quite as vivid as her picture of the war years. Throughout, she draws her distinctions with a sure hand. The extraordinary episode of the rescue of the ex-Confederates by the testimony of Belle Watling and her girls may not please Miss Mitchell's Atlanta audience but it has the convincing ring of folk-lore. And the post-war attitude of a dozen different types of human being, from Rhett Butler's to Ashley Wilkes's, is surely and deftly done—as is the amazing incident of Archie the ex-convict, who acted as chaperone and bodyguard to the ladies of Atlanta during Reconstruction days.

It is only one of a score of such incidents, for Miss Mitchell paints a broad canvas, and an exciting one. And, in spite of its length, the book moves swiftly and smoothly—a three-decker with all sails set. Miss Mitchell has lost neither her characters in her background nor her background in her characters, and her full-blooded story is in the best traditions of the historical novel. It is a good novel rather than a great one, by the impalpables that divide good work from great. And there is, to this reviewer, perhaps unjustly, the shadow of another green-eyed girl over Scarlett O'Hara—as Rhett Butler occasionally shows traces both of St. Elmo and Lord Steyne and Melanie's extreme nobility tends to drift into Ameliaishness here and there. Nevertheless, in **"Gone With the Wind,"** Miss Mitchell has written a solid and vividly interesting story of war and reconstruction, realistic in detail and told from an original point of view.

> *Stephen Vincent Benét, "Georgia Marches Through," in* The Saturday Review of Literature *(© 1936, copyright renewed © 1963, Saturday Review Magazine Co.; reprinted by permission), Vol. XIV, No. 10, July 4, 1936, p. 5.*

JOHN PEALE BISHOP (essay date 1936)

[*As a West Virginia born poet, Bishop is sometimes associated with Southern Renaissance authors such as Allen Tate and Robert*

Penn Warren, though Bishop's verse is not significantly concerned with Southern themes or subjects. Competent and formalistic, Bishop is usually regarded as an exemplary minor American poet. He also published short stories, a novel, and critical essays. In the brief excerpt below, Bishop considers Gone with the Wind *Mitchell's adaptation of the traditional picaresque novel, but in the end criticizes it for its negative moral implications.*]

Miss Margaret Mitchell has adapted the picaresque novel to her own purposes, presenting in *Gone with the Wind* a rogue's-eye view of the Civil War and Reconstruction. But since the unscrupulous rascal who must traditionally form the center of such a novel is not only a young woman, but also—at least by virtue of her upbringing—a Georgia lady, adventures must come to her; she cannot go far out of her way for them. They come to her in devastating plenty with the war and continue throughout the carpetbag dictatorship.

Scarlett O'Hara is the child of a gently bred Creole mother from the seacoast and of a riproaring, hard-riding Irishman on the make, whose stiff head for liquor and sure hand for poker have won him a large plantation in the Georgia uplands. For the critical uses of the novelist, therefore, she is well placed; for though she is born to a position in the planter class, she takes after her father and is never completely of it. Besides, this is a new country, red lands rich for cotton, but only a generation before cleared of Indians. It is constantly threatened by seedling pine and blackberry brambles and ready to slip back to wilderness. And Atlanta, where much of the action takes place, has at this time all the rawness of a frontier town; conventions appropriate enough to old settlements like Charleston and Savannah must here appear trivial.

Scarlett, in any case, could not be assimilated. Mean, superstitious and unsurpassably selfish, only in girlhood does she even superficially wear the manners of her apparent class; their emotions she never shares. Any necessity of the spirit is beyond her; the most she knows of the mind is a low peasant cunning, which values nothing beyond her own precious skin and the land and money that will allow it not to perish. To hold the one and procure the other, she kills a thieving Yankee soldier, robs his corpse, engages in several marriages, buys mills, exploits convict labor, cheats, and indifferently sends several to their deaths.

Scarlett is matched with another rogue, her male counterpart, a renegade aristocrat originally from Charleston, as reprehensible as she in morals, but much her superior by reason of his romantically cynical intelligence. Miss Mitchell uses the two of them to assert indirectly the virtues of the society whose destruction they witness. By this device, she has clearly hoped to avoid sentimentality in treating a subject she fears as sentimental. A greater novelist would have had no such dread; Tolstoy is not afraid of Prince André's enthusiasm for the Tsar. And Miss Mitchell is somewhat hampered in the long run by the emotional inadequacy of her heroine, as well as the limitations of her mind. Scarlett undergoes the war, but reacts neither to its pity nor its terror. And she is too stupid to know that there are larger issues involved than her own survival.

Gone with the Wind is one of those thousand-page novels, competent but neither very good nor very sound. The historical background is handled well and with an extraordinary sense of detail. The moral problem is less sure in its treatment. It is this: In a society falling apart, upon what terms can the individual afford to survive? Scarlett wants only to last and takes any terms life offers. Miss Mitchell seems to approve of her persistence. But she also implies that civilization consists pre-cisely in an unwillingness to survive on any terms save those of one's own determining. (pp. 253-54)

John Peale Bishop, "War and No Peace" ('Gone with the Wind' by Margaret Mitchell)," in The New Republic (© *1936 The New Republic, Inc.), Vol. LXXXVII, No. 1128, July 15, 1936 (and reprinted in* The Collected Essays of John Peale Bishop, *edited by Edmund Wilson, Charles Scribner's Sons, 1948, pp. 253-54).*

MALCOLM COWLEY (essay date 1936)

[*Cowley has made several valuable contributions to contemporary letters with his editions of important American authors (Nathaniel Hawthorne, Walt Whitman, Ernest Hemingway, William Faulkner, F. Scott Fitzgerald), his writings as a literary critic for* The New Republic, *and, above all, for his chronicles and criticism of modern American literature. Cowley's literary criticism does not attempt a systematic philosophical view of life and art, nor is it representative of a neatly defined school of critical thought, but rather focuses on works—particularly those of "lost generation" writers—that he feels his personal experience has qualified him to explicate and that he considers worthy of public appreciation. The critical approach Cowley follows is undogmatic and is characterized by a willingness to view a work from whatever perspective—social, historical, aesthetic—that the work itself seems to demand for its illumination.*]

"Gone with the Wind" is an encyclopedia of the plantation legend. Other novelists by the hundreds have helped to shape this legend, but each of them has presented only part of it. Miss Mitchell repeats it as a whole, with all its episodes and all its characters and all its stage settings—the big white-columned house sleeping under its trees among the cotton fields; the band of faithful retainers, including two that quaintly resemble Aunt Jemima and Old Black Joe; the white-haired massa bathing in mint juleps; the heroine with her seventeen-inch waist and the high-spirited twins who came courting her in the magnolia-colored moonlight, with the darkies singing under the hill—then the War between the States, sir, and the twins riding off on their fiery chargers, and the lovely ladies staying behind to nurse the wounded, and Sherman's march (now the damyankees are looting the mansion and one of them threatens to violate its high-bred mistress, but she clutches the rusty trigger of an old horse pistol and it goes off bang in his ugly face)—then the black days of Reconstruction, the callousness of the Carpetbaggers, the scalawaggishness of the Scalawags, the knightliness of the Ku Klux Klansmen, who frighten Negroes away from the polls, thus making Georgia safe for democracy and virtuous womanhood and Our Gene Talmadge—it is all here, every last bale of cotton and bushel of moonlight, every last full measure of Southern female devotion working its lilywhite fingers uncomplainingly to the lilywhite bone.

But even though the legend is false in part and silly in part and vicious in its general effect on Southern life today, still it retains its appeal to fundamental emotions. Miss Mitchell lends new strength to the legend by telling it as if it had never been told before, and also by mixing a good share of realism with the romance. She writes with a splendid recklessness, blundering into big scenes that a more experienced novelist would hesitate to handle for fear of being compared unfavorably with Dickens or Dostoevsky. Miss Mitchell is afraid of no comparison and no emotion—she makes us weep at a deathbed (and really weep), exult at a sudden rescue and grit our teeth at the crimes of our relatives the damyankees. I would never, never say that she has written a great novel, but in the midst of triteness and sentimentality her book has a simple-minded courage that suggests the great novelists of the past. No wonder it is going like the wind. (pp. 161-62)

Malcolm Cowley, "Going with the Wind," in The New Republic (© 1936 The New Republic, Inc.), Vol. LXXXVIII, No. 1137, September 16, 1936, pp. 161-62.

BELLE ROSENBAUM (essay date 1937)

The American people are not a nation of book readers.

We have been accused of this time and again, perhaps with some justification. We read a great many newspapers and magazines, but Mr. R. L. Duffus, who surveyed the reading habits of the average American, found that he averages only seven books per year—two of which he buys. . . . He spends more money on greeting cards than he does on books. But he bought *Gone with the Wind.*

It is still a complex affair, this appetite for a long romantic story of the Civil War, but some reasons obtrude. It is a simple book, bereft of obscenity, lacking the inductive vagueness of the stream-of-consciousness school, yet frankly realistic and concerned with a woman who, in all sincerity, is a harlot. It states its story without comment, without lectures on abnormal psychology. Nevertheless, these things are present. All the modern improvements are in the book; but they are not pointed up. Scarlett O'Hara and Rhett Butler retained a touch of Joyce, Hemingway, Fitzgerald, and the aftermath of the Civil War was interpreted in modern terms with Scarlett O'Hara emerging as the modern prototype of Thackeray's immortal Becky Sharp. (pp. 69-70)

If you wonder why *Gone with the Wind* is so popular, think what a Dickens, a Thackeray, or a Fielding could do for America—for the greatest single chunk of people ever made simultaneously literate—a chunk of people yearning for a tale well told, for the sake of its telling, by a teller who loves the tale and the art of telling it. There has never been any other secret to popular literature. Once in a while a writer stumbles on it. (p. 70)

Belle Rosenbaum, "Why Do They Read It?" in Scribner's Magazine (copyright, 1937, by Charles Scribner's Sons; copyright renewed 1965; reprinted with permission of Charles Scribner's Sons), Vol. CII, No. 2, August, 1937, pp. 23-4, 69-70.

HOLMES ALEXANDER (essay date 1938)

[*An historical novelist and a biographer of several important figures in American history, Alexander wrote the following defense of* Gone with the Wind *in response to Bernard De Voto's article in* The Saturday Review of Literature *(see additional bibliography) entitled "Fiction Fights the Civil War." In that essay De Voto discusses the wave of Civil War novels in the 1930s and emphasizes that* Gone with the Wind *may be one of the best sellers of Civil War fiction, but it is "far from the best."*]

Sir:—Your leading article in the issue of December 18 raises or rather resurrects a matter which has puzzled me and I know has puzzled American book readers for more than a year.

I refer to the downright snobbish treatment by the whole reviewing brotherhood of Margaret Mitchell. . . . At Christmas time last year the Sunday *Times Review* printed a feature article which rather scornfully analyzed **"Gone with the Wind"** and concluded that its chief ingredient was "emotional content"

(sex, I suppose), and that its sale was a fluke. At this Christmas season, with the book past its peak, you take the trouble to kick it in the face.

What's eating you people anyhow? Strangely enough this same issue of Dec. 18 seems to give some clue. The editorial expressed no small contempt for the un-"professional" writer. Is it because Miss Mitchell still has the debutante's blush on her writing instead of the cosmetic shine of a tired hack? If she splits infinitives, so does Hemingway. Her historical slips are no worse than Shakespeare's. Her Southerners are no more "theatrical" than Sinclair Lewis's Main Streeters from Zenith.

Indeed the very faculty style so disparaged in your editorial seems to have victimized Miss Mitchell in your piece about Civil War fiction. Her book, you say, is "hardly important" "as a novel." It has "too little thought and no philosophical overtones . . . no eye and no feeling for human character . . . the effects of melodrama is [*sic!*] offensive."

Now this is not only schoolroom criticism but it is cheap snobbery. I do not know what can keep a novel from being "important" when it is read by every eighth person in the country, and discussed by nearly every one who reads at all. There are, of course, more intrinsic values than popularity. A book can be a good novel without being great, but it is a dirty trick to spurn a chicken because it does not happen to be a turkey. Why condemn a book for not being what it was never supposed to be?

Need an adventure novel have "thought and philosophical overtones?" Then "Northwest Passage" and "Mutiny on the Bounty," to mention only two, must be trash. Is "eye and feeling for human character" to be judged by monkish reviewers only? But it is odd that Miss Mitchell's characters, like Dickens's before her, have got into the mouths of John and Jane Doe. I have heard people who seldom read a book refer to a man as "the Rhett Butler type." I have sat in on debates and heard it hotly argued whether or not Hepburn or Crawford could "play Scarlett." If Miss Mitchell does not have the "feel" of her characters, then Roosevelt has no radio appeal, for the judges are the same in both cases. If Scarlett and Rhett do not "live," then Becky Sharp is a puppet and Mr. Micawber is Charlie McCarthy.

As for the "offensive melodrama," that is the snootiest crack of all. Was the offense that, unlike so many long novels, this one lasted till the last page? Have you no praise for craftsmanship, even if it is un-"professional"? "Anthony Adverse," with all its "philosophical overtones," trailed off at the end in a most amateurish manner. And "Northwest Passage" never lived up to its first three hundred pages. Offended readers closed **"Gone with the Wind"** and shouted: "Encore."

There is more harm in this snobbishness than a mere expression of bad manners. Margaret Mitchell is a gifted story teller. She can create characters to set tongues wagging, she can swing a plot and make it crackle, she has the courage of patient endeavor, she is a "natural" if there ever was one. She is twice as "important" as the clever back-biters who review because they cannot write. I have no quarrel with personalities. I do not know Miss Mitchell. But I think, and I am not alone, that whoever discourages her from writing more and more novels has committed a literary murder. You print an article by Mr. Elliot Paul which pities the sensitive soul of poor Ernest Hemingway. And you keep on nagging the lady.

Holmes Alexander, "Holmes Alexander to the Defense: 'Gone with the Wind'," in The Saturday Review of Literature (© *1938, copyright renewed* © *1965, Saturday Review Magazine Co.; reprinted by permission*), *Vol. XVII, No. 11, January 8, 1938, p. 9.*

BERNARD DeVOTO   (essay date 1938)

[*An editor of* The Saturday Review of Literature *and longtime contributor to* Harper's Magazine, *DeVoto was a highly controversial literary critic and historian. A man whose thought enraged much of America's literary establishment during the 1930s and 1940s, he was frequently motivated by anger at authors he considered ignorant of American life and history. As a critic, he admired mastery of form and psychological subtlety in literature. His own work is characterized by its scholarly thoroughness and by its vigorous, infectious style. DeVoto was "profoundly interested" in American history and authored several historical works, notably the Pulitzer Prize-winning* Across the Wide Missouri (1947). *The following excerpt is taken from DeVoto's rebuttal to Holmes Alexander's letter to* The Saturday Review (*see excerpt above*). *Concerning DeVoto's unfavorable criticism, Edward P. J. Corbett (see excerpt below) maintains that perhaps DeVoto's "reputed antipathy for popular books" rendered him an unfair critic of* Gone with the Wind.]

[Mr. Holmes Alexander's] emotions have a high B.T.U. content but they have made him careless and incoherent. He is so excited that he can't read what honest printing says, and his prose goes badly awry. A lot of what he says is going to seem silly when he looks at it again in the calm of a historian's study. . . .

He says that the faculty style seems to have victimized Miss Mitchell. He means, probably, that it victimized us. (Our editorial on reference books recommended "Webster's Collegiate Dictionary": every historian ought to have it.) How did it victimize us? Well, Mr. Alexander quotes a clause which he thinks we wrote in our article on Civil War fiction, "the effects of melodrama is [*sic!*] offensive." If his emotions had been less vehement he would have seen that what we wrote was "its page by page reliance on all the formulas of sentimental romance and all the effects of melodrama is offensive." Reliance . . . is. The sentence is all right, and we have recommended Curme's "College English Grammar," though deep-breathing exercises would be just as helpful here. And one should check one's quotations.

Convinced that the most austere criticial judgment is just a personal opinion rationalized, we don't like to argue, but Mr. Alexander insists on misrepresenting us. (Or is his emotion pure chivalry, in response to what he regards as an attack on a lady?) He asks if we have no praise for craftsmanship. If he will read "English '37," which we ran on this page for eleven weeks last summer, he will see what our praise is, and it may clarify his ideas about craftsmanship. . . . He suggests that we may be committing a literary murder by discouraging Miss Mitchell from writing more and more novels. That shows his awe of criticism, which has no power to deter anyone from doing anything, and his lack of experience with writers, who aren't foolish enough to act on what critics say.

"Need an adventure novel have 'thought and philosophical overtones'?" No. But we are discussing **"Gone with the Wind"** in relation to a half-dozen other novels which deal with similar themes, all of them in our opinion much better novels. We gave at some length our reasons for considering it inferior to them, and nothing in Mr. Alexander's letter disposes us to confess error. He takes issue with us, when he bothers to consider what we actually said, in regard to its melodrama and

its characters. He thinks that melodrama is all right. We do too, but we don't like such a high concentration of it in a novel which undertakes to present the realities of human experience. We don't like so much of it in any single book, and we don't like Miss Mitchell's inclusiveness. She uses practically all the time-worn situations and conventions of melodrama, and averages about five "East Lynne" curtains per hundred pages. We wish she had used fewer of them or worked up more combinations of her own.

We are not disposed to argue about character, either. Certainly not with Mr. Alexander, who can perceive no essential difference in vital characterization between Becky Sharp and Scarlett O'Hara. That gives the measure of his literary judgment, and the defence rests.

We protested when **"Gone with the Wind"** got the Pulitzer Prize in a year when at least a dozen better novels were published, but we have tried to avoid the general debate. Miss Mitchell is an expert storyteller and that counts heavily in her favor, even though the story she chooses to tell is full of hackneyed situations and effects. She has written a popular novel which Mr. Alexander accurately classifies when he mentions the public interest in Crawford and Hepburn as possible Scarletts. Fifty years ago he could have heard people describing handsome and rhetorical acquaintances as "the St. Elmo type" but that hardly makes Augusta Evans the equal of Thackeray. **"Gone with the Wind"** is a lively book which will hold anyone's interest over long stretches of prose, and it is full of vivid scenes rendered with dash and verve. But it is basically wish-fulfillment literature. . . . Its sentiments are strong and lively but also commonplace and frequently cheap. Its total effect is a falsification of experience. There is nothing morally wrong with that kind of literature—if Mr. Alexander will turn to our issue of October 9, 1937, he will find us discussing it in its own terms. We recognize the success of **"Gone with the Wind"** in its own class and, if we thought anyone would be interested, would analyze it in detail. But in our article on Civil War fiction we were talking about a wholly different kind of literature. We were comparing Miss Mitchell's book with better and more serious novels, with novels that have to be taken seriously. We said that it cannot stand comparison with them, as literature, and it can't. Maybe Mr. Alexander should read the novels we were talking about. . . .

The old crack about back-biters who review because they cannot write does not impress us. Consumer's Research cannot make automobiles but is qualified to report on their use. It offers a service to the consumer and so do we. Our job is to read books and tell our subscribers what we think of them. It is a job that requires us to read them with some care. We recommend the same care to Mr. Alexander. He skimmed our article too fast; maybe he missed some of the evidence in **"Gone with the Wind."**

Bernard DeVoto, "Shallow Waters," in The Saturday Review of Literature (© *1938, copyright renewed* © *1965, Saturay Review Magazine Co.; reprinted by permission*), *Vol. XVII, No. 11, January 8, 1938, p. 8.*

JAMES D. HART   (essay date 1950)

Although *Gone with the Wind* was in great part popular because it was a particularly dramatic historical novel, it was a novel first of all. Some of its appeal derived from the usual romantic aspects of historical fiction: the portrayal of a lost cause, an unattainable ideal, and a charming way of life that was gone. The action, crowding exciting event upon exciting event, was also representative of the usual historical novel, but *Gone with the Wind* placed its emphasis as much on the private individual as on the panorama. . . . [It] represented the shift from the tradition of *When Knighthood Was in Flower* to that of accepted realism in contemporary fiction. Scarlett O'Hara and Rhett Butler, the two strong figures, and Melanie Hamilton and Ashley Wilkes, the two weak ones, were products of external characterization rather than psychological motivation, yet they gave the appearance of reality in manners and dialogue, seeming to be shaped by inner stresses and social forces rather than by prefabricated temperaments. The discussion of character, therefore, was as great as that of action, making a dual appeal. Readers, when they come by the millions, are less tutored and less demanding than those who have read much fiction, and to them it seemed that Miss Mitchell's characters were as accurately portrayed as her authentic Atlanta topography. Scarlett, being a heroine unusually wilful, mean, and selfish for popular fiction, was credited with being peculiarly real; and Rhett Butler was thought as real as Clark Gable, as indeed he was.

With the success of *Gone with the Wind* the historical novel was even more firmly established as a popular genre. The year after its publication, four of the five best-selling works of fiction were historical novels. (pp. 263-64)

> *James D. Hart, "Little Man, What Now?" in his* The Popular Book: A History of America's Literary Taste *(copyright 1950 by Oxford University Press, Inc.; renewed 1977 by James D. Hart; reprinted by permission of Oxford University Press, Inc.), Oxford University Press, New York, 1950, pp. 246-88.* *

EDWARD WAGENKNECHT   (essay date 1952)

[*Wagenknecht is an American biographer and critic. His works include critical surveys of the English and American novel and biocritical studies of Charles Dickens, Mark Twain, and Henry James, among many others. His studies of Dickens and Twain employ the biographical technique of "psychography," derived from American biographer Gamaliel Bradford, who writes of this method: "Out of the perpetual flux of actions and circumstances that constitutes a man's whole life, it seeks to extract what is essential, what is permanent and so vitally characteristic." In later works Wagenknecht has focused more on the literary than biographical aspects of his subjects, though he states: "I have no theories about writing except that I think people should write about what they care for."*]

The need to escape from an America which seemed, during the years of the Great Depression, inexplicably to have failed to fulfill all its golden promises must, in the nature of the case, have encouraged many readers to retreat to the past. Many persons found themselves fighting as bitter a battle for survival as Scarlett O'Hara herself after the Civil War. It was exhilarating to watch Scarlett fight and win; even if she did not always employ the most genteel means, at least she did not lie down and die. Futilitarianism and deflation of values had been very smart during the 'twenties, when our economic future seemed secure, but they would not do now. And as the depression years passed on into the war years, with their bitter policy debates and their conflicts of fundamental principles, Americans more and more felt the need of returning to the Rock Whence We Were Hewn and of re-examining the basic postulates upon which American thinking and living had been based since the birth of the nation. There were even times when

the historical novel almost seemed to supply a "retreat" in the religious sense of the term, and when enlightenment, not swashbuckling, became the object of the quest.

Both [Hervey Allen's novel *Anthony Adverse*] and Margaret Mitchell's [*Gone with the Wind*] occasioned a good deal of sniping. Much of this was thoroughly picayunish, the inevitable result, in an envious world, of overwhelming success. *Gone with the Wind* was the fastest-selling novel in literary history; by the summer of 1949, when a drunken driver killed its author in the streets of Atlanta, it had sold 6,000,000 copies in thirty languages, not including pirated editions. During the war the Nazis banned it as far as their influence extended, yet it is said that Hitler insisted upon viewing the film when a print turned up in occupied Paris. People who have no standards of their own are always obliged to apply curiously irrelevant criteria to the assessment of literature. To the man in the street "success" is the somewhat vulgar guarantee of excellence, but the super-aesthete is no more intelligent when he assumes that any work which exerts a very wide appeal must necessarily be second-rate. (pp. 425-26)

> *Edward Wagenknecht, "Novelists of the 'Thirties," in his* Cavalcade of the American Novel: From the Birth of the Nation to the Middle of the Twentieth Century *(copyright © 1952 by Henry Holt and Company, Inc.; copyright renewed © 1980 by Edward Wagenknecht; reprinted by permission of the author),* Holt, Rinehart and Winston, 1952, pp. 409-48.* *

EDWARD P.J. CORBETT   (essay date 1957)

[*Corbett discusses the disparity between some of the early negative commentary on* Gone with the Wind *and the immense popular reaction to the novel. Bernard De Voto's criticism (see excerpt above and additional bibliography) is cited as representative of the overall reaction of professional critics to* Gone with the Wind.]

It is interesting to go back now to the reviews that appeared within a few weeks after **GWTW** [*Gone with the Wind*] was published and to see what the reviewers said about the book then. For the most part, the attitude of the critics was grudging if not downright supercilious. The critics, to a man, granted that Margaret Mitchell had written a captivating story. Most of them acknowledged her success in creating lively, vivid characters. Some of them acclaimed the accuracy of the historical and sociological details in the novel.

But after conceding these virtues (one is tempted to cry out, "what more could anyone ask of a novel?") many reviewers threw in the punitive *but*—and the paragraphs that followed were filled with depreciatory adjectives, like "slick," "melodramatic," "verbose," "superficial," "sentimental," "banal."

This critical reaction to **GWTW** is a good example of the bifurcation in taste that has developed in our time between critics and readers. There was a time, certainly, when the books acclaimed by the critics were the books that readers took most to heart. There was a time, in other words, when the "great" novels—the novels, for example, of Scott, Dickens, Thackeray, and Trollope—were the most "popular" novels. As time went on, however, good taste did not keep pace with the growing literacy. As a result, we frequently find today that the very books the critics denigrate are the books which become runaway best-sellers. The critics can hardly be blamed for their suspicion of the best-seller: they have too often seen the potboiler become the book of the year.

The popular reaction to *GWTW* is a clear example of how the people ignore the strictures of the critics. As events proved, the weaknesses pointed out by the critics (undeniable weaknesses in most cases) did not become stumbling blocks for most readers. Many of the reviewers, for instance, deplored Miss Mitchell's style. Her style, they said, was ungrammatical, pedestrian and garrulous. Upon reading that criticism, most readers, I think, would say to themselves, "Now that's something I didn't notice when I was reading the novel." If one were to go back to the novel and study passages with a view to style, one would find solecisms and jumbled syntax; one would see that Margaret Mitchell had often used three words where she might have got by with one; that her style *was* undistinguished, in the sense that it lacked rhythmical and tonal graces, that it was often jejune, and that it had none of those distinctive marks which would identify it as Margaret Mitchell's style and no one else's.

But when all these defects are acknowledged, how much has the total impact of the novel been impaired? Very little, really. It is significant that most readers were not bothered by—if they even noticed—the banality of Miss Mitchell's style. What that seems to argue is that she had employed, perhaps all unconsciously, a perfect vehicle for the telling of her story. With a little straining, one might even make out a case for the appropriateness of the style for this particular story.

The adverse critics of the novel are perhaps best represented by Bernard De Voto [see excerpt above and additional bibliography below]. . . . The main point that De Voto made in [his initial] article was that *GWTW* was only one, and not the best by any means, of a crop of novels about the Civil War. For him, *GWTW* was "important as a phenomenon but hardly as a novel." (pp. 524-25)

Mr. De Voto here levels an accusation against Miss Mitchell's book which, if it could be made to stick, could keep *GWTW* from being a novel in the Great Tradition. Defenders of *GWTW* would find it difficult to argue with Mr. De Voto, however, since what he objects to is not melodrama *per se* but just too much of it. Arguments about *degree* are always futile. Questions of *too much* can be decided—if they can be decided at all—only by a poll of opinion; and there Mr. Alexander [see excerpt above] would have the overwhelming majority on his side. Perhaps Bernard De Voto's reputed antipathy for popular books disqualified him as a fair critic of this book. . . .

Gone with the Wind appealed to all kinds of readers—to men and to women, to old and to young, to the romantic and to the realist, to sophisticated readers and to uninitiated readers. There are few other novels in our time about which that claim could be made. And the appeal was of a very special kind. Whenever I have mentioned *GWTW* to others, I have invariably met with one of two responses: "I could hardly put the novel down once I started it" or "I can remember the exact circumstances under which I read the novel." *GWTW* was so long that it could hardly be finished in one sitting—though a New York taxi-driver claimed the record for having finished the book in a little over 18 hours—but it was so absorbing that people stayed up until two and three o'clock in the morning until they finished it. (p. 525)

The stature of *GWTW* unquestionably dwindles when it is set up against Tolstoy's *War and Peace*. *GWTW* pales, too, when it is compared with such great American novels as *Moby Dick, Huckleberry Finn, The Scarlet Letter,* even *The Red Badge of Courage.* Maybe this touchstone method of assessment is our truest index that *GWTW* is not a great novel. But great or not,

Gone with the Wind may very well be one of the few books from the 20th century that the great mass of readers will assure of survival into the next age. It would not be the first time that the people had made a "classic" in despite of the critics and the academicians. (p. 526)

> Edward P.J. Corbett, "'Gone with the Wind' Revisited," in America (reprinted with permission of America Press, Inc.; © 1957; rights reserved), Vol. XCVII, No. 21, August 24, 1957, pp. 524-26.

ROBERT Y. DRAKE, JR.   (essay date 1958)

[In the excerpt below, Drake argues that Gone with the Wind *is an "epic" novel and, therefore, exempt from elements—such as psychological insight and character analysis—found in "literary" fiction.]*

Miss Mitchell's work has little of the subtlety of presentation that characterizes the more "literary" Civil War novels, little of the "awareness" of reality that one finds in a novel like Stark Young's *So Red the Rose*, little of the complexity of the imagination of William Faulkner or the art of Robert Penn Warren. And yet I am inclined to think that its very lack of subtlety and self-consciousness is in its favor. For the society it presents (in an epic sweep, covering both War and Reconstruction) was essentially unself-conscious, as the life of tradition always is, as opposed to the analytic and introspective. And it seems to me that in a treatment as broad in scope as Miss Mitchell's is, it is altogether proper that its style maintain the detachment of the folk tale or the epic. For Miss Mitchell's novel is primarily a *story*, in which things happen to people, not, as is the case with so much modern fiction, a *study* in which people happen to things. I am oversimplifying, of course; but the point I wish to make is that *Gone with the Wind* is an epic treatment of an epic theme. And we must not look for the subtlety or conscious craftsmanship in it that we demand in more "literary" fiction.

For, truly, Margaret Mitchell, who said she was ten before she knew the South lost the War, made no pretension to being a "literary" novelist. Brought up on Civil War tales, educated briefly at Smith, trained as a newspaper woman, she later retired into devoted wifehood, wrote her book; and there, as far as she was concerned, was an end on it. In some respects—and I say this in fear and trembling—she resembled the pre-Nobel Prize Faulkner, who disdained to talk or write "critically." But, in spite of all its "critical" weaknesses, her book has, in a little over twenty years, firmly established itself in the hearts of people everywhere as *the* Civil War novel. And it is the considered advice of this layman to the "literary" practitioners of the art of the novel that, since they cannot lick her and, for reasons of conscience or art, let us say, cannot join her, they had at least better give her another look.

The chief conflict in *Gone with the Wind* is essentially what Donald Davidson has elsewhere called the conflict between tradition and anti-tradition. This conflict appears in many different forms and focuses throughout the novel, and it is its principal unifying theme. The *status quo* is represented, of course, in the planter families like the O'Haras and the Wilkeses, along with all the other "county" families. I used to think it was a weakness in the novel that Gerald O'Hara should be an Irish Roman Catholic immigrant, married to a Roman Catholic Charleston aristocrat; surely, he was no "typical" Southerner. Miss Mitchell's artistic decorum is vindicated, though, by modern historical scholarship, which has shown that the Old South was a far more fluid society than was once thought—with greater "social mobility." Thus, I believe Miss Mitchell was bent on demonstrating that part of the Southern society's vigor and strength as a traditional society was derived from its adaptation and integration of diverse national stocks and traditions to serve a unified order. (It is to be noted that it is Gerald O'Hara's daughter who brings the more "typical," inbred Wilkes family through the War and Reconstruction). This is what Grandma Fontaine tries to tell Scarlett the day of Gerald's funeral, that their strength as a family lies in their adaptability. We're buckwheat, she asserts, not wheat; buckwheat can bend with the wind.

The old order, the life of tradition, is, of course, represented in Ashley Wilkes and his wife, Melanie Hamilton. The Wilkeses are always sending off for books of poetry, taking European tours, and marrying their cousins. Their plantation, Twelve Oaks, is everything romanticists would like to believe about the Old South. And yet when the War and defeat come, and with them a peace more terrible still, they are dependent on the kindness of others for their very existence. Melanie, of course, is the ideal of Southern feminine graciousness, the great lady personified, as is Ellen O'Hara, Scarlett's mother; but there is a toughness in her that is surprising. She it is who, though she may starve, cannot compromise her principles. (pp. 142-44)

The chief focus of the conflict between tradition and anti-tradition is, of course, within the character of Scarlett O'Hara. From the very beginning we see this conflict beginning to emerge, growing in intensity until it reaches its climax in the rundown fields of Twelve Oaks, only to have its direction completely reversed at the end of the book. We know that Scarlett has a "sharp intelligence," which, in accordance with the precepts of Southern ladyhood, she struggles to hide under a countenance "as sweet and bland as a baby's." To all outward appearances she is the daughter of a coastal aristocrat, her mother; but, as Rhett tells her, to her indignation, the current that really flows in her vitals has its source in some not too remote Irish peasant ancestor. Pragmatic to the bone, she seems concerned with none of the Southern "principles" which Ashley, Melanie, and even Rhett would fight and die for. She is bent only on survival—at all costs. In the memorable climactic scene in the devastated grounds of Twelve Oaks she vows solemnly that she will never go hungry again. (pp. 146-47)

There is little subtlety or complexity in Scarlett's character, but that is quite proper in the heroine of an epic. The conflict within Scarlett may well be characterized as one between simplicity (anti-tradition) and complexity (tradition), between her "romantic love" for Ashley and her real inclination toward Rhett. But, as the novel moves toward its close, she gains progressively in insight; and finally, at the death of Melanie, which is the book's "catastrophe," she learns what it is that she really wants, only to lose it at the moment of this realization. And the insight, toward which the novel has been moving, is thus achieved. (pp. 147-48)

In the death of Melanie, who embodies a "living" tradition, Scarlett realizes at last that it is only "dead" tradition which she has loved in Ashley. It is only in Rhett that there is real vitality, as the dying Melanie makes her see. But now it is too late. Scarlett, who is only beginning to see life in its complexity, imagines that she can really start over again, that the past really can be wiped out. "My darling," says Rhett, "you're such a child. You think that by saying, 'I'm sorry,' all the

errors and hurts of years past can be remedied, obliterated from the mind, all the poison drawn from old wounds. . . ." Ironically, it is now, when she is closer to reality than she has ever been, that she loses Rhett, the "reality" she has really been seeking in the "idealistic" Ashley. But in that loss there is a gain in maturity and a growth in spirit. (p. 148)

And so at the novel's end Scarlett stands alone, having lost Melanie, "who had always been there beside her with a sword in her hands, unobtrusive as her own shadow, loving her, fighting for her with blind passionate loyalty, fighting Yankees, fire, hunger, poverty, public opinion and even her beloved kin." She has lost Ashley, whom she finds she has never really loved; and she has lost Rhett, on whose love she has unconsciously relied and whom she did not come to love until it was too late. But there is something left—Tara and all that it stands for, Tara and Mammy, "the last link with the old days." "We shall manage—somehow," she had told Ashley a few hours before when Melanie died. Now, again, she is ready to "manage," for "tomorrow is another day." But this catch-phrase is no longer a rationalization for a desire to escape the complexity of experience. She is now deliberately choosing to return to Tara and the life of tradition which she has loved all along, unconsciously, in Tara. Like Rhett, she has been redeemed into the life of tradition. In that contrast she will find solace and perhaps even some remedy for her griefs. (pp. 148-49)

This, then, is what "happens" in *Gone with the Wind,* an epic treatment of the fall of a traditional society. It is structurally, by its very nature, one-sided. The Yankees are quite properly portrayed as deep-dyed villains, as in the case of General Sherman, whose machinations all occur off-stage but whose menace is distinctly and oppressively felt in the wartime chapters, or in the instance of Jonas Wilkerson, the former O'Hara overseer who marries the poor-white, Emmie Slattery, and ironically tries to become master of the acres he once rode as overseer. In this respect *Gone with the Wind* is no more non-partisan than the *Aeneid.* But it dramatically demonstrates, as the *Aeneid* did before it, that you cannot destroy a traditional society simply by destroying its machinery. The strength of such a society does not lie, ultimately, in outward forms or institutions but, rather, in the "knowledge carried to the heart," the intangibles by which it lives. *Gone with the Wind* states once more, in dramatic terms, the hoary truth that, though you may lick a people, you cannot "reconstruct" them.

I know of no other Civil War novel with as much "breadth" in conception as *Gone with the Wind.* What it lacks in "depth" and in "art" it compensates for in the clarity and vitality of its presentation of the diverse and yet unified issues involved, in sustained narrative interest, and in the powerful simplicity of its structure. The conflict which it dramatizes is as old as history itself. It has been presented more skillfully before, and no doubt will be again. But it will never be done more excitingly or appealing than it is here. (pp. 149-50)

Robert Y. Drake, Jr., "Tara Twenty Years After," in The Georgia Review *(copyright, 1958, by the University of Georgia), Vol. XII, No. 2, Summer, 1958, pp. 142-50.*

W. J. STUCKEY (essay date 1966)

[*In the following excerpt, taken from a comparison of the five novels nominated for the 1937 Pulitzer Prize, Stuckey examines the character of Scarlett O'Hara, concluding that her "self-in-*

terest'' and "disregard for basic human decency" cannot be justified in the name of historical necessity and survival.]

In 1937 the Pulitzer jury had available two very good novels from which to choose: Faulkner's *Absalom, Absalom!* and Dos Passos' *Big Money.* If these books were too difficult or experimental for the jurors' taste, there was also Santayana's *The Last Puritan,* a good book that also had the virtue of being high on the best-seller list. But the Pulitzer jury had its sights fixed on the biggest of commercial big game: *Gone With the Wind.* It was the most discussed, the "largest," the most popular book of several decades, and these qualities doubtless weighed heavily in the jury's scales. And yet it would be a mistake to dismiss the award to *Gone With the Wind* as the apotheosis of the super-popular. The Pulitzer jurors doubtless thought they saw something important in Margaret Mitchell's historical romance—something that seemed to them wholesome, powerful, and fundamentally American. Edward Wagenknecht's comment on Scarlett O'Hara and the function of the historical novel in the 1930's [see excerpt above] may provide a possible clue as to what that something was. . . . (pp. 106-07)

Professor Wagenknecht . . . [explains] in explaining the psychological "need" which he believes *Gone With the Wind* supplied American Audiences in the 1930's. . . . "It was exhilarating to watch Scarlett fight and win: even is she did not always employ the most genteel means, at least she did not lie down and die." *Gone With the Wind,* in fact, is a story praising vicious individualism. (pp. 107-08)

Scarlett is the daughter of a well-bred South Carolina mother and a rich self-made planter. The Civil War ruins the O'Haras and everyone but Scarlett is willing to slide into genteel poverty. . . . Scarlett turns opportunist. She puts off the mask of the Southern aristocrat and takes to herself the role that had made her Irish immigrant father the success he had been before the war. But being a mere woman in a society that is bankrupt and still dominated by men who are either stupid or idealistic— and in any case ineffectual—Scarlett must use the only means available to her for saving the family plantation: sex. She will seduce her sister's fiance in order to get his money. To show that this decision is not an easy one for her heroine, Miss Mitchell has Scarlett fight a quick battle with the

> . . . three most binding ties of her soul—the memory of Ellen [her mother], the teachings of her religion and her love for Ashley. She knew that what she had in her mind must be hideous to her mother even in that warm faroff Heaven where she surely was. She knew that fornication was a mortal sin. And she knew that loving Ashley as she did, her plan was doubly prostitution. . . .
>
> (p. 108)

Miss Mitchell's basic technique is visible in her creation of Scarlett O'Hara. Scarlett is presented as a strongwilled, overbearingly beautiful and passionate woman. Such a goddess clearly is a law unto herself. Readers who might themselves hesitate to indulge in such unchristian tactics as Scarlett employs, or thinks of employing, might nevertheless thrill at the sight of this beautiful, statuesque daughter of a Southern gentlewoman flinging aside the old inhibitions. And for more thoughtful readers who might find driving personal ambition insufficient basis for immoral action, Miss Mitchell provides an intellectual rationale: history. Scarlett, like other successful Pulitzer individualists before her, is, in part, a child of the

times. She does what under the circumstances must be done if she is to succeed. Pioneer times have come to the South again and gentility will not do. Grandma Fontaine, who remembers the days prior to the war and before her family became aristocrats gives Scarlett the formula for survival and supplies the rationale for Scarlett's tooth-and-fang code of morality:

> We play along with lesser folks and we take what we can get from them. And when we're strong enough, we kick the necks of the folks whose necks we've climbed over. That, my child, is the secret of survival.

Scarlett, too, refuses to be one of the lesser folks. She wants not only to survive, but to prevail and will use any means at hand to gain her ends—charm, sex, and, when she gets it, money. And Scarlett wins—wins the economic battle at least, though she loses the battle of the heart. Before the book is over and Rhett Butler walks out of her life, there are many stormy scenes in which Scarlett, rocked by tempestuous emotions, is pulled between her love for the weak, idealistic Ashley Wilkes (i.e., the old South) and self-seeking Rhett Butler, the war profiteer and adventurer (i.e., the new South). Scarlett realizes finally that it is not Ashley she loves but rather her counterpart—dynamic, opportunistic Rhett.

Before the final curtain comes down, however, Rhett Butler's character is given a thick coating of whitewash. He is endowed with a hitherto unsuspected tragic past, the useful foreknowledge that the South will lose the war (more historical justification!), and a deep, though hidden feeling of patriotism for his native region. When it becomes apparent to everyone else that the South is going to lose the war, then for some unexplained reason Rhett enlists in the Confederate Army. After the war, for equally unaccounted-for reasons, he generously donates some of his gold (made by war profiteering) in order to drive the carpetbaggers out of the South. Rhett also wins his way into the good graces of conventional Atlanta ladies (and no doubt conventional ladies everywhere) by becoming a model family man. In a way, he is, at the end of the book the society-preserving "woman" of the novel, and Scarlett is the ruthless, go-getting "male." As Rhett Butler storms out of Scarlett's presence, Scarlett stands firm, though alone, determined to win back Rhett Butler's love and devotion.

It is an interesting coincidence that in *Absalom, Absalom!*, which appeared the same year as *Gone With the Wind,* Faulkner deals so differently with material that is similar to Margaret Mitchell's. Thomas Sutpen acquires a plantation, just as Scarlett O'Hara's father had. He too builds a house, buys slaves, and attempts to found a dynasty in the old Southern planter tradition. But Faulkner's "rugged individualist" fails in the execution of his grand design—not because of history—but because Sutpen's design, like Scarlett's, is based on injustice and brutality. Miss Mitchell goes to great lengths to justify Scarlett, but the justification is just a vast transparency of rationalization invented to excuse and glamorize piracy, coldly calculated self-interest, and violent disregard for basic human decency, all in the name of historical necessity and survival.

Some daily reviewers attempted to place *Gone With the Wind* in the "older" tradition of the English novel; but while one can hear distant echoes of Fielding, Thackeray (especially), and Emily Brontë in *Gone With the Wind,* Miss Mitchell's art most noisily proclaims its indebtedness to the literature of wish fulfillment—the bosomy and sub-pornographic historical romance, the sentimental novel, and the Hollywood extravaganza. (pp. 109-11)

W. J. Stuckey, "New Brands of Individualism," in his The Pulitzer Prize Novels: A Critical Backward Look *(copyright 1966 by the University of Oklahoma Press, Publishing Division of the University), University of Oklahoma Press, 1966, pp. 94-121.**

FLOYD C. WATKINS (essay date 1970)

[*Watkins is a professor at Emory University in Atlanta and the author of several books on Southern literature. In the following excerpt, he harshly criticizes Mitchell's* Gone with the Wind *for presenting a "false picture" of Southern culture during antebellum and postbellum times.*]

Good historical novels in some way are meditative. They are not written merely to make history come alive. Mere dramatization or fictionalizing of history may be a service to history—if it is accurate enough—but it is a disservice to literature. It is unnecessary because one may know much factual history without the embroidery of art. There must be, however, a limit to meditation. Obsessive interest in archetypes and mythology ruins the brew, and the contemporary and the humanity in the work are obscured. When a novel is false to historical fact and also false to the human heart in the contemporary age, then it must be simply a poor novel. Despite an immediate popularity which excelled that of all other books, that is the category of *Gone with the Wind*—a bad novel. It creates a myth which seems to ease the hunger of all extravagantly Southern and little romantic souls, but it propagandizes history, fails to grasp the depths and complexities of human evil and the significances of those who prevail. *Gone with the Wind* is what William Dean Howells called vulgar literature: "what is despicable, what is lamentable is to have hit the popular fancy and not have done anything to change it, but everything to fix it; to flatter it with false dreams of splendor in the past, when life was mainly as simple and sad-colored as it is now. . . ."

Never has a book been more praised than *Gone with the Wind* for what it omits. A friend of mine in the business office of Emory University became heated in anger recently when I told him that *Gone with the Wind* is a bad book partly because of what it leaves out. It is a good book, he maintains, because it tells a good story and does not expose itself to the nit-picking analyses of scholars and pedants. As a child, Margaret Mitchell evaluated a book about the Rover Boys: "The story is all that matters. Any good plot can stand retelling and style doesn't matter." And Stephens Mitchell, the brother of the novelist, asserts that she "repeated this early opinion, almost word for word," not long before she died. (pp. 89-90)

The real difficulty in criticizing *Gone with the Wind* seems to be coping with half-criticism. All it has to be is a good story. Now, the real question is whether this is possible. Ultimately, no one can prove the impossibility. Unfortunately, it is a matter of faith and taste rather than knowledge. That *Gone with the Wind* does need more analysis may be shown by claims for excitement, for tragedy, and for profound tradition and meaning—all these in what is said to be a simple story. How is one to judge whether these may be in a simple story if "story" and "simplicity" are the main characteristics? Obviously, one cannot. And that is why, perhaps, little direct frontal assault has ever been made on the novel which has outsold any other fiction. The critic faces a difficult task and a hostile audience of nations of readers. (pp. 90-1)

There are many works about history and the Civil War which accomplish things that by comparison indicate *Gone with the Wind* is no better than it should be. The Pulitzer Prize Committee chose *Gone with the Wind* over Faulkner's *Absalom, Absalom!*, published in the same year; and Faulkner believed that *The Unvanquished* was used as a threat in Hollywood's maneuverings about the production and casting of *Gone with the Wind*. These two novels alone contain much which can never be found in the gaudier romance. There is history in the works of Faulkner and Miss Mitchell, but the depths of humanity appear only in Faulkner. In Scarlett's marriages and aspirations and Rhett Butler's ruthlessness there are parallels to [Faulkner's] Sutpen. But no one in *Gone with the Wind* is capable of Sutpen's tragic failure.

Gone with the Wind lacks true depth for one reason because it leaves evil out of the garden of Tara. The "clumsy sprawling building," the old oaks, the lawn "reclaimed from weeds," the "avenue of cedars," and the slave quarters have "an air of solidness, of stability and permanence" until the Yankees come. In shallow romantic fiction except for occasional bad manners all evils flow entirely from without. The houses of great literature fall before enemies, and usually they simultaneously crumble or at least struggle from within. Consider the complex forces in the Sutpen mansion as Sutpen builds it almost with his bare hands and as it is burned by its founder's mulatto descendant. And compare the house of the seven gables and even the establishments of the Montagues and the Capulets. It is almost as if *Gone with the Wind* shares the simplicity and the callousness of its heroine, who endured struggles which "passed over her without touching any deep chord within her. . . ."

The determined and vengeful Drusilla in *The Unvanquished* is a greater enigma and tragedy than Miss Mitchell's willful and selfish Scarlett, and Bayard Sartoris's struggles in killing Grumby and renouncing the sword are deeper than any of the petty issues of the "sub-pornographic" romance *Gone with the Wind*. With Scarlet we enjoy being titillated by the hope of sexual promiscuities for the sake of material security, and then foolishly we are disappointed that she did not keep her Rhett in the end. Faulkner's Drusilla is unsexed by the loss of a lover in war; John Sartoris is violently destroyed with some justification and Bayard is redeemed by his courage and conviction in renouncing violence. *Gone with the Wind* has no character with their consistency, sacrifice, courage, and suffering. No prominent character except for the weak Ashley and the too-perfect Melanie is constant in depth and integrity. Romantic stereotypes cannot even confront the decisions of great characters created by a great and noble mind.

Movements through the city during the burning of Atlanta magnificently but superficially portray the shiftings about of small men caught in terrible forces, but *Gone with the Wind* never catches all the complexity of the Negroes marching for freedom and "homemade Jordan" in *The Unvanquished*, caught in a tangle of forces they cannot comprehend, rejected by the very soldiers who freed them, understood by some of the owners from whom they flee. The battle of Atlanta in *Gone with the Wind* is good pageantry, but its accomplishment stops precisely there. The victor is victor in romantic fiction, but Faulkner's greater work shows a victor overrun by those he liberated and harassed by those he defeated. In contrast, Margaret Mitchell's novel, in the words of her brother, "struck a blow for her Southland." The freed slave here is just another mean nigger who causes an uprising by the Ku Klux Klan, punishment of Southern whites by the Yankees, and the death of another of Scarlett's husbands. In Faulkner, he is a massive physical force or a minor character and a political issue. The great drama of the forces of history appears in Faulkner's work, but not in Miss Mitchell's. This is negative criticism, almost pure judgment. But the wise critic can make it from a perspective and with taste which cannot be shared by the large popular audience which admired *Gone with the Wind*. In the final analysis, pure assertion must have some critical place. Fiction has often fought the Civil War, and the soldiers in Warren's *Wilderness* and *All the King's Men* and in Crane's *Red Badge* engage in profounder personal and massive struggles. It is possible to bury one's head among the rapidly shuffling pages and insist that *Gone with the Wind* is good because it is an engaging story, excellently told; but when proof is not forthcoming, the same claim can also be made about "Marse Chan," *The Little Shepherd of Kingdom Come*, and Thomas Dixon's *The Clansman*. Damning a novel with faint praise because of what it does not contain is inadequate criticism, but at least it is a beginning point.

But all the errors of *Gone with the Wind* are not of omission. Much in the novel is bad, false to the facts of rural and Southern life particularly, false to history, and, worst of all, false to human nature. Grandiloquent claims have been made for the historical accuracy of *Gone with the Wind*. Miss Mitchell, we are told, "did write the truth, and because she did her novel is an authentic historical study as well as a fascinating love story." And her biographer wrote in 1965 that "So far as can be determined, there is not even a minute error of fact in the novel." (pp. 91-4)

Factual errors in *Gone with the Wind*, however, do exist, though most of them are negligible. The most obvious mistakes lie in the field of pyronomics. One burning Southern plantation home has its fire remarkably extinguished: "The wooden wing of Mimosa had burned and only the thick resistant stucco of the main house and the frenzied work of the Fontaine women and their slaves with wet blankets and quilts had saved it." . . . John Carter, a fire investigator for the city of Atlanta, comments that their methods of fire-fighting were "surely impractical" if not impossible. "Three years of stored cotton" go up in flame which lights "up the place lak it wuz day . . . , and it wuz so bright in this hyah room that you could mos' pick a needle offen the flo." . . . But loose cotton burns with a tiny blue flame, and baled cotton only smolders. (p. 94)

But many errors are more serious than factual errors though less definite. Romances of the Civil War and Southern history and the admiration for romances have had a pernicious influence. Southern readers—and foolish romantic readers anywhere—dream of an impossible past, expect more of the present than can be realized, ignore an authentic culture while praising a false culture that never existed. . . . (pp. 95-6)

Formal manners and dress in *Gone with the Wind* give a false picture of the old South, idealize its flaws, and suggest that people who are perfect in the social proprieties are also perfect or nearly so in their human relations. Scarlett's "seventeen-inch waist, the smallest in three counties" . . . , may be possible. But it surely is improbable considering her buxom flesh. Even on weekdays she wears stays "laced too tightly to permit much running." . . . Maybe on certain streets in older towns such as Charleston and New Orleans this might be the fashion, but so much style in Jonesboro, Georgia, seems most unlikely. The rather stereotyped Irish head of the O'Hara plantation, Gerald, wears a cravat when he goes on a trip to buy a slave—even on a weekday. . . . And before he married, this rough, florid forty-three-year-old bachelor had a valet who served his "meals with dignity and style." . . . These formalities sit better in the *Ladies Home Journal* or with Peggy Marsh in

Atlanta in the 1920's than with an Irish farmer in Clayton County before the Civil War.

Perhaps *Gone with the Wind* is one of the last books to be openly patriotic and popular in our time. It defies all the lessons of restraint which Miss Mitchell could have learned from the early Hemingway, and it blatantly defends what Stephens Mitchell called "the Southland." It is sentimental and patriotic and melodramatic—and shallow, enough to make shallow readers, even radical modern integrationists, suspend their disbelief. The home guard, the militia, and home-front patriots sing the "Bonnie Blue Flag," and tears come with "a deep hot glow in eyes." . . . Ashley and Miss Mitchell define the Civil War and the cause of the war in a sentimental fashion which is altogether foreign to the twentieth century except among some readers of a vast popular audience. "Perhaps," Ashley says, "that is what is called patriotism, love of home and country. . . . I am fighting for the old days, the old ways I love so much but which, I fear, are now gone forever, no matter how the die may fall." . . . Sentimentally, but truly, they are gone with the wind; and not all the weeping and wailing can bring them back. Obviously, Miss Mitchell satirizes Scarlett's chivalric dreams, but by creating characters like Scarlett and Ashley and making them admirable, Miss Mitchell also is a victim of their sentimentality. Given the plot and characters, there is no way to make "Marse Chan" or *Gone with the Wind* truly realistic. Ashley is "a young girl's dream of the Perfect Knight. . . ." And every female heart that ever dreamed of Walter Scott or soap opera falls victim along with Scarlett.

The irony of defeat . . . is conveyed mainly through the character of Rhett Butler. No patriot, Rhett predicts defeat. He even sees the flaws of the Confederacy, represented by the contract holders who sell "shoddy cloth, sanded sugar, spoiled flour and rotten leather to the Confederacy." . . . But Rhett is not enough to remove the stigma of sentimental patriotism. Truth breaks in to encourage the woebegone reader: "But even with this loss on the top of the others, the South's spirit was not broken. True, grim determination had taken the place of high-hearted hopes, but people could still find a silver lining in the cloud." . . . Such triteness is followed by tear-jerking sorrow over the retreating army. Even the sardonic Rhett finally makes a patriotic speech (and it is only half-comic) before going to join the Confederate Army. There is a "malicious tenderness" in his voice as he speaks to Scarlett. . . . Rhett is a tough guy who could get along well with the roughest of Hemingway's characters, but when he softens he is a blithering patriotic old sentimentalist, for all his rough ways with women. And his sentimentality is as false as the falsest thing of the sea. He goes to war purely for feeling, not because the South had any kind of true cause. (pp. 96-8)

An oversimplified regionalism in *Gone with the Wind* is the source from which nearly all evils flow. There has been all too much of this in Southern fiction. *To Kill a Mockingbird*, for example, a Pulitzer prize winner as was *Gone with the Wind*, divides humanity into good blacks and good white Southern liberals versus bad white Southerners. *Gone with the Wind* is on the opposite side. Yet both books take sides so superficially that one wonders if the authors would not have switched sides with the times. (p. 99)

The most unbelievable character in the book, perhaps the heroine, is Melanie Wilkes. Typically, the chief goodness belongs to a woman; the novel, after all, was written by a woman; and in the plantation tradition the South was a matriarchy, with fumbling but kindly men and competent and altogether loving women. Miss Mitchell explicitly attributes complete goodness to Melanie: "In all her sheltered life she had never seen evil and could scarcely credit its existence, and when gossip whispered things about Rhett and the girl in Charleston, she was shocked and unbelieving." . . . (The narrow puritanism of the novel at times is indicated by things like the equation here of evil and immorality which is only sexual.) Melanie's trivial flaw is that she is physically so "small-hipped" that she has great difficulty bearing a child. Attended only by Scarlett during the birth of her baby while the Battle of Atlanta is raging, she says, " 'Don't bother about talking, dear. I know how worried you are. I'm so sorry I'm so much trouble'." . . . If Scarlett is all a repressed Atlanta debutante and matron might wish to be in her most fleshly moments, Melanie is what Miss Mitchell knew a woman ought to be. But she is so perfect that she is not a sound basis for good fiction. She contains no evil. She sins too little.

Gone with the Wind is far too prudish to be a good novel. Miss Mitchell flirts with the risque. Four times Scarlett is called one kind of piece or another, and I suggest that Miss Mitchell would have enjoyed protesting her innocence while appreciating the innuendos. Except for offstage trips to Belle Watling's brothel, there is no true piece in *Gone with the Wind.* The point of the love scenes between Rhett and Scarlett even during their marriage is Scarlett's frigidity. The chief sexual characteristic of the women in the novel is an unhealthy curiosity about the life of prostitutes. . . . But prudishness becomes even more incredible. The devoted Melanie does not wish to have to be so frank in a letter as to tell her husband that she is going to have a baby. . . . Scarlett delivers the baby. Later, she kills a soldier who is looting Tara and asks Melanie for her shimmy to "wad it around his head" in order to avoid leaving a bloody trail. . . . Melanie's face turns crimson, but all of Scarlett's bluntness and directness do not prove that the "nicey-nice" way is wrong. Girls are auctioned off to dance with men and to make money for the Southern cause, but their reaction is too ridiculous to appear in any believable novel. When Maybelle Merriwether was bid on, she "collapsed with blushes against Fanny's shoulder and the two girls hid their faces in each other's necks and giggled. . . ."

Gone with the Wind is narrowly patriotic, prudish, melodramatic, and sentimental. (pp. 100-01)

Gone with the Wind is much more than a simple story. It also consists of melodrama, sentimentality, perfect characters, evil and good in black and white, anti-Negro racism, discursive essays on history and politics usually at the beginning of a chapter in the manner of Theodore Dreiser, writing in the spirit of a chamber of commerce, artificial dialogue, exaggerated Negro dialect almost at times in the speech of Irwin Russell's Negroes. The flaws of *Gone with the Wind* are not merely those of omission. It is a simple story, almost simple-minded at times. Great literature can occasionally be popular, and certainly popular literature can occasionally be great. But with a few notable exceptions, such as the Bible but not *Gone with the Wind,* greatness and popularity are more likely to be contradictory than congenial. (p. 103)

> Floyd C. Watkins, " 'Gone with the Wind' As Vulgar
> Literature," in The Southern Literary Journal (copy-
> right 1970 by the Department of English, University
> of North Carolina at Chapel Hill), Vol. II, No. 2,
> Spring, 1970, pp. 86-103.

JAMES BOATWRIGHT   (essay date 1973)

[*In the excerpt below, Boatwright re-examines* Gone with the Wind *nearly forty years after its publication. He concludes that*

though the novel has its strong points, it nevertheless fails to convince the reader of its sincerity—largely because of its "sentimentality of vision" and "narrowness of perception."]

It seemed like a good idea at first, a piece on *Gone with the Wind,* the most phenomenal of best sellers, not so much a book as a literary Act of God, unexplainable but cataclysmically there. . . .

The novel is folklore now, a part of the culture (of many cultures, of the global village?). Its success has to be evidence of something—of reading habits and tastes, of the topology of fantasy, of the possibilitites of promotion and advertising. Nothing with so much aggresive presence can be insignificant, so, as I have said, it seemed like a good idea to write an essay about *GWTW,* now that the world it came from and the world we inhabit might be different planets. That meant, of course, rereading *GWTW.* For a month I doggedly kept at it and must sorrowfully report that reliving those stirring days as described in the 862 pages of the paperback edition is mostly a tedious exercise in totin' a weery load.

Hard words from someone brought up on the book as I was and as my generation in the South was. (p. 29)

Where has the old magic gone? Who do I now find myself, like Prissy, wandering distractedly and mournfully complaining of de weery load? The book has undeniable strengths, and Malcolm Cowley, when he reviewed it [see excerpt above] . . . , was moved to admit that it "has a simple-minded courage that suggests the great novelists of the past," this admission pretty much wrenched from him after he presents a catalogue of its defects. . . . Cowley's "simple-minded courage" seems to me just right, but I would add *energy* to that praise, an energy of conception and organization that I found really admirable this time around. Mitchell absorbed great quantities of historical and sociological fact from newspapers and various specialized studies, and she worked them into the narrative with wonderful smoothness and assurance. She generalizes with the confidence of a good journalist or sociologist about the blockade, the progress of Sherman's troops, the clothes the ladies wore, what the visiting customs of cousins were, and the generalizations seem to sprout naturally from the narrative, are rooted in the lives of the major characters.

That same energy marks some of the big, heavily plotted climactic scenes. Everybody remembers the last hours in Atlanta, when Melanie is in labor, the doctors are busy with the dying, Prissy dawdles maddeningly on her desperate errands, and Scarlett shows her fierce strength and determination in the face of stifling heat, Prissy's incompetence, Melanie's screams— it all works up to an atmosphere of genuine urgency and terror. . . .

And there are other good things: the faithful attention to place, when it's accompanied by feeling and understanding, moves and convinces (when the feeling and understanding aren't there, the prose slides into what sounds like a Jaycee pamphlet on Growing Atlanta). Despite the book's length and occasional aimless wandering, it has coherence and there are signs of an ordering imagination, seeking for a shape beneath the accidents of experience. Scarlett's nightmare of homelessness and Ashley's comparison of the South's destruction to *Götterdämmerung* both suggest that the center of our desire is a sacred place, implacably threatened by private and public disaster. (p. 31)

And yet, and yet . . . reading the book now *is* a burden, the hopelessly bad outweighing the honestly good. *GWTW* is much too long . . . and a great many readers of the book and viewers of the film have persistently and legitimately complained about the second half, After the War. The telling of the story, the author's control of point of view, is frequently uncertain: it's disconcerting not to be able to winnow out Margaret Mitchell's opinions from Scarlett's. And where is the famous Southern humor and irony, the broad comic swipes and grotesque exaggeration that have come to be the identifying birthmarks of our literature? It's all deadly earnest, without distancing or wit except when the Nigras shuffle on or Aunt Pitty flutters by (although there is one delicious moment when Margaret Mitchell produces the *ur*-version of the Tom Swiftie: "'Pride! Pride tastes awfully good, especially when the crust is flaky and you put meringe on it,' said Scarlett tartly.")

The language of the narrative voice is generally functional and sure-footed and Margaret Mitchell was pleased with what she saw as the *stylelessness* of her book ("no fine writing . . . no philosophizing . . . a minimum of description . . . no grandiose thoughts, no hidden meanings, no symbolism, nothing sensational . . . ,") but it stumbles to its knees when MM forgets her rigorous precepts, when she veers into the metaphoric or poetic: "Scarlett felt the fox of wrath and impotent hate gnaw at her vitals"; "Now he had set his varnished boots upon a bitter road where hunger tramped with tireless stride and wounds and weariness and heartbreak ran like yelping wolves"; "Confronted with the prospect of negro rule, the future seemed dark and hopeless, and the embittered state smarted and writhed helplessly," etc., etc.

These language problems are minor, though: the gaping crater at the center of the book is the sentimentality of vision, the narrowness of perception and sensibility that inevitably affect everything: dialogue, characterization, incident, meaning. Like most of us, I suppose, Margaret Mitchell saw herself as a "realist" and was distressed that a Macon garden club had somehow got the notion before publication that *GWTW* "was a sweet lavender and old lace, Thomas Nelson Pagish story of the old south as it never was." MM may have believed with some justice that she had pictured the South more realistically than most earlier *romanciers* (her journalistic training gave her a healthy respect for solid fact, and she is good with *things*—houses, dresses, guns, towns), but the figures in her landscape, their emotions and inner lives, their motives and actions are preposterous and unintentionally comic—the fantasies of a fatally genteel and superficial imagination. The dialogue is a sure sign of this: Ashley and Melanie mouth an unbelievable Victorian pastry, Scarlett and Rhett endlessly repeat their first "witty" repartee, Gerald O'Hara and Rene Picard speak wiz ze foreign accents that Hollywood has instructed us in. The only vigor is found in the speech of the blacks, a minstrel show vigor, usually aimed toward an indulgent chuckle.

The surest evidence of the limitations of MM's sensibility crops up whenever the furthest reaches of the interior life must be exposed. All the stops are pulled out, and it's a strong reader who won't become queasy with embarrassment when he encounters these parodies of ladies' mag prose:

> Her eyes met his, hers naked with pleading,
> his remote as mountain lakes under gray skies.
> She saw in them defeat of her wild dream, her
> mad desires. . . . At his touch, he felt her change
> within his grip and there was madness and magic
> in the slim body he held and a hot soft glow
> in the green eyes which looked up at him. . . .
> Her body seemed to melt into his and, for a
> timeless time, they stood fused together as his

lips took hers hungrily as if he could never have enough.

The biggest disappointment on coming back to *GWTW* is not discovering that it is a camp classic, with all this ridiculous melting and glowing, the rolling eyes and heaving sighs. One could skip over that if the fine courage and rebellious badness of Scarlett and Rhett that made the adolescent heart jump survived with "My dear, I don't give a damn," with the closing chapter. But 25 years have taken their toll, and steadier, soberer eyes regard that pair at the end. When closer attention is paid to what *really* happens, we have to admit the saddest falling off of all, the cruelest fantasy. It turns out that they weren't bad, irresponsible, selfish, free—some grand Promethean figures—they were going through a *phase*. When Scarlett finally comes to realize her roots are at Tara, when Rhett tries to return to society's embraces for dear Bonnie's sake (by joining the church, patching matters up with Atlanta's *grandes dames*) and has long second thoughts about Charleston and its quieter, more lasting values, what we witness is not transformation through suffering (although both characters have certainly suffered plenty) but a simple victory for the home folks. What was billed as *conflict* ends in mechanical, predictable collapse, a rigged contest, the sheepish return to the fold of a chastened Scarlett and Rhett. What seemed to be a real issue in the book, freedom—of Scarlett and Rhett, of the Negroes—turns out to be no issue. Freedom, as the home folks know, is a *delusion* (Margaret Mitchell on blacks during Reconstruction: "the better class of them [scorned] freedom"). The world of this novel (of the novel of the popular imagination?) is truly deadend and claustrophobic because it flirts with the terrible ambiguities of freedom without ever really believing in its possibility. It sets up the illusion of danger and choice, trots out the dramatic gestures of Scarlett and Rhett, it titillates the audience, but that audience finds out what it has known all along. Once again it is comforted, assured of the rightness of its ideas of safety and propriety, secure in a cozy domestic sense that has blanked out the potentialities of tragedy. Rhett will come to Tara some day, won't he? Readers plagued Margaret Mitchell with this question, but it hardly needs asking. (pp. 31-2)

James Boatwright, "Totin' de Weery Load," in The New Republic *(reprinted by permission of* The New Republic; © *1973 The New Republic, Inc.), Vol. 169, No. 9, September 1, 1973, pp. 29-32.*

DAWSON GAILLARD   (essay date 1974)

[*Gaillard views* Gone with the Wind *as a* bildungsroman *("novel of development") of Scarlett O'Hara's personal evolution, emphasizing "the clash between the old form, the Southern Lady, and its antagonist, the New Woman."*]

[Why] does Rhett Butler leave Scarlett O'Hara. Why does he *really* leave? Why did Margaret Mitchell apparently feel compelled to separate these two people in spite of their being suitable to one another as romantic characters? And why just at the moment that Scarlett discovers that her supposed love for Ashley Wilkes has been a girlhood habit?

When we start seeking literary answers to such questions, we turn to the work and the traditions that shaped it. (p. 9)

Like the South in which she lives, Scarlett endures a violent disruption of the pattern of life that she has enjoyed. And along with endurance, knowledge of herself comes to Scarlett. Because of the disruption she learns the harsher realities of life and of her own nature.

The end of the war brings Scarlett to a moment of reflection: "Somewhere, on the long road that wound through those four years, the girl with her sachet and dancing slippers had slipped away and there was left a woman with sharp green eyes, who counted pennies and turned her hands to many menial tasks, a woman to whom nothing was left from the wreckage except the indestructible red earth on which she stood." . . . Besides the red earth, something else was left: her girlhood image of Ashley Wilkes. The memory of him and his fineness offers to Scarlett a view of herself that mitigates the harsh self-portrait of her post-war nature. It is in Ashley that she can imagine herself the lady her mother was and whom Scarlett wants to emulate—when she has world enough and time. By holding onto her girlhood image of Ashley, she holds onto a world of innocence and childhood long past. However, by the end of the novel, Scarlett has faced herself in her completeness—her harsher characteristics and her idealism. She also learns the difference between childish romantic love and finds that she has loved Rhett all along, as an adult loves, not as a girl loves.

Like many epic heroes, Scarlett is tested. She survives trial by fire and hunger. Unlike these same heroes, she loses. Her stature is not ennobled, but is diminished, by the means that she chooses to accomplish her successes. The author seemed to feel that Scarlett must be punished for something—her punishment is losing her man, the patriarchal grail, in spite of her successful *rite de passage*. To an audience of the book and the movie, Scarlett's losing Rhett is equivalent to watching Oedipus gouge out his eyes. What has her flaw been and what attitude toward it does the author have? The answer to the second question is buried more carefully than is the answer to the first.

In his study *Allegory*, Angus Fletcher says that "in discussing literature generally we must be ready to discern in almost any work a small degree of allegory." Fletcher also makes the point, "At the heart of any allegory will be found this conflict of authorities. One ideal will be pitted against another: its opposite. . . ." The literary critic is ready to discern a small degree of allegory, but what about the mass reading audience of *Gone with the Wind?* Probably not. The genre of romantic, popular fiction does not force us to dip beneath the surface story.

I suggest that there are two temporal perspectives in the novel because of the time in which the novel is set and the time in which the novel was written. On the surface story line, set in the 1800's, is Scarlett's maturation within the context of the time and place in which she lived. At this level, Mitchell could seemingly endorse traditional values which Scarlett violates. But woven into the novel is the time perspective of the 1930's. By ferreting out "a small degree of allegory," we can see what the dual time perspective suggests about the author's attitude. We also have explicit comments in the novel which are possibly forgotten in its huge bulk. Margaret Mitchell could endorse traditional values while simultaneously undermining them in the novel. (pp. 10-11)

Margaret Mitchell's choice to dramatize regional conflicts gave her a broad screen on which to include other conflicts: a social conflict between old and new social forms within the Southern region, then within a particular state, and—psychologically—a conflict of old and new social forms within one individual. What she leaves her audience feeling is nostalgia (what a shame social changes occur to disrupt people's lovely lives) and pride (look how strong people can be in the face of these changes); nostalgia and pride—ingredients of popular, romantic fiction.

And there is one other feeling left after we complete the novel—virtuousness, signalled by a noise: "*tsk, tsk,* Scarlett." The audience feels morally purged; we're clean; we know not to imitate Scarlett in all her ways. And Rhett's leaving feels somehow right to us. Scarlett's ways have shaken the surface foundations of traditional society, but they remain firm.

Since childhood, I have known the warning of the willful Scarlett O'Hara's drama, the warning of her courage, stubbornness, fire, and utter ruthlessness which allowed her to save Tara. Now, why should this epic heroine, this female protagonist of a *bildungsroman* become a warning? She *survived*, damn it, and had Tara to boot. In fact, the imagery of the last scene presents Tara as a kind of grace, a boon. . . . Margaret Mitchell does not take everything from her heroine, then; she even offers a pleasant reward. Still, at the end of the novel we are not happy. Rhett is *gone*. Perhaps our emotions have been misplaced. Perhaps we should be glad he is gone.

At the point of interesection between the surface conflict of authorities and an allegorical conflict stands the image of a popularly accepted regional paradigm of social behavior: the Southern Lady. (This image of the Southern white woman is not only an image that appears in fiction, but is also a norm that appears in society.) . . . This paradigm is harmonious with the larger national literary and social context because of the popularly accepted norms of what is a woman's place in a man's world.

Margaret Mitchell's novel dramatizes the clash between the old form, the Southern Lady, and its antagonist, the New Woman. On both the surface and the allegorical levels the Southern Lady dies; Scarlett slays the dragon within her; Mitchell slays Melanie. My speculation is that Mitchell wanted to criticize the mythic social mode of behavior that had governed her area of the country and national popular literature, but to criticize without offending her audience (and also without completely admitting to herself what she was doing). As most authors are, Mitchell is divided into all of her characters. But I suggest that she identified strongly with both Melanie and Scarlett. It is Melanie who dies, however. The dynamics are set for the survival of Scarlett from the second paragraph of the novel in which the turbulence and lustiness of life are imaged in her green eyes. On the sub-surface of the novel, the author can criticize the old forms with impunity by having her heroine, in the surface drama, receive some punishment for working against the old, accepted forms of social behavior.

Melanie Wilkes is the old order. Like Ashley, she is an anachronism as a result of the disruption of the war. In the main story line the Southern Gentleman as an efficacious norm of behavior is more explicitly rendered as passing away than is the Southern Lady. The audience feels (watching Melanie's becoming the magnetic center of the old world remnants) that the Southern Lady at its mythic best will remain to give soul-power to the society, refinement to counteract a seedy invasion from outside the region. Peering through the curtain of the surface drama, do we find nostalgia or necessity manifested by Melanie's death?

On the surface, the author may seem to feel—and may wring from us—nostalgia. However, just as the dynamics for Scarlett's survival are built into the novel, so are the dynamics for Melanie's decease. Within the context of popular sentimental fictional patterns, Mitchell's choice to do Melanie in is a necessity of audience expectation. The frail woman must die; her death is in the ground rules of the genre. There is something else in the novel, however, not superimposed upon it from outside, something that lessens the tinge of nostalgia that can accompany necessity. In Chapter XL, Grandma Fontaine tells Scarlett, "It's the way your mother would have acted if she'd lived. Melly puts me in mind of your mother when she was young." Melanie is typologically Scarlett's mother; allegorically the parent dies so that the child may grow. At this level, Melanie's death, the death of the old order, is a necessity without grief. (pp. 12-14)

To me it seems that Margaret Mitchell wanted to write a success story, a *bildungsroman* about a woman who was successful in breaking away from the life of self-effacement her mother had lived, in working counter to the existing patriarchal system as she matures from a young, frivolous girl to a twenty-eight-year-old serious-minded woman. The key is in what one defines as "successful." In the literary tradition of the United States, establishing social and psychological independence was usually achieved by acquiring financial independence. But for a woman financial independence carries with it the danger of negative consequences. Scarlett's aunt voices the accepted mores when she writes to complain that Rhett has informed her of Scarlett's daily visits to her store: "Scarlett, this must stop. . . . Think how your little children will feel when they grow older and realize that you were in trade!" . . . (p. 15)

[Even] on the surface level of the novel's drama Mitchell suggests that to continue the tradition of the Southern Lady is to encourage hypocrisy and to cripple the society, especially the women. The narrator tells us in the first chapter that Scarlett learned "how to conceal from men a sharp intelligence beneath a face as sweet and bland as a baby's." We are also told that Scarlett's "manners had been imposed upon her by her mother's gentle admonitions and the sterner discipline of her mammy; her eyes were her own." . . . In the man's world that her mother—and Melanie—knew, dissembling was crucial for survival, socially, psychologically, and financially. Scarlett breaks the rules. (pp. 15-16)

To answer one question I asked earlier, Scarlett's "frighteningly vital" personality, the personality that enabled her to succeed in saving Tara, is her flaw as much as are her girlhood illusions about Ashley. Her personality is a violation of the code of the Southern Lady. She carries her burden, but does not retain her ladylike charm, which means her bland sweetness, her deference to others, including Rhett.

In the context of the passing of the myth of the Southern Lady, Rhett Butler would seem to be the ideal hero for the rebellious Scarlett. He does say cynically that "ladies have seldom held any charms for me . . . they never have the courage or lack of it to say what they think." . . . And he does support Scarlett in her business, telling her, "All you've done is to be different from other women and you've made a little success of it. As I've told you before, that is the one unforgivable sin in any society. Be different and be damned! Scarlett, the mere fact that you've made a success of your mill is an insult to every man who hasn't succeeded. Remember, a well-bred female's place is in the home and she should know nothing about this busy brutal world." . . .

What happens? Why does Rhett's response change from understanding to rejection, from the "good guy" in the earlier chapters to the tough guy of the final chapter where he says his immortal line (changed only slightly in the movie): "My dear, I don't give a damn"?

Rhett has, it seems, a special definition of woman-wife that Scarlett violates. Secure in his own success, financial and psychological, he can scorn society; he can tell Scarlett that she

has insulted men who have not succeeded and support her in her financial quests. However, he also tells her that the house is his, he is master of it, and he does not want her Yankee friends in it. As long as Rhett defies the Southern code, he can allow relaxations in female mores to occur. But when he begins to seek social acceptance for his daughter, he falls back into the traditional patterns and expectations of man's place and woman's place. And when Rhett leaves his wife, we feel that his leaving is justifiable.

On the surface, Margaret Mitchell seems to uphold these traditional values and expectations by suggesting that Rhett's leaving is a mark of his strength, his moral right, his ethical privilege. But softly, there is something else in Rhett's departure scene, something that is consistent with the attitude only subtly evident in the total bulk of the novel, the attitude suggested in Mitchell's departure from the role of story-teller to comment on an older civilization's values, the attitude suggested by the allegorical necessity of the death of the old order, the Southern Lady.

In the final chapter of the novel, Rhett tells Scarlett why his feelings for her have changed: "I wanted you to play, like a child—for you were a child, a brave, frightened, bull-headed child. I think you are still a child. No one but a child could be so headstrong and so insensitive. . . . I like to think that Bonnie was you, a little girl again." . . . Rhett tells Scarlett this after she admits that her image of Ashley has been a little girl's illusion. . . . In discarding the illusion, the image from the past, Scarlett discards completely her girlhood; she becomes an adult, the point toward which the novel has been moving. And by becoming an adult, Scarlett loses Rhett. . . . Rhett wanted, in other words, to be the master . . . , the father of the child-woman, allowing her the benvolence of his paternity. The picture of Rhett smiling at coy Scarlett visually freezes the relationship that Rhett wanted to freeze socially.

In the final scene between two adults ("This was the first time he had ever talked to her in this manner, as one human being to another, talked as other people talked, without flippancy, mockery or riddles"), in this final scene, Scarlett matures. The Southern Lady as myth is dead; dead too is she as a viable social pattern of behavior. Times have brought changes that call for new modes of behavior. The female parent, the old order has passed away. Scarlett, the woman, is free to exert her own vital self; she is emancipated. And only completely so after Rhett leaves. What Margaret Mitchell implies—and I am not certain that she was fully conscious of doing so—is that when the woman-wife-child created by the Southern Lady myth awakens to her complete selfhood and matures, the parent-man walks out.

Viewing the novel as containing, and even moving towards, this suggestion should cause us to reconsider our feelings that the surface drama and our traditional expectations force from us: that Rhett's leaving is sad. We should, instead, be pleased. He's *got* to go as long as he feels that Scarlett should have remained a child. His leaving is not a mark of strength, but of weakness and of blindness, the blindness that tradition has produced.

Recently in *The American Scholar* . . . , an essay entitled "How a Girl Can Be Smart and Still Be Popular" by Clara Clark concluded by saying that "literature which is still overwhelmingly produced by males, has not been very helpful in providing the young girl with the *Bildungsroman* that would show her how to combine the compassionate virtues with the expansion of ego-strength that is her due as a human being." . . . The punishment Scarlett must endure because of her violations of social mores exemplifies the failure to which Clara Clark refers. Margaret Mitchell wanted her heroine to break away from traditional behavior patterns, but could not have her do so unconditionally and compassionately. Be different and be damned! (pp. 16-18)

> Dawson Gaillard, " 'Gone with the Wind' As Bildungsroman; or, Why Did Rhett Butler Really Leave Scarlett O'Hara?" in The Georgia Review (copyright, 1974, by the University of Georgia), Vol. XXVIII, No. 1, Spring, 1974, pp. 9-18.

LESLIE A. FIEDLER   (essay date 1979)

[*Fiedler is a controversial and provocative American critic. While he has also written novels and short stories, his personal philosophy and insights are thought to be more effectively expressed in his literary criticism. Emphasizing the psychological, sociological, and ethical context of a work, rather than its literary qualities, Fiedler's criticism often views literature as the mirror of a society's consciousness. Similarly, he believes that the conventions and values of a society are a powerful determinant of the direction taken by its authors' works. The most notable instance of this critical stand in Fiedler's work is his reading of American literature, and therefore American society, as an infantile flight from "adult heterosexual love." This idea is developed in his most important work,* Love and Death in the American Novel, *along with the view that American literature is essentially an extension of the Gothic novel. Although Fiedler has been criticized for what are considered eccentric pronouncements on literature, he is also highly valued for his adventuresome and eclectic approach which complements the predominantly academic tenor of contemporary criticism. In the excerpt below, taken from his* The Inadvertent Epic: From "Uncle Tom's Cabin" to "Roots," *Fiedler maintains that* Gone with the Wind *should not be measured by past scholarly standards, but should be assessed in terms of "literature as popular culture."*]

The millions who first read, then saw **Gone With the Wind** responded to it not as literature but as myth; remembering not even the original author, much less those responsible for adapting her novel to the screen, but the actors who embodied her *personae*: Clark Gable, already mythic before he was cast as Rhett, and Vivien Leigh, who became mythic from the moment she became Scarlett.

To most of those millions, ignorant or indifferent to history, the Defeat of the Confederacy and the Burning of Atlanta, represented a legend not of the ante-bellum past but the mid-Depression present. Though she had begun her novel in the 'twenties, Miss Mitchell finished it under the shadow of the great collapse of 1929; and as she revised it for publication, unemployment, strikes and the threat of violence possessed the streets of our desolate cities; while overseas Nazis and Communists goosestepped and chanted, evoking the menace of conquest and war. Small wonder then that it became the most popular work of the age.

Yet no history of our literature in the 'thirties, written then or since, considers it worthy of mention side by side with the novels of James T. Farrell, John Dos Passos, John Steinbeck, Nathanael West or Henry Roth. Dismissed contemptuously to the underworld of best-sellerdom, it is recalled, if at all, as evidence of the decline of taste in an age of Mass Culture. In Gershom Legman's *Love and Death*, for instance, a hysterical attack on comic-books and best-sellers which appeared in 1948, it is condemned, along with such forgotten pot-boilers as *Forever Amber* and *Duchess Hotspur*, as one more debased celebration of the "Bitch Heroine." "The message . . ." Legman cries out in righteous indignation, "is hate. Nothing more. Hate, and the war between the sexes, set, symbolically enough—. . . to the tune of *That's Why the Ku Klux Klan Was Born*."

In an important sense, Gershom Legman is right. **Gone With the Wind** is as much a sado-masochistic work as *Uncle Tom's Cabin, The Clansman, The Birth of a Nation* and *Roots*, for like them, it is based on a fantasy of inter-ethnic rape as the supreme expression of the violence between sexes and races. In the continuing underground epic of which it is a part, it scarcely matters whether white men are shown sexually exploiting Black Girls or Black men murderously assaulting white ones; only that the male rapist be represented as unmitigatedly evil and the female victim as utterly innocent. This simplistic feminist mythology, Margaret Mitchell qualifies somewhat by making her White female more predatory bitch than passive and helpless sufferer. Nonetheless, it is only the White Woman she is able to imagine threatened; even her passing reference to "slave concubinage," as we have seen, avoiding the mythologically loaded word "rape."

Of the three attempted rapes of Scarlett which dominate the book, however, a Black Man is involved in only one; and even in that instance, he is provided with a rather ineffectual white accomplice. The other two rapists, the first foiled by Scarlett herself, and the second successful because in some sense she collaborates in her violation, are mythological threats to the Southern lady of quite different kinds: the first, a Union Soldier, and the second, a Husband. Both scenes, however, end in the counter-climax of death; the latter stirring in us pity as well as terror; the former terror mitigated only by self-righteous satisfaction, as Scarlett shoots in the face at point-blank range the Union Soldier who dares assault her in her own home. Miss Mitchell takes great pains to make the scene as effective as it is central: "All alone, little lady?" the blue-coated invader asks suggestively, and before she or the reader quite knows what is happening, it is all over. " . . . Scarlett ran down the stairs and stood . . . gazing down into what was left of the face . . . a bloody pit where the nose had been, glazing eyes burned with powder. . . " That scene was equally well rendered in the movie version, so well rendered, in fact, that the first-night audience in Miss Mitchell's native Atlanta rose to its feet and cheered.

The second White-White rape, however, that of Scarlett by Rhett Butler, elicited more tears than cheers, when it eventuated in an aborted pregnancy on the great staircase which the film made as mythological as those protagonists themselves. First, however, Scarlett achieves in the arms of Rhett, her husband still though long since banned from her bed, what is apparently the only orgasm of her life, unless she had earlier achieved one blowing the head off the Yankee soldier. (Miss Mitchell is so cagey about such matters that it is hard to be sure.) Nonetheless, this time, too, death is the fruit of love, as Rhett forces her to stumble on the same stairs where he began the assault, and she loses the child she has conceived in his brutal but satisfactory embrace.

Only in a third encounter, occurring midway between the other two, is the would-be-rapist what [Thomas Dixon's *The Clansman*] had taught Miss Mitchell was the proper mythological color. And it remains, therefore, an archetypal scene, however undercut by the author's insistence that Scarlett may have provoked the attempt at rape, deliberately or foolishly. For a moment, Miss Mitchell seems on the verge of suggesting, in fact, that *all* such outrages arise not out of the lustful obsession with white female flesh that presumably afflicts all Black men, but in part at least out of the troubled erotic dreams (cued half by fear, half by wish) of Southern White women. In the end, however, the language and tone Miss Mitchell uses in describing the attack are scarcely distinguishable from those of Dixon, as in a kind of nightmare transformation her faithful Negro retainer, Big Sam, turns into a Black Rapist. . . . This time, too, Big Sam has been no more successful in his attempt at righteous murder than was Scarlett; so that the final act of revenge is left, as is proper to the anti-Tom tradition, to the white riders of the Ku Klux Klan.

It is, however, not her penchant for violence which has kept Margaret Mitchell from critical recognition. To many pious opponents of violence in the arts, her sadism remains as invisible as it apparently was to her, camouflaged by what they take to be her "good intentions." They remember not the terror which moves them below the level of full consciousness, but the heroism of Scarlett, and especially the high romance of her troubled relationship with Rhett Butler. The single line, for instance, that most readers and viewers of *Gone With the Wind* can quote is the one Rhett speaks as he leaves her, perhaps forever, "My dear, I don't give a damn." For elite critics, on the other hand, whom the s-m overtones of Hemingway do not trouble at all (as they did, in fact, trouble Miss Mitchell), the low piety and high romance of her novel aggravate rather than mitigate its violence.

What they cannot finally forgive her is her failure to redeem melodrama with high style and pretentious philosophizing, her giving away of the secret they try so desperately to keep: the fact that *all* literature which long endures and pleases many does so largely by providing the vulgar satisfactions of horror, sexual titillation and the release to tears. This is why *The Literary History of the United States*, for example, devotes not a single line of all of its fourteen hundred odd pages to a discussion of *Gone With the Wind* as literature, merely reporting the statistics of its sales at home and abroad, as if it were an event in the market place and not the Republic of Letters. (pp. 63-7)

[There] persists in me a sneaky inclination to believe that Scarlett O'Hara, despite the mythic dimensions she has achieved over the past forty years, does not deserve to be mentioned in the same breath with other archetypal figures out of our literature, like Natty Bumppo, Captain Ahab, Daisy Miller or Hester Prynne, much less their European prototypes like Odysseus, Aeneas, Hamlet, Don Quixote, Medea, Jocasta or Emma Bovary.

Yet I would be hard-pressed to defend such hierarchical distinctions, which depend on what I am convinced is a definition of literature no longer viable in a mass society. And I am willing to follow wherever the logic of my anti-elitist position takes me, even if this means the redemption not just of works I have always, however secretly, loved, *Gone With the Wind, The Birth of a Nation, Uncle Tom's Cabin* but even of such a prefabricated piece of commodity literature as Alex Haley's *Roots,* subsidized by *Readers Digest* and blessed by the *P.T.A.* and, therefore evoking in me an initial distrust I find it harder to overcome. (pp. 69-70)

Leslie A. Fiedler, "The Anti-Tom Novel and the Great Depression: Margaret Mitchell's 'Gone With the Wind'" (a revision of the Massey Lectures; radio broadcasts on CBC in October, 1978), in his The Inadvertent Epic: From "Uncle Tom's Cabin" to

BLANCHE H. GELFANT (essay date 1980)

[*In her psychological reading of* Gone with the Wind, *Gelfant finds the mystery of the novel's wide appeal in its "reconciling of irreconcilable desires," especially sexual desires.*]

Mitchell's statements about the simplicity of *Gone With The Wind* [see excerpt above] invite us to overlook the complex involutions within it that critics have regularly overlooked, as though the mystery of why or how a novel entertains us were entirely solved. If we try to explore this mystery—and no novel suits this purpose better than *Gone With the Wind*—we discover intricate complications of character, theme, setting, and plot—complexities which contain, I believe, the secret of the novel's universal appeal: of this novel in particular and of novels generally. Secrets are *Gone With The Wind's* explicit concern—hinted at, withheld, hunted, and exposed. The story begins with the Tarleton twins telling Scarlett their secret, and ends with Rhett telling her his—that he has always loved her. Love is a mystery that Scarlett has always skirted but never solved, one of many mysteries in the novel, all of them sexual, and all hidden behind the novel's *closed doors,* a detail of setting which appears so recurrently that it becomes an obsessive symbol, autonomous and dreamlike rather than incidental. Reality in the novel is frequently transmuted into dream or so confused with it that finally Scarlett asks, "Was she dreaming again or was this her dream come true?" Her sleeping dream—the nightmare of a child who is lost in the fog—seems impossible to reconcile with her heroic accomplishments. But the reconciling of irreconcilable desires is, I believe, the ultimate secret of *Gone With The Wind*—a secret it shares with great fiction, which accomplishes this same end in muted and much more difficult ways. *Gone With The Wind* fulfills the reader's irreconcilable desires openly, again and again, in a manner that makes gratification immediately accessible. For this reason it remains our most popular novel. It may also prove one of our most complex—crude, undoubtedly, and styled by clichés, but nonetheless intricate and relevant to our understanding of the mysterious motives of fiction.

Of course, every reader can find in *Gone With The Wind* a simple but compelling story of survival. When it first appeared, Americans could enjoy its immediacy and distance, seemingly incompatible qualities. Dealing with social collapse, the novel immersed contemporary readers in poverty, struggle, dispossession, and loss, problems immediate to the thirties but displaced to an historical past in which they had already been resolved. *Gone With The Wind* showed that survival depended upon *gumption,* the novel's homely word for courage, a word that evokes childishness and difficulty as it makes us gulp—as though we were swallowing a sticky gumdrop. Strained swallowing, however, is better than choking, as an old survivor, Grandma Fontaine, tells Scarlett at her father's funeral. . . . Survival seems a clear unequivocal theme in *Gone With The Wind,* until we move into the murky circumstances surrounding Scarlett's survival. Then we stumble upon a dark mysterious figure inevitably there. Whenever Scarlett's gumption fails, when she needs money, rescue, consolation, or challenge, one of the novel's closed doors opens and Rhett Butler appears.

Only Rhett, a man she "hated," can save her from "doom," Scarlett thinks, as Atlanta falls to the enemy. The Yankees are coming; rebel defenders have set the city aflame and are fleeing; it is "the end of the world." Now that the excruciating ordeal of helping Melanie through childbirth is over, Scarlett's self-control collapses. Fear overwhelms her, turns her into an hysterical child who wants "to bury her head in her mother's lap. . . . If only she were home! Home with mother!" She summons Rhett Butler, who appears magically to lead her through the burning city and the dangerous countryside until she can go on safely alone. As always, Rhett supports her when she is helpless, but encourages her to be strong—so that her victories in the novel involve an interesting combination of dependence and self-reliance. When she arrives at Tara, she is a survivor (though she left as a child), and she makes an appropriate if unexpected literary allusion to shipwreck: "Tara might have been Crusoe's island," she thinks, "so still it was, so isolated." Unlike Crusoe's lush island, however, Tara is a ruin that reinforces in Scarlett the sense of helplessness that had her crying for her mother on the long journey home. "Mother! Mother!", she called, wanting "the kind arms of Tara and Ellen." Like the red soil of Tara, Ellen Robillard O'Hara, the novel's *great lady*, provides Scarlett with an unfailing source of comfort; indeed, mother and earth were intertwined in many early images of the novel, so that Scarlett's desire for Tara becomes almost naturally both double and indivisible. . . . *Gone With The Wind*, like *Robinson Crusoe*, appeals to the child who survives in us all. Unconsciously, Mitchell may have been suggesting this appeal when she described her novel as a "simple story of some people who went up and some who went down." Children would respond readily to such a nice clear-cut movement (like that of a see-saw), but mature readers might suspect that this simplicity is superficial; they already know that beneath its simplicity, *Robinson Crusoe* is complex. So, I believe, is *Gone With The Wind*, which appeals to us on several different and contradictory levels, gratifying our wish for fact with American history; for moral improvement, with examples of personal courage; and for escape from reality and moral constraint, with fantasy. The fantasy underlying *Gone With The Wind* can be traced back to early feelings of helplessness and omnipotence, strong but irreconcilable feelings which every child experiences and later usually forgets—or, more precisely, remembers in the most disguised ways. *Gone With The Wind* revives these childhood emotions, once so intense and dangerous, and makes them safe to recall; not only safe but deeply pleasurable because we can suspend judgment of our self while we indulge in fantasies that belong to another, to a helpless but yet omnipotent woman who is reliving for us the child's divisive drama of growing up within a family.

Throughout the novel, Scarlett O'Hara maintains an inviolate sense of family, manipulating others to maintain herself as either the child of the family or the mother. Her childishness is reflected in her dependence, a continual reliance upon Ellen, Mammy, Melanie, Will Benteen, Archie, and of course, Rhett: "How wonderful to be a man and as strong as Rhett, she thought. . . . With Rhett beside her, she did not fear anything." At the same time, she knows men would be wise to fear her power, for she can make them do whatever she wants, make Charles Hamilton and Frank Kennedy, both promised to others, marry her, make Ashley Wilkes betray Melanie by declaring his love, make Rhett Butler lose his proud imperturbability. She can manipulate men, but her real adversary is

hunger; to fight this grim and implacable foe, she needs the magical power of metamorphosis, a power that belongs to women in fairytales. Only by changing herself—from a helpless little girl, or a flirtatious Southern belle, or a hapless victim of war—can she survive the vicissitudes of change that have swept away her security and broken her family. Scarlett transforms herself constantly, playing the different and conflicting parts which allow her to care for her ruined father and her sisters Careen and Suellen, for Ashley's family as for her own; for Mammy Pork, Dilcey and Prissy; for Aunt Pittypat and all her aunts in Charlestown who would starve to death discreetly without her help. Like Robinson Crusoe, she is essentially alone, for at Tara she finds her mother dead, her sisters sick, and her father "a little old man and broken." Out of necessity—her own and her family's—Scarlett becomes simultaneously a child and mother at Tara: like little Beau who nurses at Dilcey's breast, she lays her tired head on the "broad, sagging breasts" of her Mammy; but she cannot rest there. With Ellen gone, Tara needs a strong woman, and on the night of her return, without hesitation, Scarlett takes up maternal duties she keeps for the rest of the novel. (pp. 5-9)

When Scarlett catches the roving eye of Rhett Butler, who is almost twice her age, she is sixteen; only fourteen when she falls in love with Ashley Wilkes. Women married young in antebellum Georgia, an historical fact that becomes evocative of fantasy in the novel—a fantasy of incest and doubling, of forbidden or impossible relationships. This fantasy revolves around childlike women, epitomized by Melanie Wilkes (originally intended to be *Gone With The Wind*'s heroine). Melanie is introduced as "a tiny, fraily built girl, who gave the appearance of a child masquerading in her mother's enormous hoop skirts." She remains a frail girl, her breasts undeveloped, her body unable to deliver a child; and yet she mothers everyone, taking care of those who ostensibly protect her—Ashley, Scarlett, and Rhett. "She's like mother," Scarlett thinks as Melanie lies dying, a convenient time for unwelcome revelations: "Everyone who knew her has clung to her skirts." Melanie's death, like Ellen's unmasks the novel's disguised characters, the paternal husbands who are children to the child-wives who constantly mother them. In effect, *Gone With The Wind* relies upon surprise, the delight and terror of children who like to dress up as adults and to see adults undressed. Trouble unmasks characters who cry and run for comfort to mothers and fathers, but parents are also childish, like blustering helpless Gerald O'Hara and genteel Ashley Wilkes. Without Melanie, Ashley lapses into helplessness and is relegated, like Gerald without Ellen, to Scarlett's care. Marriage in the novel, especially the exemplary marriages of Gerald and Ellen, and Melanie and Ashley, involves a complicitous relationship between a helpless loving child and an omnipotent parent. This is the relationship Rhett Butler tries, at times desperately, to duplicate. (pp. 9-10)

Turning upon the mystery of desire, *Gone With The Wind* is an involuted novel that pursues one of the great themes of modern American literature. Desire impels the characters of Theodore Dreiser, F. Scott Fitzgerald, and Saul Bellow, whose gargantuan Henderson reiterates the phrase dear to Scarlett's heart: "*I want, I want!*" The mystery of what she wants, however, remains hidden behind the novels' *closed doors*, within *secrets* Scarlett feels compelled to discover:

> "If you'll promise, we'll tell you a secret," said Stuart. "What?" cried Scarlett, alert as a child at the word.

This childish exchange at the beginning of *Gone With the Wind* initiates Scarlett's plot to "get" Ashley (which soon entangles Rhett), for Stuart Tarleton's secret entails Ashley's engagement to Melanie. To Scarlett, this social ritual is also a secret rite preparing for intimacies between a man and woman that Scarlett does not understand. She needs her mother to explain, but Ellen is off on her own secret mission which Scarlett discovers by eavesdropping: she stands outside her parents' bedroom door and, like a child of an imagined primal scene, overhears them whisper about sex. "Curiosity" is "sharp" in Scarlett, as in any child, and sustained because she cannot find out what she wants to know. Ellen's genteel code prohibits mention of sex (though it hints at a married woman's mysterious trials); and Scarlett herself represses sexual desire by imagining Ashley as a shining knight to be adored romantically, that is, from afar. Nevertheless, his appeal is profoundly sexual, for he embodies the titillating mystery of the *closed door*. The language that tells us this is explicit if clichéd, the cliché resonating with sexual overtones: "The very mystery of him excited her curiosity like a door that had neither lock nor key." At Twelve Oaks, Scarlett draws Ashley into a "semidark room" from behind a "partly opened door" that "automatically" he closes. "Who are you hiding from?" Ashley asks, not unoblivious to her sexual excitement, "a tenseness about her, a glow in her eyes . . . rosy flush on her cheeks":

> "What is it?" he said, almost in a whisper . . .
> "What is it?" he repeated. "A secret to tell me" . . .
> "Yes—a secret. I love you."

To Scarlett, love is both a secret to tell and *secret*—hidden, inaccessible, beyond understanding. However, someone else hidden in the room seems to understand love—Rhett Butler. Concealed in semidarkness, he is the real secret locked from Scarlett behind closed doors (had she understood that, *Gone With The Wind* might have moved swiftly to a single "happy ending"). (pp. 18-19)

Victorian in its adherence to sexual fidelity, *Gone With The Wind* exposes the "other" side of Victorianism: its prurience. The novel titillates the reader with sexual secrets that titillate its well-bred ladies—pregnancy, prostitution, rape. Melanie nearly swoons when Rhett notices her "condition," and Scarlett tries to hide hers by smothering under a lap robe. She is "horrified" when Rhett says the word *pregnancy:* "I'm not a gentleman to have mentioned the matter . . . [but] pregnant women do not embarrass me as they should . . . [I] treat them as normal creatures. . . . It's a normal state and women should be proud of it, instead of hiding behind closed doors." When Dr. Meade gets beyond Belle Watling's closed doors, his wife plies him with questions (which the reader now shares): "What did it look like? Are there cut-glass chandeliers . . . red plush curtains . . . full-length gilt mirrors? And were the girls—were they unclothed?" These avid questions leave Dr. Meade "thunderstruck" at "the curiosity of a chaste woman concerning her unchaste sisters," a *devouring* curiosity shown by matrons and "innocent and well-bred young women" like Scarlett. . . . Sexual curiosity vies with sexual fear in the novel, producing an ambivalent desire for exposure and concealment, the essence of Victorian prurience.

As in a Victorian novel, the men of *Gone With The Wind* are punished for their sexuality, for the passion that Scarlett insinuates into their lives. Her first two husbands die. Her third, worn out by marriage, becomes "a swarthy sodden stranger disintegrating under her eyes." Ashley is demoralized. . . . In

devastating both Ashley and Rhett, Scarlett becomes the novel's *deadly woman*, a green-eyed Lamia whom we must reconcile with Scarlett the lost child. This *femme fatale* represents sexual fears so profound that they exceed the novel's private and cultural fantasies to underlie universal myths; but impossible though it may seem, *Gone With The Wind* overcomes even primal fears. Deadly as she can be, Scarlett is finally thwarted when she loses both Ashley and Rhett, her divided lovers who have merged two opposite and mutually exclusive mythoi in the novel into one. (pp. 25-6)

As a study of war, *Gone With The Wind* shows that reconciliation between opposites is impossible: irreconcilability is the meaning of any war, and in particular, of civil war. Symbolically, the Civil War in America was a family affair; brother fought against brother, as we know; but if separation, and even opposition, within a family is inevitable, its union, a union of blood, is irrefrangible. Just as loss demands recovery in *Gone With The Wind,* division eventuates in union. American history supports *Gone With The Wind* as a fiction of inevitable reconciliation by showing us that opposites are not only reconcilable but in fact already united. The novel goes further by making victory the sequel to defeat (and perhaps history confirms this, too, now that a citizen of once vanquished Georgia has become a President of the United States). Mitchell was always proud of the authenticity of her war scenes; its battles are unmitigated in their violence, the devastation to the land and the appalling loss of life unromanticized. But a strong sense of victory emerges from the novel, for the more brutally the South is defeated, the more triumphant its characters and readers can feel in its recovery. We are reconciled to horror because we see that it is transitory, that it can be transcended in the long and durable flow of history that the novel traces. While Stark Young's Civil War novel, *So Red the Rose,* ends with a vision of "the darkness and the field where the dead lay," *Gone With The Wind* ends with Scarlett's renewed hope in *tomorrow*. That hope does not obliterate the waste of war, which we recover every time we read the novel, but it does release us from a haunting image of death.

If *Gone With The Wind* makes our worst fears manageable, fears of war, rape, chaos, hunger, death, it also gratifies our most infantile wish, the one Scarlett expressed—that we get everything we want. As a fantasy of total gratification, the novel shows us how in addition to all the reconciliations already discussed, even an inviolate division between races can be reconciled with union—the union of mother and child, as it exists between Mammy and Scarlett, and of husband and wife, as in disguised form it exists between Aunt Pittypat and Uncle Peter. . . . (pp. 27-8)

Beginning with division—with Scarlett poised between the Tarleton twins, divided men about to fight in a divided nation— *Gone With The Wind* ends with doubling. We need not choose between contrarieties because we can possess them both in our imagination where they have become one. Scarlett herself personifies a union of opposites; as a divided woman, she is both a peasant and aristocrat; lost child and Lamia; victim and survivor; hussy and heroine; country girl and city woman; earth goddess ("like Antaeus," Rhett says) and entrepreneur; child and mother. Unlike the Tarleton women, whom she envies for their "single-mindedness," she is fated to conflict by the mixture within her blood of "Irish peasant" and "overbred Coast aristocrat"; her character epitomizes her times, both in a state of internal conflict. Because her conflicts seem impossible to resolve, she is confused, uncertain, and unpredictable, but also resilient and fascinating. She wants *everything*, and is everything to her readers—child, mother, and elusively sexual woman, all of these aspects of her being and more in irrepressible conflict. That she should divide others as she herself is divided, is inevitable. She alienates Atlanta by precipitating "a feud that would split the town and the family for generations." The order she tries to establish is inseparable from disorder; and both are pleasing to us as readers. We share her chaotically conflicting impulses and safely enjoy seeing them gratified and punished; sympathizing with her, we also repudiate her, so that we too become divided characters. We give Scarlett our emotional allegiance, but we overlay it with intellectual disdain.

When Rhett calls Scarlett "a child crying for the moon," he means of course that she wants the impossible; but the impossible has become more and more difficult for us to define, while our desires for the moon have become less outlandish. Because Scarlett reaches for the moon, she is forever attractive and forever dangerous. She keeps our unfulfilled dreams alive, while she shows that dreams which do come true may bring death. She does in fact make Rhett's dream come true—the dream that she will someday love him; but by the time she loves him, his "deathless love" has died—and so have their two children. Only the intensity of their mistimed desire for each other lasts and becomes our memory of their romance. Sexual desire, the secret that with Scarlett we seek behind closed doors, is not only prurient in the novel but proper, for desire sustains its characters and makes their survival possible. When survival seems impossible, as recurrently in history it does, we find it imagined for us in fictions which fulfill the wishes that reality denies—a wish for the moon, a wish for romance, a wish for romance to merge indivisibly with history, a wish to feel the impelling intensity of desire that makes Scarlett O'Hara so immediately and permanently alive. (pp. 28-9)

The child fantasizes impossibilities that the adult knows are unattainable—as I know that my wish to penetrate the secret of *Gone With The Wind*'s popularity can never be entirely fulfilled. Residual mystery is the critic's pleasure, exciting him with the promise of new discoveries tomorrow. The reader's pleasure is a fulfillment of impossible desires. *Gone With The Wind* unites child and adult into one reader, and then by the divisions in its form and its characters, divides and at the same time doubles the reader's response, doubles his pleasure. As fiction, it achieves the child's impossible desire for everything, and if this gratifies us, it also makes us ashamed of our childishness, ashamed of enjoying a novel that is not "great," only compelling and indelible, only uniquely and universally popular. (pp. 30-1)

> *Blanche H. Gelfant, "'Gone with the Wind' and the Impossibilities of Fiction," in* The Southern Literary Journal *(copyright 1980 by the Department of English, University of North Carolina at Chapel Hill), Vol. XIII, No. 1, Fall, 1980, pp. 3-31.*

ELIZABETH FOX-GENOVESE (essay date 1981)

[*Fox-Genovese views Mitchell's depiction of the South's transition from a pastoral to an urban society in* Gone with the Wind, *along with Scarlett O'Hara's development from a dependent Southern "lady" to a self-possessed and responsible "woman," as representative of the course of American culture as a whole.*]

Gone With The Wind as a whole transforms a particular regional past into a generalized national past. In this respect, it contributes to integrating southern history into national history even as it reestablishes the South, with all its idiosyncracies, as an only slightly special case of an inclusive national destiny. Mitchell's antebellum South manifests features characteristic of the nation as a whole. Even prior to the war, the cavalier tradition is shown as infused with the blood of Irish immigrants. As W. J. Cash does in *The Mind of the South,* Mitchell emphasizes the assimilation of the various gradations of the white elite—specifically excluding poor "white trash"—into a rural precursor of the industrial middle class.

Throughout the novel, Mitchell explicitly underscores her interest in the rise of Atlanta and the emergence of a business culture in the South. She returns regularly to the excitement and importance of Atlanta as a raw, growing, bustling city, the outgrowth of the railroads. She directly points to the similarities between Atlanta and Scarlett: "Atlanta was of [Scarlett's] own generation, crude with the crudities of youth and as headstrong and impetuous as herself. . . ." The two were roughly the same age and grew up together. (p. 397)

Atlanta, not the "old days," emerges as the victor in *Gone With The Wind.* Tara, which initially figures as a dynamic, frontier plantation—the locus of vitality—ends as a place of retreat. In the early pages of the novel, Gerald O'Hara confidently points to the land as the only reliable source of wealth. Even during the war, Scarlett recalls and echoes his view. But by the war's end, Scarlett must turn to the city to raise the money to pay the taxes on Tara. And the section of the novel devoted to Reconstruction takes place in the city. When, at the conclusion, Scarlett thinks of returning to Tara, she thinks only of a temporary refuge. With only the slightest exaggeration, it could appear as the typical house in the country to which busy city-dwellers repair for rest and refreshment. In this sense, it blends imaginatively with those New England farm houses that had also once encompassed productive labor. In Mitchell's rendition, the Civil War becomes a national turning point in the transition from rural to urban civilization. And this reading permits her to incorporate the South into a shared national drama.

This vision of Atlanta as symbol of a general urban vitality conflates the destiny of the city with the defense of middle-class values. Mitchell reserves her endorsement for an enterprising, indigenous, southern bourgeoisie—for those who can adapt to the times without sacrificing the essence of their values. Her merciless depiction of the Yankees as rapacious, dishonest, political parasites identifies them as predators, not true capitalists. Yankees are those who manipulate and stir up Negroes and poor whites. She reserves her rage for those who came South to milk the victim. She never denies the possibility of honest Yankee businessmen, comparable to their southern counterparts. But she does intend to make the country as a whole understand "what the South endured in the days of Civil War and Reconstruction."

Atlanta stands for the dynamism of the New South. At the core of the novel lies Mitchell's fascination with the way in which a new world emerges from the ashes of the old. Time and again, she returns to the problem of a dying civilization in confrontation with one being born. How, she asks, does one make money from the collapse of a society? Who makes the money? How does one survive, adapt, and prosper in the wake of a major social upheaval? Historically, economically, and socially, Atlanta provides the lynchpin of *Gone With The Wind.* By the novel's close, all of the major characters have tied their destinies to that of the city. Similarly, the character of Scarlett provides the novel's identificatory core. For against the collapse of the Old South and the birth of the New, the novel chronicles Scarlett's coming of age—her painful assumption of the burdens of southern womanhood. The historical cataclysm, however, transforms Scarlett's saga from the account of establishing a personal identity as a woman into an investigation of how to become—or whether to become—a lady.

The terms "woman" and "lady" evoke mature female identity, but in different forms. "Woman" suggests at once a more inclusive and more private female nature, whereas "lady" evokes the public representation of that nature. To be a lady is to have a public presence, to accept a public responsibility. But the essence of that presence and that responsibility consists in recognizing and maintaining a sexual division of labor that relegates any proper woman to the private sphere. No lady would admit that she, and not her husband, ran the plantation. No lady would admit to being hungry in public. No lady would admit to sexual desire or pleasure.

In Mitchell's account, the Civil War and Reconstruction forced the issue of how one remains a lady under new historical conditions. Changing times permit and even require new modes of behavior. At the same time, no society would survive did not its female members internalize certain standards and responsibilities. In *Gone With The Wind* the special case of appropriate female behavior and values in the collapse of a civilization is overdetermined by the private drama of a girl who grows to womanhood under tumultuous conditions. Mitchell provides ample evidence that Scarlett would have had trouble with or without the war. But without the war, social structures and norms would have provided a corset for her unruly impulses. (pp. 397-99)

Scarlett stands apart in *Gone With The Wind,* not merely because she is the central character, but because for her alone among the female characters do the years of the war and its aftermath render problematical the question of appropriate gender role—the definition of being, the aspiration to become, a lady. Any understanding of Scarlett's personality must take account of the other characters who, by responding to the pressures of the times, relate to her and provide both the context and the measuring stick for her responses. Mitchell once claimed that her novel had been written entirely "through Scarlett's eyes. What she understood was written down; what she did not understand—and there were many things beyond her comprehension, they were left to the reader's imagination." Mitchell's claim will not withstand even a cursory reading of her text. Possibly, she believed that she had written from Scarlett's point of view. But if so, she confused her own identification with Scarlett and had trouble differentiating her function as presenter of Scarlett's vision from her function as commentator on Scarlett. In any event, whatever the source of Mitchell's ambivalence about sexuality, gender identity, and gender role, it reaches schizophrenic proportions. Her relationship with Scarlett, her own creature, exemplifies her dilemma of identification and judgment. (pp. 399-400)

Mitchell makes scant effort to redeem Scarlett from the stark self-interest and greed of her chronicled behavior. On the contrary, from the opening pages of the novel in which upland Georgia basks in the glow of antebellum serenity, she establishes the fundamental contours of Scarlett's grasping personality. The self-conscious manipulation with which Scarlett pursues her prey foreshadows precisely the resources she will muster in her pursuit of financial security during Reconstruction. Her marriage to Rhett Butler and the ensuing hold on material security do not suffice to transform her into a real lady. But then Scarlett lacks any vital understanding of what it is to be one.

Through Scarlett, Mitchell exposes the hypocrisy of being a lady or a gentleman. Time and again, she shows Scarlett chafing under the constraints of correct behavior and utterance. No one, in Scarlett's view, could believe the phrases that govern polite interchange. Repeatedly, she mentally dismisses Melanie as "mealy-mouthed." Yet Mitchell also shows Scarlett raging because Rhett cannot be counted on to be a gentleman. In the scene of the charity bazaar in Atlanta, Scarlett worries that Rhett cannot be trusted to observe the gentleman's code and keep his mouth shut. A few pages later, during the same scene, Scarlett flares up at the hypocrisy of required ladylike conduct. Finally, in the name of the Cause, Rhett bids for Scarlett as his partner to lead the opening reel. Scarlett, aching to dance, furious at the imprisonment of her mourning, joins him, feet tapping "like castenets," green eyes flashing. This one scene captures all the contradictions of Mitchell's attitudes. For the codes against which Scarlett rebels also provide her protection: she festers at their demands, but fears a world that will not provide her the respect the codes are designed to ensure. If she does not always wish to meet the requirements of being a lady, she should not wish to be treated as one.

Mitchell thus remains ambivalent about Scarlett's difficulties. She regularly calls attention to Scarlett's natural vibrancy. . . . Mitchell seems to hold civilization responsible for repressing healthy and attractive female vitality, but her novel as a whole offers a more complex reading of the relation between female vitality and civilization. Vitality serves as a code word for sexuality, and Mitchell harbored conflicting attitudes towards the proper relation between sexuality, gender identity, and gender role.

Her confusion on this matter endows the novel with a complexity that transcends Scarlett's stereotypical features. For indisputably, if in an occasionally perverse way, Scarlett invites identification. The dynamics of that identification turn upon Scarlett's proximity to young bourgeois women of the twenties and thirties. Her career raises questions of appropriate female behavior in a changing world. Her internal life reverberates with overtones of the early twentieth-century crisis in the bourgeois family and the received notions of fitting female behavior. Much of the force of the novel as an affirmation of acceptable, middle-class social attitudes depends upon Scarlett's psychological plausibility. Scarlett herself is caught in a war between the socially ordained role into which she is expected to fit and her own natural impulses. The war in Scarlett, as perhaps in Mitchell herself, is fierce, for she lacks that solid bridge between the two—a strong identity as a woman—which might permit her to weather the storms of social change. But the acceptance of herself as a woman, Mitchell implies, would have required a resilient identification with another woman, presumably her mother, that would have nurtured her initiation into female sexuality and generativity.

As Scarlett herself comes to understand at the close of the novel, the only women she has ever loved and respected are her mother and Melanie. Tellingly, Scarlett omits Mammy from this company despite compelling claims. As Rhett (who along with Ashley represents the voice of objective judgment) categorically affirms, both Ellen and Melanie were genuinely great ladies. Scarlett's tragedy lies in her inability to understand the meaning of being a lady. (pp. 400-02)

Mitchell remains preoccupied with those features of being a lady that survive social upheaval. If the role of lady is constructed and carries serious responsibilities, how much of that role can be taken to persist through change? Or, to put it differently, does being a lady possess an essence that remains constant as manners change? The sections of the novel that describe Scarlett's early forays into the world of business betray what could be interpreted as a strong feminist approval of the self-reliance, business skills, and survival abilities of the heroine. By Mitchell's day, the South had a tradition of resilient women who, with or without their menfolk, had seen their families through the difficult postbellum decades and had reestablished family fortunes. Scarlett's economic success need not have contravened her standing as a lady. Scarlett runs into trouble not for adapting to new times, nor for displaying a vigorous individualism, but for transgressing those boundaries at which individualism becomes greed and adaptation a threat to any viable social order. For Mitchell, those limits seem to have come with the employment of convicts, the systematic betrayal of business's own standards of probity, and female intrusion—however inadvertent—into the political domain. But if Mitchell shows Scarlett's irresponsible actions as bearing heavy consequences, she does not show Scarlett experiencing pain or guilt as a result of them. The social dimensions of superego sanctions are delineated, but Scarlett has not internalized them. Her own responses remain determined by whether she gets what she wants: at the center of Scarlett, the apparent woman, lingers a demanding and frightened child. In presenting Scarlett as emotionally immature and willful, Mitchell validates the legitimacy of social constraints on female lives. In presenting Scarlett as so personally immune to the normal emotional responsibilities for her socially inappropriate behavior, Mitchell questions the psychological foundations for socially prescribed roles. She remains, in short, deadlocked on the social possibilities for and the social legitimacy of the free expression of female nature. (pp. 403-04)

Gone With The Wind originated in and spoke to a particular moment in American culture. Its very status as a novel, straddling the worlds of elite and mass culture, captured the dilemma of a bourgeois society that struggled to preserve its own values against internal rebellion and to engage the allegiance of a broad and heterogeneous popular base. Not unlike the new languages of radio, film, and advertising, it appeared to offer Americans an image of themselves at once specific enough to invite identification and general enough to encompass national diversity. Mitchell's re-creation of the 1860s, so faithful in its historical detail, bound the destruction of an ordered world to the birth of modern America. Structurally equated as the two great opportunities for making a fortune, the building-up and breaking-up of civilizations emerge as cyclical recurrences in human affairs. That philosophical distance in no way detracts from the poignancy and drama of the carefully documented tale. Nor does it ever soar to encompass the full range of human destinies. Rather, it subsumes a purportedly traditional society under the aegis of bourgeois norms. And this fusion, in turn, promises the persistence of those norms in a world that is outstripping its original social base.

No one more compelling portrayed the relation between the past and the future of the nation and the South than Mitchell. But, for her, the binding up of wounds required a shared bourgeois ethic, and could ill afford the luxury of mourning a "feudal" past. Under the bourgeois rubric, the nation could be understood as the destiny of the South, and the South as a

generalized, rural, national past. Perhaps it is a final, fitting irony that the magnetic core of Mitchell's vision of a revitalized bourgeois order lay in the unconscious life of a most disorderly girl. (p. 411)

> *Elizabeth Fox-Genovese, "Scarlett O'Hara: The Southern Lady As New Woman," in* American Quarterly *(copyright 1981, Trustees of the University of Pennsylvania), Vol. 33, No. 4, Fall, 1981, pp. 391-411.*

ADDITIONAL BIBLIOGRAPHY

DeVoto, Bernard. "Fiction Fights the Civil War." *The Saturday Review of Literature* XVII, No. 8 (18 December 1937): 4-5, 15-16.*
 Discussion of the Civil War in fiction, with several short negative comments on *Gone with the Wind*. These few comments, however, prompted historian Holmes Alexander to write an impassioned defense of Mitchell's novel. (Alexander's essay and DeVoto's rebuttal are excerpted above.)

Edwards, Anne. *Road to Tara: The Life of Margaret Mitchell*. New Haven, Conn.: Ticknor & Fields, 1983, 369 p.
 Most recent detailed biography. For her in-depth study, Edwards drew upon the hundreds of letters written by Mitchell and interviews with Mitchell's friends and acquaintances. Previous to this biography, Edwards was contracted by Richard Zanuck and David Brown to write the continuation of *Gone with the Wind;* completed in 1978, the work is waiting for film adaptation.

Farr, Finis. *Margaret Mitchell of Atlanta: The Author of "Gone with the Wind."* New York: William Morrow & Co., 1965, 244 p.
 First thorough biography; includes many photographs.

Groover, Robert L. "Margaret Mitchell, the Lady from Atlanta." *The Georgia Historical Quarterly* LII, No. 1 (March 1968): 53-69.
 Biographical sketch.

Hicks, Granville. "*Margaret Mitchell's 'Gone with the Wind' Letters: 1936-1949.*" *The New York Times Book Review* (3 October 1976): 10, 12, 14.
 Reviews a collection of Mitchell's personal letters which chronicle her career from the publication of *Gone with the Wind* until her death thirteen years later.

Jones, Marian Elder. "Me and My Book." *The Georgia Review* XVI, No. 1 (Spring 1962): 180-87.
 Recollection of Mitchell during one of her first speaking engagements as a celebrated author.

Mathews, James W. "The Civil War of 1936: *Gone with the Wind* and *Absalom! Absalom!*." *The Georgia Review* XXI, No. 4 (Winter 1967): 462-69.*
 Compares early reviews of Mitchell's *Gone with the Wind* and William Faulkner's *Absalom! Absalom!*, both Civil War novels written in 1936, each with a distinctive view of the South.

Mott, Frank Luther. "Giants of the Thirties." In his *Golden Multitudes: The Story of Best Sellers in the United States*, pp. 253-61. New York: The Macmillan Co., 1947.*
 Discusses popularity of *Gone with the Wind* as a novel and film.

Schefski, Harold K. "Margaret Mitchell: *Gone with the Wind* and *War and Peace.*" *Southern Studies* XIX, No. 3 (Fall 1980): 243-60.*
 Comparative study of Mitchell's *Gone with the Wind* and Leo Tolstoy's *War and Peace*. In this insightful examination of the two novels, Schefski postulates that Tolstoy would have approved of *Gone with the Wind* because both authors shared a "belief in simplicity and infectiveness as the two most essential criteria of an artistic work."

(José) Amado (Ruiz de) Nervo

1870-1919

Mexican poet, novelist, short story writer, dramatist, and essayist.

Along with the Nicaraguan poet Rubén Darío, Nervo is considered the most important poet of the *Modernismo* movement in Spanish-American literature. His novels and short stories also place him among this movement's leading fiction writers, though these works are less concerned with the aesthetic principles of *Modernismo*. The Spanish-American *modernistas*, a pejorative term from the viewpoint of the literary establishment of Spain, sought to free Spanish poetry from its strict adherence to fixed poetic forms. These poets were directly influenced by the experimentalism of the French Symbolists, whose formal innovations, including *vers libre*, had earlier deviated from a long-established tradition of poetic forms in their own country's literature. Nervo's early collections, such as *Perlas negras* and *Poemas*, display in particular the influence of the Symbolist poet Paul Verlaine. Later in his career, Nervo was concerned less with aesthetics as such than with philosophical and spiritual investigations, specifically the search for rational substantiation of the existence of God and personal immortality.

Nervo, the oldest of seven children, was born in Tepic on the Pacific coast of Mexico, a wild, rugged area where his Spanish ancestors had settled. From his youth he received religious training, and it seemed likely that his pious temperament and enthusiasm for the traditions of the Church would lead him to the priesthood. While he went as far as entering a seminary, an experience which provided the background for his novel *El bachiller*, Nervo eventually elected to follow literary interests which had developed along with his religious aspirations. He moved to Mexico City, where he worked on various newspapers. He also wrote for the *Revista azul*, the *modernista* literary journal which took its name from Darío's *Azul*, a collection of poetry and prose often regarded as the inaugural work of the *Modernismo* movement. It was through the editor of the *Revista azul*, poet Gutiérrez Nájera, that Nervo was introduced to the work of Paul Verlaine. Nervo later helped found the *Revista moderna*, which succeeded Nájera's publication as the leading journal of *Modernismo*. In 1900 Nervo traveled to Paris, where he lived with Darío and associated with important Symbolist writers, including Jean Moréas, whose "Symbolist Manifesto" declared many of the principles of the movement. In 1905 Nervo took the examination to enter the Mexican diplomatic service and for the next thirteen years worked in Madrid as secretary to the Mexican legation. He ended his diplomatic career as minister to Argentina and Uruguay, dying in Montevideo not long after assuming this post.

In many of Nervo's major works, the influence of a specific literary figure or movement is clearly visible. His earliest publications were the novels *El bachiller* and *Pascual Aguilera*, both of which remain his best known works of fiction and each of which is modeled on the French Realist and Naturalist novels of Guy de Maupassant and Émile Zola. While Nervo employed the technique of these literary schools, he did not share their social designs or materialist ideology, and his first two novels exhibit a distinctive thematic concern of his work: the obstacle

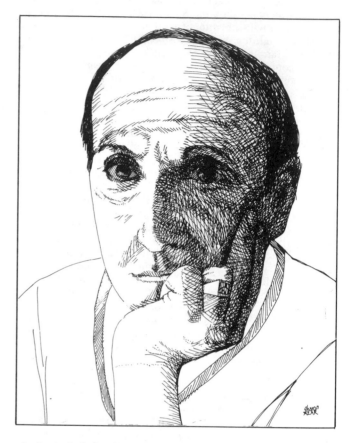

of physical desire in the search for spiritual transcendence. The title character of *Pascual Aguilera* destroys himself and others by force of an unregulated passion and a temperament devoid of spirituality. In *El bachiller*, the "bachelor" is a seminarian whose sexual awakening undermines his intentions for a religious vocation; though he finally overcomes his sensual nature, it is only by means of self-castration. A later novel, *El donador de almas*, less brutally and more abstractly explores the themes of physical versus spiritual love in a fantasy that recalls the ethereal romantic affairs common in the stories of Edgar Allan Poe. In his study of Poe's influence on Hispanic literature, John Eugene Englekirk examines at length Nervo's kinship with the American author, noting their mutual concern with death, abnormal psychology, and both scientific and supernatural explanations of life.

Like his fiction, Nervo's poetry displays his assimilation of various artistic styles and reflects his studies in philosophy and mysticism. The early collections *Perlas negras* and *Poemas* express his affinity for Verlaine and demonstrate the defining traits of much Symbolist poetry: mysticism, melancholy, and a poetics that valued the musical quality of words above their meaning. Following this Symbolist phase, Nervo looked back to the Parnassian poets of the earlier nineteenth century, and he began to style his poems in the highly formalized manner of this movement. At the same time that his work followed the currents of French literature, Nervo was pursuing personal subjects dictated by his religious concerns. Isaac Goldberg has commented that eventually Nervo "reached a stage where he recognized no arbitrary schools or rules of art; he had found himself and expressed his personality in poems that glowed with a strange new beauty." Nervo himself wrote: "I support only one school, that of my deep and eternal sincerity." These statements principally apply to the celebrated collections of the poet's maturity, including *En voz baja, Serenidad, Elevación,* and *La amada inmóvil.*

The poems of these volumes, like the prose of Nervo's philosophical writing in such works as *Plenitud (Plenitude),* reflect various spiritual and intellectual conflicts which the poet attempted to resolve throughout his life. While he had left behind much of the dogma of traditional Christianity, he struggled to reconcile its basic beliefs in God and personal survival after death with the spirit of scientific materialism that emerged in the nineteenth century. Challenged by such French intellectuals as Ernest Renan and Hippolyte Taine, and by the sceptical *Científicos* who dominated the intellectual life of Mexico at the time, Nervo sought to broaden his understanding of both natural and supernatural existence by intense study in philosophy and mysticism. He was especially receptive to the works of Henri Bergson, whose concept of "creative evolution" gave Nervo hope for a personal existence beyond the confines of the physical body, and to the mystical writings of Maurice Maeterlinck, who supported Nervo's belief in the presence of a transcendent realm of being, however indefinite it may be in nature. Nervo also incorporated into his thought the doctrines of the Hindu and Buddhist religions, especially those focusing on renunciation of the material world.

After the death in 1912 of Anne Dailliez, a woman whom Nervo deeply loved, the author intensified his search for a divine plan of existence which could be both rationally and emotionally accepted—a quest which motivated much of the mystical poetry and prose of Nervo's last volumes. Most critics agree that he never settled into a fixed doctrine of belief, and his works are variously read as Christian or Hindu or humanist in their essence. It is more the intensity of his spiritual quest and the quality of his poems that appeals to Nervo's admirers, rather than the coherence of his thought. Nervo, as Esther Turner Wellman has written, "stands or falls, not as a philosopher, but as an intense lyric artist who has emotionalized philosophy."

PRINCIPAL WORKS

El bachiller (novel) 1895
Pascual Aguilera (novel) 1896
Místicas (poetry) 1898
Perlas negras (poetry) 1898
Poemas (poetry) 1901
El éxodo y las flores del camino (poetry and prose) 1902
El donador de almas (novel) 1904
Las voces (drama) 1904
Los jardines interiores (poetry) 1905
Almas que pasan (short stories) 1906
En voz baja (poetry) 1909
Ellos (short stories) 1912
Serenidad (poetry) 1914
El diamante de la inquietud (novel) 1917
Elevación (poetry) 1917
Plenitud (essays) 1918
  [*Plenitude,* 1928]

El estanque de los lotos (poetry) 1919
La amada inmóvil (poetry) 1920
  [*Confession of a Modern Poet* (partial translation), 1935]
Obras completas. 28 vols. (poetry, novels, short stories, dramas, and essays) 1920-22
Cuentos misteriosos (short stories) 1921
"Leah and Rachel" (short story) 1963; published in *Spanish American Literature since 1888*
"Let's Speak of Writers and Literature" (essay) 1965; published in *The Modern Mexican Essay*

Translated selections of Nervo's poetry have appeared in the following publications: *Some Spanish American Poets; The Modernist Trend in Spanish American Poetry; Anthology of Mexican Poets from the Earliest Times to the Present Day; Hispanic Anthology;* and *Anthology of Mexican Poetry.*

ISAAC GOLDBERG (essay date 1920)

[As a critic, Goldberg's principal interests were the theater and Spanish-American writing. His Studies in Spanish-American Literature *(1920) and* Brazilian Literature *(1922) are credited with introducing neglected writers to English-language readers.]*

[Nervo] carried on the potent French influences that have revivified Spanish poetry on both sides of the ocean, without becoming a victim to the less artistic forms of that renovation; like the new spirits of Spanish America, he had reached a stage where he recognized no arbitrary schools or rules in art; he had found himself and expressed his personality in poems that glow with a strange, new beauty. . . . A splendid independence, a wise ignorance, that may be purchased only at the price of so much slavery to the quest of beauty, so much study of its elusive structure! "I know nothing of literature, nor of accented or unaccented vowels, nor of rhythms. . . ." Nothing,—except what only the wise know how to forget! And what a deep remark of Darío's it was, when, in referring to Nervo's skill, he mentioned a "modernism—let us call it such, that benefited only those who deserved it!" (pp. 75-6)

Profoundly affected by French influence, [Nervo] did not permit it to rob him of his poetic self; he was possessed of an inquisitive mind that now shook him in his religious beliefs, introducing the canker-worm of doubt; now enticed him into bold conceptions that ranged freely in space and time, dwelling in dreams of superhumanity; yet, as one of his noted fellow-poets, Urbina, has put it, "his autumn is filled with roses." Much of his poetry possesses an ineffable tenderness, especially such as appears in the first part of his collection called *En Voz Baja* (In a Soft Voice). Not only are the thoughts such as may be spoken only in a soft, sweet voice, but the very hush of passionate confiding, the soft breath of airy wishes, the deep sense of holy silences, the poignant, haunting memories of a past suddenly evoked, rise like incense from its pages.

Nervo, in some of his aspects, possesses a lyric introspection that seems, by some fourth-dimensional gift of thought, to penetrate into lives we only half dream of living; he feels the feverish hurly burly of modern life, yet is a man of his times and has faith in his age. His comparisons are not only things of beauty, but conveyers of beauty as well. He is not the empty, if beautiful urn of so many Parnassians; he can fashion beautiful urns and fill them with intoxicating wine.

For an example of Nervo's poetry—and it is hardly necessary to add that an example or two cannot hope even to suggest the innumerable beauties of his varied productions—we may choose a notable and a noble poem which is of especial timeliness today, when the air is so peopled with modern Columbuses en route to new discoveries. *Pájaro Milagroso* **(Miraculous Bird)** was written in 1910, after a flight in an aëroplane. To Nervo's soaring imagination (the unintentional pun possesses substance!), the aëroplane becomes a colossal white bird that realizes the dream of generations, reconquering for man, the fallen angel, the wings that he lost in his struggle with the gods. (pp. 77-8)

> Isaac Goldberg, "The 'Modernista' Renovation," in his Studies in Spanish-American Literature *(copyright, 1920, by Brentano's), Brentano's Publishers, 1920, pp. 1-100.*

JOHN EUGENE ENGLEKIRK (essay date 1934)

[In his study Edgar Allan Poe in Hispanic Literature, *Englekirk devotes one of the most extensive chapters to the influence of Poe on Nervo's short stories.*]

Amado Nervo reveals himself in his fundamental and most characteristic traits as a spiritual brother of Poe. Very early in life he manifested an interest in psychological and metaphysical problems; in his preparation for the monastic life these problems were ever uppermost in his mind, for they present themselves in his earliest published works. He wrote many short stories on cases of abnormal psychology. He believed in dual personality. Throughout life his cherished belief, often expressed in both poetry and prose, was the hope of reincarnation. From his tenacious clinging to a faith in the perpetuation of life, he turned to every possible avenue that might reveal the truth of that doctrine. He sought the company of "mediums." He read all he could obtain on spiritualism, mesmerism, and the like. He would gladly believe in fantasms, if only to come in contact with spiritual existence. He turned more and more to a belief in the ideal world, in the reality of dreams. But to fathom this spiritual existence, he must have quiet and solitude; and alone, with "El gran Silencio," he sought an answer to the problems that perplex every great man in his struggle to comprehend the meaning and significance of life. Through this feverish desire to survive, he encountered the sinister thought of inevitable death. Would death mean the complete annihilation of this existence he so enjoyed and the perpetuation of which he so longed for? He lived, consequently, in constant fear of Death as he sought to verify the truth of after-life. The great crisis of Nervo's life came with the death of Anna. It was then that he was put to the great test. That was the decisive struggle between his fear of Death and his faith in the belief that "*los muertos* no es que hayan muerto: se fueron antes" ["The spirits of the dead do not experience death: in life they did."]. *Elevación* and *Serenidad* testify to the great victory and peace that came to Nervo as a result of this trial.

But Nervo did not limit himself to "mediums" alone in his search for the truth. He manifested an unusual interest in the sciences and especially in astronomy; and therefore, on his balcony exposed the starry night of Madrid, he would peer hour after hour into the heavens above in search of what might lie beyond the realms of scientific knowledge. He hoped, as he himself confessed, that through science he might come to understand the great Beyond. . . . (pp. 248-49)

Finally, as a poet, confused, afraid, and apart, he poured the beauteous product of his mystic nature into molds of every manner of rhyme and rhythm. But his was poetry for the finer ear, for Nervo sang always "en voz baja." He was not a poet of the masses.

Such, in brief, was the complex nature of Nervo. We can now readily understand why he should have been attracted to Poe with whom he had so much in common. It is little wonder that almost everything that Poe wrote should have struck a responsive chord in the soul of the sympathetic Mexican poet. (pp. 249-50)

One is rather surprised to find so little of Poe in Nervo's **Cuentos misteriosos**. Three stories of the collection remind one quite forcibly of such tales as "Ligeia" and "The Facts in the Case of M. Valdemar," but there is no tangible evidence of any direct influence. These tales are **"Los congelados," "Muerto y resucitado,"** and **"La novia de Corinto."**

Mis filosofías, Almas que pasan, and *Ellos* reveal, perhaps more than all other works of Nervo, the depth of Poe's influence. These short tales and brief sketches contain frequent references to Poe and occasional allusions to his stories; a few were definitely prompted by certain of Poe's tales; but in none of them is there a base imitation of the North-American's work or the attempt to follow any special phase of his art. Nervo is here in all his own originality, but it is a Nervo who in spirit, in technique, and in subject matter explains why he should have been captivated by Poe's works. He proves himself to be a true "hermano espiritual" ["spiritual brother"] of Poe.

In these odd bits of prose, for they can scarcely be called tales, Nervo essays almost everything to insure their success with the periodical public;—like Poe, he lived by the sale of these contributions. He follows his usual trend; he writes about scientific speculations, about the mysterious presence of the unknown elements in life, and above all, about death.

Nervo's pseudo-scientific tales are very suggestive of Poe's work in that genre. His passion to penetrate the beyond impelled him to study the heavens in the hope of solving the eternal enigma. It was then that he would recall Poe's efforts and Poe's tales of human progress into the unknown. Out of those speculations and contacts grew such tales as **"Las nubes," "El hombre a quien le dolía el pensamiento," "La última guerra,"** and **"Dos rivales."** In **"Las nubes"** Nervo claims, with the scientific assurance of Poe, that some distant day, through forces that are now at work, complete evaporation will come to pass, and a rarity indeed will be the passing of a fleecy cloud through heavens of an uncontaminated blue. . . . In **"La última guerra"** Nervo conceives the fantasy of an interrupted cycle of human life that springs anew from the more advanced ranks of the animal kingdom to annihilate the existing race that has arrived "at the divine serenity" of perfection and for whom nothing remains but to die sweetly. (pp. 254-56)

Those tales in which Poe's influence is even more decidedly marked, however, are the ones that voice the poet's constant thoughts and dread of death. The volume *Ellos* is the supreme expression of this fear. . . . That Poe's tales of physical horror and of life after death influenced these short sketches of Nervo is unquestionable. This influence is often not so much a matter of theme as it is of technique. Nervo, now in all earnestness and again veiling his true feelings behind a lighter mood, sought to render an effect à la Poe. But in this he failed largely because he was not as seriously intent as was Poe upon the absolute domination of his readers' credulity and emotions. Although

Nervo taxes one's credulousness, he does so in a spirit of humor, good will, and understanding that adds much to the quality of his tales. (pp. 257-58)

[It] is not surprising that Nervo turned to mesmerism in an effort to master death and to penetrate the mysteries of the afterlife. He too attests to the universal popularity and influence of Poe's metaphysical tales "Mesmeric Revelation" and "The Facts in the Case of M. Valdemar," for he acknowledges that his tale **"El resucitador y el resucitado"** was prompted by them. Nervo does not imitate Poe. His tale is light, entertaining, and congenial. He does not attempt the profundity of a metaphysical discussion, nor does he seek to create an effect of loathsome horror. His story is but a tribute to the ingenious mind of Poe and a confession that no one can ever hope to surpass the portrayal of physical disgust and foul horror as depicted by the creator of Valdemar.

In spite of Nervo's yearning and willingness to believe that "todo es ilusión, hasta la muerte misma, que es la ilusión por excelencia, la última ilusión de la vida" ["all is illusion, including death, which is the most excellent illusion, life's ultimate illusion"], he cannot rid himself of that horrible fear of death. Were not Poe's tales of horror and death instrumental in the intensification of such a dread as expressed in Nervo's **"El miedo a la muerte"**? (pp. 259-60)

"El automóvil de la muerte" is one of Nervo's best tales. It belongs in the category of Poe's tales of horror and of death. Its style and technique are especially reminiscent of "The Cask of Amontillado" and "The Tell-Tale Heart." But Nervo is above mere imitation; he has here assimilated Poe's style and has made it his own. Nervo's capital sentence is brief, suggestive of what is to follow, and holds our interest immediately. . . . It may be most favorably compared to the opening lines of the two above-mentioned tales by Poe. Poe thus begins "The Cask of Amontillado": "The thousand injuries of Fortunato I had borne as best I could; but when he ventured upon insult, I vowed revenge." "The Tell-Tale Heart" opens in much the same way: "True!—nervous—very, very dreadfully I had been and am! but why will you say that I am mad? The disease had sharpened my senses—not destroyed—not dulled them. *Above all was the sense of hearing acute.*" In such introductions lies much of the secret of Poe's art; Nervo was quick to profit through that discovery. Nervo's tale moves forward rapidly. All details but those necessary to bring about the single desired effect are omitted. In this, Nervo has adhered most carefully to the principles advocated by Poe for the perfect short story. The ending is most effective as we too, after following the automobile of death through the swift dark night, stare with the people of the well-lighted garage at the indescribable, inexplicable *that* on the leather of the cushions. But behind it all, one cannot fail to sense the genial mood of Nervo. . . . (pp. 261-62)

That he learned not a little from Poe as to technique and style is obvious. To what extent his themes may have been suggested by those of Poe is rather difficult to determine because of the poets' close spiritual kinship. Even though Nervo occasionally borrowed from the American, he never failed to add his own stamp of originality and thus produce something that was unmistakably his own. (p. 263)

> *John Eugene Englekirk, "Poe's Influence in Spanish America," in his* Edgar Allan Poe in Hispanic Literature *(copyright, 1934 by Hispanic Institute of Columbia University), Instituto de las Españas en los Estados Unidos, 1934, pp. 152-417.**

G. DUNDAS CRAIG (essay date 1934)

[Nervo's] long association with Darío was due to a deep sympathy with Darío's aims and ideals, a sympathy which finds expression in the poem, **Homenaje,** written on the occasion of Darío's death. . . . What Amado Nervo most admired was evidently the clear-cut imagery, the precision and delicacy of [Darío's] workmanship, such that each poem

> twinkled with diamond sparks,
> Myriads of topaz-lights, and jacinth-work
> Of subtlest jewellery;

and this delicacy of workmanship he was eminently successful in reproducing in his own work.

Thus we find in Amado Nervo the same fondness for experimenting with new metrical effects as in Darío, the same sensitiveness to the musical quality of words and rhythms, the same felicity of phrase, and the touch of melancholy characteristic of the Modernist school—though he wears his rue with a difference.

Yet there are elements in the work of Amado Nervo that are hardly perceptible in that of Darío. For example, his early poems display a certain pantheistic sentiment, as in *La hermana agua* and *Viejo estribillo*. . . . Later, in *El puente*—the fanciful title reminds one of *The Pulley*, by George Herbert, another mystic—he comes very close to the thought of Wordsworth. (p. 277)

Parenthetically we may note that this mention of Wordsworth is somewhat remarkable, as it would seem from the writings of other poets that almost the only poetical work in English known in Spanish America is that of Walt Whitman or of Edgar Allan Poe. It is also an evidence of the broad culture of Amado Nervo. . . . Nervo, however, did not attain to this power of mystic absorption without struggle. Like Darío, like Verlaine, he experienced the seductions of the flesh and the torments of a stylite; but the combat between the soul and the body, the spiritual and the material, Christ and Pan, which in Darío ceased only with death, had in the Mexican poet an earlier and happier ending. In 1914, he wrote:

> Siento que estoy in las laderas
> de la montaña augusta de la Serenidad;
>
> ["I feel that now I stand
> On the slopes of the stately mounts, Serenity . . ."]

and, having attained this peace of mind, he was able at last to comprehend the meaning of things. . . . (p. 278)

[The poem *El día que me quieras,* from the posthumous collection *El arquero divino*] is, I think, unique in modern Spanish-American poetry, for if there is one thing more remarkable than another in the poetical work of this period, it is the note of melancholy, tending usually to become morbid. Here there is nothing of that kind. Instead, we have the spontaneous welling up of a spirit at peace within itself, and able to look out upon the world and find all things good. This is the happiest poem of the period under consideration.

This, however, is not the prevailing tone of Nervo's work. Dominating its transparency of form and its almost overpowering sweetness is the note of an ascetic melancholy. This is not the melancholy of Milton, austere and majestic, . . . nor yet the melancholy of Darío and Burns, which found its source in a pained reflection over the past and an equally painful anticipation of the future, . . . nor even the whimsical melancholy of Jaques. Nervo's melancholy is a wistful and expectant longing for the great revelation that is to come. . . . (p. 279)

Closely allied to this melancholy is the sense of mystery in outward nature and in human life. Something of this power of suggesting the mysterious is found in the poem, *Tel qu'en songe,* where the reiteration of the phrase, "en los sueños" ["in our dreams"], has a very curious effect. So in nature he finds secret meanings which he attempts to interpret to men. (pp. 279-80)

As has been already hinted, Nervo's life was not without its struggle. In *Delicta carnis* . . . he portrays the conflict of the flesh and the spirit with a vividness and power of introspection in which, I think, he excels Darío. *La montaña* . . . shows a marked difference of feeling. By force of will he has gained a serene outlook upon life. . . . In this mood his insight into the heart of things is deepened; he finds God everywhere, in nature and in his fellow-men; and from this springs a well of sympathy for all mankind.

For some years before his death Nervo was attracted by the teachings of Buddhism, and some of his later poems show this influence very strongly. . . . In complete renunciation of desire of every kind he has found Nirvana. Yet not quite. . . . (p. 280)

The whole struggle is figured forth allegorically in *La conquista* (in *El estanque de los lotos,* the last volume published in the poet's lifetime). In this poem, the hero, Miguel, whose love has been rejected by Helena, at first determines to win her, come what may; later, counseled by "una voz augusta, nunca jamás oída" (the voice of the "dios interior"), that fortifies him with a strange mixture of the philosophies of Buddha and Schopenhauer, he, reaches the point where all desire is quenched, love's power over him ceases, and he finds his real happiness in the single life devoted to contemplation. One feels, however, that the scales were rather unfairly weighted against the lady, who was only eighteen while her lover was forty. Had Miguel been twenty years younger, one doubts whether either Buddha or Schopenhauer would have counted for more than two grains of sand in the balance. (pp. 280-81)

> G. Dundas Craig, "Amado Nervo," in his The Modernist Trend in Spanish-American Poetry: A Collection of Representative Poems of the Modernist Movement and the Reaction (copyright © 1934 by the Regents of the University of California; reprinted by permission of the University of California Press), University of California Press, 1934, pp. 276-81.

ESTHER TURNER WELLMAN (essay date 1936)

[*Wellman's critical study of Nervo, from which the following excerpt was taken, is an analysis of the artistic and philosophical influences on the author's work.*]

Amado Nervo might be reduced to three words, *scepticism* and *mysticism* finally swallowed up in *love!* In fact his final philosophy might be synthesized into a single word, for in Nervo all values were eventually transvaluated by *love.* To him love was an absolute which made all other values subservient to it. A generalization that eventually overmasters his emotion, his thought and his form. Here is the only string upon which the scattered beads of his art may be strung. Love is the organizing idea—and the only idea under which he was ever able to handle the chaos of experience.

The simplicity of design is almost beyond belief. His philosophy of life is little more than a set of directions for living,

with love as the simplifying principle. Nervo wonders why it is that after Jesus untangled us once, we are forever getting all tangled up again. (pp. 217-18)

It might be urged that his oversimplification of life is pathetically naïve. For instance, he never doubted but that a pure love ethic would solve all the problems of the universe. And once the center of his philosophy was fixed, it radiated in all directions and he took it to apply everywhere. He never anticipated the slightest difficulties—neither in its application nor in its content. The infinite amount of problems which Jesus did not face directly never occurred to him. That Jesus does not define the specific duties in the content of love never bothered him. Everything to Nervo proceeded from a feeling more powerful than rules—from love. Jesus' teaching placed the emphasis upon the motive of an action, not the action itself. Therefore the outward act was less significant than the inward attitude. Nervo followed by driving sharply into motives. And a statement of the motive was a statement of his whole philosophy. (pp. 218-19)

Yet for all the disadvantages of oversimplification, this interiority of love gave to Nervo's philosophy such plasticity and powers of adaptation, that it was capable of almost indefinite renewal. Its applicability to everything was characteristic of Nervo's personal demand for universality. His transcendental talent swept everything off into the infinite. And whatever he accidentally picked up with his baggage which was incapable of such flights, he finally dropped along the way. Whatever passes through Nervo's thought becomes universal. The same thing happened to Christianity that happened to everything else. He blew off all the dust which had accumulated upon the original essence. Frankly Nervo refuses to accept from Christianity all the paraphernalia which it has accumulated throughout the ages. He will accept only those universal aspects of Christianity . . . which are the same in other religions. . . . (pp. 219-20)

Anything that is true anywhere, Nervo felt, must be true everywhere. That is to say that truth is not truth unless it is grounded in the laws of the universe. And that like sunlight it cannot be kept in one little town, and shut off from the rest of the world. And he was convinced that the only universal truth that we know, so far, at least in the realm of spirit is love. That love is at the heart of the universe. That it is the unifying cosmic force. That love, at least in the realm of spirit, like radiant energy in cosmic space (whether both are the same he does not know) is more universal than any known force. That love, the integrating force in all relationships, is God permeating the entire world. (p. 220)

Love is the first clear step in Nervo's ultimate philosophy. And although it might be urged that like Pragmatism his teaching was a method and not a philosophy, nevertheless there are moments such as in the above quotation, when his ethical art is on the point of passing over into a cosmic creed. Undoubtedly Nervo found rest from his own uncertainty in this universal conception of love. And this is where he finally satisfied his life-long hunger and thirst for belief. (p. 221)

Nervo's vast human sympathies had brought his philosophy down from the clouds. His scepticism and mysticism were drowned in his humanism. He went a step further, however. The fundamental law of love was universal in its application. And his philosophy passed over from a way of life into what amounted to an actual program for humanity. He was caught in the social consciousness of our epoch. He would not leave the world to stew in its own juice. His place was in the thud and surge of life. For he was consumed with the conviction that the revolutionary principle of Love must be unflinchingly applied to the whole tangle of social and economic problems. He believed that love should widen itself to the full limit of its possibilities. That every field of human experience should be brought under its dominion. This drew him on and on toward horizons of which he had no previous idea. It was a practical philosophy to be applied to the constructive tasks of humanity. In all his later books he is frankly out for a new world wherein dwelleth righteousness. He was rethinking the world. Creating it in his own image. His imagination could not be contained within the goals of history. And he dreamed of War, Race, and Industry merged in a higher synthesis—the kingdom of pure love. (pp. 274-75)

Three words—Scepticism, Mysticism, and Universal Love—sum up the whole of Nervo's philosophy. But the greatest of these is Love. Could Nervo have been a thorough-going sceptic, or a thorough-going mystic, he might have been satisfied. But he was caught in a tragic impasse and would give himself to neither. He ultimately satisfied both these warring tendencies within himself, as he did everything else, by transcending into another realm. Scepticism and Mysticism were taken up into a higher synthesis which contradicted neither. His Humanism never interfered with his Scepticism. And he ultimately satisfied his life-long hunger for Reality by accepting truth on the human level, which was the only place where he could scientifically test it. This led Nervo to distrust both intellect and emotion and gradually he came more and more to proclaim the force of the will. In this mysterious region where the experts are at war—how can a poet know? It may be, however, that one of the tragedies of Nervo's thought was the old traditional psychology that dissected man into the Platonic compartments of thinking, feeling and willing, instead of seeing him as a whole. Possibly his great error was in thinking it possible to separate the human spirit, and to set emotion to war against thought, without disintegration. Possibly his tragedy may have come from separating what should never have been separated. Possibly he should have trusted the totality of his spirit, and have distrusted either emotion, or thought, or will, whenever divorced from each other. Who can tell? One thing is certain, that Nervo's life was one of mortal anguish over the puzzling contradictions which he found in life. And what could be more puzzling to a student than the paradox to be found in Amado Nervo himself? His dominant intuition of unity which saw the universe as a whole, and yet at the same time feeling his own spirit chopped up into parts. . . . [He] was ultimately forced to the position of a Humanist.

It is not only a final philosophy which emerges from out the welter and mass of Nervo's contradictions. Certain steadfast attitudes toward the totality of things also appear often enough to be typical. For instance, in Nervo's Humanism, as well as in his Mysticism, and his Scepticism, his genius is essentially spontaneous. The "soul vomiting" of a subjective poet is always there. One feels that intensity of an artist. He cannot look at things with detachment. He was a meteor (he himself confesses it), rather than a star. And it is because of a lyric heart laid bare that outlines so clearly emerge of a Nervo always and forever concerned with mystery. We traced this through his Scepticism and through his Mysticism. But he was finally forced to accept truth on the only level where he could scientifically test it—on the human level. And this represents his most definitive and ultimate thought. He never stops seeking, however. For Nervo was a Bergsonist who hoped and waited for whatever

emergent evolution might evolve in the future. He lost all interest in the past. His search, therefore, though never carried on in any systematic way, was nevertheless consistent in one aspect only. His contemporary consciousness always pounced upon the *dernier cri*. His conviction that truth was universal, made him receptive to every philosophy. But he drank from so many contradictory sources that he suffered from intellectual indigestion. This situation was met in the way characteristic of his peculiar genius by his trick of transcending what could never be solved. His whole philosophical pilgrimage was one of wider and wider integrations until he finally reached the extreme limit of his final philosophy. A code of ethics which contradicted neither his Scepticism, nor his Mysticism, and yet which in a measure satisfied both. A way of living which was universal enough to admit all religions and all philosophies. Such was the life of Mexico's poet-philosopher. He could not give himself entirely to philosophy because he was born a poet. And he could not give himself entirely to poetry because his whole life was consumed with a passion for Reality. This was the distinctive stamp of his personality. This was the essence of all his work. . . . Nervo, like Spinoza was a "God-intoxicated man." (pp. 277-80)

Such outstanding professors as Pedro Henríquez Ureña, Antonio Caso, and Julio Jiménez Rueda—all have named Amado Nervo as one of the six greatest poets in Mexican literature. The six are: Nájera, Othón, Nervo, Díaz Mirón, Urbina, and González Martínez.

But Nervo transcends Mexican literature and must be classified with such names as Nájera, Casal, Silva, Darío, Herrera y Reissig, Chocano, Valencia, Lugones, Gonzáles Martínez, and Jaimes Freyre, as one of the leaders of the Modernista Movement in Spanish literature. (p. 280)

But Nervo, again, not only transcends Mexican literature. He also transcends Spanish literature. Something in Nervo refuses to be classified anywhere. (pp. 280-81)

There are two Amado Nervos. In his first manner he epitomizes his period. In the second he transcends it. The first Nervo belongs to Spanish literature. The second to the Universe. In the first, Nervo the poet swallows up the mystic. In the second, the mystic swallows up the poet. The first Nervo is an artist. The second one a saint.

Now it is illuminating to follow the shifting of public opinion regarding these two Amado Nervos. During his life-time Nervo's fame in the Republic of Mexico rested almost entirely upon the first Nervo. Mexican anthologies frankly chose from the artist. And the Mexican intellectuals preferred the Modernista lyrist. . . . But the Modernista Movement was largely taken up with form, and Nervo's interest . . . shifted from form to philosophy. Here his emotion, thought, and form became universal. His philosophy of universal love not only led him to the intellectual internationalists. Nervo could not even be contained in this world and his cosmic consciousness led him to proclaim himself a citizen of the Infinite. The same thing happened to his thought. He exercised the same weakness toward all philosophies which he did toward people. He was far too kind to all. The same thing happened in form. Like his French master, Francis Jammes, another Franciscan after his own heart, he would belong to no literary schools in order that he might belong to all of them. It is universality which characterizes Nervo in his second manner. . . . Nervo did not even publish in Mexico. (pp. 281-83)

The opposite was true of the first Nervo. Of Nervo the artistic and literary artist. He wrote for Mexico. Was published in

Mexico. And his prestige and irradiation rested almost entirely upon his Modernismo. Outside of the few who knew his writings in the Southern Continent, the Republic of Mexico was largely unconscious of the fact that one of her poets had conquered the whole Spanish-speaking world by his Franciscan universality. The first Nervo had many followers because form is easy to imitate. The second had few because such lofty ideals of purity and renunciation are too difficult to follow. And yet the legend of Amado Nervo is based almost entirely upon the second. After 1919, Nervo was lifted up into what has amounted to an apotheosis. It was the year when the Spanish-speaking nations of the new world went "Nervo mad."

"Can a pacifist come out of Mexico?" is perhaps just as natural a question as, "Can any good thing come out of Nazareth?" Over and over Nervo has been accused of being unpatriotic. Whether he was or was not depends entirely upon what content is given to the word "patriotism." If by "patriotism" is meant the love of one's country, then Nervo of all Mexicans was most patriotic. But if by "patriotism" is meant a chauvinistic hatred of all the rest, then Nervo was not patriotic. (p. 284)

Nervo in his final and universal self was a travelled man, and much too intelligent for hate. He had read too much philosophy from all the nations and from all the ages for ethnocentrism to take root. He sought truth rather than victory. History passed before him as a rosary of hatreds, and Nervo's cosmic consciousness transcended history. During the Mexican Revolution and during the World War he was a lonely figure, lean, ivory, aloof, like a towering gargoyle brooding over a ghastly abyss where humanity had reverted to cannibals and men were tearing each other to pieces below. Nervo did not fall in submissively behind any of the Revolutionary "istas" of Mexico. Not a word can be found in his twenty-nine volumes in favor of any of them. Before the endless divisions of Mexico, Nervo held up his nightly journeys through his telescope from one star to another, for he had always been a Don Quixote of the heavens. He was at home both on earth and in the sky. It would not even be accurate to say that Nervo was more cosmopolitan than Mexican, for in speaking of Nervo one must take into consideration the whole universe. And this is the central and overshadowing fact of Nervo in his second manner. What he actually did was to take transcendentalism from world philosophies and world literature and implant it in the soil of Spanish America.

He projects all his sentiments against a timeless background. This is why his work does not bear a distinctive Mexican hallmark, and why he is so quietly appropriated by the most bitter and contradictory camps as one of their own number. While he lived, humanity was his province and he suffered for it. But now that he is gone it is by all humanity that he is claimed. Nervo has woven the most contradictory material into one amazing texture. *E Pluribus Unum*—one out of many, might be his universal theme. This has made him one of the most quotable of Mexican poets, because every one can find himself reflected somewhere. He is regarded as something of a secular Bible, with the same advantage and disadvantage that Nervo in his universality can be made to say almost anything simply by suppressing certain passages and focussing the spotlight on others. For instance, I have before me on my desk three works. One by a Mexican Catholic, one by a South American Theosophist, and another by a North American Presbyterian, each claiming Nervo exclusively as their own. In

certain aspects they are all correct. In others they are all wrong for

> Truth is always polychrome.
> One fact taken all alone
> Isolated from its home
> Is often false. Remember this:
> It must be told in synthesis!

The same thing is true of all the *páginas de devoción*, proclaiming Nervo either as a sceptic or mystic, depending upon the temper of the writer. The truth is neither the one nor the other but includes both. (pp. 285-87)

> *Esther Turner Wellman, in her* Amado Nervo: Mexico's Religious Poet *(copyright, 1936 by Hispanic Institute of Columbia University), Instituto de las Españas en los Estado Unidos, 1936, 293 p.*

G. W. UMPHREY   (essay date 1949)

[*The author of several critical essays on Nervo, Umphrey here examines the influence of Hindu philosophy on the Mexican poet. While Umphrey concludes that "Hindu philosophy penetrated [Nervo's] life and writings much more deeply than the orthodox Christians are willing to believe," a later essay by Roderick A. Molina (see excerpt below) emphasizes his Christian, more specifically Franciscan, themes.*]

Amado Nervo's approach to Hindu philosophy was slow, and was not due, at first, to any conscious thought of finding in it the solution of the spiritual problems that were besetting him. During his Modernistic period, he, like his fellow craftsmen, sought the strange and exotic wherever he could find it; and apparently the rich imagery and symbolism of Oriental literature appealed to him more than the better known mythology of Greece and Rome. As early as 1898, in *Perlas Negras,* he made reference to the favorite flower of Buddha, the lotus; but since the symbolism is still that of the Homeric legend, the reference has slight significance when compared with the many later references to the *flor del loto* as the Buddhist symbol of spiritual purity uncontaminated by materialism. Six years later, in *Místicas,* he gave to one of the poems a title, *Transmigración,* the importance of which could easily be exaggerated; the Hindu doctrine merely serves as a literary device for the expression of the poet's fictitious experiences in faraway times and places. The exoticism is that of other Modernistic poets who played with the idea of reincarnation: Rubén Darío, for example, in *Metempsicosis;* or José Santos Chocano, in *Avatar.*

Nor should we consider the Pantheism of the best of his early poems, *La Hermana Agua* . . . , as proof of Hindu influence. It is true that Pantheism tinges almost all Oriental religions; but it is not, of course, exclusively Oriental, since many of the poets and mystics of Western civilization are decidedly Pantheistic. The Pantheism of *La Hermana Agua,* the exaltation of self-abnegation and sacrifice as symbolized in the joyous, humble service of Sister Water, differs little from that of Saint Francis, that saintly man of Assisi who held in the heart of Amado Nervo a place not much lower than that of Christ. *La Hermana Agua* "is no more pantheistic than the still small voice of *Thanatopsis,* or the speaking stars of David's *Nineteenth Psalm,* or a dozen Biblical texts which are intended to teach submission to divine will and guidance."

In another poem, *Implacable,* written at about the same time, there is stronger evidence of Hindu influence. In the spiritual crisis through which he was passing, brought about by a more worldly mode of living, a new scientific curiosity and a more persistent questioning of religious doctrines, he called upon Doubt . . . to cease pursuing him or to give him some consolation for his lost faith; but Doubt, the implacable, had little consolation to offer him. . . . Unwilling to become the victim of implacable Doubt, he turns for aid to the Supreme Being, whoever it may be. . . . (pp. 133-34)

Just as the Hindu theory of reincarnation is used in *Implacable*, not merely as literary ornamentation but as an essential part of the main theme, so in *Las Voces* . . . the Buddhist doctrine of the attainment of spiritual happiness through complete renunciation of human desire. In this dramatic poem the poet Angel (Nervo), weakened and saddened by youthful excesses, goes to Nature for consolation; but she, speaking with the *voices* of birds, flowers, stars, fountains, has nothing to offer him but hostility and contempt. Later in life, after he has gained serenity of spirit by renunciation, detachment from worldly joys and sorrows, self-abnegation and charity, he returns to Nature; and the same voices that had been so antagonistic give him now a glad welcome. . . . Here we have the very essence of Buddhism, the suppression of desire as the only way to final peace and serenity; and the philosophy underlying the whole poem is Buddhistic rather than Christian. The Pantheism upon which the mechanism of the poem is based is not necessarily Oriental; it is, however, entirely in accord with the Buddhist doctrine that pervades the poem. (pp. 134-35)

From 1904 until his death in 1919 the spiritual life of Amado Nervo oscillated between Hinduism and Christianity. Several volumes of his poetry and prose are permeated with the spirit of Christianity (*Serenidad, La Amada Inmóvil, Elevación, Plenitud* . . .); and various literary critics, by carefully selecting their evidence, have presented him plausibly as the Christian poet *par excellence* in modern Spanish-American literature. But scattered through these same volumes and in the volume entitled *El estanque de los lotos* . . . , there is a sufficient number of poems to prove that he was decidedly Hinduistic in the eclectic religious philosophy that finally gave him the spiritual serenity that he desired. (pp. 135-36)

The first of the Hindu teachers to absorb the attention of Nervo and the one who exerted the greatest influence upon his personal philosophy and mode of living was the Buddha Siddharta Gautama. The great love and compassion of Buddha for his fellow men and the idealism of his doctrines of morality were in harmony with the Christian virtues that were gradually changing the pattern of Nervo's own life. The Middle Path that Buddha taught was, moreover, the kind of life that Nervo was trying to follow; in public, he was an efficient diplomat, an active journalist and a poet of distinction; in private life, he chose solitude and meditation. He did not become an ascetic, and his love of humanity and deep yearning to give moral and spiritual aid to his readers still remained the inspiration for much of his poetry and prose; but his growing detachment from worldly affairs and his faith in renunciation as the only means of attaining peace of mind and serenity drew him closer to the central doctrine of Buddhistic philosophy.

In the first of the four sections of *El estanque de los lotos, La Conquista*, Nervo tells the story of a middle-aged poet scholar who falls in love with a young woman; his love unrequited, he listens to an inner voice, that of Krishna; and, unlike Faust, decides to seek serenity and happiness through suppression of desire. When finally the young woman offers him her love, he discovers that it is merely an illusion of Maya and no longer desirable; knowing reality, he attains Nirvana. (pp. 136-37)

The fifty-eight poems of the second section of *El estanque de los lotos*, entitled *Los Lotos*, composed over a period of four years and therefore contemporary, many of them, with the Christian poems of *Elevación* . . . and the prose aphorisms of *Plenitud* . . . , are mainly Buddhistic in tendency. His conception of Nirvana varies from poem to poem and seldom reaches that of complete repose through personal annihilation. At times, when meditation fails to give him the desired serenity, he goes so far as to seek emancipation from thought itself, as well as from sensation and desire. . . . Usually, however, Nirvana becomes synonymous with serenity attained through meditation; and in several poems he makes the Buddhist doctrine less repugnant by combining with it the Brahmanic theory of identity of the human spirit with that of the Supreme Being, the happy emancipation of the individual spirit from the need of reincarnation and its final absorption in Brahma (God). (pp. 137-38)

The enigmas of life and death are the ever-recurring themes of the prose and poetry of Amado Nervo and in few of the thirty volumes of his *Obras Completas* do we fail to find some reference to his tireless quest for spiritual reality. During his early provincial life, at home or in a seminary, he found spiritual satisfaction in the Christian doctrine; when wider acquaintance with modern thought began to weaken his religious faith, he decided that the priesthood was not his true vocation. In Mexico City and in Paris success soon came to him in journalism and literature, and for a few years he tried to take life as he found it, refusing to heed the inner voice that kept telling him that without spiritual growth and some religious belief there could be no real satisfaction or happiness. He then probed more deeply into the natural sciences that had made him skeptical of his religious beliefs; they gave him much information about the material world; they afforded him no help in his quest for spiritual truth. Then he turned to the great religious philosophers, particularly the mystics of all ages and countries; they could not answer all his questions, but they did convince him that spiritual reality should be sought only by spiritual means. (pp. 142-43)

Western civilization has produced many notable mystics; their influence and his own conviction that the mystic approach to spiritual problems is the only one possible would account for the mysticism that modified the poetic content of Nervo's writings during his last fifteen years. Nevertheless, in view of the fact that his favorite philosophers of the last hundred years were Emerson, William James, Schopenhauer, Maeterlinck, Bergson, all of them inclined toward mysticism and all sympathetic to Hindu philosophy, and in view of the fact that this philosophy did influence him in some of its other aspects, it may safely be said that the intuitive cognition that is so characteristic of the monistic religions of India confirmed, at least, Nervo's belief in meditation and intuition as the only means of discovering spiritual truth. (p. 143)

There are two extreme points of view regarding the religious life of Amado Nervo. Orthodox Roman Catholics would have us believe that his life consisted essentially of a spiritual evolution from the religious faith of youth, through the skepticism of his middle years, to the restored orthodox Christianity of his later years. They cannot ignore entirely the numerous references to Hindu philosophy and the scores of poems suffused with Buddhist and Brahmanic doctrine; these they explain away as a poet's use of exotic material for literary purposes. On the other hand, some critics find in these same references and poems proof of their contention that there was in his last years a definite turn from Christianity to Hinduism.

There can be no doubt that Hindu philosophy penetrated his life and writings much more deeply than the orthodox Christians are willing to believe; that through its influence his religious creed was simplified by the elimination of non-essential precepts of Roman Catholicism. His admiration for the idealistic life and teachings of Gautama Buddha was great; but it did not lessen his intense love of Christ. He was inclined to accept the Hindu doctrines of Maya, Identity of the human soul and the Supreme Being, Karma and Reincarnation; but only in so far as they did not conflict too seriously with what he considered to be the essential principles of Christianity. The religious philosophy that he finally formulated for his own guidance and that became the source of much of his later poetry was religious eclecticism, essentially Christian, a Christianity based on love of God, of Christ, and of humanity; a Christianity freed from non-essential dogmas and strengthened by the spiritual truths that he had learned from the religious mystics and teachers of India. (p. 145)

> G. W. Umphrey, "Amado Nervo and Hinduism," in Hispanic Review, Vol. XVII, No. 2, April, 1949, pp. 133-45.

RODERICK A. MOLINA, O.F.M.   (essay date 1949)

[*Complementing George W. Umphrey's essay on the importance of Hindu philosophy in Nervo's works, Molina examines the influence of Christian thought on the Mexican author.*]

Amado Nervo's affection for religious themes is projected so frequently and so intimately in all his work that literary critics have constantly classified him among the number of the mystical poets—those privileged beings who aspired to union with God through love, and who expressed their sublime thoughts in poetic form.

From his very youth, Amado Nervo was characterized by an ascetical seriousness—almost that of an El Greco portrait—a nostalgia, as it were, for the supernatural, that surrounded all his person and activities and permeated his work. This hunger for the divine is evinced in a very special manner in his *Serenidad* and *Elevación*, and above all in *Plenitud*. These works have made Amado Nervo an almost legendary personage, whose brow is crowned with the aura of sainthood.

The religious theme is found so frequently in the literary work of Amado Nervo that one considers it to be autobiographical. Now that thirty years have passed since his death, it is fitting to analyze his art—so easy to classify and so difficult to analyze—in order to find a better explanation of it for ourselves and to determine more exactly whether or not Amado Nervo was really a mystical poet and if he actually found his inspiration in the school of Saint Francis of Assisi.

The tremulous sobbing and weeping of Amado Nervo have been interpreted in very different ways. For us, they are only the revelation of a soul who abandoned the path that had been traced out for him by his vocation, and who, engaged in the battle with life's passions, succumbed for a while, until, like another prodigal son, he returned in the maturity of his faculties, that were by now tempered by suffering, to his Father's house.

Love is the principal *motif* in the work of Amado Nervo. The tender emotions aroused by a smile, a perfume, or a prolonged glance are for him the occasions for sentimental memories. They are like flowers found along the wayside and treasured among the pages of a book. One day, paging through the book

after long years, they have the power of evoking again the almost forgotten emotion. But love in Amado Nervo is also like a tranquil and fraternal sentiment, possessing a depth of gravity and a religious emotion that reminds us of the strophes of St. Francis' "Canticle of the Sun".

The literary career of Amado Nervo began without loss of time. His first writings appeared at the period when the work of Gutiérrez Nájera marked the beginning in Mexico of a reaction, both intellectual and artistic, that was to have a decisive influence upon Hispanic American literature. From Gutiérrez Nájera, Amado Nervo learned to appreciate the poetry of Verlaine, acquiring from the symbolists and the decadents the sense of color and of shading and a more profound sensitivity to the musical possibilities of words, which he later poured forth in his *Perlas Negras* and in *Místicas.* In 1900, Nervo went to the World's Fair in Paris as correspondent for the Mexican newspaper *El Imparcial,* and there he became an intimate friend of Rubén Darío. (pp. 173-75)

During this period of companionship with Rubén Darío, Amado Nervo's poetry began to shine forth with new beauty, enamored of the French poets. His poetry of that epoch is unforgettable; it was authentic; it was embellished, moreover, with expressive and musical forms, with graceful rhythms that combine with the turns of a dance, with a pleasant arrangement of metrical structures, and with an air of sadness, elegantly hidden and reserved. If he could have chosen his own career—Nervo himself tells us—he would have chosen that of organist. In a poem dedicated to the King of Bavaria, entitled **"Un Padre Nuestro"**, he manifests his great admiration for Wagner. Perhaps we must understand his words in this sense when he says·that he has not invented any new metric form; but he, as well as Darío and the Argentine, Lugones, by the application of clever fluctuation and the use of new registers, obtains the effect of delicate musicality and a new sensitiveness that are captivating. In *Místicas,* his art is one that is in perpetual flow and continual transformation. The Alexandrine verses of **"La Hermana Agua"**, in *Poemas,* lend an exquisite musical tone to the theme treated therein with esthetic devotion and a fervent, ecstatic adoration before the beauty of nature, which make his song flow like a spring of enchanting freshness. . . . The imitative harmony of the poem **"El metro de doce"**, from *Jardines Interiores,* where the verses enumerate the syllables as he describes the dodecasyllabic form, achieves the effect of dancing joyfulness. Nervo obtains this effect by breaking up the trochaic rhythm native to the Spanish language by the use of anapests. (pp. 176-77)

Nervo gives a very modernistic and extraordinarily vibrating effect to the strophes of **"Mi Verso."** . . . This aristocracy of style, the selectness of thought, the novel manner of developing his themes, the rich variety of rhyme—all of these make Amado Nervo a profoundly original poet. These qualities change him into a prince of the "blue country" of fantasy, into a magician who weaves into fans of silk and lace the forms of delightful figures and landscapes.

About the year 1910, the poetry of Nervo undergoes a strange transformation. He ceases, for the most part, to pay homage to his own century—the century of confusion—and begins to speak in a lower tone, or, in the words of the title of his outstanding work of this period, *En voz baja.* (pp. 177-78)

All those who have written about Amado Nervo have considered him to be a mystic poet. It must be admitted, however, that the spiritual path of the poet is not as clearly marked nor as precisely outlined as that of his literary development. The latter is crystal clear; the former often deviates off on tangents and detours. Attempting to clarify this difficult problem, one must not forget that Amado Nervo was forced to earn his own living early in life, because of the death of his father. And for lack of training in a clear and solid philosophy, his work often suffers from a confusion of thought. His youthful study of philosophy is the bitter fruit of a spoiled vocation, which was ruined by indiscriminate and undigested reading, as well as an excessively lyrical temperament incapable of mental serenity and scientific objectivity. When Amado Nervo attempts to explain the intricate problems of philosophy, he is beyond his depth. If to all this is added the great admiration and devotion the poet had for the world of his day, it explains, quite possibly, the waves of confusions and the sea of contradictions that overwhelmed Amado Nervo's thinking. A recent writer [Esther Turner Wellman (see excerpt above)] finds that the poet drank from such contradictory fountains of thought "that he suffered from intellectual indigestion." Amado Nervo undeniably sought to be a man of his own century, the century of philosophical confusion, the century of the fusion of the most diverse schools of religious fashions and fads. "In modernness, no one gets ahead of me. I live with my feet placed solidly in my century and my eyes firmly sighted on the future." But those years toward the end of the nineteenth century and the beginning of the twentieth were ones of feverish intellectual activity. Nervo described this restless movement as follows: ". . . all of us who read have a new philosophical, cosmogonal or religious system at breakfast every day, with another one still newer for lunch, and the newest of all at dinner." Engulfed in this mental whirlpool, Nervo began to devour all the writings of Taine and Renan. He came to accept Bergson's opinion that science would evolve the religious formula of the future, and he thought that perhaps the present century might see the dawn of a universal religion that would be eminently scientific. In his poem **"Al Cristo"**, he describes his feelings at this period of his life, when he was drifting about in the darkness, without any sure guide, because the faith of his forebears no longer cast its peaceful glow over his path. In this intellectual confusion he had recourse to all the errors of those times—to Darwinism, spiritism, theosophism and pragmatism. This, however, was only a transitory stage in his spiritual orbit. Grown weary of living far from his Father's house, he returned after ten years of restless seeking, "like the sad prodigal", to the peace of his true spiritual heritage.

Nervo's was, in every way, a religious temperament. He was one of those men so intent upon the divine that they can only find their happiness when they have solved for themselves, both theoretically and practically, the problem of God. It is difficult to distinguish in his literary work that which is authentically and truly autobiographic from that which is merely literary artifice. We believe that there is a great deal of this latter in Nervo's works. There are many places in his works wherein he seems to be posing, projecting himself in his poems in a striking and attractive manner, as it were, allowing himself the pleasure of seeing his own reflection in the echo of the popular applause.

Nevertheless, the greater part of his work is the sincere expression of the heart-rending struggle going on within his very soul. *La Amada Inmóvil* is the story of this painful, interior conflict, of an illicit love which, having been lost by death, results in the author's return to realities that are not perishable. Only after the poet's death have we come to know how deeply Nervo was affected by the death of Anne Cécile Louise Dailliez, the young French maid of extraordinary delicacy and beauty, whom he loved so much. She of the golden hair, white skin, blooming complexion and the dignity of a princess—for so does Nervo describe her for us in his *Gratia plena*. . . . (pp. 178-81)

From *La Amada Inmóvil*, which is a poem composed in the form of a diary, only one logical conclusion can be deduced, if one leaves aside the artistic surface of its construction and the moments of confusion that agitated his mind: Amado Nervo had found his way through suffering and he was turning back, after the tragic search for his lost faith, back to his Father's house. Master Eckhardt, who Nervo cites in this work, had said: "Suffering is the swiftest steed to ride to perfection". The suffering poet's dedication of *La Amada Inmóvil* is a trustworthy testimony of the transformation that had taken place in his soul. . . . (pp. 181-82)

The richest and deepest chord, the one which Amado Nervo has played with the greatest confidence and with the greatest feeling, in all the succession of his songs, is the one he found in suffering and sorrow at the loss of his earthly love on January 7, 1912. The masterpieces which he wrote after that tragedy, *Serenidad* . . . , *Elevación* . . . and *Plenitud* . . . , glow with moments of authentically mystic poetry, for now the poet is ardently striving to reach and possess God, through love. (p. 182)

Toward the end of his public life he published *El estanque de los lotos*, which shows the strong attraction that doctrinal analogies had for him and the seduction of symbolism that he had noticed in his reading of Hindustanic literature. After a reflective reading of this work, we are convinced, as was the noted Mexican critic, Alfonso Junco, that in it Amado Nervo seems to have been touched with the same affectation for Buddhistic fantasies as were so many other writers of his day, not that they, or he, really believed in these Oriental doctrines, but rather in a spirit of literary romanticism and to give their work a certain poetic emphasis and interpretation of hazy aspirations of the soul. Nervo made these excursions in the field of religions as he had done with a succession of philosophies, very much in a passing way. (p. 184)

If we may compare the literary compositions of Amado Nervo to a great symphony made up of many diversified themes, literary, religious and social, then we may also say that throughout this symphony there vibrates, repeatedly, sweetly and harmoniously, the Franciscan note. It would be difficult to explain the origin of Nervo's marked affection for Franciscanism with any precise historical data. Dr. Wellman, who has carefully assembled all possible facts bearing on the development of the poet's human and artistic personality, suspects that he did not become acquainted with St. Francis in the Church, but that he "discovered" his favorite Saint in the works of Renan and in the Parnassian literature which he read so avidly in those days at the turn of the century. It seems more logical and more natural to the present writer to suppose that for psychological reasons, his early background, family-life and education, Amado Nervo first found his Franciscan inspiration in Mexico itself, without its having been necessary for him to recur to later and more exotic sources, although admitting that these may well have confirmed and enlarged his acquaintance with matters Franciscan. (pp. 185-86)

This interest in Franciscan themes is very evident in all the work of Amado Nervo. But it is in his *La Hermana Agua* that we find the best expression of the poet's Franciscan sentiments and it is here, more than in any others of his works, that Nervo's poetic genius reaches its peak. In his introduction to this poem, he says:

A trickle of water that falls from an imperfect spout; a trickle of soft, clear water that runs happily all through the night and every night near my bedroom, that sings of my solitude and accompanies me in it; a trickle of water—what a simple thing! And, nevertheless, these ceaseless and resounding drops have taught me more than books.

"The holy soul" of Sister Water spoke to him, and he learned her lesson in loving meditation and he pointed it out in his poem, a lesson which might be summed up thus: "to be docile, to be crystal-pure."

> I know that whoever reads it [*La Hermana Agua*] will feel the gentle pleasure that I felt in hearing it from the lips of Sister Water, and this will be my guerdon in the contest, until my bones rejoice in the grace of God.

The poem finds its inspiration in that crystalline strophe of St. Francis' "Canticle of the Sun." . . . (p. 189)

This work of Nervo's in 234 verses, is true poetry, in which the Mexican author sought to sing the praises of Sister Water in lyric commentary. It is completely saturated with the Franciscan spirit, which he herein proves to have understood. The form of the poem, although it does not lack technique and polish, is notable for its purity, and rests on a basis of religious emotion and mysticism. Its literary vestiture has an immediate purpose. Like one who is not in a hurry, he tarries to listen to the pleasant message of the water "which flows under the earth", and of that which flows upon it, as well as that of the snow, the ice, the hail, the steam, the mist. And from all its forms he hears the query: "Poet, you who by the grace of heaven has come to know us, will you not sing with us?" And he replies: "Yes, I'll sing, sister voices." Thus, in an authentically Franciscan way, he has caught sight of the divine irradiation of created things, clear reflections of the beauty of God, as a means of perfection and of elevation to the Creator of all being.

Nervo shares in the tendency of Mexican poets to give a sort of pantheistic flavor to his development of the theme; but his religious and Franciscan sentiment recognizes the worth of humble things and magnifies them, recognizing their spiritual dimensions as things that have come from the hand of God by an express act of His will. This clarity of view is one of the secrets of St. Francis' soul. And for Nervo, too, the various transformations of Sister Water are so many fundamental characteristics whereby one may reach back to the beneficent Hand that created them. For this reason, amid the sea of doubts in which his spirit is tossed, the poet turns to God to ask, as did St. Paul on the road to Damascus, "Lord, what wilt thou have me do?" (p. 190)

Variety is not the outstanding note in Nervo's philosophy—it is rather monotonous and without originality. It is limited to a repetition of the ideas of confused intellectuals, with no precise distinction between what is orthodox and what is unorthodox. His model is the Archer, Apollo, constantly winging arrow after arrow at any and every cultural mark that presents itself to his view. But never, not even in the darkest days of spiritual prostration, does he lose sight of the profound beliefs of the Catholic faith that he learned in his childhood and early youth.

The aphorism, "Every one writes as he is", is usually true only when the one who writes really has a personality of his own. Amorphous and apathetic people have no style of expression—they can only state facts. But in the case of Amado Nervo there is no doubt; as soon as we begin to read his works, we are aware of his very individual personality, with its qualities of sweetness and aspiration for good. (pp. 194-95)

> Roderick A. Molina, O.F.M., "Amado Nervo: His Mysticism and Franciscan Influence," in The Americas (copyright 1949 by The Academy of American Franciscan History), Vol. VI, No. 2, October, 1949, pp. 173-96.

OCTAVIO PAZ (essay date 1952)

[*An author of works on literature, art, anthropology, culture, and politics, Paz is primarily recognized as one of the greatest modern Spanish-American poets. Early in his career he met André Breton, founder of Surrealism, and Paz's work shares the Surrealist quest for personal freedom and the high value placed on love relationships. Paz's poetry is characterized as visionary and experimental, and his critical writings on literature are regarded with respect.*]

Modernism is not merely the assimilation of parnassian and symbolist poetry. In discovering French poetry, Spanish-American modernism also discovered the Spanish classics, forgotten or betrayed in Spain. Above all, it created a new language which became the vehicle, in an extremely fertile period, of some great poets: Rubén Darío, Leopoldo Lugones, Julio Herrera y Reissig. . . . Every revolution possesses or creates a tradition. Darío and Lugones invented their own. Gutiérrez Nájera and Amado Nervo never knew that they had one, and that is why the meaning of the modernist revolution escaped them. The modernism of these two poets is nearly always exoticism, that is to say, they were constantly re-creating themselves in the most decorative and superficial elements of the new style. (pp. 33-4)

In his modernist period, Amado Nervo manipulates, without taste but with freshness and authenticity, the stock-in-trade of symbolism. Later, he decided to do without it. In fact, he simply executed a change of garment; the symbolist garb, which suited him, was discarded for the mantle of the religious and moral philosopher. Poetry lost by the change, but neither religion nor ethics gained anything. (p. 34)

> Octavio Paz, "Introduction to the History of Mexican Poetry," in Anthology of Mexican Poetry, edited by Octavio Paz, translated by Samuel Beckett (translation copyright ©1958 by Indiana University Press; originally published as Anthologie de la poésie Mexicaine, edited by Octavio Paz, translated by Guy Lévis Mano, Éditions Nagel, 1952), Indiana University Press, 1958, pp. 23-44.*

CARLOS GONZÁLEZ PEÑA (essay date 1955)

Three stages mark the development of Amado Nervo's poetic production. Belonging to the first are [*Black Pearls, Poems, The Exodus and Wayside Flowers: Lira Heroica, The Inner Gardens*]. . . . In this period the poet was influenced by French symbolism, but this did not prevent him from revealing even then a fully formed personality, original and very much his own. "I acknowledge only one school," he was to declare later, "that of my own deep and eternal sincerity." He is bold, fastidious; he boasts of the freedom with which he breaks the rules of verse; he delights in subtleties, emotions, words, and rare rhythms. There is in him, underneath the lordly elegance, tenderness and a welling up of feeling. He loves life, and he peers into its mystery. His restless youth, a flower that had opened in the perfumed smoke of the altars, was whipped by doubt and held a long debate between "the cursed flesh that kept him from heaven" and the mystic desires born in his home and altered now in the homesickness for his seminary days. For a moment it would seem that mysticism triumphs. But this mysticism is more literary and external than private and profound; it depends, above all, on the golden brilliance of the liturgy; it speaks to us of the reflection of the candles on the priests' vestments; of missals and breviaries, with the red initials standing out; of gleaming vessels for the Host; of many-hued cathedral windows; of adorned altars, over-flowing chalices, lofty domes.

Nervo's second phase comes, it would seem, when he separates himself from the dazzling outer world in order to question the deep inner "I." A love encountered suddenly, in the flesh, gives him tranquillity and serenity; and then his first personality is purified and refined: he turns to naturalness and simplicity. It is the hour of the appearance of *In a Low Voice* . . . and *Serenity* . . . , the two golden fruits of his maturity, which the autumn sun illuminated. In these books a preoccupation with the beyond is predominant; in them is clarified the pantheistic hope that he had already suggested in the earlier period in *"La Hermana Agua"* (*"Sister Water"*). The poet had reached, as Rubén Darío expressed it, "one of the most difficult points in poetic mountain-climbing: the level ground of simplicity, which is found between the very high peaks and the very deep abysses." "The pompous style" frightened him, he himself said, though he exaggerated when he alluded to his earlier poetry; "the extravagance of the showy adjectives" dismayed him; he searched for "the discreet tone, the half shading, the soft colors"; he knew, at last, how to say what he wished, in the way he wished; no longer did words drive him; "he had won dominion over them."

He was destined to go even farther along this road in his third period. The sudden breaking off of the love that filled his life, the contemplation of death, and the sorrow before irreparable loss led him to complete resignation and an expression of the most eloquent, if not the purest, asceticism. He aspired to elevate his soul and that of the world with books—as he says playfully, though it is unnecessary to take him literally—"without rhetoric, without method, without technique, without literature." And such are *Elevation* . . . ; *Plenitude* . . . , a work written in prose, as if the poet, for greater simplicity, had rejected the artifice of rhyme; and, lastly, *The Lotus Pond,* the final collection of poems that Nervo published during his life. *The Constant Lover* and *The Divine Archer* were published posthumously. . . . (pp. 299-301)

Nervo's prose work is most varied. In addition to essays, chronicles, and articles, it includes the beautiful study of *Juana de Asbaje* . . . and several novels and stories. . . . [The] literary renown of Nervo began with *El Bachiller,* a short novel of bold naturalism. This was followed by *Pascual Aguilera,* a story of pronounced regional flavor; the novelesque fantasy *The Giver of Souls;* and, finally, the short stories collected under the title *Souls That Pass.* . . . Many years were to pass before Nervo returned to the cultivation of fiction; but in 1916 appeared *The Unselfish Devil;* and other short novels followed in sequence: *The Diamond of Restlessness, A Lie, A Dream, The Sixth Sense, Amnesia,* and *Mysterious Stories.* In this man, who was above all a poet, there was also an original novelist: in the first novels and stories that he wrote (all being of Mexican character, but

the stories to a greater degree), Nervo is revealed as a most delicate observer and painter of landscapes; the novels of the second period, with the strong initial nationalism lost, belong entirely to the cosmopolitan writer. His prose is nervous, full of vivacity; the evolution toward purity and simplicity proceeded much more rapidly in it than in his poetry. (p. 301)

> *Carlos González Peña, "From 1867 to 1910: Poetry" (1955), in his* History of Mexican Literature, *translated by Gusta Barfield Nance and Florene Johnson Dustan (translation © 1943: University Press in Dallas, Southern Methodist University; © 1968: Southern Methodist University Press: Dallas; originally published as* Historia de la literatura mexicana, *ninth edition, Editorial Porrúa, 1966), revised edition, Southern Methodist University Press, 1968, pp. 267-306.**

JOHN S. BRUSHWOOD   (essay date 1966)

Amado Nervo was, beyond question, the best writer of fiction among the *modernistas,* and one of the very few capable of producing novels. Yet even his tended to be short. His first, *El bachiller* . . . , concerns a young man's struggle between worldly and spiritual love. Trained for the priesthood, he is faced with the temptation of physical love. In a dramatic moment at the end of the novel, he castrates himself to avoid being seduced. This ending is described in the literary histories as horrible, revolting, and improbable. Indeed it is so unacceptable to most people that one has to read the novel to find out what happens. Not surprisingly, it created quite a furor in 1895. The resolution of the problem is indeed sensational, but those who criticize it do not give the author enough credit for the psychological development that creates the protagonist's impasse. If it is not entirely credible, it at least shows the author's willingness to probe human reactions.

The second novel, *Pascual Aguilera* . . . , is a considerably more sophisticated effort of the same kind. It uses the same theme of the *"hacendado's* privilege" that is found in *Nieves* and in *Perico.* But Nervo's novel is psychological rather than social. Pascual—to keep the record straight—is the son of the *hacendado* rather than the master himself, but he assumes the right to take his pleasure with the peasant bride. Nervo develops the character of Pascual with extreme care. Sometimes his explanation of the basis of his protagonist's actions becomes positively textbookish. He omits no detail that will support the case, and the frankness with which he treats sex must have been earthshaking in the world of Delgado. Pascual is unsuccessful in his plan to possess the young bride, but he loses control of himself so completely that he rapes his stepmother. Nervo, not satisfied with having exploded this bomb under the chairs of his complacent contemporaries, then reveals that the stepmother enjoyed the experience and explains why.

The impact of *Pascual Aguilera* cannot be appreciated fully unless we recall that it was published just three years after Delgado's *Angelina,* and before *La siega* and *Los parientes ricos.* Nervo's book is always a surprise too for readers of his gentle, and frequently soporific, poetry. The motivation behind the writing of *Pascual Aguilera* was not a desire for sensationalism, but an interest in investigation. Nervo's was one of the most searching minds of his time. He explored everything, was interested in everything. Scientific discoveries particularly fascinated him, and in many stories he tried interpreting them in human terms. Every piece of information seemed to move him to speculation, with the human condition always the laboratory. (pp. 146-47)

John S. Brushwood, "A Certain Elegance (1892-1906), in his Mexico in Its Novel: A Nation's Search for Identity (copyright © 1966 by John S. Brushwood), University of Texas Press, 1966, pp. 137-58.*

DOROTHY BRATSAS (essay date 1968)

Much consideration has been given to Amado Nervo, the Mexican Modernist poet, but relatively little has been given to his prose fiction. Many critics have pointed out the numerous themes used by Nervo but little has been done to demonstrate Nervo's use of psychological character study as a means of exploring a specific idea. In Nervo's three earliest novels, [El Bachiller, Pascual Aguilera, and El donador de almas], . . . he used the techniques of the psychological novel to describe the conflicts arising between wordly and spiritual love.

The three protagonists represent distinct psychological types. Felipe of El Bachiller is hypersensitive, pensive, religious, and lives in a subjective world restricted to his fantasies, illusions, prayers, and books. His excessive idealism contributes to his feeling of displacement in society. His fear of being disillusioned, of never being able to attain an ideal love in secular life, and his obsessive desire for solitude contribute to his decision to study for the priesthood. Felipe's intense neurotic personality feeds on his self-introspection and soon inhibits the little semblance of normality left to him. His religious zeal contributes to his development of a morbid fear of physical gratification. He even denies himself food and water in his mortification of the flesh. Chastity becomes an obsession. This morbid fear of sex results in his self-emasculation when he is confronted with making a choice between worldly and spiritual love.

Felipe's rejection of life represents the extremist position to the one maintained by his uncle and Asunción. They represent the life force and point out that salvation and union with God may be attained in other ways as acceptable as entering the priesthood. Felipe's inability to see the intrinsic difference between worldly and spiritual love contributes to his committing a crime more offensive to God by not following his natural desires and by not accepting life's responsibilities.

Pascual Aguilera is Felipe's antithesis. He is brutal, crude, unsophisticated, and salacious. All of his interests are physical and material rather than spiritual, intellectual or artistic. He personifies primitive man whose physical needs motivate every action. His entire life has been preoccupied with gratifying his morbid sexuality. Pascual is as pathologically obsessed as Felipe, and his neurosis contributes to his death. His frustrations and anger precipitate an hysterical outburst, because he is thwarted in his attempts to possess Refugio. Her marriage to Santiago precipitates a psychotic episode culminating in his attack on his stepmother. Pascual dies from the excesses of his hysteria.

The principal point Nervo makes in Pascual Aguilera is that the hero is not only depraved because of heredity but that his and man's destruction is because of sex. Nervo feels that sex impedes man's progress and the ideal state is one based on intellect rather than physical contact. The basis for humanity's ills and human suffering is mankind's great sin, "espíritu de fornicación".

The two protagonists destroy themselves because they are emotionally incapable of handling their problems. The other characters, representing normal society, in the two novels are directly affected by the problems created by the two disturbed heroes. Asunción in El Bachiller and doña Pancha in Pascual Aguilera represent the normal, healthy world in which the pathological does not function. Yet, these normal members of society suffer and are victimized by man's selfishness. Nervo is sympathetic to the problems of the Mexican woman and her role in marriage. He laments the treatment she receives from the male, while selfishly pursuing his gratification of the flesh without giving her the consideration she deserves.

In El donador de almas Nervo continues the development of his thesis that worldly love is not possible because of man's intrinsic shortcomings. The hero, Rafael, is the most stable protagonist of the three novels although he shares some characteristics with Felipe: he is refined, cultivated, sensitive, and somewhat neurotic. Rafael is also possessed of the monomaniacal desire to find the perfect woman for a perfect relationship. He remains frustrated in his search until he is given a soul, Alda. The novel is a fantasy describing the psychological interplay of the two protagonists, one representing the flesh and the other the spirit. The ensuing conflicts and crisis arising between the two produces some fascinating dialogues on worldly and spiritual love.

Through his characters Nervo states that the soul is a sexless, immortal entity fortunately not governed by the emotional problems of the organism housing it. Therefore, spiritual union can be realized—but a physical manifestation of love is not successful because it is motivated by self-love. . . . (pp. 244-46)

Love creates many conflicts, and love between the sexes is no more than an enchanting form of hate that has existed since time immemorial and will continue to exist. . . . (p. 246)

Rafael and Alda maintain an ideal relationship as long as she remains a free spirit not restricted to living on earth, and is permitted to experience and see the beauties of the universe. Alda refuses to remain with Rafael. She says that if man on earth would develop a love for his fellow man as strong as the one for himself then she might consider returning, for utopia would then exist.

The primary theme of all three works is love, worldly and spiritual. All three protagonists are neurotic, and their neuroses are of varying degrees of severity. Pascual is primitive man always motivated by his physical needs. Felipe and Rafael are idealists in search of perfect love. Neither can achieve a satisfactory relationship on earth, because neither is capable of establishing a relationship compatible with their standards. Therefore, one turns to religion and the other to developing an intellectually perfect cerebral relationship with his captive soul, Alda. Two succeed in destroying themselves and the third in losing his captive spirit because of their human frailties.

The various ideas expressed by Nervo through his characters in these three novels are repeated in his non-fictional prose and in his poetry. Wordly love, because of its physical manifestations, prevents the complete union of man and his loved one. It is a primitive and destructive emotion as seen in a person like Pascual Aguilera. Man is imperfect because of this sexual drive or espíritu de fornicación as Nervo calls it. It causes man's destruction. Felipe exemplifies this view. He cannot separate his love for God from his love for a terrestrial being. His conflict precipitates him into committing a crime against nature, graver than the one committed by Pascual. Because of his intrinsic self-centeredness, man cannot love unselfishly. A perfect relationship must be completely reciprocal, and this condition can never exist because man is hindered by his physical desires. Nervo's ideal state is a sexless one. The best possible relationship is an intellectual marriage between individuals as seen in *El donador de almas*. Only after death can one expect to achieve this *camino de perfección* or *escala de perfección* as Alda calls it. In life after death, when two beings are not bound by their physical selves, they can enjoy a perfect union. (pp. 247-48)

> *Dorothy Bratsas, "The Problem of Ideal Love in Nervo's Novels," in* Romance Notes, *Vol. 9, No. 2, Spring, 1968, pp. 244-48.*

ADDITIONAL BIBLIOGRAPHY

Báez, C. Rangel. "The Poetry of Ideas in Darío and Nervo." *Inter-America* VIII, No. 1 (October 1924): 29-38.*
   Contrasts Rubén Darío, the poet of "life, action, love," with Nervo, the poet of "abstraction, asceticism, contemplation."

Irving, T. B. "Love and Woe (Amado Nervo, 1870-1919)." *Salon 13* III, No. 1 (March 1962): 27-34.
   Biographical sketch containing a number of translations from Nervo's poetry.

Umphrey, George W. "Amado Nervo and Maeterlinck: On Death and Immortality." *The Romanic Review* 40, No. 1 (February 1949): 35-47.*
   Finds Nervo and Maurice Maeterlinck similar in their unfearful attitude toward death, but divergent in their conceptions of an afterlife: Maeterlinck considers various propositions but ultimately suspends judgment, while Nervo accepts the Christian doctrine of personal immortality.

May Sinclair

1865?-1946

(Born Mary Amelia St. Clair Sinclair; also wrote under pseudonym of Julian Sinclair) English novelist, novella and short story writer, essayist, biographer, poet, and critic.

Sinclair was one of the earliest authors to incorporate the theories of modern psychology into her fiction. In novels such as *The Divine Fire, The Three Sisters,* and *Mary Olivier* she utilized the psychoanalytic concepts of Sigmund Freud to explore the subtle consequences of sexual sublimation. These and other works represent a revolt against religious hypocrisy and against Victorian sexual and social values, treating subjects previously thought unacceptable for women writers. Although recognized in her own time as an important writer and thinker, Sinclair's reputation severely declined after her death.

Born in Rock Ferry, Cheshire, Sinclair was educated at home and at the Cheltenham Ladies' College, where the headmistress encouraged her to write professionally. At first inclined to poetry, Sinclair published the collection *Nakiketas, and Other Poems* pseudonymously in 1886. Her first novel, *Audrey Craven,* was published more than a decade later, a period during which she developed interest in the growing field of psychology. She did not gain popular and critical recognition in England until after her novel *The Divine Fire* became a success in the United States in 1904; thereafter, her works consistently attracted a larger readership in America than in her own country. A prolific writer, Sinclair wrote steadily for over thirty years, gaining critical notice as a perceptive and innovative artist. As a friend of Ezra Pound and other members of the Imagist group, and as a student of the theories of Freud and of C. G. Jung, she was abreast of contemporary developments in literature, philosophy, and psychology. In a 1918 review of Dorothy Richardson's novel *Pointed Roofs,* Sinclair became the first person to apply William James's term "stream of consciousness" to a literary method. Before World War I, Sinclair was a suffragette, and during the war years she served in an ambulance unit on the Belgian front. Her wartime experiences provided material for two novels, *The Romantic* and *The Tree of Heaven.* Her career ended in the early 1930s, when invalidism restricted her activities and rendered her unable to write.

Steeped in modern psychological thought, Sinclair's fiction is concerned with unconscious desires and the results of their suppression, and with the mental harm wrought by despising fleshly needs while exalting spiritual ideals. Closely associated with these concerns is Sinclair's stream of consciousness method, which was utilized most successfully in the semiautobiographical *Mary Olivier.* Considered by many critics to be her greatest work, *Mary Olivier* bears the influence of Dorothy Richardson and of James Joyce, and examines one of Sinclair's recurring motifs: the socially sacrosanct—but to the author, potentially crippling—value of self-sacrificing love. In several novels, the life of the literary artist as well as society's tempering influence on creativity are explored, notably in *The Creators* and in *Far End.* A convinced spiritualist, Sinclair also wrote a number of short stories on psychic phenomena, examining the relationship between the supernatural and the psychological.

The seriousness and realism of Sinclair's fiction has led some critics to find her art overburdened by psychological concerns. Others, such as Theophilus E. M. Boll and Heywood Broun, have praised Sinclair for the controlled sense of humor and irony which underlays her works. Broun, for example, has described *Mr. Waddington of Wyck* as "perhaps the finest study of a windbag known to literature." Sinclair's skill in writing convincing dialogue, in creating interesting characters, as well as her narrative skill have also been highly praised. In addition, scholars believe that through her work in joining art with psychology, Sinclair deeply influenced the thought and poetry of her young American friend, T. S. Eliot. Recent critics have hailed Sinclair as a pioneering feminist writer; not only were her works concerned with the smothered lives of tradition-bound women (and men), but they frankly presented alcoholism, adultery, and other subjects that were hitherto rarely considered by women writers.

After a career during which her writings were widely read, Sinclair has been little discussed for the past fifty years. But the advent of the feminist movement in the early 1970s and a continued interest in stream of consciousness fiction have prompted periodic reprintings and reappraisals of Sinclair's works. She remains today an obscure but important figure in the development of modern world literature.

(See also *TCLC.* Vol. 3 and *Contemporary Authors,* Vol. 104.)

PRINCIPAL WORKS

Nakiketas, and Other Poems [as Julian Sinclair]   (poetry)
   1886
Essays in Verse   (poetry)   1892
Audrey Craven   (novel)   1897
Mr. and Mrs. Nevill Tyson   (novel)   1898; also published
   as *The Tysons (Mr. and Mrs. Nevill Tyson)*, 1906
The Cosmopolitan   (novella)   1901; published in *Two Sides
   of a Question*
Superseded   (novella)   1901; published in *Two Sides of a
   Question*
The Divine Fire   (novel)   1904
The Helpmate   (novel)   1907
The Judgement of Eve   (novella)   1907
The Immortal Moment: The Story of Kitty Tailleur   (novel)
   1908; also published as *Kitty Tailleur*, 1908
The Creators   (novel)   1910
The Flaw in the Crystal   (novel)   1912
The Three Brontës   (biography)   1912
The Combined Maze   (novel)   1913
The Judgement of Eve, and Other Stories   (novella and
   short stories)   1914
The Three Sisters   (novel)   1914
The Belfry   (novel)   1916; also published as *Tasker Jevons:
   The Real Story*, 1916
A Defence of Idealism: Some Questions and Conclusions
   (essay)   1917
The Tree of Heaven   (novel)   1917
Mary Olivier   (novel)   1919
The Romantic   (novel)   1920
Mr. Waddington of Wyck   (novel)   1921
Anne Severn and the Fieldings   (novel)   1922
Life and Death of Harriet Frean   (novel)   1922
The New Idealism   (essay)   1922
Uncanny Stories   (short stories)   1923
Arnold Waterlow   (novel)   1924
A Cure of Souls   (novel)   1924
The Dark Night   (poetry)   1924
The Rector of Wyck   (novel)   1925
Far End   (novel)   1926
The Allinghams   (novel)   1927
History of Anthony Waring   (novel)   1927
Tales Told by Simpson   (short stories)   1930
The Intercessor, and Other Stories   (short stories)   1931

THE ATHENAEUM   (essay date 1892)

The first of Miss May Sinclair's **'Essays in Verse'** is a "Philosophical Dialogue" in which the philosophies put into the mouths of five dull disputants are thin and threadbare, as if from text-book epitomes, and the arguments and illustrations are no other than what have been hackneyed, to almost meaninglessness, in the service of their respective schools. If this essay had been written in prose, as such essays should be, its writer—unless very juvenile—must have perceived its superficiality and want of original thought, and would, it must be supposed, have preferred suppressing it and waiting to produce some abler treatise on philosophic themes. But the disguise of measured lines has deceived her as much as to the philosophy as it has as to the poetry of her essay—**'Guyon'** by name. The

second essay, **'Two Studies from the Life of Goethe,'** is in two soliloquies: the first, and much the longer, is the startlingly ambitious effort to present Goethe, on the text of his love-story with Frederike eight years before, intently analyzing his own intellectual and moral nature and baring his soul to himself— an effort as to which *"non ragionam"*: the second soliloquy is dated seven years earlier than the first, and is Frederike's expression of love-lorn grief and of excuse for Goethe. . . . Frederike's monologue is, as might be foreseen, less unsuccessful than Goethe's; the simplicity and quiet pathos of the theme have a poetry in themselves, and Miss Sinclair has treated it simply: indeed, because of its simplicity it might fairly be called a poem if it were not for the bane of disturbing versification. It is, like Goethe's monologue and the philosophical dialogue, in blank verse; and Miss Sinclair is one of those prosaic metrists, fortunately now rare, who treat blank verse as an arrangement for getting words into lines, with the privilege to the arranger of beginning and ending the lines anywhere the words will measure in. **'Margery,'** last of the contents, has the advantage of not being in blank verse—with the exception, however, of two bits, in one of which, called an Introduction, the blank verse has little resemblance to that of the preceding essays and much of it is good. This is the more fortunate that the Introduction contains a noteworthy description of the Cambridgeshire fens—a description that gives grounds for thinking, what the pieces already spoken of leave very dubious, that Miss Sinclair has poetic possibilities among her evidently high intellectual gifts. There are portions of **'Margery'** which continue this impression, although **'Margery,'** a collection of lyrical pieces to shape a story, as Lord Tennyson's 'Maud' is shaped, is (unintentionally no doubt) so reminiscent of 'Maud' that it cannot be taken as betokening what it might betoken if its origin were quite independent. **'Margery'** is inartistically put together—some of its fragments, including the Introduction, are irrelevant and seem to have been inserted merely to find a place for them; it ceases with sudden impotence, leaving its story untold and scarcely at all suggested; and, endeavouring to supply the deficiency by the poor old device of an after-many-years epilogue, it appends as "Conclusion" a moralizing soliloquy which has barely an inferential connexion with the earlier records of the poem and does not in itself convey the story to which we must, by guesswork, suppose it to refer. Yet there are indications, and some fulfilments, in **'Margery'** which make it impossible to read it and not wish that Miss Sinclair would, reserving disquisitions and expositions for treatment in prose, write verse in which she could give free play to all the true poetic instinct she may possess.

> *A review of "Essays in Verse," in* The Athenaeum,
> *No. 3385, September 10, 1892, p. 350.*

THE ATHENAEUM   (essay date 1897)

The name of May Sinclair, on the title-page of **'Audrey Craven,'** is, so far as we are aware, unknown. Judging from this volume, it seems possible that it may not always be so. The story is not without fulfilment as well as promise. If it were followed by something stronger we should not feel surprised. It is free from pretentious and ambitious airs. The interest does not merely depend on the material being "very modern." The workmanship is good of its kind, the handling light and agreeable. Some quality in it points to a good deal of original observation and experience fused into fictional form. An understanding of some phases of life and character carefully, but not descriptively developed, touches of unforced humour, and a good deal of feeling are no bad equipment. The heroine is not built upon the too, too familiar and wearisome lines of many of the genus. . . . The girl's lack of intelligence under her brilliant appearance is what is best and most cleverly conveyed. The author seems to have clearly apprehended, and therefore clearly represented, the creature. Her essential incompleteness, intense artificiality, and innate self-consciousness are well suggested. The poverty of her nature, and especially the utter lack of humour that lies at the bottom of most of her folly and wrongdoing, are not overdone. It is a portrait, not the slavish photograph, of a woman. Many who are not self-deceivers will recognize some of Audrey in themselves. It is not a beautiful, but it is still less an entirely uninteresting nature. The artist brother and sister are pleasantly drawn, so are their relations with a good commercial uncle. One or two other characters are less successful, but there is more to praise than to blame.

A review of "Audrey Craven," in The Athenaeum, *No. 3639, July 24, 1897, p. 122.*

FREDERIC TABER COOPER (essay date 1912)

[*An American educator, biographer, and editor, Cooper served for many years as literary critic at* The Bookman, *a popular early twentieth-century literary magazine. He drew upon several of his reviews of Sinclair's books to compile the following survey of her career to-date.*]

The difficulty which must be faced in attempting to write a critical estimate of the work of May Sinclair, considered as a whole, is that this is precisely the way in which it refuses to be considered. Her novels are hopelessly, irremediably incommensurate; they have no common denominator; they reveal nothing in the way of a logical progression, of mental or spiritual growth from book to book, from theme to theme; *The Tysons, The Divine Fire, The Helpmate,* the three conspicuous volumes of three separate periods, might, so far as any sequence in thought or method is concerned, be the product of three different brains, striving diversely towards three several artistic ideals. The first is merely a clever character study of an exceptional man and woman, whose union inevitably leads to tragedy; the second is a prose epic of genius battling for recognition, a myriad-sided picture of modern life, flung before us with spendthrift prodigality; the third is a deliberately calculated problem novel, in which the finer realities of speech and action are sacrificed at the shrine of the author's purpose. In certain qualities of style, no doubt, it would be easy, if such proof were required, to show that as a matter of fact all the volumes which bear the signature of May Sinclair actually have emanated from her pen. Certain felicitous phrasings of description, certain luminous flashes of subtle understanding, leave the imprint of a distinctive hall-mark on all her writings. It is not the faltering hand of the artist, but the difference in the nature and magnitude of the inspiration behind the work that has made her successive volumes so astonishingly uneven, so impossible to measure one against another.

The plain and unwelcome truth which forces itself home with obstinate persistence, in proportion as one studies Miss Sinclair's literary productions, is that for the purposes of serious criticism, she is the author of just one book. Her other volumes are full of interesting promise; *The Divine Fire* is big with achievement; her other volumes are written from her head; but *The Divine Fire* came at white heat from her very heart and soul. The very qualities that stamp it as of the first magnitude are many of them conspicuously absent alike from her earlier

and subsequent books. In her recent work, especially, she tends more and more to speak as one having authority, and her theories of life persist in looming up larger than the specific human tale she has to tell; while the great triumph of *The Divine Fire* lies precisely in the absence of any such intrusion on the author's part, in its splendid and unvarying impersonality.

It was really quite curious, this sudden and bewildering fruition of unsuspected genius. It came absolutely unheralded. There was nothing in its predecessors, nothing in the uneven ability of *The Tysons* or the more finished art of a less pretentious tale such as *Superseded,* that would give even a hint of the cycloramic sweep of treatment, the breadth of vision, the deep, comprehensive human sympathy of *The Divine Fire,*—just as, despite the lavish praise of her admirers, there is no promise in anything she has since done that she will ever again rise to similar heights, ever duplicate her masterpiece. Nor is there anywhere a hint that she has the ambition to attempt it. Having once achieved a novel of the epic type, vibrant with the surge of human passions, the turmoil of civic life, she seems content to fling aside the formula, reject the spacious canvas and bold, virile brush-stroke, and content herself with the subtler, more etching-like precision of intimate home portraiture, the secret infelicities of married life. . . . There are pages in *The Tysons, The Helpmate* and *The Judgment of Eve* in which the veil of intimate mysteries is snatched aside and human frailty so uncompromisingly labeled that the reader instinctively casts a conscious glance around him, in order to be assured that he is alone. This is a feeling that has come to me a score of times in reading Miss Sinclair's books; and the oddest thing of all is that there is just one volume that never for an instant casts even a shadow of this sort of sense of trespassing on forbidden ground, namely, *The Divine Fire.* And this is not because of any lack of boldness in theme, any cowardly closing of the eyes to the actualities of life; on the contrary, the book has that full share of human error and weakness that is inevitable in any cross-section of life, cut boldly and on a large scale. But because the book is conceived on so high a plane, because in fact it has around it a halo of the sacred fire, the sins of the flesh are dwarfed to their proper relative value as factors having their significance in the development of human destinies, not as something to be whispered, with innuendoes, from behind a fan.

In order to see more plainly the gulf, both in workmanship and in ideas, that lies between *The Divine Fire* and all her other books, let us examine certain representative volumes of Miss Sinclair's earlier and later period somewhat briefly, reserving a more detailed analysis of her crowning work for the last. . . . *Audrey Craven,* which, I understand, is, with the exception of some *Essays in Verse,* her earliest published volume, is also the most easily negligible. It has cleverness and a certain kind of humor; and it relates, in a vein of light satire, the history of a young woman whose "long quest of the eminent and superlative" ends in the anti-climax of marriage with a nonentity. . . . (pp. 252-56)

Mr. and Mrs. Nevill Tyson, which in the American edition suffered an unfortunate abbreviation of title, is, in spite of certain crudities, a book of much more serious import. Nevill Tyson is of plebeian birth,—his father kept a tailor shop at an early stage in his career,—and a cosmopolitan by education. He has lived largely by his wits, and seen much service in peace and in war, always just missing the achievement of fame or fortune. Suddenly, fate plays upon him the curious prank of forcing him into the position of country gentleman, a rôle difficult of fulfilment for a man who has scant liking for the country and lacks certain essentials of gentle breeding. . . . [If] he could have brought himself to marry a clever woman with an unassailable position, all might have gone well. But instead he chose to marry little Mollie Wilcox, a mere nobody with whom, scandal-mongers insisted, he had struck up an acquaintance in a public railway carriage,—but ''an adorable piece of folly,'' none the less, ''an illusion and a distraction from head to foot; her beauty made a promise to the senses and broke it to the intellect.'' ''My husband says I am the soul of indiscretion,'' she confesses blithely, while he, with more candor than good taste, says openly, ''My wife has about as much intellect as a guinea-pig, and the consequence is that she is not only happy herself, but the cause of happiness in others.'' (pp. 257-58)

Up to a point, the book is an admirable little study of an ill-assorted marriage, made hopeless from the start by a man's monumental selfishness and the meddling of scandal-loving neighbors. But what follows is too violent, too extreme, too needlessly cruel; it lacks the restraint that is the key-note of good art. . . . Nevill, after drinking too freely, causes a lamp to overturn, and his wife rescues him, at the cost of scars which destroy her beauty forever. There are a few brief weeks when the man thinks that he can rise above himself and repay her sacrifice with a lasting devotion; but the daily sight of that disfigured face is more than his ''fastidious nerves'' can bear; so he raises a volunteer company and sets off for the Soudan, where he dies a hero's death, after having slain his wife by his desertion as surely as though he had put a bullet through her heart. The trouble with the book is that it is overdrawn; the woman is a little more than human, the man a little less. The end is melodrama, the ''brutal, jubilant lust of battle,'' and a ''wooden cross in the shifting sands.'' It is amazing how readily an obsequious bullet, at the author's beck and nod, consents to cut short a misspent life at the psychological moment.

It is pleasant to turn from the amateurishness of *The Tysons* to a much more modest bit of work which, nevertheless, in its own way is very nearly flawless. There is so much simple pathos, so much genuine human nature in *Superseded* that only a writer of the first rank could have wrought such deft effects of light and shade from such slight material. It is merely the humble tragedy of a timid, colorless, inefficient school-teacher whom Fate originally thrust into a niche that she could never adequately fill; and then, after she has spent her strength for years in the pitiful struggle to do what is demanded of her, unexpectedly thrusts her out to an old age of helplessness and want. . . . It would be difficult to point out another story in English which portrays with such quiet strength the pathos of inefficient old age, the anguish of discovering that one has outlived one's usefulness.

Superseded originally appeared just three years before *The Divine Fire,* the same interval of time that intervened before the appearance of Miss Sinclair's next novel, *The Helpmate.* Towards this volume I must confess to an antagonism incompatible with the judicial impartiality of criticism. It is a well-intentioned book, built upon an interesting thesis; but, because its chief characters are faultily conceived, it is an offensive book as well as an unconvincing one. With the central theme, that the narrow-mindedness of the so-called good woman has been the moral ruin of many a man, as surely as though she were a bad woman, I have no quarrel. I simply fail to see that

in the present volume Miss Sinclair has chosen a case that proves her contention. (pp. 260-63)

The author wants us to espouse her hero's cause, and instead, with almost everything he says or does, he alienates our sympathy. Of course, a marriage so ill-assorted [as that of Walter and Anne Majendie] is bound to turn out disastrously; but the stumbling-block will not be a youthful error long since expiated; it will be the intolerable contact with little daily vulgarisms, the hourly verbal clumsiness, the monumental incapacity to understand the finer and subtler temperament of the woman. The underlying idea of the book is undeniably big; the situation at the end of ten years of marriage that has been a mockery of the word is poignant with tragedy. . . . And as [Walter] lies hovering between life and death, [Anne] has long hours in which to learn her own narrowness, long hours in which to repeat over and over the words of Lady Cayley, whom she scorned and who has ventured to tell her the truth:

> Look at it this way. He has kept all his marriage vows—except one. You have broken all yours—except one. None of your friends will tell you that. That's why *I* tell you. Because I'm not a good woman, and I don't count.

It is because this situation is so big in possibilities, and the principle involved so vital an issue in hundreds of marriages, that it is hard to pardon Miss Sinclair her amazing lack of perception in blurring the issue by the needless complications of a special case, and narrowing down to a mere lack of breeding a question that ought to have hinged upon the relative magnitude of two souls.

The Immortal Moment, while far slighter in scope and significance than *The Helpmate,* is artistically a much finer piece of workmanship. It is seldom that a story brings to the reviewer such a sense of impotence to do it justice within the space of a single paragraph. One can, of course, assert its admirable technique, its rare truth of characterization; its logical analytical development; but mere assertion, no matter how emphatic, lacks convincing power. What Miss Sinclair's book deserves is a detailed and painstaking analysis of the kind that takes much time and space. For, after all, stripped to its bare skeleton, *The Immortal Moment* seems a curiously inadequate framework upon which to fashion a story of any considerable magnitude. (pp. 267-70)

Miss Sinclair first became a figure of importance in contemporary fiction upon the appearance of *The Divine Fire,* and that without it her importance to-day would be, if not negligible, at least greatly diminished. In that one book at least she arose to rare heights. It is one of those big, many-sided, kaleidoscopic books which paint metropolitan life, the good and the bad together, with bold, sweeping brush-strokes,—the sort of book which it is almost as hard for a woman to achieve as it is for a woman to compose a symphony. The impression that you bring away from *The Divine Fire* is, first of all, an impression of a multitude of human beings, and at the same time not an impression of a crowd,—because, in a crowd, few faces stand out distinct from the rest, while in *The Divine Fire* there is a host of faces, every one of which you recognize because they are so carefully and admirably individualized. The picture is painted on a wide canvas; and there is no mistaking the assured touch with which the seamy side of journalistic and Bohemian London are flung before us. (pp. 271-72)

[In the character of Keith, Miss Sinclair] has shown us a genius, one of the finest and rarest sort, and she has convinced us that he is all she claims for him; she has succeeded in making him plausible, she has even ventured upon the supreme audacity of showing us fugitive specimens of his verse, and yet escapes an anti-climax. Savage Keith Rickman lives so firmly in our memory as an English poet of the first magnitude that it would not be at all surprising, indeed, it would seem in a way a merited tribute to the novelist's genius, if more than one absent-minded reader should search for the name of Rickman in anthologies of English verse.

These are the reasons why it is difficult to discuss Miss Sinclair's other volumes more than half-heartedly, why it has seemed best to omit some of them altogether from discussion. They suffer too much from contrast. One by one, they add their cumulative evidence to the growing conviction that *The Divine Fire* is likely to enjoy permanently its isolated splendor among Miss Sinclair's contributions to fiction. (pp. 278-79)

> Frederic Taber Cooper, *"May Sinclair," in his* Some English Story Tellers: A Book of the Younger Novelists *(copyright © 1912 by Henry Holt and Company), Holt, Rinehart and Winston, Publishers, 1912, pp. 252-79.*

T. S. ELIOT (essay date 1922)

[*Perhaps the most influential poet and critic of the first half of the twentieth century, Eliot is closely identified with many of the qualities denoted by the term Modernism: experimentation, formal complexity, artistic and intellectual eclecticism, and a classicist view of the artist working at an emotional distance from his creation. He was a friend of Sinclair, who, evidence suggests, played a key role in the development of his poetic theory. Below, he offers guarded praise for* Life and Death of Harriet Frean.]

In Miss Sinclair's [*Harriet Frean,* the psychoanalytic] method seems to have been carried about as far as it will go; and because it is a scientific method, and rests upon a dubious and contentious branch of science, I doubt whether even Miss Sinclair can carry it much further. . . . The conclusion of Miss Sinclair's book . . . extracts as much pity and terror as can be extracted from the materials: but because the material is so clearly defined (the soul of man under psychoanalysis) there is no possibility of tapping the atmosphere of unknown terror and mystery in which our life is passed and which psychoanalysis has not yet analysed. So that if I may predict, it is that Miss Sinclair will find herself forced to proceed from psychotherapy even to the supernatural, or at least to that transfinite world with which Henry James was in such close intercourse. (p. 330)

> T. S. Eliot, *"London Letter," in* The Dial *(copyright, 1922, by The Dial Publishing Company, Inc.), Vol. LXXIII, September, 1922, pp. 329-31.*

HARRIET MONROE (essay date 1924)

[*As the founder and editor of* Poetry, *Monroe was a key figure in the American "poetry renaissance" which took place in the early twentieth century.* Poetry *was the first periodical devoted primarily to the works of new poets and to poetry criticism, and from 1912 until her death Monroe maintained an editorial policy of printing "the best English verse which is being written today, regardless of where, by whom, or under what theory of art it is written." Below, she examines* The Dark Night, *a novel-in-verse.*]

When the imagists first donned the robes of print, and the "new movement" was really new, May Sinclair was in close

touch with the group headed by Ezra Pound in England, and was profoundly sympathetic with their ideas of poetic art. So it is not surprising to find this novelist making a test of them after these ten or twelve years, trying her hand at a new kind of novel told in a free verse stripped and disciplined by contact with their austere rules. (p. 99)

[*The Dark Night*] is the history of a woman's soul, and incidentally of her marriage. The incidents are not unusual—two women, and a man who wavers between them and finally returns to his forgiving wife in weakness rather than in strength. The two minor characters in the triangle are purposely left rather shadowy—they do not matter much except as their infidelity strains the wife, the narrator, to agony, and deepens the chords of music in her spirit.

The harmony between this character and her—as it were, involuntary—chanting of the story, is the remarkable thing about this book. The poem is a fine solo played by delicate caressing hands on some soft and lovely instrument—one of the old ones, perhaps a dulcimer—an instrument with depths and overtones, played in just the right rich and rusty environment, at just the right half-lit purple-colored hour. The piece, as it progresses to its controlled and shapely climax, is manifestly of a severe austerity devoid of ornament; but he who calls it simple is in danger of missing subtleties of technical handling and rarities of emotional motive. The art which conceals art is present here, and it leaves nowhere any trace of excess, unless the blindness of the hero at the end may be a stroke of sentimentally exaggerated color.

The central theme of the tale is love, not of man, but of God. (pp. 99-100)

It is evident that Miss Sinclair found prose inadequate to the expression of religious rapture. In accepting the finer, more exacting medium for her difficult theme, she approached her task with a kind of holy awe, casting away all the luxuries and indulgences of her prose style. It may well be that this brief scant tale represents more travail of the spirit than any of its author's novels. And perhaps it achieves a higher reach into clearer air. (p. 101)

> Harriet Monroe, *"Sacred and Profane Love," in* Poetry *(© 1924 by The Modern Poetry Association; reprinted by permission of the Editor of* Poetry*), Vol. XXV, No. 11, November, 1924, pp. 99-101.*

WILLIAM LYON PHELPS (essay date 1926)

[*Phelps spent over forty years as a lecturer at Yale. His early study* The Beginnings of the English Romantic Movement *(1893) is still considered an important work and his* Essays on Russian Novelists *(1911) was one of the first influential studies of the Russian realists. From 1922 until his death in 1943 he wrote a regular column for* Scribner's Magazine *and a nationally syndicated newspaper column. Below, he relates St. Paul's words on sexuality and marriage to* Far End, *in a review of that novel and a discussion of Sinclair's career. (First Corinthians 7:7, written by the unmarried Apostle and cited by the critic, reads as follows: "I wish that all men were as I am. But each man has his own gift from God; one has this gift, another has that.")*]

With the frankness so characteristic of the Bible in general and of Saint Paul in particular, we find in the seventh chapter of the First Letter to the Corinthians (who needed it) the apostle's advice to bachelors, widows, wives, and husbands. . . . The seventh verse would be a good text for May Sinclair's novel,

"The Helpmate," and the whole chapter may be profitably read after finishing her latest novel, **"Far End."** . . .

Just as Browning's three noble ladies who were competing for the prize in a love contest appointed a priest as referee, he being out of it and therefore unprejudiced, so *Miss* May Sinclair has certain advantages in contemplating the married life. We do not need the genius of Bacon to tell us why the spectator sees mistakes that the players do not. She has in two previous novels, **"The Helpmate"** and **"The Judgment of Eve,"** admonished respectively the wife and the husband. In **"Far End,"** which is a short, episodic novel, she gives the history of a modern marriage, its fair morning, its cloudy, stormy afternoon, its calm evening.

The war comes in, as it did in **"The Belfry"** and in **"The Tree of Heaven,"** but this is not a war novel, and altho two characters are eliminated by it, that limitless catastrophe is not essential to the story. There are really only four persons who count; the husband, the wife, the pretty stenographer, who steals the man's senses, and the vampirical widow, who steals his mind. Thus the wife is twice and doubly deceived. . . .

May Sinclair's masterpiece is **"The Three Sisters."** . . . Since that time her novels have been largely composed of satire, disillusion, and Freudian physics and metaphysics. **"Mr. Waddington of Wyck"** was a terrific exposure of conceit and bombast; **"Life and Death of Harriet Frean"** was a study of self-sacrifice, with the dynamics reversed; **"Ann Severn and the Fieldings"** seemed tarred with the Freudian brush. This story is a clear, running stream, unmuddied with philosophical obscurities, and absolutely objective.

Miss Sinclair was deeply engrossed in the study of speculative philosophy and metaphysics when she was hardly out of her teens, and she has been interested in these themes—particularly idealism—all her life. She has written philosophical works, and she has not been able to keep them out of her novels. I think her preoccupation with philosophy has seriously damaged some of her works of art, especially **"Mary Olivier."** But, like all true thinkers, she has been more interested in concrete examples than in abstract themes; furthermore, she is a born story-teller, who by practise has become a consummate artist. One has only to compare **"The Divine Fire"** with **"Far End"** to see her immense progress.

This tale is superb in its concision; in two hundred pages of large print Miss Sinclair has given us more of actual life than many of our novelists present in five hundred pages of tormenting type. Furthermore, she has succeeded in the conversational parts in omitting the tiresome "said she," "he rejoined," "she wailed," "he hissed," etc. The dialog comes to the reader straight from the page as it comes from the lips of actors on the stage. Just take a look at pages 118 and 119, and see how different is their facial expression from that of ordinary novelized conversations.

Not the least interesting thing in the story is the house itself, from which the novel takes its name, with which it opens, and with which, after much turbulence, it closes. There may not be much in a name, but there is sometimes everything in a place.

> *William Lyon Phelps, "May Sinclair, H. L. Mencken, and Saint Paul" (reprinted by permission of The Literary Estate of William Lyon Phelps), in* The Literary Digest International Book Review, *Vol. IV, No. 11, October, 1926, p. 671.**

JOSEPH WOOD KRUTCH (essay date 1927)

[*Krutch is widely regarded as one of America's most respected literary and drama critics. Noteworthy among his works are* The American Drama since 1918 *(1939), which analyzes the most important dramas of the 1920s and 1930s, and* "Modernism" in Modern Drama *(1953), in which he stressed the need for twentieth-century playwrights to infuse their works with traditional humanistic values. A conservative and idealistic thinker, he was a consistent proponent of human dignity and preeminence of literary art. His literary criticism is characterized by such concerns: in* The Modern Temper *(1929) he argued that because scientific thought has denied human worth, tragedy had become obsolete, and in* The Measure of Man *(1954) he attacked modern culture for depriving humanity of the sense of individual responsibility necessary for making important decisions in an increasingly complex age. In the following essay he reviews* History of Anthony Waring.]

Miss Sinclair is one of the relatively few contemporary novelists who have continued to practice the art (as distinguished from the trade) of fiction long after the more elementary motives for doing so have passed away. It is obvious that she ceased, sometime since, to have what is called in common parlance "anything to say." It is obvious, that is, that she is no longer moved either by that impulse to social protest which once tinged even her work or by any less definite need to communicate an individual attitude toward life, and hence obvious, too, that if she continues to write novels she does so merely because she is still intrigued by the practice of what we may call, without thereby implying any praise or blame, a "pure art." Each of her recent books has been, more conspicuously than it has been anything else, an exercise, and though that does not mean that any has been carelessly or mechanically written—indeed, the reverse is true—it does mean that we can read them only because we are interested in her method and can judge them only by its success. She has deliberately chosen people and events as little extraordinary as possible and deliberately imposed upon herself the task of conferring upon them whatever distinction they may seem to possess entirely by her manner of writing their story.

The **"History of Anthony Waring"** carries her particular experiment still further, and its direction is exactly the opposite to that taken by other experimental novelists. While their works have become longer, more complicated, and less direct, hers have grown shorter, simpler, and more completely straightforward. Here one hundred and thirty-one pages, printed in large type and with lavish margins in every possible direction, serve to tell the story of a life from the nursery to the deathbed. There are paragraphs four words long and whole chapters shorter than a single paragraph of this review. Everything not absolutely necessary has been eliminated and the whole is told in words each one of which would be comprehensible to a child just finished with its primer. Simplification could be carried no further, but here at least simplification defeats its purpose, and even as an experiment the result is negative since it proves either that what Miss Sinclair is attempting to do cannot be done or else it proves nothing at all. . . .

Miss Sinclair seems to have edited or abridged her own words with fatal results. She seems to have gone over them, asking if this or that might not be omitted, and to have taken so many things away that nothing is left.

One may be amazed that the **"History of Anthony Waring"** is not flatter than it is; one may grant that it is better than either **"Far End"** or **"The Allinghams,"** but one must conclude nevertheless that the author has not been able either to say or to imply anything very significant in words so few and so simple. Even the mood which the book provokes is not the mood which it seems probable that Miss Sinclair intended. She is not exactly a bitter person; one knows that the impression which she wishes to give of life is not an impression of futility; and yet when the whole earthly existence of a hero is recorded in a book which a child could read and understand in an hour the effect is almost inevitably that. . . .

I do not say that a novel no longer than this one might not possibly be made to seem adequate and more; but I do believe that it would have to retain at least some one of the various things which Miss Sinclair has left out even if it were only a language less simple than hers. Either condensation would have to be achieved by packing in instead of cutting out or the fewness of the incidents chosen would have to be compensated for by some extraordinary vividness which the mere competence of Miss Sinclair does not achieve. She is, to put it bluntly, never intense enough to justify her brevity and her novel is no more than a mere synopsis.

> *Joseph Wood Krutch, "An Impoverished Art," in* The Nation *(copyright 1927 The Nation magazine, The Nation Associates, Inc.), Vol. CXXV, No. 3252, November 2, 1927, p. 481.*

CLIFTON FADIMAN   (essay date 1932)

[*Fadiman became one of the most prominent American literary critics during the 1930s with his often caustic and insightful book reviews for the* Nation *and the* New Yorker *magazines. He also managed to reach a sizeable audience through his work as a radio talk-show host from 1938 to 1948. In the following review, Fadiman seems to find in* The Intercessor, and Other Stories *the fulfillment of the speculations stated a decade earlier by T. S. Eliot (see excerpt above).*]

Miss Sinclair's stories will appeal to a very special class, consisting probably of a small group of highly literary ladies given to polite adventuring in the Behind the Beyond. With a skill one would like to see applied to more corporeal subject matter, Miss Sinclair continues that rather *fanée* tradition established by Poe and E.T.A. Hoffmann and carried on in our own day by Algernon Blackwood and Arthur Machen. The trouble with Miss Sinclair's ghosts and night noises and haunted houses and karma-like chains of coincidence and dreamy-eyed Swamis is simply that (evidently) she believes in them. If she didn't (Poe didn't), her stories might be convincing. Since the advent of the New Physicists rationalism is of course unfashionable; nevertheless the present stick-in-the-mud reviewer admits unblushingly that he read **"The Intercessor and Other Stories"** without a single shiver. (p. 549)

> *Clifton Fadiman, "Short Stories—Mostly Bad," in* The Nation *(copyright 1932 The Nation magazine, The Nation Associates, Inc.), Vol. CXXXIV, No. 3488, May 11, 1932, pp. 548-49.**

WILLIAM C. FRIERSON   (essay date 1942)

[*Frierson discusses Sinclair's naturalistic vision and her psychological examinations of her characters.*]

Miss Sinclair is a novelist with naturalistic vision who is primarily concerned with expressing a revolt against Victorianism. She knows people and their ways, and is none the worse

for having read Henry James, for she is not bound by James's Victorian restraints while she follows him in delineating the presence of evil in supposedly nice persons. She presents us with case histories of frustration, of oppression, of useless sacrifice. Even in pre-Freudian days she concentrated upon the vast difference between conscious and unconscious motives, upon delusion, and upon the varieties of what was later to be known as sublimation. Oppression in her novels takes various forms. It is often imposed by unconsciously selfish parents. Often the oppression is the oppression of ideas. Rarely it is circumstance. Everywhere she implies the need of sanity and self-fulfillment.

Let us consider *The Helpmate* . . . as representative of one of her more complex novels. (p. 158)

In its essentials it is a naturalistic vision of the evils of piety, but the story as told by Miss Sinclair is highly colored by exceptional circumstance. It is really a connected series of dramatic situations arranged to demonstrate the view that religious ideals may be vicious, that they may engender self-deception and become a form of man's inhumanity to man. The effort of the author is, in the word of Wells, "to ventilate the issues" in one situation after another. And the author is not too scrupulous about logicality. The discovery of the husband's fatal past is, of course, an old stage trick. The plot hinges upon an accident—the husband's indirect responsibility for the death of the child. And, finally, there is no particular reason why a mixture of heavy drinking and Lady Cayley should have produced apoplexy. The novelist is revaluing ideals, and so long as motive and character are sound, a certain liberty is demanded in the presentation of incident. The novel still fulfills the naturalistic requirement of being a cosmic commentary—it is perhaps less cosmic than a naturalistic novel, and more of a commentary.

Stripped to their essentials the novels of May Sinclair are often naturalistic in theme. (pp. 159-60)

Yet naturalistic themes are not, in the end, satisfying to Miss Sinclair. Like Wells, whose influence she acknowledges, she would find a way out. Perhaps the way out in *The Life and Death of Harriet Frean* . . . is not too comforting. Harriet sacrifices her chance for happiness and is compensated by the joy that comes from contemplating her own beautiful act, although the sacrifice is bad for all concerned. Anne in *Anne Severn and the Fieldings* . . . gives up her husband to the woman he loves because she would hate herself if she did otherwise, and because by giving up her husband in this manner she would really win his love. In a story, **"The Cosmopolitan,"** a girl runs away from an oppressing father in order to find fulfillment with the man she loves.

I have mentioned only a few of May Sinclair's novels. She published twenty-four of them and six volumes of stories between 1897 and 1927. She wrote mostly about the conceptions that people needed to be released from. Her work was largely protest, but sound protest. After getting off to a slow start she became a popular novelist, and her work had a very wide influence. (pp. 160-61)

> *William C. Frierson, "The Years 1900-1915," in his* The English Novel in Transition: 1885-1940 *(copyright 1942 by the University of Oklahoma Press), University of Oklahoma Press, 1942, pp. 143-82.**

LIONEL STEVENSON   (essay date 1967)

[*A respected Canadian literary critic, Stevenson was also the author of several biographies, each highly acclaimed for the au-*

thor's scholarship, wit, and clarity. Below, he surveys Sinclair's career.]

[Until] she was almost forty [May Sinclair] was confined by the customary duty of conscientious spinsters, the care of a demanding mother; but she struggled resolutely to expand her range of knowledge and to find a literary medium. A pseudonymous book of immature verse came out when she was twenty-three and another volume of poetry six years later. The poems reveal something of the emotional tensions and mental confusions through which she was fighting her way. Then at the age of thirty-four she published her first novel. . . . (pp. 258-59)

Audrey Craven is a quiet but perceptive study of a young woman who impresses those around her with her beauty and charm, but who is revealed as innately stupid, indiscreet, and vain. The author's style is unpretentious but effective, and a pleasant undertone of humor makes the portrait a tolerant record of human foibles rather than a censure of feminine conceit. Her next book was again uneventful but psychologically convincing, and then came *Two Sides of a Question,* consisting of a pair of novellas dealing sympathetically with the distresses of lonely women. The subdued tone of these books won critical approval but no public acclaim, and May Sinclair seemed to be established as a minor modern Jane Austen, observing the restricted world of bourgeoise women.

She broke out of the stereotype with *The Divine Fire,* which not only centered upon a male character but undertook the more demanding task of depicting a genius. . . . [In some respects her hero] resembles the protagonists in novels of Gissing, but unlike them he learns to control his weaknesses and eventually wins success.

The power of this novel resides in the honest acceptance of Keith Rickman's drinking and womanizing without impugning his essential integrity, which is set off against the pettiness of a sophisticated critic. The literary establishment of avaricious publishers and subservient journals is sharply satirized. The intensity of feeling throughout the story, which derives from the likeness of Rickman's career to May Sinclair's own long struggle toward literary discipline, is responsible for the book's main flaw, a tendency to didacticism and inflated rhetoric. (p. 259)

When her next novel, *The Helpmate,* was serialized in the *Atlantic Monthly,* its frank picture of marital discord evoked such outraged protests that the editor issued a *caveat.* The subversive voice of Bernard Shaw can be detected when the self-righteous wife is informed plainly that whereas her husband has broken only one of the marriage vows, she has violated all the others. In her next novel, however, the author readjusted the balance: in *The Judgment of Eve* it is the peevish husband who earns contempt for regarding his wife as a mere chattel. . . .

Her next significant novel, *Combined Maze,* faces the problems of love and marriage for young people in a formal society controlled by parental conventions of caste and financial advantage. Miss Sinclair was by now firmly committed to the great "revolt from the family" in which most of her contemporaries were following in the footsteps of Samuel Butler by assailing the most sacrosanct article of the Victorian creed, the authority of parents. This was obvious in the first of the major novels of her literary maturity, *The Three Sisters.* (p. 260)

During the war years she published two novels. *Tasker Jevons* (American title, *The Belfry*) concludes with somewhat melodramatic scenes based on three weeks that she spent at the front with an ambulance unit during the first months of the war. The model for the eponymous hero, again a cockney with literary gifts, but depicted less sympathetically than Keith Rickman, was apparently Arnold Bennett. *The Tree of Heaven* returns to the theme of family tyranny, though in a less somber tone than in *The Three Sisters.* (p. 262)

With her interest in psycho-analysis, Miss Sinclair was fully aware of how Dorothy Richardson and James Joyce were exploring methods for translating it into fiction; it was she who knew William James's psychological writings well enough to borrow from him the phrase "stream of consciousness" to describe the new technique. Four years after *A Portrait of the Artist* and *Pointed Roofs,* and in the same year as Virginia Woolf's second novel, she brought out her own version of a psycho-analytical story, *Mary Olivier.*

This novel, which traces its heroine's life from childhood to maturity, is largely autobiographical. Mary Olivier's father secretly dislikes his children as rivals for his wife's attention. Mrs. Olivier, like Virginia Woolf's Mrs. Ramsay, dominates the family by her maternal kindness and placid femininity; but the unhealthy results are far from the idyllic serenity of *To the Lighthouse.* The eldest son acquires a mother-fixation that inhibits any normal sexual life; and the only daughter, who gradually comes to realize that her mother unconsciously hates her, nevertheless cannot bring herself to escape the maternal net and seek a husband.

Growing up under the shadow of a family taint of perversion and insanity, Mary accepts the current theories of heredity, as formulated by Haeckel, Maudsley, and other biological determinists. May Sinclair was unalterably opposed to this gloomy fatalism; she believed in the supremacy of the individual will, and during these same years she published two treatises on Idealism. Hence she shows Mary Olivier, the only member of the family endowed with determination and intellect, as gradually rejecting the scientific doctrines she had studied in favor of the German idealists, and achieving self-mastery, while at the same time she never submits to her mother's suffocating possessiveness. One is reminded of Lawrence's Paul Morel and Joyce's Stephen Dedalus by her obdurate refusal when her mother beseeches her to conform to religious orthodoxy. Yet there is a strong tinge of mysticism in Mary's make-up: in childhood she experiences moments of "sudden secret happiness," and later in life these become states of ecstatic faith which are more like visionary trances than are the moods of illumination in some of Virginia Woolf's heroines.

Being more concerned with the *ego* than with the *id,* May Sinclair did not transcribe the disjointed associational flow in her heroine's mind as did Dorothy Richardson; but much of the book is an intimate record of Mary Olivier's inner thoughts. . . . (pp. 262-63)

In the twenties May Sinclair was at the height of her fame, widely acclaimed as "the leading English woman novelist" or "the greatest writer of psychological fiction" and mentioned respectfully in the same breath with the Brontës and George Eliot. During the decade she published ten novels and two novellas (one in verse), as well as three volumes of short stories. All were competent enough to maintain her reputation, but none added anything significantly new to what she had already achieved. *The Romantic* reverts to the theme of *Tasker*

Jevons in portraying a pathological coward facing the ordeal of battle action in the war. *Mr. Waddington of Wyck* and *A Cure of Souls* are Meredithian comedies of male egoism. *The Life and Death of Harriet Frean* is the most depressing of her portraits of sex-starved women, for Harriet remains under her mother's domination without Mary Olivier's inner fortitude. In *Ann Severn and the Fieldings* the parallel with *Mary Olivier* is even closer, the main difference being that the candid and generous heroine is only a foster-daughter in the family, so that the emotional needs of the three sons are all transferred to her as a substitute for their egocentric mother. One begins to be aware that the author was becoming progressively more obsessed with her own early unhappiness. Subsequent novels, however, *Arnold Waterlow, The Rector of Wyck, The Allinghams,* imply a mellower attitude of affection toward selfish characters.

When illness put an end to May Sinclair's career about 1930, she vanished from the literary scene with astonishing celerity. (p. 264)

> Lionel Stevenson, "A Group of Able Dames," in his The History of the English Novel: Yesterday and After, Vol. XI *(copyright ©, 1967 by Barnes & Noble, Inc.; by permission of Barnes & Noble Books, a Division of Littlefield, Adams & Co., Inc.), Barnes & Noble, 1967, pp. 257-97.*

SYDNEY JANET KAPLAN   (essay date 1975)

[*Kaplan closely examines the autobiographical* Mary Olivier *as a mirror of Sinclair's "feminine consciousness."*]

Mary Olivier's "feminine consciousness" resembles in some respects the characteristics Dorothy Richardson combined in her portrayal of Miriam Henderson. Mary is like Miriam in that she is ambivalent about her role as a woman, intellectual, rebellious, and mystical. But all of these qualities are related to a tremendous sense of oppression and restriction in the case of Mary Olivier. Mary certainly has the inquisitive spirit that marks Miriam Henderson, but May Sinclair shows us the development of her feminine consciousness through a different method and out of a quite different body of beliefs about the nature of human emotions.

She came to the writing of fiction from a background heavy with the burden of her extensive reading in philosophy and biology. (p. 56)

From the biological sciences she took the notion of determinism. If one starts with the concept of a seed or germ containing all the components of the full-grown plant or animal, one discovers an inherent determinism there. If one adds to it the necessity provided by environmental conditions, the human being is not left with much "freedom." And then, if one compounds these difficulties by adding to them the inescapable conflicts built into the race by those basic urges and fears so imaginatively described by Freud, the construct of "character" which emerges reflects these overpowering external controls. Thus it is not surprising to discover how much more closely and tightly controlled is Mary's consciousness compared with Miriam Henderson's.

Since May Sinclair brings that whole body of deterministic theories to bear upon Mary, her life is thus circumscribed by environment and heredity, and these enforced limitations are described as inescapable. The struggle for power may take place on the most personal levels as well as social ones, especially within the family, with all those Oedipal difficulties arising during child-raising, the struggle for dominance within one's sexual identity, the establishing of sexual roles. Thus Mary Olivier struggles desperately against her mother's domination. The woman restricts Mary's creativity and expressions of sexuality, forces her to give up her own life in order to devote it to hers. But this is what she has to do; her character is also determined. Consequently Mary does not hate her mother, although she is aware of the woman's horrifying power over her. Mary also realizes that she can do nothing about it; her fate is out of her own hands.

As a result Mary never achieves the freedom in her daily life that is so remarkable with Miriam. Miriam leaves—actually is forced to leave her family—and in so doing becomes independent and strong. Mary is forced to stay and gradually gives up the strong-willed passions of her youth as she cares for her domineering mother and retreats further into the life of the mind. Her one chance for fulfillment comes when she nears middle age and falls in love with a famous writer who returns her love and wishes to marry her. But she insists she cannot marry Richard because she will not leave her mother. Conditions force Mary's actions; Miriam always insisted upon changing conditions. Thus on some levels *Mary Olivier* is a protest novel. That is, it protests the conditions which force talented and intelligent women to live empty lives. This social sense is quite different from the intensely personal "pilgrimage" Dorothy Richardson was describing.

After all, Dorothy Richardson was in pursuit of the freedom of the consciousness rather than the limitations which are placed upon it. She was looking at the innumerable perceptions which change from moment to moment, at life seen in the concrete, in the particularities, never in terms of totalities; she believed this was the essence of the feminine consciousness. May Sinclair, on the other hand, was not existentialistic. Her writings in philosophy were about idealism. She was influenced by Freudian and Jungian studies in symbolism; consequently she was interested in the recurring nature of experience as it is revealed through symbols. Therefore, although *Mary Olivier* is also a deeply personal novel, its more detached point of view and more organically unified construction tend to symbolize both character and conditions and give them larger implications. The pressures of heredity and environment and natural drives seem to work toward the creation of a type rather than an individual. One might say that May Sinclair's characters, in general, do not have the amorphous, erratic, idiosyncratic personalities which are so evident in *Pilgrimage*.

Therefore, if one is to analyze the feminine consciousness in *Mary Olivier,* one must be aware that it is to be interpreted generally as well as specifically. Miriam Henderson is Miriam Henderson at every minute and every second that she lives for us; she is never "Woman" or even "Intellectual Woman." Mary is a *type* of woman as well as a particular woman. But what seems to make this novel stronger than so many of her others is the precision of May Sinclair's characterization of Mary. Some critics attribute this to the autobiographical nature of the work, insisting that May Sinclair was working out through Mary her own life and problems—a question not at issue here. Autobiographical or not, Mary Olivier has the power of a realized character.

In 1897 May Sinclair asserted that the three "dominating myths of modernity" were "Custom, Circumstance and Heredity," and throughout her fiction one can see these "myths" in operation. They precede her interest in consciousness itself, but they are eventually used to modify and direct her concept of consciousness when it appears. What is relevant to the purpose of this study is how these concepts from Naturalism are involved with the feminine character and the behavior of women in her novels. There sexual role seems to determine a woman's direction in life, and this is treated as a fact of nature by May Sinclair, as the following passage from an essay written in 1912 indicates: "That only one sex should pay is Nature's economy. It happened to be woman. And you are bound, on a one-sided arrangement of this sort, to get, in sexual relations, a profounder feeling, a finer moral splendour, a superior sex virtue in the sex that pays."

In the relations between men and women, May Sinclair implies, there are always dominant and subordinate roles. The woman has of course been the one to give in, to give up her own claims for autonomy in favor of her husband. By sticking closely to the biological interpretation of woman's role, May Sinclair seems to be saying here that self-sacrifice on the part of the woman is inevitable, and that this self-sacrifice gives the woman the moral edge.

In nearly every one of May Sinclair's novels there is a character who gives up the chance for self-fulfillment in order to help someone else. Although this is a man in a few cases, it is usually a woman who "pays," as it is the determinism of sex which complicates the issue of power. Thus one finds women in her novels who "pay" by subordinating themselves to domineering and insensitive husbands, women who "pay" by giving in to their sexual drives outside marriage and are punished by society, and women who go further and even remove themselves from sexual relations altogether, in order to realize a more "noble" ideal, giving up a lover to someone else, a sister or friend. But nobody sacrifices so much of herself as Mary Olivier, for she has more energy and talent and sensitivity than any of the other characters. In fact, her intelligence exemplifies what May Sinclair described as nature's tendency "to produce better and better, and larger and more complex brains, in response to larger and more complex needs, and on the upward lines of her own evolution." Mary is one of a new breed of "doubly vital women," with superior mental and physical capabilities, so that in terms of natural selection, her refusal to marry is unfortunate indeed. (pp. 57-60)

Mary Olivier's "feminine consciousness" grows partly out of how she is treated because of her sex and how her sexual feelings influence her thinking. The only girl in a family with three sons, her first conflicts grow out of her jealousy over her mother's preference for the boys, especially the eldest, Mark. She longs for her mother's love and is tormented by its absence all her life. As a child she builds a tower out of bricks, but her mother is too busy looking at her brother's snowman to pay attention:

> Something swelled up, hot and tight, in Mary's body and in her face. She had a big bursting face and a big bursting body. She struck the tower, and it fell down. Her violence made her feel light and small again and happy.
>
> "Where's the tower, Mary?" said Mamma.
>
> "There isn't any tar. I've knocked it down. It was a nashty tar." . . .
>
> (pp. 60-1)

Mary's anger at her mother, and the association of that anger with the destruction of a masculine symbol (May Sinclair uses obviously "Freudian" symbols frequently), are what make the passage significant. But one must also keep in mind that the incident figures in Mary's memory years after the event. She has singled out this scene and recorded it, an indication that she probably understands how it has influenced her. The scene reveals how Mary learns to minimize, and in fact to turn against, her own accomplishments. She is at the stage where she must give up her active strivings (Freud would say that she must give up her masculine strivings for her mother—and in this case the tower is perfectly fitting as a symbol), but the giving up is accompanied by hostile feelings toward the mother. Mary has to accept that she is a girl and, since she is a girl, that she comes last in her mother's affections. She also learns that she will receive attention only negatively, through contrary actions rather than through her creativity.

Not only is Mary jealous here of her mother's interest in the boys, especially Mark, but that very jealousy is turned inside out and allows her to feel passionate feelings for the very person who has caused her the most grief. She falls in love with her brother Mark and thus identifies herself with her mother, who loves him more than anyone. Here Mary deviates from the classic Freudian pattern, where the love for the mother is turned to the father. Since Mary's father is so ineffective (he later becomes an alcoholic), neither the mother nor Mary can focus their sexual desires upon him, and so the brothers take his place. In fact, the poor man frequently reveals his jealousy of his sons and remarks upon his wife's preference for them over himself and Mary.

Once when Mary was a very small child she said, "I shall paint pictures and play the piano and ride in a circus. I shall go out to the countries where the sand is and tame zebras; and I shall marry Mark and have thirteen children with blue eyes . . .". Mary not only wants to assume her mother's role and "marry" her brother (since her mother did, at least unconsciously, carry out this kind of Oedipal relationship with her son), but since she wants her mother's love so badly she also wants to *be* her brother. Naturally, this is what produces the tremendous conflict she feels within her feminine role. During much of her girlhood and adolescence she struggles against being a girl, and a continuous battle with her mother over her rebellion is the result. . . . (pp. 61-2)

Mary's lack of sexual realization, while primarily related to this confusion in role—love-hate for her mother, desire for her brother—is also connected with the fear of sex itself, transmitted to her through her mother's Victorian views, and more deeply through her belief that she has inherited her Aunt Charlotte's weakness. Any attempt at asserting her feminine desires is thwarted when her mother insists on comparing them with Aunt Charlotte's warped version of those desires. Thus the image of the dead baby in the closet is also connected with a dream that Mary had during the same night her aunt went permanently insane. Aunt Charlotte symbolizes sexual repression, but she is also a symbol of fear for Mary; Mary is afraid that she will end up like her aunt, that within herself is this same frightening drive for sex, this uncontrolled passion which becomes a sickness. Mary's fears here relate clearly to the theme of determinism and provide the most obvious example of that theme in *Mary Olivier*. (pp. 63-4)

Mary's interpretation of her own inner development includes not only memories of experiences, but memories of experiences on a deeper level of consciousness, a level which is only discernible through dreams and fantasies. Here May Sinclair's familiarity with Freudian case histories and dream analyses makes its presence felt. She gives us a layer of consciousness that is available only through symbols and cannot be expressed directly as thoughts. In her earlier novels May Sinclair used dreams as the only way in which consciousness is presented directly to the reader. In *Mary Olivier* and the novels which follow, she uses dreams also to circumvent improprieties, for after all May Sinclair may be considered a very proper novelist. (p. 65)

Mary's sexual life is thwarted by all of these inhibitions: role confusion, love for her brother, obsession with her mother, and fear of an insanity related to sexuality. Later her fiance gives her up when she grows into a rather graceless, scholarly woman. She is unable to behave like the conventional "good" girl, and she cannot become a free, emancipated woman because it would hurt her mother. She remains then at home, as years go by, developing the "masculine" side of her self, her intellect. . . .

May Sinclair does not see Mary's life as a wasted one because she was able to redirect her biological drives into creative ones. (p. 66)

Concomitant with May Sinclair's portrayal of the determinism of sex is the problem of creativity. True to her biological image—the growth of the seed—is a concept of the genius who also conforms to an organic principle. In her closed world of necessity, genius is the only way one can overcome environmental determinism, although even these individual overcomings of destiny may be illusory if genius itself is predetermined. It is a gift of the environment, a sudden flowering which derives from some confluence of the genes over which the individual has no control. (pp. 66-7)

Mary Olivier sublimates rather than represses [her sexual life] but this distinction is not a simple one with her because her "feminine consciousness" is produced more by inhibitory factors than growth-encouraging ones. Her sense of self is obscure; she must search for it. She finds it difficult to separate her true being from the illusory one made up of connections with others—that self which is always in relation to something else; she sees herself as made up of many "persons that were called Mary Olivier." . . . She is her mother's daughter, her brother's sister, herself as a growing girl, and even something else. She calls that other self "her secret happiness" which "had nothing to do with any of these Mary Oliviers." . . .

Her "secret happiness" is the key to her feminine consciousness, and later it is revealed as the only possible way for Mary to achieve "being." And it is at the beginning of Mary's search for identity as well as at its end. The more she thinks about her own "self," the more she wonders why she is told to forget about it, why she must suppress it. . . . (pp. 68-9)

[Her] assertive desires always reflect that active part of her that her mother tried to suppress in order to make her "feminine." And it is this notion of femininity as passivity which seems to give her the most trouble. As Miriam Henderson also discovered, it is usually the basis for confusion and hostility. In order to do anything in the world, it is necessary to use active impulses. In order to be the conventional woman, the wife and helpmate of the nineteenth-century image of woman, it is necessary to be passive and quiescent. Mary builds a tower and knocks it over. She learns to play the piano and gives it up to please her parents. She has an affair with a man when she

nears forty and leaves him in order to stay with her mother. She acts and then she retreats. All along she was capable of dynamic activity and strong sexual feelings. She had physical strength, in fact more of it than her brothers did. She lived with more imagination and verve. She should have been the one to travel and explore, to realize all her potentialities. Sexually, she was capable of fulfillment. The following passage hints at her ability to experience that fulfillment. It is not an overtly sexual passage (May Sinclair never does that—sexuality must be revealed through symbol and inference, never direct statement); instead, we have something that stands for it: "She let go the rail and drew herself up. A delicious thrill of danger went through her and out at her fingers. She flung herself into space and Mark caught her. His body felt hard and strong as it received her. They did it again and again. That was the 'faith-jump.' You knew that you would be killed if Mark didn't catch you, but you had faith that he would catch you; and he always did." . . . Mary is able to lose herself without fear. She can take daring chances. This is the kind of faith necessary for sexual orgasm—the ability to let oneself go and trust in the other, to let oneself die. This faith resembles religious faith, putting oneself in the hands of God. And eventually Mary is forced to choose that faith over the other. After a brief but ideal sexual relationship with Richard, a period where she is perfectly happy and fulfilled, she gives him up. Her long years of self-sacrifice and suppression have given her a life primarily of the mind. So much time had been devoted to fantasies, dreams, and unfulfilled wishes that when the real experience occurred, and she had her chance, she could not totally accept it. She needed to go on, by this time, and complete the direction her consciousness was taking. It would take her to the limits of egotism and beyond. It would take her out of herself at last.

The feminine consciousness as it emerges here—as in *Pilgrimage*—is primarily involved with the search for reality, reality as it can be perceived only by a woman. The major struggle with Mary, as it is revealed through her consciousness, is the struggle to become herself. And that "self," a feminine self, as Dorothy Richardson's Miriam also discovers, is found only in giving itself up. A profoundly mystical interpretation of life lies beneath the surface of this novel. Mary achieves "reality" only when she is able to lose herself. This Christian concept of salvation is directly related to the "femininity" which makes it possible. It comes easier to one who has been forced by environment and by determined sexual role to give up and to give in at every turn. A person whose life is spent fighting for the merest shreds of self-respect and independence of mind may more easily accept a relinquishment of self because that person knows that the self made up of experiences is so illusory. Mary Olivier understands her own process of self-making and, at the end, needs to get beyond the self she has created. She fought for it, won it in a lonely battle, and the battle forced her to accept a defeat that is also a victory: "When you lay still with your eyes shut and made the darkness come on, wave after wave, blotting out your body and the world, blotting out everything but your self and your will, that was a dying to live; a real dying, a real life." . . .

But the new living must not be made up of the conflicts of the old, but in life that is without struggle, without ego. That old life and its conflicts were primarily related to sex: sexual role, sexual desire, and sexual conditioning. "Reality" must be a going beyond sex.

The feminine consciousness, then, in *Mary Olivier* becomes finally the ultimate passivity. It is the passivity Miriam Henderson achieved at moments in *Pilgrimage,* the passivity that allows one to be completely open to God and at one with all creation. Mary has glimpses of it throughout her life. It is what she calls her "secret happiness." (pp. 69-71)

Her experience comes on by itself; it is not worked at, called for, in any way. It comes as a gift, a sudden seeing of the world as it is. In order to convey its essence, it is necessary for every detail to be described with precision, to show it in its individuality, in its very uniqueness, like "the rings of wine-red roses on the grey carpet." Yet the attempt is not completely successful because May Sinclair's use of similes and metaphors forces her to make comparisons, and ideally, in a mystical vision objects are comprehended because of their essential uniqueness, not because of their similarities. "Furniture shining like dark wine" is comparative. Yet perhaps May Sinclair is also trying to give the sense of correspondence, which is also a part of mystical awareness. Incidentally, the word "wine" may be symbolic, in fact symbolic in two directions. Traditionally it relates the experience to Christianity, and personally it refers to Mary's father, who was an alcoholic. However, any symbolism here appears incomplete and perhaps irrelevant. (p. 72)

The *kind* of mystical experience that Mary undergoes . . . is characteristic of her personality. It is related to everyday things. It is a reaction against her sense of isolation and of feeling unloved by her mother, for whom she longs without limits. She has, then, a totally impersonal experience and it makes her happy. She does not try to *own* the objects she sees, nor does she blend herself in with them. But when she comes upon her mother and is forced to feel the separation between them, she experiences suddenly the fear of losing what has just happened. She becomes afraid that "she should jar her happiness and spill it." When the mystical awareness becomes self-conscious, when there arises the need to prolong it, to hold on to it, to possess it, then it must dissipate. For that kind of self-awareness is opposed to the nature of the experience. (p. 73)

Mary's "secret happiness" recurs sporadically, especially during adolescence. . . . The sensation of standing still in time, breathless, seeing into the essential nature of things, becomes bound up with the desire for completeness, for becoming one with them. The "thrill" then takes on sexual undertones. Mary begins to discover her femininity and wants it fulfilled, and she associates the perfection of that fulfillment with what she previously experienced as her "secret happiness."

By the time Mary reaches maturity, and after she has suffered disappointments which might have embittered her, she begins to place the mystical experience in its perspective as freedom in her life. . . . (pp. 73-4)

Contained within this sense of oneness and freedom is the way the self is released. It has "got out of the net." In fact, it is the only way in which the determinism of heredity and environment can be overcome. It is an idea that is not restricted in its application to women but is a possibility for everyone. What is "feminine," however, is the acceptance which always overcomes Mary, her need to sacrifice herself so continuously.

Mary Olivier ends with Mary trying to make the connection between determinism and freedom clear in this very special sense. Her final realization involves, quite simply, accepting the will of God. . . . (pp. 74-5)

Sydney Janet Kaplan, "May Sinclair," in her Feminine Consciousness in the Modern British Novel (©

1975 by The Board of Trustees of the University of Illinois; by permission of the author and the University of Illinois Press), University of Illinois Press, 1975, pp. 47-75.

DIANE F. GILLESPIE (essay date 1978)

[Gillespie explicates Sinclair's philosophical and literary theories of the stream of consciousness.]

May Sinclair's borrowed phrase, "Stream of Consciousness," reverberates widely and wildly through criticism of modern fiction. In spite of attempts to define both "consciousness" and "stream," usage in discussions of the novel remains problematic. Most users agree that the phrase refers not to a single technique but, rather, to a category of fiction identified by psychological subject matter and utilizing several techniques and devices. Users disagree, however, about the levels of non-verbal and verbal consciousness and the degrees of author intervention the term encompasses; a work labeled "stream of consciousness" in one study, therefore, may be denied the label in another. (p. 134)

May Sinclair was aware of this imprecision when, in 1918, she applied William James's metaphor to Dorothy Richardson's novels. . . . But, while Sinclair's pioneering use of the phrase has been acknowledged, her recognition of its limitations has not. Sinclair's reference to "Miriam Henderson's stream of consciousness going on and on" in Richardson's work exists in a metaphysical context: by not intervening between herself and her material, by "identifying herself with this life which is Miriam's stream of consciousness," Sinclair says, Richardson gets "closer to reality than any of our novelists who are trying so desperately to get close." Sinclair's emphasis on reality in her critical and philosophical writings as well as in her fiction illuminates not only the history of a critical term but also her own mind and art.

Sinclair's definition of reality is inseparable from her definition of consciousness. That definition bears some resemblance to that of William James. He compares consciousness to a stream when he explains the third of his "five characters in thought." First he observes that "every thought tends to be part of a personal consciousness" and that "within each personal consciousness thought is always changing." His third observation is that "within each personal consciousness, thought is sensibly continuous." Every consciousness, he says, even after a time gap, feels that it is the same consciousness. Moreover, changes within the consciousness are gradual. Therefore

> consciousness . . . does not appear to itself chopped up in bits. Such words as "chain" or "train" do not describe it fitly as it presents itself in the first instance. It is nothing jointed; it flows. A "river" or a "stream" are the metaphors by which it is most naturally described. *In talking of it hereafter, let us call it the stream of thought, of consciousness, or of subjective life.*

In context, then, the metaphor suggests to James the consciousness's sense of its own unity and continuity.

Sinclair did not use James's comparison casually. A student of philosophy, she wrote two books on the subject. *A Defense of Idealism* was published in 1917, the year prior to the essay on Richardson. More serious in tone and rigorous in method,

The New Idealism appeared in 1922. That Sinclair should have borrowed the metaphor from a philosopher with whose views she fundamentally disagreed is, however, curious. Although eclectic, her borrowings usually reflect a consistent, if evolving, metaphysical position. James could propose a comparison she considered sufficiently apt only because she detected basic contradictions in his thinking.

Sinclair's two books of philosophy are primarily responses to the threat to a particular form of metaphysical idealism posed by the "new realists," a group of thinkers which includes not only William James, but also men as diverse as Samuel Butler, Henri Bergson, Bertrand Russell, S. Alexander, and Alfred North Whitehead. Sinclair readily acknowledges that these men are justified in attacking traditional idealism if they identify it with solipsism or subjective idealism. The destruction of that position, she says, is relatively easy and not worth dwelling upon were the new realists not so ready to assume that they had destroyed all other idealist positions with the same arguments. . . . Sinclair insists that the new realists come to terms with idealists who either do not insist that the external world is entirely dependent for its existence upon the individual consciousness or who do not consider the issue to be of significance. . . . (pp. 134-35)

Sinclair thinks she can resolve many of the disagreements between the idealists and the realists. The major problem is that they talk about one kind of consciousness when they mean another. *A Defense of Idealism,* in which Sinclair points out the dilemmas of the realists with whom she disagrees, is a negative version of *The New Idealism,* in which she offers her alternative. This second book was published four years after the essay on Richardson, but, because it clearly is implicit in the first book, it is useful in understanding Sinclair's uncertainties about the stream metaphor. In *The New Idealism,* she alters some of the terminology of the philosophers with whom she deals in the earlier book. Their controversies about differences between primary and secondary qualities and about the existence of a universal consciousness become, in the later book, distinctions among primary, secondary, and ultimate consciousness. Primary consciousness is the contents of the mind apart from any awareness of or reflection upon them. . . . The realists, Sinclair insists, make the mistake of assuming that only objects in the external world can give to consciousness any objective content. She notes that, on the contrary, consciousness can be conscious of itself. Sinclair calls the mind's ability to make an object of its primary content, secondary consciousness. It includes "observation, reflection and meditation; judgment, inference, and every form of reasoning, syllogistic or empirical; believing, disbelieving and opining; imagining." . . . (p. 136)

Sinclair makes a further distinction. Secondary consciousness is dependent upon primary consciousness, but both are dependent upon what she calls ultimate consciousness, or God. . . . This very general concept of God is an outgrowth of Sinclair's flexible and inclusive idea of the unchanging self, not of the traditional Christian God whom she rejects. The concept is closer to the God of Pantheism to whom she is attracted but about whom she remains ethically in doubt. . . . Sinclair counters the realists' certain objection to her "dragging in of God" . . . by insisting that, while realism is justified when it denies "the human subjectivity of experience," it is not justified when it denies "the spiritual nature of reality." . . . To do so is to ignore those intense moments during which practically everyone perceives not only their integrity as selves, but also a larger spiritual dimension of which that integrity partakes.

Sinclair's interest in the stream metaphor as well as her doubts about its ability to communicate accurately her developing tri-level view of consciousness are evident in *A Defense of Idealism,* published shortly before the essay on Richardson. That book contains several specific comments on the comparison. To Sinclair as to James, "stream" suggests not only flux but also unity. . . . She recognizes, however, that the metaphor may be more misleading than illuminating, that it does not suggest unity sufficiently well. It is likely to suggest, not what she later calls secondary and ultimate consciousness, but merely primary consciousness. Her reference at one point to "a stream of sensations" . . . suggests that, at times, she too associates the metaphor with the contents of the mind apart from reflection. She observes, therefore, that "the unity of consciousness," which she refers to as a fact, "can certainly not be accounted for or explained on the simple theory of consciousness as a stream or streams, or as any sequence or even conglomeration of merely 'associated states.'" . . . Numerous philosophers admit as much. One, who cannot find the necessary unity in the idea of a stream, suggests "'psychical dispositions' as a substitute for a soul" or an unchanging self. Sinclair objects that either these dispositions are part of the stream of consciousness and, thus, do not solve the problem of unity, or they are "'extra mental realities.'" . . . Many thinkers, she concludes, "look upon consciousness both as a stream and as something essentially disjointed." In this statement, Sinclair opposes the continuity that is one connotation of the word "stream" to the ceaseless change that is another. When the latter is perceived, she says, philosophers "all cry aloud" for unity. An additional problem is that "a stream of consciousness, even with central whirlpools in it of psychical dispositions, cannot have periods or even moments of unconsciousness without ceasing to exist." . . . Unity must be attributed to something else, to some concept of a unified self.

As a description of consciousness, therefore, "stream" creates as many problems as it solves. (pp. 136-37)

In her philosophical writings, Sinclair examines the accuracy of the stream metaphor as a description of consciousness and, ultimately, of reality. When she applies it to literature, she associates it with a particular decision about point of view. She defends Richardson as an artist; nevertheless, technical matters are of interest to her primarily when they result in a more accurate presentation of reality as she defines it in her philosophical writings. After the essay on Richardson, however, she no longer uses the stream metaphor in her essays to describe recent developments in the novel; it does not communicate adequately her view of consciousness, and perhaps, too, it does not readily suggest its opposite. She distinguishes, instead, between the "analytic" psychological novelist and the "synthetic" psychological novelist. The former analyzes the thoughts and emotions of his characters; the latter, refusing like Richardson and Joyce to play "God Almighty," presents those thoughts and emotions directly.

That Sinclair should have perceived relationships between her philosophical studies and art is not surprising. The author of over thirty short stories and twenty-four novels as well as numerous poems, Sinclair saw art and metaphysics as inseparable. Because many of her characters are philosophers or artists or, frequently, both, her metaphysical and aesthetic ideas emerge in her fiction. Her one additional use of the stream metaphor appears, in fact, not in her essays, but in her characterization of an experimental novelist. He is one of several psychological novelists who appear in Sinclair's fiction. The analytic psychological novelist characters, whom she also calls "Realists," are of two types. The first, because he distrusts his intuition and imagination, does not create his characters; instead, he plagiarizes them from the external world. Refusing to recognize the unity and centrality of the individual consciousness or self, he presents these people as products of elemental forces over which they have no control. The second kind of analytic psychological novelist in Sinclair's fiction also analyzes the thoughts and emotions of his characters; he does trust his inner resources, however, and creates characters at the smallest suggestions from the external world. His trust in his own perception corresponds to a trust in a similar potential in all men, and to a tendency to present characters, whatever their failings, who have some unified sense of themselves. The first kind of analytic psychological novelist, like the realist in metaphysics, leaves out the self in his consideration of the artist's role and in the analyses of his characters. The second, as if heeding the injunctions of the new idealist in metaphysics, views the individual consciousness, his own and that of his characters, as unified and central.

The second kind of analytic psychological novelist would be most likely to try, at least once in his career, the synthetic psychological novel. The stronger his belief in the unity of the individual consciousness, the less likely he is to find necessary the imposition of one consciousness, the artist's, upon another, the character's. He is more likely to attempt to present directly his character's thoughts and feelings. Christopher Vivart, Sinclair's novelist-character in *Far End* . . . moves from a novel on metaphysics to an experimental novel in which he limits himself and his reader to the consciousness of a single character. Writing about a philosopher who switches his allegiance from the idealist to the realist position, Vivart retains his neutrality on the subject. Writing his experimental novel in 1919, however, he indicates a preference for the idealists' position. Not only does he defend what he is doing as art, but he also describes his experiment much as Sinclair described Richardson's in 1918: "'It's presentation, not representation, all the time,'" Vivart says. "'There's nothing but the stream of Peter's consciousness. The book is a stream of consciousness, going on and on: it's life itself going on and on.'" Vivart, like his creator, uses the metaphor within a specific metaphysical context.

He uses it, too, as an artist theorizing about his own work. As one of Sinclair's other artist characters observes, the artist is most concerned with producing art. He has a philosophy of art and, since the function of art is "'to disentangle the reality from the appearance and show it,'" he has a metaphysics. But his ideas may be neither original nor well-articulated. To such a usage Sinclair ultimately consigns William James's stream metaphor. She herself, however extensive her philosophical pursuits, is an artist theorizing about her own work. Her use of the stream metaphor in 1918 describes and defends not only Richardson's work but also *Mary Olivier*. That novel, which appeared one year later, in 1919, is Sinclair's own attempt to present reality directly by immersing herself in the consciousness of a single character. Unlike Richardson, however, Sinclair apparently did not think that one decision about point of view is the inevitable result of her metaphysical position. Throughout her career as a novelist, she continues to use the unobtrusive omniscient authorial voice as well as the center of consciousness, in the manner of Henry James, to communicate her pervasive concern with the unified self.

At the beginning of the essay on Richardson, Sinclair says that Richardson's work, and, by extension, Sinclair's own, cannot be classified according to the neat distinctions "between idealism and realism, between subjective and objective," that dominated nineteenth-century criticism. Her reference to "Miriam Henderson's stream of consciousness," then, is an attempt primarily to suggest the metaphysical complexities inherent in such writing. Aware of the metaphor's limited ability to communicate the view of consciousness central to her developing new idealism, Sinclair still chose to use it. That she recognized the importance in Richardson's work of a central, unified inner reality is indicated by the brief discussion of Richardson's form of mysticism that concludes the essay. When she applied the stream metaphor to Richardson's work, therefore, she must have meant it to suggest not only the main character's consciousness aware of itself as unified in the manner of William James, but also the larger source of that unity which she later called ultimate consciousness. It is also possible that Sinclair considered the ambiguous metaphor appropriate even with, perhaps because of, its weaknesses. Her generalizations about Richardson's work were based only upon the three sections of *Pilgrimage* published before 1918. Sinclair refers several times to Miriam's senses and sensations. At this early stage in that character's mental development, sensation does take precedence over reflection or, to use the later terminology, primary consciousness does take precedence over secondary. Miriam does experience the ecstatic moments during which she perceives ultimate reality, but she is less likely to reflect upon them as part of a meaningful pattern than she is in later sections of the work.

The fact that Sinclair's attempt to communicate the metaphysical complexities inherent in Richardson's work was misunderstood by Richardson and rendered even more confusing by later critical usage, then, is due primarily to the multiple and contradictory associations we have with the word "stream." Sinclair herself abandoned it, except as part of her characterization of a novelist who makes a similar experiment around the time of the essay on Richardson and of *Mary Olivier*, Sinclair's own experiment along those lines. To her the metaphor suggested, at best, a view of reality which she labeled the new idealism; it suggested, as well, the choice of a point of view effective for communicating the unity and centrality of the self. At worst, however, the stream metaphor suggested a flow of sensory impressions through a consciousness that was merely a passive receiver. Like Richardson, Sinclair concluded that if "stream" does not communicate the unity of the self sufficiently well, it ought to be at least modified and, preferably, discarded. To later writers and critics who have found the metaphor convenient in precisely the ways Sinclair found it ambiguous or who have little interest in the exact nature of the psychological subject matter to which the term points, the metaphysical context in which she first used it is merely a historical curiosity. That context, however, is central to sensitive discussions of characterization and form in Sinclair's own stories and novels. Such discussions have yet to emerge with the frequency at least some of her work merits. (pp. 138-40)

Diane F. Gillespie, "May Sinclair and the Stream of Consciousness: Metaphors and Metaphysics," in English Literature in Transition *(copyright © 1978 Helga S. Gerber), Vol. 21, No. 2, 1978, pp. 134-41.*

REBECCAH KINNAMON NEFF   (essay date 1980)

[*In an essay which primarily traces Sinclair's influence on T. S. Eliot, Neff provides the following examination of* Mary Olivier,

The Dark Night, *and* Flaw in the Crystal *as psychological literature.*]

The once popular British novelist May Sinclair was a pioneer in psychological fiction. (p. 82)

Both *Mary Olivier,* clearly an offshoot of Joyce's technique in *Portrait of the Artist As a Young Man* and Dorothy Richardson's in *Pilgrimage,* and the earlier (also autobiographical) **"Flaw in the Crystal"** examine the relationship between mysticism and the unconscious. This is also the subject of *The Dark Night,* and, indeed, of much of Sinclair's short fiction, in which evil in the form of unsublimated passion is related to a psychic experience. (p. 87)

[Sinclair's *A Defense of Idealism* contains] her discussion of the repulsive qualities of Western mysticism. Among the visions and fantasies of the Christian mystics she cites the "intense and amorous impetus" of John of the Cross. In agreement with modern theories of psychoanalysis, Sinclair viewed the "old" Mystic Way—better known as negative mysticism—as potentially damaging to the psyche because under this impulse it moves backward and inward rather than forward and outward. Since the condition is characterized by withdrawal, the libido, rather than being "transformed," is "transferred from a human and bodily object to a divine and spiritual one." That is, the sexual instinct is imperfectly sublimated into the mystical longing for union. The problem with the Christian mystic, Sinclair concluded, is that he cannot transcend the flesh, whereas the Oriental mystic can. As a hope for the future of Western mysticism, she proposed a rejection of the "naif and obstinate dualism" that pervades Christian theology. . . .

Although the structure of *The Dark Night* follows closely the negative process outlined by John of the Cross's commentary on his own poem, *The Dark Night of the Soul,* Sinclair offers an alternative to total self-abnegation. Her poem begins with the narrator, Elizabeth, describing her mystical "Awakening." . . . This initial "strange joy" antedates Elizabeth's falling in love with the poet Victor Rendal, in whom she recognizes one who, like herself, "knows the hushed peace and unearthly ecstasy" and has experienced the Absolute—"has seen God as the beauty of tree and flower / In gardens stilled with light." . . . Elizabeth believes in the purity of Rendal's illuminations as much as in her own; however, the "crystal soul" is, alas, flawed by desire, as is often true of the crystalline souls in Sinclair's fiction. But Elizabeth's story differs markedly from those of her predecessors, namely Agatha Verrall of **"Flaw in the Crystal"** and Mary Olivier. Whereas both Agatha and Mary renounce marriage for the sake of protecting the purity of their psycho-spiritual powers, and in doing so inadvertently confirm the relation between sexual repression and the psychic state of heightened consciousness which is frequently described as a "mystical" experience, Elizabeth enters joyfully into the marital relation without fear of sacrificing her visions.

In the course of her relationship with Rendal, Elizabeth experiences both a "dark night of the senses," a state of detachment and emptiness in which the senses are made subject to spirit, and a "dark night of the spirit," which is marked by the customary feelings of alienation and despair. Feeling doubly betrayed after the discovery of her husband's infidelity, because Rendal's mistress is her own young niece and ward, Monica, Elizabeth faces the necessity of spiritual purification: the "three-tongued flame of jealousy, lust, and hate" must be replaced by what the Spanish mystic calls "the burning fire of

love." This is the "dark night which quenches all desire." Purged of base emotions and desires, and motivated by pure, "safe," love, Elizabeth rescues Rendal, Monica, and their child from the threat of poverty: "I have given them my house in St. John's Wood, / To live in forever." The lines startle by the aptness of the place name on both the symbolic and literal levels: Sinclair herself owned a house in St. John's Wood.

Elizabeth finds satisfaction in her generosity: "Out of my hell / I have built up heaven." Sinclair's affirmative mysticism as approached by the New Way is thus a renunciation not of the world and the flesh, but of the seeker's need for the world and his attachment to it. Although to experience "awareness," to "know" Ultimate Reality, requires a willingness to admit "the illusory nature of time and of material happenings," it does not necessitate hostility toward things of this world. . . . Severe asceticism, contemplation, and meditation find no place in New Mysticism. Sinclair thought these methods of inducing heightened consciousness psychologically harmful: "the mystic consciousness presents in a marked degree the pathological phenomena of 'dissociation'." . . . Yet a way of achieving those moments of union and illumination without risking damage to the psyche is by the process of what Sinclair calls "letting go," the obliteration of the senses in preparing the soul for union with God. . . . (pp. 89-91)

Significantly, Elizabeth, eventually reunited with her husband, finds that her mystical moments in the garden are not disturbed by the renewal of her conjugal relations. Rather than rejecting the "love of created beings," as prescribed by John of the Cross, Elizabeth welcomes it as a conjunct of her spiritual revelations. Indeed, she takes delight in both sorts of ecstasy, the erotic and the spiritual, whether experienced in "secret" (Elizabeth makes much of her silent, secret life before she met Rendal) or shared with her husband. And she considers both as an anticipation of the ultimate ecstasy of the moment of complete reunion with the Absolute. As she watches by the side of her dying grandmother, Elizabeth thinks of her own eventual death and prays that she might be given "the bright, sharp ecstasy" of that ultimate surrender of the self. In accord with New Mysticism, Elizabeth solves the problem of the conflict between body and soul by denying the conflict. She need not renounce her carnal self in order to affirm her spiritual Self, for while the Self exists on two planes—the temporal and the timeless—the physical self belongs only to the world of material reality. Thus duality is an illusion which disappears in the world beyond time. (p. 91)

The power of suggestion and the ability to exercise the will fascinated Sinclair, as did the Jungian concept of the "collective unconscious"; many of her stories demonstrate this fascination in some form. Another recurrent feature of her fiction is fear, especially fear of the unknown. In conjunction with this fear there is usually some experience or vision of evil through which the subject receives "secret" or "forbidden" knowledge. (p. 96)

In her autobiographical novel, *Mary Olivier,* Sinclair records Mary's reaction to the discovery that

> There were no independent separate entities, no sacred inviolable selves. They were one immense organism and you were part of it, you were nothing that they had not been before you. It was no good struggling. You were caught in the net, you couldn't get out. . . .

Sinclair eventually resolved her personal search for a way out of the ancestral net by an acceptance of the concept of the many in the One. The only escape from the ceaseless "round of births" of the self is for the individual to will himself out of the pattern and into infinity— to be reunited with the Higher Self. In Sinclair's fiction, then, the karma appears in modern guise as subliminal, self-limiting memories out of the collective unconscious. Sinclair expressed enthusiastic approval of Jung's psychological theories; in her early stories of the supernatural she anticipated modern theories of psychoanalysis. (p. 97)

There is something very like karma at work in **"Where Their Fire Is Not Quenched,"** the initial story in *Uncanny Stories*. Like Jones [in **"Jones's Karma"**], Harriot Leigh wills her own life—and her afterlife, a perpetual, carnal hell, which Sinclair imagined as the worst of all possible hells. Harriot's private hell is described as "a repetition of a sin" willed upon herself on her deathbed by her refusal to confess her love affair with Oscar Wade; in other words, she refuses to surrender a repressed memory. In the transfinite world Harriot's psyche wanders backward along the corridors of memory in an effort to get beyond the memory of desire to innocence, but that is impossible. . . . Harriot Leigh is doomed to a hell of her own making because she never learned how to escape from the net of sense. (p. 98)

In at least three of Sinclair's *Uncanny Stories* characters other than the protagonist are granted the power to view the ghosts that haunt those they love. It is tacitly assumed that their psychic visions result from some sort of psycho-physical sympathy. Sinclair utilizes this device in **"The Token," "The Victim,"** and in a much more complex manner in **"The Flaw in the Crystal."** (p. 100)

[In **"The Flaw in the Crystal,"**] Agatha has a mysterious and secret "Gift" which she uses to cure the nervous condition of Rodney's wife, Bella. Although he is unaware of Agatha's curative power, Rodney seeks her company on weekends at her country retreat as a relief from the strain of living with his ill wife. Soon after the story begins, the happy (but presumably chaste) weekends are interrupted by the arrival of Milly and Harding Powell, friends of Agatha. They, too, have come to the country for reasons of health: Harding suffers from some dreadful and mysterious mental disorder. . . . Through Agatha's agency Harding miraculously recovers his sanity, yet in the process Agatha's power is threatened by the interference of sexual passion in her relation with Rodney. The "crystal" vessel must remain pure and whole for the effective transmission of the healing force. When it becomes flawed through self-interest, the power becomes strangely inverted and the agent's own mental stability is endangered. (pp. 100-01)

As in the other Sinclair stories, Agatha's "crystal serenity" is threatened by the intimacy of her relation with Harding Powell; in particular, it makes her conscious of her relation with Rodney Lanyon, which is not as sexless as she had imagined. To recover her curative powers Agatha must purge her mind of this corrupting vision and of its agent, Harding Powell. She must "let go" of the sensual hold he has gained over her unconscious and reenter the center of energy in the "charmed circle" of the extra-physical realm of consciousness. At that "still point" she regains her lucidity of mind: "poised in the unspeakable stillness, beyond death, beyond the movements, the vehemences, the agitations of the world." (p. 102)

Both Sinclair and Eliot, like so many others of their time, were uncomfortable with the tradition that interprets the temporal world as a reflection of man's fallen nature; consequently, both sought a more congenial philosophy that would allow for a positive view of the human condition. Coming to terms with this essentially modern dilemma, they met on the ground of Sinclair's "New Mysticism," a way of transcendence that affirms man's spiritual nature by extending his capacity for contact with the Real in moments of heightened consciousness. Because they provide a temporary release from the self-perpetuating desires of the ego, these moments of mystic reunion prefigure the ultimate reunion of the *atman* with *Atman*. Consequently, liberation from the karma of self-willing, what Sinclair described as "the ceasing of the sorrow of divided life," comes not from attempts to escape the self, but from an acceptance of the at-one-ness of the finite self with the Infinite Self.

Although Sinclair acknowledged that of the "four great forms of Sublimation—Religion, Art, Science and Concrete Activity," religion offers the greatest possibility of spiritual progress, she contented herself with second-best, Art; she believed that while the artist risks betraying herself through her art, the risk is worth taking for the "redemptive" value her art might have for others. . . . Here I confirm what I have asserted elsewhere: that by acknowledging not only the value of the inner life as a proof of the objective reality of the subliminal self, but also the value of myth and symbol in bridging the gulf between the conscious and the unconscious, May Sinclair anticipated the psychological assumptions of modern literature and provided an exemplar for modern poets. (pp. 106-07)

> *Rebeccah Kinnamon Neff, " 'New Mysticism' in the Writings of May Sinclair and T. S. Eliot," in* Twentieth Century Literature *(copyright 1980, Hofstra University Press), Vol. 26, No. 1, Spring, 1980, pp. 82-108.**

JUDY COOKE (essay date 1980)

[*Cooke discusses two of Sinclair's most interesting novels,* Mary Olivier *and* Life and Death of Harriet Frean.]

'And the evening would go on, soundless and calm, with soft, annihilating feet, with the soft, cruel feet of oblivion.' Thus Mary Olivier, looking back on a life sacrificed to 'holy Mamma', the tyrant who has denied her emotional fulfilment and whose own life is drawing slowly to a close. Mary makes certain of painful truths: her suitor was sent packing without her knowledge and she herself recalled from school not because of her religious doubt, as she was told, but because her parents resented her success. Now middle-aged, she has one last chance of happiness. The habit of a lifetime is too strong; she renounces her lover and returns to watch obediently beside her mother's bed.

This would be a bleak, familiar story, however well told, were it not for a counter movement in the narrative by which the heroine's tragedy as a woman becomes her triumph as a writer. Very early on, Mary learns how to fight back. A child of the 1860s, she is force-fed Christianity of the kind that celebrates 'a fountain filled with blood / drawn from Emmanuel's veins'. She is revolted and afraid but fascinated, nonetheless, by the sheer power of language; moreover, she can sometimes persuade Mamma to read the bit about 'the silver cord . . . the golden bowl'. Braving ridicule, she borrows her brother's Greek textbook; she educates herself, reads Kant and Spinoza, ventures even further into Heine, Goethe and Schopenhauer. By the time she is in her forties we see her discovering Walt Whitman, writing her own poetry and publishing a translation of Euripides. It is a touching portrait; Mary has one possibility of independence, takes it and survives.

May Sinclair possessed a number of the novelist's virtues: an observant eye, an ironic awareness of what freedom costs, an ear for the inner rhythms of family debate. Like Dorothy Richardson she was an innovator, seeking a prose style which would communicate the very ebb and flow of consciousness. [Her] autobiographical study of ambivalent love [*Mary Olivier*] is both sad and compelling; first published in 1919, the wider implications make it a crucial text in literary feminism. (pp. 557-58)

With [May Sinclair's] wide-ranging abilities and interests, why has she been forgotten? Perhaps because she came to fiction late and thus published her best books in the Twenties, when the literary sky was full of rising stars. . . . Mary Olivier's character may be set alongside that of Maggie Tulliver; the short novel *Life and Death of Harriett Frean* . . . is imaginative and shrewd. As Jean Radford points out in her excellent introduction, Mary's story was one of sublimation, whereas Harriett's story is a study of repression, clinically exact. Harriett is the only child of doting parents, stifled by an upbringing in which there is no room for punishment, since 'she would always have to do what they wanted; the unhappiness of not doing it was more than she could bear'. . . .

In the course of this succinct and chilling narrative, a world decays. Harriett sees her father disgraced and her mother die of cancer. She can never accept that her own sacrifices have been meaningless, that what she practised as morality was merely cruel. The man who loved her makes a disastrous marriage. The maid who cares for her is dismissed unjustly and consequently loses her baby. Harriett takes no blame; she is like the blue ornamental egg displayed in her parents' drawing-room, hollow, sterile, of no use. Reality threatens to intrude at last in a specialist's diagnosis. 'Harriett felt nothing but a strange, solemn excitement and exultation . . . she had what her mother had.' The book is a little masterpiece, a disturbing analysis of English class and character. (p. 558)

Judy Cooke, "Pleasing Mamma," in New Statesman *(© 1980 The Statesman & Nation Publishing Co. Ltd.), Vol. 99, No. 2560, April 11, 1980, pp. 557-58.*

ADDITIONAL BIBLIOGRAPHY

Adcock, A. St. John. "May Sinclair." In his *Gods of Modern Grub Street: Impressions of Contemporary Authors*, pp. 273-80. London: Sampson Low, Marston & Co., 1923.
    A useful biocritical overview of Sinclair's life and work.

Allen, Walter. "The Twenties: British—2." In his *The Modern Novel in Britain and the United States*, pp. 14-17. New York: E. P. Dutton & Co., 1965.*
    Surveys Sinclair's career and finds *Life and Death of Harriet Frean* to be the author's masterpiece.

Atherton, Gertrude. "The Changing Genius of May Sinclair." *The Literary Digest International Book Review* I, No. 1 (December 1922): 11-12, 69.
    A review of *Anne Severn and the Fieldings* and discussion of the weaknesses of Sinclair's changing technique.

Braybrooke, Patrick. "May Sinclair." In his *Philosophies in Modern Fiction*, pp. 53-7. 1929. Reprint. Freeport, N.Y.: Books for Libraries Press, 1965.

An essay criticizing Sinclair as a pessimist, who "writes of a world of shadows, and sees it to be a world of shallow people who are merely interested in their own ambitions and comforts."

Brewster, Dorothy, and Burrell, Angus. "Post-Freudian Apron-Strings: *Mary Olivier* and *Sons and Lovers*." In their *Dead Reckonings in Fiction*, pp. 215-23. New York: Longmans, Green and Co., 1924.*
    A psychological examination of *Mary Olivier* and D. H. Lawrence's *Sons and Lovers*, and comparison of the two novels.

Broun, Heywood. "A Group of Books Worth Reading." *The Bookman*, New York LIV, No. 4 (December 1921): 393-97.*
    A short review of praise for *Mr. Waddington of Wyck*.

Chesterton, G. K. "The Weird Sisters." *The New York Times Review of Books* (22 September 1912): 515.
    Reprints a generally favorable review from the London *Nation* of *The Three Brontës*.

Chevalley, Abel. "Miss May Sinclair." In his *The Modern English Novel*, translated by Ben Ray Redman, pp. 198-207. New York: Alfred A. Knopf, 1925.
    A survey of Sinclair's works, including a lengthy discussion of *The Three Sisters*.

Gorsky, Susan. "The Gentle Doubters: Images of Women in English-women's Novels, 1850-1920." In *Images of Women in Fiction: Feminist Perspectives*, rev. ed., edited by Susan Koppelman Cornillon, pp. 28-54. Bowling Green: Bowling Green University Popular Press, 1973.*
    A short study of several of Sinclair's works from a feminist viewpoint.

Kaplan, Sydney. "'Featureless Freedom' or Ironic Submission: Dorothy Richardson and May Sinclair." *College English* 32, No. 8 (May 1971): 914-17.*
    An examination of the lives and self-fulfillment of Sinclair's Mary Olivier and Richardson's Miriam Henderson, which finds their intellectual and sexual development achieved at the expense of otherwise suppressed lifestyles.

Mansfield, Katherine. "The New Infancy" and "Ask No Questions." In her *Novels and Novelists*, edited by J. Middleton Murry, pp. 43-5, pp. 285-90. New York: Alfred A. Knopf, 1930.*
    Reprints early, unfavorable reviews of *Mary Olivier* and *The Romantic*.

Mencken, H. L. "Mainly about Novels." *The Smart Set* XXXII, No. 4 (December 1910): 163-68.*
    Reviews *The Creators*, which Mencken terms a "brilliant but unpleasant novel." The critic states that Sinclair "has a hand for effective dialogue; her grip upon her characters is firm; she knows the London she is describing."

Myers, Walter L. "General Aspects of Recent Characterization: The Incongruous." In his *The Later Realism: A Study of Characterization in the British Novel*, pp. 58-77. Chicago: The University of Chicago Press, 1927.*
    Examines Sinclair's method of grafting elements of the unconscious sex drive into her fiction, and how this method mars her works.

Steell, Willis. "May Sinclair Tells Why She Isn't a Poet." *The Literary Digest International Book Review* II, No. 7 (June 1924): 513, 559.
    A brief interview with Sinclair, in which she discusses her books, her publishers, and her domestic life.

Stragnell, Sylvia. "A Study in Sublimations." *The Psychoanalytic Review* X, No. 2 (April 1923): 205-13.
    An approving synoptic review of *Anne Severn and the Fieldings*. The critic, a psychologist, examines the book as a creative depiction of sexual sublimation and concludes that "Miss Sinclair's book is as fine a plea for self-knowledge, for faith in human potentialities, as has yet been written."

Swinnerton, Frank. "Post-Freud: May Sinclair, Dorothy Richardson, Rebecca West, E. M. Forster, D. H. Lawrence, James Joyce." In his

The Georgian Literary Scene: 1910-1935, pp. 295-327. London: Hutchinson, 1969.*

  Comments on the groundbreaking effect of Sinclair's work.

Tynan, Katharine. "Life's Many-Coloured Twist." *The Bookman*, London XLIV, No. 259 (April 1913): 30-1.

  A review of *The Combined Maze*, described by the critic as "the height of [Sinclair's] achievement."

Wellington, Amy. "An Artist of the Supernormal." *The Dial* LXIII, No. 749 (13 September 1917): 195-98.

  Analysis of two supernormal works, *The Flaw in the Crystal* and "The Intercessor," acknowledging Sinclair as an important contributor to this type of literature.

Arthur (William) Symons

1865-1945

English critic, essayist, poet, short story writer, dramatist, and editor.

While Symons initially gained notoriety as an English decadent of the 1890s, he eventually established himself as one of the most important critics of the modern era. Along with Aubrey Beardsley, he edited *The Savoy* magazine—a periodical that shocked many Victorian readers by its neglect of conventional morality in its efforts to revitalize the arts. As a member of the iconoclastic generation of fin de siècle aesthetes that included Beardsley and Oscar Wilde, Symons wholeheartedly assumed the role of the world-weary cosmopolite and sensation hunter, composing verses in which he attempted to depict the bohemian world of the modern artist. He was also a gifted linguist whose sensitive translations from Paul Verlaine and Stéphane Mallarmé provided young English poets—such as William Butler Yeats—with an introduction to the poetry of the French Symbolists. However, it was as a critic that Symons made his most important contribution to literature. Symons's critical works belie the theory that the English decadence was an inconsequential interlude between the great Victorian literary era and the modern period. Some critics now believe that Symons's 1899 study *The Symbolist Movement in Literature* laid the foundation for much of modern poetic theory. T. S. Eliot, Ezra Pound, and James Joyce were all indebted to Symons's remarkable gift for defining the elusive qualities of Symbolism, and for his timely articulation of the aims and techniques of the Symbolist writers.

Symons was born in Milford Haven, Pembrokeshire, in Wales, to parents of Cornish descent. His father was a Wesleyan minister whose vocation necessitated the frequent uprooting of the family. During the course of these wanderings, Symons acquired the extensive knowledge of French and Italian that eventually led him to undertake translations from Verlaine, Mallarmé, and Gabriele D'Annunzio. Symons's itinerant childhood was extended into a lifelong love of travel. As a young poet, Symons argued with Yeats that a rootless existence was absolutely necessary to the writing of poetry because only in isolation and through wide experience could an artist hope to achieve breadth of vision. Symons recorded his impressions of his journeys in numerous travel essays, some of which are collected under the titles *Cities* and *Seacoasts and Islands*.

By the time he had reached adolescence, Symons was aware that the rigorous type of Methodism practiced by his parents was overwhelming him with an incapacitating sense of guilt, as well as conscious and subconscious fears of retribution for sin, and persistent nightmares. Under the burden of these emotional pressures, Symons became estranged from his father, and soon thereafter abandoned religious belief altogether. Thus, when he encountered the writings of Walter Pater, he anxiously began to explore the possibility that art might serve as an alternative to religion as a means of discovering coherence and intensity in personal experience. However, in spite of Symons's eventual identification with the "art for art's sake" philosophy of Pater and the decadents, and the often self-consciously "immoral" subject matter of his poems, his early fears never wholly left him. In 1908, at the

peak of his literary career, he suffered a mental breakdown, due largely to what Arnold B. Sklare summarized as his "inability to reconcile Epicurus with Wesley." Symons's own account of his illness and the two years he spent in mental institutions is contained in his *Confessions: A Study in Pathology*. Upon his recovery, Symons retired to Wittersham, Kent, where he remained until his death in 1945. Although he continued to write, the material dating from this later period lacks the original insights and clarity of expression that distinguished his earlier work.

Symons's first book, a study of the poetry of Robert Browning, was published when he was twenty-one. As one of the founding members of The Browning Society, Symons was an enthusiastic admirer of the poet, and his book, *An Introduction to the Study of Robert Browning*, not only established aesthetic principles on which much of Symons's later criticism is based, it also proved so astute an analysis that it is today still regarded as one of the best introductions to the work of Browning. By 1890, Symons had settled in London, and his articles for *The National Review* and *Harper's Magazine* were receiving favorable attention in literary circles. In 1891, he joined the Rhymers' Club and met Yeats, Lionel Johnson, Ernest Dowson, and other young poets whose ideas about the role of poetry were similar to those that Symons had heard discussed among the Symbolists in France in 1889. These writers desired to purify the language of poetry by eliminating rhetoric, decorative flourishes, and "poetic" diction. Their aim was to create verse that could communicate the subtlest nuance of a subjective response or a personal vision. Symons's knowledge of the French Symbolists benefited his English contemporaries by providing them with an appropriate vocabulary with which to define their new aesthetic—a vocabulary that communicated their concern with dreamlike states, imagination, and a reality that exists just beyond the boundaries of the senses. Yeats, in particular, was indebted to the Symbolists and to Symons for helping him to discover the mystical direction his own verse would ultimately develop.

Symons's earliest book of poems, *Days and Nights,* was published in 1889, prior to his acquaintance with the Symbolists, and before his association with the Rhymers' Club. The optimistic tone of the poems in this volume, taken together with Symons's experimental use of the dramatic monologue, reveal that Symons was still very much under the influence of Browning at the time *Days and Nights* was written. Similarly, the subtlety and adroit technique of Symons's later poetry are also lacking in *Days and Nights.* One of the few important resemblance's between this early collection and Symons's later efforts arises from the poets's persistent use of subject matter calculated to offend Victorian prudery—a practice that Symons defended with the typically "decadent" argument that whatever is within the realm of human experience is a suitable subject for art. Symons's next volumes, *London Nights* and *Silhouettes,* contain many of his finest poems, such as "Javanese Dancers" and "La Mélinite: Moulin Rouge." But Symons's poetry is often neglected by critics today, who dismiss it as dated, or find it monotonous in its lack of emphasis. Even Symons's fellow Rhymer Lionel Johnson complained about the insubstantial, emotionally vague, impressionistic nature of Symons's verse, describing it as "a London fog, the blurred tawny lamp-light, the red omnibus, the dreary rain, the depressing mud, the glaring gin shop, the slatternly shivering women, three dextrous stanzas telling you that and nothing more." However, Johnson also recognized and praised Symons's technical mastery, and his ability to experiment with verse forms borrowed from other languages. Those modern critics who admire Symons's verse generally concur with Johnson's assessment of its merits. They appreciate Symons's poetry for its delicate perfection of form, its simplicity, and for its use of urban settings previously uncommon in English poetry. Symons's "impressionism" also left its mark on modern verse, as critics observe in T. S. Eliot's use of fragmented, impressionistic imagery in such poems as "The Love Song of J. Alfred Prufrock."

Symons's most notable fiction is contained in a collection of short stories entitled *Spiritual Adventures,* a deliberate evocation of Pater's *Spiritual Portraits.* The *Spiritual Adventures* explore the theme of disillusion, and the manner in which the artist, the lover, and the man of religious vision all attempt to escape, through their respective passions, the oppressive awareness of their ultimate mortality. Symons saw this need for some form of escape as the central dilemma of human existence and the ultimate motive behind even the noblest ideals. There are autobiographical overtones in many of the selections in *Spiritual Adventures,* the most conspicuous of which are found in the story "Seaward Lackland," about a homeless Methodist minister who loses his sanity.

Symons's dramas, such as *Cleopatra in Judaea* and *The Harvesters,* are among his least interesting works. On the whole,

Symons's impressionistic approach, which succeeded in his poetry and prose, was incompatible with the dramatic need for some measure of action and emotional conflict. Although T. Earle Welby praised *The Harvesters* as a minor masterpiece, most critics believe that Symons's dramas suffer from clichéd plots, and are too purely poetic in conception to be successful as stage productions. However, as John Munro points out, Symons's plays are fascinating for what they reveal about his state of mind in his later years. The central characters in all the dramas are, like Symons, alienated from their environment.

The Symbolist Movement in Literature and Symons's other critical works, such as *Studies in Seven Arts,* represent his foremost literary achievement. As a critic, Symons has been universally praised for his depth of scholarship, his sensitivity, his thoroughness, and his ability to perceive "the simplest and enduring aspect" of the work of art in question. Although some critics over the years have found Symons's style "irritatingly vague," others have recognized that the "delicacies and insinuations" that make up his critical prose are merely the product of his subjective approach to his material. *The Symbolist Movement in Literature* appeared in the same year as Sigmund Freud's *Interpretation of Dreams.* While at the time of its appearance Symons's book was praised for making the work of the new French writers accessible to the English public, critics today recognize the deeper significance of Symons's accomplishment. As Richard Ellmann has pointed out, both Freud's masterpiece and Symons's *Symbolist Movement* "gave a name to the preoccupation with modes of half-uttered or half-glimpsed meaning which was a principal direction in modern thought." Symons had discerned that the concept of a symbol as a vehicle by which a "hitherto unknown reality was suddenly revealed" could become the basis for the entire modern aesthetic. He was also among the first to discuss in his criticism the idea that a supreme moment of vision may have the capacity to achieve a symbolic function. As critics John Munro and Karl Beckson point out, as early as 1886 in his *Study of Robert Browning,* Symons was discussing Browning's unique ability to "flash the truth out at one blow." Later in *The Symbolist Movement in Literature,* Symons described Impressionism and Symbolism in similar language: the "Impressionist would flash upon you in a new, sudden way so exact an image of what you have just seen, just as you have seen it," while the Symbolist "would flash upon you the soul of that which can be apprehended only by the soul—the finer sense of things unseen, the deeper meaning of things evident." These statements by Symons anticipated and set the stage for James Joyce's concept of an artistic "epiphany," T. S. Eliot's "moment in time," and Virginia Woolf's "moment of being."

In view of Symons's remarkable critical achievement in *The Symbolist Movement in Literature* alone, his importance to the development of literary thought in the twentieth century is clear. As Ellmann said of him: "Symons imported into modern literature the word 'symbol' much as Wordsworth, a hundred years before had pressed upon romantic literature the word 'nature'."

(See also *Contemporary Authors,* Vol. 107 and *Dictionary of Literary Biography,* Vol. 19: *British Poets, 1880-1914.*)

PRINCIPAL WORKS

An Introduction to the Study of Browning (criticism) 1886
Days and Nights (poetry) 1889

WALTER PATER   (essay date 1887)

[*Pater was a primary influence on many of the authors who rose to prominence in the 1890s. Through private correspondence and through critical reviews, such as the one excerpted below, Pater encouraged Symons in his career as a poet and man of letters.*]

[It] is very probable that an Introduction to the study of [the works of Robert Browning], such as this of Mr. Symons ["**An Introduction to the Study of Browning**"], will add to the number of his readers. Mr. Symons's opening essay on the general characteristics of Mr. Browning is a just and acceptable appreciation of his poetry as a whole, well worth reading, even at this late day. We find in Mr. Symons the thoughtful and practised yet enthusiastic student in literature—in intellectual problems; always quiet and sane, praising Mr. Browning with tact, with a real refinement and grace; saying well many things which every competent reader of the great poet must feel to be true; devoting to the subject he loves a critical gift so considerable as to make us wish for work from his hands of larger scope than this small volume. His book is, according to his intention, before all things a useful one. Appreciating Mr. Browning fairly, as we think, in all his various efforts, his aim is to point his readers to the best, the indisputable, rather than to the dubious portions of his author's work. (pp. 41-2)

> *Walter Pater, "Browning" (originally published as his review of "An Introduction to the Study of Browning," in* The Guardian, *November 9, 1887), in his* Essays from "The Guardian", *Macmillan and Co., Limited, 1914, pp. 39-51.*

J. M. GRAY   (essay date 1889)

In the really excellent Prologue with which Mr. Symons opens his volume of poems [*Days and Nights*] he pictures Art, as some have imagined her, living withdrawn and apart from the stress and stir of actual life,

> On some far peak,
> The home of clouds, the sanctuary of stars,

regardless of man and his ways; and from this conception he turns to the truer one of Art, concerned in all things human, finding nothing that is human alien to her. . . .

It is accordingly with the "**Days and Nights**" of human life that the volume deals, with its times of joy and its times of stress and tragedy. Evidently Mr. Symons is a cultured and careful writer. His culture is hinted at by the variety of languages with which the translations in the volume deal—one of them, by the way, a rendering of the "Winnowing Song" of Du Bellay, that thing of "pure effect," as Mr. Pater has happily styled it. (p. 266)

As is almost inevitable in the work of a young poet in this over-cultured age, many of the pieces of the book are, in style and manner, distinctly derivative, showing clear traces of the influence of this or that poetic master. Poems like "**Red Bredbury's End**" and "**Margery of the Fens**" recall Mr. Tennyson in "The Grandmother"; "**A Revenge**" is strongly suggestive of Mr. Browning's "A Forgiveness"; and "**Night and Wind**" seems an exquisite echo of the strange despairing songs—the "Alas, so Long!", the "Adieu," and the "Insomnia"—of Rossetti's second volume. Mr. Symons's fine sonnet sequence, "**A Lover's Progress**," would hardly have been produced had not Shakspere's sonnets preceded it; and, perhaps we should not be altogether wrong if we were to assert that "**Fauns at Noon**" owes something of incitement, or of example, to even so very modern a poet as Michael Field. Mr. Symons has served many poetic masters, has learned from many poetic teachers—yet he cannot be said to have copied previous work in any servile or unintelligent fashion; and his poems, even when we can readily trace the source of their inspiration, and lay our hand upon the model, after which, they have been shaped, claim, by the dexterity of their handling and their independent beauty and impressiveness, an undoubted right to exist. (pp. 266-67)

> *J. M. Gray, in his review of "Days and Nights," in* The Academy, *Vol. 35, No. 885, April 20, 1889, pp. 266-67.*

RICHARD Le GALLIENNE   (essay date 1892)

[*At the time this article was written, Le Gallienne was himself regarded as one of the decadents, though he also acted as one of their critics. He was one of the contributors to Symons's notorious magazine* The Savoy.]

'Paris, May, 1892.' Thus Mr. Symons dates his dedication [in his '**Silhouettes**'] to a lady of his acquaintance. That mere superscription means much. Viewed symbolically there is in it a world of pathos. There is always pathos when any one yearns towards a particular class of life, or centre, as it seems, of 'tone,' with a feeling that there is the ideal state, to be outside of which is to be 'provincial,' *borné,* and other dreadful things. It is the dairymaid's superstition of the 'gentleman,' the parvenu's of the 'upper ten,' the outcast's of 'society.' What 'Budmouth' in Mr. Hardy's *Return of the Native* was to Eustacia Vye, Paris is to Mr. Symons and many young men of the same school. Had Mr. Symons lived earlier he would doubtless have dated his preface from Alexandria. To be 'in the movement' at all costs, in contradistinction to being 'of the centre,' is the aim of these ardent young men. Looking through Mr. Symons's 'contents' his titles prove no less characteristic: **'Pastel,' 'Morbidezza,' 'Maquillage,' 'Nocturne,' 'The Absinthe Drinker,' 'From Paul Verlaine.'** But, for all that, he is much simpler than he supposes, and there are in his book many delicate and beautiful things. His poems, indeed, look much slighter than they are. Fragile they seem, and often are, but sometimes it is with the seeming fragility of wrought iron. They are full of careful observation, and a strenuous art which has measured its form by its matter to a word. To this more self-conscious art, they sometimes add the unbidden charms of passion and song. (pp. 181-82)

These poems have both strength and charm. Many other poems prove that Mr. Symons has a genuine gift of impressionism. Mr. Whistler and M. Verlaine are evidently the dominant influences with him at present, as Browning, and perhaps Mr. Meredith, were in his first book. *Silhouettes* is a marked artistic advance on *Night and Days,* but Mr. Symons's next volume will be more crucial. It will be all the better if he will let himself go a little more, and not keep so self-conscious an eye upon his art, which by this time may safely be trusted to act instinctively. (p. 183)

> *Richard Le Gallienne, ''Arthur Symons'' (1892), in his* Retrospective Reviews: A Literary Log, 1891-1893, Vol. 1 *(reprinted by permission of The Society of Authors as the Literary Representatives of the Estate of Richard Le Gallienne), John Lane/The Bodley Head, 1896, pp. 181-83.*

W. B. YEATS (essay date 1895)

> [*The leading figure of the Irish Renaissance and a major poet in twentieth-century literature, Yeats was also an active critic of his contemporary's works. As a critic he judged the works of others according to his own poetic values of sincerity, passion, and vital imagination. In his review of* London Nights, *excerpted below, Yeats offers what has become the most widespread estimation of Symons's poetry: that within the limits placed upon it by its urban subject matter and pale moods, it is accomplished, often highly successful work. For a similarly qualified viewpoint see William Archer's essay (excerpted below), and for more favorable reappraisals see Benjamin De Casseres's and Edward Baugh's essays (excerpted below).*]

A famous Hindu philosopher once told me that one day, when he was a very young man, he walked on the bank of a great Indian river, reading a volume of erotic Sanscrit verse. He met a Hindu priest, and showed him the book, with the remark, ''A book like this must be very bad for the world.'' ''It is an excellent book, a wonderful book,'' said the priest, taking it from him, ''but your calling it bad for the world shows it is bad for you,'' and thereupon dropped the book into the great river. Before the reviewing of Mr. Symons' **'London Nights'** has come to an end, it is probable that a number of people will, if the Hindu priest spake truth, have borne witness against themselves, for the bulk of it is about musical halls, and what its author names ''Leves Amores,'' and a little is a degree franker than Mr. Swinburne's 'Poems and Ballads'; and yet, though too unequal and experimental to be called ''an excellent book, a wonderful book,'' it contains certain poems of an ''excellent'' and ''wonderful'' beauty peculiar to its author's muses. A great many of the poems are dramatic lyrics, and Mr. Symons' muses have not enough of passion, or his rhythms enough of impulse, to fuse into artistic unity the inartistic details which make so great a part of drama; he is at his best

when simply contemplative, when expounding not passion, but passion's evanescent beauty, when celebrating not the joys and sorrows of his dancers and light o' loves, but the pathos of their restless days. But in either mood he is honest and sincere, and honesty and sincerity are so excellent, that even when about immoral things, they are better for the world than hectic and insincere writing about moral things. . . .

At once the charm and defect of the book is that its best moments have no passion stronger than a ''soft joy'' and a ''pale desire''; and that their pleasure in the life of sensation is not, as in Mr. Davidson's music-hall poems, the robust pleasure of the man of the world, but the shadowy delight of the artist. When it broods, as it does far too often, upon common accidents and irrelevant details, it is sometimes crude, sometimes not a little clumsy; but it is wholly distinguished and beautiful when it tells of things an artist loves—of faint perfume, of delicate colour, of ornate and elaborate gesture. . . .

On the whole, then, Mr. Symons must be congratulated upon having written a book which, though it will arouse against him much prejudice, is the best he has done; and none who have in their memory Shelley's 'Defence of Poetry' will condemn him because he writes of immoral things, even though they may deeply regret that he has not found an ampler beauty than can be discovered under ''that subtle shade.''

> *W. B. Yeats, ''That Subtle Shade'' (reprinted by permission of the Literary Estate of W. B. Yeats), in* The Bookman, London, *Vol. VIII, No. 47, August, 1895, p. 144.*

ARTHUR SYMONS (essay date 1896)

> [*In his preface to the second edition of* Silhouettes, *excerpted below, Symons answers those critics who condemn his poetry with the charge of immorality, and he explains his preference for writing predominantly on themes of the modern city rather than on traditional themes inspired by nature.*]

An ingenious reviewer once described some verses of mine as ''unwholesome,'' because, he said, they had ''a faint smell of Patchouli about them.'' I am a little sorry he chose Patchouli, for that is not a particularly favourite scent with me. If he had only chosen Peau d'Espagne, which has a subtle meaning, or Lily of the Valley, with which I have associations! But Patchouli will serve. Let me ask, then, in republishing [in the second edition of **''Silhouettes''**], with additions, a collection of little pieces, many of which have been objected to, at one time or another, as being somewhat deliberately frivolous, why art should not, if it please, concern itself with the artificially charming, which, I suppose, is what my critic means by Patchouli? All art, surely, is a form of artifice, and thus, to the truly devout mind, condemned already, if not as actively noxious, at all events as needless. That is a point of view which I quite understand, and its conclusion I hold to be absolutely logical. I have the utmost respect for the people who refuse to read a novel, to go to the theatre, or to learn dancing. That is to have convictions and to live up to them. I understand also the point of view from which a work of art is tolerated in so far as it is actually militant on behalf of a religious or moral idea. But what I fail to understand are those delicate, invisible degrees by which a distinction is drawn between this form of art and that; the hesitations, and compromises, and timorous advances, and shocked retreats. of the Puritan conscience once emancipated and yet afraid of liberty. However you may try to convince yourself to the contrary, a work of art can be judged only from two standpoints: the standpoint from which its art is measured entirely by its morality, and the standpoint from which its morality is measured entirely by its art.

Here, for once, in connection with these **"Silhouettes,"** I have not, if my recollection serves me, been accused of actual immorality. I am but a fair way along the "primrose path," not yet within singeing distance of the "everlasting bonfire." In other words, I have not yet written **"London Nights,"** which, it appears (I can scarcely realise it, in my innocent abstraction in aesthetical matters), has no very salutary reputation among the blameless moralists of the press. I need not, therefore, on this occasion, concern myself with more than the curious fallacy by which there is supposed to be something inherently wrong in artistic work which deals frankly and lightly with the very real charm of the lighter emotions and the more fleeting sensations.

I do not wish to assert that the kind of verse which happened to reflect certain moods of mine at a certain period of my life is the best kind of verse in itself, or is likely to seem to me, in other years, when other moods may have made me their own, the best kind of verse for my own expression of myself. Nor do I affect to doubt that the creation of the supreme emotion is a higher form of art than the reflection of the most exquisite sensation, the evocation of the most magical impression. I claim only an equal liberty for the rendering of every mood of that variable and inexplicable and contradictory creature which we call ourselves, of every aspect under which we are gifted or condemned to apprehend the beauty and strangeness and curiosity of the visible world.

Patchouli! Well, why not Patchouli? Is there any "reason in nature" why we should write exclusively about the natural blush, if the delicately acquired blush of rouge has any attraction for us? Both exist; both, I think, are charming in their way; and the latter, as a subject, has, at all events, more novelty. If you prefer your "new-mown hay" in the hayfield, and I, it may be, in a scent-bottle, why may not my individual caprice be allowed to find expression as well as yours? Probably I enjoy the hayfield as much as you do; but I enjoy quite other scents and sensations as well, and I take the former for granted, and write my poem, for a change, about the latter. There is no necessary difference in artistic value between a good poem about a flower in the hedge and a good poem about the scent in a sachet. I am always charmed to read beautiful poems about nature in the country. Only, personally, I prefer town to country; and in the town we have to find for ourselves, as best we may, the *décor* which is the town equivalent of the great natural *décor* of fields and hills. Here it is that artificiality comes in; and if any one sees no beauty in the effects of artificial light, in all the variable, most human, and yet most factitious town landscape, I can only pity him, and go on my own way.

That is, if he will let me. But he tells me that one thing is right and the other is wrong; that one is good art and the other is bad; and I listen in amazement, sometimes not without impatience, wondering why an estimable personal prejudice should be thus exalted into a dogma, and uttered in the name of art. For in art there can be no prejudices, only results. If we are to save people's souls by the writing of verses, well and good. But if not, there is no choice but to admit absolute freedom of choice. And if Patchouli pleases one, why not Patchouli? (pp. 161-64)

Arthur Symons, in his preface to his Silhouettes *(reprinted by permission of the Literary Estate of Arthur Symons), second edition, L. Smithers, 1896 (and reprinted as "Preface to the Second Edition of 'Silhouettes': Being a Word on Behalf of Patchouli," in* Aesthetes and Decadents of the 1890's: An Anthology of British Poetry and Prose, *edited by Karl Beckson, Vintage Books, 1966, pp. 161-64).*

WILLIAM ARCHER (essay date 1902)

[*A dramatist and critic, Archer is best-known as one of the earliest and most important translators of Henrik Ibsen and as a drama critic of the London stage during the late nineteenth and early twentieth-centuries. Archer valued drama as an intellectual product and not as simple entertainment. For that reson he did a great deal to promote the "new drama" of the 1890s, including the work of Ibsen and Bernard Shaw. Throughout his career he protested critical overvaluation of ancient drama, claiming that modern drama was in many ways equal to or better than Elizabethan or Restoration drama. Similar in prescience to his dramatic criticism is his* Poets of the Younger Generation, *one of the first critical studies of many important modern English poets, including A. E. Housman, Arthur Symons, and William Butler Yeats. In the following excerpt from that book, Archer commends Symons for his technical accomplishments, but describes him as "a man of one mood—a sensual melancholy," feeling that Symons's poetry is chiefly interesting as a study of erotic psychology. Archer's qualified approval compares with the tone of Yeats's essay (see excerpt above) and contrasts with Benjamin De Casseres's and Edward Baugh's essays (see excerpts below).*]

Mr. Arthur Symons has ranged far and wide through many provinces of literature in search of "emotions and sensations;" but the form of his poetical utterances has been mainly shaped by two influences: the early and transitory influence of Browning, and the later and abiding influence of Verlaine. Mr. Symons himself, I imagine, must look back with wonder, and perhaps not without a smile, to the days of his *Days and Nights* . . . , when he used to Browningise at large in dramatic fragments, monologues, and character-portraits, such as *Red Bredbury's End, A Brother of the Battuti,* and *A Village Mariana.* (p. 409)

To find the real Symons, we must turn to *Silhouettes . . . , London Nights . . . ,* and *Amoris Victima. . . .* Here we encounter a distinct personality, an individual note, and a restricted, but far from insignificant, technical accomplishment. Unfortunately, the individual note is at the same time insistently monotonous. The poet, even in recording his many moods, reveals himself as a man of one mood—a sensual melancholy. His verses impress us, one and all, as the metrical diary of a sensation-hunter; and though he disclaims all concern with morality, he is a moralist in spite of himself, inasmuch as the picture he presents of a sensation-hunter's life is distinctly deterrent. I do not doubt that a good deal of Mr. Symons's work—the *Amoris Victima* sequence, for example—is dramatic. In other words, Mr. Symons does not merely record his own actual sensations and experiences, but gives them an imaginative extension; working out in detail the data they provide, the possibilities implicit in them. This, however, is not true drama. It is only self-dramatisation, Byronism. The poet never projects himself into another personality, but only enacts his own part in imaginary circumstances. Therefore the element of drama in Mr. Symons's work does not make it any the less like a diary. These three booklets might be grouped together under the title of Turgueneff's first book: *Memoirs of a Sportsman;* and one is harassed with doubts as to whether the memoirs are always quite sportsmanlike.

As documents in erotic psychology, they are undoubtedly curious and valuable; and that, to be sure, is what they set forth to be. "I do not profess," says Mr. Symons in his preface to **London Nights** (second edition), "that any poem in this book is the record of actual fact; I declare that every poem is the sincere attempt to render a particular mood which has once been mine, and to render it as if, for the moment, there were no other mood for me in the world. . . . If it be objected to me that some of them are moods I had better never have felt, I am ready to answer, 'Possibly'; but I must add, 'What of that? They have existed; and whatever has existed has achieved the right of artistic existence.'" So be it; in so far as Mr. Symons has achieved artistic beauty and potency in the expression of his moods, I admit the validity of his argument. None the less must one be permitted to observe that as all his moods (with the exception of a few brief nature-impressions) are connected with the satisfaction or non-satisfaction of one particular appetite, or play around the means of ministering to that appetite, their record becomes, in the long run, a trifle cloying. We are apt to cry, "Comfort me with apples, for I am sick of love."

In the expression of his moods, Mr. Symons often attains real beauty, seldom a very high potency. He writes very well—fluently, gracefully, without the slightest harshness or vulgarity of form; but his poems seldom take hold of us very strongly, thrill our imagination, or imprint themselves on our memory. To be fair, I ought to drop the plural pronoun, and say that I find Mr. Symons's verse, as a rule, lacking in that barb, that sting, which is the sign of true inspiration. One reads him with pleasure, admiring the even competence of his workmanship; but the element of the miraculous, of unaccountable beauty and predestinate fitness, seldom makes itself felt. Therefore, it is very difficult to select from his poems. All are characteristic; all have a certain merit; there is none which imposes itself as an indispensable trait in the portraiture of his talent. (pp. 412-13)

There is one poem, as it seems to me, in which Mr. Symons, without prejudice to his individuality, outsoars his limitations, and attains to really large and passionate utterance. It is the **Magnificat** in **London Nights.** . . . The same quality of work, if not in such high perfection, appears in several of the poems of **Amoris Victima,** on the whole, I think, Mr. Symons's strongest and most sustained effort. (p. 417)

It is possible that the psychological insight displayed in **Amoris Victima,** and indeed throughout Mr. Symons's work, has been bought at the expense of more strictly poetic qualities, and is intimately associated with the limitations of his method. He is too sedulously self-observant ever to let himself go in that fine frenzy, that paroxysm of the imagination, which is an essential condition of the creative miracle. Perhaps it is only in the very greatest spirits that keen introspection can co-exist with the highest imaginative impulse and energy. Mr. Symons is too critical of his moods, too conscious that they *are* moods, to find the most poignant expression for them. The pulse which has always a finger upon it may beat rapidly, but not strongly, contagiously. (pp. 417-18)

> William Archer, "Arthur Symons," in his Poets of
> the Younger Generation, *John Lane/The Bodley Head,*
> *1902 (and reprinted by Scholarly Press, 1969[?]),*
> *pp. 409-20.*

MAX BEERBOHM (essay date 1903)

[*Though he lived until 1956, Beerbohm is chiefly associated with the fin de siècle period in English literature, more specifically*

with its lighter phases of witty sophistication and mannered elegance. His temperament was urbane and satirical, and he excelled in both literary and artistic caricatures of his contemporaries. "Entertaining" in the most complimentary sense of the word, Beerbohm's criticism for The Saturday Review—*where he was a long-time drama critic—everywhere indicates his scrupulously developed taste and unpretentious, fair-minded response to literature.*]

Mr. Arthur Symons, whose new book [**"Plays, Acting and Music"**] is my theme, must certainly be deemed an occasional critic of drama. He has gone, in his time, to many theatres, and written about what he saw in them; but he has not lingered in them exclusively; still less has he regarded them as his goal. . . . Yet in one branch of theatrical criticism, Mr. Symons is more knowing, more meticulous, than almost any of the regular critics. Theatrical criticism concerns itself with two arts, dramaturgy and acting. The ordinary critic devotes all his intelligence to the first, partly because it is the more important, and partly because, being itself a form of literature, it can more easily be written about. Many of our dramatists can get useful hints from many of our critics. But our mimes can derive no benefit save such pride as there is for them in knowing that they are "admirable," or have "never done anything better." . . . On the other hand, I can imagine that the eminent mimes who in this book are so very sensitively and acutely appreciated might hail Mr. Symons as a wizard, in that he knows better than they how they make their every effect, and which of their effects is right, which wrong, and the why and the wherefore of all their fluid and elusive art. I can imagine that any young mime, reading attentively what Mr. Symons has to say of Coquelin and Bernhardt and Hading and many others, would derive real profit for his or her own work. I do not agree with all Mr. Symons' estimates. But the point is that they are estimates—keen and patient observations, made from a sound basis of first principles, and not merely the usual peppering of fortuitous epithets.

One reason why this book is so fresh and welcome is that we see for the first time the Pateresque manner and method of criticism applied to current dramatic art. "Pateresque" is no slight on Mr. Symons. I use it merely because "Symonsesque" would not, at present, be so quickly indicative. . . . Superficially, no doubt, Mr. Symons has indulged in some conscious imitation. His frequent "Well!" for the resumption of an argument is a conscious echo. But for Pater, again, he would not be so shy of showing us his sense of humour—would not swathe his jests in such solemn wrappers before venturing to slip them into his scheme. Nor would he so multiply his commas. But his conscious imitation does not go far. Essentially, he is himself, and that self merely happens to have been Pater's—a sensitive, fastidious, ever-ruminating self. The quietism of his style is, not less than Pater's, a genuine growth from within. The most salient point of likeness between the two men, that which is at once their cardinal strength and their cardinal weakness, is that for each of them (as, indeed, for every quietist) art matters more than life, and form in art more than meaning. Life was too harsh, chaotic an affair for the timid and exacting soul of Pater. He could not relish or digest it till art had minced it for him. He seldom mentioned it directly. . . . Not vivid, therefore, not very bracing and filling, is the impression he transmits. When Mr. Symons deals directly with life, we suffer from a similar inanition. Life has no formal curves and harmonies. It is not an art Mr. Symons thinks that it is, if you can but see it rightly, and that he is therefore in duty bound not to omit it from his syllabus. "As life too is a form of art," he says in his preface, "and the visible world the chief store-house of beauty, I try to indulge my curiosity by the study of places and of people.'' But the result of this very discreet and tentative attitude is that Mr. Symons hardly conveys through his writing that his subject is alive and kicking. When he writes, as he often has written, of the cities that he has visited, and tells us, with very delicate art, of the many impressions they made on him, I always feel that they are, somehow, cities of the dead. I do not feel that pervasive animation which is the keynote of a city's life. "Dear God! the very houses seem asleep," and Mr. Symons, a still and solitary figure, muffled, seems to be crooning over them a delicious lullaby. In this book he naïvely convicts himself of incapacity to write about actual things. . . . Even when, as in this book, Mr. Symons is dealing with life only as filtered through art, his innate quietism is sometimes a stumbling-block. Thus he argues that Sir Henry Irving was an ideal Coriolanus because "he never ranted." The truth, of course, is that Sir Henry failed as Coriolanus because he was incapable of that harsh robustness which is the very essence of the part. However, I do not deplore such errors. They are the necessary defects of a quality. If Mr. Symons were not such a quietist, he would not be, on the whole, so patient and penetrating an art-critic. He would not, moreover, be himself. A definite self—that is what one most needs in a critic. . . . Every quality has its defect, and it is only by eclectic reading that we can behold that monster, the perfect critic. (pp. 273-76)

Max Beerbohm, "An Aesthetic Book" (originally published in The Saturday Review, *London, September 19, 1903), in his* Around Theatres *(reprinted by permission of Mrs. Eva Reichmann), revised edition, Rupert Hart-Davis, 1953, pp. 273-76.*

BENJAMIN DE CASSERES (essay date 1903)

[*De Casseres was an American poet and critic whose writings militantly celebrated individualism and derided any political or philosophic system that suppressed the individual. He considered critical writing an art, and his work is characterized by a verbally lush rhetorical style. De Casseres held "logic to be one of the lowest forms of mental activity and imagination the highest"; hence, his critical judgements are usually founded on spontaneous intuition. "I think in images, flashes, epigrams. Creators should spurn Reason as an eagle would spurn a ladder." In opposition to the reserved and heavily qualified praise which most critics give Symons's poetry, De Casseres calls it "supremely great." For the more common critical view see the essays by William Butler Yeats and William Archer excerpted above; for a similar, highly laudatory estimate of Symons's poetry see Edward Baugh's essay excerpted below.*]

In Symons's poetry there is that delirious worship of beauty that has been stigmatized as decadent. It is in reality an aesthetic neo-platonism that beholds beauty as an idea independent of the object in which it is reflected. It is an eternal form hidden in the soul and streams upon the world unmuddied, ether-clear. Upon a background of nothingness it paints a gorgeous universe. It lends the odor in the flower, the hues of the sunset, and when the soul it has named as its own dreams of women, it enters the universe of Love, where it laves in ideal passions. . . .

[Symons's] is supremely great poetry—the apotheosis of soul and flesh; and only the mentally unwashed can see the base in it. Because of this absolute belief in the reality of the inner life—which is everywhere the dominant note in Symons's poetry; because of this supersensuous view of the real, the small-est personal action is laden with a significance which is not present to the ordinary observer, with his eye for "facts." . . .

The dolorous strain in Symons's poetry is not the cry of anguish that proceeds from the disillusionment of experience. It is not the cry of Job fallen from a high estate, smitten with boils and demanding the revocation of the irrevocable; rather is it the cry of the stoic soul who has realized in thought the agony of the world and has imaginatively drained the goblet of life to its lees of pain; a Leopardi who sits at home and listens to Sorrow and Care sweeping the strings of his soul. He need not walk forth, for he knows intuitively that events will tally with his thought and life but verify his divinations. (p. 355)

A hatred of his finite personality pervades all his poetry. He dissects himself with knife and scalpel. He has grown to hate his lower instincts, passions, and desires. That he is linked to the vices of race and is the victim of those rending conflicts common to the human being is for him a profound tragedy. His transgressions are magnified and judged impersonally by the higher spirit that dwells within him. From this spiritual Olympus he sees his pettier self caught in the net of evil; his body, willy-nilly, plunged into the stews by lower impulses which the ages have erected into a stratified hierarchy. This duality of being, this vision of the self by the self, is the motive for one of his most beautiful poems, **"The Dogs."** The "dogs" are the desires that assail him, the baying hounds of the instincts that are forever tugging at the leash of inhibition. These impulses are always upon him, and in spite of his present negation of them he knows intuitively that one day his soul shall be their meat. He rises in a fine mystic strain, which recalls Rossetti at his best, to a perception of the supersensuous world and cries to his guardian angels to succor him in his battle; his soul, in its transcendental flight, has passed into the upper white lights of spiritual illumination and seeks cleansing at God's very throne; looking down, he sees his desires assembling for a new assault on his soul and he asserts again in closing that they will yet rend his spirit. . . .

Of such is the poetry of dreamy introspection. The man of action oozes life; the dreamer absorbs it. Action but exhibits the profile of the soul; to see the inner self full-length and face to face one must retire to the adytum of the temple. To behold the spirit of life one must live the life of the spirit. On the gloomy background of the panorama of the world the poetic dreamer rises, gaunt in figure, channel-browed, eyes laden with veiled fires. He stands gestureless, and dominates the world through an omnipotent sixth sense. The material universe passes through his brain and is sieved in the process. The human drama is not a drama of things, but a drama of rapidly changing relations, darting, snake-like currents of being on which mosaics of flesh and blood unite and dispart. To stigmatize the poets who possess this wonderful vision as "decadent" is but the shriek of an age that is spiritually impotent, an age that must logically believe Kipling its greatest poet and Clark Russell its greatest novelist. (p. 356)

Benjamin De Casseres. "Arthur Symons: An Interpretation," in The Critic, *New York, Vol. XLIII, No. 4, October, 1903, pp. 353-56.*

PAUL ELMER MORE (essay date 1904)

[*More was an American critic who, along with Irving Babbitt, formulated the doctrines of New Humanism, or Neo-humanism, in early twentieth-century American thought. The New Humanists were strict moralists who adhered to traditional conservative val-*

ues in reaction to an age of scientific and artistic self-expression. In regard to literature, they believed that the aesthetic qualities of a work of art should be subordinate to its moral and ethical purpose. More was particularly opposed to Naturalism, which he believed accentuated the animal nature of humans, and to any literature, such as Romanticism, that broke with established classical tradition. His importance as a critic derives from the rigid coherence of his ideology, which polarized American critics into hostile opponents (Van Wyck Brooks, Edmund Wilson, H. L. Mencken) or devoted supporters (Norman Foerster, Stuart Sherman, and, to a lesser degree, T. S. Eliot). He is especially esteemed for the philosophical and literary erudition of his multi-volumed Shelburne Essays *(1904-21). More was the first critic to develop at length the idea that the real theme of Symons's poetry was escape from the knowledge of mortality through the pursuit of illusion. This idea has since been expanded upon by such modern critics as Kerry Powell (see excerpt below).]*

[The volumes of Arthur Symons's ***Collected Poems***] are made up of selections from five previously published works, viz.: [***Days and Nights; Silhouettes; London Nights; Amoris Victima;*** and ***Images of Good and Evil***] . . . , to which is added a sheaf of new poems, ***The Loom of Dreams.*** In one respect the substance of these successive books is the same; from beginning to end we are in a land of dreams—dreams always, whether fair or gloomy, or the haunting remembrance of dreams. The introductory poem of the first book is a sonnet that describes the delicious sense of drowning in the gulf of opium, and in like manner the last poem of all closes with these words in the mouth of Faustus:

> When Helen lived, men loved, and Helen was:
> I have seen Helen, Helen was a dream,
>
> (p. 129)

But if the substance of all these poems is woven on the same loom of dreams, there is still . . . a profound change in their colour and texture as we proceed. Passing over the first book, from which only a few disconnected poems have been chosen, and these evidently written before the author had arrived at maturity of self-consciousness, we come to the collection entitled ***Silhouettes,*** which will probably appeal to the largest circle of readers although they can hardly be called the strongest specimens of Mr. Symons's work. Yet even these poems can never attain to any wide popularity, nor can they ever have much weight with practical intelligences that shun the evanescent world of revery where the real and the unreal meet and blend together in indistinguishable twilight. For this atmosphere is one of indulgent brooding; their warp and woof are of the stuff of dreams woven by a mind that turns from the actual issues of life as a naked body cowers from the wind. The world is seen through a haze of abstraction, glimmeringly, as a landscape looms misty and vague through the falling, fluttering veil of the rain. Indeed it is noteworthy, how many of the poems descriptive of nature or of the London streets are drenched with rains and blown by gusty winds. . . . (pp. 129-30)

And human nature is viewed through a like mist, a mist of tears over laughter, as it may look to one who dreams deliberately while the heart is young and the haunting terror of the awakening seems still something that can be held aloof at his own sweet will. Love is the constant theme, not the great passion of strong men that smites and burns through the world, but the lighter play of emotions that dally and wanton over their own flowering beauty. And these women, to whom the poet's love goes out, girls of the dancing hall and the street, still young and very fair, are only a Western reading of that symbol of nature that dances before the watching soul of the Orient. Their faces steal into the heart with the witchery and insubstantiality of music. . . . They are not moral and they are not immoral, for they bear no relation to the claims of the soul; they are the figures of a fleeting illusion, a mere blossoming of the flesh yet undefiled. . . . So new is the illusion as yet, so fresh this vision of dreams under the spell of white loveliness, that it passes unscathed through the fires of lust. . . . (pp. 131-32)

The illusion is fair and wonderful; it revels in sweet fragrances and the unforgettable odours of shaken hair; even the artificiality of this desired beauty, its falsities of rouge and pearl-powder, seem but a touch of added spice to make its allurement more pungent. What though he who observes and translates this beauty into rhymes knows that it is only illusion? and what though he who reads and for a while surrenders himself to its sweet intoxication knows it is only illusion? Because the watcher in his real heart penetrates this illusion and knows that it must so soon slip back into the hideous reality, into the painted and haggard ugliness of the flesh that is only flesh and grows old, therefore he feels a greater tenderness for this "frail duration of a flower," and a wistfulness deeper than comes to one who has something of his own spiritual hope to throw over the vanishing loveliness. . . . And joined with this tenderness for what must pass away, there is an undercurrent of regret for his own joys that endure so little a space; there is even now, while dreams are the only reality to him, a troublous suspicion rising at intervals that the substance is slipping from his grasp, and this suspicion deepens his regret for the actual past into regret for the evanescent present shadow of things. . . . (pp. 132-33)

The poignancy of this tenderness and regret is something a little different from the sigh that runs through so much poetry for passing things; it is the result of a foreboding, half welcome, half dreaded, that the illusion of this beauty is a treachery, a snare set by some unseen tempter to hold a man from his true happiness. More than once Mr. Symons compares this illusion to the smile of Leonardo's Mona Lisa, whose haunted meaning no man, unless it be perhaps Walter Pater, has ever interpreted: . . .

> Close lips that keep the secret in,
> Half spoken by the stealthy eyes,
> Is there indeed no word to win,
> No secret, from the vague replies
>
> Of lips and lids that feign to hide
> That which they feign to render up?
> Is there, in Tantalus' dim cup,
> The shadow of water, nought beside?

The shadow of water, indeed, and nothing more. There lies the pity of it all. Suppose the thirsty watcher of the play suddenly becomes aware that the pageant is insubstantial shadows, and that the cup of this world's delight which he longs to raise to his lips is empty and holds only the shadow of water—what then? And suppose that the watcher has no desire in his heart save this one desire of the world's delight—what then? That is the terrible disillusion of the flesh, a cruel mockery of the true awakening; and for the man on whom it falls—as it must some day fall on every man of insight, either the false disillusion or the true awakening—there is nothing left but the endless rage of endeavour to hold fast an illusion which no longer deceives, or the sullen apathy of despair, or the unthinking submission to his ever coarsening appetites. You will hear the first note of this coming disillusion in the inevitable cry of satiety: . . .

> All has been ours that we desired,
> And now we are a little tired
> Of the eternal carnival.

With this word of weariness we pass from the book of *Silhouettes* to the *London Nights,* published only three years later, and the change is as marked as it is significant. On the light illusion, the shimmering web of dreams that spun themselves almost of their own accord, begins to fall the lengthening shadows of the actual world. The transient note of satiety becomes more persistent, and an ever greater effort of the will is required lest the fluttering curtain of illusion be blown away and so discover the naked reality which the watcher dreads to behold. The watcher begins to grow conscious that he is himself a part of that nature, weary a little and saddened by the satiety which must continue—for how long?—its dance of forced gayety. (pp. 134-36)

What we have to observe now is [an] . . . "impotence of rage" spending itself in the effort to preserve the fading illusion, or at least to save some part of that illusion's pleasure. To accomplish this all the colours must be heightened and all the emotions sharpened, though by doing so the very daintiness and subtlety of impressions which formed the fascination of the illusion are stript away and the deprecated end is hastened. (p. 136)

Yet even here we are far from the simple passion of the flesh, the passion, for example, of Catullus for his Lesbia, in which there is no talk of souls that turn into bodies but only the natural cry of a man of strong animal appetites and strong unperverted intellect. The morbidness and decadence of Mr. Symons's verse are shown, indeed, in this very hankering after food which to suit a jaded appetite must be unwholesomely spiced with appeals to what is called the soul. He shrinks instinctively from the outright passion of a Catullus, and chooses instead— what?. . . "a delicate Lust." . . . In this same way he cannot pause to find comfort in the homely associations of a love that is less a passion than a quiet haven from the vexations of life. You will find in these volumes nothing corresponding, for example, to the gentle verses of Tibullus counting up the treasures of his love and pastoral content while the morning rain washes on the roof. On the contrary you will find an artificial passion which requires every conceivable stimulus to preserve it from passing into sheer disgust. . . . The morbid unrest that troubles this pallid hothouse flower is the attraction most of all sought by the watcher—anything to break the monotony of the awakening which to him is death. Even the sense of shame is welcomed if only it will lend a little poignancy to this desire that grows chill, if only it will for a moment continue the illusion that something in the watcher stands apart from the play and is above it. . . . (pp. 137-38)

And shame at least is ready at hand. Out of this ecstasy of unrest, this morbid curiosity, this terror of satiety, there does spring at last a love that is genuine in its way, a pale amorphous passion, for one whom he calls Bianca. It is a love the telling of which haunts the imagination (so, indeed, it was meant to do) as something not of this world or the other, a thing unclean not with the taint of the untroubled body, but of the body that tortures itself maddeningly to escape from its own insufficiency and masquerade as the soul. . . . And the conclusion of the tale is this—"So Bianca satisfies my soul!" It is better to draw the veil of silence over this scene of painfully-won illusion.

There are things it were good for a man, even for a decadent poet, not to have written, and these poems to Bianca, with their tortuous effort to find the soul in the ambiguities and unclean curiosities of a swaying will are of them. They are a waste of shame.

The outcome of such an "ecstasy of unrest" is not difficult to foresee, and is the theme of the two following books of the collection, *Amoris Victima* and *Images of Good and Evil*. When the illusion is dispelled, when the ambiguity is found to be merely a deception of the flesh and the curiosity has spent itself in a vain endeavour to discern what does not exist, what can remain but the desolation of emptiness?. . . And so the first poems in this book which he calls *Amoris Victima* are filled with regrets that at least come nearer than any others in the collection to showing the agony of a genuine passion broken and defeated by some infirmity of the lover's will. . . . (pp. 139-41)

But this sigh of passionate regret for what seems the loss of a real happiness is but a transient note of honest self-deception. What follows is the bitter cry of the long struggle, resumed half-heartedly, between illusion and disillusion. I do not wish to dwell at length on this struggle, for it is not entirely pleasant reading, however great its psychological interest may be. Through it all runs the memory of the past, but a memory of shame and not of simple regret. . . . The thoughts that follow such memories are to the poet like hideous Harpyes, beaked and taloned, that gather about him in the darkness of his soul. And the desires that torture him are the cruel voice of the flesh from which an illusion has been torn away, save the persistent denial of relief that makes of their disillusion a mere mockery of the true awakening. . . . (pp. 141-42)

In the ocean of these degrading memories, haunting thoughts, and impuissant desires, the poor soul (let us call it soul) of the poet is tossed alternately from the exaltation of terror to the depths of indifferent despair. He learns at last that "to have fallen through dreams is to have touched hell!" As with King Richard dreaming on Bosworth Field, shadowy images rising from what has been and clamorous of what is to be, torment him with a power greater than any reality of life. The body and substance of this terror is a vision of emptiness, of the dark void, that must swallow up the watcher when the growing disillusion is made complete. . . .

> And something, in the old and little voice,
> Calls from so farther off than far away,
> I tremble, hearing it, lest it draw me forth,
> This flickering self, desiring to be gone,
> Into the boundless and abrupt abyss . . .

It is not strange that this outcast self should make the whole world of God to be a shadow of its own mood, and that this mood should assume the likeness of insomnia:

> Who said the world is but a mood
> In the eternal thought of God?
> I know it, real though it seem,
> The phantom of a haschisch dream
> In that insomnia which is God.

There, I think, is the last word to distinguish this false awakening from the true. From such an agony of insomnia there can be but one relief, the repose of utter oblivion and the escape from self in perfect death. Such in the end and nothing else is the pleading cry of the disillusioned watcher.

But again this paroxysm of rebellion spends itself in a little time, and in its place comes the sigh of lonely indifference and impotence. And I know not which of these alternating moods should remain as the last impression of this tragic history. "There are grey hours when I drink of indifference," he says; and "all things fade Into the grey of a twilight that covers my soul with its sky." And again: "The loneliness of the sea is in my heart, And the wind is not more lonely than this grey mind." All the wonted rapture of the world fades into the grey of this impotent listlessness. . . . (pp. 142-44)

Always while reading these poems, which are the first full and sincere expression of decadence in English, with their light and fair illlusion passing gradually into the terror of disillusion, I have heard running through my memory three lines of old John Ford which contain the very essence of the right illusion of art (for art, as we have seen, has its true and necessary illusion of joy as well as this false illusion of sadness); and involuntarily these lines would sound out as an echo or countertone to the painfulness of Mr. Symons's lament. They are like a breath of fresh air let into a murky chamber:

> Since my coming home I've found
> More sweets in one unprofitable dream
> Than in my life's whole pilgrimage.

There would be a world of significance in comparing this "coming home" with the wandering of that "flickering self" in the void places of despair.

And yet I would not leave the world despair as the last comment on these poems, which, no matter what their sadness and morbidness may be, stand quite apart from the ordinary versifying of the day. They have, whatever may be said, a great psychological interest for one who is curious to study the currents of modern thought. Mr. Symons impresses us as being absolutely sincere, as being the only genuine and adequate representative in English of that widespread condition which we call decadence. And sincerity in verse is a quality of inestimable value. But more than that: these poems are now and again so instinct with original perception of beauty and so lilted with cadences of sweetness, as to be remarkable in themselves apart from thier psychological interest. Toward the end of the second volume, and in the little book of recent poems that close the collection, there forces its way at times, through the turbulent cries of dull desires and stinging regrets, a recurrent note of the first simple delight in nature,—a note which one would gladly accept as prophetic of a new life to arise out of the tragedy of despair. The repose for which the poet sighs in ["Rest", one of the last poems in the volume,] is at least a better and more wholesome thing than the impious oblivion of his earlier craving. . . . (pp. 144-45)

> *Paul Elmer More, "Arthur Symons: The Two Illusions," in his* Shelburne Essays, first series *(copyright, 1904 by Paul Elmer More; reprinted by permission of G. P. Putnam's Sons), Putnam's, 1904, pp. 122-46.*

ARTHUR WAUGH (essay date 1919)

Mr. Symons calls his three plays [*The Death of Agrippina, Cleopatra in Judaea* and *The Harvesters*] "Tragedies"; and one who is so loyal to the best tradition would probably be content to accept the old Aristotelian definition of tragedy, which has yet to be supplanted. No critic has hitherto contrived to better that ramifying description; and even the newest tragedies are modelled on the old pattern, with the same demands for high

seriousness, completeness, scope, and beauty, working through the media of pity and of terror. Yet, if the whole definition be accepted, one of Mr. Symons's tragedies must be admitted to be misnamed, while another fails on the ground of scope, and [the other] must be described as a tragic fragment rather than a tragedy complete. Yet, even with this concession, every one of the plays will be found rich in poetry and dramatic power. **"Cleopatra in Judæa,"** to take the slightest first, is not indeed tragic in any accepted sense of the term, but it is alive with drama and with character. (pp. 110)

Less original in fancy, but truer to the formal definition of tragedy, is the tragic fragment **"The Death of Agrippina."** The theme has been freely used by English poets, but Mr. Symons gives it a characteristically individual turn. He pictures Nero as a wanton weakling, redeemed from contempt by possessing the pathetic imagination of the poet. His imagination is his torment and his curse. He is urged by Poppæa to kill his mother, and yields out of very impotence of heart. But he is no such stuff as murderers are made of, and having, like Hamlet, become harnessed to a deed too exigent for his strength, he is left, like Macbeth, haunted by the perpetual vision of his sin. Henceforth he will know no peace. Agrippina will absorb his solitude. (pp. 111-12)

But the perfection of the poet's resource is seen in the masterpiece of the book, the completely tragic and noble drama of **"The Harvesters."** Here Mr. Symons has at his disposal all the elements of tragedy: a theme of sufficient scope, high seriousness of purpose, completeness of scheme, and a technical command over his medium which fills the poem with passages of rare beauty and sheer power. It is to be doubted if he has ever before produced any work of equally sustained and vivid force. The plot itself is familiar enough. The scene is laid in Cornwall at the beginning of the nineteenth century. Mary Raven, a farmer's daughter, has been betrayed by her lover, Peter Corin, and is "in trouble." The father suspects the truth, and tells the girl that, if she comes to shame, he will indeed continue to give her house and home, but will never speak one word to her again. (pp. 112-13)

It is a plain story, but the poet invests it with all the intensity of a life-and-death conflict of ideals. The Cornwall of a century ago is seen to be dominated by two sombre and deathly principles—a boorish brutality, and an inhuman, inflexible hatred of what is socially recognised as sin. (p. 113)

"The Harvesters" is a drama of deep beauty, unforced pathos, and strong human conflict. The touches of insight and character which dignify it are innumerable, and its broad, untrammelled outlook is wedded to a simple, direct, and sensitive gift of poetic expression. It challenges the world of affectation, and asserts, by merit of example, the impregnable virtues of craftsmanship and restraint. In a word, in conforms to the true tradition, and at the same time presents a criticism of life, which resolves itself into the perennial struggle between old and new ideals of conduct. The tragedy of parentage, as old as "Lear." returns to torture every passing generation. Its conflict is rooted in the simplest elements of human nature: it is the same, inevitable struggle of Tradition and Change once more. (p. 115)

> *Arthur Waugh, "The Tragedies of Mr. Arthur Symons," in his* Tradition and Change: Studies in Contemporary Literature, *Chapman and Hall, Ltd., 1919, pp. 108-15.*

T. EARLE WELBY (essay date 1925)

[*Welby's* Arthur Symons: A Critical Study, *from which the following excerpt was taken, is among the most valuable and comprehensive works on the author.*]

In English poetry, for the most part, love is an affair of honest sentiment. That it can turn against itself is but rarely admitted in a poetry reluctant to strike the note of *odi et amo*. Its doubts are seldom of itself, or torturing; the lover does but doubt whether his love will be returned, whether he is worthy of love. That love may be a kind of insanity or sickness, that it may be an inverted hate or a treacherous truce between opponents indispensable to each other, are ideas as unusual with us as they are usual with the poets of Latin countries. . . . Yet the maladies of love, and its cruelty, have had poets with us: Shakespeare in certain of the sonnets; Donne eminently; the Meredith of "Modern Love"; Patmore at times, for all his air of being the apologist of domesticity; Swinburne, though love comes to him chiefly as cerebral excitement, with the metres throbbing in his head; Mr. Symons. A very few other poets might be partially brought in: Browning in a way; Rossetti in a way; more pertinently, the less familiar Keats.

In a criticism of Keats in *The Romantic Movement in English Poetry*, Mr. Symons has written:

> Have you ever thought of the frightful thing it is to shift one's centre? That is what it is to love a woman. One's nature no longer radiates freely from its own centre, the centre itself is shifted, is put outside one's self. Up to then one may have been unhappy, one may have failed, many things may have seemed to have gone wrong. But at least there was this security; that one's enemies were all outside the gate. With the woman one loves one admits all one's enemies. Think: all one's happiness to depend upon the will of another, on that other's fragility, faith, mutability; on the way life comes to the heart, sould, conscience, nerves of someone else, no longer the quite sufficient difficulties of a personal heart, soul, conscience, and nerves. . . .
>
> (pp. 34-5)

Turn to Mr. Symons's verse and you will find the equivalent of this passage of prose. . . . Look at the last of the *Spiritual Adventures* and you will see, through the highly morbid temperament predicated there, how love comes as an almost intolerable thing to the one who feels himself being minutely taken possession of by a tyranny not the less tyrannical for being benevolent. Of such fears and impotent rebellions, as of the doubts, desperate casuistries, acrid revulsions of love, Mr. Symons, in much of his maturest work, is the poet.

And he is very largely the poet of love remembered. Sight and memory count for almost as much in his poetry as in the otherwise utterly different poetry of Wordsworth. It is not only that he looks back on old experience, actual or imaginary. When the present, one would suppose, would be most absorbing, he is found projecting himself years forward in order to be able to gaze back at it. The present is appreciated as it will be when it is the past. As in some verses of light love . . . he values the situation not for what it is, but for what it will be in retrospect when a perfume will call it up, so he can hardly praise a woman's beauty until he supposes himself to be recalling it years later. (pp. 36-7)

Love, with this poet, is almost always the "desire of things unborn or things long dead''. . . .

There is scarcely ever happiness in this love; at best, the luxury of remembering, which may not easily be distinguished from its torture. Self-centred, this lover feels that love is an abdication, a transfer of the key of one's inmost citadel, and into what insecure keeping!. . .

Love is the enemy, the troubler of the peace to which one may have attained as a materialist or as a dweller in one's ivory tower. (p. 38)

Love is a glory, certainly, but it is incidentally a humiliation from the masculine point of view, an upsetting of values about which one may laugh one's self into philosophy, but which, all the same, will now and then seem intolerable. (p. 39)

Amoris Victima he entitled the first volume in which passion, with all its implications, became his subject. In those poems, written in 1895-1896, and in **"Divisions on a Ground,"** 1897-1898, **"An Epilogue to Love,"** 1900-1904, and a few single pieces in the volumes entitled *The Fool of the World* and *Knave of Hearts,* we have some of the subtlest dissections of love, as it is felt by a modern, very sensitive, very self-centred nature, that have ever been written. These poems, bound together, would take their place with Benjamin Constant's "Adolphe," the treatise of Stendhal, the poems of Donne, of Patmore, and how few other books of prose and verse, among the authorities on the subject. We pride ourselves on our psychological curiosity, our appreciation of psychological literature, and we allow these extraordinary, painful, minutely truthful poems by Mr. Symons to be lost in the mass of his verse, and suppose him to be merely the poet of alcoves.

But my concern is with the poetry, as such, and I wish to draw attention, first of all, to the almost incredible lucidity of all this work. You could hardly have a more difficult subject; it is in part Donne's, Meredith's; but put these poems beside most of Donne's, or almost any of the pieces in "Modern Love," and you will be astonished by the limpidity of the writing. Here, if you like, is proof that verse is simpler than prose. It is from Browning, no doubt, that Mr. Symons had the hint to make verse vocal, but it is only the best part of the lesson that he has learned. There are no contortions, few parentheses and those the most natural, no breaks in the music, no lapses into the deplorably conversational. Only, the voice in most of these poems is a recognisably human voice, and it speaks from the heart, or from the troubled nerves, with the most natural modulations and pauses. . . . [Except] for a passage in the final section of the *Amoris Victima* volume, where rhetoric comes in with conventional substance, could verse be more consistently kept on the level of the voice with which a man tells his secrets? There is in the writing little of what would immediately and generally be recognised as beauty. Here and there, but probably not till a second reading, there may be detected and detached a phrase or epithet separately admirable, and we may suppose one reader in ten disengaging from the context, for its imaginative truth, a line or two in this poem or that. . . . (pp. 41-3)

But there is really no separable decoration in these poems. Their style, to use such a word as Mr. Symons would himself employ, is "lean"; their texture is closely woven; and even the most readily to be felt part of their beauty, the beauty of rhythm, is not so much in couplets or short passages as in the modulations of the voice, the delicate and natural distribution of emphasis, the flow and pause and return on itself of each confession as a whole.

They suffer, inevitably, from the old confusion between subject and expression, and because they deal so much with love as a malady or an insanity are presumed to be themselves dissolved in sick luxury or infirm in æsthetic purpose. But actually, there is in them a clear-sighted and resolute aim, with an exceptional economy and lucidity in the use of words, and at times a tensity which hardly anyone in our time has rivalled. Let us not deceive ourselves. A poet might undertake to put love in its place as after all not quite the whole of life, might aspire to a more philosophical or more nobly enduring attitude towards it, and yet not give us one-tenth part of the evidence we have here of the poet's mastery of himself and of his art. The tension on these delicate lines is enormous, though it is never betrayed by the snapping of one thread in all this cobweb spun with a suicidal energy.

There are other poems of modern love by Mr. Symons which claim attention. . . . In one or two of these the influence is less Donne, with whom he has a certain affinity, . . . or Browning, from whom he took no more than a hint, than Coventry Patmore. . . . They amount to little more than the loan, the adaptation, in a way the bettering, of a method of varying the length of the line in a form not unlike that of some of Patmore's Odes. Perhaps the most beautiful instance of his originality in something superficially like imitation is **"The Ecstacy,"** from the group of poems entitled **"The Loom of Dreams,"** produced between the dates of *Images of Good and Evil* and *The Fool of the World.* (pp. 43-5)

The emotion of "reverence in extreme delight" to which this poem is devoted, and which came to this poet late and with all the value of surprise, is in other poems written about 1900 and later. It is present in that poem **"Love in Action,"** which, with the exception of Donne's beautiful, extravagant, and notorious "elegy," is the most audacious poem of love in the language, and which has all the tact in which Donne was deficient. (p. 46)

The poet of a certain agitating kind of modern love has become, at moments, the poet of love in its eternal aspects and qualities, and, as in **"The Shadow,"** can say something essential about it. . . . (p. 50)

The commonest and least justified derogatory criticism of Mr. Symons as a poet is that he dates, and from the little English decadence. (p. 121)

The duration, the literary importance, and the influence of the decadence, with us, have all been frequently exaggerated.

Mr. Symons for a few years seemed to have his place in it, but he had begun writing well before it developed, he did much of his finest work after it was at an end, and always he stood in an important sense aloof. With its curiosity, its concern to capture passing impressions and moods, its desire to be modern, to accept as material the artificiality of modern life, he was in sympathy; of the cruder part of its moral error he was the severest critic. "It pleased some young men in various countries," he wrote in 1897 in the Introduction to *The Symbolist Movement in Literature,* "to call themselves Decadents, with all the thrill of unsatisfied virtue masquerading as uncomprehended vice. . . . But a movement which in this sense might be called Decadent could but have been a straying aside from the main road of literature. Nothing, not even conventional virtue, is so provincial as conventional vice; and the desire to

bewilder the middle classes is itself middle-class." (pp. 122-23)

Well, the critic . . . is broader, is more nearly the whole man, than the poet in Mr. Symons, but the two coexist, and that they do so in harmony, co-operating to make his imaginative world, is his distinction. A few minor aberrations apart, they are not out of accord; and though at one time Mr. Symons wrote some pieces of verse open perhaps to mild reproach on his own principle, he was decadent only as Baudelaire was. In the great bulk of his poetry, that is, certainly in all the finest of it, if he at all used the material offered by the decadence in its widest sense, by the sophisticated, corrupted, self-doubting life of his age, and not merely of the 'nineties, he did so otherwise than as a decadent. For he had, though not quite from the beginning, that power which, I must repeat, only Baudelaire of the other poets of the decadence has possessed; the power of organising his material, of making his world. The artificial, the ephemeral, the ambiguous, the perverse, when you consider his poetry as a whole, and still more when you consider his entire work in verse and prose, is not presented in isolation by its dupe, but is related, tacitly, to the whole of a world in which the natural, the permanent, the unequivocal, the normal have some, if not quite their due place. (pp. 123-24)

Will anyone tell me how to date a dozen of the best songs and brief lyrics made by Mr. Symons? They connect him on the one hand with the Elizabethans, and on the other with Verlaine, and are his own. They belong, beyond possibility of question, to the eternal now of our poetry. Take one of the slenderest of them, a song for the lute, written for Madame Dolmetsch. It is, with reason, in one respect archaic, but unobtrusively; and it is, in another respect, unobtrusively modern. Take a lyric like the beautiful **"Rest."** . . . With what passing mode does that conform? **"The Crying of Water,"** . . . and its companion piece, **"The Crying of the Earth,"** . . . have a music in part, perhaps, learned from Mr. Yeats, but each has qualities proper to Mr. Symons, and the former, at any rate, is a thing of rare poignancy. **"Wind in the Valley,"** if you like, has slightly Meredithian imagery. . . . But it suggests neither discipleship nor date. In such things, in **"Wind at Night,"** in **"Night,"** in **"Think of nothing but the day,"** in **"Veneta Marina,"** in **"Her eyes say Yes, her lips say No,"** in **"The Barrel-Organ,"** something that it has always been natural to do in English lyric verse is done in a way that is both old and new.

The diction, as always in the verse of Mr. Symons but especially in the songs and concentrated lyrics, is pure; the construction of the sentences of a distinguished simplicity; the writing delicately taut, the music coaxed out of words instead of extorted from them. There are no tricks, of the 'nineties or of any other period; there are no baits for the public of that day or any. Simplicity, in the fine meaning of the word, can hardly go farther than in **"Montserrat,"** which is one of its author's chief successes in this kind, and which relies so little on verbiage that it actually contains only three words of more than one syllable. Brevity, with completeness, can hardly go farther. . . . (pp. 126-28)

[These] are very minor miracles, but they are miracles, not effects the knack of which was learnable in the 'nineties. And it is with the songs and certain of the shortest lyrics, in which Mr. Symons is obviously dependent on the sheer poetry in him for every second of the minute or two they take in the reading, that the hostile critic can most easily be refuted.

It is on these things that the anthologist of the future will most probably seize. They are the most indisputable part of his poetic achievement, as the often slightly perverse hymns of that "religion of the eyes" which he practised are the most novel part of it, and as the poems of modern love are psychologically the most important. (p. 129)

T. Earle Welby, in his Arthur Symons: A Critical Study, *Adelphi Company Publishers, 1925, 147 p.*

LOUIS J. BRAGMAN   (essay date 1932)

[In the following excerpt, Bragman considers the genesis of Symons's mental breakdown and the way in which it is reflected in his works.]

Arthur Symons, poet, critic, dramatist, biographer, translator, and editor, has been called the English literary jack-of-all-trades. (p. 346)

Symbolic literature, a leading exponent of which he has been in England for many years, he once defined as a literature in which "the visible world is no longer a reality, and the unseen world no longer a dream." A childhood tainted with many glaring factors making for inadequate adjustment and the improper facing of reality: an actual psychosis at forty-one; an extreme exoticism in his relations with his fellow-men; a trend of mind and behaviour patterned after and closely linked with the decadence of Verlaine and Baudelaire and others: an alliance with the literature of escape; a prose and a poetry filled with perverse and pathological implications—these are the components in the life of Arthur Symons that make a psychological study of his personality an epitomization of the psychology of abnormal literature.

His favourite word, says [Francis] Gribble, is 'escape'; his favourite phrase, 'escape from reality.' Of John Addington Symonds, he wrote, reflecting unconsciously his own reactions: "All his work was in part an escape from himself." Of Ernest Dowson's indulgence in squalid debaucheries he wrote: "It was his own way of escape from life." Somehow and somewhere, summarizes Gribble, the escape from life must be found if sanity is to be preserved—that is his constant pose.

But Arthur Symons found his escape not only in his madnesses, but also in the world of symbolic expression. What is the secret of the meaning of symbolism for him as an avenue of escape?

Symbolism, says [Edward J. Kempf in his *Psychopathology*], represents an effort to relieve repressions, for "when perfect reality cannot be obtained, a substitute is adopted or accepted." Whereas realistic literature aims at facing life frankly; romanticism at retreating into the world of day-dreams; impressionism, by its subservience to form, at saying rather than suggesting; decadence at revolting into chaos:—symbolism attempts to spiritualize literature. Description is banished, "that beautiful things might be evoked magically. . .the regular beat of verse broke that words might fly upon subtler wings." Reverting from the burdens of reality, a return to the unconscious longings and language becomes possible.

Symons quotes Comte to the effect that "a symbol might be defined as a representation which does not aim at being a reproduction." Carlyle asserts that "it is in and through symbols that man, consciously or unconsciously, lives, works, and has his being." The chief purpose of a symbol is to conceal the real idea from the consciousness of the individual. Is not this the meaning of a psychosis? (pp. 346-47)

Is it not true, then, of the psychoses equally with symbolic literature that each deals with the cultivation of private phantasies in the face of contemporary reality? How might this apply to the life and works of Arthur Symons? How far did he meander outside the House of Dreams?. . .

In 1865 Arthur Symons was born, in Wales, "not only like a Fiend hid in a Cloud, but a Serpent of Sorts, cruel, nervous, excitable, passionate, restless, never quite normal and, from the fact that I have never known what it is to have a home, as most children know it, my life has been in many ways a wonderful, in certain ways a tragic one; an existence, indeed, so inexplicable even to myself, that I cannot fathom it."

His parents were deeply religious, and seemed to live in continual communication with another world. His father was a "dryly intellectual, despondent person, whose whole view of life was coloured by dyspepsia, which he was never without, and the sick headaches which laid him up for a whole day, every week or every fortnight." He never seemed to have the same sense of life as his wife or son. Although Symons respected his ability, his character, and his scholarship, they were never close; they seemed to have nothing in common. He was severely indulgent to his son, was never unkind or unreasonable, but could never make himself interesting—on the contrary, bored the son exceedingly. There was no ingratitude, no dislike, but rather a little more than indifference. (p. 348)

His mother, on the other hand, had some of the joy of life, yet the thought of what his parents meant by salvation had no attraction for him. This is depicted in **"A Prelude to Life,"** which by inference and comparison can be interpreted as autobiographical, "from the nature of the emotions which they dissect, and from the kind of insight shown in the dissection. Methodism, and the hell-fire which blazes around Methodism, and the madness which is akin to it, are themes to which he recurs as if they had a special fascination for him; themes, too, on which he writes like a man who has acquired his knowledge, not from without, but from within—who has not merely observed but felt." The story of Seaward Lackland [in Symons's *Spiritual Adventures*] is specifically the story of a preacher whom Methodism drove to madness. A further example is the writer in *Extracts from the Journal of Henry Luxulyan,* who has a nervous breakdown.

All the indications are, says Gribble, that Methodism made him before art and literature began to mould him, that when he speaks of an escape from life he means primarily an escape from galling Methodism, and secondarily from "the ineffaceable mark which Methodism has branded on his mind." There would seem to be no doubt that *Spiritual Adventures* is a record of his strange and overwhelming early conditioning experiences thinly disguised as fiction. (pp. 348-49)

He hated his school teachers, particularly when he heard his parents explain to them that he was backward and was to be treated carefully. Once he began to learn, he learned quickly. Yet he never made friends at school, living there, as well as at home, his own life, doing as he pleased, rebelling against belief and orthodoxy, reacting vigorously against his overzealous parents, whose stress on the need for salvation pulled him away from every trace of piety. Cut off from "whatever is stable and of long growth in the world," he very early took up the study of literature in order to set up a barrier of words between himself and people in general. . . . (p. 349)

Introspective, self-contained, from as early a time as he could recall, he had no very clear consciousness of anything external to himself:

I never realized that others had the right to expect from me any return for the kindness which they might show me or refuse to me, at their choice. . . .I was very fond of my mother, but I felt no affection towards anyone else, nor any desire for the affection of others. To be alone, and to live my own life for ever, that was what I wanted. . . .People in general left me no more than indifferent. . .they meant no more to me than the chairs on which they sat. I was unconscious of my human relationship to them.

Although he never had any definite illness, he was always in frail health. As a youth he walked in his sleep, and had many nightmares. These were dreams of abstract horror, containing the disturbing element of sex. He dreamed of "infinite spirals, up which I had to climb, or of ladders, whose rungs dropped away from me as my feet left them, or of slimy stone stairways, into cold pits of darkness, or of the tightening of a snake's coils around me, or of walking with bare feet across a floor curdling with snakes."

At nine he was totally ignorant of everything in the world. His mind was restless, and although physically ignorant, he recalled that he was permeated with a sort of 'naïve corruption.' All the interest he had never been able to find in the soul, he discovered in what he vaguely apprehended of the body. . . . (p. 350)

He says that his vague notions of sex soon became precise, and also became a torture. When he first read Rabelais and the Poems and Ballads of Swinburne he was absolutely ignorant of his body: "I looked upon the relationship of man and woman as something essentially wicked; my imagination took fire, but I was hardly conscious of any physical reality connected with it."

This then was his childhood, learning by himself various languages, reading and studying, and beginning to think of devoting himself to literary work, not to express himself, but to write for the sake of writing. At thirteen, "already the poet of bought dreams," he wrote a piece on opium. On his fifteenth birthday he produced a monologue called *Mad* [never published], which he thinks had a certain vigour. Then he began to make contacts with people, to plunge, as Baudelaire says, into "the bath of the multitude," for he was beginning to realize, for the first time, by reading literature, and learning from the lives and deeds of others, that there was another escape from these people, besides a solitary flight into books. "If a book," he said, "could be so like a man, there were men and women, after all, who had the interest of a book as well as the warm advantage of being alone." Leaving home, he lived in London for five years, afflicted with "a search without an aim," which grew to be almost a torture to him.

His world and his companions were exotic; he met most of the wonderful artists of his time, and lived in the most wicked and wanton quarters of cities with their depraved and perverted inhabitants. . . . He developed great strength of will and an obstinate nature, with an inflexible belief in himself. He never learned what a compromise meant, or making the best of things if those things were all he wanted. He acquired a flaming temperament which had to prey on something if it was not to prey mortally on himself. He pictured himself as the typical neurasthenic artist: "I have always been highly strung, over-nervous, over-excitable, over-sensitive, and the least jar on my nerves always upsets me. I hate total darkness as much as men who are on the point of being hanged hate hell."

He lived, he writes, a kind of double life, inward and outward, both jumbled together in an inextricable confusion. Finally, he says, he always liked "the mystery of madness."

Then, at forty-one, he learned what true madness is like. (pp. 350-51)

"I inherited madness," he says, "from certain ancestors." This is by way of prelude, as he relates in his *Confessions*, to the definition of the manner in which his psychosis began. He had suffered for some time from recurrent spells of amnesia. Then, in September, 1908, a thunderbolt from hell fell upon him, and for a time destroyed his reason. He compares his experiences with those of his fictional character, Christian Trevalga, a pianist who lost his mind. Giving all to music, Christian shunned human relationship, and his madness resulted. Thus: "I have only felt. . . .I have never thought, and I have felt only one thing acutely, music."

Sound began to overtake this character, like a slave who has overcome his master. "**Music in Venice**," describing the various types of music overheard in that city, is called by Symons a document in which his own madness is most evident; although it contains, in itself, nothing noteworthily pathological. It was in Bologna that his nerves approached the breaking-point. He writes:

> I was over-excited and overstrained; several misadventures had occurred in the previous years which had greatly and deeply upset me. I had become irritable and extravagant. Even then my eyes were hurting me. I was troubled by one crisis after another, over which I had no control. My nerves reacted on my imagination: reacted, almost recoiled, on my body. Too many burdens had been imposed upon me by I know not how many task-masters. I was hallucinated, obsessed.
>
> (p. 352)

It was noticed by the people who kept the hotel he was in, and by the woman he was with, that Symons was in a state of intense exasperation. After a violent scene in which he refused to go back to England, he made his way alone to Ferrara. After a sleepless night there he wandered into the countryside, seemingly to escape something. Frightened, he writes, by a terrible inner tension, he ran on blindly, falling into ditches, sleeping in haystacks. After several days he was seized by the police and thrown into a dungeon, as a madman, his identity unknown. Beaten and starved by his jailers, he was finally rescued by the Italian ambassador, and placed in a quiet sanatorium near Bologna, where he improved.

Then, he says, the Demon of Restlessness, which had always driven him, seized him more tightly and furiously than ever before. He had been very uneasy and wanted to go to Perugia to dream on its heights. But horrible imaginations racked his brain; he seemed on fire; and as he wandered along the streets he saw the most dreadful shapes and shadows. He was, at this time, excited, assaultive, and confused.

In November, 1908, he was taken to London, where he spent one and a half years in asylums. He was very apprehensive, suffered from fears and terrors, was delirious, and hallucinated, with a feeling "of fearful isolation." He said to his wife: "You and I will people the world with men children." And to a woman friend: "I am planning a map of the world; I shall divide it into small divisions; each shall have a King and a Queen; I have not yet decided as to what these shall be. . . .I am the Pope in Rome."

He speaks of his psychosis as a break between his reason and his sense of reality; he lost tangible hold of everything; he half-forgot his own existence—the memories of things past and present. But he was not altogether oblivious, for he had lucid moments, when something of his former self returned—if only in flashes. At one time he supposed he had invented colour on colour, using boxes of paints; later he developed the idea that he could compose music.

In the spring of 1909 he had a severe attack of pneumonia, which reduced him to a mere skeleton, during which time he was "an absolute lunatic." He writes of his experiences twenty years later, clearly but bitterly, as one describes a nightmare after waking. But to this time, believing he had "survived what no living man has ever survived," he still harbours resentment against what he terms unfair treatment. . . . (pp. 352-53)

The wrath that he vents is directed mainly against those who persisted in keeping him in restraint. In his detailed description of the treatment accorded him, however, nothing can be discovered that is not consistent with the general care of psychotic individuals of his day. His chief resentment seems to have been kindled, and was apparently still kept burning, by the fact that it was considered necessary to lock him up. The doctors, he says, did him a fearful wrong, "which I have never forgotten, which I shall never forgive." One unpardonable crime was related to the *snoring* proclivities of his attendants, who slept in the room next to his; another was the deprivation of all but his bed clothes; and a third was the turning out of the lights after ten o'clock. . . .

He compares his experiences with those of Charles Reade, who, in *It is Never Too Late to Mend,* describes the horrors of an asylum; with Peacock's *Nightmare Abbey,* in which he found the equivalent of his wild imaginings in the madhouse; also with the psychotic experiences of Gérard de Nerval, whose *Le Reve et la Vie,* he says, is an outstanding narrative of madness, unique as madness itself. (p. 354)

During his attack in the asylum, Symons wrote verse, prose essays, stories, satires, sonnets, and songs. He translated from Balzac, Baudelaire, Gautier, and de Nerval. He composed a one-act play in blank verse, called *The Death of Marlowe.* His odes were absurd, he says, and his passion for writing was volcanic. He made experiments in all directions: "I wrote many corrupt things which were valueless. It is inevitable for one who is in confinement, who hates it more than he hates hell, to be obsessed with ideas of sex and of the perversities of sex."

Then, gradually "those fiends who were the keepers and the mad people they watched over became somewhat more human," and he found his mental faculties slowly returning to normal. (pp. 354-55)

As he finally regained his health he wrote: "That exit of mine was so sharp an awakening from one state to another that it led me across that narrow bridge of one step which lies between the Heaven I hoped for and the Hell I had left."

It has been said of his temporary psychosis that it was a part of his life of literary suggestion and imitation. He sees in himself certain traits which he discovered in the poets and authors he admired. He tells of choosing a hotel in Bologna where Byron had lived, and how he re-lived Byron's life; and of selecting another hotel which was "such as those Baudelaire was too often obliged to frequent." Like the men he would emulate, he became mad. (p. 355)

Yet the supreme artist, he says, is the farthest of all men from this danger, because of his supreme comprehension. His imagination is really vision. It is only the vague dreamer, the insecure artist, and the uncertain mystic, who, seeing only the shadows, fail to recognize the outlines. In this regard:

> The madness of Gérard de Nerval, whatever physiological reasons may be rightly given for its outbreak, subsidence, and return, I take to have been essentially due to the weakness and not the excess of his visionary quality, to the insufficiency of his imaginative energy, and to his lack of spiritual discipline. . . .Here is one who has gazed at light till it has blinded him, and for us all that is important is that he has seen something, not that his eyesight has been too weak to endure the pressure of light overflowing from the world beyond the world. . . .Madness, then, in him, had lit up, as if by lightning-flashes, the hidden links of distant and divergent things. . . .We owe to the fortunate accident of madness one of the foundations of what might be called the practical aesthetics of Symbolism.

Of Villiers de L'Isle-Adam, the Don Quixote of idealism, he says that "life to him was the dream, and the spiritual world the reality." Arthur Rimbaud, who invented the colour of the vowels: A, black; E, white; I, red; O, blue; and U, green; and who regulated the form and movement of every consonant, he quotes as saying: "I ended by finding something sacred in the disorder of my mind." (p. 356)

Stéphane Mallarmé "was obscure, not so much because he wrote differently, as because he thought differently, from other people; his mind was elliptical." To the student of psychology, few more interesting cases could be presented than the development of Huysmans. He was "led by what are called 'mysterious ways'; the world has always appeared to him to be a profoundly uncomfortable, unpleasant, and ridiculous place. . . .He endeavoured to clothe the mystical conceptions in a concrete form. . . .His work is largely determined by the *maladie fin de siècle*—the diseased nerves that, in his case, have given a curious personal quality of pessimism to his outlook on the world."

Symons, in characterizing the Symbolists, says further:

> We find our escape from the sterile, annihilating reality in many dreams, in religion, passion, art; each a forgetfulness, each a symbol of creation; religion being the creation of a new heaven, passion the creation of a new earth, and art, in its mingling of heaven and earth, the creation of heaven out of earth. . . .The prophets who have redeemed the world, and the artists who have made the world beautiful, and the lovers who have quickened the pulses of the world, have really, whether they knew it or not, been fleeing from the certainty of one thought: that we have, all of us, only our one day; and from the dread of that other thought:

that the day, however used, must after all be wasted.

Symons, in thus elaborating on the psychology of the literature of escape, asserts that he has "endeavoured to consider writers as personalities under the action of spiritual forces, or as themselves so many forces." But does he not mean 'psychopathological' rather than 'spiritual'? When he writes of Ernest Dowson, he refers to him as "stepping out of a paradise in which pain becomes so lovely, he can see the beauty which is the other side of madness, and in a sonnet, *To One in Bedlam,* can create a more positive, a more poignant mood, with fine subtlety." William Blake, he says, had the irresponsible rapture of madness, the wild beauty of the madman's scattering brain. . . . (pp. 357-58)

Of Emily Brontë, he says: "Her poems are all outcries, as her great novel, *Wuthering Heights,* is one long outcry. A soul on the rack seems to make itself heard at moments, when suffering has grown too acute for silence."

Rousseau's unburdening of himself he calls the last, most effectual manifestation of that nervous, defiant consciousness of other people which haunted him all his life. . . .

As the protagonist of those *who write with their nerves,* the key to this inner logic is readily manifest in the life of Arthur Symons. (p. 358)

At the age of thirteen, it has been stated, Symons, "already the poet of bought dreams," composed a piece on opium. At a later date, in the company of John Addington Symonds, he tried the effect of haschisch, "that slow intoxication, that elaborate experiment in visionary sensations." That he lived in a land of self-induced dreams is apparent in his *Poems.* . . . The introductory sonnet describes "the delicious drowning in a gulf of opium." That he needed some soporific is evident, since his was a world of weariness, in which he manifested a satiety and a hankering of a jaded appetite for strange food. (pp. 358-59)

Another sonnet is called *The Opium Smoker* [and a poem is entitled *The Song of the Poppies.* Another is called *The Absinthe Drinker.*] (p. 359)

These poisonous drugs, Symons says, have shown him "shadows hot from hell." In the very essence of them he found "a disordered Demon whose insanities make one's very flesh ache." (p. 360)

That Symons followed the example of Baudelaire and others not only into the world of drugs and dreams, but also into the Garden of the Flowers of Evil, where abounds a life of sensual perversity, is revealed in many of his poems. [T. Earle] Welby says: "Symons at one time devoted many poems to recording the sensation procured by frequent change of sleeping accommodations and company, and has always been ready to write of questionable interiors, artificial paradises, bought dreams."

In a review of one of his recent works, it was stated that: "The monograph on Toulouse-Lautrec reveals a tedious and repetitious obsession with sex. One scents most disagreeably some sort of senile greensickness. Mr. Symons avows himself a devotee of perversity."

London Nights contains many pieces against which the charge of immorality was directed. Here is to be found "the cool, deliberate cult of sensations—the cult of every refinement of voluptuousness is evidently the philosophy of life. . .that lies behind Mr. Symons' poems. This cult of the sensual ends in

an atrophy of natural feelings, in which only something forbidden, strange, perverted, has savour and sting." In these poems he writes of the "chance romances of the streets," with "a morbid sensuality ever in search of some new incentive, which it finds in states of feeling outside healthy human experience."

In *Amoris Victima,* passion is the pervading subject. In *The Knave of Hearts* one finds many poems in which Lesbia plays the chief rôle. His **"Bianca"** verses are replete with hints of perverse sexuality. . . .

Symons, like Baudelaire, seeks to paint exceptional depravity, and although it may seem that he is merely posing at times, anxious to appear a much more abandoned sensualist than he is, yet there is no doubt that he endeavours at all time to apotheosize flesh. Bianca, he reiterates, satisfies his soul. He deals, he insists, with a typical phase of modern love. . . . (p. 361)

Paul Elmer More says that Symons reproduces in English the peculiar modes of thought and emotion which are attributable to French decadence, and the distinguishing mask of which is illusion, "the false *illusion* of life which from some degeneracy of the will makes it impossible for the victim to hold fast the distinction between the flesh and the spirit, which, in fact, loses sight of the spirit altogether and sets up in its place some poor masquerading of the flesh" [see excerpt above].

In spite of an avowed literary genius, Arthur Symons has never won a large circle of readers. This may be because of his "delight in torturing self-analysis, in tracing the inner emotions to their source"; perhaps, too, because of his tendency towards subtlety and morbidity. But he has seemingly always felt a self-sufficiency which has carried him beyond the need for public recognition: "If, in addition to that mere human right— the right to assistance—one is convinced one is a man of genius, the right becomes more plainly evident, and if, in addition, one has a divine message for the world, what further need be said?"

The so-called schizoid individual, with his restricted fields of interest, requires satisfaction from highly coloured contrasts. This is based chiefly on a poor hold on reality and a need for morbid stimulation, almost, in order to retain his interest. It is through this morbid stimulation that Arthur Symons obtained his satisfactions as an antidote for the harshness of life. In this fashion a psychopathic literature complements a psychopathic personality. His "visible world is no longer a reality, and the unseen world no longer a dream." (pp. 361-62)

Louis J. Bragman, "The Case of Arthur Symons: The Psychopathology of a Man of Letters," in The British Journal of Medical Psychology, Vol. XII, Part IV, 1932, pp. 346-62.

T. S. ELIOT (essay date 1950)

[*Perhaps the most influential poet and critic of the first half of the twentieth century, Eliot is closely identified with many of the qualities denoted by the term Modernism: experimentation, formal complexity, artistic and intellectual eclecticism, and a classicist view of the artist working at an emotional distance from his creation. He introduced a number of terms and concepts that strongly affected critical thought in his lifetime, among them the idea that a poet must be conscious of the living tradition of literature in order for his work to have artistic and spiritual validity. Another of Eliot's concepts, the "objective correlative," is often cited as a major contribution to literary analysis. In* The Sacred Wood,

Eliot defined the objective correlative as "a set of objects, a situation, a set of events which shall be the formula of (a) particular emotion" and which have the ability to evoke that emotion in the reader. In general, Eliot upheld values of traditionalism and discipline, and in 1928 he annexed Christian theology to his overall conservative world-view. In his essay "The Perfect Critic," excerpted below, Eliot considers Symons as a critical impressionist.]

[Mr. Arthur Symons] is a representative of what is always called "æsthetic criticism" or "impressionistic criticism." And it is this form of criticism which I propose to examine. . . . Mr. Symons, the critical successor of Pater, and partly of Swinburne (I fancy that the phrase "sick or sorry" is the common property of all three), *is* the "impressionistic critic." He, if anyone, would be said to expose a sensitive and cultivated mind—cultivated, that is, but the accumulation of a considerable variety of impressions from all the arts and several languages—before an "object"; and his criticism, if anyone's would be said to exhibit to us, like the plate, the faithful record of the impressions, more numerous or more refined than our own, upon a mind more sensitive than our own. A record, we observe, which is also an interpretation, a translation; for it must itself impose impressions upon us, and these impressions are as much created as transmitted by the criticism. I do not say at once that this is Mr. Symons; but it is the "impressionistic" critic, and the impressionistic critic is supposed to be Mr. Symons.

At hand is a volume [*Studies in Elizabethan Drama*] which we may test. Ten of these thirteen essays deal with single plays of Shakespeare, and it is therefore fair to take one of these ten as a specimen of the book:

> *Antony and Cleopatra* is the most wonderful,
> I think of all Shakespeare's plays . . .

and Mr. Symons reflects that Cleopatra is the most wonderful of all women:

> The queen who ends the dynasty of the Ptolemies has been the star of poets, a malign star shedding baleful light, from Horace and Propertius down to Victor Hugo; and it is not to poets only . . .

What, we ask, is this for? as a page on Cleopatra, and her possible origin in the dark lady of the Sonnets, unfolds itself. And we find, gradually, that this is not an essay on a work of art or a work of intellect; but that Mr. Symons is living through the play as one might live it through in the theatre; recounting, commenting:

> In her last days Cleopatra touches a certain elevation . . . she would die a thousand times, rather than live to be a mockery and a scorn in men's mouths . . . she is a woman to the last . . . so she dies . . . the play ends with a touch of grave pity . . .

Presented in this rather unfair way, torn apart like the leaves of an artichoke, the impressions of Mr. Symons come to resemble a common type of popular literary lecture, in which the stories of plays or novels are retold, the motives of the characters set forth, and the work of art therefore made easier for the beginner. But this is not Mr. Symons' reason for writing. The reason why we find a similarity between his essay and this form of education is that *Antony and Cleopatra* is a play with which we are pretty well acquainted, and of which we have, therefore, our own impressions. We can please ourselves with our own impressions of the characters and their emotions; and we do not find the impressions of another person, however sensitive, very significant. But if we can recall the time when we were ignorant of the French symbolists, and met with *The Symbolist Movement in Literature,* we remember that book as an introduction to wholly new feelings, as a revelation. After we have read Verlaine and Laforgue and Rimbaud and return to Mr. Symons' book, we may find that our own impressions dissent from his. The book has not, perhaps, a permanent value for the one reader, but it has led to results of permanent importance for him.

The question is not whether Mr. Symons' impressions are "true" or "false." So far as you can isolate the "impression," the pure feeling, it is, of course, neither true nor false. The point is that you never rest at the pure feeling; you react in one of two ways, or, as I believe Mr. Symons does, in a mixture of the two ways. The moment you try to put the impressions into words, you either begin to analyse and construct, to "ériger en lois," or you begin to create something else. It is significant that Swinburne, by whose poetry Mr. Symons may at one time have been influenced, is one man in his poetry and a different man in his criticism; to this extent and in this respect only, that he is satisfying a different impulse; he is criticizing, expounding, arranging. You may say this is not the criticism of a critic, that it is emotional, not intellectual—though of this there are two opinions, but it is in the direction of analysis and construction, a beginning to "ériger en lois," and not in the direction of creation. So I infer that Swinburne found an adequate outlet for the creative impulse in his poetry; and none of it was forced back and out through his critical prose. The style of the latter is essentially a prose style; and Mr. Symons' prose is much more like Swinburne's poetry than it is like his prose. I imagine—though here one's thought is moving in almost complete darkness—that Mr. Symons is far more disturbed, far more profoundly affected, by his reading than was Swinburne, who responded rather by a violent and immediate and comprehensive burst of admiration which may have left him internally unchanged. The disturbance in Mr. Symons is almost, but not quite, to the point of creating; the reading sometimes fecundates his emotions to produce something new which is not criticism, but is not the expulsion, the ejection, the birth of creativeness. (pp. 2-6)

T. S. Eliot, "The Perfect Critic," in his The Sacred Wood: Essays on Poetry and Criticism, *(reprinted by permission of Methuen London), seventh edition, Methuen & Co. Ltd., 1950 (and reprinted by Methuen, 1960), pp. 1-16.**

RUTH ZABRISKIE TEMPLE   (essay date 1953)

[In her book-length study The Critic's Alchemy, *from which the following excerpt is taken, Temple comprehensively treats a subject of central importance to Symons's work: the relationship between French Symbolism and late nineteenth-century English literature.]*

Symons' first account of Symbolism was published in *Harper's Magazine* for November, 1893, as **"The Decadent Movement in Literature."** His second formed the initial chapter of *The Symbolist Movement in Literature,* which was published in 1899. The two differ in their emphasis: the second lays more stress on the aspect of Symbolism that partakes of mysticism. In the interval he had been finding his way, aided by Yeats, in that direction—a direction less natural, as he admits in the dedication of the book to Yeats, to himself than to the Irish poet.

> Still, as I am, so meshed about with the variable
> and too clinging appearances of earthly things,
> so weak before the delightfulness of earthly
> circumstance, I hesitate sometimes in saying
> what I have in my mind, lest I should seem to
> be saying more than I have any personal right
> to say.

There is, indeed, something tentative about the later essay, whereas the earlier spoke with the nineties vocabulary and enthusiasm for the perverse tone and style of the new literature. This was the aspect of that literature which Symons as poet found most naturally congenial, as his own verse and his translations of Verlaine show. He defines the literature of decadence, in 1893, following Gautier, Verlaine, and Pater, as the literature of beautiful disease. It is divided into two branches which have in common the search for essence: the *verité vraie.* Impressionism seeks the essence of the visible world, Symbolism of the spiritual. After this preliminary distinction, Symons concerns himself only with Impressionism and names its representatives, who are, with few exceptions, the authors to reappear in the chapters of the later *Symbolist Movement.* Goncourt is the inventor of impressionistic prose; Verlaine of the poetry of Impressionism. Their English equivalents are Pater and Henley.

As Symons followed the developing course of French literature, however, he came to minimize decadence as a literary manifestation. Even before the date of the *Symbolist Movement* he had decided that *decadent* was a term applicable to style only. He writes, in an essay on George Meredith (1897): "What Decadence, in literature, really means is that learned corruption of language by which style ceases to be organic, and becomes, in the pursuit of some new expressiveness or beauty, deliberately abnormal." In the introduction to the *Symbolist Movement* he limits decadence in the same way to an ingenious deformation of language and suggests further that it was the preoccupation of a moment only—a noisy moment in literary history while the serious movement of Symbolism was in preparation.

In this essay, which is less systematic and much shorter, Symbolism occupies the foreground. It is a permanent technique, now merely become self-conscious, and become so as reaction against the literature of exteriority, of form, namely that off-shoot of Romanticism known as Realism. Under the head of Realism, Symons includes all the immediately preceding literature, from Flaubert to Taine, not omitting Zola; from Baudelaire to Heredia. In his anxiety to classify, Symons has here become somewhat confused. He is constrained to admit, of course, that Symbolism like Realism is concerned with form and then tries to save the mark by explaining that Symbolism perfects form to annihilate it. The term *impressionism* recurs only as applies to Goncourt's style. Symons' error is a failure to distinguish the artist's delight in the visible world from the philosophical and literary doctrine of materialism and a disposition to regard *form* as absolute and invariable. His later essays on art indicate a truer apprehension of the common elements of Symbolism in literature and Impressionism in painting, those parallel movements of reaction against Realism. Both exploit, not the reality of mere appearance, but something beneath and beyond appearance. (pp. 153-55)

It is on the technique, not the theory, of Symbolism that Symons is best in the introduction to his essays in this book. (A far better exposition of the theory in its philosophical aspect is Yeats's, published the next year.) In the essays themselves Symons has illuminating things to say both of technique and of theory. His choice of authors for inclusion shows a remarkable awareness of the strain of Symbolism as it developed with certain of the earlier Romantics and of its various significant revelations later in the century. (pp. 155-56)

Symons is consistently aware that he is writing on a movement, and so attempts to find in each author studied the core of Symbolism. What this common element is, he has told us in the initial chapter, with a penetration that is rare indeed for a critic writing on a theory difficult and new as well as foreign and even in some sense uncongenial. The facile expedient of filling space with biographical facts Symons has generally avoided. His chapters are not of equal merit, to be sure, but those on Laforgue, Verlaine, and Mallarmé—not the least among the poets—are distinguished.

If Symons' reputation as critic were to depend only on the *Symbolist Movement,* it should be secure. (p. 173)

Since it was one of Symons' critical principles that the critic should concern himself only with work which he could treat sympathetically, this may account for the centering of his interest on those of his contemporaries who professed an ideal of poetry not unlike his own. We find him discussing chiefly the French poets whose work can, Symons thinks, be labeled "modern" in its exclusive concern with the poet's states of mind and in its technique of simplicity, directness, music, and evocation. Besides this limitation in the range of the French poetry that he discusses, there is in his criticism an emphasis on the common elements of that poetry, although according to his own salutary percept the critic should first of all indicate diversity. Perhaps because he was not a novelist, Symons' criticism of the novel shows a greater flexibility of appreciation, a larger capacity for evoking the quality of diverse works and talents than does his criticism of poetry. (The authoritative study of Baudelaire as critic shows that his art criticism is more important than his criticism of poetry.) Although this part of his work has not been my concern here, a fair estimate of the man as critic must take account of his wide and various comments on the novel. He preferred the French to the English novel, regarding the former as the more serious artistic enterprise, and he did perhaps as much for it as for French poetry in England. His essays appeared in periodicals or as the introductions to English translations, by himself or others. In many of these essays he fulfills excellently the function of the impressionist critic: he re-creates in a flexible and straightforward style the experience that the work of art has been for him—a reader of keener sensitivity and wider historical information than the average—and he re-creates it in such a way that the average reader's curiosity is aroused to procure for himself this rewarding experience. If anyone doubts this, let him make the experiment of reading *Studies in Prose and Verse,* another neglected book of Symons. There he will find fresh and provocative comments on the work even of authors by now so thoroughly explored as Meredith, Zola, the Russian novelists, Pater, Maupassant. (pp. 176-77)

Symons is content to reflect—as he reflects works of art—the generalizations on art and criticism of Coleridge, of Pater, of Poe and Baudelaire. From these he had gathered certain definite ideas about the critic's business. It is, first of all, to distinguish what is essential and unique in a writer, but with care to judge each work of art as a whole. Then, the critic must explain why we are affected as we are by works of art, and, in order to study in this way causes through effects, he must know how to allow for his own emotional and mental variations, for not otherwise can he be a safe guide. (Clearly, this presupposes an objective theory of art: the work of art is a real object possessed of qualities which may be apprehended or misapprehended. Such a theory is implicit in the criticism of Pater and of Baudelaire and even of Wilde, though Wilde's explicit statements deny it.) Finally, with a discerning intolerance of the insignificant, the critic must concern himself only with the first-rate.

In a foreword to *Plays, Acting and Music* Symons announced that he was engaged in the enterprise of expressing a theory or system of aesthetics of all the arts, and he "placed" his publications with regard to this scheme. The *Symbolist Movement* . . . had initiated the series by applying the system to literature. *Plays, Acting and Music* . . . dealt with the stage and music; the forthcoming *Studies in Seven Arts* . . . would include painting, sculpture, architecture and the dance. Living is also an art for this disciple of Pater, and *Cities* . . . would deal with the visible world, *Spiritual Adventures* . . . with the world of people. Symons hastens to clear himself from the charge of abstract systematization: his aim in all this is to be as concrete as possible, to study first principles only as operative in life and art.

It may seriously be questioned that this was more than an *a posteriori* classification for groups of essays which had been written, not to illustrate any system, but because they corresponded to the very diverse interests of the author. But the concern for theory, first of all and, secondly, the attempt to relate all the arts to one system of aesthetics distinguish Symons among English critics and had no doubt been stimulated by his frequenting of French literature. Like Baudelaire's, his critical faculty displays itself to good advantage on painting and on music. And in the fashion of the time he freely describes one art in terms of another.

Whatever the degree of realization of his system of aesthetics, it contributed at least to his critical seriousness. He is not one of the Englishmen who are critics by accident or courtesy, who read for pleasure and write about books to enjoy this pleasure a second time in retrospect. He cannot read, he declares, without the approval of an unconscious, if not indeed definitely conscious, criticism. Yet he condemns the ranks of dogmatic critics, whose whole business is the description and comparison of books, mere praise and blame.

Symons' critical practice does not belie his theory. The mere acknowledgment of principles, more or less consistently adhered to, distinguishes his work form that of such critics as Edmund Gosse, who professed the high calling with gentlemanly deprecation of its intellectual rigors, and from that of George Moore, who had no theory and did not indeed pretend to be a critic. Symons' thorough knowledge of French literature, the knowledge of an "insider," enabled him to provide for many English readers not simply information but acquaintance—as good as it may be at second hand—with that literature, and so, one may suppose, provoked the reading of French literature. One may regret that his own preferences as poet limited his criticism to a restricted group of figures in contemporary French poetry, but at least these were not the second-rate, and Symons' judgments and interpretations, besides having the support of competent French opinion of the period, have been remarkably sustained by time. Surely no single English critic did so much to acquaint the English with the work of Verlaine and Mallarmé and with the new poetic movement, Symbolism. (pp. 178-79)

Ruth Zabriskie Temple, "Arthur Symons," in her The Critic's Alchemy: A Study of the Introduction of French Symbolism into England *(copyright © 1953 by Ruth Zabriskie Temple; reprinted with the permission of the author), Twayne Publishers, Inc., 1953, pp. 121-81.*

FRANK KERMODE   (essay date 1957)

[*Kermode is an English critic whose career combines modern critical methods with expert traditional scholarship, particularly in his work on Shakespeare. In his critical discussions of modern literature, Kermode has embraced many of the conceptions of structuralism and phenomenology. Kermode characterizes all human knowledge as poetic, or fictive: constructed by humans and affected by the perceptual and emotional limitations of human consciousness. Because perceptions of life and the world change, so does human knowledge and the meaning attached to things and events. Thus, there is no single fixed reality over time. Similarly, for Kermode, a work of art has no single fixed meaning, but a multiplicity of possible interpretations. In fact, the best of modern writing is constructed so that it invites a variety of interpretations, all of which depend upon the sensibility of the reader. Kermode believes his critical writings exist to stimulate thought, to offer possible interpretations, but not to fix a single meaning to a work of art. True or "classic" literature, to Kermode, is thus a constantly reinterpreted living text, "complex and indeterminate enough to allow us our necessary pluralities." Kermode's observation that Symons was a crucial figure in the development of modern poetics is elaborated upon in Derek Stanford's essay excerpt below.*]

When we come to consider how the twentieth century has used [the ideas of the French Symbolists], we are obliged, I think, to regard Arthur Symons as crucial. He, more explicitly and more influentially than any of his contemporaries, saw how to synthesise the earlier English tradition—particularly Blake, on whom he wrote a good, and in this connexion revealing, book—with Pater and those European Symbolists he knew so well. Symons also had a considerable part in the associated revival of interest in Donne and the Jacobean dramatic poets. But above all he wrote the book out of which the important poets of the early twentieth century learnt the elements of French Symbolist poetic. (p. 107)

English poetry and criticism have been changed by his book *The Symbolist Movement in Literature* . . . , and that is as much as a critic can achieve. As I have said, it was the first book of its kind, and the work from which other important poets besides Yeats learnt the elements of the subject; and it was certainly none the worse for Symons's knowledge of Blake. That *The Symbolist Movement* is absolutely a good book I suppose nobody would suggest. It is scrappy, lacking the pertinacity we have come to expect from critics; it is often disagreeably imprecise. As a simple exposition of its subject it has of course been superseded. But it is a very good place to look if one wants to know how French Symbolism struck a well-informed, avant-garde Paterian in the 'nineties; and considering that the character of modern poetry has been, to a remarkable degree, formed by that contact, we may well think it worth while to do so.

Symons's book is dedicated to Yeats, and his prefatory letter, insisting upon the European diffusion of the new movement, calls Yeats "the chief representative of that movement in our country". It also refers to the author's own growing interest in what he calls Mysticism, which he evidently regards as a related subject, and of which he treats Yeats as a master. This is an interesting connexion, and I shall return to it. Of course Symons had much better have said Magic, and the allusion is to Yeats's interest in occult theologies of the hermetic and cabbalistic tradition. 'Tradition' is the right word, for there are recognisable affinities between Hermes Trismegistus, the Neo-Platonists, Agrippa, Boehme, Swedenborg and Blake on the one hand, and the alchemists and theurgists of the Renaissance, with their curious descendants, on the other. Symons did well to mention the connexion between Magic and Symbolism early. It is an important one, by no means as isolated from the concerns of modern poetry as might appear; this will emerge as we consider his book.

It begins with a short and inadequate introductory chapter of a theoretical nature, which is probably most interesting when related to Symons's own poetry. Then a chapter apiece is devoted to the more important Symbolists from de Nerval to Huysmans and Maeterlinck. Some of these essays are of small value, but there are scattered observations of interest, and the chapter on Mallarmé is a more serious effort. (pp. 108-09)

[Symons writes] with uncritical adulation of Verlaine, treating him (no wonder it was thought dangerous) as the pattern of Pater's perfect man as he deduced him from the original conclusion of *The Renaissance*. It was Verlaine who broke the rhetorical tradition of French poetry, who wrote poems "which go as far as verse can go to become pure music", in whom "the sense of hearing and the sense of sight are almost interchangeable". We may remember that Yeats's view of Verlaine was almost identical with this; personally, as well as in his poetry, the French poet stood for much that Yeats admired. Symons, strangely enough, makes a pair, a sort of Yeatsian antithesis, of Rimbaud and Verlaine, "the man of action" and "the man of sensation". . . . (p. 114)

The essay on Mallarmé is more important. Symons distinguishes three periods in this author: the first of clear and beautiful poems, the last of "opaque darkness", and a middle period, represented by the *Hérodiade* and *L'Après-midi d'un Faune,* which he regards as the summit of the poet's achievement, for "every word is a jewel . . . every image is a symbol, and the whole poem is visible music". What I should like here to direct attention to is what he had to say about the last period. On Symons's view, this is the expression of a devotion to silence, an isolated, solipsist poetry. And I think it is greatly to Symons's credit that he saw in these last works of Mallarmé a certain danger latent in Symbolist poetic. I think he may have communicated this understanding to Yeats, who, from the earliest days right up to the time when he made little jokes about nobody really understanding what he was talking about, was always concerned with the danger of stepping over into uncommunication, into an area where the magic bond between poet and audience should be broken. What Mallarmé aspired to, according to Symons, was a liberation of the soul of literature from "the body of that death"; in other words, to the idea of the autonomous Image, free of discursive content. The purpose of all his care was "to evoke, by some elaborate, instantaneous magic of language, without the formality of an after all impossible description", this image—again we hear the inescapable language of magic; but behind Symons's remarks there is an undoubted commonsense.

In effect, he accuses the poet of going too far in his pursuit of the ultimate aim, "to be, rather than to express". He was perfectly aware of the difficulty, which he elsewhere discusses, of working, in an art that aspired to the condition of music, with words that derive their meanings in unmusical ways, and

this seemed to him to set limits to the Symbolist aspiration, limits which Mallarmé had transgressed. The language in which he makes his accusation is drawn, whether accidentally or not I cannot say, from the terminology of the old controversy over alchemy. "To say that he had found what he sought is impossible; but (is it possible to avoid saying?) how heroic a search, and what marvellous discoveries on the way!" Mallarmé is the alchemist; he does not find the Stone, but he stumbles, in his search for it, on such fascinating compounds that we are very willing, in Donne's phrase, to glorify his pregnant pot. But the result of his efforts in the later poems, the final stages of the projection, is merely that 'the work', as an alchemist would say, returns to chaos. A poem like *Un Coup de Dès* achieves an obscurity practically impenetrable to any but the poet, and only the discoveries 'on the way' remain; these of course are great discoveries. Symons saw the dangers, but he also saw the whole future of poetry in Mallarmé's achievement: "It is on the lines of that spiritualising of the word, that perfecting of form in its capacity for allusion and suggestion, that confidence in the eternal correspondences between the visible and invisible universe, which Mallarmé taught, and too intermittently practised, that literature must now move, if it is in any sense to move forward."

So Symons, in prophesying the immediate future of poetry, prophesied also its dangers. He was acutely aware of the Symbolist paradox that art is both concrete and obscure. "All art hates the vague," he says in the essay on Maeterlinck; yet the Mallarméan method holds out little hope of avoiding an obscurity, an impermeability to the ordinary senses of the reader, which may well seem indistinguishable from the vague and indeed the obscurantist, so that the artist loses an audience and wins more hatred and suspicion. Symons welcomed the novels of Huysmans, partly because they tended to prove that Symbolism could 'make sense'; he would not have been surprised that the novel has, in some ways, had more success than poetry in post-Symbolist times. The dangers attending poetry he saw clearly. They were not merely technical. The poetry of isolation, defying philosophical and moral assumptions, and breaking the rule that it 'ought' to 'say' something, would alienate the potential audience still further, and be called obscure because of this failure in communication. The doctrine of correspondences does not in itself conduce to clarity, but Symons was not so much afraid of an exquisite Gongorism as of the failure to remember how limited words were for the purpose. He does not say so, but it looks as if he had some feeling that the symbol must deign to be domesticated in a structure with some appearance of logic, that the 'work' should cease before the whole apparatus blows up *in fumo*. It is the Mallarméan fault of pressing on to that semantic explosion, or near it, that is responsible for the fact that 'obscurity' rather than 'concreteness' is the first word that occurs to a literate non-specialist public when it thinks of modern poetry. When poetry is by definition *inexplicable* (Nerval said it of his sonnets, and poets have been saying it ever since) only an act of magic can effect communication. . . . But there was, as Symons feared, a point beyond which irrational disorder ought not to go, if the miracle was to have any chance of happening.

It is hardly too much to say that the Symbolist movement was not only the cause of many of the varieties of modern obscurity, but also of the critical techniques that have been evolved in order that such poetry may be inoffensively discussed; and of course these techniques have been applied to other poetry on the assumption that it is basically (if it is any good) Symbolist in character—a view shared, though very differently implemented, by critics as far apart as Symons and Mr. Cleanth Brooks. (pp. 114-16)

One might, if one were arguing for an upward estimate of Arthur Symons, contend that he foresaw the probable nature of the problems that would face poets like Pound. Certainly these problems are inherent in the nineteenth-century revaluation of the power and function of the Image, and we must now go on to consider some of the later developments in that effort of revaluation, between Symons and our own time. (p. 118)

> Frank Kermode, "Arthur Symons," in his Romantic Image (© 1957 by Routledge & Kegan Paul Ltd.), Routledge & Kegan Paul, 1957, pp. 107-18.

RICHARD ELLMANN (essay date 1958)

[*Ellmann is the author of the definitive biography of James Joyce. He has also written widely on early twentieth-century Irish literature, most notably on William Butler Yeats and Oscar Wilde. Ellmann discusses the importance of Symons's book* The Symbolist Movement in Literature, *explaining that "Symons imported into modern literature the word 'symbol' much as Wordsworth, a hundred years before, had pressed upon romantic literature the word 'nature'."*]

Literary movements pass their infancy in revolutionary disaffection, but mature when they achieve a terminology. Late in the nineteenth century the problem was to find the term. In 1899 two new books, one psychological and one literary, fastened on the word *symbolism:* Freud's *Interpretation of Dreams,* which appeared in Vienna in November, and Symons' **The Symbolist Movement in Literature,** published in September in London. Although unlike in method, both recorded the search for a psychic reality which had little to do with exterior reality. Symons' book, like Freud's, gave a name to the preoccupation with modes of half-uttered or half-glimpsed meaning which, as we can see clearly enough now sixty years have passed, was a principal direction in modern thought.

When Symons wrote his book readers in England and the United States were only beginning to be aware of the writers he discussed. The magically operative word "symbolism" brought to a sudden focus the rumors that had drifted slowly into England chiefly from France since 1875. . . . Rumors had come also from Ireland since 1887, when W. B. Yeats arrived in London at the age of twenty-two, his mind crowded with occult symbols, eager to defend them with extravagance and cunning. The French reports were a little sinister, of corrupt lives, enigmatic and probably immoral works, and those from Ireland were at once crepuscular and provincial, so that it remained easy, until Arthur Symons' book appeared, to ignore them. The official view, heard commonly in France and England after the death of Hugo in 1885 and then of Browning and Tennyson a few years later, was that poetry was dead. . . . Symons suddenly joined issue with this attitude of resignation. He found poetry decidedly alive and on its way to embracing, more and more completely, this new-old doctrine of symbolism. Writers who had been hesitating towards a new conception of literature—impersonal where the romantics had been personal, reticent where the romantics had been indiscreet, esoteric where the romantics had been popular—saw their intentions suddenly clarified into the philosophy of a school. Unlike the Pre-Raphaelites, who had been skimpy of theory, the symbolists were prodigal of it, in their gnomic way. (pp. vii-viii)

That it should have been Symons who wrote the first book in English expressly devoted to the French symbolists was not

strange. . . . His early volumes of verse suggest an almost frantic search for deeper emotions than he was able to attain, along with a sophisticated curiosity about all feelings. . . . Books, especially foreign books, attracted him as much as poised women; he responded to them all urbanely. His critical articles, witty, informed, sensible, and graceful, as befitted a friend and admirer of Pater, and somewhat lacking in emphasis too, were soon appearing in the *Athenaeum* and elsewhere. (pp. ix-x)

What Symons lacked as a critic was the ability to generalize (his remarks are better than his conclusions), yet paradoxically the importance of his book on symbolism was its ruling generalization. That the movement should be called "symbolist" was a point still blurred in France, and Symons did not at first acknowledge it. In an essay of 1893 he preferred, while dismissing the question of the name as of no great consequence, to use the term "decadent" rather than "symbolist." . . . It was W. B. Yeats who seems to have persuaded Symons that the season was not autumn but spring, and encouraged him to see symbolism as the soul's heroic recovery of authority over the body and the material world. (pp. x-xi)

Mostly under Yeats's influence, then, as it seems, Symons decided to publish a book on the French writers as members of a movement. Yeats's phrase, "the symbolical movement," was too general; by calling it "the symbolist movement" Symons made it more special, topical, and doctrinaire. With this theme he hoped to establish the outlines of an esthetic system that could bind the separate essays he had published between 1895 and 1898 on Huysmans, Mallarmé, Nerval, Rimbaud, Villiers, Verlaine, and Maeterlinck. He retouched them, added an essay on Laforgue, then wrote an introduction and conclusion to embody the new insight Yeats had helped him to reach, the perception of a singleness of purpose among these disparate talents.

Symons does, it is true, use the term "symbolism" rather loosely. In the essays on Nerval and Villiers symbolism is primarily the perception of a reality which is opposite to the world of appearance; in the essays on Mallarmé and Maeterlinck this reality is not opposed to appearance, but is just barely over its borders; with Rimbaud and Verlaine, on the other hand, symbolism is the perception of world of appearance with a visionary intensity; with Huysmans symbolism is the understanding of the organic unity of the world of appearance. Symons includes among the symbolists those who reject the world, those who accept it so totally as to see it with new eyes, and those who regard it under the aspect of eternity. He is less adroit than Yeats in manipulating the contrasting values of the words "appearance" and "reality," and understands vaguely, if at all, the Yeatsian view of the interpenetration of the two worlds. Yet a stricter definition of terms would have raised problems of application to particular authors that still perplex the literary historian.

In our day, when critical prose has become the straightest line between two points, some of Symons' subtleties in his book may be overlooked. His style is made up of delicacies and insinuations. Considering as he does that symbolist literature is "a sacred ritual," he treats each of his authors as a renunciant, who gives up contentment for the sake of his soul and art. Although occasionally Symons supplies a date, his portraits are almost timeless, and could be set in his book of fictitious *Spiritual Adventures* without looking very different from the characters there. These men are so strange that it seems almost problematical that they lived at all. Symons discovers them, and they discover him, finally turning, or almost turning, into aspects of his own mind struggling for expression, then dying out. Their lives seem to pass in a dream; their odd or immoral behavior simply makes the dream richer. At the end, so personal is the book, so intricate the bond of writer and reader, we are willing to concede Symons' extraordinary conclusion, that these symbolist writers may help to reconcile us to death. (pp. xii-xiv)

There are moments in literature when the important thing is to suspect, to hint, to leap, and there are moments when the important thing is to conclude, to bring together, to bind. Symons found a moment of the second soft, and, with his marvellous adaptability, took possession of it. The result was to import into modern literature the word "symbol" much as Wordsworth, a hundred years before, had pressed upon romantic literature the word "nature." Since 1899 the French symbolists have steadily affected even writers who have not read them, and for this fortunate exchange Arthur Symons, who was among those who read them first, was chiefly responsible. (pp. xv-xvi)

Richard Ellmann, "Introduction" (copyright © 1958, by E. P. Dutton & Co., Inc.; reprinted by permission of the publisher, E. P. Dutton, Inc.), in The Symbolist Movement in Literature *by Arthur Symons, revised edition, Dutton, 1958, pp. vii-xvi.*

EDWARD BAUGH (essay date 1965)

[*While not as unrestrained in his praise of Symons's poetry as Benjamin De Casseres (see excerpt above), Baugh credits Symons's with greater poetic powers and accomplishments than do standard critical appraisals, such as those of William Butler Yeats and William Archer (see excerpts above).*]

It was as a poet that Symons wished to be chiefly remembered. Ironically, even during the nineties his criticism began to overshadow his poetry, and eventually the poetry faded from view. This unjust neglect of the poetry was due partly to the tyranny of labels such as *'fin-de-siècle'* and 'decadent', by means of which the poetry was too easily dismissed. Besides, the poetry of Dowson and Johnson, whose literary talents were not as various as Symons's, has been graced with a special fascination by their early, tragic deaths. And the comments which Yeats made on the nineties during his later years have encouraged us to think of Dowson and Johnson as *the* representative poets, and of Symons as *the* critic, of that period.

Symons's poems fill three volumes of his *Collected Works*. . . . By comparison with his poetic talent, the output was disproportionately large. But there are at least a hundred pieces which are worth preserving, which can always give delight, and which achieve, within their narrow range, a kind of perfection. These pieces belong almost entirely to the period 1890-1908. In the poetry which he wrote before this period—represented by *Days and Nights* . . . , his first book of verse—he had not yet found his own true voice; in the poetry which he wrote after this period, the voice became distorted and corrupted, as a result of the mental breakdown which he suffered while travelling in Italy in the autumn of 1908. (pp. 71-2)

His most remarkable and distinctive verse is to be found mainly in *Silhouettes* . . . and *London Nights*. . . . These volumes are also the ones in which he preserves most fully the flavour of 'the Beardsley period'. He makes a unique contribution to English poetry in slight but delicate monuments to fleeting sensations of beauty, to powder and patchouli and the 'charm

of rouge on fragile cheeks'. He finds his distinctive voice in a blending of Pater, his acknowledged master, of the early Verlaine, and of Impressionist painting, of which he was one of the first advocates. And nowhere is he more himself, and at the same time more expressive of the spirit of the nineties, than in the poems concerning the ballet and the dancer. In celebrating the ballet-girls of the music halls he helped to free poetry from the bondage of Victorian prudery and 'respectability'. A few of these poems are fully accomplished, displaying a mastery of rhythm and form, and intensifying the moment's sensation into a kind of epiphany. I think, for example, of **'Javanese Dancers'**, **'The Primrose Dance: Tivoli'**, and **'La Mélinite: Moulin Rouge'**. One of the most rewarding is **'Nora on the Pavement'**, which moves from an impressionistic to a symbolic conception of the dancer, who undergoes a transfiguration into what Symons would call 'a living symbol'; we see her transcending the merely spectacular, becoming truly individual, achieving self-fulfilment, no longer just a dash of colour in the pattern woven by the *corps-de-ballet*. . . . As in **'La Mélinite'**, variation in verse length and an intricately varied pattern of repetition, rhyming on the same word, alliteration and internal rhyme (note the rhyming of the beginning of the second line of each stanza with the end of the fourth line) help to evoke a direct, sensuous awareness of 'the evasive, winding turn of things', the 'continual slight novelty' of the dance. 'Nora' is a succinct embodiment of all the ideas in **'The World as Ballet'**. . . . (pp. 72-4)

Symons's poems on the dance, as he saw it performed in the music halls of London and Paris, those 'garish temples of modernity' as Max Beerbohm called them, were also an expression of a conscious attempt at an urban poetry, 'the poetry of cities', to use his own phrase. . . . He himself contributed to the development of English poetry by making lyrical the gas-lit night-world of music-hall and pub, 'the heat and the fumes and the footlights', 'the blue-grey smoke of cigarettes', and the flash of 'the bright train' 'with all its squares / Of warm light where the bridge lay mistily'. But it isn't only in the use of urban material in these early poems that he strikes a modern note; he also manages at times to suggest a sensibility, a tone, which is peculiarily modern. Take, for example, **'At the Cavour'**, which recalls the café studies of Degas and Toulouse-Lautrec. . . . It isn't very far from here to Prufrock-land. Note how the use of 'cigarettes', new to English poetry at that time, interfuses the *fin-de-siècle* and modern qualities of the poem.

The modern quality, such as it is, of *Silhouettes* and *London Nights* is also partly due to that 'simplicity' of language at which Symons deliberately aimed. The aim was one which he shared with Yeats—to write lyric poetry which, without any loss in intensity, would speak a direct, 'natural' speech. . . . Pound [in his preface to *The Poetical Works of Lionel Johnson*] gave the impression that the poetry of his generation differed sharply from the poetry of the nineties. . . . Symons, like Yeats, contradicts such an impression, in intention as in achievement; and Eliot acknowledged a debt to this feature of Symons's poetry in a radio talk which celebrated the centenary of [John] Davidson's birth.

Symons fell deeply in love with a girl who danced in the ballet at the Empire theatre, and that love was to inspire his poetry throughout the rest of his life. Out of the anguish which attended the ending of the liaison, he produced *Amoris Victima*. . . . The achievement, as a whole, does not measure up to the ostensible profundity of the experience which inspired it. But there are a few excellent passages, and the work is interesting as a new, experimental departure in Symons's development, and one which foreshadows certain developments in twentieth-century poetry. This experimental feature lies chiefly in the overall conception and construction. The book is really one long poem made up of fifty-five short ones, all arising out of the unhappy love affair. In a prefatory note, Symons explained that he wished the book

> to be read as a single poem, not as a collection of miscellaneous pieces. . . . Each poem is, I hope, able to stand alone, but no poem has been included without reference to the general scheme of the book, the general psychology of the imaginary hero.

The wish is justified. The whole is held together as an integral unit not only by 'the general psychology of the imaginary hero', but also by a narrative thread which is not systematically laid out (in other words, the work is not constructed in terms of the narrative), but is revealed in hints at odd moments. No linear time-scheme is followed. As the work unfolds, we get glimpses backwards and forwards into time, now of a moment of remembered bliss, now of a brief meeting after the irrevocable decision to part, now of the imagined future lives of the lovers. By the time we reach the end we have divined the whole story and learnt something of the personalities of the two lovers.

The oblique telling of an unhappy love-story in a sequence of short poems, each of which is a complete lyric in itself, had already been done brilliantly by Meredith in *Modern Love*, which is the chief literary progenitor of *Amoris Victima*. But Symons goes beyond Meredith in the form and construction of the work. In *Modern Love* the individual poems are all identical in form. *Amoris Victima* achieves a pregnant novelty by varying its verse forms. The total effect is orchestral; the work is a kind of symphony, and in this respect it looks forward to the adventures of Eliot, Pound and their heirs. The nineties, with a concentration on the lyric, put an end to the tradition of the long narrative poem such as the great Victorians had written. In *Amoris Victima*, Symons, himself an eloquent champion of the lyric, suggests the way in which poets were later to attempt the long poem.

Unfortunately, much of *Amoris Victima* suffers from aridity of content, and the frequent changes of mood, showing little development, eventually constitute monotonous repetition. The anguish might have been more telling were it not stretched out so long. But there are moments of splendour in the final 'movement', 'Mundi Victima', which Yeats called 'a long ecstasy of sorrow, a long revery of that bitter wisdom which comes only to those who have a certain emotional distinction'. In this section the poet contrives a climactic effect partly by using the heroic couplet; and he makes it flow with an easy, near-conversational, yet dignified rhythm which owes little to the nimble, epigrammatic cut-and-thrust of Dryden or Pope, or to the knotty, shouldering strength of Donne. It is to Shelley's 'Julian and Maddalo', which Symons praised highly, that we must go for the most likely model. . . . In *Amoris Victima* Symons began to abandon the markedly nineties mood of *Silhouettes* and *London Nights*. The reviewers had attacked him for the 'decadence' of his verse, for his being too concerned with private and fleeting sensations, with the artificial and the tawdry, with morbidity and what he himself called 'the perverse charm of the sordid'. In *Images of Good and Evil* . . . there is not much trace, as far as content is concerned, of the poet who had helped to make *The Yellow Book* notorious. Now we even

find him writing devotional verse, under the influence of St. Theresa and St. John of the Cross, and there is an increasing interest in the universal themes of Time and Mortality. Now the imagery derives mainly from nature—wind, tree and sea. This tendency is continued in *The Fool of the World* . . . , in which he turns from 'the poetry of cities' in order to make 'Amends to Nature'. The products of this reversion, strongly influenced by the Elizabethan lyricists, to the traditional mainstream of English nature poetry, do not generally attain distinctiveness. But in a lyric like **'Time and Beauty'**, which also bears the stamp of the Elizabethans, he manages to infuse a certain freshness into the imagery and, largely because of the diction and the intelligent use of pauses, to convey, under the conventional 'body' of the poem, a sense of 'passionate intensity' . . . . In a few other tenderly grave love lyrics (e.g. **'Perfect Grief'**, **'Fear'**, **'Vanitas'**) he achieves a kind of timeless, anonymous, yet forceful speech. Significantly enough, we find him at this time praising Bridges for writing lyrics which are 'very personal, but personal in a way so abstract, so little dependent on the accidents of what we call personality, that it seems the most natural thing in the world for him to turn to a style which comes to him with a great, anonymous tradition'.

The three selections from Symons which Yeats put into *The Oxford Book of Modern Verse* are all translations. Yeats's choice was at one and the same time a slight on Symons's ability as original poet and a tribute to his ability as translator. Today the translator is much better known than the original poet, partly because the translations are most fruitfully discussed as a complement to the criticism. What I have been mainly concerned with here is giving the original poet his due. The translations which deserve our praise deserve it because they are the translations of a poet. And they are particularly praiseworthy because generally chose the hardest way: to stay as close as possible to the original, its form and spirit, and at the same time produce something which would be a poem in its own right. (pp. 74-9)

> *Edward Baugh, "Arthur Symons, Poet: A Centenary Tribute," in* A Review of English Literature *(© Longmans, Green & Co. Ltd. 1965), Vol. 6, No. 3, July, 1965, pp. 70-80 [the first excerpt of Symons's work used here was originally published in his* Poems *(reprinted by permission of William Heinemann Ltd.), Heinemann, 1902; the second excerpt was originally published in his* Amoris Victima *(reprinted by permission of the Literary Estate of Arthur Symons), Leonard Smithers, 1897, George H. Richmond and Co., 1897].*

DEREK STANFORD (essay date 1966)

> [*Stanford develops Frank Kermode's observation (see excerpt above) that Symons was a crucial figure in modern poetics.*]

Symons' contribution to the theory of modern poetics would seem to be undeniable, while being at the same time hard to locate with any satisfactory and specific precision. A wavy, uncertain but indelible line does, however, exist between Symons' criticism and the proceedings of Pound and Eliot as poets.

Contemporary literary criticism has singled out imagery as the element of most interest in verse; and in his stimulating "Reflections on a Literary Revolution" in his work entitled *Image and Experience* . . . , Graham Hough has traced the connections between the Symbolist and the Imagist Movements. He has shown how the religion of the symbol in the French and English writers of the 1890s gave way to a cult of the image among a number of avant-garde poets from about 1912; and how the theory and practice of the image was strengthened by Ezra Pound's "discovery" of the Chinese written character, or *ideogram* as he was to call it. (pp. 348-49)

Governing the use of them all is a certain aesthetic exclusiveness: a desire on the part of the poet to present his state of mind, his feeling about his subject, without recourse to discursive thinking. Eliot has assumed that "there is a logic of the imagination as well as a logic of concepts"; and it is this former type of logic that the Symbolist and Imagist poets have preferred. They wished to dispense with all save the phenomenal element in poetry—to leave out all the abstract, expository, or argumentative matter. Symbolist and Imagist poems were to be essentially high-voltage poetry, with all the low-voltage connective equipment omitted. (p. 349)

The image, the symbol, the ideogram—all are variations of those "epiphanies," or bodily showings which James Joyce spoke about in *Stephen Hero*. They are cardinal to an understanding of modern literature's concern with the sensuous manifestations of thought—with the "this-ness" or quiddity of things or ideas.

Symons, as a practising critic, was at the center of the Symbolist Movement. The trouble starts when one tries to discover just what he understood by its leading concept. The extraordinary thing is that one can search *The Symbolist Movement in Literature* without encountering one single definition of the symbol by Symons himself. It is clear, nonetheless, that he was aware of its central importance. As an epigraph to his "Introduction" he quotes Carlyle as saying that "it is in and through Symbols that man, consciously or unconsciously lives, works, and has his being," and that "those ages, moreover, are accounted the noblest which can the best recognize symbolical worth, and prize it highest." Paraphrasing Comte d'Alviella's book, *The Migration of Symbols*, he tells us that "gradually the word extended its meaning, until it came to denote every conventional representation of idea by form, of the unseen by the visible." (The word "conventional" here, one might remark, makes the definition quite inapposite if applied to the symbol in Symbolist poetry.) Later, in his chapter on "Huysman as a Symbolist" he proclaims that "truth can be reached and revealed only by symbols." And that is about the long and the short of it. Elsewhere, he speaks often of symbols; but never with any precise intent to examine their function or define their nature.

To associate Symons in any exact fashion with the theoretical aspect of modern poetics is certainly no easy matter. The attempt, however, has been made by Frank Kermode who asserts in *The Romantic Image* [see excerpt above] that Symons "more explicitly, and more influentially than any of his contemporaries, saw how to synthesize the earlier English tradition—particularly Blake . . . with Pater and those European Symbolists he knew so well." Such a claim might take some showing; but Kermode is not content. He wishes also to suggest that Symons' part in the revival of Donne (along with his interest in the Jacobean dramatists and the Symbolists) "makes intelligible a habit that came to dominate twentieth-century criticism in its historical phase." "Intelligible" perhaps is rather a misnomer. Nowhere did Symons praise the "metaphysical conceit" as a type of figurative expression nor suggest that in some way it anticipated Symbolist procedure. Indeed, he disapproved of Donne's method. (pp. 351-52)

Kermode is on a safer wicket when he claims that Symons saw the dangers of Symbolism as well as its achievements. Like Yeats, he was always aware of the limits of communication. He knew that a work of art must preserve the balance between communication and expression; and that the artist who becomes his one and only reader has somehow failed in his task and duty. Because the expressionist element was more developed in Symbolist verse than in other poetries, Symons understood how it could easily fall prey to obscurity. (p. 352)

To maintain, as Kermode does, that Symons sought to synthesize Blake and the Symbolists is something not readily evident. What is more apparent is that Symons saw the shortcomings of Blake's method just as he saw the limitations of Mallarmé. Of the former's *Prophetic Books* he observed in **The Romantic Movement in English Poetry:** "He is concerned now only with his message . . . and he has ceased to accept any mortal medium, or to allow himself to be penetrated by the sunlight of earthly beauty, he has lost the means of making that message visible to us. It is a miscalculation of means, a contempt for possibilities: not, as people were once hasty enough to assume, the irresponsible rapture of madness."

"A miscalculation of means, a contempt for possibilities"—a good deal of modern poetry, inscribed in its wayward subjective shorthand, could be written off in those two phrases. Symons, in the van of the nineties, would prove a conservative influence today. (p. 353)

Derek Stanford, "Arthur Symons and Modern Poetics" (copyright, 1966, by Derek Stanford), in The Southern Review, *n.s. Vol. 2, No. 2, Winter, 1966, pp. 347-53.*

JAN B. GORDON (essay date 1969)

[*Gordon discusses Symons's short fiction.*]

Although Arthur Symons' prescriptions about the role of art have long been viewed as the quintessence of the yellow nineties, his oft-neglected short fiction is just as interesting, if for no other reason, than because it marks a kind of culmination in his career. Published in 1905, only three years prior to the initial symptoms of Symons' madness, the *Spiritual Adventures* provides imaginative variations upon the themes that had long preoccupied their author: the perpetual threat of imprisonment by the randomness of nature; the necessity of a mediating mask; and, ultimately, a progressive loss of selfhood which characterizes the conversion to art.

Symons prefaces his *Spiritual Adventures* with an autobiographical sketch, "A Prelude to Life," detailing his growth from infancy through adolescence. The most directly personal of the stories, the reflective voice that speaks in "A Prelude" sets it apart from the omniscient author found in the other eight stories. The most striking feature of the youth's childhood is the antiphony set up by the conflicting religious views of his parents. The father's Non-conformist convictions initiate the youth into an atomized, fluid universe: ". . . what seemed so real and so permanent to me, was but an episode in existence, a little finite part of eternity." . . . In contrast, the boy's mother is entirely worthy of his admiration, for she has succeeded in uniting the moments of her existence; present, past, and future are part of the simultaneity of experience: "life was everything to her, and life was indestructible." . . . Without the organizing structure of any formal religion, she has brought about a union of the permanent and the mutable by converting her life into art. Through her guidance, the boy develops an insatiable curiosity about the myriad forms of life around him, and the **"Prelude"** concludes, like so many Victorian autobiographies, with a pilgrimage from rural Warwick to the hurly-burly of London. In the sea of faces that occupy the metropolis, the adolescent attempts to unite the fluidity of appearances into a religion of art—facial expression becomes, for him, part of a "religion of eyes." . . . It is the initial step in converting experience into an aesthetic. Yet, lurking behind any fantasy of converting life to art is the boy's remembrance of a mad uncle who, unable to preserve the sanctity of self when confronted with the randomness of experience, spends his life lying nude in the garden of the childhood house. Yeats' choice of madman or saint would seem to be, similarly, the alternatives for Symons' aesthetic soul; in its prophecy of insanity, **"A Prelude to Life"** was accurate enough.

As Barbara Charlesworth has suggested [see excerpt above], Symons' first story in the collection is only quasi-autobiographical. By comparing the story to the account of Symons' childhood in [Roger] Lhombreaud's biography, it is clear that Symons has refashioned the events of his growth into art. By calling it a "prelude," the author has caused life to approach the condition of music, that state which Symons, like Pater, felt to be the highest manifestation of art. Even more important is the way **"A Prelude to Life"** introduces the themes which reappear in the succeeding stories. Each of the protagonists in the remaining *Spiritual Adventures,* like the youth alone in the city, must attempt to reconcile the permanence of the "self" against the vagaries of random sensation. Self-isolation or a conversion at the altar of art become way stations in the life pilgrimages of Symons' personalities.

In **"Esther Kahn"** Symons takes as his subject a young Jewess from the Liverpool slums. Not unlike the adolescent Symons of **"A Prelude to Life,"** she finds herself trapped by the urban squalor of dockside surroundings. When she is introduced to the drama as a spectator, Esther's native Hebraism with its accompanying concern for moral conduct is brought into conflict with the Hellenic mask of art. . . . Upon securing a part in a play ironically entitled "The Wages of Sin," Esther Kahn comes to confuse life and art. She seizes upon her love for the playwright, Haygarth, as an agent for preserving the parallel development of her artistic and her human existence: "Her art kept pace with her life; she was giving up nothing in return for happiness; but she had come to prize the happiness, her love, beyond all things." . . . (pp. 105-06)

Upon Haygarth's betrayal of Esther for a young peasant girl of startling physical beauty, the promising actress comes to feel that her body "has been broken in two." . . . The fragmentation that accompanies the bifurcation of life and art is initiated, as "every nerve in her body lived with a separate life." . . . The disappearance of love from her life hastens the conflicting demands, and only by converting her art to a commentary upon life can she hope for a measure of unity. In the last act of the play, after the manner of the Lady of Camellias, she takes the part of a betrayed woman whose lover never appears. Only in this masochistic act can art be given any relevance. Initially, Esther Kahn performed as a complement to her ego, a way of escaping from an environment that was indifferent to "performance" of any kind. Yet the best art is seen to be dissociated from the ego, and this can be accomplished only through the paradox of identifying being and doing.

This inverted pygmalionism means, of course, that self-renunciation becomes an anodyne for the conflicting claims of life and art. As this particular "Adventure" concludes, Esther is the pose of sainthood—the perfect expression of the self dying into art.

As one proceeds in his reading of the *Spiritual Adventures,* an awareness grows that even the characters' names are important to the general theme. Although **"A Prelude to Life"** makes a recurrent use of the narrative ego in the pronoun "I" through which Symons refers to his own youth, the names of the figures in each of the succeeding stories become progressively more abstract. From Esther Kahn through the allegorical Christian Trevalga and finally to Seaward Lackland, the youth of the penultimate story whose birth had taken place on a stormy night while his father was at sea, Symons seems to be progressively renouncing private identity in order that his figures might be that which they do. (pp. 106-07)

[The] negation of self either through the attenuation of the imagination or a voluntary self-destruction is a constant feature in the pilgrimages of Symons' artists. In each of the short stories there is a typical nineties figure who either functions as an artist or whose activity is analogous to creation. **"Peter Waydelin"** is precisely such a figure. The victim of a disease that claims his life at twenty-four, Waydelin, a painter of brutally realistic canvas, meets the narrator of the story at Bognor, where "nature deals with material so much in the manner of art." . . . He is fascinated by the endless dialectic between nature and the supernatural. Yet, even at their initial meeting, the narrator of the story is unsure whether Waydelin's ideas about art are indicative of a coherent theory or personal enslavement. For Waydelin, all artists commence their careers by seeing too much, and he favors substituting a reductive vision which atomizes experience so that the eye is trained to see each thing "single." Only in this way can beauty be humanized—can we avoid the necessity of "quot[ing] Turner to apologize for a sunset." . . . (p. 108)

Sometime later the narrator [clearly a persona of the Symons who also visited Russia in the middle of the summer] returns to find his friend ill in a dingy flat with a grotesque wife who ministers to her husband's every need. Waydelin has "fitted in theories with my facts; and that is how I came to paint my pictures." . . . The narrator becomes aware that "some obscure martyrdom has been going on", and it is clear that Peter Waydelin has begun to imitate his own art in an effort to free the ego from its imprisonment. Although the unusual circumstances of his death give **"Peter Waydelin"** a more ironical tone than either **"Esther Kahn"** or **"Christian Trevalga,"** the stages of the life pilgrimage are very similar. Using the mind to formalize aesthetic response, these artists inevitably find themselves imprisoned by self-consciousness. The expense of humanizing random sensation by structuring it is the discovery that the external world is but self-projection.

The fact that Waydelin at least partially wills his own deterioration becomes the index to his aesthetic crisis. Convinced that you have to die in order to be appreciated," . . . Waydelin literally controls the aesthetic response to his own death by requesting his wife's presence. As his last canvas, Waydelin paints his deformed wife's grief-stricken response to his own death, thus electing to compete with this painting by turning life into art. Such is the only means of "proving" his aesthetic on his own terms. At the same time, such a decision is the ultimate extension of his reductionist vision; one may see each thing "single" only by negating the fragmenting intelligence, achieving in the process a uniquely organic theory of the origins of art!

Each of Symons' *Spiritual Adventures* seems to gather up the themes of the preceding story, distancing it through the allegorical mode. What makes Waydelin's episode such a splendid example is the way in which it becomes almost an allegory of Decadence itself. Unable to plumb the depths of the grotesque with his palette, the painter organizes his life so as to achieve the necessary self-sacrifice. One of the more amazing features of this particular tale is its literalization of the masturbatory aesthetic of the *fin de siècle,* through which the alienated artist achieves at least a measure of integration. Having inherited the romantic awareness that the ideal woman of the imagination— those alluring Alastors and Epipsychidions—remain illusory precisely because they are projections of the ''self,'' the Decadents achieve a unique inversion. With full knowledge that the image projections are self-generative and hence as illusory as the ''self,'' many of the artists parody the convention. Rather than a static art object at the center of a sea of mutability in the wheel-like pattern so carefully noted by G. Robert Stange, the roles are reversed so that the mutable artist dies into the work of art. The painting itself then becomes the record of the limitation of the imagination. The similarities with Wilde's novel are striking. There, Hallward's portrait becomes the mutable, grotesque record of Dorian's self-reflexiveness. Like Peter Waydelin who vanishes survived only by a horribly ugly wife, Dorian Gray degenerates into the permanence of art which has become the sole bizarre record of self-sacrifice. Waydelin's final act, in a sense, appears as a metaphor for a process which began with self-parody and culminates in self-negation. It was to be a metaphor used often, and one suspects consciously, in the nineties.

This metaphoric process is translated into a broader theory of cultural rebirth involving the familiar figures of Dionysus and Apollo. For Peter Waydelin remarks that he is a devotee of Dionysus Zagreus, the Bacchic God who underwent self-mutilation on a descent into the nether world only to be refashioned as the eternally youthful Apollo. The myth was popular in the nineteenth century, particularly after Nietzsche used it as a literalization of the creative process in *The Birth of Tragedy.* There, the narcissistic nature of the loss of individuation is imaged as a self-negating activity involving at least a symbolic emasculation. Of course, Dionysus and Apollo are variant types of the same God—''doubles'' who alternate a yearly existence in sequential six-month tenures. Even in his mythic fantasies, Symons' artist mirrors his own divided sensibility. (pp. 108-10)

It is appropriate that in the final story [''**The Journal of Henry Luxulyan**''] Luxulyan should relate in all its intricacy the self being overwhelmed by the fragmentary nature of experience. In fact, fragments of preceding *Spiritual Adventures* find their way into Luxulyan's diaries, in his reminiscence of a love affair with a member of the Kahn family. At last, he writes only in order to ''give himself a sense of companionship'' . . . as a complement to self-fragmentation and a charismatic self-sacrifice to his ''double.'' With Luxulyan's lapse into insanity, his own sense of identification disappears, and the intrusion of the persona becomes a commentary upon the process by which a loss of individuation becomes the expense of artistic creation: ''I had so singularly little feeling of personality . . . I seem to have become so suddenly imprisoned, that I wonder if Balzac was right. The world, ideas, sensations, all are fluid, and I flow through them like a gondola carried along by the

current.'' . . . At least, with the absence of selfhood, Luxulyan literally burns with ''that gem-like flame'' that Pater used, not to describe the life of self-indulgence, but the transformation into a diaphanous figure, so common in the pictorial art of the nineties. He then exists as a cultural ''light,'' fulfilling the demands of his very name. (pp. 112-13)

Like his fictional Henry Luxulyan, Symons too lapses into schizophrenia symptomized by the same word repetition that is such a curious feature of Luxulyan's ''Journal.'' Language itself becomes but a mirror of its own genesis. This feature of the Decadent consciousness was by no means unique to Arthur Symons. Ernest Dowson falls in love with Adelaide Foltinowicz long after the innocent child has appeared as a motif in his art. Oscar Wilde comes to lead a double existence complete with the Hebraic-Hellenic pen name ''Sebastian Melmoth'' long after the ''double'' has been allegorized in *The Picture of Dorian Gray.* What seems to be at stake is the entire relationship between formal structure and psychological states; by synchronizing the two, the Decadents hoped to avoid the imprisonment of self by the structure of empirical reality. When Symons accompanied his last poetry, so heavily laden with the imagery of crucifixion and martyrdom, with the apologia of the saint and called it *Confessions: A Pathological Study,* he was fulfilling Wilde's dictum that ''life should imitate art'' rather than the other way around.

The structure of literature itself would not seem to have gone unaffected, for Symons' *Spiritual Adventures* belongs to a unique genre that became increasingly prevalent in the *fin-de-siècle.* Like the short stories of Ernest Dowson, the *Imaginary Portraits* of Walter Pater, and even, to a lesser extent, Joyce's ''The Dead,'' the tales are populated by aesthetes whose lives follow the same linear pattern. In order to humanize experience, they initially develop a reductionist aesthetic that fragments nature into its discrete ''moments.'' Many of Symons' critical essays from the same period reveal an effort to formulate a theory of art that would cross media-barriers; to fail at an aesthetic of mixed-media is to surrender to a concentration upon the ''facts of nature.'' Ultimately, the artistic self is unable to escape the threat of atomization, and what began as an aesthetic issue is resolvable only as a crisis of consciousness itself. At least one manifestation of the resulting pluralism is the appearance of the doppelgänger in so much late Victorian literature, ranging from Stevenson's *Dr. Jekyll and Mr. Hyde* to Beardsley's ''hair-line'' phase. Like Yeats, Symons became fascinated with the dance as the symbolic representation of a self-surrender that would achieve unity. In ''**The World as Ballet**,'' only dancing is capable of ''dissolv[ing] the will into slumber.''

Certainly, the transitional nature of a genre that exploits the conversion from life to art becomes a commentary upon the autobiographical sensibility of the Victorians. Commencing with an attempt to define the nature of consciousness, the Victorian autobiographical novel typically concludes by visualizing autobiography as art. In a sense, *The Portrait of an Artist as a Young Man* literalizes this shift, complete, of course, with a ten year frame. Like Arthur Symons' *Spiritual Adventures* that began with defining the ego [in ''**A Prelude to Life**''] and concludes with an aesthetic confession [''**The Journal of Henry Luxulyan**''], the journey that links Mill's *Autobiography* or Dickens' *David Copperfield* to Joyce's novel appears more or less continuous. (pp. 113-14)

Jan B. Gordon, ''The Dialogue of Life and Art in Arthur Symons' 'Spiritual Adventures','' in English

Literature in Transition *(copyright © 1969 Helga S. Gerber), Vol. 12, No. 3, 1969, pp. 105-17.*

JOHN M. MUNRO (essay date 1969)

[*Munro's* Arthur Symons *is a book-length introduction to Symons's life and works. In the following excerpt, Munro contends that Symons's chief value lies in his place in literary history: his influence and "the way [his career] exemplifies the archetypal Romantic pattern."*]

To say that the work of Arthur Symons has been undeservedly neglected is to invoke one of the most shopworn clichés of literary scholarship, but it is nonetheless true. Certainly he is not a great writer, and it is equally true that, after 1908, he published very little worthy of serious consideration. It is also true that, in spite of the breadth of his interests and the variety of subjects he wrote about, his range is exceedingly limited. This limitation was recognized by the reviewer of Symons' translations from Baudelaire when he pointed out in the *Times Literary Supplement* that, although Symons was ever mindful of the aspiration of all art to the condition of music, he ought to have looked further back than Pater to Plotinus, with whom the idea originated; for the Neo-Platonist had maintained that it was necessary for there to be "base clowns and indecent drunkards in perfect drama, because perfect drama was the revelation of the unity of the world, in and through its infinite variety." In Symons' world there are no "base clowns" and "indecent drunkards." His is a world from which all the raw, animal elements have been excluded, and he presents instead nervous, rose-tinted shadows, who caper suggestively in a perfumed and melancholy twilight—all pale reflections of himself.

Yet, in spite of obvious limitations, Symons did achieve a few things of permanent value. A number of his graceful lyrics, such as those from *Silhouettes* and *London Nights,* have passed into the standard repertoire of Victorian poetry anthologists. Some of his criticism, particularly his *Introduction to the Study of Robert Browning* and *The Symbolist Movement in Literature,* is both perceptive and sound, and even today may be read with profit by those who seek useful introductions to the writers concerned. His translation, notably from the French, is on the whole good but, in the case of Verlaine, excellent. And in *Spiritual Adventures* his perceptive investigations into human psychology in general and into the artistic sensibility in particular compare favorably with Pater's *Imaginary Portraits,* on which they were, in fact, modeled. (pp. 136-37)

Yet Symons' reputation must rest less on his own work . . . than on the influence he exerted on others. And when one considers that Eliot, Pound, and Yeats all spoke highly of him, while Joyce also was heavily indebted to him, his importance cannot readily be underestimated. The fact that he bridged the chasm between the Victorians and some of the greatest figures of the twentieth-century literary scene is also worth remembering, for it helps us to place the 1890's more accurately in the history of the development of English literature. Symons' literary career, perhaps more clearly than that of any of his contemporaries, shows us that the artistic sensibility did not go into hibernation at the end of the nineteenth century to reawaken somewhere around the time of World War I; it was, in fact, very much alive all the time.

Perhaps the most fascinating aspect of Symons' career, however, is the way it exemplifies the archetypal Romantic pattern, particularly as it is manifest in the careers of Wordsworth and Coleridge. Both these writers sought transcendence through an imaginative contemplation of the outward forms of nature; both at one stage in their lives penetrated to that visionary ecstasy which they had been seeking; and both experienced a falling away from Paradise in their later years. Symons too followed the Promethean pattern, mounting to the heavens in an attempt to steal the sacred fire, only to be cast down and chained to the rock of insanity and the subsequent debilitation of his artistic faculties. Wordsworth and Coleridge also paid for their vision, it is true, the one being condemned to spin out the remainder of his days in the composition of pedestrian literary exercises, the other in turgid rationalizations of the very force which had enabled him to perceive the visions of his earlier poetry.

For Symons the Gods reserved a fate more cruel, a living death of remembrance of things past without the consolation of knowing that at least he had "fed on honey-dew, and drunk the milk of Paradise." Like Berlioz, about whom Symons had written in *The Saturday Review,* Symons' "failure" was like the fall of Icarus; his wings melted from him at a great height, and there was no one to lift him after his fall. His tireless ambition carried him again and again into the unattainable skies, and again and again he felt under him the hardness of the inhospitable earth. (pp. 137-38)

John M. Munro, in his Arthur Symons *(copyright ©1969 by Twayne Publishers; reprinted with the permission of Twayne Publishers, a Division of G. K. Hall & Co., Boston), Twayne, 1969, 174 p.*

IAN FLETCHER (essay date 1970)

[*Fletcher's article is an exploration of the development of the motif of the dancer in Symons's poetry. Fletcher attempts to show that Symons influenced Yeats as well as being influenced by him in the use of the dancer as a symbolic representation of the function of art.*]

In the early 1920s, in one of his autobiographical fantasias, Ford Madox Ford made this high claim for the influence of Arthur Symons on what was then the 'forward' movement in English poetry:

> Consider the gap there would be in a whole *genre,* if Mr. Symons had never written. I might call him, rather than myself, the doyen of free verse. . . .

[As] a man who had himself lived through the gap he was talking of, the gap in English poetry between late Pre-Raphaelitism and early Imagism, [Ford] could speak, in this instance, with some authority. Like all men who live through such a gap, Ford could feel it, but not explain it; though he instinctively, and rightly, felt that Symons's influence supplied a hidden continuity. We on the other hand have not lived through the gap, but, historically distant from it, feel we can explain it. (p. 46)

Much of Symons's work can be grasped in terms of tensions between his early revivalism (vividly depicted in *Seaward Lackland,* one of the exercises in autobiographical exploration contained in *Spiritual Adventures,* that were themselves part of his search for an identity) and impressionism; between naturalism and the occultism of Yeats in the years when they particularly associated. Symons rejected revivalism, for its group fervours were related to that 'metaphysics' Pater had taught him to distrust. This rejection marked the first stage of his alienation: Seaward Lackland, the young Methodist lay preacher in *Spir-*

itual Adventure never actually dedicates himself to God in the sight of the community, but oppressed by the sense of sin determines to cut himself off from man and God by committing the unnamed sin against the Holy Ghost, though insisting that his action is determined by love of God: a parable of the poet as rebel mystic.

Basing his life on Pater's *Renaissance* was to intensify Symons's isolation and self-consciousness. The impressionist pays a high price for the freedom of aesthetic intensity: all sense of neighbourliness, of life beyond the veil, is dissolved: 'each mind keeping as a solitary prisoner its own dream of a world'. For Pater, the only vehicle of communication lay in the senses, for they were all that men possessed in common, and it was finally through Anglo-Catholic ritual that he had attempted to redeem himself from the 'flux'. Symons was not attracted to high ecclesiastical gestures: the 'flux' with its evasive glitter absorbed him, and the dance, stylized, self-conscious, provocative, came to represent for him the perfect emblem of life in the modern city, for it dramatized his own isolation. Yet through his association with Yeats, the dance later became for Symons not spectacle merely, but participation, and, in some sense, religious.

It was towards naturalism that Symons first reacted and this note dominates his first book of poems, *Days and Nights*. . . . The themes here are mainly contemporary and urban. Symons enjoys extreme situations and his experience of nonconformity provides material that is treated in the melodramatic spirit of Henry Arthur Jones. Elsewhere, he indulges in the religious pornography his non-conformist background made voluptuous for him: a woman pleads before the crucifix and then resigns herself to her lover's embraces; in *Red Bredbury's End*, a dying man is anxious to see a minister, but his son will not allow it, for that would involve the confession of a murder in which both father and son are implicated. That Symons should turn to prose because of such psychological casuistries, was one of Pater's suggestions in a review of *Days and Nights* largely through doubts about the capacity of modern poets to control contemporary data. *Vie de Bohème,* however, is one of Symons's successes in precisely that field. . . . The shrug in the voice: 'the smiles / grew chilly as the best spring evenings do,' the confidence of tone, the suggestion of nuances, the ease of the topical references, all suggest the 'new' poetry of twenty years later. *Vie de Bohème* stands half-way between Browning and Eliot, and like the early Eliot owes something to Laforgue's *Complaintes* (1886). Still, though one admits all this, sentimentalized irony remains the note rather than Laforgue's cold frivolity: the values are not superbly mocked, other values are not suggested in Eliot's manner by trenchant omission.

In a prevalent naturalist context, another poem, *Flos Florum* . . . , strikingly prefigures Yeats's Rose poems of the 90s. Rhythm and vocabulary here are Yeatsian, though there is no symbolism and the moral is a Paterian *carpe diem*. . . . (pp. 48-50)

In 1889, Symons paid his first visit to Paris and his second book *Silhouettes* . . . , as its title indicates, reveals a new approach to contemporary life: the black and white of poetry. By 1891, he had become a member of the Rhymers' Club and was on familiar terms with Yeats. Yeats's *Autobiographies* record one of Symons's remarks at this time: 'we are concerned only with impressions'; but the word is ambiguous. It looks back to Pater's *Conclusion* to the *Renaissance;* but when the poet applies the criteria of Pater's *Preface* the range of the word extends to something that suggests analogues from painting:

> analyse, and spearate from its adjuncts, the virtue by which a picture, a fair personality in life, or a book, produces this impression . . . [the] end is reached when he has disengaged that virtue and noted it as a chemist notes some natural element.

Much of *Silhouettes* can be read as a delicate set of Paterian exercises in distinguishing appearance from reality; reality consisting simply in these 'beautiful changes', the chance integrities of light, colour and mood. What survive from *Silhouettes* are the images. . . . Yet Symons cannot maintain this role of impassive recorder, like an imagist poet; he must comment, often banally, on the order invoked. It is only later that acute visual effects cohere with the creation of mood indirectly through rhythm, so that the poet can be present indirectly. For, by this time, Symons had begun to come under the influence of symbolism, in the sweeter and scaled down version of Verlaine, Verlaine's somnambulistic rhythms which promised the lyrical dissolution of that 'discourse' the Rhymers so detested. *Dieppe— Grey and Green* is one of the successful silhouettes and, dedicated to Sickert, attempts to reproduce that master's muted palette. . . . Still, as Wilbur Urban remarked, Symons's grey 'epiphanies,' though sensed through a variety of scenes and actions, remain fatally subdued to the 'achromatic thinness of a mood'. The divination of beauty in odd places is limited by the narrowness of the temperament that divines.

London Nights . . . is unified as a volume by the capital itself established as a fugitive set of aspects, made and remade every night and morning. Effect of civilized corruption, fog collaborates vividly with gaslamps hanging 'like rotting fruit' to produce a momentary illusion of the beautiful. Within this world, Symons searches for identity. . . . (pp. 51-2)

His life was artificial enough at this time, with its constant playgoing, visits to Music Halls, circular discussions of literature under the coved ceilings of smoky-crocketed public-houses. And the beauty of artifice and illusion out of doors had its counterparts within, for it is in *London Nights* that Symons's obsession with dancers and the dance begins. Yet the dance here is essentially a spectacle for soliary enjoyment, on the level of the 'fatal art of the acrobat'. *Javanese Dancers,* his first poem on this central topic, was written as early as 1889, after his first visit to Paris. The hypnotism of the dance is cleverly evoked through the metre. . . . Though some sinister sacerdotalism is hinted at, it is with the routine coolness of the anthropologist.

It was during Symons's visit to Paris in 1892 that he discovered the European equivalents of these ritual dancers: Nini-Patte-en-l'Air, La Goulue, and La Mèlinite, with their ominous solipsist quality:

> Enigmatically smiling
> Back to a shadow in the night.

But they are also valued for their 'science of concupiscence' and this excitingly contrasts with a self-analysing gravity. As a contemporary remarked:

> Apparently (Symons) set out quite early in life to shock himself; and I cannot believe that he has ever failed. Indeed, I have seen him walking about Saint Martin's Lane in a mackintosh,

shuddering at the depths he has discovered in his soul: a soul as deep as a soup-plate.

Symons was always trailing himself round corners to catch himself at some trivial vice, trying to assimilate himself to his own myth of the 90s, and he preserves a naïvely caressing attitude to the image of himself established at this time: a nocturnal beast let loose in the Strand. His real position is rather the inverted sacramentalist's (he often writes on the theme of Amor as God of Death, 'the kiss of the spouse, gustation of God, and ingression into the divine shadow' equated ironically or blasphemously with 'the little death' of physical love: there is perhaps some influence of Wagner's _Tristan_). . . . Yet it is not merely mock-innocence with lubricious gestures that excites Symons. In an article written in 1897, he associates his Parisian dancers with the decadent myth of _chute_ and _finis latinorum_. Nini Patte-en-l'Air's cold art transforms her into 'a Maenad of the Decadence', as she dances with 'a sort of learned fury'. Yet she is hardly a Maenad, for her art is painfully erudite, it is not 'free' in the same sense as the dancing of Jane Avril or Loie Fuller. . . . [He] prefers ballet with its cross-flare of gaslights and footlights, its painted figures and its diaphanous but somewhat mechanical order (the dancers of Degas rather than those of Moreau). Ballet's illusion mimics the illusion of life. But the 'free' dancer does not depend on scenery, music, dramatic interest; she depends merely on her own body, and her dance can be readily associated with possession by god or demon. To admire the 'free' dance is to pass from 'decadent' admiration of artifice to symbolist recognition of Mallarmé's 'l'incorporation visuelle de l'idée'. From a frivolous spectacle, the dance was transformed for Symons into something quasi-religious. (pp. 52-4)

[The] more we examine Symons's work, the more we realize that the 1890s are not, as they are commonly supposed to be, a self-enclosed period, but a continuum which must be re-enacted if we are to 'distance' the 'modern' movement in English poetry.

The sad later history of Symons is the sad iteration of old themes: he could never get beyond what he had learned in the 1890s. In the Autumn of 1908, he suffered his own 'crack-up', so identifying himself with the 'Tragic Generation' whose legend he had helped to create, and all development was at an end. That delicate mechanism, so long engaged in distinguishing reality from appearance, now helplessly confused them. His account of his amnesia and flight, _Confessions_, is one of the classics of madness (particularly as it appeared in _Life and Letters_, purified by Desmond MacCarthy of its literary incrustations). Even in the labyrinths of madness, as Yeats remarks in one of his letters, Symons talked sanely of literature. And in the mental hospital, he was hounded still by his dancers: a learned Greek professor confined there would exhaust himself with Dionysiac leaps and monotonous stamping, which he insisted was the rhythm of the angels. When Symons emerged, after a year and a half's confinement, only his past was left to him; his work became a protracted parasitism on that past and in 1920 he reverted to the theme of the dancer for the last time in faded tones. Yet though criticism will have its icy points against his work, the wreckage is full of glittering hints. (pp. 59-60)

> Ian Fletcher, _"Explorations and Recoveries—II: Symons, Yeats and the Demonic Dance,"_ in London Magazine (© London Magazine 1970), Vol. 7, June, 1970, pp. 46-60 [the excerpts of Symons's poetry used here were originally published in his Poems

(reprinted by permission of William Heinemann Ltd.), Heinemann, 1902].*

KERRY POWELL (essay date 1977)

[Powell considers the subject of aesthetic escapism that was also examined in Paul Elmer More's essay excerpted above.]

In his discussions of French authors—from Gérard to Maurice Maeterlinck—Symons invests in each some of the mysticism he has to expend in [_The Symbolist Movement_]. He views Gérard de Nerval, in effect, as sharing the outlook of Baudelaire's "Correspondances" in which seemingly antagonistic elements of life—light and dark, spirit and sense, infinity and the finite—are knit together in some mysterious unity. Of Gérard's account of his madness, _La Rêve et la Vie_ (which became the model for Symons' _Confessions,_ years later, after his own mental collapse), Symons decides that the author simply had gazed at the "light" until he was blinded and "realized that central secret of the mystics . . . 'As things are below, so are they above'.". . . In the _Axel_ of Villiers de l'Isle-Adam he recognizes the spiritual realm as the main concern of the dramatist, and in the lyrics of Verlaine and his protegé Rimbaud the physical world is perceived, Symons believes, with such intensity that the experience becomes spiritual "by some strange alchemical operation of the brain.". . . Moreover Verlaine's motto, "rien que la nuance," represents an effort to reject mere descriptive rhetoric and introduce a poetry of evocative suggestion focusing on "the impression of the moment" and forming _"romances sans paroles."_ . . . Joris Karl Huysmans (obviously Symons is more concerned with the author of _La Cathédral_ than of _A Rebours_) is regarded approvingly as one who expresses "the affirmation of an eternal, minute, intricate almost invisible life, which runs through the whole universe.". . .

Notwithstanding Symons' praise of the mystical component in Symbolism, his book certainly manifests a less confident tone in this regard than we have seen so far. Like D'Albert in Gautier's _Mademoiselle de Maupin_, Symons in his own quest for transcendental significance is ultimately swamped by frustration and doubt in spite of his stated conviction that, for others if not for himself, the search has been successful. . . . For example, while on one hand maintaining that Gérard de Nerval's madness lights up the hidden links of a cosmic unity in which "un Dieu caché" can be discovered, Symons also points out that Gérard was "very tired of life" (how so, if life is a treasure-house of divine correspondences in which the poet, albeit through symbol, alone possesses the key?).

Symons' analysis of Axel, like Villiers' own characterization of his dramatic hero, assigns to the titanic figure as much disgust for life as enthusiasm for some ineffable spiritual reality. So far does Symons carry this perception, indeed, that he underscores Villiers' recognition of the "illusion" of materiality and his belief that "it must be the whole effort of one's consciousness to escape from its entanglements, to dominate it, or to ignore it, and one's art must be the building of an ideal world beyond its access.". . . But while Axel rejects life as an illusion, Symons leaves unsettled the question whether the proud young Count of Auersperg—or Symons himself, for that matter—regards the artist as attempting anything more than the improvisation of a competing illusion, more attractive perhaps, but no truer, than life itself. The language is less evasive with regard to Jules LaForgue, who Symons believes "has constructed his own world" wherein "frivolity becomes an escape from the arrogance of a still more temporary mode of being, the world as it appears to the sober majority."... Apparent in this estimate of LaForgue's poetry, with its Pierrots and "fantastic puppets," is Symons' eager approval of escape from daily reality without his pausing long to inquire whether the haven one escapes into is only the author's own fanciful illusion. And Symons has to acknowledge—as anyone must who reads Maeterlinck—that for this "mystic," at least, the unseen reality beyond our daily routine is frequently "a thing merely or mainly terrifying,"... so that, in effect, one tends the inner light at the risk of being terrified by what it illuminates. Maeterlinck's dramas, where "he has shown us people huddled at a window, out of which they are almost afraid to look, or beating at a door, the opening of which they dread," form a powerful argument, if only implicitly, for the need of escape even if at the expense of ignoring physical fact and spiritual reality alike.

At last, in Symons' "Conclusion," comes a passage in which the critic recoils in terror from the "unknown"—surprisingly, since in "The Author's Introduction" he described with seeming composure the mission of the artist to articulate, through symbols, the "unseen reality" and the "unknown sea." Man's salvation, however, now lies not in fashioning symbols wherewith to express and apprehend the unseen world, but in cloaking with illusion this and any other form of reality and in blinding himself to the facts of his own situation. The artist thus provides escape from reality—from the shadowy and "baseless fabric" of our physical existence and the vast, ominous spiritual darkness which surrounds us on all sides—and offers mere forgetfulness as the only remedy for what and where we are and for the momentous, disquieting fact of our mortality. "Our only chance" writes Symons, "lies in the measure of our success in shutting the eyes of the mind and deadening its sense of hearing, and dulling the keenness of its apprehension of the unknown."... One will encounter nowhere a more emphatic renunciation of all that Symons seemed to endorse, at the beginning of the book, when he invoked with almost religious reverence the words "Mysticism" and "Symbolism." He continues: "To live through a single day with that overpowering consciousness of our real position, which in the moments in which alone it mercifully comes, is like blinding light ... would drive any man out of his senses."... (pp. 158-60)

Nothing makes the burden of human life supportable, Symons argues, but "the compromises of our intelligence," for "We can forget so much, we can bear suspense with so fortunate an evasion of its real issues."... Art, we are told, represents just such a "compromise of intelligence," for with regard to death and our anticipation of it, "we find an escape from its sterile annihilating reality in many dreams, in religion, passion, art; each a forgetfulness, each a symbol of creation.... Through art, in other words, as in those other nondiscursive phenomena—religion and passion—we make symbols whereby we transcend the spectacle of material existence. But what, specifically, has been thus symbolized? "Creation," Symons asserts; and if we pause to wonder what, actually, has been created, Symons assures us in the same breath: "forgetfulness." The symbol, therefore, rather than providing mystical insights, has become a means by which the self acts out its own illusions and finds temporary refuge from the terrors of life—and death. (p. 161)

To understand Symons' *The Symbolist Movement,* then, we need not simply to trace his arguments but to be aware that for the author art is a "symbolic" performance whose goal is

escape and forgetfulness of objective reality through illusion. In spite of the book's arguments for a mystical Symbolism, its real utility for Symons, as the "Conclusion" aptly demonstrates, is to provide a stage whereon he can play the role of a mystic, much as Dorian Gray undertakes the same part, for a season only, in Wilde's novel. For Symons, for Wilde, and for other so-called Decadents, literature is more importantly an exercise in dramatic self-projection, and the symbol, like Symons' bewitching music hall dancer, functions mainly to deaden impressions of the everyday world and renew the artist's heart and mind in a realm of almost solipsistic illusion. *The Symbolist Movement* thus was written by a man weary of external reality, but who had nothing healthy or substantive with which to replace it; he turns from materiality to encounter, instead of God or an Over-Soul, either mere vacuity or, perhaps, a spiritual order even more ominous than the natural one he has renounced. The symbol, no longer a medium for eternity looking through time, as for Coleridge and Carlyle, becomes now, above all, a charm for dreaming oneself into forgetfulness; instead of providing "some embodiment and revelation of the Infinite," it clears "a path or temporary escape from the vicissitudes of life and death alike. (p. 166)

Kerry Powell, "Arthur Symons, Symbolism, and the Aesthetics of Escape," in Renascence *(© copyright, 1977, Marquette University Press), Vol. XXIX, No. 3, Spring, 1977, pp. 157-67.*

LAWRENCE W. MARKERT (essay date 1982)

[*Markert discusses the influence of Charles Lamb's critical writings on Symons's aesthetic theories.*]

R. V. Johnson, in his essay, "Aesthetic Traits of Charles Lamb," has touched in general on some of the significant ways in which Lamb anticipates late nineteenth century aestheticism, particularly in terms of the inevitable separation of life and art that became so crucial during this period. Lamb's influence, however, is especially strongly felt within the context of dramatic literature and theory; for, as Lamb rightly saw, on the stage the conflict between real people and imaginary lives becomes paramount....

In relation to the dominant dramatic mode of this time, the discordancy Lamb describes is quite significant. Realistic stage conventions disallow for an imaginative and aesthetic presentation which, as Lamb implicitly states, is necessary to adequately depict great drama, especially the works of Shakespeare. Arthur Symons, in turn, takes up Lamb's observations about the theatre and develops a theory of dramatic presentation which is clearly allied with the artistic ideals of aestheticism....

The influence of Lamb on Symons is, no doubt, due in part to Pater's prior appreciation of him. (p. 147)

Symons continues this same line of thinking in his own appreciation of Lamb as an aesthetic critic. Throughout his essays on drama, acting and dramatic theory, he continually alludes to Lamb in order to focus his arguments, particularly in relation to his own concern with the creation of beauty. He abstracts from Lamb a number of traits appropriate to aestheticism. In **"Sicilian Actors,"** for example, he refers to Lamb's famous essay, "On the Tragedies of Shakespeare, Considered with Reference to their Fitness for Stage Representation," in order to evolve a discussion of whether the beauty of a play, associated with the imaginative world its language is able to evoke, is not lost in the stage production. . . . Realistic imitation is, for Lamb, the lowest form of art, if art at all. Whether a play of Shakespeare's can be adequately performed depends on whether the quality of the production is dominated by the "corporal dimension" rather than the imaginative. In **"The Price of Realism"** Symons elaborates much the same point, criticizing the modern anti-artistic endeavor to be real. . . . (p. 148)

Symons always seems to lean in the direction of pure aestheticism, but he also tries, often, to balance aestheticism with an equal interest in reality. There is a sense in which a purely disembodied voice would become, to use Ortega Y Gasset's term "dehumanized." In **"Literary Drama"** Symons describes a less aloof aestheticism, one more aptly defined as aestheticized reality. Ibsen, therefore, figures significantly:

> The poetic drama, if it is to become a genuine thing, must be conceived as drama, and must hold us, as a play of Ibsen's holds us, by the sheer interest of its representation of life. It must live, and it must live in poetry, as in its natural atmosphere. The verse must speak as straight as prose, but with a more beautiful voice. . . .

The confusion implicit in this passage is somewhat inevitable. As Jan B. Gordon [see excerpt above] says about dance, Symons' ideal is to "aestheticize the randomness of human existence, to transmute life into artifice without losing the qualities of either."

Other aspects of Lamb's theories equally find their way into Symons' discussion of an overall art of the theatre. Lamb, as we have seen, centers his argument on a contrast between imagination and the limiting characteristics of stage presentation. (pp. 149-50)

[The] objection Lamb makes involves the intrusion of too much life. How much body, how much surface reality, should be mixed with what is the imaginative and artistic essence of the work? The intellectual, and even the moral, attributes of the drama are identified with its artistic qualities. Reading is a form of experience which allows for an almost ideal appreciation of literature, whereas viewing a play seems too harshly to tie us down to the surface characteristic of reality. He continues this observation in "Barrenness of the Imaginative Faculty": "By a wise falsification, the great master of painting got at their true conclusions; by not showing the actual appearances, that is, all that was to be seen at any given moment by an indifferent eye, but only what the eye might be supposed to see in the doing or suffering of some portentous action.". . . The artist creates the ideal circumstances so that the spectator may experience the essential action of the work, and this creation involves a wise falsification of the real. In other words, as Lamb says from another point of niew, when we see a play produced within the tradition of realistic stage conventions "we have only materialized and brought down a fine vision to the standard of flesh and blood.". . . Symons makes much the same point in **"Pantomime and the Poetic Drama"**:

> All drama, until one comes to poetic drama, is an imitation of life, as a photograph is an imitation of life; for this reason it can have, at best, but a secondary kind of imaginative existence, the appeal of the mere copy. To the poetic drama nature no longer exists; or rather, nature becomes, as it has been truely said nature should become to the painter, a dictionary. Here

is choice, selection, combination: the supreme interference of beauty.

It is evident, in fact, that both Lamb and Symons develop their aesthetic ideals based upon a belief in the value of "the supreme interference of beauty." (p. 151)

> *Lawrence W. Markert, "The Art of the Theatre: Charles Lamb, Arthur Symons and Edward Gordon Craig," in* English Literature in Transition *(copyright © 1982 Helga S. Gerber), Vol. 25, No. 3, 1982, pp. 147-57.**

ADDITIONAL BIBLIOGRAPHY

Atherton, James S. "The Structural Books." In his *The Books at the Wake: A Study of Literary Allusions in James Joyce's "Finnegans Wake,"* pp. 27-58. New York: The Viking Press, 1960.
> Discusses the use Joyce made of some of Symons's critical theories when writing *Finnegans Wake*.

Beckson, Karl, and Munro, John M. "Symons, Browning and the Development of the Modern Aesthetic." *Studies in English Literature, 1500-1900* X (1970): 687-99.
> Examination of Symons's *An Introduction to the Study of Robert Browning*. The authors point out how observations that Symons made in his *Study of Browning* and reiterated in *The Symbolist Movement in Literature* helped to shape modern aesthetic theory.

Burdett, Osbert. "The Poetry of the Period" and "The Prose Writers." In his *The Beardsley Period: An Essay in Perspective*, pp. 154-92, 193-247. New York: Boni and Liveright, 1925.
> Examines Symons's work in the context of the fin de siècle period.

Charlesworth, Barbara. "Arthur Symons." In her *Dark Passages: The Decadent Consciousness in Victorian Literature*, pp. 96-119. Madison and Milwaukee: The University of Wisconsin Press, 1965.
> Biocritical study of Symons's *Spiritual Adventures*.

Gibbons, Tom. "Modernism in Poetry: The Debt to Arthur Symons." *The British Journal of Aesthetics* 13, No. 1 (Winter 1973): pp. 47-60.
> Examines the influence that Symons's critical views had on W. B. Yeats, T. S. Eliot, and Ezra Pound, and on the development of modern poetry.

Gordon, Jan B. "The Danse Macabre of Arthur Symons's 'London Nights'." *Victorian Poetry* 9, No. 4 (Winter 1971): pp. 429-43.
> An examination of Symons's use of the metaphor of the dance. Gordon also attempts to construct a psychological portrait of Symons based on an analysis of his aesthetic principles.

Gribble, Francis. "The Pose of Mr. Arthur Symons." *The Fortnightly Review* LXXXIV, No. CCCCXCIX (July 1908): pp. 127-36.
> Explains the undercurrent of escapism in Symons's aesthetic theories.

Harris, Wendell V. "Identifying the Decadent Fiction of the Eighteen Nineties." *English Literature in Transition* 5, No. 5, (1962): pp. 1-13.*
> Attempts to identify the distinguishing features of decadent literature.

Holdworth, R. V. Introduction to *Arthur Symons: Poetry and Prose*, by Arthur Symons, edited by R. V. Holdworth, pp. 9-24. Manchester, England: Carcanet Press, 1974.
> Discussion of Symons's poetry and his role in the decadent movement.

Lhombreaud, Roger. *Arthur Symons: A Critical Biography*. London: Unicorn Press, 1963, 333 p.
> Contains many excerpts from Symons's letters. The biographical material is more substantive than the critical observations.

Pater, Walter. "A Poet with Something to Say." In his *Sketches and Reviews*, pp. 134-41. New York: Boni and Liveright, 1919.
    Review of Symons's *Days and Nights*. Pater compares Symons's poetry with Robert Browning's.

Starkie, Enid. "The Yellow Nineties." In her *From Gautier to Eliot: The Influence of France on English Literature, 1851-1939*, pp. 101-28. London: Hutchinson and Co., 1960.
    A general investigation of "the prevalence and extent of the influence of France on English literature, between the Second Empire and the Second World War." Starkie credits Symons's *The Symbolist Movement in Literature* with "guiding many people towards French literature for the first time."

Urban, Walter Marshall. "Arthur Symons and Impressionism." *The Atlantic Monthly*. 114, No. 3 (Sept. 1914): pp. 384-93.
    Discussion of the impressionistic detachment of appearance from reality in Symons's work.

(Count) Leo (Lev Nikolaevich) Tolstoy

1828-1910

(Also transliterated as Lyof; also Nikolayevich; also Tolstoi, Tolstoj, Tolstoï) Russian novelist, short story and novella writer, essayist, dramatist, and critic.

Tolstoy is regarded as one of the greatest novelists in the history of world literature. His *Voina i mir (War and Peace)* and *Anna Karenina* are almost universally considered as all-encompassing documents of human existence and supreme examples of the realistic novel. Commentary on these novels frequently mentions Tolstoy's feat of successfully animating his fiction with the immediacy and variousness of life. Particularly esteemed are his insightful examinations of psychology and society, along with the religious and philosophical issues which occupied him later in his career.

Tolstoy was born and lived throughout his life on his family estate near Moscow. After attending the University of Kazan, he returned to the estate and continued his education through personal study. He later served in the army in the Caucasus, at this time working on his first novel, *Detstvo (Childhood)*. This work gained notice in Russian literary circles, and elicited favorable reaction from Ivan Turgenev and Fyodor Dostoevsky. The novel also displays autobiographical elements that would come to dominate Tolstoy's later work. Short stories like "Nabey" ("A Raid") were the literary result of his experiences in the Caucasus, and his military service in the Crimean War is chronicled in the Sevastopol sketches. Subsequent short stories and short novels, including "Dva gusara" ("Two Hussars"), "Tri smerti" ("Three Deaths"), and *Kazaki (The Cossacks)*, reveal a more characteristic concern with issues of morality and the ideal of simple ways of life untainted by the complexity and temptations of society.

War and Peace has often been called the greatest novel ever written, both for the grandeur of its conception and the vividness of its plot and characterizations. Commentators point out that this work does not restrict itself to a single hero or point of view but ranges over all strata of human affairs, its subject being the whole of life. Tolstoy's characters are both realistically individualized figures and representatives of human types. From historical theory Tolstoy borrowed the idea of "the great man" in order to refute the notion that world events are primarily influenced by a few powerful individuals. For this theory he substituted his own conclusion that human life is determined by natural law and is not subject to the will of individuals, who in essence have no free choice. The passages of *War and Peace* in which Tolstoy elaborates his historical concepts are thought by some critics to be the weakest parts of the novel.

Because *War and Peace* intricately examines the lives of many unrelated characters, early critics characterized the novel as disjointed. While later critics have perceived a greater unity in *War and Peace* than previously supposed, most agree that Tolstoy's next work, *Anna Karenina*, displays a more purposeful structure. Henry James called these novels "loose, baggy monsters" of stylelessness, but Tolstoy stated of *Anna Karenina* ". . . I am very proud of its architecture—its vaults are joined so that one cannot even notice where the keystone is."

Evidence has shown that both of Tolstoy's most important works went through numerous reworkings and revisions, and critics are now more likely to emphasize Tolstoy's structural subtleties and stylistic nuances. Thematically, *Anna Karenina* parallels its heroine's moral and social conflicts with Constantine Levin's internal struggle to find meaning and guidance for his life. Levin's struggle is often said to be an embodiment of Tolstoy's moral dilemma.

But *Anna Karenina* reflects only the beginning of Tolstoy's crisis of meaning. In *Ispoved (A Confession)* he outlined a spiritual upheaval that caused him to question the basis of his existence. His attempt at a solution to this crisis took the form of a radical Christianity whose doctrines ultimately included nonresistance to evil and total abstinence from sex. The artistic repercussions of his conversion are spelled out in *Chto takoe iskusstvo (What Is Art?)*. The major concern of this essay is to distinguish bogus art, which he called an elitist celebration of aesthetics, from universal art, which successfully "infects" its recipient with the highest sentiment an artist can transmit— that of religious feeling. This conception of art led Tolstoy to dismiss most of history's greatest creators, including William Shakespeare and Richard Wagner, and to repudiate all of his own previous work save for two short stories. During this phase of his career Tolstoy began writing his many moral and theological tracts, for which he was eventually excommunicated. His pamphleteering on social, political, and economic subjects also resulted in the censorship of his work by the government.

While critics have traditionally granted Tolstoy's post-conversion writings a lesser stature than those of the earlier phase, many of these works have an artistic worth and interest in their own right. At this point in his career, Tolstoy was concerned with producing two types of fiction: simple tales written in a folk tradition for uneducated readers and more literary works focusing on his moral preoccupations of this period. The folktales, such as "Brazhe iepko, a bozhe krepko" ("Evil Allures but Good Endures"), were designed as examples of "universal art" and have often been praised for delivering their didactic point in an artful manner. Much the same estimation has been accorded Tolstoy's literary fiction of this time, including *Smert Ivana Ilyicha* (*The Death of Ivan Ilyich*) and *Kreitserova sonata* (*The Kreutzer Sonata*). If the moral stance of these fictional tracts on death and sex has been criticized as simplistic or severe, the two works have also been considered among the best examples of Tolstoy's art of storytelling. Of *The Kreutzer Sonata*, Anton Chekhov wrote: "You will hardly find anything as powerful in seriousness of conception and beauty of execution." However, Tolstoy's longest work of his post-conversion period and his last major novel, *Voskresenie* (*Resurrection*), is considered far less successful than the early masterpieces *War and Peace* and *Anna Karenina*. Although Tolstoy's genius for description and characterization are still evident in this work, the intrusion of social and moral issues is regarded as detrimental to the novel's artistic value. Among the later novels, *Khadzhi Murat* (*Hadji Murád*) is more often viewed as the work which shows the extent and endurance of Tolstoy's narrative power.

During his later period Tolstoy also produced a number of dramatic works in an attempt to express his post-conversion ideas in a genre outside fiction. Like many of his other works, these dramas are often highly regarded for their vivid and compelling sense of realism, and for the sincere and sometimes overwhelming urgency of the author's concerns. The chief work among these plays is *Vlast tmy* (*The Power of Darkness*). The somber action of the drama—adultery, murder, religious torment—culminates in the redeeming vision of Christian faith which was a spiritual focus of the elder Tolstoy. Bernard Shaw called *The Power of Darkness* "a true tragedy," while describing Tolstoy's other dramas as "terrible but essentially comedic" in their dissection of a subject through methods of satire and almost superhuman powers of analysis. In the social comedy *Plody prosvesh cheniya* (*The Fruits of Enlightenment*), the object of Tolstoy's criticism is aristocratic society, and in the unfinished drama *I svet vo tme svetit* (*The Light That Shines in Darkness*) it is the author's own life. The latter play is of particular interest for Tolstoy's view of his spiritual conversion and its effect on the people around him.

As a religious and ethical thinker Tolstoy has been criticized for the extremism, and sometimes the absurdity, of his ideas. However, he has also been admired for the gigantism of his ambition to discover absolute laws governing humanity's ethical and spiritual obligations amid the psychological and social complexities of the world. Whatever form Tolstoy's doctrines took, they were always founded on his expansive humanitarianism and based on one of the most intensive quests for wisdom in human history. Although Tolstoy ultimately believed that art should serve a religious and ethical code, he himself serves primarily as a model of the consummate artist, and his two greatest works are exemplary of the nature and traditions of the modern realistic novel.

(See also *TCLC*, Vol. 4; *Contemporary Authors*, Vol. 104; and *Something About the Author*, Vol. 26.)

PRINCIPAL WORKS

Detstvo (novel) 1852
  [*Childhood* published in *Childhood and Youth*, 1862]
Otrochestvo (novel) 1854
  [*Boyhood* published in *Childhood, Boyhood, Youth*, 1886]
Sevastopolskiye rasskazy. 2 vols. (sketches) 1855-56
  [*Sebastopol*, 1887]
Yunost (novel) 1857
  [*Youth* published in *Childhood and Youth*, 1862]
Semeinoe schaste (novel) 1859
  [*Family Happiness*, 1888]
Kazaki (novel) 1863
  [*The Cossacks*, 1878]
Polikushka (novel) 1863
  [*Polikouchka*, 1888]
Voina i mir (novel) 1869
  [*War and Peace*, 1886]
Anna Karenina (novel) 1877
  [*Anna Karenina*, 1886]
Ispoved (essay) 1882
  [*A Confession*, 1885]
V chiom moya vera (essay) 1884
  [*What I Believe*, 1885]
Smert Ivana Ilyicha (novella) 1886
  [*Iván Ilyitch* published in *Iván Ilyitch, and Other Stories*, 1887; also published as *The Death of Ivan Iliitch*, 1888]
Vlast tmy (drama) 1888
  [*The Dominion of Darkness*, 1888; also published as *The Power of Darkness* in *Plays*, 1910]
Plody prosvesh cheniya (drama) 1889
  [*The Fruits of Enlightenment*, 1890]
Kreitserova sonata (novella) 1890
  [*The Kreutzer Sonata*, 1890]
Khozyain i rabotnik (novella) 1895
  [*Master and Man*, 1895]
Chto takoe iskusstvo (essay) 1898
  [*What Is Art?*, 1898]
Otetz sergii (novella) 1898
  [*Father Sergius* published in *Father Sergius, and Other Stories and Plays*, 1911]
The Novels and Other Works of Lyof N. Tolstoi. 22 vols. (novels, novellas, short stories, dramas, essays, and sketches) 1899-1902
Voskresenie (novel) 1899
  [*Resurrection*, 1899]
I svet vo tme svetit [first publication] (unfinished drama) 1911
  [*The Light That Shines in Darkness*, 1912]
Khadzhi Murat (novel) 1911
  [*Hadji Murád* published in *Hadji Murád, and Other Stories*, 1912]
Zhivoy trup (drama) 1911
  [*The Living Corpse*, 1912]
L. N. Tolstoi: polnoe sobranie proizvedenie. 90 vols. (novels, novellas, short stories, dramas, essays, and sketches) 1928-58
Tolstoy's Letters. 2 vol. (letters) 1978

MATTHEW ARNOLD (essay date 1887)

[Arnold was one of the most important English critics of the nineteenth century. Although he was also a poet and, more significantly, a commentator on the social and moral life in England, Arnold was essentially an apologist for literary criticism. He argued that the major purpose of the critic was to inform and liberate the public at large, and to prepare the way—through the fostering of ideas and information—for his or her country's next creative epoch. Arnold was a forceful advocate of the doctrine of "disinterestedness" in all critical activities—the need for flexibility, curiosity, and a non-utilitarian approach to culture and art. He was severely critical of what he considered the spiritual death of Victorian England; nonetheless, he was optimistic that art—which he saw us classless and universal—could save modern society from materialism. Arnold's critical methodology called for the rejection of both the personal estimate and the historical estimate of art; the first assumes the value of something based on subjective criteria; the second distorts the value of a creative work by over-emphasizing its influence on historical developments. Instead, he advocated—though often failed to achieve it in his own writing—the "real estimate" of the creative object. The real estimate demands that the critic judge a work of art according to its own qualities, in and of itself, apart from the influence of history and the limitations of subjective experience. In the following excerpt, Arnold offers an early consideration of what has remained a central concern in Tolstoy criticism: the division between such early works as Anna Karenina *and the later religious and moral writings which reflect his spiritual crisis, a period whose beginning is marked by* A Confession. *For later views on this subject see Boris Eikhenbaum's and Philip Rahv's essays excerpted below.]*

Count Leo Tolstoi is about sixty years old, and tells us that he shall write novels no more. He is now occupied with religion and with the Christian life. His writings concerning these great matters are not allowed, I believe, to obtain publication in Russia, but instalments of them in French and English reach us from time to time. I find them very interesting, but I find his novel of *Anna Karénine* more interesting still. I believe that many readers prefer to *Anna Karénine* Count Tolstoi's other great novel, *La Guerre et la Paix.* But in the novel one prefers, I think, to have the novelist dealing with the life which he knows from having lived it, rather than with the life which he knows from books or hearsay. If one has to choose a representative work of Thackeray, it is *Vanity Fair* which one would take rather than *The Virginians.* In like manner I take *Anna Karénine* as the novel best representing Count Tolstoi. (pp. 257-58)

But the truth is we are not to take *Anna Karénine* as a work of art; we are to take it as a piece of life. A piece of life it is. The author has not invented and combined it, he has seen it; it has all happened before his inward eye, and it was in this wise that it happened. . . . The author saw it all happening so—saw it, and therefore relates it; and what his novel in this way loses in art it gains in reality.

For this is the result which, by his extraordinary fineness of perception and by his sincere fidelity to it, the author achieves; he works in us a sense of the absolute reality of his personages and their doings. Anna's shoulders, and masses of hair, and half-shut eyes; Alexis Karénine's updrawn eyebrows, and tired smile, and cracking finger-joints; Stiva's eyes suffused with facile moisture—these are as real to us as any of those outward peculiarities which in our own circle of acquaintance we are noticing daily, while the inner man of our own circle of acquaintance, happily or unhappily, lies a great deal less clearly revealed to us than that of Count Tolstoi's creations. (pp. 260-61)

[In Levine] we are told that many traits are to be found of the character and history of Count Tolstoi himself. Levine belongs to the world of great people by his birth and property, but he is not at all a man of the world. He has been a reader and thinker, he has a conscience, he has public spirit and would ameliorate the condition of the people, he lives on his estate in the country, and occupies himself zealously with local business, schools, and agriculture. But he is shy, apt to suspect and to take offence, somewhat impracticable, out of his element in the gay world of Moscow. (p. 264)

Levine, as I have already said, thinks. Between the age of twenty and that of thirty-five he had lost, he tells us, the Christian belief in which he had been brought up, a loss of which examples nowadays abound certainly everywhere, but which in Russia, as in France, is among all young men of the upper and cultivated classes more a matter of course, perhaps, more universal, more avowed, than it is with us. Levine had adopted the scientific notions current all round him; talked of cells, organisms, the indestructibility of matter, the conservation of force, and was of opinion, with his comrades of the university, that religion no longer existed. But he was of a serious nature, and the question what his life meant, whence it came, whither it tended, presented themselves to him in moments of crisis and affliction with irresistible importunity, and getting no answer, haunted him, tortured him, made him think of suicide. (pp. 277-78)

Now on one of his bad days he was in the field with his peasants, and one of them happened to say to him, in answer to a question from Levine why one farmer should in a certain case act more humanely than another: 'Men are not all alike; one man lives for his belly, like Mitiovuck, another for his soul, for God, like old Plato.'—'What do you call,' cried Levine, 'living for his soul, for God?' The peasant answered: 'It's quite simple—living by the rule of God, of the truth. All men are not the same, that's certain. You yourself, for instance, Constantine Dmitrich, you wouldn't do wrong by a poor man.' Levine gave no answer, but turned away with the phrase, *living by the rule of God, of the truth,* sounding in his ears. (pp. 279-80)

[In] Levine's religious experiences Count Tolstoi was relating his own, and the history is continued in three autobiographical works. . . . : *Ma Confession, Ma Religion,* and *Que Faire.* Our author announces further, 'two great works,' on which he has spent six years: one a criticism of dogmatic theology, the other a new translation of the four Gospels, with a concordance of his own arranging. The results which he claims to have established in these two works, are, however, indicated sufficiently in the three published volumes which I have named above.

These autobiographical volumes show the same extraordinary penetration, the same perfect sincerity, which are exhibited in the author's novel. As autobiography they are of profound interest, and they are full, moreover, of acute and fruitful remarks. I have spoken of the advantages which the Russian genius possesses for imaginative literature. Perhaps for Biblical exegesis, for the criticism of religion and its documents, the advantage lies more with the older nations of the West. They will have more of the experience, width of knowledge, patience, sobriety, requisite for these studies; they may probably be less impulsive, less heady.

Count Tolstoi regards the change accomplished in himself during the last half-dozen years, he regards his recent studies and the ideas which he has acquired through them, as epoch-making in his life and of capital importance. . . . (pp. 282-83)

The novel of *Anna Karénine* belongs to that past which Count Tolstoi has left behind him; his new studies and the works founded on them are what is important; light and salvation are there. Yet I will venture to express my doubt whether these works contain, as their contribution to the cause of religion and to the establishment of the true mind and message of Jesus, much that had not already been given or indicated by Count Tolstoi in relating, in *Anna Karénine,* Levine's mental history. Points raised in that history are developed and enforced; there is an abundant and admirable exhibition of knowledge of human nature, penetrating insight, fearless sincerity, wit, sarcasm, eloquence, style. And we have too the direct autobiography of a man not only interesting to us from his soul and talent, but highly interesting also from his nationality, position, and course of proceeding. But to light and salvation in the Christian religion we are not, I think, brought very much nearer than in Levine's history. I ought to add that what was already present in that history seems to me of high importance and value. Let us see what it amounts to. (pp. 284-85)

[In] Count Tolstoi's religious philosophy there is very little which is abstract, arid. The idea of *life* is his master idea in studying and establishing religion. He speaks impatiently of St. Paul as a source, in common with the Fathers and the Reformers, of that ecclesiastical theology which misses the essential and fails to present Christ's Gospel aright. Yet Paul's 'law of the spirit of life in Christ Jesus freeing me from the law of sin and death' is the pith and ground of all Count Tolstoi's theology. Moral life is the gift of God, is God, and this true life, this union with God to which we aspire, we reach through Jesus. We reach it through union with Jesus and by adopting his life. This doctrine is proved true for us by the life in God, to be acquired through Jesus, being what our nature feels after and moves to, by the warning of misery if we are severed from it, the sanction of happiness if we find it. Of the access for *us*, at any rate, to the spirit of life, us who are born in Christendom, are in touch, conscious or unconscious, with Christianity, this is the true account. Questions over which the churches spend so much labour and time—questions about the Trinity, about the godhead of Christ, about the procession of the Holy Ghost, are not vital; what is vital is the doctrine of access to the spirit of life through Jesus.

Sound and saving doctrine, in my opinion, this is. It may be gathered in a great degree from what Count Tolstoi had already given us in the novel of *Anna Karénine.* But of course it is greatly developed in the special works which have followed. (pp. 285-86)

All this is but development, sometimes rather surprising, but always powerful and interesting, of what we have already had in the pages of *Anna Karénine.* And like Levine in that novel, Count Tolstoi was driven by his inward struggle and misery very near to suicide. What is new in the recent books is the solution and cure announced. Levine had accepted a provisional solution of the difficulties oppressing him; he had lived right on, so to speak, obeying his conscience, but not asking how far all his actions hung together and were consistent. . . . (pp. 291-92)

Count Tolstoi has since advanced to a far more definite and stringent rule of life—the positive doctrine, he thinks, of Jesus. It is the determination and promulgation of this rule which is the novelty in our author's recent works. He extracts this essential doctrine, or rule of Jesus, from the Sermon on the Mount, and presents it in a body of commandments—Christ's commandments; the pith, he says, of the New Testament, as the Decalogue is the pith of the Old. (p. 292)

Jesus paid tribute to the government and dined with the publicans, although neither the empire of Rome nor the High finance of Judea were compatible with his ideal and with the 'new earth' which that ideal must in the end create. Perhaps Levine's provisional solution, in a society like ours, was nearer to 'the rule of God, of the truth,' than the more trenchant solution which Count Tolstoi has adopted for himself since. It seems calculated to be of more use. I do not know how it is in Russia, but in an English village the determination of 'our circle' to earn their bread by the work of their hands would produce only dismay, not fraternal joy, amongst that 'majority' who are so earning it already. 'There are plenty of us to compete as things stand,' the gardeners, carpenters, and smiths would say; 'pray stick to your articles, your poetry, and nonsense; in manual labour you will interfere with us, and be taking the bread out of our mouths.'

So I arrive at the conclusion that Count Tolstoi has perhaps not done well in abandoning the work of the poet and artist, and that he might with advantage return to it. But whatever he may do in the future, the work which he has already done, and his work in religion as well as his work in imaginative literature, is more than sufficient to signalise him as one of the most marking, interesting, and sympathy-inspiring men of our time—an honour, I must add, to Russia, although he forbids us to heed nationality. (pp. 298-99)

> *Matthew Arnold, "Count Leo Tolstoi" (originally published in* The Fortnightly Review, *n.s. Vol. XLII, No. CCLII, December, 1887), in his* Essays in Criticism, second series, *Macmillan and Co., Limited, 1888 (and reprinted by Macmillan, 1921), pp. 253-99.*

MAURICE BARING   (essay date 1910)

[*During the early twentieth century, Baring—along with G. K. Chesterton and Hilaire Belloc—was considered one of the most important Catholic apologists in England. He was proficient in a number of different genres, but is remembered mainly as a novelist. He also wrote several acclaimed books on Russian and French literature and introduced English readers to the works of Anton Chekhov, Ivan Turgenev, Leo Tolstoy, and other prominent Russian authors.*]

In his *Childhood and Youth,* Tolstoy gives us the most vivid, the most natural, the most sensitive picture of childhood and youth that has ever been penned by the hand of man. And yet, after reading it, one is left half-unconsciously with the impression that the author feels there is something wrong, something unsatisfactory behind it all.

Tolstoy then passes on to describe the life of a grown-up man, in *The Morning of a Landowner,* in which he tells how he tried to work in his own home, on his property, and to teach the peasants, and how nothing came of his experiments. And again we have the feeling of something unsatisfactory, and something wanting, something towards which the man is straining, and which escapes him.

A little later, Tolstoy goes to the Caucasus, to the war, where life is primitive and simple, where he is nearer to nature, and where man himself is more natural. And then we have *The Cossacks,* in which Tolstoy's searchlights are thrown upon the primitive life of the old huntsman, the Cossack, Yeroshka, who lives as the grass lives, without care, without grief, and without reflection. Once more we feel that the soul of the writer is dissatisfied, still searching for something he has not found.

In 1854, Tolstoy took part in the Crimean War, which supplied him with the stuff for what are perhaps the most truthful pictures of war that have ever been written. But even here, we feel he has not yet found his heart's desire. Something is wrong. He was recommended for the St. George's Cross, but owing to his being without some necessary official document at the time of his recommendation, he failed to receive it. This incident is a symbol of the greater failure, the failure to achieve the inward happiness that he is seeking—a solid ground to tread on, a bridge to the infinite, a final place of peace. (pp. 84-6)

[His] discontent with his position, both intellectual and social, was in reality quite unfounded.

After the Crimean War, Tolstoy went abroad. He found nothing in Western Europe to satisfy him. On his return he settled down at Yasnaya Polyana, and married; and the great patriarchal phase of his life began, during which every gift and every happiness that man can be blessed with seemed to have fallen to his lot. It was then that he wrote *War and Peace*, in which he describes the conflict between one half of Europe and the other. He takes one of the largest canvases ever attacked by man; and he writes a prose epic on a period full of tremendous events. His piercing glance sees through all the fictions of national prejudice and patriotic bias; and he gives us what we feel to be the facts as they were, the very truth. No detail is too small for him, no catastrophe too great. He traces the growth of the spreading tree to its minute seed, the course of the great river to its tiny source. He makes a whole vanished generation of public and private men live before our eyes in such a way that it is difficult to believe that these people are not a part of our actual experience; and that his creations are not men and women we have seen with our own eyes, and whose voices we have heard with our own ears.

But when we put down this wonderful book, unequalled as a prose epic, as a panorama of a period and a gallery of a thousand finished portraits, we are still left with the impression that the author has not yet found what he is seeking. He is still asking why? and wherefore? What does it all mean? Why all these horrors, why these sacrifices? Why all this conflict and suffering of nations? What do these high deeds, this heroism, mean? What is the significance of these State problems, and the patriotic self-sacrifice of nations? We are aware that the soul of Tolstoy is alone in an awful solitude, and that it is shivering on the heights, conscious that all round it is emptiness, darkness and despair.

Again, in *War and Peace* we are conscious that Tolstoy's proud nature, the "Lucifer" type in him, is searching for another ideal; and that in the character of Pierre Bezuhov he is already setting up before us . . . the model which we should seek to imitate. And in Pierre Bezuhov we feel that there is something of Tolstoy himself. Manners change, but man, faced by the problem of life, is the same throughout all ages; and, whether consciously or unconsciously, Tolstoy proves this in writing *Anna Karenina*. Here again, on a large canvas, we see unrolled before us the contemporary life of the upper classes in Russia, in St. Petersburg, and in the country, with the same sharpness of vision, which seizes every outward detail, and reveals ever recess of the heart and mind. Nearly all characters in all fiction seem bookish beside those of Tolstoy. His men and women are so real and so true that, even if his psychological analysis

of them may sometimes err and go wrong from its oversubtlety and its desire to explain too much, the characters themselves seem to correct this automatically, as though they were independent of their creator. He creates a character and gives it life. He may theorise on a character, just as he might theorise on a person in real life; and he may theorise wrong, simply because sometimes no theorising is necessary, and the very fact of a theory being set down in words may give a false impression; but, as soon as the character speaks and acts, it speaks and acts in the manner which is true to itself, and corrects the false impression of the theory, just as though it were an independent person over whom the author had no control.

Nearly every critic, at least nearly every English critic, in dealing with *Anna Karenina*, has found fault with the author for the character of Vronsky. *Anna Karenina*, they say, could never have fallen in love with such an ordinary commonplace man. Vronsky, one critic has said (in a brilliant article), is only a glorified "Steerforth." The answer to this is that if you go to St. Petersburg or to London, or to any other town you like to mention, you will find that the men with whom the Anna Kareninas of this world fall in love are precisely the Vronskys, and no one else, for the simple reason that Vronsky is a man. He is not a hero, and he is not a villain; he is not what people call "interesting," but a man, as masculine as Anna is feminine, with many good qualities and many limitations, but above all things alive. Nearly every novelist, with the exception of Fielding, ends, in spite of himself, by placing his hero either above or beneath the standard of real life. There are many Vronskys to-day in St. Petersburg, and for the matter of that, *mutatis mutandis*, in London. But no novelist except Tolstoy has ever had the power to put this simple thing, an ordinary man, into a book. . . . Yet, all the time, in *Anna Karenina* we feel, as in *War and Peace*, that the author is still unsatisfied and hungry, searching for something he has not yet found; and once again, this time in still sharper outline and more living colours, he paints an ideal of simplicity . . . in the character of Levin. Into this character, too, we feel that Tolstoy has put a great deal of himself; and that Levin, if he is not Tolstoy himself, is what Tolstoy would like to be. But the loneliness and the void that are round Tolstoy's mind are not yet filled; and in that loneliness and in that void we are sharply conscious of the brooding presence of despair, and the power of darkness.

We feel that Tolstoy is afraid of the dark; that to him there is something wrong in the whole of human life, a radical mistake. He is conscious that, with all his genius, he has only been able to record the fact that all that he has found in life is not what he is looking for, but something irrelevant and unessential; and, at the same time, that he has not been able to determine the thing in life which is not a mistake, nor where the true aim, the essential thing, is to be found, nor in what it consists. It is at this moment that the crisis occurred in Tolstoy's life which divides it outwardly into two sections, although it constitutes no break in his inward evolution. The fear of the dark, of the abyss yawning in front of him, was so strong that he felt he must rid himself of it at all costs. . . . This terror was not a physical fear of death, but an abstract fear, arising from the consciousness that the cold mists of decay were rising round him. By the realisation of the nothingness of everything, of what Leopardi calls "l'infinita vanità del tutto," he was brought to the verge of suicide. And then came the change which he describes thus in his *Confession:* "I grew to hate myself; and now all has become clear to me." This was the preliminary step of the development which led him to believe that he had at last found the final and everlasting truth. "A man has only got not to desire lands or money, in order to enter into the kingdom of God." Property, he came to believe, was the source of all evil. "It is not a law of nature, the will of God, or a historical necessity; rather a superstition, neither strong nor terrible, but weak and contemptible." To free oneself from this superstition he thought was as easy as to stamp on a spider. He desired literally to carry out the teaching of the Gospels, to give up all he had and to become a beggar.

This ideal he was not able to carry out in practice. His family, his wife, opposed him: and he was not strong enough to face the uncompromising and terrible saying which speak of a man's foes being those of his own household, of father being divided against son, and household against household, of the dead being left to bury their dead. He put before him the ideal of the Christian saints, and of the early Russian martyrs who literally acted upon the saying of Christ: "Whoso leaveth not house and lands and children for My sake, is not worthy of Me." Tolstoy, instead of crushing the spider of property, shut his eyes to it. He refused to handle money, or to have anything to do with it; but this does not alter the fact that it was handled for him, so that he retained its advantages, and this without any of the harassment which arises from the handling of property. His affairs were, and still are, managed for him; and he continued to live as he had done before. No sane person would think of blaming Tolstoy for this. He was not by nature a St. Francis; he was not by nature a Russian martyr, but the reverse. What one does resent is not that his practice is inconsistent with his teaching, but that his teaching is inconsistent with the ideal which it professes to embody. He takes the Christian teaching, and tells the world that it is the only hope of salvation, the only key to the riddle of life. At the same time he neglects the first truth on which that teaching is based, namely, that man must be born again; he must humble himself and become as a little child. It is just this final and absolute surrender that Tolstoy has been unable to make. Instead of loving God through himself, and loving himself for the God in him, he hates himself, and refuses to recognise the gifts that God has given him. It is for this reason that he talks of all his great work, with the exception of a few stories written for children, as being worthless. It is for this reason that he ceased writing novels, and attempted to plough the fields. And the cause of all this is simply spiritual pride, because he was unwilling "to do his duty in that state of life to which it had pleased God to call him." (pp. 87-94)

The question is, has a human being the right to do this, especially if, for any reasons whatever, he is not able to make the full and complete renunciation, and to cut himself off from the world altogether? The answer is that if this be the foundation of Tolstoy's teaching, people have a right to complain of there being something wrong in it. . . . The cry of his youth, "I have no modesty," remains true of him after his conversion. It is rather that he has no humility; and, instead of acknowledging that every man is appointed to a definite task, and that there is no such thing as a superfluous man or a superfluous task, he has preached that all tasks are superfluous except what he himself considers to be necessary; instead of preaching the love of the divine "image of the King," with which man is stamped like a coin, he has told us to love the make of the coin by hatred of His handiwork, quite regardless of the image with which it is stamped. (pp. 94-5)

Yet, whatever the mistakes of Tolstoy's teaching may be, they do not detract from the moral authority of the man. All his life

he has searched for the truth, and all his life he has said exactly what he thought; and though he has fearlessly attacked all constituted authorities, nobody had dared to touch him. He is too great. This is the first time independent thought has prevailed in Russia; and this victory is the greatest service he has rendered to Russia *as a man.* (pp. 97-9)

Maurice Baring, "Tolstoy and Tourgeniev," in his Landmarks in Russian Literature *(reprinted by permission of the Estate of Maurice Baring), Methuen & Co., Ltd., 1910, pp. 77-115.**

BORIS EIKHENBAUM   (essay date 1924)

[*Eikhenbaum is one of Tolstoy's most prominent critics. As a member of the Russian Formalist school of criticism, he analyzes Tolstoy's early works in terms of their reaction to the previous Romantic style in Russian fiction. Like Philip Rahv (see excerpt below), Eikenbaum also refuses to see Tolstoy's works as divided evenly between those written before and after the spiritual crisis of his fifties. For an early consideration of this subject see Matthew Arnold's essay excerpted above.*]

Tolstoy began as a liquidator of romantic poetics, a destroyer of established canons. He revolutionized the material, the devices, the form. Instead of a richly metaphorical style, instead of emphatic musical syntax—a simple, though laborious and almost clumsy phrase; instead of a diffuse flow of feeling and emotionally colored landscapes—minute detailed description, dissection, and analysis of psychic life; instead of in intricate plotting—parallelism of several lines, linked rather than interwoven.

From the very outset, Tolstoy perceived himself against the backdrop of a disintegrating romantic art. Bypassing the fathers, he returns to the grandfathers, to the eighteenth century. . . . Already in his early diaries he pokes fun at romantic landscapes. . . . (p. 97)

Tolstoy consistently fractures romantic clichés. He deglamorizes and parodies the figures of romantic warriors patterned after Marlinskij and Lermontov. The traditional "poetic" Caucasus, too, is deglamorized: "For in Russia they picture the Caucasus as something majestic, with everlasting virgin ice fields, rushing torrents, daggers, felt cloaks, Circassian girls—all this sounds strange and wonderful, but, in fact, there is nothing jolly about it. If they at least knew that we have never been on the virgin ice fields, and that there would be nothing jolly about being there, and that the Caucasus is divided into provinces: Stavropol, Tiflis, and so on" (**"A Wood Feeling"**). Significantly, Tolstoy long remains silent about the most "poetic" of subjects, love; the critics wait impatiently for his first novel with love interest. . . . A wedding serves here not as a denouement, which is usually the case in novels, but as a beginning of the story proper. This is an intentional departure from the canon. (p. 98)

Tolstoy jettisons the very genre of the romantic novella with its central hero and love-centered plot. He gravitates toward the large forms. His works written prior to *War and Peace* are merely preliminary studies that elaborate individual states of mind, scenes, or devices. Having exhausted within the large form the devices of minute description, Tolstoy turns to a new mode—the folk tale. These two junctures in his creative evolution are accompanied by violent crises. It is still widely assumed that Tolstoy's career is divided into two periods—before and after **"A Confession"**—and that in the latter period Tolstoy became a moralist.

That is not so. Tolstoy's entire life is punctuated by crises, and this is by no means an idiosyncratic phenomenon. Art itself was in the throes of a crisis. Romantic poetics had ground to halt. Art had to take a new look at life in order to claim a new legitimacy. Early on, Tolstoy gets into the habit of interrupting his artistic work for the sake of completely extraneous schemes—he clearly needs this kind of diversion. Already in 1855 Tolstoy conceives a "great, colossal" thought, to the implementation of which he is prepared to devote his whole life, a notion of founding "a religion that corresponds to the development of humanity, the religion of Christ, but cleansed of faith and mystery."

At the core of all Tolstoy's crises lies the search for new artistic forms and for their new rationale. That is why **"A Confession"** was followed by the tract on art, on which Tolstoy worked for fifteen years. . . . The way was prepared for that tract by another crisis—the crisis of the sixties—which critics unjustly neglect when they speak of the seventies as the turning point. This crisis is discernible already at the end of the fifties, when Tolstoy enters the milieu of St. Petersburg literati, stunning everyone by his sharp paradoxes and his intolerance. He spurns all cannons, all authorities and traditions. (pp. 98-9)

Tolstoy's pedagogical activity [at his Jasnaja Poljana school] emerged from a deep-seated artistic quest. Almost unwittingly Tolstoy changes from a teacher into an experimenter. His essay **"Who Should Learn from Whom How to Write: Peasant Children from Us, or We from Peasant Children?"** . . . is no less significant an artistic pamphlet than his future tract on art. Tolstoy contrasts the compositions of Sëmka and Fed'ka [two peasant boys at Tolstoy's school] with all of Russian literature, where he cannot find anything to match them. He is delighted by their vividness and precision. He is moved and stunned by the force of this naïve creativity that owes nothing to literary tradition.

This stance foreshadows Tolstoy's imminent shift to primitivism. Instead of plots, Tolstoy gives his students proverbs that serve as a sort of canvas for the weaving of a pattern, for interlacing details into a simple and lucid design. He already dreams in this period of producing such work himself: "Among my unrealizable dreams are a number of works—neither stories nor yet descriptions based on proverbs." The shift to deliberate primitivism is affirmed once and for all in the tract **What Is Art?** There Tolstoy inveighs chiefly against the "triviality," that preoccupation with detail, for which his critics once took him to task, labeling it a device of imitativeness. "In literary art, the device of imitativeness consists in describing down to the smallest detail the external aspect of a character, the clothes, gestures, voices, and settings of the protagonists, together with all the chance occurrences one finds in life. . . . Take away from the best novels of our time the details. What will remain?" He is drawn to modes of "folk art and children's art that were not considered truly artistic—jests, proverbs, riddles, songs, dances, children's games, and mimicry." Characteristically, he finds that these "primitive" genres present much more of an artistic challenge than does a "verse epic on Cleopatra or a painting about Nero burning Rome, a symphony in the manner of Brahms or Richard Strauss, or an opera like Wagner's." Tolstoy feels keenly the impossibility of using traditionally "poetic" material. "Maidens, warriors, shepherds, hermits, angels, devils in all their guises, moonlight, thunderstorms, mountains, seas, precipices, flowers, flowing tresses, lions, a lamb, a dog, a swallow, a nightingale,"—these are the clichés he lists, clichés deemed poetic because "previous artists used

them frequently in their works." Not surprisingly, he contrasts *Hamlet* as interpreted by Rossi with a description of a theatrical production among a "savage tribe," the Voguls, where the entire play consists in the hunter's pursuit of deer.

Tolstoy marks a crisis in Russian artistic prose. In the new flowering of verse that followed in his wake maidens, moonlight, storms, seas, flowers, and swallows were subjected to a new poeticization. Tolstoy is at once a destroyer and a consummator. Is not he the one to whom we might return in our quest of a new "non-poetic" art? (pp. 100-01)

> *Boris Eikhenbaum, "On Tolstoy's Crises," translated by Carol A. Palmer (originally published under a different title in his* Skov' literaturu, Voprosy poètiki, 1924), in *Twentieth-Century Russian Literary Criticism, edited by Victor Erlich (copyright © 1975 by Yale University), Yale University Press, 1975, pp. 97-101.*

D. S. MIRSKY (essay date 1926)

[*Mirsky was a Russian prince who fled his country after the Bolshevik Revolution and settled in London. While in England, he wrote two important and comprehensive histories of Russian literature,* A History of Russian Literature *and* Contemporary Russian Literature. *In 1932, having reconciled himself to the Soviet regime, Mirsky returned to the U.S.S.R. He continued to write literary criticism, but his work eventually ran afoul of Soviet censors and he was exiled to Siberia. He disappeared in 1937. In the following excerpt, Mirsky provides a survey of Tolstoy's works after 1880.*]

Tolstóy's writings after 1880 are divided by a deep cleft from all his earlier work. But they belong to the same man, and much of what appeared at first new and startling in the later Tolstóy existed in a less developed form in the early Tolstóy. From the very beginning we cannot fail to discern in him an obstinate search for a rational meaning to life; a confidence in the powers of common sense and his own reason; contempt for modern civilization with its "artificial" multiplication of needs; a deeply rooted irreverence for all the functions and conventions of State and Society; a sovereign disregard for accepted opinions and scientific and literary "good form"; and a pronounced tendency to teach. But what was disseminated and disconnected in his early writings was welded after his conversion into a solid consistent doctrine, dogmatically settled in every detail. (p. 294)

The teaching of Tolstóy is a rationalized "Christianity," stripped of all tradition and all positive mysticism. He rejected personal immortality and concentrated exclusively on the moral teaching of the Gospels. Of the moral teaching of Christ the words, "Resist not evil," were taken to be the principle out of which all the rest follows. He rejected the authority of the Church, which sanctioned the State, and he condemned the State, which sanctioned violence and compulsion. Both were immoral, like every form of organized compulsion. His condemnation of every form of compulsion authorizes us to classify Tolstóy's teaching, in its political aspect, as anarchism. (p. 295)

Tolstóy's conversion was, largely, the reaction of his fundamental rationalism against the irrationalism into which he had allowed himself to drift in the sixties and seventies. His metaphysics may be summed up as the identification of the principle of life with reason. . . . But for all its rationalism, Tolstóy's religion is in a sense mystical. . . . [In] all his more remarkable later works "conversion" is described as an essentially mystical experience. It is mystical in that it is personal and unique. It is the result of an intimate revelation, which may or may not be prepared by previous intellectual development, but is essentially, like every mystical experience, incommunicable. In Tolstóy's own case, as described in *A Confession,* it is led up to by his whole previous intellectual life. But all purely intellectual solutions to the essential question were unsatisfactory, and the final solution is represented as a series of mystical experiences, repeated flashes of inner light. The civilized man lives in a state of unquestioning sin. The questions of meaning and justification arise against his will—as the effect of fear of death—and the answer comes as a ray of inner light—the process described thus more than once by Tolstóy—in *A Confession,* in *The Death of Iván Ilyích,* in the *Memoirs of a Madman,* in *Master and Man.* The necessary conseqeunce of this fact is that the truth cannot be preached, but may only by discovered for oneself. This is the doctrine of *A Confession,* which does not attempt to demonstrate, but only to narrate and to "infect" (pp. 296-97)

The first of Tolstóy's works in which he preached his new teaching was *A Confession.* . . . *A Confession* is altogether on a higher level than the rest—it is one of the world's masterpieces. It is a work of art, and Tolstóy's biographer would give proof of too much simple-mindedness if he used it as biographical material in the strict sense of the word. (pp. 299-300)

Tolstóy's other moral and religious writings are not on a level with *A Confession,* though they are written in the same admirable Russian, sometimes with even greater elegance and precision. . . . *What Are We to Do?* is a kind of continuation of *A Confession,* but on a less mystical and more social plane. It is the story of Tolstóy's experience in the slums and night refuges of Moscow soon after his conversion. His religious views were systematized in a series of works, of which the first, *What I Believe,* was written in 1883-4. This was followed by a *Critique of Dogmatic Theology, The Kingdom of Heaven Is Within Us, An Exposition of the Gospels,* and *The Christian Doctrine. What I Believe* is the most comprehensive of his dogmatic writings. What he gave in *A Confession* in the form of a personal experience, in its process of becoming, is here crystallized and stabilized into a settled doctrine. *The Christian Doctrine* . . . is an exposition of the same doctrine in a still more logical and fixed form, after the manner of a catechism. It is a source of infinite pleasure to those who admire most in Tolstóy his lucidity and his skill at definition and precise statement. *The Exposition of the Gosepels* has less of this quality and more of a very farfetched and not always bona fide interpretation. In *The Critique of Dogmatic Theology* he is a polemist well versed in all the little tricks of argumentative tactics, a cunning fencer, and consummate ironist. Ridicule and an appeal to common sense are his favorite polemical methods. "This is unintelligible nonsense," is his knock-out argument. His minor tracts are numerous and touch on a great variety of points of detail, or on topics of current interest. Such is *Why Do People Intoxicate Themselves?* denouncing drink and tobacco. Such is *I Cannot Be Silent,* a violent invective against the Russian government and the numerous executions during the suppression of the First Revolution.

The first stories he wrote after *A Confession* were a series of edifying short stories for the people. They were published in 1885 and the following years by the firm Posrédnik, founded for the special purpose of popularizing Tolstóy's teaching. They were written with regard to the existing conditions in Russia,

that is, they were meant to satisfy the censor. Consequently they contain no violent and overt satire of the Church and State. The moral is always plainly present, often in the title—*Evil Allures, but Good Endures, God Sees the Truth but Waits*—but is not always peculiarly Tolstoyan. . . . One of the best is *Two Old Men,* the story of two peasants who set out on a pilgrimage to Jerusalem in fulfillment of a vow. (p. 304)

Later on, as his fame grew and he began to have a public all over the world, he wrote popular stories of a new kind, more universal and generalized. They approach still nearer to his ideal of being comprehensible to all men. Such are his adaptations from the French—*Françoise* (Maupassant's *La Vierge-des-Vents* pruned of realistic excrescences), *The Coffee-House of Surat,* and *Too Dear,* and his still later stories, *King Essarhadon, Work, Death, and Sickness,* and *Three Questions.* In these he approaches the style of the parable, which he had used with such powerful effect in *A Confession,* and of the oriental apologue.

The stories written with a view to the educated reader are different in manner: they are much longer, much fuller of detail, more "psychological," altogether nearer in style to his earlier work. There are problem stories, written not so much to teach as to communicate his own experience. They may be grouped into two categories, stories of conversion and stories on the sexual problem. The first group consists of [*The Memoirs of a Madman, The Death of Iván Ilyích,* and *Master and Man*]. . . . In all these stories the subject is the conversion of the dark and unregenerated educated or rich man before the face of death or madness. *The Memoirs of a Madman* is very much akin to *A Confession.* . . . In *The Death of Iván Ilyích* the hero is not a thinking and seeking man like Tolstóy of the *Confession* or like the madman. He is an ordinary, vulgar, average man of the educated classes, a judge (the class Tolstóy detested most of all). (pp. 304-05)

The "sexual" stories are [*The Kreutzer Sonata* and *The Devil*] . . . . The first, a study of jealousy and a diatribe against the sexual education of young men and women in modern society, is a powerful production but hardly a perfect work of art. It is not sufficiently concentrated; its preaching is not always artistically "necessary"; its manner strangely enough reminds one of the untidy and excited manner of Dostoyévsky. *The Devil* is more satisfactory. . . .

Of all Tolstóy's late narrative works, the one that attracted the greatest attention and became most widely known, and is consequently, more often than not, taken as typical of his last period, was *Resurrection.* . . . It is a novel in three parts—by far the longest of all his stories since 1880, almost comparable in length with *Anna Karénina* and *War and Peace.* This is the sole reason why it has usurped a principal position among his later work and is so often quoted by the side of the two earlier novels. It has often been used to prove that Tolstóy's genius declined after he became a preacher. If the imaginative work of his last thirty years is to stand or fall according to the merit of *Resurrection,* it will be in somewhat bad case, for it is quite obvious that *Resurrection* is very much inferior to *War and Peace* and *Anna Karénina.* But it is also much inferior to *Master and Man,* to *Hajjí Murád,* and to *The Living Corpse.* In spite of its size it is by no means the work into which Tolstóy put the most work and care. (pp. 306-07)

If in *Resurrection* Tolstóy is at his worst, in its twin novel he is at his best. *Hajjí Murád* was begun in 1896 and completed in 1904. It was published after his death. In it he tried to give a story that would answer to his ideal of "good universal," not religious, art. *Hajjí Murád* is a masterpiece of the highest order. (pp. 307-08)

Hajjí Murád, as well as *The Memoirs of a Madman* and *The Devil*, was published only in 1911, in the collected edition of Tolstóy's posthumous works. This collection also includes several plays and many other stories and fragments. One of these is *Father Sergius* . . . , the story of an aristocrat who became a monk and a hermit—a powerful study of spiritual pride and, once again, carnal desires. It is also an excellent example of Tolstóy's later rapid and "essential" narrative manner. Still better in this respect is *The False Coupon* . . . , the admirably constructed story of a succession of evils diverging from one initial evil action to converge by a contrasting succession of good actions towards the common salvation of all concerned. It is impossible to list all the numerous minor stories and fragments of these wonderful three volumes. But one at least must be mentioned: one of the shortest—*Alësha Gorshók*. . . . It is a masterpiece of rare perfection. It is the apotheosis of the "holy fool," who does not himself realize his goodness. (pp. 308-09)

Tolstóy's plays all belong to the period after 1880. He had not the essential qualities that go to the making of a dramatist, and the merits of his plays are not of the strictly dramatic order. (p. 309)

The dogmatic followers of Tolstóy were never numerous, but his reputation among people of all classes grew immensely. It spread all over the world, and by the last two decades of his life Tolstóy enjoyed a place in the world's esteem that had not been held by any man of letters since the death of Voltaire. (p. 311)

> D. S. Mirsky, "The End of a Great Age," in his Contemporary Russian Literature: 1881-1925 *(copyright 1926 by Alfred A. Knopf, Inc.; reprinted by permission of the publisher), Knopf, 1926, G. Routledge & Sons, 1926 (and reprinted in his* A History of Russian Literature Comprising "A History of Russian Literature" *and* "Contemporary Russian Literature," *edited by Francis J. Whitfield, Knopf, 1949, pp. 291-332).**

D. S. MIRSKY (essay date 1927)

[*In the following excerpt from his study of Russian literature, Mirsky provides a survey of Tolstoy's works before 1880.*]

From the beginnings of his diary to the time he wrote *War and Peace,* writing was to Tolstóy above all a struggle to master reality, to found a method and a technique of reducing it to words. To this, from 1851, he added the problem of transforming notation of fact into literature. Tolstóy did not achieve it at a single stroke. His first attempt at imaginative writing, a fragment entitled *An Account of Yesterday,* is apparently the beginning of an account of an actual twenty-four hours spent by him, with no invention, nothing but notation. It was only to be fuller and less selective than the diaries and subordinated to a general design. In point of detail the *Account* is almost on a Proustian if not a Joycean scale. . . . For all his pioneering courage, Tolstóy did not have the audacity to continue in this line of extensive notation. It is almost a pity he did not. The sheer originality of *An Account of Yesterday* remains unsurpassed. If he had continued in that line, he would probably have met with less immediate recognition, but he might have ultimately produced an even more astounding body of work.

In the light of *An Account of Yesterday, Childhood* seems almost a surrender to all the conventions of literature. Of all Tolstóy's writings it is the one where extraneous literary influences (Sterne, Rousseau, Töpfer) are most clearly apparent. But even now, in the light of *War and Peace, Childhood* retains its unique and unfading charm. It has already that wonderful poetry of reality which is attained without the slightest aid of poetical device, without the aid of language (the few sentimental, rhetorical passages rather tend to destroy it), by the sole help of the choice of significant psychological and real detail. (p. 254)

In all he wrote after *Childhood* and up to *War and Peace* he continued his forward movement, experimenting, forging his instrument, never condescending to sacrifice his interest in the process of production to the artistic effect of the finished product. This is apparent in the sequels of *Childhood—Boyhood* . . . and *Youth* . . .—when the poetic, evocative, atmosphere of *Childhood* becomes thinner and thinner and the element of sheer untransformed analysis protrudes more and more. It is still more apparent in his stories of war and of the Caucasus: [*A Raid, Sevastópol in December, Sevastópol in May, Sevastópol in August, A Wood Felling*]. . . . In them he set out to destroy the existing romantic conceptions of those two arch-romantic themes. To be understood in their genesis, these stories have to be felt against their background of romantic literature, against the romances of Bestúzhev and the Byronic poems of Púshkin and Lérmontov. (p. 255)

In the stories written in the second half of the fifties and early sixties Tolstóy's center of interest is shifted from analysis to morality. These stories—*The Memoirs of a Billiard Marker, Two Hussars, Albert, Lucerne, Three Deaths, Family Happiness, Polikúshka,* and *Kholstomér, the Story of a Horse*—are frankly didactic and moralistic, much more so than any of the stories of his last, dogmatic period. The main moral of these stories is the fallacy of civilization and the inferiority of the civilized, conscious, sophisticated man, with his artificially multiplied needs, to natural man. On the whole they mark an advance neither, as the war stories did, in Tolstóy's method of annexing and digesting reality, nor in his skill in transferring the raw experience of life into art (as in *Childhood* and *War and Peace*). . . . *Lucerne,* for its earnest and bitter indignation against the selfishness of the rich (which, it is true, he was inclined at that time to regard, semi-Slavophilwise, as a peculiarity of the materialistic civilization of the West) is particularly suggestive of the spirit of his later work. As a sermon in fiction it is certainly one of the most powerful things of its kind. The nearest approach to complete artistic success is *Two Hussars,* a charming story that betrays its purpose only in the excessively neat parallelism between the characters of the two Hussars, father and son. . . . Lastly, *Kholstomér, the Story of a Horse* is certainly one of the most characteristic and curious of all Tolstóy's writings. It is a satire upon civilized mankind from the point of view of a horse. (pp. 256-57)

Apart from the rest of his earliest work stands *The Cossacks* . . . . [It] is probably his masterpiece before *War and Peace.* . . . The main idea is the contrast of his sophisticated and self-conscious personality to the "natural men" that are the Cossacks. (p. 257)

Tolstóy's first literary work after his marriage was the (posthumously published) comedy *A Contaminated Family.* It shows already the conservative trend of his married mind. It is a satire of the nihilist, ending in the triumph of the meek, but fundamentally sensible, father over his rebellious children. It is a masterpiece of delicate character drawing and dialogue. It contains more genuine and good-humored humor than any other of his works. (p. 258)

War and Peace is, not only in size, but in perfection, the masterpiece of the early Tolstóy. It is also the most important work in the whole of Russian realistic fiction. If in the whole range of the European novel of the nineteenth century it has equals, it has no superiors, and the peculiarities of the modern, as opposed to the pre-nineteenth-century, novel are more clearly seen in it than in such rivals as *Madame Bovary* or *Le Rouge et le Noir*. It was an advanced pioneering work, a work that widened, as few novels have done, the province and the horizon of fiction. . . . In many respects *War and Peace* is a direct continuation of the preceding works of Tolstóy. The methods of analysis and of "making it strange" are the same, only carried to a greater perfection. . . . The glorification of "natural man," of Natásha and Nicholas Rostóv at the expense of the sophisticated Prince Andrew, and of the peasant Platón Karatáyev at the expense of all the civilized heroes, continues the line of thought of *Two Hussars* and of *The Cossacks*. The satirical representation of society and of diplomacy is completely in line with Tolstóy's disgust at European civilization. However, in other respects it is different from the earlier work. First of all it is more objective . . . . But the most wonderful difference of *War and Peace* from the earlier stories are the women, Princess Maria and especially Natásha. There can be no doubt that it was his increased knowledge of feminine nature, due to marriage, that enabled Tolstóy to annex this new province of psychological experience. The art of individualization also attains to unsurpassable perfection. . . . The roundness, the completeness, the liveness of the characters, even of the most episodic, are perfect and absolute. (pp. 258-59)

The transformation of reality into art is also more perfect in *War and Peace* than in anything that preceded it. It is almost complete. The novel is built along its own laws (Tolstóy has let escape him some interesting hints as to these laws) and contains few undigested bits of raw material. The narrative is a miracle. . . .

The philosophy of the novel is the glorification of nature and life at the expense of the sophistications of reason and civilization. It is the surrender of the rationalist Tolstóy to the irrational forces of existence. (p. 260)

There are two conceivable strictures on *War and Peace*, the figure of Karatáyev, and the theoretical chapters on history and warfare. Personally I do not admit the validity of the latter drawback. It is an essential of Tolstóy's art to be not only art, but knowledge. And to the vast canvas of the great novel the theoretical chapters add a perspective and an intellectual atmosphere one cannot wish away. I feel it more difficult to put up with Karatáyev. In spite of his quintessential importance for the idea of the novel, he jars. He is not a human being among human beings, as the other two ideally natural characters, Natásha and Kutúzov, are. He is an abstraction, a myth, a being with different dimensions and laws from those of the rest of the novel. He does not fit in. (p. 261)

Anna Karénina is in all essentials a continuation of *War and Peace*. The methods of Tolstóy are the same in both, and the two novels are justly named together. What has been said of the personages of *War and Peace* may be repeated of those of *Anna Karénina*. . . . Perhaps there is even a greater variety and a more varied sympathy in the characters of *Anna Karénina*. . . . But Lëvin is a much less happily transformed Tolstóy than are his emanations in *War and Peace*, Prince Andrew

and Pierre. . . . Another difference between the two novels is that *Anna Karénina* contains no separate philosophical chapters, but a more obtrusive and insidious moral philosophy is diffused throughout the story. The philosophy is less irrational and optimistic, more puritan, and is everywhere felt as distinct from and alien to the main groundwork of the novel. The groundwork has the idyllic flavor of *War and Peace*. But in the philosophy of the novel there is an ominous suggestion of the approach of a more tragic God than the blind and good life-God of *War and Peace*. The tragic atmosphere thickens as the story advances towards the end. The romance of Anna and Vrónsky, who had transgressed the moral and social law, culminates in blood and horror to which there is no counterpart in the earlier novel. . . . He was never again to write a novel like these two. After finishing *Anna Karénina* he attempted to resume his work on Peter and the Decembrists, but it was soon forsaken, and instead, two years after the completion of his last idyl, he wrote *A Confession*.

Anna Karénina leads up to the moral and religious crisis that was so profoundly to revolutionize Tolstóy. Before he began it he had already begun to cast his eyes on new artistic methods—abandoning the psychological and analytical manner of superfluous detail and discovering a simpler narrative style that could be applied not only to the sophisticated and corrupt educated classes, but to the undeveloped mind of the people. The stories he wrote for the people in 1872 (*God Sees the Truth* and *The Captive in the Caucasus*, which by the way, is merely a translation into unromantic terms, a sort of parody, of the poem of Púshkin) already announce the popular tales of 1885-6. (pp. 261-63)

> *D. S. Mirsky, "The Age of Realism: The Novelists (II)," in his* A History of Russian Literature from the Earliest Times to the Death of Dostoyevsky (1881) *(copyright 1926, 1927, 1949 © 1958 by Alfred A. Knopf, Inc.; reprinted by permission of the publisher), Knopf, 1927 (and reprinted in his* A History of Russian Literature Comprising "A History of Russian Literature" and "Contemporary Russian Literature," *edited by Francis J. Whitfield, Knopf, 1949, pp. 245-90).**

BERNARD SHAW (essay date 1932)

[*Shaw is generally considered the greatest and best-known dramatist to write in the English language since Shakespeare. Following the example of Henrik Ibsen, he succeeded in revolutionizing the English stage, disposing of the romantic conventions and devices of the "well-made play," and instituting the theater of ideas, grounded in realism. During the late nineteenth century, Shaw was also a prominent literary, art, and music critic. In 1895, he became the drama critic for* The Saturday Review, *and his reviews therein became known for their biting wit and brilliance. During his three years at* The Saturday Review, *Shaw determined that the theater was meant to be a "moral institution" and an "elucidator of social conduct." The standards he applied to drama were quite simple: Is the play like real life? Does it convey sensible, socially progressive ideas? Because most of the drama produced during the 1890s failed to approach these ideals, Shaw usually assumed a severely critical and satirical attitude toward his subjects. Although he later wrote criticism of poetry and fiction—much of it collected in* Pen Portraits and Reviews *(1932)—Shaw was out of sympathy with both of these genres. He had little use for the former, believing it poorly suited for the expression of ideas, and in his criticism of the latter he rarely got beyond the search for ideology. As Samuel Hynes has noted, Shaw was driven by a rage to better the world. A Fabian socialist, he wrote criticism which is often concerned with the humanitarian and political intent of the work under discussion. Like E. M. Cioran's essay (see excerpt below), Shaw's review of Tolstoy's dramas points out the destructive rather than the morally positive quality of his later works.]*

In its tragedy and comedy alike, the modern tragi-comedy begins where the old tragedies and comedies left off; and we have actually had plays made and produced dealing with what happened to Ibsen's *dramatis personae* before the first act began.

Tolstoy is now easily classed as a tragi-comedian, pending the invention of a better term. Of all the dramatic poets he has the most withering touch when he wants to destroy. His novels shew this over and over again. A man enters a house where someone lies dead. There is no moralizing, no overt irony: Tolstoy, with the simplicity he affects so well, just tells you that the undertaker has left the coffin lid propped against the wall in the entrance hall, and that the visitor goes into the drawing room and sits down on a *pouf*. Instantly the mockery and folly of our funeral pomps and cemetery sentimentalities laugh in our faces. (pp. 263-64)

This terrible but essentially comedic method is the method of all Tolstoy's plays except the first, **The Powers of Darkness,** which is, on the whole, a true tragedy. His **Fruits of Culture,** coming long before Granville-Barker's *Marrying of Ann Leete* or the plays of Tchekov, is the first of the Heartbreak Houses, and the most blighting. He touches with his pen the drawing room, the kitchen, the doormat in the entrance hall, and the toilet tables upstairs. They wither like the garden of Klingsor at the sign of Parsifal. **The Living Corpse** is as alive as most fine gentlemen are. But gentry as an institution crumble to dust at his casual remark that unless a gentleman gets a berth under Government as soldier or diplomatist, there is nothing left for him to do but to kill himself with wine and women. It is a case of "God damn you, merry gentlemen: let all things you dismay."

But Tolstoy's masterpiece is his **Light Shining Through Darkness.** In it he turns his deadly touch suicidally on himself. The blight falls on him ruthlessly. That the hero of Sevastopol becomes a second-rate dug-out is nothing. That the Levine of Anna Karenina becomes a common domestic quarreller is hardly noticed. It is the transfiguration of the great prophet into a clumsy mischievous cruel fool that makes the tragi-comedy. Mr. Aylmer Maude, in his biography of Tolstoy, holds the scales very fairly between husband and wife, and gives no quarter to the notion that a great man can do no wrong; but where he is respectfully critical Tolstoy himself is derisively merciless. He does not even pay himself the compliment of finishing the play. He left the last act unwritten, but with precise instructions as to how he was to be shot in it like a mad dog by the mother of the young man he had ruined by his teaching as he ruined everyone else who listened to him.

Nevertheless Tolstoy does not really give the verdict against himself: he only shews that he was quite aware of the disastrousness of his negative anarchistic doctrine, and was prepared to face that disastrousness sooner than accept and support robbery and violence merely because the robbers and militarists had acquired political power enough to legalize them. It must be assumed that if everyone refused compliance, the necessities of the case would compel social reconstruction on honest and peaceful lines. His own notions of such reconstruction did not go apparently beyond an uncritical acceptance of Henry George's demonstration of the need for land nationalization; and he does not seem to have foreseen that any reconstruction whatever

must involve more State compulsion of the individual than the present system, which relies for its unofficial but omnipresent compulsion on the pressure of circumstances brought about by the destitution of the proletariat. Tolstoy, like the rather spoiled aristocrat, natural and artificial, that he was, could not stand compulsion, and instinctively refused to give his mind to the practical problem of social reconstruction on his principles: that is, how to organize the equitable sharing among us of the burden of that irreducible minimum of exertion without which he must perish: a matter involving, as Lenin has discovered, a considerable shooting up of the recalcitrant. Like many other prophets, he preached the will without finding the way. Therefore his influence was extremely dangerous to individual fools (he included himself among the number in **Light Shining Through Darkness**); but he is a great Social Solvent, revealing to us, as a master of tragi-comic drama, the misery and absurdity of the idle proud life for which we sacrifice our own honor and the happiness of our neighbors. (pp. 264-66)

> *Bernard Shaw, "Tolstoy: Tragedian or Comedian?" (a revision of a speech made at the Tolstoy Commemoration at Kingsway Hall, London, on November 30, 1921), in his* Pen Portraits and Reviews *by Bernard Shaw (reprinted by permission of The Society of Authors on behalf of the Bernard Shaw Estate), revised edition, Constable and Company Limited, 1932 (and reprinted by Scholarly Press, Inc., 1971), pp. 260-66.*

CLIFTON FADIMAN   (essay date 1942)

[Fadiman became one of the most prominent American literary critics during the 1930s with his often caustic and insightful book reviews for the Nation *and the* New Yorker *magazines. He also managed to reach a sizeable audience through his work as a radio talk-show host from 1938 to 1948.]*

I hope merely to set Tolstoy's masterpiece before the reader in such a way that he will not be dismayed by its labyrinthine length or put off by its seeming remoteness from our own concerns.

War and Peace has been called the greatest novel ever written. These very words have been used, to my knowledge, by E. M. Forster, Hugh Walpole, John Galsworthy, and Compton Mackenzie; and a similar judgment has been made by many others. (p. 176)

Let us . . . try to discover together why it is a great novel.

The first thing to do is to read it. A supreme book usually argues its own supremacy quite efficiently, and *War and Peace* is no exception. Still, we may be convinced of its magnitude and remain puzzled by certain of its aspects—for no first-rate book is completely explicit, either.

On finishing *War and Peace* what questions do we tend to ask ourselves? Here is a very simple one: What is it about? (p. 177)

[We] are forced in the end to make the apparently vapid judgment that the subject of *War and Peace* is Life itself. (p. 178)

We do not know what Tolstoy had in mind as the main subject of *War and Peace,* for he stated its theme differently at different periods of his career. Looking back on it, as a fairly old man, he said that his only aim had been to amuse his readers. . . . More seriously, Tolstoy at times spoke of *War and Peace* as a picture of the wanderings of a people.

But whatever he thought its subject was, he transcended it. In one sense he put into this book everything that interested him, and everything interested him. That he managed to make it more than a collection of characters and incidents is equivalent to saying that in addition to being a man with a consuming interest in life he was also an artist who was not content until he had shaped that interest into harmonious forms.

Now, there are some who would demur, who feel that it is precisely in this quality of form that *War and Peace* is defective. (pp. 178-79)

Suppose we admit at once that there is no classic unity of subject matter as there is, for instance, in the *Iliad*. . . . This simple unity Tolstoy does not have. But a profounder unity I think he does have. When we have come to feel this unity, the philosophical and historical disquisitions cease to seem long-winded and become both interesting in themselves and an integral part of the Tolstoyan scheme. We are no longer disturbed as we should be if such digressions appeared in a work of narrower compass. We accept the fact that mountains are never pyramids.

Let us see whether we can get this clear. In the course of one of his digressions Tolstoy writes, "Only by taking an infinitesimally small unit for observation (the differential of history, i.e., the individual tendencies of men) and attaining to the art of integrating them (i.e., finding the sum of these infinitesimals) can we hope to arrive at the laws of history." . . . [In] this sentence, perhaps, is concealed the theme of the book: the movement of history which Tolstoy must examine by observing "the individual tendencies of men," on the one hand, and by attempting to "integrate them," on the other. Putting it in another way, we may say that it is not enough for Tolstoy to examine the individual lives of his characters as if they were separate atoms. He must also sweep up all these atoms into one larger experience. Now, this larger experience is the Napoleonic campaign. But the campaign itself, which fuses or enlarges or focuses the lives of Andrew and Natásha and Pierre and the rest, must itself be studied, not merely as a background—that is how an ordinary historical novelist would study it—but as thoughtfully as Tolstoy studies each individual life. In order fully to understand this focusing experience he is forced to elaborate a theory of history to explain it. And so he is forced to understand the major historical characters, such as Napoleon, Kutúzov, and the others, who are the dramatic symbols of the experience.

The result of this integration may not please everyone, but the integration is there. When one reflects upon the task, one is driven to concede, I think, that Tolstoy, in his attempt to understand history through human beings and human beings through history, is undertaking the greatest task conceivable to the creative novelist of the nineteenth century, just as Milton, attempting to justify the ways of God to man, undertook the greatest poetical theme possible to a man of his century. (pp. 179-80)

War and Peace is so vast that each reader may pick out for himself its literary qualitites he most admires. Let us select three: its inclusiveness, its naturalness, its timelessness.

The first thing to strike the reader is the range of Tolstoy's interest and knowledge. (p. 181)

At first glance the inclusiveness seems so overpowering that one inclines to agree with Hugh Walpole when he says that *War and Peace* "contains everything," or with E. M. Forster who is no less sure that "everything is in it." Naturally, these statements cannot be literally true. But it is true to say that when we have finished *War and Peace* we do not feel the lack of anything. It is only when one stops short and makes a list of the things Tolstoy leaves out that one realizes he is a novelist and not a god. We get very little awareness, for example, of the Russian middle class which was just beginning to emerge at the opening of the nineteenth century. Also, while Tolstoy does describe many peasants for us, the emphasis is thrown disproportionately on the aristocratic class with which he was most familiar. Another thing: obeying the literary conventions of his period, Tolstoy touches upon the sex relations of his men and women with great caution—and yet, so true and various is his presentation of love that we hardly seem to notice his omissions. That, after all, is the point: we do not notice the omissions, and we are overwhelmed by the inclusiveness. . . It is Tolstoy's attitude toward his own tremendous knowledge that makes him great rather than merely encyclopedic. (p. 182)

The key word here is "love." One of the most penetrating comments ever made about *War and Peace* is Mark Van Doren's, "I think he can be said to have hated nothing that ever happened." This exaggeration contains a profound truth. Tolstoy's love for his characters in *War and Peace* is very different from the mystic and, some would say, morbid sentimentality of his later years. It is more like the enthusiasm of a young man for everything he sees about him during the period of his greatest vigor. . . .

At his best Tolstoy seems to write as if Nature herself were guiding his pen. . . .

There is no formula to explain how Tolstoy does this. All we know is that he does it. (p. 183)

The constant impression of naturalness one gets from reading Tolstoy comes partly from his lack of obsessions. He does not specialize in a particular emotion, as Balzac, say, specializes in the emotions deriving from the desire for money. Perhaps we may say that if Tolstoy has an obsession, it is a passion for showing people *merely living*. . . .

It is because his eye is always on the central current of life that his perceptions seem so inevitable. (p. 184)

Tolstoy's natural sympathy overleaps the boundary of sex; his women are as convincing as his men. Indeed, he has a special talent for the presentation of women at their most female. . . .

We think of certain Tolstoyan scenes as other men would do them and then we realize the quality of his supremacy. (p. 185)

It is *normal*. Tolstoy is the epic poet of the conscious and the "normal," just as Dostoevski, complementing him, is the dramatic poet of the subconscious and the "abnormal." His instinct is always to identify the unnatural with the unpleasant. . . .

This almost abnormal normality in Tolstoy makes him able to do what would seem a very easy thing but is really very hard: describe people engaged in *nothing but being happy*. (p. 186)

The inclusiveness of *War and Peace*. Its naturalness. Finally, its timelessness. . . .

[Even] when his characters seem almost pure representatives of their class, they still have a permanent value as symbols. . . .

Here is a book, too, that seems to deal with people caught in a particular cleft of history. As that limited epoch recedes, we might suppose the people should dim accordingly. Yet this is not the case. It is impossible to say just how Tolstoy manages to give the impression both of particularity and universality. (p. 187)

War and Peace may not have a classic form. But it does have a classic content. It is full of scenes and situations which, in slightly altered forms, have recurred again and again, and will continue to recur, in the history of civilized man. . . .

It is as if the human race, despite its apparent complexity, were capable of but a limited set of gestures. To this set of gestures only great artists have the key. (p. 188)

Also the very looseness of the book's form, the fact that it has neither beginning nor end, helps to convey the sense of enduring life. (p. 189)

Has *War and Peace*, then, no defects? It has many. It is far from being a technically perfect novel, like *Madame Bovary*. . . . There are also many places in the narrative where the pace lags. Certain characters in the crowded canvas tend to get lost in the shuffle and never become entirely clear. . . . At times, so complex is the panorama that the reader has difficulty following the story, just as we have difficulty in following everything happening in a three-ring circus. Some of these defects seem to disappear on a second or third or fourth reading. Some are permanent. But none of them is so great nor are all of them taken together so great as to shake *War and Peace* from the pinnacle it occupies. Flaubert cannot afford to make mistakes. Tolstoy can. (pp. 189-90)

The insights in Tolstoy are at their best enormously moving and exactly true. But they rarely give us that uneasy sense of psychic discovery peculiar to Dostoevski. (p. 190)

So far in these comments I have emphasized those qualities— inclusiveness, naturalness, timelessness—that make *War and Peace* universal rather than Russian. But part of its appeal for us, I think, derives from the fact that though there is nothing in the book that is incomprehensible to the American or the Western European, everything in it, owing to its Russian character, seems to us just a trifle off-center. This gives the novel a piquancy, even a strangeness at times, that it may not possess for the Russians. (pp. 190-91)

There are certain central motives in *War and Peace* that are particularly (though not uniquely) Russian. The motive of moral conversion is a case in point. (p. 191)

In *War and Peace,* with varying degrees of success, the characters study themselves. All their critical experiences but lead them to further self-examination. (p. 192)

The purpose, if we may use so precise a word, of the regeneration experience is to enable the characters to attain to Pierre's state: "By loving people without cause, he discovered indubitable causes for loving them." In this sentence, a sort of moral equivalent of the James-Lange theory, lies the essence, the center, the inner flame, of the prerevolutionary Russian novel. It is only after one has pondered its meaning that one can understand what lies back of the sudden changes in Tolstoy's and Dostoevski's characters. (pp. 192-93)

The conflict in the soul of the Russian aristocrat derived not only from the conflict of cultures within him but from the moral falsity of his social position. Although Tolstoy—and this is one of his omissions—does not lay great stress on it, the

Russian upper class in varying degrees suffered from a guilt-feeling arising from the institution of serfdom. (pp. 194-95)

Much of the soul-searching in *War and Peace,* though it would seem to pivot only on each individual's personal problems, is in part a result of this vague pervasive guilt-feeling. Perhaps, indeed, a large part of the genius of the prerevolutionary Russian novel comes from the conflict born of this sense of guilt.

Finally, the Russian sought spiritual regeneration because he found no outlet for his idealistic energies in the state itself. (p. 195)

I have made these perhaps hackneyed comments in order to show that Tolstoy is a Russian novelist first and a universal novelist only by accident of genius. . . . He wrote as a Russian about Russian people—indeed about his own family, for many of the characters in *War and Peace* are transcripts from reality. But he wrote about them not only as Russians but as people. And therein lies part of the secret of his greatness.

There remains for us at least one more aspect of *War and Peace* to consider—that is, Tolstoy's view of men, war, history, and their interrelationships. (pp. 195-96)

Tolstoy's theory of history is that there is no theory of history. Or, to put it more cautiously, if there are grand laws determining the movement and flow of historical events, we can, in the present state of our knowledge, only guess at them. Until our vision and our knowledge are so extended that they reveal these underlying laws, the most intelligent thing for us to do is at least to deny validity to all superficial explanations of historical experience. (p. 196)

In *War and Peace* he attacks those theories which were popular in his own time. . . .

It is part of the purpose of *War and Peace* to prove that there is no such thing as chance and no such thing as genius. (p. 197)

For Tolstoy the fate of battles therefore is decided less by prefabricated strategies than by the absence or presence of what he calls "moral hesitation," or what we would call morale. (p. 200)

Were Tolstoy alive today would he moderate his views because the character of warfare has changed so radically in the interim? (p. 201)

Tolstoy, I think, would reply that any change is only apparent and only temporary. He would say that human nature is a constant, that it will rise to the surface despite all the deformation, the drill, the conditioning, the dehumanizing to which is may be subjected.

It is a constant, then, in war. It is a constant in peace. And it is a constant in *War and Peace*. (p. 202)

> *Clifton Fadiman, in his foreword to* War and Peace *by Leo Tolstoy, translated by Louise Maude and Aylmer Maude (copyright © 1942, 1969 by Simon and Schuster, Inc.; reprinted by permission of Simon and Schuster, Inc.), Simon & Schuster, 1942 (and reprinted in a shortened form as "'War and Peace'," in his* Party of One: The Selected Writings of Clifton Fadiman, *The World Publishing Company, 1955, pp. 176-202.*

PHILIP RAHV (essay date 1957)

[*Rahv came to the forefront of American literary criticism during the 1930s when he helped found the left-wing periodical* Partisan

Review. *Born in the Ukraine, Russia, Rahv retained his socialist upbringing throughout his life. He is essentially a social realist and historical critic of literature. In all his work he focuses on the social, cultural, and intellectual milieu which influences art and is in turn influenced by it. For Rahv, criticism is a living relationship of author, reader, and work, and not simply the study of dead works by dead men and women. In opposition to a common view of Tolstoy's development, Rahv argues that "there is no real discontinuity in his career" between the works written before and after his spiritual crisis. For a similar position on this critical issue, see Boris Eikhenbaum's essay excerpted above. For an early consideration of this subject see Matthew Arnold's essay excerpted above.*]

[From] the very first Tolstoy instinctively recognized the essential insufficiency and makeshift character of the narrowly aesthetic outlook, of the purely artistic appropriation of the world. His personality was built on too broad a frame to fit into an aesthetic mold, and he denied that art was anything more than the ornament and charm of life. He came of age at a time when the social group to which he belonged had not yet been thoroughly exposed to the ravages of the division of labor, when men of his stamp could still resist the dubious consolations it brings in its train. Endowed with enormous energies, possessed of boundless egoism and of an equally boundless power of conscience, he was capable, in Leo Shestov's phrase, of destroying and creating worlds, and before he was quite twenty-seven years old he had the audacity to declare his ambition, writing it all solemnly down in his diary, of becoming the founder of "a new religion corresponding with the present state of mankind; the religion of Christ but purged of dogmas and mysticism—a practical religion, not promising future bliss but giving bliss on earth." No wonder, then, that while approaching the task of mastering the literary medium with the utmost seriousness, and prizing that mastery as a beautiful accomplishment, he could not but dismiss the pieties of art as trivial compared with the question he faced from the very beginning, the question he so heroically sought to answer even in his most elemental creations, in which he seems to us to move through the natural world with splendid and miraculous ease, more fully at home there than any other literary artist. Yet even in those creations the very same question appears now in a manifest and now in a latent fashion, always the same question: How to live, what to do?

In 1880, when Turgenev visited Yasnaya Polyana after a long estrangement, he wrote a letter bewailing Tolstoy's apparent desertion of art. "I, for instance, am considered an artist," he said, "but what am I compared with him? In contemporary European literature he has no equal. . . . But what is one to do with him. He has plunged headlong into another sphere: he has surrounded himself with Bibles and Gospels in all languages, and has written a whole heap of papers. He has a trunk full of these mystical ethics and of various pseudo-interpretations. He read me some of it, which I simply do not understand. . . . I told him, 'That is not the real thing'; but he replied: 'It is just the real thing'. . . . Very probably he will give nothing more to literature, or if he reappears it will be with that trunk." Turgenev was wrong. Tolstoy gave a great deal more to literature, and it is out of that same trunk, so offensive in the eyes of the accomplished man of letters, that he brought forth such masterpieces as *The Death of Ivan Ilyich* and *Master and Man,* plays like *The Power of Darkness,* also many popular tales which, stripped of all ornament, have an essential force and grace of their own, and together with much that is abstract and overrationalized, not a few expository works, like *What Then Must We Do?.* which belong with the most

powerful revolutionary writings of the modern age. For it is not for nothing that Tolstoy was always rummaging in that black trunk. At the bottom of it, underneath a heap of old papers, there lay a little *mana*-object, a little green twig which he carried with him through the years, a twig of which he was told at the age of five by his brother Nicholas—that it was buried by the road at the edge of a certain ravine and that on it was inscribed the secret by means of which "all men would cease suffering misfortunes, leave off quarreling and being angry, and become continuously happy." The legend of the green twig was part of a game played by the Tolstoy children, called the Ant-Brothers, which consisted of crawling under chairs screened off by shawls and cuddling together in the dark. Tolstoy asked to be buried on the very spot at the edge of the ravine at Yasnaya Polyana which he loved because of its association with the imaginary green twig and the ideal of human brotherhood. And when he was an old man he wrote that "the idea of ant-brothers lovingly clinging to one another, though not under two arm-chairs curtained by shawls but of all mankind under the wide dome of heaven, has remained unaltered in me. As I then believed that there existed a little green twig whereon was written the message which would destroy all evil in men and give them universal welfare, so I now believe that such truth exists and will be revealed to men and will give them all it promises." It is clear that the change in Tolstoy by which Turgenev was so appalled was entirely natural, was presupposed by all the conditions of his development and of his creative consciousness. In the total Tolstoyan perspective the black trunk of his old age represents exactly the same thing as the green twig of his childhood.

Even the crude heresies he expounded in *What is Art?* lose much of their offensiveness in that perspective. In itself when examined without reference to the author's compelling grasp of the central and most fearful problems of human existence, the argument of that book strikes us as a willful inflation of the idea of moral utility at the expense of the values of the imagination. But actually the fault of the argument is not that it is wholly implausible—as a matter of fact, it is of long and reputable lineage in the history of culture—as that it is advanced recklessly and with a logic at once narrow and excessive; the Tolstoyan insight is here vitiated in the same way as the insight into sexual relations is vitiated in *The Kreutzer Sonata.* Still, both works, the onslaught on modern love and marriage as well as the onslaught on the fetishism of art to which the modern sensibility has succumbed, are significantly expressive of Tolstoy's spiritual crisis—a crisis badly understood by many people, who take it as a phenomenon disruptive of his creative power despite the fact that, in the last analysis, it is impossible to speak of two Tolstoys, the creative and the noncreative, for there is no real discontinuity in his career. . . . Thus *My Confession,* with which Tolstoy's later period opens and which appeared immediately after *Anna Karenina,* is unmistakably a work of the imagination and at the same time a mighty feat of consciousness.

Six years after writing *What is Art?* Tolstoy finished *Hadji Murad* . . . one of the finest nouvelles in the Russian language and a model of narrative skill and objective artistry. Is not the song of the nightingales, that song of life and death which bursts into ecstasy at dawn on the day when Hadji Murad attempts to regain his freedom, the very same song which rises in that marvelously sensual scene in *Family Happiness,* a scene bathed in sunlight, when Masha, surprising Sergey Mikhaylych in the cherry orchard, enjoys for the first time the full savor of her youthful love? *Hadji Murad* was written not less than forty-five years after *Family Happiness.* And in *The Devil*—a moral tale, the product, like *The Kreutzer Sonata,* of Tolstoy's most sectarian period and extremest assertion of dogmatic asceticism—what we remember best is not Eugene Irtenev's torments of conscience, his efforts to subdue his passion, but precisely the description of his carnal meetings in the sundrenched woods with Stepanida, the fresh and strong peasant-girl with full breasts and bright black eyes. The truth is that in the struggle between the old moralist and the old magician in Tolstoy both gave as good as they got. (pp. 89-93)

Tolstoy has been described as the least neurotic of all the great Russians. . . . Tolstoy is above all an artist of the normal— the normal, however, so intensified that it acquires a poetical truth and an emotional fullness which we are astounded to discover in the ordinary situations of life. . . . Even in Tolstoy's treatment of death there is nothing actually morbid. . . . Nothing could be more mistaken than the idea that Tolstoy's concern with death is an abnormal trait. On the contrary, if anything it is a supernormal trait, for the intensity of his concern with death is proportionate to the intensity of his concern with life. . . . It is due to this metaphysical simplicity that he was unable to come to terms with any system of dogmatic theology and that in the end, despite all his efforts to retain it, he was compelled to exclude even the idea of God from his own system of rationalized religion. Thus all notions of immortality seemed absurd to Tolstoy, and his scheme of salvation was entirely calculated to make men happy here and now. It is reported of Thoreau that when he lay dying his answer to all talk of the hereafter was "one world at a time." That is the sort of answer with which Tolstoy's mentality is wholly in accord.

The way in which his rationalism enters his art is shown in his analysis of character, an analysis which leaves nothing undefined, nothing unexplained. (pp. 93-4)

Unlike most of his contemporaries, Tolstoy did not pass through the school of Romanticism. . . . Insofar as he has any literary affiliations at all they go back to the eighteenth century, to Rousseau, to Sterne, to the French classical drama, and in Russia to the period of Karamzin, Zhukovsky, Novikov, and Radichev. He has their robustness and skepticism. . . . The contrast between Dostoevsky and Tolstoy, which Merezhkovsky and after him Thomas Mann have presented in terms of the abstract typology of the "man of spirit" as against the "man of nature," is more relevantly analyzed in terms of the contradiction between city and country, between the alienated intellectual proletariat of the city and the unalienated patriciate-peasantry of the country.

Much has been written concerning the influence of Rousseau on Tolstoy, but here again it is necessary to keep in mind that in western literature we perceive the Rousseauist ideas through the colored screen of Romanticism while in Tolstoy Rousseau survives through his rationalism no less than through his sensibility. (pp. 95-7)

Compared with Pierre, Prince Andrey, or Levin, Olenin [in *The Cossacks*] is a weak hero, but he is important in that in his reflections he sums up everything which went into the making of the early Tolstoy and which was in later years given a religious twist and offered as a doctrine of world-salvation. The primacy which the issue of happiness assumes in Olenin's thoughts is the key to his Tolstoyan nature. "Happiness is this," he said to himself, "happiness lies in living for others. That is evident. The desire for happiness is innate in every man; therefore it is legitimate. When trying to satisfy it self-

ishly—that is, by seeking for oneself riches, fame, comforts, or love—it may happen that circumstances arise which make it impossible to satisfy these desires. It follows that it is these desires which are illegitimate, but not the need for happiness. But what desires can always be satisfied despite external circumstances? What are they? Love, self-sacrifice." In these few sentences we get the quintessence of the Tolstoyan mentality: the belief that ultimate truth can be arrived at through common-sense reasoning, the utilitarian justification of the values of love and self-sacrifice and their release from all otherworldly sanctions, the striving for the simplification of existence which takes the form of a return to a life closer to nature—a return, however, involving a self-consciousness and a constant recourse to reason that augurs ill for the success of any such experiment.

Tolstoy's art is so frequently spoken of as "organic" that one is likely to overlook the rationalistic structure on which it is based. This structure consists of successive layers of concrete details, physical and psychological, driven into place and held together by a generalization or dogma. (pp. 98-9)

Parallelism of construction is another leading characteristic of the Tolstoyan method. In *War and Peace,* in the chronicle of the lives of the Bolkonsky and Rostov families, this parallelism is not devised dramatically, as a deliberate contrast, but in other narratives it is driven toward a stark comparison, as between Anna and Vronsky on the one hand and Kitty and Levin on the other in *Anna Karenina.* . . . (p. 99)

His early *nouvelles* can certainly be read and appreciated without reference to their historical context, to the ideological differences between him and his contemporaries which set him off to confound them with more proofs of his disdain for their "progressive" opinions. Still, the origin of *Family Happiness* in the quarrels of the period is worth recalling. At that time (in the 1850's) public opinion was much exercised over the question of free love and the emancipation of women; George Sand was a novelist widely read in intellectual circles, and of course most advanced people agreed with George Sand's libertarian solution of the question. Not so Tolstoy, who opposed all such tendencies, for he regarded marriage and family life as the foundations of society. Thus *Family Happiness*, with its denigration of love and of equal rights for women, was conceived, quite apart from its personal genesis in Tolstoy's affair with Valerya Arsenev, as a polemical rejoinder to George Sand, then adored by virtually all the Petersburg writers, including Dostoevsky.

The faith in family life is integral of Tolstoy. It has the deepest psychological roots in his private history, and socially it exemplifies his championship of patriarchal relations. It is a necessary part of his archaistic outlook, which in later life was transformed into a special kind of radicalism, genuinely revolutionary in some of its aspects and thoroughly archaistic in others. *War and Peace* is as much a chronicle of certain families as an historical novel. The historical sense is not really native to Tolstoy. His interest in the period of 1812 is peculiarly his own, derived from his interest in the story of his own family. He began work on *Anna Karenina* after failing in the attempt to write another historical novel, a sequel to *War and Peace*. And *Anna Karenina* is of course the novel in which his inordinate concern with marriage and family life receives its fullest expression. (pp. 99-100)

So much has been made here of the rationalism of Tolstoy that it becomes necessary to explain how his art is saved from the ill effects of it. (p. 100)

Now there is only one novel of Tolstoy's that might be described as a casualty of his rationalism, and that is **Resurrection**. The greater part of his fiction is existentially centered in a concrete inwardness and subjectivity by which it gains its quality of genius. In this sense it becomes possible to say that Tolstoy is much more a novelist of life and death than he is of good and evil—good and evil are not categories of existence but of moral analysis. And the binding dogmas or ideas of Tolstoy's fiction are not in contradiction with its existential sense; on the contrary, their interaction is a triumph of creative tact and proof of the essential wholeness of Tolstoy's nature. The Tolstoyan characters grasp their lives through their total personalities, not merely through their intellects. Their experience is full of moments of shock, of radical choice and decision, when they confront themselves in the terrible and inevitable aloneness of their being. (p. 101)

It is exactly this "standing face to face with life," and the realization that there are things in it that are irreducible and incomprehensible, which drew Tolstoy toward the theme of death. Again and again he returned to this theme, out of a fear of death which is really the highest form of courage. Most people put death out of their minds because they cannot bear to think of it. Gorky reports that Tolstoy once said to him that "if a man has learned to think, no matter what he may think about, he is always thinking of his own death. All philosophers were like that. And what truths can there be, if there is death?" That is a statement of despair and nihilism the paradox of which is that it springs from the depths of Tolstoy's existential feeling of life; and this is because the despair and nihilism spring not from the renunciation but from the affirmation of life; Tolstoy never gave up the search for an all-embracing truth, for a rational justification of man's existence on the earth.

The fact is that Tolstoy was at bottom so sure in his mastery of life and so firm in his inner feeling of security that he could afford to deal intimately with death. . . . His secret is that he is the last of the unalienated artists. . . . It is thanks to this unalienated condition that he is capable of moving us powerfully when describing the simplest, the most ordinary and therefore in their own way also the gravest occasions of life. . . . (pp. 102-03)

But, of course, even Tolstoy, being a man of the nineteenth century, could not finally escape the blight of alienation. In his lifetime Russian society disintegrated; he witnessed the passing of the old society of status and its replacement by a cruelly impersonal system of bourgeois relations. Tolstoy resisted the catastrophic ruin of the traditional order by straining all the powers of his reason to discover a way out. His so-called conversion is the most dramatic and desperate episode in his stubborn and protracted struggle against alienation. His attack on civilization is essentially an attack on the conditions that make for alienation. The doctrine of Christian anarchism, developed after his conversion, reflects, as Lenin put it, "the accumulated hate, the ripened aspiration for a better life, the desire to throw off the past—and also the immaturity, the dreamy contemplativeness, the political inexperience, and the revolutionary flabbiness of the villages." Still, the point of that doctrine lies not in its religious content, which is very small indeed, but rather in its formulation of a social ideal and of a utopian social program. (pp. 103-04)

Philip Rahv, "Tolstoy: The Green Twig and the Black Trunk," in his Image and Idea: Twenty Essays on Literary Themes *(copyright 1949, 1952 by Philip Rahv; copyright © 1957 by Philip Rahv; reprinted by permission of the Literary Estate of Philip Rahv), revised edition, New Directions, 1957, pp. 87-104.*

E. M. CIORAN   (essay date 1964)

[*Cioran is the author of several collections of philosophical essays which have been praised for their elegant and severe considerations of Western society and for their explorations of the limits of skepticism. Among his most frequently treated subjects is death and the impasse it presents to any body of thought that seeks to attribute a degree of value and meaning to life. Excerpted below is Cioran's analysis of Tolstoy's view of death as indicated by* The Death of Ivan Ilyich *and other works. While Cioran views the "salvation" of Ivan Ilyich as illusory, essays by John Donnelly and Robert Wexelblatt (see excerpts below) arrive at opposing conclusions.*]

If Tolstoy was always preoccupied by death, it became a besetting problem for him only after the crisis he passed through during his fiftieth year or thereabouts, when he began, in a panic, to question himself as to the "meaning" of life. But life, as soon as one is obsessed by what it may signify—life disintegrates, crumbles: which sheds a light on what it is, on what it is worth, on its wretched and improbable substance. Must one assert with Goethe that the meaning of life resides in life itself? A man haunted by such a problem will find this difficult, for the good reason that his obsession begins precisely with the revelation of the *meaninglessness* of life.

Some have tried to explain Tolstoy's crisis and his "conversion" by the exhaustion of his gifts. The explanation does not hold up. Certain works of the final period, like *The Death of Ivan Ilyich, Master & Man, Father Sergius, The Devil,* have a depth and a density no exhausted genius could have displayed. Tolstoy did not dry up, but he shifted his center of interest. Reluctant to brood further upon the external life of men, he chose to consider them only from the moment when, subject to a crisis too, they were led to break with the fictions in which they had lived heretofore. Under these conditions, it was no longer possible for him to write great novels. The pact with appearances which he had signed as a novelist he now denounced and tore up, to turn toward the *other* side of things. The crisis he entered, however, was neither so unexpected nor so radical as he thought when he wrote: "My life stopped." Far from being unforeseen, it actually represented the outcome, the exasperation of an anguish from which he had always suffered. (If *The Death of Ivan Ilyich* dates from 1886, all the themes it deals with are to be found in *Three Deaths,* from 1859.) But his early, "natural" anguish, being devoid of intensity, was tolerable, whereas the anguish he experienced later was scarcely so. The idea of death, to which Tolstoy was sensitive from childhood, has nothing morbid about it in itself; the same is not true of the obsession, the unwarranted development of this idea which then becomes fatal to the practice of life. This is doubtless the case if one accepts the viewpoint of life . . . But may one not conceive of a need for truth which, faced with the ubiquity of death, rejects every concession, as well as every distinction between normal and pathological? If only the fact of dying counts, one must draw the consequences without bothering about any other considerations. This is not a position to be adopted by those who unceasingly bemoan their "crisis," a state aspired to; on the contrary, by the true solitary who would never sink to saying "my life stopped," for that is precisely what he wants, what he pursues. But a Tolstoy, rich and famous, gratified by all that the world can bestow, stares bewildered at the collapse of his old certainties and strives in vain to banish from his mind the recent revelation of meaninglessness which invades, which overwhelms him. What amazes and baffles him in his case is that for all his vitality (he worked, he tells us, eight hours a day without feeling tired, and reaped in the fields as well as any peasant), he had to resort to various subterfuges to keep from killing himself. Vitality constitutes no obstacle to suicide: everything depends on the direction it takes or is given. Tolstoy himself observes, moreover, that the power which impelled him to self-destruction was similar to the one which had previously attached him to life—with this difference, he adds, that it now exerted itself *in the opposite direction*.

To search for the gaps in Being, to rush headlong to destruction in an excess of lucidity, to undermine and destroy oneself is not the privilege of the anemic; powerful natures, once they enter into conflict with themselves, are much more susceptible to this process; to it they bring all their passion, all their frenzy; indeed, it is such natures who suffer "crises" which we must regard as a punishment, for it is not normal that they should devote their energy to devouring themselves. Once they have attained the zenith of their career, they will asphyxiate under the weight of insoluble problems or collapse into a vertigo apparently stupid but actually legitimate and essential, the kind that seized Tolstoy when, in utter confusion, he kept murmuring to himself: "What's the use?" or "And then what?"

A man who has had an experience analogous to that of Ecclesiastes will remember it forever; the truths he will have gained from it are as irrefutable as they are impracticable: banalities ruinous to balance, *maddening* commonplaces. In the modern world, no one has had the intuition of inanity which so gratifyingly counters the hopes crammed into the Old Testament so distinctly as Tolstoy. Even when he sets himself up, later on, as a reformer, he cannot *answer* Solomon, the being with whom he has most points in common: were they not both great sensualists struggling with a universal disgust? This is a conflict with no outcome, a contradiction of temperaments, from which derives perhaps the vision of Vanity. The more inclined we are to take pleasure in everything, the more disgust persists in keeping us from doing so, and its interventions will be vigorous in direct proportion to the impatience of our thirst for pleasure. "Thou shalt not enjoy!"—such is the command it utters at each encounter, upon every forgetful occasion. Existence has a flavor only if we keep ourselves in a gratuitous intoxication, in that state of inebriation without which the self possesses nothing positive. When Tolstoy assures us that before his crisis he was "drunk with life," he means that he was simply *alive*, in other words, that he was drunk as is every living being *as such*. Then comes the sobering up, which assumes the image of fatality. What is to be done? One has the means to be drunk, but one cannot be so; in full vigor, yet one is not *in* life, one does not belong to it any longer; one breaks through it, discerns its unreality, for the sobering up is clearsightedness and awakening. And to what does one awaken, if not to death?

Ivan Ilyich wanted to be petted and comforted; more miserable than his hero, Tolstoy compares himself to a fledgling fallen from the nest! His drama compels sympathy, though we cannot subscribe to the reasons he alleges in order to explain it. The "negative" part is, in him, far more interesting than the other. If his questions rise from the deepest part of his being, the same is not true of his answers. That the perplexities he suffered during his crisis verged on the intolerable is a fact; instead of trying to rid himself of them for this motive alone, he chooses to tell us that, being the characteristic of the rich and the idle

and never of the *moujiks*, they are devoid of any intrinsic significance. Obviously he underestimates the advantages of satiety, which permits certain discoveries forbidden to indigence. (pp. 144-48)

In order to justify his cult of the *moujiks* Tolstoy invokes their detachment, their readiness to depart from this life without bothering about futile problems. Does he appreciate them, does he really love them? Rather he envies them, believing them less complicated than they are. He supposes they glide into death, that for them death is a comfort, that in the middle of a snowstorm they surrender like Nikita, while Brekhunov resists, struggles. "What is the easiest way to die?"—that is the question which has dominated his maturity and tormented his old age. The simplicity he has ceaselessly sought he has found nowhere, except in his style. He was too ravaged to achieve it. Like every tormented spirit, exhausted and subjugated by his sufferings, he could love only trees and animals, and only those men who by some characteristic were akin to the elements. From their contact he expected—no doubt about it— to wrest himself from his habitual pangs and to proceed toward an endurable, even a serene agony. To reassure himself, to encounter peace at any cost is all that mattered to him. We see now why Ivan Ilyich could not be allowed to die in disgust or in dread. "He sought his former accustomed fear of death and did not find it. 'Where is it? What death?' There was no fear because there was no death. In place of death there was light. 'So that's what it is!' he suddenly exclaimed aloud. 'What joy!'"

Neither this joy nor this light carry conviction; they are extrinsic, they are imposed. We are reluctant to admit that they can alleviate the darkness in which the dying man is struggling: nothing moreover prepared him for this jubilation, which has no relation to his mediocrity, nor to the solitude to which he is reduced. On the other hand, the description of his agony is so oppressive in its exactitude that it would have been almost impossible to end it without changing its tone and level. "'Death is finished,' he said to himself. 'It is no more.'" Prince André wanted to be convinced of the same thing. "Love is God, and to die means that I, a particle of love, shall return to the general and eternal source." More skeptical about Prince André's final divagations than he was to be later on about those of Ivan Ilyich, Tolstoy adds: "These thoughts seemed to him comforting. But they were only thoughts. Something was lacking in them, they were not clear, they were too one-sidedly personal and rationalizing; they lacked reality." Unfortunately those of poor Ivan Ilyich lacked it quite as much. But Tolstoy has come a long way since **War & Peace:** he has reached a stage where at all costs he must elaborate a formula for salvation and abide by it. That imposed light and joy—how can we help feeling that he dreamed of them for himself and that, quite as much as simplicity, they were forbidden to him? No less *dreamed of* are the last words he makes his hero speak about the end of death. Let us compare with this end which is not an end, with this conventional and arbitrary triumph, the genuine and authentic hatred which this same hero feels toward his family:

> In the morning when he saw first his footman, then his wife, then his daughter, and then the doctor, their every word and movement confirmed to him the awful truth that had been revealed to him during the night. In them he saw himself—all that for which he had lived— and saw clearly that it was not real at all, but a terrible and huge deception which had hidden

both life and death. This consciousness intensified his physical suffering tenfold. He groaned and tossed about, and pulled at his clothing which choked and stifled him. And he hated them all on that account.

Hatred does not lead to deliverance, nor is it clear how one leaps from abomination of the world and self-loathing into that zone of purity where death is transcended, "finished." To hate oneself and the world is to give both too much credit, and disqualifies one for emancipation from either. Self-hatred, above all, testifies to a capital illusion. Because he hated himself, Tolstoy believed he was no longer living a lie. Now, unless one devotes oneself to renunciation (of which he was incapable), one can live only by lying and by lying to oneself. Which is what Tolstoy did, moreover: is it not a lie to assert, *trembling*, that one has conquered death and the fear of death? This sensualist who incriminated the senses, who always opposed himself, who enjoyed persecuting his inclinations, applied himself with perverse ardor to taking a path opposed to what he was. A voluptuous need to torment himself drove him toward the insoluble. He was a writer, the first of his time; instead of deriving some satisfaction from the fact, he *invented* a vocation for himself, that of the Good Man, at every point alien to his tastes. He began to interest himself in the poor, to help them, to bemoan their condition, but his pity—alternately despairing and indiscreet—was merely a form of his horror of the world. Sullenness, his dominant characteristic, occurs in those who, convinced they have taken the wrong turn and missed their true destination, regret having remained *beneath* themselves. Despite his considerable *oeuvre*, Tolstoy had this feeling; let us not forget that he had come to regard his works as frivolous, even harmful; he had created them, but he had not created himself. His sullenness resulted from the interval separating his literary success from his spiritual frustration.

Sakyamuni, Solomon, Schopenhauer—of these three melancholics he so often quotes, the first went furthest and is doubtless the one Tolstoy would have preferred to resemble: he might have managed it, if disgust for the world and oneself sufficed to grant access to Nirvana. But then, Buddha left his family when he was very young (one cannot imagine him trapped in conjugal dramas, surrounded by his household, irresolute and moody, cursing everyone for keeping him from carrying out his grand design), while Tolstoy would wait for decrepitude to make his escape—that spectacular and painful episode. If the discrepancy between his doctrine and his life bothered him, he nonetheless lacked the strength to do anything about it. How would he have gone about it, given the incompatibility between his concerted aspirations and his deepest instincts? In order to measure the scope of his torments (as they are revealed, notably, in *Father Sergius*), we should recall that he strove in secret to *imitate* the saints and that of all his ambitions this one was the most imprudent. By proposing a model so disproportionate to his means, he inevitably inflicted further disappointments upon himself. If only he had meditated upon the verse of the Bhagavad-Gita, according to which it is better to perish by one's own law than to obey another's! And it is precisely because he sought salvation elsewhere than on his own path that in his so-called "regeneration" period he was even more miserable than before. With a pride like Tolstoy's, the pursuit of charity was a mistake: the more he aspired to it, the more grim he became. His radical incapacity to love, combined with an icy clearsightedness, explains why he cast upon all things, singularly upon his characters, a gaze without complicity. "Reading his works, one never has an impulse to laugh

or even smile," noted one Russian critic toward the end of the last century. Conversely, we have quite failed to understand Dostoevsky if we do not realize that humor is his chief quality. He is carried away, he forgets himself, and since he is never cold, he reaches that temperature, that degree of fever where, reality being transfigured, the fear of death is meaningless, since one has risen above it. He has transcended it, triumphed over it, as suits a visionary, and he would have been quite incapable of describing a deathbed with that clinical precision in which a Tolstoy excels. We may add that the latter is, moreover, a clinician *sui generis:* he never studies anything but his own ills and, when he treats them, brings to the work all the acuity and all the vigilance of his terrors.

It has often been remarked that Dostoevsky, sick and impoverished, ended his career with an apotheosis (the speech on Pushkin!), whereas Tolstoy, fortune's darling, was to conclude his in despair. Upon reflection, the contrast in their dénouements is quite in order. Dostoevsky, after the rebellions and ordeals of his youth, thought of nothing but *serving;* he reconciled himself if not with the universe at least with his country whose abuses he accepted and justified; he believed it was Russia's destiny to play a great role, he believed she was even to save humanity. The former conspirator, now established and pacified, could without imposture defend the Church and the State; in any case, he was no longer *alone*. Tolstoy, on the other hand, was to become more and more so. He plunged into desolation, and if he spoke so much of a "new life," it was because life itself escaped him. The religion he believed he was rejuvenating he was in fact undermining. Combating injustice, he went further than the anarchists, and the formulas he advanced were of a demoniac or laughable excess. What accounts for so much extravagance, so much negation is the revenge of a mind which could never bring itself to accept the humiliation of dying. (pp. 149-54)

E. M. Cioran, "The Oldest Fear: Apropos of Tolstoy," in his The Fall into Time, *translated by Richard Howard (translation copyright © 1970 by Quadrangle Books; reprinted by permission of Times Books/ The New York Times Book Co., Inc.; originally published as* La chute dans le temps, *Editions Gallimard, 1964), Quadrangle Books, 1970, pp. 141-54.*

F. R. LEAVIS   (essay date 1967)

[*Leavis is an influential contemporary English critic. His critical methodology combines close textual criticism with predominantly moral, or social-moral, principles of evaluation. Leavis views the writer as that social individual who represents the "most conscious point of the race" in his or her lifetime. More importantly, the writer is one who can effectively communicate this consciousness. Contrary to what these statements may suggest, Leavis is not specifically interested in the individual writer per se, but more concerned with the usefulness of his or her art in the scheme of civilization. The writer's role in this vision is to promote what Leavis calls "sincerity"—or, the realization of the individual's proper place in the human world. Literature which accomplishes this he calls "mature," and the writer's judgement within such a work he calls a "mature" moral judgement. From the foregoing comments it should be clear that Leavis is a critic concerned with the moral aspects of art, but a number of his contemporaries, most notably René Wellek, have questioned the existence of a moral system beneath such terms as "maturity" and "sincerity." Leavis's refusal to theorize or develop a systematic philosophy has alienated many critics and scholars from his work.*]

Anna Karenina one of the great European novels?—it is, surely, *the* European novel. The completeness with which Tolstoy, with his genius, was a Russian of his time made him an incomparably representative European, and made the book into which his whole experience, his most comprehensive 'relatedness,' went what it is for us: the great novel of modern—of our—civilization. The backwardness of Russia meant that the transcendent genius experienced to the full, taking their significances with personal intensity, the changes that have produced our modern world. In a country in which serfdom has been recently abolished, the characters of *Anna Karenina* travel as a matter of course by railway between the two capitals. The patriarchal landowner participates in a cosmopolitan culture, and, using French and English in intercourse with members of his own class, is intellectually nourished on the contemporary literature and thought of the West. Anna herself, having had at the outset of the book the shock of the fatal accident that marks her arrival at Moscow, ends her life under the iron wheels. The apparition of the little peasant with the sack who horrifies her, and is so oddly associated with the wheels and the rails, acts on our imagination as a pregnant symbol and a sinister augury (he is seen, too, later in a nightmare by Vronsky). The disharmonies, contrasts, and contradictions are challenging in a way that makes the optimisms of Progress impossible for Tolstoy—as the inability of Levin, the earnest and public-spirited, to see a duty in Zemstvo-attendance very characteristically intimates. *Anna Karenina*, in its human centrality, gives us modern man; Tolstoy's essential problems, moral and spiritual, are ours. (p. 32)

> F. R. Leavis, "'Anna Karenina,'" in his Anna Karenina and Other Essays (© F. R. Leavis 1933, 1944, 1947, 1950, 1951, 1952, 1955, 1958, 1961, 1963, 1964, 1967; reprinted by permission of the author's Literary Estate and Chatto & Windus), Chatto & Windus, 1967, pp. 9-32.

R. F. CHRISTIAN   (essay date 1969)

[*Christian's study of Tolstoy, from which the following excerpt on* A Confession *and* Resurrection *is taken, is a comprehensive survey of his works.*]

The last part of *Anna Karenina* leads logically into Tolstoy's *Confession,* which in turn is the prelude to his numerous religious treatises expounding his beliefs, his revised version of the Sermon on the Mount and his attempt to express in artistic form in his last full-scale novel, *Resurrection,* the true message of the Gospels as he understands them, stripped of their theological excrescences and purged of their supernatural mystique. . . . Christianity, however, was only one field of exploration, and it was not long before he extended his researches eastwards. His reading embraced the Vedas, the Upanishads, Confucius, Mencius and Lao Tzu. He came to believe that the most important task of his life was to synthesise the wisdom of East and West. . . . [The *Confession*] is the clearest, most relentless and most devastating statement we have of its author's spiritual pilgrimage. None of the great confessional literature from St Augustine to Rousseau can match Tolstoy's short work for power, eloquence, concise if not always logical thought, and the ability to convey with colloquial simplicity the grandeur and nobility of biblical language. (p. 213)

There is no doubt that his confession was torn from his soul in a moment of acute despair. As he said when writing it: 'This is not a work of art, and it is not for publication.' And yet he did publish it (not in Russia, where it was banned in 1882, but in Geneva in 1884), and it is precisely because it is a work of art and not a tract that it still retains its appeal today. For if

one applies to it the criteria of hard logic and common sense (as Tolstoy liked to do when he was leading for the prosecution and not the defence), its arguments leave much to be desired. When Tolstoy tries to show the inability of philosophers to answer his questions, he cites only those philosophers and religious thinkers whose views support his case that life is meaningless and that death is better than life. . . . His numerous generalisations supported by 'for the most part' or 'almost all' (believers for the most part are stupid, cruel and immoral . . . unbelievers for the most part are intelligent, upright and moral . . . almost all writers are immoral and worthless . . .) and his oversimplifications of the sort 'All that people truly believe in must be the truth', his exaggeration of his own vices or his idealisation of the faith of the common people: all belong as much to the realm of his art as to life. Indeed, at the time of writing his *Confession* and accusing himself of lying, theft, adultery, drunkenness, violence and even murder, he was telling his friend Strakhov: 'Write your biography. I keep meaning to do the same. Only one must aim to make all one's readers feel disgusted with one's life.' While it is hard to deny Tolstoy's sincerity, it is equally hard to deny his artifice. Concealed by the colloquial language, the omitted pronouns, the seemingly casual 'and', 'but', 'thus', 'and so', lie the carefully constructed runs of threes, the sets of nouns and verbs, sometimes five or six in number with no conjunctions, the rhetorical appoggiaturas and the conscious literary exploitation of the parable, the long simile or the dream.

Turgenev, while impressed by what he thought was Tolstoy's sincerity and conviction, if not his art, criticised the book because it led to the most gloomy negation of human life; 'a sort of nihilism' he terms it, thinking perhaps of Bazarov in his own *Fathers and Sons*. His remark is open to more than one interpretation. Tolstoy, like Bazarov, was contemptuous of authority and its hallowed principles. Both men tended towards puritanism, both had more than a touch of self-righteousness and contempt for human weakness. Both were to reject art, though for different reasons; both give the impression of being uncompromisingly honest with themselves; both get away with one-sided, weighted arguments because of their stark simplicity and apparent sincerity. But if Bazarov, the rationalist and materialist, believes in science, knowledge and the primacy of the mind, Tolstoy uses his immense powers of reason and his vast knowledge to exalt faith above science and rationalism. If Bazarov was a nihilist because he only wanted to destroy ('to clear the site'), Tolstoy was emphatically not so, because he was groping towards a positive faith which could give him the strength to lead a moral life, the sanction for which was to be at least in part the precepts and example of Christ.

If we regard nihilism in a wider context than that of Bazarov, we shall find more justice in Turgenev's remark. On the one hand Turgenev feared that Tolstoy's peasant-oriented, Christ-based morality would mean the end of civilised life as he himself understood it. . . . On the other hand he may have sensed Tolstoy's leanings towards Buddhism and Nirvana, the axiom that death is better than life and that faith is only a temporary palliative by means of which to endure the short time before the inevitable passage into nothingness—the feeling Prince Andrew has before his death when he wonders whether God is the Great All or Nothing. And yet there is no hopelessness in Tolstoy's work, only an endless seeking which provides that quality of ambiguity and lack of finality so important to a work of art, but inappropriate in a propaganda treatise. (pp. 215-17)

Ten years were to elapse between Tolstoy's first draft of the *Confession* and the opening chapters of *Resurrection*. Another ten years were to pass before *Resurrection* was published in 1899. . . . 'I began to think how nice it would be', he said in 1891, 'to write a novel *de longue haleine,* illuminating it with my present view of things and collecting all my ideas together in it.' He wanted to begin with an invective against the whole legal system and its absurdity. He wanted, moreover, to contrast the 'two extremes of true love with its false middle,' the youthful innocent love of Maslova and Nekhlyudov and their married love with extra-marital sexual relations and prostitution. But while his intentions were abundantly clear, he was disturbed by the effect they might have on the novelist's concern with problems of psychology, structure and composition. . . . 'Novels end with the hero and the heroine getting married. They ought to begin with this and end with their getting "unmarried", i.e. becoming free. (pp. 218-20)

The beginning and ending of his own novel proved particularly troublesome to Tolstoy. (p. 220)

The difficulty of keeping so many objectives in view, and the constant and growing tension between propaganda and art inevitably left their mark. As his crisis receded, Tolstoy's views crystallised and hardened, and when he returned to *Resurrection* for the last time he no longer had the breadth of human sympathy, the vast apprehension of reality or the restless spirit of enquiry which animated *War and Peace.* Critical opinion is often shifting, but no serious critic would deny that Tolstoy's last novel is a vastly inferior work of art to the two great novels which preceded it.

The reader whose appetite for Tolstoy has been whetted on *War and Peace* will be struck more by what is missing in *Resurrection* than by what is there. Gone are the domesticity, the poetry of 'marriage and the hearth', the ballroom, the salon, the charm, vivacity and graciousness of the best representatives of upper-class society and with them the complement of aristocratic life—hunting, coursing, and the outdoor activities of the country gentleman. Psychologically speaking, there is a striking absence of motivation for character development. (p. 221)

Missing too from *Resurrection* are the richness and variety of the parallel and contrasting themes of the earlier novels. In *Resurrection.* . . . Tolstoy, while exploiting transition and antithesis, prefers to work with a single plot line and to impart unity to the novel by the central theme of guilt and expiation.

The new theme of expiation is in marked contrast with *Anna Karenina,* for Anna can never redeem her lapse; she is fighting a losing battle from the start. Indeed there are many new departures in *Resurrection.* . . . In subject matter, though not of course treatment, *Resurrection* has more affinity with Dostoevsky's fiction than with Tolstoy's earlier novels. The theme of humanity among convicts calls to mind *The House of the Dead.* . . . Tolstoy's theme of guilt and expiation weaves together two strands and fuses an individual and a class problem. The story of the fall and regeneration of two individuals is complicated by the fact that one is an aristocrat and the other is not. . . . Tolstoy handles the theme of crime and punishment by showing the conflicting attitudes to both of the individual and the state. (pp. 222-23)

Resurrection has been called the most synthetic of Tolstoy's novels. In one sense this can be taken to refer to the synthesis of the indiviudal and the class problem. In another sense it may mean the synthesis of its author's social, political and religious opinions, for it contains the essence of his mature views on most of the fundamental questions of life. (p. 223)

In *Resurrection* it is the law which is the arch offender, and in attempting to achieve an artistic synthesis of his material Tolstoy knits together the three strands of Nekhluydov, Maslova and the pursuit of justice. He divides his novel into three parts. Part 1 is the offence, the trial, the verdict and the discrediting of the law; its satire is directed against legal institutions. Part 2 is the attempt to use the law to right the law and its target is the bureaucracy. Part 3 purports to show that it *is* possible to change human beings; and ruthless satire gives way to an attempt to understand and live with the victims of state oppression.

The tripartite division of the novel provides a good structural foundation, but the building of the individual sections is uneven. It is the first part which has the most cohesion. A brief examination of Part 1 will show how Tolstoy tried to 'mount' his story, still using his favourite devices of juxtaposition and antithesis. The novel opens on what should be a joyful note. It is spring. The trees are in leaf. The birds are singing. The sun is shining. But it is spring in a big city—a contradictory notion—where men have desecrated natural beauty, disfigured the land and learned to cheat and torment each other. This is the cue to introduce Maslova in jail and for the author to tell her story in narrative form without mentioning her seducer's name. Immediately afterwards, Nekhlyudov's life of luxury is contrasted with Maslova's squalid existence before the two come face to face in court. He recognises her; she does not recognise him. A vicious satire on the court and its proceedings juxtaposes those in authority and those in their power. Then Tolstoy turns the clock back ten years and 'in his old manner' writes the best chapters in the novel, prefaced by the simple statement: 'The relations between Nekhlyudov and Maslova had been as follows.' In a typically Tolstoyan climax, light and darkness are contrasted as the beautiful description of Easter, the snow, the church music, the bright clothes and the Easter greetings is followed abruptly by the sordid manoeuvres of seduction, the girl's resistance having been carefully eroded to the point where she becomes a not unwilling accomplice. . . . (pp. 224-25)

A stroke of the pen, ten years pass and we are back in court to witness the miscarriage of justice. . . . The verdict pronounced, Nekhlyudov leaves for a sumptuous dinner at his prospective fiancée's; Maslova returns to her cell to hunger and humiliation. The scene shifts to the jail as Nekhlyudov tries to obtain permission to visit Maslova, and in yet another pointed juxtaposition of incompatibles the strains of a Liszt rhapsody 'so unsuitable to the place' float from the prison warden's house. As Maslova lies awake in prison Tolstoy recalls through her thought processes the occasion when, already pregnant, she ran through the wind and rain to the railway station to catch a glimpse of Nekhlyudov passing through by train. Once again we have the familiar antithesis: Nekhlyudov laughing and joking inside the brightly lit carriage, Maslova standing weeping in the dark. . . . (pp. 226-27)

Her thoughts: that people live only for their own pleasure and that all talk about God and righteousness is so much deception, lead straight into the most vicious of all Tolstoy's satires—the prison chapel service—the epitome of all that is inappropriate and unnatural. (p. 228)

As the novel progresses, however, the structural synthesis is not maintained. The imbalance caused by the constant urge to denounce, the oversimplification, the crude irony and obstinate refusal to allow more than one point of view, the diminished sympathy and human understanding, all overshadow the occasional brilliant evocation of atmosphere, poignant scenes and wealth of realistic detail conveyed in direct and forceful language which are the hallmark of the mature Tolstoy. Most people will agree that 'the best qualities of *Resurrection* are not characteristic of the later Tolstoy; they are rather, in a minor degree, those of *Anna Karenina* and *War and Peace*'. Unfortunately the urge to point a moral, discreet in the two earlier novels, becomes overt and offensive in *Resurrection,* which, in the last resort, is not a search, but an analysis of society in the light of revealed truth. (p. 229)

> *R. F. Christian, in his* Tolstoy: A Critical Introduction *(© Cambridge University Press 1969), Cambridge at the University Press, 1969, 291 p.*

JOHN DONNELLY   (essay date 1978)

[*Whereas E. M. Cioran reads Tolstoy's* The Death of Ivan Ilyich *as indicative of a nihilistic vision of life (see excerpt above), Donnelly believes this story expresses a highly optimistic view of both life and death.*]

It is a curious paradox that the meaning of life is often found in the meaning of death. Presumably a man's death takes place when he suffers irreversible loss of those characteristics essential to his personhood, so that in determining when such a loss occurs, one is also determining what properties are regarded as essential to constitute a person's life. Leo Tolstoy's *The Death of Ivan Ilych* vividly depicts such a paradox through the dramatic unfolding of the moral reappraisal of Ivan Ilych's life in his dying stages. Ilych as the vernacular has it *found himself in dying,* discovering what existentialists term *authenticity* upon careful reflection on the meaning of death. Despite what appeared to be an agonizing, painful dying process, replete with pathetic self-pity on the part of his hypocritical loved ones and professional insensitivity on the part of his attending physicians, Ilych had domination over death at the end. "'Let the pain be. And death . . . where is it?' He sought his former accustomed fear of death and did not find it. 'Where is it? What death?' There was no fear because there was no death. In place of death there was light. 'So that's what it is!' he suddenly exclaimed aloud. 'What joy!'" . . . (p. 116)

[Both] Tolstoy and Ilych (that is, the Ilych in the last two hours of his drawn-out dying period) were much too sanguine about the human condition and the prospects for attaining moral integrity in this life. In short, I believe the Tolstoyan lesson to be drawn from Ilych's dying is not a realistic expectation, although it is devoutly to be wished. "At that very moment Ivan Ilych fell through and caught sight of the light, and it was revealed to him that though his life had not been what it should have been, this could still be rectified." . . .

Tolstoy seems to be suggesting that a man is dead not just when he suffers irreversible loss of neocortical activity, or when he satisfies the 1968 Harvard Medical School criteria for brain death—but most importantly a person is dead when stripped of his autonomy regardless of how operative his cerebral functions. While there is clearly a normative element in any proposed definition of death, the normative component of Tolstoy's suggestion is all-pervasive. . . . Tolstoy seems to be saying that a person may have ceased long before a human being does—even if that same human being is physiologically well-functioning.

Tolstoy appears to be maintaining then that questions about whether a man has a soul or not, or whether a man is dead or not, are not simply empirical inquiries but rather questions about the kind of life he is living. Offering a somewhat secularized version of Kierkegaard's *Purity of Heart,* death is viewed as alienation from virtue; immortality as union with various conduct. (p. 117)

A man is dead for Tolstoy, I suggest, when he either chooses to renounce his integrity and the complex set of moral practices and beliefs associated with and constitutive of that integrity, or when he has his integrity violated against his wishes. Given such a state of affairs we say "the man has lost his soul"— even though in the descriptive and more properly metaphysical sense his soul (incorporeal substance, discarnate personality, etc.) may be quite intact.

There are obviously some difficulties attached to such a normative definition of death, the most obvious being the host of slippery-slope pitfalls contained therein. However, any justified fears about such thin-edge-of-the wedge arguments seem more forceful with regard to currently formulated biological definitions of death than to Tolstoy's highly normative definition. That is, current biological accounts of death all speak of *irreversible* cessation of either neocortical activity or spontaneous brain function, etc., and consequently add a note of finality to their practical ramifications. But Tolstoy's account remains more tentative inasmuch as the man who loses his autonomy may not have suffered an irreversible loss, as but witness Ilych's moral conversion. . . .

I believe, *given* Tolstoy's proposed analysis of death, that it would be unrealistic for most persons to expect to attain moral integrity (except for death-bed moral conversions where any cause for optimism is quickly relinquished by recalling Aristotle's caveat that one swallow does not make a spring, and I take it Tolstoy considers it merely fortuitous that Ilych was in that situation), so that in some sense *pace* Ilych death has dominion over us. (p. 118)

Most people, I suspect, will become functionaries who will continue through life much like Tolstoy's Ivan Ilych did as "capable, cheerful, good natured, and sociable—though strict in the fulfillment of what [they] considered to be [their] duty; and [they] considered [their] duty to be what was so considered by those in authority." . . .

I hope, however, that that rare moment may arise (only sooner) when like Ivan Ilych (on his deathbed) each person may ask if his heteronomous life (if applicable) had not been a mistake.

It may be true, as Tolstoy's normative portrayal of Ilych implies, that Ilych lived dying and died living, but for most of us, if there be no God, our lot in all likelihood will be to live dying and eventually to die. (p. 127)

> *John Donnelly, "Death and Ivan Ilych," in* Language, Metaphysics, and Death, *edited by John Donnelly (reprinted by permission of the publisher; copyright © 1978 by Fordham University Press), Fordham University Press, 1978, pp. 116-30.*

ROBERT WEXELBLATT   (essay date 1980)

[*While E. M. Cioran and John Donnelly provide philosophical readings of* The Death of Ivan Ilyich *(see excerpts above), Wexelblatt compares this story with Franz Kafka's* The Metamorphosis. *The transformation of Gregor Samsa into an insect in Kafka's novella, and Samsa's eventual death, is contrasted with the more realistically told and more optimistically concluded fate of Ivan Ilyich.*]

Who does not agree that Kafka's is the art of neurosis, nightmare, symbol, and the unheard-of, or that Tolstoy has a knack for the materially real and socially typical? To be blunt, *The Death of Ivan Ilych* is the story of what happens to everyone, while *The Metamorphosis* is a tale of what has never yet happened to anyone.

Of course there are other, more circumstantial, differences too. For instance, Gregor is a bachelor and younger than the middle-aged paterfamilias, Ivan. Samsa is a travelling salesman, Ivan a jurist. Ivan is Russian, Gregor—? But these are relatively trivial matters, like the fact that Tolstoy supplies a devastatingly detailed biography of his bourgeois Everyman and Kafka doesn't. Somewhat more consequential perhaps are the facts that Ivan's family problems have to do with his being married, Gregor's with his celibacy—that is, with the condition of being a son and a brother—and that Ivan is "saved" in the end, while Gregor isn't. These are of obvious importance, especially the last, and yet these differences are just the sort one would expect, given any familiarity with the artists' personal situations and concerns at the time they wrote.

It is actually the most obvious difference of all that is also the most interesting to ponder: viz., that Tolstoy's story is realistic and Kafka's is not. This is as much a matter of subject as of treatment. After all, death is for us a thoroughly realistic contingency, unlike entomological metamorphosis. Tolstoy writes about the one eventuality that will occur to us all. Kafka, by selecting an impossible fate for Gregor Samsa, makes of his case the symbol for all experiences of this kind. Thus, in the end, both the realism and the symbolism pay off in universal currency.

But even such fundamental differences can be mitigated. Certainly we all must die, and may even go through a Tolstoyan criticism of our lives because of it. Nevertheless, the home-truth of mortality is generally kept as distant by us as it was by Ivan. And Tolstoy knows his reader. Prometheus, says Aeschylus, gave men "blind hopes" in precisely this way: by removing the exact knowledge of their deaths. And why, if not because the illusion of immortality is the condition of putting all the rest of Prometheus' technological gifts into effect, and therefore ultimately of building up some version of that civilization for which Tolstoy is gunning? In seeking to expunge the blindness and sublimate the hopes, Tolstoy renders the ordinary incomprehensible. His story intends to make us think that it is not only "Caius" who dies, but also Ivan and therefore we as well. Such an intention is not only aimed at transforming us, like a fire-and-brimstone sermon, but also at transforming reality.

Likewise, we all may change. An accident could make us quadruple amputees overnight; we might grow out our beards or hair, not to mention altering our politics, quitting our jobs, falling into a depression or even taking up thinking. Who can be sure that even the merest change of mind or heart might not cause us also to sound to our families or employers as if we too had "no human voice"? We may suddenly discover music, art, religion, solitude, guilt—and any one of these might make us in some degree as Gregor. Ivan's fate is ours, but we are reluctant to believe it. Gregor's fate is unbelievable, but it may well be ours. Thus the familiar can become unintelligible and the unintelligible may also light up the commonplace. And this, I think, is just what happens in *The Death of Ivan Ilych* and *The Metamorphosis*. (pp. 603-05)

The similarities between these two works may be either accidental, deliberate, or something outside the usual classifications. . . . But in any case, it is through an examination of the congruences themselves that an answer must be sought. (p. 611)

The illness and the metamorphosis correspond as causes because they produce identical effects. For instance, it is due to the changes occurring in Ivan during his illness that he is gradually isolated from the "human circle" of his family and friends. Just so, Gregor is outcast—though more radically and instantaneously—by change. . . . Notice here that the same meaning which Tolstoy conveys through a careful piling up of realistic detail leading to a portrayal of middle-class actuality Kafka hurls at us directly and all at once, through the symbol. . . . Thus it is not quite enough to say that both Tolstoy and Kafka confront their characters with "extraordinary situations." Death and metamorphosis are both situations, but not merely out-of-the-way occurrences. Properly speaking, these are situations of absurdity. . . . It is through the impact of death on Ivan's flesh and Ivan's brain that we are to learn Tolstoy's lesson, but Kafka shows us his truth nakedly, without the need even for psychological realism. (pp. 611-12)

The conformism that robs both Ivan and his house of their individuality is reflected in the interchangeability of his colleagues. The same point is made more directly by Kafka simply by having the three lodgers be identical in appearance, attitude, and behavior—carbon copies of one another. . . . The Samsas' initial response to hearing Gregor's unintelligible voice is to call aloud for a doctor and a locksmith. The hope of picking the lock of the mystery which has taken place in Gregor's room is equivalent to that of discovering a physiological cure for what is really a spiritual ailment. And both are equivalent to Ivan's dealings with his several doctors, and his hope of escaping death through them. But it is absurd to think that medical science can treat a symbol or that the key to transcendence can be procured from a smith. (p. 613)

The major elements of what must be called the redemption of Ivan Ilych include: the establishment of a valid subjectivity, the appreciation and acceptance of new and especially of neglected values, and the renunciation of a materialistic, possessive existence bound up with things. These are the ultimate achievement of Ivan and the spiritual peaks which Gregor Samsa fails—hard to say how nearly—to attain. But in making our comparison it is the formal repetition, consisting in a subtle series of gestures and responses, which is initially eye-catching. It is as if a less adept acrobat should attempt to imitate the greatest stunt of his master and, somehow in the process, question and parody success by failure. (p. 615)

Perhaps Kafka only intended to suggest a religious backdrop for the story. All the same, when he learns of Gregor's death, Mr. Samsa says: "Well, now thanks be to God." He then crosses himself "and the three women followed his example." This not only echoes the end of the Mass ("The Mass is ended. Thanks be to God."), but is reminiscent of Tolstoy's making "It is finished" Ivan's last words. Even the "three women" standing over Gregor's corpse recall the three explicitly mentioned in the Gospels as having attended at Jesus' death. Mr. Samsa's gesture may also reflect that scene in Tolstoy's prologue in which Peter Ivanovich awkwardly crosses himself when entering the room where his friend's corpse is laid out: "All he knew was that at such times it is always safe to cross oneself."

The much briefer coda of *The Metamorphosis*, comprising all that happens after Gregor's death, corresponds to the opening of *Ivan Ilych* in that it shares the same underlying action. (p. 625)

What is possible for Tolstoy in what Randall Jarrell has called "the most existential" of stories is not possible for Kafka. As perhaps this exploration of the congruences between the two novellas shows, it is not even possible for Kafka to take the possibility quite seriously. Almost exactly between the two works falls, "as lightly and heavily as a guillotine," the beginning of our own century, on the spiritual state of which this contrast may be taken as a commentary. (p. 628)

> Robert Wexelblatt, "The Higher Parody: Ivan Ilych's Metamorphosis and the Death of Gregor Samsa," in The Massachusetts Review *(reprinted from* The Massachusetts Review, The Massachusetts Review, Inc.; © 1980), Vol. XXI, No. 3, Fall, 1980, pp. 601-28.*

SYDNEY SCHULTZE (essay date 1982)

[*Schultze's* The Structure of "Anna Karenina," *from which the following was excerpted, provides an in-depth examination of the source materials, use of language, themes, images, and characters in this work.*]

Anna Karenina was conceived and written during one of the most difficult periods of Lev Tolstoi's long, turbulent life. In early September, 1869, Tolstoi suffered a sudden, severe depression. According to the fictionalized account of his experience in **"Notes of a Madman,"** he awoke one night to find himself in the presence of Death. The horror and despair he felt that night are echoed in Anna Karenina's thoughts just before her suicide. The next decade brought Tolstoi close to death again and again. . . . Tolstoi's spiritual struggle with philosophy and religion during this time increased his unrest.

Tolstoi's work on his new novel was scarcely more satisfying. Neither while he was writing nor after he finished it did Tolstoi have much good to say about *Anna Karenina*. (p. 3)

What actually emerged, despite Tolstoi's marked lack of enthusiasm, was one of the finest novels of Western literature. Among Tolstoi's own works, *Anna Karenina* occupies a special place. While *War and Peace* is often considered his best work, a case can be made for *Anna Karenina* as well. Its construction is tighter, its language more elegant, its excesses fewer. To a Tolstoi scholar, its position as the major transitional work from his early to his late period, from the point of view of both form and, to some degree, content, renders it immensely important for an adequate understanding of his works as a whole.

On the superficial level of the story, *Anna Karenina* stands midway between *War and Peace* and *Kreutzer Sonata*. *War and Peace* ends with the bliss of Pierre and Natasha's early married life; *Anna Karenina* examines marriage in all its stages; *Kreutzer Sonata* begins after the difficulties of marriage have already terminated in death. Philosophically, *Anna Karenina* bridges *War and Peace* and *Confession,* picking up the gloomier aspects of determinism in *War and Peace* and foreshadowing the arguments in *Confession.* Stylistically, *Anna Karenina* bridges the *War and Peace* period and the post-*Confession* period. Already at the time he was writing *Anna Karenina*, Tolstoi was known for his stylistic innovations. However, *Anna Karenina* marks an advance over *War and Peace* with its well-defined scenic construction and simpler language. Tolstoi's new tighter

construction is not just a result of the smaller scope of *Anna Karenina*. In fact, at the time Tolstoi was beginning *Anna,* he revised *War and Peace,* removing several long digressions from the text and placing them at the end in a separate section. Even in *Anna,* however, Tolstoi makes short excursions into issues of the day, a practice which he was to continue in *Resurrection.*

Tolstoi drew heavily from his own life for *Anna Karenina.* Obviously, the tone and subject matter echo the unsettled state of his own mind. Tolsoi also relied on events, places, and people he knew for much of the material in *Anna Karenina.* For instance, Levin is modeled on Tolstoi himself. His name is based on "Lev," and his religious search is much like Tolstoi's. Some of the events in the novel (the proposal, the search for a wedding shirt, the wedding), recall real episodes in Tolstoi's life. (pp. 4-5)

It is generally accepted that Tolstoi got his epigraph from Schopenhauer, whose ideas Tolstoi sympathized with.

Anna Karenina's simplified language owes a debt to Tolstoi's study of Greek, which may also have contributed some elements to the plot. Other sources for *Anna Karenina* may be found among the works that Tolstoi read in the late 1860s and the early 1870s. Tolstoi was known to admire English novels, and some readers find reflections of these works in *Anna Karenina.* (pp. 5-6)

Clearer is the influence of Dumas *fils,* author of the play *La Femme de Claude* (1873) and the pamphlet *L'Homme-femme* (1872). . . . Among other possible French sources for *Anna Karenina* might be mentioned Meilhac and Halévy's play *Frou-Frou,* whose story line includes an adulterous affair, a horse race, and the death of the heroine.

Tolstoi credits Pushkin with providing him an opening scene for *Anna Karenina.* . . . Pushkin's beginning *in medias res* did indeed inspire such a beginning in the rough draft of *Anna Karenina,* but the final version finds this episode in Part II, chapter 6. Tolstoi wrote two people letters that month about the delights of rereading Pushkin, in particular the *Tales of Belkin,* which he calls a "treasure." His wife tells us that he once called Pushkin his "father."

Tolstoi found many things in Pushkin besides an opening line. His style in particular was appealing in its simplicity. Twenty years earlier, Tolstoi thought, after having read *Captain's Daughter,* that Pushkin's mode of expression was dated, his tales barren of details of emotion. But he did not fault the style. And in 1897, he was still praising the virtues of Pushkin's clarity, simplicity, and brevity.

The very plot has often been seen as a continuation of Pushkin's *Eugene Onegin.* While Tatyana spurns the young Onegin and stays with her older husband at the end of the poem, Anna's story begins with her acceptance of Vronsky's attentions. It has been said that Tolstoi confirms the rightness of Tatyana's decision to put duty ahead of love. In the early plans for *Anna Karenina,* Anna was even called Tatyana.

On February 24, 1870, more than three years before Tolstoi began writing *Anna Karenina,* Sofia Tolstaya noted in her diary the following: "Last night he said to me that he had imagined a type of woman, married, from high society, but lost. He said that it was his job to make this woman only pitiful and not guilty—and that as soon as he had imagined this type, all the characters and male types he had imagined previously found their place and grouped themselves around this woman. 'Now it has all become clear to me,' he said." (pp. 6-7)

Early on, the novel was named *Molodets-baba,* which suggests Dumas's hyphenated title *l.'Homme-femme (Man-Woman).* Anna is called Tatyana Stavrovich, later Nana Karenina. In some places in the drafts, Anna is unattractive and vulgar, while the early Karenin and Vronsky are positive characters. By the final version, Anna has become more appealing in both appearance and personality, while Karenin and Vronsky are both treated more unsympathetically. The second story line, featuring Levin and Kitty, is not included in the first plans for the novel. When Levin finally appears, he is called Neradov, which means "Not-glad." (p. 7)

Since *Anna Karenina* was published a hundred years ago, readers have never stopped discussing the issues raised in the story. Perhaps of all the issues, the question of Anna's guilt, or the "wrongness" of her actions, has generated the greatest amount of discussion. (p. 10)

Some readers cite social causes for Anna's tragedy: the immutable laws of society and morality cause Anna's death. Often society is seen as an agent of God which causes her destruction. Some have wondered why Anna does not leave society altogether. According to Shklovsky, Anna submits to living within the confines of society because she needs Vronsky, and Vronsky cannot imagine living outside society. Other readers, including D. H. Lawrence, feel that by prohibiting Anna from living outside society, Tolstoi puts theory above life and betrays his heroine. Lawrence feels that Anna and Vronsky should create a "new colony of morality," free of society.

Psychological reasons are also offered for Anna's downfall. One critic adduces a Freudian explanation: Anna, ravaged by guilt feelings generated by her betrayal of her father-substitute, is impelled to seek self-punishment. Some critics find Vronsky immature or inadequate; others find Anna immature. Blackmur feels Anna lacks strength (see *TCLC,* Vol. 4); another reader finds her too traditional. Lukács attributes Anna's death to her penchant for ruthlessly drawing every conclusion, eschewing compromise. Another reader feels that Anna lacks faith in the meaning of life. Eikhenbaum finds Anna guilty before Life, because she lives by her will, her whim, her passion. She suffers, while Betsy and Stiva do not, because they live outside any ethical system or morality.

Most of these disparate views can be, and have been, supported by evidence from the novel. Tolstoi is without peer among novelists in his ability to convey the mercurial nature of our emotional lives, and the complexity and ambivalence of our characters. His penetrating dissection of social, political, and spiritual life is unsurpassed. It is no wonder that so many readers have found evidence to support so many different interpretations. (pp. 10-11)

Soviet readers often look at the novel as an illustration of class problems. According to this view, the social structure and morals of society prevent the best members of that society, like Anna, from attaining happiness. Other readers see the central concern as a search for the nature of life and life's laws; still others see it as the story of Anna's moral development.

Tolstoi speaks of the family as being his central concern in *Anna Karenina.* (p. 11)

In an attempt to find some clue to the primary concern of the novel, some readers have pointed to the title, or to the epigraph. It has been suggested that the novel was titled *Anna Karenina* because the Anna-Vronsky story is more dramatic and sensational than the Levin-Kitty or Stiva-Dolly stories. Actually, of course, the best reason for the title is the obvious one: the novel since its inception was the story of Anna, and despite the growth in size and importance of the Levin plot, it never supplants the Anna plot or even ranks in reader interest equal to the Anna plot.

Pointing at the epigraph, "Vengeance is mine, and I will repay" (*Mne otomshchenie, i az vozdam*), to explain the novel completely is little more useful than pointing at the title. Many readers have rightly noted that since the epigraph was affixed to the novel in the very early stages, before the novel was fully developed, the epigraph is no longer appropriate as a key to the whole novel. This fact, however, has not stopped some critics from devoting an inordinate amount of time to discussing the epigraph's implications. (p. 12)

Tolstoi supported Gromeka's interpretation in *Russian Thought (Russkaia mysl').* Gromeka states that there is no absolute freedom in sexual love, but there are laws man accepts or rejects, and on the choice depends his happiness or unhappiness. Since the family is the only satisfactory basis for love, to destroy a family is to cause unhappiness. His friend the poet Fet says "Count Tolstoi points at the 'az vozdam' not as at a teacher's whining birch rod, but as at the chastening power of things, as a consequence of which the person directly causing an upset in the home will suffer first of all." (pp. 12-13)

There seems to be a promise of vengeance, and a proscription against vengeance wreaked by society and the reader, but beyond this, the meaning of the epigraph can be read several ways, none of them provable conclusively.

It is Tolstoi's habit of showing, rather than preaching, that has given rise to so much controversy over interpretations of the novel. . . . V. V. Chuyko in 1875 predicted that many would not like *Anna Karenina* because it did not "instruct." Readers both in Russia and abroad have appreciated this quality in Tolstoi. Chekhov in a widely quoted letter says that Tolstoi has solved no problems, but satisfies completely because all problems are correctly stated. William Lyon Phelps sees the Russian mind as a sensitive plate, which "reproduces faithfully. It has no more partiality, no more prejudice, than a camera film; it reflects everything that reaches its surface." In the sense that Tolstoi records emotions and events impartially, Phelps's observation is true.

These comments bring to the fore another problem tackled by Tolstoi critics: that of form. Chekhov, as his statement shows, understood that the process of writing was for Tolstoi a selective one. He exercised choice in determining the materials used to present the problems. Phelps is wrong when he says that the Russian mind, if Tolstoi is an example, "reflects everything." It does not. Phelps was only one of several Western critics to misunderstand Tolstoi in this fashion. Henry James calls Russian novels "loose baggy monsters," "fluid pudding," and he deplores their "lack of composition, their defiance of economy and architecture." Similarly, French critics compared *Anna Karenina* with *Madame Bovary,* and found the Russian novel artless and chaotic. (pp. 13-14)

What is the keystone? Is it anything beyond the parallel development of Anna and Levin? . . .

Goldenveizer reports that Tolstoi said that a work of art must have a kind of focus, incapable of being expressed in words. The content of a good work of art can in its entirety be expressed only by itself. (p. 15)

In other words, Tolstoi seems to be saying that the author has various ideas with one focus, determined by his attitude to the ideas, and his whole creation is an attempt to work out these united ideas. While it would take a recital of the work to express the ideas fully, perhaps the key holding the ideas together might be found.

Of course, many readers have hazarded a guess at the identity of the key. Some see it as simply Tolstoi's overall view of life. Others see it as a search for an escape from lying and falsehood. Still others see it as a picture of the age. Some, realizing the presence of two stories in the novel, view the key as the opposition between unhappy and happy love or unhappy and happy families. And some readers have realized that the key must somehow relate not just to the presence of two stories but to the intricate interweaving of the two.

Tolstoi himself gives advice to critics. "We need people who will show the senselessness of searching out separate thoughts in an artistic production and will constantly lead readers in that endless labyrinth of links in which the essence of art consists, and to those laws which serve as a basis of these links."

If we follow Tolstoi's suggestion and plot a path through the labyrinthine links of *Anna Karenina,* we should be rewarded with new insights into the traditional problems, mentioned earlier, of Anna's guilt, of the central concern of the novel, and of the novel's form. Indeed, in and of itself, the study of the novel's construction is rewarding because the book is so beautifully crafted. (pp. 15-16)

> *Sydney Schultze, in his* The Structure of "Anna Karenina" *(© 1982 by Ardis Publishers), Ardis, 1982, 181 p.*

ADDITIONAL BIBLIOGRAPHY

Bayley, John. *Tolstoy and the Novel.* New York: Viking Press, 1966, 316 p.
    Examines Tolstoy's major fiction with respect to the traditions and devices of the nineteenth-century European novel, focusing primarily on *War and Peace.*

Crosby, Ernest Howard. *Tolstoy and His Message.* New York: Funk and Wagnall's, 1904, 93 p.
    Identifies the origins of Tolstoy's spiritual crisis and summarizes his religious, philosophical, and moral views.

Davie, Donald, ed. *Russian Literature and Modern English Fiction.* Chicago: University of Chicago Press, 1965, 244 p.*
    Includes essays on Tolstoy by George Saintsbury, George Moore, D. S. Merezhkovsky, and D. H. Lawrence.

Eikhenbaum, Boris. *Tolstoi in the Sixties.* Translated by Duffield White. Ann Arbor: Ardis, 1982, 255 p.
    Account of Tolstoy's life and works during the 1860s, culminating in a biocritical examination of *War and Peace.*

Fausset, Hugh I'Anson. *Tolstoy: The Inner Drama.* New York: Harcourt, Brace & Co., 1968, 320 p.
    Examines the effect wrought on Tolstoy's writing and personal life by an inner struggle between instinct and consciousness.

Fedin, Konstantin. "The Genius of Leo Tolstoy," *The Atlantic Monthly* 205, No. 4 (June 1960): 85-6.
    Discusses as characteristic Tolstoy's device of testing the moral value of his hero at the decisive point of life and death.

Gorky, Maxim. "Reminiscences of Leo Tolstoy." In his *Reminiscences,* pp. 4-68. New York: Dover, 1946.

Personal recollection of young Gorky's friendship with the aged Tolstoy.

Greenwood, E. B. *Tolstoy: The Comprehensive Vision.* New York: St. Martin's Press, 1975, 184 p.
    Study designed "to outline the striving on the part of Tolstoy and of many of his characters for a comprehensive vision which holds the many-sided confusion of life in a single luminous intuition."

Gunn, Elizabeth. *A Daring Coiffeur: Reflections on "War and Peace" and "Anna Karenina."* Totowa, N.J.: Rowman and Littlefield, 1971, 146 p.
    Reveals the inconsistency of Tolstoy's dictum—that one must not judge others—by reviewing several novels in which Tolstoy himself moralizes at length.

Jepsen, Laura. *From Achilles to Christ: The Myth of the Hero in Tolstoy's "War and Peace."* Tallahassee, Fla.: Jepsen, 1978, 179 p.
    A study revealing archetypal patterns in Homer's *Iliad* and Tolstoy's *War and Peace.*

Jones, Malcolm, ed. *New Essays on Tolstoy.* Cambridge: Cambridge University Press, 1978, 253 p.
    Collection of essays by British scholars, including Henry Gifford, A. V. Knowles, W. Gareth Jones, E. B. Greenwood, and F. F. Seeley. The editor states that each essay "constitutes a reassessment of some aspect of Tolstoy's legacy to the modern reader. . . ."

Knowles, A. V., ed. *Tolstoy: The Critical Heritage.* London: Routledge & Kegan Paul, 1978, 457 p.
    Compendium of early criticism on Tolstoy's major works, especially useful for its translation of Russian critics.

Lamm, Martin. "Leo Tolstoy." In his *Modern Drama,* pp. 182-93. Oxford: Basil Blackwell, 1952.
    Descriptive survey of Tolstoy's major dramas.

Lavrin, Janko. *Tolstoy: An Approach.* New York: Macmillan Co., 1946, 166 p.
    Introduction to Tolstoy's fiction and philosophy.

Matlaw, Ralph E., ed. *Tolstoy: A Collection of Critical Essays,* Englewood Cliffs, N.J.: Prentice-Hall, 1967, 178 p.
    Includes seminal essays by B. M. Eikhenbaum, Georg Lukács, R. F. Christian, R. P. Blackmur, and Lev Shestov.

Maude, Aylmer. *Tolstoy and His Problems.* London: Grant Richards, 1902, 220 p.
    Designed to elucidate Tolstoy's ideas on art, religion, politics, and economics among other subjects.

Maude, Aylmer. Introduction to *Recollections and Essays,* by Leo Tolstoy, translated by Aylmer Maude, pp. vii-xxviii. London: Oxford University Press, 1937.
    Descriptive survey of the essays in this volume, with a rebuttal to critics of *What Is Art?*

Merejkowski, Dmitri. *Tolstoi As Man and Artist: With an Essay on Dostoïevski.* New York and London: G. P. Putnam's Sons, 1902, 310 p.*
    Analyzes Tolstoy's life and work in relation to his religious ideology. This study also examines Tolstoy's use of narrative detail and discusses the importance of art and religion in the thought of Tolstoy and Dostoevsky.

Nordau, Max. "Tolstoism." In his *Degeneration,* pp. 144-71. New York: D. Appleton and Co., 1895.
    Sees Tolstoy as an example of "degeneracy" for his views on sexuality and religion.

Orwell, George. "Lear, Tolstoy and the Fool." In his *Shooting an Elephant and Other Essays,* pp. 32-52. New York: Harcourt, Brace & World, 1950.
    Examination of Tolstoy's critique of Shakespeare.

Phelps, William Lyon. "Tolstoi." In his *Essays on Russian Novelists,* pp. 170-214, New York: Macmillan Co., 1922.
    Critical overview of the major fiction.

Redpath, Theodore. *Tolstoy*. London: Bowes & Bowes, 1960, 126 p.
  Survey of Tolstoy's thought and fiction.

Reeve, F. D. "*Anna Karenina* (Tolstoy)." In his *The Russian Novel*,
pp. 236-73. London: Frederick Muller, 1967.
  Anna Karenina analyzed as a combination and reversal of the
  themes of "Family Happiness" and *War and Peace*.

Russell, Robert. "From Individual to Universal: Tolstoy's *Smert' Ivana
Il'Icha*." *The Modern Language Review* 76, No. 3 (July 1981): 629-
42.
  Explains how the individual, Ivan Ilyich, becomes a prototype of
  a social class which demands ordinariness through conformity.

Slonim, Marc. "Leo Tolstoy." In his *The Epic of Russian Literature:
From Its Origins through Tolstoy*, pp. 309-46. New York: Oxford
University Press, 1950.
  Biographical sketch with an examination of major works and
  themes.

Symons, Arthur. "Tolstoi on Art." In his *Studies in Prose and Verse*,
pp. 173-82. New York: Dutton, 1922.
  Discussion of Tolstoy's theories of art which acknowledges the
  integrity of his argument while bemoaning the narrowness of his
  vision.

Troyat, Henri. *Tolstoy*. Garden City, N.Y.: Doubleday & Co., 1967,
762 p.
  Biography emphasizing the development of Tolstoy's philosophical and ethical beliefs.

Zweers, Alexander F. *Grown-up Narrator and Childlike Hero: An
Analysis of the Literary Devices Employed in Tolstoi's Trilogy "Childhood," "Boyhood" and "Youth."* The Hague: Mouton, 1971, 165
p.
  Includes a survey of the critical literature on the trilogy and compares it to other treatments of childhood found in Russian literature.

Charles (Walter Stansby) Williams

1886-1945

English novelist, poet, essayist, dramatist, biographer, and critic.

Williams was a writer of supernatural fiction, a poet whose best works treat the legends of Logres (Arthurian Britain), and one of the central figures among the literary group known as the Oxford Christians. The religious, the magical, and the mythical are recurrent concerns in his works, reflecting his devout Anglicanism and lifelong interest in all aspects of the preternatural. Williams's novels, which include *War in Heaven*, *All Hallows' Eve*, and *The Place of the Lion*, depict the earth as a battleground in a cosmic struggle between the forces of good and evil, and present the author's conception of the natural and supernatural realms as spheres separated by a permeable boundary. Though not as well known as his novels, Williams's Arthurian *Taliessin through Logres* and *The Region of the Summer Stars* are considered by some critics to be among the most original works in twentieth-century English poetry. During the tenure of his friend C. S. Lewis as a Fellow at Oxford's Magdalen College, Williams became a guiding force of the Oxford Christians or "Inklings," a group of like-minded writers who met weekly in Lewis's rooms to discuss literature and to read works in progress to each other for critical advice and mutual enjoyment. Although his works are not today as well known as those of his fellow-Inklings Lewis and J.R.R. Tolkien, Williams was an important source of encouragement and influence among the group, and his death brought about its demise.

Williams was born in London to a financially straitened middle-class family and raised in the Anglican faith. The city of London and the Church of England were beloved by Williams throughout his life and are central elements in much of his fiction. Forced by his family's lack of money to curtail his education at the University of London, in 1908 Williams secured an editorial position at the London office of the Oxford University Press, where he worked for the rest of his life. During the same year he met Florence Conway, whom he later married and to whom he wrote many love poems which celebrate a central, Dantean tenet of his vision: that love is a sacrament enabling fellowship with God. Throughout his professional life, Williams considered himself to be primarily a poet, and during the early years of his career he published only poetry, much of it evidencing the influence of Dante and, in its style, of G. K. Chesterton. During his late twenties, Williams became interested in Rosicrucianism and magic, and joined the Hermetic Order of the Golden Dawn, a secret society devoted to the acquisition of occult knowledge. Although he did not remain with the group, Williams later drew upon his acquired knowledge of "Magia" (white magic) and "Goetia" (black magic) for subject matter in his novels. By 1930, when the first of these—*War in Heaven*—was published, Williams had established himself as a minor poet and critic, and as an outstanding lecturer on the major English poets at evening literature classes in London. His "supernatural thrillers," as his novels were called, attracted a wide audience and introduced the author to two notable admirers: T. S. Eliot, who, as a director of Faber and Faber, published several of Wil-

liams's novels; and C. S. Lewis, whose own *Allegory of Love*, with its high praise for Dante's fusion of erotic and divine love, delighted Williams and initiated the two writers' friendship.

At the outbreak of World War II, with London menaced by the Nazi *Luftwaffe*, the staff of the Oxford University Press's London office was evacuated to Oxford, where Williams was soon introduced by Lewis into the Inklings. In addition to Lewis, Tolkien, and Williams, the ever-changing group included Lewis's brother Warren, the noted philosopher Owen Barfield, and a dozen others, most of whom attended but irregularly. During one period of several months, members listened as the group's three principals read aloud from concurrent works in progress: Tolkien from *The Fellowship of the Ring*, Lewis from *Perelandra*, and Williams from *All Hallows' Eve*; novels which are recognized today to be among their authors' most accomplished works. Through the offices of Lewis and Tolkien, Williams was able to serve at Oxford as a lecturer on English poetry, attracting enthusiastic audiences at each appearance and receiving an honorary M.A. from the university in 1943. When he died suddenly after a seemingly minor operation, Warren Lewis noted in his journal that "the blackout has fallen, and the Inklings can never be the same again."

Although his poetry and novels represent Williams's chief contribution to English literature, such theological books as *He*

Came Down from Heaven and *The Descent of the Dove: A Short History of the Holy Spirit in the Church* (the latter a key influence in W. H. Auden's conversion to Christianity), as well as the critical work *The Figure of Beatrice: A Study in Dante* are important for their explicit statements of the author's beliefs. Three of these tenets, central to his thought and pervasive in his imaginative works, include what Williams termed the Affirmative Way, coinherence, and exchange or substitution. The Affirmative Way, a life-embracing concept which appears most notably in *The Place of the Lion* and in the two volumes of "Taliessin" poems, is that of approaching God through recognizing the divine essence in nature, in all created works, and in all circumstances, particularly in erotic love. This belief is exemplified by Beatrice, whom Williams (and Dante) found a "God-bearer," or one who inspires her admirer to continue the search for God. "For Williams," explains Agnes Sibley, "any person in love is very close to God, for he sees in his beloved a perfection that only God sees as well." Conversely, lost souls, to Williams, are characterized by their retreat from the outer world into totally loveless self-absorption—the Negative Way. Central to coinherence, a concept similar to Leo Tolstoy's theory of complicity, is the belief that all persons are accountable to each other for their decisions and actions. Persons cognizant of this relationship seek to live responsibly and lovingly with all others. Closely related to coinherence is Williams's theory of exchange, which is based on the atonement of Jesus Christ. Since, according to orthodox Christian doctrine, Jesus gave up his divine nature to assume human form and later sacrificed his sinless life through bearing the sins of humanity, so, according to Williams, should each person seek to bear the spiritual and physical suffering of others. Exchange and coinherence are defined in *The Image of the City* and are imaginatively presented most vividly in *All Hallows' Eve* and *Descent into Hell*. The city is idealized throughout Williams's seven complete novels as a center of life where the author's three interrelated beliefs are widely realized, but where the resultant harmony goes largely unnoticed. Williams did not fail to perceive suffering and ugliness in the world, but he believed that God's purposes are accomplished in spite of and with the seeming agency of evil, a concept derived by Williams from one of his major influences, the Scottish fantasist George MacDonald.

Concerning Williams's fiction, William Lindsay Gresham has remarked that "reading him we feel like the blind man who was given his sight and saw people like trees walking." In his novels and dramas, common, unsuspecting characters from the natural world encounter—with surprise and then acceptance—beings from the supernatural realm; the reader is likewise intended to be startled by these strange and unexpected confrontations, and thereby awakened to their symbolic value. Natural and supernatural characters are caught up together in the struggle between good and evil. In *War in Heaven*, one of Williams's most popular novels, the opposing forces converge on a humble church, each seeking to possess the Holy Grail, which has long stood unnoticed among the church's ornaments. Despite their interesting plots, the novels, as well as the dramas and "Talliessen" poems, have never attracted a wide audience for, due to Williams's difficult style, they require closer attention than most readers are willing to devote to them. Of Williams's verse, Anne Ridler wrote, "It is not a poetry for all moods; it is one, also, to which you must wholly submit in order to enjoy it. But I am sure that his cycle has its place in the tradition of English visionary poetry." Recently Agnes Sibley, agreeing with Ridler's appraisal, added "that to all of Williams's writings 'you must wholly submit'."

Williams's role as an influence is most markedly evident in the work of C. S. Lewis, whose controversial *Preface to "Paradise Lost"* and apocalyptic novel *That Hideous Strength* advance ideas held by Williams. Since the 1940s, when his novels were first published in the United States, Williams's own works have attracted a small, though enthusiastic audience. Sibley has written of Williams that "even if he never becomes known to great numbers, he will surely be rediscovered in each generation by those whom Arnold Bennett calls 'the passionate few'."

(See also *TCLC*, Vol. 1 and *Contemporary Authors*, Vol. 104.)

PRINCIPAL WORKS

The Silver Stair (poetry) 1912
Poems of Conformity (poetry) 1917
Divorce (poetry) 1920
Windows of Night (poetry) 1924
Poetry at Present (criticism) 1930
War in Heaven (novel) 1930
Many Dimensions (novel) 1931
The Place of the Lion (novel) 1931
Three Plays (dramas) 1931
The Greater Trumps (novel) 1932
Reason and Beauty in the Poetic Mind (criticism) 1933
Shadows of Ecstasy (novel) 1933
Thomas Cranmer of Canterbury (drama) 1935
Seed of Adam (drama) 1936
Descent into Hell (novel) 1937
He Came Down from Heaven (essay) 1938
Taliessin through Logres (poetry) 1938
The Death of Good Fortune [first publication] (drama) 1939
The Descent of the Dove: A Short History of the Holy Spirit in the Church (essay) 1939
The House by the Stable [first publication] (drama) 1939
Terror of Light [first publication] (drama) 1940
Grab and Grace; or, It's the Second Step [first publication] (drama) 1941
The Three Temptations [first publication] (drama) 1942
The Figure of Beatrice: A Study in Dante (criticism) 1943
The Region of the Summer Stars (poetry) 1944
All Hallows' Eve (novel) 1945
The House of the Octopus [first publication] (drama) 1945
The Image of the City and Other Essays (essays) 1958
Collected Plays (dramas) 1963
The Noises That Weren't There (unfinished novel) 1970-71; published in journal *Mythlore*

THE NATION, London (essay date 1917)

There is something so engaging in Mr. Williams's title ["**Poems of Conformity**"], so comfortably secure from the Titan brood of Jove-Defiers, who . . . pile their Pelions on their Ossas, as if they were card-castles, that he makes us anxious not to pay too much attention to the rather glaring faults of his method. And he possesses compensating qualities—an ardent religious feeling, intricacy of fancy, the power of evoking and interrelating complex imagery and a subtlety of diction which is

by no means a fancy-dress garment for a corresponding hol-
lowness of thought. Nevertheless, Mr. Williams overdoes it;
the seventeenth-century mystical poets (particularly Donne) have
gone to his head. It was not unnatural for them to employ the
language of technical theology as the interpreter of the divine
rapture and the pilgrim's staff of passionate discovery. But Mr.
Williams makes the double mistake both of following too closely
their terminology and of devoting it to much narrower ends
than they ever did. Sacerdotal imagery was fresh to them, and
they used it exquisitely and legitimately to serve the poetic and
not the theological purpose; with us, it is superannuated for
other technical facilities. . . . In [simple] cadences (such as
the carol form), when his thought is pinned down to greater
precision, where it is less a tracery and more a meaning, Mr.
Williams is much more effective. . . . (pp. 618, 620)

> "Ida's Shady Brow," in The Nation, London, Vol.
> XXI, No. 24, September 15, 1917, pp. 618, 620.*

ALLEN TATE (essay date 1925)

[*Tate's criticism is closely associated with two American critical
movements, the Agrarians and the New Critics. The Agrarians
were concerned with political and social issues as well as literature, and were dedicated to preserving the Southern way of life
and traditional Southern values. In particular, they attacked
Northern industrialism as they sought to preserve the Southern
farming economy. The New Critics, a group which included Cleanth
Brooks and Robert Penn Warren, among others, comprised one
of the most influential critical movements of the mid-twentieth
century. Although the various New Critics did not subscribe to a
single set of principles, all believed that a work of literature had
to be examined as an object in itself through a process of close
analysis of symbol, image, and metaphor. For the New Critics,
a literary work was not a manifestation of ethics, sociology, or
psychology, and could not be evaluated in the general terms of
any nonliterary discipline. However, Tate adhered to a different
vision of literature's purpose than did the other New Critics. A
conservative thinker and convert to Catholicism, Tate attacked
the tradition of Western philosophy which he felt has alienated
persons from themselves, one another, and from nature by divorcing intellectual from natural functions in human life. For
Tate, literature is the principal form of knowledge and revelation
which restores human beings to a proper relationship with nature
and the spiritual realm. Though this vision informs much of his
work, Tate is like T. S. Eliot in that an appreciation of his criticism
is not wholly dependent upon an acceptance of his spiritual convictions. His most important critical essays are on modern poetry,
and on Southern traditions and the legacy of the Civil War. In
the following essay, he scathingly reviews Williams's volume of
poetry* Windows of Night.]

[Without] a single major talent to assimilate those elements of
the historical literary experience suited to a new scientific construction of the universe, or to the social implications of that
construction, English poetry may be said merely to discourse
in three principal tendencies, each with a history: the Wheels
group, at its best in Eliot, whom it doesn't formally include;
the Georgians, from whom Wheels revolted about ten years
ago; and the Conservationists, whose cosmic and rhetorical
machinery was scrapped by the revolutionist Mr. Masefield,
a founder of Georgianism, in 1911, when he "threatened"—
according to Stephen Phillips—"the standards of English Poetry." The history is indispensable: Mr. Charles Williams can
be understood only as an anachronism; but he deserves, for
that extrinsic reason, to be understood. . . .

For Mr. Williams's verse belongs to this last and conservative
tendency. . . . [In *Windows of Night*] Mr. Williams conceives

the poet as Vates, as seer of good and evil, of their joint or
divergent progress in successive generations of the heart of
Man. He scolds modern Doubt in many lines, some of them
graceful in a synthetic melody put together from the rhetorical
Victorian poets, nearly all of them devoid of artistic value—
empty of the vitality attached to words only by a very alert
experience of either books or living. For Mr. Williams, experience, which ordinarily participates in every creative intuition of a good poet, were better silent before the superior
incentive of Inspiration. . . . The use of Mnemosyne [as a
symbol of inspiration] makes a capital point. As the type of
degenerate artist Mr. Williams, having inherited a symbol,
ignores its status as such and turns it into an efficient entity;
so that the symbol of memory, like the "efficient God" in the
Occasionalism of Malebranche, is supposed to work for the
poet in defection of the psychological operations of memory.
Mr. Williams would fail to see that James Joyce and Proust,
without invoking Mnemosyne, are the only writers of this century who have creatively defined her. His production is fundamentally a piece of ironical levity unconsciously performed,
set against the English tradition in all its distinguished phases:
solemn, it lacks seriousness altogether. Dullness comes close
to vulgarity. (p. 209)

> Allen Tate, "Rhetoric, Mysticism, Poetry," in The
> New Republic (© 1925 The New Republic, Inc.),
> Vol. XLIV, No. 567, October 14, 1925, pp. 209-10.*

STEPHEN SPENDER (essay date 1933)

[*Spender is an English man of letters who rose to prominence
during the 1930s as a Marxist lyric poet and as an associate of
W. H. Auden, Christopher Isherwood, C. Day Lewis, and Louis
MacNeice. Like many other artists and intellectuals, Spender
became disillusioned with communism after World War II, and
although he may still occasionally make use of political and social
issues in his work, he is more often concerned with aspects of
self-knowledge and depth of personal feeling. His poetic reputation has declined in the postwar years, while his stature as a
prolific and perceptive literary critic has grown. Spender believes
that art contains "a real conflict of life, a real breaking up and
melting down of intractable material, feelings and sensations which
seem incapable of expression until they have been thus transformed. A work of art doesn't say 'I am life, I offer you the
opportunity of becoming me.' On the contrary, it says: 'This is
what life is like. It is even realer, less to be evaded, than you
thought. But I offer you an example of acceptance and understanding. Now, go back and live!'" Below, Spender critically
rends* Reason and Beauty in the Poetic Mind.]

[*Reason and Beauty in the Poetic Mind*] would be excellent as
a present from parents who wish to ensure that their children
will detest poetry for their whole lives. . . . [For] the most
part, [Williams'] arguments amount to no more than a paraphrase of "The Prelude," parts of "Paradise Lost," and Keats'
"Odes," expressed in a suggestive way which might be helpful
to students who are anxious to know what these poems are
"about." . . .

The paraphrases of poems which occupy most of this book are
written in a language sometimes familiar and sometimes high-
falutin, which shames the authors in their graves. . . .

One of Mr. Williams' more interesting suggestions is that a
satiric verse of Swift, "Poor Pope will grieve a month," "reminds us of later Shakespeare, though it has less power, and
deals with less intense things, with outer habits rather than
inner life." So when he does commit himself to a statement,

like a sports' dog after a lame duck, he hastens to retrieve it. (p. 941)

This is the kind of criticism which goes far to explain why so many people detest poetry. It speaks of poets as though they were superior beings incapable of experiencing the feelings of ordinary people; it translates simple and direct poetry, which easily explains itself, into high-flown and indirect language. In trying to elevate poetry, it puts it on the shelf.

It is typical of Mr. Williams' method that he has no sense of contemporary poetry, and he seemingly has even less sense of the contemporary scene. Speaking of the Elizabethans he writes: "In those morally spacious days the highest spiritual and political authorities took a hand in the game of death with a realism inconceivable by our more puritanical generation." Has Mr. Williams ever heard of the Great War? Has he ever thought what Macbeth would have to say of some of our European Dictators? If he had answered these questions, perhaps he would have written of the poetry of the past as though it had some bearing on the present, and not as though it were dead, boneless and cremated. (p. 942)

> *Stephen Spender, "Why People Hate Poetry," in* The Spectator *(© 1933 by* The Spectator; *reprinted by permission of* The Spectator*), Vol. 151, No. 5504, December 22, 1933, pp. 941-42.*

T. S. ELIOT   (essay date 1939)

[*Perhaps the most influential poet and critic of the first half of the twentieth century, Eliot is closely identified with many of the qualities denoted by the term Modernism: experimentation, formal complexity, artistic and intellectual eclecticism, and a classicist view of the artist working at an emotional distance from his creation. As a critic, Eliot generally upheld values of traditionalism and discipline, and in 1928 he annexed Christian theology to his overall conservative world-view. Of his criticism, he stated: "It is a by-product of my private poetry-workshop: or a prolongation of the thinking that went into the formation of my verse." As Williams's publisher and good friend, Eliot favorably reviewed* The Descent of the Dove.]

It is necessary . . . to collate what are superficially different kinds of work, in order to see what Mr. Williams is about; and even then, it is very difficult to classify this extraordinary and eccentric spiritual acrobat. One may say that the centre of Mr. Williams's interest is mystical or ascetical theology: in the widest sense—for **He came down from Heaven** contains some profound remarks on Romantic Love and the *Vita Nuova*. But he enjoys all the privileges of being a *lay* theologian; he can use his own form, such as that of thrillers as thrilling as any, and he can speak in the language of contemporary conversation. Indeed, it may prove that one of his greatest contributions to his science is a refreshment of the terminology in which it is expressed.

The sub-title of the present book [**The Descent of the Dove: A Short History of the Holy Spirit in the Church**] indicates that it is in a certain sense a history of the Church. It is not, of course, a history of ecclesiastical politics or constitution. To the reader who is not interested in, or does not recognise the identity of the Holy Ghost, the book is still very interesting, as a kind of review of the points of emphasis which Mr. Williams considers important in the last nineteen hundred years: to such a reader the book will be interesting as a survey of Mr. Williams's mind. Such a reader will enjoy the review and appreciate the many good things by the way, but he will have missed the

author's intention, which is to chronicle the points of crisis and decision, at which the Church (in its widest sense) has been guided by the Holy Spirit. That is to say, Mr. Williams would wish his book to be judged, not as his "personal" impression of the history of the Church, but as an essay according to criteria quite as objective as those of the ordinary historian. His standpoint is certainly not Protestant, but it is Catholic in a larger sense than that usually attributed by Protestants to Catholicism, for it allows him to consider without prejudice the contributions of heretics and schismatics, as well as those of saints and popes. Popes, indeed, have no very conspicuous place as individuals in this book, for they are not here important as occasional "great men" in the affairs of the world, but as more or less satisfactory vehicles of the Holy Spirit. . . . One of Mr. Williams's most remarkable virtues of sensibility, in fact, is a capacity for understanding certain modes of feeling which have become extinct. It is a pleasure to find that this capacity of his operates on Montaigne as well as on Dante. (pp. 864, 866)

Whether there are any historical errors in this History of the Holy Spirit in the Church, the present reviewer is incompetent to detect: but he is sure that, if there are, they are not of importance. It might be easier to find omissions. The later history of the Eastern Church receives no attention, nor does the mysticism of Eckhart and his followers (though Boehme is mentioned for his influence upon William Law). But such omissions Mr. Williams would probably be able to justify or extenuate. He gives St. John of the Cross his due place, and the suggestion of the importance of the Great Schism in preparing a way for schism in the sixteenth century gives matter for much reflection. This is not only a valuable book, but a very readable one for those who consider themselves outside of the Church as well as for those in it; and it has a further use in that it provides a helpful introduction to the earlier books of the same author. . . . (p. 866)

> *T. S. Eliot, "A Lay Theologian," in* The New Statesman & Nation *(© 1939 The Statesman & Nation Publishing Co. Ltd.), n.s. Vol. XVIII, No. 459, December 9, 1939, pp. 864, 866.*

C. S. LEWIS   (broadcast date 1949)

[*Lewis is considered one of the foremost Christian and mythopoeic authors of the twentieth century. Indebted principally to George MacDonald, G. K. Chesterton, Charles Williams, and the writers of ancient Norse myths, he is regarded as a formidable logician and Christian polemicist, a perceptive literary critic, and—most highly—as a writer of fantasy literature. A traditionalist in his approach to life and art, he opposed the modern movement in literary criticism toward biographical and psychological interpretation. In place of this, Lewis practiced and propounded a theory of criticism which stresses the importance of the author's intent, rather than the reader's presuppositions and prejudices. Below Lewis, a fellow-Inkling and one of Williams's best friends, offers a general and favorable discussion of his friend's novels.*]

The complaint often made against [Williams's stories] is that they mix what some people call the realistic and the fantastic. I would rather fall back on an older critical terminology and say that they mix the Probable and the Marvellous. We meet in them, on the one hand, very ordinary modern people who talk the slang of our own day, and live in the suburbs: on the other hand, we also meet the supernatural—ghosts, magicians, and archetypal beasts. The first thing to grasp is that this is not a mixture of two literary kinds. That is what some readers suspect and resent. They acknowledge, on the one hand, 'straight' fiction, the classical novel as we know it from Fielding to Galsworthy. They acknowledge, on the other, the pure fantasy which creates a world of its own, cut off in a kind of ring fence, from reality; books like *The Wind in the Willows* or *Vathek* or *The Princess of Babylon,* and they complain that Williams is asking them to skip to and fro from the one to the other in the same work. But Williams is really writing a third kind of book which belongs to neither class and has a different value from either. He is writing that sort of book in which we begin by saying 'Let us suppose that this everyday world were, at some one point, invaded by the marvellous. Let us, in fact, suppose a violation of frontier. (pp. 46-7)

No doubt, the first and simplest approach to Williams's stories is to note and enjoy the lights which they cast on this side of the frontier, on our normal experience. His story *The Place of the Lion* seems to me to throw a light which I dare not neglect on the world that I myself chiefly inhabit, the academic world. The heroine, Damaris Tighe, is an extreme example of the complacent researcher. She is studying medieval philosophy and it has never once occurred to her that the objects of medieval thought might have any reality. As Williams tells us, she regarded Abelard and St Bernard as the top form in a school of which she was not so much the headmistress as the inspector. Then comes the supposal. How if these objects were, after all, real? How if they began to manifest themselves? How if this research-beetle had to experience what it so glibly catalogued? Even those who do not feel at the end of the book that we know any more about the Platonic Forms may well feel that we know more about ourselves as researchers—have seen, as if from outside, the fatuous assumption of superiority which will certainly dominate all our thinking about the past if we take no measures to correct it.

So again in *All Hallows' Eve* the strange sufferings to which Betty is subjected disengage for us her quite possible, yet now seldom imagined, character of wholly undefended and incorruptible innocence. To put it in another way, I find that when I read her history the word *victim,* after so many years of commonplace usage, is restored in my mind to its ancient, sacred and sacrificial dignity, and my vision of the everyday world proportionately sharpened.

That, indeed, is only one instance of a curious effect which Williams's supposals often have. They render possible the creation of good characters. . . . In Williams we are . . . off our guard. We see his good people in strange circumstances and do not think much of calling them good. Only on later reflection do we discover what we have been surprised into accepting.

I will go back to that point in a moment. Meantime I must repeat the claim or the confession (whichever you call it) that this illumination of the ordinary world is only one half of a Williams story. The other half is what he tells us about a different world. . . . And if we think a man is guessing very well indeed we begin to doubt whether 'guessing' is the right word.

I would hesitate to claim that Williams was a mystic. If a mystic means one who follows the negative way by rejecting images, then he was, consciously and deliberately, the very reverse. The choice between the two ways, the legitimacy, the dignity, and the danger, of both, is one of his favourite themes. But I am convinced that both the content and the quality of his experience differed from mine and differed in ways which oblige me to say that he saw further, that he knew what I do

not know. His writing, so to speak, brings me where I have never gone on my own sail or steam; and yet that strange place is so attached to realms we do know that I cannot believe it is mere dreamland.

It is a thing impossible to illustrate by short quotations, but I can point to passages where I have felt it in especial force. One comes in the last chapter of *All Hallows' Eve,* where Lester, who has been, in the physical sense, dead for many days, looks up and discovers (I cannot explain this without telling the whole story) that a still more final separation is at hand. Then come the words 'All, all was ending; this, after so many preludes, was certainly death. This was the most exquisite and pure joy of death. . . . Above her the sky every moment grew more high and empty; the rain fell from a source beyond all clouds.' (pp. 50-2)

You may, of course, ask me how Williams should know. And I am not suggesting that he knows in one sense—that he is giving me factual details about the world beyond death or on the brink of death. What I am quite sure of is that he is describing something he knows which I should not have known unless he had described it; and something that matters.

But I am horribly afraid lest what I said earlier about his good characters should leave anyone under the impression that he was a moralist. . . . The truth is, it is very bad to reach the stage of thinking deeply and frequently about duty unless you are prepared to go a stage further. The Law, as St Paul first clearly explained, only takes you to the school gates. Morality exists to be transcended. We act from duty in the hope that someday we shall do the same acts freely and delightfully. It is one of the liberating qualities in Williams's books that we are hardly ever on the merely moral level.

One little fact is significant; the unexpected extension he gives to the idea of courtesy. What others would regard as service or unselfishness he regards as good manners. That, taken by itself, might be a mere verbal trick: I mention it here only as a convenient shorthand symbol for the whole attitude. For courtesy can be frolic or ceremonial—or both—where unselfishness is lumpish and portentous. And that sublimation of merely ethical attitudes is at work through all his writing. His world may be fierce and perilous; but the sense of grandeur, of exuberance, even of carnival, the *honestade* and *cavalleria,* are never lost. (pp. 52-3)

> C. S. Lewis, "The Novels of Charles Williams" *(originally a radio broadcast on the Third Programme of the BBC on February 11, 1949), in his* On Stories and Other Essays on Literature, *edited by Walter Hooper (copyright © 1982 by the Trustees of the Estate of C. S. Lewis; reprinted by permission of Harcourt Brace Jovanovich, Inc.; in Canada by William Collins Sons & Co Ltd), Harcourt Brace Jovanovich, 1982 (also published in England as Of This and Other Worlds by C. S. Lewis, edited by Walter Hooper, Collins, 1982, pp. 46-54).*

DOROTHY L. SAYERS   (essay date 1949)

[*A noted mystery writer, essayist, and translator of Dante's works, Sayers became acquainted with Williams through the Inklings and through their mutual roles as Christian apologists.*]

The accent of Charles Williams is unique. Although he follows in the great tradition whose activity runs down through Dante and Donne from St. Paul, exploring and expounding the Affirmative Way, he remains a wholly original mind, and the first encounter with him is apt to be startling and unforgettable. To read only one work of Charles Williams is to find one's self in the presence of a riddle—a riddle fascinating for its romantic color, its strangeness, its hints of consciousness; but to read all is to become a free citizen of that world, and to find in it a penetrating and illuminating interpretation of the world we know.

The works of his maturity—the six novels, the "Taliessin" poems, the later plays, the theological and critical books—form as it were a complete body of doctrine, and each of them is a key to unlock the treasures of the rest. The salient points of that doctrine—the mutual coinherence of all men within the Divine Unity; the efficacy of substituted love; the knowledge of good in its opposite identity of evil; the restoration of the good by the surrender of the will and the acceptance of judgment; the affirmation of the validity of all temporal images of the eternal—may be called Christian truisms.

Their names in religion are the Communion of Saints, the Atonement, the Fall, the Redemption and the Incarnation. In the idiom of Charles Williams those ancient truths take on a new and searching actuality.

"**Many Dimensions**" . . . is the first of the novels in which that idiom makes itself heard with absolute certainty and control. The handling is freer and the doctrine more clarified than in "**Shadows of Ecstasy**" or "**War in Heaven**," which preceded it. The action, as in all the novels, takes place upon the borderline between the two worlds, the gateway by which the eternal irrupts into the temporal, being here the Stone of Solomon. The theme is the irresponsible loosing into the natural world of the supernatural powers hidden in the Stone, the disastrous attempt to exploit them in the service of the self, and their return to the place appointed through the surrender and sacrifice of the self.

Incidentally, this theme, which appears also with variations in "**War in Heaven**," "**The Place of the Lion**," "**The Greater Trumps**" and "**All Hallows' Eve**" may seem to have more than a merely "spiritual" significance to a generation which, by exploiting nuclear fission, has succeeded in unloosing directly into history the very force by which God unmakes the universe.

The writing is rather less colorful and more restrained than in "**The Place of the Lion**," "**All Hallows' Eve**," or in that masterpiece of horror and tenderness, "**Descent Into Hell**"—rightly so, since the central symbol of the book is Justice, embodied in the attractively dry and humorous figure of Lord Arglay, Lord Chief Justice of England. He and his secretary Chloe alone serve ends which are beyond the self, and so are able to make of themselves a passage for the return of the Powers. The other characters, eager only to exploit the Stone, whether for frankly commercial or for apparently harmless and altruistic ends, produce the inevitable havoc and go, each after his manner, to their own place.

In the novels of Charles Williams the gateway between the worlds opens always upon familiar things: the divine manifestations take place in an English village, in a London suburb, a villa residence. The instruments of power are commonplace people—secretaries, shop assistants, minor poets, government officials, clerks, railway porters, insignificant maiden ladies. It is for this reason that the tales, in spite of the fantastic incidents and the tremendous affirmations, are so curiously convincing. Having read them, one steps out into the street half convinced that the first passer-by may prove to be an angel in disguise, an envoy of Hell, or a peculiar vehicle of the celestial glory. And so, very likely, he is.

> Dorothy L. Sayers, "Between Two Worlds," in The New York Times Book Review (© 1949 by The New York Times Company; reprinted by permission), August 21, 1949, p. 7.

CHAD WALSH   (essay date 1951)

[*Walsh, an ordained Episcopal priest and English professor, is perhaps best-known as a scholar of C. S. Lewis's life and work. Below, he succinctly discusses Williams's beliefs and his seven "supernatural thrillers."*]

The seven novels [of Charles Williams] vary a great deal in tone and skill. The earliest, "**War in Heaven**" . . . , is a gay, almost Chestertonian tale of the struggle between the forces of light and the forces of darkness for possession of the Holy Grail. The last, "**All Hallows' Eve**," . . . moves much more quietly and gravely, and makes up in depth for what it lacks in sparkle.

"**The Place of the Lion**" . . . is a tour de force in which all earthly things begin to be absorbed back into their Platonic archetypes. Individual lions melt into one vast Platonic lion, and all other creatures are in danger of the same fate. The book has some memorable characters, such as the charming and irritating bluestocking, Damaris, and the theme is of great philosophic interest. Yet, on the whole, the plot does not possess as great vitality and illusion of reality as most of the other novels. However, underneath all the differences—the mark of a writer whose development was cut short at the age of 58—there is a striking similarity of theme.

In each of them there is the cosmic background. Every character is, willy-nilly, an actor in a drama with unlimited stakes. To put it mildly, each must constantly choose between good and evil. Still, there is nothing shallowly moralistic about Williams' understanding of this. Good is not obedience to a set of rules but rather a reaching out in love; a sharing in God's most basic attribute. Evil is the drawing in, the refusal to take part in the man-to-man and man-to-God exchange of love.

In order to dramatize this war of the soul and render it tangible, Williams made extensive use of magic in most of the novels. The deck of Tarot cards in "**The Greater Trumps**" (which engenders a snowstorm that shows no sign of ever stopping) and the infinitely divisible stone in "**Many Dimensions**" (which gives evil men a disastrous control over time and space) are among the devices he employs to bring about universal crises in which the most obtuse character must choose sides.

This is the underlying theme of them all—the cosmic struggle, with each of us plunged into it. Yet Williams' way of viewing the human situation is controlled by several key concepts, of which "the theology of substituted love" (as he called it) is the most basic. This is roughly equivalent to "the communion of saints" in the Apostles' Creed.

By it Williams meant that no one person is an isolated individual. Each is mysteriously linked to the others, and all to God, so that in a supernatural but thoroughly practical way each can take upon himself the burdens of anyone else. The load that is too heavy for my shoulder will be light on yours; I in turn will carry your load. This makes human existence rather like a gaily serious game (''gaily serious'' well describes Williams). The object is always to be trading burdens. And time itself is no barrier to the exchange.

Another of the concepts comes from the very high view that Williams held of the material world—stars, planets, animals, human bodies. This sets him apart from many of the medieval mystics, who were inclined to look upon matter as the prison-house of the spirit. It also distinguishes him from a considerable number of modern religious writers, such as Evelyn Waugh and Aldous Huxley, who reveal more than a lurking suspicion that the human body is the creation or the abode of the evil one. Williams' insight into the relationship between the material and the spiritual was a sacramental one: things seen are the outward expression of things unseen.

This made of Williams a determined defender of romantic love. Indeed, he liked to call himself a ''romantic theologian,'' but—as C. S. Lewis is careful to point out—this means not a person who is romantic about theology but one who is theological about romance.

Williams, like Dante, regarded romantic love as a stepping stone toward the infinitely greater love of God. The lover looks upon his beloved and sees her as she essentially is, as though the hand of the Creator were fresh upon her and the Fall of Man had never intervened. The experience is a spiritual revelation in itself, and a passport and invitation to the final experience: the beatific vision.

Williams' permanent worth as a novelist is difficult to assess because of a lack of writers with whom he can be compared. Certainly he had a breathtaking narrative sense: the ability to tell an exciting story and hold the reader from beginning to end. The main technical quarrel one might have with him would be over his extreme use of magic as a plot device. Sometimes it gets thick and clutters up the action. This is especially so in **''All Hallows' Eve,''** where the unearthly beauty of the story is chopped up by the interminable machinations of Simon the magician.

However, it seems a safe prophecy that Williams, though still little known to book club readers, will rank with the major novelists of his period—rank in his own right and also because his particular vision of reality will likely have far-reaching influence on the novels written during the coming decades. (His influence on C. S. Lewis' interplanetary romances is obvious enough, and I think I detect it in Anthony West's tale of the after-life, ''The Vintage.'') Coming as he did at a time when the serious religious novel was experiencing a rebirth, he stands as one of its pioneers and shapers.

What his angle of vision was I have tried to indicate. T. S. Eliot thus summarizes it: ''To him the supernatural was perfectly natural, and the natural was also supernatural. And this peculiarity gave him that profound insight into Good and Evil, into the heights of Heaven and the depths of Hell, which provides both the immediate thrill and the permanent message of his novels.''

Of course, it may be that the current trend toward religious fiction will dwindle away, and that the four walls and low ceiling of naturalism will close in again upon the modern novel. However, the signs point the other way. The second story of reality seems to be coming back into the picture for a prolonged stay. Williams is one of the most experienced guides to what is there. Yet he knows the first story equally well. In his novels he simply knocks down the ceiling, so that both kinds of reality

can mingle without hindrance. And having done this, he is able to lead the reader into a universe more spacious than most moderns have had the insight or daring to explore. (pp. 1, 19)

Chad Walsh, ''The Supernatural Was Also Natural,'' in The New York Times Book Review (© 1951 by The New York Times Company; reprinted by permission), March 11, 1951, pp. 1, 19.

NORTHROP FRYE   (essay date 1951)

[*Frye has exerted a tremendous influence in the field of twentieth-century literary scholarship, mainly through his study* Anatomy of Criticism *(1957). In this key work, Frye makes controversial claims for literature and literary critics, arguing that judgements are not inherent in the critical process and asserting that literary criticism can be ''scientific'' in its methods and its results without borrowing concepts from other fields of study. Literary criticism, in Frye's view, should be autonomous in the manner that physics, biology, and chemistry are autonomous disciplines. In the following essay, Frye favorably reviews the first North American edition of* Shadows of Ecstasy.]

Charles Williams' **Shadows of Ecstasy** is an intellectual thriller, and its ancestors are Lytton and Rider Haggard—it is by *Zanoni* out of *She*, if my grammar is right. The hero, or villain, Nigel Considine has, by a super-yogi discipline, enabled himself to live indefinitely (two hundred years and going strong), and has begun an attempt at a ''second evolution of man,'' politically the resurgence of Africa, and psychologically the calling up of the unawakened powers of passion and will, which has for its ultimate goal the return from death. Because this program is the result of a human will to power, Considine is a kind of Antichrist, and we are supposed to pick up a great variety of allusions to different aspects of Antichrist as we go on. If we get them all—they include the Bible, Caesar, Constantine (whose name the hero echoes), Yeats' Byzantium, Dante's Emperor, Milton's Satan and the superman of Nietzsche and Shaw—we get quite a liberal education.

It is a good thriller, written with humor and relaxation, with more respect for the art of fiction, more tolerance of irony, and less didactic hectoring than are usual with Williams. The fantasy has its own logic, and the characters and setting are studied carefully enough to give us the comfortable sense of a familiar world taking a holiday from routine. It is not giving anything away to say that the Galilean conquers, but though the author's Christian dialectic determines the solution, it does not try to force the reader's assent, and so avoids the disadvantages of melodrama. The losing side gets our sympathy and a chance to put on a good show: we do not feel pushed around nor do we get claustrophobia from a closed system of thought. In all these respects **Shadows of Ecstasy** offers a remarkable contrast to a better known but far cruder version of the same story, **All Hallows Eve,** where the Aunt-Sally epithet ''morbid'' seems to me for once appropriate. (pp. 616-17)

Northrop Frye, ''Novels on Several Occasions,'' in The Hudson Review (copyright © 1950 by The Hudson Review, Inc.; reprinted by permission), Vol. III, No. 4, Winter, 1951, pp. 611-19.*

NATHAN COMFORT STARR   (essay date 1954)

[*Starr examines Williams's treatment of Arthurian themes and credits him with helping restore vitality to the legends of Logres.*]

Some day—and his admirers hope it will be soon—Charles Williams' power as an author will be made plain by a systematic study of all his works. . . . Widely read, particularly in theology and literature, he suggests Coleridge in the breadth and grasp of his mind and in the darting play of his thought. Yet in other ways, in his humility and his stability of character, he was as unlike the other as possible.

In 1930, Williams took his place in the first rank of modern Arthurians with *War in Heaven,* the most deeply moving piece of prose fiction to spring from the legend in modern times. . . . (pp. 158-59)

The struggle in the book is the ancient one. (p. 159)

Yet though heaven and hell come to grips in Williams' novel, they do so on earth, in a quiet British village and at the present time. From a passing remark in an archaeological work about to be published, Archdeacon Davenant, vicar of Fardles, discovers that an ancient chalice in his church is the Holy Grail. This fact also becomes known to the publisher of the book, Gregory Persimmons, who has long been interested in black magic. It soon becomes evident that he is a part of satanic schemes to capture and destroy the Grail. There follows a series of swift adventures, in which the excitement of the best detective fiction is shot through with diabolical incantation on the one side and Christian faith on the other. (pp. 159-60)

Within the relatively brief compass of the 256 pages of *War in Heaven* there lies a whole world of excitement, physical, emotional, and spiritual. Probably never before in Grail literature had the issues of conflict been more vividly presented.

This conflict helps to distinguish Williams' novel from earlier works, chiefly those of Arthur Machen. In Machen the supremacy of the Grail is an established fact; its position is threatened only by the blindness of men and not by satanic power. Therefore, its eucharistic function is almost solely that of revealing hitherto uncomprehended Grace. *War in Heaven,* on the other hand, emphasizes the spiritual conflict found in the Bible and Milton; the devil strives desperately on earth "because he knoweth that he hath but a short time." In the war against evil, the Grail becomes a living symbol of unleashed spiritual power, its force lying not only in its essence, but also in its dynamic capacity. (pp. 160-61)

Williams could not have convinced us of the incredible unless he had been sure . . . that heaven and hell are closer to us than we ever imagine. As a matter of fact, Williams believed that the natural and the supernatural world are one and indivisible; he moved as easily and as naturally in one as in the other. T. S. Eliot makes this point clearly in one of his essays. He speaks of Williams' "extra perceptiveness," his "extended spiritual sense." (p. 164)

This familiarity with other worlds is a vital part of Williams' strength as a writer, for it places him at the center of a world of events and issues hardly dreamt of in our philosophy. Within this larger world Williams moves confidently, meeting its problems with mental and emotional elasticity. This confidence is particularly clear in his attitude toward evil. . . . T. S. Eliot says of him, "He was not puritanical, because he was not frightened by evil." This is not to say that he minimized it. To him evil is a spiritual reality; it is not caused by a dislocation of genes or hormones or by a set of psychopathic fixations. It is a gigantic negative force aimed at the reduction of the cosmos ordained by the Divine Will, and it operates through the degradation of fallible human beings. Yet the man who knows

what it is and who tries to understand God's grace, as Williams did, can not be injured or paralyzingly frightened by it. He will seek to understand it more and more, the better to combat it.

War in Heaven brings evil before the reader in a frightening way. It would be hard to forget the scene in which Persimmons leagues himself with sinister powers. Yet as always, Williams does not rely on melodrama; the whole episode in underwritten, and the usual apparatus of diabolical compacts is completely missing. The author simply wishes to understand as fully as possible what is happening, both inwardly and outwardly, as Persimmons applies the satanic ointment. What is happening terrifies the reader more than it does the author, for to him, good and evil are both essentially simple. He believes that if they are approached with this conviction fearlessly, the one can be exalted and the other cast down.

The Grail is the instrument of victory in this gigantic conflict— a development virtually unique in the history of the legend. The eucharistic significance of the Cup had been restored by Arthur Machen, yet it remained for Williams to make it a weapon of universal power. This means a certain shift in emphasis: the Sacred Vessel is not simply to be sought and found, but rather to be *preserved* against an onslaught undreamed of by the Fisher-King. The ancestral voices prophesying war in our age of global conflict and spiritual skepticism sound loud and clear in *War in Heaven.*

The ancestral voices are heard again in Charles Williams' poems, in which he leaves the England of his own experience and turns to Arthur's Britain. These poems appear in three collections: *Three Plays* . . . , which includes five incidental Arthurian verses, and *Taliessin Through Logres* . . . and *The Region of the Summer Stars* . . . , which deal wholly with the legend.

The songs in *Three Plays* are very different poems from those in the other two volumes, for the Taliessin who sings them sees few of the theological and legendary mysteries which moved him later. The early pieces are only the first intimations of spirituality. As in Williams' later poems, Taliessin, the Welsh seer, is appalled by the chaos of Logres before the coming of Arthur, and goes to the Emperor in Byzantion for aid and comfort. Then follows the triumphant crowning of the King. Yet the Grail, which is the *raison d'être* of Williams' Arthuriad, is mentioned only obliquely in the song which describes Galahad's ceremonious installation in King Arthur's bed. Occasionally in these poems, however, one finds Williams' authentic power. . . . And the account of Galahad's stately bedding has the imaginative grasp of the Grail hero's unique position which is the shining center of the later poems. Even so, the songs in *Three Plays* are inferior to *Taliessin Through Logres* and *The Region of the Summer Stars.* True, they are easier to understand and are more traditional in the use of meter and rhyme. What they chiefly lack is the full sweep of Williams' imagination; that was to come abundantly before very long. Father Gervase Mathew, one of his close friends, writes interestingly of his growth:

> He had become increasingly sacramental in his attitude towards material things. During his last years there was a curiously incandescent quality both in what he wrote and what he was; in teaching, writing and friendship he had gained the power first to illuminate and then by that illumination to perceive.

It is important to remember that Williams had a double advantage as an Arthurian. He was a scholar as well as a man of vaulting, illuminative imagination. His friends were struck by the breadth and depth of his knowledge. . . . He came to the Arthurian legend not only as a creator but also as a scholar. . . . His studies gave him a grasp of the Grail legend and its deep implications which helped him immeasurably.

The poems in *Taliessin Through Logres* and *The Region of the Summer Stars* comprise parts of an uncompleted Arthurian cycle. (pp. 165-68)

Williams holds to the traditional outline of the story. Within that outline, however, the treatment is brilliantly individual. In fact *Taliessin Through Logres* and *The Region of the Summer Stars* stand alone in the long record of Arthurian literature. And it is not enough merely to say that Williams places the sacramental Grail at the heart of the story. Others had done that before him. Seldom if ever before, however, had it been done with such imaginative power. Williams' serene belief in divine mysteries, even in the face of monstrous evil, gives daring and exciting expansiveness to the poems. The universe and our world become one; human experience is harmonized and interpenetrated by the miraculous. (p. 170)

The poems are reflections on (or of) characters acutely sensitized to otherworldly influences. Yet Williams' people are not unreal. In spite of ellipticality which makes the poems far from easy reading, in spite of Williams' unconventional method of characterization, his people are individuals. Each person in the story is seen in an enlarged frame of reality, his own actions but the outward (and least important) element in the supernatural relationship which gives him his reason for being.

The doctrine of reciprocity between two worlds, which Williams develops into an elaborate theological pattern beyond the scope of this book, helps to make his characters persons rather than abstractions, and, what is more, gives the best of them a serene sense of balance. (pp. 173-74)

This belief gives an unself-conscious decorum to Williams' world. It accounts for his spontaneous and unsensual recognition of delight in body as well as spirit. . . . True to his doctrine of interchange Williams gives new force to the relation of father and son. (pp. 174-75)

There is nothing "romantic" in the music we seem to hear; it is stately, yet full of light and movement, stylized yet graceful, orderly without constriction. As it first strikes the ear it may sound disharmonic, but as we listen again and recall the themes from which it springs, we seem to catch the music of the spheres. . . . (p. 177)

Williams' poems brilliantly illustrate the experimental, reconstructive temper of the best modern Arthurians. From the old legend, which he knew well as a scholar, he extracted the spiritual core; on this basis he developed a profoundly religious cycle. His originality both in conception and style is amazing, so much so that readers of his poems will doubtless have trouble with symbolism and expression which sometimes baffle even C. S. Lewis, his friend and commentator. It is not everyone, as Edna St. Vincent Millay discovered, who can easily apprehend "light anatomized." Yet there is a world of difference between Williams and some of the other cryptic poets of our time, between the obscurity which conceals the commonplace and that which shadows forth vast cloudy symbols. In Williams the epic proportions of the legend have been extended far beyond Malory's concept of a collapsing temporal kingdom. The scope is now Miltonic; the struggle primarily concerns man's responsibility under divine law. The two worlds of heaven and earth become one. And if in fusing them into transcendental reality Williams leads us into a third heaven which we never made, we should remember that out of the Summer Stars comes the mandate without which human life has no reason for being. (p. 178)

Nathan Comfort Starr, "The Spiritual Land of Logres," in his King Arthur Today: The Arthurian Legend in English and American Literature, 1901-1953 *(copyright, 1954, by the University of Florida), University of Florida Press, 1954, pp. 144-88.*

ROBERT CONQUEST   (essay date 1957)

[*Conquest is a poet, science fiction writer, and Kremlinologist who is best known for his poetry anthology* New Lines *(1956) and his study* The Great Terror: Stalin's Purges of the Thirties *(1968). The first work established Conquest, as well as the other poets represented therein—Kingsley Amis, Philip Larkin, Thom Gunn, Elizabeth Jennings, John Wain, Donald Davie, and John Holloway—as writers of "the Movement": a group of English poets whose traditionalist form stood in contrast to the surrealism of much of Europe's post-World War II literature. The author of several works on Soviet Russian policy, Conquest has received particular praise for* The Great Terror, *which has been called the most complete, scholarly, and damning book written to-date on the Stalinist terror. Below, he attempts to show that, in his thought and works, Williams was a totalitarian writer—a viewpoint which is disputed by Valerie Pitt (see excerpt below).*]

The effects of totalitarian thought on art have been examined by various writers—for instance in George Orwell's 'The Prevention of Literature'. The trouble is that it is very difficult to find really illuminating examples, which alone can show us the full pathology of the infection. The art of the totalitarian countries themselves, since the first establishment of such regimes, has been wholly contemptible—or at least, what good has been produced has been good precisely in so far as its authors did not put forward, or accept, the viewpoint of the state and their art avoided representation of its ideals. And it is only in a writer who has both a talent to ruin and actually ruins it, that the process can be properly traced.

In Charles Williams (as I hope to show) we find what is so difficult to track down in the totalitarian states—a genuine writer who has fully accepted a closed and monopolistic system of ideas and feelings, and what is more, puts it forthrightly with its libidinal component scarcely disguised.

Can such a parallel be drawn? I think so. After all we are dealing here with those aspects of totalitarianism which are not connected with the form of the state, but with men's minds and hearts. Our formal criteria might be: (*a*) the complete acceptance of a closed system of ideas; (*b*) the manipulation of this system as the only intellectual exercise; (*c*) the treatment of the outsider with a special sort of irritated contempt, which conceals, or sometimes betrays, other emotions; (*d*) the subordination of all ordinarily autonomous spheres of thought and feeling to the *a priori*: a lack of humility in the presence of the empirical.

In the case of Williams this ideological strait-jacket is religious. But for our critique this is not the essential. Nor, of course, is most religious, or mystic, thought of this nature. But humility and pity, the Christian virtues proper, are missing from Williams. . . . (pp. 32-3)

The characteristic failure of totalitarian thought is perhaps that the particular is treated *merely* as a representation of the general, an aspect of a 'higher', ordained process. . . . I would call any system of ideas which is self-consciously complete and final (except as to details to be discovered within it or by its own methods), and which is regarded as suitable for imposition on the whole human race, as in emotional effect totalitarian. An examination of Williams's work justifies this generalization in detail.

It is only necessary to deal with . . . Williams's masterpiece—with the series of poems **'Taliessin through Logres'** and **'The Region of the Summer Stars.'** . . . (pp. 33-4)

I think it is legitimate criticism to feel that the symbolism is too elaborate and complicated for poetry; or, to put it more exactly, *oversubtilized.* . . . It is difficult to deal with Williams without at least some account of his symbolism; yet a brief description may rightly be resented by his apologists as inaccurate and incomplete. With this caveat, one can say broadly that the overt action is that of Taliessin, the poet, and of the main personalities of Malory's Arthur story. It takes place in a Britain—'Logres', the old word is used—which is in some sense part of the Empire centred on Byzantium. (pp. 34-5)

[As] God's transcendence appears as Byzantium, his immanence is represented by Sarras, the distant island of the Trinity, which, however, figures only as a goal. The numinous is also manifested in the forest of Broceliande, the realm of Nature, of unorganized energy, good in essence, but able to lead to both good and bad. Beyond it is the castle of Carbonek, the home of the Holy Grail. The centre of the whole work is the attempt of Logres to be united with Carbonek and to attain the Grail and the Second Coming of Christ.

On the other side of the world is the diabolical counterpart of the emperor—the 'headless Emperor' in P'o-lu [quotation deleted]. . . . Nothing is accidental in Williams: these tentacles, the absence of true manipulative organs, represent evil's lack of 'accuracy'. We shall come to this point later.

The attempt to attain grace fails. The 'Manichaean' Muslim takes Constantinople; the barbarian hordes of disorder advance from the north, and in Logres itself Arthur commits incest and Mordred plans to set himself up as an egotist emperor like him of P'o-lu. But some hope remains—Taliessin forms a 'Company', the Pope goes on praying, and an offensive of P'o-lu's tentacles is fought to a standstill by Broceliande's roots.

There are several other levels of image, and an enormous amount of reservation and refinement to this layout. I have briefly expressed the main currents. (pp. 35-6)

The Arthurian cycle, even without Williams's additions and elaborations, is a very complicated series of episodes. And when everything is worked in to compose part of a highly involute and self-reflexive symbolic pattern, there is just too much of it for poetry; it becomes mainly a complex intellectual parlour game. And this tends to turn the verse into a series of set-pieces without internal development. At the same time the hierarchical, 'Byzantine' attitude is reflected in the style; the gnomic authoritative utterance, well though Williams uses it at times, turns monotonous.

These are superficial manifestations of deeper faults: but before going into those, we should look at the high quality of Williams's verse at its most effective. (pp. 36-7)

There are many passages where the fine potential, technically—though not merely technically—of Williams is manifest. [quotations deleted] (p. 37)

One might also cite his skilled use of a recurrent image, as in the long poem **'The Calling of Taliessin'**, where 'the summer stars' is very effectively repeated again and again. But I do not want to examine the technique of Williams's verse rigorously either in its brilliance or its faults. Many lines in such a long work are, doubtless, inessential failures—some of them through misuse of a various-based technical skill. But a large proportion of the failures in detail, and above all the failure as a whole, derive from a central error. (p. 38)

For the tendency to terrorism is itself . . . clearly marked. Pleasure in and justification of corporal punishment is found throughout, as is the thesis that force should be used to bring in unbelievers. [quotations deleted] (p. 39)

Humanity is treated as simply subject and subordinate to dogma. The barbarian is made a slave, 'compelled to come in' and whipped, and this is represented as thoroughly desirable. . . .

And this is central to his whole position. The main symbol of order, used time and again, is the hazel rod, which is quite explicitly meant to represent both a measuring implement and a means of flogging the unruly [quotation deleted]. . . . (p. 40)

On this level refinement of thought and standards of culture are not relevant. As Orwell says, 'An adolescent in a Glasgow slum worships Al Capone . . . A *New Statesman* reader worships Stalin. There is a difference in intellectual maturity, but none in moral outlook.'

The appeal of totalitarianism is certainly linked with the impulse to power and to cruelty. This was rather crude and obvious in Hitlerism. Stalinism, in the form it is presented to intellectuals at least, has a more complex, and subtler, attraction. The adept is enabled to satisfy both his less reputable instincts and his 'humane' superego at the same time. He has the thrill of applauding a brutality which, he is simultaneously able to satisfy his conscience, is the most truly humane action possible in the circumstances. His own tendencies to blind, 'disciplined', self-sacrifice are only the obverse of the same sado-masochism. (pp. 40-1)

A further characteristic of Williams's verse is his identification of the idea of accuracy with order, religion and art; words like 'precision', 'define', 'accurate', 'balance', are frequent in the favourable contexts, while their opposites are usual epithets for the inimical world of 'chaos'. In so far as this is a quasi-scientific justification for 'order' (and the hazel-rod is described as being for measurement and punishment as if these were somehow almost identical) it resembles the similar claims to scientific sanction made by totalitarian political theorists, and gives an 'objective'-seeming basis for force and cruelty. But Williams uses this imagery of precision with comparative discretion. . . . In so far as it operates apart from these unpleasant origins and intentions, it is a good and effective micro-vocabulary, words as suited to his careful manner of emphasis as are other favourite words expressive of weight, majesty and clarity—'stress', 'mere', 'grand', 'style', 'study', 'massive', 'tincture'. This last, certainly, leads into a dull and heavy 'imperial' vocabulary—to 'porphyry', 'largesse', 'glory', 'propolitan', 'ban'.

And there is a further overlap, into the vocabulary of scholasticism: 'twy-nature', 'identity', 'contingent', 'substantial', which is worse still. For it is intended as more than a mere verbal form and its failure lies in its seriousness. . . . [While] it may produce good metaphor or image, it makes a bad and dull general proposition in poetry. For example:

> in the space between
> The queen's substance and the queen

might be a vivid occasional remark, but is ruined when one sees that it is taken to have a serious direct meaning. (pp. 41-2)

One of the poems is dedicated to the proposition that poets do not make love. . . . [Theological] analysis of sexual love form's a large part of the cycle. . . . All this helpful advice and condemnation of straightforward experiences of sex comes particularly strangely from those who see nothing odd in the libido's involvement in much less pleasant mental and moral attitudes.

Still, Williams is sometimes interesting and moving on the numinous aspect of sexual love, especially when he is closest to the undeniable experience and furthest from the contortions of fitting it to his system. There are, though, astonishing grotesqueries. Thus, he maintains that menstruation is a suffering linking women with Christ's sufferings, in some sense accounting for their tendency to be divine. (p. 42)

[Williams's] hierarchial attitude is essential to the position. In Logres it is not just an accident of the period setting that society is based on slaves (not all barbarians incidentally—there are Caucasians and others too), and rises, through Lords, to King Arthur. Nor is position in society based on virtue. Slaves are put in the stocks for brawling; but Arthur, Guinevere, Lancelot, Morgause, Mordred are considerably more sinful. And Sir Kay, who appears to be in charge of punishment, will offer to let even a slave off if she seems to be a friend of one of the Lords. The gentleman ranker, Gareth, is soon restored from latrine orderly to his proper station. And so on.

The only answer to why the leaders are at the top is that such happens to be the will of God. And it is said that they should not be vain about their position, though few of them pay much attention to this. The will of God has been replaced in modern parallels by 'the nation' or 'the revolution' or 'history', but the effect seems to be much the same. (pp. 44-5)

It is difficult to see the absolute necessity to the theme of this submissive slavery and rigid hierarchy. If difference alone were implied . . . that could surely have been met in other ways. But this is only true if we take the theme to be religion, salvation. For Williams . . . the interest is elsewhere—on the manipulation of . . . [the] system of intellectual abstractions and the forcing of humanity and of events in general into its mould. The total acceptance of an ideology as providing an answer to everything is the opposite of what Lewis's enemy Keats saw as the essential for a poet—'negative capability': Keats also noted (of Dilke) that it is a weakness of the mind and not a strength to feel that one must have settled opinions about everything.

It is worse than that Williams merely 'to faction gave up what was meant for mankind', for this process of surrendering his talent has at the same time turned the talent itself sour. Partly guilty of being the unconscious source of his system, partly deriving from the exigencies of the system itself, the psychology of totalitarianism—of hierarchy and of sadism—is the essential of his work and ruins it irretrievably. [C. S.] Lewis comments [of Williams]:

> The modern world . . . has poets not a few;
> but they seldom see beauty in policemen.

No, indeed. (pp. 45-6)

Robert Conquest, "The Art of the Enemy" (originally published in a similar form in Essays in Criticism, *Vol. VII, No. 1, January, 1957), in his* The Abomination of Moab *(© 1979 by Robert Conquest; reprinted by permission of the author), Maurice Temple Smith, 1979, pp. 32-48.*

VALERIE PITT (essay date 1957)

[*Writing several months after the appearance of Conquest's controversial article in* Essays in Criticism *(see excerpt above), Pitt was one of four critics who attempted to refute Conquest's claim that Williams's vision and works exhibit the characteristics of a totalitarian writer.*]

Charles Williams's friends have done him a great disservice. It is tactless, in the present state of literary opinion, to plug a poet so esoteric in subject and manner. (p. 330)

But Mr. Conquest's article is another matter. His object is ideological and not literary and, that being so, he does not play fair. It is not clear whether the enemy of his title is a Chester-Bellocian monster, part Williams, part Lewis, called the Anglo-Oxford School (though Williams was only at Oxford at the end of his life, and Lewis is not an Anglo-Catholic), or, behind the monster, the brutal fascism of the Nicene Creed. If the latter, is theological polemic rally the province of *Essays in Criticism*? More importantly, Mr. Conquest deploys his attack from an ambush of non-committal, although he is as much the creature of his own attitudes as Charles Williams was of his. Mr. Conquest is concerned with literary, not with philosophical values, and will not be so irreverent of human experience as to mix with metaphysics and defined principles, for there is an absolute value in experience which dogma and definition, by limiting, destroy. But this is itself a principle, and not withstanding his own views Mr. Conquest accepts the Freudian explanations of human behaviour; more than that, he attaches to certain kinds of action moral and not merely clinical descriptions. (pp. 330-31)

Mr. Conquest, however, not merely believes, he is obsessed by his views. . . . The opposition between dictatorship and the free mind bulks very large in his system, and he cannot see the opposition between order and anarchy in Mr. Williams's is not the same thing. *Abusus non tollit usum.* The policeman, that he attaches such bitter significance to in the last lines of his article, is not an Ogpu or an S.S. man, but a metropolitan copper directing the traffic, and Arthur comes, in *Taliessin through Logres,* to direct activity to its proper social use. . . . Williams apprehended these normal activities with an imaginative intensity of which I think they are not really capable, and which could be dangerous. Still, I suppose that Mr. Conquest would not consider deliverance from the caprice of motorists, or even of wide boys and razor gangs, although undesirable for the free mind.

But, he objects, this is an order not experienced but imposed from above. It is hierarchical, rigid, and tied to a closed system of ideas. One begins to wonder if one is reading the same poet. Of course Mr. Williams believes in hierarchy, but his conception of it is altogether more subtle and less rigid than Mr. Conquest, with an eye on totalitarian abuses, will allow. . . . It was Williams's contention that poets meant what they said, and that when Wordsworth, for instance, speaks of the awareness of 'similitude in dissimilitude', or says that the observation of affinities / In objects where no brotherhood exists / To common minds', is an activity resembling that of creation, he is describing common poetic experience. It is on this kind of experience that Williams's love of order was founded, and it is this which governs his poetic expression.

'Correspondence and the law of similitudes' governs, for instance, the passage about the slave drawing water about which Mr. Conquest makes so much fuss. It is not because she is a slave, but because of the grace of her movement that she creates in Taliessin's mind the awareness of his journey through the Empire, and again her bodily movement is fused with the trumpet sound announcing the arrival of the woman with whom he falls in love. . . . A woman's body is not wantonly made the image of the Empire: it becomes its symbol because, in the perception of lover or of poet, the human body reveals that unity in difference which is the centre of order. But the Body as a symbol of community is, of course, a Christian symbol. . . . Hierarchy, for Mr. Conquest, I suspect means aristocratic power, for Williams it was a matter of function within a living organism, of which the outer form may as easily be republican as aristocratic. (pp. 331-33)

There remains the charge of brutality and its libidinal content. The charge of perversion rests on an explanation of human behaviour I myself don't consider adequate, but even in Mr. Conquest's terms 'the slave's discipline' is a remarkably abstract means of satisfying a perverted instinct. It is never actually used, and rarely mentioned more than fleetingly. I can't but consider Williams to be very unwise in pushing his physical symbolism to the point which Conquest describes, and I agree with him, as grotesque. But it is physical and not sexual imagery; that is, it is concerned not with sexual behaviour but with the sexual fact that human = man/woman. (pp. 333-34)

But 'the slaves discipline' is a means of coercing the barbarian into the Empire. We come back again to the fact that the Empire and a human body symbolise each other. . . . Though there may be within such society a point in restraint, not of one but of all classes, there is no point at all in exterior compulsion to, or exclusion from, this kind of unity, which exists, if at all, by the free consent of its members. (p. 334)

Mr. Conquest, one feels, would have been more profitably employed in considering that note of 'electness' which certainly appears in Williams's work, and which, unfortunately, is not peculiar to him or to his friends. It is the tone not of the masters, but of an inbred and persecuted minority, protective and defensive, rather than exclusive, and is the outward and visible sign of a fissiparous culture. Every egghead brotherhood, every new 'movement' has it. Mr. Conquest speaks of Williams's rejection 'of much of the learning and sentiment which forms the common tradition of our present culture'; by common tradition he means 'what I and my friends accept', and what *I* most complain of in his work is wilful ignorance that his position is as particular as anyone else's. Orthodoxy, in fact, is his doxy; heterodoxy, Mr. Williams's. It is very tiresome and not very helpful in the business of literary criticism to take this 'holier than thou' attitude about theological positions. What one is interested in is whether Williams has or has not created a real means of communicating the quality of experience which arises from his being that kind of a Christian. His success or

failure might be instructive, but these sectarian squabbles seem to make that kind of criticism very nearly impossible, whether in Williams's case or any other. (pp. 334-35)

> *Valerie Pitt, "The Art of the Enemy: I," in* Essays in Criticism, *Vol. VII, No. 3, July, 1957, pp. 330-35.*

J.R.R. TOLKIEN   (letter date 1965)

[*Tolkien is famous as the author of the mythopoeic* Lord of the Rings *trilogy (1954-56) and of its much simpler prequel,* The Hobbit *(1938). With his friend C. S. Lewis and with Charles Williams, Tolkien was also a central member of the Oxford Christians or "Inklings." A longtime professor of medieval English literature and philology at Merton College, Oxford, Tolkien was of quite conservative literary tastes; for years he campaigned to keep "modern" (nineteenth and twentieth-century) English literature off the curriculum at Merton. Like Lewis, he disliked nearly all the formal developments in twentieth-century writing, and his reading tended toward the traditional and the epic, his favorite literature being the ancient Norse sagas. Unlike Lewis, who greatly admired Williams and his work, Tolkien only tolerated Williams's presence among the Inklings for the sake of his good friend Lewis. Williams was too unorthodox in his Christian beliefs to suit Tolkien, a devout Roman Catholic who once referred to Williams as a "witch-doctor." Below, Tolkien reveals his thoughts about Williams to Dick Plotz, "Thain" of the Tolkien Society of America.*]

I knew Charles Williams only as a friend of C. S. L[ewis] whom I met in his company when, owing to the War, he spent much of his time in Oxford. We liked one another and enjoyed talking (mostly in jest) but we had nothing to say to one another at deeper (or higher) levels. I doubt if he had read anything of mine then available; I had read or heard a good deal of his work, but found it wholly alien, and sometimes very distasteful, occasionally ridiculous. (This is perfectly true as a general statement, but is not intended as a criticism of Williams; rather it is an exhibition of my own limits of sympathy. And of course in so large a range of work I found lines, passages, scenes, and thoughts that I found striking.) I remained entirely unmoved. Lewis was bowled over. (pp. 361-62)

> *J.R.R. Tolkien, in an extract from his letter to Dick Plotz on September 12, 1965, in his* The Letters of J.R.R. Tolkien, *edited by Humphrey Carpenter with Christopher Tolkien (copyright © 1981 by George Allen & Unwin (Publishers) Ltd. Reprinted by permission of Houghton Mifflin Company. In Canada by George Allen & Unwin (Publishers) Ltd.), Houghton Mifflin, 1981, Allen & Unwin, 1981, pp. 359-62.**

BARBARA McMICHAEL   (essay date 1968)

[*McMichael examines Williams's concept of damnation as it is presented in one of the author's strongest novels,* Descent into Hell.]

[Charles Williams] tried in a series of supernatural "mystery" novels to embody his thought in an exciting way. Although all of the novels are exciting in the concepts of the writer's thought which they reveal and in their handling of the supernatural, several of them are not completely successful. In *War in Heaven, Many Dimensions, The Greater Trumps,* and *Shadows of Ecstasy,* Williams does not quite achieve a unity of complex intellectual ideas with the mystery novel form, and many of his characters appear as unreal as the supernatural events which engage them. In the other three novels, *The Place of the Lion, Descent Into Hell,* and *All Hallows Eve,* Williams does manage to merge form and content into a unified whole, creating for his reader a vivid experience of both story and idea. Their unified effect is achieved partially because Williams' characters in these novels are more adequately realized than in the other four. While the details of the damnation or salvation of the characters in these three novels are supernatural, the substance of them is at least recognizably human. Especially well presented is the corruption of the human will by its own desires, the process of damnation. The concept of this process is a major theme of Williams' work as a whole, and it is perhaps nowhere more clearly presented than in the character of Lawrence Wentworth, whose journey to damnation gives Williams the title for *Descent Into Hell.* An examination of Wentworth's damnation should, therefore, offer some valuable insights into this aspect of Williams' thought.

Basically Williams sees the process of damnation as an intensification of self. The individual who consistently insists, as Aldous Huxley puts it in *The Perennial Philosophy,* on the "intensification of his own separateness and selfhood" makes himself "impervious to the divine." Such an individual by this insistence on self cuts himself off from God and hence from all hope of salvation. He has chosen to do so, and his damnation comes as a result of his own choice. Williams emphasizes that the individual damns himself. Freedom of choice has been given him, and of his own free will, man is damned because he will not accept salvation. Cutting oneself off completely from the cosmos cannot, in fact, be done. The sense of individual separateness is an illusion. For Charles Williams it follows, then, that being damned consists of choosing to exist in a state of illusion. Hell is composed of those who will not admit reality. From insistence upon oneself as the center of all things, one moves into the final illusion that only self exists. The insistence on the aloneness of self leads to the agony of hell, the complete void.

The character of Lawrence Wentworth in *Descent Into Hell* exemplifies this concept of damnation. When Wentworth is first introduced in the novel, he is a normal human being. He is even, perhaps a little above the average, for he is, Williams says, "the most distinguished living authority on military history (perhaps excepting Mr. Aston Moffatt)." Wentworth has reached that time in life when man begins to feel the restlessness of youthful goals secured and to seek for new goals to satisfy himself. "He was not much over fifty, but his body was beginning to feel that its future was shortening, and that perhaps it had been too cautious in the past." . . . There are three factors in Wentworth's life which could open new goals for him, three routes, as it were, to a new fulfillment. First, there is Aston Moffatt, Wentworth's only rival for prominence in the field of military history. Moffatt and Wentworth are engaged in a dispute over the details of a march of Edward Plantagenet's cavalry. The dispute presents to Wentworth an opportunity to devote himself to a pure and disinterested scholarship, an unselfish devotion to truth for the sake of truth and not for the sake of Wentworth's reputation. Or the dispute could present Wentworth with the opportunity to admit that scholarship is not his true interest, and so free him to seek elsewhere for his true goal. A choice between reality and illusion, between selfless study and selfish interest is before him. The choice which he makes at this point might constitute for him the first step on a journey to enlightenment and so salvation. Wentworth does not so choose. . . . The temptations of scholarship as well as its rewards were well known to Wil-

liams and are examined elsewhere in his work. There is, for example, the character of Damaris Tighe in *The Place of the Lion.* There, as in Wentworth's case, the conclusion is not difficult to draw; scholarship can offer an admirable way to truth and selflessness if it is pursued for its own sake out of a disinterested love for one's subject. Scholarship, on the other hand, if pursued for selfish interest as Wentworth pursues it and as Damaris Tighe for a time pursued it, can offer one of the quicker roads to hell. Research, by its very nature, is a solitary thing. As such, it tends to cut one off from much of that purely social contact with others which often serves to keep the ego in its place. Scholars of reputation too often receive adulation or unquestioning respect from those ignorant of the scholar's field, and the ego-centered image of the self may grow dangerously as a result.

Had Wentworth chosen to see his interest in history for what it was, an interest in his own reputation, there was open to him an opportunity for another choice between selfishness and love of something outside of self. He is attracted to a young woman, Adela Hunt. . . . She is, however, involved with a man, Hugh Prescott, nearer her own age. Prescott is a forceful personality. He, too, senses Wentworth's interest in Adela and determines to assert his dominant position. He persuades Adela to go to a play with him and to tell Wentworth that she cannot attend the regular gathering on a pretext. Wentworth suspects that the two are together. This circumstance offers Wentworth yet another point of choice. He could admit the reality of his desire; he could have then made an active effort to win Adela. Perhaps he could have made such a choice if his feelings for Adela were for the girl herself. But what Wentworth has desired from Adela is not the girl herself but the image of himself which having Adela would give him. It is a very common failing of man to fasten his own desires onto the nearest likely object, to love not another but only the reflection he sees of himself in another. . . . When he reaches the conclusion based on their mutual absence from his gathering that Hugh and Adela are together, Wentworth is defeated. The defeat is as real as the battle although one may choose to insist that neither exists. (pp. 59-62)

The third way open to Wentworth is a record of movement in a recurring dream. In the dream Wentworth "was climbing down a rope; he did nothing but climb down a rope." . . . The smooth white rope of the dream hangs in a void of darkness; it is fastened above and below, but both ends are hidden from Wentworth's sight. He climbs steadily downward, and although Wentworth has no sensation of movement, Williams makes it clear that the descent is a willed thing, not a sliding but a climbing. Williams does not develop the dream as a possible way for Wentworth in the concrete way that he does develop the relationships with Aston Moffatt and Adela Hunt. He uses the dream as symbol and pattern of Wentworth's deterioration, expanding upon it, referring back to it, allowing it to recur at various stages of the novel. Thus, the dream serves the reader as an explanation of what is going on, and the question arises of whether it could not so have served Wentworth. Williams does not stress this idea and makes no overt use of dream symbolism in the novel, yet the implication of the dream as a way is there, for Williams does explain that Wentworth refused to acknowledge this intrusion into consciousness of the forces of the unknown depths of his being. Wentworth chooses to ignore the dream as he has chosen to ignore all unpleasantness, all things which are not as he wills them to be. Williams makes the content of the dream so obvious that the reader must feel as he reads that a man of Wentworth's intelligence and learning could understand its warning if he wished. He would not even have to see the dream as a reference to anything supernatural for it to prove effective to him. The mere idea of descent coupled with the dream's recurrence could serve as a warning.

The warnings are many on the path to hell; the opportunities to turn back and to renounce self and the illusion of self come often. Williams emphasizes the various choices of his characters at various times in the novel in order to emphasize his thesis that the will of man is always free to choose and that its choices constitute its destiny. The supernatural details of Lawrence Wentworth's damnation are different from the experiences of most men. . . . Yet how close and how real are the desires of the self which Williams' supernatural beings embody. (pp. 62-3)

Lawrence Wentworth chooses to neglect the three ways opened to him to a new life. Disinterested scholarship, love for a woman, acknowledgment of the warning of his deram, all three or any one of these offer to him a pathway out of the illusion of the dominance of self to that realization of the need for the sacrifice of self which offers to man the only hope for joy and meaning in life. . . . The choice of man according to Williams is thus simply a choice between sacrifice of self to the unity of all being or a choice to intensify self and insist on its separateness. For Williams this is the choice between reality and illusion, between heaven and hell.

The major time of choice is brought to Lawrence Wentworth as it is to most men by events outside his control. He goes out to spy on Adela and Hugh on the night they have not come to his gathering and discovers that they have lied to him. . . . One morning of that week of waiting, he reads in the morning newspaper that Aston Moffatt, his scholastic rival, has been awarded a knighthood. . . . While this is the major opportunity for Wentworth to choose salvation, it is not the last such opportunity for him. Even further along the road of damnation than this, man may still turn back. (pp. 63-4)

So damnation comes to man naturally—a little thing, a small point of honor, and like Wentworth man may choose without even consciously knowing he has chosen. Each such choice removes man further from his humanity, and only in his humanity lies the hope of his salvation from the inhuman state of infinite illusion. Neither a machine, nor a phantasm, nor a man devoted to the world of shadows can know salvation according to Williams. Not only those elements of his humanity which man calls good can save him. Fear may often be the instrument of salvation. So, Williams rather surprisingly states, can hatred. . . . Here we see that for Williams man's intentions are of primary importance. If he cannot manage the noble act, the grand deed, he can perhaps manage an intention toward these things, and that intention in itself has redemptive power. . . . A man need not have religious faith to recognize the truth that the individual ego is not the center of the cosmos.

It is, however, exactly this glaring truth which the beings who occupy hell in Williams' vision of hell do refuse to recognize. . . . Maturity, after all, consists in the ability to see the self as it is in relationship to things as they are. For Lawrence Wentworth, hell consists of Lilith and the succubus and finally of only Wentworth himself. For mankind in the twentieth century, hell consists of a world gone mad in the despair of lives lived without meaning. This is the madness each man encounters every day in wars, and in empty cocktail party chatter, in restless pleasure seeking, and in sexual relationships devoid of any concept of love between the partners, in endless attempts to use other people as instruments for the gratification of the self. Insanity—or damnation—consists in the refusal to admit the facts of existence. (pp. 65-6)

And so he has finally nothing. In choosing the intensification of selfhood, he has rejected everything else. The individual self is not inexhaustible. As Wentworth proceeds into himself, that self is destroyed. . . .

For Williams as for Dante to whom he alludes several times in the novel, hell is imaged as a place composed of concentric circles. For Williams the human soul may move or descend through the outer circles, those closest to man's humanity and so still recognizably human, into the inner or deeper circles, those farthest removed from the human condition. In his dream Wentworth climbs unceasingly down his white shining rope. There is a downward progression in hell. (p. 67)

It is important within the framework of Williams' thought that man understand the possibility of damnation and that as far as he is capable reconcile it to the concept of the goodness of God and the unity of all things in God. . . . The idea of the unity of all things in one God forms a basic part of Williams' thought as well as of the thought of many of the mystics of all religions whom he admired. (p. 68)

Yet there is, for Williams, a circle of hell further and deeper than Gomorrah. This is the hell which Lawrence Wentworth finds at the end of the rope of his dream. . . . In three pages of vivid and frightening prose, Williams carries Wentworth through the final phases of his journey. (p. 70)

Ultimately the vision of Charles Williams, like the vision of the Christian mythology which he accepted, is more concerned with heaven than with hell. Yet an understanding of hell is probably necessary for salvation. (pp. 70-1)

Barbara McMichael, "Hell Is Oneself: An Examination of the Concept of Damnation in Charles Williams' 'Descent Into Hell'," in Studies in the Literary Imagination *(copyright 1968 Department of English, Georgia State University), Vol. 1, No. 2, October, 1968, pp. 59-71.*

GLENN E. SADLER (essay date 1970)

[*Sadler, a noted specialist in the life and work of George MacDonald, provides the only critical commentary to-date on Williams's uncompleted eighth "supernatural thriller,"* The Noises That Weren't There. *The fragment of this novel was printed in three successive numbers of* Mythlore, *the periodical of the Mythopoeic Society, which is devoted to "the study, discussion, and enjoyment of myth, fantasy & imaginative literature, especially the works of J.R.R. Tolkien, C. S. Lewis, & Charles Williams."*]

The three chapters which remain (in typescript) [of **"The Noises That Weren't There"**] are of interest, I think, to those who have taken the Way of the City throughout Williams' seven published metaphysical thrillers. The conventional but witty conversations (some of which were recorded, says Mrs. Williams, while her husband was riding the London tube) in them, the intermingling in them of natural and supernatural things and occurrences (this time of a haunted house, filled with postponed sounds, which has in it the nude "dissolving, sandy" body of a young woman) reminds us of Williams' fondness for the theme of interpenetration and coinherence. And of course there is in this novel fragment the image of the City; it is Williams' last journey through it. . . .

Glenn E. Sadler, in his introduction to "The Noises that Weren't There," in Mythlore *(copyright © by The Mythopoeic Society; reprinted by permission of The Mythopoeic Society, P.O. Box 4671, Whittier, CA 90607), 1970, Vol. 2, No. 2, Autumn, 1970, p. 17.*

DORIS T. MYERS (essay date 1971)

[*Myers examines the literary treatment of women by the principal Oxford Christians from a feminist perspective, and finds Williams to be the most progressive of the three.*]

One of the feats possible to those who write fantastic stories is to remake the world. . . . [One] type of world-remaking fiction, easier to recognize than to define, plays on our conviction that all life is stranger and more wonderful than the fustian of daily existence and this is the sort of fiction written by "the Oxford Christians": J.R.R. Tolkien, C. S. Lewis, and Charles Williams. (p. 13)

Since each of the three creates a world virtually *ex nihilo,* each is free to postulate any sort of relationship between the sexes that he wishes. Thus to the women's liberationist looking for some new vision of what could be, the "other-worldly" novels of the Oxford Christians are of great interest. (p. 14)

The worlds created by Charles Williams are indisputably different [from those of Lewis and Tolkien]. Although his best work of criticism is probably *The Figure of Beatrice,* which deals with Dante's spiritual and literary pilgrimage in the service of a lady, Williams never advocates the sort of chivalric adoration offered to the eleven ladies in *The Lord of the Rings.* On the contrary, Williams' lovers regard the failure to recognize human weakness in the beloved as a failure to love fully. Anthony Durant in *The Place of the Lion* calls his beloved "a very detestable, selfish pig and prig," but in the next breath he says, "You are the Sherbet of Allah, and the gold cup he drinks it out of."

Neither does Williams ever create a wholly masculine, epic world such as the hrossian society of *Out of the Silent Planet* or the masculine fellowship of the Ring. In one of his novels, *War in Heaven,* the primary emotional interest is the deep friendship of a duke, an archdeacon, and a publisher's assistant who band together to save the Holy Grail, but even this book contains an important female character.

Neither does Williams portray women as invariably subject to men, although, like C. S. Lewis, he loved Milton and recognized the principle of hierarchy. In Williams' novels women often serve men, but men also are subject to women. It all depends on the circumstances. In *Shadows of Ecstasy* the wife waits on the sidelines while her husband follows a compelling new prophet in search of an ultimate spiritual experience, but in *Many Dimensions* it is a girl who searches and a man, her employer, who waits on the sidelines to serve and encourage her. For Williams the principle of hierarchy is modified, not by phony housework-sharing arrangements like the one in *That Hideous Strength,* but by a literal practice of the Biblical injunction to "Bear ye one another's burdens, and so fulfill the law of Christ." This practice, which Williams called "the doctrine of co-inherence," is dramatized in his best-known and perhaps best novel, *The Descent into Hell.* The heroine, Pauline Anstruther, is haunted by a fear of meeting her double. Peter

Stanhope offers to suffer the fear for her, so that if she meets the apparition she need not be afraid of it. In turn Pauline suffers fear for her ancestor, John Struther, who was burned at the stake in the Marian persecutions. Because she, centuries later, was bearing his burden of fear, he was enabled to go to his martyrdom fearlessly.

As a contrast to co-inherence and an example of the perversion of hierarchy Williams presents the historian Lawrence Wentworth, who wants his beloved, Adela, to be a reflection of himself, completely subservient to his will. There comes to him a succubus, an image of Adela, who performs his erotic desires so completely that he loses all interest in and capacity to perceive the real world. The description of the false Adela's coy submission to Wentworth parodies Milton's description of Eve's submission to Adam: "The shape of Lawrence Wentworth's desire had emerged from the power of his body . . . [She] clung to him, pressing her shoulder against him, turning eyes of adoration on him, stroking his fingers with her own." For Williams the woman who comes from the man's side to serve him adoringly is an auto-erotic illusion—Lilith rather than Eve.

Even when Williams seems on a superficial level to be using a feminine stereotype, he avoids falling into traditional attitudes. *The Place of the Lion* is superficially a variation on the shrew-taming plot, but Williams handles it without descending to the suburban, lady's-magazine bathos of Tolkien or the patronizing masculine superiority of Lewis. Damaris Tighe is writing a doctoral thesis, and it, like Jane Studdock's in *That Hideous Strength,* is not a very good one. But instead of attributing its faultiness to Damaris' unwomanly behavior, Williams shows that the thesis is bad for the same reason that Lawrence Wentworth's scholarship is bad—because Damaris is more concerned with publication and winning arguments than with acquiring real knowledge. Her relationship with Anthony Durrant is unsatisfactory, not because women should create children rather than books, but because her interest in him is selfish. He edits a journal in which she hopes to publish. Her change of heart, unlike those of Éowyn [in Tolkien's *The Return of the King*] and Jane, involves no rejection of her previous ambition, but rather a truer, more whole-hearted devotion to scholarship. . . . The taming of Damaris involves submission to Anthony, but also to philosophy.

Williams shared the religious commitment and literary predilections of his friends, but he completely escaped their narrow, stereotyped attitudes toward women. He depicts women in their traditional roles—wife, mother, old maid aunt, bluestocking, secretary—but spiritually they are as free and responsible as men, and the "good" men characters treat them as equals. Williams' attitude is so unusually "liberated" that critics comment on his poor characterization of women. It is true that Williams' women are often stiff and awkwardly drawn, but so are his men. His inability to write realistic conversation makes both male and female characters seem precious and wooden, but he is realistic in that his men and women have the same capabilities, whether for abysmal selfishness or exalted strength and nobility. None of the three authors uses his opportunity in creating new worlds to suggest major revisions of the present social system, but Williams does suggest an attitude, a change of heart, which would make a different social system worthwhile. And despite his "ghoulies and ghosties and long-legged beasties," the fictional world of Charles Williams is better for women—for people—than the worlds of Tolkien and Lewis. (pp. 17-19)

Doris T. Myers, "Brave New World: The Status of Women according to Tolkien, Lewis, and Williams," in The Cimarron Review *(copyright © 1971 by the Board of Regents for Oklahoma State University), No. 17, October, 1971, pp. 13-19.**

HUMPHREY CARPENTER (essay date 1978)

[*Carpenter, a biographer of Tolkien and of W. H. Auden, examines differences and similarities in the thought and work of Tolkien, Lewis, and Williams.*]

Was there any such thing as a 'common Inklings attitude'? Can the group of friends who met on Thursday nights really be called with any significance 'The Oxford Christians'? Or is any attempt to search out important links between the work of these people really, as Lewis himself put it, 'chasing after a fox that isn't there'? (p. 167)

[Like Lewis, Williams] certainly could and sometimes did turn his hand to the intellectual justification of Christianity—for example, in his book *He Came Down From Heaven,* where he shows himself quite as capable as Lewis of closely reasoned argument on the subject of doctrine and belief. But that was not where Williams's heart lay. His vision of Christianity was idiosyncratic for two reasons: first because he was a poet, and many of his writings on theology are in fact poetic vision rather than rational argument; and second because of his interest in the neo-magical fringes of the Church. His principal doctrines—Co-inherence, Romantic Theology, Substituted Love—reflect his early involvement with Rosicrucianism and the Golden Dawn. As a result there is scant resemblance between the breezy outdoor Chestertonian Christianity of Lewis and the esoteric world occupied by Williams and his disciples. (p. 168)

It might be supposed that Williams and Lewis had something in common as literary critics. Certainly Williams's Milton lectures at Oxford were the germ of Lewis's *Preface to Paradise Lost.* But apart from this it is surprisingly hard to find any similarity in their literary criticism. Indeed their attitudes reveal themselves as fundamentally different. Lewis liked to maintain that literature is ultimately no more than a recreation, though a very valuable one. In the essay 'Christianity and Literature' he declared that 'the salvation of a single soul is more important than the production or preservation of all the epics and tragedies in the world'. Though Williams, as a Christian, would perhaps have agreed with this with his rational mind, it is difficult to believe in his assenting to it emotionally. To him, great poetry was a thing of supreme importance, essential to a full spiritual life, and indeed itself a source of supernatural power. 'Love and poetry are powers,' he declared through the mouth of Roger Ingram in *Shadows of Ecstasy;* elsewhere in the same novel Ingram declares that Milton's verse is a form of 'immortal energy'. This is very far from Lewis's view of such things.

What remains that can be called a 'common Inklings attitude'? Certainly it seems a significant link that Tolkien, Lewis and Williams all wrote stories in which myth plays an important part. Yet each of the three uses myth in quite a different way. Williams takes the already existing Arthurian myth and uses it as a setting for metaphysical odes. Lewis uses the Christian 'myth' and reclothes it for his didactic purposes. Tolkien invents his own mythology and draws stories of many different kinds from it. The distinction needs to be emphasised as much as the similarity. On the other hand there is, of course, the belief shared by Tolkien and Lewis that myth can sometimes convey truth in a way that no abstract argument can achieve:

a very important notion behind both men's work, and an idea that was certainly shared in some degree by Williams.

Where else might the 'fox' of shared ideas be found? Possibly in the area of magic and the occult. . . . [In] Charles Williams's novels the crucial events occur in the plane of the supernatural, while the terminology of magic and occult practices is part of Williams's basic vocabulary. He and Tolkien had nothing whatever in common in the way they used the supernatural in their stories. (pp. 170-71)

We are being driven to look for the fox in some rather unlikely places, and the next one looks distinctly unpromising: the fact that Tolkien, Lewis and Williams felt, to some extent, alienated from the mainstream of contemporary literature. (p. 172)

Williams's . . . early poetry and verse-dramas were scarcely modern in character, having a strong tendency towards the pastiche of earlier styles. Those poets who made a mark on him in his early work included Chesterton, Yeats, and Lascelles Abercrombie, as well as such diverse people as Kipling, the Pre-Raphaelites and Macaulay. His attitude to Eliot was at first largely one of puzzlement. Yet in his book *Poetry at Present* . . . he was characteristically quick to find virtues in poets whose work was distinctly modern, and by that time he was aware that if he wished to achieve anything more than minor success as a poet he must find a more modern style. 'Better be modern than minor,' says a character in *War in Heaven,* and it was with this in mind that Williams set about remodelling his verse-rhythms. Yet, despite the apparent modernity of much of *Taliessin through Logres,* his style resembled Gerard Manley Hopkins far more than (say) Eliot, while his diction remained largely formal and never became thoroughly colloquial. He was perhaps never a true modern in his poetry.

As to prose, Williams's novels, or at least the early ones, are more like the Fu Manchu thrillers of Sax Rohmer or Chesterton's *The Man Who Was Thursday* than 'serious' modern fiction. Williams, however, did read widely among contemporary writers, partly because of his work as a reviewer; and he was always finding virtues in authors whose ideas were very different from his own. In an essay for the journal *Theology* in 1939 he examined D. H. Lawrence's attitude to sex, and recorded his admiration of Lawrence's glorification of the physical body, though he pointed out that Lawrence stopped short of developing this glorification to what he himself thought out to be its true (and Dantean) end. This essay, reprinted in *The Image of the City,* precisely expresses how much more subtle Williams's mind was than Lewis's when confronted with such issues. After reading what Williams has to say about Lawrence it is merely irritating to listen to Lewis's occasional snorts of disapproval about him. (pp. 173-74)

Whether or not the Inklings can with any justification be called 'a circle of incendiaries', it must be remembered that the word 'influence', so beloved of literary investigators, makes little sense when talking about their association with each other. Tolkien and Williams owed almost nothing to the other Inklings, and would have written everything they wrote had they never heard of the group. . . . As Lewis put it, 'To be sure, we had a common point of view, but we had it before we met. It was the cause rather than the result of our friendship.' (p. 175)

Humphrey Carpenter, "'A Fox That Isn't There'," in his The Inklings: C. S. Lewis, J.R.R. Tolkien, Charles Williams, and Their Friends *(copyright © 1978 by George Allen & Unwin (Publishers) Ltd. Reprinted by permission of Houghton Mifflin Com-*

pany. In Canada by George Allen & Unwin (Publishers) Ltd.), Houghton Mifflin, 1978, Allen & Unwin, 1978 (and reprinted by Ballantine Books, 1981, pp. 166-87).

AGNES SIBLEY (essay date 1979)

[*Sibley completed her Twayne study of Williams's work shortly before her death in 1979. In the following excerpt, she examines the author's dramas.*]

[*The Death of Good Fortune*] is a short play with the theme that "All luck is good"—that is, whatever happens to people, though it may seem unfortunate, disastrous, or purely evil, is actually sent from God and is capable of producing good in the recipient. (p. 8)

Do most people today believe that all luck is good? Obviously not, but then most of the world is not turned to God. God, as Williams understands Him, contains within Himself all good and also what looks like evil. Evil, under God, is always capable of being recognized as good or love. Therefore, the human distinction between good and evil must not exist on God's level. The opposites that we see—good and evil, dark and light, innocence and experience—are transcended by God, and His greater synthesis can be accepted by man through faith and a developed imagination. (p. 10)

A first step to be taken is to accept that the meaning and purpose of life can only be found in God; in and by himself man is helpless. Paradoxically, he can achieve his full stature as a spiritual being only by seeing that as a separate individual he is nothing—he comes to his full powers not on his own but by entering into his part of God's glory. The understanding of one's own "nothingness" is a central theme in Williams's first successful play, *Thomas Cranmer of Canterbury.* . . . (pp. 10-11)

Thomas Cranmer (1489-1556), made Archbishop of Canterbury by Henry VIII, was of a studious, gentle nature, a man of peace who was thrust by circumstances into the turmoil of the Reformation. . . . Cranmer was accused of heresy after Henry's death and burned at the stake by Queen Mary. (p. 11)

Just before his death [in the play] he finds something better than his personal being, for he turns away from self and flees into God's love.

He is brought to this saving knowledge of his own powerlessness by the Skeleton, the enigmatic character who so puzzled the first reviewers of the play. What does he represent? (p. 12)

There are . . . suggestions that the Skeleton, for all his sinister aspect, is a presentation of the view not of either side but of the God that both sides claim. (p. 13)

The Skeleton suggests Christ or God also in the way that he sees into the future; he knows and declares Cranmer's fate and the fate of everyone. . . .

[The] audience begins to see that the Skeleton is speaking the same doctrine as that of Mary in *The Death of Good Fortune*— no matter what the luck, the change of time or place, the Christian is to give thanks. The Skeleton's astringent personality is somehow a glimpse of the quality of Christ's love. (p. 14)

Near the end, Cranmer prays, "What shall I then? despair? thou art not despair. / Into thee now do I run, into thy love." . . .

His running into God's love is in the mind of the audience at the very end, when only the burning is left to be done, and the Skeleton's urgent word, "Speed!" is echoed by Cranmer and everyone present as they all hurry out. (p. 17)

The chief idea of *Cranmer,* the need to see one's own personal nothingness, is again a theme in *The House of the Octopus,* a play with a twentieth-century setting. Here the spirit of God, who brings a man to see his sin of self-sufficiency, is called the Flame. . . . The Flame serves somewhat the same purpose as the Skeleton in *Cranmer,* presenting another aspect of the action and also taking part in it. (p. 18)

In this play, as in *Cranmer,* Williams presents the story of apparent failure—Christians overcome by a harsh, opposing force and losing their lives. But in both plays the inner drama is all-important; what seems outwardly like failure is the triumph of spirit, brought about in both plays by the characters' realization of their own weakness. (p. 20)

Williams's concern with the Church as an entity capable, like the individual, of both good and evil, is evident again in *Judgement at Chelmsford,* a pageant play written for the celebration of the twenty-fifth anniversary of the diocese of Chelmsford in Essex. (p. 22)

Looking at the play as a depiction of the soul's journey to God, we see the early scenes of witch-hunting as images of Hell, with the soul of man intent on gain through the selfish exploitation of others' fears. Likewise, the Reformation scenes show the soul insisting on its own "right"; it is self-centered and blind. In the episode of the hungry peasants the soul is content with its own good, heedless of the needs of others.

In the scene of the martyrdom of St. Osyth the Accuser says that it is he who shows the blessed martyrs to Chelmsford. He tells her, "The more you know me, sweet, the more you know them." . . . In other words, judgement, represented by the Accuser, always implies penitence, and with penitence comes a greater knowledge of God and the people of God. (pp. 23-4)

The play has many affirmations, such as one by St. Osyth about her vision of the City, beginning, "I saw the City where Love loves and is loved." . . . The City, one of Williams's favorite images, is the place where no person or institution will try to dominate others, where nobody will feel his own righteousness, but where all will be a part of Christ's glory, a vast web of interrelationships having a mathematically precise beauty. Here everyone will live a rich, creative life from the Creator and will practice exchange, as do Anthony and Alayu in *The House of the Octopus;* and here all luck will be seen to be good. Acknowledging one's own nothingness, then, is not an end in itself, but a preliminary to becoming part of the glory. (p. 25)

An analysis of *Seed of Adam* must begin with Williams's own statement in the synopsis of the play that he wrote for the program notes. He says, "This nativity is not so much a presentation of the historic facts as of their spiritual value. The persons of the play, besides being dramatic characters, stand for some capacity or activity of man." . . . (p. 26)

What Adam is searching for Mary has already found. Her universal goodwill reflects the all-encompassing love of God, even before the angel Gabriel comes to her. Williams implies, in fact, that the angel appears because she is ready. She represents man's intuitive knowledge of God's love, peace, and joy; and it is this openness to spiritual truth that makes possible the birth of Christ—in Bethlehem in history, and in the soul at all times. (p. 27)

For Williams, as we have seen, the true Christian believes all luck to be good, and he accepts his own nothingness, realizing that he is significant, not in and of himself, but as part of the "glory." How can this insight be made practical in daily life? The answer is given in the four plays now to be analyzed.

The first of these, *The House by the Stable,* is another nativity play. . . .

In this simple allegory Williams has given the root cause of man's original alienation from God. It is pride that makes him feel self-sufficient and almost shuts out any vision of heavenly glory. (p. 30)

At the climax of the play Man, engrossed in the dice game, yet keeps hearing voices, something outside himself; and when he finally rouses himself and calls for Gabriel to explain the voices, he is delivered from the clutches of Pride and Hell. . . .

As a continuation of the story of Man, Pride, and Hell, [*Grab and Grace; or, It's the Second Step*] is even more lively and quick-moving than *The House by the Stable.* (p. 31)

The title of this play is perfect. "Grab" suggests the slapstick quality of some of its humor, and "Grace," besides being one of the characters, indicates God's loving concern for erring Man, as it is seen at the climax of the action. (p. 32)

The "second step" mentioned in the title is what Faith calls "the perseverance into the province of death." . . . Man, in finally sending Pride away, suffers a kind of death. The second step is a death to self, willingly undertaken. (p. 33)

Even more clearly than in *Grab and Grace,* Williams shows in *The Three Temptations* that man must make a conscious choice of God. A new life is necessary. . . . (p. 34)

The Three Temptations emphasizes not only the pain of choice, but man's willful, stubborn refusal to give up anything that makes him comfortable or assured. The three particular ways in which people hold on to comfort, i.e., prefer themselves to Christ, are embodied in the three rulers. . . . And these three—money, fame, religion—are the temptations offered to Christ by the Evil one. All of these he rejects in favor of a self-denying, difficult path along which he has no personal gain but allows God to work *through* him. (p. 35)

Terror of Light is a very interesting play, containing several ideas that run through most of Williams's work. The most noticeable of these is that of exchange, which is related to the "nothingness" that is a theme in all the plays. Living in Christ, we look to others for our help, and in turn we are divinely enabled to help those who look to us. (p. 38)

The moving energy of the play is the light named in the title. Like the Flame in *The House of the Octopus,* it represents the Holy Spirit—but unlike the Flame, the light is not a character in the play; rather, it is an invisible force felt by the characters. (pp. 39-40)

Agnes Sibley, in her Charles Williams (copyright © 1982 by Twayne Publishers; reprinted with the permission of Twayne Publishers, a Division of G. K. Hall & Co., Boston), Twayne, 1982, 160 p.

GLEN CAVALIERO (essay date 1983)

[*An English poet, critic, and former Anglican cleric, Cavaliero is a member of the Faculty of English at Cambridge. A well-read critic, he is the author of acclaimed studies of the works of E. M Forster, John Cowper Powys, and of the rural tradition in the early twentieth-century English novel. In the following excerpt from his recent critical study of Williams's works, Cavaliero provides a general overview of the author's canon.*]

[Charles Williams] tends to be regarded as a brilliant oddity, the minor prophet of a dwindling cult. But to study his work with care is to be rewarded by an intellectual vision that is both sane and liberating. If the surest standard for assessing a writer's achievement is, as C. S. Lewis has argued, the quality of reading it elicits, then Williams remains a figure to be reckoned with.

Even in his lifetime he was considered eccentric, not only, as might be expected, by the clergy, but also by the London literary circuit. . . . (p. 158)

In the Western Church likewise, Williams's ideas, both in style and content, have become unfashionable. His emphasis on the power of poetic language contradicts the current simplistic preference of intelligible communication to appeals to the imagination and the heart (fundamentalist appeals to the emotions are altogether another thing). . . . In Williams's own day his use of language was suspect, even as sympathetic a reviewer as the philosopher E. I. Watkin complaining of 'a terminology distracting and irritating, and a seemingly flippant manner which sometimes jars'. (pp. 158-59)

His own enthusiasm also could get in the way. (p. 159)

Verbal mannerisms, and the assumption that what he is talking about is known and accepted, also obtrude discomfortingly in Williams's various essays and reviews. . . . Stimulating though most of Williams's occasional writings are, such a self-enclosed vocabulary has the effect of dissociating him from his contemporaries, even from those who share his religious faith.

Williams's achievement as a critic goes largely disregarded: it is in any case secondary to his theological concerns. But his perceptions are acute. . . . Along with Chesterton, Virginia Woolf and V. S. Pritchett, Williams was a critic who made an analytic tool out of metaphor; it is an achievement which touches the quick of life when more abstract discourse merely talks about doing so. But, where his theological insights are concerned, only G. Wilson Knight among contemporary critics really pursues a line conformable to Williams's own. (pp. 159-60)

With the exception of his verse play *The Witch* and some of the early poems, there is not one [of his writings] that does not reflect the peculiar quality of his mind and voice. Their limitations are self-evident: Williams reveals little interest in his contemporaries, and all his concerns are turned inward to his self-propagating personal myth. To that extent he is a supplementary, not an authoritative, writer. But, where his myth itself dictates the terms of discourse, he reveals his creative power. This happens in the novels, poetry and plays, and, because of the coincidence of myth and subject-matter, the theology.

In the novels Williams's art moves towards an ever more perfect fusion of natural with supernatural, so that in *Descent into Hell* and *All Hallows' Eve* he is able to express his vision of coinherence in a way that overcomes the potential limitation implied in the use of occult symbolism. The magical elements do, certainly, make the novels compare unfavourably as parables of grace with those of William Golding, beside whose psychological penetration and feeling for physical actuality they seem cerebral and rarefied; nor does Williams attempt to integrate theological doctrines with the contemporary world in the way that Golding seeks to do in *Pincher Martin* (1956) and *Free Fall* (1959). Yet the intellectual complexity and denseness of organisation in Williams's novels invite comparison with Golding's work. . . . The intellectual possibilities of the myths and symbols Williams employs afford his powers of analysis full scope; and, since the symbols are of their nature omnipotent and all-embracing, they can offset the flimsy characterisation by enveloping and subsuming it. Even so, the tension between natural and supernatural remains uneasy. There is an uncomfortable disparity between the grandeur of the novels' themes and the frequently trivial or reductive way in which they are presented.

These faults are least apparent in *The Place of the Lion,* where the characters are little more than cyphers acting out their parts in conformity with the dictates of the celestial invasion. . . . Similarly, in *Many Dimensions,* Lord Arglay is often either arch or pompous; his addressing his secretary as 'Child' is tiresome, while his 'O la la!' would be more appropriate in a novel by Ronald Firbank. Where the Stone is concerned, the dialogue turns scriptural and plummy. (pp. 160-62)

The worst instances of this kind of thing occur in *The Greater Trumps,* where the emphasis is more interior and psychological. . . . Williams's own over-anxiety not to be too solemn betrays him into sprightliness and whimsy. (p. 162)

The line between success and failure is more finely drawn in the character of Sybil [in *Shadows of Ecstasy*]. She shows a greater self-awareness than her predecessors among Williams's 'saints'. . . . But Sybil has no social role to play: she is a leisured lady, though one 'adult in love'. Williams portrays her interior life with a sure hand. . . . Sybil lives in accordance with a mystical quietism familiarised as the practice of the presence of God; but the obfuscating effect of conventional terms no longer comes between us and the experience described. (pp. 162-63)

All of which is to say that Williams was not an instinctive novelist, in the generally accepted sense of that term. His two final novels succeed because in them he ceased trying to be one. For what is most memorable in all of them is the sense of the transcendent as it shines through the world of space and time. In this respect the books are genuinely original and impressive. Especially striking is the way in which the supernatural manifestations are seen as being precisely that—supernatural. They do not engage with the world of appearances, they take it over. . . . And through his narrative technique Williams, not himself a mystic, is able to present dramatically the conclusion of all visionary experience that spiritual reality co-inheres in material reality. So too he is able to coin, in terms of his various myths, memorable epigrams of redemption. . . . A language for religious experience is being evolved that is specifically symbolic and allusive: no confusion between appearance and reality being raised about or by it, the balance between belief and scepticism can be verbally contained.

The logical outcome of this process is found in *Descent into Hell.* Williams's treatment of occult themes had been moving towards an all-inclusive vision that may be termed multispatial. (p. 164)

Only when read in the context of his total output [do his novels'] significance become apparent.

The first six reveal an evolving awareness of human power-drives as they are confronted with the inevitable constrictions of human existence. . . . He did not embrace religious belief because it consoled or even inspired him: rather, he saw it as the necessary accommodation of the self to fact. In his criticism, biographies and plays he concentrates on personal experience; but in the novels the individual dramas are given a wider setting. The metaphysical imagery provides an impersonal set of counters with which to set out the rules of the game.

For a game, in one sense, is what Williams saw life as being—a game for the individual, a dance in reality. The apparent frivolity of the image should not lead one to underrate it: rather it arises from one of Williams's principal beliefs, that the entire creation is necessarily superfluous to God. . . . He substitutes for the interplay of psychological characteristics found in the mainstream of English fiction, the interplay of spiritual currents and religious understanding; and is thus able to write religious novels that are neither merely tracts nor sociological studies of belief. (p. 165)

Williams uses the occult novel in terms of its own premises, not simply to entertain, but to reveal what lies hidden under the cloak of a logical impossibility. . . .

In their evolution, therefore, the novels work out the perspective from which the theological books and Arthurian poems were written. Less personal in concern and presentation than the plays, they provided imaginative testing grounds for Williams's beliefs about the relation of the individual to the community, of the power-drive to human limitation, and at a deeper level of God's justice to his love. . . .

These beliefs, however, are most subtly presented in Williams's treatment of the Arthuriad. Here the close interconnections, the pursuit of a kind of twentieth-century version of medieval analogies, result in a more wide-ranging, complex and intellectually satisfying model of reality than is to be found in the self-appointed limitations of the novels. (p. 166)

Williams . . . avoids a specifically humanistic treatment. His world is an abstract world made tangible by a subtle and effective deployment of physical details. Colourful and sensuous passages are interwoven with the narrative and dogmatic elements—often a telling adjective or phrase does the work of whole lines of more formal description. These sudden intensities, flickering amid the hard substance of the poetry like sparkles of quartzite, are furthered by the employment of internal rhyming and the use of the Homeric adjective—'sea-weighed', 'green-pennon-skirted', 'rain-dark'—with an accompanying compression of phrase that can fuse metaphor and simile with piercing effect. . . . (p. 167)

The use of imagery is similarly effective at the intellectual level. Williams uses an associative method of notation, which resembles that of Eliot and Ezra Pound. But, instead of referring to an ongoing historical process, he builds up a metaphysical world, a pattern or diagram that both reflects and interprets the physical dimension. (p. 168)

Taliessin through Logres does indeed remain alien to the twentieth-century point of view. . . . Williams makes few concessions to the normal romantic temper. The gorgeousness of imagery is treated with a fine austerity, the story is uncoloured by personal emotion. The poems' style, being at once declamatory and compact, is in marked contrast to most other poetry written at the time or since. Williams's vision is iconographical, static; he seems to be unaware of process. Relativity in time eludes him—hence for many people the curiously unreal nature of his imaginative world. (pp. 168-69)

The best indication of Williams's purpose is the use of Byzantium as a focal symbol. . . . Formalised, disciplined by its mythological imagery, and resplendent with colour, [Williams's poetry] is ideally suited to convey the ordered world of heavenly perfection which Byzantine art proclaims. . . . It is Williams's achievement to have written a poetry of transcendence which makes transcendence known through the very formalised, materialistic nature of its imagery. . . . (p. 169)

The same principle holds good for Williams's treatment of the theme of Britain. His Logres, while embodying the traditional notion of an ideal Britain (ideal through function rather than through attributes) goes far beyond contemporary developments of the theme. (pp. 169-70)

Charles Williams replaces nostalgia with belief: his Arthuriad derives from and is shaped by Christian doctrine. In this he differs from those of his contemporaries who make use of mythological material. (p. 170)

[Williams's Logres] is intended to be a diagram of what truly is, rather than a refuge from what is not. Williams makes no attempt at collocating or conjoining the natural and the supernatural. His world is a deliberate abstraction, a working model of reality, whose laws are intellectually apprehended. Indeed, it is in Williams's studies in history rather than in his poetry that we find him depicting the supernatural in relation to the natural: and the progress of his entire work is towards a fusion of the two. The difference between them is a matter not of kind but of dimension. (pp. 170-71)

For the Arthurian poems are not ideograms or versified theological treatises. They call for an intuitive reading, not mere passive receptivity. They also demand a response in keeping with their premises, a blend of perceptive wit and imaginative reason. . . . For Williams's technique of interlinked associative symbolism calls not only for an imaginative use of intelligence (common enough in contemporary practice) but also for an intelligent reliance on imagination. If his poems are anachronistic it is because they are ahead of, rather than behind, their time. (p. 172)

He saw in literature, theology and history symbols of an existence to which romantic experience points, and it is his linking of that experience to the formulations of Christian theology which is his distinctive achievement as an apologist. . . .

It is . . . appropriate . . . to compare his work with that of C. S. Lewis and J.R.R. Tolkien. However, his approach to myth is essentially different from theirs. Whereas Lewis was primarily a teacher and Tolkien a storyteller, Williams was a poet. . . . In Williams's work, . . . the Christian myth is undisguisedly the theme: all his writing springs from his assent to it. (p. 173)

His sense of the total mutual dependence of every aspect of reality makes it possible for him to recognise both the validity of scientific method (he is notably sympathetic to Bacon's aims) and to the findings of poetic intuition: he will have no schism between the two, for both are methods of discriminating among connections which make reasoning life possible. . . .

Williams's sense of coinherence makes for comprehensiveness and catholicity: it also permits, not to say insists on, the knowledge that nothing that is affirmed can escape the possibility that it may for truth's sake have to be denied. . . .

It is this particular poise which is the distinguishing mark of Williams's mature work, and which makes it so rewarding. (p. 174)

The theological vision which underlies and unifies Williams's work is expressed with a subtlety and intentness which make that work more satisfactory as a whole than in its parts. In this respect his total output can best be regarded as itself an image, a vision of the incommunicable in terms of a creative meditation on formulae which are, at the most, algebraic symbols for reality. What is impressive about his vision is its consistency and comprehensiveness; it is a total view of life emerging from a variety of occasional writings, and it rings true not so much from intellectual plausibility as from emotional conviction. His religious writing is persuasive because its source is identical with the source of his secular concerns. It has the authenticity of art.

The development of Williams's powers as an artist parallels and indeed mediates his ability as a theologian. This can be seen most clearly in his treatment of the crisis of contradictory knowledge. . . . In the biographies the crisis is examined through actual historical figures; and as a result Williams develops a sense of history as myth which allows for his vision of interpenetrating worlds both in his later novels and verse, and in his theology.

The plays objectify the crisis through personifications, *Thomas Cranmer* bridging the gap between myth and history in its domination by the figure of the Skeleton. This particular dramatised embodiment enables Williams to portray the crisis as itself the manifestation of God's redemptive purpose. Successive figures—the Third King, the Accuser, the Flame—take the concept further, into the realisation that all luck is good and the Kingdom here and now. (pp. 174-75)

Logres both is and is not; alike in the Arthurian kingdom of Williams's imagining and in the Christian Church of his experience and researches, that truth holds good. From its vantage point the poise of his last books was achieved. . . . The final creative period is thus one of ease and lucidity—lucidity, not simplicity: and the theology and the poetry illuminate each other.

The unique interest, then, of Williams's thought over all this field of speculation and deduction lies in its formation and nourishing through his parallel enquiries into the springs of poetry and human action. (p. 176)

The values which he puts forward, values native to the artist, of all-inclusiveness (suggested by the term 'coinherence') and humility before the created order (suggested by 'absolute relativity') issue in theological terms as a sense of interrelatedness and tolerance. It is this roundedness and balance which makes his theology so satisfying. (pp. 176-77)

His assumption that theological statements and symbols are intellectual clothing for, and safeguards of, the deeper poetic truths of myth, gives his writings an honesty and self-vindicating fervour which makes them accessible to those who, while responsive to his imagination, do not subscribe to his beliefs. If nature and grace are categories of one identity then the experience of their fusion in Williams's work is the measure of his achievement both as apologist and poet. (p. 177)

> *Glen Cavaliero, in his* Charles Williams: Poet of Theology *(copyright © 1982 by Glen Cavaliero; used by permisson),* William B. Eerdmans Publishing Company, 1983, 199 p.

D.J.R. BRUCKNER (essay date 1983)

[*Bruckner, reviewing Cavaliero's book (see excerpt above), provides a general and helpful appraisal of Williams's achievement.*]

[Williams] wrote many volumes of poetry, criticism, biography, theology and plays that influenced some important writers, among them T. S. Eliot, W. H. Auden, C. S. Lewis and J.R.R. Tolkien.

His novels are the easiest of his books to read, but even in them there are traps for the unwary. I am partial to **"The Place of the Lion,"** in which Platonic ideas keep bursting through the illusion of reality, and one finds the Lion of Strength and the Eagle of Wisdom and many such characters erupting into suburban London; and to **"All Hallow's Eve,"** in which two women killed in a bombing raid find themselves in a London of the dead that coexists with the London of the living, both within an eternal London. And **"Descent into Hell,"** which Eliot published for Williams in 1937, may be the most perfect spiritual thriller in English. The plot is about people performing a play but also about heaven and hell, and the characters in the novel pass in and out of history, eternity and different planes of existence without much warning to the reader, since the different planes exist simultaneously on the London hill where the action occurs. An inattentive reader can get lost quickly.

Eliot thought that much of Williams's vision of the world was simply beyond language. But his language embodied it perfectly in one play, **"Thomas Cranmer of Canterbury,"** written for the Canterbury Festival of 1936 (Eliot's "Murder in the Cathedral" was the 1935 festival play). It is a morality play, but Williams gave it great dramatic force by compressing his hero's lifetime search for salvation into rapid episodes, some of only a few lines. Its final dialogue, between Cranmer, the 16th century archbishop who is about to be executed, and a skeleton that undergoes many transformations, strips away time and reveals Cranmer searching in eternity for God, Who is just on the other side of the skeleton. . . .

Williams's reverence for poetry was sometimes ridiculous, as when he argued that great poets and saints knew the truth about everything. But two of his books, **"The English Poetic Mind"** and **"Reason and Beauty in the Poetic Mind,"** send one back to familiar poets in a new frame of mind, again and again; and his **"Figure of Beatrice"** is a book that simply enchants one into understanding Dante. His use of poetic imagery in critical writing and of metaphor as a vehicle of critical thought give his writing about poets a resonance that is rare in criticism.

Possibly his excessive reverence for poets is related to the fact that much of his own poetry is not very good. Certainly his minor poems, which lapsed into oblivion in his own lifetime, were not. And, from my youth I recall two large volumes of Arthurian verse legends as too complicated and clogged. Now, however, in an urbane, witty, learned and sympathetic book, "Charles Williams: Poet of Theology," Glen Cavaliero, a poet who teaches at Cambridge University, cites passages from Williams's Arthurian poems that convince me I was wrong. . . .

To understand fully what Williams is saying in all his other work, one has to look at his three books of theology. **"The Descent of the Dove"** (Auden re-read it every year) is a visionary account of history as an operation of divine salvation. **"Witchcraft"** is an examination of the underside of that same vision which ranks with some of the most haunting writings of the ancient fathers of the church. And in **"He Came Down From Heaven"** all history spreads out in both directions from the crucifixion of Jesus as a single divine act. . . .

The odd world he created in his books may be a bit tough to get into, but the effort is worthwhile. His world turns out to be our own familiar one transformed into a place of trial and of stern enchantment; it is also a good deal of fun. For all his seriousness, he was a poet who approached his own vision with amused irony. If he were around now and noticed that he was being neglected, he would probably write a book about that, in which neglect would become an eternal prototype or idea whose wicked laughter would be heard only by simple and saved souls.

> *D.J.R. Bruckner, "The Poet of Theology," in* The New York Times Book Review *(© 1983 by The New York Times Company; reprinted by permission), April 3, 1983, p. 27.*

ADDITIONAL BIBLIOGRAPHY

Barclay, Glen St. John. "Orthodox Horrors: Charles Williams and William P. Blatty." In his *Anatomy of Horror: The Masters of Occult Fiction,* pp. 97-110. New York: St. Martin's Press, 1978.*
> Discusses the reasons for the failure of Williams's fiction, citing his major problems with dialogue and with characterization.

Eliot, T. S. "The Significance of Charles Williams." *The Listener* XXXVI, No. 936 (19 December 1946): 894-95.
> Claims that Charles Williams is an "unusual genius" who experiences and writes about the activities of the supernatural within reality.

Eliot, T. S. Introduction to *All Hallows' Eve,* pp. ix-xviii. New York: Pellegrini & Cudahy, 1948.
> A valuable biocritical introduction to Williams and his work.

Hartley, L. P. "The Novels of Charles Williams." *Time & Tide* 28, No. 22 (14 June 1947): 628, 630.
> Considers *The Place of the Lion, War in Heaven,* and *All Hallows' Eve* to be examples of both Williams's excellence and his gradual loss of novelistic skill.

Howard, Thomas T. *The Novels of Charles Williams.* New York and Oxford: Oxford University Press, 1983, 220 p.
> An excellent critical reading of Williams's seven novels, by the author of the highly acclaimed *The Achievement of C. S. Lewis* and *Christ the Tiger.*

Lewis, C. S. Preface to *Essays Presented to Charles Williams,* edited by C. S. Lewis, pp. v-xiv. London and New York: Oxford University Press, 1947.
> Eulogistic essay by a close friend and fellow member of Williams's Oxford literary circle.

Manlove, C. N. "The Liturgical Novels of Charles Williams." *Mosaic* XII, No. 2 (Winter 1979): 161-81.
> Studies Williams as a liturgical writer who champions the idea of the coinherence, presents the supernatural within the natural, and portrays Christian formalism in his literature.

Maynard, Theodore. "The Poetry of Charles Williams." *The North American Review* CCX, No. 766 (September 1919): 401-11.

Praises the early poems and briefly discusses Williams's belief that human love is one of many roads to faith.

Moorman, Charles. "Sacramentalism in Charles Williams." *The Chesterton Review* VIII, No. 1 (February 1982): 35-50.
    States that Williams was inspired by imaginative visions rather than ideas. Coinherence and exchange become "sacramental expressions" of a totally interdependent universe.

Sayers, Dorothy L. "Charles Williams." *Time and Tide* 31, No. 48 (2 December 1950): 1220.
    Reviews the 1950 reprint of *He Came Down from Heaven* (bound with his *The Forgiveness of Sins*) and a new edition of *The Region of the Summer Stars*. Sayers was a close friend and devotee of Williams.

Sayers, Dorothy L. "The Poetry of the Image in Dante and Charles Williams." In her *Further Papers on Dante*, pp. 183-204. New York: Harper & Brothers, 1957.
    Compares the works of Williams and Dante. A concluding contrast is Dante's interest in "common human sin" and Williams's in "trespass upon the borders of two worlds"—that of spirit and that of time and space.

Shideler, Mary McDermott. *The Theology of Romantic Love: A Study in the Writings of Charles Williams*. New York: Harper & Row, 1962, 243 p.
    In-depth analysis of Williams's poetic theology.

William Butler Yeats

1865-1939

Irish poet, dramatist, essayist, critic, short story writer, and autobiographer.

Yeats is considered one of the greatest poets in the English language. Although his interest in Irish politics and his visionary approach to poetry often confounded his contemporaries and set him at odds with the intellectual trends of his time, Yeats's poetic achievement stands at the center of modern literature. Yeats's poetry evolved over five decades from the vague imagery and uncertain rhythms of *The Wanderings of Oisin, and Other Poems,* his first important work, to the forceful, incantatory verse of the *Last Poems.* His remarkable creative development in his final years, at an age when most poets are content to reiterate old themes, illustrates a lifelong determination to remake himself into his ideal image of the poet: a sacerdotal figure who assumes the role of mediator between the conflicting forces of the objective and the subjective worlds. Though he was never drawn to extremist political views, Yeats was devoted to the cause of Irish nationalism. He played an important part in the Celtic Revival Movement, founding an Irish literary theater, the Abbey, with the help of Lady Augusta Gregory and J. M. Synge. Yeats also promoted the Irish literary heritage through his use of material from ancient Irish sagas in his poems and dramas. He desired to invoke the hidden Ireland of heroic times, believing that only by "expressing primary truths in ways appropriate to this country" could artists hope to restore to modern Ireland the "unity of culture" that he felt was needed to bring an end to his country's internal division and suffering. In addition to the myths and history of Ireland, magic and occult theory were also important elements in Yeats's work. Related to his belief in the power of the imagination and his view of the poet as kindred to the magician and the alchemist, was his interest in spiritualism, theosophy, and occult systems. Many of the images found in his poetry are derived from Rosicrucianism and his own occult researches as described in the prose work *A Vision.*

Yeats was born in Dublin. His father, Jack Yeats, was the son of a once affluent family whom Oscar Wilde's father, Sir William Wilde, described as "the cleverest, most spirited people I ever met." For as long as he lived, Jack Yeats, himself an artist, exercised an important influence over his son's thoughts about art. Yeats's mother, Susan Pollexfen, was the daughter of a successful merchant from Sligo in the west of Ireland. Many of the Pollexfens were intense, eccentric people interested in faeries and astrology. From his mother, Yeats inherited a love of Ireland, particularly the west of Ireland near Sligo and Rosses Point, and an interest in folklore.

Yeats received no formal education until he was eleven years old, when he began attending the Godolphin Grammar School in Hammersmith, England. He continued his education in Ireland at the Erasmus Smith High School in Dublin. Generally, he was a disappointing student—erratic in his studies, prone to much daydreaming, shy, and poor at sports. In 1884, Yeats enrolled in the Metropolitan School of Art in Dublin, where he met the poet George Russell (A.E.). Russell shared Yeats's enthusiasm for dreams and visions; together they founded the

Dublin Hermetic Society for the purposes of conducting magical experiments, and promoting their belief that "whatever the great poets had affirmed in their finest moments was the nearest we could come to an authoritative religion and that their mythology and their spirits of water and wind were but literal truth." This event marked the beginning for Yeats of a life-long interest in occult studies, the extent of which was only revealed by the examination of his unpublished notebooks after his death. Following his experience with the hermetic society, Yeats joined the Rosicrucians, Madam H. P. Blavatsky's Theosophical Society, and MacGregor Mathers's Order of the Golden Dawn. He frequently consulted spiritualists, and engaged in the ritual conjuring of Irish gods. Yeats found occult research a rich source of images for his poetry, and traces of his esoteric interests appear everywhere in his poems. "The Rose upon the Rood of Time," for example, takes its central symbol from Rosicrucianism, and "All Soul's Night" describes a scrying ceremony.

In 1885, Yeats met the Irish nationalist and Fenian leader John O'Leary, who was instrumental in getting Yeats's first verses published in *The Dublin University Review* and in directing Yeats's attention to native Irish sources for subject matter. Under the influence of O'Leary, Yeats took up the cause of Gaelic writers at a time when much native Irish literature was in danger of being lost due to England's attempts to anglicize Ireland through a ban on the Gaelic language. O'Leary's ardent nationalism and resolute opposition to violence also impressed Yeats and were instrumental in shaping political views that he held for the rest of his life. Perhaps the most fateful day in Yeats's life was January 30th, 1889, when he met Maud Gonne, an agitator for the Nationalist cause whose great beauty and reckless destructiveness in pursuit of her political goals both intrigued and dismayed him. He immediately fell in love with her. He began accompanying her to political rallies, and though he often disagreed with her extremist tactics, he shared her desire to see Ireland freed from English domination. During this period he wrote the drama *Cathleen ni Houlihan* for Gonne, and she was featured in the title role in its initial production. Yeats considered the play, which is about a noblewoman who sells her soul to the devil in order to save starving peasants, as appropriately symbolic of the activities to which Gonne had dedicated her life. Although Gonne's repeated refusals to marry Yeats brought him great personal unhappiness, their relationship endured through many estrangements, including her brief marriage to Major John MacBride. Nearly all of the love poetry that Yeats wrote during his career is addressed to her. In his verses she is associated with Helen of Troy, whose capriciousness led to the destruction of a civilization. To Yeats she represented an ideal, and throughout his life he found the friction between them, as well as their friendship, a source of poetic inspiration.

It was not until 1917 when he was fifty-two years old that Yeats finally married. On their honeymoon his young wife, Georgie Hyde-Lees, discovered that she had mediumistic abilities and through the technique of automatic writing could receive communication from a visionary realm. Her efforts over many months produced the notes and materials on which Yeats based the text of *A Vision*—his explanation of historical cycles and a theory of human personality based on the phases of the moon. Late in his life, when decades of struggle by the Irish nationalists had finally culminated in the passage of the Home Rule Bill, Yeats became a senator for the Irish Free State. He left the senate in 1928, due to failing health, in order to devote his remaining years to poetry. He died in 1939.

In his earliest poetic works, such as *Mosada*, Yeats took his symbols from Greek mythology. After meeting John O'Leary, he turned instead to Irish mythology as a source for his images. The long narrative poem, "The Wanderings of Oisin" was the first he based on the legend of an Irish hero. In spite of its self-consciously poetic language and typically pre-Raphaelite rhythms, the poem's theme—the disagreement between Oisin and St. Patrick—makes it important to an understanding of the later Yeats. The sense of conflict between vision and corporeal realities, as symbolized by the saint and the hero, is the most essential dichotomy in Yeats's poetry. Throughout his poetic career Yeats's chief concern was the disparity between the imaginative individual's need to seek immortality through renunciation of the world of "mire and blood," and the instinctive human love of what perishes. In his poems he sought to resolve this disparity. He believed such a resolution was necessary because he felt the world of pure forms was impotent without its connection to life, but he also recognized that only through imagination could the raw materials of life be transformed into something enduring. For Yeats, the role of the artist was the same as that of the alchemist: he must effect a transformation that obscures the distinction between form and content, between "the dancer and the dance." This theme is most effectively expressed in the late poems "Sailing to Byzantium" and "Byzantium." As Yeats grew older and

more sure of his themes, his approach to the techniques of poetry changed. Recognizing that faery songs were less suited to the tragic themes that preoccupied him than were more realistic narratives, he began, with the poems of *In the Seven Woods*, to write verses describing actual events in his personal life or in the history of Ireland. One of his most famous lyrics, "Easter 1916," about a rebel uprising that resulted in the martyrdom of all who participated, belongs to this latter group. In his maturity, Yeats wrote little narrative poetry. Instead he adopted the dramatic lyric as his most characteristic form of expression. Under the influence of Ezra Pound, he simplified his diction and modified his syntax to more closely reflect the constructions of common speech. In works such as *Responsibilities, and Other Poems; The Wild Swans at Coole;* and *Michael Robartes and the Dancer,* his verses began to take on the rhetorical, occasionally haughty tone that readers today identify as characteristically Yeatsian. Critics agree that Yeats's poetic technique was impeccable. It was this mastery of technique that enabled him to perfect the subtle, forceful, and highly unusual poetic meter that he used to create the effect of a chant or an incantation in such poems as "The Tower."

Yeats considered his dramas an aspect of his plan to revitalize Irish culture. He wanted to create dramas that were symbolic and austere—a reflection not of life, but of "the deeps of the mind." The form that such dramas should take and the manner in which they should be staged eluded him for many years. In his early works, such as *The Shadowy Waters* and *The Land of Heart's Desire,* he found that conventional stage techniques and realistic characters were not suited to the poetic portrayal of spiritual truths and psychological realities. It was not until Ezra Pound introduced him to the ancient Nō plays of Japan that he found a form he felt was suited to the heroic and tragic subjects that he wished to depict. In *Four Plays for Dancers,* as well as in subsequent works such as *Purgatory,* Yeats experimented with techniques borrowed from the Nō, such as ritualized, symbolic action and the use of masks. These plays contain some of his finest verse, and critics now believe that Yeats's approach to drama anticipated in many ways the abstract movements of modern theater.

Yeats's prose style in his essays and *Autobiographies* was influenced by his early admiration of Walter Pater. The detached and elegant *Autobiographies* have long been a source of controversy among critics. In the *Autobiographies* Yeats provides a sensitive, if sometimes ironic, view of his age, but reveals little about his own life and thoughts. Even his close friend, George Russell, in reviewing the *Autobiographies,* criticized Yeats for these omissions. Nonetheless, the *Autobiographies* are a valuable source of information about Yeats's views on art and his theories of personality. In *The Celtic Twilight,* his collection of folktales from the west of Ireland, Yeats endeavored to record the folk legends of Irish peasants in a simple and dignified manner, rather than in the patronizing and comic way such materials were often treated by English writers. Yeats not only wished to preserve these legends, he also wanted to make them more widely available to the Irish people, who had lost touch with ancient Irish traditions. He sought in this way to promote the "unity of culture" that he believed could only be achieved in modern Ireland through an increased awareness of Ireland's heroic past.

Yeats was awarded the Nobel Prize in literature in 1923. However, for many years his intent interest in subjects that others labelled "archaic" and perceived as an affront to their modernity, delayed his recognition among his peers. At the time of his death in 1939, Yeats's views on poetry were overlooked as eccentric by students and critics alike. This attitude held sway in spite of critical awareness of the beauty and technical proficiency of his verse. Yeats had long stood opposed to the notion that literature should serve society. As a youthful critic he had refused to praise the poor lyrics of the "Young Ireland" poets merely because they were effective as nationalist propaganda. Now, in maturity, he found that despite his success, his continuing conviction that poetry should express the spiritual life of the individual alienated him from those who believed that a "modern" poet must take as his themes social alienation and the barreness of materialist culture. As Kathleen Raine wrote of him: "against a rising tide of realism, political verse and University wit, Yeats upheld the innocent and the beautiful, the traditional and the noble," and in consequence of his disregard for the concerns of the modern world, was often misunderstood. As critics became disenchanted with the modern movement, Yeats's Romantic dedication to the laws of the imagination and art for art's sake became more acceptable. Critics today are less concerned with the validity of his occult and visionary theories than with their symbolic value as expressions of timeless ideals and a need for order. Yeats's interest in arcana is considered a manifestation of the truth of Wallace Stevens's statement that "poets are never of the world in which they live."

(See also *TCLC*, Vol. 1; *Contemporary Authors*, Vol. 104; *Dictionary of Literary Biography*, Vol. 10: *Modern British Dramatists, 1900-1945*; and Vol. 19 *British Poets, 1880-1914*.)

PRINCIPAL WORKS

Mosada (poetry) 1886
The Wanderings of Oisin, and Other Poems (poetry) 1889
The Countess Cathleen and Various Legends and Lyrics (poetry) 1892
The Celtic Twilight (folklore) 1893
The Land of Heart's Desire (drama) 1894
Collected Poems (poetry) 1895
The Wind among the Reeds (poetry) 1899
The Shadowy Waters (drama) 1900
Cathleen ni Houlihan (drama) 1902
Ideas of Good and Evil (essays) 1903
In the Seven Woods (poetry) 1903
Plays for an Irish Theatre. 5 Vols. [first publication] (dramas) 1903-05
Stories of Red Hanrahan (short stories) 1904
Discoveries (essays) 1907
The Unicorn from the Stars [with Lady Isabella Augusta Gregory] (drama) 1907
Poetry and Ireland [with Lionel Johnson] (essays) 1908
The Green Helmet, and Other Poems (poetry) 1910
**Plays for an Irish Theatre* [first publication] (dramas) 1913
Responsibilities, and Other Poems (poetry) 1914
At the Hawk's Well (drama) 1916
On Baile's Strand (drama) 1916
The Wild Swans at Coole (poetry) 1917
Per Amica Silentia Lunae (essay) 1918
The Player Queen (drama) 1919
Michael Robartes and the Dancer (poetry) 1920
Four Plays for Dancers [first publication] (dramas) 1921
Four Years: 1887-91 (memoir) 1921
Later Poems (poetry) 1922

The Cat and the Moon and Certain Poems (poetry) 1924
A Vision (essay) 1925; also published as *A Vision* [*enlarged edition*], *1937*
***Autobiographies* (memoir) 1926; also published as *Autobiographies* [enlarged edition], 1938
The Tower (poetry) 1928
The Winding Stair (poetry) 1929
The Dreaming of the Bones (drama) 1931
Words for Music Perhaps, and Other Poems (poetry) 1932
The Collected Poems of W. B. Yeats (poetry) 1933
The Collected Plays of W. B. Yeats (dramas) 1934; also published as *The Collected Plays of W. B. Yeats* [enlarged edition], 1952
The King of the Great Clock Tower (poetry) 1934
Wheels and Butterflies (drama) 1934
A Full Moon in March (poetry and dramas) 1935
The Herne's Egg (drama) 1938
New Poems (poetry) 1938
Purgatory (drama) 1938
Last Poems and Two Plays (poetry and dramas) 1939
On the Boiler (essays and poems) 1939
The Death of Cuchulain (drama) 1949
The Letters of W. B. Yeats (letters) 1954
The Complete Poems (poetry) 1957
W. B. Yeats: Essays and Introductions (essays) 1961

*This work also includes the drama *At the Well of the Saints* by J. M. Synge.

**This work is a revision of the earlier *Plays for an Irish Theatre*.

***This work includes the memoirs *Reveries over Childhood and Youth* and *The Trembling of the Veil*. The enlarged edition of 1938 also includes the memoirs *Dramatis Personae, Estrangement, The Death of Synge,* and *The Bounty of Sweden*.

KATHARINE TYNAN (essay date 1887)

[*Tynan, an Irish poet and novelist, was an early member of the Celtic Revival and a friend of Yeats.*]

The voice in ["**Mosada**"] seems to us a new voice, wonderfully clear, rich, and soft in its minor tones, for it has this one point of agreement with modern music that it is pitched in a minor key. We are glad to welcome a new singer in Erin, one who will take high place among the world's future singers if the promise of this early work be fulfilled, or if, indeed, the performance of the future be equal to that of to-day. The young poet follows no master, and reminds us of no elder poet. This poem is rich with colour, alive with dramatic feeling, and the stately measure of the blank verse never halts or is disconcerted. (p. 166)

It is full of such beauty . . . —beauty rapt and exalted, the very spirit of poetry; it is strong and joyful with the consciousness of power. If it were the work of an old poet, it would be beautiful work; being the work of a very young one, it has far greater value. Of Mr. Yeats' future position as a poet, great things may be prophesied. . . . (p. 167)

Katharine Tynan, "Three Young Poets," in The Irish Monthly, *Vol. 15, March, 1887, pp. 166-68.*

[OSCAR WILDE]   (essay date 1889)

[*Wilde was one of the most prominent Irish literary figures of the late nineteenth century. Perhaps more than any other author of his time, he is identified with the nineteenth-century "art for art's sake" movement, which defied the contemporary trend that subordinated art to ethical instruction. For Wilde, originality of form was the only enduring quality in a work of art.*]

Books of poetry by young writers are usually promissory notes that are never met. Now and then, however, one comes across a volume that is so far above the average that one can hardly resist the fascinating temptation of recklessly prophesying a fine future for its author. Such a volume Mr. Yeats's **"Wanderings of Oisin"** certainly is. Here we find nobility of treatment and nobility of subject matter, delicacy of poetic instinct, and richness of imaginative resource. Unequal and uneven much of the work must be admitted to be. Mr. Yeats does not try to "out-baby" Wordsworth, we are glad to say, but he occasionally succeeds in "out-glittering" Keats, and here and there in his book we come across strange crudities and irritating conceits. But when he is at his best he is very good. If he has not the grand simplicity of epic treatment, he has at least something of that largeness of vision that belongs to the epical temper. He does not rob of their stature the great heroes of Celtic mythology. He is very naïve, and very primitive, and speaks of his giants with the awe of a child. . . . (p. 73)

> [*Oscar Wilde*], *in an extract from his review of "Three New Poets: Yeats, Fitzgerald, LeGallienne," in* Pall Mall Gazette, *July 12, 1889 (and reprinted in* W. B. Yeats: The Critical Heritage, *edited by A. Norman Jeffares, Routledge & Kegan Paul, 1977, pp. 72-3).*

WILLIAM WATSON   (essay date 1892)

[*Watson, an English poet, believed that a writer should be an integral part of the social and intellectual life of an era and contribute to decisions of public policy. One of his primary aims as a poet was to elucidate current affairs; for that reason, he wrote much occasional poetry. He was alien to the aesthetic temper of the 1890's and, in fact, held more imaginative realms of poetry to be the province of the second-rate.*]

It may be laid down as an art-maxim of general application that to fail in the attainment of any given end is disastrous in direct proportion to the ambitiousness of the means employed. [In *The Countess Kathleen and Various Legends and Lyrics*] Mr. Yeats's artistic means are ambitious; he fails to produce any kind of effect, and the disaster is accordingly considerable. To supplement his human puppets—we cannot say his human beings, for being they have none, in the sense of life or life-likeness—he invokes the aid of all manner of supernatural and elemental agencies, spirits and fairies, and what not, together with *sowlths* and *tevishes*, whatever they may be, for we unblushingly confess our ignorance of their nature or attributes. There are also a great many *sheogues*, and we do not feel in the least called upon to know what a *sheogue* is like—in fact, we would much rather not be told. How many legs has it? There is also a peasant who nods by the fire 'telling old shannachus.' Now, we should really like to have heard a shannachu. Why didn't Mr. Yeats let us have one? It would have been worth a world of sheogues. The fact is—to drop into seriousness for a moment, with many apologies—the supernatural in poetry has no excuse for itself except where, as in "The Ancient Mariner," for instance, it bites its way into the reader's consciousness and compels imaginative belief by the sheer despotism of imperious genius. All Mr. Yeats's grotesque ma-

chinery of sowlths and tevishes and sheogues leaves us without a shudder; his fantasies are stage-properties of the most unillusive kind. . . . Mr. Yeats seems to be under the delusion that imaginative belief can be compelled by the employment of baldly material detail, as when he talks of "Michael looking down from Heaven's door-post." Sometimes he certainly has a kind of extravagant picturesqueness, as when he makes the waves of the sea clash like cymbals, but what does "the long-hoarding surges" mean? And he has literally no idea of versification: witness his excruciating trick—a favourite one with him—of making the second foot of a blank verse line trochaic. A man who can do this could commit—but one must not be libellous in so respectable a journal.

> *William Watson, in his review of "The Countess Kathleen and Various Legends and Lyrics," in* The Illustrated London News *(© 1892 The Illustrated London News & Sketch Ltd.; reprinted by permission of Illustrated London News & Sketch Ltd.), Vol. CI, No. 2787, September 10, 1892, p. 334.*

LIONEL JOHNSON   (essay date 1892)

[*Johnson, an English poet of Irish descent, was a friend of Yeats. Johnson's poetry reflects a deep interest in medieval literature and thought and demonstrates two major influences: Walter Pater's aestheticism and the poetry of the Celtic Revival.*]

Mr. Yeats has published two volumes of verse: *The Wanderings of Oisin* and *The Countess Kathleen*. Doubtless it is difficult to speak with perfect security about the first books of a living writer; but I feel little diffidence in speaking of these two volumes. In the last two or three years much charming verse has been published by many writers who may make themselves distinguished names; but nothing which seems to me, in the most critical and dispassionate state of mind, equal in value to the poems of Mr. Yeats. Irish of the Irish, in the themes and sentiments of his verse, he has also no lack of that wider sympathy with the world, without which the finest national verse must remain provincial. Yet, for all his interests of a general sort, his poetry has not lost one Irish grace, one Celtic delicacy, one native charm. . . .

The distinction of Mr. Yeats, as an Irish poet, is his ability to write Celtic poetry, with all the Celtic notes of style and imagination, in a classical manner. Like all men of the true poetical spirit, he is not overcome by the apparent antagonism of the classical and the romantic in art. Like the fine Greeks or Romans, he treats his subject according to its nature. Simple as that sounds, it is a praise not often to be bestowed. Consider the "Attis" of Catullus: how the monstrous, barbaric frenzy of the theme is realised in verse of the strictest beauty. It is not a Latin theme, congenial to a Latin nature: it is Asiatic, insane, grotesque; its passion is abnormal and harsh. Yet the poem, while terrible in its intensity of life, is a masterpiece of severe art. It is in this spirit, if I may dare so great a comparision, that Mr. Yeats has written: his poetry has plenty of imperfections, but it is not based upon a fundamental mistake; he sees very clearly where success may be found. When he takes a Celtic theme, some vast and epic legend, or some sad and lyrical fancy, he does not reflect the mere confused vastness of the one, the mere flying vagueness of the other: his art is full of reason. So he produces poems, rational and thoughtful, yet beautiful with the beauty that comes of thought about imagination. It is not the subjects alone, nor the musical skill alone, nor the dominant mood alone, but all these together that make these poems so satisfying and so haunting. They have that natural felicity which belongs to beautiful things in nature, but a felicity under the control of art. (p. 278)

In these poems, the immediate charm is their haunting music, which depends not upon any rich wealth of words, but upon a subtle strain of music in their whole quality of thoughts and images, some incommunicable beauty, felt in the simplest words and verses. Collins, Blake, Coleridge, had the secret of such music; Mr. Yeats sings somewhat in their various ways, but with a certain instinct of his own, definitely Irish. The verse is stately and solemn, without any elaboration; the thought falls into a lofty rhythm. Or the verse is wistful and melancholy, an aërial murmur of sad things without any affectation. . . .

In all the poems, even the most mystical in thought, there is a deep tone of sympathy with the world's fortunes, or with the natures of living things: a curiously tender gladness at the thought of it all. . . . His ballads are full of this natural sentiment, shown rather in their simple mention of facts and things, as an old poet might mention them, than in any artificial simplicity. There is humour in this verse: a sense of the human soul in all things, a fearless treatment of facts, a gentleness towards life, because it is all wonderful and nothing is despicable. And through the poems there pierces that spiritual cry, which is too rare and fine to reach ears satisfied with the gross richness of a material Muse. . . . There is much to distress some readers in Mr. Yeats's poems. Cuchullin, to them, is less familiar than King Arthur, and they know nothing about the Irish symbolism of the Rose, and much fearless simplicity seems to them but odd and foolish. All writers of distinction, who have a personal vision of life, and thoughts of their own, and a music of unfamiliar beauty, must lay their account with ridicule or misapprehension. But a very little patience will overcome all difficulties. It is impossible to read these poems without falling under their fascination and taking them home to heart. (p. 279)

> *Lionel Johnson, in his review of ''The Countess Kathleen and Various Legends and Lyrics,'' in* The Academy, *Vol. 42, No. 1065, October 1, 1892, pp. 278-79.*

[FRANCIS THOMPSON] (essay date 1899)

[*Thompson was one of the most important poets of the Catholic Revival in nineteenth-century English literature. Like other writers of the fin de siècle period, his poetry and prose is noted for rich verbal effects and a devotion to the values of aestheticism.*]

Mr. W. B. Yeats is well known as one of the most active and prominent leaders of that movement in present literature which goes by the somewhat high-flown title of the Celtic Renaissance. . . . [It] is a plain fact, dependent on no flourish of trumpets, that at present Ireland has a number of workers who have made their mark in the more refined and fastidious pursuits of literature.

None among them has a more genuine, more distinctive and personal note than Mr. Yeats. His first book, *The Wanderings of Oisin,* some years ago made that evident, and he has not receded from the promise then given. His work has been slender in quantity. Since he collected his previously published verse into one by no means bulky volume of *Poems,* his total product in verse and prose is included in five small books. . . . But it has quality; it is artistic and conscientious. His prose inclines to a poetised style: it is good of its kind, but not eminently good. With all its poetic infusion, it has nothing tawdry. With

all its self-conscious artistry, the note is not forced: its rhythm is a true prose-rhythm, with none of that terrible bastard movement—like blank verse gone very much to the bad—which makes most writing of this sort anathema. . . . Yet it is not sufficient for a reputation.

That reputation must rest on Mr. Yeats's poetry. Here he stands quite alone: a poet he is, and—to our thinking—a poet only. In everything else which he writes he suggests the poet. As poet he suggests nothing outside poetry—the simple essence; not poetic embodiment of this thing or that, but just poetry. In this respect he belongs natively to the same order as Coleridge and Spenser and Shelley. . . . Not that Mr. Yeats is as one of these; not his a large or wide gift. It is, in truth, an exceedingly contracted gift; but a gift it is, authentically his and no man else's. Whether from singular self-judgment or the good-hap of simple sincerity, Mr. Yeats has practically recognised this. He has known that his gift was small, he has known that his gift was narrow; he has known that his gift was *his* gift—or he has acted as if he knew, which comes to the same thing; and he has held to it and within it, unswerving and contented as the blackbird on the bough. . . .

This gift of Mr. Yeats, so one and individual, is easy to feel, not easy to state: it is not the gift of any poet before him. . . . To the peculiar *aura,* the effluence of his poetry, if we were asked to attach the phrase ''Celtic magic'' our conscience would not take alarm. Certainly, if it be not *the* magic—on which let Celts pronounce—it is *a* magic which merits a distinctive phrase.

It is an inhuman beauty, a haunting of something remote, intangible, which the poet himself only feels, but cannot trace to its source. In proportion as he becomes, or tries to be, definite this power passes from him. It is when he is obeying the dictates of an emotion, a sentiment, as insubstantial and uncapturable as a gust of the night, that he achieves this most delicate and evanescent charm. With a true instinct of his own prevailing quality he calls this latest book *The Wind Among the Reeds.* No less frail and mysterious than such a wind is the appeal of Mr. Yeats's best verse. (p. 501)

The very finest examples are contained in his collected *Poems* —namely, **''The Lake Isle of Innisfree''** and **''The Man Who Dreamed of Fairyland''.** The first expresses in most daintily sweet verse the appeal of remembered solitary water and reedy isle to a born dreamer stranded in city streets. The second embodies in finely haunting verse Mr. Yeats's most constant mood—the call upon the visionary's heartstrings of the legendary country, where is ''the light that never was on sea or land''. On the whole, it is Mr. Yeats's best poem. And it should be; for he is himself ''the man that dreamed of fairyland.'' All his poetry is one plaintive cry for a domain set apart from ''life's exceeding injocundity''. We are not pronouncing whether this is a wholesome or desirable frame of mind. Perhaps we have other views. We merely state the case. And since every poet is best when he expresses his dominant love, Mr. Yeats is always at his best when he is dealing with the world of fays or spirits. At such times his lightness of touch is exquisite. It is hard to say where the fascination lies. It is as much in the music as the apparent words—a true test in lyrics of this kind, which are sensitive rather than intellectual. . . . In this sense Mr. Yeats has always been a mystic. He has always ''dreamed of fairyland''. But in this new volume there are signs that he desires to be a mystic in a more recondite sense. The old Irish mythology, which always attracted him, he has taken up the study of in its symbolic meanings, and endeavours to import it into his verse as a vehicle for the expression of modern and personal ideas.

Frankly, we view this development with alarm. It would always be a perilous experiment, because (unlike the language of Greek or Biblical religion) Irish mythology is so unknown to English readers. But Mr. Yeats's treatment of it increases the difficulty. He frequently uses this mythological imagery in a sense of his own, though in his elaborate notes he acknowledges himself doubtful about the correctness of his interpretation—that he is, in fact, guessing at the meanings of the symbols he uses. But how shall the reader follow this arbitrary use of symbolism, or be certain where the poet himself is uncertain? The only road out is the clumsy expedient of explanatory notes. This is not the true use of symbolism, and from a purely poetical standpoint is quite inartistic. It creates wanton difficulty. Mr. Yeats should at any rate be clear to the few who understand the system of mythological imagery. But his arbitrary use of it often leaves even them in the dark. "I use this to signify so and so," is the formula. But he should not "use it to signify" anything. He should use it (if he needs it) for what it does signify; and if he is unsure what it signifies, he should not use it at all. It is wantonness to darken his poetry by employing recondite imagery, which he confesses elaborately he is doubtful about the meaning of. Frankly, there is more ingenuity than insight in much of it.

This we have said with some emphasis, because it is a feature which threatens to mar Mr. Yeats's poetry; and his poetry is too good for us to see it marred with equanimity. But it is the trick of an artist unduly enamoured of a new medium for its own sake, and he will grow out of it. (pp. 501-02)

> [*Francis Thompson*], *"Mr. Yeat's Poems," in* The Academy, *Vol. 56, No. 1409, May 6, 1899, pp. 501-02.*

ARTHUR SYMONS (essay date 1900)

[*While Symons initially gained notoriety as an English decadent of the 1890s, he eventually established himself as one of the most important critics of the modern era. His* The Symbolist Movement in Literature *(1899) provided his English contemporaries with an appropriate vocabulary with which to define their new aesthetic—one that communicated their concern with dreamlike states, imagination, and a reality that exists just beyond the boundaries of the senses. Symons also discerned that the concept of the symbol as a vehicle by which a "hitherto unknown reality was suddenly revealed" could become the basis for the entire modern aesthetic. A proper use of the symbol "would flash upon you the soul of that which can be apprehended only by the soul—the finer sense of things unseen, the deeper meaning of things evident." This anticipated and influenced James Joyce's concept of an artistic "epiphany," T. S. Eliot's "moment in time," and laid the foundation for much of modern poetic theory. In the following excerpt, Symons discusses several characteristics of Yeats's verse, particularly those reflecting the ideals of aestheticism and Symbolism. For a less favorable discussion of Yeats's Symbolism, see the essay by William Archer excerpted below.*]

Mr Yeats is the only one among the younger English poets who has the whole poetical temperament, and nothing but the poetical temperament. He lives on one plane, and you will find in the whole of his work, with its varying degrees of artistic achievement, no unworthy or trivial mood, no occasional concession to the fatigue of high thinking. It is this continuously poetical quality of mind that seems to me to distinguish Mr Yeats from the many men of genius. A man may indeed be a poet because he has written a single perfect lyric. He will not be a poet of high order, he will not be a poet in the full sense, unless his work, however unequal it may be in actual literary skill, presents this undeviating aspect, as of one to whom the act of writing is no more than the occasional flowering of a mood into speech. And that, certainly, is the impression which remains with one after a careful reading of the revised edition of Mr. Yeats' collected poems and of his later volume of lyrics, **"The Wind among the Reeds."** The big book . . . contains work of many kinds; and, among mainly lyrical poems, there are two plays, **"The Countess Cathleen"** and **"The Land of Heart's Desire."** **"The Countess Cathleen"** is certainly the largest and finest piece of work which Mr Yeats has yet done. Its visionary ecstasy is firmly embodied in persons whose action is indeed largely a spiritual action, but action which has the lyrical movement of great drama. Here is poetry which is not only heard, but seen; forming a picture, not less than moving to music. And here it is the poetry which makes the drama, or I might say equally the drama which makes the poetry; for the finest writing is always part of the dramatic action, not a hindrance to it, as it is in almost all the poetical plays of this century. In the long narrative poem contained in the same volume, **"The Wanderings of Oisin,"** an early work, much rewritten, a far less mature skill has squandered lyrical poetry with a romantic prodigality. Among the lyrics in other parts of the book there are a few which Mr Yeats has never excelled in a felicity which seems almost a matter of mere luck; there is not a lyric which has not some personal quality of beauty; but we must turn to the later volume to find the full extent of his capacity as a lyric poet.

In the later volume, **"The Wind among the Reeds,"** in which symbolism extends to the cover, where reeds are woven into a net to catch the wandering sounds, Mr Yeats becomes completely master of himself and of his own resources. Technically the verse is far in advance of anything he has ever done, and if a certain youthful freshness, as of one to whom the woods were still the only talkers upon earth, has gone inevitably, its place has been taken by a deeper, more passionate, and wiser sense of the "everlasting voices" which he has come to apprehend, no longer quite joyously, in the crying of birds, the tongues of flame, and the silence of the heart. It is only gradually that Mr Yeats has learnt to become quite human. Life is the last thing he has learnt, and it is life, an extraordinarily intense inner life, that I find in this book of lyrics, which may seem also to be one long "hymn to intellectual beauty."

The poems which make up a volume apparently disconnected are subdivided dramatically among certain symbolical persons, familiar to the readers of **"The Secret Rose,"** Aedh, Hanrahan, Robartes, each of whom, as indeed Mr Yeats is at the trouble to explain in his notes, is but the pseudonym of a particular outlook of the consciousness, in its passionate, or dreaming, or intellectual moments. It is by means of these dramatic symbols, refining still further upon the large mythological symbolism which he has built up into almost a system, that Mr Yeats weaves about the simplicity of moods that elaborate web of atmosphere in which the illusion of love, and the cruelty of pain, and the gross ecstasy of hope, became changed into beauty. Here is a poet who has realised, as no one else, just now, seems to realise, that the only excuse for writing a poem is the making of a beautiful thing. But he has come finally to realise that, among all kinds of beauty, the beauty which rises out of human passion is the one most proper to the lyric; and in this volume, so full of a remote beauty of atmosphere, of a strange beauty of figure and allusion, there is a "lyrical cry" which has never before, in his pages, made itself heard with so penetrating a monotony.

There are love-poems in this book which almost give a voice to that silence in which the lover forgets even the terrible egoism of love. Love, in its state of desire, can be expressed in verse very directly; but that "love which moves the sun and the other stars," love to which the imagination has given infinity, can but be suggested, as it is suggested in these poems, by some image, in which for a moment it is reflected, as a flame is reflected in trembling water. (pp. 230-32)

To a poet who is also a mystic there is a great simplicity in things, beauty being really one of the foundations of the world, woman a symbol of beauty, and the visible moment, in which to love or to write love songs is an identical act, really as long and short as eternity. Never, in these love songs, concrete as they become through the precision of their imagery, does an earthly circumstance divorce ecstasy from the impersonality of vision. This poet cannot see love under the form of time, cannot see beauty except as the absolute beauty, cannot distinguish between the mortal person and the eternal idea. Every rapture hurries him beyond the edge of the world and beyond the end of time.

The conception of lyric poetry which Mr Yeats has perfected in this volume, in which every poem is so nearly achieved to the full extent of its intention, may be clearly defined; for Mr Yeats is not a poet who writes by caprice. A lyric, then, is an embodied ecstasy, and an ecstasy so profoundly personal that it loses the accidental qualities of personality, and becomes a part of the universal consciousness. Itself, in its first, merely personal stage, a symbol, it can be expressed only by symbol; and Mr Yeats has chosen his symbolism out of Irish mythology, which gives him the advantage of an elaborate poetic background, new to modern poetry. I am not sure that he does not assume in his readers too ready an acquaintance with Irish tradition, and I am not sure that his notes, whose delightfully unscientific vagueness renders them by no means out of place in a book of poems, will do quite all that is needed in familiarising people's minds with that tradition. But after all, though Mr Yeats will probably regret it, almost everything in his book can be perfectly understood by any poetically sensitive reader who has never heard of a single Irish legend, and who does not even glance at his notes. For he has made for himself a poetical style which is much more simple, as it is much more concise, than any prose style; and, in the final perfecting of his form, he has made for himself a rhythm which is more natural, more precise in its slow and wandering cadence, than any prose rhythm. It is a common mistake to suppose that poetry should be ornate and prose simple. It is prose that may often allow itself the relief of ornament; poetry, if it is to be of the finest quality, is bound to be simple, a mere breathing, in which individual words almost disappear into music. Probably, to many people, accustomed to the artificiality which they mistake for poetical style, and to the sing-song which they mistake for poetical rhythm, Mr Yeats' style, at its best, will seem a little bare, and his rhythm, at its best, a little uncertain. They will be astonished, perhaps not altogether pleased, at finding a poet who uses no inversions, who says in one line, as straightforward as prose, what most poets would dilute into a stanza, and who, in his music, replaces the aria by the recitative. How few, it annoys me to think, as I read over this simple and learned poetry, will realise the extraordinary art which has worked these tiny poems, which seem as free as waves, into a form at once so monumental and so alive! Here,

at last, is poetry which has found for itself a new form, a form really modern, in its rejection of every artifice, its return to the natural chant out of which verse was evolved; and it expresses, with a passionate quietude, the elemental desires of humanity, the desire of love, the desire of wisdom, the desire of beauty. (pp. 233-35)

Arthur Symons, "Mr. W. B. Yeats" (1900), in his Studies in Prose and Verse, *JM Dent & Sons Ltd, London, 1904, pp. 230-35.*

WILLIAM ARCHER (essay date 1902)

[*A dramatist and critic, Archer is best-known as one of the earliest and most important translators of Henrik Ibsen and as a drama critic of the London stage during the late nineteenth and early twentieth-centuries. Archer valued drama as an intellectual product and not as simple entertainment. For that reason he did a great deal to promote the "new drama" of the 1890s, including the work of Ibsen and Bernard Shaw. Similar in prescience to his dramatic criticism is his* Poets of the Younger Generation, *one of the first critical studies of many important modern English poets, including A. E. Housman, Arthur Symons, and William Butler Yeats. In the following excerpt from that book, Archer notes that Yeats's early Celtic themes were an outgrowth of his personality and beliefs, and not affectations of a current style. He also praises Yeats's simplified diction but, unlike Arthur Symons (see excerpt above), decries the elements of Symbolism appearing in his works.*]

It is easy, or so it seems to me, to make too much of the influence of race upon literature. On the one hand, he would be a bold man who should postulate absolute purity of race for any mother's son in this mingle-mangle of a Western world. "It's a wise child who knows his own great-great-great-great-grandfathers." On the other hand, I would engage to take a child of guaranteed Saxon ancestry and make him a Kelt of the Kelts by bringing him up in Keltic country and under exclusively Keltic influences. . . . I am not disputing, be it observed, the existence of marked and potent race-characteristics. On the contrary, I assert their existence and their stength, but suggest that they are transmitted rather in the atmosphere than in the blood, and are at least as much a matter of tradition as of heredity. (p. 531)

It is with Mr. Yeats that, so far as I know, the genuine spirit of Irish antiquity and Irish folk-lore makes its first entrance into English verse. Irish poets before him have either been absorbed in love, potheen, and politics—as Mr. Yeats himself puts it, they have "sung their loudest when a company of rebels or revellers has been at hand to applaud"—or (like Goldsmith and Moore) they have become to all intents and purposes Anglicised. Even William Allingham's fairies, pleasant little people though they be, are rather Anglo-Saxon Brownies than Keltic Sheogues. In Mr. Yeats we have an astonishing union of primitive imagination and feeling with cultivated and consciously artistic expression. He does not manipulate from outside a dead and conventionalised mythological machinery. The very spirit of the myth-makers and myth-believers is in him. His imaginative life finds its spontaneous, natural utterance in the language of the "Keltic twilight." This is no literary jargon to him, but his veritable mother-tongue. When he deals with Catholicism, you see in his mental processes a living repetition of what occurred when the first missionaries evangelised Hibernia. You see the primitive pagan assimilating the Catholic mythology to his own spiritual habits and needs, and attaching purely pagan concepts to Christian names and terms. His moral ideas are enlarged, no doubt; his metaphysics are practically unaffected. Christianity, in Mr. Yeats's poems, is not a creed, but a system of folk-lore. You do not trouble about its historical basis, you neither accept nor reject its dogmas. It is part and parcel of the innumerable host of spiritual entitites and influences which beleaguers humanity from the cradle to the grave. Belief in these entities and influences is no more a matter of intellectual determination, of voluntary assent, than belief in the air we breathe. It is part of our constitution: innate, inevitable. Mr. Yeats's religion (I speak, of course, of Mr. Yeats the poet, not of the theoretical mystic and editor of Blake) is not "morality touched with emotion," but rather superstition touched with morality. It is "older than any history that is written in any book."

Mr. Yeats has in some measure simplified the task of criticism by collectiing in a single book of *Poems* . . . all that he "cares to preserve out of his previous volumes of verse." The previous volumes were three: *The Wanderings of Oisin and other Poems* . . . , *The Countess Cathleen, and Various Legends and Lyrics* . . . , and a little play called *The Land of Heart's Desire*. . . . (pp. 532-33)

[In] whatever form Mr. Yeats chooses to write, his genius is essentially lyrical. His epic poem, *The Wanderings of Oisin* consists of three long lyrical ballads, as who should say three *Ancient Mariners* bracketed together. The charm of his two dramas lies in the "lyric cry" which runs through them. There are touches of character in them, no doubt, but no character-development or clash of will with will. They show the melancholy race of mortals at the mercy of vague and for the most part malevolent external powers, and their chief beauty lies in single speeches, easily detachable from their context, each of which is a little lyric in itself. . . . The whole play might be called a dialogue in folk-songs.

But before examining the plays more closely, let us glance at Mr. Yeats's epic, *The Wanderings of Oisin*. And here it must be said that the curious crispness, delicacy, and artful simplicity of his style is the result of patient effort and slow development. His verse has now a peculiar, indefinable distinction, as of one tiptoeing exquisitely through a fairy minuet; whereas ten years ago its movement was often flat-footed and conventional enough. *The Wanderings of Oisin,* as it now stands, is very different from the poem originally published under that title. (pp. 534-35)

[In its original form, the poem] is pretty, indeed, and fancifully decorative, with unmistakable foretastes of the poet's maturer quality; but it is nerveless, diffuse, and now and then commonplace. Everything of value is retained in the later version; some exquisite touches are added. . . . (p. 537)

[Every] change tends to heighten the racial colour of the passage (if I may call it so) and make it more characteristically Keltic. The first form might have been the work of an Englishman cleverly applying the method of *Christabel* to an Irish subject; the second form is Irish to its inmost fibre. . . . Magical and mysterious though the subject be, the design is perfectly definite, and is picked out, so to speak, in washes of brilliant, translucent, almost unharmonised colours. The picture is illuminated rather than painted, like the border of an ancient manuscript. It is characteristic of the Keltic imagination, though it may dwell by preference in the mist, to emerge at times into a scintillant blaze of light and colour. (pp. 538-40)

[*The Wanderings of Oisin* is] a singularly beautiful and moving poem, in which the high-hearted bravery and the wistful beauty

of the old Irish myth-cycle find the most sympathetic of interpreters.

In Mr. Yeats's first book there were several brief dramatic sketches of no very notable merit. One of them reappears, considerably altered, in the *Anashuya and Vijaya* of [*Poems*]. . . . The scene of another was laid in Spain, of a third in some Arthurian region; not one of them was located in Ireland. But Mr. Yeats draws his true strength from his native soil. In these early experiments the conventionality of the verse was particularly noticeable. It showed scarcely a trace of individual accent, and was not to be distinguished from the blank verse of the scores of stillborn "poetic dramas" which every year brings forth. No sooner had Mr. Yeats returned to Ireland and chosen a dramatic motive from Irish folk-lore, than his individuality asserted itself not only in the idea and structure of his work but in its rhythms as well. *The Countess Cathleen* has undergone stringent revision since its first appearance; and here, as in *The Wanderings of Oisin,* the changes—and especially the rounding-off of metrically defective lines—have all been for the better. But even in its original form the poem was full of a weird impressiveness which was then new to dramatic literature. (pp. 541-42)

A melancholy theme indeed is that of *The Countess Cathleen*. It can be told in a few words: The land is famine-stricken; Satan sends two demons in the guise of merchants to buy the souls of the starving peasants; the Countess Cathleen will sacrifice all her vast wealth, her "gold and green forests," to save the people; but the emissaries of hell (the heavenly powers being apparently asleep) steal her treasure, becalm her ships, delay the passage of her flocks and herds; so that at last there is nothing for her to do but to sell her own soul and feed the people with the proceeds. The absolute impotence, the practical non-existence, of the powers of good, and the perfect ease with which the powers of evil execute their plots, render the play depressing almost to the point of exasperation. It is true that at the end an Angel intervenes, and gives us to understand that Cathleen's soul is safe, because

> The Light of Lights
> Looks always on the motive, not the deed,
> The Shadow of Shadows on the deed alone.

But this is a tardy consolation to the reader, who feels, moreover, that Satan is not quite fairly dealt with, being baulked by a quibble, not openly encountered and vanquished. Oppressive melancholy, however, is the note of the folklore from which Mr. Yeats draws his inspiration; though in his delightful little book of prose, *The Celtic Twilight,* he seems inclined to contest the fact. Be this as it may, *The Countess Cathleen* (especially in its revised form) is as beautiful as it is sad. The blank verse has a monotonous, insinuating melody which is all its own, arising not only from the dainty simplicity of the diction, but from the preponderance of final monosyllables and of what the professors of Shakespearometry call "end-stopped" lines. Mr. Yeats eschews all attempt to get dramatic force and variety into his verse by aid of the well-known tricks of frequent elisions, feminine endings, periodic structure, and all the rest of it. And herein he does well. No rush and tumult of versification could suit his mournful fantasies so perfectly as this crooning rhythm, this limpid melody, which seems, as Cyrano de Bergerac would say, to have a touch of the brogue in it. (pp. 543-44)

Mr. Yeats's pure lyrics and ballads, too few in number, are full of beauty and charm. I can only refer to a few of those which have most impressed me: the dedication *To Some I have Talked with by the Fire, To the Rose upon the Rood of Time, When You are Old, The White Birds, To Ireland in the Coming Time, The Lake Isle of Innisfree . . . , The Stolen Child,* and *The Ballad of Father O'Hart.* Other readers may prefer other poems; these are the ones which have taken most hold upon me. (pp. 553-54)

In [*The Wind Among the Reeds* and *The Shadowy Waters,* Mr. Yeats's] peculiar gifts of imagination and of utterance are seen at their best. He extracts from a simple and rather limited vocabulary effects of the rarest delicacy and distinction. There is a certain appearance of mannerism, no doubt, in Mr. Yeats's individuality. One can scarcely turn a page of these books without coming upon the epithets "dim," "glimmering," "wandering," "pearl-pale," "dove-grey," "dew-dropping," and the like. His imagery is built up out of a very few simple elements, which he combines and re-combines unweariedly. The materials he employs, in short, are those of primitive folk-poetry; but he touches them to new and often marvellous beauty. What in our haste we take for mannerism may be more justly denominated style, the inevitable accent of his genius. (p. 555)

One other word, and I have done. It appears from the notes to *The Wind Among the Reeds,* rather than from the poems themselves, that Mr. Yeats is becoming more and more addicted to a petrified, fossilised symbolism, a system of hieroglyphs which may have had some inherent significance for their inventors, but which have now become matters of research, of speculation, of convention. I cannot but regard this tendency as ominous. His art cannot gain and may very easily lose by it. A conventional symbol may be of the greatest interest to the anthropologist or the antiquary; for the poet it can have no value. If a symbol does not spring spontaneously from his own imagination and express an analogy borne in upon his own spiritual perception, he may treasure it in his mental museum, but he ought not to let such a piece of inert matter cumber the seed-plot of his poetry. (pp. 556-57)

> William Archer, "William Butler Yeats," in his Poets of the Younger Generation, *John Lane/The Bodley Head, 1902 (and reprinted by Scholarly Press, 1969?), pp. 531-57.*

HORATIO SHEAFE KRANS (essay date 1904)

[*Krans's article discusses Yeats's use of native Irish materials in his early poetry. For more critical comments on this subject see the essays by William Archer, Yeats, and Vivian de Sola Pinto excerpted above and below.*]

The chief inspiration of the literary revival is the love of the legends and romances that belong to the Gaelic past of Ireland, and the desire to make their strange beauty known to the modern world. No one sets a higher value upon the ancient creations of the Irish imagination than Mr. Yeats, and no one knows better than he the need and use of getting them into English. He is eager to interest the people of to-day in the old nobility—the heroic temper, the courtesy, the generosity, the faithfulness among friends, and the courage in the face of enemies, which are the cardinal virtues of Celtic romance. This task he has essayed in lyrics and narrative poems, in plays, and in prose tales. Of the poems that draw on Gaelic sources some, it would seem, aim to reproduce the heroic spirit, while others run the author's own sentiment, which is akin to the gentle, dreamy moods of Irish romance, into the mould of the Gaelic stories. Notable among the poems of the former group are "**The Death**

of Cuhoolin," "On Baile's Strand," and "The Old Age of Queen Maeve."

In "**The Death of Cuhoolin**" and "**On Baile's Strand**," the first a short poem in rhymed couplets, the second a one-act play in mixed blank verse and prose—here to be considered as a revival of romance, not as a drama—the situations and characters come from the Red Branch cycle. Each tells of the combat between Cuhoolin and his son, and of the death of both. A father and son, neither knowing his relationship to the other, engage in single combat, and the son is slain. The father discovers the youth's identity, and, maddened by his grief, dies battling with the waves of the sea. The situation is essentially that of Arnold's "Sohrab and Rustum." But neither the poem nor the play has anything like the sweep and depth of emotion of Arnold's narrative. Neither seems to have responded well to the heroic spirit, and, though they both deal with one of the most tragic situations of Irish literature, neither has captured the grand note of primitive tragedy that is heard in the romances. Nor have they the peculiar charm of those poems that are deeply coloured by the poet's personality.

If the heroic note did not ring clear in "**The Death of Cuhoolin**" and "**On Baile's Strand**," the same criticism is not likely to be made of "**The Old Age of Queen Maeve**," which speaks, in a blank verse of grave and dignified cadence, and in a diction of noble simplicity, of the great spirit, high courage, and firm mind of Queen Maeve. Through this poem echoes of the poetry of the hero age are heard. (pp. 53-6)

In "**The Old Age of Queen Maeve**" may be recognised that kinship of spirit between the poetry of the Irish heroic age and the Homeric epics, which students of the Gaelic have so often remarked. But this poem and others of the same kind are rather appreciations of the temper of ancient Irish literature than embodiments of it. They belong to the poetry of an age of thought, revolting against itself, and imitating the poetry of an age of action.

It is when the beautiful old stories are used as a frame for the poet's own sentiment and point of view that they make their strongest appeal. The blank-verse poem, "**Fergus and the Druid**," is a good instance of Mr. Yeats's way of putting his own stamp upon what he borrows. According to Lady Gregory's rendering of the situation, Fergus lays down his sceptre against his will and under constraint from the men of Ulster. Mr. Yeats plants his own idea in the heart of the situation by changing the motive of the King's abdication. The Fergus of his poem longs to escape the duties and responsibilities of kingship, and is glad at last to change his crown for the bag of dreams offered him by the druid. (pp. 58-60)

"**The Madness of King Goll**," the story of the monarch, who, according to the legend, went mad, and hid himself in a valley near Cork, comes straight from Mr. Yeats's standpoint. He is no stranger to the mood that runs through all the veins of the poem, and gives life to every haunting line—the mood of eager, awed expectancy in which the King, alert to catch the mystic messages from the spirit world that everywhere closes in upon him, sees keen eyes peer at him from the night, hears the tramp of unseen feet, and cannot hush the voices in the winds and waters, in which cry the powers who are busy shaping the lives of men. Here nature is presented, in the true Celtic spirit, as haunted by mysterious presences, that seem to speak to man of his origin and destiny. (pp. 61-2)

The story of Baile and Aillinn has more than once been put into English, but never with a freer sweep of lyrical emotion or more melodiously than in the poem of Mr. Yeats's that takes its name from this famous pair of lovers. It is a ballad-like poem, in rhyming couplets that happily escape the monotony of movement incident to this kind of verse. The argument tells the story in a word:

> Baile and Aillinn were lovers, but Aengus, the Master of Love, wishing them to be happy in his own land among the dead, told to each a story of the other's death, so that their hearts were broken, and they died.

A trend of feeling that finds its way often into Mr. Yeats's poetry has a place in the rendering of this old tale—a discontent with the world as it is, and a preoccupation with dreams of a better, in the light of which the actual world is a faded and dusty thing. From the standpoint of this poem the tragic fate of Baile and Aillinn is a happy thing. . . . (pp. 64-5)

No Irish tale has found a finer form in English verse than that which Mr. Yeats has given to the story of Oisin (Ossian), as told in **"The Wanderings of Oisin,"** the poem that gave his first published volume its title. Dominated by a mood thoroughly characteristic of the poet, it is, the dramas excepted, his longest and most sustained flight, and has a romantic witchery and beguilement unsurpassed if not unequalled elsewhere in his work. Though abounding in lyrical passages and enlivened by dramatic dialogue, **"Oisin"** is narrative in form. It tells of the love of the Princess Niam, an immortal woman, for Oisin; of how she carried him, bound by the spell of her beauty, riding over the green sea, to spend three hundred years with her in the Land of the Ever-Young. (pp. 66-7)

The romantic charm of the world into which Niam and her lover ride is what makes the first impression in **"The Wanderings of Oisin."** One need go but a little way into the poem for the assurance that the poet is free of a kingdom in that world of romance in which Malory and Spenser, each in his own way, rules a realm. Nor would it be fanciful to maintain that the intellectual traditions, if not the blood, of the race that gave romance and the realm of fairy to European literature are still potent here. The mythic country of everlasting youth is the world conjured into being by the romantic magic of the Celtic imagination, a world strange in its personages, in its happenings, and in its landscape and pageantry. Niam, whom Oisin met and loved, is a creature of a spiritual life as intense as the fairy woman in Keats's "La Belle Dame Sans Merci." The passage that introduces her is a masterly piece of romantic portraiture. . . . Quite as memorable in another way is the demon of the second book of the poem, who wanders in that vast rocky hall whose description recalls the pictures in "Hyperion." . . . The landscape and pageantry in Oisin are as fine in their way as the portraiture. . . . (pp. 67-70)

The romantic beauty of **"Oisin"** is what makes the first impression. After this will be remarked the dominant unity of the mood. Here the poet has found a way to weave upon the old frame of legend a tapestry of rich poetic texture, whose pictured story tells of his own longing for a life of the spirit, free from mortal limitations, from the chains of custom and convention, and from the hard tyranny of time, and change, and death. This mood, here one of wistful longing, is in much of Mr. Yeats's work, and, growing more militant and aggressive, later becomes at one with the Celt's spirit of immemorial revolt against the tyranny of the real. (pp. 72-3)

The music of the poem, which is in rhymed verses of different length, is strikingly fine—not the music of the mere accomplished versifier, but that of a poet of rare melodic faculty, who never permits his verse to slip into the insistent jingle and slipshod melody that are the pitfalls of long rhymed poems. Now and then in the music, as in the diction and the phrasing, there are echoes of Keats, of Shelley, of Coleridge, and of Tennyson—pleasant assurances that the poet has enriched his spirit and formed his art in the school of the masters. Gaelic in subject and inspiration, **"Oisin"** evinces a remarkable literary faculty, romantic beauty, and musical skill of a high order, and reveals a complete poetic temperament. A poem of generous length, there is yet no lapse in sentiment, style, or music from the levels of pure poetry. It is this sustained poetic quality that has given Mr. Yeats his distinction among the poets of the younger generation. **"Oisin"** and the other poems based upon Irish romance are one more illustration of the adaptability of the old legends to the purposes of modern poetry; and in them the Gaelic stories have a new flowering. They render the spirit of the heroic age for the most part on one side—not in its virile passion, in its triumphant, buoyant, or poignantly tragic note, but when it is softly dreaming of happy worlds beyond, of love, and feasts, and phantom, bloodless fights; or when it stands awe-struck at the touch of supernatural powers. (pp. 77-9)

> *Horatio Sheafe Krans, in his* William Butler Yeats and the Irish Literary Revival *(copyright 1904 by McClure, Phillips & Co.; reprinted by permission of Doubleday & Company, Inc.) McClure, Phillips, 1904, 196 p.*

JOHN BERRYMAN   (essay date 1936)

[*The poet John Berryman wrote this essay on Yeat's dramas while he was still an undergraduate at Columbia University. It originally appeared in the* Columbia Review. *Berryman acknowledged Yeats as his own most important early influence stating, "I began work in verse-making as a burning, trivial disciple of the great Irish poet William Butler Yeats."*]

The twenty-one plays in [*The Collected Plays of William Butler Yeats*] represent the work of forty-two years, from *The Countess Cathleen* in 1892 to *The Words upon the Window-pane* in 1934; and a chronological reading of them suggests many problems. (p. 245)

The striking fact about this body of work . . . is its triviality, considered in the tradition of English dramatic literature. The volume is apparently arranged to culminate in the two "modern versions" of Sophocles' *Oedipus the King* and *Oedipus at Colonus,* and these are unquestionably the most full-bodied, the most satisfactory plays Yeats has written. With four exceptions, the others are all brief and relatively thin, if interesting and even excellent in special ways. In only one, *The Hour-Glass,* is anything like dramatic tension achieved; the rest relate delightfully and inconsequentially the legends of the Irish heroic age, of Cuchulain and Emer of Conchubar, of Deirdre, of angels and demons, the cats and the Shape-Changers, beggars and fools and kings.

It is clear that Yeats has not been concerned, as Shakespeare (we assume) was concerned, with the creation of recognizable and individual character. The people in his plays are typical or symbolic or mythical (and, as such, acceptable), or they are necessary figures to speak his lines in the interests of presentation and description. No one of them can be discussed apart from his immediate context and said to exist in his own right. They are, in fact, simple as a morality mask is simple; such inconsistencies as we note are the product of typical change or dramatic indirection—verbal ambiguity with a plastic end in view. Nor has Yeats been interested, clearly, in representation of the natural world, except in *The Words upon the Window-pane,* where realistic conversational prose serves to lend verisimilitude to his revelation of Swift's spirit through a medium. What then was Yeats doing in these plays?

The answer is threefold, insofar as we can discover it. He wanted, first, to hear his poetry spoken, and spoken under the most emphatic conditions obtainable—those of the theatre; probably he knew also that the discipline of dramatic verse would be good for his early luxuriance and imprecision, as indeed it was. He wanted to re-create the body of Irish legend and myth, seeing this re-creation as a necessary step in the nationalist movement of the early nineteen hundreds and believing that the theatre was the most popular and thus the most adequate means. And he wanted, particularly in his later plays, but to a degree in all, to dramatize his beliefs and doubts and preoccupations. These intentions, if I have stated them correctly, will describe the limits within which he has worked. His failure to achieve perfection within these limits must be ascribed to something else: Yeat's habit of mind is not dramatic but meditative. He speaks naturally, in other words, in reflection, not (as Congreve and Molière and O'Neill undeniably do) in terms of situation and action. Thus only is it possible to account for the fact that Yeats, who is probably the greatest living poet and who has worked in the theatre for forty-five years with all his intelligence and energies, has not written great plays or anything like great plays. (pp. 245-46)

In *The Countess Cathleen* a single atmosphere, of ominous and imminent disaster, is established and maintained more effectively than in any other play here of similar length; the incongruous salvation of Cathleen, which Yeats himself has recently deplored, is unfortunate, but it does not destroy the mood. Emphasis by contrast Yeats has secured in only one case, the brief *On Baile's Strand.* The heroic strife between the great king Conchubar and Cuchulain, who speak in blank verse, is enclosed in the framework of the Fool and the Blind Man, who begin and end the play, speaking a nervous and idiosyncratic prose; the device is not wholly successful, but it is notable, for it represents Yeats's only effort to attain this kind of complexity; actually it is only a rudimentary step in the direction of the highly individual, unmistakable accent of Shallow and Hamlet, Lear's Fool, and the Bastard Faulconbridge.

The Unicorn from the Stars and *The Player-Queen* are more recognizably dramatic pieces than any other original plays Yeats has written, particularly the latter, which is a very charming fantastic comedy in two long scenes, with little supernatural and legendary reference. The other play is allegorical, probably with a basis in legend; standing alone, it is too confused to admit of a single interpretation. Martin, the young dreamer who is led from his work by visions of great white unicorns trampling vineyards, remains an inexplicable shadow, and even his death is ambiguous.

Owing to Yeats's constant revision of all his plays, we find a remarkable uniformity of style here. As in his poetry, we see his vocabulary becoming more concrete, dependent on nouns rather than on adjectives, the unit of sound within the line briefer; and the later plays are written in a prose which differs in a similar way from the prose of *Cathleen Ni Houlihan.* . . . But the change in the verse of the plays is as nothing to the complete remodelling of his style in his later poems. (pp. 246-47)

Yeats may have realized this: the six plays since 1920 have been entirely in prose, except for songs and choruses.

Yeats wrote the first of what he calls his "dance plays" in 1917, and he has used the form five times since (or six, if we include *The King of the Great Clock-Tower,* . . . which is not included in this volume and is hardly worth independent comment, despite three beautiful lyrics, for it resembles the others closely). The term is hardly appropriate, for although dances do occur in two of them, gesture and action are almost completely subordinated to speech. . . . Such action as there is takes place within [a] limited space; at the end the Musicians unfold and fold [a] cloth . . . singing, in order to allow the players to leave the scene unobserved.

This narrow and almost private form is clearly very different from the dance dramas of Egypt and medieval Europe, but the at-once-implied classification of "ritual" is very useful; it may help us to understand the function and the real value of Yeats's work in these plays. Let us take "ritual" to signify a code or form of ceremonies, the formal character imposed on any experience as it is given objective existence by the imagination working in craft; the experience attains independent aesthetic vitality precisely through and by its limitation. Coming nearer to Yeats, we can say that this effective form will be meditative and single, that the experience will be largely from the body of myth and personal belief, and that the vitality will be dependent not at all on reference but on the skill and accuracy of insight as it is objectified.

It was appropriate and even inevitable that Yeats, a self-conscious and deliberate artist, should evolve some such form as this, as his most satisfactory means of expression, apart from the personal lyric. In agreeing to work within the narrowest possible "dramatic" limits, he at once lessened the probability of failure by obviating the necessity of using techniques not natural to him, and emphasized his accustomed talent by letting it work alone to the fullest advantage and with an appropriate subject matter.

His most important device, which allows him to establish and control almost in his own person the mood or system of reference of a given play, is the singing. . . . Thus, in *Calvary* these songs are so important that the play might be incomprehensible without them. (pp. 248-49)

The songs serve as a frame, an intelligible and coherent structure on which the action depends, as brickwork on girders.

Another important feature of the ritual is the use of masks; they figure more or less significantly in all six of the dance plays, but particularly in *The Only Jealousy of Emer,* which is impossible to conceive in anything like its present form without masks. The body of the renowned Cuchulain, "that amorous, violent man," has been washed ashore, and Emer, his wife, watches beside it; she sends for his mistress, Eithne Inguba, the woman he loved last, for Cuchulain is not dead: Bricriu of the Sidhe, the company of evil powers, has entered into him and dispossessed his spirit. All the players are masked, and the masked Ghost of Cuchulain crouches near the bed. Bricriu calls up a Woman of the Sidhe to take Cuchulain away, unless Emer will renounce forever his love; the Ghost and the Woman go out, but under the hypnotic urging of Bricriu in the Figure of Cuchulain, Emer gives up her claim and the Figure\ sinks back, to be awakened as the living Cuchulain by Eithne Inguba. Heroic and distorted masks are in large part responsible for the strange power of the play when it is read; in performance the effect of their rigid impersonality while passionate speech comes from their lips must be startling. More broadly, the stylized terms in which Emer's sacrifice is enacted are not merely the conductor but the cause of the play's strength and beauty.

The Dreaming of the Bones is the only dance play with a contemporary setting. A young Irish patriot, escaping through the hills after the fighting in Dublin in 1916, meets two strangers with heroic masks, a man and a young girl; they take him to the ruined Abbey of Corcomroe, where the dreaming bones of the dead wander in torment, and tell him the story of Dermot and Dervorgilla, who brought the Norman into Ireland to fight for them and who must wander until one of their race says, "I have forgiven them." Unknowing, the young man curses that pair, and when he learns, as they dance, their identity, he is yet stern. . . . This is perhaps the simplest and most compact of all the plays; great emotional intensity is secured through a curious and eerie relaxation of the verse: the players dream rather than speak, except when the young man's angry hatred lashes out against a seven-hundred-year-old treachery. A very interesting device, which illustrates the freedom that can be obtained through strict adherence to ritual, is used here and again in *The Cat and the Moon:* symbolic progress, action represented by the direction, "They go round stage once. The Musicians play." Any mode of writing, however narrow when it was adopted, is constantly available to intelligence for de-published in velopment in subtlety and scope; and, frequently, the more restricted the imagination, the more splendid its activity. (pp. 250-51)

> *John Berryman, "The Ritual of W. B. Yeats" (reprinted by permission of Farrar, Straus and Giroux, Inc.; copyright 1936 by Columbia Review; copyright © 1976 by Kate Berryman; originally published in* The Columbia Review, *Vol. 17, May-June, 1936), in his* The Freedom of the Poet, *Farrar, Straus and Giroux, 1976, pp. 245-52.*

W. B. YEATS (essay date 1937)

[*In the following excerpt, Yeats discusses the nature of his poetry and the influences of Celtic legend, his Irish heritage, and other poets on his work.*]

A poet writes always of his personal life, in his finest work out of its tragedy, whatever it be, remorse, lost love, or mere loneliness; he never speaks directly as to someone at the breakfast table, there is always a phantasmagoria. Dante and Milton had mythologies, Shakespeare the characters of English history or of traditional romance; even when the poet seems most himself, when he is Raleigh and gives potentates the lie, or Shelley 'a nerve o'er which do creep the else unfelt oppressions of this earth,' or Byron when 'the soul wears out the breast' as 'the sword outwears its sheath,' he is never the bundle of accident and incoherence that sits down to breakfast; he has been reborn as an idea, something intended, complete. . . . He is part of his own phantasmagoria and we adore him because nature has grown intelligible, and by so doing a part of our creative power. 'When mind is lost in the light of the Self,' says the Prashna Upanishad, 'it dreams no more; still in the body it is lost in happiness.' 'A wise man seeks in Self,' says the Chandogya Upanishad, 'those that are alive and those that are dead and gets what the world cannot give.' The world knows nothing because it has made nothing, we know everything because we have made everything.

It was through the old Fenian leader John O'Leary I found my theme. His long imprisonment, his longer banishment, his magnificent head, his scholarship, his pride, his integrity, all that aristocratic dream nourished amid little shops and little farms, had drawn around him a group of young men; I was but eighteen or nineteen and had already, under the influence of *The Faerie Queene* and *The Sad Shepherd,* written a pastoral play, and under that of Shelley's *Prometheus Unbound* two plays, one staged somewhere in the Caucasus, the other in a crater of the moon; and I knew myself to be vague and incoherent. He gave me the poems of Thomas Davis, said they were not good poetry but had changed his life when a young man, spoke of other poets associated with Davis and *The Nation* newspaper, probably lent me their books. I saw even more clearly than O'Leary that they were not good poetry. I read nothing but romantic literature; hated that dry eighteenth-century rhetoric; but they had one quality I admired and admire: they were not separated individual men; they spoke or tried to speak out of a people to a people; behind them stretched the generations. I knew, though but now and then as young men know things, that I must turn from that modern literature Jonathan Swift compared to the web a spider draws out of its bowels; I hated and still hate with an ever growing hatred the literature of the point of view. I wanted, if my ignorance permitted, to get back to Homer, to those that fed at his table. I wanted to cry as all men cried, to laugh as all men laughed, and the Young Ireland poets when not writing mere politics had the same want, but they did not know that the common and its befitting language is the research of a lifetime and when found may lack popular recognition. (pp. 509-11)

Behind all Irish history hangs a great tapestry, even Christianity had to accept it and be itself pictured there. Nobody looking at its dim folds can say where Christianity begins and Druidism ends; 'There is one perfect among the birds, one perfect among the fish, and one among men that is perfect.' I can only explain by that suggestion of recent scholars—Professor Burkitt of Cambridge commended it to my attention—that St. Patrick came to Ireland not in the fifth century but towards the end of the second. The great controversies had not begun; Easter was still the first full moon after the Equinox. Upon that day the world had been created, the Ark rested upon Ararat, Moses led the Israelites out of Egypt; the umbilical cord which united Christianity to the ancient world had not yet been cut, Christ was still the half-brother of Dionysus. A man just tonsured by the Druids could learn from the nearest Christian neighbour to sign himself with the Cross without sense of incongruity, nor would his children acquire that sense. The organised clans weakened Church organisation, they could accept the monk but not the bishop. (pp. 513-14)

Into this tradition, oral and written, went in later years fragments of Neo-Platonism, cabbalistic words—I have heard the words 'tetragrammaton agla' in Doneraile—the floating debris of mediaeval thought, but nothing that did not please the solitary mind. Even the religious equivalent for Baroque and Rococo could not come to us as thought, perhaps because Gaelic is incapable of abstraction. It came as cruelty. That tapestry filled the scene at the birth of modern Irish literature, it is there in the Synge of *The Well of the Saints,* in James Stephens, and in Lady Gregory throughout, in all of George Russell that did not come from the Upanishads, and in all but my later poetry. (pp. 514-15)

Our mythology, our legends, differ from those of other European countries because down to the end of the seventeenth century they had the attention, perhaps the unquestioned belief, of peasant and noble alike; Homer belongs to sedentary men, even to-day our ancient queens, our mediaeval soldiers and lovers, can make a pedlar shudder. I can put my own thought, despair perhaps from the study of present circumstance in the light of ancient philosophy, into the mouth of rambling poets of the seventeenth century, or even of some imagined ballad singer of to-day, and the deeper my thought the more credible, the more peasant-like, are ballad singer and rambling poet. Some modern poets contend that jazz and music-hall songs are the folk art of our time, that we should mould our art upon them; we Irish poets, modern men also, reject every folk art that does not go back to Olympus. Give me time and a little youth and I will prove that even 'Johnny, I hardly knew ye' goes back. (p. 516)

If Irish literature goes on as my generation planned it, it may do something to keep the 'Irishry' living, nor will the work of the realists hinder, nor the figures they imagine, nor those described in memoirs of the revolution. These last especially, like certain great political predecessors, Parnell, Swift, Lord Edward, have stepped back into the tapestry. It may be indeed that certain characteristics of the 'Irishry' must grow in importance. When Lady Gregory asked me to annotate her *Visions and Beliefs* I began, that I might understand what she had taken down in Galway, an investigation of contemporary spiritualism. For several years I frequented those mediums who in various poor parts of London instruct artisans or their wives for a few pence upon their relations to their dead, to their employers, and to their children; then I compared what she had heard in Galway, or I in London, with the visions of Swedenborg, and, after my inadequate notes had been published, with Indian belief. . . . I am convinced that in two or three generations it will become generally known that the mechanical theory has no reality, that the natural and supernatural are knit together, that to escape a dangerous fanaticism we must study a new science; at that moment Europeans may find something attractive in a Christ posed against a background not of Judaism but of Druidism, not shut off in dead history, but flowing, concrete, phenomenal.

I was born into this faith, have lived in it, and shall die in it; my Christ, a legitimate deduction from the Creed of St. Patrick as I think, is that Unity of Being Dante compared to a perfectly proportioned human body, Blake's 'Imagination,' what the Upanishads have named 'Self': nor is this unity distant and therefore intellectually understandable, but imminent, differing from man to man and age to age, taking upon itself pain and ugliness, 'eye of newt, and toe of frog.'

Subconscious preoccupation with this theme brought me *A Vision,* its harsh geometry an incomplete interpretation. The 'Irishry' have preserved their ancient 'deposit' through wars which, during the sixteenth and seventeenth centuries, became wars of extermination; no people, Lecky said at the opening of his *Ireland in the Eighteenth Century,* have undergone greater persecution, nor did that persecution altogether cease up to our own day. No people hate as we do in whom that past is always alive, there are moments when hatred poisons my life and I accuse myself of effeminacy because I have not given it adequate expression. It is not enough to have put it into the mouth of a rambling peasant poet. Then I remind myself that though mine is the first English marriage I know of in the direct line, all my family names are English, and that I owe my soul to Shakespeare, to Spenser and to Blake, perhaps to William Morris, and to the English language in which I think, speak, and write, that everything I love has come to me through English; my hatred tortures me with love, my love with hate.

I am like the Tibetan monk who dreams at his initiation that he is eaten by a wild beast and learns on waking that he himself is eater and eaten. This is Irish hatred and solitude, the hatred of human life that made Swift write *Gulliver* and the epitaph upon his tomb, that can still make us wag between extremes and doubt our sanity. (pp. 517-19)

Style is almost unconscious. I know what I have tried to do, little what I have done. . . . The English mind is meditative, rich, deliberate; it may remember the Thames valley. I planned to write short lyrics or poetic drama where every speech would be short and concentrated, knit by dramatic tension, and I did so with more confidence because young English poets were at that time writing out of emotion at the moment of crisis, though their old slow-moving meditation returned almost at once. Then, and in this English poetry has followed my lead, I tried to make the language of poetry coincide with that of passionate, normal speech. I wanted to write in whatever language comes most naturally when we soliloquise, as I do all day long, upon the events of our own lives or of any life where we can see ourselves for the moment. I sometimes compare myself with the mad old slum women I hear denouncing and remembering; 'How dare you,' I heard one say of some imaginary suitor, 'and you without health or a home!' If I spoke my thoughts aloud they might be as angry and as wild. It was a long time before I had made a language to my liking; I began to make it when I discovered some twenty years ago that I must seek, not as Wordsworth thought, words in common use, but a powerful and passionate syntax, and a complete coincidence between period and stanza. Because I need a passionate syntax for passionate subject-matter I compel myself to accept those traditional metres that have developed with the language. Ezra Pound, Turner, Lawrence wrote admirable free verse, I could not. I would lose myself, become joyless like those mad old women. . . . If I wrote of personal love or sorrow in free verse, or in any rhythm that left it unchanged, amid all its accidence, I would be full of self-contempt because of my egotism and indiscretion, and foresee the boredom of my reader. I must choose a traditional stanza, even what I alter must seem traditional. I commit my emotion to shepherds, herdsmen, cameldrivers, learned men, Milton's or Shelley's Platonist, that tower Palmer drew. Talk to me of originality and I will turn on you with rage. I am a crowd, I am a lonely man, I am nothing. Ancient salt is best packing. (pp. 521-22)

W. B. Yeats, "A General Introduction for My Work" (1937), in his Essays and Introductions *(reprinted with permission of Macmillan Publishing Company; in Canada by Michael B. Yeats, Anne Yeats and Macmillan, London, Ltd;* © *Mrs. W. B. Yeats, 1961), Macmillan, 1961, pp. 509-26.*

A. E. [pseudonym of GEORGE WILLIAM RUSSELL] (essay date 1938)

[*A key figure of the Irish Literary Renaissance, A. E. contributed more to the movement through his personality than through his artistry. He was a gifted conversationalist, a popular lecturer, and a generous man who brought many of the members of the Renaissance together. Along with his lifelong friend Yeats, J. M. Synge, and Lady Gregory, A. E. founded the Abbey Theatre, where the dramas of Yeats, Synge, and Sean O'Casey debuted.*]

What I regard as the chief defect in Yeats' autobiographies will, I think, be considered by others as their main virtue. The poet tells us but little about his internal life, but much about the people he has met, and as he has met many famous people of his time . . . his memories of these will be, for most readers, the chief interest in the memoirs. I hold that there is only one person that a man may know intimately, and that is himself. If he be a man of genius, what he could tell us about his own inner life would be of much more value than anything he could tell us of the external life of others, no matter how notable these people may have been. I read the *Reveries Over Childhood and Youth,* and into this river of beautiful prose there hardly falls an image of the imagination which was then wandering in *The Island of Statues,* or with Oisin in Tir na n-óg. His mirror reflects almost everything his eye has seen, but nothing of the imagination which was to make so rare a beauty and which must then have been in its rich springtime. The external world evolves its patterns before his eye, but of the involution of the spirit into the bodily nature bringing with it its own images and memories of another nature, there is but little, and I read this biography as I would look at some many-coloured shell, from which the creature inhabiting it, who might have told us about its manner of being, had slipped away leaving us only the miracle of form to wonder at. I am inclined to prophesy a reaction from the objective treatment of life in literature, and that the age which follows ours may value a writer only for what he can report on the inmost mysteries of his life, with the thought that from his candle we may set fire to our own. But of its kind, this mirroring of notable personalities in another, as notable as any he writes about, has unusual distinction. The prose in its cool, luminous flowing is a delight to follow. His portraits of his contemporaries are always interesting. If I do not recognise myself or my friends in the chapter he has devoted to us, I can understand how we may have appeared like this to another. But it is because I know myself and my friends so much better than the poet could have known us, and because I see the chasm between our inner life and the outer which he describes, that I am inclined to suppose, though I may be in error, that there is a wide gulf between the inward and the external life of others whom he portrays. I say this without reflecting in any way upon either the memories or the sincerity of the writer, which is made obvious in many passages relating to himself. But I return to my original conviction, that no true portrait can be made by any, save of themselves, though the doing of this would require extraordinary qualities in the writer, which not even a Rousseau had in the necessary fullness. (pp. 95-6)

> *A. E. [pseudonym of George William Russell], "Autobiography," in his* The Living Torch, *edited by Monk Gibbon (reprinted with permission of Russell & Volkening, Inc., as agents for the author; in Canada by Colin Symthe Ltd, Gerrards Cross, Bucks, England; © 1938 by A. E.), Macmillan Publishing Company, 1938, pp. 95-6.*

CLEANTH BROOKS (essay date 1939)

[*Brooks is the most prominent of the New Critics, an influential movement in American criticism which also included Allen Tate, R. P. Blackmur, and Robert Penn Warren, and which paralleled a critical movement in England led by I. A. Richards, T. S. Eliot, and William Empson. Although the various New Critics did not subscribe to a single set of principles, all believed that a work of literature had to be examined as an object in itself through a process of close analysis of symbol, image, and metaphor. For the New Critics, a literary work was not a manifestation of ethics, sociology, or psychology, and could not be evaluated in the general terms of any nonliterary discipline. For Brooks, metaphor was the primary element of literary art, and the effect of that metaphor of primary importance. Brooks's most characteristic*

essays are detailed studies of metaphoric structure, particularly in poetry. According to René Wellek, "Brooks analyzes poems as structures of opposites, tensions, paradoxes, and ironies with unparalleled skill." For Brooks, irony is the most important of these elements and, as Wellek notes, "indicates the recognition of incongruities, the ambiguity, the reconciliation of opposites which Brooks finds in all good, that is, complex poetry." Brooks's criticism strongly influenced critical writing and the teaching of literature in the United States during the 1940s and 1950s. In the following excerpt, Brooks explicates Yeats's mythic system and theory of history as presented in A Vision. *For another discussion of* A Vision, *see the essay by Allen Tate excerpted below.*]

William Butler Yeats has produced in his *Vision* one of the most remarkable books of the last hundred years. It is the most ambitious attempt made by any poet of our time to set up a "myth." The framework is elaborate and complex; the concrete detail constitutes some of the finest prose and poetry of our time. But the very act of boldly setting up a myth will be regarded by most critics as an impertinence, or, at the least, as a fantastic vagary. And the latter view will be reinforced by Yeats's account of how he received the system from the spirits through the mediumship of his wife.

The privately printed edition of *A Vision* appeared so long ago as 1925, but it has been almost completely ignored by the critics even though there has been, since the publication of *The Tower* . . . , a remarkable resurgence of interest in Yeats's poetry. Indeed, Edmund Wilson has been the only critic thus far to deal with *A Vision* in any detail. His treating it in any detail is all the more admirable in view of his general interpretation of the significance of Yeats's system. For Wilson . . . considers the symbolist movement as a retreat from science and reality; and Yeats's system, with its unscientific paraphernalia, its gyres and cones, its strange psychology described in terms of Masks and Bodies of Fate, and most of all its frank acceptance of the supernatural, is enough to try the patience of any scientific modernist. A very real regard for the fineness of Yeats's later poetry has kept him from carrying too far the view of Yeats as an escapist. But to regard the magical system as merely a piece of romantic furniture is to miss completely the function which it has performed for Yeats.

The central matter is science, truly enough, and Edmund Wilson is right in interpreting the symbolist movement as an antiscientific tendency. But the really important matter to determine is the grounds for Yeats's hostility to science. The refusal to accept the scientific account in matters where the scientific method is valid and relevant is unrealistic, but there is nothing "escapist" about a hostility to science which orders science off the premises as a trespasser when science has taken up a position where it has no business to be. For example, Victorian poetry will illustrate the illegitimate intrusion of science, and Yeats in his frequent reprehension of the "impurities" in such poetry—far from being a romantic escapist—is taking a thoroughly realistic position. The formulas which Edmund Wilson tends to take up—scientific, hard-headed, realistic; antiscientific-romantic, escapist—are far too simple. (pp. 173-74)

[All] poetry since the middle of the seventeenth century has been characterized by the impingement of science upon the poet's world. Yeats, after a brief enthusiasm for natural science as a boy, came, he tells us, to hate science "with a monkish hate." (p. 174)

It is easy, when one considers the system as expressed in *A Vision* to argue that Yeats's quarrel with science was largely that the system of science allows no place for the supernatural—

visions, trances, and incredible happenings—which began to manifest itself to Yeats at a very early period in his life. Undoubtedly Yeats wished for an account of experience which would make room for such happenings. But if we insist on this aspect of the matter, as most critics have done, we neglect elements which are far more important. Granting that Yeats had never had a single supernatural manifestation, many of his objections to science would have remained. The account given by science is still abstract, unconcerned with values, and affording no interpretations. Yeats wished for an account of experience which would surmount such defects: as he once put it, a philosophy which was at once "logical and boundless." The phrase is an important one. Had Yeats merely been content to indulge himself in fairy tales and random superstitions, he would never, presumably, have bothered with a system of beliefs at all. A philosophy which was merely "boundless" would allow a person to live in a pleasant enough anarchy. The "logical" quality demands a systematization, though in Yeats's case one which would not violate and oversimplify experience.

The whole point is highly important. If Yeats had merely been anxious to indulge his fancy, not caring whether the superstition accepted for the moment had any relation to the world about him—had he been merely an escapist, no system would have been required at all. For the system is an attempt to make a coherent formulation of the natural and the supernatural. The very existence of the system set forth in *A Vision* therefore indicates that Yeats refused to run away from life.

But if he refused to run away from life he also refused to play the game with the counters of science. For the abstract, meaningless, valueless system of science, he proposed to substitute a concrete, meaningful system, substituting symbol for concept. As he states in the introduction to *A Vision,* "I wished for a system of thought that would leave my imagination free to create as it chose and yet make all it created, or could create, part of the one history, and that the soul's." Or if we prefer Mr. Eliot's terms, Yeats set out to build a system of references which would allow for a unification of sensibility. Yeats wanted to give the authority of the intellect to attitudes and the intensity of emotion to judgments. The counsel of I. A. Richards is to break science and the emotions cleanly apart—to recognize the separate validity and relevance of "statements" (scientific propositions) on the one hand and of "pseudo-statements" (unscientific but emotionally valid statements) on the other.

Yeats, on the contrary, instead of breaking science and poetry completely apart, has preferred to reunite these elements in something of the manner in which they are fused in a religion. His system has for him, consequently, the authority and meaning of a religion, combining intellect and emotion as they were combined before the great analytic and abstracting process of modern science broke them apart. In short, Yeats has created for himself a myth. (pp. 174-76)

It is because most of us misunderstand and distrust the myth and because we too often trust science even when it has been extended into contexts where it is no longer science that most of us misunderstand the function of Yeats's mythology. A further caution is in order. Yeats has called his system "magical," and the term may mislead us. . . . Yeats obviously does not propose to use his system to forecast the movements of the stock market, or to pick the winner of the Grand National. The relation of the system to science and the precise nature of Yeats's belief in it will be discussed later. For the present, the

positive qualities of the myth may be best discussed by pointing out its relation to Yeats's poetry.

The system may be conveniently broken up into three parts: a picture of history, an account of human psychology, and an account of the life of the soul after death. The theory of history is the easiest aspect of the system. It bears a close resemblance to Spengler's cyclic theory. (Yeats takes notice of this, but he points out that his system was complete before he had read Spengler.) Civilizations run through cycles of two thousand-odd years, periods of growth, of maturity, and lastly, of decline; but instead of Spengler's metaphor of the seasons, spring-summer-autumn-winter, Yeats uses a symbolism drawn from the twenty-eight phases of the moon. . . . Yeats further complicates his scheme by dividing his cycle into two subcycles of twenty-eight phases and one thousand-odd years each. The phases 15 of these two subcycles which make up the two thousand years of Christian civilization are, for example, Byzantine civilization under Justinian and the Renaissance. Our own period is at phase 23 of the second subcycle; the moon is rapidly rounding toward the dark when the new civilization to dominate the next two thousand years will announce itself—"the Second Coming."

The full moon (phase 15) symbolizes pure subjectivity, the height of what Yeats calls the "antithetical" which predominates from phase 8 (the half moon of the first quarter) to the full moon and on to phase 22 (the half moon of the last quarter). The dark of the moon ("full sun") symbolizes pure objectivity, the height of what Yeats calls the "primary," which dominates from phase 22 to phase 8. The critical phases themselves, 8 and 22, since they represent equal mixtures of primary and antithetical, are periods of great stress and change. So much for the four cardinal phases. Each of the various twenty-eight phases, indeed, is assigned a special character in like manner.

An account of phase 23 will be sufficient illustration—all the more since this phase is the subject of several of Yeats's poems. Yeats regards phase 22 as always a period of abstraction. Synthesis is carried to its furthest lengths and there comes "synthesis for its own sake, organization where there is no masterful director, books where the author has disappeared, painting where some accomplished brush paints with an equal pleasure, or with a bored impartiality, the human form or an old bottle, dirty weather and clean sunshine" (*A Vision*). In the next phase, phase 23, which the present world has already entered upon (Yeats gives the year of transition as 1927) "in practical life one expects the same technical inspiration, the doing of this or that not because one would, or should, but because one can, consequent license, and with those 'out of phase' anarchic violence with no sanction in general principles."

It is a vision of this period which Yeats gives us in what is perhaps the best known of his historical poems, **"The Second Coming."** . . . (pp. 176-79)

In **"Meditation in Time of Civil War"** Yeats gives another vision of the same period. . . . In Section VII of this poem the poet has a vision of abstract rage, "The rage-driven . . . troop" crying out for vengeance for Jacques Molay, followed by a vision of perfect loveliness—ladies riding magical unicorns. But both visions fade out and

> Give place to an indifferent multitude, give place
> To brazen hawks. Nor self-delighting reverie,
> Nor hate of what's to come, nor pity for what's
>   gone,

Nothing but grip of claw, and the eye's complacency,
The innumerable clanging wings that have put out the
    moon.

The moon is used as a symbol of the imagination in its purity, of the completely subjective intellect. It has this general meaning in many of Yeats's poems—for example, in the poem, **"Blood and the Moon,"** where it is played off against blood (which is comparable to the sun, or the dark of the moon) as a symbol of active force—of the objective, or the primary.

An examination of the various meanings of blood in this poem will indicate how flexible and subtle the "meanings" attached to one of Yeats's concrete images can be. The symbol first occurs in the phrase, "A bloody, arrogant power." The tower on which the poet stands has been built by such a force and the symbolic meaning of the term is partially indicated by the characterization of the power as "bloody," shedding blood. But the meaning is extended and altered somewhat in the reference to Swift's heart: "in his blood-sodden breast" which "dragged him down into mankind." Blood here is associated with elemental sympathy, though the reference to Swift's particular quality of sympathy qualifies it properly—a sympathy grounded in one's elemental humanity which cannot be escaped and which—from the standpoint of the pure intellect—may be said to drag one down. The third reference to blood occurs in the phrase, "blood and state," and a third connection emerges—the connection of blood with nobility and tradition.

These references, it is important to notice, do not so much define the meaning of the symbol as indicate the limits within which the meaning (or manifold of meanings) is to be located. That meaning emerges fully only when we reach the last two sections of the poem where the symbols of blood and moon enter into active contrast: action contrasted with contemplation, power with wisdom, the youth of a civilization with its age. . . . The development is very rich, and even though the poet in the last stanza has apparently reduced his meaning to abstract statement, the meaning is fuller than the statement taken as mere statement. We must read the lines in their full context to see how their meaning is made more complex, and, if one likes, more "precise" by the development of the symbols already made. . . . The poem itself is a very fine example of the unification of sensibility. As we have said, the poem refuses to be reduced to allegory—allegory which is perhaps the first attempt which man makes to unite the intellect and the emotions when they begin to fall apart—Spenser's *Faerie Queene*, for example. Moreover, the poet has repudiated that other refuge of a divided sensibility, moralization following on a piece of description—Tennyson's *Princess*, for instance. One can imagine how the poem would probably have been written by a Victorian: The old man standing upon the tower surveys from its vantage point the scene about him; then the poet, having disposed of the concrete detail, moralizes abstractly on the scene to the effect that wisdom and power are incompatibles. Instead, Yeats has confidence in his symbols; the concrete and the abstract, thought and feeling, coincide. The poet refuses to define the moralization except in terms of the specific symbols and the specific situation given.

A more special and concentrated example of Yeats's contemplation of the cyclic movement of history is revealed in his **"Two Songs from a Play."** These poems really represent his account of "the First Coming," the annunciation to Mary of the birth of Christ, the dynamic force which was to motivate the two thousand year cycle of Christian civilization (pp. 179-82)

The celebrated poem, **"Leda and the Swan,"** is of course related to this same general theme, for the annunciation to Leda is felt by the poet to have ushered in the cycle of classic civilization. Leda and her swan are thus parallel to Mary and her dove. The power with which Yeats handles the old myth resides in part in the fact that his own myth allows him to take the older one in terms of *myth*, reincorporating it into itself. **"Leda and the Swan,"** far from being merely a pretty cameo, a stray *objet d'art* picked up from the ruins of the older civilization, has a vital relation to Yeats in his own civilization of the twentieth century. (One may observe in passing that the section on history in *A Vision* includes the finest rhythmic prose written in English since that of Sir Thomas Browne.)

Remembering Yeats's expressed desire for a system which would make all history an imaginative history, "and that the soul's," one is not surprised to find that Yeats employs the symbolism of the moon also to describe the various types of men. Men are classified on the basis of their mixtures of the subjective and objective. There are not twenty-eight possible types of men, however, but only twenty-six; for phase 1, complete objectivity, and phase 15, complete subjectivity are not mixtures. These phases are therefore supernatural or superhuman and may characterize an age though not an individual person. Several possible misapprehensions may be anticipated here: The phase of an age does not determine the phase of men living in that age. A man of phase 20, for example, like Shakespeare, may live in some other historical phase than 20—Yeats assigns him, as a matter of fact, to historical phase 16. Moreover, the determination of a man's personality by the nature of his phase is by no means absolute. He is also influenced by his environment. The historical phase thus qualifies the individual phase.

The faculties involved in Yeats's system of psychology are four rather than the Aristotelian three. In Yeats's system, Man possesses: Will; Mask (image of what he wishes to become or reverence); Creative Mind (all the mind which is consciously constructive); and Body of Fate (physical and mental environment). One need not enter here into the modes for determining the precise relations of the four faculties to each other in a given personality. One relationship among them, however, is of great importance. The four faculties are divided into two sets, and each member of the pair is opposite to the other. A man is classified under the phase to which his Will belongs. The Mask is always opposite to this phase. Thus, if we imagine the twenty-eight phases of the moon drawn in the form of a circle, a man whose Will is of phase 17, will have his Mask directly across the circle at phase 3; in the same way, a man with Will at phase 18, will have his Mask at phase 4. Creative Mind and Body of Fate are paired in oposition in like manner.

The interplay of tensions among the four faculties is very intricate, and this also cannot be treated here. The important thing to notice, one repeats, is this: that the psychology is founded on the conflict of opposites. The basic form of the whole system is the gyre, the one end of which widens concomitantly as the other narrows. Will and Mask are fixed in such a relation in one gyre; Creative Mind and Body of Fate, in another. "All things are from antithesis," Yeats observes, "all things dying each other's life, living each other's death." Will and Mask, desire and the thing desired, among the other elements of Yeats's system, bear such a relationship.

The relationship of Will and Mask especially illuminates Yeats's theory of the artist. Men of the antithetical or subjective phases (8 to 22) must strive in their work to realize the Mask which is the opposite of all that they are in actual life. The poem, "**Ego Dominus Tuus**," gives an exposition of this view. (pp. 183-85)

The case of Yeats himself, who apparently considers himself a man of phase 17, will also illustrate. He says of himself in his **Autobiographies** that he is "a gregarious man, going hither and thither looking for conversation, and ready to deny from fear or favor [his] dearest conviction." Frequently he chides himself for his interest in politics. Yet the Mask, the antiself of man of phase 17, hates "parties, crowds, propaganda" and delights in "the solitary life of hunters and of fishers and 'the groves pale passion loves.'" In his own great later poetry it is the "proud and lonely things" which he celebrates, and typically the fisherman. . . .

So much for antithetical men, men whose Will is at phases dominantly antithetical; but primary men, on the other hand, men of phases 22 to 8, "must cease to desire *Mask* and Image by ceasing from self-expression, and substitute a motive of service for that of self-expression. Instead of the created *Mask* [they have] an imitative *Mask*. . . ." (p. 186)

If Yeats may appear to the reader to have fallen into a mechanical determinism quite as rigid as the scientific determinism which he tried to escape, and one which is fantastic to boot, one should notice that Yeats allows a considerable amount of free will. For each man of every phase, there is a False Mask as well as a True Mask—a course of action which is fatal for him to pursue as well as a course which he should pursue. Shelley, for example, (like Yeats, a man of phase 17 and "partisan, propagandist, and gregarious") too often sought his False Mask and wrote "pamphlets, and [dreamed] of converting the world." (p. 187)

[One] may observe that Yeats accounts for the subconscious in his myth of the Daimon. "The *Four Faculties* are not the abstract categories of philosophy, being the result of the four memories of the *Daimon* or ultimate self of that man. His *Body of Fate,* the series of events forced upon him from without, is shaped out of the *Daimon's* memory of the events of his past incarnations; his *Mask* or object of desire or idea of the good, out of its memory of the moments of exaltation in his past lives; his *Will* or normal ego out of its memory of all the events of his present life, whether consciously remembered or not; his *Creative Mind* from its memory of ideas—or universals— displayed by actual men in past lives, or their spirits between lives." The man's Will is the Daimon's Mask; his Mask, the Daimon's Will; and so likewise with Creative Mind and Body of Fate. The mind of the man and his Daimon are thus related as the narrow and wide ends of a gyre are related. And Yeats had already told us in "**Anima Mundi**," that the Daimon "suffers with man as some firm-souled man suffers with the woman he but loves the better because she is extravagant and fickle." Moreover, "the Daemon, by using his mediatorial shades, brings man again and again to the place of choice, heightening temptation that the choice may be as final as possible . . . leading his victim to whatever among works not impossible is the most difficult." Man must not refuse the struggle. To do so is to fall under automatism and so be "out of phase." But the most powerful natures may occasionally need rest from the struggle and may fall into such an automatism temporarily without becoming out of phase.

Yeats has apparently described such a rest in his own life in his fine but obscure poem, "**Demon and Beast**." (pp. 189-88)

But man not only is influenced by his Daimon; he may also be influenced by the dead, and partake in the *Anima Mundi,*

the great collective memory of the world. Here one comes upon the third division of Yeats's system, that which deals with the life after death. To deal with Yeats's highly complicated account very summarily, one may say that Yeats holds that the soul after death goes through certain cycles in which it relives its earthly life, is freed from pleasure and pain, is freed from good and evil, and finally reaches a state of beatitude. Unless it has finished the cycle of its human rebirths, it then receives the Cup of Lethe, and, having forgotten all of its former life, is reborn in a human body.

The soul remains in existence, therefore, after the death of the body, and under various conditions disembodied souls may communciate with the living—for example, in dreams—though on waking, the dreamer has substituted for the dream, some other image. The reader will remember that in *A Packet for Ezra Pound* Yeats claims, like Kusta Ben Luka in the poem, "**The Gift of Harun Al-Rashid**," to have received this system of thought itself from the spirits through the mediumship of his wife.

The relation of the artist to the souls of the dead is apparently a highly important one for Yeats, and two of Yeats's finest poems, the "Byzantium" poems, depend heavily upon a knowledge of this relationship.

Byzantium, as Mr. R. P. Blackmur has pointed out, is the heaven of man's mind. But more especially it is a symbol of the heaven of man's imagination, and pre-eminently of a particular kind of imagination, the nature of which Yeats suggests for us in the following passage from *A Vision*. (pp. 188-89)

> I think that in early Byzantium, maybe never before or since in recorded history, religious, aesthetic and practical life were one, that architect and artificers—though not, it may be, poets, for language had been the instrument of controversy and must have grown abstract— spoke to the multitude and the few alike. . . .
>
> [In Byzantium of this period] . . . all about . . . is an incredible splendor like that which we see pass under our closed eyelids as we lie between sleep and waking, no representation of a living world but the dream of a somnambulist. Even the drilled pupil of the eye, when the drill is in the hand of some Byzantine worker in ivory, undergoes a somnambulistic change, for its deep shadow among the faint lines of the tablet, its mechanical circle, where all else is rhythmical and flowing, give to Saint or Angel a look of some great bird staring at miracle.
>
> (pp. 189-90)

The poem ["**Sailing to Byzantium**"] can be taken on a number of levels; as the transition from sensual art to intellectual art; as the poet's new and brilliant insight into the nature of the Byzantine imagination; as the poet's coming to terms with age and death. The foregoing account of the development of the symbols in the poet's personal experience will not in itself explain the fineness of the poem, or even indicate its aesthetic structure: it will not indicate, for example, the quality of self-irony in his characterization of himself as a "monument of unageing intellect" or as a "tattered coat upon a stick" or the play of wit achieved in such a phrase as "the artifice of eternity." The account given will, for that matter, do no more than indicate the series of contrasts and paradoxes on which the poem is founded—it will not assess their function in giving the poem its power. But it may indicate the source of the authority which dictates the tone of the poem. The real importance of the symbolic system is that it allows the poet a tremendous richness and coherency. (p. 192)

The system, in these terms, is an instrument for, as well as a symbol of, the poet's reintegration of his personality. It is the instrument through which Yeats has accomplished the unification of his sensibility.

A brief summary of the general function of Yeats's system may be in order here. We have already spoken of the advantages which the poet gains by using concrete symbols rather than abstract ideas and of traditional symbols which make available to him the great symbolism out of the past. The system, to put it concisely, allows Yeats to see the world as a great drama, predictable in its larger aspects (so that the poet is not lost in a welter of confusion), but in a pattern which allows for the complexity of experience and the apparent contradictions of experience (so that the poet is not tempted to oversimplify). The last point is highly important and bears directly on the dramatic aspect of the system, for the system demands, as it were, a continually repeated victory over the contradictory whereby the contradictory is recognized, and through the recognition, resolved into agreement. Yeats's finest poems not only state this thesis but embody such a structure, and his increasing boldness in the use of the contradictory and the discordant in his own poetry springs directly from his preoccupation with antithesis.

It is easy to see, at least from our vantage point of the present, the effect of this emphasis in making possible Yeats's break with Victorianism. The prime defect of Victorian poetry was that it subordinated the imaginative act of assimilating the incongruous to the logical act of matching the congruent. Yeats, in trying to write from his antiself, in trying to be all that he naturally was not—whatever we may think of his Doctrine of the Mask—broke away from Victorian optimism, decorum, and sentimentality, and disciplined his dramatic powers.

One may cite text and verse in corroboration. For example, in a highly illuminating passage in **"Anima Hominis,"** Yeats has written: "The other self, the anti-self or the antithetical self . . . comes but to those who are no longer deceived, whose passion is reality. The sentimentalists are practical men who believe in money, in position, in a marriage bell, and whose understanding of happiness is to be so busy whether at work or play, that all is forgotten but the momentary aim." The antiself, then, is incompatible with sentimentality. And in **"Hodos Chameliontos"** Yeats writes of two such men who sought reality, Dante and Villon, saying of them that "had they lacked their Vision of Evil, had they cherished any species of optimism, they could but have found a false beauty. . . . They and their sort alone earn contemplation, for it is only when the intellect has wrought the whole of life to drama, to crisis, that we may live for contemplation, and yet keep our intensity." "Their sort" of poets is that to which Yeats himself must be certainly assigned. And his insistence on the dramatic element is fundamental. . . . Active virtue, as distinguished from the passive acceptance of a code, is therefore theatrical, consciously dramatic, the wearing of a mask. . . . Wordsworth, great poet though he be, is so often flat and heavy partly because his moral sense, being a discipline he had not created, a mere obedience, has no theatrical element."

So much for the general nature of Yeats's myth and for its relation to his own great poetry; and now, one further reference

to the vexing question of Yeats's belief in his system. "The saner and greater mythologies," as Richards says, "are not fancies; they are the utterance of the whole soul of man and, as such, inexhaustible to meditation." The statement can be claimed for Yeats's myth. We have already uttered a warning against the use of the misleading term "magic" for Yeats's system. Magical in the sense that it proposes to use unscientific means to accomplish ends better accomplished by scientific means the system is not. Properly speaking it is a world-view or a philosophy—an "utterance of the whole soul of man" having for its object imaginative contemplation.

Yeats, as we have seen, apparently has no objection himself to referring to his system as a myth, but we are to remember that in calling it this, he is not admitting that it is trivial, or merely fanciful, or "untrue." And this is doubtless why Yeats, in answering the question of whether or not he believes in his system, can only reply with a counter-question as to whether the word "belief," as the questioner will use it, belongs to our age. For the myth is not scientifically true, and yet though a fiction, though a symbolical representation, intermeshes with reality. It is imaginatively true, and if most people will take this to mean that it is after all trivial, this merely shows in what respect our age holds the imagination. (pp. 200-02)

> *Cleanth Brooks, "Yeats: The Poet As Myth-Maker,"*
> *in his* Modern Poetry and the Tradition *(copyright,*
> *1939, by The University of North Carolina Press),*
> *University of North Carolina Press, 1939, pp. 173-*
> *202.*

LOUIS MacNEICE (essay date 1941)

[*MacNeice was an Irish poet who came to prominence during the 1930s. He is often discussed in conjunction with W. H. Auden and Stephen Spender, but his work was never as political as that of the other two poets. The Poetry of W. B. Yeats, from which the following excerpt is drawn, is an important study of Yeats's entire career.*]

The Wild Swans at Coole contains several poems which are obscure because they imply an esoteric world system. This system Yeats was working out from 1917 on, partly through 'spirit messages' obtained by his wife when she was in a state of trance, partly through the folk-beliefs, the Indian and cabbalistic philosophy, which he had been exploring since his youth. Some of his new poems he wrote, according to himself, 'as a text for exposition'. The exposition is to be found in *A Vision,* first published in 1925. This book is the most ingenious, the most elaborate, and the most arid of his writings. He attached vast importance to it. Although from one angle a romantic individualist, even an anarchist, he had always had a desire to docket the universe. He did not fancy himself beating his wings in a void. He could say 'An aimless joy is a pure joy,' thinking of the tramps in Synge, but would then go further back and argue that there is a *point* in being aimless; fool, libertine, vagrant, are following the path of the stars. Being unable to accept the established religions or to understand the professional philosophers, he had begun with a vague predilection for psychic experiences which he could not co-ordinate and ended by producing a system which professed to be a blue print for reality but was actually a sop to his own conscience; hating scientists and rationalists he set out to be scientifically irrational. He succeeded in writing a book more unreadable than most orthodox philosophy. Here and there in the book are statements which give him away. He recounts that when his wife began transmitting the messages from the spirits, he made them an offer that he would spend the rest of his life 'explaining and piecing together those scattered sentences'. 'No,' was the answer, 'we have come to give you metaphors for poetry.' (pp. 112-13).

A.E.'s comment on *A Vision* was: 'It is of much more importance to us to have experience than to have philosophies.' But Yeats, although he paid lipservice to experience, was never one of those who write as the bird sings. Both his themes and his images were selected rather than spontaneous. His life was not a series of unexpected illuminations punctuating the irrelevant darkness of every day; it was rather a sustained and conscious effort to illuminate that darkness and make it relevant. He was no Rimbaud or Blake. His writing was not, in the narrower sense, 'inspired'; Inspiration for him was a sort of First Cause which had set him on a road where he had to look after himself. Hence his longing for rigid symbols. The French Symbolists wanted their symbols fluid because for them each experience was unique, the component parts of a complex of sensation and thought must not be separable from the whole and in a poem representing such a complex the individual words must only exist in and for the poem. To write by these standards a poet must have unusual physical sensitivity or a habit of genuinely mystical experience. Yeats, I think, had neither. As a poet he was as deliberate as Virgil. He wanted to dig out from history, or from what he called the Great Memory, a set of properties which would serve him as Virgil was served by the leavings of the Greeks. (p. 113)

The world of *A Vision* is determinist. Where D. H. Lawrence said 'Not, I, not I, but the wind that blows through me,' Yeats would have said 'Not I but the stars,' meaning an inexorable cycle which binds the individual. It is not however the stars themselves which govern the individual, for Yeats writes approvingly in *A Vision*: 'Ptolemy must have added new weight to the conviction of Plotinus that the stars did not themselves affect human destiny but were pointers which enabled us to calculate the condition of the universe at any particular moment and therefore its effect on the individual life.' This concession does not mitigate his determinism. Freedom for Yeats, as for Engels, was a recognition of necessity—but not of economic necessity, which he considered a vulgarism. Yeats's necessity is even more rigorous than the Communist's. The Communist can die for his cause in the belief that he is part of an inevitable forward process. For Yeats the inevitable process is not forwards but round and round, like his favourite Indian symbol of eternity, a serpent with its tail in its mouth. . . . Yeats however continued to blend into his system a sort of Berkeleian idealism, founded on the principle that things only exist in and for a perceiving mind. This mind, for Yeats, is not so much the mind of God as the super-mind of humanity of which all individual human minds are partial manifestations. . . . This view is essentially monist and refuses to recognize any pure objectivity because such objectivity implies too great a separateness in the objects concerned. (pp. 113-14)

A large section of *A Vision* consists of a classification of human types. Yeats disregards psychology as much as he disregards economics. According to his friends he was a poor judge of men, could be deceived by charlatans. Lacking intuitive knowledge of people he declined also to accept the explanations offered by professional psychologists. As in the other sections of *A Vision* he wants the vigour of an *a priori* philosophy but he wants vigour without logic. He would have thought it an indignity that a man's life should be conditioned by a word of his nurse's overheard when he was in a pram. If life is to be conditioned by accidents, the accidents must be supernatural.

Where he most nearly approaches psychology is in his basic principle that a man desires his opposite; he had observed this in himself—the contemplative man envying the life of action. This being so, a man's poetry, which is the expression of his desires, tends to be in a sense the contradiction of his life. He had written earlier, in *Per Amica Silentia Lunae:* 'When I think of any great poetical writer of the past . . . I comprehend, if I know the lineaments of his life, that the work is the man's flight from his entire horoscope, his blind struggle in the network of the stars.' In a sense then the poet as poet can escape up to a point from determinism. (p. 115)

This idea of the quarrel with ourselves, of the artist's search for his opposite, appears in *The Wild Swans at Coole* in the poem *Ego Dominus Tuus*. . . . The examples given here are Dante who, being himself lecherous and irresponsible, 'set his chisel to the hardest stone' and built a world upon Beatrice; and Keats whose 'art is happy, but who knows his mind?' The pursuit of one's opposite is also connected by Yeats with reincarnation. . . . The poet is always quarrelling with himself, perhaps because he half remembers himself in a past life as having been some one different. The quarrel is partly, but only partly, resolved in his poetry. He knows, however, that, to put it vulgarly, there is still time for everything; this is not his only day.

How far he really believed these doctrines it is, as I have said already, difficult to say, but they make a good vehicle for that cosmic pride which is common among artists. The artist is proud to be of the world but it enrages him to know himself such a small part of it. . . . [Yeats] preferred to think of history as an enormous kaleidoscope where each man in the changing but recurring patterns can play all the different rôles: only there must be no fusion, the pattern is always the pattern. *A Vision* with its seemingly arbitrary complexities is to be regarded as a diagram for something which Yeats knew to be unknowable; that he knew how any such diagram must be unjust to its concrete subject is proved by those poems which are professedly on the same theme; here what was static becomes dynamic, what was abstract concrete. That the diagram is merely ancillary to the poetry is admitted at the end of his introduction to *A Vision* . . . : 'Some will ask whether I believe in the actual existence of my circuits of sun and moon. . . . I regard them as stylistic arrangements of experience comparable to the cubes in the drawing of Wyndham Lewis and the ovoids in the sculpture of Brancusi. They have helped me to hold in a single thought reality and justice.'

The Wild Swans at Coole was followed by *Michael Robartes and the Dancer*. . . . *The Tower,* where his new poetry reached considerable greatness, did not follow till 1928 but some of the poems in it were written much earlier, some as early as 1919 and 1920. This was the period of the Troubles in Ireland; Yeats himself was troubled spiritually and physically.

His reaction to the Irish rebellion was, as I said, equivocal. (pp. 115-17)

This book contains three poems of homage to the martyrs of the 1916 rising. They are typical products of one who was not a man of action. . . . The man of action must not qualify, must not have any doubts. Yeats qualifies continually. Even in the patriotic memorial poem, *Easter 1916,* he suggests:

Was it needless death after all?

His attitude is still slightly patronizing and at the same time envious. He represents the rebels as ordinary enough men transformed by an ideal. (p. 118)

It was men like the Gaelic enthusiast, Pearse, and the dockhand balladist, Connolly, who made the rising and Yeats admits—admiringly—that they were transformed by it. But their hearts, he goes on, were thereby turned to stone. . . . [One] suspects that he is admiring the ritual of idolaters whose sacrifices he thinks are perhaps unnecessary.

The same book contains a great prophetic poem, **The Second Coming,** which is based upon his cyclic philosophy of gyres and reincarnation but which, allowance being made for this parable convention, can be taken as a direct prophecy of imminent disaster. There have been many such poems since the Great War, by such different poets as D. H. Lawrence and W. H. Auden, but Yeats differs from the others in that he implies that even the coming anarchy has its place in a pattern; the strong movement of the verse is appropriate to a poet who does not really expect the triumph of flux. . . . This [poem] has been taken by Mr Stephen Spender (in *The Destructive Element*) to refer to the coming of fascism. It is doubtful whether Yeats meant his prophecy so precisely, but 'the blood-dimmed tide' does represent that upsurge of instinctive violence which, other outlets being barred, finds a natural outlet in fascist mobmania. That the rise of this tide is heralded with a certain relish is attributable to the fact that Yeats had a budding fascist inside himself. With a fatalism parallel to that of the Marxists he felt that the world was ripe for the rule of 'the worst'. Paradoxically, perhaps, he felt that this would give the individual freedom as prison has been known to give it to prisoners and the Roman Catholic Church to Catholics; he never made the idea of freedom contingent on democracy. In his introduction to **The Words upon the Windowpane** . . . he justifies his own (perhaps sadistic, perhaps masochistic) determinism: 'though history is too short to change either the idea of progress or the eternal circuit into scientific fact, the eternal circuit may best suit our preoccupation with the soul's salvation, our individualism, our solitude.' Yet he himself—or the larger part of him—looked back longingly to an earlier 'phase of the moon', to 'the ceremony of innocence'. It is this ceremony which governs his **Prayer for my Daughter.**

It is interesting to compare **The Second Coming** with T. S. Eliot's crying in *The Waste Land*. Eliot, anti-Bolshevik like Yeats, is obsessed, as he admits in a note, with 'the present decay of eastern Europe', with the enervation of the general European tradition. But the passionate intensity of the worst holds no compensation for him. For him this is not merely a necessary turn of the wheel; it is the end, sheer dissolution. . . . The mere difference in versification between Eliot and Yeats represents here an essential difference in attitude; for Eliot both hope and heroism have vanished with regular metric, with punctuation. When the Auden school appeared, who were nominally affiliated to Communism, they showed much superficial resemblance to Eliot but, below the surface, they were actually nearer to Yeats; their early poetry was most often gloomy but it was more the gloom of tragedy than of defeatism, of nihilism. Like Yeats they opposed to the contemporary chaos a code of values, a belief in system, and—behind their utterances of warning—a belief in life, in the dignity, courage, and stamina of the human animal. Falling towers—yes. But, they suggest (their Marxist premises leading in the same direction as Yeats's) when a tower falls something comes up in its place. (pp. 119-120)

> *Louis MacNeice, in his* The Poetry of W. B. Yeats *(copyright, 1941, by Oxford University Press, New York, Inc.; reprinted by permission of the Literary Estate of Louis MacNeice), Oxford University Press, New York, 1941 (and reprinted by Faber and Faber, 1967, 207 p.).*

ALLEN TATE (essay date 1942)

[*Tate's criticism is closely associated with two American critical movements, the Agrarians and the New Critics. The Agrarians were concerned with political and social issues as well as literature, and were dedicated to preserving the Southern way of life and traditional Southern values. The New Critics, a group which included Cleanth Brooks and Robert Penn Warren, among others, comprised one of the most influential critical movements of the mid-twentieth century. Although the various New Critics did not subscribe to a single set of principles, all believed that a work of literature had to be examined as an object in itself through a process of close analysis of symbol, image, and metaphor. For the New Critics, a literary work was not a manifestation of ethics, sociology, or psychology, and could not be evaluated in the general terms of any nonliterary discipline. However, Tate adhered to a different vision of literature's purpose than did the other New Critics. A conservative thinker and convert to Catholicism, Tate attacked the tradition of Western philosophy which he felt has alienated persons from themselves, one another, and from nature by divorcing intellectual from natural functions in human life. For Tate, literature is the principal form of knowledge and revelation which restores human beings to a proper relationship with nature and the spiritual realm. In the excerpt below, Tate discusses Yeats's* A Vision *not as a philosophical system, but as an extended metaphor expressing Yeats's disenchantment with the modern world and his attempt to preserve vanishing traditions.*]

The profundity of Yeats's vision of the modern world and the width of its perspective have kept me until this occasion from writing anything about the poetry of our time which I most admire. The responsibility enjoins the final effort of understanding—an effort that even now I have not been able to make. The lesser poets invite the pride of the critic to its own affirmation; the greater poets—and Yeats is among them—ask us to understand not only their minds but our own; they ask us in fact to have minds of a related caliber to theirs. And criticism must necessarily remain in the presence of the great poets a business for the ant-hill: the smaller minds pooling their efforts. For the power of a Yeats will be given to the study of other poets only incidentally, for shock and technique and for the test of its own reach: this kind of power has its own task to perform.

Ours is the smaller task. The magnitude of Yeats is already visible in the failure of the partial, though frequently valuable, insights that the critics have given us in the past twenty years. There is enough in Yeats for countless studies from many points of view, yet I suspect that we shall languish far this side of the complete version of Yeats until we cease to look into him for qualities that neither Yeats nor any other poet can give us; until we cease to censure him for possessing "attitudes" and "beliefs" which we do not share. Mr. Edmund Wilson's essay on Yeats in the influential study of symbolism *Axel's Castle* [see *TCLC*, Vol. 1] asks the poet for a political and economic philosophy; or if this is unfair to Mr. Wilson, perhaps it could be fairly said that Mr. Wilson, when he was writing the essay, was looking for a political and economic philosophy, and inevitably saw in Yeats and the other heirs of symbolism an evasion of the reality that he, Mr. Wilson, was looking for. (If you are looking for pins you do not want needles, though both will prick you.) Mr. Louis MacNeice's book-length study of Yeats [see excerpt above] says shrewd things about the poetry, but on the whole we get the impression that Yeats had bad luck in not belonging to the younger group of English poets, who had a monopoly on "reality." (The word is Mr. MacNeice's.) Those were the days when not to be a communist was to be fascist, which is what Mr. MacNeice makes Yeats out to be. (Yeats liked the ancient "nobility," of which for Mr. MacNeice, Wall Street and the City offer examples.)

I cite these two writers on Yeats because in them we get summed up the case for Yeats's romanticism, the view that he was an escapist retiring from problems, forces, and theories "relevant" to the modern world. While it is true that Yeats, like every poet in English since the end of the eighteenth century, began with a romantic use of language in the early poems, he ended up very differently, and he is no more to be fixed as a romantic than Shakespeare as a Senecan because he wrote passages of Senecan rhetoric. If one of the historic marks of romanticism is the division between sensibility and intellect, Yeats's career may be seen as unromantic (I do not know the opposite term) because he closed the gap. His critics would then be the romantics. I do not think that these squabbles are profitable. It is still true that Yeats had a more inclusive mind than any of his critics has had. (pp. 214-16)

The picture of a perfect culture that [Yeats] gives us in Byzantium (which in the poem of that name becomes something more than mere historical insight) where men enjoy full unity of being has too many features in common with familiar Western ideas to be seen as an eccentric piece of utopianism. Byzantium is a new pastoral symbol and will be taken as that by anybody who sees more in the pastoral tradition than ideal shepherds and abstract sheep. The annunciation to Leda offers historical and philosophical difficulties; yet in spite of Yeats's frequently expressed belief that he had found a new historical vision, the conception is not historical in any sense that we understand today. It is a symbol established in analogical terms; that is, our literal grasp of it depends upon prior knowledge of the Annunciation to the Virgin. The "Babylonian mathematical starlight" is self-evidently clear without Yeats's scattered glosses on it: it is darkness and abstraction, quantitative relations without imagination; and I doubt that Yeats's definitions make it much clearer than that. If Leda rejected it, we only learn from Yeats's "system" that the coming of Christ brought it back in; for an entire cultural cycle can be predominantly antithetical or predominantly primary, at the same time that it goes through the twenty-eight phases from primary to antithetical back to primary again.

In [a] letter to Dorothy Wellesley occurs a sentence which sounds casual, even literally confessional; there is no harm done if we take it at that level; there is merely a loss of insight such as we get in Mr. MacNeice's *The Poetry of W. B. Yeats,* in which Yeats's myth is dismissed as "arid" and "unsound." . . . [Yeats] writes: "In my own life I have never felt so acutely the presence of a spiritual virtue and that is accompanied by intensified desire." The literal student of *A Vision,* coming upon statements like this, may well wonder what has become of the determinism of the system, which, with an almost perverse ingenuity, seems to fix the individual in a system of co-ordinates from which he cannot escape. Mr. Cleanth Brooks [see excerpt above] believes that some measure of free will lies in Yeats's conception of the False Mask, which some unpredictable force in the individual may lead him to choose instead of the True Mask. I believe this is only part of the explanation.

Does not the true explanation lie in there being *no* explanation in terms of the system? . . . Mr. MacNeice at this point en-

lightens us almost in spite of himself: "Freedom for Yeats, as for Engels, was a recognition of necessity—but not of economic necessity, which he considered a vulgarism." Yes; and he would have considered psychological necessity, or any inner determinism no less than an outer, economic determinism, a vulgarism also. But in the phrase the "recognition of necessity" we get a clue to Yeats's own relation to his system and to what seems to me the right way to estimate its value. He only wanted what all men want, a world larger than himself to live in; for the modern world as he saw it was, in human terms, too small for the human spirit, though quantitatively large if looked at with the scientist. If we say, then, that he wanted a *dramatic* recognition of necessity, we shall have to look at the system not as arid or unsound or eccentric, which it well may be in itself, but through Yeats's eyes, which are the eyes of his poetry.

If we begin with the poetry we shall quickly see that there is some source of power or illumination which is also in us, waiting to be aroused; and that this is true of even the greater number of the fine poems in which the imagery appears upon later study to lean upon the eccentric system. I would say, then, that even the terms of the system, when they appear in the richer texture of the poems, share a certain large margin of significance with a wider context than they have in the system itself. May we say that Yeats's *A Vision,* however private and almost childishly eclectic it may seem, has somewhat the same relation to a central tradition as the far more rigid structure of *The Divine Comedy* has to the Christian myth? I dare say that Mr. Eliot would not chide Dante for accepting a "lower mythology." Perhaps the central tradition in Dante and Yeats lies in a force that criticism cannot specifically isolate, the force that moved both poets to the dramatic recognition of necessity; yet the visible structure of the necessity itself is perhaps not the source of that power. I do not say that Yeats is comparable in stature to Dante; only that both poets strove for a visible structure of action which is indeed necessary to what they said, but which does not explain what they said. I believe that Mr. Eliot should undertake to explain why Arnold's Higher Mythology produced poetry less interesting than Yeats's Lower Mythology, which becomes in Yeats's verse the vehicle of insights and imaginative syntheses as profound as those which Arnold talked about but never, as a poet, fully achieved. Myths differ in range and intensity, but not I take it as high and low; for they are in the end what poets can make of them. (pp. 217-19)

A Vision has been described by more than one critic as a philosophy; I speak of it here as a "system"; but I doubt that it is a system of philosophy. What kind of system is it? Yeats frequently stated his own purpose, but even that is a little obscure: to put myth back into philosophy. This phrase may roughly describe the result, but it could not stand for the process; it attributes to the early philosophers a deliberation of which they would have been incapable. . . .

In what sense is *A Vision* a myth? There are fragments of many myths brought in to give dramatic and sensuous body to the framework, which attains to the limit of visualization that a complex geometrical picture can provide. (p. 220)

It is clear visually with the aid of the diagrams; but when Yeats complicates it with his Principles and Daimons, and extends the symbol of the gyres to cover historical eras, visualization breaks down. It is an extended metaphor which increasingly tends to dissolve in the particulars which it tries to bring together into unity.

When we come to the magnificent passages on history in **"Dove or Swan"** all the intricacies of the geometrical metaphor disappear; and the simple figure of historical cycles, which Yeats evidently supposed came out of his gyres, is sufficient to sustain his meaning. Again Yeats's "system" overlaps a body of insight common to us all.

I would suggest, then, for the study of the relation of Yeats's "system" to his vision of man, both historical and individual, this formula: As the system broadens out and merges with the traditional insights of our culture, it tends to disappear in its specific, technical aspects. What disappears is not a philosophy, but only a vast metaphorical structure. In the great elegy, **"In Memory of Major Robert Gregory,"** we get this couplet:

> But as the outrageous stars incline
> By opposition, square, and trine—

which is the only astrological figure in the poem. Yet it must not be assumed that Yeats on this occasion turned off the system; it must be there. Why does it not overtly appear? It has been absorbed into the concrete substance of the poem; the material to be symbolized replaces the symbol, and contains its own meaning. I would select this poem out of all others of our time as the most completely expressed: it has a perfect articulation and lucidity which cannot be found in any other modern poem in English. (pp. 220-21)

[The] remarkable feature of the system, as I see it, is that it is not a mythology at all, but rather an extended metaphor, as I have already pointed out, which permits him to establish relations between the tag-ends of myths eclectically gathered from all over the world. For example, there is nothing in the geometrical structure of the system which inherently provides for the annunciation to Leda; it is an arbitrary association of two fields of imagery; but once it is established, it is not hard to pass on through analogy to the Annunciation to the Virgin.

Thus it is difficult for me to follow those critics who accept Yeats's various utterances that he was concerned with a certain relation of philosophy to myth. Any statement about "life" must have philosophical implications, just as any genuine philosophical statement must have, because of the nature of language, mythical implications. Yeats's doctrine of the conflict of opposites says nothing about the fundamental nature of reality; it is rather a dramatic framework through which is made visible the perpetual oscillation of man between extreme introspection and extreme loss of the self in the world of action. The intricacies of Yeats's system provide for many of the permutations of this relation; but it cannot foresee them all; and we are constantly brought back to the individual man, not as a symbolic counter, but as a personality rich and unpredictable. Yeats's preference for the nobleman, the peasant, and the craftsman does not betray, as Mr. MacNeice's somewhat provincial contention holds, the "budding fascist"; it is a "version of pastoral" which permits Yeats to see his characters acting above the ordinary dignity of men, in a concrete relation to life undiluted by calculation and abstraction. I can only repeat here that the "system" is perpetually absorbed into action. If Yeats were only an allegorist, the meaning of his poetry could be ascertained by getting hold of the right key. The poetry would serve to illustrate the "system," as the poetry of the Prophetic Books fleshes out the homemade system of Blake.

Mr. Eliot's view, that Yeats got off the central tradition into a "minor mythology," and Mr. Blackmur's view, that he took "magic" (as opposed to religion) as far as any poet could [see *TCLC*, Vol. 1], seem to me to be related versions of the same fallacy. Which is: that there must be a direct and effective correlation between the previously established truth of the poet's ideas and the value of the poetry. (I am oversimplifying Blackmur's view, but not Eliot's.) In this difficulty it is always useful to ask: *Where* are the poet's ideas? Good sense in this matter ought to tell us that while the ideas doubtless exist in some form outside the poetry, as they exist for Yeats in the letters, the essays, and *A Vision,* we must nevertheless test them in the poems themselves, and not "refute" a poem in which the gyres supply certain images by showing that gyres are amateur philosophy. . . . [The] opening lines of **"The Second Coming"** . . . make enough sense apart from our knowledge of the system; the gyre here can be visualized as the circling flight of the bird constantly widening until it has lost contact with the point, the center, to which it ought to be able to return. As a symbol of disunity it is no more esoteric than Eliot's "Gull against the wind," at the end of "Gerontion," which is a casual, not traditional or systematic, symbol of disunity. Both Mr. Blackmur and Mr. Brooks—Mr. Brooks more than Mr. Blackmur—show us the systematic implications of the symbols of the poem **"Byzantium."** The presence of the system at its most formidable cannot be denied to this poem. I should like to see, nevertheless, an analysis of it in which no special knowledge is used; I should like to see it examined with the ordinary critical equipment of the educated critic; I should be surprised if the result were very different from Mr. Brooks's reading of the poem. The symbols are "made good" in the poem; they are drawn into a wider convention (Mr. Blackmur calls it the "heaven of man's mind") than they would imply if taken separately.

I conclude these notes with the remark: the study of Yeats in the coming generation is likely to overdo the scholarly procedure, and the result will be the occultation of a poetry which I believe is nearer the center of our main traditions of sensibility and thought than the poetry of Eliot or Pound. Yeats's special qualities will instigate special studies of great ingenuity, but the more direct and more difficult problem of the poetry itself will probably be delayed. This is only to say that Yeats's romanticism will be created by his critics. (pp. 222-24)

Allen Tate, "Yeats's Romanticism: Notes and Suggestions" (copyright, 1942, by Allen Tate), in The Southern Review, Special Issue: W. B. Yeats, *Vol. 7, No. 3, Winter, 1942 (and reprinted as "Yeats's Romanticism," in his* On the Limits of Poetry: Selected Essays, 1928-1948, *The Swallow Press, 1948, pp. 214-24).*

JAMES STEPHENS (essay date 1942)

[*A member of the Irish Literary Renaissance and friend of Yeats, Stephens is best known for his tales and poems based on Irish folklore and mythology.*]

[If] I were asked what modern poet is best to be acquainted with, and best worth carrying, then I should plump for Willy Yeats. As Wordsworth was the most individual and personal poet of his time, so Yeats is the most individual and personal poet of our day. There are very few poets of whom it can be said, "Who touches this book touches a man": it can be said of Donne and Wordsworth, and curiously, Yeats. All other poets are, as it were, writing on another than the personal plane, and, very properly, forgetting themselves in a meditation on God and man and nature, so that one could easily conceive that in general, poets have no personal life at all.

Wordsworth in almost every poem is present, and is speaking personally to his personal friend, the reader, and there is more of the individual and communicative quality to be found in Yeats than in any other modern poet I know of. Shelley and Keats are not writing about you and me and themselves, and our own hills and vales and neighbours. They are writing about other and further and stranger matters. They are not good poets for hard, homeless times like ours. Yeats' poems often smell of the ground he walked on, and sound of the people he was interested in, or angry with, or hoping to get his own back upon. (p. 68)

> *James Stephens, ''W. B. Yeats'' (1942; © Iris Clare Wise 1962, 1964; reprinted by permission of The Society of Authors on behalf of Mrs. Iris Wise), in his* James, Seumas & Jacques: Unpublished Writings of James Stephens, *edited by Lloyd Frankenburg, The Macmillan Company, 1964, pp. 67-72.*

VIVIAN DE SOLA PINTO (essay date 1965)

[*In this survey of Yeats's work de Sola Pinto praises Yeats for his continual development as a poet, but decries his use of native Irish materials as ''mere antiquarianism.''*]

The mythology which Yeats used extensively in his early poems was the great body of Gaelic heroic legend which had been presented to English readers of the late eighteenth century in the faked prose ''epics'' of Ossian by the Scottish schoolmaster Macpherson, and which was available for a young poet a hundred years later in the more scholarly and authentic versions published by Standish O'Grady and Douglas Hyde. This mythology had never been wholly forgotten in Ireland and for the young Yeats it had the fascination that Greek mythology had for the men of the Renaissance. For him it was no mere antiquarianism but something which he wholly absorbed and made part of his imaginative life as Milton absorbed the Hebrew sagas and Keats the Greek myths. ''Might I not'', he wrote, ''with health and good luck to aid me, create some new *Prometheus Unbound,* Patrick or Columbkell, Oisin or Finn in Prometheus' stead, and instead of Caucasus, Cro-Patrick or Ben Bulben?'' This ambition to treat heroic themes on a large scale was very different from the spirit of the English Rhymers with their concentration on short, highly wrought poems. In 1905, he complained that ''modern literature and above all poetical literature is monotonous in its structure and effeminate in its continual insistence on certain moments of strained lyricism.'' His own much-anthologized early lyrics include exquisite examples of this strained lyricism. . . . [For] instance, in *When you are old* he pictures Maud Gonne as an old woman nodding by the fire. . . . As John Davidson recognized, there was, however, in the young Irishman too much ''blood and guts'' for him to remain satisfied for long with poetry of this kind.

Very early in his career he attempted to treat legendary material on a large scale. *The Wanderings of Oisin* is a long romantic narrative poem full of echoes of Morris, Shelley, Coleridge, Keats and Sir Samuel Fergusson. As he admitted later, ''it has the overcharged colour inherited from the romantic movement''. Yet the mythology of Niam and Angus, the Fenians and the Danaans is fresh and has ''the beauty and wonder of altogether new things''. Moreover, the conflict between the old Celtic bard, Oisin (Macpherson's ''Ossian'') and St. Patrick is no mere piece of romantic antiquarianism but a symbol of a permanent and unresolved conflict in the European mind between the ideal of the artist and that of religion.

The same theme is treated dramatically in the short play called *The Land of Heart's Desire* where the conflict is placed in a peasant setting. The struggle for the soul of the girl Mary Bruin is a tragic theme because it is a struggle between two powers both of which are respected by the poet. . . . Yeats always preferred the world of the poetic imagination to the world of religion, but he knew that Mary Bruin's choice was a dangerous one. From the beginning his faery world was not the tinsel of the English Victorian imagination, but a world which was at once terrible and beautiful. (pp. 90-2)

The Countess Cathleen, his first full length play, was originally written when he was little more than a boy but was repeatedly altered and revised. It is in the traditional English Shakespearian form and is full of Pre-Raphaelite decoration. Nevertheless, there are also touches of sharp realism which contrast with the literary flavour of the speeches about Celtic mythology. . . . The Countess is a highly idealized Maud Gonne and Aleel the Poet is doubtless an equally idealized Yeats, but the central theme is no mere romantic fancy. The demon merchants who buy the souls of the starving peasants clearly represent the commercialism of Yeats's own day which was corrupting the minds of men all over Europe, and Shemus's mad song, when he has sold his soul, is the work of a poet who had already grasped the significance of the crisis of the modern world. (p. 92)

Yeats began as a late Romantic and Pre-Raphaelite with the additional advantage of contact with Irish mythological tradition and folk culture. What is remarkable about his whole career is his sustained power of development. He could not remain a poet of the Celtic Twilight. In the second phase of his work represented by *The Wind among the Reeds* . . . and *The Shadowy Waters* . . . he is making the Voyage Within, withdrawing as much as possible from the contemporary world and enriching his inner life by concentrating on purely visionary themes. This phase of his work is comparable with Hopkins's arduous spiritual training as a Jesuit. The religion which served as a means to purify and intensify Yeats's inner life was Symbolism and the high priest of the great French Symbolist movement was Stephane Mallarmé. (pp. 92-3)

Yeats accepted wholeheartedly Mallarmé's conception of 'pure' poetry. In his essay on **''The Symbolism of Poetry''** he called for ''a return to the way of our fathers, a casting out of descriptions of nature for the sake of nature, of the moral law for the sake of the moral law, a casting out of all anecdotes and of that brooding over scientific opinion that so often extinguished the central flame in Tennyson''. (p. 93)

Instead of the private symbols of Mallarmé, which are always, in part, at least, unintelligible, Yeats uses the images of Celtic mythology in his symbolic poems. These are at once more precise than Mallarmé's inventions and also have a richness of association which Mallarmé's symbols lacked. In his earlier works Yeats had used the ancient Irish myths simply as stories; in the poems in *The Wind among the Reeds* he uses them to express his own states of mind. Thus in *The Song of Wandering Aengus* he takes the story of the ancient Irish hero who dreamed of a wonderfully beautiful maiden and searched for her throughout Ireland. Yeats turns the story into a symbol (not an allegory) of the search of the poet for an unattainable beauty. . . . (p. 94)

This poem contains echoes of Morris's *Nymph's Song to Hylas,* but it is at once more precise and richer in texture than Morris's vague nostalgic poem. The symbolism is perfectly intelligible but it has the magic of song and is not dimmed by any prosaic moralizing. In some poems, however, in this collection Yeats uses symbols which have no precise or intelligible meaning but which live by their own power and intensity. Such a poem is *The Cap and the Bells* which is founded on a dream. No intellectual meaning can be attached to this jester who sends his soul in the shape of "a straight blue garment" and his heart in the shape of "a red and quivering garment" to the young queen. Nevertheless it is an impressive and moving poem and the symbols have a great emotional intensity. . . . (pp. 94-5)

In his note on *The Cap and the Bells,* Yeats wrote, "The poem has always meant a great deal to me, though, as is the way with symbolic poems, it has not always meant quite the same thing. Blake would have said, 'the authors are in eternity', and I am quite sure they can only be questioned in dreams". This note shows that Yeats's symbolism (unlike that of Mallarmé) is connected with a belief in occult influences and magic.

Yeats's most ambitious and elaborate symbolist work is the dramatic poem called *The Shadowy Waters.* He tried to adapt it for performance on the stage but never succeeded. It is essentially undramatic, a magnificent lyric in dialogue where all the characters speak with the voice of the poet. The image of a private ship sailing into unknown seas had haunted Yeats from his boyhood. The story of the pirate Forgael, the queen Dectora whom he captures and bewitches and the birds with human heads who follow his ship has no meaning that can be translated into intellectual terms, but like the jester and the queen in *The Cap and the Bells* these characters are highly successful symbols of emotional states that defy analysis. *The Shadowy Waters* is a great hymn to the romantic conception of a love that passes human understanding. . . . The rich music of the last lines of the play is one of the most splendid of all expressions of this ideal of romantic love. . . . *The Shadowy Waters* is the culmination of Yeats's symbolist poetry. Reading Mallarmé many years later he wrote "this was the road I and others of my time went for certain furlongs. . . . It is not the way I go now but one of the legitimate roads". Some of the poems in the collection called *In the Seven Woods* . . . are still in the symbolist manner but in [*Adam's Curse*] at least there is a new note of sharp satire and realism. . . . (pp. 95-6)

At the end of the collection Yeats placed the remarkable poem called *The Happy Townland,* which might be called his farewell to Symbolism. In one sense of the term he always remained a symbolist, but the Symbolism of the school of Mallarmé was too inhuman a doctrine to provide a permanent home for his rich and vital personality. In *The Happy Townland* he uses the popular Irish myth of a faery world of ideal happiness where men are freed from the cares of material existence, but now instead of conceiving it in the vague misty manner of his early poem, he paints it in sharp, brilliant colours and concrete forms. . . .

The happy townland is a place of danger as well as beauty and the traveller is warned. . . . (p. 97)

This poem is a turning point in Yeats's development. He had made the Voyage Within and had discovered the beauty of the Inner Life, but he had also discovered that it was a terrible, inhuman beauty . . . "the world's bane". This discovery made him the master and not the servant of the terror.

After Yeats had made his great exploration of the inner life under the guidance of the Symbolists, circumstances enabled him to make the Voyage Without in the stimulating atmosphere of Dublin in the opening years of the twentieth century, the Dublin of Mr. Bloom and James Joyce's youth, of the Gaelic League and the early days of Sinn Fein and above all of the Abbey Theatre and the Irish literary movement of which he was the acknowledged leader. The aesthetic recluse of the Rhymers' Club, the student of the occult and adept of the Order of the Golden Dawn, the guest of Lady Gregory at Coole, now became a public figure in Dublin, dramatist, orator, wit and conversationalist. (pp. 97-8)

The genius of Synge made an enormous impression on Yeats at this time. The younger writer's "harsh, heroical, clean, windswept view of things" was exactly the stimulant that was needed by a poet who was growing weary of romantic idealism and the inhumanity of symbolist doctrine. The fullest expression of Synge's genius is, of course, to be found in his plays, but his handful of short poems must be reckoned as an important contribution to the poetry of the modern crisis. . . . Nothing could be more unlike Yeats's early poems about "white beauty", "pearl pale hands" and "cloud-pale eyelids".

During the first six years of the twentieth century Yeats worked hard at writing plays for the Abbey Theatre. These plays were part of the means by which he was trying to create a new 'unity of life' for the whole Irish people based on their traditional heroic legends. The best of them are the two fine tragedies, *On Baile's Strand* . . . and *Deirdre*. . . . Unlike *The Shadowy Waters* and even *The Countess Cathleen* they are essentially acting plays written for the stage by a poet who is also a man of the theatre. Yeats was too subjective and too lyrical to be a great dramatist yet he had a passion for the theatre and never ceased from experimenting in the drama up to the end of his career. To make plays that would act well he had to write clearly and concisely and to discipline his imagination by constructing shapely and effective plots. The clarity and directness of the speeches in these plays is very different from the romantic vagueness of his earlier work. . . . In spite of their great merits, these plays suffer from the fact that they are built on an illusion. Yeats believed when he wrote them that by using the Gaelic legends he could "bring the old folk life to Dublin . . . and with the folk life all the life of the heart." In other words he thought he could create an audience like the audience of Shakespeare or Sophocles in twentieth-century Dublin. Actually, the legendary material, whatever it may have been among the peasants in Galway or Kerry, was mere antiquarianism in the Dublin of Mr. Bloom. For Yeats himself the world of the old Irish sagas was a dream world providing a refuge from the ugliness of contemporary life. This is not the material out of which great drama can be made. All Yeats's plans seemed to have failed in the years immediately preceding the First World War. Synge had died, an unhappy and disappointed man. The Abbey Theatre gave up the attempt to become the ideal "People's Theatre" of his dreams, and under the management of Lennox Robinson concerned itself chiefly with realistic plays, "objective with the objectivity of the office and the workshop, of the newspaper and the street, of mechanism and of politics". Finally, after a bitter struggle the Dublin Corporation rejected Sir Hugh Lane's proposals for a great Irish Gallery of Modern Art. Some of Yeats's contemporaries thought his literary career was at an end. Actually the most important phase of it was only just beginning. Like Dante and Milton he only started to write his greatest poetry when all his projects in the sphere of action had ended in complete disaster.

The beginning of the new Yeats is to be found in the poems published with *The Green Helmet*. . . . From these poems the romantic decoration, the mythology and the vague incantatory music of his earlier works have been almost entirely banished.

In their place there is terse, unadorned language and rhythms of an almost Wordsworthian simplicity. The emotion communicated by Yeats's earlier lyrics is nearly always vague and remote. In the poems published with *The Green Helmet* there is a new immediacy and concreteness. For instance the poem called *No Second Troy,* unlike the early poems on Maud Gonne, makes the reader share not a vague general emotion but a particular experience. . . . The fourth line of this poem illustrates the new concreteness of this phase of Yeats's poetry and also a new power of including in poetic experience material from daily life which had hitherto been avoided. The poem is not a contemplation of abstract love but a successful attempt to show what it is like to love a particular beautiful woman who is also a political agitator.

The turning point in Yeats's development was the publication of the volume of poems called *Responsibilities.* . . . In these poems he widens the scope of his subject matter to include ironic commentary on contemporary affairs. The splendid elegy on O'Leary is poetry made out of the stuff of contemporary life, and of the poet's contempt for its sordid spirit of money-grubbing. . . . Now instead of the remote mythology of Gaelic legend he creates a new mythology out of the memory of the patriots of eighteenth-century Ireland who still lived in the popular imagination. . . . Here the language is that of common speech but, as in Synge's poems, it is ennobled by sheer intensity of passion. Yeats has come out of the ivory tower of symbolism, but he has brought with him a power capable of transforming contemporary actualities into the material of high poetry. The poem called *A Coat* is at once a searching self-criticism and a manifesto of a new art which would no longer evade actualities. . . . Yeats was in Dublin at the time of the Rebellion of Easter 1916. He was deeply moved by the heroism and the martyrdom of the insurgents. He had little sympathy with their political methods, but with a true poet's insight he saw that the whole Irish scene was transformed by the tragedy of their execution. Now he no longer writes of contemporary Ireland with scorn or irony but of the common life of Dublin irradiated by the magnificence of tragedy. . . .

> "There's nothing but our own red blood
> Can make a right Rose Tree."

The Rose, which in Yeats's early poems was a symbol of an unattainable dream world has now become a symbol of a living political idealism. Yeats's political poems are not magical incantations or exorcisms like Kipling's. They are sane, clear-eyed and unsentimental. He is not afraid to call one of the martyrs "a drunken vainglorious lout". He even suggests that their death may after all be "needless", "For England may keep faith". It is the moderation and sanity which gives such tremendous power to his celebration of the heroism of the men who died in April 1916.

Yeats's most memorable and important poetry was not written till he was over fifty. It is to be found in the series of volumes which he published in the years immediately following the end of the First World War: [*The Wild Swans at Coole, Michael Robartes and The Dancer, The Tower* and *The Winding Stair*]. . . . In these years he was reading widely in the philosophers, Plato, Plotinus, Vico, Hegel, Croce and Whitehead, and he was particularly impressed by the idealism of George Berkeley, the Irish eighteenth-century bishop, "God-appointed Berkeley who proved all things a dream". From about 1920 onwards he was working out the curious and elaborate system of occult thought which he expounded in the prose work called *A Vision.* . . . The lady whom he had married in 1916 was a medium and with her he had conducted various experiments in spiritualism. He could not be content with the illogical dualism of the average modern man who accepts scientific naturalism with one part of his mind and belief in a divinely revealed religion with the other. On the other hand he could not accept the traditional Christian theology. As he himself wrote, he had an essentially religious mind; his mind was also orderly and logical. So, like William Blake, he constructed a system of belief out of his own private experiences. This is the system of *A Vision,* a doctrine of reincarnation, according to which all the types of humanity are arranged in a cycle or "Great Wheel" consisting of twenty-eight phases corresponding to the phases of the moon. Every soul has to pass through these twenty-eight phases and history is simply a cyclic repetition of the phases of the Great Wheel. The system is further complicated by the division of each soul into four "faculties": "will", "mask", "creative mind" and "body of fate". It is strange to find Yeats elaborating this fanciful yet inhuman and abstract system of determinism accompanied by various romantic mystifications at the very time when his personality was acquiring an unrivalled richness and power through a new vital contact with humanity and the contemporary world. He himself was fond of quoting Goethe's saying that "a poet cannot have too much philosophy but he ought to keep it out of his poetry". Yeats did not keep the "philosophy" of *A Vision* out of all his later poems, but those in which he used it directly such as *Ego Dominus Tuus, The Phases of the Moon* and *The Double Vision of Michael Robartes,* in spite of notable passages, are artistic failures. The "philosophy" seems to have been chiefly valuable not as the material for poetry but as a kind of map of the inner life, a spiritual framework like that which Catholicism provided for Hopkins. The power and intensity of the best poems in his later volumes was certainly due to a synthesis of a realistic and humorous view of life with the strengthened visionary power arising from his occult adventures. Soon after the first version of *A Vision* was published he wrote of it as something which he had to get out of his system before the poetry he wanted to write would be possible: "I have not . . . dealt with the whole of my subject . . . but I am longing to put it out of my reach that I may write the poetry it seems to have made possible. I can now, if I have the energy, find the simplicity I have sought in vain. I need no longer write poems like *The Phases of the Moon*. . . . Nor spend years . . . striving with abstractions". *A Vision* did not provide a new mythology for Yeats's later poetry but it provided a background which illuminates the dynamic myths of his maturity with a visionary radiance.

In this poetry the vague figures of Celtic legend and the tragic heroes of 1916 are replaced partly by the great men of Protestant eighteenth-century Ireland, Swift and Berkeley, Goldsmith and Burke, partly by the figures who had played a significant part in Yeats's own experience, Lionel Johnson, "that loved his learning better than mankind", "that enquiring man John Synge" and "old George Pollexfen, in muscular youth well known to Mayo men". Yeats remained a symbolist in his later poetry but he now moved to a far wider and deeper conception of symbolism, which was his interpretation of Platonic idealism particularly in the form in which it was restated by Berkeley. He now saw the whole material world as a symbolic dramatization of eternity and he was free to choose his symbols from the whole range of his reading and personal experience. Two of the most impressive are Byzantium, the holy city, which is at once an idealized Ireland and a timeless paradise, and the image of himself as a terrible and dynamic old man for whom old age is not decrepitude but a spiritual adventure. This is the old poet of *Sailing to Byzantium,* a poem where he achieves a true 'unity of life', 'an organic thing . . . the flow of flesh under the impulse of passionate thought'. The subject of this poem is really the same as that of *The Song of Wandering Aengus* and *The Shadowy Waters,* the quest for a timeless existence transcending the world of sensuous experience. But now this theme is embodied not in the vaguely beautiful symbols of romantic love but in images which (to use Ben Jonson's phrase that Yeats was fond of quoting) are ''ramm'd with life''. . . . Against [the] ''richly concrete evocation of instinctive life'' the figure of the old poet is seen, at once slightly ridiculous and yet frightening. . . . (pp. 98-106)

In the *Song of Wandering Aengus* the poet's imagination is not capacious enough to include laughter. In *Sailing to Byzantium* he can laugh at the absurdity of the scarecrow body of the old man and yet retain his dignity and seriousness. The laughter is drowned in the noble music that announces the voyage to the 'holy city of Byzantium', no dim wraith like the ''glimmering girl'' of the earlier poem but the concrete splendour of the Byzantine mosaic representing a timeless world that lives with a life more intense than that of the ''dying generations'' of the first stanza. . . .

Sailing to Byzantium . . . should be read in conjunction with its sequel, *Byzantium* written four years later. The first poem is a picture of a voyage from the material world to the holy city of eternity; the second is a vision of the city from the inside where the soul is imaged first as a walking mummy and then as the Emperor's golden bird, whose ''glory of changeless metal'' is contrasted with the ''complexities of mire and blood''. Here Byzantium is a Purgatory as well as a Paradise, a place of cleansing flames. . . . (p. 107)

Sailing to Byzantium is a meditation on timeless existence or eternity. *Among Schoolchildren,* the other great achievement of Yeats's maturity, is a meditation on existence in time, the world of becoming. As *Sailing to Byzantium* can be related to *The Song of Wandering Aengus, Among Schoolchildren* can be related to the early poems on Maud Gonne such as *When you are old.* . . . In that poem Yeats, following Ronsard, had imagined his mistress in old age sitting by the fire and remembering his love, and had then allowed his mood of vague desire to lead him to the sentimental image of Love on the mountains hiding his face ''amid a crowd of stars''. In *Among Schoolchildren* he starts with a vivid picture of himself as an elderly senator of the Irish Free State inspecting a convent school. Again there is ironic humour both in the glimpse of the education of the children and in the self-portrait. . . . The sight of the girls recalls Maud Gonne, not imagined in a vague romantic old age, but as she actually was when, ''bent above a sinking fire'', she told the poet of ''a harsh reproof or trivial event, that changed some childish day to a tragedy''. . . . The ageing Maud Gonne is no mere fantasy but a living woman whose fading beauty is contrasted with the freshness of childhood. . . . Beside the pathos of this portrait is set the mockery of the old poet in his official mask of respectability. . . . This record of personal experience is the prelude to a series of questionings on the mystery of life. First there is the paradox of the suffering of the mother in travail for ''a shape upon her lap'' which must turn at last into the ''comfortable kind of old scarecrow'', ''that shape with sixty or more winters on its head''. Then the theories of the philosophers are set forth in dancing lyrical music and dismissed with flashing wit. . . . Finally the nuns like the mothers are shown worshipping images, though theirs are lit by candles and ''keep a marble or

a bronze repose''. These ''Presences'' symbolize ''all heavenly glory'' and yet they too are:

> Self-born mockers of man's enterprise.

The last stanza answers all the questionings by showing a beauty which is perpetual growth and movement, the wholeness of life which defies analysis. . . .

> O body swayed to music, O brightening glance,
> How can we know the dancer from the dance?

This is poetry in which the outer and inner lives are brought together in a unity which includes realism, wit, lyrical beauty and philosophic meditation. It is not a synthesis in which we feel a sense of terrible effort and strain as we do in much of the best work of Hopkins, but it seems to arise easily and naturally from the poet's mind. . . . In a few great poems Yeats achieved this triumphant wholeness of poetic life. His great ambition of creating a 'unity of life' for the whole Irish nation was shattered by the vulgarity and insensitiveness of the modern world. In his old age he gloried in being unpopular, identifying himself deliberately with aristocracy and wealth, the life of the great country houses—which was indeed little more than an empty memory in the twentieth century—and flirting with fascism, which he seems at first to have mistaken for the beginning of a new aristocratic civilization. He had, he writes, a conception that had freed him ''from British Liberalism and all its dreams'', but he was never completely emancipated from nineteenth-century romanticism in spite of his rejection of romantic diction and romantic imagery. In his early poems he uses the vague and beautiful images of flowers, stars, birds and mythical figures as an escape from the ugliness of his age. In his later poetry he uses the more realistic images of drunkards and lechers, Crazy Jane and Tom the Lunatic and finally the figure of the mad, reckless old poet in that splendid piece of bravado, *The Statesman's Holiday.* . . . There is much more vitality here than in the poetry of the Celtic Twilight, but it is really only another kind of defiant protest against that ugliness and vulgarity which Yeats called Whiggery. . . . Both are the work of an isolated and therefore incomplete genius, and, in this sense, Yeats's work, like that of Hopkins, if judged by the highest standards, can be called, as L. C. Knights has called it, ''a heroic failure''. (pp. 107-11)

> *Vivian de Sola Pinto, ''Yeats and Synge,'' in her* Crisis in English Poetry, 1880-1940 *(© V. de S. Pinto 1958 and 1961), fourth edition, Hutchinson University Library, 1965, pp. 85-111.**

HAROLD BLOOM   (essay date 1970)

[In The Anxiety of Influence *(1973), Bloom formulated a controversial theory of literary creation called revisionism. Influenced strongly by Freudian theory, which states that ''all men unconsciously wish to beget themselves, to be their own fathers,'' Bloom believes that all poets are subject to the influence of earlier poets and that, to develop their own voice, they attempt to overcome this influence through a process of misreading. By misreading, Bloom means a deliberate, personal revision of what has been said by another so that it conforms to one's own vision: ''Poetic influence—when it involves two strong, authentic poets—always proceeds by a misreading of the prior poet, and act of creative correction that is actually and necessarily a misrepresentation. The history of poetic influence . . . is a history of anxiety and self-serving caricature, of distortion, of perverse, wilful revisionism.'' In this way the poet overcomes the fear that his poetry will be inferior to that of his predecessors and creates his own voice. Bloom's later books are applications of this theory,*

extended in Kabbalah and Criticism *(1974) to include the critic or reader as another deliberate misreader. Thus, there is no single reading of any text, but multiple readings by strong poets or critics who understand a work only in ways that allow them to assert their own individuality or vision. In addition to his theoretical work, Bloom is one of the foremost authorities on English romantic poetry and has written widely on the influences of Romanticism in contemporary literature. His* Yeats *is considered one of the best and most detailed analyses of Yeats's important poems. Although Bloom rejects Yeats's deterministic philosophy and denial of free will, his readings of Yeats's poems are eminently fair and do not depend upon philosophic objections. In the following excerpt, Bloom discusses "The Second Coming."*]

Increasingly [*The Second Coming*] is seen as Yeats's central poem, and not only by exegetes, but by whatever general literary public we still have. The Johnsonian respect for the common reader must enter into any fresh consideration of *The Second Coming*. Though I will indicate limitations of the poem, my concern here is not with its limitations, but with the nature of its power. My prime subject . . . is Yeats's Romanticism, particularly with regard to the austere and terrible melancholy of Poetic Influence within that tradition. As much as any other poem by Yeats, *The Second Coming* bears its direct relation to Blake and Shelley as an overtly defining element in its meaning. The poem quotes Blake and both echoes and parodies the most thematically vital passage in Shelley's most ambitious poem, *Prometheus Unbound*, as a number of critics have remarked.

The manuscripts of *The Second Coming*, as given by Stallworthy, are something of a surprise in relation to the poem's final text. Yeats is writing (according to Ellmann) in January 1919, in the aftermath of war and revolution. His mind is on the Russian Revolution and its menace, particularly to aristocrats, to *antithetical* men. In a way instantly familiar to a student of Blake and Shelley, as Yeats was, the Revolution suggests an apocalypse, and the time of troubles preceding it. But unlike his Romantic precursors, Yeats is on the side of the counter-revolutionaries, and his apocalyptic poem begins by seeing the intervention against revolution as being too late to save the ceremoniously innocent: "The germans are . . . now to Russia come / Though every day some innocent has died." In his grief for these innocents, Yeats laments the absence of those Blake had satirized as Albion's Angels, the champions of reaction: "And there's no Burke to cry aloud no Pitt." With no one to lead them against revolutionary violence: "The good are wavering," while the worst prevail.

Donald Davie has remarked that the title of Yeats's poem is a misnomer, since Christ's advent was not for Yeats the First Coming. I wish to go further, and suggest that the title is not only a misnomer, but a misleading and illegitimate device for conferring upon the poem a range of reference and imaginative power that it does not possess, and cannot sustain. The poem should have been called *The Second Birth*, which is the wording Yeats first employs in its drafts: "Surely the great falcon must come / Surely the hour of the second birth is here." Two lines later Yeats first cried out "The second Birth!" and later in revision altered "Birth" to "Coming." As he revised, Yeats evidently thought of associating his vision in the poem both with Christ's prophecy of his Second Coming and with Revelation's account of the Antichrist. I propose the argument that the poem, even as he revised it, does not justify this portentous association. It remains a poem about the second birth of the *antithetical* Divinity or spirit, and a few verbal changes did not alter the poem's conception enough to give a full coherence to its intended irony of reference. Kierkegaard, in the thirteenth

thesis of the defense of his *The Concept of Irony* says that irony is like vexation over the fact that others also enjoy what the soul desires for itself. This is worth remembering in judging the irony of *The Second Coming,* and in brooding upon Poetic Influence.

Yeats's poem is a vision not of the Second Coming, but of the Second Birth of the Sphinx, not of Thebes but of Memphis, not the Riddler and Strangler but the one-eyed Divinity of the Sun: "An eye blank and pitiless as the sun," as the draft has it. This is the male Sphinx who had haunted Yeats ever since he had read Shelley's *Ozymandias* in his youth, as distinct from the female Sphinx who had served as a Muse of Destruction for the poets and painters of his Tragic Generation. The Egyptian Sphinx is a kind of demonic parody of one of the Cherubim of Ezekiel's vision, the Cherub taken by Blake as the archetype of his Urizen, whose "stony sleep" in *The Book of Urizen* is used by Yeats in the poem as a description of the dormant state-between-births of his "shape with lion body and the head of a man."

In *The Book of Urizen* that Giant Form falls, unable to bear the battle in heaven he has provoked. To ward off the fiery wrath of his vengeful brother Eternals, he frames a rocky womb for himself.

> But Urizen laid in a stony sleep
> Unorganiz'd, rent from Eternity
>
> The Eternals said: What is this? Death
> Urizen is a clod of clay.

During this stony sleep, Urizen writhes in his rocky womb, going through seven ages of creation until he emerges in a second birth as fallen man, man as he is, as we are. This is man become the Sphinx of Egypt, a demonic parody of what man was, the Living Creatures or Cherubim of Ezekiel's vision.

Yeats's poem then is about the second birth of Urizen or the Egyptian Sphinx, but in a context of revolutionary and counter-revolutionary violence, the literary context of Shelley's *Prometheus Unbound,* among other Romantic apocalypses. We need not believe that Yeats's use of Shelley here is any more unintentional than his use of Blake. The moral climax of Act I of *Prometheus Unbound* is the speech of the last Fury to the crucified Titan. The Furies have shown Prometheus visions of the failure of the French Revolution, and the failure of Christ's sacrifice. But the last Fury unfolds a worse torment.

> In each human heart terror survives
> The ravin it has gorged: the loftiest fear
> All that they would disdain to think were true:
> Hypocrisy and custom make their minds
> The fanes of many a worship, now outworn.
> They dare not devise good for man's estate,
> And yet they know not that they do not dare.

What follows is Shelley's central insight; an insight of the Left that Yeats proceeds to appropriate for the Right:

> The good want power, but to weep barren tears.
> The powerful goodness want: worse need for them.
> The wise want love; and those who love want wisdom;
> And all best things are thus confused to ill.
>
> The best lack all conviction, while the worst
> Are full of passionate intensity.

Other echoes of Shelley are at work also, before *Ozymandias* and *The Book of Urizen* are recalled. "Things fall apart; the centre cannot hold" takes us to the tremendous lament for Mutability from *The Witch of Atlas*, when the Witch rejects all natural love:

> The solid oaks forget their strength, and strew
> Their latest leaf upon the mountains wide;
> The boundless ocean like a drop of dew
> Will be consumed—the stubborn center must
> Be scattered, like a cloud of summer dust.

Because the center cannot hold, natural love cannot endure, and the Witch will not accept the unenduring. Prometheus, the figure of endurance, can scarcely bear the condition that Yeats grimly accepts, the rending apart of power and knowledge, of good and the means of good. Both Shelley and Yeats are noting the weakness of their own camps; Shelley sees the spiritual schizophrenia of his own revolutionary intelligentsia, and Yeats, writing still *before* the rise of Fascism, sees the lack of fervor of the ruling classes. In a dubious afterthought, Yeats later claimed **The Second Coming** as a prophecy of Fascism, but if this was so, then the moral urgency we have assigned to prophecy would have to be reviewed. Conor Cruise O'Brien is the inevitable authority on the politics of Yeats, and he reminds us that "The *Freikorps* on the Polish-German border were at this time trying to do exactly what the Black and Tans were doing in Ireland and the *Freikorps* were the direct and proudly acknowledged predecessors of Hitler's Nazis." The *Freikorps*, I would assume, are the Germans who are "now to Russia come" of Yeats's draft, and clearly this is for Yeats his *antithetical* defence against the *primary* "blood-dimmed tide." The greater terror to come, the apocalyptic shape or Egyptian Sphinx to be reborn, may frighten the poet as he does us, but what I hear in the poem is exultation on the speaker's part as he beholds his vision, and this exultation is not only an intellectual one. But this is where critics must disagree in reading, and discussion needs to be conducted more closely.

Christianity, largely irrelevant to the poem, is dragged into its vortex by Yeats's title, and his change of the Second Birth into the Second Coming. This has resulted in some critical arbitrariness, such as Jeffares's comment on the poem's opening:

> The falcon represents man, present civilisation,
> becoming out of touch with Christ, whose birth
> was the revelation which marked the beginning
> of the two thousand years of Christianity.

A juxtaposition of this interpretative remark with the two opening lines is not encouraging. All those lines tell us is that the falconer has lost control of his falcon, not because the bird wills disobedience, but because it has spun too far out to hear its master. Powerful as the ensuing lines may be, they are not wholly coherent, in terms of following upon this initial image. It seems likelier that the falconer, rather than the falcon, represents man, and the falcon his mastery of nature, now in the act of falling apart. The center is man; he cannot hold the falcon to an imposed discipline, and the widening gyre is therefore one with the loosing of anarchy upon the world. Anarchy is "mere" because the value-systems that could judge it portentous are being overwhelmed. What seems to me the poem's first real difficulty enters with "the ceremony of innocence." What is it? By the most legitimate rules of interpretation, one looks nearest to hand. If the best lack all conviction, it is because conviction must be ceremonious (in Yeats's view), and the rituals by which conviction is taught to "the best" are not being observed. Yeats is a ritualist in Pater's manner, where

the ritual may be the best part of the belief, the only operative technique for fostering conviction. Radical innocence, according to the matched poem, **A Prayer for My Daughter,** is the soul's solipsistic knowledge of its own autonomy, and is born only out of ritual, "where all's accustomed, ceremonious." The question then becomes, why does the falconer's loss of control over the falcon betoken a lapse in the maintaining of ritual, and we thus face a dilemma. Either the opening image reduces to an emblem of ceremony, which trivializes the entire poem, or else it does refer to man's mastery over nature, in which case Yeats has not provided any demonstration that a loss of such mastery necessarily leads to the abandonment of elitist ritual. Either way, an aesthetic difficulty exists, which critics continue to evade.

With the second stanza, heretofore evaded difficulties crowd upon the detached reader, if he can resist not only Yeats's heroic rhetoric but also the awed piety of the exegetes. The poet (or poem's speaker) says "surely" revelation, the uncovering of apocalypse, is at hand, but what *in the poem* justifies that "surely"? Mere anarchy does not always bring on revelation, and we would all of us be scarred with multiple apocalypses by now if every loosing of a blood-dimmed tide had compelled a final reality to appear. Presumably the poet's repetition of "surely" merely indicates his own uncertainty, but nothing in the poem justifies the subsequent and merely misleading outcry that the Second Coming, with all of its traditional reverberations, is upon us. In fact the Second Birth of the Sphinx of Egypt, *even in the poet's personal vision* or private apocalypse, is what comes upon him, and us. This is not unimpressive in itself, and the most indisputable lines in the poem proclaim the origin and nature of the vision. Difficulty enters again when the vision ends, and Yeats claims an access of knowledge, if not of power, on the basis of his vision. He claims to know one thing, and pretty clearly a related fact, by presenting the second part of his knowledge as a climactic rhetorical question. For twenty centuries the Sphinx or Urizen, demonic parody of angelic or imaginative man, has been vexed to nightmare by the Incarnation, by the perpetual image of a myth of *primary* salvation (how to keep **A Vision's** terms out at this point, I do not know). This nightmare of Christian history is over, even as Enitharmon's dream of the Christian centuries ends in Blake's *Europe*, when Orc is re-born as the French Revolution. The Egyptian Sphinx is the rough beast who slouches toward Bethlehem to be re-born, not born, in place of the re-birth of Christ. Once the initial shock is set aside, Yeats's closing image is surely replete with difficulties. Christian apocalypses do not visualize the Child born again at Bethlehem; that is not the Christ of Revelation. There is imagistic desperation in Yeats's closing rhetorical lunge. Has he earned his ironic reversal of his own arbitrary use of the Christian reference? And is his closing image coherent in itself? In what sense will the rough beast be "born" at Bethlehem? Clearly, not literally, but is it legitimate then to use "born" for what would actually be a demonic epiphany?

The power of **The Second Coming** is not called in question by these smaller questions, but perhaps its artistry is. Winters was justified in observing that

> . . . we must face the fact that Yeats's attitude toward the beast is different from ours: we may find the beast terrifying, but Yeats finds him satisfying—he is Yeats's judgment upon all that we regard as civilized. Yeats approves of this kind of brutality.

But Winters was too idealistic when he concluded from this that a great poem could not be based, even in part, on "a homemade mythology and a loose assortment of untenable social attitudes." Much major poetry has been founded, in part, upon such odd materials. And one needs to dissent from Winters's judgment that the ideas of *The Second Coming* are "perfectly clear." There is a puzzle about the entire poem, which is why Yeats risked as much arbitrariness and incoherence as the poem possesses. The reason is somewhere in the dark area that the still undeveloped critical study of poetic influence must clarify. Yeats's swerve away from his precursors, in *The Second Coming* as elsewhere, is in the direction of a Gnostic quasi-determinism. The meaning of *The Second Coming* turns upon Yeats's deliberate misinterpretations of apocalyptic poems like Blake's *The Book of Urizen, Europe,* and *The Mental Traveller,* and of Shelley's *Prometheus Unbound* and *The Witch of Atlas. A Vision* deliberately associates *The Second Coming* and *The Mental Traveller,* and Yeats's late essay on *Prometheus Unbound* explicitly chides Shelley for not sharing the attitude of the speaker of *The Second Coming*:

> Why, then, does Demogorgon . . . bear so terrible
>   a shape? . . .
> Why is Shelley terrified of the Last Day like a
>   Victorian child?

What *The Mental Traveller* reveals is the hopelessness of cycles, unless the Imagination dares to break through them. As for Demogorgon, his shape is not terrible, and does not trouble the sight, because he is a formless darkness, the agnostic's vision of historical reversal. Yet he does speak, unlike Yeats's Sphinx, and what he says is a considerable contrast to *The Second Coming*:

> To defy Power, which seems omnipotent;
> To love, and bear; to hope, till Hope creates
> From its own wreck the thing it contemplates;

To do this, Demogorgon simply concludes, is to be free. What the contrast between Shelley and Yeats, or Blake and Yeats, suggests is the problem not of humaneness in apocalyptic poetry, but of freedom even in the context of apocalypse. To Yeats, like any other Gnostic, apocalypse is the fiction of disaster, and *The Second Coming* is an oracle of an unavoidable future. What is a Last Judgment for, in the vision of Yeats's precursors? "A Last Judgment is not for the purpose of making Bad Men better but for the Purpose of hindering them from oppressing the Good with Proverty & Pain."

There is something in the power of *The Second Coming* that persuades us of our powerlessness. Other poems of Advent by Yeats, including *Leda and the Swan,* share in this characteristic. The common reader suffers many mysteries, whose very menace makes for an augmented influence upon him. It is hardly the function of criticism to deny these mysteries, but it need not be the role of criticism to celebrate them. If the good time yet comes, as the faith of Blake and Shelley held it must, *The Second Coming* may impress the common reader rather less than it does now. (pp. 317-25)

Harold Bloom, in his Yeats *(copyright © 1970 by Oxford University Press, Inc.; reprinted by permission), Oxford University Press, New York, 1970, 500 p. [the first excerpt of Yeats's work used here was originally published in his* The Collected Poems of W. B. Yeats *(reprinted with permission of Macmillan Publishing Company; in Canada by Michael B. Yeats, Anne Yeats and Macmillan, London, Ltd; copyright, 1924 by Macmillan Publishing Co., Inc., renewed 1952 by Bertha Georgie Yeats), Macmillan, 1956; the second excerpt was originally published in his* Essays and Introductions *(reprinted with permission of Macmillan Publishing Company; in Canada by Michael B. Yeats, Anne Yeats and Macmillan, London, Ltd; © Mrs. W. B. Yeats, 1961), Macmillan, 1961].*

SEAMUS HEANEY   (lecture date 1978)

[*Heaney is one of the most prominent contemporary Irish poets.*]

Yeats would never have been 'content to live' merely, because that would have meant throwing words away, throwing gesture away, throwing away possibilities for drama and transcendence. From the beginning of his career he emphasized and realized the otherness of art from life, dream from action, and by the end he moved within his mode of vision as within some invisible ring of influence and defence, some bullet-proof glass of the spirit, exclusive as Caesar in his tent, absorbed as a long-legged fly on the stream.

Whatever Yeats intends us to understand by **'Long-legged Fly',** we cannot miss the confidence that drives it forward and the energy that underlies it, an energy that exhilarates in the faith that artistic process has some kind of absolute validity. There is a kind of vitreous finish on the work itself that deflects all other truths except its own. Art can outface history, the imagination can disdain happenings once it has incubated and mastered the secret behind happenings. In fact, we can sense a violence, an implacable element in the artistic drive as Yeats envisages and embodies it. . . . If the act of mind in the artist has all the intentness and amorousness and every bit as much of the submerged aggression of the act of love, then it can be maintained that Yeats's artistic imagination was often in a condition that [can] only be properly described as priapic.

Is this, then, exemplary? (pp. 99-100)

Personally, I find much to admire in the intransigence of the stance, as I find much to commend and imitate in the two things that Yeats was so often determined to set at loggerheads, his life and his work. . . . What is finally admirable is the way his life and his work are *not* separate but make a continuum, the way the courage of his vision did not confine itself to rhetorics but issued in actions. Unlike Wallace Stevens, for example, that other great apologist of the imagination, Yeats bore the implications of his romanticism into action: he propagandized, speechified, fund-raised, administered and politicked in the world of telegrams and anger, all on behalf of the world of vision. His poetry was not just a matter of printed books making their way in a world of literate readers and critics; it was rather the fine flower of his efforts to live as forthrightly as he could in the world of illiterates and politicians. . . . I admire the way that Yeats took on the world on his own terms, defined the areas where he would negotiate and where he would not; the way he never accepted the terms of another's argument but propounded his own. I assume that this peremptoriness, this apparent arrogance, is exemplary in an artist, that it is proper and even necessary for him to insist on his own language, his own vision, his own terms of reference. This will often seem like irresponsibility or affectation, sometimes like callousness, but from the artist's point of view it is an act of integrity, or an act of cunning to protect the integrity. (pp. 100-01)

[Yeats's] poetry is cast in a form that is as ear-catching as the man was eye-catching, and as a writer, one is awed by the achieved and masterful tones of that deliberately pitched voice, its bare classic shapes, its ability to modulate from emotional climax to wise reflection, its ultimate truth to life. Nevertheless, the finally exemplary moments are those when this powerful artistic control is vulnerable to the pain or pathos of life itself. (p. 109)

What Yeats offers the practising writer is an example of labour, perseverance. He is, indeed, the ideal example for a poet approaching middle age. He reminds you that revision and slogwork are what you may have to undergo if you seek the satisfactions of finish; he bothers you with the suggestion that if you have managed to do one kind of poem in your own way, you should cast off that way and face into another area of your experience until you have learned a new voice to say that area properly. He encourages you to experience a transfusion of energies from poetic forms themselves, reveals how the challenge of a metre can extend the resources of the voice. He proves that deliberation can be so intensified that it becomes synonymous with inspiration. Above all, he reminds you that art is intended, that it is part of the creative push of civilization itself: from **'Adam's Curse'** to **'Vacillation'** and on until the last poems, his work not only explicitly proclaims the reality of the poetic vocation but convinces by the deep note of certitude registered in the proclamation itself. . . . But it is not this vaunting of the special claims of art and the artist that is finally to be saluted. Rather, it is Yeats's large-minded, wholehearted assent to the natural cycles of living and dying, his acknowledgement that the 'masterful images' which compel the assent of artist and audience alike are dependent upon the 'foul rag-and-bone shop of the heart', the humility of his artistic mastery before the mystery of life and death. There are several poems where this tenderness towards life and its uncompletedness is at odds with and tending to gain sway over the consolations of the artificial work. The tumultuousness and repose of a poem like **'Sailing to Byzantium'** comes to mind, although there the equilibrium between the golden bird of art and the tattered scarecrow of life is just held, as it is held and held in mind, contemplated and celebrated in **'Among School Children'**. I am thinking, however, of quieter poems, more intimate, less deliberately orchestrated pieces, such as 'What Then?'. . . . [Two other poems] ask, indirectly, about the purpose of art in the midst of life and by their movements, their images, their musics they make palpable a truth which Yeats was at first only able to affirm abstractly, in those words which he borrowed from Coventry Patmore: 'The end of art is peace.'

The first is [**'Meditations in Time of Civil War'**]. . . . What we have is a deeply instinctive yet intellectually assented-to idea of nature in her benign and nurturant aspect as the proper first principle of life and living. The maternal is apprehended, intimated and warmly cherished and we are reminded, much as Shakespeare might remind us, of the warm eggs in the nest shaking at the impact of an explosion. The stare at Yeats's window and the temple-haunting martlet in Macbeth's castle are messengers of grace.

And if the maternal instincts are the first, perhaps they call us back at the very end also. Yeats lies under Ben Bulben, in Drumcliff Churchyard, under that dominant promontory which I like to think of as the father projected into the landscape, and there is perhaps something too male and assertive about the poem that bears the mountain's name [**"Under Ben Bulben"**] and stands at the end of the *Collected Poems*. If I had

my choice I would make the end of that book more exemplary by putting a kinder poem last, one in which the affirmative wilful violent man, whether he be artist or hero, the poet Yeats or the headhunter Cuchulain, must merge his domineering voice into the common voice of the living and the dead, mingle his heroism with the cowardice of his kind, lay his grey head upon the ashy breast of death.

I would end with **'Cuchulain Comforted'**, a poem which Yeats wrote within two weeks of his death, one in which his cunning as a deliberate maker and his wisdom as an intuitive thinker find a rich and strange conclusiveness. It is written in *terza rima*, the metre of Dante's *Commedia*, the only time Yeats used the form, but the proper time, when he was preparing his own death by imagining Cuchulain's descent among the shades. We witness here a strange ritual of surrender, a rite of passage from life into death, but a rite whose meaning is subsumed into song, into the otherness of art. It is a poem deeply at one with the weak and the strong of this earth, full of a motherly kindness towards life, but also unflinching in its belief in the propriety and beauty of life transcended into art, song, words. (pp. 109-13)

Seamus Heaney, "Yeats As an Example?" (originally a lecture given at University of Surrey in 1978), in his Preoccupations: Selected Prose, 1968-1978 *(reprinted by permission of Farrar, Straus and Giroux, Inc. and Faber and Faber Ltd, London; copyright ©1980 by Seamus Heaney), Farrar, Straus and Giroux, 1980, pp. 98-114.*

M. L. ROSENTHAL   (essay date 1978)

[*Rosenthal, a noted Yeats scholar, discusses Yeats's use of the modern literary innovation of the poetic sequence in his* Nineteen Hundred and Nineteen *and* Meditations in Time of Civil War.]

[The modern poetic sequence] is both our characteristic form of the long poem and the outstanding development, going back at least as far as Whitman, in our poetry for over a century. Intimate, fragmented, open, and emotionally volatile, it meets the needs of modern sensibility so naturally that its evolution has gone all but unnoticed. Ordinarily it consists of a grouping of mainly lyric poems and passages, rarely uniform in pattern, that tend to interact as an organic whole. It usually includes narrative, dramatic, and ratiocinative elements, but its ordering is finally lyrical, a succession of *affects*—that is, of units of phrasing that generate specific intensities of feeling and states of awareness. Because of these separate radiating centers, the sequence meets Poe's significantly modern objection to the idea of a long poem: namely, that it is impossible because of the limited duration of any one surge of emotional energy.

In addition, the sequence is openly improvisational and tentative in structure, a condition in fact of all art but often papered over by the conventions of set forms. (p. 27)

Sometimes the speaker is *in extremis*. More often he or she is oppressed by what Delmore Schwartz called "the burden of consciousness," locked in Laocoön-like struggle with a moribund yet murderous civilization. Seeking to objectify itself, the speaking sensibility calls up sunken dimensions of its consciousness from the depths, moving through confusions and ambiguities toward a precarious balance. The process is as much cultural as psychological. The heroic or tragic aspect of the sequence lies in its protagonist's effort to pit personal, historical, and artistic memory or vision against anomie and alienation. In short, the modern poetic sequence has evolved out of a serious need for a poetry even more encompassing than even the greatest single lyric poem. (p. 28)

Yeats's **"Nineteen Hundred and Nineteen"** was written the year of its title and published two years later. **"Meditations in Time of Civil War"** was written in 1923 and published in 1924. When Yeats included them both in his volume *The Tower* . . . , he placed them together but in the reverse order of their composition. From their titles alone one can see that he composed them under the pressure of political events, and if one reads through the thirteen poems that comprise them their reciprocity is clear—they are a single constellation, or twin-sequence. The immediate context of **"Meditations,"** which is the more concretely personal and local of the two, is postwar Ireland during the "troubles." That of **"Nineteen Hundred and Nineteen"** is the whole turbulence of modern history during the Great War and just after. (An earlier title, in fact, was "Thoughts upon the Present State of the World.") Once the sequences were reversed in order, the second seemed to take off naturally from the first into its more encompassing orbit of passionately tragic vision. One would surely have thought that Yeats had written them that way from the start. (pp. 28-9)

In any case, once he had completed the sequences and reversed their order, the dynamics of their movement seemed inevitable. . . . In combination, they take on a complex simultaneity . . . , an organic body of awareness of the tidal flow of feeling that is the subjective undertow of history. The speaker is at once caught up in the world he is observing and apart from it, staring transfixed at an apocalyptic moment in the cyclical rise and fall of civilizations. **"Meditations"** opens ironically with a comment on the helpless abdication of responsibility by the traditional gentry, contrary to all surface appearances. (pp. 29-30)

The rise in intensity between this poem, **"Ancestral Houses,"** which sets the **"Meditations"** going, and the nightmare vision of history at the end of **"Nineteen Hundred and Nineteen"** marks the main curve of movement in the double sequence. The movement completes itself in the archetypal images of recurrent terror that appear in the final poem. . . . (p. 30)

In between **"Ancestral Houses"** and Poem VI of **"Nineteen Hundred and Nineteen"** (whose individual poems are untitled) the movement has three major phases. **"Ancestral Houses"** is a wry overture on the many-sided theme of the brutal discrepancy between reality and dream on which all the poems play. In its relatively low-keyed way it opens us to the stronger music to follow. The rest of **"Meditations"** then takes us through the first two phases in the major movement of the sequences. The first brings us into the poet's self-enclosed fantasy of creating anew, in his own home and family, the obsolete realm of aristocratic dedication forgotten by his country's great families. The second shows the crushing of that fantasy by the violence of history. The third phase is developed in the whole of **"Nineteen Hundred and Nineteen,"** a complex little structure in itself. Poem I recapitulates the emotional discovery of **"Meditation,"** but at a stormier and more cosmic level, and the remaining five poems relate this state of awareness to a number of others—particularly to the ultimate image of the "solitary" individual human soul as a swan that "has leaped into the desolate heaven."

This image appears in Poem III, the point of deepest internalization of all the motifs of the twin-sequence into the dreaming knowledge of the speaking self. Man seeks to re-create himself socially through politics, and personally through art,

and in both instances comes up against the intransigence of impersonal process. Such is the bearing of the symbolic argument presented in Poem III—but the language and spirit are of a magnificent, doomed adventure . . . . (pp. 30-1)

The state of balance reached [in Poem III] compresses within a few lines the main oppositions of both sequences, from the furthest reach of the most daring dreams to the most fumbling sense of personal inadequacy. The idea that any illusion of fixing reality in a perfect form diverts the soul's attention from its true state—an impossible readiness for potentiality amidst utter objective chaos—is itself an oxymoron identifying mature wisdom with introvert withdrawal. Yeats had put the matter less philosophically and glamorously in the down-to-earth explanation of his own nature at the close of **"Meditations"**:

> The abstract joy,
> The half-read wisdom of daemonic images,
> Suffice the ageing man as once the growing boy.

But it is toward the balance of Poem III and then around it that the sequences move—toward the state in which, though the word "triumph" can still be used, it is valued less than the precious solitude of the human soul face to face with mutability and death.

I have suggested that the first stage of this movement comes in **"Meditations,"** after **"Ancestral Houses"** has prepared the way. In a group of three serious yet whimsically eccentric poems, **"My House," "My Table,"** and **"My Descendants,"** Yeats talks of his country home in an old Norman tower and imagines that he and his family have somehow taken over the role of the failed aristocracy. Their form of *noblesse* will be a fusion of simplicity, aestheticism, high meditation, and what he elsewhere calls "the ceremony of innocence." **"My Table,"** for instance, is focused on a samurai sword in the poet's study. To him it speaks with silent eloquence of heroic family traditions and of a mystical link between one's love of beautiful craftsmanship and one's moral élan—the right to "pass Heaven's door." **"My Table,"** with its succession of rhyming couplets in a single unbroken stanza, is the most urgently incantatory of these opening poems. The speaker is willing himself into the exalted mentality of a forgotten time and an exotic culture, an idealized ancient Japan where art and beauty, élite responsibility, and religious duty were one. The sword is an emblem of the violent world of the past whose need to be transformed into its opposite led to such ideals; as an aesthetic object it embodies the opposite condition as well.

Here I must go back for a moment to **"Ancestral Houses."** It provided a dark opening for the first movement, and its initial acidly elegiac tonalities are intimately bound up with the lyrical development of the motif of failed dreams in all the poems. The passage ("Surely among a rich man's . . .") . . . ends with the outcry "Mere dreams, mere dreams!" Indeed, what is striking about this poem is not so much its specific theme; most of us, after all, have never had any illusions about the virtues of "great" families. But that outcry, and the atmosphere of bleak disappointment that goes with it and with the poem's repeated ironies toward the present masters of "ancestral houses," gives us the first, most crucial context for the word "dreams" among the many in the twin-sequence. The irony is especially strong in the poem's use of the term "rich man" to degrade the contemporary aristocracy. Homer's genius, the poem goes on to say, was inspired by a genuinely aristocratic spirit, the "abounding glittering jet." But our modern experience imposes a changed metaphor; for us there is only a "marvellous empty sea-shell," separated from its sources that lie in "the obscure dark of rich streams." This last image, symbolic of the psyche itself, implies that we must re-create our meanings anew from the mysterious springs in racial memory. "Bitter and violent" founders of great lines in the past, we are told, created the dream of beauty and civilization because unhappy with their own lives. (pp. 32-4)

All those bitter, violent founders were like the samurai whose passion and discipline "My Table" exalts in the emblem of the beautiful sword. "Ancestral Houses" clearly implies that only artists themselves in their vision-haunted intensity can now summon the will and imagination to live for such dreams. The three poems that follow—"My House," "My Table," and "My Descendants"—act out this role. "My House" shows the poet as the true aristocratic inheritor, laboring in his tower like *"Il Penseroso's* Platonist" to conjure up visions of the "sweetness" and "gentleness"—transcendent joy and knowledge. (pp. 34-5)

In "My House" and "My Table" Yeats successively dons two masks of visionary wholeness from the past, that of Milton's "Platonist" and that of the Japanese warrior-aesthete. He does so only partially, for it is more a matter of summoning up their worlds than actually calling himself Milton or a samurai. . . . Still, Yeats's imagination is . . . reaching into an alternative state of being to his own literal self. Having gone so far out of himself, as it were, he grows gentler and more humanly familiar in "My Descendants." This poem shows him at his most exposed and personal in these four opening poems— quietly happy despite the pomposity of the first two stanzas, in which his aristocratic play-acting grows solemnly egotistical for the moment. Both tones, the pompous and the intimately relaxed, are appropriate before the sledgehammer blow falls of the next poem, "The Road at My Door." When that happens, the darker spirit that has been hovering over the poems all along comes into its own. "The Road at My Door" and the two poems that follow it and complete the "Meditations"— "The Stare's Nest by My Window" and "I See Phantoms of Hatred and of the Heart's Fullness and of the Coming Emptiness"—show reality crashing in on the poet's mad but engaging dream. In them he is forced to face his weakness and accept his isolation after all.

But the crucial moment of confrontation between his inner world and the destructive tidal wave of history comes in "The Road at My Door." The emotional heart of "Meditations" lies in the situation of this poem and of its central metaphor, "the cold snows of a dream." The most acutely personal poem in the twin-sequence, it also places the speaker in his impersonal historical setting, the period of the "troubles" in Ireland. The topical allusions speak for themselves. (pp. 35-6)

The "Irregulars" and the "brown" troops were rival bands of soldiers. The former belonged to the Irish Republican Army, which started the civil war against England, refusing the Dominion status agreed to by the Provisional Free State government to whose National Army the brown troops belonged. That much footnoting at least seems useful, for this is the one poem in the sequences whose emotional character is somewhat unclear if one does not know certain facts. It is important to know that the Irregular and the brown Lieutenant belong to warring factions, for that fact makes the speaker's failure to express sympathy with either one significant. The poem is full of precise detail and ambiguous feeling. *Perhaps* the speaker has a certain admiration for the highspirited Irregular although he is a happy killer—one cannot quite tell. When he complains to

the Free Staters about the weather, *perhaps* he implies a worse complaint, against Ireland's miseries. And after each band in turn has left his door and returned to the outside world of murderous action and he is left alone, "caught/In the cold snows of a dream," he may be referring to more than his own unbreakable isolation and practical ineffectiveness. He may be suggesting, as well, the rigid rival idealisms of political struggle and even the opiate dream that universal peace and order prevailed in the world—the dream that had lulled the peoples before the outbreak of the Great War and all the subsequent revolutionary struggles throughout Europe.

All this is part of the poem's muted structure of ambivalences, of the way it is packed with mounting, impossible pressure. Even the affectionate phrase the speaker uses for the moorhen's chicks that he "counts" to calm his nerves—"those feathered balls of soot"—seems to reflect that pressure. "Balls of soot" carries a penumbral suggestion of bullets and fire. And his sudden confession that he needs to "silence the envy in my thought" shows his ambivalent, near-hysterical feeling. It seems he cannot altogether repress a primitive if unworthy chagrin at not being the sort of man who "Comes cracking jokes of civil war" himself.

The politics of "The Road at My Door" is the politics of sensibility in the context of history. The poem thus embodies the whole tendency of "Meditations" and readies us for the further intensities and wider tragic scope of "Nineteen Hundred and Nineteen." Its real character lies in its movement from the robust, startled half-ironies of the first stanza to the veiled, passive complaining of the second and finally to the chill, incontrovertible self-characterization of the third. The successive images spring out at us, exploding the speaker's solitary dreaming and knocking into oblivion the noble self-image so carefully built up in the preceding poems. He is left, at the end, with no certainties save the unresolved anguish of his private state and the equally unresolved terror and chaos of the external world.

The next poem, "The Stare's Nest by My Window," provides an acerbic burning away of the ambiguities of "The Road at My Door." Here there is no hint of admiration for swashbuckling killers, and the sequence is locked into a position of depressive transcendence, beyond political partisanship and firm in its private attitude. The speaker's uncertainty is now transferred from the paralyzed inner state of the preceding poem to something more outward and empirical. . . . (pp. 36-8)

Part of the genius of the poetic sequence as a form, and of this pair of sequences in particular, lies in its hospitality to contradictory moods and attitudes that correct or modify one another. One more instance comes in the next poem, which concludes "Meditations." Here we are back in the midst of the poet's fantasies. . . . The title of the poem shows, however, what the two preceding poems have discovered but have not stated—how permeated dream-reverie is with "phantoms" distilled from life, projections that hardly speak of unmitigated ecstasy: "I See Phantoms of Hatred and of the Heart's Fullness and of the Coming Emptiness." The poem presents images of mob fury and counter-images of supernatural erotic female beauty, then replaces both with a prophetic symbol of impersonal destruction—"brazen hawks" with "innumerable clanging wings that have put out the moon."

By the end of "Meditations," then, we have been taken to a place very like the arena of dark germinal consciousness. . . . Out of this terror the unknown future will be born. The sequence became vibrantly painful once it touched the naked facts of Ireland's agony, in **"The Road at My Door."** **"The Stare's Nest by My Window,"** equally painful, begins the shift to reconciliation that is completed, for the time being, in the final poem of **"Meditations."** There the dreaming mind reasserts itself, but without illusions now either about bringing practical life under meaningful control or about the poet's superiority to other men. Notice, for example, the self-mocking buffoonery of Yeats's echoing of Wordsworth's slightly solemn style in his closing sentence, and the absolute humility of [the] ending generally. . . . (pp. 38-9)

The final note here is both humble and self-regarding, the poet's reconciliation with his own image as the unheroically abstracted and introspective man he must be. It stands in beautiful counterpoint to the music of the preceding poem as established in its opening stanza. . . . (p. 40)

The feeling of defeat, the feeling of possibility, are in imperfect balance in [*The Stare's Nest by My Window*] . . . as at the end of the closing poem. The tower's loosening masonry is a literally observed detail but also an obvious symbol of the dissolving dream-structure of the earlier poems. The stares (starlings) have built a nest there but it is empty now. Crumbling wall and empty nest are a double image of the speaker's condition—yet at the same time the honey-bees are actually building in the same place. "Come build in the empty house of the stare" is a harsh parody of the poet's past hopes and efforts. But there is a further implication. If there must be cyclical change, let it result in the sweetness and fragrance of honey-bees. (Remember the "sweetness" and "gentleness" of which founders dreamed.) These images from nature are a quiet counter-note to the major horror and depression of the sequence, a note picked up again in the equally subdued Wordsworthian passage at the end of the next poem.

Still, it is a true reassertion, a persistence of open sensibility in the face of acknowledged disaster, in both passages. . . . It reveals how we "sail after knowledge" even when lost in pursuit of the dream, for the pursuit itself opens us to the grim uncertainties that make up knowledge. If this is a riddle, and a not particularly happy one, nevertheless **"Nineteen Hundred and Nineteen"** *leaps* into it like the swan into desolate heaven and makes a kind of triumph of confronting our blindness and inability to penetrate the universe.

The leap begins with Poem I, which as I have suggested recapitulates the emotional dynamics of **"Meditations"** but alters the context. (pp. 40-1)

The new key of **"Nineteen Hundred and Nineteen"** is the one I have described, the leap into man's desolate existential state as the poet's major ground of awareness. The difference from **"Meditations"** will be clear if we compare the two opening poems. Each of them establishes the dominant emotional set of its sequence, and despite the larger scope of the former they parallel one another in form and thought. Both are in Yeats's modified ottava rima, holding him to a firm pattern which he nevertheless adapts to his idiom. The only poems in the twin-sequences to use this stanza, both are modern versions of an ancient poetic mode: the lament against mutability. Where **"Ancestral Houses"** laments the dead spirit of Ireland's ruling gentry, Poem I of **"Nineteen Hundred and Nineteen"** laments the disappearance, in time's fullness, of everything we cherish. . . . (pp. 41-2)

The subdued tone of [the poem's] beginning, its air of dispassionate contemplation, belies its elemental sadness. The feeling makes for a special turn on the Romantic longing for the unattainable; the regret here is that, having reached perfection in certain ways, we cannot sustain it. The phrase "ingenious lovely things" rings through the poem with the memory of lost perfections and is reinforced by "sheer miracle" and, later, "famous" and "golden" and even "ornamental." Against this joyous language suggesting we are loved by smiling gods stands the word "gone" at two strategic points: the end of the first line and the beginning of the final couplet. The only active principle in the stanza is a destructive one—"the circle of the moon / That pitches common things about."

Free of any narrow local base, Poem I gathers into itself the revulsion-laden political awareness of **"Meditations."** Its range, though, is the whole of history, summed up in a single line: "Man is in love and loves what vanishes." The disillusionment of **"Ancestral Houses"** was only a prelude to the helpless, heartbroken music of this poem, whose vision is of the self-betrayal, not only of a social class, but of mankind through the ages. . . . In much the same way the glimpse of "that dead young soldier in his blood" in **"The Stare's Nest by My Window"** is recalled but surpassed by an even more shocking image in Poem I, where it is imbedded too in language of philosophical despair over what humanity—"we"—can permit itself to be and do:

> a drunken soldiery
> Can leave the mother, murdered at her door,
> To crawl in her own blood, and go scot-free. . . .
>   (pp. 42-3)

Anyone who has been shocked out of his dreams by such knowledge as this, says the poem, "has but one comfort left: all triumph would / But break upon his ghostly solitude." What was seen in the closing poems of **"Meditations"** as the self-indulgence of an impotent dreamer now becomes, through a conversion of spiritual energy, his one great strength. He can internalize, in the images of his art, the inhuman cyclical progression that life has forced him to confront. Poem II, for example, gives us an image of exotic dancers whose whirling movement recalls to the speaker the ancient concept of the "Platonic Year," a period of centuries marking vast cycles of fated change in human life. . . . (pp. 43-4)

But it is Poem III especially, with its swan-image and its image of "the labyrinth" that man has made "in art or politics," and Poem VI with its images of Herodias's daughters returning and other, grosser archetypes that complete the transorming conversion of defeat into a kind of power. . . . [It] is interesting that both closing poems in Yeats's double sequence introduce the motif of the impersonal power of sexuality. At the end of **"Meditations"** we see female "phantoms of the heart's fullness" who are lost in entrancement by their own bodily loveliness and "sweetness." At the end of **"Nineteen Hundred and Nineteen"** the comparable figures are more compelling and energetic, and also vicious. In addition to Herodias' daughters with their evil "amorous cries, or angry cries" there is the "love-lorn Lady Kyteler" wooing her succubus, an "insolent fiend," with a phallic, black-magic ritual. What seemed an image of war-terror at the start of the poem—"Violence upon the roads: violence of horses"—becomes by the end a symbol of vehement, mindless supernatural forces. This last poem does precisely what Poem III says the solitary soul must do. Its wings, "half spread for flight," are ready in the face of these mindless phantoms of reality and imagination either "to play, or to ride / Those winds that clamour of approaching night." (p. 44)

M. L. Rosenthal, "'Structure and Process': Yeats's Civil War Sequences," in his Sailing into the Unknown: Yeats, Pound, and Eliot *(copyright © 1978 by M. L. Rosenthal; reprinted by permission of Oxford University Press, Inc.), Oxford University Press, New York, 1978, pp. 26-44 [the excerpts of Yeats's poetry used here were originally published in his* The Collected Poems of W. B. Yeats *(reprinted with permission of Macmillan Publishing Company; in Canada by M. B. Yeats, Anne Yeats; copyright by Macmillan Publishing Co., Inc., renewed 1956 by Bertha Georgia Yeats), Macmillan, 1949].*

MARY HELEN THUENTE　(essay date 1980)

[In this excerpt from her well-researched study W. B. Yeats and Irish Folklore, *Thuente analyzes and evaluates Yeats's* The Celtic Twilight *utilizing standards established by modern folklorists for determining the value of folk materials.]*

Yeats's sense of the significance of his early attempts to collect Irish folklore and of the resulting collection, *The Celtic Twilight,* is apparent in a statement he made in 1903: 'When I was a boy I used to wander about at Rosses Point and Ballisodare listening to old songs and stories. I wrote down what I heard and made poems out of the stories or put them into the little chapters of the first edition of **"The Celtic Twilight,"** and that is how I began to write in an Irish way.' The nature and significance of *The Celtic Twilight* and Yeats's developing use of Irish folklore can best be understood when the collection is analysed as folklore. . . . (p. 120)

Considering the preference for legends which Yeats had shown in his first two anthologies [*Fairy and Folk Tales of the Irish Peasantry* and *Representative Irish Tales*], it is not surprising that he included only legends and no folk tales or myths in the first edition of *The Celtic Twilight.* Any preference that Yeats had for legends over the other genres of oral narrative, folk tale and myth, was also encouraged by the nature of materials available to him in oral tradition in and around Sligo. Because of their simpler and more anecdotal form, legends survived among the peasantry after lengthier and more complex forms of narrative like folktales and myths had died out. Legends also crossed over into English much more easily than folktales and ancient hero tales whose complex plots were ornamented with lengthy and obscure passages known as 'runs' which were difficult to translate into English. Because Yeats did not speak Irish, the English-speaking informants he used were much more likely to give him fairy legends and beliefs even if he had preferred folktales and tales from ancient Irish mythology.

Although his earlier anthologies had been composed chiefly of previously published folklore, *The Celtic Twilight* includes only those materials which Yeats had collected himself or that he had heard secondhand from an oral informant or a written report. Yeats's reliance on oral materials in *The Celtic Twilight* represents a deepening sense of the essentially oral nature of folklore. Moreover, he not only used oral materials, but recorded them as accurately as possible. In contrast to most of his predecessors in the publication of Irish folklore, Yeats was able to declare at the beginning of *The Celtic Twilight,* 'I have therefore written down accurately and candidly much that I have heard and seen, and, except by way of commentary, nothing that I have merely imagined.' However, Yeats's qualifying phrase 'except by way of commentary' makes it clear that the unvarnished oral traditions which Yeats has so 'accurately' recorded are to be accompanied by his comments.

Yet his commentary was not to be either arguments concerning the truth or falsehood of folk belief or philological data such as had appeared in the editorial comments with which his predecessors had prefaced and annotated their materials. Instead, Yeats's 'commentary' would involve the presentation of his own visions and beliefs. He declared in the sentence which succeeded the one just quoted: 'I have, however, been at no pains to separate my own beliefs from those of the peasantry, but have rather let my men and women, dhouls [sic] and faeries, go their way unoffended or defended by any argument of mine.' Yeats had scrupulously avoided including his own beliefs in *Fairy and Folk Tales,* of which he had written to Katharine Tynan in 1888: 'All will go well if I can keep my own unpopular thoughts out. . . . I must be careful in no way to suggest that fairies, or something like them, do veritably exist, some flux and flow of spirits between man and the unresolvable mystery.' Yeats had indeed maintained a strict silence concerning his own beliefs in that anthology, but descriptions of his persoanl visionary experiences abound in *The Celtic Twilight.*

However, rather than criticise Yeats for thus 'embellishing' the authentic oral materials he had collected, the reader should realise that Yeats was simply using himself as an informant. Although he had chosen to present only the visionary experiences of Irish peasants in *Fairy and Folk Tales,* his presentation of such materials had developed considerably by 1893 and now included descriptions of how he and his friends, and even how middle-class clerks, had had contact with the fairies. Such a presentation of folklore, no matter how accurately Yeats recorded legends and beliefs from his informants, has not found much favour with the scientific folklorists of today. Richard Dorson has described *The Celtic Twilight* as 'a musing, introspective diary playing with the shadowy folk beliefs of fairy powers'. However, such a judgement applies recent collecting standards to *The Celtic Twilight* without giving adequate credit to Yeats's sincerity in presenting his personal visionary experiences as the equivalent of those he recorded from his peasant informants. Folklorists today obviously use much more objective standards in collecting. Yeats recorded his materials as accurately as he could but he believed, or tried very hard to believe, in what he recorded as a folklorist. As a result he could not and did not approach his own beliefs and visionary experiences any differently than those of his peasant informants: he thus collected from them and himself and his juxtaposition of the two kinds of materials is not without rhetorical effect. The personal visionary experiences which Yeats incorporates into his accounts of peasant visions and beliefs reinforce their reality and vice versa. Yeats's visionary perspective is also characteristically Irish. According to a recent essay by Dáithi Ó hÓgáin, 'The Visionary Voice: A Survey of Popular Attitudes to Poetry in Irish Tradition', the ancient Irish concept of the poet as having visionary powers and of his poetry as a verbal manifestation of occult knowledge survived in peasant traditions.

The visionary experiences which Yeats records also represent an early attempt to record what folklorists today call 'memorats'—first or secondhand accounts of encounters with supernatural creatures. *The Celtic Twilight* is filled with such 'memorats'. (pp. 121-24)

The vivid presence of Yeats's voice, of his own beliefs and experiences in *The Celtic Twilight,* is all the more surprising because one of his major editorial emendations in tales he had included in *Fairy and Folk Tales* had been to remove the narrative device of an interlocutor. He becomes an interlocutor in

The Celtic Twilight where he is by turn collector, interlocutor, informant. Although the removal of an interlocutor from tales Yeats used in *Fairy and Folk Tales* had improved the sense of immediacy in those selections, the presence of Yeats's personal voice in *The Celtic Twilight* increases rather than decreases the immediacy of his materials. . . . Yeats's personal voice is an integral part of the immediacy of his essays. Moreover, any folklore collector inevitably becomes an interlocutor because his function is to question and engage his informant in conversation. Yeats is simply recording his own part of the interviews with informants or acting as his own informant.

In *The Celtic Twilight* Yeats thus displayed an awareness of the effectiveness of the personality of the narrator, whether the peasant or himself, in the transmission of folklore decades before contemporary folklorists did. Yeats's careful descriptions of Mary Battle's and Paddy Flynn's personalities indicate he appreciated the significance of the storyteller's personality. His own vivid personal voice in *The Celtic Twilight* actually makes the collection resemble what folkorists today call a 'tale-telling event' in which the personality of the narrator naturally intrudes on and becomes a part of his materials. (pp. 124-25)

Other features of Yeats's presentation of his materials in *The Celtic Twilight* both contradict and foreshadow methods used today. Folklorists today are expected to include data identifying their informant and the context in which they collected their material. *The Celtic Twilight* has been criticised for lacking such data because Yeats named and described only some of his informants. However, what seems at first glance to be due to careless, incomplete recording methods is again traceable to Yeats's personal involvement with his own materials and is most likely a conscious effort to protect his informants. A basic tenet of Irish fairy belief was that one should never talk about or reveal one's experiences with the fairies because the fairies jealously guarded their privacy and would punish anyone who revealed things about them. Consequently, Yeats's informants were often reluctant to speak of their experiences of the fairies. (p. 126)

In *The Celtic Twilight* Yeats usually identifies by name only those informants who have died. (p. 127)

When Yeats did identify his informants and subjects in *The Celtic Twilight* by name, he was deliberately vague as to the locale. The anecdotes in the essay about **'Village Ghosts'** all concern people identified by name, but all these ghosts 'inhabit the village of H——, in Leinster'. Other informants are simply identified as 'an old Miller at Ballylee' or, 'a doubter in Donegal'. Such vagueness about informants, even if attributable to a desire on Yeats's part to 'protect' the identity of his informants, also represents a literary technique which, whether it is intentional of not, has significant repercussions on the presentation of Yeats's materials. The accuracy of Yeats's materials could, of course, never be checked. By not tying his materials to a specific informant Yeats also enhanced their mystery which, because they could possibly be traced to innumerable people and places in the West of Ireland, seemed all the more general and universal. Yeats's sense that such beliefs and legends were ancient and ultimately anonymous, that they belonged to tradition and not to a single informant, also helps to explain why he did not wish to present them as the property of a specific Irish peasant or locale. (pp. 127-28)

Although Yeats was deliberately vague about the specific identity or locale of his informants, he carefully created the impression that the experiences and beliefs he recorded had occurred to real people in real places. . . . Yeats is quite masterful at conveying a sense of reality about his informants while refraining from actually revealing their identity, as when he describes his informant in the essay **'Kidnappers':** 'I heard it from a little old woman in a white cap, who sings to herself in Gaelic, and moves from one foot to another as though she remembered the dancing of her youth.' Occasionally Yeats hints at the context in which an item was collected. . . : 'One night as I sat eating Mrs H——'s soda-bread, her husband told me a longish story. . . .' Yeats often 'quotes' common opinion rather than specific informants. In such cases, he usually associates the beliefs he narrates with actual places which he does describe in detail: 'At the northern corner of Rosses is a little promontory of sand and rocks and grass: a mournful, haunted place. No wise peasant would fall asleep under its low cliff, for he who sleeps here may wake "silly", the "good people" having carried off his soul.' In such passages objective description imperceptibly shades into personal impressions and beliefs. The word 'may' can be read either as 'sometimes' in the sense that it can actually sometimes be carried off by the fairies, or as 'perhaps' in the sense that 'maybe' such reports are true. (pp. 128-29)

The question inevitably arises as to how generalised such beliefs and visionary experiences actually were in and around Sligo. To his credit, later collectors have generally found similar materials in the West of Ireland. W. Y. Evans-Wentz, who had been influenced no doubt by Yeats's materials but who possessed his own extensive and firsthand knowledge of Irish oral tradition, found in 1911 that 'the Ben Bulbin country in County Sligo', the locale of much of Yeats's material in *The Celtic Twilight,* was especially full of fairy lore and that the fairies were seen by his Sligo informants rather than merely heard and felt. (p. 129)

[As] respected an Irish folklist as E. Estyn Evans has recently published an essay on nineteenth-century Irish peasant beliefs which suggests that traditional beliefs remained relatively strong well into the late nineteenth century in rural Ireland, despite the famine, increased anglicisation and other social upheavals. According to Evans, a keen sense of and a reliance on pagan supernatural beliefs was actually encouraged by the disappearance of external features of traditional folk life such as language and customs: 'I see the crisis in the middle of the nineteenth century as marking in many ways the end of pre-history. At the same time the tensions produced by the fundamental changes in rural society brought about by the Famine appear to have resulted in secret recourse to supernatural forces during the second half of the century and, in some parts of the country, well into the present century. However, Evans does comment that it was a 'secret recourse' to such pagan beliefs and many informants may not have been willing to yield their secret beliefs to Yeats. Indeed, he frequently remarks on how difficult it was to get informants to discuss the fairies. Theoretically he should have been able to find many potential English-speaking informants around Sligo. In 1891, a census year, only one-third of the population of the western seaboard counties spoke Irish. Whether or not these English-speaking informants would speak of fairy lore was another matter.

The fact that Yeats did not know Irish undoubtedly restricted the number of his potential informants because folklore, especially narrative, does not always cross over into English. He ultimately employed the same informants—Biddy Hart and her husband, Paddy Flynn, Mary Battle—again and again which implies his actual sources were few. (pp. 130-31)

Most of Yeats's sources, even the nameless ones, are referred to as 'old': In *Fairy and Folk Tales* we are told 'Paddy Flynn is very old'; Biddy Hart is referred to as 'old Biddy Hart' in *Irish Fairy Tales*. The majority of the other informants he quotes in *The Celtic Twilight* in 1893 and 1902 are also old. . . . Yeats is obviously recording the remnants of a dying tradition. . . . The question of senility inevitably arises when such elderly informants are used. Years's description of Paddy Flynn 'asleep under a hedge smiling in his sleep' can suggest simple-mindedness as easily as visionary powers. Yeats admits that his informant in the second section of the essay **'Happy and Unhappy Theologians'** is thought by other villagers to be 'a little crazed', and Yeats refers to 'half-mad and visionary peas-ants' in **'A Visionary'**. Likewise, Yeats says of 'old Martin Roland' who was dead when Yeats wrote **'Friends of the People of Faery'** in 1897: 'His neighbours were not certain he really saw anything in his old age, but they were all certain that he saw things when he was a young man.' . . . In any event, Yeats found informants to be relatively scarce and many of the Sligo peasantry probably did not share his credulity about the visions and beliefs he collected. (pp. 131-32)

The Celtic Twilight develops as well as continues approaches to Irish folklore which Yeats had used in *Fairy and Folk Tales*. In that anthology he had presented fairy lore as a uniquely Irish phenomenon, experienced solely by the peasantry who en-countered fairies much more frequently than any other kind of spirit. Yeats's perspective in *The Celtic Twilight* is much less pointedly Irish, less concerned with only peasants and much less concerned with the fairies. One essay, **'The Last Glee-man'**, does not even mention the fairies, any visionary expe-riences or rural Ireland. Yeats obviously found it unnecessary to be as militantly nationalistic as he had been when he com-piled *Fairy and Folk Tales*. . . . Having successfully propa-gandised its nationalistic significance as a uniquely Irish cul-tural and literary tradition, Yeats could begin to expand its significance by revealing its more universal and philosophical implications. So in *The Celtic Twilight* the visions and beliefs of the peasantry are linked to those of Yeats and his friends. (p. 132)

> *Mary Helen Thuente, in her* W. B. Yeats and Irish Folklore *(© Mary Helen Thuente, 1980; by permis-sion of Barnes & Noble Books, a Division of Little-field, Adams & Co., Inc.), Barnes & Noble, 1981, 286 p.*

JAY CANTOR (essay date 1981)

[*Cantor discusses the elegiac tone of Yeats's work as the poet's response to, and affirmation of, an era of political upheaval in Ireland.*]

Perhaps there comes a certain time in the life of a nation when it wrestles with an angel to gain its name. In this time a people feel they must find what they will worship and who they are; it is the moment of beginnings, the revolutionary moment. A people then discovers (or recovers—the origin sometimes be-comes a second founding) their identity. (It is a time of high talk; in later ages the language seems too unironic, the speech of patriotic pageants. "The whole race is a poet that writes down / The eccentric propositions of its fate," Wallace Stevens wrote, in "Men Made out of Words." But it is perhaps only in such revolutionary moments that the race, its politicians or its poets, feels this.

The revolutionary moment is intensely poetic and intensely political. For Ireland, Yeats said in his Nobel Prize acceptance speech, this time began with the death of Parnell. . . . The revolutionary moment is something that troubles one as if from underground, in the dark, unconsciously, as the word gestation suggests; the nation is something created by a people as a child or dream is created. ("Is there a nation-wide multiform rev-erie," Yeats asks, "every mind passing through a stream of suggestion, and the streams acting upon one another, no matter how distant the mind, how dumb the lips?") The moment, the time, is, Yeats says, the beginning of modern Irish literature and of the Irish Revolution—they may diverge later, but they were conceived at the same time and take their impetus from the same origin.

This is a rare moment in the life of a nation. It presents its writers with great possibilities: to have their words matter. . . . The artist is contesting something large: the future identity of his country, the shape of the national will, what will be valued, what reviled. (pp. 19-20)

Ireland was fortunate in its writers. "Few historians," Conor Cruise O'Brien writes in an essay on Yeats's politics, "would challenge Yeats's estimate in his Swedish address of the impact of Parnell's fall and death, or his summary account of a process in which he himself played an important part. His historical sense was keen, as his political sense was also. For he not only saw in retrospect the crucial importance of the death of Parnell. He saw it *at the time*, immediately, and he saw in it his op-portunity, and took that opportunity . . . he made Parnell a symbol, almost a god."

This seizing of the occasion was not simple literary opportun-ism on Yeats's part (as O'Brien sometimes makes it sound), say to gain more readers by making his remarks topical. He wanted his words to matter, and that meant they must come at the right time; there is a strategy, a cunning, to poetry become politics, and politics become poetry. It was not simply oppor-tunism because such times *are* a kind of poetry. Each day brings forth, in Yeats's terms, symbols, prophecies. . . . Such times, it seems, almost heal the writer's isolation—that dis-tance he often feels between the nature of his role and the world of events, of prose, the political world. Did Yeats make Parnell a symbol, "almost a god," or did he find a symbol, one made by that "multi-form reverie" of the people? The politician is already a symbol, I think; the nation is creating a new world by metaphor. In the revolutionary moment the poet can feel in his own words, in the process that gives birth to those words, the archetypal creative fiat that is then the true nature of both politics and poetry. (pp. 20-1)

Yeats also took part in this struggle. [Yeats offered] the Irish a version of themselves to behold and so become. His was an Ireland of the past, of folk tales and stately mansions. (They were, Yeats indicates, in some way the same world; both the aristocracy and the peasants shared a habit of thought, an or-dered tradition, a world of "intuitive knowledge.") . . .

Yeats's style underwent a striking transformation. (p. 24)

But what is equally striking in Yeats's poetry is not what changes, but what remains the same. The thematic tone of much of his greatest poetry, the tonality of ideas, attitudes, and postures taken, remain, I think, consistent throughout his work. That tone, which he describes in **"The Autumn of the Flesh,"** "Man has wooed and won the world, and has fallen weary, and not, I think, for a time . . . " is a tone that one would describe as elegiac: "The elegiac presents a heroism unspoiled by irony, a diffused resigned melancholy sense of the passing of time, the old order changing and yielding to a new one." (p. 25)

Autumn is the season in . . . [the] elegy, **"The Wild Swans at Coole,"** the characteristic time for Yeats's poetry. . . . Autumn is the characteristic time for Yeats's apprehension of the revolutionary moment, an always failing return to origin. It is close of day; the end of the cycle for Yeats. . . . What is richest and most alive, most lovely, least anxious, most vivid, most present, is, for Yeats, in the past, recaptured only in memory, speaking to us as one of the things of memory might. **"The Wild Swans at Coole"** is calm and reflective, regretful, detached from present time, elegiac: the characteristic phrase, I think, is "All's changed . . . "

"All's changed . . . " The phrase recurs when Yeats revisits **"Coole Park and Ballyee, 1931."** . . . (pp. 25-6)

"But all is changed . . . " The poet here in this later poem is as masterfully elegiac, but less unperturbedly so. Now there is a "darkening flood" to be feared, or "blood-dimmed tide" (as he named it in **"The Second Coming,"** a somewhat earlier poem). A new note haunts Yeats's poetry, near a kind of terror; yet the tone remains elegiac (and it is one facet of his art to be true to both these feelings). A consciousness, a style of consciousness, one that does not shift about, is going under, being drowned; but this going under (I think we can feel in the last verse) is not only defeat, it is also exaltation, for the dying world is most beautiful as it is most utterly lost; and the poet is at the peak of his powers because he has remembered it, has sung it even in the face of this catastrophe that will overwhelm him, will overwhelm poetry. For to face the end, the apocalypse, the darkening flood, is also to feel most strongly *oneself* in the very bitterness of the last moment.

And this elegiac exultation was characteristic too of a certain style of politics of the time, one that saw itself as facing the decline of the West, as facing the barbarian hordes of the East, the rising tide of the masses, that knew itself as aristocratic because of its distance from this "mass of interchangeable people." Its time was also autumn. And this is the time that Yeats himself evokes for this politics, in discussing his feelings for fascism: "Italy, Poland, Germany, then perhaps Ireland. Doubtless I shall hate it (though not so much as I hate Irish democracy) but it is September and we must not behave like the gay young sparks of May or June."

Yeats looked to the past because, first of all, it was in the past that a certain myth (but it was not yet "myth," it was, he thought, a lived reality) and way of life were in congruence. The objects men lived among in this lost world were not dead things, but spoke to us of ourselves as symbols do. It was a "total world," an ordered world, a world "instinct with piety" (as Proust called his personal lost world) in which things were unalien to us, all a single indivisible whole. It is this world that Yeats holds before himself, this world that he meditates on in time of civil war—it is disappearing, always disappearing, even as it is named—this world, our ancestral home. . . . (pp. 26-7)

This world, where Being is present to us, and "Life overflows without ambitious pains: / And rains down life until the basin spills" is the inherited glory of the rich. But the world of industry, of mechanical shapes, has caused it to go under, has turned it to a world of fragments, where ambitious men, seeking only their own profit, rule. A symbol is an emergence from this lost world: it is the voice of the dead. "The aura we feel

in a symbol," Denis Donoghue writes of Yeats's symbolism, "is the presence of the supernatural in the natural; the souls of the dead are understood as living in places which are sacred because of that residence . . . Belief in reincarnation is endorsed by assent to tradition; Symbolism is the hermeneutics of that faith." It is the race itself that through the Great Mind gives us symbols. Symbols are for Yeats the creative words of the race, but the race of the past, the dead. "The dead living in their memories are, I am persuaded, the source of all that we call instinct, and it is their love and their desire, all unknowing, that makes us drive beyond our reason, or in defiance of our interest it may be." The emergence of the symbol is no longer the creative work of the revolutionary moment, but the imposition of the past; the nation—essentially passive (symbols aren't made, but received)—only calls up the voices of the dead, brings blood to their ghosts. The dead will occupy them, and by this occupation, the visionary moment turns the present into the past. (pp. 27-8)

To recapture the lost world in the visionary moment is the poet's work; it is to bring two lenses together (self and antiself) inside the Self (the only place they can be brought together now; the heart is moved "but to the heart's discovery of itself"), to a focus where mythic consciousness and reality seem to meet for a moment, and the world becomes our home, a place of self-contained satisfaction and mastery. "Yet I am certain," Yeats wrote, "that there was something in myself compelling me to attempt creation of an art as separate from everything heterogeneous and casual, all character and circumstance, as some Herodiade of our theater, dancing seemingly alone in her narrow moving circle." This world—all that is heterogeneous and casual—falls away from the dancer, within the circle of her self. "And all about lives but in mine own / Image, the idolatrous mirror of my pride, / Mirroring this Herodiade diamond eyed."

From this self-contemplation the dancer (the poet) may give forth a gesture; a gesture that she will not herself—outside the circle of her dance—understand. . . . (pp. 28-9)

The gesture of the poet or the dancer is to us an elegy—the visionary moment falls away, back into a past that leaves the present bitter, empty, longing. The visionary moment contains within itself a mourning.

Yeats looks for the lost world everywhere, but finds it only in fragments, in broken sentences, moments of memory and prophecy. . . . (p. 29)

The emergence of the symbol, of the prophecy, is for Yeats, the destruction of the present moment; the self is moved into a future time in which he looks back on the destruction of what is (though not the destruction of the observing self); the symbolic prophecy makes of this world a dying world, a fit subject for elegy. The world enters the poem only as a figure of the past. And again this prophecy of destruction, of time closing, is not only an elegy, but an exultation, the exultation of being present at one's own funeral, singing one's own death, and so surviving it, savoring it (for it is within the imagination). The Yeatsian world is one of "brooding memory and dangerous hope," but the dangerous hope turns all into the realm of memory. All is possessed in loss, contained within the self, even one's own death.

This elegiac tone, one might think, would cut one off from contesting the nation's political future, the nation's identity. However, it is close to the ideologies of both left and right that have dominated the political thought of this century, for we are nostalgic for a total world, a world of order, completeness, unity of Being. Recurrently nations have wished to imagine the future in the image of a lost past, a reconciliation with the dead, an atonement; a future in which our souls will be occupied by immortal ancestral voices; one in which our lost father speaks to us directly. (pp. 29-30)

Elegy—longing for the past—does not seal one off from the world of politics either on the right or the left. Yeats, more than all but a few of the writers of his time, (Pound and Brecht come to mind, though each had only partially the chance Yeats had to matter most directly) took the largest risks, led his deepest life in public—even when his poetry complained of the savage effects of too much public life. It was his genius, his generosity in the use of himself, to find the public within the private, to find that place (a place clearly of bad dreams, terrifying apparitions, disgust, regret, extremities of hope and savagery) within oneself where one's quarrel with the world, and one's quarrel with oneself can truly be apprehended as the same skirmishing; and out of this apprehension he constructed some of the enduring political prophecies for his (our, any) time; mistakes worth wondering at, places where the road comes recurrently, and forks off, and history goes wandering in error again.

"All's changed . . . " The phrase finds its greatest exaltation in **"Easter, 1916."** The revolution, the political identity of the nation, will not come from the stately mansions, but from the little streets (and their leaders) as they are hurled upon the great. Yeats turns here to the task of ennobling those little men, of taking them up into his imagination, his rhetoric, his traditional grand manner. (p. 31)

Yeats takes figures of the Easter Rebellion up into his imagination, numbering them in his verse. But this also means taking them up into the past, the past that is the very substance of Yeats's language, his high style and his poetic method. In this poem, elegy and epic are as close to being one as—in this world—they can be. The figures of the rising are no longer comic; they have ceased to play a part; Being and becoming. Being and appearance are one in the dignity of death. . . . The epic wholeness in this fallen world can be regained only in memory, after the event, in death, as story. The figures of **"Easter, 1916"** are exalted in the poem, and yet the very substance of the poem reveals that its politics are those of elegy, and of an activism that can only have as its end, elegy, which is to say, death. The poem insists that, regretfully, there is something about politics and about fanaticism (they were for Yeats—not always figuratively—the same) that makes one unliving, that "too long a [political] sacrifice can make a stone of the heart." ("The revolutionary," Nechayev said, "is a doomed man." He is one who imagines himself already dead.) But the poem itself shows that it is sacrifice, not metaphorical but actual physical sacrifice that is ennobling. The figures are beautiful not in victory, but in defeat; the exultation is felt in tragedy, in death. (p. 32)

"All's changed . . . " The phrase in **"Easter, 1916"** seems at first to have reversed its meaning; the men are changed into something beautiful; it is not a lament over the fallen state of the world. But the figures are transformed, their terrible beauty released, made actual, only by their joining the lost world at the moment of their dying. In an elegy, Northrop Frye says, the subject of the poem is "idealized and exalted into a nature spirit or dying god." Possession by the dead has become death itself; dying they are united with the god. The poet survives to number them in his verse, for now that they are lost they are poetic figures. The poet survives: elegy is the song of a survivor. (p. 33)

> Jay Cantor, "History in the Revolutionary Movement: 'Men Made Out of Words'," in his The Space Between: Literature and Politics (copyright © 1981 by Jay Cantor), The Johns Hopkins University Press, 1981, pp. 19-58.*

ADDITIONAL BIBLIOGRAPHY

Bloom, Harold. "Yeats, Gnosticism and the Sacred Void." In his *Poetry and Repression: Revisionism from Blake to Stevens*, pp. 205-34. New Haven: Yale University Press, 1976.
>   Discusses the origins of gnosticism, as well as Yeats's use of it.

Bohlmann, Otto. *Yeats and Nietzsche: An Exploration of the Major Nietzschean Echoes in the Writings of William Butler Yeats*. London and Basingstroke: Macmillan Press, 1982, 222 p.
>   Explores Yeats's use of Nietzschean concepts such as "Unity of Being," the *Übermensch*, and the cyclical nature of history.

Bornstein, George. *Transformations of Romanticism in Yeats, Eliot and Stevens*. Chicago: University of Chicago Press, 1976, 263 p.*
>   Discussion of Yeats's part in the continuance of the Romantic tradition. There are references to Yeats throughout the book.

Bradley, Anthony. *William Butler Yeats*. New York: Frederick Ungar Publishing Co., 1979, 306 p.
>   Describes the plays as well as the Irish and Japanese source materials that Yeats used in writing them. Many photos from performances at the Abbey Theatre are included.

Ellmann, Richard. *Yeats: The Man and the Masks*. New York: The Macmillan Co., 1948, 331 p.
>   Excellent biocritical study by a prominent American critic and Yeats scholar.

Fallis, Richard. *The Irish Renaissance*. Syracuse: Syracuse University Press, 1977, 319 p.*
>   History of the Irish Renaissance that provides a cultural and historical background to Yeats's era.

Flannery, Mary Catherine. *Yeats and Magic: The Earlier Works*. New York: Barnes and Noble, 1977, 165 p.
>   Traces Yeats's growing awareness of occult phenomena and increasing involvement with occult societies and parallels this spiritual awareness with his developing awareness of himself as a poet.

Frazier, Adrian. "The Ascendency Poetry of W. B. Yeats." *The Sewanee Review* LXXXVIII, No. 1 (January-March 1980): 67-85.
>   Examines the historical period in which Yeats wrote and the manner in which historical events influenced the selection of themes and subject matter for his poetry.

Friedman, Barton R. *Adventures in the Deeps of the Mind: The Cuchulain Cycle of W. B. Yeats*. Princeton: Princeton University Press, 1977, 151 p.
>   On the Cuchulain cycle as a "paradigm of Yeats's dramatic career." Friedman endeavors to show that "Yeats succeeded where his Romantic precursors had failed in finding ways of staging 'the deeps of the mind'."

Frye, Northrop. "The Rising of the Moon." In his *Spiritus Mundi*, pp. 245-74. Bloomington: Indiana University Press, 1976.
>   An analysis of Yeats's *A Vision*.

Gibbon, Monk. *The Masterpiece and the Man: Yeats As I Knew Him*. London: Rupert Hart-Davis, 1959, 226 p.
>   Biography based largely on personal reminiscences of Yeats's young cousin, Monk Gibbon. Gibbon was also acquainted with A. E., George Moore, Maud Gonne, and other notable Irish artists and politicians.

Hone, Joseph. *W. B. Yeats: 1865-1939*. London: Macmillan and Co., 1943, 504 p.

Biography generally regarded as the finest available. Hone had the help of both Mrs. W. B. Yeats and Maud Gonne in preparing the text, as well as access to all of Yeats's unpublished papers.

Jeffares, A. Norman. *A Commentary on "The Collected Poems of W. B. Yeats."* Stanford: Stanford University Press, 1968, 563 p.

Line by line explications of each poem in Yeats's *Collected Poems*.

Lynch, David. *Yeats: The Poetics of the Self*. Chicago: The University of Chicago Press, 1979, 192 p.

Psychoanalytic study of Yeats based on the most recent psychological theories of narcissism. Lynch uses these theories as a starting point for an analysis of Yeats's poetry and his philosophies.

Moore, Virginia. *The Unicorn: William Butler Yeats's Search for Reality*. New York: The Macmillan Co., 1954, 519 p.

Examination of Yeats's religious beliefs and occult researches. Moore's volume contains many excerpts from Yeats's unpublished notebooks and records of his magical and Rosicrucian experiments.

Murphy, William M. *Prodigal Father: The Life of John Butler Yeats*. Ithaca, N.Y.: Cornell University Press: 1978, 649 p.*

Biography of Yeats's artist father, whose philosophy and personality markedly influenced his son's career. There are many references to W. B. Yeats throughout the text.

Reid, Forrest. *W. B. Yeats: A Critical Study*. London: Martin Secker, 1915, 257 p.

Early survey containing criticism of the poems written before 1899, the lyrical dramas, the earliest plays written for the Abbey Theatre, and the prose sketches in *The Celtic Twilight*.

Scott, Clive. "A Theme and Form: 'Leda and the Swan' and the Sonnet." *The Modern Language Review* 74, Part 1 (January 1979): 1-11.

On Yeats's experiments with the sonnet form and mythological materials.

Symons, Arthur. "Mr. W. B. Yeats." In his *Studies in Prose and Verse*, pp. 235-41. New York: E. P. Dutton, 1904.

Survey of Yeats's very early dramas.

Taylor, Richard. *The Drama of W. B. Yeats: Irish Myth and the Japanese Nō*. New Haven: Yale University Press, 1976.

Scholarly study of the influence of the Nō plays of Japan on Yeats's dramas. Particular attention is paid to the influence of Ezra Pound and the work of Ernest Fenollosa in directing Yeats's attention to the study of the Nō.

Weygandt, Cornelius. *Yeats and the Irish Renaissance: English Poetry of Today against an American Background*. New York: Russell and Russell, 1937, 460 p.*

An American view of early twentieth-century English poetry, with extensive references throughout to Yeats.

Appendix

THE EXCERPTS IN TCLC, VOLUME 11, WERE REPRINTED FROM THE FOLLOWING PERIODICALS:

The Academy
America
American Literature
American Mercury
American Quarterly
The American Society Legion of Honor
  Magazine
The Americas
The Arena
The Athenaeum
The Bookman, *London*
The Bookman, *New York*
Books Abroad
The British Journal of Medical Psychology
Cesare Barbieri Courier
Chūōkōron
The Cimarron Review
CLA Journal
The Columbia Review
The Crisis
The Critic, *London*
The Critic, *New York*
Criticism
Critique: Studies in Modern Fiction
The Dial
Educational Theatre Journal
Encounter
English Journal
English Literature in Transition
Essays in Criticism
The Evening Sun, *Baltimore*
The Fortnightly
The Fortnightly Review
Forum
Forum Italicum
The Freeman
The Georgia Review
German Life & Letters
The German Quarterly
The Germanic Review
The Guardian

Harper's New Monthly Magazine
Harvard Journal of Asiatic Studies
Hispanic Review
Horizon
The Hudson Review
The Hungarian Quarterly
The Illustrated London News
The Irish Monthly
Italian Quarterly
James Joyce Quarterly
Journal of American Studies
The Journal of Negro History
The Journal of Southern History
Kentucky Foreign Language Quarterly
Life and Letters To-Day
The Literary Digest International Book
  Review
The Literary Review
London Magazine
The Massachusetts Review
The Michigan Daily Sunday Magazine
The Mississippi Quarterly
Modern Austrian Literature
Modern Drama
Modern Fiction Studies
The Modern Language Journal
Monatshefte
Mythlore
The Nation
The New England Quarterly
The New Hungarian Quarterly
New Orleans Times-Democrat
The New Republic
The New Review
New Statesman
The New Statesman & Nation
New York Evening Post
New York Herald Tribune Book Review
New York Herald Tribune Books
The New York Times
The New York Times Book Review

The New Yorker
Nineteenth-Century Fiction
The North American Review
Novel: A Forum on Fiction
Nyugat
The Old Northwest
The Outlook
Pall Mall Gazette
Partisan Review
Philologica Pragensia
PHYLON
Poet Lore
Poetry
Prairie Schooner
The Quarterly Journal of Speech
Renascence
A Review of English Literature
Richmond Times-Dispatch
Romance Notes
Russian Literature Triquarterly
The Saturday Review
The Saturday Review of Literature
Scribner's Magazine
Slavic Review
The Slavonic and East European
  Review
The Smart Set
The Southern Literary Journal
The Southern Review
The Spectator
Studies in Black Literature
Studies in the Literary Imagination
The Tennessean, *Nashville*
Theatre Arts Monthly
The Times Literary Supplement
Twentieth Century Literature
The Virginia Magazine of History and
  Biography
Wisconsin Studies in Contemporary
  Literature
The Yale Review

THE EXCERPTS IN TCLC, VOLUME 11, WERE REPRINTED FROM THE FOLLOWING BOOKS:

A. E. The Living Torch. *Edited by Monk Gibbon. Macmillan, 1938.*

Abramson, Doris E. Negro Playwrights in the American Theatre, 1925-1959. *Columbia University Press, 1969.*

Aiken, Conrad. Collected Criticism. *Oxford University Press, 1968.*

Anderson, David D. Louis Bromfield. *Twayne, 1964.*

Anderson, Sherwood. Introduction to The Work of Stephen Crane: "Midnight Sketches" and Other Impressions, Vol. XI, *by Stephen Crane. Edited by Wilson Follett. Knopf, 1926, Russell & Russell, 1963.*

Andreas, Osborn. Henry James and the Expanding Horizon: A Study of the Meaning and Basic Themes of James's Fiction. *University of Washington Press, 1948.*

Archer, William. Poets of the Younger Generation. *John Lane/The Bodley Head, 1902, Scholarly Press, 1969[?].*

Arnold, Matthew. Essays in Criticism, second series. *Macmillan, 1921.*

Auden, W. H. Forewords and Afterwords. *Edited by Edward Mendelson. Random House, 1973.*

Baldwin, Charles C. The Men Who Make Our Novels. *Rev. ed. Dodd, Mead, 1924.*

Bangerter, Lowell A. Hugo von Hofmannsthal. *Ungar, 1977.*

Barclay, Glen St. John. Anatomy of Horror: The Masters of Occult Fiction. *Weidenfeld and Nicholson, 1978.*

Baring, Maurice. Landmarks in Russian Literature. *Methuen, 1910.*

Barry, Philip. You and I: A Comedy in Three Acts. *Brentano's, 1923.*

Barthes, Roland. New Critical Essays. *Translated by Richard Howard. Hill and Wang, 1980.*

Beckson, Karl, ed. Aesthetes and Decadents of the 1890's: An Anthology of British Poetry and Prose. *Vintage Books, 1966.*

Berg, A. Scott. Max Perkins: Editor of Genius. *Pocket Books, 1979.*

Bergson, Frank. Stephen Crane's Artistry. *Columbia University Press, 1975.*

Berryman, John. Stephen Crane: A Critical Biography. *William Sloane, 1950, Octagon Books, 1975.*

Berryman, John. The Freedom of the Poet. *Farrar, Straus and Giroux, 1976.*

Beucler, André. Poet of Paris: Twenty Years with Leon-Paul Fargue. *Chatto & Windus, 1955.*

Bishop, John Peale. The Collected Essays of John Peale Bishop. *Edited by Edmund Wilson. Charles Scribner's Sons, 1948.*

Bloom, Edward A., and Bloom, Lillian D. Willa Cather's Gift of Sympathy. *Southern Illinois University Press, 1962.*

Bloom, Harold. Yeats. *Oxford University Press, 1970.*

Bone, Robert. Down Home: A History of Afro-American Short Fiction from Its Beginnings to the End of the Harlem Renaissance. *G. P. Putnam's Sons, 1975.*

Bonnerjea, René. Introduction to Poems, *by Endre Ady. Translated by René Bonnerjea. Dr. Vajna & Bokor Publishers, 1941.*

Brooks, Cleanth. Modern Poetry and the Tradition. *University of North Carolina Press, 1939.*

Brooks, Van Wyck. The Pilgrimage of Henry James. *Dutton, 1925.*

Brown, E. K. Willa Cather: A Critical Biography. *Edited by Leon Edel. Knopf, 1953.*

Brown, John Mason. Upstage: The American Theatre in Performance. *Norton, 1930, Kennikat Press, 1969.*

Brown, Morrison. Louis Bromfield and His Books: An Evaluation. *Essential Books, 1957.*

Brown, Sterling. The Negro in American Fiction. *Associates in Negro Folk Education, 1937.*

Brushwood, John S. Mexico in Its Novel: A Nation's Search for Identity. *University of Texas Press, 1966.*

Cabell, James Branch. Joseph Hergesheimer: An Essay in Interpretation. *Bookfellows, 1921.*

Cady, Edwin H. Stephen Crane. *Twayne, 1980.*

Cantor, Jay. The Space Between: Literature and Politics. *Johns Hopkins University Press, 1981.*

Carpenter, Humphrey. The Inklings: C. S. Lewis, J.R.R. Tolkien, Charles Williams, and Their Friends. *Houghton Mifflin, 1978, Allen & Unwin, 1978, Ballantine Books, 1981.*

Cather, Willa. Willa Cather on Writing: Critical Studies on Writing as an Art. *Knopf, 1949.*

Cather, Willa. Introduction *to* The Work of Stephen Crane: "Wounds in the Rain and Other Impressions of War," Vol. IX, *by Stephen Crane. Edited by Wilson Follett. Knopf, 1926.*

Cavaliero, Glen. Charles Williams: Poet of Theology. *William B. Eerdman, 1983.*

Christian, R. F. Tolstoy: A Critical Introduction. *Cambridge University Press, 1969.*

Cioran, E. M. The Fall into Time. *Translated by Richard Howard. Quadrangle Books, 1970.*

Cohen, Morton. Rider Haggard: His Life and Works. *Hutchinson, 1960.*

Conrad, Joseph. Last Essays. *Edited by Richard Curle. Doubleday, Page, 1926.*

Conrad, Joseph. Preface *to* The Red Badge of Courage, *by Stephen Crane. William Heinemann, 1925.*

Cooper, Frederic Taber. Some English Story Tellers: A Book of the Younger Novelists. *Holt, Rinehart, and Winston, 1912.*

Craig, G. Dundas. The Modernist Trend in Spanish-American Poetry: A Collection of Representative Poems of the Modernist Movement and the Reaction. *University of California Press, 1934.*

Crews, Frederick C. The Tragedy of Manners: Moral Drama in the Later Novels of Henry James. *Yale University Press, 1957.*

Davidson, Donald. The Spyglass: Views and Reviews, 1924-1930. *Edited by John Tyree Fain. Vanderbilt University Press, 1963.*

Davis, Arthur P. From the Dark Tower: Afro-American Writers, 1900 to 1960. *Howard University Press, 1974.*

Donnelly, John, ed. Language, Metaphysics, and Death. *Fordham University Press, 1978.*

Dukes, Ashley. Modern Dramatists. *Frank Palmer, 1911, Charles H. Sergel, 1911.*

Edgar, Pelham. Henry James: Man and Author. *Houghton Mifflin, 1927.*

Eliot, T. S. The Sacred Wood: Essays on Poetry and Criticism. *7th ed. Methuen, 1960.*

Ellin, Stanley. Introduction *to* The Conjure-Man Dies: A Mystery Tale of Dark Harlem, *by Rudolph Fisher. Arno Press, 1971.*

Ellmann, Richard. Introduction *to* The Symbolist Movement in Literature, *by Arthur Symons. Rev. ed. Dutton, 1958.*

Englekirk, John Eugene. Edgar Allan Poe in Hispanic Literature. *Instituto de las Españas en los Estados Unidos, 1934.*

Erlich, Victor, ed. Twentieth-Century Russian Literary Criticism. *Yale University Press, 1975.*

Evans, Arthur R., ed. On Four Modern Humanists: Hofmannsthal, Gundolf, Curtius, Kantorowicz. *Princeton University Press, 1970.*

Fadiman, Clifton. Party of One: The Selected Writings of Clifton Fadiman. *World, 1955.*

Fadiman, Clifton. Foreword to War and Peace, *by Leo Tolstoy. Translated by Louise Maude and Aylmer Maude. Simon & Schuster, 1942.*

Fiedler, Leslie A. The Inadvertent Epic: From "Uncle Tom's Cabin" to "Roots." *Canadian Broadcasting Corporation, 1979.*

Flexner, Eleanor. American Playwrights: 1918-1938. *Simon & Schuster, 1938.*

Ford, Ford Madox. Portraits from Life: Memories and Criticisms of Henry James, Joseph Conrad, Thomas Hardy, H. G. Wells, Stephen Crane, D. H. Lawrence, John Galsworthy, Ivan Turgenev, W. H. Hudson, Theodore Dreiser, Algernon Charles Swinburne. *Houghton Mifflin, 1937, Greenwood Press, 1974.*

France, Anatole. On Life & Letters, fourth series. *Edited by Frederic Chapman. Translated by Bernard Miall. Dodd, Mead, 1924.*

Frierson, William C. The English Novel in Transition: 1885-1940. *University of Oklahoma Press, 1942.*

Garnett, Edward. Friday Nights: Literary Criticism and Appreciations. *Knopf, 1922.*

Gassner, John. The Theatre in Our Times: A Survey of the Men, Materials and Movement in the Modern Theatre. *Crown, 1954.*

Geismar, Maxwell. Henry James and the Jacobites. *Houghton Mifflin, 1963.*

Gloster, Hugh M. Negro Voices in American Fiction. *University of North Carolina Press, 1948.*

Goldberg, Issac. Studies in Spanish-American Literature. *Brentano's, 1920.*

Gosse, Edmund. French Profiles. *Rev. ed. William Heinemann, 1913.*

Graham, Kenneth. Henry James: The Drama of Fulfilment; An Approach to the Novels. *Oxford at the Clarendon Press, 1975.*

Gumilev, Nikolai. Nikolai Gumilev on Russian Poetry. *Edited and translated by David Lapeza. Ardis, 1977.*

Hamburger, Michael. Introduction to Selected Writings of Hugo von Hofmannsthal: Poems and Verse Plays, Vol. 2, *by Hugo von Hofmannsthal. Edited by Michael Hamburger. Translated by John Bednall and others. Pantheon Books, 1961.*

Hammelmann, H. A. Hugo von Hofmannsthal. *Bowes & Bowes, 1957.*

Hart, James D. The Popular Book: A History of America's Literary Taste. *Oxford University Press, 1950.*

Harwell, Richard. Introduction to Lee, *by Douglas Southall Freeman. Charles Scribner's Sons, 1961.*

Hatfield, Henry. Crisis and Continuity in Modern German Fiction: Ten Essays. *Cornell University Press, 1969.*

Heaney, Seamus. Preoccupations: Selected Prose, 1968-1978. *Farrar, Straus and Giroux, 1980.*

Hearn, Lafcadio. Essays in European and Oriental Literature. *Edited by Albert Mordell. Dodd, Mead, 1923.*

Hemingway, Ernest. Introduction to Men at War: The Best War Stories of All Times. *Edited by Ernest Hemingway. Rev. ed. Crown, 1955.*

James, Henry. Essays in London and Elsewhere. *Harper & Row, 1893.*

Jeffares, A. Norman, ed. W. B. Yeats: The Critical Heritage. *Routledge & Kegan Paul, 1977.*

Jones, Llewellyn. American Writers on American Literature. *Edited by John Macy. Liveright, 1931.*

Kafka, Franz. Letters to Friends, Family, and Editors. *Translated by Richard Winston and Clara Winston. Schocken, 1977.*

Kaplan, Sydney Janet. Feminine Consciousness in the Modern British Novel. *University of Illinois Press, 1975.*

Katz, Joseph, ed. Stephen Crane in Transition: Centenary Essays. *Northern Illinois University Press, 1972.*

Kayser, Wolfgang. The Grotesque in Art and Literature. *Translated by Ulrich Weisstein. Indiana University Press, 1963.*

Kazin, Alfred. On Native Grounds: An Interpretation of Modern American Prose Literature. *Reynal & Hitchcock, 1942.*

Keene, Donald. Landscapes and Portraits: Appreciations of Japanese Culture. *Kodansha, 1971.*

Kermode, Frank. Romantic Image. *Routledge & Kegan Paul, 1957.*

Kipling, Rudyard. Rudyard Kipling to Rider Haggard: The Record of a Friendship. *Edited by Morton Cohen. Hutchinson, 1965.*

Klaniczay, Tibor; Szauder, József; und Szabolcsi, Miklós. History of Hungarian Literature. *Edited by Miklós Szabolcsi. Translated by József Hatvany and István Farkas. Collet's, 1964.*

Kossman, Rudolf R. Henry James: Dramatist. *Wolters-Noordhoff, 1969.*

Krans, Horatio Sheafe. William Butler Yeats and the Irish Literary Revival. *McClure, Phillips, 1904.*

Kraus, Michael. The Writing of American History. *University of Oklahoma Press, 1953.*

LaFrance, Marston. A Reading of Stephen Crane. *Oxford University Press, 1971.*

Leavis, F. R. Anna Karenina, and Other Essays. *Chatto & Windus, 1967.*

Le Gallienne, Richard. Retrospective Review: A Literary Log, 1881-1893, Vol. I. *John Lane/The Bodley Head, 1896.*

Lemaitre, Jules. Literary Impressions. *Translated by A. W. Evans. Daniel O'Connor, 1921.*

Lerner, Michael G. Pierre Loti. *Twayne, 1974.*

Lewis, C. S. On Stories and Other Essays on Literature. *Edited by Walter Hooper. Harcourt Brace Jovanovich, 1982.*

Lewisohn, Adéle. Introduction to Edgar Allan Poe, *by Hanns Heinz Ewers. Translated by Adéle Lewisohn. Huebsch, 1917.*

Lowell, Amy. Introduction to The Work of Stephen Crane: "The Black Riders and Other Lines," *Vol. VI, by Stephen Crane. Edited by Wilson Follett. Knopf, 1926, Russell & Russell, 1963.*

Lubbock, Percy. The Craft of Fiction. *Cape, 1921.*

MacNeice, Louis. The Poetry of W. B. Yeats. *Oxford University Press, 1941, Faber and Faber, 1967.*

Malone, Dumas. Introduction to George Washington, a Biography: Patriot and President, Vol. 6, *by Douglas Southall Freeman. Charles Scribner's Sons, 1954.*

Mansfield, Katherine. Mystery and Adventure. *Edited by J. Middleton Murry. Knopf, 1930.*

Mansfield, Katherine. Novels and Novelists. *Edited by J. Middleton Murry. Knopf, 1930.*

Martin, Ronald E. The Fiction of Joseph Hergesheimer. *University of Pennsylvania Press, 1965.*

Maslenikov, Oleg A. The Frenzied Poets: Andrey Biely and the Russian Symbolists. *University of California Press, 1952.*

Mencken, H. L. A Mencken Chrestomathy. *Knopf, 1949.*

Meyers, Jeffrey. Homosexuality and Literature 1890-1930. *Athlone Press, 1977.*

Michaud, Regis. Modern Thought and Literature in France. *Funk & Wagnalls, 1934.*

Miles, David H. Hofmannsthal's Novel "Andreas": Memory and Self. *Princeton University Press, 1972.*

Miller, Henry. The Books of My Life. *Peter Owen, 1952.*

Mirsky, D. S. Contemporary Russian Literature: 1881-1925. *Knopf, 1926, G. Routledge & Sons, 1926.*

Mirsky, D. S. A History of Russian Literature from the Earliest Times to the Death of Dostoyevsky. *Knopf, 1927.*

Mirsky, D. S. A History of Russian Literature Comprising ''A History of Russian Literature'' and ''Contemporary Russian Literature.'' *Edited by Francis J. Whitfield. Knopf, 1949.*

Mitchell, Margaret. Margaret Mitchell's ''Gone With the Wind'' Letters, 1936-1939. *Edited by Richard Harwell. Macmillan, 1976.*

Miyoshi, Masao. Accomplices of Silence: The Modern Japanese Novel. *University of California Press, 1974.*

More, Paul Elmer. Shelburne Essays, first series. *Putnam's, 1904.*

Moses, Montrose J. and Brown, John Mason, eds. The American Theatre As Seen by Its Critics: 1752-1934. *2d ed. W. W. Norton, 1934.*

Munro, John M. Arthur Symons. *Twayne, 1969.*

Nagel, James. Stephen Crane and Literary Impressionism. *Pennsylvania State University Press, 1980.*

Natan, Alex, ed. German Men of Letters: Twelve Literary Essays, Vol. III. *Wolff, 1964.*

Nathan, George Jean. The Theatre Book of the Year, 1942-1943: A Record and an Interpretation. *Knopf, 1943.*

Norris, Frank. The Literary Criticism of Frank Norris. *Edited by Donald Pizer. University of Texas Press, 1964.*

Oates, Joyce Carol. New Heaven, New Earth: The Visionary Experience in Literature. *Vanguard Press, 1974.*

O'Brien, James. Dazai Osamu. *Twayne, 1975.*

Olgin, Moissaye J. A Guide to Russian Literature (1820-1917). *Harcourt Brace Jovanovich, 1920.*

Pater, Walter. Essays from ''The Guardian.'' *Macmillan, 1914.*

Paz, Octavio, ed. Anthology of Mexican Poetry. *Translated by Samuel Beckett. Indiana University Press, 1958.*

Peacock, Ronald. The Poet in the Theatre. *Routledge & Kegan Paul, 1946, Hill and Wang, 1960.*

Peña, Carlos González. History of Mexican Literature. *Translated by Gusta Barfield Nance and Florene Johnson Dustan. Rev. ed. Southern Methodist University Press, 1968.*

Phelps, William Lyon. Introduction to The Work of Stephen Crane: ''Whilomville Stories,'' Vol. V, *by Stephen Crane. Edited by Wilson Follett. Knopf, 1926.*

Pinto, Vivian de Sola. Crisis in English Poetry, 1880-1940. *4th ed. Hutchinson University Library, 1965.*

Pizer, Donald. Realism and Naturalism in Nineteenth-Century American Literature. *Southern Illinois University Press, 1966, 1976.*

Poggioli, Renato. The Poets of Russia: 1890-1930. *Harvard University Press, 1960.*

Pritchett, V. S. The Living Novel & Later Appreciations. *Rev. ed. Random House, 1964.*

Pritchett, V. S. The Tale Bearers: Literary Essays. *Random House, 1980.*

Rahv, Philip. Image and Idea: Twenty Essays on Literary Themes. *Rev. ed. New Directions, 1957.*

Randall, John H., III. The Landscape and the Looking Glass: Willa Cather's Search for Value. *Houghton Mifflin, 1960.*

Rapin, René. Willa Cather. *McBride, 1930.*

Reményi, Joseph. Hungarian Writers and Literature: Modern Novelists, Critics, and Poets. *Edited by August J. Molnar. Rutgers University Press, 1964.*

Rimer, J. Thomas. Modern Japanese Fiction and Its Traditions: An Introduction. *Princeton University Press, 1978.*

Robinson, William H., Jr. Introduction to The Walls of Jericho, *by Rudolph Fisher. Columbia University Press, 1969.*

Roppolo, Joseph Patrick. Philip Barry. *Twayne, 1965.*

Rosenthal, M. L. Sailing into the Unknown: Yeats, Pound, and Eliot. *Oxford University Press, 1978.*

Rosset, Barney, ed. Evergreen Review Reader: 1957-1961. *Grove Press, 1979.*

Sandburg, Carl. The Letters of Carl Sandburg. *Edited by Herbert Mitgang. Harcourt Brace Jovanovich, 1968.*

Sandison, Alan. The Age of Kipling. *Edited by John Gross. Simon & Schuster, 1972.*

Saurat, Denis. Modern French Literature: 1870-1940. *J. M. Dent & Sons, 1946, Kennikat Press, 1971.*

Schneider, Daniel J. The Crystal Cage: Adventures of the Imagination in the Fiction of Henry James. *Regents Press of Kansas, 1978.*

Schroeter, James, ed. Willa Cather and Her Critics. *Cornell University Press, 1967.*

Schultze, Sydney. The Structure of "Anna Karenina." *Ardis, 1982.*

Shaw, Bernard. Dramatic Opinions and Essays with an Apology by Bernard Shaw, Vol. I. *Brentano's, 1907.*

Shaw, Bernard. Pen Portraits and Reviews by Bernard Shaw. *Rev. ed. Constable, 1932, Scholarly Press, 1971.*

Sherman, Stuart. Critical Woodcuts. *Charles Scribner's Sons, 1926.*

Sherwood, Robert E. Preface to Second Threshold, *by Philip Barry. Harper & Brothers, 1951.*

Sibley, Agnes. Charles Williams. *Twayne, 1982.*

Sievers, W. David. Freud on Broadway: A History of Psychoanalysis and the American Drama. *Hermitage House, 1955, Cooper Square, 1970.*

Simmons, Ernest J. An Outline of Modern Russian Literature (1840-1940). *Cornell University Press, 1943.*

Sinclair, Upton. Money Writes! *Albert & Charles Boni, 1927.*

Skinner, R. Dana. Our Changing Theatre. *Dial Press, 1931.*

Slonim, Marc. Modern Russian Literature: From Chekov to the Present. *Oxford University Press, 1953.*

Slonim, Marc. From Chekov to the Revolution: Russian Literature, 1900-1917. *Oxford University Press, 1962.*

Solomon, Eric. Stephen Crane: From Parody to Realism. *Harvard University Press, 1966.*

Stallman, Robert Wooster. Introduction to The Red Badge of Courage: An Episode of the American Civil War, *by Stephen Crane. The Modern Library, 1951.*

Starr, Nathan Comfort. King Arthur Today: The Arthurian Legend in English and American Literature. *University of Florida Press, 1954.*

Stephen, James Kenneth. Lapsus Calami and Other Verses. *Edited by Herbert Stephen. Macmillan and Bowes, 1896.*

Stephens, James. James, Seumas & Jacques: Unpublished Writings of James Stephens. *Edited by Lloyd Frankenburg. Macmillan, 1964.*

Stevenson, Lionel. The History of the English Novel: Yesterday and After: Vol. XI. *Barnes & Noble, 1967.*

Stork, Charles Wharton. Introduction to The Lyrical Poems of Hugo von Hofmannsthal, *by Hugo von Hofmannsthal. Yale University Press, 1918.*

Stouck, David. Willa Cather's Imagination. *University of Nebraska Press, 1975.*

Stuckey, W. J. The Pulitzer Prize Novels: A Critical Backward Look. *University of Oklahoma Press, 1966.*

Symons, Arthur. Preface to Silhouettes, *by Arthur Symons. 2d ed. L. Smithers, 1896.*

Symons, Arthur. Studies in Prose and Verse. *Dutton, 1904.*

Tate, Allen. On the Limits of Poetry: Selected Essays, 1928-1948. *Swallow Press, 1948.*

Temple, Ruth Zabriskie. The Critic's Alchemy: A Study of the Introduction of French Symbolism into England. *Twayne, 1953.*

Thuente, Mary Helen. W. B. Yeats and Irish Folklore. *Barnes & Noble, 1981.*

Tolkien, J.R.R. The Letters of J.R.R. Tolkien. *Edited by Humphrey Carpenter. George Allen & Unwin, 1981, Houghton Mifflin, 1981.*

Tymn, Marshall B. Horror Literature: A Core Collection and Reference Guide. *Bowker, 1981.*

Ueda, Makoto. Modern Japanese Writers and the Nature of Literature. *Stanford University Press, 1976.*

Van Ghent, Dorothy. The English Novel: Form and Function. *Holt, Rinehart and Winston, 1953.*

Wagenknecht, Edward. Cavalcade of the American Novel: From the Birth of the Nation to the Middle of the Twentieth Century. *Holt, Rinehart and Winston, 1952.*

Wagenknecht, Edward. The Novels of Henry James. *Ungar, 1983.*

Wake, Clive. The Novels of Pierre Loti. *Mouton, 1974.*

Walcutt, Charles Child. American Literary Naturalism, a Divided Stream. *University of Minnesota Press, 1956.*

Ward, J. A. The Search for Form: Studies in the Structure of James's Fiction. *University of North Carolina Press, 1967.*

Waugh, Arthur. Tradition and Change: Studies in Contemporary Literature. *Chapman and Hall, 1919.*

Weatherford, Richard M., ed. Stephen Crane: The Critical Heritage. *Routledge & Kegan Paul, 1973.*

Welby, T. Earle. Arthur Symons: A Critical Study. *Adelphi Company Publishers, 1925.*

Wellman, Esther Turner. Amado Nervo: Mexico's Religious Poet. *Instituto de las Españas en los Estados Unidos, 1936.*

Welty, Eudora. The Art of Willa Cather. *Edited by Bernice Slote and Virginia Faulkner. University of Nebraska Press, 1974.*

White, E. B. Poems and Sketches of E. B. White. *Harper & Row, 1981.*

Williams, C. E. The Broken Eagle: The Politics of Austrian Literature from Empire to Anschluss. *Barnes & Noble, 1974.*

Williams, Harry T. The Selected Essays of T. Harry Williams. *Louisiana State University Press, 1983.*

Wilson, Edmund. Classics and Commercials: A Literary Chronicle of the Forties. *Farrar, Straus and Giroux, 1950.*

Wilson, Edmund. The Shores of Light: A Literary Chronicle of the Twenties and Thirties. *Farrar, Straus and Young, 1952.*

Wilson, Edmund, ed. The Shock of Recognition: The Development of Literature in the United States Recorded by the Men Who Made It. *Farrar, Straus and Cudahy, 1955.*

Woollcott, Alexander. Woollcott's Second Reader, *edited by Alexander Woollcott. Viking Press, 1937.*

Yeats, W. B. Essays and Introductions. *Macmillan, 1961.*

Cumulative Index to Authors

Cumulative Index to Nationalities

Cumulative Index to Critics

Critic Index

Critic Index